The Cambridge Handbook of Sociopragmatics

Sociopragmatics is a rapidly growing field and this is the first ever handbook dedicated to this exciting area of study. Bringing together an international team of leading editors and contributors, it provides a comprehensive, cutting-edge overview of the key concepts, topics, settings and methodologies involved in sociopragmatic research. The chapters are organised in a systematic fashion, and span a wide range of theoretical research on how language communicates multiple meanings in context, how it influences our daily interactions and relationships with others, and how it helps construct our social worlds. Providing insight into a fascinating array of phenomena and novel research directions, the Handbook is not only relevant to experts of pragmatics but to any reader with an interest in language and its use in different contexts, including researchers in sociology, anthropology and communication, and students of applied linguistics and related areas, as well as professional practitioners in communication research.

Michael Haugh's research interests centre on the role of language in social interaction. He has published widely in pragmatics on topics such as (im)politeness, face, conversational humour and metapragmatics. He is an elected Fellow of the Australian Academy of Humanities and co-editor of the new *Cambridge Elements in Pragmatics* series, as well a former co-editor in chief of the *Journal of Pragmatics* (2015–2020).

Dániel Z. Kádár has a research background in cross-cultural, intercultural and historical pragmatics, as well as linguistic politeness and impoliteness, interactional rituals and Chinese pragmatics. He is Research Chair in both China and Hungary. He is Co-Editor of *Contrastive Pragmatics*.

Marina Terkourafi is interested in the interface of language with society and has published widely in all areas of pragmatics, including post-Gricean, sociocultural, historical and experimental pragmatics. She is currently Professor and Chair of Sociolinguistics at Leiden University in the Netherlands and co-editor-in-chief of the *Journal of Pragmatics*.

CAMBRIDGE HANDBOOKS IN LANGUAGE AND LINGUISTICS

Genuinely broad in scope, each handbook in this series provides a complete state-of-the-field overview of a major sub-discipline within language study and research. Grouped into broad thematic areas, the chapters in each volume encompass the most important issues and topics within each subject, offering a coherent picture of the latest theories and findings. Together, the volumes will build into an integrated overview of the discipline in its entirety.

Published titles

The Cambridge Handbook of Phonology, edited by Paul de Lacy
The Cambridge Handbook of Linguistic Code-switching, edited by Barbara E. Bullock and Almeida Jacqueline Toribio
The Cambridge Handbook of Child Language, Second Edition, edited by Edith L. Bavin and Letitia Naigles
The Cambridge Handbook of Endangered Languages, edited by Peter K. Austin and Julia Sallabank
The Cambridge Handbook of Sociolinguistics, edited by Rajend Mesthrie
The Cambridge Handbook of Pragmatics, edited by Keith Allan and Kasia M. Jaszczolt
The Cambridge Handbook of Language Policy, edited by Bernard Spolsky
The Cambridge Handbook of Second Language Acquisition, edited by Julia Herschensohn and Martha Young-Scholten
The Cambridge Handbook of Biolinguistics, edited by Cedric Boeckx and Kleanthes K. Grohmann
The Cambridge Handbook of Generative Syntax, edited by Marcel den Dikken
The Cambridge Handbook of Communication Disorders, edited by Louise Cummings
The Cambridge Handbook of Stylistics, edited by Peter Stockwell and Sara Whiteley
The Cambridge Handbook of Linguistic Anthropology, edited by N.J. Enfield, Paul Kockelman and Jack Sidnell
The Cambridge Handbook of English Corpus Linguistics, edited by Douglas Biber and Randi Reppen
The Cambridge Handbook of Bilingual Processing, edited by John W. Schwieter
The Cambridge Handbook of Learner Corpus Research, edited by Sylviane Granger, Gaëtanelle Gilquin and Fanny Meunier
The Cambridge Handbook of Linguistic Multicompetence, edited by Li Wei and Vivian Cook
The Cambridge Handbook of English Historical Linguistics, edited by Merja Kytö and Päivi Pahta
The Cambridge Handbook of Formal Semantics, edited by Maria Aloni and Paul Dekker
The Cambridge Handbook of Morphology, edited by Andrew Hippisley and Greg Stump
The Cambridge Handbook of Historical Syntax, edited by Adam Ledgeway and Ian Roberts
The Cambridge Handbook of Linguistic Typology, edited by Alexandra Y. Aikhenvald and R. M. W. Dixon
The Cambridge Handbook of Areal Linguistics, edited by Raymond Hickey
The Cambridge Handbook of Cognitive Linguistics, edited by Barbara Dancygier
The Cambridge Handbook of Japanese Linguistics, edited by Yoko Hasegawa
The Cambridge Handbook of Spanish Linguistics, edited by Kimberly L. Geeslin

The Cambridge Handbook of Bilingualism, edited by Annick De Houwer and Lourdes Ortega

The Cambridge Handbook of Systemic Functional Linguistics, edited by Geoff Thompson, Wendy L. Bowcher, Lise Fontaine and David Schönthal

The Cambridge Handbook of African Linguistics, edited by H. Ekkehard Wolff

The Cambridge Handbook of Language Learning, edited by John W. Schwieter and Alessandro Benati

The Cambridge Handbook of World Englishes, edited by Daniel Schreier, Marianne Hundt and Edgar W. Schneider

The Cambridge Handbook of Intercultural Communication, edited by Guido Rings and Sebastian Rasinger

The Cambridge Handbook of Germanic Linguistics, edited by Michael T. Putnam and B. Richard Page

The Cambridge Handbook of Discourse Studies, edited by Anna De Fina and Alexandra Georgakopoulou

The Cambridge Handbook of Language Standardization, edited by Wendy Ayres-Bennett and John Bellamy

The Cambridge Handbook of Korean Linguistics, edited by Sungdai Cho and John Whitman

The Cambridge Handbook of Phonetics, edited by Rachael-Anne Knight and Jane Setter

The Cambridge Handbook of Corrective Feedback in Second Language Learning and Teaching, edited by Hossein Nassaji and Eva Kartchava

The Cambridge Handbook of Experimental Syntax, edited by Grant Goodall

The Cambridge Handbook of Heritage Languages and Linguistics, edited by Silvina Montrul and Maria Polinsky

The Cambridge Handbook of Arabic Linguistics, edited by Karin Ryding and David Wilmsen

The Cambridge Handbook of the Philosophy of Language, edited by Piotr Stalmaszczyk

The Cambridge Handbook of Sociopragmatics

Edited by
Michael Haugh
University of Queensland

Dániel Z. Kádár
Hungarian Research Institute for Linguistics/Dalian University of Foreign Studies

Marina Terkourafi
Leiden University

CAMBRIDGE
UNIVERSITY PRESS

University Printing House, Cambridge CB2 8BS, United Kingdom

One Liberty Plaza, 20th Floor, New York, NY 10006, USA

477 Williamstown Road, Port Melbourne, VIC 3207, Australia

314–321, 3rd Floor, Plot 3, Splendor Forum, Jasola District Centre, New Delhi – 110025, India

79 Anson Road, #06–04/06, Singapore 079906

Cambridge University Press is part of the University of Cambridge.

It furthers the University's mission by disseminating knowledge in the pursuit of education, learning, and research at the highest international levels of excellence.

www.cambridge.org
Information on this title: www.cambridge.org/9781108844963
DOI: 10.1017/9781108954105

© Cambridge University Press 2021

This publication is in copyright. Subject to statutory exception and to the provisions of relevant collective licensing agreements, no reproduction of any part may take place without the written permission of Cambridge University Press.

First published 2021

Printed in the United Kingdom by TJ Books Limited, Padstow Cornwall

A catalogue record for this publication is available from the British Library.

Library of Congress Cataloging-in-Publication Data
Names: Haugh, Michael, editor. | Kádár, Dániel Z., 1979- editor. | Terkourafi, Marina, editor.
Title: The Cambridge handbook of sociopragmatics / edited by Michael Haugh, University of Queensland ; Dániel Z. Kádár, Hungarian Research Institute for Linguistics/Dalian University of Foreign Languages ; Marina Terkourafi, Leiden University.
Description: Cambridge ; New York : Cambridge University Press, 2021. | Series: Cambridge handbooks in language and linguistics | Includes bibliographical references and index.
Identifiers: LCCN 2020046748 (print) | LCCN 2020046749 (ebook) | ISBN 9781108844963 (hardback) | ISBN 9781108949309 (paperback) | ISBN 9781108954105 (epub)
Subjects: LCSH: Pragmatics. | Sociolinguistics.
Classification: LCC P99.4.P72 C3654 2021 (print) | LCC P99.4.P72 (ebook) | DDC 306.44–dc23
LC record available at https://lccn.loc.gov/2020046748
LC ebook record available at https://lccn.loc.gov/2020046749

ISBN 978-1-108-84496-3 Hardback

Cambridge University Press has no responsibility for the persistence or accuracy of URLs for external or third-party internet websites referred to in this publication and does not guarantee that any content on such websites is, or will remain, accurate or appropriate.

Contents

List of Figures	page ix
List of Tables	x
List of Contributors	xi
Acknowledgements	xiii

1	Introduction: Directions in Sociopragmatics *Michael Haugh, Dániel Z. Kádár and Marina Terkourafi*	1
Part I	**Fundamentals of Sociopragmatics**	13
2	Sociopragmatics: Roots and Definition *Jonathan Culpeper*	15
3	Inference and Implicature *Marina Terkourafi*	30
4	Speaker Meaning, Commitment and Accountability *Chi-Hé Elder*	48
5	Social Actions *Arnulf Deppermann*	69
6	Stance and Evaluation *Maarit Siromaa and Mirka Rauniomaa*	95
7	Reflexivity and Meta-awareness *Jef Verschueren*	117
8	Participation and Footing *Elizabeth Holt and Jim O'Driscoll*	140
9	Conventionalization and Conventions *Dániel Z. Kádár and Juliane House*	162
10	Synchronic and Diachronic Pragmatic Variability *Anne Barron*	182
11	Activity Types and Genres *Dawn Archer, Piotr Jagodziński and Rebecca Jagodziński*	206
12	Social Groups and Relational Networks *Diana Boxer and Florencia Cortés-Conde*	227
Part II	**Topics and Settings in Sociopragmatics**	247
13	Face, Facework and Face-Threatening Acts *Maria Sifianou and Angeliki Tzanne*	249
14	Relationships and Relating *Robert B. Arundale*	272
15	Analysing Identity *Pilar Garcés-Conejos Blitvich and Alex Georgakopoulou*	293

16 (Im)politeness and Sociopragmatics *Jonathan Culpeper and Michael Haugh* 315
17 Affect and Emotion *Laura Alba-Juez* 340
18 Power *Michiel Leezenberg* 363
19 Morality in Sociopragmatics *Pilar Garcés-Conejos Blitvich and Dániel Z. Kádár* 385
20 Conversational Humour *Marta Dynel and Valeria Sinkeviciute* 408
21 Gesture and Prosody in Multimodal Communication *Lucien Brown and Pilar Prieto* 430
22 Digitally Mediated Communication *Chaoqun Xie and Francisco Yus* 454
23 Workplace and Institutional Discourse *Meredith Marra and Shelley Dawson* 475
24 Service Encounter Discourse *J. César Félix-Brasdefer and Rosina Márquez Reiter* 496
25 Argumentative, Political and Legal Discourse *Anita Fetzer and Iwona Witczak-Plisiecka* 520
26 The Pragmatics of Translation *Juliane House* 544

Part III Approaches and Methods in Sociopragmatics 567
27 Interpersonal Pragmatics *Miriam A. Locher and Sage L. Graham* 569
28 Sociocognitive Pragmatics *Istvan Kecskes* 592
29 Conversation Analysis and Sociopragmatics *Rebecca Clift and Michael Haugh* 616
30 Corpus Pragmatics *Svenja Adolphs and Yaoyao Chen* 639
31 Variational Pragmatics *Klaus P. Schneider* 663
32 **Historical Sociopragmatics** *Magdalena Leitner and Andreas H. Jucker* 687
33 **Emancipatory Pragmatics** *Scott Saft, Sachiko Ide and Kishiko Ueno* 710
34 **Cross-Cultural and Intercultural Pragmatics** *Troy McConachy and Helen Spencer-Oatey* 733
35 Second Language Pragmatics *Elly Ifantidou* 758

Index 780

Figures

1.1	Sociopragmatics at the intersection of linguistics and sociology	page 3
1.2	General pragmatics, pragmalinguistics and sociopragmatics	4
1.3	Sociopragmatics at the intersection of sociolinguistics and pragmatics	5
1.4	Key anchors of sociopragmatics	7
2.1	General pragmatics, pragmalinguistics and sociopragmatics	21
10.1	Focus of research on intralingual pragmatic variation	187
16.1	Componential analysis of the reporting of taking offence	330
16.2	Adverbs by which *offensive* is pre-modified: American and Australian English compared	332
21.1	Coordinating eyebrow movements with hand gestures	435
21.2	Two types of epistemic gestures	437
22.1	Sources of identity as triangles	466
27.1	Physical position of interdisciplinary discharge round participants	582
30.1	Distribution of speech functions in the MWE	651
30.2	A screenshot of ELAN	652
30.3	An instance of embedded in stroke phase	655
30.4	Gesture–speech functional profile for the MWEs	656
32.1	Relations between clans and their leaders in the Campbell–Buchanan conflict	695
35.1	General pragmatics, pragmalinguistics and sociopragmatics	760

Tables

2.1	Levels of context in pragmatic description	page 26
16.1	Instantiations of the first-order versus second-order distinction in politeness research	321
21.1	Main findings of sociopragmatic research on gesture and prosody	446
25.1	Argumentation strategies in expert–lay talk shows	529
25.2	Ordinary and 'new ordinary people'	529
25.3	A typology of situations in which English legal language is used	532
30.1	All the concordance lines of *do you know what I mean* in NMMC	642
30.2	Collocates to the left of *why don't you* in CANCODE	643
30.3	Frequency of variations of *(do) you know/see what I mean*	648
30.4	Gesture phases co-occur with the MWEs as checking understanding	654
30.5	Gesture types co-occurring with the MWEs as a combination of checking understanding and discourse marker	655
30.6	Gesture types co-occurring with the MWEs as a discourse marker	656
34.1	Parameters for analysing social activities	736

Contributors

Svenja Adolphs, *University of Nottingham, UK*
Laura Alba-Juez, *UNED, Spain*
Dawn Archer, *Manchester Metropolitan University, UK*
Robert B. Arundale, *University of Alaska, Fairbanks, USA*
Anne Barron, *Leuphana University of Lüneburg, Germany*
Diana Boxer, *University of Florida, USA*
Lucien Brown, *Monash University, Australia*
Yaoyao Chen, *Macau University of Science and Technology, Macau*
Rebecca Clift, *University of Essex, UK*
Florencia Cortés-Conde, *Goucher College, USA*
Jonathan Culpeper, *Lancaster University, UK*
Shelley Dawson, *Victoria University of Wellington, New Zealand*
Arnulf Deppermann, *Leibniz-Institut für Deutsche Sprache, Germany*
Marta Dynel, *University of Łódź, Poland*
Chi-Hé Elder, *University of East Anglia, UK*
J. César Félix-Brasdefer, *Indiana University, USA*
Anita Fetzer, *University of Augsburg, Germany*
Pilar Garcés-Conejos Blitvich, *University of North Carolina, USA*
Alexandra Georgakopoulou, *King's College London, UK*
Sage L. Graham, *University of Memphis, USA*
Michael Haugh, *University of Queensland, Australia*
Elizabeth Holt, *University of Huddersfield, UK*
Juliane House, *University of Hamburg, Germany*
Sachiko Ide, *Japan Women's University, Japan*
Elly Ifantidou, *National and Kapodistrian University of Athens, Greece*
Piotr Jagodziński, *Manchester Metropolitan University, UK*
Rebecca Jagodzińska, *Lancaster University, UK*
Andreas H. Jucker, *University of Zurich, Switzerland*
Dániel Z. Kádár, *Hungarian Research Institute for Linguistics, Hungary / Dalian University of Foreign Studies, China*

Istvan Kecskes, *State University of New York, Albany, USA*
Michiel Leezenberg, *University of Amsterdam, The Netherlands*
Magdalena Leitner, *University of Zurich, Switzerland*
Miriam A. Locher, *University of Basel, Switzerland*
Rosina Márquez Reiter, *Open University, UK*
Meredith Marra, *Victoria University of Wellington, New Zealand*
Troy McConachy, *University of Warwick, UK*
Jim O'Driscoll, *University of Huddersfield, UK*
Pilar Prieto, *ICREA-Pompeu Fabra University, Catalonia, Spain*
Mirka Rauniomaa, *University of Oulu, Finland*
Scott Saft, *University of Hawai'i, USA*
Klaus P. Schneider, *Bonn University, Germany*
Maria Sifianou, *National and Kapodistrian University of Athens, Greece*
Valeria Sinkeviciute, *University of Queensland, Australia*
Maarit Siromaa, *University of Oulu, Finland*
Helen Spencer-Oatey, *University of Warwick, UK*
Marina Terkourafi, *Leiden University, The Netherlands*
Angeliki Tzanne, *National and Kapodistrian University of Athens, Greece*
Kishiko Ueno, *Tokyo City University, Japan*
Jef Verschueren, *University of Antwerp, Belgium*
Iwona Witczak-Plisiecka, *University of Łódź, Poland*
Chaoqun Xie, *Zhejiang International Studies University, China*
Francisco Yus, *University of Alicante, Spain*

Acknowledgements

We would like to sincerely thank all the reviewers of chapters in the volume, who helped us and the authors immeasurably. Our thanks also go to Valeria Sinkeviciute and Nathaniel Mitchell, who both contributed editorial assistance at various stages of this project, and to our Editor Helen Barton for her unwavering support and encouragement that helped us see the project through to completion. Finally, we would like to acknowledge a grant from the Chiang Ching-kuo Foundation (RG029-P-25) that supported work by the first editor on this volume, and a Hungarian Academy of Sciences Momentum (Lendület) Research Grant (LP2017/5) that supported work by the second editor.

1

Introduction

Directions in Sociopragmatics

Michael Haugh, Dániel Z. Kádár and Marina Terkourafi

1.1 The Genesis of the Present Handbook

Pragmatics is generally defined as the study of the *use* of language. It is a rapidly growing field that is associated with numerous international conferences, more than a dozen specialist journals, and a number of book series with international publishers. It is thus not surprising that there are already a number of one-volume handbooks of pragmatics on the market, as well as two well-established handbook series.[1] What is perhaps surprising, however, is that in the case of one-volume handbooks of pragmatics, topics in linguistic and cognitive pragmatics still seem to predominate. The apparent preference for such topics in single-volume handbooks can be explained, in part, by the philosophical origins of pragmatics as a discipline in the 1970s. Pragmatics as a field, however, has expanded significantly beyond those origins.

This was recognized early on by Leech (1983) and Thomas (1983), who proposed a distinction be made between *pragmalinguistics* (the study of the meanings conveyed by different linguistic forms and strategies) and *sociopragmatics* (the study of users' perceptions of the contextual factors, including perceived sociocultural norms, underlying the interpretation and performance of communicative acts as (in)appropriate). Both of these areas typically address topics, such as implicature, speech acts, deixis, politeness and so on, albeit from a more cognitive, linguistic or social perspective. The latter, however, adds further topics to the mix, including face, relationships, identities, power, emotion, stance and humour, to mention but few. A glance through recent issues of leading journals in the field shows that many of the articles published are concerned with topics from this second

---

[1] The latter include the *Handbook of Pragmatics Online* published by John Benjamins (ed. by Östman and Verschueren, since 1995) and the *Handbooks of Pragmatics* series published by Mouton de Gruyter (ed. by Bublitz et al., since 2011).

set suggesting that they are active loci of research in which students should also be trained. Yet, questions of linguistic and cognitive pragmatics have generally received the lion's share of attention in previous handbooks.[2]

In making this point we are in no way intending to diminish the valuable contribution that the currently available handbooks of pragmatics have made to the field. They are important and clearly vital for advancing debate and understanding pragmatics scholarship. There is, however, in our view, also room for further elaboration of other topics that figure prominently in pragmatics research. Indeed, this handbook was conceived to complement the coverage of linguistic and cognitive aspects of pragmatics in the previously published *Cambridge Handbook of Pragmatics* (Allan and Jasczcolt 2012). We thus initially started out by identifying areas of pragmatics that we felt had not received enough attention in extant handbooks of pragmatics. In other words, we started out with a 'negative' definition of sociopragmatics as areas of pragmatics that were *not* covered in previous handbooks. However, it quickly became apparent to us that approaching the design of the handbook in this way could only get us so far. A different approach was needed.

A handbook can attempt to do two things. It can represent an attempt to systematize a field and lay out key elements of its orthodoxy. The aim is to organize and define the field in question. Alternatively, a handbook can represent an attempt to chart out a field of inquiry in order to stimulate further dialogue and showcase its richness. The aim in the latter case is thus not to codify or prescribe, but rather to lay out the various directions in which a field has been developing. This handbook falls clearly into this second camp. Our goal with it has been to map the territory occupied by sociopragmatics, a field which has been developing a distinct identity in its own right 'in the wild', so to speak. That said, charting the boundaries – or, rather, the outer edges – of a field is also a work in progress. As the field continues to grow, we expect that new topics will be added to it. We therefore caution that this is only a first attempt at representing the richness of sociopragmatic research and, indeed, welcome future works that will expand the field in new, possibly unanticipated directions.

In the following section, we move to consider more carefully the scope of sociopragmatics, and how it can be framed in different, albeit largely complementary ways. We then offer, in Section 3, an overview of the contents of the handbook proper, explaining how we have brought together a range of different research areas, topics and approaches under the

---

[2] In the most extreme case, there is not one single chapter devoted to topics in sociopragmatics (Horn and Ward 2004), something which generated some controversy at the time (Mey 2005). But even when there have been attempts to strike some kind of balance, chapters focusing on topics in sociopragmatics remain few and far between. For example, in Allan and Jaszczolt (2012) there are just two chapters out of 31 that deal directly with issues in sociopragmatics, while in Huang (2017) only four chapters out of 30 focus on sociopragmatics. There is greater balance in Barron et al. (2017), but the depth of coverage of sociopragmatics is limited due to the sheer breadth of topics in pragmatics a general handbook needs to cover.

umbrella of 'sociopragmatics'. We conclude with a brief discussion of the place of sociopragmatics with respect to the broader field of pragmatics.

1.2 The Scope of Sociopragmatics

This volume is, to our knowledge, the first handbook of sociopragmatics. However, since our aim has not been to codify or prescribe, but rather to chart existing and new directions, we have taken a broadly inclusive and open-ended approach to what we consider sociopragmatics to be. Some of the chapters in this handbook offer explicit definitions of sociopragmatics, others do so only implicitly, remaining largely tacit on the matter. Our preference is for an organic, bottom-up conceptualization of the field to emerge through researchers engaging with this collection of chapters, rather than trying to advocate for a one-size-fits-all definition of sociopragmatics. This preference is also rooted in the observation that, while there is clearly an overall direction in which the field is moving, different shades and nuances emerge when one starts to consider seriously the scope of 'sociopragmatics' – what the field encompasses and its theoretical and methodological underpinnings.

One way of scoping out sociopragmatics is to examine its disciplinary antecedents. The roots of pragmatics generally lie in the work of ordinary language philosophers (Austin, Grice, Searle, and the later Wittgenstein) and attempts to theorize the abstract, context-general principles by which we use language to mean and do things in the world. Attention to the role of social variables with respect to the operation of such principles featured very early on in this work as well (e.g. Austin [1962] 1975; Brown and Gilman 1960; Lakoff 1973; Leech 1977). This places sociopragmatics at the intersection of linguistic and social concerns, which can be approached from multiple perspectives, as shown in Figure 1.1.

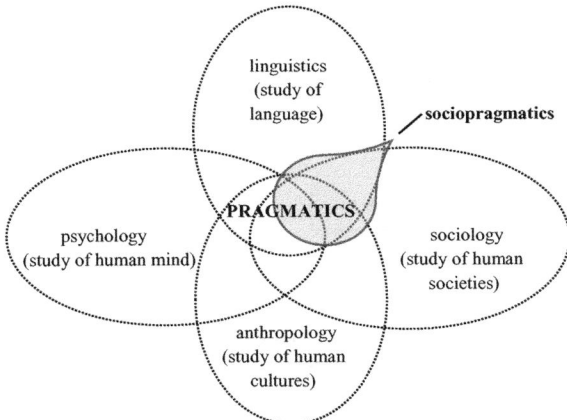

Figure 1.1 Sociopragmatics at the intersection of linguistics and sociology. Adapted from Haugh and Culpeper (2018: 220).

From this very broad perspective, sociopragmatics focuses on the role of social conditions and variables in determining the use of language to mean and do things in the world. It thus lies at the intersection of linguistics and sociology, a space also traditionally occupied by sociolinguistics, while also taking in aspects of anthropology and (social) psychology.

A first pass at delimiting the scope of this rather broad conceptualization of sociopragmatics is to follow the original distinction between pragmalinguistics and sociopragmatics as distinct avenues of research, which fall under, but are somewhat separate from, general pragmatics, as argued by Leech (1983). On this view, pragmalinguistics examines the relationship between forms and the meanings they can express, while sociopragmatics examines the distribution of form/meaning pairs in different contexts and the extent to which they are appropriate to those contexts. The latter is most closely aligned with sociology, as represented in Figure 1.2, echoing the view of sociopragmatics as lying at the intersection of linguistics and sociology we saw in Figure 1.1.

As the account of sociopragmatics developed by Leech (1983) and Thomas (1983) is arguably rather under-developed, particularly with respect to the role of culture in the production and interpretation of pragmatic meanings (Chapter 2), an important goal of the present handbook is to flesh this out more fully and offer grounds to develop this further. This has already been done in some quarters of sociopragmatics, particularly in cross-cultural and intercultural pragmatics (Chapter 34) and second language or interlanguage pragmatics (Chapter 35).

A second view is to regard sociopragmatics as arising from a fusion between (classical) pragmatics and (classical) sociolinguistics, as represented in Figure 1.3. Holmes (2018) most clearly articulates this view. She describes pragmatics as involving the study of the use of language in context, specifically, "how individuals use linguistic resources to produce and interpret meaning in interaction, and sometimes to change relationships" (11). Sociolinguistics, on the other hand, involves the study of

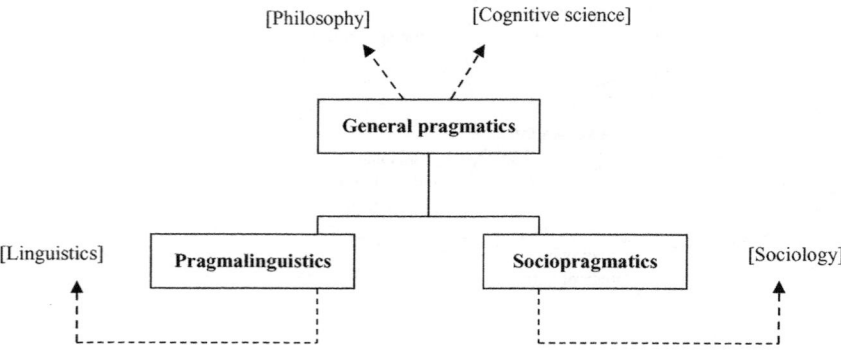

Figure 1.2 General pragmatics, pragmalinguistics and sociopragmatics. Adapted from Leech (1983: 11).

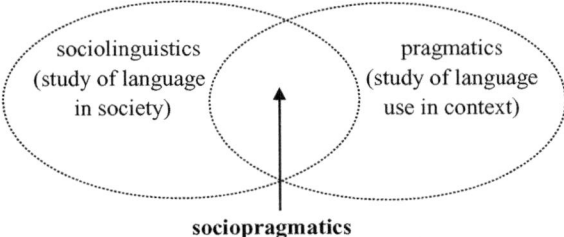

Figure 1.3 Sociopragmatics at the intersection of sociolinguistics and pragmatics.

language in society, resulting in descriptions of variation in the linguistic resources available in speech communities, and "systematic accounts of how social variables influence linguistic choices from among those resources" (Holmes 2018: 11). On this view, sociopragmatics involves "identifying and analysing evidence for societal norms and how they are subscribed to and contested" (Holmes 2018: 15).

This view draws particular attention to the importance of norms and interaction, in addition to the already well-attested focus on users and the social dimension of language use seen in the two approaches above. This approach also tends to privilege discourse analytic approaches, such as interactional sociolinguistics.

A final possibility is to take our lead from published articles and volumes over the past couple of decades and present a bottom-up view of what sociopragmatics encompasses based on what people have analysed. This leads us to adopt, in this handbook, social, interactional and normative dimensions of language use as the three key anchors of sociopragmatic research.

A focus on the social side of pragmatics, in contrast to its linguistic side, means we are interested in speakers first and utterances second. This means engaging with the subjectivities, social identities and individual positionings of speakers as they arise in interaction with others: speakers are not treated as isolated individuals (as they might in a processing account of individual cognition), but as members of various groups, with those membership(s) being attested and contested in interaction. It also means examining the intersection of language and sociocultural phenomena, that is, teasing out the processes by which language use impacts on and interfaces with the social world. There are, of course, significant differences in the ways in which the "social" (or sociocultural) is theorized and operationalized in sociopragmatic research. For instance, a sociolinguistic view of the social dimension of language use tends to focus on social and cultural variables (Labov 1966; Chapter 10), while a sociological view tends to conceptualize it through the lens of the social or moral order (Goffman 1969; Garfinkel 1967; see also Chapter 19).

A focus on interaction means we are interested in discourse first and utterances second. The primary aim is to examine the production and interpretation of meaning in situated contexts, and the choices of speakers and recipients in the accomplishment of those meanings. The emphasis is on both local and meso-level contexts (i.e. what are variously called activity types, speech events, genres and so on – see Chapter 11). There are, of course, significant differences in the ways in which "interaction" is theorized and operationalized in sociopragmatic research. For instance, a discourse analytic view tends to focus on the indexical properties of interaction (Silverstein 1976), while a conversation analytic view emphasizes the sequential properties of interaction (Sacks et al. 1974). As Arundale (Chapter 14) notes, different views of interaction impact the ways in which social elements of language use, such as relationships, are conceptualized. For this reason, it is difficult to analyse social dimensions of language use without considering interactional aspects, and vice versa.

Finally, a focus on the normative side of pragmatics draws attention to the ways in which language use is both constituted through and constitutive of norms, that is, common or preferred ways of using language. A key focus in sociopragmatics is on evaluation and issues of '(in)-appropriateness' or '(un)acceptability' of certain forms of interactional behaviour within and across groups, as well as on the maintenance, exploitation and contestation of those norms within and across groups. Once again there are, of course, significant differences in the ways in which "norms" are theorized and operationalized in sociopragmatic research. For instance, in some approaches the focus is primarily on statistical norms, that is, examining what is most frequently done, or what are also variously called empirical or descriptive norms of language use. In other approaches, the focus is primarily on moral norms, that is, examining how people talk about what should be done, or what are also variously called injunctive or prescriptive norms (Deutsch and Gerard 1955). A mark of sociopragmatic research is that it attempts to elucidate the relationship between the two (see also Chapters 9 and 16), and for this reason it is difficult to analyse social and interactional dimensions of language use without also considering its normative dimensions, and vice versa.

The view of sociopragmatics we have sketched above is represented in Figure 1.4. We caution that this representation is intended to be neither exhaustive nor prescriptive. Instead, our aim is simply to draw attention to some common threads that can be found across research in sociopragmatics to date. We also note that these three anchors of sociopragmatics are broadly compatible with the two main approaches to delimiting sociopragmatics we discussed earlier in this section. This is important because all of these understandings of sociopragmatics are represented across the chapters in this volume.

We hasten to add that this emphasis on analytical anchors, and the fact that there is no one grand theory of sociopragmatics, should not be taken to mean that the field itself is atheoretical. Nevertheless, we do see a need for

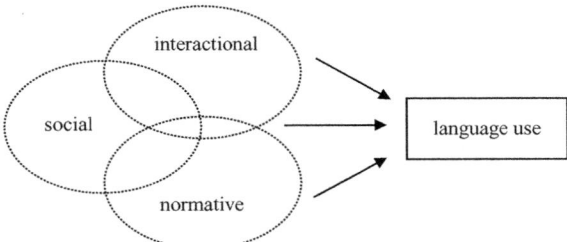

Figure 1.4 Key anchors of sociopragmatics.

more explicit theorization in sociopragmatics. As the discussion above suggests, and the chapters in this volume attest, many theoretical developments in sociopragmatics have built on concepts and theories borrowed from cognate disciplines. Perhaps the time is now ripe to move from empirical studies to theorization, developing theories which build on other areas but nevertheless address the three key anchors of sociopragmatics we highlight here, thus treating sociopragmatics as an area requiring theorization in its own right.

Drawing attention to the social, interactional and normative ends of pragmatics also makes more pronounced the need to extend our research in pragmatics to a much greater range of languages than has traditionally been the case. There are more than 6,000 languages spoken in the world, although many of these are currently endangered. By extending sociopragmatics research to a broader range of the world's languages we can test the theoretical and conceptual apparatus that has been developed, contributing to our understanding of not only what makes each language and culture unique, but importantly what also lies in common and ultimately unites us all.

1.3 Overview

This handbook is aimed at both students who have studied linguistics or pragmatics and need an up-to-date account of the field, as well as researchers wishing to gain an advanced overview of different areas within sociopragmatics. The contributors, who were all chosen for their specific expertise and contributions to sociopragmatics, were asked to provide accessible summaries of key concepts, issues and ongoing research on significant areas within sociopragmatics. Many of the chapters also feature original case studies that illustrate how one can undertake research in sociopragmatics. As the purpose of this handbook is to showcase research and directions in sociopragmatics, it is expected that readers will not necessarily review the book from cover to cover, but will rather consult specific chapters depending on their needs and areas of interest. Efforts have therefore been made to cross-reference other chapters where relevant in order to guide readers and assist them in expanding their knowledge of the field.

The handbook is divided into three parts: "Fundamentals" (Part I), "Topics and Settings" (Part II) and "Approaches and Methods" (Part III). Notably, while some of the chapters cover areas that are highly developed, and so involve summarizing a fairly large extant literature in a way that speaks to the specific concerns of sociopragmatics (e.g. implicature, politeness and impoliteness, cross-cultural pragmatics), other chapters break new ground, identifying gaps and areas that are ripe for further study (e.g. affect and emotion, morality, CA and sociopragmatics). In both cases, however, the emphasis is on illustrating key concepts and issues through data, exemplifying the significant emphasis that is placed on empirical analysis in the field.

Part I, "Fundamentals", offers coverage of some of the key theoretical and conceptual tools drawn upon in sociopragmatic analyses. The emphasis in this part is on introducing these concepts, while the next two parts exemplify their application to the study of particular phenomena and settings. Both foundational notions in pragmatics (inference and implicature, speaker's meaning, speech acts and social actions, conventions), as well as notions originally developed in other disciplines including sociology (footing), anthropology (reflexivity), and sociolinguistics (communities of practice, stance), are featured in this part, highlighting from the outset the interdisciplinary origins of the field. At the same time, their relevance to sociopragmatics is highlighted through case studies that are intended to show how these concepts can be put to use as tools for sociopragmatic research. Although most of the examples are drawn from (varieties of) English, examples from other languages, such as German and Finnish, are also discussed, setting the tone for the description of multiple varieties and languages, a thread that runs throughout this handbook. Indeed, as we observed earlier, we see the presence of multiple varieties and languages as serving not only a descriptive but also a theoretical goal in sociopragmatics, as it can serve to propel theory development in the field. As such, it has been our distinct goal in this handbook to be inclusive, not only with respect to theoretical and topical perspectives, but also with respect to the languages and language varieties represented.

The topics covered in Part II of this handbook are centred on the interactional formation and negotiation of interpersonal relationships, an area that has continued to remain at the forefront of sociopragmatic research over many decades. The "interpersonal" focus of sociopragmatics (Leech 1983: 79) traditionally consists of research on either types of interpersonal behaviour, such as politeness and humour, or on socio-psychological and societal factors that both underpin and are accomplished through interpersonal behaviour, such as identity and face. Part II, "Topics and Settings", brings this research together by addressing (1) key topics in sociopragmatics, spanning (im)politeness and humour through to morality and power; and (2) key settings of sociopragmatic research, spanning digitally mediated and multimodal forms of communication through to workplaces, service encounters and discourse in translation. Although the chapters in this part include well-studied topics, such as face and (im)-politeness, and less-studied ones (at least from a sociopragmatics angle), such as emotion, morality and power, we are well aware that the current selection is far from exhaustive. Indeed, it could not be, as researchers continue to approach new topics from a sociopragmatic angle on a regular basis. Our goal here was on achieving representativeness rather than exhaustiveness. Our selection of key settings thus focuses on the most popular and widely studied contexts of sociopragmatic research to date, including multimodal communication, digitally-mediated communication, workplace and institutional discourse, service encounters and discourse, argumentative, political and legal discourse, and discourse in translation. What makes research on these settings particularly relevant to the reader, in our view, is their relevance for our ordinary lives. Along with English, the examples and analyses in this part draw on various other languages, including Arabic, Chinese, Korean and Spanish. As noted earlier, this demonstrates a long-term aspiration of the field to describe the sociopragmatics of languages around the world.

The final part of the handbook, Part III, "Approaches and Methods", features a number of key areas that contribute to sociopragmatics, spanning well-established ones, such as second language pragmatics and cross-cultural/intercultural pragmatics through to emerging ones, such as CA-informed sociopragmatics and corpus sociopragmatics. Many of these represent areas of research in their own right, with their own distinct sets of methods and theoretical commitments. In other words, we are not seeing these necessarily as sub-fields of sociopragmatics, but rather as areas that make important contributions to the range of research approaches and methods that are used in sociopragmatics. These range from an explicit commitment to the use of multiple methods (e.g. interpersonal pragmatics; historical sociopragmatics; variational pragmatics), through to a commitment to a particular, clearly circumscribed set of methods (e.g. corpus pragmatics; CA), although a common touch point in terms of methodology across these different approaches is the frequent use of various forms of discourse analysis. Other chapters also draw attention to the need to broaden the scope of sociopragmatics, to be inclusive of different cultural perspectives (e.g. emancipatory pragmatics; cross-cultural and intercultural pragmatics). Overall, the chapters in this part collectively demonstrate the wide range of approaches and methods that are drawn upon in sociopragmatics research, which, once again, draws attention to the necessarily interdisciplinary theoretical and methodological outlook of the field.

We admit, however, that while we have aimed to be inclusive and open-ended in our coverage, this is not necessarily complete. We have only been able to include passing reference to important topics or approaches that are potentially relevant to sociopragmatics, such as social cognition or ethnopragmatics, while other areas that we think are of considerable importance, such as the sociopragmatics of endangered languages, still remain to be adequately charted, and so were not included. In the end, some hard choices had to be made in order to keep the overall length of the volume manageable. We anticipate that in future handbooks, the new directions currently being developed will inevitably result in new topics, settings and approaches also being explored. We look forward to seeing those seeds come to fruition.

1.4 Closing Thoughts

The present handbook began as an attempt to address what we felt to be a significant gap in relation to the coverage of topics in extant handbooks of pragmatics, especially when viewed against the background of research published in this field. However, we would like to stress that, while naming a field through the development of a handbook can inadvertently emphasize points of difference over points of commonality, we are all interested in language use. As such, our view is that more, not less, dialogue with researchers in linguistic and cognitive pragmatics is what is needed. Pragmatics involves not only social, but also cognitive and linguistic perspectives on language use. The superordinate field of pragmatics will only progress when we find ways to bring these perspectives together (perhaps in new ways). Bringing together different disciplinary perspectives in productive ways inevitably begins from mutual understanding. In articulating what is encompassed by sociopragmatics through this handbook, and complementing previous handbooks that cover the more linguistic and cognitive end of pragmatics, we are attempting to put in place solid grounds for such dialogue to proceed. By the time our task was completed, we felt ourselves that we had learnt a lot from bringing together the various strands of research in sociopragmatics under a single 'home'. We hope that readers of this volume will share in this feeling and that this handbook will offer much needed coherence to this corner of pragmatics, as well as push the field forward through the contributions of leading scholars featured in its pages.

References

Allan, K. and Jaszczolt, K. M. (eds.). (2012). *The Cambridge Handbook of Pragmatics*. Cambridge: Cambridge University Press.

Austin, J. L. ([1962] 1975). *How to Do Things with Words*. 2nd ed. Edited by J. O. Urmson and M. Sbisà. Cambridge, MA: Harvard University Press.

Barron, A., Grundy, P. and Gu, Y. (eds.). (2017). *The Routledge Handbook of Pragmatics*. London: Routledge.

Brown, R. and Gilman, A. (1960). The pronouns of power and solidarity. In T. A. Sebeok, ed., *Style in Language*. Cambridge, MA: MIT Press, pp. 253–76.

Brown, P. and Levinson, S. C. (1987). *Politeness: Some Universals in Language Usage*. Cambridge: Cambridge University Press.

Bublitz, W., Jucker, A. H. and Schneider, K. P. (eds.). (2011–). *Mouton Handbooks in Pragmatics*. Berlin: Mouton de Gruyter.

Deutsch, M. and Gerard, H. (1955). A study of normative and informational social influences upon individual judgment. *The Journal of Abnormal and Social Psychology, 51*, 629–36.

Garfinkel, H. (1967). *Studies in Ethnomethdology*. Englewood Cliffs, NJ: Prentice Hall.

Goffman, E. (1969). *The Presentation of Self in Everyday Life*. New York: Doubleday.

Haugh, M. and Culpeper, J. (2018). Integrative pragmatics and (im)politeness theory. In C. Ilie and N. R. Norrick, eds., *Pragmatics and Its Interfaces*. Amsterdam: John Benjamins, pp. 213–39.

Haugh, M., Kadar, D. and Mills, S. (2013). Interpersonal pragmatics: Issues and debates. *Journal of Pragmatics, 58*, 1–11.

Holmes, J. (2018). Sociolinguistics vs. pragmatics. In C. Ilie and N. R. Norrick, eds., *Pragmatics and Its Interfaces*. Amsterdam: John Benjamins, pp. 11–32.

Horn, L. and Ward, G. (eds.). (2004). *Handbook of Pragmatics*. Oxford: Blackwell.

Huang, Yan (ed.). (2017). *The Oxford Handbook of Pragmatics*. Oxford: Oxford University Press.

Labov, W. (1966). *The Social Stratification of English in New York City*. Cambridge: Cambridge University Press.

Lakoff, R. (1973). The logic of politeness; or, minding your p's and q's'. *Papers from the Ninth Regional Meeting of the Chicago Linguistic Society, 8*, 292–305.

Leech, G. (1977). Language and tact (Series A, Paper No. 46). Linguistic Agency University of Trier.

Leech, G. (1983). *Principles of Pragmatics*. London: Longman.

Marmaridou, S. (2011). Pragmalinguistics and sociopragmatics. In W. Bublitz and N. R. Norrick, eds., *Foundations of Pragmatics*. Berlin: Mouton de Gruyter, pp. 77–106.

Mey, J. (2005). What is in a (hand)book? Reflections on a recent compilation: Review of Horn, R. Laurence and G. Ward (eds.), The handbook of pragmatics. *Intercultural Pragmatics, 2*, 347–58.

Mey, J. L. (2012). Societal pragmatics. In C. A. Chapelle, ed., *The Encyclopedia of Applied Linguistics*. Chichester: John Wiley, pp. 1–6.

Östman, J.-O. and Verschueren, J. (1995–). *Handbook of Pragmatics Online*. Amsterdam: John Benjamins.

Sacks, H., Schegloff, E. and Jefferson, G. (1974). A simplest systematics for the organization of turn-taking for conversation. *Language, 50,* 696–735.

Silverstein, M. (1976). Shifters, linguistic categories and cultural description. In K. Basso, H. Selby and A. Henry, eds., *Meaning in Anthropology.* Albuquerque: University of New Mexico Press, pp. 11–55.

Thomas, J. (1983). Cross-cultural pragmatic failure. *Applied Linguistics,* 4(2), 91–112.

Part I
Fundamentals of Sociopragmatics

2

Sociopragmatics

Roots and Definition

Jonathan Culpeper

2.1 Introduction

What one thinks sociopragmatics is depends on what one thinks pragmatics is. There are, of course, multifarious views on what constitutes the latter. As a starting point, Section 2.2 airs some of these views and considers where sociopragmatics might sit within them. The foundations of sociopragmatics, as it is usually understood today, are usually deemed to be in the work of Geoffrey N. Leech (e.g. 1983) and Jenny Thomas (e.g. 1981, 1983). This chapter does not deviate from this view. However, it is intriguing to consider whether there might be elements associated with sociopragmatics in foundational pragmatics works. Consequently, Section 2.3, on the foundations of sociopragmatics, begins with a glance at J. L. Austin's ([1962] 1975) work on speech acts. The bulk of that section is devoted to the important distinction made between pragmalinguistics and sociopragmatics. It also notes how that distinction has been adopted as a useful approach in certain sub-fields of pragmatics, including cross-cultural pragmatics, inter-cultural pragmatics and variational pragmatics. Finally, Section 2.4 focuses on context. Leech (1983: 10) states that sociopragmatics deals with 'more specific "local" conditions on language use'. This is an important defining feature of sociopragmatics. But it is inadequately specified – how specific is specific? How local is local? Section 2.4 airs some of the issues and argues that the key level of context for sociopragmatics is somewhere in the middle of the micro–macro continuum.

2.2 Positioning Sociopragmatics in Pragmatics

One well-worn way of viewing pragmatics is in terms of the Continental European view and the Anglo-American view. These geographical labels perhaps give some vague indication of where practitioners of these views are located, but disguise the variety of views held within those locations and have nothing to say about some large swathes of the world that are 'big' in pragmatics, Japan being a particular case in point, yet are neither in Continental Europe, the United Kingdom or the United States. It is better, in my view, to label these the 'broad view' and the 'narrow view'. In the former, pragmatics is conceived as the huge superordinate field, with linguistics a sub-field, along with psychology, sociology and so on. The biennial conferences organized by the International Pragmatics Association reflect the diversity of the broad view. As Verschueren (1999: 7) puts it, pragmatics is a 'general cognitive, social, and cultural perspective on linguistic phenomena in relation to their usage in forms of behaviour'. Note the incorporation of the word 'social'. The key point is that if pragmatics itself is already social, then sociopragmatics, one might argue, is redundant. Much the same could be said of Jacob Mey's (1998: 724) description of pragmatics in the *Concise Encyclopedia of Pragmatics*, where pragmatics is 'societally oriented and societally bound linguistics'. However, in 2010 Mey established the journal *Pragmatics and Society*. How are the contents of this journal distinguished from pragmatics in general? The scope statement states:

> *Pragmatics and Society* puts the spotlight on societal aspects of language use, while incorporating many other facets of society-oriented pragmatic studies.... It is concerned with how language use and social normativity influence and shape each other, for instance, in education (the teaching and acquisition of first and second languages), in political discourse (with its manipulative language use), in the discourse of business, and in all kinds of discriminatory uses of language (gender- and class-based or other) (https://benjamins.com/catalog/ps).

Despite his earlier statement, 'society-oriented pragmatic studies', or societal pragmatics, seems to be distinguished as a sub-group in broader (social) pragmatics by its emphasis on relatively macro social issues, societal practices and values, institutionalized and hegemonic discourses and so on. As Mey (2012: 2) states:

> while 'pragmatics is defined as the study of language in human communication as determined by the conditions of society' (Mey, 2001: 6), societal pragmatics emphasizes the social conditions under which we live and use language, and tries to determine in what specific ways these conditions respectively facilitate or obstruct, indeed, 'make and break', our use of language.

Societal pragmatics is also distinguished by a critical agenda: 'Societal pragmatics sees it as its primary task to "unmask" manipulative use of language' (Mey, 2012: 3). One might wonder: should sociopragmatics be accommodated somewhere on this 'pragmatics to social' dimension? If so, should it be towards the more macro end? Where would the boundary be?

Is it in fact synonymous with societal pragmatics? This issue will be further aired later in this chapter.

A way of approaching the narrow view of pragmatics is to consider Charles Morris' (1938: 6–7) three-way semiotic distinction:

- Syntax (or syntactics) = mono relationship (relationships between linguistic signs)
- Semantics = dyadic relationship (relationships between linguistic signs and the things in the world that they designate)
- Pragmatics = triadic relationship (relationships between linguistic signs, things they designate, and their users/interpreters)

Morris' pragmatics incorporates the same components as syntax and semantics, but in addition connects with users and interpreters – it connects with context. So, pragmatics in this view is a component within a theory of language. This view of pragmatics is exemplified by the papers in Horn and Ward's (2004) *Handbook of Pragmatics*. As one might imagine, the focus is on more formal, philosophical and cognitive aspects. The discussion is of reference, deixis, (in)definiteness, information structure, implicature and inferencing, presupposition, formal aspects of speech act theory, and so on. Context is generally restricted to references to the 'user' or the 'interpreter', their purported intentions, inferential paths and so on. It is most certainly micro in focus. Does this view of pragmatics accommodate sociopragmatics? In their introduction, Horn and Ward (2004: xi) state that they 'largely restricted' their coverage of pragmatics to this narrow view. Despite the length of the volume – 842 pages – sociopragmatics is not mentioned in the index. It is perhaps too 'socio', too macro, to be accommodated.

Thus far, it seems difficult to find the pragmatic space that sociopragmatics inhabits. Part of the problem is that dichotomies such as continental European versus Anglo-American or micro versus macro are not particularly helpful. They are not, of course, the only ways of viewing pragmatics. Culpeper and Haugh (2014) set out to map a middle ground, referring to it as 'integrative pragmatics'. It is characterized by engagement with data (both informing and being informed by data), and a particular focus on interaction (a focus that is partly inspired by Clark 1996 and Thomas 1995). It incorporates both user (first-order) and observer (second-order) perspectives, thus allowing a holistic approach. For example, it could highlight a micro conventionalized formula, but equally how a specific meaning potential emerged in interaction. Slightly more recently, Félix-Brasdefer (2015) articulated a 'pragmatic-discursive approach', which has some similarities to integrative pragmatics. Integrative pragmatics, and pragmatic-discursive pragmatics for that matter, were not designed with sociopragmatics in mind. Nevertheless, as will become clear in the following sections, sociopragmatics could be a happy sibling in the middle ground of pragmatics.

2.3 Sociopragmatics: Foundations

2.3.1 Austin: A Precursor?

The rather thin treatment of J. L. Austin's ([1962] 1975) work on speech acts in Horn and Ward (2004) – a few sections in a couple of chapters – might hint at work that is too social for the micro-pragmatics agenda. His focus was on the 'circumstances' of a particular occasion of use. This is very much part of his notion of felicities, circumstances that must be in place for a speech act to be 'happy'. For example, if I said 'I now pronounce you man and wife' to a random couple on a UK bus, it will fail to have any effect (aside from them thinking I was mad!), because I am not empowered as a priest or registrar to perform a marriage, the context is not appropriate, and so on. This focus on a particular occasion of use is typical of sociopragmatics. Austin (1975: 8, original emphasis) writes:

> Speaking generally, it is always necessary that the *circumstances* in which the words are uttered should be in some way, always, *appropriate*, and it is very commonly necessary that either the speaker himself or other persons should also perform certain *other* actions, whether 'physical' or 'mental' actions or even acts of uttering further words.

Interestingly, as sociopragmatics developed, the idea of being appropriate became associated with sociopragmatics (see Section 2.3.2). Note also in the quotation that Austin accommodates '*other* actions ... uttering further words'. This is very different from John Searle's (e.g. 1969) approach to speech act theory, with its theorizing about single speech acts. For Austin, constellations of actions are at the heart of sociopragmatics. Furthermore, Austin factors in social concepts throughout. Consider two brief examples from Austin (1975:28):

> 'I pick' is only in order when the object of the verb is 'a player', and a command is in order only when the subject of the verb is 'a commander' or 'an authority'.

Picking involves selecting players for a team and illustrates a mapping between the performative and a role in a particular activity; commanding illustrates a mapping between a speech act and a social role with power. Roles, activities, social dimensions, such things are the stuff of sociopragmatics.

Before leaving Austin, it is worth using his words to help clarify why we are talking about socio*pragmatics* and not socio*linguistics*.

> for a procedure to be *accepted* involves more than for it merely to be the case that it is *in fact generally used*, even actually by the persons now concerned; and that it must remain in principle open for anyone to reject any procedure – or code of procedures – even one that he has already hitherto accepted – as may happen with, for example, the code of honour. One who does so is, of course, liable to sanctions; others refuse to play with him or say that he is not a man of honour. (Austin 1975: 29; *original emphasis*)

Austin is discussing a number of things here. One is the difference between acceptability as a morally sanctioned 'ought' (a code of honour is a set of social oughts sustained by a particular community) and regularity of experience (norms of habit) (for further discussion of this, see Culpeper 2011: 33–6). But what I wish to focus on is the possibility of rejecting a procedure. We have a choice, and, having made one choice, we can change to another if we wish. These possibilities allow us to generate pragmatic meanings. In Austin's example, choosing the code of honour and then rejecting it can lead to an interpretation that the person merits sanctions – refusal to engage ('to play with him'), negative identity attributions ('he is not a man of honour'), and so on.

Thomas (1995: 185, original emphasis) makes a parallel point when elaborating on what she sees as the demarcation between sociolinguistics and pragmatics:

> we could say that sociolinguistics is mainly concerned with the systematic linguistic correlates of relatively *fixed* and *stable* social variables (such as region of origin, social class, ethnicity, sex, age) on the way an individual speaks. Pragmatics, on the other hand, is mainly concerned with describing the linguistic correlates of relatively *changeable* features of that same individual (such as relative status, social role) and the way in which the speaker exploits his/her (socio)linguistic repertoire in order to achieve a particular goal.
>
> Sociolinguistics is static, offering a 'snapshot' of the language of a particular community at a particular moment in time. Pragmatics is dynamic, describing what a speaker from that community does with those resources, how he or she uses them to change the way things are or in order to maintain the status quo. Pragmatics is parasitic upon sociolinguistics, taking the sociolinguistic description of an individual's repertoire as a point of departure: sociolinguistics tells us what linguistic resources the individual has, pragmatics tells us what he or she does with it.

Of course, one should remember here that Thomas' work was published in 1995, bringing together research generated in the 1980s, and both fields have developed so that they are closer than they used to be (for a recent discussion of the sociolinguistics-pragmatics interface, see Holmes 2018). Some branches of sociolinguistics, and indeed pragmatics, have changed in response to the development of social constructionist approaches (notably to gender; see e.g. Eckert and McConnell-Ginet 2003) and discursive approaches (notably pioneered in discursive psychology; see e.g. Edwards and Potter 1992). These branches most certainly view language as dynamic; it is their *sine qua non*. Nevertheless, the point is true of much of traditional sociolinguistics, and in particular sociolinguistics of the Labovian kind. It is also true that much of pragmatics focuses on dynamic matters – the way in which meanings shift in tandem with shifts in context, including the ebb and flow of conversation – though not all areas of pragmatics do to the same degree, some areas of formal pragmatics being less dynamic in this sense.

2.3.2 Sociopragmatics and Pragmalinguistics

As Marmaridou (2011) elaborates, the term pragmalinguistics seems to have been used since at least the 1970s for functional aspects of language use. It was not, however, positioned in contrast to sociopragmatics – an important definitional development – until we arrive at the work of Geoffrey N. Leech and Jenny Thomas. Thomas (1981: 13) attributes the notion of 'sociopragmatics' to 'Leech (1981)'. That is, in fact, a prepublication draft of Leech (1983). In turn, Geoffrey Leech (1983: 18n13) attributes the distinction between 'pragmalinguistics' and 'sociopragmatics' to Thomas (1981), an MA thesis supervised by Leech. That attribution could have been an act of generosity and modesty on his part. The detail of who did what is lost in the jointly constructed discourses of supervisor and supervisee. Where Leech has a clearer role is in also positioning pragmalinguistics and sociopragmatics in the field of pragmatics.

Leech (1983: 11) makes the following three-way distinctions:

> *General pragmatics*: 'the general conditions of the communicative use of language';
>
> *Sociopragmatics*:[1] 'more specific "local" conditions on language use'; and
>
> *Pragmalinguistics*: 'the particular resources which a given language provides for conveying particular illocutions'.

These areas are arranged in a diagram (Leech 1983: 11), showing the relationships amongst them. This is reproduced in Figure 2.1, with the addition of 'philosophy' and 'cognitive science' at the top of the diagram.

Note that pragmalinguistics and sociopragmatics are separate from general pragmatics, which is distinguished from the latter by the fact that it 'exclude[s] more specific "local" conditions on language use' (1983: 10). An important issue here is what exactly constitutes '"local" conditions'. We will return to this in Section 2.3.3. Regarding sociopragmatics, Leech (1983: 10) states,

> It is clear that the Cooperative Principle and the Politeness Principle operate variably in different cultures or language communities, in different social situations, among different social classes, etc.... pragmatic descriptions ultimately have to be relative to specific social conditions. In other words, socio-pragmatics is the sociological interface of pragmatics.

---

[1] In his 1983 book, Leech writes 'socio-pragmatics' with a hyphen. In more recent years, it is generally solid.

```
                    [Philosophy]    [Cognitive science]
                           ↖          ↗
                            ╲        ╱
                        ┌─────────────────┐
                        │ General pragmatics │
                        └─────────────────┘
                                │
                    ┌───────────┴───────────┐
[Grammar]   ┌───────────────┐       ┌───────────────┐   [Sociology]
            │ Pragmalinguistics │   │ Sociopragmatics │
   ↑        └───────────────┘       └───────────────┘        ↑
   │                │                         │              │
   └────────────────┘                         └──────────────┘
```

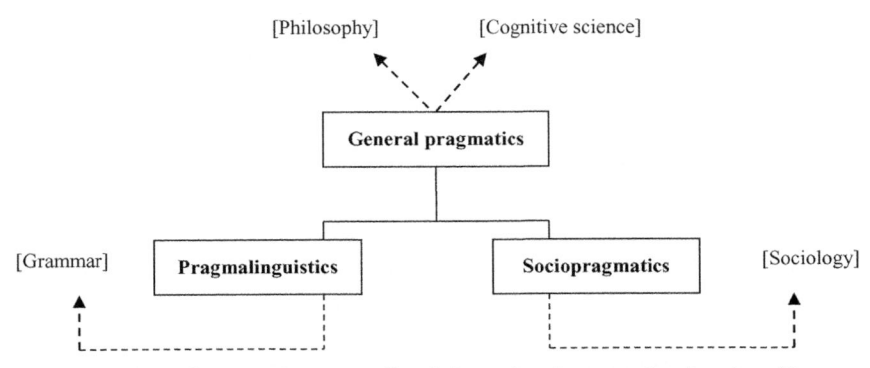

Figure 2.1 General pragmatics, pragmalinguistics and sociopragmatics. Developed from Leech (1983: 11). (Reproduced with permission of Informa UK Ltd through PLSclear)

More recently, Leech (2014: 14), in reference to the pragmatics of politeness, describes sociopragmatics as involving 'the various scales of value that make a particular degree of politeness seem appropriate or normal in a given social setting'. Note the idea of being deemed appropriate. Leech's earlier statement referring to 'language use' (Leech 1983: 10) reflects the pragmatics of that time, which was very much concerned with a speaker-oriented view of pragmatics, that is to say, the speaker making choices in their use of language. In this more recent quotation, we clearly are dealing with understanding and evaluation, things that the hearer does. Leech is not, of course, rejecting his earlier view of sociopragmatics, but rather discussing sociopragmatics in the context of politeness. Nevertheless, the fact that he is now doing this demonstrates that he is attuned to shifts in pragmatics that have reduced the ascendancy of the speaker in the processes of making meaning. Pragmalinguistics, on the other hand, concerns 'such phenomena as the range of the lexico-grammatical resources of the language, their meanings, the degree of pragmaticalization, their frequency, and how they are deployed as linguistic strategies of politeness' (Leech 2014: 14).

General pragmatics relates to the 'general conditions of the communicative use of language' (Leech 1983: 10), and, I would argue, concerns the more philosophical or cognitive sides of pragmatics. The three areas together are viewed by Leech as complementary areas of study within pragmatics as a whole. Of course, just as noted with Thomas (1995) at the end of the previous section, the academic world has changed since the early 1980s. For instance, the field of social cognition, interfacing with cognitive science and sociology, has grown significantly in strength, and can provide input into sociopragmatics (see Chapter 28).

The concepts of pragmalinguistics and sociopragmatics are explored in Thomas' early work dealing with 'pragmatic failure' in the context of cross-cultural pragmatics. According to her:

> while pragmalinguistic failure is basically a *linguistic* problem, caused by differences in the linguistic encoding of pragmatic force, sociopragmatic failure stems from cross-culturally different perceptions of what constitutes appropriate linguistic behaviour. *(Thomas 1983: 99)*

Two points are noteworthy here. One is that sociopragmatics is identified with cultures rather than Leech's '"local" conditions'. I shall discuss both views on the key aspects of context for sociopragmatics in the following section. The other is that the notion of sociopragmatics is seen as a means of identifying (in)appropriate linguistic behaviour. Thomas' work did much to propel sociopragmatics into the fields of cross-cultural pragmatics and inter-language pragmatics. Moreover, in those fields we often find studies investigating what is sociopragmatically appropriate.

Thomas (1983: 104) claims that sociopragmatic issues are 'social before they are linguistic'; and presumably pragmalinguistic issues are linguistic before they are social. However, she states that there is no 'absolute distinction' between them – 'they form a continuum and there is certainly a grey area in the middle' (Thomas 1981: 49). Minimally, Thomas (1981: 50) claims that they are a 'useful heuristic'. Marmaridou (2011: 84) notes that

> Leech's principles of general pragmatics are to be held constant and form the basis, or the ground, against which all other language-and culture-specific pragmatic variables can be studied as distinct figures. This position lends itself to cross-linguistic and cross-cultural comparisons of communicative behaviour with obvious applications for language teaching/learning and testing. Moreover, the distinction proposed within this framework seems compatible with the aims and methods of the study of discourse and historical pragmatics in particular.

The areas of second language pragmatics and cross-cultural pragmatics, and also historical pragmatics, have indeed seen many studies deploy the pragmalinguistic/sociopragmatic distinction (see Chapters 32, 34 and 35). To these areas, we should also add that of variational pragmatics (see Chapter 31). However, it cannot be said that it is a straightforward distinction to make as a methodological approach, even when operating at the apparent extremes of the continuum. Marmaridou (2011: 93–4) elaborates on the difficulty of diagnosing whether a particular area is due to pragmalinguistic or sociopragmatic issues:

> If politeness markers are missing from an utterance, this could be either because the learner does not know these markers, or because she is not aware that these markers should be used in the particular situation. The former indicates pragmalinguistic, whereas the latter sociopragmatic, inadequacy. Therefore, it is difficult to devise a test that would assess pragmalinguistic knowledge to the exclusion of sociopragmatic knowledge, or the reverse. The problem seems more acute when testing

pragmatic strategies, such as indirectness. While the linguistic expressions used to encode indirectness belong to the pragmalinguistic level, the social target to which they are addressed is a sociopragmatic matter.

2.3.3 Sociopragmatics and Context

As already mentioned, Leech (1983: 10) stated that sociopragmatics deals with 'more specific "local" conditions on language use'. 'Specific' here obviously contrasts with the 'general' of general pragmatics. This is of some help in delimiting sociopragmatics. However, it is important to understand it as meaning a specific *occasion* of use and not just the one-off *specifics* of an occasion. A social constructionist or discursive approach might focus on the specifics of an occasion, and how they together construct particular potential for meanings. A sociopragmatic approach might do that too, but would not shy away from encompassing the more general elements that are deployed. Janet Holmes has made this point in a number of publications. She notes that 'the patterns, generalizations, and norms of speech usage which emerge from quantitative analyses provide a crucial framework which informs and illuminates the way in which individual speakers use language' (Holmes 1998: 325). Writing about the sociopragmatic analysis of politeness, Holmes and Schnurr (2005: 122) comment:

> Attention to context, to the community of practice in which people are participating ..., awareness of the dynamic and negotiated nature of interaction, and of the constantly shifting assessments participants make when engaged in talk – these are all considerations which have improved the quality of the socio-pragmatic analysis of politeness.... But there is also a place for generalisation, and for the identification of patterns in linguistic behaviour.

Indeed. Pragmatics is partly about conventions and norms, which can be exploited to generate meanings, and sociopragmatics is no different. All this, one might note, is in tune with a kind of middle-ground pragmatics, as outlined at the end of Section 2.2.

But what of 'local'? 'Local' is a relative notion – how local is local? Here, we return to the micro–macro dimension aired in Section 2.2. Hoye (2006: 25), discussing applications of pragmatics, refers to the micro–macro distinction:

> 'Micro-pragmatics' looks at the day-to-day context of communication between individuals and groups situated in their local contexts. At the same time, local practices need to be seen against the societal backgrounds and institutional settings in which they occur (i.e. 'macro-pragmatics').

Thus, micro-pragmatics is aligned with the local. However, recollect that sociopragmatics is not accommodated within the kind of micro-pragmatics practised in Horn and Ward (2004). Moreover, Hoye (2006: 25) goes on to attribute a particularly narrow remit to the micro and the local:

> With its focus on the sentence/utterance level of discourse, micro-pragmatics is concerned primarily with the local constraints of the immediate context, such as: deixis and the indexing of personal, temporal, and locative features; reference and the textually directed function of anaphora and cataphora; and word order and the sequencing/clustering of particles and their discourse function to modify illocutionary force, to facilitate the management of conversation or to highlight salient parts in a stretch of discourse.

This is certainly narrower than Leech or Thomas would envisage. For example, they would include issues of politeness within sociopragmatics, as indeed Leech (1983) did with his Politeness Principle, but that is not accommodated within the vision of micro-pragmatics articulated immediately above, or for that matter in Horn and Ward (2004).

Thomas' decision to place 'culture' at the heart of the definition of sociopragmatics, and without elaboration, is no less problematic. Is culture a macro contextual notion? It could be. But in fact culture is variable in terms of level of abstraction. Popular cultural labels concern hemispheres (i.e. Eastern/Western), nations, institutions, social groups (e.g. working class), and so on. Moreover, the notion of culture itself offers a definitional nightmare. Cultures are multiple and constantly undergoing change, and people shift in and out of particular cultures (see e.g. Wright 1998; Gudykunst and Kim 2003); they are not reducible to a relatively short list of stable features passed on from generation to generation – something that would reflect an essentialist view.

In my view, some of the above problems can be eased by taking the view that sociopragmatics is most at home in the medial or meso level of context. Various language scholars have suggested three levels of context. For example, Dittmar (1997: 99–100) posits that sociolinguistics falls into 'social dialectology' (i.e. 'variationist sociolinguistics'), 'interactional sociolinguistics' and the 'sociology of language'. Halliday makes a three-way distinction: 'text', 'context of situation' and 'context of culture' (see e.g. Halliday and Hasan, 1989: 44–7). Fairclough (1992: chapter 3), discussing Critical Discourse Analysis, elaborates a 'three-dimensional conception of discourse', comprising 'text' (formal linguistic features), 'discursive practice' (a type of social practice involving the production and interpretation of texts) and 'social practice' (actions relating to social structures, e.g. ideologies, institutions, power relations). From scholars who would think of themselves as contributing to pragmatics, we should mention Levinson (1995) and also Terkourafi (e.g. 2005a). Levinson (1995) proposes three levels or layers of meaning. In between the traditional distinction coded meaning and speaker meaning, he suggests there is utterance-type meaning, that is, stereotypical meaning based on 'general expectations about how language is normally used' (93). The background to this proposal lies in Grice's (1989) distinction between particularized and generalized implicatures. Particularized implicatures are nonce inferences worked out from scratch on the basis of the particular context the utterance appears in; generalized implicatures have a more stable association with particular linguistic forms (cf. Grice 1989: 37). Levinson's contribution was to characterize generalized implicatures as the level of meaning between particularized implicatures and fully conventionalized (non-defeasible) implicatures. One might wonder what all this has to do with sociopragmatics. An early trace of the idea of a third level of meaning can be found in Levinson's work on activity types (examples of which include an interview, lecture, trial, service encounter, chat), a contextual notion that is very much a meso level. According to Levinson (1992: 970), understanding what activity type is involved will 'help to determine how what one says will be "taken" – that is, what kinds of inferences will be made from what is said.' (See also Mooney 2004: 903–5 for a discussion of how activity types can contextualize the workings of the Cooperative Principle.) However, it was Terkourafi (e.g. 2005a) who forged a clear connection with central sociopragmatic concerns, notably, politeness.

Terkourafi (e.g. 2005a) split generalized implicatures into two according to their relationship with context. One sub-category involves implicatures that are weakly context-dependent, requiring a minimal amount of contextual information relating to the social context of use in which the utterance was conventionalized to some degree; the other, as described by Levinson, involves implicatures that are even more weakly context-dependent – their meaning is presumed in a variety of contexts. This gives us the following categories:

Particularized implicature (utterance-token meaning derived in nonce context)	→	Generalized implicature I (utterance-type meaning presumed in minimal context)	→	Generalized implicature II (utterance-type meaning presumed in all contexts *ceteris paribus*)	→	Coded meaning (sentence meaning)

Terkourafi argues that, whilst politeness can involve full inferencing in a nonce context, as leading works on politeness argue (e.g. Brown and Levinson 1987), what lies at its heart is a generalized implicature of the first type given above. Her argument is neatly summarized here (Terkourafi 2005b: 251, original emphasis):

> Politeness is achieved on the basis of a *generalised implicature* when an expression *x* is uttered in a context with which – based on the addressee's previous experience of similar contexts – expression *x* regularly co-occurs. In this case, rather than engaging in full-blown inferencing about the speaker's intention, the addressee draws on that

previous experience (represented holistically as a frame) to derive the proposition that "in uttering expression *x* the speaker is being polite" as a generalised implicature of the speaker's utterance. On the basis of this generalised implicature, the addressee may then come to hold the further belief that the speaker *is* polite.

In all these cases, I would argue that it is the middle area involving the medial or meso level of context that is closest to sociopragmatics. Table 2.1 presents one way of conceiving of different degrees of contextual abstraction in pragmatic description.

Needless to say, these levels do *not* exist in isolation but interact with other levels. Cultures, for example, interact with activity types, which interact with particular speech acts, which in turn interact with particular linguistic forms; in other words, as already noted, there is a sense in which cultures are present at all levels. It is the contextual level represented by activities that is the middle or meso level that is so important for sociopragmatics, not least of all because it acts as a bridge between the micro and the macro. As Linell and Thunqvist (2003: 431), writing about activity types, argue: 'it can be seen as a meso-level concept in providing a link between the micro and macro levels of sociological description, thus working against micro–macro dualism' (cf. Layder 1994). In my view, sociopragmatics should primarily, though not exclusively, concern itself with the medial level of context (or aspects that compose it). It links more micro, linguistically oriented considerations (the typical focus of pragmalinguistics) and more macro, sociologically oriented considerations (the typical focus of, for example, Critical Discourse Studies). The argument about levels and sociopragmatics here is broadly in tune with Holmes' (2018: 28) positioning of sociopragmatics:

> sociopragmatics productively explores the relationship between macro-level sociolinguistics concerns and micro-level interactional sociolinguistic concerns, providing a myriad of new insights into the ways in which individuals are constantly negotiating complex social identities in everyday face-to-face interaction.

Table 2.1 *Levels of context in pragmatic description*

Level of context	Descriptive focus	Associated descriptive concepts
Macro	Sociocultural phenomena across interactions	E.g. ideologies, cultures, nationalities, genders, ages
Meso	Situated interaction	E.g. activity types, frames, genres, discourses, social practices
Micro	Use and interpretation of specific forms	E.g. speech acts, discursive practices
-	Linguistic form	E.g. modal verb, interrogative structure, rising intonation, vowel

Note: Developed from Culpeper et al. (2008: 320).

2.4 Conclusion

In this brief conclusion, I bring together some of the elements discussed in this chapter to propose a possible definition of sociopragmatics:[2]

> Sociopragmatics is positioned on the more social side of pragmatics, standing in contrast to the more linguistic side. It is focussed on the construction and understanding of meanings arising from interactions between language (or other semiotic resources) and socio-cultural phenomena. It is centrally concerned with situated interaction, especially local, meso-level contexts (e.g. frames, activity types, genres). It often considers norms emerging in such contexts, how they are exploited by participants, and how they lead to evaluations of (in)appropriateness.

This is not intended as a radical departure from the original statements of scholars like Leech and Thomas, but instead largely an updating in the light of developments since they wrote. Moreover, it is not intended as a prescriptive definition.

This definition avoids two pitfalls in current understandings of sociopragmatics. It avoids the excessively broad understanding in which sociopragmatics becomes very difficult to distinguish from pragmatics generally, especially if we accept that all pragmatics has a social aspect. It also avoids the broad understanding in which sociopragmatics becomes aligned with macro sociocultural units and takes on a critical agenda (an understanding that would make it difficult to distinguish from Critical Discourse Studies). The phenomena falling under the sociopragmatics espoused in this chapter are not restricted to one method of study. In fact, multi-method studies would provide a more complete picture. For example, corpus methods, adapted for local meso level contexts, could tease out norms; qualitative analyses could describe exploitations of norms; analyses of metalanguage could reveal evaluations of appropriateness; and so on.

References

Austin, J. L. ([1962] 1975). *How to Do Things with Words*. 2nd ed. Edited by J. O. Urmson and M. Sbisà, Cambridge, MA: Harvard University Press.

Bucholtz, M. and Hall, K. (2005). Identity and interaction: A socio-cultural linguistic approach. *Discourse Studies*, 7(4/5), 585–614.

Brown, P. and Levinson, S. C. (1987). *Politeness: Some Universals in Language Usage*. Cambridge: Cambridge University Press

Clark, H. H. (1996). *Using Language*. Cambridge: Cambridge University Press.

---

[2] I proposed a definition of sociopragmatics in Culpeper (2010). This is compatible with what I said there but considerably expanded.

Culpeper, J. (2010). Historical sociopragmatics. In A. H. Jucker and I. Taavistainen, eds., *Historical Pragmatics*. Vol. 5 of *Handbooks of Pragmatics*. Berlin: Mouton de Gruyter, pp. 69–96.

Culpeper, J. (2011). *Impoliteness: Using Language to Cause Offence*. Cambridge: Cambridge University Press.

Culpeper, J., Crawshaw, R. and Harrison, J. (2008). 'Activity types' and 'discourse types': Mediating 'advice' in interactions between foreign language assistants and their supervisors in schools in France and England. *Multilingua*, 27, 297–324.

Culpeper, J. and Haugh, M. (2014). *Pragmatics and the English Language*. Basingstoke, UK: Palgrave Macmillan.

Dittmar, N. (1997). *Grundlagen der Soziolinguisti*. Tübingen: Max Niemeyer Verlag.

Eckert, P. and McConnell-Ginet, S. (2003). *Language and Gender*. Cambridge: Cambridge University Press.

Edwards, D. and Potter, J. (1992). *Discursive Psychology*. London: Sage.

Fairclough, N. (1992). *Discourse and Social Change*. Cambridge: Polity Press.

Félix-Brasdefer, J. C. (2015). *The Language of Service Encounters: A Pragmatic-Discursive Approach*, Cambridge: Cambridge University Press.

Grice, H. P (1989). *Studies in the Way of Words*. Cambridge, MA: Harvard University Press.

Gudykunst, W. B. and Young, Y. K. (2003). *Communicating with Strangers*. 4th ed. New York: McGraw-Hill.

Halliday, M. A. K. and Hasan, R. (1989). *Language, Context, and Text: Aspects of Language in a Social-Semiotic Perspective*. Oxford: Oxford University Press.

Holmes, J. (1998). Women's role in language change: A place for quantification. In N. Warner, J. Ahlers, L. Bilmes, M. Oliver, S. Wertheim and M. Chen, eds., *Gender and Belief Systems: Proceedings of the Fourth Berkeley Women and Language Conference, 1996*. Berkeley: Berkeley Women and Language Group, pp. 313–30.

Holmes, J. (2018). Sociolinguistics vs. pragmatics. In C. Ilie and N. R. Norrick, eds., *Pragmatics and Its Interfaces*. Amsterdam: John Benjamins, pp. 11–32.

Holmes, J. and Schnurr, S. (2005). Politeness, humor and gender in the workplace: Negotiating norms and identifying contestation. *Journal of Politeness Research*, 1(1), 121–49.

Horn, L. and Ward, G. (eds.). (2004). *Handbook of Pragmatics*. Oxford: Blackwell.

Hoye, L. F. (2006). Applying pragmatics. In J. L. Mey, ed., *Concise Encyclopedia of Pragmatics*. Amsterdam: Elsevier, pp. 24–7.

Layder, D. (1994). *Understanding Social Theory*. London: Sage.

Leech, G. N. (1983). *Principles of Pragmatics*. London: Longman.

Leech, G. N. (2014). *The Pragmatics of Politeness*. Oxford: Oxford University Press.

Levinson, S. C. ([1979] 1992). Activity types and language. In P. Drew and J. Heritage, eds., *Talk at Work: Interaction in Institutional Settings*. Cambridge: Cambridge University Press, pp. 66–100.

Levinson, S. C. (1995). Three levels of meaning. In F. R. Palmer, ed., *Grammar and Meaning: Essays in Honour of John Lyons*. Cambridge: Cambridge University Press, pp. 90–115.

Linell, P. and Thunqvist, D. P. (2003). Moving in and out of framings: Activity contexts in talks with young unemployed people within a training project. *Journal of Pragmatics, 35*, 409–34.

Marmaridou, S. (2011). Pragmalinguistics and sociopragmatics. In W. Bublitz and N. R. Norrick, eds., *Foundations of Pragmatics*. Vol. 1 of *Handbooks of Pragmatics*. Berlin: Mouton de Gruyter, pp. 77–106.

Mey, J. L. (1998). Pragmatics. In J. L. Mey, ed., *Concise Encyclopedia of Pragmatics*. Amsterdam: Elsevier, pp. 716–37.

Mey, J. L. (2001). *Pragmatics: An Introduction*. 2nd ed. Oxford: Blackwell.

Mey, J. L. (2012). Societal pragmatics. In C. A. Chapelle, ed., *The Encyclopedia of Applied Linguistics*. Chichester, UK: John Wiley, pp. 1–6.

Mooney, A. (2004). Co-operation, violation and making sense. *Journal of Pragmatics, 33*, 1601–23.

Morris, C. W. (1938). Foundations of the theory of signs. In O. Neurath, ed., *International Encyclopedia of Unified Science*, Vol. 1, No. 2. Chicago: University of Chicago Press, pp. 1–59.

Searle, J. R. (1969). *Speech Acts: An Essay in the Philosophy of Language*. Cambridge: Cambridge University Press.

Terkourafi, M. (2005a). Pragmatic correlates of frequency of use: The case for a notion of 'minimal context'. In S. Marmaridou, K. Nikiforidou and E. Antonopoulou, eds., *Reviewing Linguistic Thought: Converging Trends for the Twenty-first Century*. Berlin: Mouton de Gruyter, pp. 209–33.

Terkourafi, M. (2005b). Beyond the micro-level in politeness research. *Journal of Politeness Research: Language, Behaviour, Culture, 1*(2), 237–62.

Thomas, J. A. (1981). Pragmatic failure. Master's thesis, University of Lancaster.

Thomas, J. A. (1983). Cross-cultural pragmatic failure. *Applied Linguistics, 4*(2), 91–112.

Thomas, J. A. (1995). *Meaning in Interaction: An Introduction to Pragmatics*. London: Longman.

Verschueren, J. (1999). *Understanding Pragmatics*. London: Hodder Arnold.

Wright, S. (1998). The politicization of 'culture'. *Journal of the Royal Anthropological Institute, 14*(1), 7–15.

3

Inference and Implicature

Marina Terkourafi

> Whether or not it involves the use of a language or some other code, human communication is inferential communication
>
> Sperber and Wilson (2008: 87)

3.1 Introduction

The notions of inference and implicature are central to pragmatics, so much so that they can be used to define the pragmatic enterprise itself. Meaning which does not come from the words themselves (is not encoded) but rather from how they are used (is inferred) is considered pragmatic meaning per excellence. Both inference and implicature can be used to describe the latter type of meaning. While similar, inference and implicature are not synonymous, yet they can be hard to distinguish and even harder to keep apart. This chapter presents an overview of the various understandings of these two terms, focusing especially on their intertwining as well as how and why we may (wish to) keep them apart. We begin by drawing three distinctions between the possible meanings of these terms at increasingly finer levels of granularity, which also allows us to begin to place them in various pragmatic frameworks. We then move on to discussing the main mechanisms involved in their generation according to these frameworks. The chapter ends with considering recent developments that challenge some of the earlier distinctions, pushing them in new directions.

3.2 Key Concepts and Theories: Definitional Issues

To help us begin to tease apart the various meanings of 'inference' and 'implicature', in this section I draw three distinctions, shifting from coarser to finer levels of granularity as I do this. The three distinctions are (a) between inference in a broad sense and inference in a narrow sense, (b) between inference (in a narrow sense) and implicature and, finally, (c) between inference and implicature as both process and product. Of these, the first distinction concerns only inference, since this is the older and more general term, having been around since at least the late 1500s (OED, s.v. 'inference'). Implicature, on the other hand, is a newer term, having been introduced only in the second half of the twentieth century as a term of art in the philosophy of language, a status which it retains to this day (OED, s.v. 'implicature').

3.2.1 Inference in a Broad and in a Narrow Sense

A first distinction can be drawn between inference in a broad sense, which refers to the process of linking premises with conclusions, and inference in a narrow sense, which refers to meaning that is not encoded in the speaker's words but may be derived from them by following some reconstructible steps. Inference in a broad sense is part of the study of reasoning and is studied most prominently in psychology and in logic. Logic in particular aims to model particular types of inference: the classic modes of deduction (inference from what applies in general to specific instances), induction (inference from specific instances to what applies generally) and, more recently, abduction (inference to the best explanation) are all different types of inference.[1] It is also clear that inference in a broad sense can take as input any type of information (including visual, aural, and other stimuli), and this can further include stimuli that are non-agentively produced, in the sense that they are not intentional but can still be informative. The well-known joke of a mathematician, a physicist, and an engineer riding on a train through Scotland and seeing a black sheep can serve to illustrate this.

(1)   A mathematician, a physicist and an engineer are riding on a train through Scotland. The engineer looks out the window, sees a black sheep, and exclaims, "Hey! They've got black sheep in Scotland!" The physicist looks out the window and corrects the engineer, "Strictly speaking, all we know is that there is at least one black sheep in Scotland". The mathematician looks out the window and corrects the physicist, "Strictly speaking, all we know is that one side of one sheep is black in Scotland".

The engineer's way of thinking is a case of inductive reasoning, the physicist is reasoning abductively, while the mathematician, at the other extreme, refrains from drawing any inferences from the perceptually

---

[1] Of these, deductive inference is truth preserving, while inductive and abductive inferences are both probabilistic (likelihood-enhancing in the former case and ignorance-preserving in the latter). On some accounts, entailment is also a type of (truth preserving) inference, although unlike these three modes, entailment describes things from the language's (the system's) perspective while deduction, induction and abduction do so from the user's perspective. Implicature, on this account, is a type of defeasible (not necessarily truth preserving) inference (for more details, see Woods 2010: 218).

available information. The sheep's black fleece is of course not a case of the sheep trying to influence in any way what casual observers think and it is non-agentive in this sense; that is simply the way the sheep is. Information about its appearance can however be informative for observers, who can use it to draw conclusions about the world. This example also nicely illustrates the fact that observers may draw different inferences from the same perceptually available information.

While logic is interested in relationships between propositions, cognitive psychology studies how people derive these relationships. Cognitive psychology is therefore also interested in a wide array of non-demonstrative inferences,[2] including those that result from categorization (*if one cat can see in the dark, then all cats can see in the dark*), encyclopaedic knowledge (*the janitor sweeps the floor* [*with a broom*]), and meaning generation guided by principles of rationality (Noveck 2010). This last sense is closer to how 'inference' is used within pragmatics, or what we will call 'inference in a narrow sense'. The term 'pragmatic inference' to characterize this last type of inference is therefore not redundant, since there are also other types of non-pragmatic (logical, encyclopaedic etc.) inference.[3]

3.2.2 Inference versus Implicature

Inference in a narrow sense is, as we just saw, the purview of linguistic pragmatics, which treats linguistic communication as a case of *ostensive-inferential* communication and treats utterances as ostensive stimuli. An ostensive stimulus is one that is produced intentionally by a communicator in order to bring about a change in the set of assumptions held by a recipient. Ostensive stimuli are couched within a communicative intention that serves to fix the meaning communicated by the stimulus itself. A handwave produced by a worker next to some roadworks can be a signal to passing drivers to keep moving forward and it is interpreted as such by them in virtue of attributing to the worker the intention to communicate precisely that meaning to them. The same gesture made by him to chase away a buzzing fly would not be communicative at all (although it may be mistaken as such). A crucial difference between the two is the communicator's producing this stimulus for the sake of some recipient: an ostensive stimulus is formulated with a particular audience in mind. The relevant distinction parallels one made by the philosopher H. P. Grice (1957) between natural and non-natural meaning (meaning$_{NN}$). Grice's goal in proposing this was to differentiate cases where meaning attribution follows from natural necessity (*those spots mean measles, those dark clouds mean rain*) from cases where it is tied to a

---

[2] Non-demonstrative inferences are those in which the premises support the conclusion but they don't entail it. (The conclusion may still be false.)

[3] However, the modifier 'pragmatic' in front of 'implicature' *is* redundant, since 'implicature' as a term of art was introduced precisely to refer to a subcategory of defeasible inference.

communicator's intention to produce a certain effect in a hearer. Only the latter type of meaning is, according to Grice and later approaches to pragmatics, relevant to linguistic communication.

While the word 'inference' is in general use in the English language, 'implicature' is a technical term, introduced by Grice precisely to narrow down the object of investigation to a specific sub-case of meaning$_{NN}$. In Grice's account of meaning, implicatures are tied to the speaker's intention. Grice ([1969] 1989: 92) defines the speaker's intention as follows:

> 'U[tterer] meant something by uttering [expression] x' is true if and only if, for some audience A, U uttered x intending:
>
> (1) A to produce a particular response r
> (2) A to think (recognize) that U intends (1)
> (3) A to fulfil (1) on the basis of his fulfilment of (2).

Note that what this definition requires is simply that the speaker intend all of (1)–(3); whether the audience in actual fact follows suit and produces the required responses has no impact on whether the speaker meant something or not. It is clear from this definition that the speaker's intention is itself a technical term referring to a special kind of intention that is fulfilled by its recognition, what has been called a reflexive intention (Bach and Harnish 1979: xiv–xv). Grice's delimitation of speaker's meaning with reference to the speaker's intention limits this notion only to what a speaker intended a hearer to recognize, or, in other words, what the speaker is willing to be held accountable for – even if there is further content that can be derived from the speaker's utterance and the hearer derives this. Speaker's meaning (or meaning$_{NN}$) is further broken down, according to Grice, into what is said and what is implicated, which may in turn be implicated conventionally
or conversationally (via the Cooperative Principle and the maxims of conversation; Grice [1975] 1989; Section 3.3), in normal circumstances (generalized conversational implicatures) or in specific contexts (particularized conversational implicatures). What all of these sub-categories of meaning$_{NN}$ have in common is that they are intended by the speaker to be so recognized by the hearer.[4] Grice was much less concerned with meaning that the hearer may derive from the speaker's utterance but was not intended (or else envisaged) by the speaker herself.[5] However, it is clear that such meaning exists and later accounts have been preoccupied with finding ways to talk about it.

Paradigmatic work in this vein has been carried out within Relevance Theory (Sperber and Wilson [1986] 1995). A first distinction drawn within RT that is relevant to our purposes is between explicatures and implicatures. An explicature is the hybrid product of decoding and inference, while an

---

[4] Or at least not consciously not intended by her. This qualification is important to accommodate the category of generalized conversational implicatures which are generated in normal circumstances without taking the speaker's intention into account although they may be canceled by it.

[5] For Grice this would simply not be meaning$_{NN}$.

implicature is the product of inference alone. Thus, cases of disambiguation and reference assignment, for instance, which would have been part of 'what is said' for Grice, are explicatures in RT. Implicatures, on the other hand, are independent propositions derived by combining the explicature with elements of the context on the presumption that the speaker produced her utterance intending it to be optimally relevant (balancing cognitive effort against effects achieved) for the hearer. Thus, in the exchange

(2)   A: Have you been able to return to Mary the money you owe her?
      B: I haven't been to the bank.

the proposition that B hasn't used the services of a financial institution (including an ATM) is an explicature of B's utterance (involving various processes of reference assignment to 'I', disambiguation of *bank* as 'financial institution' and subsequent adjustment of this concept to include facilities where one may obtain financial services such as an ATM, and narrowing of *be at + PLACE* to 'being at a place for the purpose of undertaking the activities that are stereotypically undertaken there'), whereas the proposition that B hasn't been able to return Mary the money that B owes her is an implicature of B's utterance. While this way of distinguishing explicatures from implicatures amounts to redistributing meaning between 'what is said' and 'what is implicated' in the Gricean account, both explicatures and implicatures are intended by the speaker, and in this sense, they are both part of Gricean meaning$_{NN}$.

However, RT also draws a further distinction between those implicatures that are strongly communicated and those that are weakly communicated. An implicature is strongly communicated if drawing it is necessary to make the speaker's utterance optimally relevant. So, for instance, in example (2) above, the implicature that B hasn't paid Mary back is strongly communicated by B's reply or else B's utterance would fail to provide an answer to A's question. An implicature is weakly communicated in case it is one among many that would make the speaker's utterance optimally relevant. So, for instance, when a wife tells her husband over breakfast:

(3)   "I have to work late tonight".

she could be implicating any and all of the following:

(4)   a. 'Don't wait up for me'.
      b. 'Don't make dinner for me'.
      c. 'Go ahead and have dinner without me'.
      d. 'Please feed the kids'.
      e. 'Please put the kids to bed'.
      f. 'Don't go worrying that something bad happened to me'.
      g. 'Don't call looking for me'.
      h. 'I will miss our favorite show on TV'.
      i. 'Please record it for me'.
      j. '...'

Items (4.a–j) are all weak implicatures of the speaker's utterance, which it would be uneconomical (not to mention tedious) for her to list one by one. As this list may be open-ended (this is what (4.j) stands for), an exhaustive listing may not even be possible; in this case, her utterance is more like an invitation for him to draw further inferences that she may be currently forgetting but is happy to subscribe to. To the extent that her husband derives at least some of these inferences, her utterance will have achieved its goal, in other words, it will have been optimally relevant. That implicatures can have this property of indeterminacy was acknowledged also by Grice ([1975] 1989: 40). However, it is only within RT that the full implications of this were drawn.

Correlating implicature strength with the extent to which an implicature is determinate, Wilson and Sperber (1986: 253) note: "The weaker the implicature, ... the weaker the speaker's responsibility for its truth, up to the point where the implicature disappears altogether and the responsibility for the assumptions used and the conclusions drawn lies solely on the side of the hearer". What this statement makes clear is that all assumptions derived by combining a speaker's utterance with a context are inferences from the speaker's utterance but only those that are intended by the speaker herself to be recognized by the listener as so intended are implicatures of her utterance. This might be schematically represented as in (5):

(5) implicature = inference + speaker's (communicative) intention

Or, as we may say, paraphrasing an older adage:[6] Speakers implicate, hearers infer.

In the same essay, Wilson and Sperber (1986: 252) write: "sometimes, a speaker can observe the principle of relevance without having any idea of the sort of context in which the utterance will be processed, or the sort of conclusions that will be derived. In these cases, the utterance will have no implicatures at all". This, however, does not mean that it will not lead to any inferences either. Listeners can (and, according to RT, will, since the principle of relevance is more of a basic communicative instinct than a social convention or something that is learnt; cf. Carston 2002) always draw inferences from what a speaker said (sometimes also if they are not among the speaker's intended audience or there is no such audience).[7]

There are a few reasons why it can be useful to maintain a strict inference versus implicature distinction along these lines, with only the latter being connected to the speaker's intention. First and foremost, as we just noted, inferences not intended by the speaker are not part of Gricean meaning$_{NN}$. As such, Grice does not offer an account of how they are derived. However, as a framework approaching communication from the hearer's perspective, RT

---

[6] "Propositions imply, people infer", cited in Woods (2010: 218).
[7] Incidentally, that is why the worker's chasing away a buzzing fly may be mistaken as a communicative handwave in the example at the start of this section.

can account for all the inferences a hearer draws from a speaker's utterance so long as the balance between cognitive effects and effort is maintained.

Another reason why it can be useful to maintain a strict inference versus implicature distinction is that implicature (as speaker intended) and inference (as hearer derived) can overlap but they are not always co-extensive. A speaker may implicate a proposition (intend the hearer to think something) that the hearer doesn't end up thinking: this does not mean that the speaker did not implicate it – although it does mean that this aborted meaning will not become part of the conversational record or 'common ground' (Clark 1996) between interlocutors. If the speaker becomes aware of this and really wants the hearer to get it, she will have to try harder – possibly by repeating her utterance or making this content more explicit.

Conversely, a hearer may infer a proposition that the speaker did not intend: that does not make the speaker responsible for this meaning that she had not foreseen – although if it does become apparent to her that the hearer has derived this and it is a meaning she would like to distance herself from, she should take steps to do so, lest the inference becomes part of the conversational record that is taken for granted in later discourse. This captures the truism that speakers and listeners may not always end up entertaining the same meaning out of an utterance, which is a major advantage of an inferential model of communication over a code one. In a code model of communication (such as Shannon and Weaver 1963), any discrepancies between the meaning intended by the speaker and the one derived by the listener are considered exceptional and attributed to noise in the channel. However, in an inferential model (such as Sperber and Wilson [1986] 1995), such discrepancies are expected and attributed to the fact that communicating partners can only make hypotheses about each other's cognitive environment and take this into account within the limits of their own abilities and preferences.

3.2.3 Inference and Implicature as Process and Product

A third distinction can be drawn between inference and implicature as both process and product. As Lyons (1995: 35) makes clear, many terms in linguistics are used in this dual sense, without clear signposting of which of the two senses is meant each time. For instance, in the discussion of RT above, inference is used to refer to both a process of deriving new propositions by combining a speaker's utterance with a context as well as the products of that process, the actual propositions inferred. Implicature, on the other hand, is reserved only for a subset of those products, namely those propositions that the hearer infers and which are actually intended by the speaker. That is also why inference (as a process) can also contribute to explicatures. More generally, in RT, inference as a process can lead to implicatures as products or not. The term 'inferential process' is sometimes used to distinguish inference as process from inference as product.

Mindful of this distinction, Grice ([1975]/1989: 24) introduced alongside 'implicature', that is, the act of implying, the noun 'implicatum', that is, what is implied and was careful to maintain the distinction between the two throughout his writing. For instance, when talking about the indeterminacy of conversational implicatures, he makes clear that this is a property "that many actual implicata do in fact seem to possess" (40). Others have not always emulated this careful usage and over time the distinction has faded. The distinction between implicature and implicatum can nevertheless be useful to keep in mind, as it is possible that the same process can lead to different products or, conversely the same product can be the result of different processes. So much has become apparent in recent experimental pragmatics research, which has granted researchers the opportunity to observe the interpretation process unfold in real time. What such research, drawing among others on recordings of event-related brain potentials, has revealed is that there can be qualitative differences in the interpretation patterns of different individuals, even if the overall quantitative trends remain the same (Franke and Degen 2016; Tanner et al. 2018).

3.3 Matters of Process

That a proposition must be capable of being worked out from the information available in the speaker's utterance and the context following some reconstructible steps[8] is a requirement for pragmatic inference and in this regard, Grice once again set the scene, with his Cooperative Principle (henceforth CP) and the maxims of conversation.[9] While the maxims

---

[8] This is of course the property of calculability of conversational implicatures, which, alongside cancellability, and non-detachability, set conversational implicatures apart from conventional ones (Grice [1975] 1989: 30). Later scholars have added reinforceability, universality and non-conventionality to this list (Huang 2007). Because conventional implicatures are not calculable but have to be learnt they are not a type of pragmatic inference as this is understood in this chapter (although they can be considered a type of encyclopedic inference having to do with the lexical meaning of words).

[9] The Cooperative Principle reads: "Make your conversational contribution such as is required, at the stage at which it occurs, by the accepted purpose or direction of the talk exchange in which you are engaged". This subsumes four categories of maxims which spell out what it means to be conversationally cooperative. These are:

The maxims of Quantity

(i) Make your contribution as informative as is required (for the current purposes of the exchange).
(ii) Do not make your contribution more informative than is required.

The maxims of Quality
Supermaxim: Try to make your contribution one that is true.

(i) Do not say what you believe to be false.
(ii) Do not say that for which you lack adequate evidence.

The maxim of Relation
Be relevant.

The maxims of Manner

(falling under the four categories of Quantity, Quality, Relation and Manner) are typically honoured in the breach, meaning it is their (real or apparent) non-observance by the speaker that licenses the derivation of an implicature by the listener, the CP is always tacitly assumed to be in operation (unless explicitly opted out of; Grice [1975] 1989: 30) and provides the general background that justifies the listener thinking that the speaker meant more than what they said.

In describing how a listener goes about figuring out this additional meaning, Grice outlined five sources of information on which the listener relies (Grice [1975] 1989: 31). These are (1) the conventional meaning of the words used, together with the identity of any references that might be involved (essentially, his notion of 'what is said'); (2) the Cooperative Principle and its maxims; (3) the context, linguistic or otherwise, of the utterance; (4) other items of background knowledge and (5) the fact (or supposed fact) that all relevant items falling under the previous headings are available to both participants and both participants know or assume this to be the case. Of these, items (3) (=context, including the discourse and physical context) and (4) (=background knowledge) are especially interesting from a sociopragmatic point of view. Their inclusion among the sources of information that determine the outcome of the inferential process essentially opens up the possibility that different listeners may draw different implicatures from the same utterance – something speakers themselves may purposefully exploit, as in the case of coded communication, which is frequent in politicians' and social media discourse (Marwick and boyd 2011: 123).[10]

More often than not, however, discrepancies in world knowledge or, more generally, in what interlocutors take for granted, result in miscommunication. Some often cited examples of this come from exchanges between women and men, such as the example in (6) (from Tannen 1993: 168):

(6) (Context: A male and female co-worker are walking between buildings on a cold day)
Woman co-worker: "Where's your coat?"
Male co-worker: "Thanks mom".

Supermaxim: Be perspicuous.

(i) Avoid obscurity of expression.
(ii) Avoid ambiguity.
(iii) Be brief (avoid unnecessary prolixity).
(iv) Be orderly. (Grice [1975] 1989: 26–7).

[10] Coded communication refers to using a stimulus which speakers know different audiences will interpret differently to activate these different interpretations in the respective audiences' minds. Examples include pop singer Madonna's early image (which signaled empowerment to young women and sexual appeal to young men) and references to Christian texts in former US President George W. Bush's speeches (which appealed to his base without alienating others). In the case of coded communication, all of these inferences are implicatures of the speaker's utterance, since they are all equally intended by the speaker (formulated with different audiences in mind).

According to Tannen's analysis of this example, the man's response frames the woman's utterance as parental advice, reflecting a (male) worldview in which conversational exchanges aim at domination. The woman's utterance, however, she argues, may have been simply motivated by friendly concern as is common among peers, reflecting a (female) worldview where actions are driven by solidarity. The differences in worldviews between speaker and hearer result in different inferences being drawn by them from the same utterance. Which of these was actually intended by the speaker (and therefore an implicature of her utterance) is a question best left to psychologists or sociologists to answer. For so long as our account of meaning can reconstruct the steps by which different interpretations can be arrived at, our work will have been done.

Or will it? Grice ([1975] 1989: 31) summarizes the process of implicature derivation as follows:

> [The speaker] has said that p; there is no reason to suppose that he is not observing the maxims, or at least the CP; he could not be doing this unless he thought that q; he knows (and knows that I know that he knows) that I can see that the supposition that he thinks that q is *required*; he has done nothing to stop me thinking that q; he intends me to think, or is at least willing to allow me to think, that q; and so he has implicated that q.

One important question this account leaves unanswered is how we get from p or 'what is said' by the speaker's utterance to the specific q that the speaker thereby implicates. As Wilson and Sperber (1986: 244) note, out of any proposition, myriad others may be justifiably drawn. To give but one quick example, in (6) above, some of the (more readily accessible) inferences from the female co-worker's utterance include that she assumes that her addressee owns a coat and that he has brought it to work that day. How does the listener know which of these inferences are actually intended by her, making them implicatures of her utterance?

What Wilson and Sperber are highlighting here is the well-known frame-problem in artificial intelligence research (McCarthy and Hayes 1969).[11] This is more generally the problem of delimiting the relevant domain or universe of discourse in which to interpret the speaker's utterance and has led to various taxonomical classifications of world knowledge from general (knowledge we have because we are human and live on earth) to specific (including cultural and other routinized knowledge, and even knowledge pertaining to specific individuals), such as Schank and Abelson's (1977) four levels of themes-goals-plans-scripts. Episodic memory plays an important role in these classifications and the organization of knowledge is based on experience, making it possible for interlocutors to be operating with

---

[11] Rather than as the frame problem, Wilson and Sperber (1986) discuss this as the problem of hypothesis formation and relate it back to Fodor's (1983) discussion of global and local processes.

different knowledge structures (or frames) in mind (at least at the lower, culture-specific levels). What specific information is stored in a frame or other stereotypical data structure,[12] how this is acquired and how it is accessed during utterance interpretation remain major problems of artificial intelligence research.

Wilson and Sperber's (1986: 249) solution to this problem is to argue that the concepts encoded in the speaker's utterance provide entry points into the relevant encyclopaedic entries, thus helping the listener to delimit the appropriate search space for hypothesis confirmation and disconfirmation.[13] In this process of delimitation, the listener is guided by the presumption of optimal relevance, which states that "(a) the ostensive stimulus is relevant enough for it to be worth the addressee's effort to process it [and] (b) the ostensive stimulus is the most relevant one compatible with the communicator's abilities and preferences" (Sperber and Wilson [1986] 1995: 270). The listener then engages in a comprehension strategy that enjoins them to "(a) consider interpretations (disambiguations, reference assignments, enrichments, contextual assumptions etc.) in order of accessibility (i.e. follow a path of least effort in computing cognitive effects) and (b) stop when the expected level of relevance in reached" (Carston 2002: 143).

A similar intuition about the importance of world knowledge is captured in Neo-Gricean frameworks (Horn 1984; Levinson 2000). These frameworks recast Grice's maxims in a smaller number of heuristics or principles (three for Levinson, two for Horn),[14] which are activated automatically by specific lexical items or constructions contained in incoming utterances, amplifying their content in predictable directions. Levinson's I-heuristic, in particular, is activated by describing things in a normal, unmarked way and makes specific reference to knowledge of stereotypical relations (*They unpacked the picnic. The beer was warm*, which I-implicates 'The beer was part of the picnic'), indicating how world knowledge can be brought into the utterance interpretation process. This is less so for his other two heuristics, Q and M, which are said to be metalinguistic in nature (relying on knowledge of language rather than knowledge about the world; for instance, knowledge about scalar

---

[12] Levinson's (1992) notion of 'activity types' is another.

[13] Note, however, that their later claim that concepts can be adjusted during the utterance interpretation process (Sperber and Wilson 2008) complicates this picture considerably, possibly to the point of making it circular.

[14] The three Levinsonian heuristics are:
Q[uantity]: 'What is not said is not the case'
I[nformativeness]: 'What is simply described is stereotypically and specifically exemplified'
M[anner]: 'Marked descriptions warn "marked situation"'.
Horn's two principles are:
The Q[uantity]-principle (hearer-based): Say as much as you can (given R).
The R[elation]-principle (speaker-based): Say no more than you must (given Q).

alternates relies on a relationship of semantic entailment which is independent of context).[15]

While both Relevance theorists and Neo-Griceans acknowledge the importance of world knowledge to the outcome of the utterance interpretation process (the actual inferences drawn), there is considerable disagreement as to the temporal parameters of this process – namely at what point during the utterance interpretation process is world knowledge, including information about the context of utterance, taken into account? For Relevance Theory, all inference is local, meaning world knowledge is present at all times and comprehension draws on a set of assumptions activated by previous discourse and by the information conveyed by the incoming utterance. On this account, there are no default interpretations attached to specific expressions out of context. For Neo-Griceans, on the other hand, pre-contextual defaults (such as the interpretation 'not all' attached to utterances containing *some*) can be attached to expressions in the lexicon and filtered out in particular contexts. A middle-of-the-road solution here is that some parameters of context (such as the language spoken by the speaker, their age, gender, ethnicity and so on) may be presumptively fixed prior to interaction (while remaining open to revision later on), with other elements (intonation, gestures etc.) affecting interpretation as they become available parallel with the speech signal itself (Terkourafi 2005). These questions are currently being addressed in experimental pragmatics, from where new insights have also originated (e.g. constraint-based pragmatics; Degen and Tanenhaus 2019).

3.4 Critical Overview and Future Directions

We said earlier that for Grice, speaker's meaning is a case of meaning$_{NN}$, which crucially relies on the speaker having a certain type of communicative (reflexive) intention when producing an utterance. Whether an inference is an implicature of the speaker's utterance or not, then, depends on whether the speaker is happy to be credited as the originator of this meaning. Speakers can only take responsibility for those inferences they intended the hearer to recognize as intended by them and only those are implicatures of their utterances. While RT acknowledges the possibility of inferences that were not intended by the speaker and offers an account of how they are derived (see Section 3.2.2), it retains the notion of communicative intention as central to communication: communication requires a change in the communicators' mutual cognitive environment (i.e. in the set

---

[15] Nevertheless, recent work on scalar diversity (Van Tiel et al. 2016; McNally 2017) and work on non-entailment scales more generally (Hirschberg 1991) has shown that sentence as well as situational context can affect which expressions are considered alternates, blurring the distinction between knowledge of language and knowledge about the world in this respect.

of assumptions that they not only share but are mutually aware that they share) and inferences that are not implicatures of the speaker's utterance fall outside its scope.

This take on implicature can be problematic for two reasons. The first is that intentions can be hard to verify: as mental states, intentions are in speakers' heads so they cannot be observed directly, let alone subsequently confirmed. Indeed, deniability is one of the main reasons (though not the only one) why a speaker may choose to lead a hearer to understand something without telling them as much (Pinker et al. 2008). Also, it is not always the case that a speaker has a specific intention in mind that they have fully worked out in advance and want the hearer to recognize; speakers can also have proto-intentions and their utterances can be invitations to hearers to help clarify these (Terkourafi 2014). For this reason, the Gricean and post-Gricean accounts' reliance on intention makes the notion of implicature hard to implement empirically. This has prompted, in conversation analytic accounts, a move away from speakers' intentions towards evidence of such intentions in the conversational transcript. That evidence is not necessarily verbal: other types of cues such as gaze or even absence of a behavioural cue (silence) can be evidence of a speaker's internal mental state and stance on the situation. The notion of speaker accountability (Haugh and Jaszczolt 2012: 110, and references therein; see also Chapter 4) has been productively explored in this respect.

The second reason why tying the notion of implicature to the speaker's intention is problematic is because intention-based accounts have been criticized as Western-centric (Ameka and Terkourafi 2019). As anthropologists have been quick to point out, "even if it is true that the capacity for inferring the mental states of others is a generically human one, and plays a part in communication everywhere, it does not follow that all language ideologies will give it equal prominence, or even allow it to be openly recognized or actualized in speech" (Robins and Rumsey 2008: 414). What the experience of other cultures suggests on this point is that cultural groups vary in the extent to which they consider the speaker's intention to be the primary determinant of the meaning that the speaker must take responsibility for, another important determinant of this being the meaning encoded in the words themselves. In an older article, Matsumoto (1989) makes the point that Gricean principles apply better to English than to Japanese, where social context is encoded in obligatory grammatical choices, with the result that all the available forms carry additional meanings — what she calls "interactional implicatures" (1989: 210) — that the speaker cannot help but communicate. Similarly, based on her work with the Mopan Maya, Danziger (2011: 123) has argued for a

> symptomic set of understandings about language . . . in which sign form is taken to be necessarily related to sign content through indexical relations of cause and effect.. . . Under such a philosophy, the hearer

need seek no assistance for the task of interpretation in the context of any utterance's production – certainly not in "what is in the mind of the speaker". Utterance effect is instead believed to be achieved regardless of such circumstances.... Adherence to a Symptomic philosophy corresponds to a belief that signifiers are related 'naturally' and of necessity to their signifieds, in a way that can be ideologically contrasted with the "non-natural" [Grice 1957] relations of the arbitrary Symbol.

Despite coming from a non-Western perspective, the idea that words can produce meanings directly regardless of how the speaker may have intended them should not be so exotic to Western ears either, if we consider cases where speakers have had to apologize for what their words meant, even if they were adamant that they did not mean it themselves (the 2007 case of radio show host Don Imus is a rather (in)famous example of this; see Allan 2016: 219).

A different yet related critique, again from a non-Western angle, is discussed by Haugh (2002), this time relating to the distinction between explicatures and implicatures within RT. Using examples from Japanese, Haugh argues that the line between explicit and implicit meaning, and therefore between explicatures and implicatures, is blurred in this language by the existence of utterances that 'trail off'. What speakers do with such utterances is to leave something unsaid while simultaneously indicating that they are leaving it unsaid. Haugh discusses two possibilities in this regard: one in which the speaker does not trail off their utterance (thereby not indicating that they are leaving something unsaid) and one in which they do, using a discourse marker (*kara*, lit. 'so, therefore') that indicates that the hearer is to draw a conclusion from what the speaker said that they are hesitant to articulate themselves. Haugh furthermore argues that the second possibility is perceived as more polite than the first. Although, as Haugh convincingly argues, it is hard to tell whether the meaning that is left unsaid is communicated implicitly in the first case and explicitly in the second (where a discourse marker encoding procedural meaning guides its derivation), distinguishing explicatures from implicatures from a process angle, by considering the former to be the product of decoding + inference and the latter to result from inference alone (see Section 3.2.2), may solve this problem. Moreover, considering that at least part of the meaning comes from decoding in the second example could explain why it is considered more polite: the explicit guidance offered by the discourse marker in this case lessens the imposition on the listener's cognitive resources (Blum-Kulka 1987) reducing costs, or, conversely, shows that the speaker is at least trying to be relevant (provide an answer to a previous question and not just avoiding the topic) while avoiding any disaffiliating effects their utterance might have. While the challenge to RT may thus not be so great as envisaged, one may still find it worrisome that the distinction between explicatures and implicatures cannot be defended on intuitive grounds but only intra-theoretically. In other words, what is the status of this distinction outside the theory itself?

The final critique I would like to raise relates to the closing lines of the quote from Danziger (2011) above. There Danziger claims, based on her observations of Mopan Maya discourse, that at least on some occasions, signifiers can be linked to their signifieds in a more direct and 'natural' way than is envisaged within Grice's notion of meaning$_{NN}$. This point is also acknowledged by pragmaticians and philosophers of language, who are increasingly paying attention to the fact that all kinds of behaviour and not just that produced intentionally can give rise to inferences and that theories of meaning should also account for these types of inferences, since they constitute a type of meaning occasioned by the speaker's behaviour. A recent attempt at describing this is as "organic meaning", a type of meaning proposed by Green (2019) as meeting some, though not all, of Grice's conditions on meaning$_{NN}$ and thus lying halfway between natural and non-natural meaning in this respect.[16] As an example of organic meaning in human behaviour (most of his examples come from the animal kingdom whereby theory of mind cannot be taken for granted), Green cites uptalk – ending one's statements with rising intonation as in "My name is Jenny Smith?" – which in contemporary American English can convey an attitude of being accommodating and non-aggressive (and, I would add, potentially of a certain generation or age, gender, social class and from a certain part of the country). These meanings, which are all part of uptalk's "indexical field" (Eckert 2008) and are conveyed in specific situations, can depend on the speaker as much as on the addressee: as we have already mentioned several times throughout this chapter, addressees may well read meanings into a speaker's utterance that a speaker never intended to convey. What is relevant to our purposes is that the respective meanings can arise without the speaker wanting their signal to be taken in any particular way, or in fact thinking of their behaviour as a signal at all. I am reminded here of an incident from my student days at the centre of the Greek capital, Athens, where, after I placed my order at a fast-food restaurant, one worker turned to the other repeating my order and adding: 'make it a good one for the lass from Crete'. The island of Crete is indeed where I was brought up but I had no clue how the worker could have known that – until I realized I had used the dialectal pronunciation [oi] for 'no' (Standard Greek /oxi/). It is these unintended yet consequential aspects of our behaviour that Green's term "organic meaning" aims to capture. Increasing attention to these aspects means that not only the line between inference and implicature, but also that between natural meaning and non-natural meaning, and correspondingly between inference in the broad sense and in the narrow sense, is being scrutinized and potentially redrawn.

---

[16] For a related attempt from an RT angle, see Wharton (2003, 2009).

As this brief overview has hopefully shown, despite being foundational pillars of all pragmatics research, the notions of inference and implicature continue to be hotly debated and their boundaries are active loci of research in pragmatics and the philosophy of language. Considering that much of the research cited in this section comes from a sociopragmatics perspective, an important contribution of sociopragmatics to the study of these notions has been to question their generality: are these really culturally neutral and/or asocial, or are they as culturally imbued as Foucault (1978) has claimed all theorizing to be? With much of this research currently conducted within sociopragmatics, this is also an area whence new developments and insights can be expected to emerge.

References

Allan, K. (2016). The reporting of slurs. In A. Capone, F. Kiefer and F. Lo Piparo, eds., *Indirect Reports and Pragmatics: Interdisciplinary Studies*. Cham, Switzerland: Springer, pp. 211–32.

Ameka, F. K. and Terkourafi M. (2019). What if . . . ? Imagining non-Western perspectives on pragmatic theory and practice. *Journal of Pragmatics, 145*, 72–82.

Bach, K. and Harnish, R. M. (1979). *Linguistic Communication and Speech Acts*. Cambridge, MA: MIT Press.

Blum-Kulka, S. (1987). Indirectness and politeness in requests: Same or different? *Journal of Pragmatics, 11*, 145–60.

Carston, R. (2002). *Thoughts and Utterances: The Pragmatics of Explicit Communication*. Oxford: Blackwell.

Clark, H. H. (1996). *Using Language*. Cambridge: Cambridge University Press.

Danziger, E. (2011). Once more with feeling: A forbidden performance of the Great Speech of the Mopan Maya. *Anthropological Quarterly, 84*(1), 121–40.

Degen, J. and Tanenhaus, M. K. (2019). Constraint-based pragmatic processing. In C. Cummins and N. Katsos, eds., *Handbook of Experimental Semantics and Pragmatics*. Oxford: Oxford University Press.

Eckert, P. (2008). Variation and the indexical field. *Journal of Sociolinguistics, 12*(4), 453–76.

Fodor, J. A. (1983). *Modularity of Mind*. Cambridge MA: MIT Press.

Foucault, M. (1978). *The History of Sexuality*. New York: Pantheon Books.

Franke M. and Degen, J. (2016). Reasoning in reference games: Individual- vs. population-level probabilistic modeling. *PLoS ONE, 11*(5), e0154854. doi:10.1371/journal.pone.0154854

Green, M. (2019). Organic meaning: An approach to communication with minimal appeal to minds. In A. Capone, M. Carapezza and F. Lo Piparo, eds., *Further Advances in Pragmatics and Philosophy. Part II Theories and Applications*. Cham, Switzerland: Springer, pp. 211–28.

Grice, H. P. (1957). Meaning. *The Philosophical Review*, 66, 377–88. Reprinted in: Grice, H. P. (1989). *Studies in the Way of Words*. Cambridge, MA: Harvard University Press, pp. 213–23.

Grice, H. P. (1969). Utterer's meaning and intentions. *The Philosophical Review*, 78, 147–77. Reprinted in: Grice, H. P. (1989). *Studies in the Way of Words*. Cambridge, MA: Harvard University Press, pp. 86–116.

Grice, H. P. (1975). Logic and conversation. In P. Cole and J. Morgan, eds., *Syntax and Semantics. Vol. III: Speech Acts*. New York: Academic Press, pp. 41–58. Reprinted in: Grice, H. P. (1989). *Studies in the Way of Words*. Cambridge, MA: Harvard University Press, pp. 22–40.

Haugh, M. (2002). The intuitive basis of implicature: Relevance Theoretic implicitness versus Gricean implying. *Pragmatics*, 12(2), 117–34.

Haugh, M. and Jaszczolt, K. (2012). Speaker intentions and intentionality. In K. Allan and K. M. Jaszczolt, eds., *Cambridge Handbook of Pragmatics*. Cambridge: Cambridge University Press, pp. 87–112.

Huang, Y. (2007). *Pragmatics*. Oxford: Oxford University Press.

Hirschberg, J. (1991). *A Theory of Scalar Implicature*. New York: Garland.

Horn, L. (1984). Toward a new taxonomy for pragmatic inference: Q-based and R-based implicature. In D. Schiffrin, ed., *Meaning, Form, and Use in Context*. Washington, DC: Georgetown University Press, pp. 11–42.

Levinson, S. C. (1992). Activity types and language. In P. Drew and J. Heritage, eds., *Talk at Work: Interaction in Institutional Settings*. Cambridge: Cambridge University Press, pp. 66–100.

Levinson, S. C. (2000). *Presumptive Meanings: The Theory of Generalized Conversational Implicature*. Cambridge, MA: MIT Press.

Lyons, J. (1995). *Linguistic Semantics*. Cambridge: Cambridge University Press.

Marwick, A. and boyd, d. m. (2011). I tweet honestly, I tweet passionately: Twitter users, context collapse, and the imagined audience. *New Media and Society*, 13(1), 114–33.

Matsumoto, Y. (1989). Politeness and conversational universals: Observations from Japanese. *Multilingua*, 8, 207–21.

McCarthy, J. and Hayes, P. J. (1969). Some philosophical problems from the standpoint of artificial intelligence. *Machine Intelligence*, 4, 463–502.

McNally, L. 2017. Scalar alternatives and scalar inference involving adjectives: A comment on van Tiel, et al. 2016. In J. Ostrove, R. Kramer and J. Sabbagh, eds., *Asking the Right Questions: Essays in Honor of Sandra Chung*. Santa Cruz: University of California Santa Cruz, Linguistics Research Center, pp. 17–28.

Noveck, I. (2010). Inferential comprehension. In L. Cummings, ed., *The Pragmatics Encyclopedia*. London: Routledge, pp. 220–22.

Pinker, S., Nowak, M. A. and Lee, J. J. (2008). The logic of indirect speech. *Proceedings of the National Academy of Sciences*, 105(3), 833–8.

Robbins, J. and Rumsey, A. (2008). Introduction: Cultural and linguistic anthropology and the opacity of other minds. *Anthropological Quarterly*, 81(2), 407–20.

Schank, R. C. and Abelson, R. P. (1977). *Scripts, Plans, Goals, and Understanding: An Inquiry into Human Knowledge Structures*. Hillsdale, NJ: Erlbaum.

Shannon, C. E. and Weaver, W. (1963). *The Mathematical Theory of Communication*. Urbana: University of Illinois Press.

Sperber, D. and Wilson, D. ([1986] 1995). *Relevance: Communication and Cognition*. 2nd ed. Oxford: Blackwell.

Sperber, D. and Wilson, D. (2008). A deflationary account of metaphors. In R. Gibbs, ed., *The Cambridge Handbook of Metaphor and Thought*. Cambridge: Cambridge University Press, pp. 84–105.

Tannen, D. (1993). The relativity of linguistic strategies: Rethinking power and solidarity in gender and dominance. In D. Tannen, ed., *Gender and Conversational Interaction*. Oxford: Oxford University Press, pp. 165–88.

Tanner, D., Goldshtein, M. and Weissman, B. (2018). Individual differences in the real-time neural dynamics of language comprehension. *Psychology of Learning and Motivation*, 68, 299–335.

Terkourafi, M. (2005). Pragmatic correlates of frequency of use: The case for a notion of 'minimal context'. In K. Nikiforidou, S., Marmaridou and E. Antonopoulou, eds., *Reviewing Linguistic Thought: Converging Trends for the 21st Century*. Berlin: de Gruyter, pp. 209–33.

Terkourafi, M. (2014). The importance of being indirect: A new nomenclature for indirect speech. *Belgian Journal of Linguistics*, 28(1), 45–70.

van Tiel, B., van Miltenburg, E., Zevakhina, N. and Geurts, B. (2016). Scalar diversity. *Journal of Semantics*, 33, 137–75.

Wharton, T. (2003). Natural pragmatics and natural codes. *Mind and Language,* 18, 447–77.

Wharton, T. (2009). *The Pragmatics of Non-Verbal Communication*. Cambridge: Cambridge University Press.

Wilson, D. and Sperber, D. (1986). Inference and implicature in utterance interpretation. In T. Myers, K. Brown and B. McGonigle, eds., *Reasoning and Discourse Processes*. London: Academic Press, pp. 241–63.

Woods, J. (2010). Inference. In L. Cummings, ed., *The Pragmatics Encyclopedia*. London: Routledge, pp. 218–20.

4

Speaker Meaning, Commitment and Accountability

Chi-Hé Elder[*]

4.1 Introduction

Grice's (1989) pioneering work put 'speaker meaning' at the heart of the study of meanings in use. His work on the role of intentions in meaning generation challenged the so-called code model of meaning – the assumption that speakers use the linguistic system to encode messages, which hearers then decode using the same linguistic system – in favour of the now widespread 'inferential model', which affords speakers' intentions a significant role in both the delivery and interpretation of utterances. However, in assuming that successful communication relies on hearers satisfactorily inferring meanings that align with speakers' intended meanings, Grice's work did not address the questions of how or why hearers may derive meanings which were not intended by the speaker. This chapter looks at three divergent accounts of meaning in communication focussing on how the derivation of meaning affects what one is deemed committed to or accountable for: either by speakers themselves, by other discourse participants, or normatively irrespective of the mental states of either speaker or hearer. These considerations are important for studies in sociopragmatics as they provide the theoretical rationale for why speakers hold themselves and each other accountable for certain meanings, which in turn can shed light on why speakers may choose to formulate their utterances in certain ways over others. The different perspectives addressed in this chapter are brought together in two case studies: one on 'hinting', demonstrating the risks associated with assigning speaker intentions to individual utterances, and one on manipulating implicatures in political discourse that serves to highlight the limitations of only considering publicly available information without recourse to mental states. The chapter finishes by questioning whether,

[*] Thank you to Bart Geurts, Michael Haugh, Diana Mazzarella and Marina Terkourafi, all of whom provided detailed and insightful comments on a previous draft of this chapter.

and if so how, the seemingly conflicting approaches can be combined in a theoretically and empirically satisfactory way that can capture the different manifestations of 'meaning' from different perspectives.

4.2 Key Issues and Theories

This section begins by outlining Grice's seminal proposal for 'speaker meaning' before comparing two models of communication which utilize the notion of 'commitment' in divergent ways, namely the inferential approach (most notably in Relevance Theory, stemming from Sperber and Wilson [1986] 1995) and the commitment-based approach to communication (e.g. Austin 1975; Searle 1976; Brandom 1994; Geurts 2019a, 2019b). It then introduces a conceptually distinct approach to communication utilizing the concept of interactional achievement that makes use of the notion of 'accountability' in communication (e.g. Heritage 1984; Sanders 1987; Clark 1996; Arundale 1999, 2020).

4.2.1 Grice's 'Speaker Meaning'

Unlike philosophical approaches to language that focussed on deriving meanings of sentences from their component parts (which led to the field of formal, or linguistic semantics today), Paul Grice (1989) was concerned with explaining how speaker meaning can be due to more than simply sentence meaning. In particular, he acknowledged that 'what is said' is not all that can be communicated by an utterance, and invoked the notion of 'non-natural meaning' – intentional meaning – as the sum of 'what is said' and 'what is implicated' (see Chapter 3 for further detail). His Cooperative Principle, "Make your conversational contribution such as is required, at the stage at which it occurs, by the accepted purpose or direction of the talk exchange in which you are engaged" (Grice 1989: 26), along with the four categories of maxims – of quantity, quality, relation and manner – were a first attempt at providing a systematic general theory of utterance meaning, explaining how speakers are able to communicate more than the explicit content of what they say. It is this 'intentional meaning' that is typically equated with the notion of 'speaker meaning' in Gricean pragmatics.

Underlying the Cooperative Principle is the assumption that successful communication relies on cooperative, rational behaviour, and it is the assumption that a speaker is adhering to the maxims that allows a hearer to make certain inferences about what the speaker intends to communicate by an utterance. The flouting of, or blatant failure to fulfil, a maxim signals that an aspect of 'what is said' does not conform to the speaker's intended meaning, and it is the task of the hearer to figure out how a speaker can both be rationally abiding by the Cooperative Principle while failing to abide by the maxims that gives rise to a conversational implicature. In sum, Grice's distinction between 'what is said' and 'what is implicated', alongside the maxims for cooperative conversation, provided an objective description of how people use language by means of the principles of discourse that speakers are expected to abide by in conversation as explanatory tools, while also providing a method of evaluating whether and, if so, why a given communicative act has been successful.

Grice's philosophical account of speaker meaning has been reframed by many theorists as a more general account of communication, and scholars have since taken Grice's original work on speaker meaning broadly in two directions. On the one hand, the mechanisms that Grice describes for recognizing speaker meaning have been formulated in terms of the cognitive processes in which a hearer engages in order to infer the speaker's intended meaning (most notably in Relevance Theory; Sperber and Wilson [1986] 1995). This I call the 'inferential view' of communication, in which the theoretical goal is to explain the cognitive processes via which hearers are able to recover certain meanings from speakers' utterances. Other scholars take the view that a theory of communication should aim to explain *why*, in given circumstances, a hearer recovers a conversational implicature based on the utterance in context itself, and not necessarily *how* they do it in terms of mental processes. In this view, the attribution of speaker meaning is a matter of social commitment: what I term the 'commitment-based' approach to communication (e.g. Geurts 2019a, 2019b, stemming from Hamblin 1970; Brandom 1994). Note that these two approaches to communication will not necessarily yield different results regarding speaker meaning. Comparing their different goals, however, is nevertheless useful as it raises a range of interrelated theoretical questions whose answers have ramifications for the sociopragmatic question of which meanings speakers hold each other committed to and/or accountable for.

The foremost issue that distinguishes the two approaches lies in the extent to which speaker intentions are given precedence in the determination of meaning. The answer to this has knock-on effects for whether speaker meaning is considered to be the same as the meaning a speaker is held committed to or accountable for: to describe speakers as *committing themselves to meanings* typically presupposes an intentional view on speaker meaning, while taking speakers to be *normatively committed to meanings* in virtue of what they say is to give higher theoretical importance to the roles of norms and conventions vis-à-vis commitment to meanings. Next, if we consider implicitly communicated meanings (i.e. implicatures) to be part of speaker meaning as per Grice's formulation of non-natural meaning, this raises a further question regarding the extent to which speakers can be deemed committed to, or held accountable for (either by other speakers or normatively), those implicatures. And, once we extend the scope of inquiry beyond hearers' successful inference of speakers' intended meanings, there are further questions: first, whether a speaker can be committed to a meaning they intend to communicate even if a hearer fails to recover it; and second, whether a speaker can be held committed to meanings they communicate to hearers even in the absence of an intention to do so.

The two theoretical options described so far put the onus of speaker meaning on either the speaker's intention or on the conventions of language use. However, there is a third option which is to allow the hearer greater importance in the determining of speaker meaning. This is an option that is pursued by different schools of thought to different ends, whether in allowing the hearer's interpretation to guide the attribution of speaker meaning (as per Relevance Theory), or in allowing a hearer's uptake to guide the inferential process of meaning negotiation. This final option will be discussed with respect to approaches to communication in talk-in-interaction (e.g. Heritage 1984; Sanders 1987; Clark 1996; Arundale 1999, 2020) which, while being seemingly incompatible with philosophical pragmatic analyses of meaning in their epistemological and ontological commitments, nevertheless provide insight into how meanings are viewed between speakers themselves in the process of interaction. In the brief precis of different theoretical options to follow, we will see that all of these questions and issues cross-cut each other, yielding varying outcomes with regard to speaker meaning, commitment and accountability.

4.2.2 Communication As Inferential

Relevance Theory (Sperber and Wilson [1986] 1995) is one post-Gricean theory that aims to explain the cognitive processes that interlocutors engage in when recovering utterance meanings, thus pursuing representations of speaker meaning as a reflection of cognitive reality. As Sperber and Wilson (2002: 3) state, "pragmatic interpretation is ultimately an exercise in mind-reading, involving the inferential attribution of intentions". On this account, it is hearers' recognition and attribution of speakers' intentions that are assumed to underlie human communication. Relevance Theorists have long argued that speakers are committed to the truth of what they are understood to mean by hearers (unless otherwise indicated; see Sperber and Wilson 2002: 626; Boulat 2015), giving hearers' recovered meanings precedence in determining 'what is said'. The theoretical goal thus becomes not to explain why a hearer is able to recognize a speaker's intended meaning according to supposed norms of communication, but instead *how* a hearer infers a speaker's meaning through cognitive processes.

The quest to understand how hearers infer speakers' intended meanings is subtly different from Grice's position of explaining the relationship between uttered sentences and speakers' intended meanings in two key ways. First, Relevance Theory reduces Grice's four categories of maxims to just one principle – the principle of relevance – which assumes that hearers recover meanings through a trade-off between maximizing cognitive effects (i.e. changes to one's immediate and manifest cognitive environment) and minimizing processing effort. Second, and of greater interest here, in allowing the hearer's perspective a more privileged theoretical position than the speaker's, the hearer can sometimes assign a meaning intention to the speaker that the speaker did not actually intend.

There are some benefits to prioritizing hearers' inferred content in the study of meaning. One of the motivations for looking at hearers' recovered meanings has been revived by Sperber and Wilson (2015) who, following Grice (1989), noted that speaker meaning can in some cases be ambiguous, leaving open a broad range of possible interpretations for a hearer to recover (see Chapter 3 for further discussion). In such cases, speaker meaning can be more or less determinate, and as long as a hearer recovers a meaning that is *compatible* with the speaker's intended meaning, communication can be considered successful. So, when we acknowledge the multiplicity of potential inferences available from a single utterance, we can view implicatures as lying on a cline from strong to weak: from those that are clearly inferable, determinate in content and strongly intended by the speaker, to those that are weakly communicated and which are the responsibility of the hearer to recover. This takes the account of communication beyond those cases in which the hearer's inferred content and speaker's intended content align, allowing 'successful communication' to also encompass those cases where hearers recover meanings that a speaker may endorse – perhaps on account of the speaker having normative responsibility for the things that they say – even if they did not have a determinate intention to communicate them (see also Ariel 2016; Elder 2019).

On the other hand, there are also challenges for prioritizing hearer inferred meanings in a theory of communication. If speakers' meanings can be indeterminate, this raises the question of which meanings hearers take speakers to be committed to, as well as the degree to which speakers are held committed to those meanings. Relevance Theorists have begun to address the question of how confident a hearer can be in their assessment of the speaker's commitment, considering whether different kinds of meaning inferences commit speakers to those meanings to different extents. It is generally accepted that a speaker bears a greater degree of commitment to explicit content ('what is said') than to implicated meanings (Moeschler 2013), that hearers can be more certain of a speaker's commitment to explicit content than to implicatures (Morency et al. 2008), and that hearers are more forgiving of implicated falsehoods than they are of either explicit or presupposed falsehoods (Mazzarella et al. 2018). However, just because a speaker can be considered *less* committed to an implicature than to explicit content does not mean that speakers do not bear *any* commitment to implicated content. It is exactly because Relevance Theory assumes hearers to infer speakers' intended meanings, and by extension speaker commitments, by accessing their mental states, that hearers can hold speakers committed to implicatures as speaker intended aspects of meaning.

4.2.3 Commitment-Based Communication

The inferential view of speaker meaning discussed above assumes that speakers commit themselves to meanings via their utterances, and it is the hearer's task to access that commitment by accessing the speaker's mental state. A contrasting view is that speaker commitment is not ensured through cognitive, inferential processes, but that commitment is a normative state ensured through the conventions of language use. This view I attribute to 'commitment-based' approaches to communication. In fact, those working in the paradigm of normative, commitment-based communication insist that a commitment *cannot* be a mental state for the reason that, following Hamblin (1970: 264), "a commitment is not necessarily a belief of the participant who has it. We do not believe everything we say; but our saying it commits us whether we believe it or not". In other words, commitment is not a product of the speaker's intention and uttered content, but of the utterance alone in its socionormative environment, irrespective of the speaker's intention to communicate (but see Boulat and Maillat 2017 on different types of commitment from a Relevance Theoretic perspective).

The view that commitment is ensured through conventional, as opposed to inferential, means is often applied to properties of speech acts, for example with Austin (1975: 154) stating that speech acts "commit us to certain future conduct", and with Searle (1976: 10) describing the illocutionary point of an assertive as "to commit the speaker (in varying degrees) to something's being the case, to the truth of the expressed proposition". Note that in both cases, it is the utterance itself that is described as committing the speaker to some state of affairs, which is subtly different from the view that a speaker commits themselves to a certain meaning in virtue of what they say. It is the latter that is typically propounded by the inferential account discussed in the previous section, while the former – the utterance committing a speaker to a certain meaning – is equated with the commitment-based account discussed presently.

Building on a foundation of commitment-based approaches to communication laid by Hamblin (1970) and Brandom (1994), among others, Geurts (2019a, 2019b) has recently proposed the beginnings of a model of communication that brings together the inferential view – that the goal of a theory of communication is to explain how hearers infer speakers' mental states – and the social view, that communication is first and foremost a tool for publicly sharing and negotiating social commitments, and that what goes on in the actual minds of speakers is irrelevant to communication as a form of public action. That is, although he acknowledges that speakers and hearers will inevitably have private beliefs about what someone is committed to, he argues that commitments qua states are neither psychological nor epistemic. His principle idea builds on that of traditional speech-act theory: when a speaker produces an utterance, the speaker incurs certain social commitments, which then entitle the hearer to draw corresponding inferences. And since communication is primarily a form of social action, it is publicly negotiated commitments that take centre stage in his account, with private commitments taking a reduction in theoretical importance.

Geurts thus redefines Grice's story for why hearers are able to infer speakers' intended meanings, and in doing so moves away from the inferential account that has become the mainstay of theoretical pragmatics to one that explains how a speaker can communicate an implicature on the basis of the public commitments they make. To do this, he identifies a number of things that are presumed in the common ground, including:

(i) the speaker has said p;
(ii) the speaker observes Grice's maxims;
(iii) it would not be possible for the speaker to be observing the maxims unless they were committed to q;
(iv) the speaker has not done anything to prevent q from becoming common ground;
(v) the speaker is committed to the goal that q becomes common ground.

If all of these items are in the common ground, then it must be the case that the speaker has implicated q (adapted from Geurts 2019a: 21). This proposal moves us towards a normative account of communication that can explain not only how meanings are derived on the basis of conventional language use, but also how meanings are derived according to the norms of communication, thus allowing both explicit and implicit content in the scope of speaker meaning and commitment. However, note that in removing speaker intentions from the explanatory toolkit, a speaker can be held committed to any meanings that normatively arise from what they say. Indeed, Geurts goes so far as to stipulate that in undertaking a certain commitment, a speaker also undertakes any further commitments that can be derived from it, such as entailments, irrespective of whether the speaker is aware of them.

It is here that we see the main difference between 'meanings' as they are derived by commitment-based accounts and inferential accounts. While for inferential accounts meanings are associated with speakers' intentions and recovered via inferential cognitive processing, for the commitment-based account, it is possible for a speaker to be committed to a meaning without having awareness of being so committed. But note that the two accounts are not necessarily at odds with one another. Whether commitment is, or should be, determined by inference or by convention depends, at least in part, on theoretical desiderata: to talk of speakers committing themselves to certain meanings as per the Relevance Theoretic account (or of hearers inferring speaker commitment; see Boulat 2015 for further distinctions) denotes a psychological understanding of commitment, while disassociating commitment from belief is to take commitment in a 'contractual' way (cf. De Brabanter and Dendale 2008) as a consequence of the conventional meanings associated with particular speech acts: something independent of the speaker's mental state. It does not make sense to conflate the cognitive process of 'accessing a speaker's commitment' – where what a speaker is committed to is a proposition – with a normative view of commitment as a state shared among interlocutors.

The value of the commitment-based account of communication from a sociopragmatic perspective is exactly that communication is viewed as a form of social action with the state of shared commitments at its heart. In this respect, commitments can be, and often are, social in nature, with promises committing speakers to future actions, commissives committing speakers to future goals, and so forth. That is,

> Commitments are interpersonal relationships that are established in the wake of our social activities, and it is entirely possible to engage in the game of sharing and acting on commitments without knowing one's commitments or others', and indeed without knowing what commitments are. (Geurts 2019a: 15)

But despite the fact that a speaker can be committed to some state of affairs without awareness of that commitment, since a commitment is a relation between a speaker *and a hearer*, for Geurts it has to be accepted by both (i.e. be in the common ground) in order to count as a commitment. Admittedly, the stipulation that commitment requires acceptance may on the surface appear to invoke the mental states of speakers and hearers. However, Geurts emphasizes that acceptance does not require awareness: "even if acceptance is acknowledged specifically (which it often isn't), acknowledgements are likely to be sent and received subliminally" (Geurts 2019b: 120–21). So, although commitment-based accounts are not primarily concerned with how interlocutors come to shared commitments (à la inferential accounts), what is lacking from such normative models of communication is any explanation for how implicit, subliminal acceptance of commitments is achieved; what remains absent from the account is an explanation for how speakers come to know that their hearers have understood them, and thus on what grounds the conversational participants themselves consider communication to be 'successful' (see Arundale 2008: 239 on this point).

4.2.4 Interactional Achievement and Accountability

While commitment-based approaches to meaning are currently gaining traction in theoretically oriented linguistic accounts of communication, an alternative to intention-based models of communication has long been on offer from work in talk-in-interaction and Conversation Analysis using the concept of 'reflexive accountability' (cf. Heritage 1984: 110). Accounts of communication that make use of the idea of 'interactional achievement' include, but are not limited to, Sanders' (1987) 'strategic' theoretical model, Arundale's (1999, 2020) 'conjoint co-constituting' model and Clark's (1996) account of 'joint action'.

The main idea is that interaction follows a pervasive three-part architecture of conversational inferencing (see Heritage 1984: 254–60; Levinson 1983: 326–33). Meanings (or 'understandings') are often subject to a three-part process of conversational inference in which a speaker's utterance constitutes the first part, a hearer's response the second part, and the initial speaker's subsequent response the third part. That is, a hearer's response to an utterance makes their inference about that utterance publicly available, after which the initial speaker can respond to the hearer's displayed inference, in turn publicly displaying their confirmation or disconfirmation of the hearer's presumed understanding. Such accounts take the function of hearers' responses to speakers' utterances seriously as providing public confirmation to the speaker about how they have understood the speaker's initial utterance, and hence whether the hearer's understanding aligns with the speaker's own meaning. In this regard, speakers and hearers co-construct meanings together through a process of interactional achievement, in the spirit that

> meaning lies not with the speaker nor the addressee nor the utterance alone as many philosophical arguments have considered, but rather with the interactional past, current, and projected next moment. (Schegloff et al. 1996: 181)

So rather than a speaker committing themselves to a particular meaning, or an utterance committing a speaker to a meaning, on the interactional achievement account, accountability comes about both by the fact that a speaker has produced an utterance as well as by the hearer's interpreting of the utterance. This is because the hearer presumes agency of the speaker, and hence holds the speaker accountable for the hearer's interpreting. So in the first instance, by producing an utterance in a given sequential context, a speaker immediately publicly makes available inferences about their own utterance meaning in virtue of being held committed to what their utterance is normatively taken to mean (Jary 2013; Sanders 2015). But furthermore, any response to an utterance then makes publicly available further inferences about how that previous utterance has been understood, and in that way holds the initial speaker accountable for the meaning they have communicated in virtue of it having been made the object of a future response.

It has to be noted at this point that scholars working in talk-in-interaction tend to disfavour talking of speaker 'intentions', as inferences about meaning are made available via publicly available information as opposed to presumed mental states. However, as noted by Dynel (2016), the word 'intention' could be substituted for a notion of the speaker's projection of the hearer's interpretation, and 'intention recognition' for inferences from what the speaker says. As Dynel says, even if we avoid using the term 'intention', the resulting meaning postulation will still be the meaning the hearer ascribes to the speaker as 'intended'. In this regard, we are closer to the post-Gricean inferential accounts that aim at recovering speakers' intentions than it may appear. But where the notion of 'intention' as used in many post-Gricean accounts of meaning comes apart from Dynel's description is on how these intentions are ascribed from a theoretical point of view. Rather than inferring meanings on the basis of presumed *psychological* processes as on the inferential account, on the talk-in-interaction account, meanings are instead inferred on the basis of *observable* features of the interaction itself without recourse to postulations about speakers' mental states:

> a speaker's meaning intention is a static psychological state, defined within a rational explanation of a speaker's meaning something by a single utterance, and employed as the central concept in an explanation of communication framed within the commitments of encoding/ decoding models... On the other hand, the speaker's projecting of a recipient's interpreting in a dynamic psychological process, defined with respect to practices observable in the sequential organization of ordinary conversation, and employed within a closely linked network of other concepts in an explanation of communication is consistent with the commitments of interactional achievement models. (Arundale 2008: 253)

In this regard, the talk-in-interaction account aligns with the ontology of the commitment-based accounts discussed in the previous section, both differing in this respect from inferential accounts that promote a psychological understanding of Grice's intentional meaning. That is, what the talk-in-interaction and the commitment-based accounts have in common is the aim to derive meanings on the basis of the observable features of language in line with the social conventions associated with certain linguistic practices.

One could go so far as to deem it permissible to use the terms 'commitment' and 'accountability' interchangeably in the sense that both terms are related to a public notion of speaker meaning. However, there is some discrepancy in how these two concepts are utilized in their respective fields. Where the commitment-based approach comes apart from the interactional achievement account is in one respect in terms of how the content of what a speaker is committed to and/or held accountable for is determined. As discussed in the previous section, commitment in the commitment-based accounts, being a normative state based on the conventions of language use, can be external to the minds of the speakers who are thus committed, and hence a speaker may be committed to some meaning without awareness of being so committed. By contrast, accountability in the interactional achievement account – while a matter of public on-record negotiation – is ascribed and perceived by the participants themselves involved in the discourse. This difference has ramifications for the ways in which speakers may orient themselves to certain meanings. In view of relying on principles of normativity, the commitment-based account focuses on commitments that arise on the basis of propositional contents communicated by utterances and what they are normatively taken to mean in those contexts. By contrast, the interactional achievement account leaves open the possibility that a hearer may come to an understanding that wasn't intended or even *said*, for example due to mismatches in background assumptions, or external factors such as noise in the communicative channel.

4.3 Combining Eclectic Perspectives on Speaker Meaning, Commitment and Accountability

'Speaker meaning' is an integral component of the broader enterprise of communication, and yet it is obvious that communication does not solely rest on hearers successfully inferring speakers' intended meanings in the spirit of Grice. Rather, 'speaker' meanings can be indeterminate in intention (Terkourafi 2014; Sperber and Wilson 2015; Elder and Savva 2018), intentionally vague (Clark 1997) or even unintended but difficult to dismiss by the hearer on the basis of the speaker being held normatively accountable to what they said (Haugh 2008). In light of the increasing build-up of empirical evidence that in 'real-life' communication identifying speaker intentions vis-à-vis meanings is not always a straightforward task, it becomes necessary to locate speaker meaning in a broader account of linguistic communication in a way that involves (re-)opening the question of whose perspective should take precedence in the theorization of so-called speaker meaning.

One way to encompass such eclectic empirical evidence is to take both speaker and hearer perspectives into account in deriving utterance meanings (cf. Kecskes 2010, 2017; Sanders 1987, 2015). A motivation for such a move is that divergences in understandings of utterance meanings do inevitably arise between interlocutors, and when such cases arise, speakers and hearers need to negotiate their agreement on such meanings. Indeed, it is not that these are special cases that can be cast aside as somehow non-standard, but that meaning negotiation is a typical occurrence in everyday communication (see e.g. Haugh 2008; Kecskes 2008; Sanders 2015), and hence needs to be acknowledged in an account of communication that adequately reflects how people communicate.

Elder and Haugh (2018) have recently argued that attending to the local processes of interactionally achieving meanings provides important insights into how utterance meanings become understood as public commitments. The way in which they do this involves departing from the Gricean view that speaker meaning is dependent on a priori speaker intentions recoverable at the point of utterance, and instead involves making the leap to equate 'speaker meaning' with the meaning that is interactionally achieved between participants. That is, they use the three-part architecture of conversational inferencing offered by interactional achievement accounts to extend the Gricean, intentional notion of 'speaker meaning' to one that allows and accommodates the local processes of meaning negotiation that speakers engage in. This involves indexing meanings for both times (which allows meanings to be updated as an interaction progresses) and perspectives (i.e. both speaker and hearer), as well as including private, intentional meanings alongside publicly available ones in their model. As such, they aim to offer an empirically informed view on utterance meaning that incorporates both speakers' and hearers' perspectives, as well as the process of interactionally negotiating meanings that occurs through subsequent responses to prior utterances. 'Speaker meaning' thus takes on a broader characterization than the familiar Gricean one as it now involves speakers converging on particular meanings, sometimes over a course of utterances, which often requires complex joint inferential work, while the model also provides a framework for identifying when speakers diverge in their understandings of particular utterances.

While taking 'speaker meaning' as the meaning that is interactionally achieved between conversational participants is seemingly at odds with the post-Gricean intentional accounts of speaker meaning in philosophical pragmatics, Elder and Haugh (2018) aim to integrate both private and public inferences in a single model of communication. However, rather than assuming private inferences to be the result of accessing a hearer's mental state via cognitive processes, they trace the (presumed) private inferences that people make on the basis of inferences that they make publicly available via their responses to others' utterances. In this respect, Kecskes' (2010) socio-cognitive approach is on a similar track, in that it mandates a holistic interpretation of utterances by taking on board both speaker and hearer perspectives, combining the notion of speaker intention as a private, individual phenomenon in a broader conception of intention as one that is dynamic, co-constructed by participants and emergent and that emphasizes that both sides of the phenomenon are needed for an adequate model of communication.

Haugh (2013) provides some rationale for reconciling the inferential, mental state, account of speaker meaning with a more public view of speaker meaning. Based on his work on the practice of implicating by 'not-saying', he argues that

> when an implication is attribut*able* to, but not actually attribut*ed* to, someone, it does not count as an implicature for which they can be held fully accountable. But, since it arises from what was said, the speaker still bears some degree of responsibility for it. So we have a case of speaker meaning where what is implied *by the utterance, not the speaker* is left (partly) to the hearer, thereby reducing the *speaker's* degree of accountability for the implied meaning. (adapted from Haugh 2013: 52)

This idea is reminiscent of the notion of strongly and weakly communicated implicatures from Relevance Theory: speakers can communicate a broad range of meanings from a single utterance, to which they may hold stronger or weaker degrees of commitment. However, while in Relevance

Theory it is the hearer's responsibility to infer a speaker's commitment (and so a hearer's confidence in a speaker's commitment to different meanings can also range from strong to weak), the interactional view presents a case in favour of departing from accountability as being strongly tied to a view of speaker meaning in terms of the speaker's communicative intention. Instead, it is utterances themselves, in virtue of the linguistic elements of what is said, that take a more central role in determining the meaning(s) that can be attributed to the speaker. While proponents of both accounts would likely agree that a speaker cannot be held to be *more* committed to a meaning that they implied but did not say than to one they actually said, as Haugh (2013) says, speakers can deliberately formulate their utterances so as to modulate their commitments to certain meanings, which in turn increases or decreases the degree of accountability to which they can be held for those meanings. Viewing accountability as not only a function of speaker intentions and utterance meanings, but of utterances themselves and their meanings, provides a link between 'speaker meaning' as it is understood in Gricean terms, and the sociopragmatic question of why speakers may formulate their utterances in one way rather than another.

4.4 Case Studies

In what follows are two case studies that exemplify both the strengths and limitations of the different theoretical commitments of the accounts of communication discussed in this chapter. The case studies showcase how utterances can give rise to multiple potential meanings, but also how divergences in their sociopragmatic contextual environments can affect and/or constrain how speakers orient themselves to certain meanings that are inferable from their utterances.

4.4.1 Case Study I: Ascribing Speaker Meanings to Hinting Utterances

Requestive hinting is a pragmatic move in which a speaker makes an 'off record indirect request' (Brown and Levinson 1987): a request that is not explicitly stated. As discussed by Elder and Haugh (2018), the case of requestive hinting is a fruitful test case for teasing out different options vis-à-vis speaker meaning: precisely because speakers formulate requestive hints in such a way as to avoid explicitly spelling out the content of the request, the speaker can claim plausible deniability and hence deny that they did, in fact, perform a request in the first place (Haugh 2017). This means that attributing a priori speaker intentions to specific utterances is not always empirically justified; yet requestive hints are pervasive in everyday interactions, with hearers systematically responding as if a request has been made.

In the following example, we see Emma mention needing to go to the store (line 2), prompting Betsy to offer to get something for her (line 6).

(1) Emma has been talking about needing to go out and buy some food (as she doesn't have anything for dinner)

```
1       E:   I had a little tiny bit - piece a fish
2    →       so I don't know I may have to go to the store but you go
             ahead
3            Betsy and phone it up I think maybe
4       B:   they'll send it down
5       E:   ye[ah
6    → B:       [can I add anything for you?
7    → E:   Oh honey thanks I think I'll ah let Guy go
8       B:   [Yes
9    → E:   [Maybe (you) get some fish.
10      B:   Yes.
11      E:   I'll plan on that.
```

(adapted from Jefferson's NB:IV:2:R, available at https://ca.talkbank.org/)

Focussing on Emma's utterance "I may have to go to the store" in line 2, there are different options regarding her speaker meaning. There is first the explicit content, stating a future possibility for Emma. However, there are different options regarding her possible implicit meanings. On the one hand, it is possible that, based on the utterance alone, Emma's utterance could be interpreted as a hint – or even a request – for Betsy to go to the store for her: an inference that is calculable on Gricean principles. Indeed, Betsy's subsequent offer in line 6 to get something for Emma could function as confirmation of Betsy's inference of such a request. However, despite such a request being inferable from line 2, in line 7 Emma refuses Betsy's offer, explicitly indicating a denial of any such intention in her prior turn.

Emma's refusal in line 7 highlights the risk of attributing speaker intentions to individual utterances in abstraction from their position in the broader interaction. The case of hinting thus provides empirical grounds for including the third turn in the theoretical apparatus of speaker meaning. Rather than making claims about Emma's a priori intention to communicate a request in the first turn in line 2, her third turn in line 7 makes available her own inference about the way in which her initial utterance is being operationalized by Betsy, in turn allowing herself plausible deniability as to any initial hinting intention – even if she did, in fact, privately 'intend' for Betsy to make such an offer. So, not attributing speaker intentions to particular utterances on the basis of either the utterance itself or even the immediately subsequent utterance becomes of particular importance when we observe that meanings can be negotiated over several turns, as the third turn does the work of confirming or disconfirming a hearer's previous inference.

At this point it is important to note that deriving a negotiated 'speaker meaning' by including the third turn is not to attribute a presumed intention of the speaker on the basis of the third turn. That is, it is not the speaker's *intention* that emerges or becomes clear over the course of the interaction: as hinted at above, intentions qua speakers' private mental states can be dynamic and alter over time. Rather, it is 'meanings' that emerge over an interaction that can be procedurally attributed to a speaker's initial utterance (hence 'speaker meaning') even if those meanings do not necessarily correspond to a speaker's intention at the time of that utterance. This becomes important when we notice that utterance negotiation can occur over more turns than the canonical three-part architecture of conversational inferencing. Taking the example above, while at line 7 we might attribute to Emma a lack of intention to issue a request in line 2 on the basis of her response to Betsy's offer, we see further complexity when Emma later *accepts* Betsy's offer in line 9 in her request, "Maybe (you) get some fish". Again, while we may be hesitant to ascribe a retrospective intention of a request to Emma's utterance in line 2, her move to accept the offer at this later point in the interaction would arguably not have been possible without Emma's initial hinting utterance which led to Betsy's offer, thereby highlighting the interrelatedness of different ascriptions of meanings that arise in the incremental process of interaction.

4.4.2 Case Study II: Manipulating Implicatures in Political Discourse

It goes without saying that conversational participants are not always aligned in their communicative goals, which can result in disagreements about or manipulation of meanings in the process of interaction. As Grice (1989: 369) himself noted, "collaboration in achieving exchange of information or the institution of decisions may coexist with a high degree of reserve, hostility, and chicanery". The following example is taken from the 2016 presidential debates between Donald Trump and Hillary Clinton (moderated by Lester Holt) which showcases how the multiplicity of meanings that are available from a single utterance can be manipulated as a way of promoting one's own political agenda (see Elder 2020 for further discussion).

Immediately prior to the following example, the two presidential candidates have been discussing employment. Trump has criticized Clinton's proposal for creating jobs, to which Clinton has urged the audience to 'fact check' Trump's statements via her website. As they come to the end of the segment on employment, Trump refers back to Clinton's website, shifting the discussion as follows.

(2)

1 →	T:	You know what? It's no different than this. She's telling us how to fight ISIS. Just go to her website. She tells you how to fight ISIS on her website.
2 →		I don't think General Douglas MacArthur would like that too much.
3	H:	The next segment, we're continuing –
4 →	C:	Well, at least I have a plan to fight ISIS.
5	H:	– achieving prosperity –
6 →	T:	No, no, you're telling the enemy everything you want to do.
7	C:	No, we're not. No, we're not.

(adapted from transcripts available on Internet Archive 2016, available at http://politicaladarchive.org/debate-project/)

In line 1, Trump claims that Clinton "tells you how to fight ISIS on her website", immediately following up with a jibe in line 2, "I don't think General Douglas MacArthur would like that too much". Focussing on this latter remark, (at least) three inferable aspects of meaning can be identified. First, it communicates the explicit content regarding MacArthur's presumed opinion of Clinton's ISIS strategy. Second, it carries a strongly inferable implicature that reporting her ISIS plan on her website is not a good strategy. Finally, the indexical 'that' entails the content of the previous utterance, namely "she tells you how to fight ISIS on her website". All three of these meanings can be presumed on a single utterance basis, both through presumptions of the language system, through Gricean principles of rationality, and/or due to inferred meanings based on the speaker's presumed communicative intentions.

Clinton responds in line 4, constituting a second turn to Trump's just prior first turn. In stating "at least I have a plan", she makes available her inference that Trump's just prior turn is indeed a description of her 'plan' to fight ISIS. Moreover, her use of "at least" as a minimizer also demonstrates her understanding of his implicitly communicated jibe as it serves to reduce the strength of his prior allegation. In this instance, an appropriate response from Clinton is sufficient for the two participants to assume mutual understanding of Trump's implicated meaning. But note that while the explicit content of Clinton's response demonstrates understanding of Trump's prior turn, it also performs its own jibe through its implicit content: in putting focus on "I", she communicates her own strongly inferable implicature that Trump – as the salient alternative to Clinton – does not have a plan to fight ISIS.

Trump presents a third turn in this interaction, responding to Clinton's remark in line 6. However, while a response to her implicated meaning would demonstrate his understanding of that meaning, he does not acknowledge it, instead responding directly to the explicit content of her utterance with "No, no" to dispute her assertion "I have a plan". Here we have a case where Clinton's strongly inferable implicature was not jointly operationalized by the participants, and hence the interactional achievement account would not take it on board as Clinton's 'speaker meaning'. However, it has to be noted that just because the implicature was not acknowledged does not mean that Trump did not recognize it. As Drew (1987: 226) notes with regard to teasing, "although the only research methodology for seeing that someone has recognized a tease is through their displaying that recognizing (for example, by laughing) it cannot be inferred from an absence of such a display that they did not recognize the tease", thus highlighting the limitations of focussing solely on meanings as interactional achievements.

In response to this limitation of the interactional approach, one could highlight as a strength that it allows us – given that Clinton's implicature was strongly inferable – to account for how Trump could legitimately avoid responding to it. One explanation is that given that Clinton's jibe was only communicated implicitly, it left the explicit content of her utterance open as a potential target for Trump's next utterance – which he capitalized on in the third turn, both diverting attention from her implicitly communicated criticism while at the same time calling into question the content of her just prior utterance. In this respect, as Trump's third turn communicated no strongly inferable alternative interpretation of its own, we can also observe how Clinton was restricted to respond to the only available interpretation left open, namely the criticism of her ISIS plan.

4.5 Conclusion

This chapter has looked at conceptions of 'speaker meaning' stemming from Grice's (1989) seminal work that introduced the role of intentions as an explanatory tool, alongside accounts of communication that view meaning as socially and/or conventionally grounded avoiding equating meanings as reflections of speakers' mental states. The upshot of these different accounts of meaning is that speakers can be deemed committed to, or held accountable for, different kinds of meanings depending on the principles one subscribes to in deriving those meanings.

Relevance Theory is one example of an 'inferential', post-Gricean theory that aims to explain the cognitive processes by which hearers recover speakers' intended meanings. On this account, speakers can be held committed to both explicit and implicit meanings on account of the hearer 'accessing' the speaker's mental state via considerations of optimal relevance. On the other hand, commitment-based accounts theorize communication in view of its role as a social practice, taking speakers to be held committed to meanings based on conventions of language use. This removes intentionalism from the explanatory toolkit, as commitment is instead viewed as a normative state that is held between interlocutors. Commitment on this latter account is not limited to meanings qua propositions, but acknowledges that speakers also make a range of social commitments via their utterances.

The interactional achievement account takes an orthogonal line to either of these theoretical options, as it prioritizes both the meanings that are publicly made available by speakers, but at the same time views meaning as that which is understood and negotiated by the speakers themselves. In this sense, the interactional achievement account takes elements from both inferential and commitment-based accounts: from the latter in that it is concerned with public commitments, and from the former in that it prioritizes participant understandings. What the interactional achievement view offers to the sociopragmatic toolkit is a deontological notion of meaning in communication (e.g. Elder and Haugh 2018), as speakers are held accountable for their meanings through the responses of others, and in turn held reflexively accountable to those meanings through their own responses to those hearers' responses. This deontological notion thus provides the rationale for – assuming that speakers typically hope to be understood in the ways in which they want to be understood – why speakers may formulate their utterances in particular ways in particular circumstances.

A question that remains regards the extent to which these different conceptions of speaker meaning, that necessarily hold different epistemological and ontological commitments, are compatible. On the one hand, while the interactional achievement account provides a nuanced picture of how speakers coordinate meaning negotiation, while also offering an alternative view of 'speaker meaning' in terms of the mutually accepted operationalized meaning, it does not give any explanation of the internal, cognitive processes by which interlocutors are presumed to engage in the process of arriving at those meanings that the inferential account aims to provide. By the same token, given the potential multiplicity of meanings available from a single utterance, the three-turn model does not provide any rationale for when or why a hearer may make available inferences that pertain to explicit or implicit meanings. The two case studies showcase how utterances can give rise to a range of meanings that vary in determinacy, from strongly intended speaker meanings to more weakly recoverable inferences, but at the same time how hearers can pick up on, or even deliberately manipulate, different meanings. In this sense, the three-turn model is compatible with accounts of speaker meaning that aim to explain the relationship between explicit utterance content in its contextual environment and the meaning(s) that arise on an utterance-by-utterance basis, while at the same time leaving room in pragmatic theory for an answer to the procedural question of why a hearer is likely to pick up on certain inferences more readily than others, alongside answers to the sociopragmatic question of why a speaker may formulate their utterances in certain ways over others.

References

Ariel, M. (2016). Revisiting the typology of pragmatic interpretations. *Intercultural Pragmatics*, 13(1), 1–35.

Arundale, R. B. (1999). An alternative model and ideology of communication for an alternative to politeness theory. *Pragmatics*, 9, 119–53.

Arundale, R. B. (2008). Against (Gricean) intentions at the heart of human interaction. *Intercultural Pragmatics*, 5(2), 229–58.

Arundale, R. B. (2020). *Communicating and Relating: Constituting Face in Everyday Interacting*. Oxford: Oxford University Press.

Austin, J. L. (1975). *How to Do Things with Words*. Oxford: Oxford University Press.

Boulat, K. (2015). Hearer-oriented processes of strength assignment: A pragmatic model of commitment. *Belgian Journal of Linguistics*, 29, 19–40.

Boulat, K. and Maillat, D. (2017). She said you said I saw it with my own eyes: A pragmatic account of commitment. In J. Blochowiak, C. Grisot, S. Durrleman and C. Laenzlinger, eds., *Formal Models in the Study of Language*. Cham, Switzerland: Springer, pp. 261–79.

Brandom, R. B. (1994). *Making It Explicit: Reasoning, Representing and Discursive Commitment*. Cambridge, MA: Harvard University Press.

Brown, P. and Levinson, S. C. (1987). *Politeness: Some Universals in Language Usage*. Cambridge: Cambridge University Press.

Clark, H. H. (1996). *Using Language*. Cambridge: Cambridge University Press.

Clark, H. H. (1997). Dogmas of understanding. *Discourse Processes*, 23(3), 567–98.

De Brabanter, P. and Dendale, P. (2008). Commitment: The term and the notions. *Belgian Journal of Linguistics*, 22, 1–14.

Drew, P. (1987). Po-faced receipts of teases. *Linguistics*, 25(1), 219–53.

Dynel, M. (2016). With or without intentions: Accountability and (un)intentional humour in film talk. *Journal of Pragmatics*, 95, 67–98.

Elder, C. (2019). Negotiating what is said in the face of miscommunication. In P. Stalmaszczyk, ed., *Philosophical Insights into Pragmatics*. Berlin: Mouton de Gruyter, pp. 107–26.

Elder, C. (2020). Trump vs. Clinton: Implicatures as public stance acts. In L. N. Berlin, ed., *Positioning and Stance in Political Discourse*. Wilmington, DE: Vernon Press, pp. 71–91.

Elder, C. and Haugh, M. (2018). The interactional achievement of speaker meaning: Towards a formal account of conversational inference. *Intercultural Pragmatics*, 15(5), 593–625.

Elder, C. and Savva, E. (2018). Incomplete conditionals and the syntax-pragmatics interface. *Journal of Pragmatics*, 138, 45–59.

Geurts, B. (2019a). Communication as commitment sharing: Speech acts, implicatures, common ground. *Theoretical Linguistics*, 45(1-2), 1–30.

Geurts, B. (2019b). Commitments continued. *Theoretical Linguistics*, 45(1-2), 111–25.

Grice, P. (1989). *Studies in the Way of Words*. Cambridge, MA: Harvard University Press.

Hamblin, C. L. (1970). *Fallacies*. London: Methuen.

Haugh, M. (2008). Intention and diverging interpretings of implicature in the uncovered meat sermon. *Intercultural Pragmatics*, 5(2), 201–29.

Haugh, M. (2013). Speaker meaning and accountability in interaction. *Journal of Pragmatics*, 48, 41–56.

Haugh, M. (2017). Prompting offers of assistance in interactions. *Pragmatics and Society*, 8(2), 183–207.

Heritage, J. (1984). *Garfinkel and Ethnomethodology*. Cambridge: Polity Press.

Jary, M. (2013). Two types of implicature: Material and behavioural. *Mind and Language*, 28(5), 638–60.

Kecskes, I. (2008). Dueling contexts: A dynamic model of meaning. *Journal of Pragmatics*, 40, 385–406.

Kecskes, I. (2010). The paradox of communication – socio-cognitive approach to pragmatics. *Pragmatics and Society*, 1, 50–73.

Kecskes, I. (2017). The interplay of recipient design and salience in shaping speaker's utterance. In M. de Ponte and K. Korta, eds., *Reference and Representation in Thought and Language*. Oxford: Oxford University Press, pp. 238–73.

Levinson, S. C. (1983). *Pragmatics*. Cambridge: Cambridge University Press.

Mazzarella, D., Reinecke, R., Noveck, I. and Mercier, H. (2018). Saying, presupposing and implicating: How pragmatics modulates commitment. *Journal of Pragmatics*, 133, 15–27.

Moeschler, J. (2013). Is a speaker-based pragmatics possible? Or how can a hearer infer a speaker's commitment? *Journal of Pragmatics*, 48, 84–97.

Morency, P., Oswald, S. and de Saussure, L. (2008). Explicitness, implicitness and commitment attribution: A cognitive pragmatic perspective. *Belgian Journal of Linguistics*, 22, 197–219.

Sanders, R. E. (1987). *Cognitive Foundations of Calculated Speech*. Albany: State University of New York Press.

Sanders, R. E. (2015). A tale of two intentions: Intending what an utterance means and intending what an utterance achieves. *Pragmatics and Society*, 6(4), 475–501.

Schegloff, E. A., Ochs, E. and Thompson, S. A. (1996). Introduction. In E. Ochs, E. A. Schegloff and S. A. Thompson, eds., *Interaction and Grammar*. Cambridge: Cambridge University Press, pp. 1–51.

Searle, J. (1976). A classification of illocutionary acts. *Language in Society*, 5(1), 1–23.

Sperber, D. and Wilson, D. ([1986] 1995). *Relevance: Communication and Cognition*. Oxford: Basil Blackwell.

Sperber, D. and Wilson, D. (2002). Pragmatics, modularity and mind-reading. *Mind and Language*, 17(1-2), 3–23.

Sperber, D. and Wilson, D. (2015). Beyond speaker's meaning. *Croatian Journal of Philosophy*, 15, 117–49.

Terkourafi, M. (2014). The importance of being indirect: A new nomenclature for indirect speech. *Belgian Journal of Linguistics*, 28, 45–70.

5

Social Actions

Arnulf Deppermann[*]

5.1 Introduction

This chapter enquires into the nature of social actions. It discusses how actions are organized in social interaction and how social factors impinge on the formation and the interpretation of actions. In Section 5.2, we contrast three leading theoretical approaches to the study of social actions, namely Speech Act Theory, the Ethnography of Communication and Conversation Analysis, the latter being the vantage point which informs this chapter most. Section 5.3 deals with linguistic social action formats, i.e. linguistic resources that are used to implement specific actions. Action-meanings are often ambiguous, multi-faceted and multi-layered, because they depend on the position of an action within an action sequence, its relationship to larger goals and social factors like the deontic, epistemic or institutional status of the participants (Section 5.4). Section 5.5 lays out that the meaning of an action as a social fact is neither sufficiently defined by speakers' intentions nor by conventions, but it is subject to interactive confirmation and negotiation.

5.2 Approaches to the Study of Social Action

All linguistic action is social action, because it is necessarily addressed to some recipient, even if they are unknown or it is the agent themselves (Linell 2009). Yet the social has played rather different roles in different approaches. In Speech Act Theory (Austin 1962; Searle 1969) the focus has been on individual actions. Austin (1962) called for a linguistic phenomenology of speech acts, building on the vocabulary of action-terms that exist in a

---

[*] I am grateful to Marina Terkourafi and an anonymous reviewer for comments to prior versions of this chapter.

language. Like Wittgenstein's emphasis on the multiplicity of language games (Wittgenstein [1950] 1953: §§23–4), Austin's approach is bottom-up and opens up the possibility that speech acts may differ between cultures. Searle (1969), in contrast, argued that basic actions-types are universal and defined by the agent's intentions. Speech act categories are derived from a universal, theoretical taxonomy of speech acts. They are deductively attributed to concrete tokens of linguistic behaviour. According to Searle, action-types are defined by a specific "direction of fit" between the words and the world. They conceptually imply felicity conditions, whose fulfilment is imperative for the valid execution of a speech act. These early philosophical approaches deduced properties of the nature of actions and of specific action-types from conceptual analysis, introspection and thought-experiments. Later research in linguistic Speech Act Theory has increasingly used empirical methods (like sentence completion tasks, adequacy judgements, corpus analysis). The turn to empirical data brought the importance of context to the researchers' attention and fostered an understanding according to which "situated action [is] an action made possible and afforded by and in a particular situation" (Mey 2006: 7). Many proponents of Speech Act Theory have moved away from an understanding of speech acts as isolated, context-free, abstract types and turned to a more contextualist approach (Thomas 1995: esp. 133–42; Sbisà 2002; Fetzer 2004). The latter studies how humans use language and produce actions in a way that flexibly adapts to their ends and to the many facets of the social and material situation they are in (Verschueren 1999: 55–114). Similar to Critical Discourse Analysis (van Dijk 2015), for speech act theorists, contextual factors are mainly socio-categorical features like institutional and power relations and speakers' and addressees' membership in social categories like gender, race, ethnicity and class (Mey 2001). Dealing specifically with 'face-threatening acts', Politeness Theory (Brown and Levinson 1987) insisted on the importance of power relationships and social distance for the choice of linguistic forms in order to act in accordance with constraints of the ritual order of interpersonal relationships (Goffman 1971). More recently, there have been increasing attempts to integrate the sequential context, which has been the primary focus of Conversation Analysis (see below), into speech act–theoretic approaches (Terkourafi 2009; Fetzer and Oishi 2011; Fetzer 2017) and politeness research (Davies et al. 2011).

Ethnographic research has shown that societal and cultural aspects of actions enter into action-formation and action-ascription in various ways. They concern the very idea of what actions actually are, which actions there are and how some action-type is to be defined. Anthropological studies have shown that in some non-Western cultures, the ascription of intentionality to the agent may not play a role for ascribing meanings to actions and that the agent will be held responsible for understandings and effects of actions which they could not anticipate (Rosaldo 1982; Duranti 1988). The idea that speech act types are universal and obey uniform felicity conditions has been equally challenged by studies in Western cultures (see e.g. Kreckel 1981: 87): "What counts as a 'warning' depends on rules evolved and sustained in concrete interaction within social groups". Ethnographic approaches, such as the Ethnography of Communication (Saville-Troike 1989) and Interactional Sociolinguistics (Gumperz 1982), therefore, study actions in the context of the rules of cultural-specific speech events and social situations (Hymes 1972). They aim at the identification of contextualization conventions, which must be known in order to understand how communicative intentions, key, stance towards the addressee, and emotional meanings are communicated by linguistic cues (such as code-switching, prosody and formulaic speech; Gumperz 1982).

In contrast to Speech Act Theory and like ethnographic approaches, Conversation Analysis is interested in an emic understanding of social actions (Atkinson and Drew 1984; Schegloff 1996b). Yet, while ethnographers rely on background knowledge of larger social and cultural contexts, conversation analysts underscore the primary relevance of the sequential order of social actions (Schegloff 2007). Their analysis of social action is based on audio and video recordings of naturally occurring social interaction. They aim to identify action-meanings by means of the "next-turn proof procedure" (Sacks et al. 1974: 729), that is, by recipients' responses in interaction, and by the "procedural consequentiality" (Schegloff 1991) of actions for the further course of the interaction in which they occur. In contrast to Speech Act Theory, actions here are seen as being essentially "context-shaped" and "context-renewing" (Heritage 1984: 238). Action-meanings are shown to emerge from social negotiation and (joint) accomplishment (see Section 5.5); their empirical status can neither be warranted by reference to speaker's intentions nor to theoretical, rule-based deduction. In the following we will use the notion 'social action' (and not 'speech act') in order to index that we adopt an emic perspective on action meaning, understanding social actions as recipient-designed and intrinsically tied to their sequential context both in terms of their composition and their interpretation.

5.3 Social Action Formats

Social action formats are routine ways for the linguistic implementation of certain actions (Goodwin and Goodwin 1992; Fox 2007; Couper-Kuhlen 2014). They can be seen as a linguistic variant of the broader concept of 'practices' in Conversation Analysis (Schegloff 1997; Heritage 2010). Practices consist in using verbal and bodily resources (grammar, lexis, prosody, gaze, gesture etc.) in specific kinds of contexts for specific kinds of action. Yet, the same resource can be put to different pragmatic uses, depending on context, e.g. a *wh*-question can implement a request for information, a known-answer question, a rhetorical question or an announcement of the topic of a multi-unit turn.

Couper-Kuhlen (2014) shows for American English that a number of constructions using imperatives, modal verbs, or catenative verbs are routine means for formulating requests (imperative), offers (*do you need/want X? If you X, then Y*), suggestions (imperative; *why don't you X?*) and proposals (*I/we can/could X. Why don't we X?*). Social action formats are grammatical constructions (Fillmore 1989) with a pragmatic profile in the sense that they are idiomatic ways of performing an action. Their pragmatic meaning often cannot be derived from their semantics; moreover, social action formats are sometimes language-specific. They sometimes perform actions which have no precise equivalent in another language. Social action formats therefore are idioms, i.e. socially sanctioned, routine ways to perform an action, which often cannot be supplanted by lexical items, which would be paraphrases from a semantic point of view (Terkourafi 2002). Recent research has dealt with requests (Drew and Couper-Kuhlen 2014), apologies (Drew et al. 2016), invitations (Margutti et al. 2018), offers (Curl 2006; Kärkkäinen and Keisanen 2012), compliments (Golato 2005) and various kinds of responsive actions (Thompson et al. 2015).

Requests belong to the kinds of actions which are peculiar to the human species and its orientation to cooperation. (See Tomasello 2008 for phylogenetic and ontogenetic evidence.) The larger category of 'requests' includes instructions, directives, commands and so on. Since the 1970s, they have figured importantly in research on politeness (Brown and Levinson 1987), which considers them as face-threatening acts. According to Brown and Levinson, the choice of a direct format (imperative) versus an indirect one (*can you give me X?*) or an off-record format (*X really tastes good*) for the production of a request depends on power relationships and social distance between participants and on the degree of imposition by the request. Curl and Drew (2008) have shown that the entitlement of the requester to the service and the contingencies impinging on the grantability of a request determine the choice of request-formats (*Can you do X?* vs *I wonder if you can do X*). High entitlement (which can be related to power asymmetry and high deontic status; Section 5.4.2) licences the use of directives (Craven and Potter 2010; Antaki and Kent 2012). But there are still other factors (Drew and Couper-Kuhlen 2014; Sorjonen et al. 2017; Rossi, in press). Imperatives often index the need for an urgent response (Mondada 2017), they insist on a missing response (Craven and Potter 2010), they are used if the compliant action is simple and routine (Deppermann 2018b), and if the request is highly expectable (Zinken and Deppermann 2017). More generally, the issues of who is responsible for some task as part of a joint project and who benefits from the request (is the gain unilateral or bilateral?) are crucial for the choice of the request format (Heritage and Clayman 2014; Zinken 2016; Rossi, in press). Considerations of benefit equally decide whether an action counts as a request, an offer or a proposal (Couper-Kuhlen 2014). Recently, Kendrick and Drew (2016) have proposed the term "recruitment", arguing that there is a continuum of how assistance in social interaction is achieved. While assistance may be sought for most bluntly by a direct request, there is a gradient of increasingly indirect forms (such as stating a problem) ranging up to cues that are not accountable as requests, such as searching for an object, which can be effective in mobilizing help perhaps even contrary to the beneficiary's intention.

Grammatical properties can implement subtle differences between subtypes of an action. In his comparative study of requests, Zinken (2016) has shown how specific grammatical options in Polish, such as impersonal deontic statements and the distinction between perfective and imperfective verbal aspect, allow for tailoring requests to specific situational features, such as responsibilities in the context of a joint project or recipients' ongoing practical involvements, in culture-specific ways as compared to English.

The relationship between linguistic formats and social actions is generally characterized by the following properties:

1) Grammatical constructions as pure forms, abstracted from context, can be used for different kinds of actions (Deppermann 2011). Taken as such, they are ambiguous. Couper-Kuhlen (2014), for instance, shows that many of the verb-constructions she studied are used for more than only one action, e.g. the imperative being used both for requests, offers and suggestions, *why don't you*-formats being used for suggestions and proposals. Yet, ambiguities will be mostly limited to a small range of possible actions.
2) Grammatical constructions mostly become definite social action formats only in certain sequential contexts. They belong to a "positionally-sensitive grammar" (Schegloff 1996b). (Sequential) position and (formal) composition together define the pragmatic value of a construction as implementing or contributing to a certain type of action (Clift 2016: chapter 3).
3) Even in these defining contexts, ambiguities can arise, which, however, are even more restricted. Yet mostly, they are ruled out because of other (sequential, epistemic, social, etc.) factors (see below). If ambiguities (are likely to) arise, then speakers provide for clarifications in ensuing talk, often occasioned by obvious/putative recipients' misunderstandings or unexpected/unwanted responses (Schegloff 1984).

5.4 The Relevance of Contextual Orders to Action-Formation and Action-Ascription

There is an enormous array of situational contingencies that inform the production and understanding of actions. The most basic contextual condition for the constitution of social action and for the concept of 'action' as such, is that social actions almost never come alone, but as part of action-sequences (Atkinson and Heritage 1984). The sequential embeddedness of actions is the most immediate social context, which directly impinges on the production and interpretation of actions and which accounts for a great number of action-types. There is a long research tradition in pragmatics that shows how other contextual factors impinge on the design of social actions. Cultural conventions (Gumperz 1982), asymmetries of knowledge (Heritage 2013), social distance (Brown and Levinson 1987), institutional role-relationships (Heritage and Clayman 2010) and power-asymmetries between the interlocutors (Brown and Levinson 1987; Mey, 2001, 2006; Stevanovic and Peräkylä 2012) have all been shown to affect the production and interpretation of linguistic actions. After discussing the fundamental role of sequential position, we take a closer look at how four contextual factors matter to action-formation and action-ascription: activity type, participants' epistemic statuses, their deontic statuses and the common ground that can be taken to hold for them.

5.4.1 Sequentiality in Action-Formation and Action-Ascription

A great number of social actions gain their interpretive status as being actions of a certain kind only by virtue of the position they inhabit within sequences of interaction. Consider Extract (1) from a coaching interaction. The coach (CO) asks the coachee (CE) about his 'philosophy of life':

(1) FOLK_E_00174_SE_01_T_01_DF_01_c597–603

```
01 CO  °hh wie is denn Ihre philosophie so;
       so how does your philosophy sound like
02     ihre LEbensphilosophie;
       your philosophy of life
03     (0.6)
04 CE  meine LEbensphilosoph[ie-
       my philosophy of life
05 CO                       [ja ich mein ihre- (.)
                            well I mean your
06     ihre ARbeitsphilosophie,=
       your philosophy of work
07     =weil sie eben SACHten so-=
       because you just said
08     =das is ne FRAge der der-=
       it is a question of the of the
09     =haben sie philosoPHIE gesacht,=
       did you say philosophy
10     der,=
       of the
11 AS  =EINstellung;
       attitude
12     (0.2)
13 CO  der EINstellung;
       of the attitude
```

Almost all of the participants' actions in this extract can only be characterized by reference to their sequential position: a repair-initiation (04), an other-repair (05–06), an account for the prior utterance (07–08), a collaborative completion of a prior turn (11), an acceptance (13). All of these actions are sequentially dependent in two ways:

(1) Empirically, none of these action-tokens acquires its status as an instance of a certain type of action by virtue of some context-free linguistic property. For example, *meine lebensphilosophie* could as well be an answer, a confirmation, a collaborative completion and many more in other sequential contexts.
(2) Conceptually, action-types like 'repair-initiation', 'other-repair', 'confirmation' and so on are intrinsically sequential actions: They require that certain other actions have taken place (immediately) before so that next actions can be understood as actions of these types. Therefore, it is not possible to define an inventory of self-contained, autonomous actions. A large number of action-types are intrinsically tied to encompassing action-sequences.

Of course, not all action-types are sequentially dependent in the same way, as far as their conceptual meaning is concerned. For example, informings and assessments are action-types that can occur in all sorts of contexts. Yet, because of their sequential embeddedness, all action-tokens in interaction are both context-sensitive and context-renewing (Heritage 1984: 238ff.). Adjacency of actions plays a key role here: the precise moment in which an action is produced affords and at the same time constrains possibilities and normative expectations for action-formation and understanding. For instance, repair-initiations and confirmations by partial repeats (as in lines 04 and 13 in Extract (1); Stivers 2005) require that the trouble source, viz. the confirmable, has been produced in the immediately prior turn. If they are more remote, more explicit forms of back-referring have to be used to accomplish, e.g. repair-initiations, repair, and confirmations (Benjamin 2012; Deppermann 2015). Social actions operate on three temporal planes (Deppermann 2015): they are responsive to prior context exhibiting some understanding of it, they are a present action, and they project some future subsequent action (either by a recipient or an action-continuation by the same agent). Projections can be more or less normatively obligatory. An obligatory expectation is most clearly established by a first pair-part of an adjacency pair, such as a question making an answer due, an offer projecting acceptance/refusal, or a repair-initiation calling for a repair (Schegloff 2007; Stivers 2013). Yet, depending on the type of action, linguistic design and bodily conduct, response projection may be less strict (Stivers and Rossano 2010). Second pair-parts (like answers, compliant actions) have no clear projective force in many activity types. The three temporal planes on which actions operate can have different weight in categorizing different kinds of actions. Whereas responsive actions like acknowledgements, confirmations or compliant actions are characterized by their retrospective properties, initiating actions are categorized by reference to what they project as a response, e.g. questions, requests or repair-initiations. Other actions are more akin to traditional speech act categories, because they are defined by what they are for themselves, not including retro- or prospective aspects, e.g. informings, assessments or compliments.

The sequential organization of social interaction accounts for the infrastructure of social action in Weber's sense of taking account of the behavior of others and being oriented to it in its course (Weber [1922] 1968: 4). Social actions in interaction are reciprocal: they constitute webs of interlocking projections and responses, which create new projections again (Arundale 1999, 2020: 44–112). Social actions thus are inherently temporal and recipient-designed, displaying understanding of the partner's prior turn and anticipating next moves. Social action necessarily is joint action: the status of each individual action as a contribution to discourse depends on the recipient's uptake in the second position (Clark and Schaefer 1989; Enfield and Kockelman 2017). Sacks et al. (1974: 728–9) speak of a "next-turn proof procedure": The recipient's response shows which action and meaning is ascribed to the prior turn. Yet, the recipient's response as such is not sufficient for accomplishing intersubjectivity. It is only in the third position that the producer of the original action in first position can respond to the recipient's uptake in the second position. Third-positioned actions display an understanding of the recipient's understanding. Thereby they show if the producer of the original action accepts the recipient's understanding and considers it to be intersubjective (Schegloff 1992; Sidnell 2014; Deppermann 2015). This three-step process of reciprocal sequential actions thus provides for the basic framework of socially shared meanings of actions.

While adjacency plays a key role for constituting and understanding social actions, the cooperative nature of joint action reaches further. Actions are parts of larger projects which are implemented by sequences (Clark 1992, 1996a), but not necessarily tied to definite sequential trajectories (Levinson 2013: 118–22). Projects are informed by goals, which can be individual (getting something for free, persuading a reluctant recipient) or joint (baptizing a child, negotiating a contract). Both individual and joint projects make for hierarchical relationships between actions in interaction, some actions being prerequisites or being instrumental for other actions (Levinson 1981, 2013). In sequential terms, this hierarchical relationship can play out in pre-actions and pre-sequences (Schegloff 2007: 28–57), like pre-disagreements by way of repair-initiation or announcements of a larger preliminary to a question by formulaic social action formats like 'can I ask you a question?' (Schegloff 1980). The meaning that an individual action acquires therefore often is derived by reference to the larger goal it serves, even if a projected sequence does not materialize and the goal is not reached. There is thus a meronymical relationship between actions and larger projects viz. sequences: actions can index the whole sequence or a superordinate goal and therefore allow for cooperation by enabling anticipation (Levinson 2013: 119–27).

The hierarchical, instrumental dependency of individual actions and their meanings from remote goals gave rise to plan-based modelling of discourse in Artificial Intelligence (e.g. Schank and Abelson 1977; Cohen and Perrault 1979; Grosz and Sidner 1990; Allen 1995). They held that cooperative interaction is to reach joint goals (like buying a ticket, consuming a meal in a restaurant), which involve a number of sub-goals (like inspecting offers, making a request for a ticket, ordering a meal, paying). Individual utterances (*I'd prefer a beer*) can be interpreted unambiguously (as an order) by reference to their position in a script (Schank and Abelson 1977) and/or their instrumental relationship to next (sub)-goals. Ethnographic research by Suchman (2007), however, has shown that script- and plan-based approaches are too inflexible to capture the situated and indexical nature of human action. Although they pursue goals by acting, humans are sensitive to the ever changing (material, temporal, interactive, attentional, etc.) contingencies of actions, to unforeseen circumstances and to unexpected interlocutors' responses; they continuously find situated, creative solutions in the here and now, which do not correspond to the implementation of a deterministic script (Hutchins 1995).

Joint action is needed if goal attainment requires the interdependent actions of multiple agents, even if the goal is ultimately an individual or strategically concealed one. While Clark (1996a) and Tomasello (2008) stress that cooperation in interaction relies on shared goals, intention-reading and altruistic motivation, Charles Goodwin (2017) advocates a different idea of 'co-operative action'. According to him, 'cooperation' refers to the constant reuse and recombination of properties of prior actions (such as grammatical constructions, lexemes, rhythm, gestures) for building new actions in which various layers of semiotic resources are combined in new ways. Marjorie Harness Goodwin (1990) and Charles Goodwin (2017) show how even conflictual interactions and misunderstandings build on the use and mutual elaboration of shared resources, creating emergent effects of interactional structure building, which are not just implementations of (shared) goals and intentions. An example is format-tying in conflict talk, i.e. the reuse of the lexical resources and the syntactic structure of the opponent's prior talk:

(2)   from Goodwin (2017: 28)

```
((Eddie has been teasing Sharon about her hair))
1 Eddie:    he heh
2 Sharon:   I don't know what you're laughing at.
3 Eddie:    I     know what I am    laughing at.
4           Your head.
```

As is common for rejections in conflict talk, Eddie in line 3 reuses the syntax and most of the wording of Sharon's prior turn. The only difference lies in the absence of the negation and, of course, in the deictic shift from "you" to "I". Although the interaction is clearly conflictual, the next speaker uses the prior speaker's turn as a resource to assemble his own turn and to highlight opposition precisely by a combination of repetition and change, stressing the discrepant elements against a background of sharedness.

5.4.2 Activity Types, Deontics, Epistemics and Common Ground as Contexts for Actions

Activity types (Levinson 1979) and communicative genres (Günthner and Knoblauch 1995; Hanks 1996) importantly impinge on action-formation and action-ascription. This is most clearly the case for institutional activity types, such as classroom interaction (Koole 2015), courtroom examination (Drew 1992) and police interrogation (Edwards 2008). In institutional interaction, both the overall organization of exchanges and types of routine sequences are restricted to specific actions. Expectable and allowable contributions are tied to specific institutional roles. There are constraints on possible topics as well as on turn-design, including grammatical constructions and lexical choice for implementing specific actions. Epistemic and deontic asymmetries between role incumbents are constitutive of the interaction and specific rules of inference concerning action-ascription and communicative intentions apply (cf. Drew and Heritage 1992; Heritage and Clayman 2010: chapter 4; Drew and Sorjonen 2011).

One important aspect of interactional rights and duties is the epistemic relationship between participants (Stivers et al. 2011). Participants treat each other as having different epistemic statuses concerning certain topics, i.e. the obligation and the right to know about certain facts and procedures. Doctors, for example, are supposed to be experts for medical knowledge, while patients should be authorities on their own life-history and on their subjective experience. While 'epistemic status' concerns the state of knowledge which is (mutually ascribed) to participants (by virtue of prior knowledge or category-membership), 'epistemic stance' refers to the knowledge-claim which speakers display by the design of their actions. Epistemic stance can amount to a claim to epistemic authority (certainty, independent knowledge) or even superiority vis-à-vis their interlocutor (prior, more knowledge) versus an indication of low epistemic status (uncertainty, less or no knowledge). Epistemic stance and epistemic status have been shown to inform action-formation and action-ascription (Heritage 2012, 2013). While polar questions convey an epistemic stance of no/low knowledge (=k-minus stance), declaratives convey a state of more knowledge (= k-plus stance). Yet, the interpretation of a declarative depends on the epistemic gradient between its producer and the recipient: if the recipient inhabits a k+-status (more knowledge), the declarative will count as a question (e.g. a confirmation check); if the producer of the declarative has a k+-status, it will be understood as an assertion.

Another aspect of interactional rights and duties is the deontic relationship (Stevanovic and Peräkylä 2012, 2014). Especially institutional agents are equipped with role-related deontic rights and duties, that is, rights to decide on (their own and others') future actions and obligations to comply with others' decisions. Deontic status also impinges on action-formation and on the consequentiality of actions. For example, if a person with a high deontic status asserts some own future action, this implies that an addressee with a lower deontic status who is expected to collaborate with the speaker will produce a corresponding compliant action. In contrast, the participant with a lower deontic status will produce a request which checks the addressee's availability and willingness if they seek their collaboration in a future joint project.

Epistemic and deontic status do not have to be displayed explicitly; they are reciprocally ascribed by the participants and show up in the design and understanding of their actions. Despite being tied to socio-structural roles, they can be negotiated.

An example for the specifics of actions in institutional role-relationships are oral examinations at a university. In Extract (5), the examiner EX asks the student about methods of teaching literature.

(3)   FOLK_E_00036_SE_01_T_01_DF_01_c644

```
01 EX  °h jetz müssen wir aber zur literaTURdidaktik übergehen,=
          now we have to turn to teaching literature
02     =sie haben Eben geSAGT;
        you have just said
03     °hh man arbeitet hAndlungs und produkTIONsorientiert.=
          you work action- and production-oriented
04     =wenn man die schüler BRIEfe an einen konkreten
       adressAten schreiben lässt.
        if you make the pupils write letters to a concrete addressee
05     °hhh
06     (2.2)
07 EX  diese definition von ha pe el u ist mir !FREMD!?
          this definition of HPLU[ =action and production oriented
          literature teaching] sounds strange to me
08     °h wie defINIEren sie denn ha pe el u für den
       literaTURunterricht.
         how do you define HPLU for teaching literature
09     (0.6)
10 ST  °h ((dental click)) also ich würde noch die unterscheidung
       zwischen HANdlungso[rientierten] unterricht und
       produkTIONsorientierten (.) unterricht öhm (0.3) MAchen;
         well I would add the distinction between action-oriented and
         production-oriented teaching
```

```
11 EX                    [hm_HM,    ]
12 ST  °h und da wäre eben produktionsorientierter unterricht
          and then production-oriented teaching would just be
       literarische texte produZIERen,=
       producing literary texts
13     =also es müssen nich nur liteRArische texte sein;=
       I mean it does not necessarily have to be literary texts
14     =es können auch ähm °h texte über literatur sein,
       it could also be texts about literature
15 ST  [°h ]
16 EX  [nein;]
        no
17     (1.4)
18 ST  aber wenn man sich jetz in ne rezenSION hinein[verSETzt,]
       but if you take the position of a review
19 EX                                                 [das is n]
                                                       icht
       ha pe el U.
       that's not HPLU
20     (0.7)
21 EX  das is ein: °hhh kommunikaTIONsorientiertes
       adreSSAtenorientiertes SCHREIben,=
       this is communication-oriented, addressee-oriented
        writing
22     =sicherlich SINNvoll.=
        certainly makes sense
23     =aber das ist NICHT[handlungs und]
       produktionsorientierter literaturunterricht.
        but this is not action- and production-oriented literature
        teaching
24 ST                     [okAY;    ]
                           okay
```

The examiner starts the new topic 'methods of teaching literature' in line 01 using a variant of the topic-initiating construction *zu X* [= topic] (*über*) *gehen/kommen* ('to turn to [topic]'). This construction is employed by speakers who have the deontic right and duty to guide an institutional interaction in keeping with an agenda (Proske 2017). When the examiner says in line 07: "diese definition von ha pe el u ist mir ! FREMD!?" ('This definition of HPLU [=action- and production-oriented literature teaching] sounds strange to me"), this is not to be understood as a display of ignorance, but as a rejection of the definition that the student offered. The ensuing question "°h wie defINIEren sie denn ha pe el u für den literaTURunterricht" ('how do you define HPLU for teaching literature', 08) is not a request for information, but a known-answer question, which is to check the student's knowledge (cf. Mehan 1979; Koole 2015). Both action-ascriptions ('rejection' and 'known-answer question') can be inferred from the epistemic statuses that are characteristic of an oral examination, namely that the examiner should be knowledgeable about the topics they ask about. This inference about both the action-ascription and about the participants' reciprocal assignment of epistemic status is corroborated by the examiner's final negative assessment of the student's answer in line 23, which the student accepts without reservation.

Epistemic and deontic status are also important grounds for the recipient design of turns, which can change dynamically over the course of interaction. Sacks et al. (1974: 727) define 'recipient design' this way:

> By 'recipient design' we refer to a multitude of respects in which the talk by a party in a conversation is constructed or designed in ways which display an orientation and sensitivity to the particular other(s) who are co-participants. In our work, we have found recipient design to operate with regard to word selection, topic selection, admissibility and ordering of sequences, options and obligations for starting and terminating conversations etc.

Action-formation is also subject to recipient design. A most important factor of recipient design is common ground (Clark 1992, 1996b). Common ground includes all assumptions and knowledge (about the world, themselves, the ongoing discourse etc.) that participants consider to be mutually shared and accessible at a given moment of talk. The influence of common ground on the recipient design of actions is revealed over the course of interactional histories, when people increasingly become acquainted with each other and thereby enhance their common ground step by step.

In a micro-longitudinal study, Deppermann (2018a) shows how the format of instructions in driving lessons changes over time by virtue of repeated rehearsals of the same task. Across rehearsals, common ground about the instruction and the correct task performance accumulates. This is reflexively indexed by the fact that instructions become increasingly economical: steps of the initial instruction are left out, turn-length and argument structure are reduced, references are increasingly indexical, pronominalized or omitted, understanding-checks and verbal responses do not occur anymore. In order to illustrate these changes in action-formation over an interactional history, we show the first and the fourth occurrence of the same driving task instruction concerning how to reverse the car into a parking lot. In the first instruction, the instructor demonstrates the driving action by a toy car (representing the driving school car) and a box (representing a car parked in front of it):

(4) FAHR_02_15_33:12–33:19

```
01 INS    fährst *du SOweit,
          drive-2SG you so far
    i-h         *..........
02        (.) *BIS diese *be säule,
              until this b-column
    i-h   ....*points at b-column of toy car* points at one end of box—
          >
03 INS    wieder mit DEM-
          again with the
04        +*(0.2)$(0.35)*+
    i-g   +gazes at b-column+
    i-h   *points at b-column of car*
    s-g          $gazes upwards—>
05 INS    +mit dem $LISCHT so;
          with the light like this
    i-g   +gazes at toy car—>
                 $gazes at toy car—>
06 INS    (0.2) *eine LInie so hier ergibt,
                makes for a line kind-of here
    i-h         *draws line from one end of box to b-column of
                toy car—>>
07 INS    SIEH[ST +du ]?
          you see?
08 STU        [hm_hm; ]
    i-g              +gazes at student—>>
```

This first instruction is a complex description in declarative mode, which highlights its descriptive content as an explication of a regular procedure. The main clause exhibits three arguments (agent = "du", 'you', 01; location = "soweit", 'so far', 01; location = adverbial clause, 02–06), the adverbial clause does so as well (theme = "be säule", 'b-column', 02; counter-theme = "mit dem lischt", 'with the light', 05; result = "linie", 'line', 06). The student should not follow the instruction in situ. The action to be performed is explicitly mentioned ("fährst du SOweit (.) bis [...]", 'you drive so far until [...]') and three landmarks are provided by lexical categorization ("be säule", 'b-column', 02;[1] "mit dem licht", 'with the light', 05; "linie", 'line', 06). Pointing gestures (twice in 02, 04) and an iconic gesture (embodying the imaginary line between the b-column of the toy car and the rear light of the other car) indicate landmarks (06–08). The instruction is prosodically segmented into instalments (Clark and Brennan 1991; Svennevig 2018), i.e. small chunks. The instructor closes it with an understanding-check (06) and monitors the student's understanding (07–08).

---

[1] The 'b-column' is the middle column between the two side-windows of a car.

In stark contrast to this first instruction, the fourth instruction (only seven minutes later!) is designed as a reminder of what the student should already know.

(5)   FAHR_02_15_39:04–39:08

```
01 INS  so;
        so;
    s-h  >>turns steering wheel to the left—>
02       (0.9)
    i-g  .....
03 INS  $guck *jetzt# haste schon *deine Linie,=
        look now you've already got your line
    i-g  $looks out of right window
    i-h         *horizontal gesture along rt window*,,,,
    s-h  ————————>#
04 INS  =genAU,
        exactly
```

This time, the teacher uses only a simple main clause with two arguments (agent = "du", 'you'; result = "deine linie", 'your line', 03). The action to be performed is not mentioned anymore, but a light verb ("hast", 'have') is used. The resulting landmark, the line, is demonstrated by an iconic gesture. The next action which the student should perform is not mentioned anymore; instead, the mention of the landmark is itself action-implicative: it implies that the student has to stop and turn the steering wheel in the opposite direction. The other landmarks that make for the line (i.e. the b-column, the rear light of the car in front) are not mentioned anymore. This instruction works only as a non-first, consecutive instruction which builds on common ground, without which it could not be understood properly. The instructor uses a possessive indexical "deine linie" ('your line'), which shows that the student should know the line and its practical relevance because of her prior experience. This instruction is shorter and relies more on indexicality. It presupposes actions and relevant landmarks. It is designed as a reminder which expects the student to be able to use the common ground achieved earlier for proper understanding and for organizing her own actions.

The studies reviewed support Stevanovic's and Peräkylä's (2014: 185) claim that "without social organization, action understanding is impossible". Yet, in social interaction, there is a reflexive relationship between context and action (Gumperz 1982; Auer 1992): while action-formation and action-ascription take social context (such as epistemic and deontic asymmetries, institutional routines, common ground) into account, they reflexively enact the relevant context and "talk [it] into being" (Heritage and Clayman 2010: chapter 3). Talk confirms and reproduces social structure as well as it can alter it. Social realities (institutions, identities, relationships) can only be maintained by the repeated enactment of practices that are constitutive of social structures.

Whereas linguists tend to stress the relevance of linguistically defined action formats, conversation analysts highlight the relevance of the sequential position, and sociologists point to the influence of social structures for action-formation and -ascription. We have seen that all three dimensions are crucial, albeit to varying degrees for individual tokens of situated action. The combination of these three approaches also helps us to solve the problem of indirect speech acts (Searle 1975). Indirect speech acts often have emerged as the most conventional and most frequent ways of performing actions in certain contexts. Literal uses, in contrast, are often rare and unidiomatic and therefore even harder to understand (Gibbs 1994). Levinson (1983: 356–63) has argued that some highly recurrent indirect forms, such as requests implemented by a polar interrogative (as 'Can you pass me the salt?') have originated from pre's (pre-requests, pre-offers, pre-invitations) that ask about preconditions that must hold if the core sequence is to be successful. Due to routinization and high projectability of the core sequence, such pre's lead to compacted sequences. More generally, the social properties which recurrently apply when using certain resources of action-formation, i.e. the social actions, projected next actions, the participation framework, the activity type, speaker's stance, etc., lead to stable pragmatic connotations of those forms, i.e. action-meanings, which become idiomatic and part of our "common-sense competence" (Feilke 1994).

5.5 Action-Ascription, Responses and Intentions

For Levinson (2013), action-ascription (concerning a past or ongoing action) is the prerequisite for producing a responsive next action in interaction. He speaks of the "miracle" of action-ascription (105): people are able to respond to actions with a delay of only 200 milliseconds on average (and often already in overlap) despite the inferential complexity of the sources impinging on action-ascription, such as turn-design, sequential position, social roles, activity type, gesture, etc. Enfield and Sidnell contest this view: "A definitive categorization of conduct into action types is not required for the orderly flow of interaction" (Enfield and Sidnell 2017a: 517). They suggest that taking into account all sorts of semiotic resources which are mobilized in an action and drawing on the particulars of the context, recipients make situated inferences about expected responses and about the speaker's communicative goals (Enfield and Sidnell 2017b: chapter 1.2; see also Haugh 2017). According to their view, such inferences are sufficient for responding appropriately to an action, without any need to arrive at an action-categorization. Inferences about expected responses can be much coarser than generic speech acts; e.g. the respondent may understand that the other person wants to get them to do something, but need not make a distinction between request, command or instruction. The expected response can also be much more specific, as when expecting to respond by a specific formula, e.g. in a wedding ceremony. Explicitly categorizing an action, however, invokes the accountability of the agent, e.g. a commitment to future actions, the ability to give reasons and justifications, and often a moral assessment of the action (Enfield and Sidnell 2017a). Levinson (1981, 2013) stresses the hierarchical nature of actions, i.e. different action-ascriptions instrumentally being related to each other (e.g. describe an action in order to blame somebody else in order to defend oneself). Sidnell (2017) highlights the multiplicity of possible action-ascriptions that can be assigned to a stretch of behaviour without necessarily excluding each other.

Multiple possible action-ascriptions can give rise to misunderstandings and negotiation. This is even more the case if actions come with a design that is not a straightforward social action format, which shows the essential, yet fallible role of inference in action-ascription (Haugh 2017). Declaratives often are of that kind. An example is Extract (6). Four female friends are talking about the real first name 'Henriette' of a non-present girl, who is usually called by her nickname 'Molly' and who belongs to their peer-group as well.

(6)　　FOLK_E_00055_SE_01_T_05_DF_01_c25–38

```
01 AM  °h heißt die molly eigentlich richtig molly?
            is Molly actually Molly's real name
02 US  °h nee henriette.
            no (it's) Henriette
03 AM  (0.3) henriette.
04 US  ja des[so_n] (.) to[TAL] ANständiger name.
            well that's kinda totally decent name
05 LM         [ja;]
              yes
06 AM                         [hö-]
07 AM  ja sch[on henriette]
            well PTCL Henriette
08 US         [wenn man sie kennt dann] PASST_s gar nich. häˈ
                if you know her then it does not suit at all
09 NH  (0.2) ʔäh hä ʔäh hä hä
10 US  <<f>NE[IN- (.) ]
            no
11 AM         [((laughs))]
12 US  [<<f>NEIN> oh] GOTT-=
        no oh god
13 AM  [((laughs)) ]
14 US  =des des klingt jetz KOmisch.
            this this sounds odd now
15 US  [also NEIN NEIN-]
        I mean no no
```

```
16  NH  [°h       nein;]
             no
17      ich hab_s ja sch[on (.)    verSTANden. °h]
        I have PTCL already understood
18  US                  [weil_s einfach so_(n bis)] so_n bisschen
        so_n STEIferer name;=ja?
        because it's simply kinda kinda bit kinda more formal name,
        right?
19      und sie is ja[total die witzige   also]
        and y'know she is absolutely the humorous[person] so
20  NH               [ja henriette stimmt is so.]=ja;
                     yes Henriette correct[she] is like that yes
```

Discussing the name 'Henriette', US first states that it is a decent (reputable) name (04). She then claims that 'if you know her (= Molly), then it (= the name 'Henriette') does not suit at all' (08). NH responds with laughter, some of it consisting of glottalized laugh particles, which seem to index embarrassment or surprise (Haakana 2001; Chafe 2007). NH's and AM's laughter (11–13) seem to convey that US' turn was inapposite. US now hastens to initiate a self-repair (12/15), using expressive negative particles, and distances herself from her formulation in line 08 by stating that 'this sounds odd'. Yet, already before US manages to repair herself, NH claims that she has 'already understood' (16–17) what US meant in line 08 when saying that the name Henriette does not fit Molly. Up to that point in the interaction, both US, NH and AM produce evaluative responses to US' turn in line 08 that rely on the mutual recognition of an action-ascription that is treated as shared, although no ascription was made explicit. It is only afterwards that US explains that she considers 'Henriette' to be a rather 'formal' (lit. 'stiff') name, which is in contrast to Molly being known as a humorous person (18–19).

The treatment of US' turn in line 08 shows how an action-ascription can become ambiguous because of its sequential context (04). Having categorized 'Henriette' as a decent name, the statement that the name 'does not suit [Molly] at all', allows for a devaluating inference, i.e. a strong negative assessment about Molly. The participants' responses to line 08 implicitly negotiate this meaning, first by laughter, which may convey embarrassment and disaffiliation, but also astonishment and fun because of US' awkward formulation, then by an understanding claim and only finally by making the intended meaning explicit, which, however, is not couched in terms of an action-categorization, either. The sequence shows how important participants' inferences are for action-ascription. It also shows how other pragmatic sources than turn-design enter into the ascriptive work, here in particular the prior sequential context and the ascription of a sympathetic socio-emotional attitude by US towards Molly by virtue of being her friend. (See Stevanovic and Peräkylä 2014, who add an emotional order to the epistemic and deontic orders as a resource for action-ascription.) The latter is the basis for NH in lines 16/17 not to treat US' turn in line 08 as a deprecatory assessment of Molly, but as an action with an unproblematic communicative intention, whose precise nature, however, is not displayed. Still, NH'S understanding claim does not seem to set the record straight for US, the speaker of the problematic turn, because she explicitly clarifies her intended meaning. Yet, it remains hard to categorize which kind of action line 08 was to perform – something like 'noticing an incongruence (which is funny)' may be at issue. A generic categorization like 'assertion' or 'assessment' would be insufficient for characterizing what the turn was doing and what it projected as a response.

While it is still a disputed matter whether producing an appropriate next action always requires an (implicit) action-ascription to the prior turn, it is clear that some ascription of intentionality to the agent is necessarily involved. This does not mean that there will always be an imputation of a conscious goal or a motivating intention. Rather, a more general ascription of accountability to warrantable understandings of the action holds (Haugh 2013). Explicit intention-ascription in second position to the prior action is used to resolve coordination-problems and clarify conditions for response generation and own larger strategies of the ascriber (Deppermann and Kaiser, in press). Yet, explicit intention ascriptions in second position or self-ascription by speakers (Deppermann 2014) are rare. Intentionality has a somewhat paradoxical status in social actions in multiple senses (see Haugh 2008). While intentionality is always presupposed, it cannot be verified unambiguously by observation. Even if participants explicate their intentions or accept others' ascriptions of intentions and actions, this does not guarantee that accepted meanings have been the originally intended meanings. The accomplishment of intersubjectivity of intention and action-meanings therefore is not a process of mutual recognition of original, factual intentions. It is a process of reciprocal understanding, displaying and negotiating meanings, which are sometimes emergent. Accomplished intersubjectivity then refers to what the parties to an interaction accept as shared interpretation for all practical purposes. This (apparently) intersubjective understanding may still contain differences in interpretation, which are more or less transparent to the participants and which often play out only later (Arundale 2020).

5.6 Conclusion

In this chapter, we have shown the multiple ways in which actions in interaction are social. Actions are tailored to a social context to which their design and their interpretation is sensitive. It is both an interactive-sequential and a socio-structural and -historical context. It includes epistemic, deontic and emotional relationships as well as interactional histories. The linguistic design of utterances indexes its action-oriented nature, but it almost never works in isolation. Action-formation mostly only acquires determinate meanings in specific contexts.

Actions are not only social in being influenced by interactional and social factors. They reflexively build and index, maintain and change social realities. They are intrinsically social, because their meaning and effect depend on the collaborative uptake of recipients.

This chapter has also addressed a number of current research issues which remain to be explored in more detail: the role of interactional histories over which action-formation and -ascription change, the importance of action- and intention-ascription for the organization of social action (Depermann and Haugh 2021). And, most importantly, we have not addressed the multimodal packaging and coordination of social actions. These remain areas ripe for further exploration.

References

Allen, J. (1995). *Natural Language Understanding.* New York: Benjamin/Cummings.

Antaki, C. and Kent, A. (2012). Telling people what to do (and, sometimes, why): Contingency, entitlement and explanation in staff requests to adults with intellectual impairments. *Journal of Pragmatics, 44,* 876–89.

Arundale, R. B. (1999). An alternative model and ideology of communication for an alternative to politeness theory. *Pragmatics, 9*(1), 119–53.

Arundale, R. B. (2020). *Communicating and Relating.* Oxford: Oxford University Press.

Atkinson, J. M. and Heritage, J. (eds.). (1984). *Structures of Social Action: Studies in Conversation Analysis.* Cambridge: Cambridge University Press.

Auer, P. (1992). Introduction: John Gumperz' approach to contextualization. In P. Auer and A. Di Luzio (eds.), *The Contextualization of Language.* Amsterdam: Benjamins, pp. 1–38.

Austin, J. L. (1962). *How to Do Things with Words.* London: Oxford University Press.

Benjamin, T. (2012). When problems pass us by: Using "you mean" to help locate the source of trouble. *Research on Language and Social Interaction, 45*(1), 82–109.

Brown, P. and Levinson, S. (1987). *Politeness: Some Universals of Language Use.* Cambridge: Cambridge University Press.

Chafe, W. A. (2007). *The Importance of Not Being Earnest: The Feeling behind Laughter and Humor.* Amsterdam: Benjamins.

Clark, H. H. (1992). *Arenas of Language Use.* Chicago: University of Chicago Press.

Clark, H. H. (1996a). *Using Language.* Cambridge: Cambridge University Press.

Clark, H. H. (1996b). Communities, commonalities, and communication. In J. Gumperz and S. Levinson, eds., *Rethinking Linguistic Relativity*. Cambridge: Cambridge University Press, pp. 324–55.

Clark, H. H. and Brennan, S. A. (1991). Grounding in communication. In L. B. Resnick, J. M. Levine and S. D. Teasley, eds., *Perspectives on Socially Shared Cognition*. Washington, DC: APA Books, pp. 127–49.

Clark, H. H. and Schaefer, E. F. (1989). Contributing to discourse. *Cognitive Science*, 13(2), 259–94.

Clift, R. (2016). *Conversation Analysis*. Cambridge: Cambridge University Press.

Cohen, P. R. and Perrault, E. (1979). Elements of a plan-based theory of speech acts. *Cognitive Science*, 3(3), 177–212.

Couper-Kuhlen, E. (2014). What does grammar tell us about social action. *Pragmatics*, 24(3), 623–47.

Craven, A. and Potter, J. (2010). Directives: Entitlement and contingency in action. *Discourse Studies*, 12(4), 419–42.

Curl, T. S. (2006). Offers of assistance: Constraints on syntactic design. *Journal of Pragmatics*, 38(8), 1257–80.

Curl, T. S. and Drew, P. (2008). Contingency and action: A comparison of two forms of requesting. *Research on Language and Social Interaction*, 41(2), 129–53.

Davies, B. L., Haugh, M. and Merrison, A. J. (eds.). (2011). *Situated Politeness*. London: Continuum.

Deppermann, A. (2011). Constructions vs. lexical items as sources of complex meanings. A comparative study of constructions with German verstehen. In P. Auer and S. Pfänder, eds., *Constructions: Emerging and Emergent*. Berlin: Mouton de Gruyter, pp. 88–126.

Deppermann, A. (2014). Handlungsverstehen und Intentionszuschreibung in der Interaktion I: Intentionsbekundungen mit *wollen*. In P. Bergmann, K. Birkner, P. Gilles, H. Spiekermann and T. Streck, eds., *Sprache im Gebrauch: räumlich, zeitlich, interaktional. Festschrift für Peter Auer*. Heidelberg, Germany: Winter, pp. 309–26.

Deppermann, A. (2015). Retrospection and understanding in interaction. In A. Deppermann and S. Günthner, eds., *Temporality in Interaction*. Amsterdam: Benjamins, pp. 57–94.

Deppermann, A. (2018a). Changes in turn-design over interactional histories – the case of instructions in driving school lessons. In A. Deppermann and J. Streeck, eds., *Time in Embodied Interaction: Synchronicity and Sequentiality of Multimodal Resources*. Amsterdam: Benjamins, pp. 293–324.

Deppermann, A. (2018b). Instruction practices in German driving lessons: Differential uses of declaratives and imperatives. *International Journal of Applied Linguistics*, 28(2), 265–82.

Deppermann, A. and Kaiser, J. (in press). Intention ascriptions as a means to coordinate own actions with others' actions. In A. Deppermann and M. Haugh, eds., *Action Ascription*. Cambridge: Cambridge University Press.

Deppermann, A. and Haugh, M. (eds.) (2021). *Action Ascription*. Cambridge: Cambridge University Press.

Drew, P. (1992). Contested evidence in courtroom cross-examination: The case of a trial for rape. In P. Drew and J. Heritage, eds., *Talk at Work: Interaction in Institutional Settings*. Cambridge: Cambridge University Press, pp. 470–520.

Drew, P. and Couper-Kuhlen, E. (eds.). (2014). *Requesting in Social Interaction*. Amsterdam: Benjamins.

Drew, P. and Heritage, J. (eds.). (1992). Analyzing talk at work: An introduction. In P. Drew and J. Heritage, eds., *Talk at Work: Interaction in Institutional Settings*. Cambridge: Cambridge University Press, pp. 3–65.

Drew, P. and Sorjonen, M. L. (2011). Dialogue in institutional interactions. In T. A. van Dijk, ed., *Discourse Studies: A Multidisciplinary Introduction*, 2nd ed. London: Sage, pp. 191–216.

Drew, P., Hepburn, A., Margutti, P. and Galatolo, R. (eds.). (2016). Apologies in discourse. *Discourse Processes*, 53(1–2), 114–31.

Duranti, A. (1988). Intentions, language, and social action in a Samoan context. *Journal of Pragmatics*, 12(1), 13–33.

Edwards, D. (2008). Intentionality and mens rea in police interrogations: the production of actions as crimes. *Intercultural Pragmatics*, 5(2), 177–99.

Enfield, N. J. and Sidnell, J. (2017a). The concept of action in interaction. *Discourse Studies*, 19(5), 515–35.

Enfield, N. J. and Sidnell, J. (2017b). *The Concept of Action*. Cambridge: Cambridge University Press.

Enfield, N. J. and Kockelman, P. (eds.). (2017). *Distributed Agency*, New York: Oxford University Press.

Feilke, H. (1994). *Common-Sense-Kompetenz. Überlegungen zu einer Theorie des »sympathischen« und »natürlichen« Meinens und Verstehens*. Frankfurt am Main, Germany: Suhrkamp.

Fetzer, A. (2004). *Recontextualizing Context: Grammaticality Meets Appropriateness*. Amsterdam: John Benjamins.

Fetzer, A. (2017). Context. In Y. Huang, ed., *The Oxford Handbook of Pragmatics*. Oxford: Oxford University Press, pp. 259–76.

Fetzer, A. and Oishi, E. (eds.). (2011). *Context and Contexts: Parts Meet Whole?* Amsterdam: John Benjamins.

Fillmore, C. (1989). Grammatical construction theory and the familiar dichotomies. In R. F. Dietrich and C. F. Graumann, eds., *Language Processing in Social Context*. Amsterdam: Elsevier, pp. 17–38.

Fox, B. A. (2007). Principles shaping grammatical practices: An exploration. *Discourse Studies*, 9(3), 299–318.

Gibbs, R. W. (1994). *The Poetics of Mind: Figurative Thought, Language, and Understanding*. Cambridge: Cambridge University Press.

Goffman, E. (1971). *Relations in Public: Microstudies of the Public Order*. New York: Harper and Row.

Golato, A. (2005). *Compliments and Compliment Responses: Grammatical Structure and Sequential Organization*. Amsterdam: John Benjamins.

Goodwin, C. (2017). *Co-operative Action*. Cambridge: Cambridge University Press.

Goodwin, C. and Goodwin, M. H. (1992). Assessment and the construction of context. In A. Duranti and C. Goodwin, eds., *Rethinking Context: Language as an Interactive Phenomenon*. Cambridge: Cambridge University Press, pp. 147–89.

Goodwin, M. H. (1990). *He-Said-She-Said: Talk as Social Organization among Black Children*. Bloomington: Indiana University Press.

Grosz, B. J. and Sidner, C. (1990). Plans for discourse. In P. R. Cohen, J. Morgan and M. E. Pollack, eds., *Intentions in Communications*. Cambridge, MA: MIT Press, pp. 417–44.

Gumperz, J. J. (1982). *Discourse Strategies*. Cambridge: Cambridge University Press.

Günthner, S. and Knoblauch, H. (1995). Culturally patterned speaking practices: The analysis of communicative genres. *Pragmatics*, 5(1), 1–32.

Haakana, M. (2001). Laughter as a patient's resource: Dealing with delicate aspects of medical interaction. *Text*, 21(1–2), 187–219.

Hanks, W. F. (1996). *Language and Communicative Practices*. Boulder, CO: Westview.

Haugh, M. (2008). The place of intention in the interactional accomplishment of implicature. In I. Kecskes and J. Mey, eds., *Intention, Common Ground and the Egocentric Speaker-Hearer*. Berlin: Mouton de Gruyter, pp. 45–86.

Haugh, M. (2013). Speaker meaning and accountability in interaction. *Journal of Pragmatics*, 48(1), 41–56.

Haugh, M. (2017). Implicatures and the inferential substrate. In P. Cap and M. Dynel, eds., *Implicitness: From Lexis to Discourse*. Amsterdam: Benjamins, pp. 281–304.

Heritage, J. (1984). *Garfinkel and Ethnomethodology*. Oxford: Polity.

Heritage, J. (2010). Conversation analysis: Practices and methods. In D. Silverman, ed., *Qualitative Sociology*, 3rd ed. London: Sage, pp. 208–30.

Heritage, J. (2012). Epistemics in action: Action formation and territories of knowledge. *Research on Language and Social Interaction*, 45(1), 1–29.

Heritage, J. (2013). Epistemics in conversation. In J. Sidnell and T. Stivers, eds., *Handbook of Conversation Analysis*. New York: Wiley-Blackwell, pp. 370–94.

Heritage, J. and Clayman, S. (2010). *Talk in Action: Interactions, Identities and Institutions*. Chichester, UK: Wiley-Blackwell.

Heritage, J. and Clayman, S. (2014). Benefactors and beneficiaries: Benefactive status and stance in the management of offers and requests. In P. Drew and E. Couper-Kuhlen, eds., *Requesting in Social Interaction*. Amsterdam: Benjamins, pp. 55–86.

Hutchins, E. (1995). *Cognition in the Wild.* Cambridge, MA: MIT Press.

Hymes, D. (1972). Models of the interaction of language and social life. In D. Hymes and J. J. Gumperz, eds., *Directions in Sociolinguistics: Explorations in the Ethnography of Speaking.* New York: Winston, Holt and Rinehart, pp. 270–320.

Kärkkäinen, E. and Keisanen, T. (2012). Linguistic and embodied formats for making (concrete) offers. *Discourse Studies,* 14(5), 587–611.

Kendrick, K. H. and Drew, P. (2016). Recruitment: Offers, requests, and the organization of assistance in interaction. *Research on Language and Social Interaction,* 49(1), 1–19.

Koole, T. (2015). Classroom interaction. In K. Tracy, ed., *International Encyclopedia of Language and Social Interaction.* Hoboken, NJ: Wiley-Blackwell.

Kreckel, M. (1981). Where do constitutive rules for speech acts come from? *Language and Communication,* 1(1), 73–88.

Lerner, G. H. (1989). Notes on overlap management in conversation: The case of delayed completion. *Western Journal of Speech Communication,* 53(2), 167–77.

Levinson, S. C. (1979). Activity types and language. *Linguistics,* 17(5–6), 365–400.

Levinson, S. C. (1981). The essential inadequacies of speech act models of dialogue. In H. Parret, M. Sbisà and J. Verscheuren, eds., *Possibilities and Limitations of Pragmatics: Proceedings of the Conference on Pragmatics, Urbino, July 8–14, 1979.* Amsterdam: John Benjamins, pp. 473–92.

Levinson, S. C. (1983). *Pragmatics.* Cambridge: Cambridge University Press.

Levinson, S. C. (2013). Action-formation and ascription. In J. Sidnell and T. Stivers, eds., *The Handbook of Conversation Analysis.* Malden, MA: Wiley Blackwell, pp. 103–30.

Linell, P. (2009). *Rethinking Language, Mind, and World Dialogically: Interactional and Contextual Theories of Human Sense-Making.* Charlotte, NC: Information Age.

Margutti, P., Tainio, L., Drew, P. and Traverso, V. (eds.). (2018). Inviting in telephone calls: A cross-linguistic study of social actions in interaction. *Journal of Pragmatics,* 125, 52–199.

Mehan, H. (1979). *Learning Lessons: Social Organization in the Classroom.* Cambridge, MA: Harvard University Press.

Mey, J. L. (2001). *Pragmatics.: An Introduction.* 2nd ed. Oxford: Blackwell.

Mey, J. L. (2006). Pragmatic acts. In K. Brown, ed., *Encyclopedia of Language and Linguistics,* 2nd ed. Oxford: Elsevier, pp. 5–11.

Mondada, L. (2017). Precision timing and timed embeddedness of imperatives in embodied courses of action. In M.-L. Sorjonen, E. Couper-Kuhlen and L. Raevaara, eds., *Imperative Turns at Talk: The Design of Directives in Action.* Amsterdam: John Benjamins, pp. 65–101.

Proske, N. (2017). Perspektivierung von Handlungen und Zuschreibung von Intentionalität durch pseudokoordiniertes kommen. In A. Deppermann,

N. Proske and A. Zeschel, eds., *Verben im interaktiven Kontext. Bewegungsverben und mentale Verben im Gesprochenen Deutsch.* Tübingen: Narr, pp. 177–247.

Rosaldo, M. Z. (1982). The things we do with words: Ilongot speech acts and speech act theory in philosophy. *Language in Society*, 11(2), 203–37.

Rossi, G. (in press). *Systems of Social Action: The Case of Requesting in Italian.* Oxford: Oxford University Press.

Sacks, H., Schegloff, E. A. and Jefferson, G. (1974). A simplest systematics for the organisation of turn-taking in conversation. *Language*, 50(4), 696–735.

Sbisà, M. (2002). Speech acts in context. *Language and Communication*, 22(4), 421–37.

Saville-Troike, M. (1989). *The Ethnography of Communication.* Oxford: Blackwell.

Schank, R. C. and Abelson, R. P. (1977). *Scripts, Plans, Goals and Understanding: An Inquiry into Human Knowledge Structures.* Hillsdale, NJ: Erlbaum.

Schegloff, E. A. (1980). Preliminaries to preliminaries: "Can I ask you a question?" *Sociological Inquiry*, 50(3–4), 104–52.

Schegloff, E. A. (1984). On some questions and ambiguities in conversations. In J. M. Atkinson and J. Heritage, eds., *Structures of Social Action: Studies in Conversation Analysis.* Cambridge: Cambridge University Press, pp. 28–52.

Schegloff, E. A. (1991). Reflections of talk and social structure. In D. Boden and D. H. Zimmerman, eds., *Talk and Social Structure.* Cambridge: Cambridge University Press, pp. 44–70.

Schegloff, E. A. (1992). Repair after next turn: The last structurally provided defense of intersubjectivity in conversation. *American Journal of Sociology*, 97(5), 1295–1345.

Schegloff, E. A. (1996a). Confirming allusions: Toward an empirical account of action. *American Journal of Sociology*, 104(1), 161–216.

Schegloff, E. A. (1996b). Turn organization: One intersection of grammar and interaction. In E. Ochs, E. A. Schegloff and S. A. Thompson, eds., *Interaction and Grammar.* Cambridge: Cambridge University Press, pp. 52–133.

Schegloff, E. A. (1997). Practices and actions: Boundary cases of other-initiated repair. *Discourse Processes*, 23(3), 499–545.

Schegloff, E. A. (2007). *Sequence Organization in Interaction.* Cambridge: Cambridge University Press.

Searle, J. R. (1969). *Speech Acts: An Essay in the Philosophy of Language.* Cambridge: Cambridge University Press.

Searle, J. R. (1975). Indirect speech acts. In P. Cole and J. L. Morgan, eds., *Syntax and Semantics. Vol. 3: Speech Acts.* New York: Academic, pp. 59–82.

Sidnell, J. (2014). The architecture of intersubjectivity revisited. In N. J. Enfield, P. Kockelman and J. Sidnell, eds., *Cambridge Handbook of Linguistic Anthropology.* Cambridge: Cambridge University Press, pp. 364–99.

Sidnell, J. (2017). Action in interaction is conduct under a description. *Language in Society*, 46(3), 313–37.

Sorjonen, M.-L., Raevaara, L. and Couper-Kuhlen, E. (eds.). (2017). *Imperative Turns at Talk: The Design of Directives in Action.* Amsterdam: Benjamins.

Stevanovic, M. and Peräkylä, A. (2012). Deontic authority in interaction: The right to announce, propose, and decide. *Research on Language and Social Interaction*, 45(4), 297–321.

Stevanovic, M. and Peräkyläa, A. (2014). Three orders in the organization of human action: On the interface between knowledge, power, and emotion in interaction and social relations. *Language in Society*, 43(2), 185–207.

Stivers, T. (2005). Modified repeats: One method for asserting primary rights from second position. *Research on Language and Social Interaction*, 38(2), 131–58.

Stivers, T. (2013). Sequence organization. In J. Sidnell and T. Stivers, eds., *The Handbook of Conversation Analysis*. Oxford: Wiley-Blackwell, pp. 191–209.

Stivers, T., Mondada, L. and Steensig, J. (2011). Knowledge, morality and affiliation in social interaction. In T. Stivers, L. Mondada and J. Steensig, eds., *The Morality of Knowledge in Conversation*. Cambridge: Cambridge University Press, pp. 3–24.

Stivers, T. and Rossano, F. (2010). Mobilizing response. *Research on Language and Social Interaction*, 43(1), 3–31.

Suchman, L. (2007). *Human–Machine Reconfigurations: Plans and Situated Actions*. Cambridge: Cambridge University Press.

Svennevig, J. (2018). Decomposing turns to enhance understanding by L2 speakers. *Research on Language and Social Interaction*, 51(4), 398–416.

Terkourafi, M. (2002). Politeness and formulaicity: Evidence from Cypriot Greek. *Journal of Greek Linguistics*, 3(1), 179–201.

Terkourafi, M. (2009). On de-limiting context. In A. Bergs and G. Diewald, eds., *Context and Constructions*. Amsterdam: Benjamins, pp. 17–42.

Thomas, J. (1995). *Meaning in Interaction: An Introduction to Pragmatics*. London: Longman.

Thompson, S. A., Fox, B. A. and Couper-Kuhlen, E. (2015). *Grammar in Everyday Talk: Building Responsive Actions*. Cambridge: Cambridge University Press.

Tomasello, M. (2008). *Origins of Human Communication*. Cambridge MA: MIT Press.

Van Dijk, T. (2015). Critical discourse analysis. In D. Tannen, H. E. Hamilton and D. Schiffrin, eds., *The Handbook of Discourse Analysis*, 2nd ed. Oxford: John Wiley, pp. 466–85.

Verschueren, J. (1999). *Understanding Pragmatics*. London: Arnold.

Weber, M. ([1922] 1968). *Economy and Society: An Outline of Interpretive Sociology*. New York: Bedminster.

Wittgenstein, Ludwig ([1950] 1953). *Philosophical Investigations*. Translated by G. E. M. Anscombe. Oxford: Blackwell.

Zinken, J. (2016). *Requesting Responsibility: The Morality of Grammar in Polish and English Family Interaction*. New York: Oxford University Press.

Zinken, J. and Deppermann, A. (2017). A cline of visible commitment in the situated design of imperative turns. In M.-L. Sorjonen, L. Raevaara and E. Couper-Kuhlen, eds., *Imperative Turns at Talk*. Amsterdam: John Benjamins, pp. 27–63.

6
Stance and Evaluation

Maarit Siromaa and Mirka Rauniomaa

6.1 Introduction

This chapter sets out to review recent work on stance taking and evaluative practices relevant for sociopragmatics within fields such as interactional sociolinguistics, linguistic anthropology and systemic functional linguistics. Placing special emphasis on the study of interaction, the chapter attempts to outline the discursive turn in the study of language and social conduct: from the 1990s onwards, the focus of analysis has shifted from speakers' internal mental representations to the interactional processes that are involved in expressing personal feelings and positioning towards the current subject matter and context. Kockelman (2004: 131) characterizes the discursive turn as follows: "the turn from attitude to stance is in keeping with other trends in linguistics and anthropology: from an emphasis on the private, subjective, and psychological (attitude) to an emphasis on the public, intersubjective, and embodied (stance)". These studies establish how phenomena such as stance, attitudes and emotions are constructed and managed in everyday human social practices and are thus observable in interaction.

As noted by Kockelman (2004), the philosophical and linguistic origins of stance stem from Kantian modality as well as the concept of mood as a grammatical class. Within linguistics, studies on modality (e.g. Palmer 1979; Chafe 1986) indeed preceded the early literature on stance (e.g. Biber and Finegan 1989). On the other hand, within sociology, Goffman's (1983) theory of the interaction order, and respective participant roles (see also Chapter 8), which are used as concepts to deconstruct the speaker, as well as his theory of footing as a model for analysing the complexity of language use (Goffman 1974), drew on a long tradition of thinking within semiotics and pragmatics by philosophers such as George Herbert Mead and Charles Sanders Peirce. Kockelman (2005) traces the development of the notion of stance out of Peirce's semiotics, with the complex triadic relation of sign, object, and interpretant having informed the understanding of stance taking as a similar three-fold dialogic and emergent phenomenon (discussed further in Section 6.2).

The discursive treatment of various cognitive phenomena opened up new avenues of research in several fields, including sociology, psychology, linguistics and anthropology. Within social psychology, pioneering work by Wetherell, Edwards and Potter gave rise to the field of discursive psychology (e.g. Wetherell and Potter 1987; Potter and Edwards 2003). Similarly, at the forefront of such developments, linguists such as Du Bois and Kärkkäinen started to investigate speaker stances in naturally occurring face-to-face interaction as public and emergent instead of internal positionings (e.g. Kärkkäinen 2003, 2006; Du Bois 2007; Du Bois and Kärkkäinen 2012). These studies of *stance taking* in interaction lend support to the discursive psychological studies of cognitive phenomena: just as in the field of discursive psychology, stance-taking research in sociopragmatics focuses on the displays rather than the mental processes of speakers' discursive activities (McLaughlin 2009: 58). Within this line of work, stance taking is regarded as a dialogic and mutually reflexive process in which participants evaluate a stance object (e.g. people, artefacts, ideas or phenomena), position themselves with regard to the stance object, and align themselves, or evoke alignment with, their co-participants (see particularly Du Bois 2007). Stance taking is thus seen as an everyday, ubiquitous practice that emerges from the sequential unfolding of social interaction.

The linguistic study of evaluation has been significantly pushed forward by Martin and White's framework of appraisal (Martin and White 2005). More recently, a similar shift to that noted above for stance means that linguistic and pragmatic studies on the evaluative function of language place emphasis on the dialogic and interpersonal dimensions of evaluation and treat it as a collaborative activity that is constructed in interaction, evaluative turns building on those of prior speakers in expressing (dis)-affiliation between participants in the given situation. That is, values are seen as negotiable and situated in a specific context (Alba-Juez and Thompson 2014: 4). Similarly, in the study of (im)politeness, scholars have started to treat evaluation of politeness as situated activity that has consequences for the ongoing interaction. (See detailed discussion by Kádár and Haugh 2013.) The authors suggest, for instance, that what is perceived to be polite by people, even with similar backgrounds and within a social group, is by no means fixed. What is more, the analysis of interaction as it unfolds may enable the analyst to identify various evaluative practices that are involved in expressing (im)politeness and constructed in and through interaction, thus expanding the array of phenomena under examination.

Indeed, the increasing interest in naturally occurring discourse and especially in the detailed sequential analysis of interaction has facilitated a new sociopragmatically relevant understanding of phenomena such as stance, evaluation and (im)politeness. As many scholars have embraced this sociopragmatic perspective, the discursive turn continues to move forward in a multidisciplinary and multi-methodological front in various fields. A methodological link exists between the work done within these various fields in that they often apply the method of conversation analysis or some other discourse-oriented approach. While other methods ranging from corpus linguistics to textual analysis have been used to study stance and evaluation, this chapter focuses on work with a conversation-analytic flare as the most widely used one within the field of sociopragmatics at present.

The rest of this chapter is organized as follows. We first discuss the discursive turn in sociopragmatics in more detail in light of some of the pertinent work on stance taking and evaluation. We then map out studies that investigate stance taking in interaction as well as attempt to outline the most relevant milestones of stance-related research within a larger sociolinguistic framework. Finally, we provide a synthesis of studies that deal with evaluation as situated activity, and while doing so, touch upon some key developments within discursive psychology as well as in the study of (im)politeness and appraisal. We close the chapter with an analysis of stance taking in a sequence of conversational storytelling and with some observations about current challenges in research on stance and evaluation in sociopragmatics.

6.2 A Dialogic and Reflexive Take on Stance in Interaction

Within the field of linguistics, early studies on *stance* treat it as an expression of a single speaker's individual mental position that can be expressed in discourse through various linguistic devices (see e.g. Biber and Finegan 1989; Hunston and Thompson 2000; Scheibman 2001). In this line of work, stance is defined as "the lexical and grammatical expression of attitudes, feelings, judgements, or commitment concerning the propositional content of a message" (Biber and Finegan 1989: 92). Such markers of stance may include adverbials in framing a personal position (Conrad and Biber 2000), and adjectives and nouns as evaluative resources in encoding affect, appreciation and judgement (Martin 2000).[1] Furthermore, they may involve linguistic structures such as factive predicates and the way in which speakers "index their own stance, or attribute stance to some other participant" (Field 1997: 800–801) or certain subject–predicate combinations that speakers favour in expressing subjectivity (Scheibman 2001). More recently, Gray and Biber (2014) have provided an exhaustive discussion on the various stance markers identified by previous work and note the significance of

---

[1] Martin (2000) and Martin and White (2005) will be discussed in more detail in Section 6.3.

such work in developing an understanding of the pragmatic dimension of stance taking and evaluative practices in interaction.

As acknowledged by these studies, stance is rarely a static mental or cognitive state encoded in a fixed linguistic arrangement, but rather involves a highly social and dynamic process emerging from the sequential unfolding of interaction. To highlight this understanding of stance as collaborative activity, scholars such as Du Bois and Kärkkäinen prefer to talk about the phenomenon of stance taking (also spelled as a closed compound *stancetaking*) instead of stance. What is more, stance taking is regarded as a social phenomenon manifested in various linguistic, prosodic and embodied practices and resources in the ongoing interaction. Du Bois (2007: 163), for instance, defines stance taking as "a public act by a social actor, achieved dialogically through overt communicative means, of simultaneously evaluating objects, positioning subjects (self and others), and aligning with other subjects, with respect to any salient dimension of the sociocultural field". This definition bears a resemblance to and stems from, especially, the Peircean triadic semiotic, a linguistically and philosophically fundamental understanding of signs and meaning. The process here is investigated as situated in naturally occurring interaction arching over various distances in the turn-by-turn progression of dialogue between participants. In a similar vein, Kärkkäinen (2003, 2006) treats stance taking as essentially dialogic, interactive and intersubjective activity and goes on to show how interlocutors within larger storytelling sequences negotiate a shared stance in and through a series of assessments in two frequently occurring patterns of stance taking. First, the participants frame an initial individual stance by means of *I think* (or a similar expression), and second, they recycle each other's words, phrases, syntactic structures or prosodic patterns across a series of turns. Within such assessment sequences, the participants need to achieve at least a superficial agreement on an underlying social norm or value before closing one topic and/or moving on to another. Much of the interactionally oriented research on stance taking sees it as activity that consists of displays of stance, i.e. turns that participants take in a social situation that somehow display stances. Pioneering work on assessment activity by Goodwin and Goodwin (1987) comprises analysis of this kind: it describes an interactive process in which the participants organize their talk and embodiment in positioning and aligning themselves towards the issue at hand and towards other interlocutors by way of assessments and displays of affect.

An adjacent body of research (Du Bois 2007; Kärkkäinen 2003; Wu 2004; Haddington 2006; Keisanen 2006; Englebretson 2007; Rauniomaa 2008; Niemelä 2011) has partly both catalysed and contributed to the discursive turn in the linguistically oriented study of stance taking as a situated, pragmatic and interactional phenomenon in naturally occurring interaction. This work sees stance taking as situated activity and socially relevant positioning of oneself in view of the object of contemplation and in view of potential prior interactional turns and events. Although scholars subscribe to these central principles of stance taking, their individual definitions and understandings of stance taking are rather heterogeneous – even within a single research group. Namely they hold somewhat differing views on the pervasiveness and influence of stance taking in interaction. Some consider stance taking a highly or moderately pervasive activity that potentially affects the form of language and the organization of social actions and so treat displays of stance as more or less independent social actions enregistered in language (e.g. Du Bois 2007; Wu 2004; Englebretson 2007; Kärkkäinen 2007). Others see stance taking as sequentially emerging displays of personal positioning that are embedded in particular social actions (e.g. Ford et al. 2002; Haddington 2006; Keisanen 2006; Rauniomaa 2008; Niemelä 2011).

Researchers from the first group emphasize stance as a socially significant process that affects interaction and, to a certain degree, even the form of language. Du Bois (2007: 141), for example, sees stance as both deriving from and having consequences for social actors: the acts of stance taking have a central role in the interlocutors' display and construction of sociocultural meanings. Englebretson (2007: 69) similarly considers stance taking to occupy a rather pervasive role in language use, which in turn greatly influences language form; for example, he shows how Indonesian speakers use certain first-person-singular referring expressions to manage and index specific facets of stance taking in colloquial Indonesian speech. Likewise, Wu (2004: 3, emphasis added) suggests that "like all other actions, stance is treated as an emergent product which is shaped by, and *itself shapes*, the unfolding development of interaction". Adopting a more moderate view, Kärkkäinen (2007: 184) argues that the epistemic stance marker *I guess*, for example, acts as an intersubjective stance frame that organizes the stance-taking activity between participants.

Viewing stance as a less impelling force in interaction, Haddington (2006: 320) argues that the interlocutors produce practices and actions that are not necessarily conventionalized displays of stance but rather vehicles of stance taking. For instance, Haddington (2006) identifies three interactive gaze patterns coupled with verbal assessments that participate in and ultimately organize the overall stance-taking activity. The first gaze pattern, displaying agreement between participants, involves participants looking together at an assessable in which a participant's gaze shift towards the assessable and/or the verbal mention of it makes relevant the collaborative 'looking'. In the second gaze pattern, two participants who produce agreeing actions and recycle (each other's) linguistic material establish a mutual gaze during an agreeing 'second stance'. The third gaze pattern differs from the prior two in that a participant's cut-off gaze is treated as a disagreeing reaction to a prior display of stance. In a study of negative yes/no interrogatives and tag questions, Keisanen (2006: 53) adopts a more conversation-analytic view on stance taking, regarding it as emerging from the current social action and sequential position, so that "any linguistic or paralinguistic feature of language, or a linguistic construction for that matter, can function as a stance marker". Rauniomaa (2008: 215–17) similarly shows that recovery through repetition, i.e. repetition that is used to return to prior talk, may implement stance taking either towards an activity in progress, or towards a recipient response. Ford et al. (2002: 26) examine unattached NP-increments functioning as displays of stance that guide the recipients' uptake of the just possibly completed turn.

This latter line of thinking enables a parallel analysis of stance taking and social actions as interlaced but distinct phenomena in interaction. Niemelä (2005), for instance, establishes a pattern in which the initial storyteller (animator 1, in Goffman's terms)[2] uses voicing to animate DRS (direct reported speech) sequences that convey a certain stance, first, towards the character or figure to whom DRS is assigned and, second, towards some aspect of the story content, for example, an evaluation of a story character's appearance, temperament or conduct. For instance, in the invented Example 1, Ann is the initial storyteller assigning an animated DRS turn to her daughter in a child-like inquisitive voice quality, *Daddy, what are you doing?*

(1)
ANN: Our daughter saw Tim dangling on a ladder and getting red-faced angry trying to reach the smoke detector to change the battery, and she was just sitting there watching him like, "Daddy, what are you doing?"
TIM: Yeah like, "Why are you angry at the ceiling, Daddy?"

The fragment of DRS produced by Ann presents Tim, the father, in a particular light. In the next turn, the recipient or co-teller (animator 2) may respond with a matching animated DRS assigned to the same character or figure to display a shared stance. In Example 1, Tim contributes to the storytelling and stance taking by assigning a matching DRS turn to his daughter that is produced in a similar inquisitive tone, *Why are you angry at the ceiling, Daddy?* Together, the participants not only construct a narrative event that unfolds turn-by-turn but also formulate a shared stance.

It has been suggested that coupling the conversation-analytic approach with the theoretical orientation to stance and stance taking may be problematic because of the pervasive and abstract nature of taking a stance in interaction. Local and Walker (2008), for example, suggest that analysts should refrain from making claims based on existing theoretical assumptions about stance being encoded in the phonetic design of an utterance. They further suggest that the analysis should "reflect categories which are significant *for the participants themselves*, rather than exemplifying and confirming any pre-theoretical assumptions we may hold" (Local and Walker 2008: 4, emphasis in the original). A similar criticism has been voiced by Clift (2010: 521) in connection with the sociolinguistic study of

---

[2] The use of Goffman's categories in illustrating the findings is adopted from Goodwin (2006).

identity and stance, giving credit to and, at the same time, highlighting the potential danger of treating stance as "a mediating concept between linguistic forms and social identity". If stance is not studied by way of rigorous empirical sequential analysis, investigating what is evidenced to be meaningful for the participants, and treated as a phenomenon that is constructed in and through interaction, the concept may lose all of its explanatory power. Certainly, a close sequential analysis of interactional data allows a concurrent investigation of both stance taking and social actions (see Chapter 5) as processes that describe different aspects of various interactional and societal phenomena.

Addressing issues from the viewpoint of linguistic anthropology, Kockelman (2004, 2010) likewise brings up a concern that stance may sometimes be investigated in an unreflective manner and without clearly defined criteria to support the analyst's interpretations. Introducing the notion of *meta-stance* as "the orientations that we take toward our own and others' orientations", Kockelman (2010: 161) suggests that being constantly conscious of and taking into consideration such orientations is vital for the analytic process; otherwise the analyst risks allowing their own orientation to others' orientation play far too great a role in the interpretation of stance. In Kockelman's (2010) view, it is thus crucial to engage in ethnographic research within the given collectivity to gain an understanding of its linguistic and (inter)personal landscapes. Indeed, methodological choices may help alleviate some of the above-mentioned concerns. Ethnomethodological conversation analysis, for example, trusts the analyst as a competent member of society with access to the mundane everyday activity that takes place in the given collectivity and with an ability to take analytic distance when necessary (Garfinkel 1967). Terkourafi (2019: 1201) likewise maintains that "it is only by gaining a sound understanding of insiders' shared knowledge that we can begin to account for what happens when insiders become cultural outsiders as they encounter each other in cross-cultural communication".

6.3 From Attitudes to Evaluative Practices

Evaluation is one of the ways in which stance taking can be displayed and manifested in interaction. As Alba-Juez and Thompson (2014: 10) put it, "evaluation constitutes the *expression* of the speaker's stance or attitude; thus *evaluation* and *stance* are not exactly the same thing: From this perspective, *stance* would be a more abstract concept, and *evaluation* would be the actual verbal realization or manifestation of the stance" (emphasis in the original). Evaluation is captured by practices that are central to many fields of study, including (im)politeness, attitudes and appraisal research. Starting with the latter, studies by Martin and White (Martin 2000; Martin and

White 2005) have been key in developing appraisal theory. Drawing on the Bakhtinian idea of dialogism that "to speak or write is always to reveal the influence of, refer to, or to take up in some way, what has been said/written before, and simultaneously to anticipate the responses of actual, potential or imagined readers/listeners" (Martin and White 2005: 92), appraisal theory offers a systematic framework for studying evaluation by way of identifying and investigating the lexical resources at speakers' disposal to express affect, judgement and appreciation in written and spoken interaction. Stemming from the study of literacy and writing in school and in the workplace and media discourse, appraisal theory has taken shape by moving from one genre to another to cover various modes of written and spoken interaction (Martin and White 2005).

Furthermore, a major research area in social psychology involves investigating the ways in which people's attitudes develop and change and how attitudes affect people's behaviour (e.g. Eagly and Chaiken 1998). This line of investigation has a long-standing tradition in social psychology and views attitudes as more or less fixed perceptions that people have of the world. However, as mentioned earlier, Edwards and Potter (e.g. Potter and Edwards 2003) laid the groundwork for shifting the focus from the underlying cognitive processes in people's minds to the evaluative practices that emerge from and are shaped by the unfolding of talk in mundane everyday interactions between people. Similarly, politeness theory has branched off to a discursive direction, sometimes identified as a second-wave approach to politeness. Haugh (2007: 295), for example, calls for a careful investigation into "how (im)politeness is interactionally achieved through the evaluations of self and other (or their respective groups) that emerge in the sequential unfolding of interaction". Culpeper (2011: 394) concurs by suggesting that "pragmatic choices are not made in a vacuum but in the light of repeated experience of social situations" and that "meanings, including understandings of politeness, thus emerge in the flux of social interaction". Kadár and Haugh (2013) take the notion further by illustrating how people's individual and joint understandings of politeness are formed and shaped by the recursive use of evaluative patterns over time in specific evaluative moments of politeness in interaction.

Contributing to a similar line of investigation, a collection of articles edited by Alba-Juez and Thompson (2014: xi) traces developments in the study of values and evaluation from "ancient Greco-Latin approaches to argumentation and work on Ethics" via Habermas and Perelman to Hunston (2008) and the contributions in the volume itself (Alba-Juez and Thompson 2014). With a linguistic and pragmatic aim, these contributions examine the complexity of evaluative practices by focusing on the multiple layers of evaluative acts as well as the finely tuned nuances of both explicit and implicit evaluation, and further, are firmly committed to shedding new light on the situatedness of evaluative practices.

6.4 Stance and Evaluation Research within Sociolinguistics

Within sociolinguistic research, local micro-level instances of stance taking and evaluation in interaction are treated as indexing global macro-level sociocultural phenomena in various contexts. Potter (1998) suggests that although discursive social psychologists, for example, typically work with the 'micro' features of interaction, their interests extend beyond the detailed analysis of interaction, reflecting ideas similar to those that have been cultivated in ethnography, linguistic anthropology and sociolinguistics. Drawing on early work on the construction of large-frame ideological themes in everyday talk in various contexts, Potter (1998: 240) further suggests that "it is often at the level of specific arguments or detailed conversational patterns that 'micro' issues of ideology, social structure and social setting become important".

In keeping with Potter's (1998) understanding of the relations of micro to macro analysis of discourse, Kiesling (2009) explores the link between the everyday use of sociolinguistic language variation in interaction and the emerging larger-scale social stance-taking patterns. Similarly to Du Bois (2007) and Englebretson (2007), he views stance taking as a highly pervasive activity that potentially affects the form of language, and makes an interesting point by claiming that "any choice of linguistic form made by a speaker is based ultimately on the interpersonal or epistemic stance they wish to take with their various interlocutors at a particular time", and "that it is stances that become associated, through cultural models, with various identities (including particular speaking roles in specific situations)" (Kiesling 2009: 172). These styles, then, become connected to certain social identities, and the concept of exterior indexicality is highlighted in the process. What is more, when certain stance-related variables appear constantly and long enough in everyday discourse, over time they develop into more stable stance indexicalities. Kiesling (2009: 178) illustrates the construction of a social identity by exploring the sociolinguistic development of *dude* as an attention-getter in North American English over the past few decades, suggesting that over time, the expression has gained much wider usage and, at the same time, its laid-back stance meaning, originally associated with 'surfers' and 'stoners', has widened. With respect to language variation and stance, Kiesling's data show that speakers in an American college fraternity use the suffix *-in'* variant (instead of the *-ing* variant) in displaying certain stances and that personal style emerges from this habitual stance taking. By the same token, Bucholtz (2009) investigates developments in the way in which Mexican immigrant youth in the United States use a specific stanced attention term to construct social identity and the way in which this linguistic marker, and style, is appropriated in media advertisements. Within evaluation research, Bednarek (2014) makes use of a discourse-based corpus analysis to examine DVD blurbs that are provided on the back of television series DVD box sets and concludes that the evaluative practices in the DVD blurbs closely resemble those of advertising discourse.

An important milestone in sociolinguistic work on stance that draws sociologically meaningful macro conclusions based on micro analysis of spoken and written discourse is a collection of papers edited by Jaffe (2009: 3), which offers a definition of stance taking as a process of "taking up a position with respect to the form or the content of one's utterance". The contributions to the volume pay particular attention to speaking styles in constructing, among others, social identity and ideology. In the introduction, the concept of positionality is highlighted as a pervasive theme that runs throughout the collection of papers, while some of the contributions investigate the relation of stance to the concept of belonging in various contexts. (For a thorough review of the volume, see Kockelman 2012.) The sociolinguistic and sociocultural dimensions of stance taking are thus emphasized.

Scheibman (2007) explores the use of generalizations in spoken interaction and suggests that they make manifest speakers' understandings of belonging and not belonging in particular social groups. Conversational partners may, for example, use the generic *they* subject in *othering* a group that they themselves do not identify belonging to. In turn, Shoaps (2007) explores the presumptions of shared values in 'moral irony' that is manifested in evaluative stance taking. Stance and stance taking have been further explored in connection with various other socially consequential characteristics, such as gender, class, socioeconomic status, race, ethnicity, physical disability and/or appearance and age, in various cultural contexts and configurations. For example, by using written texts as data, Walton and Jaffe (2011) investigate the twofold nature of racialized stances in a blogger's posts and adjacent commentary; they show how the participants, on one hand, parody the way in which the privileged class operates and, on the other hand, display participation in it. In a seminal paper on indexing gender, Ochs (1992) discusses the way in which gender is constituted through specific stances and social acts. Finally, in a chapter involving a discussion on body type and size, Coupland and Coupland (2009) make a distinction between speakers taking stances and stances being projected onto someone else, critically illustrating how these local acts of stance attribution relate to wider societal discourses and especially to medical discourses dealing with the body and weight loss.

Although the body itself may be closely discussed in such research, Bucholtz and Hall (2016: 173–4) draw attention to a significant gap in sociolinguistic research involving "the theoretical relationship between language and embodiment" and call for "placing embodiment at the center of sociolinguistic inquiry". They mention, for example, the stereotypical depiction of 'gay speech' in which the specific animated speaking style is often accompanied by a wave of a limp wrist and conclude that "the iconic dimension of indexicality is therefore a central issue for an embodied socio-cultural linguistics, as shown especially in studies of the voice as well as research on style" (Bucholtz and Hall 2016: 178). Likewise, Burdelski (2013: 275) suggests that it would be particularly useful to study the socialization of politeness practices in a Japanese context as "politeness is encoded in both linguistic resources such as honorifics and non-linguistic resources such as the body". Indeed, the time seems ripe for more contributions in the interdisciplinary field studying the role of the body in stance taking, evaluation and meaning making in general, without forgetting investigations into the way that the body is talked about, i.e. what are the prevailing dominant and subversive or alternative discourses surrounding the body. Among other factors, the relative ease of making audiovisual recordings and gaining access to them, as well as their constantly improving features and quality, facilitates and invites a close detailed investigation of the embodied practices of human interaction. Such studies certainly face an array of challenges that are briefly discussed in the conclusion to this chapter.

6.5 Stance and Evaluation in Storytelling: The Case of the Sagging Face

In this section, we offer an analysis of a storytelling sequence, which have been shown to function as vehicles of stance taking (see e.g. Niemelä 2011). Our aim is to show through an original data example that the storytelling framework allows for both local and global observations into stance taking and evaluation.

Example 2 is an everyday speech event extracted from a dataset collected in a staff break room of a Finnish workplace. The social setting of the speaking event has consequences for the sequential organization of the interaction. Firstly, the three women are taking a break at work, which renders relevant their status and position at the workplace. Two of the women, Johanna and Pirkko, are established senior members of the staff, whereas Sanna is a junior member with no permanent position. Another consequential characteristic is the age of the participants: Johanna is approaching retirement, and Pirkko is middle aged with many years of working life ahead of her. Sanna, on the other hand, is at the entry phase of her career. The Finnish practices under examination here seem to work in much the same way as comparable English practices.

The participants are discussing the kinds of jewellery they own, and Johanna and Pirkko have established that they both own a lot of Kalevala jewellery (a common Finnish high-end brand). Right before the extract, Pirkko has confirmed that she has 'an insane number' of dangling earrings by Kalevala. The transcript follows common conversation-analytic conventions and includes descriptions of some embodied actions by the participants (in grey).

(2) *Your face certainly isn't sagging anywhere yet* (Finnish Workplace Data)

```
01 PIR:   mutta korvakoruja ei ennää voi vaan pittää,
          and one just cannot wear earrings anymore
02        ko jossaki vaiheessa joku sano että,
          because at some point someone said that
03        joo että sitte tietyssä iässä naisella,
          yeah at a certain age with a woman
04        <@ku naama alakaa roikkumaan,
             when face starts to sag
05        nii ei voi ennää käyttää roikkuvia korvakoruja@>.
          one cannot wear dangling earrings anymore
06 JOH:   aijja[a:]
          oh really
   joh    touches ears with both hands
07 PIR:        [ni]in [mää en oo voinu sen jälkeen-
          so I haven't been able to after that
   san             lifts mug in front of mouth
08 SAN:                [(oikeesti).
                        are you serious
09 JOH:                [pitäs-
                        should-
10        pitäskö näistä sitte luopua(h) [heh heh heh
          should one maybe give these up then
11 PIR:                                  [ei,
                                          oh no
12        mullon niinkö niitä isoja,
          I have like those big ones
   pir    draws big circle in the air next to right ear
13 JOH:   nii[sulla on niitä isoja=
          yes you have those big ones
   joh    adjusts hair above ears
14 PIR:      [mullon niitä isoja isoja.
              I have those big big ones
15 JOH:   =no: mullahan on kans kalevalakorut ni[itä] isoja.
          well my Kalevala jewelry are also those big ones
16 PIR:                                          [nii],
                                                  so
17        niitä isoja,
          those big ones
18        niin tuota (.) minun piti sitte-
          so then I had to then
19 SAN:   mm mut kyl[(nyt kai voi pitää)].
          but surely one can wear them
   san    drinks out of mug, puts it on the table,
          lowers face to palm
```

```
20 PIR:            [en voinu enää] sitt[e sen jäläkeen
                    laittaa(h)
                   I couldn't wear them anymore after that
21 JOH:                                  [eh he:
22 PIR:  eh heh[heh]
23 JOH:        [eh][.he:]
24 SAN:            [m h]
25 PIR:            [aina] alako näyttää että no nyt.
                   it started to look like now (was the time)
26       (0.3)
27 JOH:  ei sulla- ei sulla naama roiku mistään vielä.
         your- your face certainly isn't sagging
         anywhere yet.
28 PIR:  ky:llä se (.) roikkuu naamaki.
         yes (I'm afraid) my face is sagging too.
```

The extract begins when Pirkko gives a preface to her telling in the form of an account of not being able to wear her dangling earrings anymore: 'someone' has at some point said that, when 'at a certain age' a woman's face begins to sag, she should not wear dangling earrings anymore. Because of this comment, Pirkko suggests, she does not wear such earrings anymore.

Firstly, we need to consider the stance that the participant takes by telling the story here and now (see e.g. Ochs and Capps 2001; Niemelä 2011). With regard to taking a stance via storytelling, Stivers (2008: 31) proposes that "when someone tells a story, the teller provides the recipient with 'access' to an event and to the teller's stance toward that event". Storytelling also facilitates the study of the acts of stance taking in a larger sociolinguistic framework. Schiffrin (1996), for example, looks at the resources for identity work in storytelling, and Ochs and Capps (2001) explore conversational narratives as vehicles of displaying moral stances and constructing selves and communities. In Example 2, the participants negotiate their identities as 'women of a certain age' by appealing to gender norms and assumptions about the body and the process of ageing, which are in turn displayed and iterated in interaction through stylized language use.

We begin our examination of the stance-taking practices that appear in this example by looking at the prosodically animated reported speech sequence in lines 4–5. The dualistic function of direct reported speech in talk-in-interaction has been widely recognized. Besnier (1993: 161), for instance, characterizes it, firstly, as "the representation of linguistic actions" and, secondly, as "commentaries about these actions". Direct reported speech is not verbatim repetition of another person's words but instead constructed and shaped by the current teller to take a specific stance on, and evaluate, the subject at hand and sometimes also the reported speaker. These types of reports of someone else's speech or attributed thought in conversation are designed to elicit a specific kind of response from the recipient(s) and often involve a shift in prosody. As observed in this example, the storyteller, Pirkko, resorts to using an 'other voice' (see e.g. Couper-Kuhlen 1999; Niemelä 2005; Goodwin 2007) to differentiate the reporting from surrounding talk and to display the positioning and mind-set of the reported speaker. In the sociolinguistics literature, the phenomenon is discussed under the concept of *stylization* or styling the other (see e.g. Coupland 2001; Jaworski and Thurlow 2006).

In lines 4–5, the animated direct reported turn is produced in two rhythmic stanzas: *kun naama alakaa roikkumaan, ei voi ennää käyttää roikkuvia korvakoruja* 'when face starts to sag, one cannot wear dangling earrings anymore', and the prosody depicts a somewhat stern and matter-of-fact voice quality. The authoritative voicing seems to function as a distancing and disaligning element towards the content of the report. It also conveys a disaligning stance towards the reported speaker, the 'someone' who imposes rules like this on 'women of a certain age'. Indeed, a reported utterance such as this characteristically *embodies a dualistic stance by the current speaker*, first, on the subject matter at hand and, second, on the reported speaker.

However, "a story is not only in itself a display of stance" and "a storytelling sequence may, and typically does, contain evaluations or reported speech, provided by both teller and recipient(s), which function as displays of stances that align with and support the main storytelling and the main stance-taking activity" (Niemelä 2011: 43). In Example 2, the telling by Pirkko can be interpreted as a troubles-telling conveying a grievance caused by someone's normatively oriented and negatively stanced ageist commentary on the appropriate adornment of 'women of a certain age'. Here one interpretation of society's dominant norms concerning women's ageing and appearance is set up for display through a telling that contains direct reported speech. As Romano (2014) suggests, evaluation is embedded in the entire narrative from beginning to end, and that is the case here as well. The teller positions herself in view of the crux of the telling by implying that she belongs to the group of women who cannot do something because of (features related to) her age. What she conveys is a rather negative evaluation of herself as a woman with a sagging face who cannot wear dangling earrings, and possibly in this way elicits support from her co-participants.

Within the storytelling sequence, there are more specific turns, by the teller and the recipients, that display a more explicit stance on the subject matter at hand. Evaluative practices are shown to have a pivotal role in displaying and constructing speaker stances. The storytelling participants reflexively and collaboratively adjust their turns vis-à-vis the immediate social and physical stance-taking environment. Here the telling and the direct reported speech elicit affiliative responses from the participants. Explicit evaluation is observed in an expression of disbelief, *oikeesti* (line 8), which is produced by the junior member of staff, Sanna. Translated into English, *oikeesti* literally means 'for real' but carries also the meaning of 'you're kidding'. By using this, Sanna positions herself vis-à-vis the telling by Pirkko, aligning with the stance but orienting rather to the negatively stanced telling than to Pirkko's negative self-evaluation and resisting the implications of the telling.

What is more, Sanna's evaluation of the telling is multimodal in nature. She raises her mug in front of her mouth (line 8, image 1), not to drink from it but to keep it in front of her mouth, at the same time as she utters *oikeesti*. The mug-to-mouth gesture bears an uncanny resemblance to the hands-over-mouth gesture that signals surprise and associated emotions, such as disbelief or shock (see Heath et al. 2012). Likewise, the embodied features coupled with the verbal element display disbelief and bewilderment at the face of, apparently, an appalling claim. Sanna keeps the mug there for eight seconds until her next turn at talk: *mut kyl nyt kai voi pitää* 'but surely one can wear them' (line 19), which explicitly disaligns from and attempts to overturn the normative ageist assumption conveyed by the telling. After that, Sanna lowers her face to palm as if closing off the sequence of responsive evaluation (line 19, image 2). The verbal turn contains a non-specific reference, a zero-person subject in Finnish, which has been shown to "leave the conceptualizer of the situation implicit, provid[ing] a more subjective perspective on the experience than explicit personal pronouns" (Laitinen 2006: 209). Thus, the utterance can be seen as a carefully constructed turn that avoids explicit evaluation of the degree of sagging of a colleague's face. Instead, moral judgement is made on the normative constraints displayed by the telling. This is evaluative activity that, on one hand, organizes and shapes the sequential stance-taking process and, on the other hand, provides commentary and participates in larger societal discourse.

Johanna, in turn, responds to the telling by uttering *aijaa, pitäskö näistä luopua sitte* 'oh really, should one maybe give these up then' (lines 6 and 10), while touching her own earrings. Johanna thus seems to include herself in the group of women whose faces are sagging and seemingly questions whether she should also abide by the rules imposed by this 'someone' on 'women of a certain age'. Pirkko is quick to deny this and clarifies that she actually means the big (earrings), 'those big big ones' (lines 11–14). However, Johanna confirms that her Kalevala earrings are also those big ones. Considering that Johanna is approaching the age of retirement while Pirkko still has an ample number of years ahead of her in working life, and that both Johanna and Pirkko have declared that they own and wear this type of jewellery, Pirkko's entire telling could potentially be interpreted as face-threatening, albeit produced in a joking manner and followed by pulses of hearty laughter. Nevertheless, the participants do not seem to treat it as such. In fact, the responses by Johanna and Sanna alike show how they evaluate the telling as something that is unbelievable and, to a certain degree, quite ridiculous. The example thus provides an opportunity to investigate the role of evaluative practices in 'facework' and the overall dialogic nature of (im)politeness in face-to-face interaction.

This complex and multifaceted example rich in multimodal features could certainly be analysed in much more detail; however, the aim here has been to provide a glimpse into some interactional practices of stance taking and evaluation and to discuss the more explicitly sociolinguistic dimension of the example. What we see here are "culturally dominant ageist assumptions about the body and ageing" (Coupland 2013: 3). The 'someone' in Pirkko's telling embodies in a rather fascinating way such dominant discourse about societal gender and ageist norms. The example further illustrates the jointly constructed and emergent nature of bodily categorization. Johanna's turn on line 27, *ei sulla naama roiku mistään vielä* 'your face certainly doesn't sag anywhere yet', does exactly that as it continues to iterate the categorization of women into groups based on some features that are visible on their bodies: to those whose faces are sagging and those whose faces are not sagging yet. Interestingly, Sanna does not go along with the evaluation of the sagginess of Pirkko's face, which might be due to her age and/or position at the workplace but could also be interpreted as a sign of refusal to accept the norm conveyed in the telling.

6.6 Conclusion

The principal idea shared by the studies discussed in this chapter is that stance taking and evaluation emerge from and have consequences for interaction. In addition to being sequentially consequential, stance taking and evaluation have an impact on the negotiations of meaning and interpersonal positionings and relations between participants. Embracing a novel discursive viewpoint, researchers in these various fields have rather dramatically shifted the point of departure for analysis: the internal has become public; the personal has become interpersonal and social; the fixed has become fluid and emergent. Thus, studies have moved from linguistic markers to interactional practices that ultimately reach beyond the realm of language. After all, the way in which we interact with others, expressing stances and evaluations, is deeply rooted in our bodies.

Several studies have moved beyond the purely linguistic content of speech to study various paralinguistic features with regard to stance taking and evaluation. For example, the prosodic details and general phonetic features of talk, embedded and intertwined in the processes of sequential organization of conversational turns, have been shown to play a significant role in the unfolding of stance taking in interaction (see e.g. Local and Walker 2008; Couper-Kuhlen 2009). Ford et al. (2002: 32) relate prosodic features, namely the reset of pitch, to the stance-expressing function of NP-extensions (see also Wu 2004; Keisanen 2006). Prosodically animated direct reported utterances have been shown to be a sequentially relevant practice of stance taking (see e.g. Couper-Kuhlen 1999) and indeed subsequent resonant direct reported turns as vehicles of displaying a congruent stance have been established as an orderly phenomenon in interaction (Niemelä 2005).

The role of stance taking and evaluation pertaining to the body and embodiment in interaction and discourse has also received some scholarly attention recently. Among others, researchers have investigated the role of gaze in stance taking (Haddington 2006), the body in organizing the participation framework (Goodwin 2007), re-enactments (Sidnell 2006) and their bodily and space-related dimension in taking stances in storytelling (Niemelä 2011). However, these studies need to be complemented by a closer investigation of stanced and evaluative bodies on the move and relating to the surrounding environment, objects and artefacts. With the recent increase in the study of embodiment in interaction, a very timely and relevant effort would indeed be to attempt to identify those – explicit and implicit – dialogic and reflexive processes in the interacting bodies that have to do with taking stances and doing evaluation. A thorough multidisciplinary investigation is called for to disclose such reoccurring practices in versatile sites and contexts.

This type of research obviously provides a plethora of challenges for the analysts. The challenges lie especially in the amount and degree of co-occurring multimodal resources that are being employed by people to perform social actions. That is, the linguistic and bodily resources are often highly complex and finely nuanced and may contain minute yet consequential details for the unfolding of interaction and meaning making. Moreover, in the absence of clear linguistic markers of stance and evaluation, building collections of cases can be rather laborious and time-consuming, which means that such investigations typically consist of case studies. Certainly, verbal practices are studied in various contexts but the aim per se is not to look for verbal expressions, or embodied practices for that matter, that encode a specific stance. Rather, stance and evaluation often consist of implicit structural recurrent multimodal patterns and practices that need to be approached from a comprehensive angle, embracing many fine details of interaction at the same time.

To date, empirical work on stance and evaluation in sociopragmatics has been somewhat limited but perhaps the brief look into some of that work provided in this chapter will help spark ideas for future work that manages to address and solve some of the issues pointed out by critics (e.g. Kockelman 2004, 2005, 2010, 2012; Local and Walker 2008; Clift 2010) and, while doing so, will contribute to developing further the theoretical framework for the study of stance and evaluation as situated language use.

References

Alba-Juez, L. and Thompson, G. (2014). The many faces and phases of evaluation. In G. Thompson and L. Alba-Juez, eds., *Evaluation in Context*. Amsterdam: John Benjamins, pp. 3–23.

Bednarek, M. (2014). An astonishing season of destiny! Evaluation in blurbs used for advertising TV series. In G. Thompson and L. Alba-Juez, eds., *Evaluation in Context*. Amsterdam: John Benjamins, pp. 197–220.

Besnier, N. (1993). Reported speech and affect on Nukulaelae atoll. In J. H. Hill and J. T. Irvine, eds., *Responsibility and Evidence in Oral Discourse*. Cambridge: Cambridge University Press, pp. 161–81.

Biber, D. and Finegan, E. (1989). Styles of stance in English: Lexical and grammatical marking of evidentiality and affect. *Text*, 9(1), 93–124.

Bucholtz, M. (2009). From stance to style: Gender, interaction, and indexicality in Mexican immigrant youth slang. In A. Jaffe, ed., *Stance: Sociolinguistic Perspectives*. Oxford: Oxford University Press, pp. 146–70.

Bucholtz, M. and Hall, K. (2016). Embodied sociolinguistics. In N. Coupland, ed., *Sociolinguistics: Theoretical Debates*. Cambridge: Cambridge University Press, pp. 173–98.

Burdelski, M. (2013). Socializing children to honorifics in Japanese: Identity and stance in interaction. *Multilingua*, 32, 247–73.

Chafe, W. (1986). Evidentiality in English conversation and academic writing. In W. Chafe and J. Nichols, eds., *Evidentiality: The Linguistic Coding of Epistemology*. Norwood, NJ: Ablex, pp. 261–72.

Clift, R. (2010). REVIEWS - Alexandra Jaffe (ed.), Stance: Sociolinguistic perspectives (Oxford Studies in Sociolinguistics). Oxford: Oxford University Press, 2009. Pp. vii 261. *Journal of Linguistics*, 46(2), 518–22.

Conrad, S. and Biber, E. (2000). Adverbial marking of stance in speech and writing. In S. Hunston and G. Thompson, eds., *Evaluation in Text: Authorial Stance and the Construction of Discourse*. Oxford: Oxford University Press, pp. 56–73.

Couper-Kuhlen, E. (2009). Prosody. In J. Verschueren, J. Östman and S. D'hondt, eds., *The Pragmatics of Interaction*. Amsterdam: John Benjamins, pp. 174–89.

Couper-Kuhlen, E. (1999). Coherent voicing: On prosody in conversational reported speech. In W. Bublitz and U. Lenk, eds., *Coherence in Spoken and Written Discourse: How to Create It and How to Describe It*. Amsterdam: John Benjamins, pp. 11–32.

Coupland, J. (2013). Dance, ageing and the mirror: Negotiating watchability. *Discourse and Communication*, 7(1), 3–24.

Coupland, J. and Coupland, N. (2009). Attributing stance in discourses of body shape and weight loss. In A. Jaffe, ed., *Stance: Sociolinguistic Perspectives*. Oxford: Oxford University Press, pp. 227–49.

Coupland, N. (2001). Dialect stylization in radio talk. *Language in Society*, 30, 345–75.

Culpeper, J. (2011). Politeness and impoliteness. In K. Aijmer and G. Andersen, eds., *Sociopragmatics*, Vol. 5 of *Handbooks of Pragmatics*. Berlin: Mouton de Gruyter, pp. 391–436.

Du Bois, J. (2007). The stance triangle. In R. Englebretson, ed., *Stancetaking in Discourse: Subjectivity, Evaluation, Interaction*. Amsterdam: John Benjamins, pp. 139–82.

Du Bois, J. and Kärkkäinen, E. (2012). Taking a stance on emotion: Affect, sequence, and intersubjectivity in dialogic interaction. *Text and Talk*, 32(4), 433–51.

Eagly, A. H. and Chaiken, S. (1998). Attitude structure and function. In D. T. Gilbert, S. T. Fiske and G. Lindzey, eds., *The Handbook of Social Psychology*, Vol. I, 4th ed. New York: McGraw-Hill, pp. 269–322.

Englebretson, R. (2007). Stancetaking in discourse: An introduction. In R. Englebretson, ed., *Stancetaking in Discourse: Subjectivity, Evaluation, Interaction*. Amsterdam: John Benjamins, pp. 1–25.

Field, M. (1997). The role of factive predicates in the indexicalization of stance: A discourse perspective. *Journal of Pragmatics, 27*, 799–814.

Ford, C. E., Fox, B. A. and Thompson, S. A. (2002). Constituency and the grammar of turn increments. In C. E. Ford, B. A. Fox and S. A. Thompson, eds., *The Language of Turn and Sequence*. New York: Oxford University Press, pp. 14–38.

Garfinkel, H. (1967). *Studies in Ethnomethodology*. Cambridge: Polity Press.

Goffman, E. (1983). The interaction order: American Sociological Association, 1982 presidential address. *American Sociological Review*, 48(1), 1–17.

Goffman, E. (1974). *Frame Analysis: An Essay on the Organization of Experience*. London: Harper and Row.

Goodwin, C. (2007). Participation, stance, and affect in the organization of activities. *Discourse and Society*, 18(1), 53–73.

Goodwin, C. (2006). Interactive footing. In E. Holt and R. Clift, eds., *Reporting Talk: Reported Speech in Interaction*. Cambridge: Cambridge University Press, pp. 16–46.

Goodwin, C. and Goodwin, M. H. (1987). Concurrent operations on talk: Notes on the interactive organization of assessments. *Pragmatics*, 1(1), 1–55.

Gray, B. and Biber, D. (2014). Stance markers. In K. Aijmer and C. Rühlemann, eds., *Corpus Pragmatics: A Handbook*. Cambridge: Cambridge University Press, pp. 219–48.

Haddington, P. (2006). The organization of gaze and assessments as resources for stance taking. *Text and Talk*, 26(3), 281–328.

Haugh, M. (2007). The discursive challenge to politeness research: An interactional alternative. *Journal of Politeness Research, Language, Behaviour, Culture*, 3(2), 295–317.

Heath, C., vom Lehn, D., Cleverly, J. and Luff, P. (2012). Revealing surprise: The local ecology and the transposition of action. In A. Peräkylä and M.-L. Sorjonen, eds., *Emotion in Interaction*. Oxford: Oxford University Press, pp. 212–34.

Hunston, S. (2008). The evaluation of status in multi-modal texts. *Functions of Language*, 15(1), 64–83.

Hunston, S. and Thompson, G. (2000) Evaluation: An introduction. In S. Hunston and G. Thompson, eds., *Evaluation in Text: Authorial Stance and the Construction of Discourse*. Oxford: Oxford University Press, pp. 1–27.

Jaffe, A. (2009). *Stance: Sociolinguistic Perspectives*. Oxford: Oxford University Press.

Jaworski, A. and Thurlow, C. (2006). The alchemy of the upwardly mobile: symbolic capital and the stylization of elites in frequent-flyer programmes. *Discourse and Society*, 17(1), 99–135.

Kadár, D. and Haugh, M. (2013). *Understanding Politeness*. Cambridge: Cambridge University Press.

Keisanen, T. (2006). *Patterns of Stance Taking: Negative Yes/no Interrogatives and Tag Questions in American English Conversation*. Acta Universitatis Ouluensis B71. Oulu: Oulu University Press.

Kiesling, S. (2009). Style as stance: Can stance be the primary explanation for patterns of sociolinguistic variation? In A. Jaffe, ed., *Stance: Sociolinguistic Perspectives*. Oxford: Oxford University Press, pp. 171–94.

Kockelman, P. (2012). Review of "Stance: Sociolinguistic Perspectives." Edited by Alexandra M. Jaffe. Oxford: Oxford University Press. *Journal of Linguistic Anthropology*, 22(2), 105–8.

Kockelman, P. (2010). *Language, Culture, and Mind: Natural Constructions and Social Kinds*. Cambridge: Cambridge University Press.

Kockelman, P. (2005). The semiotic stance. *Semiotica, 157*, 233–304.
Kockelman, P. (2004). Stance and subjectivity. *Journal of Linguistic Anthropology, 14*(2), 127–50.
Kärkkäinen, E. (2012). On digressing with a stance and not seeking a recipient response. *Text and Talk, 32*(4), 477–502.
Kärkkäinen, E. (2007). The role of *I guess* in conversational stancetaking. In R. Englebretson, ed., *Stancetaking in Discourse: Subjectivity, Evaluation, Interaction*. Amsterdam: John Benjamins, pp. 183–219.
Kärkkäinen, E. (2006). Stance-taking in conversation: From subjectivity to intersubjectivity. *Text and Talk, 26*(6), 699–731.
Kärkkäinen, E. (2003). *Epistemic Stance in English Conversation: A Description of Its Interactional Functions, with a Focus on I Think*. Amsterdam: John Benjamins.
Laitinen, L. (2006). Zero person in Finnish: A grammatical resource for construing human reference. In M.-L. Helasvuo and L. Campbell, eds., *Grammar from the Human Perspective: Case, Space and Person in Finnish*. Amsterdam: John Benjamins, pp. 209–31.
Local, J. and Walker, G. (2008). Stance and affect in conversation: On the interplay of sequential and phonetic resources. *Text and Talk, 28*(6), 723–47.
Martin, J. (2000). Beyond exchange: APPRAISAL systems in English. In S. Hunston and G. Thompson, eds., *Evaluation in Text: Authorial Stance and the Construction of Discourse*. Oxford: Oxford University Press, pp. 142–75.
Martin, J. and White, P. (2005). *The Language of Evaluation: Appraisal in English*. Basingstoke, UK: Palgrave Macmillan.
McLaughlin, J. (2009). Discourse or cognition: An introduction to discursive psychology. *Journal of Systemic Therapies, 28*(2), 50–61.
Niemelä, M. (2011). *Resonance in Storytelling: Verbal, Prosodic and Embodied Practices of Stance Taking*. Acta Universitatis Ouluensis B95. Oulu: Oulu University Press.
Niemelä, M. (2005). Voiced direct reported speech in conversational storytelling: Sequential patterns of stance taking. *SKY Journal of Linguistics, 18*, 197–221.
Ochs, E. (1992). Indexing gender. In A. Duranti and C. Goodwin, eds., *Rethinking Context: Language as an Interactive Phenomenon*. Cambridge: Cambridge University Press, pp. 335–58.
Ochs, E. and Capps, L. (2001). *Living Narrative*. Cambridge, MA: Harvard University Press.
Palmer, F. (1979). *Modality and the English Modals*. London: Longman.
Potter, J. (1998). Discursive social psychology: From attitudes to evaluative practices. *European Review of Social Psychology, 9*, 233–66.
Potter, J. and Edwards, D. (2003). Sociolinguistics, cognitivism and discursive psychology. *International Journal of English Studies, 3*(1), 93–109.
Rauniomaa, M. (2008). *Recovery through Repetition: Returning to Prior Talk and Taking a Stance in American-English and Finnish Conversations*. Acta Universitatis Ouluensis B85. Oulu: Oulu University Press.

Romano, M. (2014). Evaluation in emotion narratives. In G. Thompson and L. Alba-Juez, eds., *Evaluation in Context*. Amsterdam: John Benjamins, pp. 367–86.

Scheibman, J. (2007). Subjective and intersubjective uses of generalizations in English conversation. In R. Englebretson, ed., *Stancetaking in Discourse: Subjectivity, Evaluation, Interaction*. Amsterdam: John Benjamins, pp. 111–39.

Scheibman, J. (2001). Local patterns of subjectivity in person and verb type in American English conversation. In J. Bybee and P. Hopper, eds., *Frequency and the Emergence of Linguistic Structure*. Amsterdam: John Benjamins, pp. 61–89.

Schiffrin, D. (1996). Narrative a self-portrait: Sociolinguistic construction of identity. *Language in Society, 25,* 167–203.

Shoaps, R. (2007). Moral irony: Modal particles, moral persons and indirect stance-taking in Sakapultek discourse. *Pragmatics, 17*(2), 297–335.

Sidnell, J. (2006). Coordinating gesture, gaze and talk in re-enactments. *Research on Language and Social Interaction, 39*(4), 377–409.

Stivers, T. (2008). Stance, alignment, and affiliation during storytelling: When nodding is a token of affiliation. *Research on Language and Social Interaction, 41*(1), 31–57.

Terkourafi, M. (2019). Coming to grips with variation in sociocultural interpretations: Methodological considerations. *Journal of Cross-Cultural Psychology, 50*(10), 1198–215.

Walton, S. and Jaffe, A. (2011). Stuff white people like: Stance, class, race, and internet commentary. In C. Thurlow and K. Mroczek, eds., *Digital Discourse: Language in the New Media*. Oxford: Oxford University Press, pp. 199–219.

Wetherell, M. and Potter, J. (1987). *Discourse and Social Psychology: Beyond Attitudes and Behaviour*. London: Sage.

Wu, R. (2004). *Stance in Talk: A Conversation Analysis of Mandarin Final Particles*. Amsterdam: John Benjamins.

7

Reflexivity and Meta-awareness

Jef Verschueren

7.1 Introduction

There is a long tradition in logic and linguistics that deals with metalanguage as opposed to so-called object language (cf. Lyons 1977: 10ff.). The latter would comprise most instances of language use, talking about non-linguistic entities, states of affairs and events. Metalanguage then serves as a cover term for linguistic resources or instances of language use that have aspects of language itself as their object. But metalinguistic awareness, the real topic of this article, is not restricted to metalanguage (see also Merz and Yovel 2000). It is an essential ingredient of whatever goes on in people's minds when language serves expressive and communicative purposes.

Human language cannot function the way it does without theory of mind, the ability to form hypotheses about others' mental states and knowledge, and to reflexively monitor (both retroactively and projectively) the meaning generation effect of one's words. This is the sociocognitive basis of a reflexive meta-level which is a pervasive dimension of all language use. This is why, in addition to interest from logicians (Tarski 1956) and linguists (Jakobson [1956] 1985), there is also a longstanding interest in metalinguistic awareness from psychologists, including those focusing on psychological development in children (e.g. Tunmer et al. 1984; Gombert 1990).

There is also a long history of philosophical discussions about reflexivity (see e.g. Babcock 1980). It is hard to resist, in this context, a furtive reference to the ancient Greek wisdom of γνῶθι σεαυτόν (*gnothi seauton*, know yourself), normatively encouraging self-reflection – wisdom ascribed to several Greek philosophers including Socrates, but probably just an instance of widespread aphorisms. Or, for that matter, reference to Descartes' *cogito ergo sum* (I think therefore I am) which reflexively equates the powers of reflexivity with the very fact of human existence.

For a phenomenon that takes centre stage in the mental processing of language use, which itself is the bread and butter of social interaction, it is not surprising that it attracted the attention of psychiatrists. From the angle of psychiatry, Ruesch and Bateson (1951) formulate a theory of communication which is proposed as "the only scientific model which enables us to explain physical, intrapersonal, interpersonal, and cultural aspects of events within one system" (5). We are, so the theory goes, biologically compelled to communicate so that communication forms the substance or the basis of both mental and social life. And since all successful communication requires correction and self-correction, a great deal of reflexivity, communication about communication, is essential. Such observations can of course be made outside of the context of psychiatry. But reflexivity involves the complex management of different levels of meaning, and when this fails, psychiatric problems may result. Hence this specific professional attention for metalinguistic awareness. In the terms of Watzlawick et al. (1967: 53): "The ability to metacommunicate appropriately is not only the *conditio sine qua non* of successful communication, but is intimately linked with the enormous problem of awareness of self and others". All of this links up to George Herbert Mead's social psychology which holds that metalinguistic awareness provides the key to an understanding of intersubjectivity in a communicative act (see Caton 1993).

While it is not possible not to communicate, it is also impossible not to 'mean'. Peter Winch (1958) may have been the first – in a critical extension of Max Weber's view of understanding (*Verstehen*) in the social sciences – to explicitly draw attention to the fundamental reflexivity of all social action. There is no way, according to Winch, to understand any form of social behaviour without grasping the concepts in terms of which the participants interpret their own behaviour. This is because all social action is 'meaningful' in the sense that it is already being interpreted by those involved. This counts *a fortiori* for verbal behaviour which somehow shows a double form of reflexivity because language provides the tools for reflecting upon itself. This observation was at the basis of one strand of metapragmatic research which was designed to gain a better understanding of aspects of language use by analysing (usually contrastively) the often lexicalized concepts available in specific languages to talk about language (see Verschueren 1985a), without assuming that explicit conceptualizations necessarily provide true accounts of the nature of language use. A lot of work under the label of 'ethnography of speaking' (e.g. Bauman and Sherzer 1974) was carried out in pursuit of this goal.

Though more fine-grained distinctions are possible,[1] I will in the remainder of this article use 'meta-awareness' as the more general term

---

[1] A useful distinction, harder to use for the following overview of research themes and topics, is the one made by Silverstein (1993) between nomic, reportive and reflexive modes of 'calibration' between meta-signs and the signs that are their targets. For an insightful use of these distinctions, e.g. in the discussion of (explicit) performativity, see Nakassis (2013).

for the phenomena involved (awareness of aspects of language or language use), and I will reserve 'reflexivity' for cases in which awareness is not just situated at a general metalinguistic level, but appears as literally reflexive awareness at the token level, albeit potentially to various degrees of 'consciousness'. It is important to keep in mind, however, that reflexivity and meta-awareness both bear on an invariably present meta-dimension of language use (see Verschueren 2000). This notion of the metalinguistic dimension is strongly relied on in a second strand of metapragmatic research, centred around the work of Michael Silverstein. I quote:

> Without a metapragmatic function simultaneously in play with whatever pragmatic function(s) there may be in discursive interaction, there is no possibility of interactional coherence, since there is no framework of structure – here, interactional text structure – in which indexical origins or centerings are relatable one to another as aggregated contributions to some segmentable, accomplishable event(s). (Silverstein 1993: 36–7)

Predating this general stance on the constant interaction between pragmatic and metapragmatic functioning, there was the more concrete experience of anthropological linguists that they "spend a great deal of time listening to people talk about what they are doing" when they are speaking, and the observation that "such metalanguage, for the analyst of culture, is as much a part of the problem as part of the solution" (Silverstein 1981: 382).[2]

Section 7.2 of this chapter will deal with metalinguistic activity types. In a sense, this is about explicit metalanguage, or metalanguage and metalinguistic utterances as objects of investigation in their own right, all necessarily involving meta-awareness, with one type (discussed in Section 7.2.4) being reflexive. By contrast, Section 7.3 will deal more directly with implicit metalanguage by focusing on specific types of indicators of meta-awareness, all of which are to a certain extent reflexive. Continuing into Section 7.4, we move towards examples of the interactional role of metapragmatic awareness. The significance of cross-cultural variability will be the subject of Section 7.5, and we will end, in Section 7.6, with a brief look at methodological challenges for the investigation of reflexivity and meta-awareness.

---

[2] The two strands of metapragmatics mentioned here emerged simultaneously but independently of each other in the early 1980's. While Silverstein and a number of his students and colleagues were developing the more general notion at the University of Chicago, a more lexically oriented version appeared at the University of California, Berkeley, in a graduate course taught by this author in collaboration with Charles Fillmore, John Gumperz and John Searle under the title *Metapragmatics; Or, the lexicalization of linguistic action* (Winter quarter 1982).

7.2 Metalinguistic Activity Types

As suggested above, I will handle a rough distinction (first introduced in Verschueren 2000) between (largely implicit) indicators of reflexive awareness (to be discussed in Section 7.3), and more explicit forms of metalanguage or metalinguistic activity types which can be isolated as easily identifiable objects of close scrutiny in their own right. Metalanguage as an object of scrutiny corresponds to Jakobson's (1971) messages referring to messages (M/M) as in various forms of quoted and reported speech, and messages referring to the code (M/C) as found whenever a word is 'mentioned' rather than 'used' (more about which later). In what follows I will distinguish between (1) talk about linguistic forms and utterances, (2) talk about language(s), (3) quoted and reported speech, and (4) self-reflexive speech. Note that, except for some of the talk about specific linguistic forms, all of these metalinguistic activity types are by definition metapragmatic since they bear on (contexts of) use.

7.2.1 Talk about Linguistic Forms and Utterances

Aspects and instances of language (use) can be put on display, as it were. Two categories of such metalinguistic behaviour were distinguished by Bateson ([1955] 1972) with the labels metalinguistic messages and metacommunicative messages. In metalinguistic messages "the subject of discourse is the language" (178). Examples would be cases of 'mention' as opposed to 'use' (a phenomenon that has attracted philosophical attention at least since Carnap 1919). While the words 'cat' and 'pup' in (1) and (2) are used referentially, in (3), (4) and (5) they are 'mentioned'; i.e. they are reflexive, lacking their usual referential value.

(1)   This cat is getting old.

(2)   They bought a new pup.

(3)   The word 'cat' has no fur and cannot scratch

(4)   'Pup' means a young dog

(5)   'Pup' is a monosyllable

Note that in writing the distinction is usually marked by scare quotes, while in spoken language there may be subtle prosodic cues; in both, the 'mention' status may be underscored by additional qualifications such as 'so-called'. When distinction markers are left out, (an attempt at) punning may be involved.

Cases of 'mention' are not necessarily restricted to single words.

(6)   "I'm not a racist, but ..." is a common way of expressing racist ideas

In (6) the phrase "I'm not a racist, but ..." is mentioned rather than used. And the same counts for the full sentences (1) through (6) in the context of this linguistics article.

Borderline cases include instances of metalinguistic negation as in (7).

(7) Peter isn't *happy* ... he's *ecstatic*

Furthermore, there is a subtle distinction between a sentence such as (4), in which the focus is on the word 'pup', and other types of definitions or circumlocutions which are also metalinguistic but which focus on a word's content rather than the word as such, as in (8).

(8) Copper is a metal

In spite of the surface similarity with (4), here the word 'copper' is really used, in contrast to (9), which is a clear case of 'mention'.

(9) 'Copper' has six letters

In contrast to such metalinguistic messages, in Bateson's terminology, there are also metacommunicative messages. "In these, the subject of discourse is the relationship between the speakers" (Bateson ([1955] 1972: 178). Examples are (10) and (11).

(10) This is play

(11) Is that a threat?

Here the focus is on communicative intent; the communication which such messages describe metalinguistically is provided with a frame of interpretation.

To perform these metacommunicative reflexive activities, most natural languages have a wide range of metapragmatic terms available. With reference to the multiple layers of meaning in ordinary human communication, Silverstein says

> If strategy requires purposive manipulation of pragmatic rules, then it may also require an overt conceptualization of speech events and constituent speech acts. (Silverstein 1976: 48)

Such overt conceptualizations may be reflected in lexical items, which is why metapragmatic terms have been extensively studied contrastively (Verschueren 1985a), lexicographically (Harras et al. 2004) and historically (Busse and Hübler 2012). When studying the use of such terms in discourse, also the conceptualization of relationships between talk and other forms of action comes in:

> In a text, the speech that is reported typically has some relationship to other action that is reported, for example, the speech may be about action that has taken place or will take place, it may be a command, it may be a lie, and so on. By studying these relationships, one gains access to what may be termed the "ethno-metapragmatic theory" the text embodies, that is, how the relationship between speech and action is conceptualized by the users of the language. (Urban 1984: 310)

Exemplifying this, Urban analyses a myth that embodies a prescriptive tale (from the Shokleng Indians of southern Brazil) about what the relationship between speech and action ought to be, and specifically about instructions and the following of instructions.

A specific tradition studying explicit comments made on language by language users goes under the label of *folk pragmatics* or more generally folk linguistics (Niedzelski and Preston 2007; Wilton and Stegu 2011). The tradition goes back to Hoenigswald (1966), who distinguished between what people say, people's unconscious reactions to what is said and people's conscious comments on language. According to Niedzelski and Preston (2007: 7), folk pragmatics does not simply consist of reflexive labelling but rather of outspoken views about aspects of language use, as in a conversation about whether or not something was polite and why (possibly even incorporating advice).

7.2.2 Talk about Language(s)

One aspect of folk linguistics/pragmatics is the way in which 'folk' perceive language variation (cf. McKenzie and Osthus 2011). A well-attested historical case showing the prominent role this may play in public life, is the long-standing controversy surrounding variation in Arabic (Daniëls 2018). Another concerns the pervasive stereotyping of foreigners' use of a language. One example of this is provided by Suzuki (2018), who gives an account of the relationship between norms of Japanese usage which are connected with a form of ethno-linguistic nationalism creating a Japanese identity which a foreigner cannot possibly belong to; she further analyses how in a novel this stereotype can be dramatically exploited by letting a non-Japanese speak so perfectly that his identity as a non-Japanese comes as a complete surprise. Here *normativity* comes in at various levels and for various purposes. An incisive analysis of what is involved can be found, for example, in Okamoto's (2018) account of normative linguistic femininity in the form of metapragmatic discourse in self-help books on Japanese women's speech.

With these analyses we have squarely entered into the domain of *language ideologies* (Kroskrity 2010; Schieffelin et al. 1992; Silverstein 1979; Woolard and Schieffelin 1994). Not only linguistic forms and utterances are talked about, but also language, languages and language use in general. The reflexive conceptions of language (use) that are involved play an important role in the organization of individual and institutional interaction in a wide range of settings, from everyday conversations to courtrooms and medical encounters.

In relation to language as a human phenomenon and its everyday use in interpersonal interaction, there are numerous – no doubt culture-specific – ideas about how it works or should work. One of the most-cited examples is Reddy's (1979) 'conduit metaphor', a naïve but widespread way of looking at verbal communication as clear output serving as clear input. Another example is the importance which many of us attach to intentionality ("I did not mean it that way"), to such an extent that it became the cornerstone of Gricean and Searlean theories of meaning. Since it has been shown that focus on intentionality is a variable (cf. Duranti's 2015 'intentional continuum'), such theoretical stances must be said to have language-ideological underpinnings.

In relation to languages, plural, there is first of all the common idea that languages are somehow natural objects that are neatly separable and homogeneous. Second, there are ideologies related to the role or desired status of specific languages. And the combination of these two factors feeds into language policies aimed at societal monolingualism (i.e. with one dominant language to be known by all) or standardization to turn language into a benevolent instrument providing equal access – a desired effect that is seriously counterbalanced by the reality that a language, handled in that way, easily serves as an instrument of power (cf. Errington 1992; Hill 2008; Kroskrity 2010).

7.2.3 Quoted and Reported Speech

A third metalinguistic activity type, probably the best-documented because of its relative (or at least apparent) simplicity and its obvious ubiquity, is quoted and/or reported speech. (See Holt 2009, Recanati 2000 or Coulmas 1986a for a good range of analyses in a number of different languages.)

The simplest form is *direct quotation* or citation, technically also known as *oratio recta*, which is a *de dicto* rendition of what was said on an earlier occasion by either the speaker or (more typically) someone else, or of what an imagined character is saying (as in a novel). Sometimes the term is also used to describe a direct verbalization of someone's thoughts. Usually it is accompanied or introduced by a descriptively used metapragmatic term.

Indirect quotation, usually called *indirect (reported) speech*, and also known as *oratio obliqua*, reports the content of what was said. This is why also the term *de re* comes up ('about the thing') in contrast to *de dicto* ('about what is said' – a translation that may be confusing in light of the definition I just gave of indirect speech). There are different degrees of 'indirectness' in indirect speech. Just consider (12) to (14).

(12)   He said "Hello!"

(13)   He said hello.

(14)   He greeted her.

Clearly, (13) is still very close to the direct quotation in (12), while (14) more clearly brings in the utterer's interpretation. Moreover, indirect speech may be ambiguous between *de dicto* and *de re* because the speaker is free to blend information from his/her own interpretation of the world with what was actually said in the reported utterance. To take an example from Coulmas (1986b), it is unlikely (though not impossible) that the utterance reported in (15) contained the same qualification of 'wife' as this indirect report.

(15)   John asked me to dance with his hysterical wife

In addition to direct quotation and indirect speech, there is an extensive literature on the so-called *free indirect style*, common in literary narratives, as in the second sentence in (16), which simultaneously represents the narrator's and the hero's points of view to the reader.

(16)   He asked her to stay. Had he not done enough for her?

It is important to notice the close relationship between these notions and Goffman's (1979) influential analytical concept of *footing*, referring to the specific personal alignment of an utterer to the content of his/her utterance as 'animator' (the person who actually produces an utterance), as 'author' (the one who chooses the words and thus the sentiments expressed), or as the 'principal' (the person whose position is established or who is presented as committed to what the words say). This, in turn, relates closely to Bakhtin's (1986) suggestion that utterances may incorporate a diversity of *voices*, i.e. the concealed or partly concealed words of others. According to the corresponding theory of *polyphony* (further developed by Ducrot 1984; see also Roulet 1996), it would even be the case that every negation incorporates a suggestion of its opposite: Nixon would not say "I'm not a crook" unless there is the assumption that others would or could make the opposite claim.

7.2.4   Self-Reflexive Speech

Language users often reflect quite explicitly upon their own utterances. There are two rough categories of this kind of verbal behaviour. The first is a mixed bag of *comment* types which may serve to situate an utterance in a wider discourse (e.g. *As I explained earlier* . . .), to mark rhetorical connections (e.g. with discourse markers such as *anyway, however*), to indicate or appeal to a degree of involvement (as with pragmatic particles such as *You know,* . . . or sentence adverbs such as *Actually,* . . . or *Frankly,* . . .), to reveal a degree of responsibility or commitment for what is said (with evidentials such as *possibly, evidently, allegedly,* or with hedges such as *sort of*), or to guide the interpreter's understanding or to prevent misinterpretation (as in *You did a great job, and I'm not being polite*).

The second category comprises Austin's (1962) *explicit performatives*, probably the only language forms which exhibit full reflexivity in the sense that they perform a speech act while (and by) describing it at the same time. It is this complete reflexivity, which makes the describing act and the described act fully coincide conceptually, that explains why you can say *I promise to come tomorrow* but not *I threaten to* . . . Threatening is an activity type which is looked upon as less than praiseworthy in mainstream western culture, so that the verb 'to threaten' carries a negative connotation which blocks the possibility of full coincidence with the act it describes (see Verschueren 1995).

7.3 Indicators of Reflexive Awareness

In addition to his M/M and M/C, Jakobson (1971) also distinguishes instances of the code referring to the code (C/C) as in proper names (the definition of which requires circular reference to the code itself because a name means that to which the name is assigned), and instances in which the code inevitably refers to aspects of the message (C/M) as in the indexical forms to be discussed shortly. All the forms reviewed in Section 7.2 are indicators of metapragmatic awareness. But while they also openly *display* such awareness, the phenomena to be studied in this section only serve as *indicators*. In other words, while Section 7.2 presented metalinguistic objects to be scrutinized (mostly explicit metalanguage), we now move to less overt or more implicit aspects of the metalinguistic or metapragmatic dimension of all language use.

We will not go into the problem of proper names (C/C). All other phenomena to be discussed here somehow relate to *contextual indexing*, the process of establishing links between utterances and aspects of their context. Why do they figure in an investigation of reflexivity? Clearly, we must assume language users' meta-awareness of a reflexive type to be able to understand their making the linguistic choices that reflect the situatedness of their own utterances.

7.3.1 Indexical Forms or 'Shifters'

Though the term had been introduced much earlier by Jespersen (1921), it is usually Jakobson (1971) and Silverstein (1976) who are referred to when 'shifters' are mentioned. The term essentially provides an alternative way to talk about deictic forms (to the study of which significant contributions were made several decades ago by linguists ranging from Benveniste 1956 to Fillmore 1997). Deictic forms have the capacity to 'shift' depending on who the participants in the communication are and how they relate to each other (person deixis and social deixis), participants' location in space (spatial deixis), and the time of communication in relation to the event or state of affairs talked about (temporal deixis).

It is important to understand that shifters or indexical forms are basically tools for reference. It was and still is quite common to distinguish a referential or predicational aspect of speech acts from their performative aspect. But as Silverstein (1976) observes, reference is as much a 'purposeful speech event' as any other speech event. Reference is not just 'used' performatively. That is why, in its purposefulness it is equally subject to reflexivity as any other purposeful functional speech event. This is the basis on which presuppositional referential indexes (shifters) have to be understood. In Silverstein's terms, "The reference value of a shifter ... depends on the presupposition of its pragmatic value" (24), or "a given shifter token is uninterpretable referentially without the knowledge of some aspect of the situation" (33).

7.3.2 Contextual Adjustment and Contextualization (Cues)

While the proper use of indexical forms or shifters is clearly a matter of contextual adjustment, this general process is not restricted to those forms. While pronoun choice (*tu* vs *vous*) may be a straightforward example of person/social deixis, the degrees of formality with which it is associated are also potentially reflected in other discourse phenomena, such as other aspects of lexical choice or even sound patterns. Because of the functional affinity of such discourse phenomena with indexical forms, Silverstein (1976) would call them 'nonreferential indexes'. It is important to note, however, that mere contextual adjustment yields easily to forms of strategic modulation. Intentional choices may disregard prescribed norms, thus changing context and creating, as it were, a new social or pragmatic reality. See, e.g., the studies of positioning self and others in interaction in Beeching et al. (2018): from forms of address – studied profusely – to Aijmer's (2018) attention-getters *look, listen, excuse me, come on*.

It is at this point that we see pragmatics moving from the notion of *context* to the process of *contextualization*. According to Auer, contextualization comprises

> all activities by participants which make relevant, maintain, revise, cancel ... any aspect of context which, in turn, is responsible for the interpretation of an utterance in its particular locus of occurrence. This notion implies a certain conceptualization of 'context' which can be characterized as flexible and as reflexive. (Auer 1992: 21)

Potentially relevant context is infinite. Processes of contextualization, language users' orientation to specific aspects of context, or contextual indexing, can also move into an infinite range of directions. Analytically, therefore, these notions would lose their usefulness if there would not be observable linguistic (and non-linguistic) choices which an utterer can make in keeping with a specific orientation to context, which an interpreter can use as input for understanding, and which a linguist can then rely on for a systematic investigation of the processes involved. Such linguistic (and non-linguistic) choices are called *contextualization cues*. In Auer's words:

> '*Contextualization cues*' are, generally speaking, all the form-related means by which participants contextualize language. Given the general

notion of a flexible and reflexive context ... it is clear that any verbal
and a great number of non-verbal (gestural etc.) signantia can serve
this purpose. (Auer 1992: 24)

Contextualization cues range from gaze and gesture to intonation patterns and forms of code-switching. One of their important properties is their habitual nature: while they form the basis for interpretations, they tend to escape conscious processing. Numerous examples, often involving intercultural communication, can be found in Gumperz (1982). One of the classics is the falling intonation with which a woman of Pakistani descent makes an offer to British workers who, expecting a rising intonation for a friendly offer, walk away from the encounter with a negative view of the woman's attitude. Another one is the symbolic code-switching from mainstream American English to Black English, with which an Afro-American student speaking to a white professor signals his belonging to fellow Afro-Americans overhearing their conversation. These examples involve variability between the communicative styles used by recognizable groups of speakers of the same language. Variability,[3] however, goes a lot further, as should be recognized by any student of pragmatics:

In the first place variability is not language specific but situation specific so that the primary unit or domain of analysis is not a language dialect or code seen as a structurally cohesive entity, but rather a situation, social encounter, or speech event.... Secondly it seems useful to speak of variable use in terms of communicative strategies that build on interactants' knowledge or on presuppositions associated with a paradigmatically organized range or repertoire of constellations of variants in order to achieve discourse level communicative goals. (Gumperz 1992: 41)

Gumperz continues:

I argue that conversational *interpretation* is cued by empirically detectable signs, contextualization cues, and that the *recognition* of what these signs are, how they relate to grammatical signs, how they draw on socio-cultural *knowledge* and how they affect *understanding*, is essential for creating and sustaining conversational *involvement* and therefore to communication as such. (42, italics added)

A *contextualization cue*, then, could be defined as any structural or formal marker of the way in which a stretch of discourse derives meaning from its

---

[3] Verschueren (1999: 59–63) defines *variability* as a first key notion for a theory of pragmatics: the property of language which defines the range of possibilities from which choices can be made when producing or understanding utterances. The other two are *negotiability* (the property of language responsible for the fact that choices are not made mechanically according to fixed form-function relationships, but on the basis of flexible principles and strategies) and *adaptability* (the property of language which enables human beings to make negotiable linguistic choices in pursuit of their communicative goals; see also Verschueren and Brisard 2002).

embeddedness in context. In the above quotation, note the heavy emphasis on (socio-)cognitive notions, highlighted by italics, which should be reminiscent of the introductory section on the socio-cognitive basis of reflexivity and meta-awareness (Section 7.1), and in particular of Winch's emphasis on the inherent meaningfulness of social action. We should add that all understanding is essentially 'framed': the variability referred to by Gumperz takes the shape of a repertoire of activity types (e.g. job interviews, academic lectures, telling a joke and the like). An *activity type* can be defined as any identifiable combination of ingredients from any set of contextual dimensions that is 'meaningful' in the sense that it provides a frame of interpretation for whatever happens in the course of specific tokens of the type (see also Levinson 1992). Established activity types play a vital role, in combination with contextualization cues, in contextual understanding. This insight did not appear all of a sudden. In intellectual history it can be traced back to Bakhtin's ([1952–3] 1986) speech genres and their social functions, as well as the power dynamics they often involve. Levinson (1992) links the notion of activity type to Wittgenstein's (1958) 'language game', presented as a concept needed to grasp the meaning of utterances, clearly requiring reflexive awareness of the contextually shaped nature of the activity which an utterance belongs to.

As multimodal approaches to conversation analysis (e.g. Goodwin 2018) have shown convincingly, gesture plays an important role as a contextualization cue in spoken interaction. But the role of gesture is not restricted to indicating metapragmatic awareness of the accompanying speech. In addition, gesture can itself metapragmatically comment on gestural behaviour. Hübler (2007), for instance, mentions a narrative stretch with gestures of boxing immediately followed by a metagesture which is "a slightly varied replication of the original gesture followed by a deictic gaze into the direction of that gesture and an amused smile", which he interprets as self-ironic "in the sense that the narrator creates a distance from his spontaneous gestural behavior by displaying an awareness of his own gestural expressivity" (111).

7.4 The Interactional Role of Metapragmatic Awareness

Every type of language use that requires multiple levels of understanding also requires metapragmatic awareness. This clearly counts for language play. Consider (17), on a poster in Paris, or (18), in a bookshop in London.

(17) Ne me tweete pas
('Do not tweet me', playful reference to *Ne me quitte pas*, 'Do not leave me')

(18) Oh what a wonderful word

Salverda (2017) adduces these examples, suggesting that processes involved in language play can be extended to any intentionally creative use of language, as in poetry, literature, good speeches. He writes:

> Taking Saussure's cue and investigating language itself as *un jeu* [a game/ play] opens the way towards a systematic linguistic study of language play phenomena and the potentialities of human language, as a clear window into the linguistic creativity of our species. (Salverda 2017: 124)

Linguistic creativity, which must be reflexively unpacked, is involved in every form of humour (consider e.g. Sinkeviciute's 2019 metapragmatic analysis of interviewees' jocular playing around with identity construction), in irony (even when marked only by a specific intonation contour), in metaphor, in the rhetorical use of parallelisms and comparisons.

In addition, there are three distinctively interactional functions that are served by indicators of metapragmatic awareness, whether of the explicit or the more implicit type. First of all, *all* indicators of metapragmatic awareness *guide listeners' or readers' interpretations*. A sarcastic intonation tells the hearer that *A great job you did!* is not to be taken literally. The response-controlling *but*-preface in *I am not a racist, but* … is intended to avert the hearer's potentially negative evaluation of what follows. Similarly, and more explicitly, metapragmatic comments intervening in ongoing talk (e.g. *I'm not kidding*) perform this function.

A second interactional function may be *to guide other's subsequent utterances*. Typical examples are political interviewers' attempts to control the direction of the interviewees' talk, as with comments such as *You're answering a different question* (Sivenkova 2013). Another well-documented case (first studied extensively by Jacobs 1999) is the surreptitious way in which metapragmatic aspects of the formulation of press releases in fact serve to 'preformulate' the news.

Third, there is also straightforward *commenting*, which may or may not overlap with one of the first two functions. Some types of commenting are clearly the opposite of preformulation. Think, for instance, of the 'reformulation' in the practice of therapists. Muntigl (2007) describes the reformulation of what a patient says as a way of reframing that makes it possible for a problem to be seen from a different point of view. Other types of comments are conscious attempts to build common ground. In the context of international project work, Penz (2007) argues that working towards a common goal in a multilingual and multicultural context requires awareness of differences in communicative repertoires that may be related to a lack of shared background knowledge, and she shows that metapragmatic comments are important aspects of attempts to overcome such hurdles. A third type of comment is evaluative. In her analyses of the metapragmatics of 'attentiveness', Fukushima (2013) addresses the issue of how hearers or beneficiaries evaluate (im)politeness. Evaluation is also involved in Márton Petykó's (2018) study of the motives ascribed by bloggers to contributors to threads whom they identify as trolls. Within a similar realm we can situate Deschrijver's (2018) fascinating study of metalanguage in *The Guardian* comment boards. Deschrijver develops an interesting measure of 'metalinguistic density', the number of times a term such as 'progressive', 'feminist' or 'sexist' would be used metalinguistically in comparison to the total number of occurrences of the term, and he identifies patterns in the clustering of metalinguistic usages of specific terms at specific moments in the development of economic reporting on specific issues.

7.5 The Significance of Cross-Linguistic Variability

Probably, the notion of contextualization cues would not have been formulated with such clarity, as in Gumperz (1982), if it had not been for his observation of the variability that may cause problems in a context of intercultural communication. As already suggested in Section 7.3.2, such problems do not simply follow from variability as such, but rather from the fact that the way in which inferences are drawn on the basis of subtle formal cues is usually habit-based and escapes conscious processing. Difficulties, however, are not restricted to everyday usage. As argued convincingly by Briggs (1986) and re-emphasized by Mertz (1993), metapragmatic problems may even come up in the intercultural use of social science interview formats, in spite of the well-wrought conscious choices they involve, just because there may be mismatches between the researcher's conceptions of language and their implications for language use, and those held by the speakers whose speech or behaviour is investigated.

In addition to this general issue, there are language-specific 'dedicated' linguistic devices reflecting meta-awareness. Here is a very brief and random sampling from the pragmatics literature.

Honorifics, the sometimes elaborate and highly language-specific systems of signalling deference, present a classical example (cf. Irvine 1995), and they characterize languages as diverse as Javanese, Nahuatl, ChiBemba and Dyirbal. The appropriateness of choices may in some cases be so closely linked to a specific social structure that an outsider can hardly ever make the right ones.

Closely related are issues of *entitlement* which may be marked formally. Not all communicative goals may be pursued equally by all members of a given speech community, so that different categories of members may have to modulate specific types of speech acts in highly conventionalized ways. Geyer's (2018) study of Japanese requesting strategies in faculty meetings in secondary schools, for instance, shows that specific linguistic choices are made to negotiate the entitlement to make certain requests; entitlement is in this case related to local institutional identity and the nature of the requested activities; the negotiation process itself, as well as the linguistic means that are deployed, are highly language and context dependent.

Discourse markers of various types vary significantly across languages. Consider, for instance, Maschler's (2009) account of Hebrew discourse markers which are said to be characterized by patterns of usage that are part of the essence of 'interacting as an Israeli'. An example is the discourse marker *nu*, for which there is no direct equivalent in English but which can sometimes be translated as 'well?', 'go on', 'so?', 'so what?' and which signals a form of interactive impatience which may be felt to be impolite by outsiders but which is rather indicative of an expected form of engagement or involvement within an Israeli Hebrew context.[4] *Particle*-rich languages such as Dutch or German offer utterances which are often hard to match in translation. When trying to render the German sentences in (19) in English, there are no corresponding particles available and the speaker of English must rely on formulas.

(19) German   English
     Ich bin ja dein Vater   I am your father, you know
     Ich bin nämlich dein Vater   You see, I'm your father
     Ich bin doch dein Vater   I am, after all, your father

Observing this contrast, Fillmore remarks:

> The pragmatic points to be made here are (1) that the German particles correspond (however imperfectly) to fairly subtle parenthetical formulaic expressions in colloquial English, and (2) that these expressions, if used in English as often as their counterparts are used in German, would produce very mannered speech. (Fillmore 1984: 133)

Thus there seem to be typological differences involved. The same goes for discourse-deictic elements such as *finally, all in all, indeed*, which Nyan (1998) calls 'metalinguistic operators'.

Beeching (2018) shows that even standard *metacommenters* which may be quite similar across closely related languages (e.g. English *sort of/kind of, like* vs French *genre, comme*, post-posed *quoi*, or *if you like/if you will* vs *si tu veux/si vous voulez*) may show regional differences and indexicalities. As an example she gives *comme* ('like') which in Canada seems to arise from English–French bilingualism, thus getting associated with a particular Canadian identity, while post-position *quoi* indexes speakers as coming from or associated with France.

There are numerous language-specific devices for *reporting speech*. Coulmas (1986a) presents case studies from Athabaskan, Yoruba, Swahili,

---

[4] It is important to realize that variability also implies changes over time. The notion of 'interacting as an Israeli', which somehow underlies this example, has undergone, still following Maschler (2009), significant changes since Katriel (1986) associated it with the straightforward, direct, and even blunt, self-named *dugri* style evoking the mythical image of the 'Sabra', the Jew born in Palestine under British mandate.

Japanese, Hungarian, Danish, French, Greek, Spanish, Caucasian languages and languages of Nepal. Lucy (1993b) draws our attention to special forms in Yucatec Maya, marking directly quoted speech, or 'quotatives', which do not take the form of full verbs of speaking but rather of affixes or particles. Hanks (1993) describes special metalinguistic labels in Mayan which serve to indicate that the speech reported on is hypothetical speech (i.e. without a real 'principal' in Goffman's terms, as opposed to real speech of which the current animator is also the principal). Apparently, these are often used to make a point, for the sake of argument or for fun, as opposed to discourse presenting one's own opinion and for which one takes responsibility.

Even seemingly trivial reflexive forms such as English *question tags* lack direct equivalents in many languages. As argued extensively by Birdsong (1989), such phenomena and the variability they involve are a common concern for language teaching and 'interlinguistic competence'.

The remaining question is whether there are any metapragmatic universals. Clearly, the fact of reflexivity is a universal property of all human languages. And probably so is the fact that languages dispose of a variety of formal indicators of metapragmatic awareness. Beyond this, most attention has gone so far to variability and contrastive research. One minor – and not so successful – attempt at identifying universal tendencies was made in Verschueren (1989), a comparative study of basic linguistic action verbs (defined as those metapragmatic lexical items which, in the same natural language, cannot be adequately defined in terms of a different lower-level linguistic action verb). Some patterns could be tentatively identified, but our understanding of language-specific notions of communication and language use is not sufficiently advanced to venture at generalizations. There is an urgent need for an inventory of metapragmatic conceptualizations which speakers of different languages live by and operate with.

7.6 Methodological Challenges

Silverstein already warned against the 'limits to metapragmatic awareness':

> It is very easy to obtain accurate pragmatic information in the form of metapragmatic referential speech for segmental, referential, relatively presupposing indexes. It is very difficult, if not impossible, to make a native speaker aware of nonsegmental, nonreferential, relatively creative formal features, which have no metapragmatic reality for him. (Silverstein 1976: 49)

This means that, in spite of the necessity to try and grasp language users' own conceptualizations of the communicative activities they are involved in, speakers' conscious reflexive awareness is not equally reliable at all levels.

A further methodological complication is that it is not always easy to distinguish analytical notions from everyday notions. This is why Eelen (2001), in his critique of politeness research, emphasized the need (already felt by others before him) to clearly distinguish between politeness1 (commonsense, lay views of politeness) from politeness2 (the scientific conceptualization needed in a theory of politeness1). Referring to Whorf, Lucy (1993a) formulates the same problem as follows:

> Although he [Whorf] suggests that overt categories are more salient for speakers when they reflect on language, he also seems to argue that covert categories can also exert suggestive influences on thought, influences which are potent precisely insofar as it is difficult to bring such categories to conscious attention.
>
> Whorf then takes the crucial additional step of suggesting that these influences do not just operate for the ordinary speaker but for scientists, philosophers, and others, who use language as a guide to reality.... Thus the use of our own language as a scientific metalanguage carries these problems into the research process itself. (Lucy 1993a: 25)

This is why paying attention to the role of knowledge, awareness, and reflexivity in the practice of (linguistic) research (as in Woolgar 1988; Kertész 1997) is so important. All this, of course, also goes back to what was already said about language ideologies (see Section 7.2.2); what is added here is their possible influence on research on language (already hinted at in Section 7.5 with reference to Briggs 1986 and Mertz 1993).

We do, however, have useful tools to avoid the major pitfalls. One of them is *ethnography*, the necessary counterpart to theorizing about verbal behaviour. Fortunately, this is still a prominent trend in pragmatics-related research, continuing and broadening the work that was once started under the flag of ethnography of speaking.

Recently, the availability of computational tools has greatly expanded the possibilities of *corpus research*. Michael Haugh (2018) advocates the tracing of common metapragmatic collocations (e.g. *just kidding*) in larger corpora as a basis for their analysis. In fact, studying their recurrence in large corpora may serve as a step towards their more detailed analysis in local instances of use.

Finally, also *experimentation* belongs to the methodological options. The very results of experimentation, however, often hinge strongly on meta-awareness and reflexivity. But smart forms of experimentation may be devised, taking into account that there are different degrees of awareness, sometimes very conscious, but sometimes well hidden – thus bringing in the important notion of salience (cf. Errington's 1985 'pragmatic salience', referring to the differential role of conscious processing in language use).

Ideally, all these approaches can be made to converge.

References

Aijmer, K. (2018). Positioning of self in interaction: Adolescents' use of attention-getters. In K. Beeching, C. Ghezzi and P. Molinelli, eds., *Positioning the Self and Others: Linguistic Perspectives*. Amsterdam: John Benjamins, pp. 177–95.

Auer, P. (1992). Introduction: John Gumperz' approach to contextualization. In P. Auer and A. Di Luzio, eds., *The Contextualization of Language*. Amsterdam: John Benjamins, pp. 1–37.

Auer, P. and Di Luzio, A. (eds.). (1992). *The Contextualization of Language*. Amsterdam: John Benjamins.

Austin, J. L. (1962). *How to Do Things with Words*. Cambridge, MA: Harvard University Press.

Babcock, B. A. (ed.). (1980). *Signs about Signs: The Semiotics of Self-Reference*. Special Issue. *Semiotica*, 30(1/2).

Bakhtin, M. M. (1986). *Speech Genres and Other Late Essays*. Edited by M. Holquist and C. Emerson. Translated by M. Holquist. Austin: University of Texas Press.

Bateson, G. (1972). *Steps to an Ecology of Mind*. New York: Ballantine Books.

Bauman, R. and Sherzer, J. (eds.). (1989). *Explorations in the Ethnography of Speaking*. 2nd ed. Cambridge: Cambridge University Press.

Beeching, K. (2018). Metacommenting in English and French: A variational pragmatics approach. In K. Beeching, C. Ghezzi and P. Molinelli, eds., *Positioning the Self and Others: Linguistic Perspectives*. Amsterdam: John Benjamins, pp. 127–53.

Beeching, K., Ghezzi, C. and Molinelli, P. (eds.). (2018). *Positioning the Self and Others: Linguistic Perspectives*. Amsterdam: John Benjamins.

Benveniste, E. (1956). La nature des pronoms. In M. Halle et al., eds., *For Roman Jakobson*. The Hague: Mouton, pp. 34–7.

Benveniste, E. (1966). *Problèmes de linguistique générale*. Paris: Gallimard.

Birdsong, D. (1989). *Metalinguistic Performance and Interlinguistic Competence*. Berlin: Springer.

Briggs, C. (1986). *Learning How to Ask: A Sociolinguistic Appraisal of the Role of the Interview in Social Science Research*. Cambridge: Cambridge University Press.

Bublitz, W. and Hübler, A. (eds.). (2007). *Metapragmatics in Use*. Amsterdam: John Benjamins.

Busse, U. and Hübler, A. (eds.). (2012). *Investigations into the Meta-Communicative Lexicon of English: A Contribution to Historical Pragmatics*. Amsterdam: John Benjamins.

Carnap, R. (1919). *The Logical Syntax of Language*. London: Routledge and Kegan Paul.

Caton, S. C. (1993). The importance of reflexive language in George H. Mead's theory of self and communication. In J. A. Lucy, ed., *Reflexive Language: Reported Speech and Metapragmatics*. Cambridge: Cambridge University Press, pp. 315–37.

Coulmas, F. (ed.). (1986a). *Direct and Indirect Speech*. Berlin: Mouton de Gruyter.

Coulmas, F. (1986b). Reported speech: Some general issues. In F. Coulmas, ed., *Direct and Indirect Speech*. Berlin: Mouton de Gruyter, pp. 1–28.

Daniëls, H. (2018). Diglossia: A language ideological approach. *Pragmatics, 28*(2), 185–216.

Deschrijver, C. (2018). Economic and financial terms in online interaction: Metalanguage in the Guardian comment boards during the 2010–2011 Euro Crisis bailouts. PhD dissertation, King's College London.

Ducrot, O. (1984). *Le dire et le dit*. Paris: Seuil.

Duranti, A. (2015). *The Anthropology of Intentions: Language in a World of Others*. Cambridge: Cambridge University Press.

Eelen, G. (2001). *A Critique of Politeness Theories*. Manchester, UK: St Jerome.

Errington, J. J. (1985). On the nature of the sociolinguistic sign. In E. Mertz and R. Parmentier, eds., *Semiotic Mediation*. New York: Academic Press, pp. 287–310.

Errington, J. J. (1992). On the ideology of Indonesian language development: The state of a language of state. *Pragmatics, 2*(3), 417–26.

Fillmore, C. J. (1997). *Lectures on Deixis*. Stanford: CSLI Publications.

Fillmore, C. J. (1984). Remarks on contrastive pragmatics. In J. Fisiak, ed., *Contrastive Linguistics: Prospects and Problems*. Berlin: Mouton, pp. 119–41.

Fukushima, S. (2013). Evaluation of (im)politeness: A comparative study among Japanese students, Japanese parents, and American students on evaluation of attentiveness. *Pragmatics, 23*(2), 275–99.

Geyer, N. (2018). Negotiating entitlement in Japanese: The case of requesting forms. In M. E. Hudson, Y. Matsumoto and J. Mori, eds., *Pragmatics of Japanese: Perspectives on Grammar, Interaction and Culture*. Amsterdam: John Benjamins, pp. 149–72.

Goffman, E. (1979). Footing. *Semiotica, 25*, 1–29.

Gombert, J. É. (1990). *Le développement métalinguistique*. Paris: Presses Universitaires de France. English translation, 1992, *Metalinguistic Development*. Hertfordshire, UK: Harvester Wheatsheaf.

Goodwin, C. (2018). *Co-operative Action*. Cambridge: Cambridge University Press.

Gumperz, J. J. (1982). *Discourse Strategies*. Cambridge: Cambridge University Press.

Gumperz, J. J. (1992). Contextualization revisited. In P. Auer and A. Di Luzio, eds., *The Contextualization of Language*. Amsterdam: John Benjamins, pp. 39–53.

Hanks, W. F. (1993). Metalanguage and pragmatics of deixis. In J.A. Lucy, ed., *Reflexive Language: Reported Speech and Metapragmatics*. Cambridge: Cambridge University Press, pp. 127–57.

Harras, G., Winkler, A., Erb, S. and Proost, K. (2004). *Handbuch deutscher Kommunikationsverben*. 2 vols. Berlin: Walter de Gruyter.

Haugh, M. (2018). Corpus-based metapragmatics. In A. Jucker, K. P. Schneider and W. Bublitz, eds., *Methods in Pragmatics*. Berlin: Mouton de Gruyter, pp. 615–39.

Hill, J. H. (2008). *The Language of Everyday White Racism*. Oxford: Wiley-Blackwell.

Hoenigswald, H. (1966). A proposal for the study of folk-linguistics. In W. Bright, ed., *Sociolinguistics*. The Hague: Mouton, pp. 16–26.

Holt, E. (2009). Reported speech. In J.-O. Östman and J. Verschueren, eds., *Handbook of Pragmatics*. Amsterdam: John Benjamins, pp. 1–19.

Hübler, A. (2007). On the metapragmatics of gestures. In W. Bublitz and A. Hübler, eds., *Metapragmatics in Use*. Amsterdam: John Benjamins, pp. 107–28.

Hudson, M. E., Matsumoto, Y. and Mori, J. (eds.). (2018). *Pragmatics of Japanese: Perspectives on Grammar, Interaction and Culture*. Amsterdam: John Benjamins.

Irvine, J. T. (1995). Honorifics. In J.-O. Östman and J. Verschueren, eds., *Handbook of Pragmatics*. Amsterdam: John Benjamins, pp. 1–22.

Jacobs, G. (1999). *Preformulating the News: An Analysis of the Metapragmatics of Press Releases*. Amsterdam: John Benjamins.

Jakobson, R. ([1957] 1971). Shifters, verbal categories, and the Russian verb. In *Selected Writings II*. The Hague: Mouton, pp. 130–47.

Jakobson, R. ([1956] 1985). Metalanguage as a linguistic problem. In *Selected Writings VII*. Berlin: Mouton de Gruyter, pp. 113–21.

Jaworski, A., Coupland, N. and Galasiński, D. (eds.). (2004). *Metalanguage: Social and Ideological Perspectives*. Berlin: Mouton de Gruyter.

Jespersen, O. (1922). *Language: Its Nature, Development and Origin*. New York: George Allen and Unwin.

Katriel, T. (1986). *Talking Straight: 'Dugri' Speech in Israeli Sabra Culture*. Cambridge: Cambridge University Press.

Kertész, A. (1997). The reflexivity of cognitive science and the philosophy of linguistics. In A. Kertész, ed., *Metalinguistik im Wandel: Die 'kognitive Wende' in Wissenschaftstheorie und Linguistik*. Frankfurt am Main, Germany: Peter Lang, pp. 197–233.

Kroskrity, P. V. (2010). Language ideologies. In J-O. Östman and J. Verschueren, eds., *Handbook of Pragmatics*. Amsterdam: John Benjamins, pp. 1–24.

Levinson, S. C. (1992). Activity types and language. In P. Drew and J. Heritage, eds., *Talk at Work: Interaction in Institutional Settings*. Cambridge: Cambridge University Press, pp. 66–100.

Lucy, J. (1993a). Reflexive language and the human disciplines. In J. A. Lucy, ed., *Reflexive Language: Reported Speech and Metapragmatics*. Cambridge: Cambridge University Press, pp. 9–32.

Lucy, J. (1993b). Metapragmatic presentationals: Reporting speech with quotatives in Yucatec Maya. In J. A. Lucy, ed., *Reflexive Language: Reported Speech and Metapragmatics*. Cambridge: Cambridge University Press, pp. 91–125.

Lucy, J. A. (ed.). (1993). *Reflexive Language: Reported Speech and Metapragmatics*. Cambridge: Cambridge University Press.

Lyons, J. (1977). *Semantics*. Vol. I. Cambridge: Cambridge University Press.

Maschler, Y. (2009). *Metalanguage in Interaction: Hebrew Discourse Markers*. Amsterdam: John Benjamins.

McKenzie, R. M. and Osthus, D. (2011). That which we call a rose by any other name would sound as sweet: Folk perceptions, status and language variation. *AILA Review*, 24, 100–115.

Mertz, E. (1993). Learning what to ask: Metapragmatic factors and methodological reification. In J. A. Lucy, ed., *Reflexive Language: Reported Speech and Metapragmatics*. Cambridge: Cambridge University Press, pp. 159–74.

Mertz, E. and Yovel, J. (2000). Metalinguistic awareness. In J.-O. Östman and J. Verschueren, eds., *Handbook of Pragmatics*. Amsterdam: John Benjamins, pp. 1–26.

Muntigl, P. (2007). A metapragmatic examination of therapist reformulations. In W. Bublitz and A. Hübler, eds., *Metapragmatics in Use*. Amsterdam: John Benjamins, pp. 235–62.

Nakassis, C. V. (2013). Citation and citationality. *Signs and Society*, 1(1), 51–78.

Niedzelski, N. and Preston, D. R. (2007). Folk pragmatics. In J.-O. Östman and J. Verschueren, eds., *Handbook of Pragmatics*. Amsterdam: John Benjamins, pp. 1–12.

Nyan, T. (1998). *Metalinguistic Operators with Reference to French*. Bern: Peter Lang.

Okamoto, S. (2018). Metapragmatic discourse in self-help books on Japanese women's speech: An indexical approach to social meanings In M. E. Hudson, Y. Matsumoto and J. Mori, eds., *Pragmatics of Japanese: Perspectives on Grammar, Interaction and Culture*. Amsterdam: John Benjamins, pp. 246–66.

Penz, H. (2007). Building common ground through metapragmatic comments in international project work. In W. Bublitz and A. Hübler, eds., *Metapragmatics in Use*. Amsterdam: John Benjamins, pp. 263–92.

Petykó, M. (2018). The motives attributed to trolls in metapragmatic comments on three Hungarian left-wing political blogs. *Pragmatics*, 28(3), 391–416.

Recanati, F. (2000). *Oratio Obliqua, Oratio Recta: An Essay on Metarepresentation*. Cambridge, MA: MIT Press.

Reddy, M. J. (1979). The conduit metaphor: A case of frame conflict in our language about language. In A. Ortony, ed., *Metaphor and Thought*. Cambridge: Cambridge University Press, pp. 284–324.

Roulet, E. (1996). Polyphony. In J.-O. Östman and J. Verschueren, eds., *Handbook of Pragmatics*. Amsterdam: John Benjamins, pp. 1–18.

Ruesch, J. and Bateson, G. (1951). *Communication: The Social Matrix of Psychiatry*. New York: W. W. Norton.

Salverda, R. (2017). "Montrer au linguiste *ce qu'il fait*": Revisiting Saussure from an experimental perspective on language play. *Cahiers Ferdinand de Saussure: Revue de Linguistique Générale*, 70, 115–27.

Schieffelin, B. B., Kroskrity, P. V. and Woolard, K. A. (eds.). (1992). *Language Ideologies.* Special Issue. *Pragmatics, 3*(2).

Silverstein, M. (1976). Shifters, linguistic categories, and cultural description. In K. Basso and H. Selby, eds., *Meaning in Anthropology.* Albuquerque: University of New Mexico Press, pp. 11–55.

Silverstein, M. (1979). Language structure and linguistic ideology. In P. R. Clyne, W. F. Hanks and C. L. Hofbauer, eds., *The Elements: A Parasession on Linguistic Units and Levels.* Chicago: Chicago Linguistic Society, pp. 193–247.

Silverstein, M. (1981). The limits of awareness. Sociolinguistic Working Paper 84.

Silverstein, M. (1993). Metapragmatic discourse and metapragmatic function. In J. A. Lucy, ed., *Reflexive Language: Reported Speech and Metapragmatics.* Cambridge: Cambridge University Press, pp. 33–58.

Sinkeviciute, V. (2019). Juggling identities in interviews: The metapragmatics of 'doing humour'. *Journal of Pragmatics.* 152: 216–227.

Sivenkova, M. (2013). On the metapragmatics of British, German and Russian political questions and answers. In A. Fetzer, ed., *The Pragmatics of Political Discourse: Explorations across Cultures.* Amsterdam: John Benjamins, pp. 21–46.

Suzuki, S. (2018). Linguistic nationalism and fictional deception: Metapragmatic stereotype on non-Japanese in Japan. In M. E. Hudson, Y. Matsumoto and J. Mori, eds., *Pragmatics of Japanese: Perspectives on Grammar, Interaction and Culture.* Amsterdam: John Benjamins. pp. 267–87.

Tarski, A. (1956). The semantic conception of truth. *Philosophical and Phenomenological Research, 4,* 341–75.

Tunmer, W. E., Pratt, C. and Herriman, M. L. (eds.). (1984). *Metalinguistic Awareness in Children: Theory, Research, and Implications.* Berlin: Springer.

Urban, G. (1984). Speech about speech in speech about action. *The Journal of American Folklore, 97*(385), 310–28.

Verschueren, J. (1985a). *What People Say They Do with Words: Prolegomena to an Empirical-Conceptual Approach to Linguistic Action.* Norwood, NJ: Ablex.

Verschueren, J. (1985b). *International News Reporting: Metapragmatic Metaphors and the U2.* Amsterdam: John Benjamins.

Verschueren, J. (1989). Language on language: Towards metapragmatic universals. *IPrA Papers in Pragmatics, 3*(2), 1–144.

Verschueren, J. (1995). The conceptual basis of performativity. In M. Shibatani and S. Thompson, eds., *Essays in Semantics and Pragmatics.* Amsterdam: John Benjamins, pp. 297–319.

Verschueren, J. (1999). *Understanding Pragmatics.* London: Edward Arnold/ Oxford University Press.

Verschueren, J. (2000). Notes on the role of metapragmatic awareness in language use. *Pragmatics, 10*(4), 439–56.

Verschueren, J. and Brisard, F. (2002). Adaptability. In J.-O. Östman and J. Verschueren, eds., *Handbook of Pragmatics.* Amsterdam: John Benjamins, pp. 1–24.

Watzlawick, P., Bavelas, J. B. and Jackson, D. D. (1967). *Pragmatics of Human Communication: A Study of Interactional Patterns, Pathologies, and Paradoxes.* New York: W. W. Norton.

Wilton, A. and Stegu, M. (eds.). (2011). Applied Folk Linguistics. Special Issue. *AILA Review, 24.*

Winch, P. (1958). *The Idea of a Social Science and Its Relation to Philosophy.* London: Routledge.

Wittgenstein, L. (1958). *Philosophical Investigations.* Oxford: Basil Blackwell.

Woolard, K. and Schieffelin, B. (1994). Language ideology. *Annual Review of Anthropology, 23,* 55–82.

Woolgar, S. (ed.). (1988). *Knowledge and Reflexivity: New Frontiers in the Sociology of Knowledge.* London: Sage.

8

Participation and Footing

Elizabeth Holt and Jim O'Driscoll

8.1 Introduction

Almost every attempt to characterize the concerns of pragmatics has, somewhere in it, *people* – what they mean, intend and understand and/or how they are affected when words are uttered. Logically, therefore, who these people are and what they are doing when the words are uttered – the roles they are playing – is a crucial aspect of this kind of study. Hence the fundamental notion of participation.

Notwithstanding the centrality of this notion, the first 'pillars' of pragmatics to emerge – speech act theory and implicature – had remarkably little to say about participation, confining themselves to the recognition that there has to be somebody to produce words and somebody to receive them. Hence speech act theory's S (for 'speaker', the producer of a bit of language) and H (for 'hearer', the receiver). In this respect, they followed a general tendency of language-related study in the middling decades of the twentieth century: just as Chomsky assumed an ideal native speaker-hearer when describing the language system, so this approach to the study of language-in-use assumed a kind of ideal interactive situation comprising only two people who do no more than attend to their communicative roles as either S or H and no complicating aspects of context intrude. It is, in other words, language-use in a human vacuum with participants functioning, as in the classic communication theory of the time (Shannon and Weaver 1949), simply as communicative nodes, with a rather particular style of conversation (neither notably formal nor informal) as the prototype.

And yet, now that pragmatics (or at least the kind addressed in this book) has expanded beyond the examination of isolated predications and considers real-life cases of the language used by actual interacting people, the notion of participation becomes even more crucial. This chapter explores the various ways in which the notions of S and H have been – and can be – unpacked and expanded to take account of the myriad possible constellations of roles when people interact.

8.2 Key Concepts and Issues: A Scalar Approach

This account of participation begins by considering what it is that participants might be participating *in*. We address this question as a matter of scale. At the most micro level, there is the single utterance; that is, any uttered (string of) words interpretable as a unit. Or, slightly wider, we may view participation during one person's whole turn at talk, which may contain several utterances. Allowing for more than one person, we can think of participation in a single verbal exchange often taking the form of an 'adjacency pair' (Schegloff 1968), or a series of verbal exchanges with a recognizable beginning and end, known in the ethnography of communication (e.g. Hymes 1977: 52) and in interactional sociolinguistics (e.g. Gumperz 1982: 164–5) as a 'speech event', and called an 'encounter' by Goffman (1964: 135; 1967: 144). Still wider now, these more-or-less bounded stretches of talk often take place as part of an event in its everyday sense, a socially recognized occasion such as a party, meal or seminar. These are labelled 'activity type' by Levinson (1979) and 'frame' by Goffman (1974), individual examples of which are called a 'speech situation' in the ethnography of communication (Hymes 1977: 52; Saville-Troike 1989: 28–9) and a 'speech event' by Levinson (1988). Widest of all, we could talk about participation when people are merely in each other's presence, which Goffman (e.g. 1963: 55–82; 1967: 144–5) calls 'unfocused interaction'.

We adopt for our purpose here four increasingly wide angles of view, four sizes of (what we call hereafter) 'aperture', which we label *utterance, talk, event* and *interaction*, respectively. We claim no special status for this four-fold division, nor for these terms. Our categories, moreover, are not substantive ones. Utterances and talk (our first two categories above) always take place in a context (our other two categories) and, as has been convincingly argued in numerous studies (e.g. Auer 2009), each affects and modifies the other. But looking through these different apertures separately allows us to present each of the specific issues involved in participation more easily. Our categories are, in other words, a discursive convenience.

Arguably, it would make sense to start our examination from the largest aperture. Other attempts at an account of the range of participant roles have done this (e.g. O'Driscoll 2009: 85–9) and it is, after all, how participants themselves experience their participation (starting with the context and then doing and saying things within it). However, taking our lead from the preoccupation of early pragmatics with the single utterance, we start with this smallest aperture.

8.2.1 Utterance

Even from this smallest of our apertures, as soon as we consider the relation of participants to what is being said, the notions of S and H are far too simplistic. This is most obvious once we allow for more than two people to be present, opening the possibility of more than one kind of H. But the apparently self-evident notion of S also turns out to be far from straightforward.

At this aperture, we imagine a stasis, adopting Levinson's (1988: 167–8, 193) concept of the 'utterance-event'; that is, any stretch of speech over which the roles of the participants remain the same. Goffman's ([1979] 1981a) deconstruction of the notions of S and H also starts this way, portraying a sort of freeze-frame (he calls it a 'cross-section') of a moment in time during which something is being said.

8.2.1.1 Producing Utterances

As Goffman (1981a: 144–6) demonstrates and others beforehand have observed (e.g. Hymes 1972), the relation of S to what gets said involves a number of distinct roles which may or may not inhere in the same person. The most obvious of these is the *animator*, the role of the 'talking machine', making the words manifest by vocal activity – or, we may add, by putting pen to paper or typing out on a keyboard. The role of selecting the words produced, that of *author*, is in principle a separate role, the animator giving voice to a script already written by someone else, as when actors speak their lines or a person gets themselves 'sworn in' to some position (e.g. court witness or holder of a public office). Now note that in each of these examples, the relation of the animator to the utterance diverges. The actor (as actor, not character) cannot be held accountable for the meanings to which s/he gives voice; that responsibility lies with the author and/or publisher. The person taking up a sworn-in role, on the other hand, becomes committed to them. Thus a third role can be identified, that of *principal* – the person 'whose position is established by the words that are spoken'(Goffman 1981a: 144).

The configuration of the roles of animator, author and principal in an utterance is what Goffman calls its *production format*. Any configuration is possible. Above we have exemplified how the animator can be principal but not author (the person being sworn in) or neither author nor principal (the actor). S/he can also be author but not principal, for example an interpreter at work. It is even possible for all three roles to be played by different people: Scollon (1996: 2) offers an example of his drafting of a letter (author role) which is then typed up by a secretary (animator) and signed by his head of department (principal).

Production format, however, involves more than simply assigning each of the three roles to identifiable individuals. When a representative of a political party is interviewed on TV, for example, s/he can clearly be identified as both animator and author of the words, but unless specific linguistic cues foreground one or the other, we must assume that both the interviewee and the party for which s/he is spokesperson have a share in the principal role. Similarly, our account here of Goffman's ideas is more than a simple relaying. The very fact that we have taken the trouble to relay them in particular must mean we think they are worthwhile, so that our position as well as Goffman's is established by them. (When mediated communication is considered, we must also allow for different animator roles as well; see Section 8.3.)

8.2.1.2 Receiving Utterances

It has been suggested by both Scollon (1996: 3–4; 1998: 257) and Haugh (2013; see also Kádár and Haugh 2013: 127–9) that roles precisely equivalent to those itemized by Goffman for S can be identified for H. The counterpart of animator would be the mere mechanical reception of the utterance. Scollon argues for the validity of this *receptor* role by observing that it is possible to re-animate an utterance (as in taking dictation from speech) without understanding it. The counterpart of Goffman's author is the role of deriving meaning from the utterance, for which both propose the term *interpreter*. The two authors diverge slightly, though, on what constitutes the counterpart of principal. Scollon's *judge* takes responsibility for the interpretation of the utterance and for 'undertaking a response' to it (Scollon 1996: 3), while Haugh's *accounter* is simply the role of 'hold[ing] the principal responsible' (Haugh 2013: 62) for what s/he says.

These proposed reception formats pertain to H's cognitive processing of and reaction to an utterance. What they do not address is H's interactive role. When there are two or more people able to receive and/or interpret and/or 'judge' (or 'account for') an utterance, they can have a number of different relations to what is said. Goffman's *participation framework* (1981a: 129–43) makes a distinction between, on the one hand, the person or people to whom S, as signalled by gaze, posture, physical proximity, terms of address or (more likely) a combination of these, is directing his/her utterance and, on the other hand, anybody else within hearing range; that is, between *addressed* and *unaddressed* participants.

The latter, unaddressed, participant role can be further deconstructed. The basic distinction here involves Goffman's notion of ratification. Sometimes, each person within hearing range of the utterance is regarded by all the others also in range, including S, to be a *ratified participant*. That is, they have all 'jointly ratified one another as authorized co-sustainers of a single ... focus of visual and cognitive attention' (Goffman 1964: 135) and are 'open to each other for talk or its substitutes' (Goffman 1967: 144). Even when unaddressed, they are understood to have rights to be able to hear the utterance and sometimes also rights, and even an obligation, to project their reaction to it, to demonstrate in some minimal way that they have been listening. Such people are *unaddressed ratified participants*. However, there may be other people within earshot – or perhaps just eyeshot – of the utterance who are not ratified in this way. For a discussion of this more peripheral role in interaction, see Section 8.2.3.2.

8.2.2 Talk

We now unfreeze the frame and consider how participant roles change in ongoing *talk*.

There is, of course, on all occasions except monologues, a purely operational way in which roles change, whereby a person who has been an H becomes S and the person who has been S becomes an H. But what interests us here is how participants' footings can shift within a single turn as a result of what is said, how it is said and/or who it is said (or appears to be said) to; that is, while S retains the animator role and H remains an H, but of a different kind.

8.2.2.1 Producing Talk

The shifting alignments which speakers can take towards their own speech within ongoing talk are explored at length by Goffman (1981b) and Levinson (1988: 184–9), both demonstrating that the former's original categories are skeletal, particularly in regard to the role of principal (and arguably in need of elaboration; see Section 8.4). Such exploration has been particularly useful when considering reported speech (Holt 2009). In the following example from a telephone conversation, Lesley reports a comment made to her while browsing around stalls at a charity sale.

```
(1)   Holt:C85:4:2-3
1   Lesley:   AND uh ↑we were looking rou-nd the ↓stalls 'n
2             poking about 'n he came up t' me 'n he said Oh:
3             hhello Lesley, (.) ↑still trying to buy
4             something f'nothing .tch! .hhhahhhhhhhhh!
```

Lesley shifts footing in line 2 to portray the comment made to her, retaining the role of animator but relinquishing those of author and principal. Several aspects of her enactment make this footing shift clear: these include the turn initial 'oh', the greeting, the vocative and the shift in intonation (as shown by the underlining indicating emphasis and the arrow indicating an upward shift in pitch).

Instances of direct reported speech such as this constitute a clear change of footing. However, in other instances the situation is more complex. For example, on occasion S may report the speech of others with a less dramatic footing shift than that involved in direct reporting. In the following instance, Emma reports criticisms of her made by her husband.

```
(2)   NB:IV:7:2
1   Barbra:   Is this been goin on lo:ng er wha:t.
2   Emma:     OH:::: I DON' T KNOW I JIS CA:N' T SEEM TUH SAY
3             BLUE IS BLUE HE AR:GUES e-WITH ME ER:: *u- (.)
4             u-SOMETHING EN: AH: DON' T DO THIS RI:GHT' n
5             THAT RI:GHT. .hhhhh I NEED hhHE:L:P.hh
```

This less overt shift of footing conveys the *kinds* of things Emma's husband says without going into detail. While she is animator but not principal, exactly who is the author is unclear, as she does not purport to enact his precise words. (The various permutation and gradations involved when one person reports what someone else said have been well explored in the discipline of stylistics; see Leech and Short ([1981] 2007) and Short (2007).) A less dramatic footing shift such as this can be useful for S when glossing recurrent comments by a third party without enacting them or the situations in which they occurred in granular detail (Holt, in preparation).

But Goffman ([1979] 1981a: 147) argues that to fully understand the fluidity of talk, we need to remember that we do not always refer to current desires, beliefs, perceptions, etc. Rather we represent ourselves using personal pronouns, thus becoming a 'figure' that 'serves as an agent, a protagonist in a described scene, a "character" in an anecdote'. This he refers to as *embedding*. In the following extract, Emma is recounting a conversation she had with her daughter (Barbara) to her sister (Lottie) about having fallen out with her husband. Using the personal pronoun *I*, she embeds a version of herself as a character in the telling.

```
(3)     NB:IV:10:45
1       Lottie:     ↓Ye:ah
2  →    Emma:       .t.hhhh So I just ↓ca:ll' Barbr' en I told
3  →                'er eh said we'd hadda problem Barbr' en
4  →                I don' know whether yer father's gun
5  →                be do:wn here en I'm aw:f'lly upset,h
6                   .hhhhhh An' in the (0.2) When he CA::LLED
7                   me,hh (0.2) u- er I called him the
8                   other ni↓*:ght.
9       Lottie:     Ye:ah,
```

Two animators can be said to be involved: the one who is physically animating the sounds that are heard, and an embedded animator, a figure in a statement who is present only in a world that is being told about, not in the world in which the current telling takes place (Goffman 1981a: 149).

Using other pronouns (e.g. *he, she*) it is as easy to embed other speakers into our utterances (and arguably the other examples of reported speech discussed above can be handled this way). This, as Goffman points out, provides a way of understanding the myriad ways in which we can convey the words of others. Embedding is a form of footing shift, and together these concepts can shed light on the complexities of interaction especially when we evoke others or our former selves in talk.

8.2.2.2 Receiving Talk

Just as S can shift footing, so can Hs, most obviously by a change in facial expression, direction of gaze and/or posture. But more interesting are cases in which Hs find the nature of their participation (potentially) shifted for them. Clark and Carlson (1982) analyse many examples where an apparently unaddressed H clearly has an integral role in the construction of ongoing talk, some of which effectively select this H to make the next contribution. Particularly intriguing are cases when S says something which projects the notion that H is not present at all. An example of such a case used by Sacks et al. (1974: 717) is reproduced thus by Levinson (1988: 166):

```
(4)   SN-4:3
1 Sharon:  You didn' come tuh talk tuh Karen?
2 Mark:    No, Karen- Karen' I' re having a fight,
3          (0.4)
4          after she went out with Keith an' not with (me)
5 Ruthie:  Hah hah hah hah
6 Karen:   Wul, Mark, you never asked me out
```

Sharon's enquiry is expressed with 'negative orientation' (Quirk and Greenbaum 1973: 193–4), allowing the interpretation that she intends to convey surprise that Mark's purpose in joining them may not have been to talk to Karen. And as Karen is present, it may be further understood to have the illocutionary force of an invitation for him to do so.

But Mark does not (choose to) draw this latter inference. Instead, he addresses first the yes/no element of the question ('no') and then the surprise element by giving a reason for his negative answer. As Levinson (1988: 167) observes, the imputation of blame to Karen can be interpreted as a challenge for Karen to respond in some way. Both he and Sacks et al. (1978: 717) interpret his utterance as picking out Karen to speak next. Observing, then, that although Karen is present (and in our terms is clearly ratified), Mark's utterance places her as neither addressee (Sharon) nor as what he calls 'audience' (i.e. unaddressed ratified participant, a role filled by Ruthie here), Levinson presents this case as an example of the need for more terms to denote particular participant roles. In this case, he suggests (Levinson 1988: 210) 'indirect target'.

But there is another, dynamic, way of analysing Mark's utterance and Karen's response to it, which arguably obviates the need for this additional category. By asserting that he does not intend to talk to Karen and referring to her twice in the third person, he acts *as if* Karen is not a ratified participant in the interaction. He is symbolically 'de-ratifying' her. And by taking up the challenge, Karen's response rebuffs this attempted repositioning of her. The fact that she takes the next turn reasserts her role as part of the ratified circle with speaking rights and her manner of doing so, which includes direct address to Mark ('you'), does so forcibly.

Nevertheless, it cannot be denied that Mark's utterance is directed to Karen, at least in part. Mark is only *pretending* to de-ratify her. It is, in fact, an example of embedding, this time not with production formats as above but with participation frameworks (see Goffman 1981a: 155.) Whether it really does point to the need for additional categories of participant is a moot point.

Examples of de-ratification without any hint of such play acting can be found. O'Driscoll (2018) analyses one such case during a pre-trial court hearing, in which the accused female is effectively shut out of the talk at various times in various ways. Despite her canonically ratified status, she is sometimes reduced to little more than a bystander (see Section 8.2.3.2) in the interaction, with none of the rights conventionally accorded a ratified participant but retaining most of the obligations of such a status. Once again, the question is therefore raised as to whether further categories of participant are needed.

8.2.2.3 Producing and Receiving Together

So far we have discussed examples whereby the footings of S or H are shifted but we have not yet questioned the assumption that S and H themselves are distinct, 'top-level' nodes which are always valid. We do so now. That Goffman presents a typology of participants rather than an 'analysis of how utterances are built through the participation of structurally different kinds of actors within ongoing courses of action' (Goodwin 2007: 17) is a starting point for Goodwin's (2007) analyses of (1) a storytelling focusing on the teller and the silent participants, and (2) interaction with a man whose verbal contributions are severely limited due to aphasia. Both lead him to highlight limitations in Goffman's approach.

In the first extract below, Ann is telling a story about her husband making a faux pas when they visited the new house of friends by asking about the wallpaper.

```
(5)
13  Ann:    Do(h)n said (0.3) dih-did they
14          ma:ke you take this[wa(h)llpa(h)p(h)er?
15  Beth:                      [hh!
16  Ann:    er(h)di[dju pi(h)ck[i(h)t ou(h)t.
17  Beth:          [Ahh huh huh [huh huh
```
                                        (Goodwin, 2007: 22)

In the terms outlined above Ann's reporting of her husband's question positions her as the animator but Don as author and principal. However, Goodwin shows how Don's presence and embodied actions during the telling are consequential to the way it unfolds. For example, as Ann begins to laugh while saying 'wallpaper', Don starts to smile, which matches Ann's escalation of laughter as she continues. Thus, the participation framework 'extends far beyond structure in her talk to encompass the embodied actions of others who are present' (Goodwin 2007: 21). It is the product of 'mutual reflexivity' which leads Goodwin to criticize Goffman's adherence to the original binary distinction between S and H, as that makes it 'impossible to investigate how utterances are built through processes of interaction that include the participants' ongoing analysis of each other. In essence the world being analysed is lodged within a single speaker's speech' (Goodwin 2007: 33).

The inadequacy of the binary distinction is highlighted even more starkly by his analysis of interaction where the speaker is located across more than one participant over a sequence of utterances. Because Chil can only produce three words – 'yes', 'no' and 'and' – he relies on others present to participate in his contributions.

(6) (The participants have been discussing snow in the area where Chil lives)
```
1  Candy:  You haven' t had that much this year have you.
           ((18 lines omitted))
2  Candy:  But la[st year. Whoo!
3  Chuck:      [mm
4  Candy:  [in the l[ast year-
5  Chil:   [yeah    [No No. No:.
6  Candy:  er the year before la[st
7  Chil:                        [Yes.
```
(Goodwin 2007: 40)

As a result of Chil's verbal participation and his embodied actions during line 5 (he makes a 'backwards' gesture with his hand) Candy produces a turn at line 6 that we might say is animated by Candy, but authored by Chil who is also the principal. However, Goodwin poses the question of whether we can refer to Chil as the author when (due to his aphasia) he lacks the capacity to produce such a turn. Arguably, we can – the author is s/he who composes the words used but does not necessarily animate them. But presumably Candy could have animated different words and as long as they conveyed the same meaning (e.g. 'the one before that / last year but one'), Chil would have still affirmed them as he does in line 7. On this latter reading, it is Candy who is the author. And yet Chil is not merely responsible for the meaning conveyed in line 6 (the defining feature of the principal role); he also plays an active role in its expression through his hand gesture: he is *prompting* Candy. The problem of assignment here hinges on what 'composing' the words entails. Perhaps a way out of it is to assign joint authorship in this case. And via this speculation, we arrive at Goodwin's central argument, which is that participation is more usefully analysed,

> not as static categories constructed by the analyst (addressee, speaker, hearer, etc.) but instead as forms of temporally unfolding interactively organised action through which participants demonstrate with precision ... their understandings of the events in progress by building action that helps to produce these very same events. (Goodwin 2007: 38)

In conversation, it is not just S who composes the meanings conveyed. In examples (5) and (6), a person conventionally designated as H has a hand in its production.

What all the cases considered in this subsection have in common is an illustration of the fluidity of participation statuses. Many of them also involve the use of indexical forms. As Sidnell (2009: 151) points out, 'participant categories are themselves instantiated through the use of deictic, or at least indexical forms: pronouns, directed gaze, bodily orientation and so on.... In practice, these forms constitute emergent and unfolding participant frameworks subject to moment-by-moment permutations and transposition'. Thus, as Irvine (1996: 136) argues, what becomes significant (as it is to participants) is 'the process by which participation structures are constructed, imagined and socially distributed'.

8.2.3 Events

Perhaps the most common lay understanding of 'participation' pertains to this aperture: a conversation, an interview, a committee meeting, a football match, a party, etc.; in other words, in some socially recognizable spate of activity which has a detectable beginning and end.

Such events comprise extended and/or attenuated stretches of talk in most of which the roles of participants frequently alternate. In them, it is possible to identify certain *patterns* of participation framework and production format which operate, or may be expected to operate, over the whole course of specific (types of) events. The patterns range from the relatively clear and rigid, as in many formal occasions, to the absence of any discernible pattern at all, as in many multi-party casual conversations (see O'Driscoll 2018: 46–8, 58). The description of who speaks or can speak when and to whom, and who hears or can hear, during such events gives us a clue to the style of participation in such events (and it might even be possible to define different kinds of event according to their typical participation framework patterns).

8.2.3.1 Social Roles

However, to identify such patterns is to describe participation in events in a mainly operational sense only. To more fully describe – and explain – the roles played by the participants at such events, we have to recognize that people at these events are acting in some kind of social capacity *from their outset*. It is for this reason that scholars have often distinguished between two levels of participant role, one referring to the relation between a participant and an utterance or ongoing talk (as discussed above) and the other referring to the relation between a participant and the event in which they are participating. The labels often used for this distinction are 'discourse roles' and 'activity (or 'social') roles', respectively (e.g. Thomas 1995; Sarangi and Slembrouck 1996; Halvorsen and Sarangi 2015). Importantly, it can be shown (e.g. Sarangi and Slembrouck 1996: 66–71) that the former are interpreted in the light of the latter and that this interpretation can extend to moral evaluation (e.g. Davies 2018; O'Driscoll 2018). That is, the footings adopted by one participant are evaluated by other participants according to their understanding of what is – and what should be – going on.

In some cases, the footing adopted is understood to be within the remit of the participant's social role. Thus, for example, Clayman (2007) shows how news interviewers recurrently shift footing to speak on behalf of the public in news interviews.

```
(7)    CBS 60 Minutes 8 March 1998
1      IE:  you don:' t talk to people the way .hh PJ: talked
2           to me.
3   →  IR:  People might be saying Hey kid. .hh You ear:n (0.2)
4   →       millions and millions of dollars, .hh Live with it.
5           (0.2)
6      IR:  Forget the respect, take your money,
7      IE:  When you' re dealing with respect: uh: money is not
8           a issue.
```
                                                          (Clayman 2007: 221)

This device has a 'strategic importance' (Clayman 2007: 243), enabling the interviewer to ask potentially aggressive questions on sensitive matters while at the same time diffusing responsibility for what the s/he is saying, thus adopting a neutral stance. There is a close relationship here between the footing adopted by the speaker and the social role s/he enacts. This footing is accepted as one of the interviewer's rights in this kind of event. Indeed, it may be considered one of his/her obligations. Likewise, a doctor/patient consultation entitles (and to some extent obliges) the doctor to ask about, and the patient to disclose, personal information which would be regarded as inappropriate in a conversation between working colleagues, even quite close friends.

In other cases, though, a participant might be considered to have strayed beyond the rights allowed by their social role. In the pre-trial hearing analysed by O'Driscoll (2018), a single word of leave-taking from the accused is considered so inappropriate by the judge that it triggers a trajectory leading to a highly undesirable outcome for both parties. Examples such as this help us to understand why Levinson's (1979) attempt to identify the defining features of different types of event ('activity types') places greatest emphasis on 'allowable contributions'.

8.2.3.2 Peripheral Participation

In 2.1.1 above, we briefly alluded to encounters which are accessible in some way to people who are not considered to be active participants in them. We now address the nature of this, more peripheral kind of participation. Consider cases of people who, while not part of it themselves, are visibly present to the ratified participants of an ongoing encounter (e.g. in the corridor at work, on the bus, on the street). Here, the talk is open to reception by such people, who are classed by Goffman (1981a) as *unratified participants*, also called *bystanders*. In some cases, such witnessing can be no more that the registering *that* something is being said. But in others, the bystander will be near enough to catch something or all of *what* is said, becoming thus an *overhearer*, or will be deliberately listening in, becoming thus an *eavesdropper*.

In explorations of the nature of peripheral participation, several typologies, of varying degrees of granularity and with conflicting terminology, have been offered (e.g. Bell 1984; Clark and Carlson 1982; Levinson 1988: 172–3; Clark and Schaefer 1992; Dynel 2010). In the identification of particular peripheral roles, a major issue which emerges is whether the classification comes from the point of view of ratified participants, especially the speaker, or from the point of view of the peripheral participants themselves. Here, we make some observations from the latter viewpoint.

Logically, a bystander has choices about how to conduct him/herself relative to the encounter (though culture-specific norms may limit them). One is to act as if the encounter was not taking place at all, or at least that s/he has no interest in it. Goffman (1963: 84) alludes on such occasions to the 'civil inattention' which appears to be the polite norm in many parts of the world. However, a moment's thought allows us to realize there are degrees of civility and degrees of inattention. At one extreme, the person may be able to 'shut out' the encounter (e.g. by reading an engrossing book), the inattention being entirely sincere; at the other extreme, s/he may be following every word of the conversation avidly while pretending not to, all civility and no inattention (in Goffman's terms, affecting the role of a mere bystander while actually eavesdropping).

Another choice for the bystander is to adopt an open stance, making no attempt to hide awareness of the encounter, perhaps even showing signs of reaction to particular utterances, thereby encouraging ratified participants to invite him/her into the ratified circle. Lastly, s/he could invite him/herself in by making a contribution to the conversation. Ratified participants sometimes give off clues as to whether they are open to such a widening of the ratified circle. However, the clearest of these is a negative one, hushed tones indicating that they have no wish to intrude on the attention of others or to be intruded upon. A 'normal' conversational volume in a confined indoor space presents problems of interpretation in this regard. Here is an example from personal observation:

(8) Cathy is sitting in a small hospital waiting room. Not many other people are there (several chairs are empty). All are silent except for two women sitting together, side on to Cathy with one empty chair between. They are talking, at what appears to be their own default conversational volume, about a minor-celebrity who had written books about how to be a good mother, in mostly derogatory terms (e.g. 'don't know how she has the nerve'). Then Cathy attempts to

'join in'. She remarks that this author's son has just killed himself, an offering which is both propositionally relevant and affiliates to the attitudinal direction of their talk. However, they totally ignore the remark and Cathy herself. Their only recognition is a later remark in their ongoing talk about the rudeness of 'some people'.

So Cathy started off as a bystander (= unratified participant) of a talking encounter of which she was a total overhearer. By making her remark, she was inviting herself into the ratified circle. However, her attempt was refused and she remained unratified. At the same time, she was clearly supposed to hear the later 'some people' remark!

As this example illustrates, the precise role of a peripheral participant in an event is just as subject to change and contestation as those of ratified participants as discussed above. Moreover, there appear to be degrees of (un) ratification. In some kinds of event, accessibility for peripheral participants is not accidental but rather expected, and in some even required. Sporting events are an example of the former, spectators of which have no right to 'join in' the action and the main actors in the arena of play feel no responsibility to make their doings visible to them. In theory, the event (e.g. the match, the race) could still take place without them. However, their ability to witness the details of the action is no accident; they *expect* to be able to do so and the organization under whose auspices the event is taking place typically makes various provisions (e.g. seating, announcements) to meet this expectation. From this point of view, they seem to be more than mere bystanders.

This degree of ratification is greater in members of the audience at what Goffman (1981a: 137–40) calls 'podium events', live performances being one type of these. Here, the active participants *do* feel the need to make their doings accessible to the audience, the main action would usually *not* take place if they were entirely absent and where in some types (e.g. stand-up comedy acts) they are directly addressed. Even when audience participation is strictly limited to attending to the action (e.g. classical music concerts), it makes little sense to classify them as mere overhearers.

Once again, then, Goffman's suggested categories seem no more than a starting point. At podium events, moreover, a consideration of various roles is not exhausted by the audience. There are often additional kinds of peripheral participant. Kádár and Haugh (2013: 88–90), for instance, suggest the label *listener-in* to denote the technical crew backstage at a rock concert. These are people who do not have the rights of the audience to contribute vocally to the encounter, and yet they have obligations relative to it which the audience does not have. (The description of participant roles in mediated events becomes even trickier; see Section 8.3.1.)

8.2.4   Interaction – with a Fuzzy Focus

Finally, from the widest perspective, we consider what Goffman calls 'unfocused interaction' as a locus of participation, which denotes mere co-presence of two or more people who can see each other and know that they are being seen. Arguably, such a tenuous connection between people does not qualify as participation at all. However, as Goffman (1963) demonstrates, people in such situations typically behave with some allowance for others' visible presence and their own visibility. Moreover, there is social significance in how people conduct themselves in unfocused interaction, as demonstrated by Rampton and Eley's (2018) study of data from CCTV cameras.

Of particular interest here are cases which, while they do not seem focused enough to fit Levinson's (1979) concept of activity type nor Goffman's notion of an encounter, seem to be something a little more focused than mere co-presence. They are situations, in other words, which lie halfway between focused and unfocused interaction. They are worth considering because specific expectations of behaviour are attached to them.

Behaviour at supermarket checkouts in Britain can serve as an example. The only focused interaction normatively ratified is between the checkout worker and the customer(s) whose purchases are being scanned through. It is focused in that there is a single, sustainable focus of attention with a recognizable beginning and ending. But consider the behaviour of the next customer(s) in line. As soon as there is space available, they are expected to place their intended purchases on the conveyor belt. They also, then, have a focus of attention very similar to, and consequent on, the behaviour of those in front of them, and in that sense they are interacting with each other. And yet there is rarely any overt extending of the status of co-participant among them. And again, little flurries of clearly focused interaction can occur.

(9) Jim is in the checkout queue. He has already put his intended purchases on the conveyor belt. The worker is scanning the purchases of the couple in front of him. Two of these items are bottles with security contraptions around their necks. The worker now tries to remove the contraptions with the aid of a device for this purpose. The task proves tricky. She repeatedly bangs the necks of the bottles into the device, harder and harder. It takes several such blows for each bottle. Jim takes increasing interest. As the struggle progresses, he not only fixes his gaze on it but makes this obvious to the worker – not just looking, but looking as though he is looking. When the worker finally frees the second bottle, she looks at Jim and says "I should be chopping down trees, shouldn't I?" Jim laughs.

In this case, then, rather than attempting to join the focused interaction already taking, Jim attempts to initiate a separate encounter with the shop worker. His attempt is successful in that the shop worker then makes a remark relevant to his 'looking'.

Two observations can be made about (9) and example (8) in Section 8.2.3.2, both indicating that it does indeed make sense to speak of participation in such circumstances. First, they show that bystanders are not merely observers; they have behavioural choices relative to the focused interaction. The second is that even this kind of participant status is subject to moral evaluation. There are normatively proper and improper ways, and locally welcome and unwelcome ways, in which to conduct oneself. Cathy's choice of behaviour – to attempt to join the encounter – was unwelcome to the ratified participants. Jim's attempt to create an encounter was welcomed. But note that this success was dependent on the fact that he was already playing a sanctioned peripheral role as 'next in the queue'. If someone else not in this position had approached the shop worker so closely and indulged in the same kind of intrusive staring, one can imagine she would have called for security instead!

8.3 Technology-Mediated Communication

Ever since the invention of writing, it has been possible for linguistic communication to take place across vast distances and with a significant time lapse between production and reception. The question therefore arises as to whether the account of participation which we have given here, which relies heavily on Goffmanian categories, can accommodate this dislocated, asynchronous kind of communication. To take production format first, a simple historical example shows that to some extent it can, once we allow for particular production roles to be shared (see Section 8.2.1.1). Consider Jucker's (2010: 195) observation that 'In the fifteenth and early sixteenth centuries [in England], letters were still carried by personal messengers and often written by amanuenses and possibly even read out to the addressee'. Here, then, we can see three different parties sharing animation, and taking distinct roles within it.

The increasing reach of broadcast mass media and the rise of new forms of technology-mediated communication in the last few decades have provoked a further need to reconsider Goffman's account. Encounters associated with specific physical situations often have set physical boundaries, are not prone to sudden, wholesale transformations and have associated with them, as we have suggested in Section 8.2.3, a specific participation framework. However, as Meyrowitz (1990) points out, our interactions now are increasingly 'interrupted by, or interwoven with, encounters with or through media' (87) and, thus 'electronic media override the boundaries and definitions of situations supported by physical settings' (90).

This challenge, then, concerns participation framework. For example, what exactly is the footing of members of the audience of a TV broadcast? As Dynel (2011) observes, it is remarkable how many scholars have designated them overhearers. Presumably, they have done so to reflect the fact that these participants have no right – in fact no ability – to have an immediate effect on the encounters they can see and hear. Indeed, given that participants at the other end of the screen have no way of knowing which particular individuals are watching or how intently they are following proceedings, they might even be described as eavesdroppers. And yet Dynel (2011) is surely right to insist they are actually ratified. The broadcast is designed for them and exists because of them; pains are taken, always by the technical staff transmitting the broadcast and often by the main actors themselves, to make sure that they *can* follow.

There is, however, considerable variation in the precise footings of audience members according to the type of event being broadcast. As one example, contrast the 'rights' of the TV viewing audience and the obligations of the speaking participants in two kinds of quite similar event: (a) a political interview on a TV current affairs or news programme and (b) a live TV broadcast of debate in a legislative assembly. In (a), this audience considers itself as entitled to hear every word spoken clearly and the speakers in the interview feel some obligation to make their talk clear to the audience. In (b), on the other hand, though viewers may also feel they have the right for proceedings to be at least audible to them, they do not necessarily feel they have a right for the talk to be intelligible to them. Moreover, this obligation for the action to be audible rests with the broadcaster, not with the speaking participants. The main concern of the latter is to make their words intelligible to the other ratified participants in the same physical space as them. Event (a) is 'for' the audience; if for whatever reason, the audience were not able to access it, it would not take place at all. Event (b), on the other hand, would take place anyway.

This example makes just one distinction. It by no means exhausts the permutations of participation framework which technology now makes possible. As Davies (2018: 125) observes, the video used for the pre-trial court hearing case examined by O'Driscoll (2018) and others (see Section 8.2.3.1) was not designed for public consumption and yet was publicly available, so that those who came across the video and watched it were indeed overhearers. However, Davies (2018: 125) points out that 'once the video has been embedded into online newspaper reportage', online readers become ratified in the 'metadiscussion' which follows online. Her study of online reactions to this case exemplifies what has been called (e.g. Kádár and Haugh 2013) 'meta-participation' in an event. The process is akin to what O'Driscoll (2013) calls 'situational transformation'.

The technology of the twenty-first century has opened up a vast and, frankly, bewildering array of possible types of participation and participation statuses. The 'affordances' (Hutchby 2014) of new media have added to our recognition of the complexities of both production and reception format and the possibilities of multiple kinds of participation in an encounter (e.g. where text messages to a TV show are discussed on air). Numerous scholars have taken up the challenges posed by these developments and have recurrently added or altered categories to better describe the complex arrangements pertaining on particular sites (e.g. Boyd 2014; Dynel 2014; Marcoccia 2004; Dynel and Chovanec 2015; Garcés-Conejos Blitvich et al. 2019).

There is no space to discuss all these efforts here. (For an excellent review and discussion, see Chovanec and Dynel 2015.) But one observation made by them is worthy of comment because it suggests a way out of the ever more-crowded forest of newly propagated participant categories, offering the hope that we might be able to catch sight of the wood for the trees again. This is that researchers are generally in agreement that communication in public media can be seen to take place at different *levels*. And in fact, the same perspective has been taken by some of those analysing participation in social media. Boyd (2014), for example, examining the participant roles of users on YouTube when watching and commenting on Barack Obama's Inaugural Address in 2009, proposes a reworking of the traditional participation framework categories on two different levels. A primary level encompasses Obama, while the comments on the speech belong to a secondary level. Both levels involve various reception roles dependent on, for example, whether a viewer of YouTube is a registered or an unregistered user. These latter two categories are argued to be more useful than the traditional distinction between ratified and unratified participants. Identifying levels of participation is also found useful by Dynel (2014) in her analysis of YouTube interaction. She proposes three levels of participatory framework: (1) the level encompassing the speaker and hearer in the posted video; (2) the level of the sender and receiver of the video; (3) YouTube speakers and hearers who post and read comments.

The notion of levels, similar to Goffman's notion of embedding in conceptualizing one framework as involved in another, offers the possibility of curtailing the quantity of participant categories that need to be identified. Instead, we can see one and the same category as appearing recursively. This *kind* of perspective – that is, of detecting two or more communicative frames in relation to each other – is in any case necessary to comprehend what people are doing in technology-mediated communication. This is because frames can often be crossed at will, with one instance of meta-participation spawning another, potentially ad infinitum. In this world, it makes little sense to see participation as pertaining to events. Rather, what people are participating in is simply (ongoing) interaction.

8.4 Conclusion: Future Directions

What are the categories of participant status that are most useful for the analysis of interaction? One way of addressing this question is that of Levinson (1988), who suggests that what is needed is a number of primitive or etic categories – more than Goffman provides – plus a 'bundle' of derivative categories, which would denote particular combinations of the former. However, it has been argued that, the particularities of encounters being *so* particular, such a procedure would lead to endless proliferation of labels (Irvine 1996; Halvorsen and Sarangi 2015; O'Driscoll 2018). Our own inclination, as implied above, is that it is more fruitful to conceive of the categories of participant status as points rather than discrete areas, not as pigeon-holes to which each participant must be assigned but rather as benchmarks near to or far from which each can be positioned at any one moment. Such a perspective, we suggest, better accommodates the changes in participants' statuses which their utterances and actions (attempt to) achieve. These changes are rarely abrupt, total relocations, as when a piece is moved on a chess board; instead, they are subtle shifts of position, often ambivalent in that they may be perceived differently by different participants (and analysts!), and often contested, as in a sort of multi-directional tug-of-war. From this perspective, it may well be that a relatively small number of roles need to be universally recognized and labelled by the analyst, lest a profusion of them causes an a priori typology to dominate the analysis so that we lose sight of the participants themselves.

This is not to say that more precise roles for individual participants cannot be identified when useful. And indeed, the fact that particular roles in Goffman's production format sometimes seem to be shared suggests that sometimes it might be. In the case of our reflexive comment on our account of Goffman's production format in Section 8.2.1, we might suggest the labels of *source* (Goffman) and *interpreter* (ourselves). And in the case of the sixteenth-century written missive mentioned at the start of Section 8.3.1, which is dictated, then conveyed and then read-aloud, we might suggest that the different animating roles might be labelled *scribe, carrier* and *reciter*, respectively – but only if it is germane to the analysis at hand. The fact that by now (as the alert reader may notice) we have at two points in the course of this chapter cited or suggested the same label for two different roles illustrates the dangers of attempting to reify roles cross-situationally. As Irvine (1996) suggests, just a handful of basic, universal roles can be sub-categorized situation-specifically, as and when the analytical occasion demands. How can roles in this conception be identified? With respect to the (cross-cultural) empirical validity of categories of participant status from a first-order perspective – that is, from the point of view of participants themselves – it may well be fruitful to investigate linguistic evidence. Both Levinson (1988) and Hanks (1990, 1996) consider grammatical categories in different languages as providing evidence for orientation to participant roles. It might also be worthwhile, we suggest, to test the categories which have been suggested by theorists against the reporting verbs used in everyday language to denote various kinds of production and reception, many of which evoke particular production formats and/or participation frameworks. For example, there is an intriguing possibility that Goffman's three production roles and their various possible combinations may be mirrored in the discourse representation verbs most frequently used in the English language. When a person 'says' something, all three roles are usually assumed to be taken by that one person; but when s/he 'tells' a story s/he has heard, s/he is animator and author but the principal role must be assigned elsewhere; and when s/he 'speaks', it is the animator role that is foregrounded, the other two roles possibly being assigned to other(s). These suggested correspondences are speculation at this point; they would need to be tested by corpus research. But clearly, English verbs such as 'announce', 'recite', and 'confide' entail – or at least imply – very divergent participation frameworks and production formats. Similar research in other languages could point to certain cultural specificities and perhaps help in the identification of relatively robust universal categories.

Whether intended as part of a pan-situational framework or as a local convenience in the analysis of one encounter, the crucial factors in identifying participant roles must surely lie with their understood (albeit negotiable and subject to manipulation and contest) rights and obligations and the relative strengths of these. We have shown that in these respects there are many more possibilities than Goffman's prototypical ratified participant, who has both rights and obligations, and his prototypical unratified participant, with none of the former and very few of the latter.

A final caveat: by framing this account of participation in terms of scalar situational locus, we have ignored one major aspect of it – the interpersonal. The nature of the relationships between the participants, both vertically (relative power, status or rank) and horizontally (relative social distance), plus the history of their previous encounters can sometimes constitute the main determiner of the content and tenor of their interaction, the assumed rights and obligations of particular individuals, and the situational and social roles they play (impressionistically identifiable as, for example, the topic selector, the talker, the joker, the confidant and so on). The influence of these interpersonal factors is of course likely to be greater in relatively informal situations. Nevertheless, it is remarkable how sometimes exactly the same group of people can play radically different roles on different occasions. Think, for example, of a group of working colleagues at a formal committee meeting and the same set of individuals in the pub afterwards. This apparently decisive influence of the situation is our justification for treating participation from this point of view.

References

Auer, P. (2009). Context and contextualization. In J. Verschueren and J-O. Östman, eds., *Key Notions for Pragmatics*. Amsterdam: John Benjamins, pp. 86–101.

Bell, A. (1984). Language style as audience design. *Language and Society*, 13(2), 145–204.

Boyd, M. S. (2014). (New) participatory framework on YouTube? Commenter interaction in US political speeches. *Journal of Pragmatics*, 72, 46–58.

Chovanec, J. and Dynel, M. (2015). Researching interactional forms and participant structures in public and social media. In M. Dynel and

J. Chovanec, eds., *Participation in Public and Social Media Interactions.* Amsterdam: John Benjamins, pp. 1–26.

Clark, H. H. and Carlson, T. (1982). Hearers and speech acts. *Language, 58,* 332–72.

Clark, H. H. and Schaefer, E. F. (1992). Dealing with overhearers. In H. H. Clark, ed., *Arenas of Language Use.* Chicago: University of Chicago Press, pp. 248–73.

Clayman, S. (2007). Speaking on behalf of the public in broadcast news interviews. In E. Holt and R. Clift, eds., *Reporting Talk: Reported Speech in Interaction.* Cambridge: Cambridge University Press, pp. 221–43.

Davies, B. (2018). Evaluating evaluations: What different types of metapragmatic behaviour can tell us about participants' understandings of the moral order. *Journal of Politeness Research, 14*(1), 121–51.

Dynel, M. (2010). Not hearing things – Hearer/listener categories in polylogues, http://mediazioni.sitlec.unibo.it.

Dynel, M. (2011). 'You talking to me?' The viewer as a ratified listener to film discourse. *Journal of Pragmatics, 43*(6), 1628–44.

Dynel, M. (2014). Participation framework underlying YouTube interaction. *Journal of Pragmatics, 73,* 37–52.

Dynel, M. and Chovanec, J. (eds.). (2015). *Participation in Public and Social Media Interactions.* Amsterdam: John Benjamins.

Garcés-Conejos Blitvich, P., Fernández-Amaya, L. and de la O Hernández-López, M. (eds.). (2019). *Technology Mediated Service Encounters.* Amsterdam: John Benjamins.

Goffman, E. (1963). *Behaviour in Public Places: Notes on the Social Organization of Gatherings.* New York: The Free Press.

Goffman, E. (1964). The neglected situation. *American Anthropologist, 66*(6, part II), 133–6.

Goffman, E. (1967). *Interaction Ritual: Essays on Face-to-Face Behaviour.* Harmondsworth: Penguin.

Goffman, E. (1974). *Frame Analysis: An Essay on the Organization of Experience.* Harmondsworth, UK: Peregrine Books.

Goffman, E. ([1979] 1981a). Footing. In *Forms of Talk.* Philadelphia: University of Pennsylvania Press, pp. 124–59. (Originally published in *Semiotica, 25,* 1–29.)

Goffman, E. (1981b). Radio talk. In *Forms of Talk.* Philadelphia: University of Pennsylvania Press, pp. 197–327.

Goodwin, C. (2007). Interactive footing. In E. Holt and R. Clift, eds., *Reporting Talk: Reported Speech in Interaction.* Cambridge: Cambridge University Press, pp. 16–46.

Gumperz, J. J. (1982). *Discourse Strategies.* Cambridge: Cambridge University Press.

Halvorsen, K. and Sarangi, S. (2015). Team decision-making in workplace meetings: The interplay of activity roles and discourse roles. *Journal of Pragmatics, 76,* 1–14.

Hanks, W. F. (1990). *Referential Practice: Language and Lived Space among the Maya*. Chicago: Chicago University Press.

Hanks, W. F. (1996). Exorcism and the description of participant roles. In M. Silverstein and G. Urban, eds., *Natural Histories of Discourse*. Chicago: Chicago University Press, pp. 160–200.

Haugh, M. (2013). Im/politeness, social practice and the participation order. *Journal of Pragmatics*, 58, 52–72.

Holt, E. (2009). Reported speech. In S. D'hondt, J.-O. Östman and J. Verschueren, eds., *The Pragmatics of Interaction*. Amsterdam: John Benjamins, pp. 190–205.

Holt, E. (in preparation). Reporting a rant: Loosely portrayed speech in interaction.

Hutchby, I. (2014). Communicative affordances and participation frameworks in mediated interaction. *Journal of Pragmatics*, 72, 86–9.

Hymes, D. (1972). Models of the interaction of language and social life. In J. Gumperz and D. Hymes, eds., *Directions in Sociolinguistics: The Ethnography of Communication*. New York: Holt, Rhinehart and Winston, pp. 35–71.

Hymes, D. (1977). *Foundations in Sociolinguistics*. London: Tavistock.

Irvine, J. T. (1996). Shadow conversations: The indeterminacy of participant roles. In M. Silverstein and G. Urban, eds., *Natural Histories of Discourse*. Chicago: University of Chicago Press, pp. 131–59.

Jucker, A. (2010). 'In curtesie was set ful muchel hir lest': Politeness in Middle English. In J. Culpeper and D. Z. Kádár, eds., *Historical (Im)politeness*. Bern: Peter Lang, pp. 175–200.

Kádár, D. and Haugh, M. (2013). *Understanding Politeness*. Cambridge: Cambridge University Press.

Leech, G. and Short, M. ([1981] 2007). *Style in Fiction: A Linguistic Introduction to English Fictional Prose*. 2nd ed. London: Pearson Education.

Levinson, S. C. ([1979] 1992). Activity types and language. In P. Drew and J. Heritage, eds., *Talk at Work*. Cambridge: Cambridge University Press, pp. 66–100. (Originally in *Linguistics*, 17, 365–99.)

Levinson, S. C. (1988). Putting linguistics on a proper footing: Explorations in Goffman' concepts of participation. In P. Drew and A. Wootton, eds., *Erving Goffman: Exploring the Interaction Order*. Cambridge: Polity Press, pp. 161–227.

Marcoccia, M. (2004). On-line polylogues: Conversation structure and participation framework in internet newsgroups. *Journal of Pragmatics*, 36(1), 115–45.

Meyrowitz, J. (1990). Redefining the situation: Extending dramaturgy into a theory of social change and media effects. In S. H. Riggens, ed., *Beyond Goffman: Studies on Communication, Institution and Social Interaction*. Berlin: Mouton de Gruyter, pp. 65–98.

O'Driscoll, J. (2009). Erving Goffman. In S. D'hondt, J.-O. Östman and J. Verschueren, eds., *The Pragmatics of Interaction*. Amsterdam: John Benjamins, pp. 79–95.

O'Driscoll, J. (2013). Situational transformations: The offensive-izing of an email message and the public-ization of offensiveness. *Pragmatics and Society*, 4(3), 369–87.

O'Driscoll, J. (2018). Dances with footings: A Goffmanian perspective on the Soto case. *Journal of Politeness Research*, 14(1), 39–62.

Quirk, R. and Greenbaum, S. (1973). *A University Grammar of English*. London: Longman.

Rampton, B. and Eley, L. (2018). Goffman and the everyday interactional grounding of surveillance. *Working Papers in Urban Language and Literacies*, 246.

Sacks, H., Schegloeff, E. A. and Jefferson, G. (1974). A simplest systematics for the organisation of turn taking for conversation. *Language*, 50(4), 696–735.

Sarangi, S. and Slembrouck, S. (1996). *Language, Bureaucracy and Social Control*. London: Longman.

Saville-Troike, M. (1989). *The Ethnography of Communication*. 2nd ed. Oxford: Blackwell.

Schegloff, E. A. (1968). Sequencing in conversational openings. *American Anthropologist*, 70, 1075–95.

Scollon, R. (1996). Discourse identity, social identity, and confusion in intercultural communication. *Intercultural Communication Studies*, 6(1), 1–16.

Scollon, R. (1998). *Mediated Discourse as Social Interaction*. London: Longman.

Shannon, C. and Weaver, W. (1949). *The Mathematical Theory of Communication*. Champaign: University of Illinois Press.

Short, M. (2007). Thought presentation twenty-five years on. *Style*, 41(2), 227–43.

Sidnell, J. (2009). Participation. In S. D'hondt, J.-O. Östman and J. Verschueren, eds., *The Pragmatics of Interaction*. Amsterdam: John Benjamins, pp. 125–56.

9

Conventionalization and Conventions

Dániel Z. Kádár and Juliane House[*]

9.1 Introduction

Our day-to-day interaction is imbued by conventions, i.e. shared understandings of meanings and practices. As Morgan (1977: 1) points out in his now classic study:

> I will argue for an account of "can you pass the salt" and similar expressions which treats them as conventional but not idioms, by establishing the necessity for distinguishing two kinds of language-related conventions: conventions of language, that jointly give rise to the literal meanings of sentences; and conventions about language, that govern the use of sentences, with their literal meanings, for certain purposes. I will suggest, in short, that "can you pass the salt", is indeed conventional in some sense, but not an idiom; rather it is conventional to use it (with its literal meaning) for certain purposes.

Morgan's second definition of convention as a phenomenon that facilitates meaning making in interaction is particularly relevant to sociopragmatics, and we will use it as our definition in this chapter. As Terkourafi (2013) points out, conventionalized expressions operate vis-à-vis routinized schemata by means of which we draw inferences about illocution. Moreover, as Escandel-Vidall (1984: 348) notes, a pragmatic norm represents a pragmatic convention, and because of this relationship between abstract descriptive norms and conventions of language use, violations of conventions are perceived as salient (see Kádár 2020).

---

[*] The authors express their gratitude to the Hungarian Academy of Sciences for funding the research visit of the second author to Budapest. Dániel Kádár also acknowledges the funding of the MTA Hungarian Academy of Sciences Momentum (Lendület) Research Grant (LP2017/5) for sponsoring the time he invested in the present project.

Conventions often concern language use that is relatively 'straightforward' to interpret and reproduce mimetically (Potolsky 2006). According to Donald (2011: 15),

> Mimesis ... produces such typically human cognitive patterns as ritual, skill, gesture, tribal identification, personal style, and public spectacle. It explains our irresistible tendency to imitate one another and conform to patterns of group behavior, especially group emotional expression.

Mimesis plays a particularly important role in the conventionalization process. Since language users very often acquire convention by mimicking each other, they often do not have to consciously 'decode' conventions, as Morgan's (1977) above-discussed case of "can you pass the salt" illustrates. When it comes to the performance of conventionalized speech acts, people more often than not understand their meaning without difficulty. This is why misunderstandings of conventional language use often become sources of humour (see e.g. Dynel 2017). Yet, conventions of language use are certainly not 'simple' for a number of reasons, which we will discuss in detail in Section 9.3.

The present chapter has the following structure. Section 9.2 overviews the key factors that make conventions complex from a pragmatic perspective. Section 9.3 summarizes facets of language use in which conventions can be particularly intriguing to study for the pragmatician. Finally, Section 9.4 looks into future areas of inquiry by means of which research on convention can be advanced.

9.2 The Pragmatic Complexity of Conventions

It is important here to make a clear distinction between the terms 'conventional' and 'conventionalized'. We will use the former to refer to the outcome of a conventionalization process and the latter to describe a pragmatic unit's degree of conventionalization in a particular context.

While the existence of conventions assumes shared pragmatic knowledge, in real-life conventions can trigger misunderstanding and pragmatic failure due to the following three factors:

1. Conventionalization is a matter of degree (cf. Terkourafi 2001). This variation of the degree of conventionalization of a particular instance of language use permeates different pragmatic units. For instance, while words in general – and formulae in particular – tend to have conventional meanings (Lyons 1977: 100), when it comes to words conventionally associated with a particular sociopragmatic engagement such as expressing impoliteness, some qualify as 'more conventionalized' than others (Culpeper 2010). Words which are less conventionalized in a particular sociopragmatic engagement may trigger ambiguity, as our

discussion of the pragmatic practice of using 'vintage' swearwords in Section 9.3.1 will demonstrate. The same issue of variation in degree of conventionalization can also be observed in the higher analytic unit of speech acts (see Section 9.3.2; see also the discussion in Section 9.4). Speech acts are traditionally understood as phenomena anchored in convention (Strawson 1964). However, as previous research has demonstrated, even within a speech act category such as requests – which are often realized in significantly conventionalized patterns – a given speech act may be expressed in innovative and unconventional ways (House 1989; see also Chapter 5). Furthermore, language users often deploy conventionalized speech acts in not strictly formulaic and formalized but still socially coded ways. Even within a cluster of different forms of expression, which all qualify as 'conventional' representations of a speech act, there may be pragmatic variations (Gibbs 1983). The highest unit of analysis, discourse, also has an intricate relationship with conventions. However, when it comes to longer chunks of interaction or monologues, there can also be variation in the degree of conventionalization of the given discourse. This degree may depend on interpersonal factors, such as the relational history between the participants and generic factors (Kádár and House 2020).

2. Convention-grounded intercultural clashes may occur as people interact by using a lingua franca such as English. The use of a lingua franca may lead to the spurious belief that we share common conventions and related pragmatic practices when in reality we do not (House 2003a, 2009). Along with contexts of using lingua francas, intercultural differences in understandings of conventions and related pragmatic practices may flare up in contexts where the speakers share the same native tongue but have different socio-economic backgrounds. For instance, Erickson and Shultz (1982) analyse cases in which differences in routine conventions for signalling listenership between Americans of European and of African descent result in the practice of European-American school counsellors "talking down" to their Afro-American peers. Thus, it is problematic to ignore the importance of often implicit but fundamental pragmatic discrepancies that culturally embedded conventions may trigger in intercultural scenarios in which the interactants use a lingua franca.

3. Conventions and related pragmatic practices are also subject to acquisition and socialization, i.e. it is not self-evident that language learners are aware of what counts as conventional in a particular context. In the context of L2 acquisition in particular, language learners are often faced with the problem that conventions that are 'self-evident' for natives of a particular language are alien to them (House 2003b; Kasper and Rose 1999). At the same time, language learners usually aim to acquire the new conventions of the culture mediated by their target language, since indicating awareness of conventions helps their

social integration. However, the problem is often that even highly proficient speakers of a target language tend to demonstrate a certain gap between their understanding and use of conventional practices (Taguchi 2011).

In sum, convention is a phenomenon of intriguing complexity, and so are interactional practices associated with conventions. Despite the fact that the raison d'être of conventions is exactly to make communication efficient and sort of 'automatized', and thereby easy to use due to knowledge of the practices associated with them, paradoxically they often trigger sociopragmatic difficulties.

9.3 Facets of Language Use with Complex Implications for Convention and Practice

9.3.1 Conventions, Practices and Time

A linguistic form may become conventional for a certain period, but it may lose this conventional character with the passing of time (cf. Pizziconi and Christie 2017). The usual pattern for such changes is that a particular word gains popularity as a conventionalized expression, and then its frequency in daily language usage may gradually decrease (see Kádár 2017). Note that some types of linguistic forms may be more 'enduring' than others; we agree with Burling (2000) on that this is a highly important evolutionary question. Since it is difficult to model how the conventionalization of a particular expression type develops in comparison to others, it is safe here to argue simply that the degree of conventionalization of many pragmatically salient expressions in meant to decline after some time. Thus, diachronic development – and time in a broader sense – is an important facet to study when it comes to conventions and practices.

A prime example of how the conventionalized value of words can change may be provided by swearwords. Let us refer here to an anecdote: A friend of the first author was riding his bike when he had a conflict with an unruly car driver. The driver cut in before the bike, and after this friend shouted at him, the driver braked and got out of his car. The cyclist realized at that moment that the driver was much larger than him, and as the driver began to swear at him, he uttered the rather archaic utterance "Darn you!" When the first author was first told about this exchange, he requested an explanation for this choice of swearword, as he felt that 'Darn you' is an old-fashioned expression to use in the scene of a conflict. The friend rationalized his behaviour by explaining that he had used this curse because he was *afraid of* the driver: by using an expression that was conventionally rude but has with time lost some of its face-threatening import, the cyclist could react to the challenge on the one hand while minimizing the risk of retribution, on the other.

Such 'vintage' swearwords are constant sources of humour exactly because – having been once conventional and thus popular – if they are used now, their use as a practice can sound dated and hence less acute. The following example, drawn from a news article, further illustrates this point:

> (1) In 1939, Rhett Butler, played by Clark Gable, ended "Gone with The Wind" with the world's most famous dismissive zinger: "Frankly, my dear, I don't give a damn". At the time, it was a bit of a shocker, even though the expletive had been uttered a year earlier in "Pygmalion".
>
> . . .
>
> So what words did they use decades ago when they wanted to blow off some steam? We asked our readers to name some of their favorite swear words from years past – and here's what they had to say. Remember any others? Let us know in comments.
>
> (1) "Frazzlin, dadgummit", said Theresa Reed.
> (2) "Heavens to Betsy!" said Marti Gilley.
> (3) "Jumpin' Jahosafat!!!" said Vicky Merling Points.
> (4) "Yikes and I still say it", said Jackie Lamothe.....[1]

Along with diachronic change, a different sense of time – related to the age of language users – also influences perception of 'appropriate' conventionalized practices. Language users often associate certain conventions and practices with a certain age group, and instances of language use that do not fit with the age group of their users may be evaluated as 'inappropriate'. To stick to the above-discussed practice of conventionalized swearing, Montagu (1967: 70) delivers the following interesting case of how expectations towards conventionalized practices of behaviour interrelate with age:

> (2) With the acquisition of speech and experience the child learns to cry less frequently and to express himself in ways that are more effective and "naughty". When he grows to adolescence, crying and childish naughtiness are abandoned for more manly forms of conduct; where one formerly wept, one now swears. This is well exemplified by an old *Punch* cartoon (2 April 1913):
>
> OLD LADY: Why are you crying, little boy?
> LITTLE BOY: Because I bea'nt old enough to swear.

This example illustrates that many language users associate certain of sociopragmatic practices with age. Because of this, if someone outside of

---

[1] www.huffingtonpost.com/2014/01/16/curse-words_n_4570641.html

the group or social unit associated with the given (perceived) conventionalized language practice deploys such forms as interactional resources, they become salient, as the following example illustrates:

(3) *Video has emerged of a young boy from the unruly British tourists pulling the finger and yelling at media and locals outside court in Hamilton today.*

   Footage captured by the Herald *shows a female walking away from the camera with a young boy by her side, flipping the bird at a* Herald *journalist following the court appearance of a 26-year-old relative.*

   When approaching the female family member for comment, the young boy turned and pulled the finger, shouting at media.[2]

When reporting on the behaviour of a family of unruly British tourists in New Zealand, many news reports devoted significant attention to the fact that the underage child of the family 'flipped the bird' at a journalist. This shows that there is a clear tension between the young age of the child and the conventions associated with the practice of making obscene gestures. While such gestures might not be more acceptable if an older person deployed them, the fact that it was a young person who behaved in such a vulgar fashion unavoidably caused surprise. Note that it was not only this gesture that caused the shock of locals: the media might have picked it up as a prime example of the uncivil behaviour of the British tourists. However, it might not have been a coincidence that it triggered particular interest, due to the age issue discussed here.

9.3.2 Conventions, Practices and Pragmatic Units

Pragmatic units provide another key facet to explore conventions and practices. Any pragmatic unit, including expressions and speech acts, may be realized in a conventionalized way but if it is embedded in an unconventionalized fashion in a largest unit of interaction, it will be evaluated as 'inappropriate'. For example, 'bloody' is a conventionally 'light' expletive (although Ardington's 2011 research has revealed that this varies across speakers of different varieties of English), which may not be noticed and as such is conventionalized in many informal settings involving speakers of British English. However, it may be improper to use it in formal contexts, in particular in settings that involve power and impression-management (such as management meetings or formal interaction between representatives of different organizations). As Blakemore (2011) has demonstrated, prosody, gesture and other non-linguistic factors closely correlate with the perception of whether a word is perceived as conventionalized or not in a given interaction. Such perceptions

---

[2] www.nzherald.co.nz/nz/news/article.cfm?c_id=1andobjectid=12191293

may also be influenced by variation across varieties of a language such as variants of world Englishes (Van Rooy 2010), dialects of a language (Ferguson 1994), particular genres (Thelwall 2008) and so on.

Moving to the higher unit of speech acts, it is also worth to investigate complexities that surround conventions and speech acts. While speech acts are traditionally understood as phenomena anchored in convention (Strawson 1964) – but see Searle's work in which speech acts are grounded in intentions – they may become ambiguous and unconventional in two different respects, which we categorize here as *formal* and *functional*.

The first, formal, type of ambiguity of speech acts fits with what has been said so far about words: there are cases when a speech act is produced in a form that counts as unconventional as a practice in a particular context. (For this issue, see Cooren's 2000 overview of Habermas.) For instance, Kádár (2020) has previously analysed a dataset of dismissals from work in which a dismissal is evaluated as offensive because the dismissed person and the observers of the dismissal perceive that the directive was realized in an unusual fashion. This lack of conventionalization contradicts with the contextual requirement of the practice of dismissing someone with dignity. That latter is a norm which conventionally triggers a formal, conventional and emphatic style in the context of dismissal. For instance, we may refer to the following example:

(4) A fragment from a news report dedicated to the inappropriate practices of some British employers)
Sacking by text was 'brutal and gutless'
9 May 2013

The sacking of a retail worker, after 19 years of service, via a 21-word text message, was 'brutal and gutless', the FW Commission has ruled.[3]

Note that example (4) represents a case when it is clear to practically everyone that the speech act has been made in an unconventional form because its brevity and the related perception that the dismissal was somehow 'tactless' contradict the broader discursive norms.

There are also more intricate cases. Ackerman's (1978) thought-provoking study of child language acquisition recounts interactions where children struggled with interpreting speech acts that were unroutinized and as such unconventional from their perspective, even when for adults these speech acts might have represented conventionalized practices. These children experienced a sense of tension between speech act and their broader expectations about the interaction. Another noteworthy phenomenon are cases when an unconventional form of speech act becomes conventional in a certain area of life. For instance, such cases may occur when

---

[3] https://workplaceinfo.com.au/termination/unfair-dismissal/cases/sacking-by-text-was-worst-brutal-and-gutless

groups/communities of practice of language users conventionalize otherwise socially unconventional forms of speech acts to express humour (Hancher 1980). Labov's (1972) ritual insults – i.e. forms of insult that transform into forms of sociality through the conventionalization process – are a prime example to mention here.

The second, functional, ambiguity of conventionalized speech acts becomes relevant if the speech act is somehow in conflict with the context in which it occurs. This phenomenon has been at the centre of a recent investigation by Kádár and House (2019), who studied a small corpus of media reports on a high-profile 'grudge match' between two mixed martial art athletes, the Dagestani Khabib Nurmagomedov (N) and the Irish Conor McGregor (M). Prior to the match, M insulted N with a religious and partly racial chain of slurs. This chain is a ritual called 'trash talk': the players of mixed marital arts are generally expected to exchange insults in Labov's (1972) sense. However, M's slurs trespassed the ritual boundaries: N himself reflected on the chain of events by arguing that "he lost his cool after defeating Conor McGregor because the Irishman disrespected his father, religion and country ahead of the fight",[4] i.e. the event transformed into a 'culture clash'. Following M's moral trespasses, the match between M and N became a *real* grudge match, escalating into a mass brawl. During the fight, M and N exchanged words which were clearly audible due to technology. A narrated excerpt of the interaction follows:

(5) The UFC [Ultimate Fighters' Championship] have released audio of Khabib Nurmagomedov's and Conor McGregor's exchanges during their Lightweight title fight at UFC 229 in Las Vegas last weekend.

Nurmagomedov defended his 155 pound belt with a convincing performance against McGregor that saw him submit the Dubliner via a neck crank in the fourth round.

Both fighters entered the fight with tensions at a high after a strenuous build up that saw a bus attack at a UFC 223 media day used as the main driver in promoting the fight.

Nuramgomedov, as he has done in previous fights, began talking to McGregor during the fight and requested that they 'Talk now' as he rained down punches on top of the former two-weight world champion.

McGregor was also picked up saying, "It's only business" at the end of the third round.

Nurmagomedov jumped out of the cage and attacked McGregor's teammates after this fight and the Russian said at his post-fight press conference that the Crumlin [Dublin] native had crossed lines during

---

[4] www.independent.ie/sport/mma/he-talked-about-my-religion-my-country-and-my-father-nurmagomedov-explains-why-he-attacked-mcgregor-team-37392589.html

the promotion of the fight, a point which McGregor seems to reference during the fight by saying 'it's only business'.[5]

Of the two utterances, N's "Let's talk now", which can be interpreted as an "Invite" (Edmondson and House 1981: 98), is a reference to M's previous moral trespasses. More interesting for us here is M's utterance "It's only business", which was understood by many fans as a speech act "Apologize" or "Excuse/Justify" (Edmondson and House 1981), and as such it was perceived to be at odds with the context and thus ambiguous, not so much in form but rather in our present functional sense. Interestingly, the post-event discussion of this utterance confirms the validity of this interpretation: There was a huge media backlash on M's perceived "apology", which illustrates the sense of ambiguity created by delivering a conventionally formulated speech act in a context in which use of this speech act is itself highly unconventional.

Note that presently there is an absence of a widely agreed upon speech act annotation scheme (although see e.g. Weisser 2014), which makes it difficult to systematically examine the relationship between a particular context, or interaction/discourse type, and expectancies of what kind of speech act realizations are regarded as conventionalized in this context. We further discuss this issue in Section 9.4.

9.3.3 Conventions, Practices and Intercultural Pragmatics

In intercultural contexts, differences may arise in understandings of what counts as a conventional meaning or practice, and so intercultural pragmatics is another key facet to consider in the present overview. A prime example of the influence of the intercultural context on conventions and practices can be found in the previously quoted study by Erickson and Shultz (1982), who analyse cases in which differences in routine conventions for signalling listenership between Americans of European and of African descent result in European-American school counsellors "talking down" to their Afro-American peers.

House (2003b: 38–9) demonstrates that such convention-based intercultural clashes may be particularly salient if language users are from different cultural backgrounds but use a lingua franca. To illustrate this point, House refers to the following interaction, which took place in German:

(6) (Brian, an American student spending a year in Germany has cooked a meal for Andi, a German friend, who has recently helped him with his German seminar paper. Brian and Andi have met several times before, both in class and at social get-togethers. Andi has just arrived.)

---

[5] www.sportsjoe.ie/mma/audio-emerges-conor-mcgregor-khabib-nurmagomedov-said-fight-180880

01	Brian:	hallo Andi wie geht's?
		hallo Andi how are you?
02	Andi:	ja prima oh prima doch ja;
		yeah fine oh fine really yeah
03	Brian:	so (0.1) es is alles fertig jetzt (0.1) ich hoffe es schmeckt dir gut (0.3)
		so everything's ready now I hope you like it
04		ich hab es selber gekocht [so weil]
		I have cooked it myself [so because]
05	Andi:	[ja prima]
		[yeah fine]
06	Brian:	isst man bei uns im Süeden
		that's what we eat in the South
07	Andi:	{in a loud voice}aber das is ja so VIEL das is ja VIEL ZU VIEL Reis
		but that's so much that is FAR TOO MUCH rice
08	Brian:	das MACHT doch nichts (0.1) ich hab es ja bezahlt und ich hab dich
		that doesn't MATTER I have paid for it and I have
09		EINgeladen (.) [du hast]
		INVITED [you have]
10	Andi:	[nein das] MACHT DOCH was DOCH DOCH denk doch an die
		[no it] DOES MATTER it does IT DOES think of the many
11		armen vielen hungernden Menschen die sowas gern essen wüerden
		poor people who go hungry and would like to eat something like that
12		[also ich]
		[well I]
13	Brian:	[ich ich] glaube ich (0.1) ich [finde]
		[I I] believe I I [I find]
14	Andi:	[ich finde] man sollte in dieser gemeinsamen Welt in der wir alle
		[I find] one should in this common world where we do all
15		doch leben (0.2) der Welt in der wir alle so UNgleich mit materiellen
		live the world in which we are all endowed with material
16		Güetern ausgestattet sind sollten wir uns zumindest in kleinem Maßstab
		goods so UNequally we should at least in small scale
17		bemüehen keine Verschwendung keine unnüetze Ver[schwendung]
		try to produce no waste no useless [waste]
18	Brian:	[also Andi] ich bin nicht ich (0.2) [glaube nicht]
		[well Andi] I am not I [don't believe]

19	Andi:	[keine Ver]schwendung zu produzieren und immer in unserem
		[no waste] to produce and always in our
20		Bewußtsein daran zu denken daß wir in der reichen westlichen Welt
		consciousness to think that we in the rich western world
21		{monologue continues for 1,5 minutes}

This example represents a case of misunderstanding emerging because of different communicative styles, and different interpretations of what counts as a convention in a particular social event, such as an invitation to a dinner. The monologous and monothematic nature of the discourse is marked. Ample use is made by Andi of the supportive move type "expander" (expanding information) in lines 2–4 in order to keep a particular topic in play. As a result of this, one gains the impression that it is one participant who clearly "hogs" the topic (Andi), with the other's (Brian's) two attempts (see turns 11 and 17) to gain the floor being overrun. Also marked (from an Anglo-point of view) is the unconventional non-reciprocity of the "how-are-you move" in line 2, and the non-concatenation of line 5 and line 6. The move in line 5 is clearly a ritual move characteristic of a conversational opening phase or phatic talk in general, which would conventionally (in certain Anglophone discourse types) be coupled with either a follow-up request for information or another remark thematically linking line 6 with line 5, opening up a chain of sequentially relevant moves as contiguous replies in Goffman's sense. By contrast, what happens in line 6 is an abrupt topic switch in the form of a complaint followed by a request in line 9, with both of these speech acts being produced at high levels of directness.

A key issue that makes convention a problem source in scenes of intercultural pragmatics is that L2 language users are often motivated to follow conventionalized practices. Unless there is a strong sense of intercultural awareness in operation in a particular scene, language users may not realize that different understandings of norms may cause problems, until a fully fledged interactional clash occurs. Tan (1999) provides a prime example for this phenomenon in her case study of interaction between members of a Chinese family where the interactants have the same native tongue. Some members of this family had lived in the United States for a long time, and when they were visited by their relatives from China, the following interaction took place:

(7) My mother thinks like ... an expatriate ... no longer patient with ritual courtesies. As if to prove her point, she reached across the table to offer my elderly aunt the last scallop from the Happy Family seafood dish. Sau-sau scowled.

"B'yao, zhen b'yao" (I don't want it, really, I don't) she cried, patting her plump stomach.

"Take it! Take it!" scolded my mother in Chinese.

"Full, I'm already full", Sau-sau protested weakly, eyeing the beloved scallop.

"Ai!" exclaimed my mother, completely exasperated. "Nobody else wants it. If you don't take it, it will only rot!"

At this point, Sau-sau sighed, acting as if she were doing my mother a big favor by taking the wretched scrap off her hands. My mother turned to her brother ... who was visiting her in California for the first time:
"In America a Chinese person could starve to death. If you say you don't want it, they won't ask you again forever".
My uncle nodded and said he understood fully: Americans take things quickly because they have no time to be polite.

(Tan 1999: 292)

A noteworthy point in this scenario is that the author's mother metapragmatically narrates the cause of the intercultural clash. What seems to be the main source of the problem here is that the participants were all ethnic Chinese, but due to her migration status the mother already found Chinese table manners annoying. While an intercultural pragmatic issue emerges in the interaction, this issue is not due to misunderstanding but rather to the mother's critical view of certain practices.

What makes conventions in intercultural scenarios particularly fluid is that (1) both our linguistic and non-linguistic behaviour continuously indicate culturally embedded pragmatic conventions and related norms (e.g. Tannen 1984), and perhaps even more importantly (2) these behaviours often triggers cross-cultural pragmatic stereotypes, which in turn influence our intercultural expectations.

9.3.4 Conventions and Language Acquisition and Socialization

Since conventions and conventional practices are acquired, L1 speakers develop awareness of convention in a gradual fashion (Garvey 1977; Schieffelin and Ochs 1986). In L2 settings, it is not always self-evident that a language user is aware of what counts as conventional in a particular context. As Bardovi-Harlig and Vellenga (2012) note, in L2 settings even conventionalized words may cause communicative difficulties. For example, they refer to the following case in which foreign learners of English chose a conventionally inappropriate response (8b) to a conventional phrase (8a) instead of the expected response (8c):

(8)
a.   Thanks for coming.
b.   You are welcome.*
c.   Thanks for inviting me.

(Bardovi-Harlig and Vellenga 2012: 85)

It is only (8c) as the conventionalized response which is acceptable. However, various learners responded with the first "You are welcome" response. While correct in some scenarios, learners tend to overgeneralize this expression onto other scenarios where it is not correct, as the example above illustrates.

Such instances of language use are relatively simple. Conventions become significantly more intricate when it comes to higher units in language acquisition. For instance, Taguchi (2006) refers to the following case:

(9) Native Speaker (NS) sample, Asking to reschedule the exam:
NS: I, look, I have a big favor to ask you. I know our exam is this week on Friday, but my friend is getting married that day. Is there any chance, like, maybe I can take it earlier or later or some other time?

L2 sample, Asking to reschedule the exam ("L" refers to "learner" and "I" refers to "interlocutor"):

1 L: Ah, so I'm here to ah, can you do me a favor? Because I heard there is gonna be test next Friday, but I do need to go to my friend's wedding. ((gap))
2 I: OK, ah, yeah, ah ((pause)) what kind of favor do you want me to do?
3 L: Ah, I hope I can do, I can shift the test date.

(cited from Taguchi 2006: 525–6)

While the advanced learner in the second case has no problems with the English language per se, when it comes to the conventionalized speech act of requesting, his behaviour frustrates the instructor because – unlike what counts as normative in Anglo-cultures – he is perceived to have unnecessarily delayed the request. From the instructor's point of view the pre-request causing the delay was unnecessary in a context in which making the request in a conventionally indirect way together with the grounder could have been sufficient.

It is relevant to note that language socialization and acquisition do not always take place in classrooms and in clear native–non-native settings (and here we should also remind ourselves that being a 'native' speaker of a language, in particular English, is often overvalued; see House 2003a). For example, Khubchandani (1997) and Planken (2005) both draw attention to the fact that conventions are often readjusted as people from different backgrounds jointly engage in language learning and begin to use the new language as a lingua franca. (See House 2003a; see also Section 9.2.2.) Hyland (2002) provides a noteworthy case study of instances where different conventional practices of 'sounding appropriate' in academic writing cause frustration for language users who do not share the dominant (usually Anglo) academic conventions. Hyland (2002: 1105) refers to the case of Chinese students who, in the course of learning academic English, indirectly expressed disagreement with the overemphasis of an impersonal style in academic writing, which was at that time deemed necessary by textbook writers:

(10)   We have to be objective in reporting our results. I don't like to be definite because my idea may be wrong and not what my supervisor believes. He might have a different idea. I think it is better to be quiet and not use 'I' but just tell what the experiment shows.

While this student, and many of her peers, accepted the 'authority' of Anglo-academic conventions, the statement "better be quiet" indicates that this is not necessarily how she would have preferred to express herself. That is, this student experienced a sense of cultural clash in terms of conventional requirements.

It is worth mentioning here that the acquisition of conventions and conventionalized practices can become a ritual process, and showcasing awareness of 'native' conventions in a particular setting often facilitates social integration. In academic research, it is not universally accepted that such integration is necessary or even desirable. However, ultimately there tends to be a desire to integrate, and often foreign language learners not only deploy language according to conventions but also ritually display their awareness of these conventionalized practices. Kádár and Haugh (2013: 239) quote the following case regarding the phenomenon of adopting a convention to indicate willingness to align with locals:

(11)   DK: Well *dun*, as *we* Yorkshire people say!

The first author (DK in the example) used to teach at a British university in Yorkshire where he made this jocular utterance to a local friend. In Yorkshire it is a conventional form of politeness to acknowledge the uniqueness of the local accent (see Mills and Kádár 2011). In the example above, DK ritually showcased his awareness of this convention by briefly switching to a clearly fake and foreign-sounding accent and indicating that he has no intention of mocking the speech partner, as he made the clearly false statement ('*we* Yorkshire people') that he is a Yorkshire person. The utterance was evaluated positively, supposedly not so much because DK could imitate the accent, but rather because he ritually demonstrated his embracing of the conventionalized practice of talking about Yorkshire accent.

9.3.5   Conventions and Rituals

Convention as normative knowledge that facilitates meaning making manifests itself in two types of pragmatic *practices*: 'convention' and 'ritual' (in the following, for the sake of simplicity, we will refer to convention and ritual practice types simply as convention and ritual). These practice types have many similar features because both of them are conventional: in fact, they represent the two ends of a pragmatic scale. As such, the convention–ritual continuum is a key facet where conventions and practices are studied.

It is not always possible – and may not even be desirable – to clearly distinguish these practice types from each other. At the same time, they need to be disentangled, so that we can analyse seemingly similar but in actual fact different pragmatic phenomena, such as engaging in chit-chat with a friend on the train (conventional behaviour) v. engaging in the same conversation type with someone's manager in the form of small-talk (ritual behaviour). Simply put, convention includes language users following what they regard as expected behaviour in a particular situation, while ritual practices are activated in contexts in which rights and obligations are important.

Convention and ritual differ in a number of ways (see also Terkourafi and Kádár 2017):

- *Complex participation framework*: Conventions can take place in practically any relationship, while ritual tends to occur in complex participation frameworks. This complexity does not mean that ritual may not occur in dyadic settings, but rather that its operation always *reflects* complex participation frameworks, in that the interactants tend to be aware of their rights and obligations whenever they perform a ritual. To refer to our example of engaging in chit-chat with a friend on the train, it is clear that such an interaction is likely to be personal. However, when it comes to small-talk with someone's manager in a context in which rank matters, the participants are aware of who and where they are, and so the conversation unavoidably transforms into what Bax (2010) defines as 'ritual performance'. Due to the prevailing rights and obligations, the speakers may not interact as 'ordinary' individuals, and the interaction is unlikely to go beyond certain conventionalized boundaries.
- *Salience*: Conventions tend to be salient (or 'marked') only for those who are outside the group or community of practice in which they operate. For example, a conventional Anglo chit-chat, and the related norm of avoiding certain (overtly personal) themes in this type of interaction, may only become salient for a participant of an interaction if this person is not familiar with this conventional practice. Rituals, on the other hand, are salient to everyone. To refer to our example of train-talk, it is literally impossible not to be aware of the fact that someone interacts with her manager (and, supposedly, one's subordinate), since a manager can also not afford to say arbitrary things in order to protect her professional 'face'.
- *Time and place*: Conventions are only loosely constrained by context, while rituals can only take place at certain times and places. For example, one may engage in a friendly chat with one's friend in any context. However, an encounter between a manager and an employee provides a distinctively ritual frame for the manager and the employee to interact. Due to norms of 'civility', they may find it difficult not to interact in the context which we use as an example here, while in the corridors of the company there would be no such pressure on them to talk. In other words, such a ritual encounter can only take place at a certain time and place.

- *'Ratification'*: Usually, ratification (in the sense of Goffman 1979) is not an issue when it comes to convention, in particular if all interactants follow situated conventional practices (and there are no formal consequences when it does not). Ritual, on the other hand, can only be operationalized by ratified personae, and non-ratified participation in a ritual tends to be sanctioned (Bell 1997). For instance, should there be family members around during an *ad hoc* conversation on a train, it would certainly not be a major issue for them to participate. However, if the same talk takes place between colleagues who are not intimate, and rights and obligations are important in the situation, then the conversational participation of family members is not self-evident and could be of a limited nature.

Note that the degree to which a particular interaction is institutionalized also influences whether a particular form of pragmatic behaviour is conventional or ritual: while this is an overgeneralization, generally, institutional interaction prefers/triggers ritual behaviour.

The boundary between convention and ritual is nevertheless blurred by a number of shared characteristics, including the following:

- *Recurrence*: Both convention and ritual are recurrent practices. Irrespective of whether a conversation on the train takes place between friends or colleagues with distant and power-driven relationship, the interactants may be aware of 'what's coming', interactionally speaking, due to the routinized nature of convention and ritual.
- *Normativity*: Both convention and ritual carry penalties in the case of non-compliance or defective performance. These penalties can range from negative evaluations to more serious ones. For instance, ignoring someone in the confined space of a train may trigger negative evaluations, since there is a normative 'pressure' on interactants in many cultures to engage in some form of chit-chat or small-talk, especially if they know each other (see also Leech's 1983 Phatic Maxim).
- *Formality and sequentiality*: Both convention and ritual have certain formal and sequential properties, which make them recognizable and differentiate them from non-conventionalized practices. Such formal and sequential properties might be explicit or implicit from the external observer's point of view, but they are definitely obvious to the participants.

9.4 Further Directions

The present chapter has examined conventions and practices, which represent key phenomena in sociopragmatics. While the existence of convention assumes a sense of sharedness and common knowledge of language use, we have illustrated that conventions can be complex and their existence can be exploited to various effects. We have also examined facets of pragmatics with particular relevance to conventions and practices, including contexts in which diachronicity or time itself is somehow important, instances in which a conventional unit is not used conventionally on the level on interaction/discourse, intercultural communication, and L2 settings. We have also discussed the convention–ritual interface.

Conventionalization and convention still remain a key area to investigate, and the following research directions are particularly relevant to future inquiries:

1. *Conventional speech act in sociopragmatic theory, in particular, (im)politeness research*: Following criticisms of politeness research before the twenty-first century, the concept of conventionalized speech act seems to have lost its significance. We believe that the speech act remains fundamental when it comes to conventionalized language use (see Kádár and House 2019, 2020). In this chapter, we have only looked into the tension between speech act and the broader context in which a speech act is evaluated as unconventional (Section 9.3.2). However, the phenomenon of speech act offers various other intriguing areas for pragmatic research on convention and conventionalization. Perhaps most importantly, future studies need to examine the relationship between forms indicating speech acts and politeness. Kádár and House (2019, 2020) have pointed out that expressions in some linguacultures are significantly more anchored in certain speech acts such as requests and apologies – and as such are more intrinsically interlinked with (im)politeness – than their counterparts in other linguacultures. Is it possible to conduct systematic explorations in order to capture this interface between form, speech act and (im)politeness?
2. *Re-examining the very notion of conventionalized speech act*: This seems to be a key task for future research, considering that current speech act theory is not sufficiently developed to describe all kinds of conventionalized language phenomena and their relationship with practices of behaviour (see also Chapter 5). We need to re-examine exactly what we mean by convention and conventionalization when it comes to speech acts. For instance, let us refer here to the case of a dismissal (example 4), which is difficult to describe as a single speech act as it is often realized through various speech act categories. Since dismissal is clearly a conventionalized practice, its study in terms of speech act theory implies that one needs to compare frequencies of speech act types through which it is realized in a corpus. Thus, in order to grasp the nature of speech act in the broader environment of discursive practices, which is essential for studying the conventional side of sociopragmatics, we need to look at speech act from new angles.

We hope that the relevance of conventions and practices to a variety of areas – spanning historical pragmatics, through intercultural inquiries, to applied linguistics – will trigger further academic interest in this area.

References

Ackerman, B. P. (1978). Children's understanding of speech acts in unconventional directive frames. *Child Development*, 49(2), 311–18.

Ardington, A. (2011). Tourist advertising of Australia: Impolite or situation-appropriate? Or a uniquely Aussie invite lost in translation. In B. L. Davies, M. Haugh and A. J. Merrison, eds., *Situated Politeness*. London: Bloomsbury, pp. 253–9.

Bardovi-Harling, K. and Vellenga, H. E. (2012). The effect of instruction on conventional expressions in L2 pragmatics. *System*, 40, 77–89.

Bax, M. (2010). Rituals. In A. H. Jucker and I. Taavitsainen, eds., *Handbook of Pragmatics, Vol. 8: Historical Pragmatics*. Berlin: Mouton, pp. 483–519.

Bell, C. (1997). *Ritual: Perspectives and Dimensions*. Oxford: Oxford University Press.

Blakemore, D. (2011). On the descriptive ineffability of expressive meaning. *Journal of Pragmatics*, 43(14), 3537–50.

Brown, P. and Levinson, S. C. (1987). *Politeness: Some Universals in Language Usage*. Cambridge: Cambridge University Press.

Burling, R. (2000). Comprehension, production and conventionalisation in the origins of language. In C. Knight, M. Studdert-Kennedy and J. Hurford, eds., *The Evolutionary Emergence of Language: Social Function and the Origin of Linguistic Form*. Cambridge: Cambridge University Press, pp. 27–39.

Cooren, F. (2000). Toward another ideal speech situation: A critique of Habermas' reinterpretation of speech act theory. *Quarterly Journal of Speech*, 86, 295–317.

Culpeper, J. (2010). Conventionalised impoliteness formulae. *Journal of Pragmatics*, 42(12), 3232–45.

Donald, M. (2011). Art and cognitive evolution. In M. Turner, ed., *The Artful Mind: Cognitive Science and the Riddle of Human Creativity*. New York: Oxford University Press, pp. 3–20.

Dynel, M. (2017). "Is there a tumour in your humour?" On misunderstanding and miscommunication in conversational humour. In R. Gioria and M. Haugh, eds., *Doing Pragmatics Interculturally: Cognitive, Philosophical, and Sociopragmatic Perspectives*. Berlin: Mouton de Gruyter, pp. 55–78.

Edmondson, W. and House, J. (1981). *Let's Talk and Talk about It: A Pedagogic Interactional Grammar of English*. Munich: Urban and Schwarzenberg.

Erickson, F. and Shultz, J. (1982). *The Counsellor as Gatekeeper: Social Interaction in Interviews*. New York: Academic Press.

Escandel-Vidall, V. (1984). Norms and principles: Putting social and cognitive pragmatics together. In R. Márquez-Reiter and M. E. Placencia, eds., *Current Trends in the Pragmatics of Spanish*. Amsterdam: John Benjamins, pp. 347–72.

Ferguson, C. A. (1994). Dialect, register, and genre: Working assumptions about conventionalization. In D. Bieber and E. Finegan, eds., *Sociolinguistic Perspectives on Register*. Oxford: Oxford University Press, pp. 15–30.

Garvey, K. (1977). Play with language and speech. In S. Ervin-Tripp and C. M. Kernan, eds., *Child Discourse*. New York: Academic Press, pp. 27–48.

Gibbs, R. (1983). Do people always process the literal meanings of indirect requests? *Journal of Experimental Psychology: Learning, Memory, and Cognition*, 9(3), 524–33.

Goffman, E. (1979). Footing. *Semiotica*, 25(1/2), 1–30.

Hancher, M. (1980). How to play games with words: Speech-act jokes. *Journal of Literary Semantics*. 9(1), 20–29.

House, J. (1989). Politeness in English and German: The functions of *please* and *bitte*. In S. Blum-Kulka, J. House and G. Kasper, eds., *Cross-Cultural Pragmatics: Requests and Apologies*. Norwood, NJ: Ablex, pp. 96–119.

House, J. (2003a). English as a lingua franca: A threat to multilingualism? *Journal of Sociolinguistics*, 7(4), 556–78.

House, J. (2003b). Misunderstanding in intercultural university encounters. In J. House, G. Kasper and S. Ross, eds., *Misunderstanding in Social Life: Discourse Approaches to Problematic Talk*. London: Longman, pp. 22–56.

House, J. (2009). Introduction: The pragmatics of English as a Lingua Franca. *Intercultural Pragmatics*, 6(2), 141–5.

Hyland, K. (2002). Authority and invisibility: Authorial identity in academic writing. *Journal of Pragmatics*, 34, 1091–1112.

Kádár, D. Z. (2017). *Politeness, Impoliteness and Ritual: Maintaining the Moral Order in Interpersonal Interaction*. Cambridge: Cambridge University Press.

Kádár, D. Z. (2020). Capturing injunctive norm in pragmatics: Meta-reflective evaluations and the moral order. *Lingua*. DOI: 10.1016/j.lingua.2020.102814.

Kádár, D. Z. and Haugh, M. (2013). *Understanding Politeness*. Cambridge: Cambridge University Press.

Kádár, D. Z. and House, J. (2019). Revisiting speech acts from the perspective of ritual: A discussion note. *Multilingua*, 38(6), 687–92.

Kádár, D. Z. and House, J. (2020). Linguistic forms, standards situations and ritual frames: A contrastive pragmatic framework. *Pragmatics*, 30(1), 142–68.

Kasper, G. and Rose, K. R. (1999). Pragmatics and SLA. *Annual Review of Applied Linguistics*, 19, 81–104.

Khubchandani, L. M. (1997). *Revisualizing Boundaries: A Plurilingual Rthos*. New Delhi, India: Sage.

Labov, W. (1972). 'Rules for Ritual Insults'. In D. Sudnow, ed., *Studies in Social Interaction*. Oxford: Blackwell/The Free Press. Reprinted in Labov, W. (1972). *Language in the Inner City: Studies in the Black English Vernacular*. Philadelphia: University of Pennsylvania University Press/Basil Blackwell, pp. 297–353.

Levinson, S. C. (1979). Pragmatics and social deixis: Reclaiming the notion of conventional implicature. In *Proceedings of the Fifth Annual Meeting of the Berkeley Linguistics Society*. Berkeley: Berkeley University Press, pp. 206–23.

Levinson, S. C. (1983). *Pragmatics*. Cambridge: Cambridge University Press.

Lyons, J. (1977). *Semantics*. Vol. 1. Cambridge: Cambridge University Press.

Mills, S. and Kádár, D. Z. (2011). Politeness and culture. In D. Z. Kádár and S. Mills, eds., *Politeness in East Asia*. Cambridge: Cambridge University Press, pp. 21–44.

Montagu, A. (1967). *The Anatomy of Swearing*. Philadelphia: University of Pennsylvania Press.

Morgan, J. L. (1977). *Technical Report 52: Two Types of Convention in Indirect Speech Acts*. Urbana: University of Illinois at Urbana-Champaign.

Pizziconi, B. and Christie, C. (2017). Indexicality and (im)politeness. In J. Culpeper, M. Haugh and D. Z. Kádár, eds., *The Palgrave Handbook of Linguistic (Im)Politeness*. Basingstoke, UK: Palgrave Macmillan, pp. 143–70.

Planken, B. (2005). Managing rapport in lingua franca sales negotiations: A comparison of professional and aspiring negotiators. *English for Specific Purposes*, 24, 381–400.

Potolsky, M. (2006). *Mimesis*. London: Routledge.

Schieffelin, B. and Ochs, E. (eds.). (1986). *Language Socialisation across Cultures*. Cambridge: Cambridge University Press.

Strawson, P. F. (1964). Intention and convention in speech acts. *The Philosophical Review*, 73(4), 439–60.

Taguchi, N. (2006). Analysis of appropriateness in a speech act of request in L2 English. *Pragmatics*, 16(4), 513–33.

Taguchi, N. (2011). The effect of L2 proficiency and study-abroad experience on pragmatic comprehension. *Language Learning*, 61(3), 904–39.

Tan, A. (1999). The language of discretion. In C. Ricks and L. Michaels, eds., *The State of Language*. Berkeley: University of California Press, pp. 25–32.

Tannen, D. (1984). The pragmatics of cross-cultural communication. *Applied Linguistics*, 5(3), 189–95.

Terkourafi, M. (2001). Politeness in Cypriot Greek: A frame-based approach. PhD dissertation, University of Cambridge, Department of Linguistics.

Terkourafi, M. (2013). Re-assessing the speech-act schema: Twenty-first century reflections. *International Review of Pragmatics*, 5(2), 197–216.

Terkourafi, M. and Kádár, D. Z. (2017). Convention and ritual (im)politeness. In J. Culpeper, M. Haugh and D. Z. Kádár, eds., *The Palgrave Handbook of Linguistic (Im)Politeness*. Basingstoke, UK: Palgrave Macmillan, pp. 171–95.

Thelwall, M. (2008). Fk yea I swear: Cursing and gender in MySpace. *Corpora*, 3(1), 83–107.

Van Rooy, B. (2010). Social and linguistic perspectives on variability in world Englishes. *World Englishes*, 29(1), 3–20.

Weisser, M. (2014). Speech act annotation. In K. Aijmer and C. Rühlemann, eds., *Corpus Pragmatics: A Handbook*. Cambridge: Cambridge University Press, pp. 84–114.

10

Synchronic and Diachronic Pragmatic Variability

Anne Barron[*]

10.1 Introduction

Pragmatic variability refers to the fact that language users have a wide range of options available to create and understand meaning (Verschueren 1999). It is present in all aspects of language use, from discourse markers, to routine formulae to implicatures to speech acts to turn-taking and beyond. To take an example from the speech act of greeting in an English-speaking context: greetings can be realized using a routine realization, such as 'good day', 'hello', 'hi', 'good morning', 'G'day', 'how are you?', 'how's the craic?', 'howreya?', 'Dear X', 'wes hal', 'deo gratias' or conceivably via a non-routine form, such as 'I didn't see you there'. Non-verbally, the handshake, high five or fist bump represent means of greeting.

The range of possible choices for language users is unstable and continuously changing. Such change can be seen on a diachronic axis, with options changing over time. The form 'wes hal', for instance, is no longer employed in present-day English, but 'wes hal' with syntactic variants was a common form in Old English. Similarly, 'deo gratias' was a common form in fourteenth- and fifteenth-century Britain not employed today (Jucker 2011). Nearer our century, 'good morning' and 'how are you?' were the most frequent greetings in nineteenth-century American English, whereas 'hi' and 'hello' dominate today (Jucker 2017). Such change is continuously taking place, and the causes of change are many and varied. Change may occur, for instance, if a speaker borrows a form from another language or creates a new idiosyncratic form or gesture to meet a particular communicative demand. Such innovative forms potentially become options in their own right in the process of language change. Take the fist bump: some trace its origins as a greeting to the context of a

---

[*] My thanks to the editors, particularly to Marina Terkourafi, and to an anonymous reviewer for their valuable comments and suggestions. The usual disclaimers apply.

boxing match in which opponents touch gloves prior to a match. Others trace them to its use by star basketballer Fred Campbell of the Baltimore Bullets in the 1970s. The use of this communication form has spread since, also due to its use by later President Barrack Obama in the context of the 2008 US election (Hamilton 2018). Currently, the fist bump is starting to replace the handshake as a greeting in colder seasons in Canada, also due to its status among medical researchers as a more hygienic alternative to the handshake (Mela and Whitworth 2014; Hamilton 2018). In sum, the pragmatic options available to speakers are unstable and dynamic. Newer options emerge over time and previous options disappear for a variety of reasons.

The variable options at our disposal in using language at any one time are constrained by their context of use. A particular choice in language use can serve to exclude other options or create new options (Verschueren 1999). An initial 'hi' as an informal greeting is more likely to trigger a reciprocal 'hi' over a more formal greeting such as 'good day'. Not only does 'hi' in this context keep the level of formality constant, but the repetition of the same form represents what is termed 'format trying', whereby parts of a previous utterance may be re-used for a variety of reasons, such as to support conversation flow or show solidarity (Goodwin and Goodwin 1987). Genre conventions also create a constraining context. 'Dear X' is more likely in the written context of email or letter-writing than in spoken communication. Similarly, the interactants within a particular context, whether familiars or strangers, whether status equals or unequals, will shape our choices (Blum-Kulka et al. 1989). Thus, the variability of language use highlights the importance of context in pragmatic analyses.

Closely related to variability is a further feature of language use, namely its 'negotiability' (Verschueren 2008). There is no one-to-one relationship between an individual form and its function. Rather, meaning generation in language use is always highly dynamic and functions only due to the adaptability of the human mind (feature of 'adaptability') (Verschueren 1999, 2008). Meaning is negotiated in context. The same form may have a different meaning in a different context. The form 'Hello', for instance, may function not as a greeting (as above), but as an attention-getter in a particular context. Finally, a change of form can trigger a change of context (Verschueren 2008), as when, for example, an informal form, such as 'hi', offered in an initial greeting, is followed not by an informal greeting, as expected, but by a more formal 'good day'. If the interactants involved are an employee and employer, the choice of a more formal greeting by the employer may consciously construct a change from an informal to a formal context. If, on the other hand, the more formal greeting is produced by a parent to a child, the use may be ironic and an attempt to add humour to the interaction. Here too, it becomes clear that studying language use always means studying language use in context and appealing to contextual clues and pragmatic principles.

Thus far, we have taken a pragmatic perspective on variability. Sociolinguists, on the other hand, relate variation in language to stylistic constraints and to underlying socio-demographic parameters. Variationist sociolinguists conceptualize a particular language choice using the concept of the variable which has different linguistic realizations (variants) (Labov 1972). They see variability as patterned and orderly and explainable via matters of style or such socio-demographic factors as region, gender, age, socioeconomic class and ethnicity. On a pragmatic level, sociolinguists have usually analysed variation in single linguistic items, such as discourse markers or general extenders. Tagliamonte (2012), for instance, found general extenders to have multiple pragmatic functions, including the creation of shared knowledge. Individual general extenders have been found to correlate with specific social classes. Thus, the general extender 'and that' correlates with working class speech, while other forms, such as 'and stuff' and 'and things' correlate rather with middle-class speech (Cheshire 2007).

When studying language change, sociolinguists attempt to understand the path of change, for instance, whether a change represents a spread of vernacular forms or a spread from a higher social class to lower social classes. Language change always involves variability. Vice versa, however, variability in language does not necessarily mean change, with variable features also remaining stable over time. Thus, part of the challenge of such research is to identify when variation in language represents a change in progress and when it represents a stable, but variable, state of language whose use is regulated by a range of parameters (D'Arcy 2013).

Although some research on pragmatic or discourse variation has been available since approximately the late 1970s, the sociolinguistic study of variation has traditionally focused on the language system, with comparatively limited research on pragmatic or discourse variation. Terkourafi (2011: 344) sees the comparatively small amount of research in this area to date as the result of the 'limiting influence [of Labov's (1972) conception of the linguistic variable] on the study of variation at other levels, especially in syntax and discourse'. We return to this point in Section 10.3, in the discussion of the pragmatic variable.

Similar to sociolinguistics, the study of pragmatic variation within pragmatics was relatively slow in emerging. Discussion was long focused on issues of universality, including the universality of theoretical frameworks and the universality of speech acts and speech act strategies. Wierzbicka's (1985) research, highlighting language-specific and culture-specific pragmatics, as well as later research conducted within the Cross-Cultural Speech Act Realisation Project (CCSARP; Blum-Kulka et al. 1989) investigating language use across cultures and across native speakers and learners, triggered a movement away from issues of universality and towards synchronic research focused on pragmatic variation across cultures (cross-cultural pragmatics), between native speakers and learners (interlanguage pragmatics), and across time (historical pragmatics).

Interest in pragmatic variability and change from a historical perspective was inaugurated in 1995 with the publication of Jucker (1995), an edited volume entitled *Historical Pragmatics*. Historical pragmatics is both synchronic and diachronic in focus, examining pragmatic norms within a particular period and pragmatic variability over time. This area of research and the related newly proposed area of historical (socio)pragmatics (Culpeper 2009) recognize that the choice of a particular option at any particular time in history will depend on and also influence the particular context of use. Given the broad view of pragmatics adopted within historical pragmatics, researchers also investigate the influence of social variation on language use, further blurring the differentiation with historical sociolinguistics (Taavitsainen and Jucker 2015).

Research on intralingual synchronic pragmatic variation across varieties or across macro-social factors, such as gender, age, socioeconomic status or ethnic identity, was slowest to emerge. Early studies focused on individual factors, such as gender (e.g. Holmes 1995), social variation (e.g. Deutschmann 2003) or region on a national level (e.g. Márquez Reiter 2003 on pragmatic variation across national varieties of Spanish). It was against the background of such initial sociolinguistic and pragmatic research on intralingual regional and social variation that variational pragmatics emerged as a field of research (Schneider and Barron 2008; Barron and Schneider 2009). Variational pragmatics is concerned with the systematic analysis of synchronic present-day pragmatic variation according to regional and social factors. It combines both the sociolinguistic and pragmatic perspective on variability and investigates the influence of macro-social factors (region, gender, age, socioeconomic class and ethnic identity) on language use and interaction as they interact with micro-social factors relating to situational uses. To return to the greeting example above, the influence of regional factors might be seen in the preferred use of 'G'day' in an Australian context (Harting 2005) and in the use of 'How's the craic?' or 'Howreya?' in an Irish context (Regan 2008). On the other hand, the influence of age and gender is evident in the use of 'G'day' in an Australian context, where it is favoured as a greeting by males and those over 30 regardless of addressee (Harting 2005).

The present chapter examines synchronic and diachronic pragmatic variability by focusing on situational, regional and social variation from a synchronic and diachronic perspective. Following an overview of synchronic and diachronic approaches to variation, with a particular focus on the fields of variational pragmatics and historical pragmatics (Section 10.2), a case study focusing on offers across the regional varieties of Irish and British English is briefly presented (Section 10.3). Key methodological and theoretical issues arising from this study, and shared by researchers working on pragmatic variation in a contrastive manner irrespective of their theoretical background, are discussed in this section. We examine how a pragmatic variable might be defined using multiple criteria, we address the influence of method on definitions of the variable as well as the potential for interdisciplinary research between diachronic and synchronic researchers. The chapter closes with a brief summary and suggestions for future research (Section 10.4).

10.2 Key Theoretical Approaches

Research on intralingual pragmatic variation may take a synchronic and/or diachronic perspective. This section details and contrasts approaches within these perspectives. Figure 10.1 provides an overview and is referred to throughout this section.

10.2.1 Intralingual Synchronic Pragmatic Variation

Intralingual synchronic pragmatic variation involves pragmatic variation within a particular language at a particular point in time. Studies of present-day synchronic variation focus on two types of variation, intralingual micro-social pragmatic variation ((a1) in Figure 10.1) and intralingual macro-social pragmatic variation ((a2) in Figure 10.1) (Barron 2005a). Micro-social pragmatic variation (a1) involves situational variation in language use and is frequently examined as a function of the factors of social distance (SD), power (P) and degree of imposition (R) as identified in Brown and Levinson's (1978, 1987) politeness theory. To these one may add conversational setting, ranging from formal settings with transactional roles to the fore to informal settings in which the focus is primarily on interactional roles (Holmes 1995). For instance, Ogiermann (2009) finds high social distance (interactions between strangers) to be associated with a strong preference for explicit apologies and intensifiers and a low use of downgrading accounts. Apologies to familiars or friends (medium/ low social distance), on the other hand, were rather characterized by a tendency to hide the offence where possible. Similarly, Deutschmann (2003), in an analysis of apologies in the British National Corpus (BNC) corpus, found that the lexeme *apologize* is typically employed in formal interactions only.

Intralingual macro-social pragmatic variation ((a2) in Figure 10.1) is concerned with synchronic variation in language use due to such macro-social factors as region, gender, age, socioeconomic class and ethnic identity. It operates on the sociopragmatic and pragmalinguistic levels, the former relating to social structure (e.g. varying assessment of social factors), the latter relating to the language used (e.g. strategies, linguistic realizations). To stay with apologies, such research might look at how an apology in a particular language (e.g. English) might be employed or formulated in a particular situation according to whether it was produced in, for instance, Jamaica, Ireland, America (region) or by a younger or an older speaker (age) or a speaker of a higher or lower socioeconomic class (socioeconomic class)

Intralingual pragmatic variation

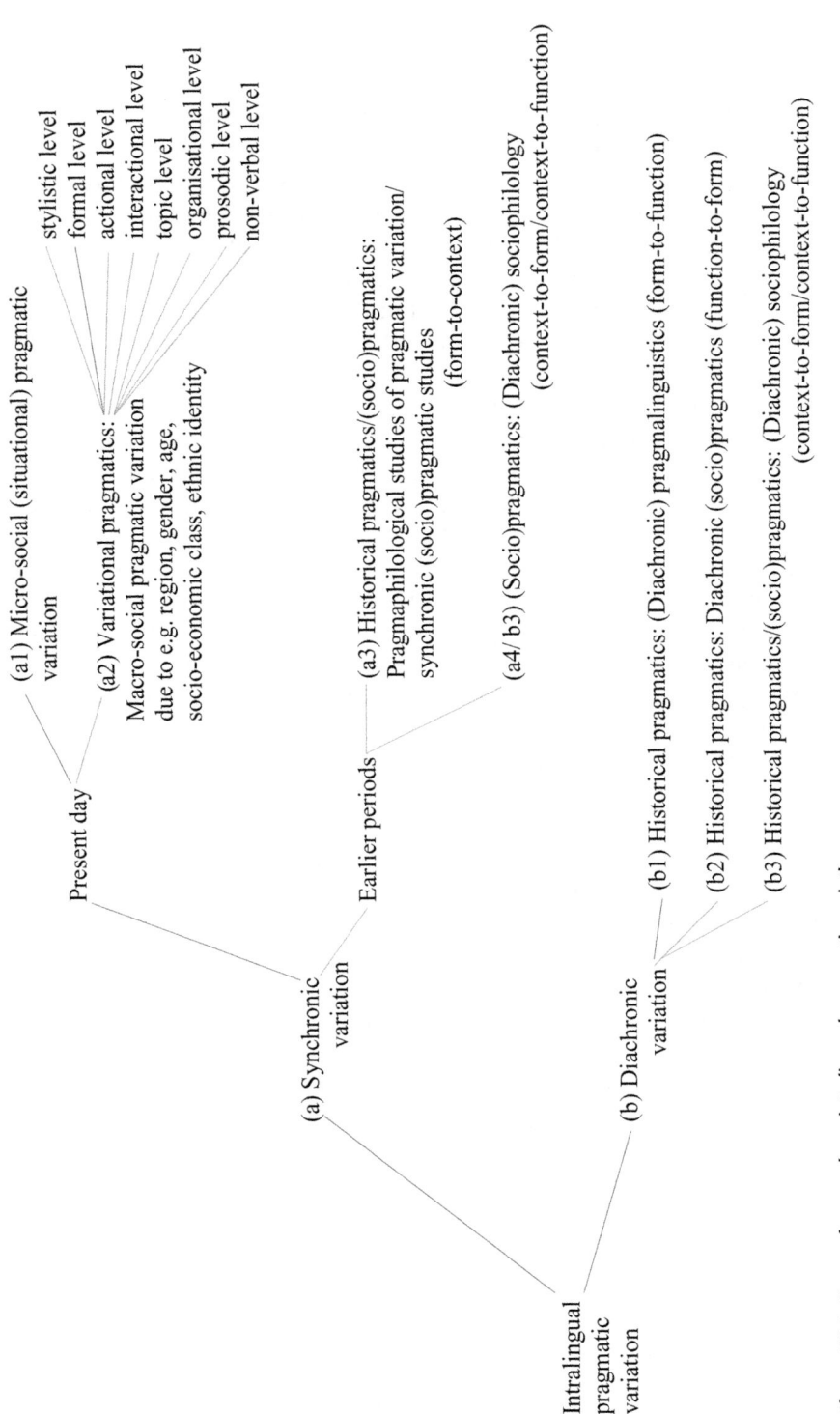

(a) Synchronic variation
- Present day
  - (a1) Micro-social (situational) pragmatic variation
  - (a2) Variational pragmatics: Macro-social pragmatic variation due to e.g. region, gender, age, socio-economic class, ethnic identity
    - stylistic level
    - formal level
    - actional level
    - interactional level
    - topic level
    - organisational level
    - prosodic level
    - non-verbal level
- Earlier periods
  - (a3) Historical pragmatics/(socio)pragmatics: Pragmaphilological studies of pragmatic variation/synchronic (socio)pragmatic studies (form-to-context)
  - (a4/b3) (Socio)pragmatics: (Diachronic) sociophilology (context-to-form/context-to-function)

(b) Diachronic variation
- (b1) Historical pragmatics: (Diachronic) pragmalinguistics (form-to-function)
- (b2) Historical pragmatics: Diachronic (socio)pragmatics (function-to-form)
- (b3) Historical pragmatics/(socio)pragmatics: (Diachronic) sociophilology (context-to-form/context-to-function)

Figure 10.1 Focus of research on intralingual pragmatic variation.

in a particular situation. Barron (in press b), for instance, finds a higher use of vocatives in apologies in Irish English relative to English English (e.g. 'I'm sorry I didn't mean to offend you in any way Lisa!'), pointing to higher levels of relational orientation in the Irish English data.

Variational pragmatics is devoted to the investigation of synchronic intralingual macro-social pragmatic variation ((a2) in Figure 10.1), i.e. to the analysis of variation in language use and interaction according to the macro-social factors of region, age, gender, socioeconomic status and ethnic identity (Barron 2014, 2015, 2017b; Schneider 2010, 2014; Chapter 31). It is broadly situated within the perspective approach (see also Chapter 2), with analyses referencing the social and cultural context of use, in particular the linguistic context (e.g. co-text of the spoken or written text, the genre), the cognitive context (e.g. assumptions and expectations of how to use language in a particular context), the social context (e.g. physical surroundings, participant roles, interpersonal situational factors, social parameters of interactants) and the sociocultural context (Fetzer 2010; cf. also De Saint-Georges 2013; Staley 2018; Barron 2019). Variational pragmatic research aims to identify a 'pragmatic core' (Schneider 2017: 320) of language patterns shared across regional and social varieties and also to systematically describe pragmatic variation across these varieties. Three principles are important in variational pragmatic research: empiricity, comparability and contrastivity – the latter two highlighting that only in contrasting language use is it possible to see what is variety-specific, variety-preferred or shared across varieties.

Variational pragmatics distinguishes eight local levels of analysis ((a2) in Figure 10.1): the stylistic (e.g. variation in T/V address forms), the formal (e.g. variation in discourse-pragmatic markers, pragmatic routines), the actional (e.g. variation in speech acts), the interactional (e.g. variation in sequential patterns), the topic (e.g. variation in content and topic management), the organizational (e.g. variation in turn-taking), the prosodic (e.g. variation in intonation, pitch) and a non-verbal level (e.g. gaze, posture) (Schneider and Barron 2008; Barron and Schneider 2009; Félix-Brasdefer 2015). Empirical analyses often combine these local levels of analysis and also investigate how particular macro-social factors interact with micro-social factors (e.g. degree of imposition), also taking genre and co-text into account. Thus, continuing with apologies, Deutschmann (2003), in his analysis of apologies in the BNC, finds the 'taking on responsibility' apology strategy to be employed to a higher extent by older speakers in informal texts and to be used to a lower extent by older speakers in formal texts. The opposite effect was recorded for younger speakers, who employed more 'taking on responsibility' strategies in formal contexts and less in informal contexts. Deutschmann (2003) explains this variation with reference to a different ranking of imposition by different age groups. Thus, here we see how macro-social pragmatic variation (here age variation) and micro-social pragmatic variation (formality level – imposition) interact.

Research explicitly conducted within variational pragmatics has increased significantly in the last number of years. In addition, there has been an increase in research on pragmatic variation within the study of pluricentric languages and, adhering to Labovian principles and frequently on the formal level, within variationist sociolinguists. The borders between these disciplines and variational pragmatics are frequently blurred and many studies positioned in one field might also have been situated within the other. Often, the positioning of a study in one discipline or another depends on research traditions, on the extent to which the social and cultural context of use is taken into account, on data types or methodologies traditionally associated with one discipline or another, on researcher aims beyond synchronic variation (e.g. for variationist sociolinguistics, the analysis of variation and change frequently go hand in hand), but also on the publication context, researcher identity issues and levels of familiarity with the differing fields. For instance, researchers traditionally engaged with pluricentric languages now work largely within a variational pragmatic framework (e.g. Norrby et al. 2015). Similarly, Dinkin (2018), a sociolinguist, has situated her work on responses to thanks in variational pragmatics using a sociolinguistic methodology. Irrespective of their preferred 'home', researchers interested in synchronic macro-social pragmatic variation, have much in common. One such shared issue is how comparability is ensured. This is the focus of the case study in Section 10.3.

Thus far this section has focused on synchronic intralingual micro-social and macro-social pragmatic variation for present-day language use. Studies of synchronic pragmatic variation in earlier periods focus on similar factors, including the relationship of language use and situational variation, genre, and social variation (e.g. social status, age). Studies of regional variation in earlier times, on the other hand, represent a research desideratum. (See Jucker and Landert 2017 for an overview.)

Studies of synchronic variation in language use in past times are carried out within historical pragmatics, most specifically within pragmaphilology ((a3) Figure 10.1). Pragmaphilologists study communicative language use in historical texts of a past period (Jucker 2010). Analyses may be focused on the works of one author (e.g. Chaucer) or on data spanning a short time period. Although pragmaphilology does not specifically focus on synchronic pragmatic variation, pragmatic variation is also analysed (e.g. Jucker and Landert 2017). Research in pragmaphilology is form-to-context oriented (cf. Figure 10.1) and combines both pragmalinguistic and sociopragmatic perspectives (Archer and Culpeper 2009). Thus, it examines utterances in their particular context of use and investigates how a particular linguistic form (pragmalinguistic side) is used in its particular context of use (sociopragmatic side). Analysts also investigate the contextual aspects of texts of a past time, noting the relationships between interactants and the situational context at hand (micro-social factors) as well as the social characteristics of the informants present (macro-social factors). In addition, pragmaphilology requires a detailed analysis of the background sociocultural context, given especially the fact that the analyst does not share the same sociocultural context as the interactants. Information is needed on sociocultural structures, such as the laws and ideologies prevailing in the context at hand, genre knowledge and knowledge of participant roles (Jacobs and Jucker 1995). In recent years, a field of research termed (historical) (socio)pragmatics has emerged with a particular interest in context (Culpeper 2009). Closely related to interactional sociolinguistics, (socio) pragmatics focuses on how pragmatic meaning is constructed in interaction. As a secondary consideration, it also relates social features to pragmatic features. From the perspective of the historical pragmatics tradition, however, which is embedded in the Continental European view of pragmatics, the term (socio)pragmatics may appear redundant given the focus of perspective pragmatics on the sociocultural context anyway (hence the brackets around socio). Hence, studies of pragmatic variation within pragmaphilology with a form-to-context focus may also be termed synchronic (socio)pragmatic studies ((a3) Figure 10.1; Włodarczyk 2016).

Synchronic variation of times past may finally be studied with a context-to-form or context-to-function focus ((a4) in Figure 10.1). Such research is carried out in sociophilology, an area belonging to the recently emerged field of (socio)pragmatics (Culpeper 2009; Archer 2017). Sociophilology – in contrast to pragmaphilology (which is synchronic) – may be either synchronic or diachronic in focus ((a4), (b3) in Figure 10.1) and takes context as the starting point, while at the same time realizing that language use may also shape context. Such studies examine how the cultural background, genre, social situation and co-text shape communicative forms and functions. The approach taken to analysing social context is more systematic than in pragmaphilology, as corpus linguistic methods are employed and the local conditions of language use coded. Archer and Culpeper (2009) is an example of sociophilology in action. Starting from a corpus of comedy plays and trial proceedings, the authors develop annotations for genre and for the social characteristics of the interactants in a systematic manner. They thus annotate for social features, such as gender, status, age and role (activity role, e.g. defendant), kinship role (e.g. wife), social role (e.g. friend), and drama role (e.g. villain). This annotation is then used to electronically retrieve data produced by speakers of particular social categories. Using keyword analysis, it is also possible to establish pragmatic norms specific to the particular local contexts examined. Findings show that male servants were addressed by both their masters and mistresses using imperative verbs and were not addressed using thou-forms. Taking the socio-historical context into account, this pattern is suggested to reflect their low status and to highlight their subordinate role vis-à-vis the protagonists in the play. In contrast, female servants were generally addressed by their mistresses using thou-forms, a convention suggested to reflect the more intimate relationship between mistresses and their maids in that socio-historical context. The intimate relationship also served as a means of communicating details of the plot and intimate details to the audience.

10.2.2 Intralingual Diachronic Pragmatic Variation

Historical pragmatics deals with pragmatic features of times past, including pragmatic features subject to variation and/ or change. In addition, it investigates intralingual diachronic pragmatic variation. As such, it tracks historical developments of communicative language use and aims to establish the general principles underlying these developments (Taavitsainen and Jucker 2010; Jucker and Landert 2017; Chapter 32).

Three types of diachronic pragmatic variation are identified. Diachronic form-to-function mappings ((b1) in Figure 10.1) and diachronic function-to-form mappings ((b2) in Figure 10.1) were identified first (Jucker 2010), while recently a further type, context-to-form/function mappings ((b3) in Figure 10.1), has been put forward (Archer and Culpeper 2009). The differences between these different types of diachronic studies lie in their starting point. Form-to-function mappings start out from forms and examine changes in their function over time. For instance, Culpeper and Demmen (2011) examine the use of 'can you' and 'could you' in eighteenth- and nineteenth-century texts. They conclude that today's conventional use of such ability-oriented enquiries to realize a request is a recent development. Due to the focus on individual forms, such as deixis, discourse markers or interjections, this strand of research is primarily pragmalinguistic in focus and has thus been termed (diachronic) pragmalinguistics. Within this area of research fall also studies which trace the grammaticalization of a particular form (Tagliamonte 2012; D'Arcy 2013).

Function-to-form mappings, also termed diachronic (socio)pragmatic studies within the historical (socio)pragmatic framework, take function as their starting point and examine changes in the forms realizing a particular communicative function in a particular context over time (Jucker 2010). Analyses of realizations of a particular speech act over time represent examples of such analyses. Finally, a third focus of diachronic pragmatics recently put forward are the context-to-form/ function mappings discussed above within the context of sociophilology (cf. synchronic pragmatic variation (earlier periods)). Such research has investigated how contextual factors, such as the genre or the activity type, participant goals, the language used and the period at hand, influenced the questioning function and its formal realizations in previous times (Archer 2017).

Despite these three distinct frameworks within diachronic pragmatics, empirical research in the area frequently straddles subcategories, with diachronic pragmalinguistic studies, for instance, also taking account of context despite their focus on the pragmalinguistic level of language. As Archer and Culpeper (2009: 287) point out, 'many papers, whilst they might emphasize one approach, also do something in relation to the other'. Part of the reason for this is the blurred division between pragmalinguistics and sociopragmatics (Włodarczyk 2016). In addition, overlaps emanate from the origins of historical pragmatics in the broad European perspective view of pragmatics (Taavitsainen 2015; Jucker and Landert 2017), given that this broad understanding of pragmatics itself deals with the social.

10.3 Critical Overview of Research through Case Study

This section examines a range of theoretical and methodological issues encountered by researchers in synchronic and diachronic investigations of intralingual pragmatic variation irrespective of their specific research tradition, using a recent project on pragmatic variation in offering according to region. The first study is a synchronic study set at the actional level within variational pragmatics. It focuses on regional pragmatic variation in the speech act of offers. Specifically, it contrasts offers in British English and Irish English using comparable corpus data, specifically, the face-to-face conversation text type of the British and Irish components of the International Corpus of English (ICE-GB and ICE-IRE) (Barron 2017a). The analysis of the Irish component is limited to data from the Republic of Ireland excluding Northern Ireland (ICE-IRE(R)). The investigation builds on a second study on offers in British English (specifically English English) and Irish English which used a production questionnaire (Barron 2005b).

The focus of both studies was on initiative offers, i.e. on offers constituting the first move in an offer sequence. In the corpus study, the initiative offers were retrieved via search strings of conventionalized offer realizations. The analysis centred on the offer strategies and forms in the corpora. Findings revealed a higher use of hospitable offers in ICE-IRE(R) relative to ICE-GB. The analysis also showed an effect of offer type on offer strategy realization. Specifically, hospitable offers in the ICE-GB and ICE-IRE(R) were found to be prototypically realized using the broad category of conventionalized preference strategies, that is, hearer-oriented strategies focused on the hearer's potential desire that the act offered is carried out (e.g. 'Do you want NP/ VP?', 'Would you like NP/ VP?', 'Need NP?'). These contrast with speaker-oriented executive strategies, focusing on the commissive nature of offers such as 'I want to VP', 'Shall I VP?', and with directive offers focusing on the directive nature of offers such as 'Close the door', e.g. 'Why don't you VP?'. The corpus analysis supported the production questionnaire findings that showed preference strategies to also be prototypical across both varieties of English in hospitable offers. In addition, both analyses revealed a variety-specific realization of one particular strategy, the 'question future act of speaker' strategy. In both British English and Irish English, this strategy was found to be realized by the conventionalized pattern 'AUX I + agentive verb?' However, pragmalinguistic variation was noted in that the modal verb employed across the varieties differed: while 'shall' is exclusively used in British English offers of this kind (e.g. 'Shall I pour out your water?'), 'will' is employed in its place in Irish English.

Research into pragmatic variation, whether synchronic or diachronic in nature, is empirical. In the following, theoretical and methodological considerations and difficulties discussed in the case study above serve to illustrate some of the challenges of empirical studies of pragmatic variation.

10.3.1 Pragmatic Variable – What Is Equivalence?

One of the first questions when beginning a study of pragmatic variation is the question of a *tertium comparationis* or 'common platform of reference' (Krzeszowski 1990: 15), which will allow different pragmatic choices to be compared. Sociolinguistic analyses of variation have traditionally adopted the Labovian concepts of variable and variant as a tool for investigating linguistic variation. Labovian sociolinguistics conceives of the variable as a linguistic feature which can be realized in two or more different ways (variants). The variants themselves represent semantic, or truth-conditional, equivalents, and thus 'say "the same thing" in several different ways' (Labov 1972: 271). They are employed by the same speaker in different situations (stylistic variation) or by different speakers in a particular situation. In the latter case, sociolinguists typically attempt to correlate variants of a particular variable with the independent variables of region, social class, gender, age and ethnicity by investigating uses and frequencies of each variant across each macro-social category (regional/ social variation). Analyses obey the principle of accountability, whereby all variants of a particular variable are isolated and all occurrences of a variant out of all possible contexts of occurrence calculated (Labov 1972; Tagliamonte 2012).

As Jucker and Taavitsainen (2012: 303) note, research on pragmatic variation within variational pragmatics and historical pragmatics 'does not usually invoke the notion of pragmatic variables at all'. However, recent years have seen numerous discussions concerning the applicability of the Labovian concepts to analyses of pragmatic variation (Pichler 2010, 2013; Schneider 2010, 2014; Terkourafi 2011, 2012; Tagliamonte 2012; Jucker and Taavitsainen 2012; Beeching and Woodfield 2015; Barron 2017b, in press a). The difficulty with applying the Labovian concept of the variable to pragmatic research is the criterion of semantic equivalence since pragmatic variants are not straightforwardly alternative ways of saying the same thing. Discourse markers, for instance, are by definition semantically bleached, having instead acquired pragmatic meaning. Thus, given that they are lacking in semantic meaning, two variant forms of a discourse marker cannot be claimed to share semantic equivalence (Pichler 2010, 2013). Similarly, different strategies in requesting or offering (e.g. the offers 'Shall I pour you some tea you?' vs 'Would you like some tea?') cannot be said to be semantically equivalent (Jucker and Taavitsainen 2012). Also, any form, even a simple 'Hello', can convey different meanings in different contexts ('Hello' as a greeting vs 'Hello!' as an admonishment).

Nonetheless, the concept of a pragmatic variable has a number of methodological advantages from which research on pragmatic variation would potentially benefit. Firstly, the use of the variable forces researchers to consider how contrastivity and comparability across data sets may be achieved in a more systematic manner than is currently the practice (Jucker and Taavitsainen 2012). Secondly, a focus on the concept of the variable and in particular on the principle of accountability makes researchers more aware that discourse-pragmatic features do not operate in a systemic vacuum. Rather, all variants of a variable are to be seen as related and analysed together rather than as frequently done, comparing frequencies of individual discourse-pragmatic features in isolation (Pichler 2013).

Given the difficulties surrounding the application of the variable/variant concept to pragmatic variation but also its potential benefits, a range of modifications of the concept have been put forward to allow its application to discourse-pragmatic variation. Functional equivalence between the variants of a pragmatic variable as a defining criterion to replace semantic equivalence is one suggestion (Lavandera 1978; Dines 1980; Schneider 2010; Jucker and Taavitsainen 2012; Cameron and Schwenter 2013; Barron 2017b). Terkourafi (2011) offers a procedural definition of the pragmatic variable drawing on the Relevance Theoretic concept of procedural meaning. This approach proposes that forms, such as 'hello', 'hi' and 'good day', have encoded instructions which guide H's inferences in a similar way. The process of inference remains stable (pragmatic variable) while the forms alternate (variants). Irrespective of the concept adopted, operationally, differing dynamics of communication across varieties means that total functional equivalence will rather be the exception, and partial equivalence the norm, as indeed long recognized in the neighbouring field of contrastive genre analysis (Eckkrammer 2002).

The concept of functional equivalence has been used to study speech acts (actional level) in both variational pragmatics and historical pragmatics (Schneider 2010). Firstly, the illocution under investigation may be seen as the variable and the speech act strategies realizing this illocution seen as variants of this variable, all representing maximum illocutionary equivalence. Similarly, the individual speech act strategy may be viewed as a variable and the linguistic realizations of this the variants realizing this functional variable. In the case study detailed above (Barron 2017a), the variable is defined via maximum illocutionary equivalence and the variants understood as the whole range of offer strategies available to realize an offer. In addition, on a sub-ordinate level, the individual offer strategies may be viewed as the variable and the variants as all realizations of this variable in the corpus. So, for instance, the variable 'question future act of speaker' strategy in Barron (2017a) was realized via the pattern 'AUX I + agentive verb?', with the auxiliary (AUX) taking the form of the modal verb 'will' or 'shall'. The analysis found the variant 'Shall I + agentive verb?' to be used exclusively in British English, and the variant 'Will I + agentive verb?' to be exclusive to Irish English.

The challenge confronting researchers is how to establish maximum illocutionary equivalence. Given the negotiability of pragmatic meaning, and thus the fact that there is no one-to-one relationship between a particular form and illocution, form cannot be taken as an indicator of illocutionary force (Terkourafi 2012; Barron 2017b). For instance, the conventionalized offer forms 'can I VP' ('can I lend you a hand?') and 'would you like to VP' ('would you like to have some tea?') may realize offers but these same forms are also used in request formulae ('can I ask you to help me?', 'would you like to help me?'). This means that illocutionary equivalence must be established within a particular context. In the rest of this section, I show with reference to the questionnaire study and the corpus study of offers that the challenges of defining the variable also depend on the data employed. In both studies, the challenge was to ensure that the forms searched for actually represented offers in both corpora. In both studies, it proved essential to define the variable on multiple levels.

Barron (2005b) studied offers in British English (specifically English English) and Irish English using a production questionnaire. Production questionnaires require informants to imagine themselves in a particular situation and complete the ensuing dialogue. A situational description common to all informants provides information concerning the micro-social and macro-social factors of relevance. The dialogue itself may already be initiated. In the classic production questionnaire (see Kasper 2000 for variations), this is followed by a gap which informants are to complete and the dialogue generally closes with a hearer response, signalling uptake (i.e. proof that the illocutionary force is recognized by H). Uptake thus generally aids in defining the variable. However, even in the absence of a hearer response, situations are designed to elicit a single speech act, for instance via implicit or explicit clues relating to the illocution or perlocution in the situational description. In Barron (2005b), a hearer response was not included in the production questionnaire items; instead an explicit direction to offer was included in the situational description (e.g. 'you offer to help'). This helped guarantee the equivalence of the illocution, as indeed also did the description of propositional content (information on that which was to be offered) in each situation. Additionally, position helped define the variable with only initiative offers included in the analysis. In sum, the propositional content related to the commissive-directive nature of offers, the position of the speech act, and explicit metapragmatic information on function (direction to offer) in the situational description ensured the establishment of illocutionary equivalence and also comparability across varieties and cultures.

When analysing naturally occurring data, as in corpus research, a number of criteria need to be employed in defining the variable. Here, however, attaining equivalence is more difficult to achieve than with controlled data. In the corpus analysis in Barron (2017a), form served as a starting point in accessing utterances functioning as offers. However, as already mentioned, form cannot be taken as an indicator of illocutionary force given the negotiability of pragmatic meaning. Thus, there was a need to differentiate offers from neighbouring speech acts, such as invitations, promises and requests among the hits returned. From the perspective of illocutionary point, offers are commissive-directives: they commit the speaker (S) to a future action A which may be implicitly or explicitly mentioned and is assumed to be beneficial to the hearer (H) (Copestake and Terkourafi 2010). In the present context, hits were examined to ascertain which forms potentially realized an offer according to this description.

In addition to illocutionary point, other supplementary criteria included position, hearer uptake, and offer type (Sidnell 2009; Copestake and Terkourafi 2010; Barron 2017a; Terkourafi 2012). As regards position, only initiative offers were considered, excluding, for instance, pre-offers and reoffers. The criterion of hearer uptake takes H's response as proof that the illocutionary force is recognized by H (Terkourafi 2002). In example (1), the uptake 'yeah yeah please' shows that A's utterance has been interpreted as an offer.

(1)   A> <#> Granny do you want tea
       C> <#> Yeah yeah please
       D> <#> I'll have a cup too thanks (ICE-IRE(R), s1a-067)

Given the conditional nature of offers, uptake, whether verbal or non-verbal (evidenced in the verbal data), was taken as an obligatory criterion in the study at hand (Sidnell 2009; but see Barron 2017b for discussion of the obligatory status). The analysis thus captured the effect of a particular utterance on the dialogue rather than focusing exclusively on a speaker's intention. This combination of criteria was chosen to facilitate the definition of the pragmatic variable of offering so as to allow offers to be contrasted across varieties. The initial criteria employed included commissive-directive illocutionary point, position and uptake. However, an initial round of analysis showed it was necessary to redefine the pragmatic variable adding a further criterion of topic. The initial analysis revealed a range of statistically significant differences between the offers used in ICE-GB and ICE-IRE(R), pointing to a higher use of preference strategies ('Would you like X?') in ICE-IRE(R) and a higher use of execution strategies ('Shall I get X?') in ICE-GB. However, an in-depth qualitative analysis of offer topic revealed these differences to relate to offer type. The analysis showed a higher frequency of hospitable offers in ICE-IRE(R) relative to ICE-GB. These hospitable offers – as also hospitable offers in ICE-GB – were realized preferentially using preference strategies. Indeed, hospitable offers in ICE-GB and ICE-IRE(R) were prototypically realized using conventionalized preference strategies. Thus, the analysis showed that the criterion of offer type was also required to guarantee comparability, and to avoid making misleading claims. To summarize, Barron (2017a) defined the pragmatic variable on the actional level using multiple criteria, namely illocutionary point, position, uptake and offer type. Redefinition of the variable was necessary during the analytical process as it was found that cross-varietal comparisons of offers that did not focus on similar offer topics did not compare like with like. This trend in defining pragmatic variables using multiple criteria is evident in other recent studies. In a recent monograph on present-day socioeconomic variation in offers, thanks responses and address terms in Los Angeles, Staley (2018) also characterizes her pragmatic variables on multiple levels, including sequential location in communicative activity (e.g. pre-offer, offer, re-offer), function as commissive-directives and offer type. (See also Barron 2019 on responses to thanks.)

10.3.2 Methodologies: Data Type

The case study described above employed corpus data, focusing in particular on spoken data. In contrast, historical pragmatics focuses frequently on written data, often out of necessity. Originally, this written data was viewed as poor data given that pragmatics traditionally favoured naturally occurring spoken data. Efforts were made to access data which would approximate authentic language use as closely as possible (cf. Taavitsainen and Jucker 2010). Currently, however, there is an appreciation that written texts themselves are communicative acts. Analysing written texts as genres is one current approach (Taavitsainen 2016; Taavitsainen and Jucker 2010). Włodarczyk (2017) is a recent (socio)pragmatic study of petitions investigating the influence of education level on how contact is initiated in this genre.

Spoken analyses in variational pragmatics take genre into account as a contextual influence. Additionally, a small number of top-down studies of spoken synchronic pragmatic variation take genre as an analytical starting point (e.g. Félix-Brasdefer 2015 on service encounters; Staley 2018 on restaurant service encounters; see also Schneider 2020). Genre-based studies of pragmatic variation in written discourse are limited (cf. Barron 2012). In her study of the written genre of death announcements in Scotland, Wales and the Republic of Ireland, Burmeister (2013) focused on region as a macro-social variable showing that genre conventions do vary across region. Yajun and Chenggang (2006) is an interesting article in this regard. They address the question of how contrastive genre analysis can be successfully combined with the study of World Englishes (regional variation in the present context), given that in the study of World Englishes 'the involvement of discoursal and rhetorical analyses are exceptions rather than regular practice'. The question whether genre conventions differ across regional and social parameters is also pertinent for variational pragmatics, not only in the area of regional variation but also in relation to gender, age, socioeconomic and ethnic variation.

Jucker and Taavitsainen (2012) suggest that genres may also function as pragmatic variables. Włodarczyk (2017), in her analysis of the genre of petitions, focused on function and position within the genre. Specifically, she examined the initiation type employed and correlated these findings with educational level. Given that Włodarczyk's (2017) texts were all written in the same socio-historical context and in response to the same government call for applications, comparability of genre is given. However, in potential analyses of genre across time or region, researchers will need to first establish genre equivalence. Not only do genre purposes differ across cultures (e.g. Eckkrammer 2002 on package inserts for medical products and obituaries across cultures), but genre labels do not necessarily reflect modern communicative purposes (e.g. job announcement vs job advertisement), and even expert members may not recognize the communicative purpose of a genre (Askehave and Swales 2001; Swales 2004). In light of such difficulties, particular effort needs to be made in the process of comparative research to establishing communicative purpose and degrees of equivalence. An openness to 'repurposing' genres after some analysis (similar to the redefining of the variable discussed above) (Askehave and Swales 2001) is vital to ensure maximum equivalence across varieties (Barron 2012).

10.3.3 Interaction of Diachronic and Synchronic Perspectives

Since its inception, there has been a strong regional focus in variational pragmatics, while in historical pragmatic research, the study of intralingual regional variation represents a research desideratum. An increase in interdisciplinary work would trigger several developments in the field. The case study of offers across two varieties of English and particularly the analysis of the variable 'question future act of speaker' strategy illustrates potential interactions between present-day synchronic and diachronic studies. As mentioned above, the analysis of this variable and its variants shed light on the use of 'will' rather than 'shall' in 'AUX I + agentive verb?' offer patterns in Irish English. Interestingly, historical linguistic work by McCafferty and Amador Moreno (2014) has revealed a major shift from 'I shall' to 'I will' in Irish English (and in other varieties of English) between the late eighteenth and late nineteenth centuries due, they propose, to an increase in literary skills among the less educated. At the same time, McCafferty and Amador Moreno (2014) find that 'shall' persisted in interrogative constructions ('shall I?') in their diachronic analysis of Irish English correspondence from 1760 to 1890, an intriguing pattern 'given that present-day Irish English generally does not use 'shall' in this clause type: the shift from 'shall' to 'will' has been total in this context, and it would be interesting to try to trace this change'. Combining present-day synchronic pragmatics with historical pragmatics, an interesting question might be when 'will I' began to be used in the 'AUX I + agentive verb?' pattern in the speech act of offers. Further research might investigate the diachronic development of 'will' and 'shall' in offers in British English but also across the varieties of English. This is just one particular example of how present-day and historical studies might work hand in hand.

10.4 Summary and Future Directions

Sociolinguists studying linguistic variation have not traditionally paid much attention to pragmatic units. Similarly, pragmaticists have not traditionally analysed correlations of socio-demographic variables with pragmatic units of language use systematically. Rather, focus in pragmatics has been on micro-social variation at the situational level, and in particular on variation due to such factors as social dominance, social distance and degree of imposition. The systematic analysis of synchronic present-day pragmatic variation according to regional and social factors has recently gained momentum with the emergence of variational pragmatics, a field of research which can be traced back to Schneider and Barron (2008) and Barron and Schneider (2009).

In addition, the historical dimension of pragmatic variation remained long neglected within historical linguistics. Interest in historical pragmatic variation can be traced back to Jucker (1995), an edited volume on historical pragmatics. The influence of macro-social variables on conventions of language use in past times and across time is also a relatively new undertaking in historical pragmatics. As Jucker and Taavitsainen (2012: 303) point out, 'this lack of interaction between studies on linguistic variation and pragmatics is even more pronounced in historical linguistics [than in pragmatics]'.

The fields of both historical pragmatics and variational pragmatics have expanded considerably since their inception and research in both is vibrant. Recent years have also seen the emergence of historical (socio)pragmatics, a field focused on the social side of language use in historical contexts. Pragmatic variation is also the focus of research in related fields, such as in studies on pluricentric languages, in variationist sociolinguistics and indeed within the broader field of contrastive pragmatics. Researchers in variational pragmatics and in historical pragmatics have much in common despite a focus on different time-frames and despite different methodological challenges in accessing data, historical linguistics being confined to texts of previous times. These common theoretical and methodological issues have been the focus of the present chapter. They include a focus on pragmatic variation according to micro-social and macro-social factors. In addition, corpus data is employed in both contexts, presenting researchers with the challenge of contextualizing decontextualized data. Similarly, the suitability of the concept of the pragmatic variable from variationist sociolinguistics for pragmatic research on variation has been debated in both variational pragmatics and in historical pragmatics, with both fields enjoying the synergies of these commonalities.

The present chapter has also put forward some areas ripe for further development and cross-fertilization of approaches. Firstly, the detailed discussion of the pragmatic variable made clear that the application and adaptation of this concept to the study of pragmatic variation is challenging and continuously developing. Recent developments on the formal and functional levels suggest defining the variable using multiple criteria. These discussions are welcomed given that, as Jucker and Taavitsainen (2012: 303–4) note, they force 'more rigorous definitions of the elements under investigation and their variants, and an even clearer understanding of how they correlate with the socio-demographic features of the users of the language'. For sociolinguists, Jucker and Taavitsainen (2012) see these discussions as leading to a greater understanding and interest in pragmatic variables, long neglected in sociolinguistic research. In the present context, we illustrated the challenge of defining the pragmatic variable on the actional level in particular and showed that in both the production questionnaire and corpus data investigated, a range of criteria, such as illocutionary point, position, uptake (or explicit naming of the illocution) and also offer type were necessary concepts. Furthermore, the case study presented above illustrated how it may be necessary to further define a pragmatic variable in the course of the analytical process.

A second possible development concerns the data used in analyses of pragmatic variation. To date, historical pragmatics focuses primarily on written data as communicative units. In contrast, variational pragmatics has to date focused almost exclusively on spoken language use and only taken genre as a starting point to a limited extent. It was suggested that further research in variational pragmatics might take written genre as an additional pragmatic variable. Such a development would involve extending the variational pragmatic framework which is currently oriented towards spoken data. The analysis of genre across varieties necessarily also poses the same challenge of achieving genre equivalence as discussed above for illocutionary equivalence. Cross-varietal genre analyses necessitate equivalence of communicative function, given that communicative function enjoys a privileged role, determining genre structure and the choice of linguistic features. Similar to the variable revision needed in the offer case study above, it may be necessary to 'repurpose' the communicative purpose of a particular genre after some analysis.

Thirdly, I have argued for further integration of present day with past perspectives on the level of the individual study. Much of current scholarship in variational pragmatics pays little heed to historical research. However, historical research can throw light on the existence of, or preferences for, pragmatic variants which can lead to additional insights on pragmatic variation, perhaps holding explanatory potential. Interdisciplinary research between variational pragmaticists and historical pragmaticists from both synchronic and diachronic perspectives therefore represents a research desideratum. An increase in interdisciplinary work would trigger several developments in both fields. We look forward to continued cross-fertilization between the fields of historical pragmatics and variational pragmatics.

References

Archer, D. (2017). Context and historical (socio)pragmatics twenty years on. *Journal of Historical Pragmatics*, 18(2), 315–36.
Archer, D. and Culpeper, J. (2009). Identifying key sociophilological usage in plays and trial proceedings (1640–1760): An empirical approach via corpus annotation. *Journal of Historical Pragmatics*, 10(2), 286–309.
Askehave, I. and Swales, J. M. (2001). Genre identification and communicative purpose: A problem and a possible solution. *Applied Linguistics*, 22(2), 195–212.
Barron, A. (2005a). Variational pragmatics in the foreign language classroom. *System*, 33(3), 519–36.
Barron, A. (2005b). Offering in Ireland and England. In A. Barron and K. P. Schneider, eds., *The Pragmatics of Irish English*. Berlin: Mouton de Gruyter, pp. 141–77.
Barron, A. (2012). *Public Information Messages: A Contrastive Genre Analysis of State-citizen Communication*. Amsterdam: John Benjamins.
Barron, A. (2014). Variational pragmatics. In C. A. Chapelle, ed., *The Encyclopedia of Applied Linguistics (EAL): Electronic Version*. Oxford: Wiley-Blackwell, pp. 1–7.
Barron, A. (2015). Explorations in regional variation: A variational pragmatic perspective. *Multilingua*, 34(4), 449–59.
Barron, A. (2017a). The speech act of 'offers' in Irish English. *World Englishes*, 36(2), 224–38.
Barron, A. (2017b). Variational pragmatics. In A. Barron, Y. Gu and G. Steen, eds., *The Routledge Handbook of Pragmatics*. Abingdon, UK: Routledge, pp. 91–104.
Barron, A. (in press a). Contrastivity and the pragmatic variables. Pragmatic variation across pluricentric varieties. Sociolinguistica.
Barron, A. (in press b). 'Sorry Miss, I completely forgot about it': Apologies and vocatives in Ireland and England. In S. Lucek and C. P. Amador Moreno, eds., *Expanding the Landscapes of Irish English: Research in Honour of Jeffrey Kallen*. Abingdon, UK: Routledge
Barron, A. and Schneider, K. P. (2009). Variational pragmatics: Studying the impact of social factors on language use in interaction. *Intercultural Pragmatics*, 6(4), 425–42.
Beeching, K. and Woodfield, H. (2015). Introduction. In K. Beeching and H. Woodfield, eds., *Researching Sociopragmatic Variability: Perspectives from*

Variational, Interlanguage and Contrastive Pragmatics. London: Palgrave Macmillan, pp. 1–16.
Blum-Kulka, S., House, J. and Kasper, G. (eds.). (1989). *Cross-Cultural Pragmatics: Requests and Apologies*. Norwood, NJ: Ablex.
British National Corpus. www.english-corpora.org/bnc/.
Brown, P. and Levinson, S. C. (1978). Universals in language usage: Politeness phenomena. In E. N. Goody, ed., *Questions and Politeness: Strategies in Social Interaction*. Cambridge: Cambridge University Press, pp. 56–289.
Brown, P. and Levinson, S. C. (1987). *Politeness: Some Universals in Language Usage*. Cambridge: Cambridge University Press.
Burmeister, M. (2013). Variability in death notices from Scotland, Wales and the Republic of Ireland: A comparative perspective. In M. Bieswanger and A. Koll-Stobbe, eds., *New Approaches to the Study of Variability*. Frankfurt am Main, Germany: Peter Lang, pp. 65–88.
Cameron, R. and Schwenter, S. (2013). Pragmatics and variationist sociolinguistics. In R. Bayley, R. Cameron and C. Lucas, eds., *The Oxford Handbook of Sociolinguistics*. Oxford: Oxford University Press, pp. 464–83.
Cheshire, J. (2007). Discourse variation, grammaticalisation and stuff like that. *Journal of Sociolinguistics*, 11(2), 155–93.
Copestake, A. and Terkourafi, M. (2010). Conventionalized speech act formulae: From corpus findings to formalization. In P. Kühnlein, A. Benz and C. L. Sidner, eds., *Constraints in Discourse 2*. Amsterdam: John Benjamins, pp. 125–40.
Culpeper, J. (2009). Historical sociopragmatics: An introduction. *Journal of Historical Pragmatics*, 10(2), 179–86.
Culpeper, J. and Demmen, J. (2011). Nineteenth-century English politeness: Negative politeness, conventional indirect requests and the rise of the individual self. *Journal of Historical Pragmatics*, 12(1–2), 49–81.
De Saint-Georges, I. (2013). Context in the analysis of discourse and interaction. In C. A. Chapelle, ed., *The Encyclopedia of Applied Linguistics*. New York: Wiley Blackwell, pp. 920–26.
D'Arcy, A. (2013). Variation and change. In R. Bayley, R. Cameron and C. Lucas, eds., *The Oxford Handbook of Sociolinguistics*. Oxford: Oxford University Press, pp. 484–502.
Deutschmann, M. (2003). *Apologising in British English*. Skrifter från moderna språk 10. Umeå University.
Dines, E. (1980). Variation in discourse – 'and stuff like that'. *Language in Society*, 9(1), 13–31.
Dinkin, A. J. (2018). It's no problem to be polite: Apparent-time change in responses to thanks. *Journal of Sociolinguistics*, 22(2), 190–215.
Eckkrammer, E. M. (2002). Textsorten im interlingualen und -medialen Vergleich: Ausschnitte und Ausblicke. In M. Drescher, ed., *Textsorten im romanischen Sprachvergleich*. Tübingen: Stauffenburg, pp. 15–39.

Félix-Brasdefer, J. C. (2015). *The Language of Service Encounters: A Pragmatic-Discursive Approach*. Cambridge: Cambridge University Press.

Fetzer, A. (2010). Contexts in context: Micro meets macro. In S.-K. Tanskanen, M.-L. Helasvuo, M. Johansson and M. Raitaniemi, eds., *Discourses in Interaction*. Amsterdam: John Benjamins, pp. 13–31.

Goodwin, M. H. and Goodwin, C. (1987). Children's arguing. In S. Philips, S. Steele and C. Tanz, eds., *Language, Gender, and Sex in Comparative Perspective*. Cambridge: Cambridge University Press, pp. 200–248.

Hamilton, E. L. (2018). Greetings! The high five and the fist bump are twentieth century, but the first handshake dates to fifth century B.C. Greece, as way to prove you were weapon free. www.thevintagenews.com/2018/04/12/hand shake/.

Harting, A. (2005). Pragmatic idioms in Australian English – A survey of gender and age-related usage of greetings, leave-takings, thanks, and apologies. *Studies in Language and Literature 松山大学*, 24(2), 53–79.

Holmes, J. (1995). *Women, Men and Politeness*. London: Longman.

International Corpus of English. http://ice-corpora.net/ice/.

Jacobs, A. and Jucker, A. H. (1995). The historical perspective in pragmatics. In A. H. Jucker, ed., *Historical Pragmatics: Pragmatic Developments in the History of English*. Amsterdam: John Benjamins, pp. 3–33.

Jucker, A. H. (ed.). (1995). *Historical Pragmatics: Pragmatic Developments in the History of English*. Amsterdam: John Benjamins.

Jucker, A. H. (2010). Historical pragmatics. In M. Fried, J. Östman and J. Verschueren, eds., *Variation and Change: Pragmatic Perspectives*. Amsterdam: John Benjamins, pp. 110–22.

Jucker, A. H. (2011). Greetings and farewells in Chaucer's *Canterbury Tales*. In P. Pahta and A. H. Jucker, eds., *Communicating Early English Manuscripts*. Cambridge: Cambridge University Press, pp. 229–40.

Jucker, A. H. (2017). Speech acts and speech act sequences: Greetings and farewells in the history of American English. *Studia Neophilologica*, 89(S1), 39–58.

Jucker, A. H. and Landert, D. (2017). Variation and change: Historical pragmatics. In A. Barron, Y. Gu and G. Steen, eds., *The Routledge Handbook of Pragmatics*. Abingdon, UK: Routledge, pp. 79–90.

Jucker, A. H. and Taavitsainen, I. (2012). Pragmatic variables. In J. M. Hernández-Campoy and J. C. Conde-Silvestre, eds., *The Handbook of Historical Sociolinguistics*. Oxford: Wiley-Blackwell, pp. 293–306.

Kasper, G. (2000). Data collection in pragmatics research. In H. Spencer-Oatey, ed., *Culturally Speaking: Managing Rapport through Talk across Cultures*. London: Continuum, pp. 317–41.

Krzeszowski, T. P. (1990). *Contrasting Languages: The Scope of Contrastive Linguistics*. Berlin: Mouton de Gruyter.

Labov, W. (1972). *Sociolinguistic Patterns*. Oxford: Blackwell.

Lavandera, B. R. (1978). Where does the sociolinguistic variable stop? *Language in Society*, 7(2), 171–82.

Márquez Reiter, R. (2003). Pragmatic variation in Spanish: External request modifications in Uruguayan and Peninsular Spanish. In L. Nuñez-Cedeño, L. López and R. Cameron, eds., *A Romance Perspective on Language Knowledge and Use*. Philadelphia: John Benjamins, pp. 166–80.

McCafferty, K. and Amador Moreno, C. P. (2014). '[The Irish] find much difficulty in these auxiliaries …putting will for shall with the first person': The decline of first-person shall in Ireland, 1760–1890. *English Language and Linguistics*, 18(3), 407–29.

Mela, S. and Whitworth, D. E. (2014). The fist bump: A more hygienic alternative to the handshake. *American Journal of Infection Control*, 42(8), 916–17.

Norrby, C., Wide, C., Lindström, J. and Nilsson, J. (2015). Interpersonal relationships in medical consultations: Comparing Sweden Swedish and Finland Swedish address practices. *Journal of Pragmatics*, 84, 121–38.

Ogiermann, E. (2009). *On Apologising in Negative and Positive Politeness Cultures*. Amsterdem: John Benjamins.

Pichler, H. (2010). Methods in discourse variation analysis: Reflections on the way forward. *Journal of Sociolinguistics*, 14(5), 581–608.

Pichler, H. (2013). *The Structure of Discourse-Pragmatic Variation*. Amsterdam: John Benjamins.

Regan, A. (2008). Current conversation patterns in the Republic of Ireland. *Journal for EuroLinguistix*, 5, 101–8.

Schneider, K. P. (2010). Variational pragmatics. In M. Fried, J. Östman and J. Verschueren, eds., *Variation and Change: Pragmatic Perspectives*. Amsterdam: John Benjamins, pp. 239–67.

Schneider, K. P. (2014). Comparability and sameness in variational pragmatics. In S. Mergenthal and R. M. Nischik, eds., *Anglistentag 2013 Konstanz: Proceedings*. Trier: Wissenschaftlicher Verlag Trier, pp. 361–72.

Schneider, K. P. (2017). Pragmatic competence and pragmatic variation. In R. Giora and M. Haugh, eds., *Doing Pragmatics Interculturally: Cognitive, Philosophical, and Sociopragmatic Perspectives*. Berlin: Mouton de Gruyter, pp. 315–33.

Schneider, K. P. (2020). Rethinking pragmatic variation: The case of service encounters from a modified variational pragmatics perspective. In J. C. Félix-Brasdefer and M. E. Placencia, eds., *Pragmatic Variation in Service Encounter Interactions across the Spanish-Speaking World*. London: Routledge, pp. 251–64.

Schneider, K. P. and Barron, A. (2008). Where pragmatics and dialectology meet: Introducing variational pragmatics. In K. P. Schneider and A. Barron, eds., *Variational Pragmatics: A Focus on Regional Varieties in Pluricentric Languages*. Amsterdam: John Benjamins, pp. 1–32.

Schneider, K. P. and Barron, A. (eds.). (2008). *Variational Pragmatics: A Focus on Regional Varieties in Pluricentric Languages*. Amsterdam: John Benjamins.

Sidnell, J. (2009). Sequences. In S. D'Hondt, J. Östman and J. Verschueren, eds., *The Pragmatics of Interaction*. Amsterdam: John Benjamins, pp. 215–39.

Staley, L. (2018). *Socioeconomic Pragmatic Variation: Speech Acts and Address Forms in Context.* Amsterdam: John Benjamins.

Swales, J. M. (2004). *Research Genres: Exploration and Applications.* Cambridge: Cambridge University Press.

Taavitsainen, I. (2015). Historical pragmatics. In D. Biber and R. Reppen, eds., *The Cambridge Handbook of English Corpus Linguistics.* Cambridge: Cambridge University Press, pp. 252–68.

Taavitsainen, I. (2016). Genre dynamics in the history of English. In M. Kytö and P. Pahta, eds., *The Cambridge Handbook of English Historical Linguistics.* Cambridge: Cambridge University Press, pp. 271–85.

Taavitsainen, I. and Jucker, A. H. (2010). Trends and developments in historical pragmatics. In A. H. Jucker and I. Taavitsainen, eds., *Historical Pragmatics.* Berlin: Mouton de Gruyter, pp. 3–30.

Taavitsainen, I. and Jucker, A. H. (2015). Twenty years of historical pragmatics: Origins, developments and changing thought styles. *Journal of Historical Pragmatics, 16*(1), 1–24.

Tagliamonte, S. A. (2012). *Variationist Sociolinguistics: Change, Observation, Interpretation.* Malden, MA: Wiley-Blackwell.

Terkourafi, M. (2002). Politeness and formulaicity: Evidence from Cypriot Greek. *Journal of Greek Linguistics, 3*(1), 179–201.

Terkourafi, M. (2011). The pragmatic variable: Toward a procedural interpretation. *Language in Society, 40,* 343–72.

Terkourafi, M. (2012). Between pragmatics and sociolinguistics: Where does pragmatic variation fit in? In J. C. Félix-Brasdefer and K. Dale, eds., *Pragmatic Variation in First and Second Language Contexts: Methodological Issues.* Amsterdam: John Benjamins, pp. 295–318.

Verschueren, J. (1999). *Understanding Pragmatics.* London: Arnold.

Verschueren, J. (2008). Context and structure in a theory of pragmatics. *Studies in Pragmatics, 10,* 13–23.

Wierzbicka, A. (1985). Different cultures, different languages, different speech acts: Polish vs. English. *Journal of Pragmatics, 9*(2/3), 145–78.

Włodarczyk, M. (2016). *Genre and Literacies: Historical (Socio)Pragmatics of the 1820 Settler Petition.* Poznań: Adam Mickiewicz University Press.

Włodarczyk, M. (2017). Initiating contact in institutional correspondence: Historical (socio)pragmatics of late modern English literacies. *Journal of Historical Pragmatics, 18*(29), 271–94.

Yajun, J. and Chenggang, Z. (2006). World Englishes and contrastive rhetoric. *English Today, 2*(2), 11–22.

11
Activity Types and Genres

Dawn Archer, Piotr Jagodziński and Rebecca Jagodziński

11.1 Introduction

The concepts of *activity type* and, to a lesser extent, *genre* have proven useful for pragmaticians when seeking both to explain the extent to which context determines language use and the way in which interactants categorize their experiences, thereby developing expectations about their communicative behaviour within a given context (Tannen 1993; Mayes 2003). As will become evident, both concepts – but especially *genre* – are used quite extensively in other disciplines too (see Section 11.2.2). Sections 11.2–11.2.4 thus explore

- Their different conceptual origins, and how they have been drawn upon within pragmatics (and related fields) since their introduction.
- Their similarities and differences with respect to one another.
- Their similarities and differences with respect to other concepts drawn upon by pragmaticians, for example, *footing*, *frames* (or *framing*), *speech events*, *speech activities*, *schemas*, *scripts*, and *prototypes* (Gumperz 1982: 166–7; Goffman 1981: 128; Tannen 1993: 3; Tannen and Wallat 1993: 76; Mayes 2003: 30–34).

Sections 11.3–11.3.2 then go on to describe a case study relating to the interview *activity type* (drawing upon Culpeper and McIntyre 2010), and a case study relating to the *genre* of biographical data statements (drawing upon Tardy and Swales 2014), following which promising areas for future research are identified (in Section 11.4).

11.2 Key Concepts and Theories

In the following sections, we first provide a working definition of the concepts of *activity type* and *genre*, outline their respective origins, and explore how they are drawn upon in the field of pragmatics as well as other (related) disciplines (see Sections 11.2.1 and 11.2.2). We then assess their similarities and differences both with respect to each other (see Section 11.2.3) and also related concepts (see Section 11.2.4).

11.2.1 The Concept of Activity Type, Its Origins and Its Use in Pragmatics

Stephen Levinson is usually credited with introducing the concept of *activity type* into pragmatics.[1] Inspired by Wittgenstein (1958), Levinson ([1979] 1992) sought to highlight that understanding the meaning of utterances requires us to also have an understanding of the activity within which the utterances occur. This assumes such activities are 'goal defined' as well as culturally recognizable, such that they place 'constraints on participants', especially in respect to what kinds of contributions are allowable (Levinson 1992: 69). They are also 'bounded' in time in some way.[2] It should be noted from the outset, however, that talk was not an essential criterion of every *activity type*, as far as Levinson was concerned. He noted additional ways in which distinct *activity types* might differ too. They might involve a single participant, such as a homework task, or several participants, such as a dinner party. They might be heavily scripted, such as a Roman Mass, or largely unscripted, such as a chance meeting on the street. They might be formal, such as a city council meeting, or informal, such as small talk between friends.

Some of the extant pragmatics studies that explore *activity types* also develop their understanding of the concept itself. Clark (1996) provides one such example. He argued that *activity types* can exhibit differences with respect to their cooperative traits and governance traits (i.e. how cooperative or egalitarian particular *activity types* are). He explains how they can 'range from cooperative activities like buying groceries to adversarial or competitive activities like playing tennis or cross-examining witnesses in court' (Clark 1996: 31), for example. He further notes how a participant (A) might play a dominant role within a given activity type, whereby they do something 'to or for B', as in the case of lecturing, or how participants might have roughly equal roles, akin to A and B doing something together, as in the case of chess playing (Clark 1996: 31). In a more recent study, Culpeper and McIntyre (2010) have argued that – and go on to demonstrate how – *activity types* (such as job interviews) can be both context-dependent and context-creating. They thus operationalize what Levinson ([1979] 1992) had only alluded to with respect to the 'inside-out' view of the context being

---

[1] But note also the similarity with some of Allwood's (1976) early work exploring *Linguistic Communication as Action and Cooperation*.

[2] One of the paradigm examples of an activity type, offered by Levinson (1979: 368), is that of teaching. Given the mention of a "task in a workshop" as another paradigm example, amongst a list (job interview, jural interrogation, football game, dinner party) all of which are also bounded in time, we are assuming that Levinson had a bounded "episode" of teaching in mind, when he mentions the latter (cf. teaching as an ongoing process, and also Gumperz 1982).

shaped by participants as well as the more frequently cited 'outside-in' view of context determining language use, when it comes to *activity types*. Culpeper and McIntyre also emphasize another point to which Levinson alluded: how the *activity type* concept constitutes an indispensable bridge or the meso-level between the micro and the macro level of analysis, thereby 'rescuing' Grice's (1975) Cooperative Principle.[3] We describe Culpeper and McIntyre's study in more detail in Section 11.3.1 (see also Section 11.2.3).

11.2.2 The Concept of Genre, Its Origins and Its Use in Pragmatics

According to Martin (1985: 248), a genre 'is how things get done, when language' or another medium 'is used to accomplish them'. Martin (1984: 24) also delineates the concept based on its characteristics, likening *genre* to 'a staged, goal-oriented, purposeful activity' or practice involving 'members of [the specified] culture'. The similarities to the concept of *activity type* are immediately apparent, and will be discussed in more detail in Section 11.2.3. Suffice it to say, both concepts are broadly concerned with the way in which we categorize our experiences, and develop thereby expectations about communicative behaviour within a given context. There are important differences too, occasioned in part by their different origins: contra *activity type*, the origins of *genre* are not associated with one scholar, for example. This may help to explain (1) why it can be difficult to delineate *genre* as succinctly as we might *activity type* (see Section 11.2.1) and (2) why genre tends to be described in terms of other concepts in consequence. Some of these concepts (*frame, prototype, style*) are noted below. These and other terms (*domains, episodes, schemata, scripts, speech events*) are also discussed in some detail in Sections 11.2.3 and especially 11.2.4.

Genre has a particularly long history when it comes to literary studies, as it can trace its roots back to ancient Greek literature, where it was used to distinguish poetry, prose and performance. Today, the concept is drawn upon by not only literary theorists (Bawarshi and Reiff 2010) but also art historians (see e.g. Belton 1996), musical theorists (see e.g. van der Merwe 1989) and linguists. Within linguistics, it has been particularly associated with the "Sydney School" of Systemic Functional Grammar (SFG) since the 1980s, thanks to researchers such as J. R. Martin, Frances Christie, Bill Cope, Mary Kalantzis, Gunther Kress and Brain Paltridge. Paltridge (1997) has linked SFG with prototype theory, for example, to allow for 'text membership within genres' to be defined 'on the basis of how closely their structural and linguistic patterns relate to' a given *genre's* prototype (Bawarshi and Reiff 2010: 39). As Barwarshi and Reiff explain, 'the relation

---

[3] See also Mooney's (2004: 903) argument for the recontextualization of Grice's Cooperative Principle with Levinson's *activity type*, in the belief that "it contextualizes the maxims and allows a clearer and more relevant construal of contributions".

between texts and genres is not simply based on features internal to both', but on what, from Paltridge's (1997: 62) perspective, equate to learned, conceptual relations between 'memory, context and frames'. Prototypes, in this case, are thus understood to provide a means of selecting, organizing and interpreting – with the aim of differentiating between – *genres* (see e.g. Lee 2001). Several historical linguists and corpus linguists have also sought to provide a means of categorizing *genres*, most notably Hans-Jürgen Diller and Douglas Biber. In his earlier work, for example, Biber (1988) was interested in the extent of linguistic variation within *genres*, which he measured along different dimensions: 'narrative versus non-narrative', 'non-impersonal versus impersonal style', and 'situation dependent versus elaborated reference'. The methods of both Biber and Paltridge have since been picked up by (and thus influenced) researchers interested in the study of English for Specific Purposes (ESP). As such, ESP researchers (many of whom are associated with the "North American" approach to genre studies) can also trace the use of genre analysis within their linguistic (sub)field to the 1980s. Particularly influential, here, is the work of John Swales (1990). As Tardy and Swales (2014: 166) note,

> genres have a communicative purpose, which may in fact serve as the key characteristic for placing discourses into generic categories. In addition *genres are socially situated.* As a rhetorical category of discourse, genre cannot be distinct from social context. Genres arise within social contexts, [and] are carried out for social purposes ranging from the relatively simple (e.g., creating a list of items to buy at a grocery store) to the more complex (e.g., outlining the terms of a business transaction). By virtue of their social situatedness, genres are necessarily dynamic, always changing. (Tardy & Swales 2014: 166, original emphasis)

The above, and Tardy and Swales' (2014: 167) observation that *'genres both shape and are shaped by the communities and contexts in which they exist'* (authors' italics), is where the overlap between *genre* and *activity type* is at its most evident (cf. Section 11.2.1; see also Section 11.2.3). For example, all of the linguistic approaches mentioned to date share 'the view that linguistic features' associated with a particular *genre* are always 'connected to social context and function' (Bawarshi and Reiff 2010: 42) in some way. Those actions 'embody goals, actions' and 'activities' that are 'repeatedly required in similar situations', moreover, thereby explaining why *genres* (like *activity types*) are *recognizable* to users (Tardy and Swales 2014: 167). Interestingly, *genres* are argued to embody 'histories and politics' too (Tardy and Swales 2014: 167), which potentially sets them apart from *activity types* (see Section 11.2.3). This political characteristic helps to explain, in addition, why a growing number of researchers are opting to combine genre analysis with critical discourse analysis. Bhatia (2008) has even outlined a framework for a critical genre analytic approach, which brings together 'an analysis of text, genre, professional practice, and professional culture', by integrating 'what he calls "text-internal features" (e.g. lexicogrammatical features, rhetorical moves) with "text-external features" (e.g. institutional discourses, actions, and voices)' (Tardy and Swales 2014: 173).

Given that *genre* is so intimately interwoven with context, it is somewhat surprising that the term is not more widely used within pragmatics than it is currently. What has kept *genre* and *activity type* apart historically, according to Tardy and Swales (2014: 165), is not only their respective origins (as noted above), but also their particular (sub-)disciplinary origins and the previous foci of these (sub-)disciplines. For example, genre analysis (as a form of discourse analysis) often traces its roots to literary studies via anthropology and folklore studies. It has thus prioritized written texts historically. Pragmatics, in contrast, traces its origins to the work of ordinary language philosophers, and has often focused on spoken data (typically, on a smaller scale). Over the past two decades, however, 'genre analysts have become increasingly interested in characterizing spoken *genres*, while pragmatists have additionally turned their attention to written texts and longer spoken utterances, especially when those texts have explicitly persuasive motivations' (Tardy and Swales 2014: 165). Tardy and Swales' (2014) study provides us with one example of a pragmatics study which has used genre analysis as an important analytical tool, and will thus be discussed in more detail in Section 11.3.2.

11.2.3 Activity Type and Genre: Similarities and Differences with Each Other

Linell (1998: 239) has suggested that, because *activity type* and *genre* overlap conceptually in several ways, teasing them apart is essentially 'a matter of definition'. As noted in Section 11.2.2, this is not a particularly easy endeavour. Indeed, linguists have suggested that both tend to be somewhat "fuzzy" concepts in practice (Levinson 1979: 368; Włodarczyk 2016: 47). Our starting point, then, will be the key points of convergence to have emerged reasonably consistently in the extant literature, namely:

(1) the sociocultural ratification of (language use within) communicative activities
(2) the cognitive organization of human experience, and
(3) act-activity co-construction.

In relation to (1), we may note that both *activity type* and *genre* are typically understood within pragmatics as having sociocultural underpinnings (Linell 1998; Linell and Thunqvist 2003). Levinson's (1979: 368) *activity type*, for instance, describes communicative activities that are both 'socially constituted' and 'culturally recognizable'. Indeed, Levinson's concluding remarks in his original paper on *activity types* describe the notion by the name, *social episodes* (393; see also Forgas 1979). He also draws upon the ethnography of speaking, and more specifically the work of Hymes (1962), stating that there are 'culturally specific' language rules in operation when it comes to particular *activity types*:

> [such that] having a grasp of [activity-specific rules] will play an important role in the reception side of communicative competence, the ability to understand what one hears. And because these activity-specific rules are more culturally-specific than other sorts, they are likely to play a large role in cross-cultural or inter-ethnic miscommunications. (Levinson 1979: 393)

Comparably, *genre* has been utilized both within and outside of pragmatics to investigate 'the relationship between language, social structure, and culture' (Mayes 2003: 18; see also Luckmann 1992). Whether and to what extent culture is foregrounded over and above social structure (or vice versa) may vary from scholar to scholar. As Włodarczyk (2016: 47) notes, for instance, some researchers within historical pragmatics see *genre* as predominantly cultural (Claridge 2012), while others approach it from more of a social perspective (see e.g. Hoey 2001). Broadly speaking, both notions therefore attempt to describe how language use is shaped by the wider sociocultural landscape in which activities are situated. That is to say, social actors need not "spontaneously" select communicative behaviours *ab novo*. Rather, they may (at least partly) rely upon existing patterns – patterns which are drawn from, and ratified by, the discourse community and/or the culture at large – as appropriate ways to speak and behave within a given activity (Luckmann 1992: 244; see also Levinson 1979: 370). In regard to (2), the concepts of *genre* and *activity type* delineate contextual resources not only in terms of social structure and culture, but also in terms of cognition (Linell and Thunqvist 2003: 410). Levinson (1979: 376), for instance, states that there are activity-specific 'rules of inference' which are, in essence, the 'mirror image' of activity-specific constraints on behaviour. To clarify, he argues that the structure of a given *activity type* sets up certain expectations in the minds of the participants about utterance function. This in turn affects the process of inferential intention-attribution – that is, how we go about interpreting an utterance's intended meaning, as well as more generally determining 'how what one says will be "taken"' (393).

Although not all genre theorists foreground cognition, Taavitsainen's (2001) frequently cited definition of *genre* (especially within historical pragmatics) does stress the organization of experience: "Genres are inherently dynamic cultural *schemata* used to *organise knowledge and experience* through language" (Taavitsainen 2001: 139–40, emphasis added). In line with this, Mayes (2003: 21, 28) states that much of the existing literature on *genre* references the 'stored knowledge' that social actors accumulate based on repeated prior experience of 'typified' (i.e. frequently repeated) activities. It is important to note, however, that (1) and (2) do not mean pragmaticians necessarily adopt a deterministic, 'outside-in' (Culpeper and Haugh 2014: 192) view of cognitive, social or cultural contextual resources when applying the concepts of *genre* or *activity type*. This brings us to point (3): the principle of 'act-activity co-constitution' (Linell 1998: 237). Wittgenstein's discussion of *language-games* and Levinson's *activity type* were both underpinned by the assumption that there is an intrinsic dialogical relationship between discourse and context (Wittgenstein 1958: 5; Levinson 1979: 368). In particular:

> activity types involve both what interactants do in constituting the activity and the corresponding knowledge – schemata – one has of that activity; they have an interactional and a cognitive side. (Culpeper and Haugh 2014: 192)

According to this view, then, context is understood not as a stable aspect of the external environment, but, rather, as a dynamic process that is brought into being in and through interaction (Linell and Thunqvist 2003: 411; see also Thomas 1995: 189). In a similar vein, many genre theorists conceptualize *genre* as (1) having both schematic (cognitive) and emergent (dynamic) aspects and (2) being both constituted and reconstituted by the actions of social actors (Hanks 1996; Miller 1984: 159; Tardy and Swales 2014). To clarify:

> a genre is inseparable from the situation in which it occurs and is constituted by regular patterns of communicative action associated with that situation. Of course, the situation and recurring patterns of action also shape the genre. (Mayes 2003: 20)

Both *activity types* and *genres* are thus understood to be developed through interaction, socioculturally ratified, in some instances 'institutionally congealed' (Linell 1998: 239), and then reconstructed online by participants, moment by moment.

Despite these areas of overlap, several scholars have explicitly argued that the two terms can and/or should be analytically distinguished along several dimensions (see e.g. Linell 1998; Linell and Thunqvist 2003; Mayes 2003; van Eemeren 2010, 2013). *Genre* and *activity type* are often differentiated at the level of generality, for example, such that *activity types* may be seen as representing specific instantiations of broader communicative *genres*. Consider van Eemeren's (2010: 143) pragma-dialectal book *Strategic Manoeuvring in Argumentative Discourse*, in which he organizes the concepts of *domain, genre, activity type* and *speech event* in descending order of specificity. Within the broad *domain* of legal communication, for instance, adjudication is an example of a *genre*. Subsumed within the latter, in turn, are the *activity types* of court proceedings, arbitration and summoning. More specifically still, the *'defense pleading at O. J. Simpson's murder trial'* (van Eemeren 2010, emphasis original) is conceptualized as an exemplar *speech event* of the *activity type* of court proceedings. While one may disagree with the finer details of how van Eemeren conceptualizes any or all of these notions, his line of argument echoes – and is echoed by – several others (Bhatia 1993, 2004; Swales 1990, 2004; van Eemeren and Garsson 2013). Swales (1990: 58), for example, describes *genre* not as a specific communicative event but as 'a class of communicative events'. Linell (1998: 238) states that 'communicative activity types can be thought of as being *organized in terms of* communicative genres' (emphasis added). Linell adds further that, while *genres* may well be associated with particular *activity types*, 'there are activity types which are arguably not so culturally fixed' – such as a discussion group arranged for the express purpose of recording an interaction – and that one may thus hesitate to label these as "full-blown" communicative *genres* (239–40). On a related note, one may differentiate between *genres* and *activity types* on the basis that the latter are explicitly described as 'bounded' (Levinson 1979: 368; see also 368n2). Although Levinson himself does not elaborate extensively upon this aspect of his definition, he touches upon the fact that *activity types* are similar in many respects to *speech events* – that is, 'units of verbal behaviour *bound in time and space*' (Gumperz 1972: 165, emphasis added). In addition, the 'paradigm examples' of *activity type* put forward by Levinson (1979: 368) are all bounded events, such as a job interview, a football game or a task in a workshop. By contrast, *genre* – as a macro-level concept – may be conceptualized not as temporally or spatially isolable, but instead as 'continuous and intertextual' (Mayes 2003: 34), hence the "historical" characteristic noted in Section 11.2.2. *Genre* thus shares more of an affinity with Gumperz' *speech activity* than with *speech event* (Gumperz 1982: 166; see also Mayes 2003; Miller 1984). There is a sense in which activity types, in turn, may evolve over time becoming more socially, culturally and historically embedded, leading to the formation of 'new and complex genres', according to Linell (1998: 243).

11.2.4 Activity Type and Genre: Similarities and Differences with Other Concepts

As discussed in Section 11.2.3, both *genre* and *activity type* as concepts encompass the organization of human experience (Culpeper and Haugh 2014; Linell and Thunqvist 2003). They thus share similarities with various terms used in linguistics, artificial intelligence, anthropology, and psychology to refer to cognitive 'structures of expectation' (Tannen 1993: 21; Tannen and Wallat 1993: 59; see also Ross 1975), including *script, schema/ schemata, prototype* and *frame*. Put simply, all of these notions are underpinned by a common principle:

> on the basis of one's experience of the world in a given culture (or combination of cultures), one organizes knowledge about the world and uses this knowledge to predict interpretations and relationships regarding new information, events, and experiences. (Tannen 1993: 16)

It is worth reiterating that Levinson (1979: 371) emphasized the central role of *'inferential schemata'* in the development of (and adherence to) structural constraints on participants' 'allowable contributions' within an *activity type*.

If we consider the words of Bartlett (1932: 201), the first psychologist to use the term *schema* to describe the constructive nature of human memory, we can see the similarities: 'The past operates as an organized mass rather than as a group of elements each of which retains its specific character'. In addition, what Levinson refers to as *inferential schemata* closely resembles a *script*, or a specific kind of schema(ta) that consists of:

> a structure that describes appropriate sequences of events in a particular context.... Scripts handle stylised everyday situations. Thus, a script is a predetermined, stereotyped sequence of actions that defines a well-known situation. (Schank and Abelson 1977: 41)

Notice how this definition characterizes scripts as involving "appropriate" sequences of events. Schema-theoretic notions, then, allow us to tap into empirical norms that contribute to politic behaviour, that is, behaviour which is 'expectable' and 'perceived to be appropriate' (i.e. 'allowable', in Levinson's terms) 'to the social constraints of the ongoing interaction' (Watts 2003: 19). Many definitions of *genre* within pragmatics emphasize its cognitive dimension in similar terms. Taavitsainen (2001: 139–40) explicitly references both *schemata* and the organization of knowledge and experience, for example (see also Section 11.2.3), while Włodarczyk (2016) mentions *sociocognitive schemes*. Drawing upon Miller's (1984: 159) definition of *genre* as 'typified communicative action associated with recurrent situations', Mayes (2003: 55) notes, in addition, that the *genre* concept demonstrates considerable areas of overlap with *schema, prototype, activity type* and *frame*. Of note, when it comes to frames in particular, is Terkourafi's (2001: 254) frame-based conceptualization of politeness as the regular occurrence of unchallenged realizations of particular acts, allowing 'expression x' to become 'the socio-historically constrained "preferred" interpretation' for the performance of a certain act in a particular community.

According to Tannen and Wallat (1993: 59) and Mayes (2003: 28), the cognitive understanding of *frame* tends to capture little of the anthropological/sociological sense of *frame* as used/discussed by Goffman (1974, 1981) and others (see e.g. Hymes 1974; Gumperz 1982). In consequence, Tannen and Wallat (1993: 59) have drawn upon some of the extant literature as a means of making a theoretical distinction between the two understandings of this term. They use *cognitive schema* to encapsulate the abovementioned 'knowledge structures', and *interactive frame* to refer to 'what is going on in [a given] interaction'. Ultimately, however, Tannen and Wallat's (1993: 59) approach is like that of Terkourafi (2001, 2009), in that they tend to engage with frame analysis in ways that incorporate both understandings of the term, based on the argument that the two work together in interaction. Levinson (1979: 371) delineates the cognitive and interactive aspects of *activity types* on a theoretical level too, of course. Specifically, structures of expectation are referred to as *inferential schemata*, and are described as the 'mirror image' of structural constraints on participants' contributions.

Interestingly, Mayes is amongst those genre theorists who question even the theoretical separation of cognitive schema from interactive frames:

> Is human knowledge actually divided in this way – one part devoted to cognitive processes and one part to social interaction? ...
> I suggest that a more natural approach would be to merge these two concepts, despite the fact that they have been dealt with separately in the literature. (Mayes 2003: 35)

The dichotomy drawn between cognition and social interaction seems, at least in part, to reflect conventions within a given (sub-)discipline, and/or researchers' predominant goals. For instance, Culpeper and McIntrye (2010: 178) note that many researchers within pragmatics who have applied the concept of *activity type* have paid less attention to the cognitive element than to the 'pragmatic interactional' element (204). Whether or not cognition and social interaction are dealt with separately on a theoretical level, *genre* and *activity type* (as well as the broader notion of *frame* encapsulated in the work of, e.g. Tannen, Terkourafi, Wallat) are all equipped to deal with both at the analysis level.

11.3 Critical Overview through Two Case Studies

11.3.1 Culpeper and McIntyre (2010)

Culpeper and McIntyre's (2010) paper begins by providing a comprehensive theoretical background of the *activity type* concept. The authors are particularly careful, here, to highlight the (often-overlooked) cognitive dimension of *activity types*, emphasizing that the notion encapsulates 'both what interactants do in constituting the activity and the corresponding knowledge one has of that activity' (178). As discussed in Section 11.2.2, then, act-activity co-constitution is a central component of the *activity type* concept: language use both shapes and is shaped by context, rather than simply statically reflecting it (Culpeper and McIntyre 2010). This aspect is emphasized by the authors throughout their paper, with a view to redressing the analytic im/balance between the traditional outside-in approach to context in pragmatics (cf. Huang 2014: 17) and the inside-out, dynamic approach which assumes that language is context-creating (i.e. shapes/produces context *in situ*). In doing so, they manage to provide an extensive theoretical supplement to Levinson's ([1979] 1992) original explication.

The cognitive aspect captured by the notion of *activity types* equates to the 'strong expectations about the functions' utterances will fulfil (Levinson 1992: 79) at certain points in an exchange. Elsewhere, Levinson (1992: 72, 97) describes these expectations as the 'set of *inferential schemata*' that participants draw upon in order to evaluate *what is said* in activity-type-appropriate ways (Levinson 1992: 72, 97, emphasis original). Consider *How are you?* In most circumstances, this would function as a phatic question. In a clearly demarcated activity such as a doctor-patient consultation, however, patients are likely to use their knowledge-based schematic inferencing and conclude that the doctor wants them to provide him or her with an assessment of their physical health and/or mental well-being.

It is worth reiterating the overlap with schema theory here (see esp. Section 11.2.4), given that Culpeper and McIntyre (2010: 179) mention that Schank and Abelson's (1977) script-based approach to schema theory has 'some particular affinities with activity types'. Succinctly put, 'schemata enable us to construct an interpretation that contains more than the information we receive from the text. We can supply, or infer, extra bits of information from our schematic knowledge' (Culpeper and McIntyre 2010: 179). The activation of a particular schema triggers speaker's expectations. Following Neisser (1976: 22), the authors define schemata as anticipations that mediate between past and present experiences. For the purposes of their study, they then operationalize Schank and Abelson's (1977) and Schank's (1982, 1999) notion of *script* and *scene*, respectively. *Scripts* are proposed to work at a more specific level of knowledge structures and, thus, determine speakers' expectations within a given activity, whereas *scenes* are said to operate at a more general level. Scenes, then, are more affiliated with the setting and participants' goals, whereas scripts 'are more focused on just the actions or one set of possible actions within the scene' (Culpeper and McIntyre 2010: 180).

The authors demonstrate how the schematic aspect of activity types can be operationalized at the level of analysis by applying it to dramatic texts. Specifically, they focus upon four extracts drawn from two screenplays: a job interview from Danny Boyle's *Trainspotting*, and a police interview from BBC's *One Foot in the Grave*. They are careful to point out that their analysis is not, technically speaking, an analysis of a job interview *activity type*, but an analysis of interview *scenes* or *scripts* (180). They go on to demonstrate, nonetheless, that particular characterizations can be 'foregrounded as a result of deviation[s] from what is expected' (204). Consider the following example from the fictional job interview in *Trainspotting*:

Man 1   Mr Murphy, do you mean that you lied on your application?
Spud   Only to get my foot in the door. Showing initiative, right?

The authors note, here, that Spud pragmatically deviates from a prototypical interview response by openly admitting to having lied on his application form. The effect of Spud's non-conformance to the interview activity type is to characterize him as 'overly confident', 'unaware of social conventions', 'inattentive', and 'unintelligent' (194–5). Thus, the 'schematic aspect of activity types' (187) helps to explain how we make particular *inferences* about a character, about that character's social role, and about 'oddities of character' (204).

In addition to their detailed explication of the cognitive dimension of the notion of *activity type*, the authors summarize the more familiar, and more widely explored, interactional dimension, which boils down to how participants interactionally constitute *activity types*. They refer, in this case, to Thomas' (1995: 190–92) comprehensive list of elements, which are designed to elaborate on what Levinson labelled 'allowable contributions' (such as participants' goals and their allowable contributions). The authors characterize the comprehensiveness of the list as a double-edged sword; that is, they may help to capture the specific nature of some *activity types*, but may also obscure the differences between them (182). Here, the authors incorporate Sarangi's (2000) notion of *discourse type*, which helps to characterize 'the forms of talk occurring within activity types' (Culpeper and McIntyre 2010: 182). The main difference between the notion of *discourse type* and that of an *activity type* centres around the fact that the latter concentrates predominantly on contextual factors, whereas the former focuses on the *forms of talk* which may include, for example, history taking and promotional talk (cf. Sarangi 2000: 3). Culpeper and McIntyre make clear that their focus is upon such 'forms of talk' in their dramatic texts. They begin by establishing the typical features of the interview (drawing heavily on the work of Button 1992). This includes explaining the linguistic structures of the interview activity type, following what Button (1992) labels 'interview orthodoxy', that is, 'the elements that we might expect to see in all variations of the interview activity type' (Culpeper and McIntyre 2010: 184). Button's elements are, broadly speaking, 'conversation-analytic sequential practices' and 'conventionalisation conventions' (Culpeper and McIntyre 2010). For example, one has to do with there being no provision for interviewee's answers that extend over several turns, or the fact that the interviewee's first answer is taken to be complete and that no corrections are (typically) allowed. Culpeper and McIntyre then go on to supplement Button's list with 'other types of knowledge which feed into the job interview schema' in the British cultural context, such as assumptions about the dress code or the appropriate register (185).

The authors operationalize the interactional component of the *activity type* concept as a means of demonstrating how it might be applied to the analysis of characterization in dramatic discourse. Consider the following extract, taken from Culpeper and McIntyre (2010: 189):

Man 2   You seem eminently suited to this post but I wonder if you could explain the gaps in your employment record?
Renton   Yes I can. The truth – well, the truth is that I've had a long-standing problem with heroin addiction. I've been known to sniff it, smoke it, swallow it, stick it up my arse and inject it into my veins. I've been trying to combat this addiction, but unless you count social security scams and shoplifting, I haven't had a regular job in years. I feel it's important to mention this.

Culpeper and McIntyre highlight that, while the register adopted by Renton remains rather formal and thus appropriate to the interview activity type, his use of taboo language – coupled with his frank admission of heroin addiction and criminal activity – conflicts sharply with the overarching goal of the job interview as an activity type (that is, to secure the job). Prior to this extract, Renton had presented himself as highly educated through his 'relatively sophisticated register' (190) and had developed a rapport with one of the interviewers as a result. At this point, however, he sharply subverts this characterization through his (inappropriate) linguistic choices. In this way, Culpeper and McIntyre demonstrate that 'a major source of humour in the extract is ... Renton's *linguistic construction of the interview*' (191; emphasis added).

When discussing these and similar extracts, Culpeper and McIntyre are careful to emphasize and draw upon the dual aspect of the *activity type* concept, with the purpose of demonstrating that both the cognitive and (pragmatic) interactional dimensions are relevant to the stylistic analysis of dramatic texts. As they note, adopting a dual-aspect activity type approach in this way can capture particular dramatic effects (such as humour and irony), as well as 'feed into both bottom-up and top-down processes of characterisation' (204). It thus offers promise as a more "holistic" analysis of drama as discourse. The authors also go on to acknowledge, however, that the interview as an activity type is 'relatively conventionalised and stable, and thus relatively easy to describe' (205). For this reason, the application of an activity type approach may not prove quite so "neat" on a less clearly demarcated activity type, and/or to data taken from real-life interaction (see also Section 11.4).

11.3.2 Tardy and Swales (2014)

As noted in Section 11.2.2, Tardy and Swales (2014) provide a useful explanation in respect to how – in spite of a previous focus on spoken versus written interaction, respectively – genre analysis and pragmatics have nonetheless moved closer together since the 1980s. For instance, they note that genre analysts have become increasingly interested in spoken genres over the course of the past two decades and that, correspondingly, pragmaticians have begun to show interest in written texts. They further note that *genre* is now considered to be an important analytical tool in examining the pragmatics of both spoken and written discourse (Tardy and Swales 2014). On a theoretical level, the authors explain that genres – like activity types – 'both shape and are shaped by the communities and contexts in which they exist' (196). Following Miller (1984), they also see genres as being socially situated, dynamic categories of discourse which are formed in order to carry out social actions and purposes (see also Swales 1990). They are understood, however, to be intertextually linked to one another rather than isolable, and note that power dynamics are embedded within genres, since they are 'reflections of the social groups that use them'.

On a more practical note, Tardy and Swales (2014: 198–206) outline the repertoire of methods that make up genre analysis. They include: text analysis (supported by corpus-based analysis), move structure analysis, comparative genre analysis (comparing linguistic, national, professional or disciplinary affiliations), diachronic genre analysis, genre system analysis (focused on genres as clusters or networks), critical genre analysis, multi-modal/visual genre analysis and the study of genre and identity (see also Barron and Schneider 2014: 11). A commonality among these methods is the goal of 'gaining insight into the social function of language' (Tardy and Swales 2014: 198). With this in mind, it is not uncommon to adopt a mixed-method approach (as part of genre analysis) that examines multimodal data, from spoken language and written texts to graphical, figurative, and numerical data (204). While the concept of *genre* has traditionally been applied to 'communities of texts' (Tardy and Swales 2014: 205), the authors note that there has also been recent interest in examining the ways in which individuals assert their identity within a given text by, for instance, subverting genre conventions (see e.g. Hyon 2008; Hyland 2008; Matsuda and Tardy 2007).

The authors go on to apply a selection of the abovementioned methods to 60 bio-statements from two linguistics journals, i.e. *Applied Linguistics* (henceforth AL) and the *ELT Journal* (henceforth ELTJ), as a means of demonstrating what kinds of insights we might gain from each (as well as collectively). Their focus upon biographical notes is due to these texts' tendency to serve two important purposes, in spite of their relatively short length (around 90 words). That is, they provide relevant background information about the author/researcher whilst establishing their (academic) credibility, identity and ethos. Tardy and Swales (2014) start by analysing textual features: in particular, they provide frequencies of the most commonly used content words in the two samples. They found, for example, that the authors' bio-notes prepared for ELTJ included the word *research* more frequently than is the case with AL. Tardy and Swales (2014: 208–9) suggest this may reflect the contributors' greater interest in conducting academic research than is the case with the ELTJ, which is aimed primarily at teachers and ELT practitioners. In addition, the authors argue that the high frequency of the nouns *university, language* and *education* likely reflect 'the importance attached to institutional affiliation and degree names' (208).

They also point to the different ways in which the contributors to both journals refer to themselves (i.e. formal titles as opposed to their first names) in the analysed notes, which might be taken to reflect how firmly they are embedded in their (hierarchical) academic culture. For instance, while the first person pronoun *I* does not appear in the bio-notes of either journal, two Anglo male authors refer to themselves by their titles (*Professor*), while two Anglo female ELTJ authors refer to themselves by their first names only. Consistent with this, the few examples of evaluative adjectives and adverbs that appear in AL only are used to emphasize scholarly strength:

> he is also **well known** for his research into teaching and learning ...
> Professor [Name] is a **prolific** writer and he has published 12 books.

Tardy and Swales (2014) go on to analyse the rhetorical moves carried out by the authors of the bio-notes. They identify six types of moves, designed to either describe position or mention publications composed altogether of 14 steps. This includes the following:

1. Describing one's professional role/position
2. Establishing formal qualifications
3. Mentioning publications
4. Describing research areas
5. Describing professional activities
6. Describing honours

(adapted from Tardy and Swales 2014: 211)

Tardy and Swales suggest that the journals' contributors use these rhetorical moves 'in order to build their credibility as a published writer, illustrating their credentials as well as their experiences that they hope are valued in the field' (Tardy and Swales 2014: 213). While the authors note that there is a high degree of similarity between the AL and ELTJ corpora, they point to several discrepancies between the samples in terms of incorporating all the possible moves. To illustrate: within the AL bio-statements, 90 per cent of statements incorporate move 4 (describing research areas), compared to only 60 per cent of ELTJ statements. Tardy and Swales (2014) argue that, once again, this reflects AL's focus on research as opposed to classroom practice. By contrast, 70 per cent of authors within the ELTJ bio-statements included move 5 (describing professional activities), compared with 50 per cent of those from AL. This places a greater emphasis on the value of being 'an active practitioner' (Tardy and Swales 2014).

The authors' third stage of analysis involves exploring identity in some detail. Here, Tardy and Swales (2014: 215) highlight how, in spite of the specific rhetorical context, the journal contributors' still exercise freedom when negotiating their self-presentations. ELTJ is, according to Tardy and Swales, more flexible here than AL, perhaps because there is more scope for emphasizing 'a teaching persona' as well as a publishing or research persona. With regard to ELTJ, this was achieved by some authors through foregrounding their practical ELT experience over and above any research expertise (215).

The authors' final piece of analysis adopts a more 'critical' approach (216). This kind of genre analysis concerns itself with the very nature of the *genre* of bio-notes, which privileges or foregrounds certain aspects of (academic) identity that are assigned certain symbolic value(s) or that may have varying symbolic capital. Needless to say, not all of these identity aspects are equally available to all journals, thereby demonstrating how 'power dynamics are embedded in genres' (Tardy and Swales 2014: 216). For example, move 1 (describing one's position) is noted as 'near-obligatory' (216) in both AL and ELTJ, though they may place differing levels of emphasis on positions versus institutional affiliations. In AL, for instance, positions like "professor", "director", or "senior lecturer" afford more prestige than "doctoral student" or "senior lecturer". In light of this, Tardy and Swales (2014) argue that certain aspects of professional identity are 'privileged' within these bio-statements, which 'reproduces the power structure that lends prestige to these characteristics' (Tardy and Swales 2014).

The authors conclude their sample analysis by emphasizing that the presented methodological approaches 'shed light on different generic patterns and features, giving the genre analyst a repertoire of complementary tools from which to choose' (Tardy and Swales 2014: 217). The theoretical portion of this paper is afforded less prominence than its methodological counterpart; the authors provide only a brief ostensive definition of *genre* based upon previously established key features of genre in the extant literature, such as its socially situated character, the concept of rhetorical action and intertextuality (see also Bakhtin 1986; Miller 1984). Such a focus is understandable and likely deliberate, given that this paper was written for the series *Handbooks of Pragmatics*. Its practical slant is therefore particularly useful for any pragmatician wishing to embark upon genre analysis.

11.4 Summary and Future Directions

This chapter has critically compared the concepts of *activity type* and *genre* with regard to both their historical and (sub-)disciplinary origins, and subsequent uses in various disciplines – but especially pragmatics – as a means of assessing their similarities and differences with regard to (1) each other and (2) concepts that share 'a considerable family resemblance' (Linell 2010: 42) to them. In the process, it has become clear that *activity type* tends to be the more popular concept of the two within the field of general pragmatics, even though there are signs that the *genre* concept is growing in use (see Section 11.3.2). There have also been attempts to combine the two, as part of a specificity scale that also includes *domain* and *speech event* (van Eemeren 2010: 143; see also Section 11.2.3). Within this scale, it is suggested that *genres* are made up of *activity types* or what Swales (1990: 58) likes to call 'communicative events', and that *activity types* are made up of *speech events* (cf. Levinson's 1979: 368 description of *social events*). This is in line with Mayes' (2003: 34) understanding of *genre* as a 'continuous and intertextual' macro-level concept (cf. Gumperz's 1982: 166 notion of *speech activity*). *Activity types* and *speech events*, in contrast, share the characteristic of being 'bound in time and space' (Gumperz 1972: 165; Levinson 1979: 368). This does not prevent *activity types* evolving over time, however, such that they become more socially, culturally and historically embedded. As they do so, Linell (1998: 243) believes they may form 'new and complex genres', which we might want to explain as moving to a different point of the specificity scale.

A related characteristic that both concepts share is their "fuzzy" nature. Indeed, Levinson (1979: 368) in particular emphasized that the boundaries of an activity type need not be clearly demarcated at all, adding further that activity types will tend to sit 'along a gradient formed by two polar types', namely 'the totally pre-packaged activity on the one hand ... and the largely unscripted event on the other'. Such fuzziness can be useful, of course, especially when our interest lies in differentiating the less prototypical members of a given *activity type* (or *genre*) from its more prototypical members (Mayes 2003: 33), as well as differentiating one *activity type* (or *genre*) from another. As Mooney (2004: 905) and LoCastro (2013: 66) both note, in identifying a given *activity type* – say, courtroom cross-examination or classroom – we provide ourselves with useful information with regard to situational constraints, and hence related expectations regarding who, what, when and how co-participants might be expected to contribute to the unfolding interaction. It is this aspect of the *activity type* concept, in particular, that leads Mooney (2004: 905) to argue for its ability to give greater explanatory power to concepts like the Cooperative Principle (Grice 1975), not least because

> Using activity types forces the analyst to reconsider the goals of [such] discourse activities ... [as it is not u]ntil one knows the "*structural properties of an activity*" that one can [suitably] understand the way in which these properties "*constrain ... the verbal contributions that are made.*" (Levinson 1979: 370, italics as in original)

As Culpeper and McIntyre (2010: 178) note, Levinson was very much aware of 'the strict constraints on contributions' with regard to a 'particular activity' and how they can lead, in turn, to 'corresponding strong expectations about the functions that ... utterances ... can be fulfilling' within a given activity type. Hence, his theoretical delineation of *inferential schemata* from structural (i.e. interactional) constraints, drawing on the metaphor of a 'mirror image' (Levinson 1979: 371). As highlighted in Section 11.2.4, this cognitive-interactional dynamic is evident in the *genre* concept too. For example, *genres* are often argued to overlap with and/or are explained with reference to other cognitive-based concepts such as schema(ta), prototype and frame (Mayes 2003: 55). Some researchers – such as Tannen and Wallat (1993: 59) – have even sought to draw on some of the latter to delineate 'knowledge structure' (i.e. cognitive schema) from 'what is going on in [a given] interaction' (i.e. interactive frame). Mayes (2003: 35), in contrast, has argued for a merging of the 'two concepts, despite the fact that they have been dealt with separately in the [extant] literature'.

One reason they may have been dealt with separately relates to the conventions within a given (sub-)discipline. A second related reason pertains to researchers' predominant goals. For example, the cognitive aspect of *activity types* (or *genres*) has received much less attention than the interactional aspect within the field of general pragmatics (be it by Levinson or others). The bias towards the interactional may be due, in part, to the well-known concern that what 'is in people's heads is accessible neither to analysts nor to interlocutors (nor even ... to those whose behaviour is under investigation)' (Grimshaw 1990: 281). 'Rather, we are all reliant on assessing plausible intentions, using the evidence available to us' (Archer 2017: 392). This is less problematic if researchers use fictional texts as their data sources, as Culpeper and McIntyre (2010) do, as the authors of such works can provide us with insights into their characters' innermost thoughts. We would contend, nonetheless, that both *activity type* and *genre* have been developed and operationalized in ways that allow future researchers to begin analysing the complex interplay between multiple dimensions of real-life data: that is, language, social structure, culture, cognition, etc. It might be necessary, however, for those researchers to traverse beyond their (sub-)disciplinary boundaries, so that they might together account for the complexities of interaction and, in particular, any representativeness of a specific *activity type* and *genre*.

References

Allwood, J. (2000). An activity based approach to pragmatics. In H. Blunt and W. Black, eds., *Abduction, Belief and Context in Dialogue: Studies in Computational Pragmatics*. Ambsterdam: John Benjamins, pp. 47–80.

Allwood, J. (1976). Linguistic communication as action and cooperation. Gothenburg Manuscripts in Linguistics 2. Göteburg.

Archer, D. (2017). Politeness. In A. Baron, Y. Gu and G. Steen, eds., *The Routledge Handbook of Pragmatics*. London: Routledge, pp. 384–98.

Bakhtin, M. (1986). *Speech Genres and Other Late Essays*. Translated by V. W. McGee. Austin: University of Texas Press.

Barron, A. and Schneider, K. P. (2014). Discourse pragmatics: Signposting a vast field. In K. P. Schnieder and A. Barron, eds., *Pragmatics of Discourse*. Berlin: Mouton de Gruyter, pp. 1–33.

Barlett, F. C. (1932). *Remembering: A Study in Experimental and Social Psychology*. Cambridge: Cambridge University Press.

Bawarshi, A. S. and Reiff, M. J. (2010). *An Introduction to History, Theory, Research and Pedagogy*. West Lafayette, IN: Parlor Press.

Bazerman, C. (1997). The life of genre, the life of the classroom. In W. Bishop and H. Ostrom, eds., *Genre and Writing*. Portsmouth, NH: Boynton/Cook-Heinemann, pp. 19–26.

Belton, R. J. (1996). *The Elements of Art. Art History: A Preliminary Handbook*. www.academia.edu/23437708/Art_History_A_Preliminary_Handbook_1996.

Bhatia, V. K. (1993). *Analyzing Genre: Language Use in Professional Settings*. New York: Longman.

Bhatia, V. J. (2004). *Worlds of Written Discourse: A Genre-Based View*. London: Continuum.

Bhatia, V. K. (2008). Towards critical genre analysis. In V. K. Bhatia, J. Flowerdew and R. H. Jones, eds., *Advances in Discourse Studies*. London: Routledge, pp. 166–77.

Biber, D. (1988). *Variation across Speech and Writing*. Cambridge: Cambridge University Press.

Button, G. (1992). Answers as interactional products: Two sequential practices used in job interviews. In P. Drew and J. Heritage, eds., *Talk at Work: Interaction in Institutional Settings*. Cambridge: Cambridge University Press, pp. 212–31.

Claridge, C. (2012). Styles, registers, genres, text types. In A. T. Bergs and L. J. Brinton, eds., *English Historical Linguistics: An International Handbook*. Berlin: Mouton de Gruyter, pp. 237–53.

Clark, H. H. (1996). *Using Language*. Cambridge: Cambridge University Press.

Culpeper, J. and Haugh, M. (2014). *Pragmatics and the English Language*. Hampshire, UK: Palgrave Macmillan.

Culpeper, J. and MacIntyre, D. (2010). Activity types and characterisation in dramatic discourse. In J. Eder, F. Jannidis and R. Schneider, eds., *Characters in Fictional Worlds: Understanding Imaginary Beings in Literature, Film, and Other Media*. Berlin: Walter de Gruyter, pp. 176–207.

Eemeren, F. H., van. (2010). *Strategic Maneuvering in Argumentative Discourse: Extending the Pragmadialectical Theory of Argumentation*. Amsterdam: John Benjamins.

Eemeren, F. H., van and Garssen, B. (2013). Argumentative patterns in discourse. In D. Mohammed and M. Lewiński, eds., *Virtues of Argumentation: Proceedings of the Tenth International Conference of the Ontario Society for the Study of Argumentation (OSSA), 22–26 May 2013*. Windsor, ON: OSSA, pp. 1–15.

Forgas, J. P. (1979). *Social Episodes: The Study of Interaction Routines*. London: Academic Press.

Goffman, E. (1974). *Frame Analysis: An Essay on the Organisation of Experience*. Cambridge, MA: Harvard University Press.

Goffman, E. (1981). *Forms of Talk*. Philadelphia: University of Pennsylvania Press.

Grice, H. P. (1975). Logic and conversation. In P. Cole, ed., *Syntax and Semantics 3: Speech Acts*. New York: Academic Press, pp. 41–58.

Grimshaw, A. D. (1990). Research on conflict talk: Antecedents, resources, findings, directions. In A. D. Grimshaw, ed., *Conflict Talk: Sociolinguistic Investigations of Arguments and Conversations*. Cambridge: Cambridge University Press, pp. 281–324.

Gumperz, E. (1972). Introduction. In J. Gumperz and D. Hymes, eds., *Directions in Sociolinguistics*. New York: Holt, Rinehart and Winston, pp. 1–26.

Gumperz, J. (1982). *Discourse Strategies*. Cambridge: Cambridge University Press.

Hanks, W. F. (1996). *Language and Communicative Practices*. Boulder, CO: Westview Press.

Hoey, M. (2001). *Textual Interaction: An Introduction to Written Discourse Analysis*. London: Routledge.

Hyland, K. (2008). "Small bits of textual material": A discourse analysis of Swales' writing. *English for Specific Purposes, 27*, 143–60.

Hymes, D. (1962). The ethnography of speaking. In T. Gladwin and W. Sturtevant, eds., *Anthropology and Human Behavior*. Washington, DC: Anthropological Society of Washington, p. 13–53.

Hymes, D. (1974). *Foundations in Sociolinguistics: An Ethnographic Approach*. Philadelphia: University of Pennsylvannia Press.

Hyon, S. (2008). Convention and inventiveness in an occluded academic genre: A case study of retention-promotion-tenure reports. *English for Specific Purposes, 27*, 175–92.

Lee, D. Y. W. (2001). Genres, registers text types, domains, and styles: Clarifying the concepts and navigating a path through the BNC jungle. *Language Learning and Technology, 5*(3), 37–72.

Levinson, S. (1992). Activity types and language. In P. Drew and J. Heritage, eds., *Talk at Work*. Mouton: The Hague, pp. 66–100.

Levinson, S. (1979). Activity types and language. *Linguistics, 17*, 365–99.

Linell, P. (1998). *Approaching Dialogue: Talk, Interaction and Contexts in Dialogical Perspectives*. Amsterdam: John Benjamins.

Linell, P. (2010). Communicative activity types as organisations in discourses and discourses in organisations. In S. Tanskanen, M. Helasvuo, M. Johansson, J. Karhukorpi and M. Raitaniemi, eds., *Discourses in Interaction*. Amsterdam: John Benjamins, pp. 33–59.

Linell, P. and Thunqvist, D. P. (2003). Moving in and out of framings: Activity contexts in talks with young unemployed people within a training project. *Journal of Pragmatics, 35*, 409–34.

LoCastro, V. (2013). *Pragmatics for Language Educators: A Sociolinguistic Perspective*. New York: Routledge.

Luckmann, T. (1992). On the communicative adjustment of perspectives, dialogue and communicative genres. In A. H. Wold, ed., *The Dialogical Alternative*. Oslo: Scandinavian University Press, pp. 219–34.

Martin, J. R. (1984). Language, register and genre. In F. Christie, ed., *Children Writing: Reader*. Geelong, VI: Deakin University Press, pp. 21–30.

Martin, J. R. (1985). Process and text: Two aspects of semiosis. In J. D. Benson and W. S. Greaves, eds., *Systemic Perspectives on Discourse, Vol. 1: Selected Theoretical Papers from the Ninth International Systemic Workshop*. Norwood, NJ: Ablex, pp. 248–74.

Matsuda, P. and Tardy, C. (2007). Voice in academic writing: The rhetorical construction of author identity in blind manuscript review. *English for Specific Purposes, 26*, 235–49.

Mayes, P. (2003). *Language, Social Structure, and Culture: A Genre Analysis of Cooking Classes in Japan and America*. Amsterdam: John Benajmins.

Miller, C. R. (1984). Genres as social action. *Quarterly Journal of Speech, 70*, 151–67.

Mooney, A. (2004). Co-operation, violations and making sense. *Journal of Pragmatics*, 36, 899–920.

Neisser, U. (1976). *Reality: Principles and Implications of Cognitive Psychology*. San Francisco: W. H. Freeman.

Paltridge, B. (1997). *Genre, Frames and Writing in Research Settings*. Amsterdam: John Benjamins.

Ross, R. N. (1975). Ellipsis and the structure of expectation. *San Jose State Occupational Papers in Linguistics*, 1, 183–91.

Sarangi, S. (2000). Activity types, discourse types and interactional hybridity: The case of genetic counselling. In S. Sarangi and M. Coulthard, eds., *Discourse and Social Life*. London: Pearson Education, pp. 1–27.

Schank, R. C. (1982). *Dynamic Memory: A Theory of Reminding and Learning in Computers and People*. Cambridge: Cambridge University Press.

Schank, R. C. (1999). *Dynamic Memory Revisited*. Cambridge: Cambridge University Press.

Schank, R. C. and Abelson, R. P. (1977). *Scripts, Plans, Goals and Understanding: An Inquiry into Human Knowledge Structures*. Hillsdale, NJ: Lawrence Erlbaum Associates.

Swales, J. M. (1990). *Genre Analysis: English in Academic and Research Settings*. Cambridge: Cambridge University Press.

Swales, J. (2004). *Research Genres: Explorations and Applications*. Cambridge: Cambridge University Press.

Taavitsainen, I. (2001). Changing conventions of writing: The dynamics of genres, text types, and text traditions. *European Journal of English Studies*, 5(2), 139–50.

Tannen, D. (1993). *Framing in Discourse*. Oxford: Oxford University Press.

Tannen, D. and Wallat, C. (1993). Interactive frames and knowledge schemas in interaction: Examples from a medical examination/interview. In D. Tannen, ed., *Framing in Discourse*. Oxford: Oxford University Press, pp. 57–76.

Tardy, C. M. and Swales, J. M. (2014). Genre analysis. In K. P. Schneider and A. Barron, eds., *Pragmatics of Discourse*. Berlin: Mouton de Gruyter, pp. 165–88.

Terkourafi, M. (2009). On de-limiting context. In A. Bergs and G. Diewald, eds., *Context and Constructions*. Constructional Approaches to Language 9. Amsterdam: John Benjamins, pp. 17–42.

Terkourafi, M. (2001). *Politeness in Cypriot Greek: A Frame-Based Approach*. Cambridge: Cambridge University Press.

Thomas, J. (1995). *Meaning in Interaction: An Introduction to Pragmatics*. London: Longman.

van der Merwe, P. (1989). *Origins of the Popular Style: The Antecedents of Twentieth-Century Popular Music*. Oxford: Clarendon Press.

Watts, R. J. (2003) *Politeness*. Cambridge: Cambridge University Press.

Wittgenstein, L. (1958). *Philosophical Investigations*. 2nd ed. Translated by G. E. M. Ansycombe. Oxford: Oxford University Press.

Włodarczyk, M. (2016). *Genre and Literacies: Historical (Socio)pragmatics of the 1820 Settler Petition*. Poznań: Adam Mickiewicz University Press.

12

Social Groups and Relational Networks

Diana Boxer and Florencia Cortés-Conde

12.1 Introduction

The study of sociopragmatics has its roots in early linguistic paradigms. In the middle of the twentieth century, in response to structuralism, two different areas of studies with differing methodologies began to examine the issue of language use (performance) as opposed to decontextualized language as an abstract system (competence): (1) sociolinguistics proposed to study the speech community in an effort to explain change and social variation; (2) pragmatics attempted to examine what speakers mean by what they say (or write). Both sociopragmatics and sociolinguistics are terms that are currently used to describe a wide range of research related to interaction, identity and culture. Sociopragmatics derives from this second tradition, pragmatics, endeavouring to account for culture-specific use. The shift now is more in the direction of sociolinguistics becoming more interactional (micro) and sociopragmatics more societally (macro) focused. The term 'social network' adopted in this chapter is intended to cover these different theoretical perspectives on social group and the explication of relational networks offered in this chapter purports to offer a partial solution to the differing terminologies taken by the varied perspectives.

Thus, there has been a theoretical shift in linguistics towards understanding language as realized in context and in relational contexts in particular. While sociopragmatics was never centrally concerned with speech communities, it has had to consider societal groups; thus, we see a new focus on the concept of Communities of Practice (CofP). As we begin to view relational networks against a backdrop of CofP, the contexts in which such networks emerge are transformed in an era of globalization, the internet and transnationalism. Indeed, the concept of CofP is highly relevant to the field of sociopragmatics.

One of the foundational problems for all of these fields of study is how to delineate the basic unit of analysis. Changes in the object of study accompany societal shifts in how social groups come together and how language divides or unites them. The convergence goes from the notion of a speech community (e.g. Hymes 1974; Gumperz 1971; Labov 1972), to social networks (Milroy and Milroy 1978, 1985), to Community of Practice (CofP) (Lave and Wenger 1991; Eckert and McConnell-Ginet 1992, 1999) to more loosely structured virtual/online/global communities that form 'light' social groups (Blommaert 2018). The evolution from the more fixed and bounded notions of social organization to the fluid and ever-changing negotiation of interaction and identities is not a linear and clear path. There is no unified field of study with a clear object and fixed methodology. The study of language as it is used in context, although having a more nuanced understanding of the 'linguistically' focused, has borrowed from different social theories to forge a stronger connection between language and society.

In his most recent work, Blommaert (2018) is critical of the lack of attention paid in both sociolinguistics and sociopragmatics to the social theory used to make that connection. Over the years, the study of language use has borrowed theoretical frameworks from sociology, cultural anthropology, social psychology, gender theory, communication theory and philosophy of language, among others. This has created a lack of a unified and clear use of terminology. The following section shows the confusion and difficulty of establishing clear boundaries for the study of relational networks that directly impact the field of sociopragmatics.

12.2 Key Concepts and Theories

12.2.1 Social Groupings and Identity

The current view of social groups held by identity researchers is that identity is fluid. If identities are neither fixed nor bound, then neither are the social groupings[1] from which they emerge nor in which they are performed. Anderson's (1983) seminal work on nationalism proposed the emergence of 'imagined communities' during the creation of nation-states in the eighteenth century. These imagined communities were bound by notions of one language, one territory and one history. Anderson's notion of imagined communities is now more salient than ever, given that social groupings have been radically changed by the advent of the internet (Blommaert 2018). Indeed, the anti-essentialist, performative constitution of groups for which Anderson argues is now becoming much more obvious. From the hegemonies that nation-states created to shape citizens' identities to make them one homogenous unit, the internet and the many virtual communities connected through it are polycentric with normative systems

---

[1] The term "social groupings" entails a dynamic look at the formation of groups as these formations are taking place.

that are both global and local. If the nation-state had perceived 'thick' social groupings bound by race, gender, ethnicity and so on, there are currently more 'light' social groups that are more ephemeral but just as important, since they give insights into socialization and identity. Blommaert (2018: 66) proposes that "we need to examine the less conspicuous forms of relationships and kinds of interactions not instead of, but alongside 'the major social formations". The shift from nation-state to globalized cultures, from more 'permanent' social formations to online social practices, creates a need for new ways of conceiving and studying social action, social groupings and identities. In this chapter we trace this shift as sociolinguistics and sociopragmatics endeavour to understand communicative practices and acts of identity (Le Page and Tabouret-Keller 1985).

Indeed, since the development and diffusion of the notions of speech community and social network (e.g. Gumperz 1971; Hymes 1974; Labov 1972; Milroy and Milroy 1978, 1985), the world has dramatically changed. Most language users now interact in an array of groups owing to the development of the ability to connect virtually, across vast geographical areas and with language users who may use a link language (in the present case, English) as a lingua franca. Globalization has changed the way we connect and the type of conversations and identities we develop through those conversations. Because of this global phenomenon, we can no longer view sociopragmatics as necessarily tied to 'dialects' grounded in geography (Rampton 2008; Blommaert 2005, 2018). The issue of 'norms' here becomes paramount. While norms are inherently important in new research thrusts in studies of (im)politeness, they are also much discussed in work on language and identity issues within social networks. This is especially true given the fluidity of such networks in current online CofPs. Normative social and linguistic behaviour is thus a critical point of analysis for these fluid contemporary social groupings.

12.2.2 Sociopragmatics, Linguistic Ethnography and Interactional Sociolinguistics

One of the most widespread methodologies for studying sociopragmatics is interactional sociolinguistics (IS), a direct sub-field of Linguistic Ethnography (LE). IS emphasizes situated communication and focuses on efforts to ascertain participants' own perceptions and interpretations of their interactional efforts. For IS, every moment is both unique and informed by previous interactions. Individuals use rhetorical strategies, semiotic material and institutional genres in systematic ways that repeat what has gone on before and also deviates from it. Analytic resources for interactional sociolinguistics are linguistics and discourse analysis (participant's resources), conversational analysis (intersubjectivity), ethnography (cultural and personal meanings), public and academic discourse (environment).

The IS methodology is particularly relevant to studying the sociopragmatics of relational networks. Grounded in the sociological principles of Durkheim, it was brought centrally into the analysis of face-to-face interaction by Erving Goffman in his efforts to locate the relationship between *self* and *society*. Gumperz et al. (1979), in their pioneering work *Crosstalk*, brought IS into focus as a method for revealing how differing sociopragmatic norms in cross-cultural communication can be fraught with misunderstandings.

Rampton (2008) discusses the usefulness of IS in the study of identities. In his view, Linguistic Ethnography's empirical scope is instrumental in illuminating issues of identity and thus the sociopragmatic use of language. Issues of identity emerge in the analysis when the analyst draws on a "mixture of linguistics, discourse analysis and ethnographic detail" (8).

The critical part of IS methodology is in the triangulation of the data; that is, the post-analysis feedback from participants in situating their own meanings of taped interactions in which they participated. This type of triangulation affords a third perspective on analysis, adding to the retrievable data in the form of audio or video recordings and to the researcher's own perspective on what was going on. Thus, both LE and IS are valuable methodologies for the study of the sociopragmatic norms of social groups and relational networks. By taking such a research perspective, we can more clearly trace the move from a structural view of language to a sociopragmatics view that takes into account relationality and the dynamic nature of identity in an era of globalization.

12.2.3 From the Speech Community, to the Social Network, to Communities of Practice

We can trace the evolution of the concept of relational networks beginning with Labov's (1966, 1972) and others' definitions of speech community, to the more recent conceptualization of 'Communities of Practice' (Lave and Wenger 1991; Eckert and McConnell-Ginet 1992) created by their very own social interactants. The issue in the latter is, with whom do you interact, and in what contexts? This concept is tied directly to the issue of relationality; that is, when, where and in what ways one connects with others in an interaction.

As we indicated above, Social Network Theory entered into the field of sociolinguistics via the important work of Leslie and James Milroy (1978, 1985), begun in Belfast. Borrowed from sociology, Social Network Theory emphasized the kinds of groups in which individuals engaged on a day-to-day basis. In the first instance, the theory examined communities like those in working-class neighbourhoods in Belfast, in which individuals interacted in multiple communicative activities with other individuals with whom they lived in close proximity, worked, socialized, worshipped and intermarried. Such communities were deemed *multiplex* (the number of capacities in which people interact with each other) and *dense* (how many ties one has in one's network) in that era and in that sort of geographical context. Individuals' identities were thus intimately tied to others with whom they interacted in multiple spheres of discourse. Social network theory was compelling for the field of linguistics, yielding direct implications for analysing the sociopragmatics of groups. People who interacted in dense and multiplex networks developed the same norms of interaction with each other that may have differed greatly from those of more peripheral individuals or individuals who (also) formed part of other networks.

Due to globalization and the consequent opening up of virtual communication, the current notion of how we interact in social groups and develop relational networks centres on Communities of Practice (CofP) (Lave and Wenger 1991; Eckert and McConnell-Ginet 1992, 1999). CofP are loosely defined social groupings that are neither fixed nor permanent. They bring together individuals with a shared interest in 'practice' with the others in the group. As is obvious, most of us are members of several relational networks or CofPs. These CofPs move beyond face-to-face communication towards the virtual sphere. We may be part of a videogamers' network, a political/activist network, a parents' group and so on. These are often communities in which membership is fluid and ever changing. We quickly acquire the sociopragmatic norms of interaction as we become members of these various CofPs.

Since it was first articulated in print (e.g. Rheingold 1993), the concept of 'virtual community' has become increasingly utilized in internet research, although it has also been criticized. The criticisms include a concern that the term has been overextended to the point of becoming meaningless – for some authors, it seems that any online group automatically becomes a 'community' – and a philosophical scepticism that virtual community can exist at all, given the fluid membership, reduced social accountability, and lack of shared geographical space that characterize most groups on the internet (cf. McLaughlin 1995). For the purposes of the present discussion, we assume that virtual community is possible, but that not all online groups constitute virtual communities. The task of the researcher then becomes to determine the properties of virtual communities, and to assess the extent to which they are (or are not) realized by specific online groups.

While we certainly continue to be part of established face-to-face networks, a large segment of people in the developed world also belong to additional virtual CofPs based upon shared personal interests. This trend is burgeoning as well in the developing world, with increased access to computers and connectivity. Herring (2004) discusses the various analytic methodologies that can be employed to study linguistic and pragmatic interactions in these online communities and considers discourse analysis the paradigm that is most appropriate to study the sociopragmatics of virtual communities.

Overall, there is widespread agreement among pragmatics scholars that the concept of Community of Practice is now most relevant to the study of relational networks in the current globalized world. Agency was not adequately acknowledged in previous theorizing about networks. The effect of dense and multiplex ties on language use/change was assumed to be more or less automatic and self-evident.

Norms emerge and can change in the practice, while membership in the community remains fluid and individuals' agency also plays a part in determining membership.

12.2.4 Politeness and Relational Networks

Closely connected with the discussion of social interactions within communities are the important concepts derived from politeness theory as it evolved from the work of Brown and Levinson (1978, 1987) and influenced by the sociology of Erving Goffman (1959, 1963). However, politeness theories did not initially take social networks and communities as a central focus of study. Later conceptualizations (e.g. Locher and Watts 2008) do indeed discuss the connection between relational work and politeness. Participants in a communicative act, even when they belong to the same community, make judgements and negotiate norms regarding social behaviour. Locher and Watts see these norms as changing over time, and thus, politeness work includes not only politeness, but also the notion of (im)politeness. They incorporate into their work notions of CofP:

> Relational work is defined as the work people invest in negotiating their relationships in interaction.... In other words, communicative acts always embody some form of relational work. Taking this approach means that we are not restricted to studying merely the polite variant of the interpersonal aspect of a communication, as Brown and Levinson ([1978] 1987) have predominantly done, but can equally focus on impolite, or rude aspects of social behavior. Relational work, in other words, comprises the entire spectrum of the interpersonal side of social practice. (Locher and Watts 2008: 78)

Culpeper (2008) likewise advocates that we must take into account the existence of (im)politeness encompassing the notion of *power* as an important aspect of relationality. Culpeper contends that there are various ways in which interactants' behaviours might be considered negative or impolite, and some of these might be considered both negative and appropriate in some sense. Much depends on the power relationship among the individuals in particular constellations of interaction. Power, in addition to social distance, figures largely into the participants' evaluations of particular forms as (im)polite in context.

With current attention on both politeness and impoliteness, we see clearly how the study of social groups and relational networks fits right into sociopragmatics. As Enfield (2009: 64) suggests, "At the core of our social world is the maintenance of relationships; these relationships are not only dyadic (that we enter with others), but relations between relationships. This relationship thinking takes communicative interactions as a key locus". What this means is that politeness is not only about interactions between two people to save face but also politeness may display the relationship that has already been established to an audience or third party. This we have termed 'relational identity display' (RID) (Boxer and Cortés-Conde 1997). We define RID as follows: in an interaction two or more individuals can display an identity for a third participant (or participants), thus showing that identities in interactions are emergent phenomena. This can be one of many ways in which relations happen between and within relationships. This thinking concurs exactly with Enfield's notion. As he states:

> Every interaction increments an interpersonal relationship by means of building common experience, and displays the nature of that relationship such that it may be evaluated by participants and onlookers. A relationship thinking approach puts this in
> the foreground. (Enfield 2009: 71–2)

The central focus of the study of (im)politeness then becomes that of interpersonal relations. According to Haugh et al. (2013), pragmatics has incorporated the relational dimension through Leech's notion of interpersonal rhetoric. He states: "Interpersonal Communication has traditionally been defined by its focus on the process of creating social relationships between at least two people by acting in concert with one another" (1). A key insight in developing a theory of interpersonal relations is Spencer-Oatey's (2002, 2003) notion of 'rapport management'. In her view, Brown and Levinson did not address the wider society in which relations flourish; their theory was indeed seen as lacking a social dimension despite addressing issues of power, distance and imposition. In other words, what is lacking has been the notion of how relations fit into wider societal networks. This is consistent with our earlier discussion of norms in CofP and in the 'light' social groupings of the internet. Spencer-Oatey's proposed notion of rapport management includes management of face (the personal and individual concerns for saving face) and management of sociality rights (the social concerns for equity and fairness). Spencer-Oatey states:

> We cannot sensibly divorce linguistic politeness from the social context in which it occurs. If we are to understand how relations are managed, including the role of language in this process, we need to have insights into the social expectancies and judgments of the people involved. (3)

Spencer-Oatey defines sociality rights as

> the "fundamental personal/social entitlements that a person effectively claims for him/herself in his/her interactions with others.... Face is associated with personal/social value, and is concerned with people's

sense of worth, credibility, dignity, honour, reputation, competence and so on. Sociality rights, on the other hand, are concerned with personal/social entitlements, and reflect people's concerns over fairness, consideration, social inclusion/exclusion and so on". (10)

Rapport management is thus inextricably interwoven with (im)politeness theory but extends it to explicate how we linguistically negotiate our social relationships within groups – and thereby our social networks. All of this is to say that as we manage rapport, we may emulate or distance ourselves from the sociopragmatic norms of the CofP in which we wish to establish rapport. In relatively stable social networks, norms are more enduring. As CofP norms emerge in specific moments of specific practice, in 'light' social groupings norms can be taken on and shed if and when one ceases to be part of that grouping.

Similar and related to the notion of rapport management is Arundale's (1999, 2010, 2020) conceptualization of Face Constituting Theory, based on current theory in the study of human communication. Grounded in Conversation Analysis (Sacks et al. 1974), Arundale's model offers a fresh conceptualization of face that goes from person-centred attributes to a social identity created by two or more persons in interaction. Face Constituting Theory of Communication is a theoretical model whose core principles are framed from the participant's rather than from the analyst's perspective. The principles of the theory not only model "the procedures and expectations in terms of which [participants] produce their own behaviour and interpret the behaviour of others as their utterances unfold in sequence" (Heritage 1984: 241), but also explain how "meaning and action are achieved in talk-in-interaction" (Arundale 1999, 2010). Arundale conceptualizes face as a social phenomenon arising in the conjoint co-constituting of human relationships, rather than as an individual phenomenon involving person-centred attributes. More specifically, face is one key aspect of the relationship between/among two or more persons as they conjointly co-constitute meanings and actions in talk-in-interaction. Thus, Arundale's model views 'face' as both relational but also as emergent, as it brings relations centre stage by not only focusing on the attributes of the persons involved but beyond this on what emerges from the relationship itself.

Both theory and method impact the study of social groups and relational networks. For methodologies, Linguistic Ethnography and its correlate, interactional sociolinguistics, are paramount in this endeavour. Rapport management and Face Constituting Theory fit logically into the notion of relational networks and CofP discussed above; we must consider both as part of the conversation on relational network theories. The notion of relational networks is indeed central to their goals, in ways in which they are not central to different (more individual-based or static) frameworks of approaching language use. As we have noted above, relational network models such as those of Spencer-Oatey and Arundale shift the focus from attributes and fixed categories to emerging relationships. Theoretical notions of politeness and impoliteness, interpersonal and intercultural pragmatics, rapport management and Face Constituting Theory, help empirical studies reveal the instantiations of sociopragmatics of relational networks. We illustrate with some case studies.

12.3 Overview of Research: Case Studies

We bring together here a sampling of case studies emanating from differing strands of research. While some are more theoretical in nature, others are more applied, and still others focus in particular on the use of relational networks in understanding the sociopragmatics of online spaces. Rather than focusing on a single case-study, we sample work from these different areas to illustrate the widespread nature of the workings of relational networks.

Early work employing IS (or microethnography) is perhaps best illustrated by the pioneering study of Erickson and Schultz (1982) in *The Counselor as Gatekeeper*. The researchers' fine-grained analysis uncovered the subtle sociopragmatics of identity that allowed (or prevented) access through the 'gate'. In this case, the gatekeepers were college counsellors who allowed students whose identities reflected their own to enter the gate; in contrast, when the social identity of the student did not mirror their own, the gatekeepers tended to keep the 'gate' shut. This early study employing IS was foundational for sociopragmatic studies that ensued.

From a theoretical perspective following in this tradition, Boxer and Cortés-Conde (1997) employed an interactional sociolinguistic/ethnographic methodology to study the functions of varied types of humour in their study 'From Bonding to Biting: Conversational Humor and Identity Display'. The various kinds of identity that impact sociopragmatic use are here disambiguated from each other. These are (1) personal identity (e.g. demographic characteristics of sex, race, ethnicity); (2) social identity (the identity one presents in interaction (e.g. parent, professor, democrat); and, most important for this chapter, (3) relational identity (RID). As indicated earlier, RID is the development and display of ingroupness, where the relation may be temporary or more permanent, but in which the norms of sociopragmatic use are part of the fluid group identity during the time that the group is interacting. It is neither fixed nor bounded. This research disentangled the type of humour that serves to bond people together from the biting kind that uses humour to soften the effects of scolding or complaining.

Bucholtz and Hall's (2004) work on "theorizing identity in language and sexuality research" played an important role in contributing to the theoretical notion of relationality. Their work focuses on gender and language, highlighting the importance of critically examining the sociopragmatics of gendered use of language in interaction. In their words, "research on identity, sexual or otherwise, is most productive when the concept is understood as the outcome of intersubjectively negotiated practices and ideologies" (469).

From a more applied perspective, one can look to case studies from the domain of workplace interactions, since much recent research on sociopragmatic norms focuses on this specific domain of interactions. The challenges in studying the sociopragmatics of the workplace have attracted interest over the years, but not until relatively recently have discourse analysts closely examined sociopragmatics in this domain. Marra (2013), for example, asserts that understanding the sociopragmatics of the workplace is a key concern in an increasingly globalized workforce.

Schnurr and Zayts (2011) provide a good example of a social constructionist perspective of identities in the workplace in their examination of the sociopragmatics of leadership. In their close analysis of what makes for leadership, they conclude that acts of identity emerge and are performed in interaction. Using a multi-method approach in their study (video recording, interview of individual participants and participant observation, document consultation), Schnurr and Zayts are able to extract the ways in which leaders engage with their teams, noting the nuanced sociopragmatics of leadership development. Identity construction is conceptualized not as a straightforward one-way process but as typically characterized by multiple and complex interactional processes.

Also in the workplace domain, Kirilova and Angouri (2018) address the notion of 'fitting in' in the modern workplace. The study focuses on issues around recruitment, access and integration in multilingual and multinational workplaces. The authors utilize interactional approaches to identity and culture stemming from Goffman's conceptions of performance, stigma, and passing (Goffman 1959, 1963) as well as Bourdieu's habitus (Bourdieu and Wacquant 1992). The authors aptly show the juxtaposition of the flexibility needed for 'fitting in' with the typical power and hegemony pressures of L2 gatekeeping events in workplace settings. Newcomers must thus balance the need for this flexibility with their own powerlessness in adjusting and attempting to fit in. It is shown that those coming in must bear the pressure to quickly adapt to local pragmatic norms.

A great deal of this focus on workplace sociopragmatics emanates from the New Zealand Workplace project headed by Janet Holmes, much of which emphasizes differing gender norms in the workplace. With this focus, Holmes and Schnurr (2006) discuss the notion of 'relational practice' from Fletcher (1999). Fletcher defines relational practice as a way of working "that springs from a relational or stereotypically feminine belief system" (163). Holmes and Schnurr found that "effective women leaders typically drew strategically on a variety of discourse strategies, encompassing both conventional masculinity as well as normative femininity, to accomplish their relational goals" (Holmes and Schnurr 2006: 42).

Their fine-tuned discourse analysis demonstrates the sociopragmatic complexity of gender identities in workplace talk. They suggest a re-examination of concepts such as 'feminine' and 'femininity', casting these "in [a] more positive light, reclaiming the potential for women and men to behave in feminine ways, and make constructive but unremarkable use of conventionally feminine discourse strategies, 'even' at work" (Holmes and Schnurr 2006: 45).

We see in the case studies listed above that the study of social networks within sociopragmatics has concentrated on the various domains of face-to-face interaction. Highlighted here are the spheres of social and workplace CofP. Studies of social networks within sociopragmatics in other domains (e.g. family, education, religious) are somewhat less numerous but nonetheless illuminating; even more illuminating perhaps for sociopragmatics in the present day are interactions in online communities.

12.3.1 Social Groups and Relational Networks in Online Communities

Harkening back to determine if an earlier theoretical concept is more apt in studying online discourse, Paolillo (2001) examined how Milroy and Milroy's (1992) Social Network theory worked in relation to linguistic variation in an Internet Relay Chat (IRC). The idea from social network theory is that standard variants correlate with weak social network ties, while vernacular variants are associated with strong network ties. Strong network ties would indicate an agreed-upon set of sociopragmatic norms of interaction. Paolillo's study found that the correlations are not neatly tied to network strength. More relevant to our current purposes here, the study found that the specific social functions of the different variables and the larger social context of IRC affects tie strength. In other words, we might say that Social Network Theory, as it was originally proposed, may not be the most relevant for applications to the newer relational networks found in online communities.

If Social Network Theory cannot be straightforwardly applied to online communities, things are not necessarily easier for the notion of Communities of Practice. We already highlighted (in Section 12.2.3) the difficulty of deciding whether an online group constitutes a recognizable CofP or not. Susan Herring (e.g. Herring et al. 1992) has proposed the term Computer Mediated Discourse Analysis (CMDA) to identify the area of online research that is most fruitful for analysing sociopragmatic phenomena. In her own words: "An important challenge facing Internet researchers is ... how to identify and describe online phenomena in culturally meaningful terms, while at the same time grounding their distinctions in empirically observable behavior" (Herring et al. 1992: 338).

Herring has contributed greatly to our knowledge of how CofPs instantiate norms of interaction within the boundaries of those very groups. Her

1992 study focused on the folk belief that women talk more than men. That research analysed an internet discussion group of academics on the topic of men's literature. The data showed that during two days when women in the group participated more than the men, several of the men unsubscribed from the group, citing as their reason for unsubscribing that the women monopolized the discussion. The authors state: "it was a 'boy' cott, a 'power play' intended to silence those women who persisted in speaking uncomfortable truths about the gender/power dynamics on the list ... threats of withdrawal occurred on and immediately following a day when the majority of messages were posted by women" (175). The study exemplifies the sociopragmatic belief that women talk more than men, which has been widely shown not to be the case. In other words, even in the academic domain, among scholars of both sexes, the perceived violation of the norm of who gets to 'talk' resulted in an attempt to silence the women's participation in the online discussion group.

Clearly, this is an early study, pre-dating a plethora of research on socially focused CMDA. More recent research reveals much about group identity, identifying discourse styles associated with several sociolinguistic variables beyond gender, e.g. participant age (see Ravert 2001), ethnicity and race (see Jacobs-Huey 1997). The inherent problem with analysing online discursive behaviour is that of inferring perceived group identity indirectly. In fact, there are severe constraints on what kinds of phenomena can be investigated via online discourse behaviours.

Notwithstanding these limitations, there is also the case for utilizing various methodologies in such analysis, including the analysis of speech behaviour. One important strand of research on sociopragmatics in virtual communities has concentrated on Interlanguage Pragmatics (ILP) and Cross-Cultural Pragmatics (CCP) (see Boxer 2002). The study of sociopramatics in these two research threads is critical for ascertaining just how language users, either as a lingua franca (in CCP) user or as a new speaker (in ILP), use aspects of the language in appropriate ways. It has long been known that while so-called native speakers tend to forgive their interlocutors' errors in grammar and pronunciation, we are less forgiving of violations of sociopragmatic norms, rendering our perceptions of the interlocutor *not* as a non-native user but rather as someone who is simply rude.

Blattner and Fiori (2011) report on the results of a pedagogical intervention, sociocultural in nature, that afforded learners guided awareness on discourse analysis tasks on the social practices in social network communities (SNCs), specifically Facebook groups. This was one way in which a SNC was constructively integrated into the classroom with the hope of widening the options available to learners and instructors. The authors' expressly stated goal was to promote sociopragmatic development through online communication that entailed interpretation and collaboration – a major goal of language itself. They indicate that clearly it is not technology itself that promotes learning, but rather the ways in which technology is employed. An important aspect of sociopragmatic development is, as we know from early SLA research, the establishment of relational networks, in this case online networks. Only with the trust that comes with feeling part of a group dynamic are language learners comfortable enough to engage in the sort of negotiated interaction that is so necessary for L2 pragmatic development.

Zappavigna (2011) terms this notion 'ambient affiliation'. The concept is informative for sociopragmatics in that it shows how online communities are being created in ways that enable one to search for only like-minded individuals. In other words, relationality in online platforms is often preconceived by the language user in selection of social groups online. Zappavigna explores how language is used to build community with the microblogging service Twitter. The study analyses the structure and meaning in a corpus of 45,000 tweets collected in the 24 hours after the announcement of Barack Obama's victory in the 2008 US presidential elections. This analysis examines the evaluative language used to affiliate in tweets, showing how a typographic convention, the hashtag, has extended its meaning potential to operate as a linguistic marker referencing the target of evaluation in a tweet (e.g. #Obama). This both renders the language searchable and is used to upscale the call to affiliate with values expressed in the tweet. We are currently witnessing a cultural shift in electronic discourse from online conversation to such searchable talk. In our ability to now search for like-minded individuals that are part of group affiliation, we self-select the 'choir' of which we desire to be part. Thus, the built-in relationality lends itself to already ingrained sociopragmatic norms.

Also concentrating on Twitter as a resource for online communication, Terkourafi et al. (2018) provide a very recent analysis of sociopragmatics that reveals uncivil speech, or in this case, perceived hate speech. Borrowing Zappavigna's notion of the affiliative function of online platforms, the authors contend that it is this very function that draws like-minded users to break the rules of what in politeness theories is typically considered appropriate speech behaviour. It offers a case-study of a real-life academic job retraction offer regarding reneging on the appointment of a new faculty member after his series of tweets criticizing Israeli military operations in Gaza. Drawing on the notion of context collapse from Marwick and boyd (2011), the authors assert that in Twitter the various social contexts are collapsed, making it difficult for users to manage issues of face and identity:

> Pragmatic theories have traditionally assumed that communicators formulate their messages with a particular audience in mind and reference this audience to circumscribe the meaning of the message itself.... However, if the audience of the message is potentially open-ended – especially if knowingly so – so will the interpretations that can be derived from it. (Terkourafi et al. 2018: 52)

With searchable talk in virtual discourse, we are able to bypass the work involved in becoming part of a social group. In contrast, there is also the inherent ability to be part of a wider and more diverse audience with no clear sharing of norms of interaction. There are clearly pros and cons to searchability, the analysis of which is philosophical and therefore somewhat beyond the scope of the present chapter. Suffice it to say that CofPs now may be pre-existing in some platforms of the virtual world, but a shared set of practices cannot be assumed for all online communication, which is much more heterogeneous and diverse, as the work of Terkourafi et al. (2018) demonstrates.

12.4 Summary and Future Directions

In this chapter we have attempted to illuminate how social groups and relational networks work to create a consensus among their members regarding sociopragmatic norms of interaction. Central to these notions are the various conceptualizations of identity. We have discussed the historical evolution of key theories upon which the sociopragmatics of relational networks are based and key methodologies that have been most fruitfully employed to research relationality.

Regarding methodologies, we have outlined the usefulness of Linguistic Ethnography and its correlate, interactional sociolinguistics as preferred means to study the sociopragmatics of relational networks. In-depth qualitative analysis of new groups can shed light on the development of shared norms in particular constellations of practice. We have offered a sampling of historically spread out case studies in order to demonstrate just how sociopragmatic norms are instantiated in various domains of interaction. These have concentrated on the spheres of social discourse and workplace discourse, with more recent research centred on online discourse. Regarding face-to-face interaction, the workplace domain is now of critical importance given the multicultural nature of workplaces in postmodernity. Transnationalism and globalization have rendered sociopragmatics a more difficult issue than ever before. When people move from one location to another that is vastly different both culturally and linguistically, identities become a matter of flux and fluidity. They are neither fixed nor permanent. This very fact makes salient the idea that identity and social groups are two concepts that go hand in hand.

The sociopragmatics of relational networks has been studied against the backdrop of the speech communities, social networks and Communities of Practice in which interactions take place. This latter notion of CofP has been most useful in present-day studies where social groups are often fluid or even ephemeral, rendering the study of sociopragmatic norms a more fuzzy area than it had been previously. When social networks were considered to be bounded by geography, we needed only to discover the domains in which interactants engaged, the individuals who were at the vanguard of linguistic diffusion, and the outcomes of a more fixed set of norms. Nowadays, with more 'light' networks prevailing in a world of virtual communities, the task is not as clear-cut. Adding to this difficulty, the current state of globalization and transnationalism renders sociopragmatics obfuscated in a shrinking planet. We assert that the planet is shrinking due to the very fluidity of movement of people from one community to another to another. This action is taking place both in real time and virtually. The question regarding sociopragmatics now is: what can we truthfully say about present-day group norms?

According to Blommaert (2018: 56), "communicative practice is always and invariably an act of identity". Blommaert's notions of 'thick' versus 'light' communities aptly illustrate just how identity and social groups are inextricable from each other. In the online/offline world there are profound identity shifts occurring moment by moment. Identities are enacted and performed in specific time-space environments, making salient the difficulty of taking into account the different contexts provided by online and offline contexts. In Blommaert's words, "The online world is a space where distinct forms of identity work can be performed, only distantly connected to what goes on elsewhere" (62).

In the discussion here we have outlined how these insights lend themselves to the broader field of social action. Examining the new array of communities from former 'thick' groups to more current 'light' communities, we are now called to engage with a deeper understanding of the range of social contexts between these two poles. Upon superficial examination, newer online communities may appear to display many of the same features of more traditional 'thick' communities. However, in Blommaert's (2018: 68) view, "if we wish to comprehend contemporary forms of social cohesion, we need to be aware of the prominent role of 'light' communities and 'light' practices of conviviality as factors of cohesion".

The notions of social groups and relational networks are therefore changing before our very eyes. With this change come issues of how relationality works in newer fluid and ever-changing groups. Initially, the sociolinguists' task was descriptive in nature. However, since the 1990s, research took a stance of going beyond describing communicative practices to understanding and ameliorating problems inherent in newer kinds of human interactions. Where groups collide in attempts to merge into new sociopragmatic realities, discourse analysts are taking a more critical approach in order to reach beyond description to what Wodak (1999) has termed 'therapy'. What is to be done about the current issues inherent in new social groups and relational networks? How are we to forge a better understanding among emerging groupings? Sociolinguistics (and thus sociopragmatics) has taken a step beyond the merely descriptive. We must now apply our theoretical and empirical findings to ameliorate social problems.

Future studies of social groups and relational networks must necessarily take into account this pressing issue, focusing on power dynamics in newer social groupings. New methodologies are now needed that take a critical perspective on sociopragmatic collision, clash and conflict.

References

Anderson, B. (1983). *Imagined communities: Reflections on the origin and spread of nationalism.* London: Verso Books.

Arundale, R. B. (1999). An alternative model and ideology of communication for an alternative to politeness theory. *Pragmatics: Quarterly Publication of the International Pragmatics Association*, 9(1), 119–53.

Arundale, R. B. (2010). Constituting face in conversation: Face, facework, and interactional achievement. *Journal of Pragmatics*, 42(8), 2078–2105.

Arundale, R. B. (2020). *Communicating and Relating: Constituting Face in Everyday Interacting.* Oxford: Oxford University Press.

Austin, J. (1962). *How to Do Things with Words.* Cambridge, MA: Harvard University Press.

Blattner, G. and Fiori, M. (2011). Virtual social network communities: An investigation of language learners' development of sociopragmatic awareness and multiliteracy skills. *CALICO Journal*, 29(1), 24–43.

Blommaert, J. (2005). *Discourse: A Critical Introduction.* New York: Cambridge University Press.

Blommaert, J. and De Fina, A. (2015). Chronotopic identities. In A. De Fina, D. Ikizoglu and J. Wegner, eds., *Diversity and Super-diversity: Sociocultural Linguistic Perspective.* Washington, DC: Georgetown University Press, pp. 1–15.

Blommaert, J. (2018). *Durkheim and the Internet: On Sociolinguistics and the Sociological Imagination.* London: Bloomsbury.

Bourdieu, P. and Wacquant, L. J. (1992). *An Invitation to Reflexive Sociology.* Chicago: University of Chicago Press.

Boxer, D. (2002). Discourse issues in cross-cultural pragmatics. *Annual Review of Applied Linguistics*, 22, 150–67.

Boxer, D. and Cortés-Conde, F. (1997). From bonding to biting: Conversational joking and identity display. *Journal of Pragmatics*, 27(3), 275–94.

Bucholtz, M. and Hall, K. (2004). Theorizing identity in language and sexuality research. *Language in Society*, 33(4), 469–515.

Brown, P. and Levinson, S. (1987). *Politeness.* Cambridge: Cambridge University Press.

Culpeper, J. (2008). Reflections on impoliteness, relational work and power. In D. Bousfield and M. A. Locher, eds., *Impoliteness in Language: Studies on Its Interplay with Power in Theory and Practice*, vol. 21. New York: Mouton Gruyter, pp. 17–44.

Eckert, P. (2006). Communities of practice. *Encyclopedia of Language and Linguistics, 2*, 683–5.

Eckert, P. and McConnel-Ginet, S. (1992). Communities of practice: Where language, gender, and power all live. In K. Hall, M. Bucholtz and B. Moonwoman, eds., *Locating Power: Proceedings of the Second Berkeley Woman and Language Conference*, vol. 2, pp. 80–99.

Eckert, P. and McConnell-Ginet, S. (1999). New generalizations and explanations in language and gender research. *Language in Society, 28*(2), 185–201.

Enfield, N. J. (2009). Relationship thinking and human pragmatics. *Journal of Pragmatics, 41*(1), 60–78.

Erickson, F. and Schultz, J. (1982). *The Counselor as Gatekeeper*. New York: Academic Press.

Fodor, J. A. and Katz, J. J. (1963). The structure of a semantic theory. *Language, 39*(2), 170–210.

Fletcher, J. K. (1999). *Disappearing Acts: Gender, Power, and Relational Practice at Work*. Cambridge, MA: MIT Press.

Goffman, E. (1959). The moral career of the mental patient. *Psychiatry, 22*(2), 123–42.

Goffman, E. (1963). *Stigma: Notes on the Management of a Spoiled Identity*. New York: Simon and Schuster.

Gumperz, J. (1971). *Language in Social Groups*. Stanford, CA: Stanford University Press.

Gumperz, J., Jupp, T. and Roberts, C. (1979). *Crosstalk*. Southall, UK: BBC/National Centre for Industrial Language Training.

Grice, H. P. (1973). Logic and conversation. In P. Cole and J. Morgan, eds., *Syntax and Semantics*, vol. 3, *Speech Acts*. New York: Academic Press, pp. 41–58.

Haugh, M., Kádár, D. and Mills, S. (2013). Interpersonal pragmatics: Issues and debates. *Journal of Pragmatics, 58*, 1–11.

Heritage, J. (1984). *Garfinkel and Ethnomethodology*. Oxford: Blackwell.

Herring, S. (2004). Computer-mediated discourse analysis: An approach to researching online behavior. In S. A. Barab, R. Kling and J. H. Gray, eds., *An Approach to Researching Online Behavior: Designing for Virtual Communities in the Service of Learning*. New York: Cambridge University Press, pp. 338–76.

Herring, S., Johnson, D. and DiBenedetto, T. (1992). Participation in electronic discourse in a 'feminist' field. In K. Hall et al., eds., *Locating Power: Proceedings of the Second Berkeley Women and Language Conference*. Berkeley: University of California Press, pp. 250–62.

Holmes, J. and Schnurr, S. (2006). Doing femininity at work: More than just relational practice. *Journal of Sociolinguistics, 10*(1), 31–51.

Hymes, D. (1974). *Foundations in Sociolinguistics: An Ethnographic Approach*. Philadelphia: University of Pennsylvania Press.

Jacobs-Huey, L. (1997). Is there an authentic African American speech community? CARLA revisited. *University of Pennsylvania Working Papers in Linguistics, 4*(1), 331–70.

Kirilova, M. and Angouri, J. (2018). You are now one of us – negotiating 'fitting in' in the workplace. In A. Creese and A. Blackledge, eds., *The Routledge Handbook of Language and Superdiversity*. London: Routledge, pp. 345–60.

Labov, W. (1966). *The Social Stratification of English in New York City*. Washington, DC: Center for Applied Linguistics.

Labov, W. (1972). *Sociolinguistic Patterns*. Philadelphia: University of Pennsylvania Press.

Lave, J. and Wenger, E. (1991). *Situated Learning: Legitimate Peripheral Participation*. Cambridge: Cambridge University Press.

Le Page, R. B. and Tabouret-Keller, A. (1985). *Acts of Identity: Creole-Based Approaches to Language and Ethnicity*. Cambridge: Cambridge University Press.

Leech, G. N. (2016). *Principles of Pragmatics*. London: Routledge.

Locher, M. A. and Graham, S. L. (2010). Introduction to interpersonal pragmatics. In M. Locher and S. L. Graham, eds., *Interpersonal Pragmatics*. Berlin: Mouton de Gruyter, pp. 1–13.

Locher, M. A. and Watts, R. J. (2008). Relational work and impoliteness: Negotiating norms of linguistic behavior. In D. Bousfield and M. A. Locher, eds., *Impoliteness in Language: Studies on Its Interplay with power in Theory and Practice*. Berlin: Mouton de Gruyter, pp. 77–99.

Marwick, A. E. and boyd, d. (2011). I tweet honestly, I tweet passionately: Twitter users, context collapse, and the imagined audience. *New Media and Society*, 13(1), 114–33.

McLaughlin, B. (1995). Aptitude from an information-processing perspective. *Language Testing*, 12(3), 370–87.

Marmaridou, S. (2011). Pragmalinguistics and sociopragmatics. In W. Bublitz and N. Norrick, eds., *Foundations of Pragmatics*. Berlin: Mouton de Gruyter, pp. 77–106.

Marra, M. (2013). English in the workplace. In B. Paltridge and S. Starfield, eds., *The Handbook of English for Specific Purposes*. Hoboken, NJ: Wiley & Blackwell, pp. 175–92.

Milroy, J. and Milroy, L. (1978). Belfast: Change and variation in urban vernacular. In P. Trudgill et al., eds., *Sociolinguistic Patterns in British English*. London: Arnold, pp. 19–36.

Milroy, J. and Milroy, L. (1985). Linguistic change, social network and speaker innovation. *Journal of Linguistics*, 21(2), 339–84.

Milroy, L. and Milroy, J. (1992). Social network and social class: Toward an integrated sociolinguistic model. *Language in Society*, 21(1), 1–26.

McLaughlin, B. (1995). Aptitude from an information-processing perspective. *Language Testing*, 12(3), 370–87.

Paolillo, J. C. (2001). Language variation on Internet Relay Chat: A social network approach. *Journal of Sociolinguistics*, 5(2), 180–213.

Ravert, R. (2001). Adolescent chat style. Unpublished manuscript, Indiana University, Bloomington.

Rampton, B. (2011). Linguistic ethnography, interactional sociolinguistics and the study of identities. In Li Wei, ed, *The Routledge Applied Linguistics Reader*. London: Routledge.

Rampton, B. (2008). Disciplinary mixing: Types and case. *Journal of Sociolinguistics, 12*(4), 525–31.

Rheingold, H. (1993). *The Virtual Community: Finding Connection in a Computerized World*. Boston: Addison-Wesley Longman.

Sacks, H., Schegloff, E. and Jefferson, G. (1974). A simplest systematics for the organization of turn-taking in conversation. *Language, 50*, 696–735.

Schnurr, S. and Zayts, O. (2011). Be (com)ing a leader: A case study of co-constructing professional identities at work. In J. Angouri and M. Marra, eds., *Constructing Identities at Work*. London: Palgrave Macmillan, pp. 40–60.

Schiffrin, D. (1996). Interactional sociolinguistics. *Sociolinguistics and Language Teaching, 4*, 307-28.

Searle, J. (1969). *Speech Acts*. Cambridge: Cambridge University Press.

Spencer-Oatey, H. (2002). Managing rapport in talk: Using rapport sensitive incidents to explore the motivational concerns underlying the management of relations. *Journal of Pragmatics, 34*, 529–45.

Spencer-Oatey, H. & Jiang, W. (2003). Explaining cross-cultural pragmatic findings: Moving from politeness maxims to sociopragmatic interactional principles (SIPs). *Journal of Pragmatics, 35*(10–11), 1633–50.

Terkourafi, M., Catedral, L., Haider, I., Kaimzad, F., Melgares, J., Mostacero-Pinilla, C., Nelson, J. and Weissman, B. (2018). Uncivil Twitter: A sociopragmatic analysis. *Journal of Language Aggression and Conflict, 6*(1), 26–57.

Wenger, E. (1999). *Communities of Practice: Learning, Meaning, and identity*. Cambridge: Cambridge University Press.

Wodak, R. (1999). Critical discourse analysis at the end of the twentieth century. *Research on Language and Social Interaction, 32*(1-2), 185–93.

Zappavigna, M. (2011). Ambient affiliation: A linguistic perspective on Twitter. *New Media and Society, 13*(5), 788–806.

Part II
Topics and Settings in Sociopragmatics

Part II

Topics and Settings in Sociopragmatics

13

Face, Facework and Face-Threatening Acts

Maria Sifianou and Angeliki Tzanne[*]

13.1 Introduction

In terms of the traditional components of the language system, the study of face falls under semantics given its rich metaphorical and metonymic extensions (e.g. Marmaridou 2011; Yu 2001). However, since face is a concept 'that has simultaneous affective (e.g. feelings of shame and pride), cognitive (e.g. calculating how much to give and receive face) and behavioral layers' (Ting-Toomey and Kurogi 1998: 190), one could argue that such a psycho-socio-anthropological concept falls squarely under sociopragmatics ('the sociological interface of pragmatics') while it does not seem to be directly related with pragmalinguistics ('the more linguistic end of pragmatics'; Leech 1983: 10, 11; see also Thomas 1983), which deals primarily with issues like speech acts, deixis, implicature and inferencing. Being a complex and multidimensional concept, 'face' is an issue of concern of various disciplines such as sociolinguistics, communication studies, sociology, anthropology, psychology, philosophy, theology, biology and medicine among others (Bogdanowska-Jakubowska 2010: 13, 53; Haugh and Bargiela-Chiappini 2010: 2073).

In pragmatics, in the last 40 or so years, the powerful influence of Goffman ([1955] 1972) and Brown and Levinson's ([1978] 1987) politeness theory, in particular, instigated extensive research on the concept of 'face'. In fact, its bond to im/politeness has been so tight that O'Driscoll (2011a: 21) talks of the routine yoking of face and politeness. This has led to ignoring the millennia long concern with face independent of politeness and outside its presumably Chinese roots (e.g. Bogdanowska-Jakubowska 2010; Ting-Toomey and Kurogi 1998). In fact, it was Brown and Levinson's ([1978] 1987) concept of 'face' which initially attracted criticism from non-western, Japanese and Chinese, in particular, scholars (e.g. Gu 1990; Ide 1989; Mao

---

[*] We thank the reviewer for their expert, detailed and constructive comments.

1994; Matsumoto 1988; Nwoye 1992). Such criticisms along with the "discursive turn" in im/politeness research (Eelen 2001; Locher 2004, 2006; Mills 2003; Watts 2003) brought with them renewed interest in the concept of 'face'. As van der Bom and Mills (2015: 187) contend, a discursive approach is 'concerned with a more contextualized, localized interpretation and a more socially focused approach, centring on judgement and interpretation'. In this context, politeness and face by extension are seen as situated, discursively negotiated phenomena rather than as static entities constructed by analysts.

Given the voluminous research on the concept of 'face' in this direction, one may wonder what more there is to be explored; yet, a volume on sociopragmatics cannot but include an exploration of this concept, which, not only appears to be relevant to both sociology and pragmatics, but it may also offer a useful link between them. Since 'face' is clearly located in sociology and 'face-threatening act' draws heavily on pragmatics, 'facework' may provide a kind of bridge connecting them. The aim of this chapter is to explore these concepts and attempt to unearth their links and sources in both pragmatics and sociology.

The following section offers a brief critical exploration of the concepts of 'face' (Section 13.2.1), 'face-threatening acts' (Section 13.2.2) and 'facework' (Section 13.2.3). Section 13.3 presents a critical overview of some of the developments that resulted from the above concerns along with the discursive turn in politeness research. More specifically, Section 13.3.1 discusses suggested finer distinctions and alternative ways of conceptualizing 'face', Section 13.3.2 deals with the appeal to return to the broader Goffmanian concept, Section 13.3.3 considers the suggested need to distinguish between lay and scientific constructs of face and Section 13.3.4 considers the suggested need to disentangle face from im/politeness. Finally, Section 13.4 concludes the discussion and suggests possible directions in the study of 'face'.

13.2 Key Concepts and Theories

13.2.1 The Concept of 'Face'

The face is a very important part of the human body and, as such, it has given rise to various metaphorical and metonymic extensions in most, if not all, languages (e.g. Marmaridou 2011; O'Driscoll 2017; Yu 2001). More specifically, the meaning of 'face' has extended from the physical object it signifies to the whole human being, including physical and non-physical aspects.

For Spencer-Oatey (2000: 14) face 'is concerned with people's sense of worth, dignity and identity, and is associated with issues such as respect, honour, status, reputation and competence'. Discussing 'face' with reference to Persian, Koutlaki (2002: 1742) sees 'pride' and 'honour' as its two basic components, including 'personality', 'character', 'self-respect' and 'social standing' but also 'esteem' and 'dignity'. According to Ting-Toomey and Kurogi (1998: 190), the notions that are relevant to 'face' are: 'respect, honor, status, reputation, credibility, competence, family/network connection, loyalty, trust, relational indebtedness and obligation'. Ukosakul (2005: 119) sees the Thai notion of face as very similar to that in Chinese, Japanese and other Asian cultures and as frequently 'associated with the sense of dignity, self-esteem, prestige, reputation and pride'. In broader terms, Ting-Toomey (2005: 73) contends that 'the concept of face is about identity respect and other-identity consideration', while being 'tied to the emotional significance and estimated calculations that we attach to our own social self-worth and the social self-worth of others'. Acts threatening these qualities of face may lead to feelings of embarrassment, shame and/or guilt, whereas acts enhancing them may lead to boosted self-esteem and pride.

Bargiela-Chiappini (2009: 307) sums up the roots of face concerns 'in values such as honour, shame and pride'. Brown and Levinson (1987: 13) themselves see face as linked to cultural notions of 'honour and virtue, shame and redemption' and, in relation to Greek, Hirschon (2001: 20) views 'face' and 'honour' as conceptual equivalents. It is worth noting that, while the above understandings of face appear to encompass a variety of different qualities, they seem to be related in sharing a core concept of honour. Reviewing research and debates on honour, Hirschon (2001: 20) distinguishes two lines of interpretation; one seeing honour as 'referring to a person's social reputation, prestige and esteem', and thus as being externally bestowed, and another taking honour to refer to 'a person's intrinsic worth and to moral integrity' and thus to be 'a moral attribute, inherent in a person's notion of self'. This distinction appears to be quite similar to the two aspects of face in Chinese: one which relates to 'honour' and 'reputation', attributed to one by others and the other which relates to 'self-respect' or 'dignity', which is more an inner feeling (St. André 2013: 70).

Even though the above discussion indicates that there is variation across cultures and research has also shown that there is variation across contexts and even among individuals (O'Driscoll 2011a, 2017; Sifianou 2012) as to the conceptualization of 'face', this focus on variation has hindered search for possible commonalities.[1]

Face is a core concept in sociology but unlike many other concepts (e.g. prestige) it is a major determinant of linguistic behaviour or 'the generative mechanism for all communicative behaviors' (Ting-Toomey and Kurogi 1998: 188). Seen in this perspective or even in its alternative, namely that linguistic behaviour in interaction generates face, it becomes apparent that its linguistic manifestations or construction are of immense significance to pragmaticists, since pragmatics at its most basic level is defined as 'the study of language use' (Verschueren 1999: 1, italics removed). Indeed, within

---

[1] But see Yu (2001: 20) who argues that if figurative meaning has a bodily base then similar extensions should be expected in many languages.

pragmatics, Goffman's sociological concept of 'face' constitutes one of the foundational pillars of Brown and Levinson's ([1978] 1987) theory of politeness. For Goffman ([1955] 1972: 319), '*face* may be defined as the positive social value a person effectively claims for himself by the line others assume he has taken during a particular interaction. Face is an image of self delineated in terms of approved social attributes – albeit an image that others may share'. Even though Brown and Levinson (1987: 61) state that their views are a combination of Goffman's and of English folk perceptions which tie face together with 'notions of being embarrassed or humiliated, or "losing face"', Brown and Levinson have developed a theoretical construct which is very distant from both Goffman's and non-academic understandings of the concept. For Brown and Levinson (1987: 66), 'face' is 'the public self-image that every member wants to claim for himself' and consists of two interrelated even though somewhat conflicting aspects: 'positive face' refers to the desire to be appreciated and approved of by at least some others and 'negative face' refers to the desire to be free from impositions.

Brown and Levinson's ([1978] 1987) theory has received both extensive support, especially in earlier publications, and a lot of criticism on a number of grounds, a substantial body of which relates to their employment of the concept of 'face'. Despite their claims to universality, the validity of the theory to account for related phenomena across various cultural contexts has been questioned (e.g. Eelen 2001; Gu 1990; Kasper 1997; Mao 1994; Matsumoto 1988; Mills 2003; Nwoye 1992; Watts 2003; Watts Ide and Ehlich 1992; but see O'Driscoll 2017). They have also been criticized for restricting Goffman's notion of 'face' and introducing a narrow and individualistic construct equating identity concerns with a positive and a negative aspect of it. However, a closer look at Brown and Levinson reveals that for them face is not just a self-image claimed but rather one 'attributed by interactants to one another' (1987: 13). So the dimension of interdependence of social beings is not completely absent from Brown and Levinson's conceptualization of 'face' (but see Arundale 2010 for an alternative view). They (1987: 60) recognize that for an interaction to succeed both self-respect and consideration for the other are needed, but focus on other-face concerns through the mitigation of what they view as, and term, Face-Threatening Acts (FTAs), discussed in Section 13.2.2.

13.2.2 The Concept of 'Face-Threatening Act' (FTA)

A foundational concept closely tied to 'face' in Brown and Levinson's ([1978] 1987) theory is that of 'face-threatening act' (FTA) whose roots are in pragmatics, and speech act theory, in particular. According to Brown and Levinson (1987: 61, 65), face-threatening acts are 'acts that by their nature run contrary to the face wants of the addressee and/or of the speaker'. They (76) suggest that the seriousness of a threat is not inherent in an act but is rather calculated on the basis of three social variables: (1) social distance (D) (i.e. the degree of familiarity shared by interlocutors), (2) relative power (P) (i.e. the social status of the speaker in relation to that of the addressee) and (3) the absolute ranking of the imposition (R) (i.e. the level of face threat of the specific act in the particular culture). Given the mutual vulnerability of face, FTAs and their minimization or avoidance emerge as highly prominent aspects of Brown and Levinson's theory. In fact, politeness is understood as minimizing or avoiding FTAs which is achieved through various facework strategies, that is, through selecting from among a number of alternatives the most appropriate ones in the specific context.

Brown and Levinson (1987: 65–8) classify FTAs according to which aspect of the speaker's or the addressee's face is threatened. Acts that appear to prevent the addressee's independence of movement and freedom of action threaten their negative aspect of face, whereas those which appear as disapproving of their desires threaten their positive aspect of face. For instance, directives (e.g. requests) are seen as prime examples of acts that threaten the addressee's negative aspect of face in that they impose on him/her and disagreements as acts that threaten his/her positive aspect in that they constitute negative evaluations of the other and thus possible disapproval.

Brown and Levinson (1987: 65) admit that they rely on their intuition to suggest that '*certain kinds of acts* intrinsically threaten face' of either or both of the interlocutors, and further add that 'we may distinguish between acts that *primarily* threaten H's face ... and those that threaten *primarily* S's face' (Brown and Levinson 1987: 67, emphasis ours; see also O'Driscoll 2017: 98; Culpeper and Terkourafi 2017: 17). They also note that since speaker and addressee cooperate to maintain each other's face, acts that threaten the speaker's face also potentially threaten the addressee's face. At this point, it is worth mentioning that nowhere in the book are non-face-threatening acts discussed nor are we given any clues as to what kinds of acts they would classify as such. On the contrary, in their illustrative classification of acts in relation to which aspect of whose face is threatened (Brown and Levinson 1987: 65–8), one finds all kinds of speech acts, including expressing thanks and paying compliments and even responding to some such acts. In this sense, despite their clarifications mentioned above, Brown and Levinson ([1978] 1987) appear to view all speech acts as primarily face threatening. This standpoint obscures the fact that some acts can be supportive of (rather than threatening) face and multidirectional and, as such, it has created problems and triggered criticism (e.g. Arundale 2010; Pizziconi 2003). In fact, 'face support is central in everyday language use' (Arundale 2010: 2093), because the expression of compassion and care is integral to human survival (Jones and Bodie 2014).

For Spencer-Oatey (2009: 137), in classifying acts as face threatening, broader issues are at stake since deciding *a priori* on the status of an act ignores 'the dynamic aspect of people's face sensitivities'. Even self-complimenting which is typically understood as breaching the self-praise avoidance principle (Pomerantz 1978) is expected and perceived as appropriate in certain contexts, such as business meetings (Spencer-Oatey 2009: 146). In a similar vein, Mills (2003: 61, 79) contends that Brown and Levinson's notion of what constitutes an FTA is sometimes perverse and further illustrates that the concept is a lot more complex than their conceptualization. This conceptualization probably stems from and/or is reinforced by their preoccupation with decontextualized acts like requests, which rather clearly (though not unexceptionally as shown below) threaten the addressee's negative aspect of face. Moreover, viewing all acts (e.g. thanking and complimenting) as primarily face threatening probably reflects the importance attached to non-imposition by the theory, where even mere verbalization of any act might be considered face threatening (e.g. Mills 2003: 60). In our view, the problematic nature of the concept of 'FTA' is most clearly evident in Brown and Levinson's last (and rather ignored) strategy ("Don't do the FTA"). This issue has been explored elsewhere (e.g. Sifianou 1997), so suffice it to say here that if acts like thanking and apologizing are seen as FTAs (or even as *primarily* FTAs), then we can come to the odd conclusion that avoiding them will be the politest way of behaving.

Holtgraves (2002: 40) illustrates how an act can have multiple implications for face as in the case of compliments which support the positive aspect of the addressee's face but can simultaneously threaten its negative aspect because recipients must provide some kind of response, usually by downgrading the compliment in order to comply with the self-praise avoidance injunction (Pomerantz 1978). As Chang and Haugh (2011: 2948) report, in some contexts, even criticisms and insults can be face-enhancing and some acts may be evaluated as both face threatening and face supportive at the same time. Even requests, which seem to be straightforward cases of threatening the addressee's negative aspect of face, on closer scrutiny, appear to be a lot more complex. Asking for help or for a favour may indicate closeness and solidarity (Fukushima 2000; Spencer-Oatey 2008) and may be even face-enhancing since one must value somebody's views, for instance, to ask for their comments (e.g. between colleagues). Even though one may argue here that the imposition is more salient, the degree of imposition cannot be assessed for any act outside a specific context. For instance, there are requests, such as those employed by customers in service encounters which cannot be seen as face threatening at all since it is part of the duties of shop assistants to serve customers.

A good example of the multidirectionality of speech acts is disagreements, in that they can affect either or both aspects of one or both interlocutors' face. On a theoretical level, Brown and Levinson's (1987: 66) contention that disagreements threaten the addressee's positive aspect of face and should thus be avoided in favour of agreements sounds plausible. However, on closer inspection, the picture appears to be a lot more complex since, as Mey (1993: 72) states, when face is threatened both of its aspects may come under attack. In the case of disagreements, such acts may threaten both aspects of the speaker's face because in disagreeing the speaker may indicate that s/he is not a person who should be liked or approved of, thus threatening his/her own positive aspect of face or conversely, if s/he feels forced to disagree in order to protect his/her own face or even help his/her addressee protect their own face in some way, s/he threatens his/her own negative aspect of face (Sifianou 2012).

Given such criticisms, in the introduction of their new edition, Brown and Levinson (1987: 1) explain their understanding of face-threatening acts as reflecting Goffman's (1971) notion of 'virtual offence' or 'worst possible reading' (Culpeper 2011: 118; O'Driscoll 2017: 98). This notion of 'virtual offence' appears to explain Brown and Levinson's overreliance on the concept of 'face-threatening acts' and to some extent justify their classification of almost all acts as face threatening but it seems to be a rather misplaced account. Goffman (1971: 118) used the concept of 'virtual offence' in relation to remedial work, that is, those exchanges which involve attempts to change the meaning of actions that are potentially offensive for the recipient and this is achieved through accounts, apologies and requests. In addition to remedial interchanges, Goffman also discusses supportive ones, such as offers in response to a request, greetings and expressions of appreciation. If conditions necessitate a supportive act but no such act is performed, then virtual offence will occur which necessitates remedy. For instance, if an offer, a compliment or a greeting among other acts is expected but not produced and this omission conveys disregard, their provision functions as a remedy for which thanks are owed (Goffman 1971: 158).

We thus believe that the problem with Brown and Levinson's ([1978] 1987) conceptualization of most of our acts as face threatening or potentially face threatening still remains. If compliments and apologies, for instance, are face-threatening acts in their worst possible reading, then one may wonder how the former can serve as devices redressing other face-threatening acts (Brown and Levinson 1987: 103) and the latter can redress the impingement on the addressee's negative aspect of face (Brown and Levinson 1987: 187). It seems that conceptualizing speech acts in isolation allows for such readings whereas seeing them in interactions reveals their complex nature and the impossibility of deciding in advance whether they are FTAs.

13.2.3 The Concept of 'Facework'

To avoid or mitigate face-threatening acts, people use what Goffman ([1955] 1972: 324) calls 'facework' and defines as 'the actions taken by a person to make whatever he is doing consistent with face. Facework serves to counteract "incidents" – that is, events whose effective symbolic implications threaten face'. Relating facework to face threats only is restrictive and for O'Driscoll (2007: 467), facework 'is widely accepted as a useful term to denote actions which have a bearing on face'. Goffman provides a number of distinctions relating to facework. One such basic distinction is that between avoidance (negative rites) and presentational (positive rites) rituals. The former refer to avoiding impinging on the other and the latter to the presentation of appreciation for and solidarity with another. These include 'ritualized offerings', also called 'supportive interchanges', such as greetings, compliments and invitations offered to others as a means of supporting social relationships (Holtgraves 1992: 142). Goffman sees poise as an important type of facework and discusses in detail two basic types of facework: the avoidance process and the corrective process. The best way to avoid threats to face is to avoid contacts in which they are likely to occur or voluntarily withdraw from them. If they do occur, there are other avoidance practices which come into play such as switching topics at opportune moments, displaying discretion, respect and politeness, using ambiguities and courtesies and overlooking the incident. In any encounter, as Goffman argues, a person will have a defensive and a protective orientation, the former directed at saving one's own face and the latter at saving the other's face and, in general, the two perspectives will be taken simultaneously. On the other hand, the corrective process is involved when a face threat is acknowledged, and attempts are made to correct the offence and re-establish the ritual equilibrium (Goffman [1955] 1972: 328).

Brown and Levinson ([1978] 1987) do not use the term 'facework' but instead discuss exclusively face threats and face redressive action in relation to politeness. By redressive action they mean 'action that "gives face" to the addressee, that is, that attempts to counteract the potential face damage of the FTA by doing it in such a way, or with such modifications or additions, that indicate clearly that no such face threat is intended or desired, and that S in general recognizes H's face wants and himself wants them to he achieved' (Brown and Levinson 1987: 69–70). Such redressive action is of two types, depending on which aspect of face (negative or positive) is being focused on. They outline five possible strategic choices for dealing with FTAs: (1) bald on record, (2) positive politeness, (3) negative politeness, (4) off record and (5) don't do the FTA. The first strategy is chosen when the threat to face is estimated to be relatively low or when other concerns are more salient than those related to face (e.g. urgency). When the face threat is estimated to be relatively very high, the last strategy is seen as the most appropriate one.

Even though for Brown and Levinson politeness is assumed to be involved only when face interests are at risk, thus being much narrower than facework (Kasper 1997: 377), the way Brown and Levinson's theory has developed may lead one to assume that facework is coterminous with politeness, so that Watts (2003: 89 and elsewhere) warns us against such a reading. In this connection, Watts (2003) and Locher and Watts (2005: 10) argue that Brown and Levinson's theory is not a theory of politeness but rather one of facework, though largely concerned with the mitigation of face-threatening acts. In fact, there is wide consensus that Brown and Levinson's understanding of face is restricted since politeness is just one of the dimensions of facework (e.g. Haugh 2013; Hernández-Flores 2008; O'Driscoll 2017; Spencer-Oatey 2008), it is 'a display of facework' (Hernández-Flores 2008: 693), especially its 'other-oriented, supportive type' (O'Driscoll 2011b). But facework is not thus restricted as it may also aim at maintaining or enhancing the speaker's face or, on the contrary, at (intentionally) attacking it, a possibility that has been extensively discussed in impoliteness scholarship (e.g. Culpeper 2011). In addition, Koutlaki (2002) and Ruhi (2010), among others, argue for the importance of considering a self perspective of face since self-presentation is significant in the management of face. Similarly, for Hernández-Flores (2008: 695), facework may be self-oriented, that is, focus on the speaker's face without 'directly affecting the addressee's face' as in self-praise or self-criticism. Moreover, politeness broadly understood is not only face-related as it also involves adherence to social norms. In this sense then, politeness is broader than facework (O'Driscoll 2011a). Haugh (2012: 118) elucidates this ambiguity when he states that we should be careful when we use the term 'facework' as it can be used in Brown and Levinson's narrower sense of "face-saving" politeness or in the broader sense of interactional moves that impact on face. Along similar lines, O'Driscoll (2011a: 23) contends that the relationship between facework and politeness can be seen from two perspectives: (1) politeness as a possible aspect of facework and (2) facework as one component of politeness.

Thus, one can conclude that there is an area of overlap between facework and politeness but the two are not coterminous.

13.3 Developments in the Conceptualization of 'Face'

Initial reactions against Brown and Levinson's ([1978] 1987) conceptualization of face concerned its duality (i.e. its positive and negative aspects). Early research emanating mostly from non-western contexts argues that face is a richer construct which involves not only social and moral but also group aspects. It is worth noting here that despite harsh criticism, this duality, modified in various ways, has survived as togetherness / apartness in a lot of later research (see O'Driscoll 2017: 106–7 for a comprehensive overview). These have been argued to be universal wants and what differs cross-culturally is their intensity and content.

Such concerns along with the discursive turn in im/politeness research have contributed to the expansion of research on the concept of 'face'. Generally speaking, the discursive approach is concerned with the contextual analysis of both politeness and impoliteness (LPRG 2011: 5). Face is now seen not as something of a more or less static nature but emergent in interaction. Going further, Arundale (2010) sees face as a relational and interactional phenomenon arising in everyday interaction, a kind of dyadic achievement. In this context, various related lines of argumentation have emerged. These include (1) suggestions for finer distinctions and alternatives, (2) the need for a return to the broader Goffmanian concept, (3) the need for a distinction between first- and second-order face and (4) the need for disentangling face from politeness. These issues will be considered in Sections 13.3.1–13.3.4.

13.3.1 Finer Distinctions and Alternatives

Even before the emergence of the discursive turn, concerns that Brown and Levinson's ([1978] 1987) conceptualization of face was restricted and thus rather unable to capture the complexities of the concept cross-culturally had led scholars to suggest modifications and refinements. For instance, Lim and Bowers (1991) argued that 'positive face' is underspecified and suggested that it has two distinct dimensions: (1) the want to be included or 'fellowship face' and (2) the want to be respected for one's abilities or 'competence face'. These may look superficially very similar but at a deeper level, they represent two very different kinds of basic human needs, the former relating to the need for belonging and inclusion and the latter to esteem needs. These along with 'autonomy face' (i.e. Brown and Levinson's 'negative face') are not just threatened but supported or threatened in interaction. Related is O'Driscoll's (2007: 474) view who advocates the confinement of the positive aspect of face to 'pertain solely to connection and belonging' and the negative aspect to 'separation and individuation'. In this way, he preserves the positive/negative relationship by retaining the term 'positive' but restricting its content to the exact opposite of the negative (something akin to Lim and Bower's 1991 'fellowship face'). O'Driscoll (2007: 480, 481) sees a further need for what he terms 'culture-specific face' and contends that this bears considerable cross-cultural and situational variation and may have little to do with the positive and the negative aspects of face. In other words, he espouses the need for an empty category which becomes culturally and situationally meaningful. Similarly, empty categories are envisioned by Bravo (2008) who expands on her earlier suggestion on 'affiliation' and 'autonomy' aspects of face. The former refers to being a member of a group and the latter to having one's own identity within a group (Bravo 2008: 566; see also Garcés-Conejos Blitvich and Bou-Franch 2019). According to Bravo, these notions are interdependent and can account for the interdependence of individuals in society. Going further, Bogdanowska-Jakubowska (2010) sees face as an empty container, which she calls 'cultural face', and which is filled with specific cultural content, the social dimension of which includes moral face, prestige face and relational face. Ting-Toomey (2009: 240) explicates a longer list of types of face which includes: 'autonomy face, approval face, status face, reliability face, competence face, and moral face'.

In order to uncover the interdependence through the discursive negotiation of face that goes on between interlocutors in interactions, alternatives such as 'rapport-management' (e.g. Spencer-Oatey 2000, 2005), 'relational work' (e.g. Locher and Watts 2005, 2008; Locher 2006) and 'face constituting theory' (e.g. Arundale 1999, 2005, 2010) have been proposed. These terms are akin to 'facework' but they are preferred to it since in early politeness research, 'facework' was restricted having been associated with the mitigation of face-threatening acts (Locher 2006: 250). Spencer-Oatey (2000, 2002 and elsewhere) proposes a sociopragmatic model of rapport-management and suggests a refinement of the concept of 'face' to include not only 'quality' and 'social identity' face and later 'relational' face but also 'sociality rights' specifically comprising 'equity' and 'association' rights. Even though these are conceptually distinct, they can be interrelated (Spencer-Oatey 2007: 652). Very briefly, 'quality face' refers to the desire of positive evaluation of one's personal qualities (e.g. competence, abilities) and 'social identity face' refers to the desire for acknowledgement of one's social identities or roles (e.g. group leader, valued customer). 'Sociality rights' are entitlements that one claims for oneself in interactions with others and are derived from personal and/or social expectancies. They include two interrelated aspects: 'equity rights', that is, one's entitlement to personal consideration from others, so as to be treated fairly by not being imposed unduly or ordered about unfairly, and 'association rights', that is, one's entitlement to social involvement with, or detachment from, others. Equity rights are seen as partly related to Brown and Levinson's ([1978] 1987) concept of 'negative face', but they are broader in scope and may not lead to face threat or loss but rather to annoyance or irritation;[2] on the other hand, 'quality face' is seen as partly related to Brown and Levinson's ([1978] 1987) concept of 'positive face'. Spencer-Oatey (2008) illustrates how all these are involved in specific instances of requests, apologies and compliments rather than being simply viewed as inherently face-threatening acts oriented to one aspect of face. In addition, she (2007: 644) suggests that, in cognitive terms, face relates to the notion of 'self-image', which includes individual, relational and collective construals of self, and is perceived as a more global and long-term construal akin to identity (Garcés-Conejos Blitvich 2013; Locher 2011). These suggestions tie in with core arguments in relation to what face is, such as its enduring or fleeting and group aspects (e.g. O'Driscoll 2017).

The relational aspect of communication is foregrounded by Locher and Watts (e.g. Locher and Watts 2005, 2008; Locher 2006) who define relational work as referring 'to the "work" individuals invest in negotiating relationships with others' (Locher and Watts 2005: 10) and elsewhere argue

---

[2] As Culpeper (2011: 62) suggests, violations of sociality rights will probably be accompanied by other-condemning emotions such as anger and contempt whereas violations of face are more likely to be accompanied by self-conscious emotions such as embarrassment and shame.

that relational work 'refers to all aspects of the work invested by individuals in the construction, maintenance, reproduction and transformation of interpersonal relationships among those engaged in social practice' (Locher and Watts 2008: 96). At the heart of their broad understanding of relational work lies Goffman's concept of 'face' which they view as negotiated rather than fixed in the social practices that interlocutors get engaged in and also as significant since 'there is no face-less communication' (Locher 2011: 188). This understanding of relational work also enables them to account for the various shades of both polite and impolite behaviour. In this context, face crucially depends on its acceptance by the other(s) one is interacting with.

In contrast to the above, Arundale (2005, 2009, 2010, 2013) rejects both Goffman's and Brown and Levinson's conceptualizations of face and offers a truly alternative relational and interactional approach to face, grounded in a different conceptualization of communication, which he calls 'Face Constituting Theory'. For him, face is conjointly co-constituted by interlocutors in interactions, that is, it is seen as an emergent property of situated relationships but not in terms of individual agency but in terms of relationships among persons (Arundale 2005: 201, 202; 2013: 292). More recently, Arundale (2013) has questioned the utility of the concept of 'face' as 'the best metaphor to use in representing either the phenomena that Goffman (1955) examined, or the broad range of social practices for relating to others in using language that are evident across cultural groups' (Arundale 2013: 282) and argues that 'scholars need to identify the best alternative to the metaphor of face to use in their work with each cultural group' (Arundale 2013: 293).

13.3.2 Return to the Goffmanian Concept of Face

Concerns similar to those which have led scholars to suggest finer distinctions and alternatives have also led other scholars to espouse a return to the Goffmanian concept (see e.g. Bargiela-Chiappini 2003; Watts 2003), since, as has been argued, it provides a better basis for the social/interpersonal aspects of face. However, as Haugh (2009: 4; see also Bargiela-Chiappini 2003) argues, even though 'a return to a more interactionally-grounded notion of face certainly holds much promise' ample evidence from folk conceptualizations of face indicates that 'a more careful examination of the implications of this proposed shift back to Goffman's notion of face is clearly warranted' as Goffman's views may reflect North American understandings.

It may be the case that, as Ruhi and Işık-Güler (2007: 708) argue, 'the use of 'face' as a technical term has biased the attention given to 'public self-image' in research on (im)politeness'. As mentioned earlier, Arundale (2013) suggested that we probably need to identify better alternatives to the concept of 'face' to explore the range of social practices for relating to others. In this direction and on the basis of Thai data, Intachakra (2012) suggests that we should move beyond the face metaphor in politeness research and offers the heart as an alternative. After all, face mostly represents the outside whereas the heart the inside, the former being a (closed or open) window to the latter for the Chinese (see also Yu, 2001) or a mirror to the soul for the Greek. Fukushima (2015) also argues for the concept of 'heart' in Japanese as better suited to account for non-linguistic (behavioural) aspects of politeness, in particular.

13.3.3 Distinction between Face1 and Face2

The issues that emerged from attempts to consider face across cultures have led scholars to suggest the need for a distinction between Face1 and Face2. This is analogous to an earlier distinction, which goes back to Watts et al. (1992) and Eelen (2001), between first- and second-order politeness with the latter referring to theoretical constructs and the former to lay conceptualizations of it (O'Driscoll 2011a; Terkourafi 2007). In this sense, some scholars have searched for a universal construct, associated with psychological processes of identity construction (St. André 2013: 78) and others have argued that face is not given but negotiated between interlocutors as they interact in specific contexts, much like politeness, and should thus be analysed from the participants' perspective rather than the analyst's (Arundale 2010; Haugh 2009: 5). Haugh (2009, 2012) argues that special care should be taken to ensure that participants' perspectives are investigated and that the analyst's perspectives are not imposed on the interpretation of an encounter. He states that this can only be grounded in the sequential development of interaction and discusses in detail why a more careful deconstruction is needed as regards both the ontological and epistemological loci of the first/second-order distinction. However, since identification of face and facework in interactional data entails judgement (Haugh 2009: 7), one should perhaps start with the analysis of interactional data which include invokings of face. Even though such invocations have been associated mostly with East Asian societies and metapragmatic discourse, they can be found in other languages (Haugh 2009: 12–13). Moreover, most of these do not constitute metapragmatic discourse but metaphorical and metonymic uses of language. For instance, a Greek person went to Athens aiming to find a job but as she did not succeed, she says "I was obliged to 'drop my face' and borrow money from my parents" (Sketchengine, elTenTen14). In a similar vein, another Greek person says "Having no other option, I 'lowered my face' and returned home" (Sketchengine, elTenTen14).

Clearly, such uses are not metapragmatic evaluative judgements about behaviour, but rather collocations used instead of other expressions as in Haugh's (2010: 13) example of the footballer who said "The loss awoke us. We had to save face after such a defeat". These are mostly used in self-reference to describe one's own emotions and feelings (e.g. embarrassment, shame or guilt) and may implicitly evaluate their own actions.

In reference to others, such collocations are usually descriptive even though they may also be evaluative of some presumably inappropriate behaviour. Furthermore, as O'Driscoll (2017: 95) avers 'face' denotes a property whereas 'politeness' a kind of behaviour. This then indicates that it is easier to unearth first-order understandings of politeness since there may be overt evaluations of behaviour but rather difficult to do so with a property like face. In other words, people do not comment in any similar way on face or facework in their interactions, unless they are specifically asked to do so by, for instance, the analyst (e.g. Garcés-Conejos Blitvich and Bou-Franch 2019). Close scrutiny of such collocations will reveal how interlocutors actually conceptualize and use the term 'face' and the gamut of its meanings that their language offers them. This approach will offer us the clear understanding of first-order notions that as Haugh and Watanabe (2009: 91–2), among others, argue, is needed for 'an understanding of the assumptions and expectations constitutive of and enacted through interaction which underlie the interactional achievement of face'.

The study of such data shows that folk understandings of face go beyond Brown and Levinson's conceptualization. As a result, as we have seen, some suggested modifications and alternatives and others a return to the broader Goffmanian concept. Such considerations are also related to voices who have argued that, despite their relationship, face and politeness should be studied separately.

13.3.4 Disentangling Face from Politeness

Despite the fact that politeness is no longer seen as the only type of facework (Section 13.2.3), the concept of 'face' has remained at the core of im/politeness research (Haugh 2013). However, as the above examples indicate and as various scholars have suggested this conflation between face/facework and im/politeness is problematic. For instance, Haugh and Bargiela-Chiappini (2010: 2073) suggest that 'the time has come for face to be theorized on its own terms' and thus face and politeness should be studied as distinct objects. For Watts (2005: xxviii), face has already 'become an area of research in its own right'. This disentangling has been a result of the problematic nature of the assumed close association between face and im/politeness. As Haugh (2013: 61) argues, 'emic understandings of face$_1$ generally do not underpin emic understandings of politeness$_1$ in many languages'. Scholars exploring im/politeness in different cultural contexts, argue in particular that politeness phenomena are more related to appropriate behaviour than to concerns of maintaining face. For instance, Hinze (2012) offers a number of examples and argues that *mianzi* and *lian* ('face' in Chinese) are not at the heart of Chinese politeness as they are separate concepts which may overlap with politeness in some instances, but they frequently operate in quite different ways. Kádár and Haugh (2013: 51) offer an interesting illustration of face being disentangled from politeness, which they take from the American comedy series *Everybody Hates Chris*.

(1) (Chris is complaining to his parents, asking them to buy him new clothes. They are both adamant against it when the narrator, the grown-up version of Chris, intervenes)

NARRATOR: *The only way I was going to get my mom to spend money on me was if not doing it would embarrass her.*
CHRIS: Mom, I'm the only black kid in the whole school. They already think I'm a crack baby. Wearing this sweater, they'll probably think we're on welfare.
ROCHELLE: Who said we were on welfare? Be home from school on time tomorrow. We're gonna go shopping.

Chris' allusion to the potential embarrassment or face threat to the family's and mother's (Rochelle's) face prompted her to offer to buy new clothes for him. As the authors (2013: 52) contend, 'despite the obvious salience of face in this interaction, it is quite clear that evaluations of politeness (or impoliteness) are not at issue here'. In Greek, too, concern with face is not always related to politeness (Sifianou 2011, 2016). An illustration of this is the headline of a newspaper article (*Vima*, 1 July 2008) which appeared in the midst of the global financial crisis and read as 'the Prime Minister "drops his face" and asks Brussels for help'. In this instance, the then Greek Prime Minister presented as dropping his face and asking Brussels for financial aid is clearly not evaluated as being rude or impolite to Brussels officials. What this headline meant is that this person did something embarrassing, threatening his face as Prime Minister because other concerns were more significant at the time. At the other end of the spectrum, as Spencer-Oatey (2005: 108) illustrates, an unhelpful or indifferent shop assistant can be evaluated as impolite but not as threatening the customer's face unless her behaviour was the result of a discriminatory attitude against him/her. Disentangling face from politeness has given rise to further issues such as the relationship between face and identity (e.g. Garcés-Conejos Blitvich 2009, 2013; Garcés-Conejos Blitvich and Sifianou 2017; Hall and Bucholtz 2013; Haugh and Bargiela-Chiappini 2010; Locher 2011; Spencer-Oatey 2007), an issue not discussed here due to space limitations.

13.4 Concluding Remarks and Future Directions

In this chapter we have tried to locate the beginnings and the development of the concept of 'face' in pragmatics. Since Brown and Levinson ([1978] 1987) presented the concept of 'face' as one of the foundational pillars of their politeness theory, many researchers were intrigued and thus work on this concept proliferated both supporting and refuting their claims. Initially, mainly in cross-cultural research, discontent was expressed with Brown and Levinson's conceptualization of face. This along with the subsequent discursive turn in im/politeness research brought further concerns as regards the concept of 'face' and its relationship to politeness.

There are many ethnographic studies of face in different socio-cultural settings (Haugh 2009) but these tend to focus on differences. However, we are in agreement with Bargiela-Chiappini (2009: 315) who contends that we should perhaps concentrate more on what emic concepts of face share, and on their common underlying norms and values (e.g. shame, honour, deference). In earlier research (Sifianou 2011, 2016), we suggested that the concept of face in Greek seems to share features with the Japanese, Chinese and Korean concepts. For instance, much like these languages, Greek has more than one term for 'face' with overlapping functions, and a range of expressions involving the term 'face'. Much as in East Asian languages, the verbs used in related collocations are those also used for possessions (e.g. *have, fall down, drop*). As in East Asian languages, face is also conceptualized as a collective possession, since a group such as a family may lose face due to wrongdoings by one of its members (see also Ervin-Tripp et al. 1995). In their comparative study, Ruhi and Kádár (2011) find noteworthy similarities between Chinese and Turkish.

It has been argued that exploring the details of the development of actual interactions will enable us to make sense of how participants themselves understand face. Haugh (2012) espouses a conversation analytic approach which will also include ethnographic information and broader sociological perspectives (see also Arundale 2010; Haugh and Watanabe 2009). This clarification is significant because it will be difficult, for instance, to decode the full meaning of a response without relevant detailed information on the interlocutors' relational history. In this connection, it should be noted that work on face appears to have concentrated on passing encounters and has sidestepped issues involved in long-term relationships where some form of face pre-exists having been established in the multitude of prior interactions. A straightforward response which to an outsider (e.g. analyst) may indicate that no offence was taken, may in fact result from a concern to avoid the eruption of conflict or may reflect the interactional style of the producer or the demands of the specific context, among others. As Locher (2011: 203) contends, it is frequently the case that when people feel offended, they may not verbalize it directly, thus such feelings may escape the analyst's attention and this may lead to inaccurate conclusions. In other words, reactions to preceding acts may not necessarily reveal how the act was perceived by the addressee.

What we would like to suggest is that performing a thorough examination of interactions containing collocations with the lexical item 'face' should be a very first step before embarking on analysing actual interactions devoid of such collocations and trying to guess the underlying facework performed. Comparative studies at this initial level can also be illuminating (e.g. Ruhi and Kádár 2011) as it is frequently through comparison that we can better understand our own uses. Constructing a theory of face, especially one that aims to be applicable across languages and cultures is a further step after investigating interactions which include face-related terms and collocations in order to better understand the different ways in which people conceptualize face. Once we obtain this information we can more confidently analyse data which lack such expressions and then proceed with theoretical constructs. As Holtgraves (2002: 59) suggests 'specification of the manifestations of face within a culture needs to be undertaken before the theory can be tested within that culture'.

However, Brown and Levinson's ([1978] 1987) influence has been so strong that it has delimited our understanding of the concept (cf. Hinze 2012) to such an extent that it may even be in conflict with our emic conceptualizations. In addition, it has marginalized the rich western tradition on the concept (but see Bogdanowska-Jakubowska 2010). In our view, such a rather neglected dimension relates to the meaning of this concept in ancient Greek where the word πρόσωπον meant face but also the mask actors wore to enact the specific character and show his/her emotions. Even though πρόσωπο 'face' does not mean mask in current use, this sense is implicit in expressions like "He showed his true/real/other face". This is not a peculiarly Greek understanding, as St. André (2013: 70) reports that '"face" is a mask that the Chinese wear' (see also Kinnison 2017; Yu 2001) and in Japanese *men* means both face and mask (Ho et al. 2004: 68). In fact, this conceptualization is familiar to us from Goffman's (1959) dramaturgical understanding of the concept. As he (1959: 19) contends, we all more or less consciously play roles always and everywhere. If the mask we wear represents our conceptualization of ourselves then this is our true self. This is an aspect of face that has received scant attention in pragmatics (Bogdanowska-Jakubowska 2010; Kinnison 2017; Locher 2004, 2011; Watts 2003) and deserves further exploration.

For the last 20 or so years, a number of scholars have been arguing in favour of an all-encompassing pragmatics which will not be restricted to linguistic, philosophical and cognitive aspects of language use but will also include social ones (e.g. Verschueren 1999). We believe that issues of politeness, face and related notions clearly point to such a broad pragmatics as they are primarily social phenomena and a narrow pragmalinguistics cannot account for them fully. People draw from social values and expectations to do facework as they co-construct their multitude of faces to perform or avoid face-threatening acts or perform face-enhancing acts, considering not only their interlocutor's face but also their own as they are located in specific situations.

References

Arundale, R. B. (1999). An alternative model and ideology of communication for an alternative to politeness theory. *Pragmatics*, 9(1), 119–53.
Arundale, R. B. (2005). Pragmatics, conversational implicature, and conversation. In K. L. Fitch and R. E. Sanders, eds., *Handbook of Language and Social Interaction*. Mahwah, NJ: Lawrence Erlbaum Associates, pp. 41–63.
Arundale, R. B. (2009). Face as emergent in interpersonal communication: An alternative to Goffman. In F. Bargiela-Chiappini and M. Haugh, eds., *Face, Communication and Social Interaction*. London: Equinox, pp. 33–54.
Arundale, R. B. (2010). Constituting face in conversation: Face, facework, and interactional achievement. *Journal of Pragmatics*, 42(8), 2078–105.
Arundale, R. B. (2013). Face as a research focus in interpersonal pragmatics: Relational and emic perspectives. *Journal of Pragmatics*, 58, 108–20.
Bargiela-Chiappini, F. (2003). Face and politeness: New (insights) for old (concepts). *Journal of Pragmatics*, 35(10–11), 1453–69.
Bargiela-Chiappini, F. (2009). Facing the future: Some reflections. In F. Bargiela-Chiappini and M. Haugh, eds., *Face, Communication and Social Interaction*. London: Equinox, pp. 307–26.
Bogdanowska-Jakubowska, E. (2010). *Face: An Interdisciplinary Perspective*. Katowice: Wydawnictwo Uniwersytetu Śląskiego.
Bravo, D. (2008). (Im)politeness in Spanish-speaking socio-cultural contexts: Introduction. *Pragmatics*, 18(4), 563–76.
Brown, P. and Levinson, S. (1987). *Politeness: Some Universals in Language Usage*. Cambridge: Cambridge University Press. Originally published as Universals in language usage: Politeness phenomena, in E. Goody, ed. (1978), *Questions and Politeness: Strategies in Social Interaction*. New York: Cambridge University Press, pp. 56–289.
Chang, W. M. and Haugh, M. (2011). Strategic embarrassment and face threatening in business interactions. *Journal of Pragmatics*, 43(12), 2948–63.
Culpeper, J. (2011). *Impoliteness: Using Language to Cause Offence*. Cambridge: Cambridge University Press.
Culpeper, J. and Haugh, M. (2014). *Pragmatics and the English Language*. Basingstoke, UK: Palgrave Macmillan.
Culpeper, J. and Terkourafi, M. (2017). Pragmatic approaches (im)politeness. In J. Culpeper, M. Haugh and D. Kádár, eds., *The Palgrave Handbook of Linguistic (Im)Politeness*. Basingstoke, UK: Palgrave Macmillan, pp. 11–39.
Eelen, G. (2001). *A Critique of Politeness Theories*. Manchester, UK: St. Jerome.
Ervin-Tripp, S., Nakamura, K. and Guo, J. (1995). Shifting face from Asia to Europe. In M. Shibatani and S. Thompson, eds., *Essays in Semantics and Pragmatics: In Honor of Charles J. Fillmore*. Amsterdam: John Benjamins, pp. 43–71.
Fukushima, S. (2000). *Requests and Culture: Politeness in British English and Japanese*. Bern: Peter Lang.

Fukushima, S. (2015). In search of another understanding of politeness: From the perspective of attentiveness. *Journal of Politeness Research*, 11(2), 261–87.

Garcés-Conejos Blitvich, P. (2009). Impoliteness and identity in the American news media: The "Culture Wars". *Journal of Politeness Research*, 5(2), 273–304.

Garcés-Conejos Blitvich, P. (2013). Face, identity, and im/politeness: Looking backwards, moving forward – From Goffman to Practice Theory. *Journal of Politeness Research*, 9(1), 1–33.

Garcés-Conejos Blitvich, P. and Bou-Franch, P. (2019). Emic conceptualizations of face (*imagen*) in Peninsular Spanish. In E. Ogiermann and P. Garcés-Conejos Blitvich, eds., *From Speech Acts to Lay Understandings of Politeness: Multilingual and Multicultural Perspectives*. Cambridge: Cambridge University Press, pp. 301–27.

Garcés-Conejos Blitvich, P. and Sifianou, M. (2017). Im/politeness and identity. In J. Culpeper, M. Haugh and D. Kádár, eds., *The Palgrave Handbook of Linguistic (Im)politeness*. Basingstoke, UK: Palgrave Macmillan, pp. 227–56.

Goffman, E. (1959). *The Presentation of Self in Everyday Life*. New York: Doubleday.

Goffman, E. (1971). *Relations in Public: Microstudies of the Public Order*. London: Allen Lane.

Goffman, E. ([1955] 1972). On face-work: An analysis of ritual elements in social interaction. In J. Laver and S. Hutcheson, eds., *Communication in Face-to-Face Interaction*. Harmondsworth, UK: Penguin, pp. 319–46.

Gu, Y. (1990). Politeness phenomena in Modern Chinese. *Journal of Pragmatics*, 14(2), 237–58.

Hall, K. and Bucholtz, M. (2013). Epilogue: Facing identity. *Journal of Politeness Research*, 9, 123–32.

Haugh, M. (2009). Face and interaction. In F. Bargiela-Chiappini and M. Haugh, eds., *Face, Communication and Social Interaction*. London: Equinox, pp. 1–30.

Haugh, M. (2010). When is an email really offensive? Argumentativity and variability in evaluations of impoliteness. *Journal of Politeness Research*, 6(1), 7–31.

Haugh, M. (2012). Epilogue: The first-second order distinction in face and politeness research. *Journal of Politeness Research*, 8(1), 111–34.

Haugh, M. (2013). Disentangling face, facework and im/politeness. *Sociocultural Pragmatics*, 1(1), 46–73.

Haugh, M. and Bargiela-Chiappini, F. (2010). Editorial: Face in interaction. *Journal of Pragmatics*, 42, 2073–7.

Haugh, M. and Watanabe, Y. (2009). Analysing Japanese 'face-in-interaction': Insights from intercultural business meetings. In F. Bargiela-Chiappini and M. Haugh, eds., *Face, Communication and Social Interaction*. London: Equinox, pp. 78–95.

Hernández-Flores, N. (2008). Politeness and other types of facework: Communicative and social meaning in a television panel discussion. *Pragmatics*, 18(4), 681–706.

Hinze, C. G. (2012). Chinese politeness is not about 'face': Evidence from the business world. *Journal of Politeness Research*, 8(2), 11–27.

Hirschon, R. (2001). Freedom, solidarity and obligation: The socio-cultural context of Greek politeness. In A. Bayraktaroğlu and M. Sifianou, eds., *Linguistic Politeness across Boundaries: The Case of Greek and Turkish*. Amsterdam: John Benjamins, pp. 17–42.

Ho, D. Y. F., Fu, W. and Ng, S. M. (2004). Guilt, shame and embarrassment: Revelations of face and self. *Culture and Psychology*, 10, 64–84.

Holtgraves, T. (1992). The linguistic realization of face management: Implications of language production and comprehension, person perception, and cross-cultural communication. *Social Psychology Quarterly*, 55, 141–59.

Holtgraves, T. (2002). *Language as Social Action*. Mahwah, NJ: Lawrence Erlbaum.

Ide, S. (1989). Formal forms and discernment: Neglected aspects of linguistic politeness. *Multilingua*, 8(2), 223–48.

Intachakra, S. (2012). Politeness motivated by the 'heart' and 'binary rationality' in Thai culture. *Journal of Pragmatics*, 44(5), 619–35.

Jones, S. M. and Bodie, G. D. (2014). Supportive communication. In C. R. Berger, ed., *Handbooks of Communication Science: Vol. 6. Interpersonal Communication*. Berlin: Mouton de Gruyter, pp. 371–94.

Kádár, D. Z. and Haugh, M. (2013). *Understanding Politeness*. Cambridge: Cambridge University Press.

Kasper, G. (1997). Linguistic etiquette. In F. Coulmas, ed., *The Handbook of Sociolinguistics*. Oxford: Blackwell, pp. 374–85.

Kinnison, L. Q. (2017). Power, integrity, and mask: An attempt to disentangle the Chinese face concept. *Journal of Pragmatics*, 114, 32–48.

Koutlaki, S. A. (2002). Offers and expressions of thanks as face enhancing acts: *tæ'arof* in Persian. *Journal of Pragmatics*, 34(12), 1733–56.

Leech, G. (1983). *Principles of Pragmatics*. London: Longman.

Leech, G. (2014). *The Pragmatics of Politeness*. Oxford: Oxford University Press.

Lim, T.-S. and Bowers, J. W. (1991). Facework: Solidarity, approbation, and tact. *Human Communication Research*, 17, 415–50.

Locher, M. A. (2004). *Power and Politeness in Action: Disagreements in Oral Communication*. Berlin: Mouton de Gruyter.

Locher, M. A. (2006). Polite behaviour within relational work: The discursive approach to politeness. *Multilingua*, 25(3), 249–67.

Locher, M. A. (2011). Situated impoliteness: The interface between relational work and identity construction. In B. L. Davies, M. Haugh and A. J. Merrison, eds., *Situated Politeness*. London: Bloomsbury, pp. 187–208.

Locher, M. A. and Watts, R. J. (2005). Politeness theory and relational work. *Journal of Politeness Research*, 1(1), 9–34.

Locher, M. A. and Watts, R. J. (2008). Relational work and impoliteness: Negotiating norms of linguistic behaviour. In D. Bousfield and M. A. Locher, eds., *Impoliteness in Language: Studies on its Interplay with Power in Theory and Practice*. Berlin: de Gruyter, pp. 77–99.

Linguistic Politeness Research Group (ed.). (2011). *Discursive Approaches to Politeness*. Berlin: Mouton de Gruyter.

Mao, L. M. (1994). Beyond politeness theory: 'Face' revisited and renewed. *Journal of Pragmatics*, 21, 451–86.

Marmaridou, S. A. S. (2011). The relevance of embodiment to lexical and collocational meaning: The case of *prosopo* 'face' in Modern Greek. In Z. A. Maalej and N. Yu, eds., *Embodiment via Body Parts: Studies from Various Languages and Cultures*. Amsterdam: John Benjamins, pp. 23–40.

Matsumoto, Y. (1988). Re-examination of the universality of face: Politeness phenomena in Japanese. *Journal of Pragmatics*, 12(4), 403–26.

Mey, J. L. (1993). *Pragmatics: An Introduction*. Oxford: Basil Blackwell.

Mills, S. (2003). *Gender and Politeness*. Cambridge: Cambridge University Press.

Nwoye, O. G. (1992). Linguistic politeness and sociocultural variations of the notion of face. *Journal of Pragmatics*, 18(4), 309–28.

O'Driscoll, J. (2007). Brown and Levinson's face: How it can – and can't – help us to understand interaction across cultures. *Intercultural Pragmatics*, 4, 463–92.

O'Driscoll, J. (2011a). Some issues with the concept of face: When, what, how and how much? In F. Bargiela-Chiappini and D. Z. Kádár, eds., *Politeness across Cultures*. Basingstoke, UK: Palgrave Macmillan, pp. 17–41.

O'Driscoll, J. (2011b). Review of F. Bargiela-Chiappini and M. Haugh (eds.). 2009. *Face, Communication and Social Interaction*. London: Equinox. *Journal of Politeness Research*, 7, 153–7.

O'Driscoll, J. (2017). Face and (im)politeness. In J. Culpeper, M. Haugh and D. Z. Kádár, eds., *The Palgrave Handbook of Linguistic (Im)Politeness*. Basingstoke, UK: Palgrave Macmillan, pp. 89–118.

Pizziconi, B. (2003). Re-examining politeness, face and the Japanese language. *Journal of Pragmatics*, 35, 1471–1506.

Pomerantz, A. (1978). Compliment responses: Notes on the co-operation of multiple constraints. In J. Schenkein, ed., *Studies in the Organization of Conversational Interaction*. New York: Academic Press, pp. 79–112.

Ruhi, Ş. (2010). Face as an indexical category in interaction. *Journal of Pragmatics*, 42(8), 2131–46.

Ruhi, Ş. and Işık-Güler, H. (2007). Conceptualizing face and relational work in (im)politeness: Revelations from politeness lexemes and idioms in Turkish. *Journal of Pragmatics*, 39, 681–711.

Ruhi, Ş. and Kádár, D. Z. (2011). 'Face' across historical cultures: A comparative study of Turkish and Chinese. *Journal of Historical Pragmatics*, 12(1/2), 25–48.

Sifianou, M. (1997). Silence and politeness. In A. Jaworski, ed., *Silence: Interdisciplinary Perspectives*. Berlin: Mouton de Gruyter, pp. 63–84.

Sifianou, M. (2011). On the concept of face and politeness. In F. Bargiela-Chiappini and D. Z. Kádár, eds., *Politeness across Cultures*. Basingstoke, UK: Palgrave Macmillan, pp. 42–58.

Sifianou, M. (2012). Disagreements, politeness and face. *Journal of Pragmatics*, 44, 1554–64.

Sifianou, M. (2016). On culture, face and politeness. Again. In E. Bogdanowska-Jakubowska, ed., *New Ways to Face and (Im)Politeness*. Katowice: Wydawnictwo Uniwersytetu Śląskiego, pp. 15–30.

Spencer-Oatey, H. (2000). Rapport management: A framework for analysis. In H. Spencer-Oatey, ed., *Culturally Speaking: Managing Rapport through Talk across Cultures*. London: Continuum, pp. 11–46.

Spencer-Oatey, H. (2002). Managing rapport in talk: Using rapport sensitive incidents to explore the motivational concerns underlying the management of relations. *Journal of Pragmatics*, 34(5), 529–45.

Spencer-Oatey, H. (2005). (Im)politeness, face and perceptions of rapport: Unpackaging their bases and interrelationships. *Journal of Politeness Research*, 1(1), 95–119.

Spencer-Oatey, H. (2007). Theories of identity and the analysis of face. *Journal of Pragmatics*, 39, 639–56.

Spencer-Oatey, H. (2008). Face, (im)politeness and rapport. In H. Spencer-Oatey, ed., *Culturally Speaking: Culture, Communication and Politeness Theory*, 2nd ed. London: Continuum, pp. 11–47.

Spencer-Oatey, H. (2009). Face, identity and interactional goals. In F. Bargiela-Chiappini and M. Haugh, eds., *Face, Communication and Social Interaction*. London: Equinox, pp. 137–54.

St. André, J. (2013). How the Chinese lost 'face'. *Journal of Pragmatics*, 55, 68–85.

Terkourafi, M. (2007). Toward a universal notion of face for a universal notion of cooperation. In I. Kecskés and L. Horn, eds., *Explorations in Pragmatics: Linguistic, Cognitive and Intercultural Aspects*. Berlin: Mouton de Gruyter, pp. 307–38.

Thomas, J. (1983). Cross-cultural pragmatic failure. *Applied Linguistics*, 4, 91–112.

Ting-Toomey, S. (2005). The matrix of face: An updated face-negotiation theory. In W. B. Gudykunst, ed., *Theorizing about Intercultural Communication*. Thousand Oaks, CA: Sage, pp. 71–91.

Ting-Toomey, S. (2009). Facework collision in intercultural communication. In F. Bargiela-Chiappini and M. Haugh, eds., *Face, Communication and Social Interaction*. London: Equinox, pp. 227–49.

Ting-Toomey, S. and Kurogi, A. (1998). Facework competence in intercultural conflict: An updated face-negotiation theory. *International Journal of Intercultural Relations*, 22(2), 187–225.

Ukosakul, M. (2005). The significance of 'face' and politeness in social interaction as revealed through Thai 'face' idioms. In R. Lakoff and S. Ide, eds., *Broadening the Horizon of Linguistic Politeness*. Amsterdam: John Benjamins, pp. 117–25.

Van der Bom, I. and Mills, S. (2015). A discursive approach to the analysis of politeness data. *Journal of Politeness Research*, 11(2), 179–206.

Verschueren, J. (1999). *Understanding Pragmatics*. London: Hodder Arnold.

Watts, R. J. (2003). *Politeness*. Cambridge: Cambridge University Press.

Watts, R. J. (2005). Linguistic politeness research. *Quo vadis*? In R. J. Watts, S. Ide and K. Ehlich, eds., *Politeness in Language: Studies in Its Hstory, Theory and Practice*, 2nd ed. Berlin: Mouton de Gruyter, pp. xi–xivii.

Watts, R. J., Ide, S. and Ehlich, K. (1992). Introduction. In R. J. Watts, S. Ide and K. Ehlich, eds., *Politeness in Language: Studies in Its History, Theory and Practice*. Berlin: Mouton de Gruyter, pp. 1–17.

Yu, N. (2001). What does our face mean to us? *Pragmatics and Cognition*, 9(1), 1–36.

14

Relationships and Relating

Robert B. Arundale

14.1 Introduction

Sociologist Georg Simmel (1950) argued that human relationships are "inseparable from the immediacy of interaction". We often think about our relationships with one another, but our relationships are realized not in our cognizing, but in our interacting with one another. Relationships are born, grow, thrive, survive and die as persons engage in talk and conduct with other persons. A relationship is a dynamic, on-going process of using language and non-language resources in relating with one another. Relationships and relating are primary social phenomena, inherent in everyday pragmatic phenomena.

This chapter characterizes current conceptualizations of the sociopragmatics of relationships and relating, against the backdrop of a much broader range of theory and research on relating in interpersonal communication than can be surveyed here (cf. Arundale 2010b; Baxter and Montgomery 1996; Braithwaite and Schrodt 2015). Recognizing both the wide range of these conceptualizations, and the diversity in their underlying assumptions, the chapter provides researchers with bases for choosing a conceptualization of relationships that will be productive in addressing their particular research questions regarding the sociopragmatics of relating in everyday interacting.

One initial clarification. In their contribution, Locher and Graham (2010; also Chapter 27) examine research within the province "interpersonal pragmatics", which they define as an interdisciplinary "perspective on the interpersonal side of language and communication", and which they indicate encompasses the issues addressed in a number of other chapters in this handbook. Because relationships are interpersonal phenomena, it might appear that examining the sociopragmatics of relationships and relating in this chapter is synonymous Locher and Graham's examining of interpersonal pragmatics. Not so. The current use of the term "interpersonal" with regard to the study of human interaction is much more encompassing than the terms "relationship" or "relational" (Haugh Kádár and Mills 2013). In short, research on relationships and relating is one among a number of other research foci in studying the "interpersonal side" of language use in human communication. I indicate that broader scope in Section 14.3.

Why focus specifically on relationships and relating? Because they are fundamental to our lives as human beings. We have no life at all apart from the prior embodied interaction of two other human beings, who in their interacting had formed some type of relationship with one another. We are nurtured in relationships with other human beings, on whom we at first depend entirely. As we develop in on-going interaction in these different relationships, we develop the language and non-language resources needed to become more independent and to interact with new individuals. And as we begin to interact with a wider range of individuals, we also begin to form, and go on forming, a diversity of relationships with one another in dyads, in families, in teams, in organizations, in communities and more. These many different relationships bind us to one another in ways essential to our continued existence as human beings. Human sociality is essential to human individuality, and vice versa, but neither comes into being apart from the relationships we form in interacting, and in relating, with one another.

14.2 Conceptual Frameworks in Research on Relationships and Relating

Metaphors, models and theories are different types of frameworks for conceptualizing phenomena. One's choice of a particular metaphor, model, or theory is consequential in one's research because it entails a particular conceptual framework that enables and constrains both how one understands a phenomenon, and how one goes about studying it. Because there are many metaphors, models and theories in use in research on relationships and relating, there are many ways of understanding them.

Following Krippendorff (2009: chapter 3) and Lakoff and Johnson (1980), employing a metaphor in everyday use or in scholarly inquiry involves identifying some well-understood phenomenon like a financial asset, a container, a living entity or a culture and adopting it as a basis for understanding a less well-understood phenomenon like a relationship. What is familiar becomes an analogue for the unfamiliar, so that one understands a relationship, for example, as an asset or investment owned jointly by the relational partners, to be managed by them in expectation of a profit rather than a loss (Bavelas 2003). Alternatively, conceptualized as a container or context, relational partners are understood to reside within, and to be shaped by and at times constrained by its boundaries (Owen 1990). Or as a living entity like a child, a relationship is born of the union between the partners, who nurture it, care for it when it is ill, support it, and seek its continuing development (Bavelas 2003). And seen as a culture, a relationship is a set of shared meanings, "interaction routines and rituals, norms and rules that organize, sequence, and control" the behaviours of the relational partners (Burleson Metts and Kirch 2000: 252). In choosing a metaphor one appropriates the structure and processes of the familiar phenomenon as the structure and processes of the less well known phenomenon, together with all of its assumptions and conceptual entailments. One is thus enabled to think of relationships in terms of economics, physical structures, organisms or cultures, but one's understanding is at the same time constrained by those conceptual analogues, at times apart from one's awareness of that constraint.

There are many models and theories of relationships and relating, as well. A model is a representation of a phenomenon in some medium, but one that abstracts only key aspects of its structure or function, and that may or may not provide an account of the phenomenon. A theory on the other hand provides an account of a phenomenon, but does not necessarily provide a representation of structure or of function. A theoretical model provides both an account and a representation. In choosing or developing a model or a theory as a conceptual framework for one's inquiry, one commits oneself to its assumptions, whether tacitly or explicitly, to its concepts and definitions, to the account it provides, and to the framework's entailments for understanding the phenomenon. Those entailments are not only conceptual, but also methodological, as in Krippendorff's (1970) detailed argument that one's conceptual framework enables and constrains one's procedures of observing, generating data, producing evidence and interpreting the results of one's inquiry. Methods incompatible with one's conceptual framework produce evidence that is incapable of warranting interpretations in terms of one's model or theory (Arundale 2013a, 2020: 362–71).

Scholars have developed many different models and theories to account for relationships and relating because they are complex, multi-faceted phenomena, one consequence being that these models and theories encompass a wide range of assumptive commitments, concepts, definitions, accounts and conceptual and methodological entailments. Although many of these models and theories employ the same terms, the understandings and accounts of "relationship" and of "relating" provided do not necessarily index the same phenomena, nor are they necessarily conceptually or methodologically compatible with one another. Yet diversity in models and theories is not inherently problematic. As Kaplan (1964: 309) argues, scholars "need not look for the *true* theory, but countenance and even encourage various theories, and without thinking of them only as so many candidates for the single post to be filled". Baxter and Montgomery (1996: chapter 9), Craig (1999, 2015) and Krippendorff (2009: chapter 1) all agree.

Yet countenancing a wide range of theories of relationships and relating requires not only awareness of the distinctions among them, but also care in choosing a particular model or theory from among the alternatives, given that doing so is consequential both in the conduct of inquiry, and in understanding relationships as created and sustained everyday social interaction. I address the issues of awareness of distinctions and care in choosing by identifying three broad dimensions for comparing current models and theories of the sociopragmatics of relationships and relating, and by illustrating their use in examining seven representative conceptualizations. The three dimensions enable one to make productive comparisons between alternative models or theories by identifying not only basic, underlying assumptive commitments, but also key concepts and entailments. Comparing assumptions, concepts and entailments is fundamental to choosing a conceptual framework to guide one's inquiry, as well as to combining compatible theoretical frameworks where useful, and to engaging in constructive critique. With regard to the conduct of inquiry on relationships, Enfield (2013: 216) argues that "if we do not make explicit the theoretical framing of ... our work, then we are withholding half the story". Krippendorff (2009: 96) argues that with regard to choosing a theoretical framework for understanding social interaction, "there is no socially neutral theory".

In examining the sociopragmatics of relationships and relating I focus principally on two or more persons engaging in talk and/or visible conduct with one another, whether co-present or not. Persons do use language in addressing others when they not co-present, as for example in print or in mediated communication, but these require different models and theories. Persons also use language in co-present situations like public speaking and live performance where there is mutual engagement of speaker and audience (Goodwin 1986), although I do not consider such one-to-many interactions. The focus here is on situations in which two or a few persons engage one another, as in relationships between friends, parents and children, romantic and married couples, family members, colleagues, business partners, providers and clients and in service encounters, small groups and teams. Note however that "friends" or "parents and children", for example, are but broad relationship categories. A particular friend or parent–child relationship is realized only as particular persons engage one another in a particular situation, every such engaging being in some measure distinct from every other. One identifies a category by abstracting across particular realizations, but relationships and relating are not abstractions. They are concrete, embodied, contingent instances of talk and conduct between persons, which implies considerable diversity across friendships, across mother-daughter relationships, across married couples and across every other relationship category one might identify.

Consider in turn each of the three dimensions for comparing theories and models.

First, *Are relationships and relating conceptualized as exogenous to, or as endogenous in interacting?* The term "relationship" is widely employed to index a context, an entity or a force that exists apart from interaction. Conceptualized in these ways, relationships are exogenous to and separate from the interaction between the relational partners, and take the form of pre-existing imperatives, scripts, or roles understood to be cued or brought into play in using language when the individual recognizes that he or she is in a particular relational situation (Arundale 2020: 258–60). The term "relationship" is also widely understood to index a psychological state such as a disposition, drive, or want, internalized by each relational partner in the process of socialization. Such states are also exogenous to interaction, and understood to guide, control, constrain or cause the partner's choices of particular language forms, nonverbal conduct, or social practices (Arundale 2020: 263–9; cf. Haugh Kádár and Mills 2013: 2–3). More simply, when relationships are conceptualized as exogenous to interaction, they are understood to be relatively static, contextual phenomena that generate the partner's use of language.

I use the term "relating", rather than "relationship", to index the dynamic processes of creating and recreating a relationship that occur between persons as they interact with one another amidst the contingencies of particular times and places. Conceptualized in this manner, relating and relationships are on-going processes endogenous to, emergent in or an integral part of interaction, not entities or states apart from interaction. A relationship is not a pre-existing context, and does not guide, control, constrain or cause the partner's choices of language forms, non-verbal conduct or social practices. Rather, it is in engaging language resources that partners constitute their relationship in the moment of interaction. Relationships are therefore episodic because they terminate when interaction terminates, although they can be created once again should the same persons interact on a subsequent occasion (Sigman 1991). Relationships are endogenous to interaction because human interaction requires at least two persons engaged in talk and conduct with one another, and because those persons are always situated with respect to or in relationship to one another in some particular manner (Arundale 2010a: 2086–8; 2020: 256–8). More simply, if relationships are conceptualized as endogenous to interaction, they are dynamic phenomena understood to be generated in the pragmatics of using language and visible conduct in the here and now of everyday interacting. Again, as Simmel (1950: 126), a relationship is "inseparable from the immediacy of interaction".

Second, *How does the model or theory link what is individual with what is social in relationships and relating?* Relationships and relating require at least two individuals, the dyad being the smallest social unit. It follows that relationships and relating always entail not only properties defined on the individuals, but also properties defined on the social unit. One possible way to link what is individual and what is social is as two or more parts belonging to a whole. Another way to link them is as a dualism: what is individual is independent of, separate from and the opposite of what is social. And they can be linked as a yin/yang dialectic: what is individual and what is social co-exist, yet are contradictory elements that mutually require one another because there is no social unit without individuals, and no individuals without social units (Arundale 2010a: 2085–6). Understood as a yin/yang dialectic, what is social and what is individual "function in incompatible ways such that each negates the other" (Baxter and Montgomery 1996: 8), but they are unified because they function interdependently in a dynamic and interactive manner. Accounts that employ models and theories that link what is individual and what is social either as part and whole, or as a dualism, have uniformly privileged one contradictory over the other, with accounts that privilege what is individual as the minimum unit of analysis being far more common than accounts that privilege the social unit. In contrast, employing a model or theory that links the individual and the social as a yin/yang dialectic requires that neither one nor the other be privileged in the account, and that the minimum unit of analysis be the social unit, conceptualized as inclusive of the individuals who compose it. Note that I use "individual" here to index a singular biological and psychological human being, as distinct from a "person" as an individual who, in communicating with other persons, becomes interdependently entwined with them in a social system.

Third, *Is what is social conceptualized as an additive or as a non-additive phenomenon?* Examining both the distinction between and the linking together of what is individual and what is social is important in comparing models and theories, but it is equally important to consider whether what is social is conceptualized as an additive or as a non-additive phenomenon. Models and theories of relationships and relating that link what is individual and what is social as part and whole, or as a dualism, uniformly conceptualize the properties of social units as the sum or the aggregate of the properties of the individual units that compose the social unit. That implies that the properties of a relationship comprising two individuals can be accounted for entirely in terms of the *additive* combination of the properties of the two or more individuals involved. In their Communicate Bond Belong theory, for example, Hall and Davis (2017) define a relationship as a tie between individuals that is stable, and that involves both mutual acknowledgement of individuality, and mutual influence (25). Relationships develop "from internal pressures to satiate a need to belong", and are "shaped by competing desires to invest and conserve social energy" (21), which together influence the individual's choices among relationally oriented actions in everyday talk like self-disclosing or gossiping. For each individual, "the result of any given communication episode varies by feelings of relatedness, which is theorized to be a proximal indicator of the need to belong being satiated" (38–9). In other words, relationships are conceptualized as venues for addressing a fundamental individual need, as shaped by individual desires and choices, and as resulting in an individual's feelings of relatedness. All of these properties are defined on individuals, so that in Hall and Davis's nomological theory, the additive combination of the behaviors and psychological states of the individuals involved is entirely sufficient to explain the mutuality and reciprocity of a relationship, or in other words, to account for what is social as an additive combination of what is individual.

The alternative is to conceptualize the properties of the social specifically as the *non-additive* or non-linear outcomes of processes occurring between the individuals who compose the social unit. That implies that the properties of a relationship are distinct from, and cannot be accounted for entirely in terms of the sum or the aggregate of the properties of the individuals, without at the same time leaving the systemic interdependence between those individuals as an unaccounted for remainder. Krippendorff (1970) and Watzlawick et al. (1967) called for this alternative conceptualization long ago, and Sawyer (2005) points to more recent arguments. In Face Constituting Theory, for example, Arundale (2010a: 2086–8; 2020: 29–32, 248–56) defines a relationship as a social system of at least two individuals engaged in sequential interaction that generates non-additive, systemic interdependence among them. That interdependence emerges between the individual's interpretings of any given utterance as those individuals construct triads of verbal and non-verbal utterances by placing new utterances next adjacent to one another's prior utterances. At the point the third utterance is added in sequence, the individual's interpretings of the given utterance become reciprocally conditional on one another's subsequent utterances. Reciprocal conditionality between the individual's interpretings is a non-additive, non-linear property that emerges only in their interaction, and that defines the social system that is their relationship (2010a: 2083–5; 2020: 79–88, 248–56). In Face Constituting Theory, each individual's independent, additive interpreting of the given utterance is necessary, but not sufficient to account for the non-additive systemic interdependence of those interpretings that emerges across the sequence of utterances they constitute conjointly. The emergent, non-additive properties that define relationships as social systems are readily apparent in everyday interacting, but only if one chooses to conceptualize the processes of interacting as generating such properties (2020: 22–9). I use the terms "social system", "emergent", and "interdependence" here specifically to index non-additive phenomena, not additive phenomena as is more common.

A further clarification may prove helpful. It is entirely possible to conceptualize the properties that characterize independent individuals as the emergent, non-additive outcomes of processes occurring in human interaction. Bucholtz and Hall (2005) represent a number of researchers who have argued not only *that*, but also *why* individual identity is constructed in interaction. But Bucholtz and Hall do not specifically conceptualize identity as an emergent, non-additive property of an individual, nor do they specify *how* identity is constructed in the sequential details of everyday language use. Antaki and Widdicombe (1998) also argue that and why identity emerges in interaction, but provide not only a conceptualization compatible with understanding identity as a non-additive outcome of interaction, but also considerable evidence of how identity emerges in the sequential details of everyday talk and conduct. Very importantly, even if one provides an account of the properties of individuals as the emergent, non-additive outcomes of interacting, such an account does not in and of itself comprise an account of the emergent and non-additive properties of a social unit like a relationship. In other words, the additive combining of the non-additive properties of two individuals does not generate an account of the non-additive properties of a social unit comprising those individuals, quite simply because non-additive properties defined on individuals are entirely distinct from non-additive properties defined on a social unit comprising those individuals (cf. Krippendorff 1970).

As I indicate in Section 14.4, there are other dimensions one might use in comparing conceptual frameworks for research on the sociopragmatics of relationships and relating. Why then focus on these three? Space is one constraint, but more importantly, these three dimensions facilitate comparisons regarding how a given model or theory conceptualizes the basic characteristics of relationships and of relating with one another. First, a dyad is the most basic social unit, but it does not exist apart from two individuals. Individuals are identifiable, embodied units, but identifying what composes the social unit has proved more elusive. Because relationships are social units comprising two or more individuals, the way in which a given model or theory conceptualizes not only *what is individual and what is social*, but also *how the individual and the social are linked with one another*, are consequential for how that model or theory accounts for relationships. Second, scholars have provided multiple accounts of what composes social units of various sizes, one long standing argument being that what is social is "emergent" as human beings engage with one another (Sawyer 2005). Yet research since the mid twentieth century across multiple disciplines has made apparent that there are both additive and non-additive senses of "emergent", and hence of what is social. Because relationships are social units, *whether one's model or theory conceptualizes what is social as additive or non-additive* is likewise consequential for how that model or theory accounts for relationships. Third, many common metaphors for relationships and relating frame them as entities or states apart from or exogenous to, but as directly causing or constraining language use among relational partners. Yet theory and research in pragmatics over the past half century have also made clear that in using language, human beings are constituting social actions with one another: promising, informing, questioning, teasing and countless more. As two or more persons constitute a promise in interacting with one another, they become situated with respect to or in relationship to one another in a manner that is distinct from their constituting a tease. It is in the processes of constituting social action in talk and conduct that persons constitute the myriad ways in which they relate with one another. In other words, constituting human relationships is endogenous to human interaction. It follows that *whether a given model or theory conceptualizes relationships as exogenous to or as endogenous in language use* is a basic distinction among the types of account one can provide regarding the sociopragmatics of relationships and relating.

14.3 Comparing Models and Theories of the Sociopragmatics of Relationships and Relating

Rapport Management. Spencer-Oatey (2007; 2015: 1286) provides a model of managing social relations in using language that focuses on managing "rapport", or "people's perceptions of (dis)harmony, smoothness-turbulence, and warmth-antagonism in interpersonal relations". The primary bases for rapport are people's face sensitivities, their rights and obligations in social groups, and their transactional and relational goals. People's face sensitivities are matters of identity, understood in terms of "individual, relational, and collective construals of self" (2007: 644). People's social rights and obligations within a social network are matters of "fitting in (or failing to fit in) with the behavioral expectations associated with the interlocutors' role rights and obligations" (2015: 1287), those expectations including matters not only of equity rights, but also of association rights or interactional and affective involvement-detachment. People (mis)manage rapport in employing various rapport management strategies, the use of which reflects sociopragmatic and pragmalinguistic conventions that vary across situations and across cultural and language groups (2000).

Fitting in with others with regard to association rights entails people's perceptions and "assessments of the affective quality they subjectively and dynamically experience in their relations with others" (2011: 3567), as distinct from their perceptions and assessments of transactional matters (2007: 647). These relational perceptions and assessments are central to one's identity at "an individual level where the focus is on self and other; a relational level where the focus is on mutuality and connection/separation between the members of interpersonally significant dyads or teams; and a group level where the focus is on membership of a group category" (2011: 3567). For Spencer-Oatey, then, relationships are exogenous to interaction in that they are conceptualized in terms of an individual's perceptions and cognitive-affective assessments of oneself vis-à-vis others as individuals, as teams or as categories. Although Spencer-Oatey (2013) identifies several relational dialectics, and argues that both social phenomena and individual cognitive phenomena are key in understanding the processes of rapport management, what is individual and what is social are conceptualized as a dualism rather than as a dialectic, and what is social in relating is conceptualized as the additive combination of two or more individual's relational perceptions and assessments (Arundale 2013b: 139–40).

Relational Work and Identity Construction. Locher (2008: 533) argues that rapport management and her concept of "relational work" both "refer to the same phenomenon – the negotiation of relations and identities in interaction". The concept of relational work is "meant to cover the entire spectrum of interpersonal linguistic behavior" and meaning, as distinct from, although not divorced from "transactional discourse" (2008: 510). More precisely, "relational work refers to the ways in which the construction of identity is achieved in interaction, while identity refers to the 'product' of these linguistic and non-linguistic processes" (2008: 511). Locher (2013: 146) draws on Bucholtz and Hall's (2005) understanding of identity as continually constructed in relational work in everyday interaction as persons become positioned as a self vis-à-vis others in various social categories, roles and stances. Identity is identified as "emergent", although neither Locher nor Bucholtz and Hall define "emergent" in terms of the non-additive properties of interaction. In subsequent work, Langlotz and Locher (2013: 92) argue the participant's emotions in interaction are also central in relational work because they are "the fundamental glue for relating".

Locher (2013: 147) argues as well that "the individual should not be lost to a focus on the emergence of the relational element only, the inclusion of socio-cognitive elements in the understanding of relational work takes care of this desideratum, as it is the individual from which the relational originates and is grounded". For Locher, then, relational work is an additive, socio-cognitive/emotive, linguistic and non-linguistic process whose principal product is a person's identity as an individual. Individuals are thus the focal, grounding parts of additive social wholes, or of relationships that are conceptualized as a self plus one or more others, positioned vis-à-vis one another. The relational work that generates the positioned identities of a set of individuals takes place in interaction, but it is the social categories, roles and stances in which individuals are positioned that define relationships. Categories, roles and stances are part of an individual's normative social knowledge, which implies that what composes a relationship is exogenous to the processes of interaction.

Language and Social Relations. Agha (2007: 9) focuses on social relations as cultural representations that "are reproduced over social groups through communicative processes that unfold one participation framework at a time". Such "cultural representations are formulated through semiotic acts", that "generate various roles (stakes, stances, positions, identities) and relationships among roles (alignments, asymmetries, power, hierarchy)" (2007: 9). These cultural representations of relationships and roles are key components of "cultural models of action", which take the form of "register formations" that involve both language and non-language forms, and that are "stereotypic ways of performing 'social acts' of enormous range and variety" (2007: 4). In Agha's account, then, relationships are culturally known, stereotypical models of linked roles that are not only created and maintained across time and space, but also engaged by persons in moments of language use (2007: 6). That persons are able to engage their culturally known stereotypical models of relationships in using language implies that those models are part of their individual knowledges. As do Spencer-Oatey and Locher, then, Agha conceptualizes relationships as pre-existing contexts and hence as exogenous to interaction. What is individual is the privileged part of and basis for what is social. And what is social is understood as an additive combination of what is individual because Agha's information transmission model of communication (2007: 67) cannot account for non-additive outcomes of interaction between individuals (Arundale 2013a).

Relationship Thinking. Enfield (2009, 2013) argues that in examining human sociality and cognition, researchers need to adopt "relationship thinking" as a heuristic stance because that is the stance that participants themselves adopt in their social lives. The central question in relationship thinking is "Why and how does this piece of behavior reflect or constitute a social relationship?" (2013: xvii). Enfield draws on concepts and principles from multiple disciplines to develop an integrated, culturally sensitive conceptual framework, analytic tools and strategy for research on the relating that takes place as participants engage every day in face-to-face, linguistic, multimodal social interaction (Arundale 2015). Enfield (2013: 29) argues that interaction is central to human sociality, and defines it as an on-going sequence of interlocking and interdependent moves, each comprising an initiating action and its responsive action. However, the encoding/decoding model of communication that he tacitly adopts in adopting a neo-Gricean position on meaning cannot account for non-additive outcomes of interaction (Arundale 2013a), hence what is social in sociality and in relationships is tacitly conceptualized as the additive combination of what is individual.

Human interaction requires extensive and specialized cognitive capacities, and Enfield (2013: 81) argues that cognition and interaction are to be studied as integral with one another, rather than as distinct phenomena. He argues as well that relationships lie at the core of human sociality, and they arise as persons interact in a continual process of fission from and fusion with one another (2013: 6). Both positions are compatible with conceptualizing what is individual as linked dialectically with what is social. For Enfield (2013: xv), "human social relations are a central locus of cause, condition, and consequence in human communicative behavior", a relationship being defined as "a set of rights and duties applying to interaction between members of a dyad" (2013: 8–9), or as "statuses" or sets of "entitlements, obligations, and dispositions in relation to one another" (2013: 60). Rights, duties, entitlements, obligations, and dispositions are cognitions and psychological states, understood to be brought into play or to cause and constrain instances of interaction, which entails that *relationship thinking* conceptualizes relationships as exogenous to interaction.

Face Constituting Theory. Human communication is commonly understood to involve a two-position sequence of an utterance and a responsive utterance (e.g. Enfield 2013: 28). In developing the Conjoint Co-constituting Model of Communicating (the CCMC, Arundale 2010a; 2020), I argue that the basic unit is a three-position sequence of an utterance and the two next adjacent utterances, such sequences continually overlapping as each new utterance is added. Unlike other three-position conceptualizations, the CCMC is a theoretical model that accounts for *how*, across each triad of utterances, the participants generate both reciprocally conditional interpretings of the first position utterance, and the non-additive properties that define them as a social system (Arundale 2010a: 2079–85; 2020: 79–88). Face Constituting Theory draws directly on the CCMC, as well as on Baxter and Montgomery's (1996; Baxter 2004) Relational Dialectics Theory, in arguing that a relationship is a non-additive social system that emerges in the dynamic processes of relating, or more specifically, in the processes of participants conjointly co-constituting non-additive interpretings of both connection with and separation from one another as they engage in everyday talk and conduct. Connection and separation form a yin-yang dialectic in that connection between persons is not possible except that they are or have been in some way separate, and separation between persons requires that they are or have been in some way connected (Arundale 2010a: 2086–7; 2020: 248–56). Connection and separation make up a culture-general conceptualization of what is understood cross-culturally as "face", that is amenable to wide variety of culture-specific interpretations (2006; 2020: 282–9; cf. Sifianou and Tzanne, Chapter 13). It follows then that as persons conjointly co-constitute interpretings of face, understood as both connection with and separation from one another, they are conjointly co-constituting relationships with one another.

In Face Constituting Theory, relationships and relating are fully endogenous to interaction because all human interaction requires at least two persons engaged in talk and conduct, those persons in all cases being situated with respect to or in relation to one another in some manner (Arundale 2020: 256–8). Relationships are non-additive social systems that are conjointly co-constituted as persons engage one another in interaction at particular times and particular places. Relationships terminate when the partner's interaction ceases, but they can be re-constituted when those persons resume interaction on subsequent occasions (Sigman 1991). What is individual in relationships is linked dialectically with what is social, because as individuals engage in communicating with one another they ongoingly constitute what is social, while at the same time constituting the social in communicating is ongoingly constitutive of individuals (Arundale 2010a: 2085; 2020: 202–6).

Speaking Relationally. As an ethnographer of communication (see Carbaugh and Boromisza-Habashi 2015), Fitch (1998: 3) approaches interpersonal relationships by examining the patterns of language use through which middle-class Columbians construct and maintain personal relationships. She considers practices of personal address and directives, as well as of constituting *palanca* (connections of power and helping), with particular attention to "the premises about personhood, relationships, and communication that lend symbolic coherence to these interpersonal practices" as persons formulate their own and interpret one another's line of action. Fitch provides a detailed case study of the use of these resources in everyday talk and conduct in a long-term personal relationship in which two women employ resources that are both relationship-specific, and at the same time "an instantiation of certain relational ideals of friendship, family, and employer/employee relationships" (1998: 143). Fitch identifies those relational ideals as an "ideology of connectedness" reflected in the understanding that "the fundamental unit of existence for Columbians is the *vinculo*": a human being is not a monadic individual but "set of bonds to others" (1998: 147).

Vinculos are characterized by the dialectic opposition of *confianza*, or trust and commonality, with *distancia*, or difference and respect between relational partners. Fitch finds evidence of this dialectic in play in a wide range of social and linguistic practices in every talk and conduct, and argues that *confianza* and *distancia* is a unique Columbian construal of Baxter and Montgomery's (1996) relational dialectic of connection and separation (Fitch 1998: 175–9). She quite clearly conceptualizes what is social as linked dialectically with what is individual, and understands relationships as endogenous to interaction, continually being formed, sustained and changed as persons engage resources in everyday talk and conduct. Fitch does not specifically identify the properties of interaction as non-additive, but the fundamental concept of the *vinculo* is entirely compatible with understandings both of interaction as having properties that are not reducible to individuals, and of individuals as defined in and emergent from interaction.

Relational Ritual. Kádár (2012, 2013) argues for a wider, discursive conceptualization of ritual practices that encompasses what he defines as "relational ritual", or "a formalised/schematic, conventionalised and recurrent act, which is relationship forcing, i.e. by operating it reinforces/transforms in-group relationships. Ritual is realised as an embedded (mini-) performance (mimesis), and this performance is bound to relational history (and related ethos). Ritual is an emotively invested action" (2012: 6–7). Formally, both widely recognized social rituals and more local in-group rituals are manifested in prescribed vocabulary, ritualized forms, and sequential rules of interaction (2012: 16). Functionally, the recurrent performance of schematic patterns of language use sustains and changes existing social networks because, following Durkheim, "by performing rituals, individuals convey their "social dependence" or express their wish to find a place in the community, hence to create new social dependences" (2012: 3). In short, relational rituals accomplish "relational work" (as Locher 2008) "directed at the participant's socio-psychological needs and wants so as to (re)-establish or maintain intra group relationships" (Kádár and Bax 2013: 74).

For Kádár, then, a relationship is a local, in-group "relational network", defined as a set of "intersecting social links between persons that collectively form the basis of an identifiable group to those persons who constitute the relational network in question" (Kádár and Haugh 2013: 43, 125). Relational networks are (re-)established and changed over time as individuals engage their knowledge of schematic patterns for language use to perform in-group rituals, and in so doing establish and sustain mutual social dependence with other persons who are members of that in-group. A relationship, or a relational network of social links, is an abstraction across recurrent ritual performances: it is exogenous in that it is both apart from and pre-exists the performances, rather than being emergent in the here and now of using language. The social linkages among persons are distinct from the knowledge of the schematic patterns required to engage in relational rituals, hence what is social and what is individual in relational rituals form a dualism. And given that relational networks are additive collectivities of individuals (Arundale 2013a), and that the mutual dependence that is established in performing rituals is an additive property of human interaction (2010a: 2079–80; 2020: 72–9), relationships are conceptualized as additive rather than as non-additive phenomena.

Each of these seven scholars seeks a conceptualization of relationships and relating that is culture-general, rather than culture-specific, but each is in some way culture bound. It is culture bound simply because no human construction can be otherwise. Understanding a relationship as a *vinculo*, as in Columbia, is distinct from understanding it as a link between two monadic individuals, as is common in North America. Fitch (1994) identifies a number of potential cultural limitations in theory and research in interpersonal and relational communication, and post-modern critiques have made evident not only that awareness of such cultural framing is a necessity, but also that claims for culture-generality need always be assessed critically in view of ethnographically informed inquiry.

The seven conceptualizations sketched above are *not* equivalent, and I have compared them only on the basis of three specific dimensions that I argue are central to defining and to identifying what makes a "relationship". One might also compare these seven conceptualizations, and others, on a number of additional dimensions, as indicated in Haugh et al.'s (2013) overview of the range of complex issues to be addressed in theorizing and in examining matters of language pragmatics in interpersonal interaction. For example,

(a) Is the conceptualization of relationships and relating framed from the observer's perspective only, or from an observer perspective that addresses how the participants themselves go about forming relationships with one another, and that seeks direct evidence in analyses of how particular participants interpret particular utterances (2013: 4–5)?
(b) How does the model or theory conceptualize the development of relationships and relating over time, particularly with regard to what makes up the "history" of a relationship (2013: 6)?
(c) If the conceptualization links social relationship phenomena with individual identity phenomena (cf. Chapter 15), of what is that link comprised (2013: 4)?
(d) How does the conceptualization of relationships and relating link phenomena at the level of the minimum dyadic social system to the broader communities of practice, relational networks, societal, cultural, or language groups within which relational partners are always embedded (2013: 6)?
(e) How does the model or theory address participant's attitudinal or emotional states, as well as their processes of evaluating relationships and relating as they engage in using language with one another (2013: 4)?

These seven distinct conceptualizations of relationships in research in sociopragmatics reflect different disciplinary perspectives: social psychology for Spencer-Oatey and Locher, linguistic anthropology for Agha and Enfield, human communication for Arundale, ethnography of communication for Fitch, and ritual studies for Kádár. Antos et al. (2008) argue for a linguistic perspective, but do not develop a specific conceptualization of relationships. There are many more such conceptualizations to be found in theorizing and in research on interpersonal and relational communication within these disciplines and others (e.g. Arundale 2010b; Baxter and Montgomery 1996; Braithwaite and Schrodt 2015).

14.4 Conceptualizations of Relationships and Relating in Inquiry and in Practice

Again, as in Section 14.2, the considerable diversity in models and theories of relationships and relating requires considerable care in choosing a conceptual framework because that framework is consequential not only in one's formulating an account of relationships and relating, but also in the conduct of one's inquiry into these phenomena. If one's conceptual framework is consequential in both of these ways, it follows that it is also consequential as one's account is engaged in informing the practices persons employ in relating with one another in everyday life. Consider these observations on consequentiality for the conduct of inquiry and for informing practice.

The conceptual framework one employs both enables, and more importantly, constrains all aspects of the conduct of one's inquiry, which implies that that framework shapes the nature of the evidence one can provide in addressing one's research questions. More specifically, and following Krippendorff (1970; cf. Arundale 2013a), how one conceptualizes a phenomenon defines what one observes as an instance of that phenomenon, those observations serving as the basis for generating one's data regarding the phenomenon. The nature of one's data both enables and constrains the types of analysis one can apply to those data, and the data and the analytic technique in turn delimit the evidence one can adduce as a warrant for one's interpretations in terms of one's model or theory.

Returning to the three dimensions of difference, choosing a model or theory that conceptualizes relationships as exogenous to interaction leads one to making observations of and generating data on entities, forces, or contexts that precede interaction, or on prior psychological states or socialized patterns that are somehow cued in the current situation. On the other hand, choosing a model or theory in which relating is conceptualized as endogenous to interaction constrains one to observing and generating data on particular, situated, evolving instances of interaction. Choosing a model or theory that frames what is individual as a part of what is social, or as a dualism, constrains one to observing and generating data on the properties of the individuals as independent units, distinct and separable from the properties of the social unit. On the other hand, choosing a conceptual framework in which what is individual is linked dialectically with what is social constrains one to observing and generating data on social units as integral with and inseparable from the interdependent individuals who compose them. And whereas choosing a model or theory that understands what is social as an additive phenomenon requires no more than observations and data on the independent individuals who compose a collectivity, choosing a framework that conceptualizes what is social as non-additive requires making observations and generating data on the properties not only of individuals, but also of the social system that emerges in the interdependencies among those individuals. These distinct forms of observation and types of data enable and constrain the techniques applicable in analysing one's data because providing a credible account requires that one's analytic techniques be consistent with the assumptions entailed in formalizing one's observations as data (see Arundale 2010b, 2013a, 2020: 362–5, 383–90; Krippendorff 1970). And because one generates evidence by applying analytic techniques to one's data, it is apparent that one's choice of a conceptual framework for understanding relationships and relating is consequential in shaping the type of evidence one can provide in support of one's conclusions with regard to one's research questions.

The conceptual framework one employs in inquiry into a human social phenomenon is also consequential as one's account is engaged to better understand and to inform everyday practices of relating with one another. All models or theories of human social phenomenon forward particular understandings of how human beings interface with one another, models and theories of relationships and relating being a primary example. Over time such models and theories become widely known and come to affect human behaviour, or at times may be applied directly in shaping social practice, as for example with models of supply and demand from economics. Scholarly conceptualizations of relationships and relating become known and come to inform everyday personal interaction through coursework, training, and workshops using a wide array of textual materials focused on interpersonal and relational communication (e.g. Duck and McMahan 2009; Stewart et al. 2005), through publications addressed to the general public (e.g. Gergen 2009; Stewart 2014), through presentation and discussion in the mass media, and through interaction with practitioners in a wide range of professions. In this latter regard, Peräklyä et al. (2005: 163) argue that "professionals who work with people have often theories, concepts, and ideals that are related to their interactions with their clients. Practitioners understand their own work (and related practices such as training or development) in terms of these theories, and much of the research around professional fields is conducted by reference to such theories". To be a professional is to engage a particular set of social practices for interacting with clients. Those practices are informed by theories, concepts, and ideals for relationships and relating, and as professionals engage with clients those conceptualizations come to inform everyday social interaction. Medicine and clinical therapy are key examples, but so too are professions like education, mediation and law.

Again with regard to the three dimensions of difference, if one adopts a model that conceptualizes relationships as exogenous and as guided by pre-existing scripts, roles, drives or wants, that frames individuals as independent selves separate from other individuals, and that understands a relationship as an additive collectivity of a self plus an other, then understanding relationships and changing practices of relating entails understanding and changing pre-existing, exogenous properties like scripts, roles, drives or wants that self-contained individuals bring with them to interaction. Understanding and changing individuals is sufficient because relationships and relating are additive phenomena. On the other hand, if one adopts a model or theory that conceptualizes relationships as endogenous to and emergent in on-going, dynamic episodes of persons engaging one another in talk and conduct, that frames individuals as interdependent with one another in a dialectical linking of what is individual with what is social, and that understands a relationship as a non-additive social system, then understanding relationships and changing practices of relating entails understanding and changing properties that are endogenous to and inseparable from the immediacy of the interaction between persons: properties of the sequential organization of the talk and conduct that the participants conjointly constitute. Understanding and changing individuals is necessary, but not sufficient because relationships and relating are non-additive, systemic phenomena.

Models and theories of relationships and relating differ considerably from one another along these dimensions and others. They enable distinct understandings of what composes a productive relationship, as well as distinct recommendations for changing relationships that are deemed less productive. Such understandings and recommendations are consequential in the everyday lives of the human beings involved, and thus have important ethical and moral implications (e.g. Arundale 2020: 226–33, 350–53; Stewart 2011). Returning to Krippendorff (2009: 96), theories of human interaction are not socially neutral, and researchers who forward models and theories of relationships and relating need accept responsibility for what their formulations entail, both in the conduct of inquiry, and beyond in their own and other's personal and professional practices (2009: 28).

References

Agha, A. (2007). *Language and Social Relations.* Cambridge: Cambridge University Press.
Antaki, C. and Widdicombe, S. (1998). Identity as an achievement and as a tool. In C. Antaki and S. Widdicombe, eds., *Identities in Talk.* London: Sage, pp. 1–14.
Antos, G., Ventola, E. and Weber, T. (2008). Introduction: Interpersonal communication – Linguistic points of view. In G. Antos and E. Ventola, eds., *Handbook of Interpersonal Communication.* Berlin: Mouton de Gruyter, pp. 1–13.
Arundale, R. B. (2006). Face as relational and interactional: A communication framework for research on face, facework, and politeness. *Journal of Politeness Research*, 2(2), 193–216.
Arundale, R. B. (2010a). Constituting face in conversation: Face, facework, and interactional achievement. *Journal of Pragmatics*, 42(8), 2078–2105.
Arundale, R. B. (2010b). Relating. In M. A. Locher and S. L. Graham, eds., *Interpersonal Pragmatics,* Vol. 6, *Handbooks of Pragmatics.* Berlin: Walter de Gruyter, pp. 137–65.
Arundale, R. B. (2013a). Conceptualizing "interaction" in interpersonal pragmatics: Implications for understanding and research. *Journal of Pragmatics*, 58, 12–26.

Arundale, R. B. (2013b). Face, relating, and dialectics: A response to Spencer-Oatey. *Journal of Pragmatics*, 58, 138–51.

Arundale, R. B. (2020). *Communicating & Relating*. New York: Oxford University Press.

Arundale, R. B. (2015). Review of *Relationship Thinking: Agency, Enchrony, and Human Sociality*, by N. J. Enfield. *Language in Society*, 44(4), 584–7.

Bavelas, J. B. (2003). Relationship metaphors. In *International Encyclopedia of Marriage and Family*. www.encyclopedia.com/reference/encyclopedias-almanacs-transcripts-and-maps/relationship-metaphors.

Baxter, L. A. (2004). Relationships as dialogues. *Personal Relationships*, 11(1), 1–22.

Baxter, L. A. and Montgomery, B. M. (1996). *Relating: Dialogues and Dialectics*. New York: Guilford Press.

Braithwaite, D. O. and Schrodt, P. (eds.). (2015). *Engaging Theories of Interpersonal Communication: Multiple Perspectives*. Thousand Oaks, CA: Sage.

Bucholtz, M. and Hall, K. (2005). Identity and interaction: A sociocultural linguistic approach. *Discourse Studies*, 7(4–5), 585–614.

Burleson, B. L., Metts, S. and Kirch, M. W. (2000). Communication in close relationships. In C. Hendrick and S. S. Hendrick, eds., *Close Relationships: A Sourcebook*. Thousand Oaks, CA: Sage, pp. 245–58.

Carbaugh, D. and Boromisza-Habashi, D. (2015). Ethnography of communication. In K. Tracy, C. Ilie and T. Sandell, eds., *The International Encyclopedia of Language and Social Interaction*. Boston, MA: Wiley, pp. 537–52.

Craig, R. T. (1999). Communication theory as a field. *Communication Theory*, 9(2), 119–61.

Craig, R. T. (2015). The constitutive metamodel: A Sixteen-year review. *Communication Theory*, 25(4), 356–74.

Duck, S. and McMahan, D. T. (2009). *The Basics of Communication: A Relational Perspective*. Thousand Oaks, CA: Sage.

Enfield, N. J. (2009). Relationship thinking and human pragmatics. *Journal of Pragmatics*, 41(1), 60–78.

Enfield, N. J. (2013). *Relationship Thinking: Agency, Enchrony, and Human Sociality*. New York: Oxford University Press.

Fitch, K. L. 1994. Culture, ideology, and interpersonal communication research. In S. A. Deetz, ed., *Communication Yearbook 17*. Thousand Oaks, CA: Sage, pp. 104–35.

Fitch, K. L. (1998). *Speaking Relationally: Culture, Communication, and Interpersonal Connection*. New York: Guilford Press.

Gergen, K. J. (2009.) *Relational Being: Beyond Self and Community*. New York: Oxford University Press.

Goodwin, C. (1986). Audience diversity, participation and interpretation. *Text*, 6(3), 283–316.

Hall, J. A. and Davis, D. C. (2017). Proposing the communicate bond belong theory: Evolutionary intersections with episodic interpersonal communication. *Communication Theory*, 27(1), 21–47.

Haugh, M., Kádár, D. Z. and Mills, S. (2013). Interpersonal pragmatics: Issues and debates. *Journal of Pragmatics*, 58, 1–11.
Kádár, D. Z. (2012). Relational ritual. In J. Östman and J. Verschueren, eds., *Handbook of Pragmatics*. Amsterdam: John Benjamins, pp. 1–40.
Kádár, D. Z. (2013). *Relational Rituals and Communication: Ritual Interaction in Groups*. Basingstoke, UK: Palgrave Macmillan.
Kádár, D. Z. and Bax, M. M. H. (2013). In-group ritual and relational work. *Journal of Pragmatics*, 58, 73–86.
Kádár, D. Z. and Haugh, M. (2013). *Understanding Politeness*. Cambridge: Cambridge University Press.
Kaplan, A. (1964). *The Conduct of Inquiry: Methodology for Behavioral Science*. San Francisco, CA: Chandler.
Krippendorff, K. (1970). On generating data in communication research. *Journal of Communication*, 20(3), 241–69.
Krippendorff, K. (2009). *On Communicating: Otherness, Meaning, and Information*. Edited by F. Bermejo. New York: Routledge.
Lakoff, G. and Johnson, M. (1980). *Metaphors We Live By*. Chicago: University of Chicago Press.
Langlotz, A. and Locher, M. A. (2013). The role of emotions in relational work. *Journal of Pragmatics*, 58, 87–107.
Locher, M. A. (2008). Relational work, politeness, and identity construction. In G. Antos and E. Ventola, eds., *Handbook of Interpersonal Communication*. Berlin: Mouton de Gruyter, pp. 509–40.
Locher, M. and Graham, S. L. (2010). Introduction to interpersonal pragmatics. In M. Locher and S. L. Graham, eds., *Interpersonal Pragmatics*. Berlin: Mouton de Gruyter, pp. 1–13.
Locher, M. A. (2013). Relational work and interpersonal pragmatics. *Journal of Pragmatics*, 58, 145–9.
Owen, W. F. (1990). Delimiting relational metaphors. *Communication Studies*, 41(1), 35–53.
Peräkylä, A., Ruusuvuori, J. and Vehviläinen, S. (2005). Introduction: Professional theories and institutional interaction. *Communication and Medicine*, 2(2), 105–9.
Sawyer, R. K. (2005). *Social Emergence: Societies as Complex Systems*. Cambridge: Cambridge University Press.
Sigman, S. J. (1991). Handling the discontinuous aspects of continuous social relationships: Toward research on the persistence of social forms. *Communication Theory*, 1(2), 106–27.
Simmel, G. (1950). *The Sociology of Georg Simmel*. Translated by K. H. Wolff. New York: Free Press.
Spencer-Oatey, H. (2000). Rapport management: A framework for analysis. In H. Spencer-Oatey, ed., *Culturally Speaking: Managing Rapport through Talk across Cultures*. London: Continuum, pp. 11–46.
Spencer-Oatey, H. (2007). Theories of identity and the analysis of face. *Journal of Pragmatics*, 39(4), 639–56.

Spencer-Oatey, H. (2011). Conceptualizing "the relational" in pragmatics: Insights from metapragmatic emotion and (im)politeness comments. *Journal of Pragmatics, 43*(14), 3565–78.

Spencer-Oatey, H. (2013). Relating at work: Facets, dialectics, and face. *Journal of Pragmatics, 58*, 121–37.

Spencer-Oatey, H. (2015). Rapport management model. In K. Tracy, C. Ilie and T. Sandell, eds., *The International Encyclopedia of Language and Social Interaction*. Boston: John Wiley, pp. 1286–91.

Stewart, J. (2011). A contribution to ethical theory and praxis. In G. Cheney, S. May and D. Munshi, eds., *The Handbook of Communication Ethics*. New York: Routledge, pp. 15–30.

Stewart, J. (2014). *U and Me: Communicating in Moments That Matter*. Chagrin Falls, OH: Taos Institute.

Stewart, J., Zediker, K. E. and Witteborn, S. (2005). *Together: Communicating Interpersonally, a Social Construction Approach*. 6th ed. New York: Oxford University Press.

Watzlawick, P., Beavin, J. H. and Jackson, D. D. (1967). *Pragmatics of Human Communication*. New York: W. W. Norton.

15
Analysing Identity

Pilar Garcés-Conejos Blitvich and Alex Georgakopoulou

15.1 Introduction

The study of identity comes with a long, multidisciplinary tradition. Edwards (2009: 20) points out that "identity... is central to all the 'human' or 'social' sciences, as it is also in philosophical and religious studies". However, as Joseph (2010: 12) notes, modern linguistics, due to its traditional emphasis on structure and representation, was slow in embracing the function of identity as central to language. Once it did, though, the number of language-based approaches to the study of identity proliferated. These can be roughly categorized into two main groups: the sociolinguistic variationist/quantitative tradition initiated by Labov (e.g. 1963, 1972) and the (primarily qualitative) discourse-analytic and social interactional tradition (e.g. Mendoza-Denton 2008: 475). The latter sees identity in anti-essentialist terms, as co-constructed by communicators in discourse and in other semiotic systems of meaning-making (Benwell and Stokoe 2006). This is the view espoused in this chapter, as we will elaborate in Sections 15.1.2 and 15.1.3. In brief, we see identity, in tune with Bucholtz and Hall (2005), as the social positioning of self and other that is inherently relational and "produced through contextually situated and ideologically informed configurations of self and other" (Bucholtz and Hall 2005: 605). From this point of view, we concur with Joseph (2004), amongst others, who sees identity as belonging as much to the individual who interprets it as to the one who constructs it.

The complexity of the concept of identity itself, as well as the multidisciplinary research that has made it a focal point, make it difficult to do the concept full justice within the scope of this chapter. Our more modest aim then is to single out key-aspects in the interconnections between sociopragmatics and influential approaches to identities within conversation analysis, discourse analysis and sociolinguistics that set out to document the emergence of identities in discourse, their context-specificity and their multiplicity. We collectively call these approaches identities-in-interaction. After we distil assumptions within identities-in-interaction research, we will provide a brief overview of studies of identity in different sub-fields of pragmatics before moving to what we view as the key-domain of productive cross-fertilization between identities and pragmatics, namely the area of politeness and concomitant face concerns. We will illustrate these areas of cross-fertilization with case studies and then we will turn to the discussion of avenues for future research.

15.2 Identities-in-Interaction

A major paradigm shift in terms of identities research within discourse studies and sociolinguistics has been that of identities-in-interaction. Work within this paradigm has amply demonstrated the emergence of identities-in-interaction, their co-construction (i.e. relationality) and their context sensitivity. A key characteristic of identities-in-interaction research is that it draws upon conversation analysis (CA) for tools and modes of analysis. One of the premises of this analysis is that 'the events of conversation have a sense and import to participants which are at least partially displayed in each successive contribution, and which are thereby put to some degree under interactional control' (Schegloff 1997: 165). Speakers' actions are, therefore, contextual and need to be investigated as such.

The notion of context here is closely associated with that of co-text which includes the ongoing sequence of events and the immediate configuration of actions in any given interaction. Interactions are seen as both shaped by this co-text and co-text-shaping: "every contribution shapes a new context for the action that will follow" (Heritage 1984: 242). Identities, too, are seen as intimately shaped by the co-text of a communication. The categorizations and associated features we attribute to other people as well as how we present ourselves as members of specific groups are seen as *indexical and occasioned*. That is, they only make sense in a local setting and they may point more or less indirectly to an aspect of this local context. In addition, this self- and other-positioning and casting *makes relevant* the identity to the interactional business going on. In this respect, the force of "having an identity" is its *consequentiality* in the interaction: what it allows, prompts or discourages participants to do next. All the above is visible in people's exploitation of the structures of conversation (Antaki and Widdicombe 1998: 3ff.).

Locating identities-in-interaction, therefore, entails the analyst attending to participant perspectives and looking to the 'characterizations that are privileged in the constitution of socio-interactional reality ..., to the endogenous orientations of the participants ..., what constitutes the relevant context' (Schegloff 1997: 167). From this point of view, identities become an outcome, a finding, a result of an analysis, as opposed to being a presupposition of analysis and a definition of what analysis should be (Schegloff 1997: 170). In turn, the analytical priorities of an interactional approach to identities involve finding where, how and why an identity claim or categorization occurs and how it relates to its co-text. Similarly, what systematicity (i.e. location, design, responses) an identity category presents and what (other) categorizations, attributions and/or activities it is linked to.

Identities-in-interaction research sees identities as emergent and jointly drafted by participants (e.g. accepted, upheld, contested, negotiated) in actual interactions and this makes them difficult to anchor on individuals. The emphasis on the local context and the interactional drafting of identities implicates a focus on the importance of identities as temporary and contingent, situation-bound, participation roles. For example, in Zimmerman's (1998) heuristic of analysing identities-in-interaction, situated/situational identities (e.g. 'doctor', 'patient') are intimately connected with discourse (or interactional identities, for example, 'questioner', 'answerer', 'inviter-invitee'), and with the sequentiality of a conversation (e.g. adjacency pairs). The links the two provide vital clues for participants' larger, transportable identities (i.e. exogenous, extra-situational). These are viewed as latent identities which travel with individuals across situations and are potentially relevant at any time in a given interaction (e.g. 'middle-aged woman').

The influence of conversation analysis in identities-in-interaction research is undeniable. That said, many studies have moved beyond the confines of conversation analysis, so as to be in a position to explore any durability and stability of identities, beyond the here-and-now of interactions (e.g. Georgakopoulou 2013a; Wortham 2010). A first point of critique of narrow conversation-analytic approaches to identities involves the difficulty they have in capturing identities that are not" oriented to" by the participants, yet they influence interlocutors' actions. As Zimmerman (1998) puts it, the importance of "apprehended" identities, tacitly noticed but not treated as immediately relevant to the interaction hand, should not be under-estimated. To tap into such apprehended identities, many analysts claim that it is necessary to go beyond the single event so as to explore the dialectic of permanency and transiency in identities. In his study of students' social identification and its connections with academic learning, Wortham (2010) for instance, traced how specific roles and identities came to be attributed to two students and then to be occupied habitually by them across an academic year. This research is an example of how identities can present both continuity across interactions as well as being partly predetermined by discourses that position individuals in specific ways. In Wetherell's (1998) terms, it is important in this respect for the analyst to uncover the participants' interpretative repertoires, which comprise a backcloth of culturally familiar themes and arguments for the realization of locally managed positions in actual interaction.

Overall, one can talk about 'strong' and 'soft' understandings of a identities as continuous versus emergent in discourse within the broad spectrum of interactional approaches to identities. According to Brubaker and Cooper (2000: 10–11), strong views place emphasis on sameness over time or across persons while soft views see identities as multiple, unstable, fragmented, negotiated etc. There is an increasing tendency within identities-in-interaction for synthesizing insights from conversation analysis, interactional sociolinguistics and linguistic anthropology with a view to producing multi-layered approaches to identities (see e.g. Bucholtz and Hall 2005). Various overlapping concepts are deployed as necessary in forging links between linguistic and sequential choices in local context and larger, extra-situational identities. For example, positioning (Bamberg and Georgakopoulou 2008), indexicality (Wortham 2010), stance (Jaffe 2009), timescales, chronotopes (Blommaert and de Fina 2017). These concepts are aimed at aiding the analysis of how linguistic forms can point to social meanings such as identity without necessarily referring to them. Similarly, they are useful for exploring the creation of links between linguistic devices and social meanings that are implicit, indirect and associative (see Ochs 1992). Much of this work is aligned with ethnographic perspectives on language and communication (e.g. Georgakopoulou 2008). These allow the study of identities as parts of social and communicative practices: recurrent and recognizable ways of (inter)acting that are conventionally associated with particular meanings, activities, participation roles and actions.

15.3 Identity in Sociopragmatics

Although, as shown above, identity has come to occupy a central position in "sister" disciplines such as sociolinguistics, linguistic anthropology, conversation and discourse analysis, it has only been peripheral to the study of pragmatics. This may be due to the fact that pragmatics inquiry, at least in its beginnings, was mostly utterance-based, while the linguistic examination of identity has invariably been located in stretches of discourse or interactions. It is then no accident that interest in identities in pragmatics has coincided with the recent development of the interdisciplinary fields of discourse pragmatics (Blum-Kulka and Hamo [1997] 2011; Schneider and Barron 2014), discursive pragmatics (Kasper 2006; Zienkowski et al. 2011), interpersonal pragmatics (Locher and Graham 2010) or, as we will see below, with the second (Eelen 2001; Locher and Watts 2005; Mills 2003) and third waves (Garcés-Conejos Blitvich 2010; Grainger 2011; Haugh 2007; Terkourafi 2005, amongst others) in im/politeness research. Such approaches present a clear overlap with identities-in-interaction research, as described above. Indeed, as Arundale (2005: 56ff.) argued, interactional pragmatics encompasses research informed by findings and methodology in conversation analysis. A case in point is interpersonal pragmatics which places identity at the core of relational phenomena. Interpersonal pragmatics is defined as the "examinations of the relational aspect of interactions between people that both affect and are affected by their understandings of culture, society, and their own and others' interpretations" (Locher and Graham 2010: 2). Importantly, as the authors point out, "the relational aspect of language is closely linked to how people shape their identities" (3).

In interpersonal pragmatics, it is often situated identities or roles that form the main focus of the analysis, for their consequences for pragmatic phenomena of interest, e.g. politeness, relational work. Relational work or relationality covers a broad range of definitions from intersubjective practices (e.g. ways of doing friendship, alignment, affiliation, creation and enhancement of rapport) which encompass the ways in which identities are interactionally drafted (Locher 2008: 510), to a more specific focus on participants' shared norms, normative expectations and evaluations (Haugh 2015). Within this framework, there has been an increasing recognition that identity work and relational work are inter-related (Haugh et al. 2015: 76) and should be co-investigated. But the exact relationships between the two remain a point of contention, as we will see below.

Furthermore, as we will discuss, discursive/interpersonal pragmatics can bring together the componential and perspectivist views on pragmatics (Mey 1993; Verschueren 1999), also known as the narrow versus wide or the micro versus macro views on pragmatics. Those who approach pragmatics from a componential perspective usually focus on deixis, implicature, presupposition, speech acts and conversational interaction (see Levinson 1983; Mey 1993; Verschueren 1999). A perspectivist view of pragmatics, however, involves seeing it as "a usage-oriented approach to certain language resources" (Verschueren 1999: 228). More specifically, in Mey's (1993: 287) words, "pragmatics places its focus on the language users and their conditions of language use. This implies ... that there are specific societal factors (such as the institutions of the family, the school the peer group and so on) which influence the development and use of language, both in the acquisition stage and in usage itself". Importantly for this handbook, Leech (1983: 10–11) divides general pragmatics into *pragmalinguistics*, related to grammar, i.e. the resources a language provides for conveying different illocutions, and *sociopragmatics*, related to sociology, i.e. the sociological interface of pragmatics, how pragmatic principles "operate variably in different cultures or language communities, in different social situations, among different social classes, etc." (10). In view of these definitions, there is clear interconnectivity between the foci of pragmatic analysis and the linguistic phenomena associated with identity construction.

When identity has been incorporated into pragmatics, however, it has mostly been from a broad view of pragmatics (*sociopragmatics*), rather than a narrow one (*pragmalinguistic view*). For example, Locher and Graham (2010: 1) state that their views on interpersonal pragmatics stem from a perspectivist view of the field. This means that studies of identity (e.g. Clark 2016; Tuan and Ran 2016; Dings 2012; Finnis 2013; Flowerdew and Leong 2010; Ige 2010; Vöge 2010) have been published in pragmatics journals or books which approach identity from a socio-constructivist perspective, as emergent and co-constructed in interaction. At the same time, transportable identities in pragmatics research (especially in cross-cultural and interlanguage pragmatics, e.g. Blum-Kulka et al. 1989; Kasper and Blum-Kulka 1993) have been presented as categorical, demographically attestable identities (e.g. gender, age, ethnicity) which can be postulated in advance of the analysis and their significance for the analysis presupposed. The focus has been on how certain groups (e.g. Americans, Chinese, Italians, the young, the old) carry out some kind of linguistic performance (usually speech acts; e.g. Comstock 2015; Gonzalez-Cruz 2014; Hlavac et al. 2015; Koning and Zhu 2017). This has also been true of politeness scholarship that has related politeness realizations broadly to identity categories, mostly language and culture groups or gender (Fukushima and Sifianou 2017; Marquez 2000; Placencia 2008; Taylor 2016). This can cause a degree of circularity: characterizing and pre-categorizing interlocutors, for instance, as Chinese or Greek, and exploring how culture shapes their interactions, somehow assumes that differences in their interactions will be down to their cultural identities. In contrast, as we have seen, in the identities-in-interaction research, which category, or combination of categories, and any associated characteristics are viewed as matters of changeable, local circumstances.

Below, we will move to the key-domain of productive cross-fertilization between identities and pragmatics, which is the area of politeness and the concomitant face concerns.

15.4 Identity and Face in Im/politeness Research

The sub-field of pragmatics in which identity as co-constructed in interaction has been examined in more detail is im/politeness studies. This is not surprising, as identity and face, a key-concept in im/politeness research, are both related to the construction and presentation of self (Goffman 1967). Interest in identity was triggered by the advent of the discursive turn within politeness (Eelen 2001; Mills 2003: Locher and Watts 2005). The main changes in this sub-field that are linked with the surge in interest in identities can be summed up as follows:

(i) The shift in interest to politeness realized in longer stretches of discourse;
(ii) An ethnographic, bottom-up understanding of politeness phenomena with a focus of participants' rather than analysists' evaluations. This aligns the field of politeness with the identities-in-interaction approach. Discursive approaches to politeness caution the analyst

against coding forms and strategies a priori of concrete analyses and according to pre-conceived theoretical categories (i.e. second-order interpretations). Instead, they favour an analytical focus on participants' emic (first order) understandings of politeness norms (Eelen 2001);
(iii) A renewed attention to face, in connection with its Goffmanian origins, thus questioning Brown and Levinson's reinterpretation.

Face, the inspiration behind the core concept in Brown and Levinson's ([1978] 1987) framework, was defined by Goffman (1967: 5) as "the positive social value a person effectively claims for himself by the line others assume he has taken during a particular contact. Face is an image of self-delineated in terms of approved social attributes". As Garcés-Conejos Blitvich (2013) has argued, Goffman conceptualized face as being tied to a line (a role, an identity).[1] However, Brown and Levinson's construal of face altered its essence, as they separated face from *line* and presented it as a primarily cognitive construct possessed by a rational person.

In the mid to late 2000s, identity started to be introduced alongside face in the definitions of im/politeness. Certain scholars also began enquiring its relationship with face and introducing im/politeness studies to the frameworks developed for the analysis of identity, arguing for their relevance to im/politeness research (see among others Spencer-Oatey 2007; Locher 2008; Garcés-Conejos Blitvich 2009, 2010, 2013). Perhaps in an attempt to maintain the "identity" and separateness of the field of im/politeness, other im/politeness scholars argued for the differences between the two (see Spencer-Oatey 2007, 2009; Arundale 2009, 2010, 2013a, 2013b; O'Driscoll 2011). According to Garcés-Conejos Blitvich and Sifianou (2017, 235), four major differences were thus established between face and identity by im/politeness scholars:

(a) Face is a social attribute; identity is an individual one.
(b) Face is relational, the result of a non-summative process; identity is the property of monadic individuals, the outcome of a summative process.
(c) Face is a punctual phenomenon; identity is a durative one.
(d) Face is invested with emotion; identity is not.

On the basis of a thorough review of identity models and scholarship, Garcés-Conejos Blitvich and Sifianou (2017) argue that the above differences cannot stand up to close scrutiny.[2] They nonetheless note that im/politeness research needs to consider the importance of relational histories (Haugh 2013) in the definition of face and the links between identities and emotion (see Garcés-Conejos Blitvich 2013), as part of this ongoing debate regarding the relations of the two concepts.

---

[1] As a matter of fact, Goffman dropped the term 'face' and substituted it unproblematically with 'identity' in the bulk of his work.
[2] It is worth noting that empirical analyses have demonstrated the difficulty of teasing face and identity apart in real interaction (see Joseph 2013; Kádár et al. 2013; Bousfield 2013, among others).

Scholars who have argued for a more multi-disciplinary approach to the study of im/politeness phenomena see identity models as a way to achieve that goal, especially due to the close relationship between face and identity in the presentation of self. Their proposed ways of advancing the field can be summarized as follows:

(a) Im/politeness manifestations/assessments can be tied to identity (co)construction, not just to face.
(b) Identity and face are inseparable, as they co-constitute each other.
(c) Im/politeness can be analysed as an index in identity construction.
(d) Models developed for the analysis of identity construction can be fruitfully applied to the study of im/politeness (Garcés-Conejos Blitvich and Sifianou 2017: 238).

A close connection between identity and im/politeness is the fact that the latter has been shown to be an indirect index of identity construction. For example, Locher (2008) argued that being perceived as polite may be one of the attributes one wants to claim as part of one's identity. For her part, Garcés-Conejos Blitvich (2009) showed how deploying impoliteness was a crucial indirect index of the identity construction of the hosts/guests/audience of cable TV news programmes. Along these lines, discourse-analytic studies have connected politeness manifestations to the construction of social identities in Japanese drama (Barke 2010) and to stereotypes of Englishness (Ajtony 2013). Similarly, swearing in story-telling has been linked to the construction of the Greek teenager identity (Karahaliou and Archakis 2015). Humour, a positive politeness strategy (Brown and Levinson 1987), has often been related to identity construction (see, among others, Rees and Monrouxe 2010; Wolfers et al. 2017). In a recent study of TV interviews with athletes and coaches, File and Schnurr (2018) explored the relationship of failed humour to identity claims. They reported a connection of humour failure with face threat and with the challenge of the public image of those who attempted the humour. The authors concluded that failed humour can damage athletes' face and identity, and thus have serious consequences for their future careers. There has also been a rapprochement between the study of participants' understandings and evaluations of their identity work, by focusing, for instance, on how identities themselves are evaluated and what moral and other dimensions such evaluations may carry for the participants (see e.g. Haugh et al. 2015: 2015).

Other scholars have begun to show how im/politeness and conflict play a crucial role in the construction of identities (see Donaghue 2018), as strategies for building the basic sense of difference upon which identities are constructed. Indeed, identity construction has often been seen in terms of a similarity/difference dialectic and of marking difference (see e.g. Hall and Du Gay 1996; Mendoza-Denton 2008). Mouffe (2005: 129), for instance, states that there cannot be a common identity without drawing a frontier; those frontiers used to be political but are currently drawn along moral categories, "between 'us', the good' and 'them', the evil ones". Thus, the 'us', for its mere existence, is dependent on a constitutive outside. This tension, often or potentially conflictual, is an inherent part of identity construction. This has also been shown by Perelmutter (2018) and by Garcés-Conejos Blitvich (2018) who looked at processes of intra-group disaffiliation within a Russian-speaking Jewish community and Latinos in the United States, respectively.

Case Study 1: Globalization, Transnational Identities, and Conflict Talk: The Superdiversity and Complexity of the Latino Identity

In this paper, Garcés-Conejos Blitvich (2018) analysed the functionality of conflict talk as an ideologically loaded, indirect index of identity construction (Kiesling 2013). The study focuses on the construction of the Latino identity: a transnational (de Fina and Perrino 2013), top-down identity, that was created in the 1970s by the Nixon administration. The data comprise the comments posted on a CNN discussion forum in response to Soledad O'Brien's question "What did you think about Latino in America?" An initial look at the corpus indicated that many Latino participants felt insulted and claimed that CNN, with its focus on illegal Latinos, had presented the community in a bad light. It was also observed that the participants' selective dissociation (Garcia-Bedolla 2003) from those views was the main process at work to carry out intragroup dissociation.

The data were then subjected to a thematic analysis and coded at the micro level to unveil the role conflictual strategies played in selective dissociation. The results of the thematic analysis showed recurrent themes that were conflictual and could potentially trigger conflict as they dealt with core issues of positive/negative group presentation. In the discussion, there was a palpable tension: posters expressed their assessment of CNN's views on the Latino identity, as they discursively struggled to position themselves as a heterogeneous group against CNN's top-down, superimposed, homogenizing presentation of Latinos in America. The analysis of how selective dissociation was carried out at the micro level also found that conflictual strategies played a major role and revealed two interesting patterns. Regarding the first, it was observed that somebody/their actions/thoughts, etc., would be associated with a negative aspect. By pointing out this negative aspect, the poster would try to make that addressee feel uncomfortable and by disagreeing with that person/action/thought, would also indicate a lack of common ground. The poster would then finally dissociate themselves from that person or group. A second pattern was identified that may reflect, pending further research, a fundamental difference between intragroup dissociation and othering processes, as described by van Dijk (1998) in his ideological square for intergroup dissociation. There was a focus on emphasizing and mitigating *our* good/bad properties/actions, respectively, rather than on emphasizing and mitigating *their* bad/good properties and actions. As shown, Latinos selectively dissociated themselves from what they perceived as the stereotypical/negative representations conveyed by CNN's documentary by emphasizing their good properties and dissociating themselves from negative representations of others, on the basis of their many educational, financial, accomplishments or their law-abiding qualities. They did this without expounding on the bad properties of other Latinos. Emphasizing their good properties and actions coincided in the corpus with repositioning themselves as neo-liberal subjects. Observing the processes that reflect and help construct superdiversity and complexity in this bottom-up way lends credence to the vital role of conflictual interaction therein.

Another mode of cross-fertilization between im/politeness and identities research has taken the form of productively drawing upon theoretical frameworks and methodologies developed for the analysis of identity construction, so as to transpose onto the study of im/politeness manifestations. A case in point is Garcés-Conejos Blitvich (2009) and Garcés-Conejos Blitvich et al. (2013), who applied Anton and Peterson's (2003) model of subject positions in identity construction in interaction. The studies showed how im/politeness ensued when the identities and positioning we are trying to construct are not verified by interlocutors. Drawing on Zimmerman's (1998) tripartite distinction to the analysis of identity (see Section 15.2), another well-established framework, Garcés-Conejos Blitvich et al. (2010) and Dobs (2014) found that im/politeness and identity are intrinsically related and co-constructed in constitutive processes. Other cases include Locher's (2008) application of Bucholtz and Hall's (2005) framework to the analysis of relational work and Miller (2013) who drew on positioning analysis (for details, see Bamberg 1997; Bamberg and Georgakopoulou 2008) to show how identity construction and relational work are co-constitutive processes in local interactions. Also drawing on positioning analysis and her small stories framework,[3] Georgakopoulou (2013b) explored the connection of identities with im/politeness, in the interactions of a group of female 13- to 14-year-old pupils in a London comprehensive school. She concluded that a discursive account of im/politeness could emphasize narrative activities and transfer tools of identity analysis to the study of im/politeness. She specifically showed how focusing on the stories' *ways of telling*, *sites* (the social spaces in which the stories were told as well as those of their taleworlds), and the roles of the *tellers* in the telling could shed light on the tellers' management of im/politeness norms in stories that narrated their interactions with users in new media environments (e.g. MySpace) as well as transgressive uses and behaviour in those environments. The study demonstrated how im/politeness norms and the participants' construction of gendered and expert (or novice) identities as social media users were interwoven in such cases.

Case Study 2: Small Stories, Positioning and Impoliteness on Social Media

In a similar vein of exploring the intersections of small stories, positioning and impoliteness, Georgakopoulou and Vasilaki (2018) focused on discussions and comments in response to political party posts on Facebook and YouTube in a three-month turbulent period of a referendum and elections in Greece (2015). The analysis

---

[3] Small stories are defined as multi-semiotic, often literally "small", multiply authored and mobile discourse activities of creating a, however incipient, plot (i.e. connections between events in specific time and place, characters, emotions and evaluations). Small stories research was first put forward as a counter-move to conventional narrative analysis and biographical research that had privileged a specific type of teller-led, past events, personal experience story, with a clear beginning, middle and an end. A case was made for the salience of stories that departed from this in everyday-life contexts and for their significance for the tellers' identity work (Georgakopoulou 2007).

brought together a combination of Culpeper's (2011) and Bousfields' (2008) frameworks for examining impolite contributions with tools for analysing (small) stories on social media. Taking into account the distinct affordances of each platform, the study explored how Facebook and YouTube commenters "bash" political leaders and perceived political opponents and attribute blame to them for the crisis, through comments that attest to specific links of doing impoliteness with storying the crisis. On-record impoliteness strategies for bashing politicians were associated with specific narrating positions in stories about the crisis and, in turn, with specific identities for the tellers: the narrator as sufferer, as witness of suffering and as spokesperson for collective suffering. In all these cases, on-record impoliteness was placed at the end of a small story and presented as legitimated and justified by the preceding account. Personal crisis stories thus served as a legitimation resource for the use of impoliteness vis-à-vis both targeted politicians and any commenters in the here-and-now exchanges, who supported them. Impoliteness was normalized as an appropriate mode of conduct for the posters, in response to their recounted dire circumstances. A key function of stories was to provide a moral ground for employing impoliteness.

A notable related finding was that all three types of impoliteness that Culpeper (2011) describes, namely affective, coercive and performative, were present in the data. The authors argued that this was linked to the widely held view that stories afford multi-participation roles and identities to their tellers, whilst also bringing together their epistemic and agentive selves, their actions and affective responses. Specifically, the role of the sufferer in the stories at hand justified the use of *affective impoliteness*, in an effort to unleash feelings of injustice and anger with the political system. In addition, the lived experience of the crisis allowed for the role of an 'expert' on the political situation to emerge. Building such implicit expertise was linked to the use of *coercive impoliteness*, as commenters attempted to gain the upper hand in the discussion with others (i.e. "pwn" them) and to prove they have the right to target the responsible politicians, who, in the offline world, are in a higher position in terms of power ranking. Finally, the use of impoliteness in this context was found to have a *performative* element, since it was used to verify the identities of sufferers and experts that the commenters tried to construct.

These findings suggest that un-instigated swearing, hostile comments, hate-speech and other conduct often described as 'flaming' and 'ranting' on social media would benefit from an examination of the co-text and the specific discourse activities (incl. stories) that such comments become part of. In addition, the findings point to a close association of impoliteness used to target public figures with the media-afforded engagement of ordinary people with political affairs as 'experts' due to personal experience.

15.5 Summary and Avenues for Further Research

The above overview shows that much progress has been made in integrating insights and concerns from identities analysis, especially the identities-in-interaction paradigm, into discursive, interactional and interpersonal pragmatics. The views of identities as co-constructed and relational phenomena, with contingency and connections with situated roles, have been influential in establishing links between identities research and mainstay pragmatics concerns, in particular, face and im/politeness. We showed how these links have resulted from creatively applying insights and modes of analysis from identities research into sociopragmatic research and vice versa.

Despite this ongoing productive rapprochement, in our view, there is much scope for discursive/interpersonal pragmatics integrating a narrow, more pragmalinguistically oriented, approach that could be fruitful in the analysis of identities, as we will explain in Section 15.4.1. We will conclude (Section 15.4.2) with suggestions for further research on the rapprochement of pragmatics and the analysis of identity.

15.5.1 Identities in Pragmalinguistic Approaches

As claimed above, discursive pragmatics can help connect the narrow view of pragmatics with the analysis of identity. According to discourse theorists (see Fairclough 2003; Gee 2005, among others), identity is at the heart of both big D-/little d-discourses. If pragmatics becomes discursive, then identity is at the heart of discursive pragmatics as well. Therefore, we can look at phenomena that have been the traditional foci of pragmatic enquiry not as ends in themselves, but as resources that interlocutors draw from, when constructing their identities. For instance, the pairing of identities with roles is an important rapprochement of traditional pragmatic concerns with the importance of relational roles and facework. It is often the case that the two come together in examining speech acts. Local cultural positions emerge, often, through the performance of specific speech acts. Along these lines, the city-foundational festivities in a medium size city in the East of Spain begin with a parade and more specifically with a declaration/proclamation made by a *pregonero*, i.e. crier, both an identity and a speech event invested with local, historical significance.

Regarding the temporary stances and roles of participants in interaction, we also see them as mostly related to the performance of specific speech acts. For example, the role of a concerned friend is often constructed through advice-giving or the role of a caregiver is frequently associated with directive speech acts. In institutional discourse, where roles are usually pre-allocated, we find that there is a co-constitutive relationship between identities and the use of certain speech acts: occupying a role thus allows participants access to certain speech acts and not others; access to those speech acts, in turn, helps position participants in certain roles. There is an emphasis in this respect on interpersonally sensitive activities with the potential for face vulnerability for the interlocutors. For example, during a physician/patient interaction, the physician usually asks questions, whereas the patient is expected to provide accurate answers. A few years ago, one of the authors was rebuked by an older physician for asking him too many questions during her visit: "I ask the questions", he stated. By usurpating a speech act he believed he only had access to, he might have felt his identity as a physician was not being verified by her, as a patient. Indeed, current views of physical/patient interaction advocate for a more equal access to questions by both roles, as patients are encouraged to be more pro-active in directing the encounter, which also lets it proceed on a more equal footing rather than on the more traditional hierarchal basis (see Basturkmen 2010). Such situations lend themselves well to the investigation of how pre-allocated, institutionally defined roles that place the interlocutors in some kind of an asymmetry (e.g. employees vs bosses, callees vs callers in call centres) shape situated speech acts, e.g. requests, apologies etc.

There was always a connection in the pragmatics literature between, especially, declaration speech acts and institutional identity: e.g. officiating a marriage ceremony, sentencing, baptizing a ship etc. have been associated with specific institutional identities, which derive their power from the institution they represent. But this connection has been, for the most part, overlooked. An interesting exception is Terkourafi's (2013) reassessment of the speech act schema. The author analysed three types of indirect speech acts between intimates and found that, along with others, a perlocutionary effect of re-affirming or testing the degree of sharedness between speaker/addressee was achieved. This was a necessary step towards recognizing the speaker's illocutionary intention. Terkourafi thus effectively established a correlation between identity and speech acts. This is an important line of enquiry with a welcome focus on how specific language and sequential choices are tied to local activities.

Bucholtz and Hall (2005: 594) argue that "identity relations emerge in interaction though several related indexical processes including (1) overt mention of identity categories and labels; (2) implicatures and presuppositions regarding one's own or others' identity position (3) displayed evaluative and epistemic orientations to ongoing talk, as well as interactional footings and participant roles; and (4) the use of linguistic structures and systems that are ideological associated with specific personas or groups". As we can see from this definition, phenomena that are at the heart of pragmatics research, such as implicatures and presupposition, as well as deixis and reference assignment, play a major role in identity construction. Introduced by Grice (1967, 1989), the notion of implicature refers to those instances in which what a speaker means goes beyond what he literally says. The study of implicature, tackled from Gricean, Neo-Gricean and Post-Gricean perspectives (for a detailed review, see Haugh 2015), was to become central to pragmatics. Indeed, it could be argued that different approaches to politeness were developed in an attempt to explain speakers' deviations from overt cooperation (Lakoff 1975 ; Leech 1983). For their part, Brown and Levinson also drew on Grice's conceptualization and saw politeness as an implicature. In the same way that implicatures are central to politeness and can be related to face concerns, their links to identity construction are clear but under-researched within pragmatics. The creation and interpretation of non-conventional, especially generalized, conversational implicatures are tied to the identity/roles of participants, i.e. the implicatum may be interpreted differently, depending on who is communicating it. Also, as Bucholtz and Hall (2005) point out, identity claims may be constructed via implicature rather than explicitly.

Another under-researched but promising area of the intersection between pragmatics and identity is presuppositions, defined as "aspects of meaning that must be presupposed, understood, taken for granted for an utterance to make sense" (Vershueren 1999: 27). Bucholtz and Hall (2005) also mention presuppositions as playing a major role in identity construction. A glimpse at the possibilities offered by presuppositions and pre-supposed knowledge in constructing identities can be obtained from studies such as Ponton (2010), who examined presuppositions in interviewers' questions to Margaret Thatcher during her time as Prime Minister. Ponton analysed how Thatcher strategically played along, ignored or objected to presuppositions, so as to present a specific kind of identity. Similarly, Flowerdew and Leong (2010) present interesting insights regarding the role of pre-supposed knowledge in the discursive construction of Hong-Kong's socio-political cultural identity.

Deixis, a quintessentially pragmatic phenomenon (see Levinson 1983; Verschueren 1999), which anchors language in its interactional context, also plays a major role in co-constructing identities. Attitudinal deixis (Verschueren 1999: 20–21) signals aspects of social status and/or forms of respect and relates to reference assignment and terms. As Chaemsaithong (2019: 92) argues,

> Reference terms constitute par excellence a communicative resource for managing impressions and positioning of self and others. For example, a person by the name of Michael Smith can be referred to in a myriad of ways, Michael, Mike, Mr. Smith, that dude, my pal, or (metaphorically) that snake. Needless to say, each label is value-laden. When choosing a term of reference, the speaker not only has to take into account her relationship with the hearer, but also has to decide how to present the referent in a situationally appropriate manner.

For their part, person deixis and deictic centre are essential to the construction of second-person or addressee and third-person and crucial to understanding different positions and alignments, such as those presented in Goffman's (1981) participation framework. This refers to how individuals produce and interpret talk and conduct. This framework has also been fruitfully applied to the analysis of understandings of im/politeness (see Kádár and Haugh 2013). Furthermore, as we have illustrated above, evaluative and epistemic orientations are constructed through different speech acts (e.g. declarations, expressives, commissives).

The above suggests that the functionality of pragmatic phenomena can be tied to the interlocutors' (co)construction of an identity. In a sense, what we are proposing here is not dissimilar to Haugh's (2015) framework for the analysis of im/politeness which alludes to traditional pragmatic notions (speech acts, speaker intentions, and Gricean implicatures) but also "reconfigures them in quite different ways as forms of social action, and thus ultimately of social practice" (Haugh 2015: 319). Situating interaction within social practice ultimately involves giving pre-eminence to an agent, to the performance of the practice, i.e. an identity (Reckwitz 2002).

15.5.2 Other Directions for Research

There is still scope for the rapprochement between identities and pragmatic research to be explored and tested out in sites and situations which provide fruitful cases of intersection between relational practices and identity work. A case in point is social media communication. Since Locher (2010) urged pragmaticists to pay more attention to computer-mediated data, several studies have taken up this plea, especially in connection with conflict and im/politeness on social media (see case studies in Section 15.3). More work needs to be done though on characterizing the range of relational practices and identities on different platforms. Identity research is currently moving to exploring the interplay between algorithms, affordances and communication, in particular how algorithms may infer and predict users' identities, what assumptions they make about them and how those shape users' communication choices and self-perceptions (see Georgakopoulou 2017, 2019). Studies have begun to show that users can be highly reflexive and aware online, developing discursive strategies to tweak and manipulate algorithms (e.g. Jones, forthcoming). Further work is needed to explore the connections between algorithmically produced identities in different types of posting and users' compliances, resistances or ways of counter-acting them. Pragmatics can play a key-role in this inquiry, which is expected to shed light on the potential and limits of the agentive aspects of participants' constructions of identities.

Another area of cross-fertilization between identities research and pragmatics that merits more scrutiny concerns the relationship between first- and second-order principles. Multi-layered approaches to identities (see Section 15.2) can benefit from the focus of pragmatics on theorizing meaning-making and providing second-order conceptualization of participants' attitudes and evaluations of self and other.

Finally, three areas that are still in need of further research are as follows:

(a) The interconnections between face and identity (but see articles in Garcés-Conejos Blitvich 2013).
(b) The moral aspects of identity construction (e.g. as attested to in evaluations) and the role of impoliteness in them (e.g. in polarized political climates).
(c) The embodied and multi-semiotic aspects of identity construction and their implications for relational work.

References

Ajtony, Z. (2013). Various facets of the English stereotype in *Downton Abbey* – A pragmatic approach. *Topics in Linguistics*, *12*, 5–14.

Antaki, C. and Widdicombe, S. (eds.). (1998). *Identities in Talk*. Thousand Oaks, CA: Sage.

Anton, C. and Peterson, V. (2003). Who said what: Subject positions, rhetorical strategies and good faith. *Communication Studies, 54*, 403–19.

Arundale, R. B. (2005). Pragmatics, conversational implicature, and conversation. In K. L. Fitch and R. E. Sanders, eds., *Handbook of Language and Social Interaction*. Mahwah, NJ: Erlbaum, pp. 41–63.

Arundale, R. B. (2006). Face as relational and interactional: A communication framework for research on face, facework and politeness. *Journal of Politeness Research, 2*(2), 193–216.

Arundale, R. B. (2009). Face as emergent in interpersonal communication: An alternative to Goffman. In F. Bargiela-Chiappini and M. Haugh, eds., *Face, Communication and Social Interaction*. London: Equinox, pp. 33–54.

Arundale, R. B. (2010). Constituting face in conversation: Face, facework, and interactional achievement. *Journal of Pragmatics, 42*(8), 2078–2105.

Arundale, R. B. (2013a). Face, relating, and dialectics: A response to Spencer-Oatey. *Journal of Pragmatics, 58*, 138–42.

Arundale, R. B. (2013b). Face as a research focus in interpersonal pragmatics: Relational and emic perspectives. *Journal of Pragmatics, 58*, 108–20.

Bamberg, M. (1997) Positioning between structure and performance. *Journal of Narrative and Life History, 7*, 335–42.

Bamberg, M. and Georgakopoulou, A. (2008). Small stories as a new perspective in narrative and identity analysis. *Text and Talk, 28*, 377–96.

Barke, A. (2010). Manipulating honorifics in the construction of social identities in Japanese television drama. *Journal of Sociolinguistics, 14*(4), 456–76.

Basturkmen, H. (2010). *Developing Courses in English for Specific Purposes*. New York: Springer.

Benwell, B. and Stokoe, E. (2006). *Discourse and Identity*. Edinburgh: Edinburgh University Press.

Blommaert, J. and De Fina, A. (2017). Chronotopic identities: On the timespace organization of who we are. In A. De Fina, D. Ikizoglu and J. Wegner, eds., *Diversity and Super-diversity*. Washington, DC: Georgetown University Press, pp. 1–14.

Blum-Kulka, S. and Hamo, M. (2011). Discourse pragmatics. In T. van Dijk, ed., *Discourse Studies: A Multidisciplinary Introduction*. London: Sage, pp. 143–65.

Blum-Kulka, S., House, J. and Kasper, G. (1989). *Cross-Cultural Pragmatics: Requests and Apologies*. New York: Ablex.

Bousfield, D. (2008). *Impoliteness in Interaction*. Amsterdam: John Benjamins.

Bousfield, D. (2013). Face in conflict. *Journal of Language Aggression and Conflict*, 1(1), 37.

Brown, P. and Levinson, S. C. (1978). Universals in language usage: Politeness phenomena. In E. N. Goody, ed., *Questions and Politeness: Strategies in Social Interaction*. Cambridge: Cambridge University Press, pp. 56–289.

Brown, P. and Levinson, S. C. (1987). *Politeness: Some Universals of Language Usage*. Cambridge: Cambridge University Press.

Brubaker, R. and Cooper, F. (2000). Beyond "identity". *Theory and Society*, 29(1), 1–47.

Bucholtz, M. and Hall, K. (2005). Identity and interaction: A socio-cultural linguistic approach. *Discourse Studies*, 7(4/5), 585–614.

Chaemsaithong, K. (2019). Person reference, identity, and linguistic violence in capital trials. *Journal of Pragmatics*, 142, 90–104.

Cheng-Tuan, L. and Yong-Ping, R. (2016). Self-professional identity construction through other-identity deconstruction in Chinese televised debating discourse. *Journal of Pragmatics*, 94, 47–63.

Clark, B. (2016). Flight attendant identity construction in inflight incident reports. *Pragmatics and Society*, 7(1), 8–29.

Comstock, L. B. (2015). Facilitating active engagement in intercultural teleconferences: A pragmalinguistic study of Russian and Irish participation frameworks. *Intercultural Pragmatics*, 12(4), 481–514.

Culpeper, J. (2011). *Impoliteness: Using Language to Cause Offence*. Cambridge: Cambridge University Press.

de Fina, A. and Perrino, S. (2013). Transnational identities. *Applied Linguistics*, 34(5), 509–15.

Dings, A. (2012). Native speaker/nonnative speaker interaction and orientation to novice/expert identity. *Journal of Pragmatics*, 44(11), 1503–18.

Dobs, A. M. (2014). Identities in conflict: Examining the co-construction of impoliteness and identity in classroom interaction. *Journal of Language Aggression and Conflict*, 2(1), 36–73.

Donaghue, H. (2018). Relational work and identity negotiation in critical post observation teacher feedback. *Journal of Pragmatics*, 135, 101–16.

Edwards, J. (2009). *Language and Identity*. Cambridge: Cambridge University Press.

Eelen, G. (2001). *A Critique of Politeness Theories*. Manchester, UK: St. Jerome.

Fairclough, N. (2003). *Analysing Discourse: Textual Analysis for Social Research*. London: Routledge.

File, K. A. and Schnurr, S. (2018). That match was "a bit like losing your virginity": Failed humour, face and identity construction in TV interviews with professional athletes and coaches. *Journal of Pragmatics*, 152, 132–44.

Finnis, K. (2013). Creating a "new space": Code-switching among British-born Greek-Cypriots in London. *Pragmatics and Society*, 4(2), 137–57.

Flowerdew, J. and Leong, S. (2010). Presumed knowledge in the discursive construction of socio-political and cultural identity. *Journal of Pragmatics, 42*(8), 2240–52.

Fukushima, S. and Sifianou, M. (2017). Conceptualizing politeness in Japanese and Greek. *Intercultural Pragmatics, 14*(4), 525–55.

Garcés-Conejos Blitvich, P. (2009). Impoliteness and identity in the American news media: The Culture Wars. *Journal of Politeness Research, 5*, 273–304.

Garcés-Conejos Blitvich, P. (2010). A genre approach to the study of impoliteness. *International Review of Pragmatics, 2*, 46–94.

Garcés-Coneos Blitvich, P. (ed.). (2013). Special issue: Face, identity, and impoliteness. *Journal of Politeness Research, 9*(1).

Garcés-Conejos Blitvich, P. (2013). Face, identity, and im/politeness: Looking backwards, moving forward – From Goffman to Practice Theory. *Journal of Politeness Research, 9*(1), 1–33.

Garcés-Conejos Blitvich, P. (2018). Globalization, transnational identities, and conflict talk: The complexity of the Latino identity. *Journal of Pragmatics, 134*, 120–33.

Garcés-Conejos Blitvich, P. and Sifianou, M. (2017). Im/politeness and identity. In J. Culpeper, M. Haugh and D. Kádár, eds., *The Palgrave Handbook of Linguistic (Im)politeness*. London: Palgrave Macmillan, pp. 227–56.

Garcés-Conejos Blitvich, P., Bou-Franch, P. and Lorenzo-Dus, N. (2010). A genre-approach to im-politeness in a Spanish TV talk show: Evidence from corpus-based analysis, questionnaires and focus groups. *Intercultural Pragmatics, 7*(4), 689–723.

Garcés-Conejos Blitvich, P., Bou-Franch, P. and Lorenzo-Dus, N. (2013). Identity and impoliteness: The expert in the talent show *Idol*. *Journal of Politeness Research, 9*(1), 97–121.

Garcia-Bedolla, L. (2003). The identity paradox: Latino language, politics and selective dissociation. *Latino Studies, 1*, 264–83.

Gee, J. P. (2005). *An Introduction to Discourse Analysis Theory and Method*. 2nd ed. New York: Routledge.

Georgakopoulou, A. (2007). *Small Stories, Interaction and Identities*. Amsterdam: John Benjamins.

Georgakopoulou, A. (2008). "On MSN with buff boys": Self-and other-identity claims in the context of small stories 1. *Journal of Sociolinguistics, 12*(5), 597–626.

Georgakopoulou, A. (2013a). Building iterativity into positioning analysis: A practice-based approach to small stories and self. Special Issue on Positioning. *Narrative Inquiry, 23*, 89–110.

Georgakopoulou, A. (2013b). Small stories and identities analysis as a framework for the study of im/politeness-in-interaction. *Journal of Politeness Research, 9*(1), 55–74.

Georgakopoulou, A. (2017). Sharing the moment as small stories: The interplay between practices and affordances in the social media-curation of lives. *Narrative Inquiry, 27*, 311–33.

Georgakopoulou, A. (2019). Designing stories on social media: A corpus-assisted critical perspective on the mismatches of story-curation. *Linguistics and Education.*

Georgakopoulou, A. and Vasilaki, M. (2018). The personal and/as the political. *Internet Pragmatics*, 1(2), 215–40.

Grainger, K. (2011). "First order" and "second order" politeness: Institutional and intercultural contexts. In Linguistic Politeness Research Group, ed., *Discursive Approaches to Politeness.* Berlin: Mouton de Gruyter, pp. 167–88.

Goffman, E. ([1955] 1967). *Interaction Ritual: Essays on Face-to-Face Behaviour.* New York: Pantheon Books.

Goffman, E. (1981). *Forms of Talk.* Philadelphia: University of Pennsylvania Press.

González-Cruz, M. (2014). Request patterns by EFL Canarian Spanish students: Contrasting data by languages and research methods. *Intercultural Pragmatics*, 11(4), 547–73.

Grice, H. P. (1967). Logic and conversation. William James Lectures.

Grice, H. P. (1989). *Studies in the Way of Words.* Cambridge, MA: Harvard University Press.

Hall, S. and Du Gay, P. (eds.). (1996). *Questions of Cultural Identity.* London: Sage.

Haugh, M. (2007). The discursive challenge to politeness research: An interactional alternative. *Journal of Politeness Research*, 3(2), 295–317.

Haugh, M. (2013). Disentangling face, facework and im/politeness. *Sociocultural Pragmatics,* 1(1), 46–73.

Haugh, M. (2015). *Im/politeness Implicatures.* Berlin: Mouton de Gruyter.

Haugh, M. and Culpeper, J. (2017). Integrative pragmatics and (im)politeness theory. In C. Ilie and N. Norrick, eds., *Pragmatics and Its Interfaces.* Amsterdam: John Benjamins, pp. 213–39.

Haugh, M., Chang, Wei-Lin M. and Kádár, D. (2015) 'Doing deference': Identities and relational practices in Chinese online discussion boards. *Pragmatics, 25,* 73–98.

Heritage, J. (1984). *Garfinkel and Ethnomethodology.* Cambridge: Polity Press.

Hlavac, J., Xu, Z. and Yong, D. X. (2015). Intercultural pragmatics at work: (Self)perceptions of intercultural behavior of Chinese and English speakers and interpreters in healthcare interactions. *Intercultural Pragmatics, 12*(1), 91–118.

Ige, B. (2010). Identity and language choice: 'We equals I'. *Journal of Pragmatics, 42*(11), 3047–54.

Jaffe, A. (ed.). (2009). *Sociolinguistic Perspectives on Stance.* Oxford: Oxford University Press.

Jones, R. (forthcoming). Discourse analysis and digital surveillance. In A. de Fina and A. Georgakopoulou, eds., *Handbook of Discourse Studies.* Cambridge: Cambridge University Press, pp. 708–31.

Joseph, J. (2004). *Language and Identity: National, Ethnic, Religious.* New York: Palgrave Macmillan.

Joseph, J. (2010). Identity. In C. Llamas and D. Watt, eds., *Language and Identities*. Edinburgh: Edinburgh University Press, pp. 9–17.

Joseph, J. (2013). Identity work and face work across linguistic and cultural boundaries. *Journal of Politeness Research*, 9(1), 35–54.

Kádár, D. Z. and Haugh, M. (2013). *Understanding Politeness*. Cambridge: Cambridge University Press.

Kádár, D., Haugh, M. and Chang, W. M. (2013). Aggression and perceived national face threats in mainland Chinese and Taiwanese CMC discussion boards. *Multilingua*, 32(3), 343–72.

Karachaliou, R. and Argiris, A. (2015). Identity construction patterns via swearing: Evidence from Greek teenage storytelling. *Pragmatics and Society*, 6(3), 421–43.

Kasper, G. (2006). Speech acts in interaction: Towards discursive pragmatics. *Pragmatics and Language Learning*, 11, 281–314.

Kasper, G. and Blum-Kulka, S. (eds.). (1993). *Interlanguage Pragmatics*. Oxford: Oxford University Press.

Kiesling, S. (2013). Constructing identity. In J. Chambers and N. Schilling, eds., *The Handbook of Language Variation and Change*, 2nd ed. Hoboken, NJ: John Willey, pp. 448–67.

Koenig, K. and Zhu, Q. (2017). Communicative constructions of space in epistemic asymmetry: The case of German-Chinese university placement interviews. *Intercultural Pragmatics*, 14(2), 239–76.

Labov, W. (1963). The social motivation of a sound change. *Word*, 19(3), 273–309.

Labov, W. (1972). *Language in the Inner City: Studies in the Black English Vernacular*. Philadelphia: University of Pennsylvania Press.

Lakoff, R. T. (1975). *Language and Woman's Place*. New York: Harper and Row.

Leech, G. N. (1983). *Principles of Pragmatics*. Harlow, UK: Longman.

Levinson, S. (1983). *Pragmatics*. Cambridge: Cambridge University Press.

Locher, M. A. (2008). Relational work, politeness and identity construction. In G. Antos and E. Ventola, eds., *Handbooks of Applied Linguistics. Issue 2: Interpersonal Communication*. Berlin: Mouton de Gruyter, pp. 509–40.

Locher, M. A. (ed.). (2010). Politeness and computer-mediated communication. Special Issue. *Journal of Politeness Research*, 6(1).

Locher, M. A. and Graham, S. L. (eds.). (2010). *Interpersonal Pragmatics*. Berlin: Walter de Gruyter.

Locher, M. A. and Watts, R. J. (2005). Politeness theory and relational work. *Journal of Politeness Research*, 1, 9–33.

Marquez Reiter, R. (2000). *Linguistic Politeness in Britain and Uruguay*. Amsterdam: John Benjamins.

Mendoza-Denton, N. (2008). Language and identity. In J. K. Chambers, P. Trudgill and N. Schilling-Estes, eds., *The Handbook of Language Variation and Change*. Oxford: Blackwell, pp. 475–99.

Mey, J. L. (1993). *Pragmatics: An Introduction*. Oxford: Blackwell.

Miller, E. (2013). Positioning selves, doing relational work and constructing identities in interview talk, *Journal of Politeness Research, 9*(1), 75–95.

Mills, S. (2003). *Gender and Politeness*. Cambridge: Cambridge University Press.

Mouffe, C. (2005). For an agonistic public sphere. In L. Tønder and L.Thomassen, eds., *Radical Democracy: Politics between Abundance and Lack*. Manchester, UK: Manchester University Press, pp. 123–32.

Ochs, E. (1992). Indexing gender. In A. Duranti and C. Goodwinm, eds., *Rethinking Context: Language as an Interactive Phenomenon*. Cambridge: Cambridge University Press, pp. 335–58.

O'Driscoll, J. (2011). Some issues with the concept of face: When, what, how and how much? In F. Bargiela-Chiappini and D. Kádár, eds., *Politeness across Cultures*. London: Palgrave Macmillan, pp. 17–41.

Perelmutter, R. (2018). Globalization, conflict discourse, and Jewish identity in an Israeli Russian-speaking online community. *Journal of Pragmatics, 134*, 134–48.

Placencia, M. E. (2008). Pragmatic variation in corner shop transactions in Ecuadorian Andean and Coastal Spanish. In K. P. Schneider and A. Barron, eds., *Variational Pragmatics: A Focus on Regional Varieties in Pluricentric Languages*. Amsterdam: John Benjamins, pp. 307–32.

Ponton, D. M. The female political leader: A study of gender-identity in the case of Margaret Thatcher. *Journal of Language and Politics, 9*(2), 195–218.

Reckwitz, A. (2002). Toward a theory of social practice. *European Journal of Social Theory, 5*(2), 243–63.

Rees, C. E. and Monrouxe, L. V. (2010). "I should be lucky ha ha ha ha": The construction of power, identity and gender through laughter within medical workplace learning encounters. *Journal of Pragmatics, 42*(12), 3384–99.

Schegloff, E. A. (1997). Whose text? Whose context? *Discourse and Society, 8*(2), 165–87.

Schneider, K. P. and Barron, A. (eds.). (2014). *Pragmatics of Discourse*. Berlin: Walter de Gruyter.

Spencer-Oatey, H. (2007). Theories of identity and the analysis of face. *Journal of Pragmatics, 29*(4), 639–56.

Spencer-Oatey, H. (2009). Face, identity and interactional goals. In F. Bargiela-Chiappini and M. Haugh, eds., *Face, Communication and Social Interaction*. London: Equinox, pp. 137–54.

Taylor, C. (2016). Mock politeness and culture: Perceptions and practice in UK and Italian data. *Intercultural Pragmatics, 13*(4), 463–98.

Terkourafi, M. (2005). Beyond the micro-level in politeness research. *Journal of Politeness Research, 1*(2), 237–62.

Terkourafi, M. (2013). Re-assessing the speech act schema: Twenty-first century reflections *International Review of Pragmatics, 5*, 197–216.

van Dijk, T. (1998). Opinions and ideologies in the press. In A. Bell and P. Garrett, eds., *Approaches to Media Discourse*. Oxford: Blackwell, pp. 21–63.

Verschueren, J. (1999). *Understanding Pragmatics*. London: Arnold.

Vöge, M. (2010). Local identity processes in business meetings displayed through laughter in complaint sequences. *Journal of Pragmatics, 42*(6), 1556–76.

Wetherell, M. (1998). Positioning and interpretative repertoires: Conversation analysis and post-structuralism in dialogue. *Discourse and Society, 9*(3), 387–412.

Wolfers, S., File, K. and Schnurr, S. (2017). "Just because he's black": Identity construction and racial humour in a German U-19 football team. *Journal of Pragmatics, 112*, 83–96.

Wortham, S. (2010). *Learning Identity*. Cambridge: Cambridge University Press.

Zienkowski, J., Östman, J. and Verschueren, J. (eds.). (2011). *Discursive Pragmatics*. Amsterdam: John Benjamins.

Zimmerman, D. H. (1998). Identity, context and interaction. In C. Antaki and S. Widdicombe, eds., *Identities in Talk*. London: Sage, pp. 87–106.

16

(Im)politeness and Sociopragmatics

Jonathan Culpeper and Michael Haugh

16.1 Introduction

Politeness and sociopragmatics were aligned in some of the earliest pragmatics works. Leech (1983), along with Thomas (1981, 1983), played a key role in founding sociopragmatics. In the context of his discussion of sociopragmatics, it is his Politeness Principle that consumes most space. The dominance of politeness and impoliteness in work on sociopragmatics has continued – witness the strong thread on (im)politeness running through this sociopragmatics volume. Our aim in this chapter is to consider the connections, indeed synergies, between sociopragmatics and (im)politeness research. Given that both areas are diffuse, this discussion is inevitably highly selective. However, we endeavour to counter-balance this selectivity by pointing the reader to other relevant chapters in this volume along the way. We begin, in Section 16.2, by going back to the roots of connections between sociopragmatics and (im)politeness. Section 16.3 contains what is necessarily a rather brief overview of (im)politeness theories, whilst in Section 16.4 we discuss some key sociopragmatic concepts that have come to play an important role in (im)politeness research, especially those that are not otherwise discussed in other chapters in this volume. In Section 16.4, we illustrate, through a case study of offence-taking, how sociopragmatics and (im)politeness now have a much broader scope, theoretically and methodologically, than the early traditional analyses of the politeness values of single utterances (often requests). We conclude by critically evaluating current developments, and laying out some possible future directions for the field.

16.2 The Fundamental Connections between (Im)politeness and Sociopragmatics

Leech (1983: 10) states that sociopragmatics is characterized by its 'more specific "local" conditions on language use'. However, Leech did not elaborate on what 'local' means (see Chapter 2). One understanding, a narrow one, is that the local pertains to a specific *occasion* of use. Whatever the case for his definition of sociopragmatics, the connection between the local, sociopragmatics and politeness is clear:

> [more specific 'local' conditions on language use] may be said to belong to the less abstract field of socio-pragmatics, for it is clear that the Cooperative Principle and the Politeness Principle operate variably in different cultures or language communities, in different social situations, among different social classes, etc. (Leech 1983: 10)

If we move to another classic of that period, Brown and Levinson (1987), the connection with sociopragmatics is less explicit but there nevertheless. Brown and Levinson (1987) position their work not within pragmatics but in (interactional) sociolinguistics. Here, compared with Labovian sociolinguistics, there is "greater concern with the linguistic expression of social relationships" (49). They note that "all the social motivations for patterns of language use must be at least mediated through the 'playing out' of social relationships in interaction" (50), and remind readers that this connects with the behaviours that they have "collected under the rubric of politeness" (50). So, whilst the label sociopragmatics is not used, it is quite clear that they are dealing with matters at the heart of sociopragmatics, as social relationships play out in local social situations.

In fact, more recently, a key proponent of interactional sociolinguistics, Janet Holmes, has been clear that her approach to politeness is a sociopragmatic one. For example, commenting on the sociopragmatic analysis of politeness, Holmes and Schnurr (2005: 122) write:

> Attention to context, to the community of practice in which people are participating ..., awareness of the dynamic and negotiated nature of interaction, and of the constantly shifting assessments participants make when engaged in talk – these are all considerations which have improved the quality of the socio-pragmatic analysis of politeness.

However, Holmes and Schnurr (2005: 122) add: "But there is also a place for generalization, and for the identification of patterns in linguistic behaviour". This does not, on the face of it, sound like a sociopragmatic matter. Is it the case that the study of politeness can involve more than sociopragmatics defined narrowly as that which pertains to a specific occasion of use?

In fact, Leech's own statements are not consistent with such a narrow definition, as here:

> one of the main purposes of socio-pragmatics, as I envisage it, is to find out how different societies operate maxims in different ways, for example by giving politeness a higher rating than cooperation in certain situations. (Leech 1983: 80)

Here the sociopragmatic and politeness concern is about generalizations in terms of a society, which is hardly a specific occasion of use. The question this raises is whether one can orientate to politeness within pragmatics without directly doing sociopragmatics, especially if taken in the narrow sense. The part of politeness studies that perhaps less obviously fits sociopragmatics is precisely that flagged by Holmes and Schnurr (2005: 122) – the stuff of generalizations and linguistic patterns does not, on the face of it, fit sociopragmatics concerns, especially if this is understood as dealing with specific local social occasions of use. However, one argument against this narrow view is put by Holmes (1996: 316) herself: "patterns, generalizations, and norms of speech usage which emerge from quantitative analyses provide a crucial framework which informs and illuminates the way in which individual speakers use language" (325). Furthermore, consider Leech's (2014: 14) relatively recent description of sociopragmatics as involving 'the various scales of value that make a particular degree of politeness seem appropriate or normal in a given social setting'. Note that what counts as 'normal' – that is, generalizations – is part of the definition. So, in this view, whilst sociopragmatics might not be about generalizations per se, it often focuses on the way in which speakers orientate to and exploit such generalizations in specific local occasions of use to generate particular meanings, take up particular social positionings, and so on.

A second argument against the narrow view of sociopragmatics relates in particular to linguistic patterns. Linguistic resources generally might be said to belong to a different area of pragmatics, that of pragmalinguistics. Discussing the pragmatics of politeness, Leech (2014: 14) argues the latter involves 'such phenomena as the range of the lexico-grammatical resources of the language, their meanings, the degree of pragmaticalization, their frequency and how they are deployed as linguistic strategies of politeness'. Significantly, he adds in a footnote that 'because pragmalinguistic politeness implies an evaluative judgement about speaker and hearer, it does involve S and H as pragmatic entities, and cannot be divorced from general considerations of context' (Leech 2014: 16). If this is so, then politeness can exist in some way in linguistic patterns. One view is that those linguistic resources are pragmaticalized in local contexts; that is, the repeated meanings that they have in those contexts become associated with the linguistic resource. It is Terkourafi's work (e.g. 2001, 2005a, 2005b) in particular that factors this in for politeness concerns (see also Section 16.3).

How (im)politeness connects with sociopragmatics thus depends on how sociopragmatics and (im)politeness are defined, especially with respect to context. Context has been a key element driving theories of (im)politeness from the very beginning (Brown and Levinson 1987; Lakoff 1973; Leech 1983). It is sometimes claimed that (im)politeness does not inhere in linguistic forms, but in situated judgements of their use in different contexts (e.g. Eelen 2001). If that is the case, then it obviously fits the narrow view of sociopragmatics. However, that narrow view does not accommodate the fact that speakers orient to and exploit generalizations in specific local occasions of use to generate particular meanings. This is important because norms, as we will elaborate in Section 16.4, are an important part of (im)politeness. More controversially for some, there are also (im)politeness scholars who accommodate a contextual aspect within their notion of linguistic form. Leech (2014) clearly does, as noted above, as part of his semantically orientated account, and Terkourafi (e.g. 2001) does within her frame-based approach. Rather than say that (im)politeness does not inhere in linguistic forms, then, it is perhaps more representative of politeness scholarship to say that (im)politeness always involves judgements of use in context. This would accommodate sociopragmatics of all hues.

16.3 A Brief History of (Im)politeness Theories

The evolution of (im)politeness studies has been described in terms of waves. Culpeper (2011) and Grainger (2011), working at the same time though unaware of each other, both drew the lines around approximately the same waves. Here, we will briefly outline the three main three waves that have been discussed to date.[1]

The first wave might be labelled 'establishment'. This took place in the period, starting in the 1970s and including the 1980s, when the classic politeness studies first appeared, including Lakoff (1973), Leech (1983) and Brown and Levinson ([1978] 1987). Early approaches to impoliteness (e.g. Culpeper 1996) also belong to this group. All these approaches oriented to speech act theory and/or conversational implicature. Therein, lay their limitations. They have been subsequently criticized for, amongst other things, being biased towards the speaker; having a limited Gricean focus (only on particularized implicatures); having a 'Western' conceptual bias; being focused only on utterances with little attention paid to broader discourse; having a limited notion of context (which is reduced to variables such as power and social distance); and paying little attention to participants' understandings.

The second wave might be labelled 'rejection'. It began to build up in the 1990s and broke through in the very early 2000s. This wave is constituted by discursive/social constructionist approaches, with notable publications including Eelen (2001), Watts et al. (1992), Watts (2003) and Mills (2003). It is worth noting that the distinction between 'politeness' and 'impoliteness' began to dissolve in the works of this wave. Though the focus remains on politeness, both politeness and impoliteness are explicitly accommodated in relation to the notions and frameworks proposed. However, these studies

---

[1] Given the sheer scope of (im)politeness research, perhaps best represented in the recent publication of a more than 800-page handbook (Culpeper et al. 2017), we suggest the reader consult other recent summaries to gain additional perspectives (e.g. Brown 2017; Terkourafi 2019a).

themselves have also been criticized, for example, for not being fully discursive (a notion like 'politic behaviour' is hardly the construction of the layperson); cutting out the analyst (because the analyst should not impose meaning); taking away the possibility of generalizing; assuming that linguistic structures have no stability of meaning; and so on.

The third wave, which commenced at the beginning of the 2000s, and continues still, is perhaps trickier to label because the scope of the field is significantly broader. From relatively few 'theoretical' frameworks, a plethora of different approaches have emerged. As Terkourafi (2019a: 2) points out,

> the older and newer theories of politeness are theories of *different things*: they draw their conceptual repertoires from different fields, use different data, and have different goals. Ultimately, they are trying to explain different phenomena.

Indeed, the same point can be made with respect to the approaches that have emerged in this period: discursive-materialist (e.g. Mills 2017); frame-based (e.g. Terkourafi 2001, 2005a); genre (e.g. Garcés-Conejos Blitvich 2010); interactional (e.g. Haugh 2013, 2015); maxim-based (e.g. Leech 2014); Neo-Brown and Levinsonian (e.g. Holmes et al. 2012; Grainger 2013); relational (e.g. Spencer-Oatey 2005); and ritual (e.g. Kádár 2017) approaches.[2] What has emerged, then, is a situation on par with the field of communication research, where there are now a vast range of different theories that each attend to different dimensions of interpersonal communication (Haugh et al. 2013). In short, there is no one grand theory of politeness that dominates because the scope of the field is simply too large for any coherent theory to realistically address.

As far as impoliteness is concerned, it is with this third wave that we begin to see the imbalance in the quantity of research efforts between politeness and impoliteness being addressed. (Substantial works include Bousfield 2008; Culpeper 2011; Bousfield and Locher 2008; and the first journal special issue devoted to impoliteness, Bousfield and Culpeper 2008.)[3] Indeed, in the last 15 or so years, there has been a dramatic increase in the blended term '(im)politeness', capturing the fact that many scholars are attending to both politeness and impoliteness issues. Needless to say, there are attendant problems with the third wave too. So many different approaches can give the appearance of it being an overwhelming jungle, especially for those new to the area. There is also no continuity of development within one approach,

---

[2] This is not a full list. It also does not include hybrid approaches. For example, Locher and Watts (2005) fits both the relational approach and the discursive approach, while Culpeper (2011, 2015) fits both the relational approach and interactional approach. Our intent here is to simply illustrate some of the diversity of third-wave approaches to (im)politeness.

[3] In fact, whilst chronologically Bousfield 2008 belong in this wave and certainly raised the profile of impoliteness research, conceptually it is in tune with the first wave of approaches.

and it is more difficult to compare across studies when they draw from different sets of theoretical assumptions.

Where does all this leave us? If we leave aside the negativity involved in such labels as 'fragmentation' or 'jungle', we can see that we have available a diverse range of approaches from which we can choose. What is important, then, is to make a careful choice. Haugh and Watanabe (2017: 73) suggest that:

> any particular theory of (im)politeness both affords and constrains our understanding of the phenomenon in question. In researching (im) politeness ... what drives one's choice of theoretical approach should ultimately be one's specific object of study and one's research questions therein, as well as one's method(s) of choice.

Can we mix and match current approaches? To an extent we can, but some approaches are not compatible with others. It is difficult to imagine a discursive-materialist approach combined with a Neo-Brown and Levinsonian approach, given that one eschews stable linguistic structures but the other one does not.

A useful (if problematic) distinction which can be brought to bear when comparing these different approaches is that between first-order politeness (politeness1) and second-order politeness (politeness2). The distinction was initially proposed by Watts et al. (1992), but has since taken on range of different understandings (e.g. Eelen 2001; Haugh 2012; Spencer-Oatey and Kádár 2016; Terkourafi 2011). Some of the key ways in which the distinction has been framed are listed in Table 16.1.

The first/second-order distinction thus encompasses at least three distinct sets of contrasting perspectives: (1) commonsense, ordinary, non-academic versus academic, technical or scientific ways of talking and thinking about (im)politeness; (2) the understandings of participants themselves versus the understandings of observers of interactions; and (3) emic understandings of (cultural) members versus etic understandings of non-members.[4] Each of these can be further characterized as we can see in Table 16.1.

Drawing such distinctions does not amount to a theory of (im)politeness, however, in spite of the way it has sometimes been (mis)used in back-and-forth critiques (cf. Brown 2017: 391–2). Rather, it constitutes a meta-theoretical tool (Haugh 2018), a means of assessing which approach, or set of approaches, one might usefully draw on to address one's specific set of research questions. The distinctions are also far from absolute. Indeed, many (im)politeness researchers now profess to draw on both perspectives (e.g. Jucker 2020: 18; Locher and Larina 2019: 875), and some even claim it is a defining feature of third wave approaches (Ogiermann and Garcés-Conejos Blitvich 2019: 7). However, it is important to

---

[4] The emic/etic distinction originates in the work of Kenneth Pike (1967).

Table 16.1 *Instantiations of the first-order versus second-order distinction in politeness research*

First order	Second order
Commonsense	Academic
• lay terms	• technical terms
• evaluative	• non-evaluative
• normative	• non-normative
User	Observer
• participant	• analyst
• what people 'do'	• why, when and how they do it
• practice	• theory
• prescriptive	• descriptive
Emic	Etic
• cultural insider	• cultural outsider
• culture internal	• culture comparative
• language specific	• language independent
• culture-specific instantiation	• abstract universal

remember that there are a lot of different research agendas encompassed within that distinction.

Indeed, one might start to wonder whether in fact there are any commonalities across these varied approaches at all. Haugh and Watanabe (2017: 67) remark that in politeness studies:

> the focus has shifted squarely to politeness as involving 'subjective judgements about the social appropriateness of verbal and non-verbal behaviour' (Spencer-Oatey 2005, 97), and (im)politeness itself is broadly conceptualised as a type of interpersonal attitude or attitudinal evaluation.... The general consensus being that a theory of (im)politeness should offer a systematic, internally coherent account of how these subjective judgements, or (inter)subjective attitudinal evaluations arise, and what role such evaluations play in interpersonal relations.

It is probably true that many scholars would accept that (im)politeness is a type of situated interpersonal attitude or attitudinal evaluation (e.g. Locher and Larina 2019: 875). Note, however, that the second half of the above quotation suggests what a theory of (im)politeness 'should' do; whether they actually do it is more doubtful. This is a likely trajectory of development for future research.

16.4 Foundational Sociopragmatic Concepts in (Im)politeness Research

As a result of different waves in theorizing (im)politeness, there are now a large number of different analytical concepts and tools used in the field.

Many of these are not endogenous to sociopragmatics, having been imported from psychology, sociology, anthropology and related fields, reflecting the interdisciplinary nature of pragmatics itself (Haugh and Culpeper 2018: 220). A number of these are already covered in other chapters in this volume, including stance and evaluation (Chapter 6), face (Chapter 13), relationships (Chapter 14), identities (Chapter 15), affect and emotion (Chapter 17), power (Chapter 18) and morality (Chapter 19). We direct readers to consult these chapters for further detail. In this section, then, we focus on those concepts that have played a particularly important role in sociopragmatic work on (im)politeness, and discuss how they have progressively developed over the course of the three successive waves of theorization in (im)politeness research. While any such list is inevitably open to contestation, we suggest that four concepts foundational to any sociopragmatic account of (im)politeness are context, strategies, indirectness and norms.[5]

16.4.1 Context

Early work on (im)politeness in sociopragmatics tended to draw on the micro–macro distinction in theorizing context. The former refers to salient aspects of the local, situated context, while the latter refers to broader global context, including belief systems, ideologies, social structure and institutions (Garcés-Conejos Blitvich and Sifianou 2019: 93). In early work on politeness, Brown and Levinson (1987), for instance, drew attention to power and social distance as key features of the micro-context, while aspects of the macro-context were generally located at the level of national cultures. The conceptualization of both micro and macro contexts have since been the subject of significant critique (e.g. Sifianou and Garcés-Conejos Blitvich 2017). Brown (2017), however, has recently argued Brown and Levinson's (1987) general point still stands:

> [we] insist[ed] on the centrality of social interaction as a significant level of social life, intermediate between the individual and society, where social/cultural facts (status, role, values, norms, rights, and obligations) are integrated with individual ones (goals, plans, strategies, communicative intentions). (390)

In short, (im)politeness is argued to play a key role mediating between the social lives of individuals and the societies in which they live. Such a claim is undoubtedly sound. Yet it is less obvious whether micro aspects of social life can be connected so straightforwardly to the macro without inadvertently reifying the latter; that is, treating social status, roles, values, norms, rights and obligations as if they have an existence

---

[5] See also Culpeper and Terkourafi (2017) for another useful overview of these key notions. As they note, face is clearly a key fifth conceptual pillar in sociopragmatic research on (im)politeness (see Chapter 13).

independent of the social interactions through which they are continually reinforced as well as contested (see Terkourafi 2019b, which addresses some of these issues).

While the (necessarily) abstract nature of the macro-context and the challenges that face the analyst in tracing its role in local, situated assessments of (im)politeness has led some to abandon the micro–macro distinction altogether, other scholars have argued that we need a greater focus on meso (lit. 'middle') aspects of context – which mediate between micro and macro aspects of context – in theorizing (im)politeness. These include: (1) schematic, 'minimal' contexts (Terkourafi 2001, 2005b), which build on the cognitive notion of 'frame' (Minsky 1975; Schank and Abelson 1977); (2) activity types (Culpeper 2011), building on the original notion proposed by Levinson (1979); (3) genres (Garcés-Conejos Blitvich 2010), drawing on the work of Fairclough (2003); and (4) communities of practice (Mills 2003), drawing on the work of Lave and Wenger (1991).

These are not, of course, equivalent or analogous notions, as pointed out in a recent discussion by Blitvich and Sifianou (2019), and they clearly do different work in the analysis of (im)politeness. We would also caution, echoing an insightful critique by Mills (2011), that sometimes such notions can be over-stretched to the point they no longer offer us any real analytical insights. Nevertheless, while caution on the part of the analyst in their application is required, meso-level concepts do have an important role to play in teasing out the role context plays in assessments of (im)politeness. Indeed, we suspect that it is at the meso-level that the most important work in theorizing (im)politeness is most likely to continue.

16.4.2 Strategies

The notion of politeness strategy is central to the framework developed in Brown and Levinson (1987). Over the years, many additional strategies have been proposed. The notion of strategy is also central to early work on impoliteness (e.g. Culpeper 1996). What is understood by a strategy in these works? Brown and Levinson (1987: 85) elaborate on their understanding of this concept:

> We continue to use the word 'strategy', despite its connotations of conscious deliberation, because we can think of no other word that will imply a rational element while covering both (a) innovative plans of action, which may still be (but need not be) unconscious, and (b) routines – that is, previously constructive plans whose original rational origin is still preserved in their construction, despite their present automatic application as ready-made programmes.

The idea of mapping out the logical, rational choices of speakers in order to achieve particular goals is typical of politeness research in that era. Brown and Levinson's (1987) framework is very much underpinned by this assumption. A "Model Person" (Brown and Levinson 1987) – that is, a rational actor – will select an appropriate superstrategy (Bald-on-record, Positive politeness, Negative politeness, Off-record, or Don't do the FTA) to counterbalance the expected face threat. Within the superstrategies Positive politeness, Negative politeness and Off-record, there are sets of "output strategies" to denote "the final choice of linguistic means to realise the highest goals" (1987: 92). For example, "claiming common ground" is a lower order strategy embedded within the superstrategy of Positive politeness.

Pragmatics has moved on. One obvious criticism of Brown and Levinson's (1987) approach to strategies is its steadfast focus on what the speaker does, as opposed to the hearer, or indeed the interaction between the two. There is also, whilst acknowledging that there is always directedness (or 'intentionality') underpinning communication, increasing realization in pragmatics that speakers do not make plans and then speak, but that plans emerge through the course of interaction (see Chapter 4). Consequently, there has been something of a shift in the way pragmaticists and discourse analysts conceive the notion of strategy. This shift reflects a general movement towards the notion of 'routines', which are in fact briefly alluded to in the quote from Brown and Levinson (1987) above. Indeed, other linguists at that time were thinking of strategies in terms of shared routines. Gumperz's (1982: 3) notion of 'discourse strategy' is a case in point:

> A general theory of discourse strategies must therefore gain by specifying the linguistic and socio-cultural knowledge that needs to be shared if conversational involvement is to be maintained, and then go on to deal with what it is about the nature of conversational inference that makes for cultural, subcultural and situational specificity of interpretation.

Note the emphasis here is on the "shared" "linguistic and socio-cultural knowledge" that enables understandings of strategies in conversation to proceed. In fact, the label 'strategy' is not always used, but other terms instead, such as 'conversational routine', 'linguistic / discoursal expression', 'situational formula', 'conventionalized expression', and so on. Of particular note here is Coulmas (1981) on conversational routines, and later Aijmer's (1996) work on conversational routines in English. Both focus on linguistic expressions that occur regularly within specific pragmatic contexts (see also Chapter 9). Such shifts have also impacted upon (im)politeness studies. Terkourafi's (e.g. 2001, 2005a) frame-based approach to politeness rejects the notion of strategy, and focuses on linguistic items conventionalized for a particular context of use. As for impoliteness, similarly, and partly influenced by Terkourafi's work, Culpeper (2011) abandoned his earlier use of the notion of strategy, and instead adopted the notion of formulae.

16.4.3 Indirectness

The assumption that politeness is a key driver of indirectness in communication (Searle 1975) came to dominate first-wave accounts of (im)politeness, as we noted in the previous section. Indirectness can refer either to: (1) some kind of *gap* between meaning that is derived largely from what is said and that which is derived primarily through inference, or (2) *mitigation* of the speaker's commitment to propositional content (Haugh 2015: 21). The latter sense of indirectness was subsequently swept up under the notion of politeness strategy, while the former has remained at the core of debates about pragmatic meaning up to the present day. Indeed, inference lies at the centre of any cognitively and interactionally plausible theory of meaning (Sperber and Wilson [1986] 1995). Thus, although the assumption that more 'indirect' communication is more 'polite', which lies at the centre of Brown and Levinson's (1987) account of politeness, has been well and truly put to bed, the role played by inference in (im)politeness most certainly has not. In standard pragmatic accounts, meanings that are derived largely through inference are termed implicatures (Grice 1975). While the mechanisms that govern such inferences vary across different theoretical accounts, the focus is by and large squarely on those that are speaker-intended.[6]

A much more nuanced account of implicature with respect to (im)politeness, however, has been developed by Terkourafi (2001, 2005b). She proposes that politeness mostly arises through conventionalized inferences in schematic, minimal contexts (giving rise to a special type of minimally context dependent generalized conversational implicature), which may be confirmed in subsequent discourse or else challenged by particularities of the context leading to effortful inference (giving rise to particularized conversational implicatures). Haugh (2017: 285) goes further with respect to the theorization of the latter in arguing that

> there is evidently a much richer inferential substrate underpinning conversational interaction than many standard accounts of implicature would generally admit. The challenge for us as ordinary participants in conversational interaction is thus to figure out what can be legitimately inferred. This process is not just a matter of 'reading off' the intentions of others, but is arguably invested with some degree of agency on the part of participants.

The existence of this rich inferential substrate, and the role of different linguistic and cultural constraints on it, has important consequences for the study of (im)politeness. Tayebi (2018: 93), for instance, offers an intriguing discussion of *tikkeh*, which refers to the "indirect communication of snide, spiteful, derogatory and disparaging remarks" in Iranian cultural contexts. Similar studies, however, are few and far between, perhaps because of the challenges inherent to "researching the unsaid", given "one needs to

---

[6] See Chapters 3 and 4 for further discussion.

show that both participants are oriented to something not occurring and deliberately kept off-stage as it were" (Levinson 2013: 115–16).

One framework for doing so is proposed by Culpeper (2011), who distinguishes between three different mechanisms by which impoliteness can be implied: form-driven, convention-driven and context-driven. An alternative framework that (re)conceptualizes implicatures as a form of social action (Haugh 2015), focuses on the systematic practices by which participants expose such inferences. For instance, through attenuating and withholding (actions by self), pre-empting (the actions of others), or prompting (action from others). However, further studies across a more diverse range of languages are needed to test the robustness of such frameworks. While the notion of indirectness has been with us from the beginning of academic studies of (im)politeness, the role of inference vis-à-vis (im)politeness across different languages and cultures has arguably yet to be fully explored.

16.4.4 Norms

It has long been recognized that norms are central to (im)politeness. To evaluate someone or their conduct as (im)polite is to make what amounts to a normative claim about conduct and how others will evaluate that conduct. The notion of norm is, of course, central to a range of different disciplines, including psychology, philosophy and linguistics, with a distinction having long been drawn between what people think should be done and what is typically done (Deutsch and Gerard 1955). The former is variously referred to as a moral, injunctive or prescriptive norm, while the latter is variously referred to as an empirical, statistical or descriptive norm (Cialdini et al. 1990; Eelen 2001). Norms are thus typically discussed with respect to ways of thinking or ways of behaving that are (presumed) to be shared across groups of people.

In sociopragmatics, the central focus is on appropriateness, that is, what conduct is considered to be suitable or fitted to a context, as well as what is considered to be proper or right conduct in that context. This is because language use is inherently reflexive: we use language bearing in mind how we think others will understand and evaluate how we are using language (see also Chapter 7). Sociopragmatic norms of language use are grounded in the presumption that what is usually or typically done is what should be regarded as good or proper. As Terkourafi (2019a: 10–11) has recently put it:

> What is frequent to our experience is automatically positively evaluated simply because that's the way we've always done it and seen it done and it didn't occur to us to do it in any other way.

A sociopragmatic norm thus formally links ways of behaving (i.e. empirical norms) with ways of thinking about conduct (i.e. moral norms). The notion of the moral order encapsulates that relationship in suggesting that what is regarded as good or proper is immanent to what is typically done (Haugh 2013; Kádár and Haugh 2013).[7] The complication, of course, is that we do not all do things in the same ways and have different experiences of what is usually or typically done, even when speaking the same (variety of) language (let alone across different linguistic or cultural settings). To study norms in sociopragmatics thus inevitably entails the analysis of variability across different people and settings, and across different languages and periods of time, and providing empirical and theoretical accounts of that variability.[8]

The variability one inevitably encounters when studying sociopragmatic norms raises questions about the scope of those norms; that is, to whom are they salient and in what circumstances? Culpeper (2008: 30), for instance, draws distinctions between, personal, cultural, situational and co-textual norms, while Holmes et al. (2011: 11) distinguish between interactional, community of practice/team, organizational, societal (or mainstream), and minority norms. These different types of sociopragmatic norms can, of course, come in conflict with each other in particular situated contexts. It has also been observed that not all sociopragmatic norms are born equal. First-order (im)politeness is typically associated with the middle classes (Allan 2016; Mills 2017). However, whether conduct that is sociopragmatically normative is regarded as (im)polite depends very much on who is evaluating that conduct. The challenge for (im)politeness researchers, therefore, is to disentangle the relationship between sociopragmatic norms and (im)politeness.

One way of doing so is through a greater focus on sociopragmatic variation vis-à-vis (im)politeness across different social groups over time. Cross-linguistic, cross-cultural, historical and variational agendas clearly have a key role to play in sociopragmatic research on (im)politeness. However, in so doing, it is important to always bear in mind that an evaluation of (im)politeness is never inevitable, but always mediated with respect to the socially-mediated agency of the parties concerned (Mitchell and Haugh 2015). In short, we cannot assume a particular configuration of social variables in a particular context will necessarily result in a particular evaluation being made by (one or more of) the parties involved. Yet while we are somewhat far from being able to propose a predictive theory of (im)politeness in light of the amount of data and analyses of data across different contexts that would need to be amassed to evidence any such theoretical claims, the search for generalizations vis-à-vis (im)politeness should continue apace. The question this raises, then, and as aired in Section 16.2, is what role should sociopragmatics, especially if conceived of in the narrow sense, with its emphasis on relatively local social contexts, play in such efforts?

In the following section, we propose that an approach that draws from both user and observer perspectives, what we term integrative pragmatics

---

[7] An alternative view of (im)politeness norms is that they can be traced back to underlying moral foundations or meta-discourse on morality (see Chapters 10 and 19 for further discussion).

[8] See Chapters 10, 31 and 32 for further discussion.

(Culpeper and Haugh 2014; Haugh and Culpeper 2018), can go some way towards reconciling these seemingly contrary agendas.

16.5 Case Study: User and Observer Perspectives in (Im)politeness Research

One of the key challenges in sociopragmatics is to demonstrate how (im)politeness norms play out in locally situated contexts, and to consider how those local dynamics can inform broader generalizations made about (im)politeness, and vice versa. In this section, we attempt to illustrate the importance of drawing from both user and observer perspectives in such research. Our case study focuses on an apparent attempt by one participant to avoid a potential impropriety through a joking deflection of appreciation from the other participant, who subsequently claims she took offence at that deflection. In other words, the attempt to avoid an impropriety by one participant is treated as an impropriety by the other. We draw from user and observer perspectives in two senses in our analysis. First, we undertake a CA-informed sequential analysis of what is inferable from *in situ* behaviour of the participants in that interaction (user perspective), and compare it with the *post facto* comments made by one of the participants in a subsequent interview (observer perspective). Second, we undertake a componential analysis of how the person takes offence in that locally situated interview (user perspective), and then consider what a corpus-based metapragmatic analysis of what is considered *offensive* by (American and Australian) speakers of English can potentially add (observer perspective).

We begin by briefly analysing the joking deflection of appreciation which occurred in an initial interaction between Tammy (an American) and Nathan (an Australian). Just prior to this, Tammy has asked what else Nathan does with his time.[9]

(1)   CAAT: AmAus13: 3:53

```
1      N:  um: ↑at the moment I've got s-:: oh I'm making
2          an iphone app.
3          (0.4)
4      T:  REally? >heh heh heh<[°ha ha°]
5                               |((smiling))  |
6  -> N:                        [well ] when I say that
7          I mean (.) I've hired £Indians to make it for me£=
8      T:  =.hh ha ha ha °£nice£ ha ha°
9          |((smiles and throws head back))|
```

---

[9] CA transcription conventions (Jefferson 2004) are used here to enable us to draw attention to particular aspects of the timing and delivery of the talk. Pseudonyms are used for all the participants, except for the interviewer, Lara Weinglass, who transcribed this data (ARC DP120100516).

As this excerpt has been analysed in some detail already (Haugh 2017: 113), here we just briefly summarize a few key observations. First, Tammy responds to Nathan informing her that he is making an iphone app by signalling surprise, thereby implying that she is impressed (lines 4–5). Second, Nathan responds, in turn, by deflecting this appreciation through downgrading his own involvement in actually making it (lines 6–7). Third, Tammy responds to this with laughter and a positive assessment (lines 8–9). From a user perspective, then, it appears they have jointly accomplished an appreciation and deflection, as Nathan navigates between the preference for agreement and preference for avoidance of self-praise in compliment sequences more broadly (Pomerantz 1978).

When we shift to an observer perspective, however, a somewhat different picture emerges. When asked by the interviewer, Lara, what she thought of Nathan in a post-recording interview, Tammy began by saying he was "nice", but when pressed on what was "nice" about him, she responded, "he wasn't like. (.) outright (.) ru:de or anything so:". To assess Nathan as "not outright rude" makes available the inference (via scalar implicature) that he may have been 'somewhat rude', a point the interviewer subsequently pursues in restating Tammy's prior assessment that Nathan "wasn't rude", as we can see in excerpt (2).

(2)   CAAT: AmAus13_Followup(Am): 19:26

```
1      L:   so nothing out of the ordinary happened you said
2           he wasn' t ru:de and
3           (0.5)
4      T:   ↑yeah [↓no]
5      L:         [bit] awkward at fi:rst (.) but
6           (0.3)
7      T:   um
8           (.)
9      L:   okay otherwise?
10     T:   yeah >okay there' s I mean< one thing .hh (.) was
11          like um (1.0) .hh h- he had said about the
12          iphone app and stuff?
13     L:   ↑o(hh)h[right]
14     T:          [how ] he' s doing that?
15          (.)
16     L:   yep
17          (.)
18     T:   and then one thing that >it< kind of (0.4) caught
19          me: (.) a bit was he sai:d um: (0.2) oh well
20          I paid some (0.6) £Indians to do it?£
21     L:   yeah.
22     T:   .hh and like (1.1) I dunno I' m (.) fr- from
```

```
23            the States like we're very (0.7) multicultural
24            [and]
25     L:     [>yeah] yeah yeah.<
26            (0.3)
27 -> T:      u:m. (.) >like I know he was just joking< but
28 ->         >that was something I was< like °↑oh (.) okay (.) so°
29     L:     >ha ha ha ha ha<
30 -> T:      maybe a bit offensive but
31            (.)
32     L:     oh: right. (.) ha ha[ha]
33     T:                         [ye] ah=
34     L:     =yeah
```

It appears that Tammy has inferred from Nathan's joking reference to Indians making the app that he "looks down" on Indians, and moreover, that Nathan has invited her to share in this attitude. This invitation from Nathan to share in this attitude is registered as "offensive" (to her) through invoking lay discourses on sensitivity about mentions of race amongst Americans (lines 22–3), and sanctioned as "offensive" (to others) (line 30), despite her explicitly acknowledging that this was delivered jokingly by Nathan (lines 27). There are two key points to note here. First, there is a discrepancy between Tammy's in situ response to Nathan's joking reference to Indians, which is a positive assessment ("nice", line 8 in excerpt 1), and her post-facto evaluation of it as "offensive". Second, her post-facto evaluation is delivered through a very delicately formulated negative assessment that is delayed within this overall sequence.

To more clearly illustrate the delicacy with which Tammy treats this taking of offence, we briefly summarize a componential analysis of the embodied formulation of talk across lines 27–30 in Figure 16.1.

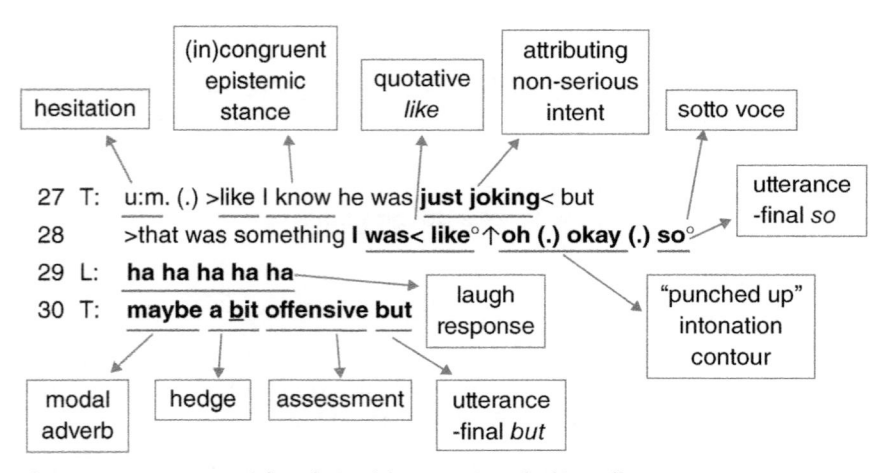

Figure 16.1 Componential analysis of the reporting of taking offence.

In line 27, the turn begins with a hesitation marker and the assessment itself is delayed until line 30, marking the assessment as dispreferred (Pomerantz 1984). The quotative 'like', which is associated with reported thought in delivering complaints and criticisms (Haakand 2007), occurs twice in lines 27 and 28: the first in reporting that she attributed non-serious intent to Nathan's mention of Indians helping him make the app; the second in reporting surprise through a 'punched up' intonation contour, and raising of her shoulders, which enacts surprise at what Nathan reportedly said (Wilkinson and Kitzinger 2006), followed by an utterance-final 'so' that attenuates the upshot of that enactment of surprise (Haugh 2015: 247–50). Notably, this second reported thought is delivered sotto voce, which frames this enactment of surprise as a somewhat delicate matter. Lara's laughing response in line 29 appears to be a move to defuse anticipated criticism (Holt 2012), which Tammy goes on to deliver in line 30. However, the negative assessment through which the criticism is delivered is mitigated by a modal adverb ('maybe') and hedge ('a bit'), alongside a back-and-forth hand gesture indicating an assessment that lies somewhere between two extremes (e.g. *not offensive* and *very offensive*). This is followed by an utterance-final 'but' that leaves the implication of this mitigated criticism hanging for Lara to reach her own conclusion (Mulder and Thompson 2008).[10]

Our point in bringing attention to this very fine level of detail is that each component of Tammy's turn (across lines 27–8 and 30) indexes an orientation to the potential delicacy of this negative assessment. The high degree of granularity in the design of this action (Schegloff 2000) thus constitutes data internal evidence that taking offence is being treated here as a dispreferred, sensitive social action. We note that this delicacy in the delivery of this criticism might stem, in part, from the fact that Tammy's conversation with Lara is for all intents and purposes also a first conversation (just as it was with Nathan). For that reason, Tammy is likely unsure just how Lara (who is also Australian) might respond to this criticism, especially since it is grounded with respect to how Americans more generally would react to Nathan's comment (lines 22–3). In short, Tammy taking offence here might prompt Lara to take offence in turn.

The broader question perhaps, however, is why this joking reference is treated as offensive by Tammy, but not so by Nathan (who did not indicate any awareness of the offence he had caused in the post-recording interview). A corpus-based analysis of the term *offensive* indicates that there may be more to this than one seemingly insensitive – from Tammy's perspective – individual. A comparative analysis of collocates of *offensive* in (North) American English and Australian English taken from the Oxford Corpus of English

---

[10] We have deliberately drawn from both CA and corpus-based studies in warranting our claims about the indexical value of each of these components of the talk by which Tammy implements this criticism of Nathan in order to demonstrate the value of both kinds of studies in evidencing analytical claims.

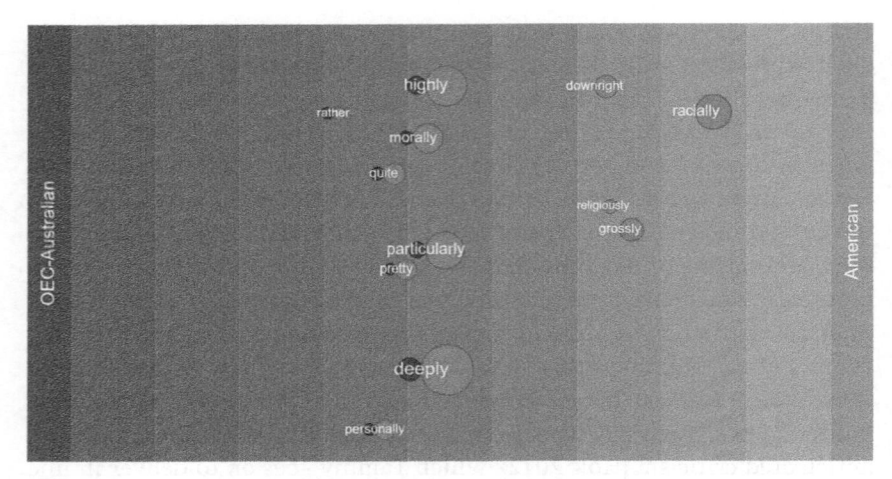

Figure 16.2 Adverbs by which *offensive* is pre-modified: American and Australian English compared.

(OEC) reveals a striking difference between these two varieties. Examining a word's collocates is one way of teasing out its meanings (Firth 1957: 11). Here we have used the program Sketch Engine to examine the target word, *offensive*, for 27 grammatical relations, and used the statistic logDice to assess the strength of the collocates within that relation.[11] Figure 16.2 captures the grammatical relations in which the distribution of collocates exhibit clear differences between American and Australian English.

The key aspect to focus on in Figure 16.2 is the positioning of the circles horizontally. This indicates whether the collocate forms a stronger collocate in the American or Australian components or whether it is somewhere in between. (Nothing can be concluded from the differing sizes of the collocate circles and text, which represents their frequencies, because this largely reflects the fact that the American sub-corpus is bigger than the Australian). A striking feature of Figure 16.2 is the collocate *racially* clearly has a stronger association with *offensive* in the American data. Examples from the American data include 'In the actual world of today's America, the dialogue is also racially offensive', and 'Moreover, the Democrats attack Brown for dissenting from a ruling that an injunction against the use of racially offensive epithets in the workplace did not violate the First Amendment'. It seems to be the case that race-related offensiveness is highly salient in the American data, but absent, at this level of granularity, in the Australian data.

Of course one cannot conclude from a study of aggregated data, as represented in the OEC, what a particular individual in a situated

---

[11] A full elaboration of the approach and method behind this analysis can be found in Culpeper and Haugh (forthcoming).

interaction might be thinking. To do so would amount to the ecological fallacy (Robinson 1950), that is, "thinking that relationships observed for groups necessarily hold for individuals" (Freedman 2001: 4028). We are also at pains to point out that we are not proposing that one group is any more or less racist than the other, or that all Australians are insensitive about mentions or race or ethnicity, while all Americans are highly sensitive. We are here dealing with what are tendencies with respect to whether mentions of race or ethnicity count as offensive. What is notable is that these differences appear to be built into the very semantics of the term across different varieties of English (Culpeper and Haugh, forthcoming).

More generally, we have aimed to show here how an indexical-sequential analysis of the taking (or not) of offence in a locally situated context can be enriched through a corpus-based quantitative analysis of an aggregated dataset of language use. Our view is that this iterative back-and-forth between user and observer perspectives (and thus between different methodological paradigms), and the emphasis placed on the meso level when attempting to make generalizations (in this case first encounters), is a hallmark of a sociopragmatics approach to (im)politeness.

16.6 Future Directions

What then does sociopragmatics bring to (im)politeness research? We have suggested that what lies at the core of the contribution of sociopragmatics to (im)politeness is the emphasis on context and its call to systematically examine the affordances and constraints that different contexts bring to bear on interaction. This entails close attention to the granular design of talk and aspects of its embodied or multimodal delivery, as well as systematic attention to the organization of context (with respect to activity types, frames, genres, practices etc.). What sociopragmatics brings to (im)politeness research is thus not only greater attention on the ways in which social relationships play out in local social situations, but a shift in focus to the meso level of analysis and theorization.

As we noted at the outset, we are not able to do justice, within the confines of this chapter, to the rich and varied set of approaches to (im)politeness that have been developed, or the nuances of the theoretical debates that the field has witnessed over the past 20 years. In lieu of such a summary, we would like to conclude this chapter by offering some thoughts on some potentially productive future directions for the field, focusing, in particular, on the issues of interdisciplinarity, data types and methods and meta-theorization.

Calls for greater interdisciplinarity in (im)politeness research are increasingly being made by a range of different scholars (e.g. Brown 2017; Kádár and Haugh 2013; Locher 2015; Terkourafi 2019a). Brown (2017: 398) goes further in arguing the lack of awareness of relevant research across disciplines is hampering development of the field:

> The hugely broad sweep of work on politeness and impoliteness, coming from different academic disciplines, with different methods, different theoretical presuppositions and priorities, and vastly different research goals, has meant that often the work of one group is quite inaccessible to another. (Brown 2017: 398)

Indeed, we would all benefit from paying greater attention to work on (im)politeness that builds on different methodological paradigms or theoretical models. However, we caution that the aim of interdisciplinary work is not to arrive at some grand overall theory of (im)politeness, but to enable cross-fertilization in ways that are meaningful to practitioners of those different disciplines.

A second call that is increasingly made is for us to broaden the range of data types we consider in (im)politeness research (Locher and Larina 2019). To some extent such a move is well under way, as (im)politeness research has moved beyond its traditional focus on face-to-face interaction to encompass a greater focus on historical data, online data, public and broadcast data and increasingly fictional data. Such a move goes hand in hand with the need for methodological innovation and greater sensitivity to ethical considerations (Locher and Bolander 2019). However, we would caution that in moving to enlarge the scope of types of data, we would do well to retain a focus on ordinary, everyday uses of language (Ogiermann and Garcés-Conejos Blitvich 2019), and to avoid theorization that is overly reliant on examples that "stand out". We would also add that there is also much to be gained from broadening the range of languages we study, as this will allow us to focus on identifying universal aspects of (im)politeness, thereby complementing the current emphasis on its culture-specific aspects (Brown 2017).

A final call that has been recently made is for a move to more systematic meta-theorization in the field. While having a diverse range of frameworks and approaches on offer certainly leaves researchers seemingly spoilt for choice, such a situation can also inadvertently lead to "sterile eclecticism" (Haugh 2018). Indeed, in navigating the complex theoretical landscape of (im)politeness research it is clear there are a number of potential pitfalls. These include rejecting theories because they are "old", following fashions and engaging in "bandwagonism", misinterpreting (and even misrepresenting) theories, or being isolationist and making theoretical claims with little heed to what else has been said in the field. There is much to be celebrated in the broadening of research on (im)politeness beyond its classic pragmatic origins. However, in so doing it is important that we do not lose touch with many of the most important insights of this initial work which have, in our view, stood the test of time.

References

Aijmer, K. (1996). *Conversational Routines in English*. London: Longman.

Allen, K. (2016). A benchmark of politeness. In A. Capone and J. Mey, eds., *Interdisciplinary Studies in Pragmatics, Culture and Society*. Heidelberg: Springer, pp. 397–420.

Bousfield, D. (2008). *Impoliteness in Interaction*. Amsterdam: John Benjamins.

Bousfield, D. and Culpeper, J. (eds.). (2008). Impoliteness: Eclecticism and Diaspora. Special Issue. *Journal of Politeness Research*, 4(2).

Bousfield, D. and Locher, M. (eds.). (2008). *Impoliteness in Language*. Berlin: Mouton de Gruyter.

Brown, P. (2017). Politeness and impoliteness. In Y. Huang, ed., *Oxford Handbook of Pragmatics*. Oxford: Oxford University Press, pp. 383–99.

Brown, P. and Levinson, S. C. (1987). *Politeness: Some Universals in Language Usage*. Cambridge: Cambridge University Press.

Cialdini, R., Reno, R. and Kallgren, C. (1990). A focus theory of normative conduct: recycling the concept of norms to reduce littering in public places. *Journal of Personality and Social Psychology*, 58(6), 1015–26.

Coulmas, F. (1981). *Conversational Routine*. The Hague: Mouton.

Culpeper, J. (1996). Towards an anatomy of impoliteness. *Journal of Pragmatics*, 25, 349–67.

Culpeper, J. (2008). Reflections on impoliteness, relational work and power. In D. Bousfield and M. Locher, eds., *Impoliteness in Language*. Berlin: Mouton de Gruyter, pp. 17–44.

Culpeper, J. (2011). *Impoliteness: Using Language to Cause Offence*. Cambridge: Cambridge University Press.

Culpeper, J. and Haugh, M. (2014). *Pragmatics and the English Language*. Basingstoke, UK: Palgrave Macmillan.

Culpeper, J. and Haugh, M. (forthcoming). The metalinguistics of offence in (British) English: A corpus-based metapragmatic approach. *Journal of Language, Aggression and Conflict*.

Culpeper, J. and Terkourafi, M. (2017). Pragmatics and (im)politeness. In J. Culpeper, M. Haugh and D. Z. Kádár, eds., *Palgrave Handbook of (Im)politeness*. Basingstoke, UK: Palgrave, pp. 11–39.

Culpeper, J., Haugh, M. and Kádár, D. (eds.). (2017). *Palgrave Handbook of (Im)politeness*. Basingstoke, UK: Palgrave.

Deutsch, M. and Gerard, H. (1955). A study of normative and informational social influences upon individual judgment. *The Journal of Abnormal and Social Psychology*, 51(3), 629–36.

Eelen, G. (2001). *A Critique of Politeness Theories*. Manchester, UK: St. Jerome.

Fairclough, N. (2003). *Analysing Discourse*. London: Routledge.

Firth, J. (1957). A synopsis of linguistic theory 1930–1955. In J. R. Firth, ed., *Studies in Linguistic Analysis*. Oxford: Philological Society, pp. 1–32.

Freedman, D. (2001). Ecological inference and the ecological fallacy. In N. J. Smelser and P. B. Baltes, eds., *International Encyclopedia of the Social and Behavioral Sciences*, vol. 6. New York: Elsevier, pp. 4027–30.

Garcés-Conejos Blitvich, P. and Sifianou, M. (2019). Im/politeness and discursive pragmatics. *Journal of Pragmatics*, 145, 91–101.

Garcés-Conejos Blitvich, P. (2010). A genre approach to the study of im-politeness. *International Review of Pragmatics*, 2(1), 46–94.

Grainger, K. (2011). 'First order' and 'second order' politeness: Institutional and intercultural contexts. In Linguistic Politeness Research Group, eds., *Discursive Approaches to Politeness*. Berlin: Mouton de Gruyter, pp. 167–88.

Grainger, K. (2013). Of babies and bath water: Is there any place for Austin and Grice in interpersonal pragmatics? *Journal of Pragmatics*, 58, 27–38.

Grice, P. (1975). Logic and conversation. In P. Cole and J. Morgan, eds., *Syntax and Semantics 3: Speech Acts*. New York: Academic Press, pp. 41–58.

Gumperz, J. (1982). *Discourse Strategies*. Cambridge: Cambridge University Press.

Haakana, M. (2007). Reported thought in complaint stories. In E. Holt and R. Clift, eds., *Reporting Talk: Reported Speech in Interaction*. Cambridge: Cambridge University Press, pp. 150–78.

Haugh, M. (2012). Epilogue: The first-second order distinction in face and politeness research. *Journal of Politeness Research*, 8(1), 111–34.

Haugh, M. (2013). Im/politeness, social practice and the participation order. *Journal of Pragmatics*, 58, 52–72.

Haugh, M. (2015). *Im/politeness Implicatures*. Berlin: Mouton de Gruyter.

Haugh, M. (2017). Implicature and the inferential substrate. In P. Cap and M. Dynel, eds., *Implicitness: From Lexis to Discourse*. Amsterdam: John Benjamins, pp. 281–304.

Haugh, M. (2018). Afterword: Theorising (im)politeness. *Journal of Politeness Research*, 14(1), 153-65.

Haugh, M. and Culpeper, J. (2018). Integrative pragmatics and (im)politeness theory. In C. Ilie and N. R. Norrick, eds., *Pragmatics and Its Interfaces*. Amsterdam: John Benjamins, pp. 213–39.

Haugh, M. and Watanabe, Y. (2017). (Im)politeness theory. In B. Vine, ed., *Handbook of Language in the Workplace*. London: Routledge, pp. 65–76.

Holmes, J. (1996). Women's role in language change: A place for quantification. In N. Warner, J. Ahlers, L. Bilmes, M. Oliver, S. Wertheim and M. Chen, eds., *Gender and Belief Systems*. Berkeley: University of California, Berkeley Women and Language Group, pp. 313–30.

Holmes, J. and Schnurr, S. (2005). Politeness, humor and gender in the workplace: Negotiating norms and identifying contestation. *Journal of Politeness Research*, 1(1), 121–49.

Holmes, J., Marra, M. and Vine, B. (2011). *Leadership, Discourse and Ethnicity*. Oxford: Oxford University Press.

Holt, E. (2012). Using laugh responses to defuse complaints. *Research on Language and Social Interaction*, 45(4), 430–48.

Jefferson, G. (2004). Glossary of transcript symbols with an introduction. In G. Lerner, ed., *Conversation Analysis: Studies from the First Generation.* Amsterdam: John Benjamins, pp. 13–23.

Jucker, A. (2020). *Politeness in the History of English: From the Middle Ages to the Present Day.* Cambridge: Cambridge University Press.

Kádár, D. and Haugh, M. (2013). *Understanding Politeness.* Cambridge: Cambridge University Press.

Kádár, D. (2017). *Politeness, Impoliteness and Ritual.* Cambridge: Cambridge University Press.

Lakoff, R. (1973). The logic of politeness; or, minding your p's and q's'. *Papers from the Ninth Regional Meeting of the Chicago Linguistic Society,* pp. 292–305.

Lave, J. and Wenger, E. (1991). *Situated Learning.* Cambridge: Cambridge University Press.

Leech, G. (1983). *Principles of Pragmatics.* London: Longman.

Leech, G. (2014). *The Pragmatics of Politeness.* New York: Oxford University Press.

Levinson, S. (1979). Activity types and language. *Linguistics,* 17(5–6), 365–99.

Levinson, S. (2013). Action formation and ascription. In J. Sidnell and T. Stivers, eds., *Handbook of Conversation Analysis.* Malden, MA: Wiley-Blackwell, pp. 103–30.

Locher, M. (2015). Interpersonal pragmatics and its link to (im)politeness research. *Journal of Pragmatics,* 86, 5–10.

Locher, M. and Bolander, B. (2019). Ethics in pragmatics. *Journal of Pragmatics,* 145, 83–90.

Locher, M. and Larina, T. (2019). Introduction to politeness and impoliteness research in global contexts. *Russian Journal of Linguistics,* 23(4), 873–903.

Locher, M. and Watts, R. (2005). Politeness theory and relational work. *Journal of Politeness Research,* 1(1), 9–33.

Mills, S. (2003). *Gender and Politeness.* Cambridge: Cambridge University Press.

Mills, S. (2011). Communities of practice and politeness. In B. Davis, M. Haugh and A. Merrison, eds., *Situated Politeness.* London: Continuum, pp. 73–87.

Mills, S. (2017). *English Politeness and Class.* Cambridge: Cambridge University Press.

Minsky, M. (1975). A framework for representing knowledge. In P. H. Winston, ed., *The Psychology of Computer Vision.* New York: McGraw-Hill, pp. 211–77.

Mitchell, N. and Haugh, M. (2015). Agency, accountability and evaluations of impoliteness." *Journal of Politeness Research,* 11(2), 207–38.

Mulder, J. and Thompson, S. (2008). The grammaticalization of *but* as a final particle in English conversation. In R. Laury, ed., *Crosslinguistic Studies of Clause Combining: The Multifunctionality of Conjunctions.* Amsterdam: John Benjamins, pp. 179–204.

Ogiermann, E. and Garcés-Conejos Blitvich, P. (2019). Im/politeness between the analyst and participant perspective: An overview of the field. In E. Ogiermann and P. Garcés-Conejos Blitvich, eds., *From Speech Acts to Lay Understandings of Politeness: Multilingual and Multicultural Perspectives*. Cambridge: Cambridge University Press, pp. 1–24.

Pike, K. (1967). Etic and emic standpoints for the description of behavior. In D. C. Hildum, ed., *Language and Thought: An Enduring Problem in Psychology*. Princeton, NJ: Van Norstrand, pp. 32–39.

Pomerantz, A. (1978). Compliment responses: Notes on the cooperation of multiple constraints. In J. Schenkein, ed., *Studies in the Organization of Conversational Interaction*. New York: Academic Press, pp. 79–112.

Pomerantz, A. (1984). Agreeing and disagreeing with assessments: Some features of preferred/dispreferred turn shapes. In J. Atkinson and J. Heritage, eds., *Structures of Social Action*. Cambridge: Cambridge University Press, pp. 57–101.

Robinson, W. (1950). Ecological correlations and the behaviour of individuals. *American Sociological Review*, 15(3), 351–7.

Schank, R. and Abelson, R. (1977). *Scripts, Plans, Goals, and Understanding: An Inquiry into Human Knowledge Structures*. Mahwah, NJ: Erlbaum.

Schegloff, E. (2000). On granularity. *Annual Review of Sociology*, 26, 715–20.

Searle, J. (1975). Indirect speech acts. In P. Cole and J. Morgan, eds., *Syntax and Semantics 3: Speech Acts*. New York: Academic Press, pp. 59–82.

Sifianou, M. and Garcés-Conejos Blitvich, P. (2017). (Im)politeness and cultural variation. In J. Culpeper, M. Haugh and D. Kádár, eds., *Palgrave Handbook of (Im)politeness*. Basingstoke, UK: Palgrave, pp. 571–99.

Spencer-Oatey, H. (2005). (Im)politeness, face and perceptions of rapport: Unpackaging their bases and interrelationships. *Journal of Politeness Research*, 1(1), 95–119.

Spencer-Oatey, H. and Kádár, D. (2016). The bases of (im)politeness evaluations: Culture, the moral order and the East-West debate. *East Asian Pragmatics*, 1(1), 73–106.

Sperber, D. and Wilson, D. ([1986] 1995). *Relevance: Communication and Cognition*. 2nd ed. Oxford: Blackwell.

Tayebi, T. (2018). Implying an impolite belief: A case of *tikkeh* in Persian. *Intercultural Pragmatics*, 15(1), 89–113.

Terkourafi, M. (2001). Politeness in Cypriot Greek: A frame-based approach. Unpublished PhD dissertation, University of Cambridge.

Terkourafi, M. (2005a). Beyond the micro-level in politeness research. *Journal of Politeness Research*, 1(2), 237–62.

Terkourafi, M. (2005b). Pragmatic correlates of frequency of use: The case for a notion of 'minimal context'. In S. Marmaridou, K. Nikiforidou and E. Antonopoulou, eds., *Reviewing Linguistic Thought: Converging Trends for the 21st Century*. Berlin: Mouton de Gruyter, pp. 209–33.

Terkourafi, M. (2011). From politeness1 to politeness2: Tracking norms of im/politeness across time and space. *Journal of Politeness Research*, 7(2), 159–85.

Terkourafi, M. (2019a). Im/politeness: a twenty-first century appraisal. *Foreign Language and Foreign Language Teaching* [外语与外语教学] (Dalian University of Foreign Languages), *2019*(6), 1–17.

Terkourafi, M. (2019b). Coming to grips with variation in sociocultural interpretations: methodological considerations. *Journal of Cross-Cultural Psychology, 50*(10), 1198–1215.

Thomas, J. (1981). Pragmatic failure, unpublished MA dissertation, University of Lancaster.

Thomas, J. (1983). Cross-cultural pragmatic failure. *Applied Linguistics, 4*(2), 91–112.

Watts, R. (2003). *Politeness*. Cambridge: Cambridge University Press.

Watts, R., Ide, S. and Ehlich, K. (1992). Introduction. In R. Watts, S. Ide and K. Ehlich, eds., *Politeness in Language*. Berlin: Mouton de Gruyter, pp. 1–17.

Watts, R., Ide, S. and Ehlich, K. (eds.). (1992). *Politeness in Language*. Berlin: Mouton de Gruyter.

Wilkinson, S. and Kitzinger, C. (2006). Surprise as an interactional achievement: Reaction tokens in conversation. *Social Psychology Quarterly, 69*(2), 150–82.

17
Affect and Emotion

Laura Alba-Juez[*]

17.1 Introduction

Human interaction is strongly loaded with – and influenced by – emotion.[1] The observations and findings of different scholars at the turn and first two decades of the twenty-first century (e.g. Ochs and Schieffelin 1989; Scherer 2009; Damasio 2003, 2018) show that we human beings are not the paragons of reason we assumed ourselves to be in previous centuries. These studies are part and parcel of what is now deemed as the great paradigm change of the twenty-first century, namely "the emotional turn" in the humanistic sciences (Le Doux 2000). As linguist George Lakoff (2016: 4) puts it, "the conceptual is inseparable from the emotional, and vice-versa", so it would be unwise to ignore or suppress the latter on the illusionary assumption of the supremacy of the former. What may have sounded unscientific a century ago is now an undeniable fact: emotion has become a pivotal factor for researchers to understand not only the workings of the human psyche, but also those of language, communication and social interaction.

The existence of affective meaning had already been noted by Aristotle (McKeon 1941), but Darwin (1872) can be said to be the first author to have studied the nature of emotion in human beings and animals from a scientific point of view, laying the foundations for later psychological theories of basic emotions such as Ekman's (2003).

The fact that human emotions can be conceptualized and expressed through language (by means of speech acts that contribute to an interpersonal network of shared affective practices) is precisely the most salient

---

[*] I owe a debt of gratitude to J. Lachlan Mackenzie as well as to the editors of this volume and the anonymous reviewers for their kindness and valuable suggestions when reading earlier versions of this chapter.

[1] The research done for this chapter has been funded by the Spanish Governemt through the EMO-FUNDETT project (FFI2013-47792-C2-1-P, PI Laura Alba-Juez). Some of the findings of this project's research can be seen in the series of videos recorded for the MOOC entitled *Language and Emotion 'at work'*: https://canal.uned.es/video/5a6f39f6b1111f39448b456a

characteristic that distinguishes them from the emotions of animals. In this chapter the focus will be placed on the linguistic, sociopragmatic (in Leech's 1983, 2014 sense of the term) approach to emotion, without disregarding the importance of the contributions coming from other disciplines. I will thus first present an overview of key theories that have addressed affect and emotion (mainly) from a linguistic and discourse-pragmatic perspective. I will then argue that a fully comprehensive picture of human emotion has not yet been painted, and for this reason a more complex, sociopragmatic, multidisciplinary and multidimensional analysis of emotion is needed. I will next outline a case study that illustrates some of the key tenets of such an approach before concluding with suggestions for future research.

17.2 Key Concepts and Main Approaches to Affect and Emotion

As with many a concept in scientific studies, there is no consensus as to the terminology employed to refer to the phenomenon of emotion. Different terms have been used to describe and define it within and across disciplines. *Affect*, *feeling*, *emotion* and *mood* are sometimes used indistinctly, but some other times these same terms are differentiated as related but distinct concepts (e.g. Tomkins 1982). It is worth noticing that in most definitions of emotion the concept of evaluation or appraisal is also present, which attests to the close relationship between the two phenomena. From the perspective of cognitive linguistics, Schwarz-Friesel (2015: 161) defines emotion as "a complex internally represented knowledge system having a primarily evaluative function within the human organism". Definitions coming from psychology, such as Frijda's (1998) or Myers' (2004) point to the fact that emotions are complex phenomena that involve not only physiological arousal, expressive behaviours and conscious experience, but also appraisal of the situation.

From the perspective of Systemic Functional Linguistics, Martin and White (2005) use the term *Affect*. In their model, Appraisal is conceived as a discourse semantic system which includes three interacting domains: ATTITUDE, ENGAGEMENT and GRADUATION (35). AFFECT constitutes one of the three subsystems of ATTITUDE, together with JUDGMENT and APPRECIATION. AFFECT here is characterized as the subsystem "concerned with registering positive and negative feelings" (42), but it is not treated independently outside the realm of evaluation. Thus, some attempts have been made to refine the Appraisal model, in particular the subsystem of AFFECT, such as those shown in Thompson (2014) or Benítez-Castro and Hidalgo-Tenorio (2019).

Another functional linguist, Monika Bednarek (2008), equally includes emotion within her account of evaluation, and makes a distinction between *emotion talk* and *emotional talk*. The former refers to what cognitive linguists describe as the verbal representation of the *conceptualization* of emotion (e.g. *She feels sad today*), whereas the latter would correspond to what cognitivists refer to as the direct *expression* of emotion, normally materialized by means of interjections, a given intonation or pitch, or any other communication feature which is (supposedly) not mediated by cognition (e.g. *Ouch! Yuk! To hell with that!!*). This distinction is indisputably useful for the appreciation of two related but different manifestations of emotion in language and communication; however, it is important to note that very often both types of talk co-occur, and it is therefore not always easy to distinguish or separate one from the other.

At the intersection of (functional) linguistics and computer science we find the approach to evaluation and emotion known as *Sentiment Analysis* (Taboada 2016), whose main task consists in extracting information from positive and negative words in the text and co-text of a given corpus. Even if this is a growing field of research, to date it is far from being able to identify and consider the effects of sociopragmatic variables such as relational work,[2] irony or humour upon the meaning finally agreed by the interlocutors in social interaction.

In contrast with functional linguists, cognitive linguists (e.g. Foolen 2012) have studied emotion in and of itself, independently of appraisal systems (although they are aware of the close connection between the two) looking into the manifestation of emotion in language, with a special focus on the lexical level of analysis. Some authors (e.g. Soriano et al. 2015) have concentrated on the use of emotive terms and emotive conceptual metaphors. Another cognitive approach to expressive language is that of Relevance Theory. Blakemore (2011), for instance, argues that expressives are best explained through an analysis that uses procedural meaning and the idea that they show one's emotions.

Many authors, such as Damasio (2018) or Wierzbicka ([1991] 2003, 2009), have shed light on the cultural aspects of emotion and the fact that they are instruments and motivators for culture. Some of these studies have raised the question whether emotions are universal or culture-specific. So, for instance, while Geeraerts and Grondelaers (1995) foreground cultural factors, Lakoff (1987) focuses on the importance of universal constraints. Bosque (2010) points to the impossibility of doing without the social and cultural component of emotions for its conceptual characterization, which he illustrates, among other things, by comparing the cultural use of the term *vergüenza* in Spanish with that of *shame* and *embarrassment* in English. In this respect Foolen (2017: 4) argues that rather than positioning the different approaches on a one-dimensional universalism-relativism

---

[2] As defined by Locher and Watts (2008).

continuum, as far as emotion is concerned, the relations between language and culture "are manifold and multidimensional".

At the intersection of social cognitive and communicative development we find the studies coming from developmental pragmatics, some of which have focused on so-called *protoconversations* (Bateson 1975; Trevarthen 1979), which are thought to be a universal feature of infant-caregiver interaction involving a range of affect, emotion, social expectations and rounds of vocal turn-taking. According to these studies, sharing emotions is a crucial action for human beings to learn the rules of conversation and turn-taking at a very early stage.

Finally, it is worth mentioning that another socially conscious approach to emotion is found in the school of *Emotiology* (Shakhovsky 2016), whose researchers have developed a field of research related to 'emotive ecology', based on the proposition that verbal actions have social importance and are closely related to the social health of the nations and that of the individuals.

This overview of approaches to emotion could never be complete due to space constraints, but even if it were complete, it would show that in spite of the great rise of emotion in the humanistic sciences of the new millennium, there is still much to be researched as far as the sociopragmatic perspective is concerned.

17.3 A Sociopragmatic Approach to Emotion

As Leech (1983: 11) states, sociopragmatic studies deal with "more socially specialized uses of language" than pragmalinguistic studies, and therefore they take into account the users' perceptions of the context, including perceived sociocultural norms, underlying the interpretation and performance of communicative acts as (in)appropriate.

The great majority of the existing linguistic accounts of evaluation and emotion have presented a semantic and/or pragmalinguistic approach to these interrelated phenomena. And even though Martin and White's (2005) Appraisal Model can be said to be the most complete and elaborate linguistic theory of evaluation (including emotion) to date, it cannot be said to account for many of the (socio)pragmatic aspects that interact with language to convey emotive meanings. In view of this, in their study and definition of 'evaluation in context', Alba-Juez and Thompson (2014) deemed it necessary to include other key discourse and sociopragmatic variables, among which we find the concept of *relational work*. Also, in an attempt to go beyond the limitations of Appraisal Theory in its treatment of the AFFECT domain, and from a more pragmatically oriented and interdisciplinary perspective which includes aspects such as expressive speech acts, irony, humour, emotional metaphors or emotional implicatures (Schwarz-Friesel 2010), Alba-Juez (2018) proposes to analyse emotions in discourse as dynamic processes, as opposed to static, basic categories, and thus treats them as complex discourse bundles having different components,[3] somewhat in line with the *component* approach to emotion (Ortony and Turner 1990). The proposal (Alba-Juez 2018: 242–3) arose from the observed fact that, if emotive discourse was to be analysed only by using the tools given by Appraisal Theory, we would not go much further than saying that, for instance, in the newspaper headline in (1) below, we have an example of negative, inscribed AFFECT (ATTITUDE) within the *insecurity* (disquiet) set of meanings (the boy in question expresses what he feels about being judged by everybody) and heteroglossic ENGAGEMENT (shown in the fact that the utterance is between quotation marks, which shows the journalist or newspaper in question do not take direct responsibility for the words uttered), with a high degree of gradability (GRADUATION) found in the word *daily*:

(1) 'I feel judged daily, by everybody': 16-year-old boys in pictures[4]

However, if we approached the analysis of this headline from a more comprehensive multidimensional and sociopragmatic perspective, we would have to consider other variables revealing deeper aspects of the intersubjective meanings directly expressed or implied: we would also have to look into its position along the emotion continuum, its mode (i.e. linguistic, paralinguistic, through images, emoticons etc.), the type of press, the political orientation of the newspaper, the emotions conveyed by means of narrative techniques, the writer's stance, the expectations related to the readers' reaction, the relationship between the text and the image of the boy accompanying it (e.g. Do image and text cohere in their emotional message?), the emotional implicatures triggered, the different alignments or *footings* (Goffman 1981) taken by the participants, or the (psychological) emotion systems being put into motion, among other things. As has recently been acknowledged by some authors (e.g. Alonso Belmonte 2019) emotions play an important part in both tabloid and hard news.

Having reflected upon all of the above, Mackenzie and Alba-Juez (2019) present some of the latest studies showing a concern for describing and analysing emotion as it occurs in different discourse systems and social interaction, and they define *emotion in discourse* as a multimodal dynamical discourse process where sociopragmatic variables such as expectations or common-ground knowledge are of paramount importance (Alba-Juez and Mackenzie 2019: 18).

Expectations and emotional implicatures work hand in hand and are crucial when analysing emotion from a sociopragmatic perspective. Even

---

[3] Russell (1991) also rejects the idea of describing emotion as a static thing, in favor of conceiving it as a sequence of subevents (causes, beliefs, feelings, physiological changes, overt actions, vocal and facial expressions, and desires).

[4] The headline is accompanied by a picture of a teenager with piercings on his eyes, nose and lips. See the article in the *Guardian*, 9 March 2019, at www.theguardian.com/artanddesign/gallery/2019/mar/09/i-feel-judged-daily-by-everybody-16-year-old-boys-in-pictures.

though implicatures can be said to be more associated to the realm of pragmalinguistic studies, the specific concept of emotional implicature (*e-implicature* for short; Schwartz-Friesel 2010) incorporates social, cultural and personal elements that go beyond the pragmalinguistic field. Consider the exchange in (2), an excerpt from a YouTube video in which a boy and a man 57 years older than him ask each other questions about how it feels to be young and older, respectively:

(2)   "*57 years apart*"
Boy: Did you fall in love? What was it like?
Man: Yeeesss, ehhh. It was different for me ... I fell in love ... /()
Boy: And did you get married?
Man: No, unfortunately ... my, my partner ... she passed away, she died. That was a sad ...
Boy: ( ) sad ...
Man: Yeah. She got sick
Boy: I'm gonna cry... (He rubs his eyes)
Man: > No, no, no. Don't. No, no, no. Ah no, these things happen Shawn; that's life ... But ... we have, eeh, I have very good memories ... VERY good memories ... And you live ... a lot of time you live in your head with memories. You can remember all the good things, and that's the important thing.

The man and the boy speak about the emotion of love, and when the man says that his partner passed away, the boy immediately says he is going to cry. This is surely not surprising to any viewer, for it has to do with deeply grounded emotional expectations.[5] The e-implicature that is normally triggered when someone says that a loved one has died is that the speaker is sad and probably suffering, which in turn may cause a similar (empathetic) feeling in his/her interlocutor(s). This reaction has to do mainly with the human experience of love and death, and how these affect us emotionally. However, these generic, unmarked e-implicatures may vary depending on the personal situation of the people involved. One could imagine a case in which the man had had a terribly bad relationship with his partner, and therefore was not sad or did not suffer when she died, in which case those who knew him well would have extracted a different emotional implicature, i.e. that he was somehow relieved. In contrast with the previous unmarked implicature, this other (more personalized) e-implicature would not be in agreement with the otherwise general expectations, and would therefore be marked.

Other authors, such as Wetherell (2012) have explored affect and emotion from a social perspective. Wetherell argues that conventional psychological research on the topic is too restrictive, and she therefore proposes the concept of *affective practice* as an appropriate unit of analysis which

---

[5] For the concept of *expectations*, see e.g. Escandell-Vidal (2017).

integrates readings of the "somatic, discursive, situated, historical, social, psychological and cultural bases of affectivity" (4). An instance of an affective practice can be observed in the case of the crowds weeping hysterically over the death of dictator Kim Jong-il of North Korea (December 2011).[6] This practice shows emotion in action as a social behaviour, but it seems to be more connected to the political expectations of the regime than to the real emotions felt by each and every person in the crowd, which, however, does not invalidate the legitimacy of the affective practice per se.

The now emerging school of *sensory pragmatics* (e.g. Bargiela-Chiappini 2013; Majid 2013) also presents a methodology of analysis that surpasses language in an attempt to understand and explain aspects of *embodied discursivity* – as could be those found in the North Korean example above – focusing on the concept of the *social body*. Sensory pragmaticians attempt to understand communication beyond the concept of *embodied interaction* used by multimodal analytical approaches. Aspects such as the role of gaze in stancetaking (Haddington 2005) or that of the body in the organization of the participation framework (Goodwin 2007) have been recently addressed, but as Siromaa and Rauniomaa suggest in Chapter 6, these studies need to be complemented by further research covering stanced bodies on the move and relating to the surrounding environment.

In what remains of this section, I will focus on the relationship between emotion and some of the areas of research that are normally included in sociopragmatic studies, such as stancetaking, (im)politeness, irony or humour.

17.3.1 Stancetaking and Emotion

As pointed out in Section 17.3, the relation between stancetaking/evaluation and emotion is a very intimate one, to the point that all theories of emotion and all theories of stancetaking/evaluation (whether coming from linguistics or psychology) respectively include evaluation and emotion as key for their characterization, and some of these approximations consider it to be so tight a relationship that they do not even distinguish one from the other. However, our view is that each of them has distinctive features. For that reason, in previous work (e.g. Alba-Juez 2018) we have extensively explored their connection in an attempt to elucidate their common and non-common textual and contextual features by, for instance, analysing different corpora to see if AFFECT is a mere type of evaluation as argued by Appraisal Theory. Our results have shown a much more complex relationship than that of hyponymy (i.e. emotion being just one class of evaluation), for emotion permeates not only the AFFECT subsystem but also the other two subsystems of ATTITUDE (i.e. JUDGEMENT and APPRECIATION), as can be seen, for example, in the simple utterance *He is a despicable person!*, where JUDGEMENT and AFFECT are clearly intertwined. Furthermore, emotion

---

[6] See e.g. www.youtube.com/watch?v=pSWN6Qj98Iw

can also be expressed through the other two main domains of the Appraisal system, namely ENGAGEMENT and GRADUATION (e.g. *HE said she is an idiot, not ME!* in a situation where ENGAGEMENT is used to minimize the negative judgment or emotion towards the person being judged and avoid responsibility for it). But despite the great overlay existing between evaluation and emotion, cases can be found, for instance, in which evaluation is devoid of emotion, as is the case of so-called *descriptive appraisal*[7] (Price 2014), which attests to the thence observed fact that despite their connection, they do not share all manners of expression and manifestation.

This previous work and that of other authors (e.g. Planalps 1999; Langlotz 2017) has also focused on the verbal, bodily and facial cues of emotional stancetaking, or on aspects such as the extent to which grammatical and discourse structures serve affective ends. Emotion and evaluation have thus been shown to permeate and be encoded at all linguistic layers. At the morphological level, for example, it is widely acknowledged in the literature that the use of diminutives in English and in many other languages is indicative of a certain evaluative-emotive quality which in many cases can be placed at the positive end of the continuum (e.g. the suffix *-ie* in *sweetie*), and in others could be identified as a sign of derision (e.g. Spanish *Pedro tiene un **puestito** en la compañía* – English: *Peter has a 'little post' in the company* – using the diminutive suffix *-ito* when referring to the position held by Pedro in the company, thus showing signs that the speaker considers it is not an important or desirable job). At the lexical level, the expressive and evaluative meanings of words are encoded in their valence. In general, notwithstanding specific discourse systems in which these general terms might not apply, in most languages the words *murder* or *death*, for instance, have a negative valence and the word *birth* a positive one. At the phonological level, the use of non-segmental prosodic features such as high pitch or creaky voice may be a sign of an emotional process having to do with sadness or suffering (see also the narrative analysed in Section 17.4). There is also evidence that stance and emotion can be expressed at the syntactic level by means of, for instance, insubordinate constructions (Evans 2007), as seen in Spanish *¡Que no quiero!* (literally: *That I do not want!*) or English *If only you knew!* At the semantic level, and by way of example, different studies (e.g. Foolen 2012) have shown that very often metaphors conceptualize emotions (e.g. *She was brimming over with rage*, the rage being conceptualized as a liquid in a container). Finally, at the pragmatic and sociopragmatic levels, a myriad of phenomena could be mentioned, many of which are illustrated in different parts of this chapter, such as e-implicatures, the use of reference and/or vocatives having an emotional implication (e.g. *darling*), or the use of expressive speech acts (e.g. *thanking* or *congratulating*).

---

[7] An example of descriptive appraisal could be the statement *This room is 4 m long*, in which a simple, objective appreciation of the measurement of the room is given, and other things being equal, there is no trace of affect or emotion in it.

Both linguists and psychologists seem to support the idea that the emotions people feel and/or express are predictable from their appraisal of the situation and conversely, that their appraisal of the situation is predictable from their emotional behaviour or expression. Thus, if I appraise a situation as dangerous, it is very likely that I will immediately after start experiencing an emotional process of fear and distress, and vice versa, if for some reason I am distressed and fearful, I may appraise a situation as dangerous.

As suggested in the introduction to this chapter, emotional stancetaking is more frequent than a "rational" person might think, and this is made patent in many social practices nowadays, such as the easiness with which some readers accept the contents of fake news (just because they would like them to be true), or in more 'serious' genres such as scientific discourse (see e.g. Sancho Guinda 2019). Taking emotional stances, therefore, is a human feature of interaction which cannot be avoided, sometimes contributing to a healthy kind of persuasion, and at other times, in contrast, to the manipulation of others' emotions and stances.

(Im)politeness is an example of a human relational mechanism through which we may also manifest our emotional stances. We now turn to this issue.

17.3.2 Emotion and (Im)politeness

When I first read Brown and Levinson's (1987) book on politeness, I could not help thinking that, even though its focus was on pragmatics and interactional sociolinguistics, this was also a treatise on *emotional intelligence*. Mayer et al. (2000: 396) define *emotional intelligence* (EI) as "the ability to perceive and express emotion, assimilate emotion in thought, understand and reason with emotion, and regulate emotion in the self and others", a definition that inevitably triggers an association with the management of sociopragmatic systems or social practices such as that of (im)politeness.[8] In their description of politeness strategies, Brown and Levinson had tacitly taken into consideration the emotions of the interlocutors and how both speakers and hearers were supposed to manage them if they wanted (or not) to avoid unwanted or hard feelings. However, only a few sociopragmatic studies on (im)politeness have pointed to the important role that emotions play in relational work (e.g. Spencer Oatey 2013; Culpeper et al. 2014; Terkourafi 2015, 2020), as well as to the existing 'emotional lacuna in linguistic analysis' (Langlotz and Locher 2013: 88) in general.

The idiom *losing face* in English refers to how our public image may be damaged, often resulting in emotional reactions, such as shame or anger. Goffman (1967) had already noticed the emotional consequences of face loss

---

[8] For a deeper treatment of the relationship between emotional intelligence, impoliteness and pragmatic competence, see Alba-Juez and Pérez-González (2019).

when, among other things, he stated that, "it is plain that emotions play a part in the cycles of response, as when anguish is expressed because of what one has done to another's face, or anger because of what has been done to one's own" (23).

When reflecting upon the difficulty with the distinction between *Politeness 1* and *Politeness 2*,[9] Terkourafi (2015: 11) assigns part of the difficulty to the fact that both notions are ultimately evaluative and that the evaluations made in dealing with (im)politeness are emotionally invested. Indeed, Culpeper (2011) remarks that impoliteness can almost universally guarantee to arouse feelings of anger and being hurt, while politeness can spark off a more varied gamut of emotions, including passing unnoticed (as could be the case when using conventionalized negative politeness, e.g. *Could you pass the salt?*). But here again it is difficult to assign features of universality: What is polite in one situation or culture may not be so in another. Smiling to strangers, for instance, is a sign of positive emotion and conviviality among most European cultures, but it can signal embarrassment or phoniness among Russians (Larina 2015). A man complimenting a woman (e.g. *You look gorgeous today!*) may trigger positive or negative emotions in the recipient (or even a third person or overhearer), depending on the expectations of the participants (e.g. a traditional vs a feminist environment).

Culpeper et al. (2014) address the question of whether different cultures experience different emotions when facing discourses deemed impolite, and they argue that the role of cognition in the mediation of emotion is essential for explaining impoliteness. They show evidence that the violations of sociality rights that sometimes impoliteness involves are not linked to anger in all cultures (as they are in English), for their data show that, for instance, the Chinese may feel sadness or a sense of being let down instead of anger. However, all (inter)cultural studies on emotion present common problems, going from the difficulty in making generalizations about what people in a given culture 'really' feel or express they feel when facing (im)politeness, to the simpler but obvious fact that it is very difficult to translate emotion terms because their semantic and pragmatic scope normally varies from one language to another, or just because some cultures may have an emotion concept playing a part in (im)politeness assessments that is inexistent in other cultures (such as those encoded in the terms *Amae* (甘え) in Japanese or *litost* in Czech), among other issues.

As Haugh (2013: 57) points out, the very essence of (im)politeness lies in the evaluative moment (of informants evaluating hypothetical speakers or utterances), and therefore impoliteness has been increasingly characterized as either an interpersonal attitude or an evaluation. In theorizing im/politeness as social practice, Haugh claims that the moral order is what grounds our

---

[9] See Watts (1989, 2003) for the distinction between Politeness 1 and 2.

evaluations of social actions and meanings as 'good' or 'bad', 'normal', exceptional', 'appropriate' or 'inappropriate', 'polite' or 'impolite' and so on.

The use (and abuse) of swear words also bears an important connection with (im)politeness and emotion, a topic that would require a more extensive treatment than is possible in a handbook article. It is worth noticing, however, that albeit swearing may at first sight always seem to be a kind of rude or impolite behaviour having to do exclusively with negative emotions, research has demonstrated that this is not always the case: swearing is highly multifunctional (Bednarek 2019) and very frequently fulfils important sociopragmatic functions associated with positive emotions, such as reinforcing group solidarity (e.g. Stapleton 2010).

Finally, it is worth mentioning that display rules (Ekman and Friesen 1975) are of special relevance in the management of both (im)politeness and emotion. These rules have to do with cultural standards learnt at a young age which determine how, when and to what extent one should express certain emotions, and they are normally used to protect one's feelings or those of another person. Therefore, they are also associated with the expectations about how others will act and react (e.g. exhibiting grief at funerals, displaying joy at parties, showing strength and self-assertion when holding a management position) in cultural, professional or personal environments. Expectations about the emotions triggered by the use of humour and irony in all these different environments are also an important part of sociopragmatic studies, a topic to which we now turn.

17.3.3 Humour, Irony and Emotion

Research on humour and irony in rhetorical studies can be traced back to the classics (Cicero 106–43 BC; Quintilian, ca AD 35–100), but their connection with evaluation and emotion has begun to be explored in depth relatively recently. Irony has been studied by many an author as a major stylistic resort within humour (e.g. Nash 1985; Attardo 2008), but they are certainly not the same thing. However, what is common to both phenomena for sure is their evaluative and emotive nature. Alba-Juez and Attardo (2014: 31) focus on the power of verbal irony as a discursive mechanism used to express different degrees and types of evaluation and/or emotion. Alba-Juez (2016: 31) argues that "humorous discourse always contains an underlying stance manifested through the use of evaluative language/discourse, gestures, prosody, laughter, or images", and thus proposes the inclusion of evaluation as an important element in any theory of humour performance. Smiling and gaze, which are often associated to different emotions, are presented as markers of humour in naturalistic conversation in Gironzetti et al. (2016). Attardo (2019)[10] points out that the emotion mostly associated with humour is that

---

[10] See also his lecture on humour and mirth within the UNED MOOC *Language and Emotion at Work*, at https://canal.uned.es/mmobj/index/id/53458

of mirth, and that the facial gestures accompanying humour furnish clues to this association. In the case of irony, however, the associated emotions are frequently found on the negative side of the emotion spectrum, the reason being that the type of verbal irony most frequently found in human interaction is negative irony or sarcasm, normally intended to criticize the interlocutor, a third party or even the speaker (ironic self-criticism). Nevertheless, the gamut of emotions accompanying irony is varied; there is, for instance, a kind of irony that intends to praise or convey positive feelings, called *positive irony* by some authors (e.g. Kaufer 1983). A prototypical example of negative irony would be the utterance *A fine friend you are!* as a reaction of the speaker towards a bad action committed by her friend, while a prototypical example of (conventionalized) positive irony would be the expression *Break a leg!* normally used in artistic environments (e.g. among actors in a theatre) to wish good luck to a colleague. In the former case, the emotion emanating from the irony is negative (the speaker is resentful against her friend), while in the latter it is just the opposite (wishing good luck to a friend involves positive empathetic feelings). But normally things are more complex in interaction, and there are many more variables to consider than just the (supposed) feelings of the speaker or the recipient of the irony. In some cases, a criticism levelled at a person by means of a sarcastic comment may raise negative feelings in the person criticized but a positive feeling of camaraderie in a third person (or group) who aligns with the ironist and considers herself a foe of the irony victim. This is very common, for instance, in parliamentary debates, when members of one political party laugh at a given member of the opposite party who is being attacked by means of funny and/or ironic comments.[11] Sarcasm or negative irony is therefore very often associated to 'impolite behaviour', while positive irony, realized by means of the *mock impoliteness* strategy (Culpeper 1996), is often associated to 'polite' behaviour.

17.4 A Sociopragmatic Case Study of Oral Narrative: Oprah Winfrey's Happiest Christmas

17.4.1 Narrative and Emotion

In their analysis of the narratives of Holocaust survivors, Schiff and Noy (2006: 398) observe that "the focus on narrative studies across the humanities and social sciences reflects a shared concern with the interpretation of subjective experience". Other authors (e.g. Rollins 2017) include the ability to understand one's own emotions and those of others as one of the most important abilities needed for telling a narrative. Here again, we are talking about empathy: sharing emotions with a narrator may make all the difference between a good and a bad narrative. And precisely taking this fact into

---

[11] See e.g. www.youtube.com/watch?v=4bhpXhxP-WU

account, Romano (2014) shows that the expression of the narrator's emotions is not an independent section but permeates the whole text of the narrative from beginning to end. Different authors (e.g. Bamberg 1997) have explored the various discourse strategies used by narrators to express evaluation and/or emotion. These include expressive phonetics (e.g. lengthening of vowels, syllables or words, changes in pitch, pauses, deep respiration), expressive lexis, profusion of details, repetitions, the insertion of dialogue or the use of certain discourse markers, among others. Other researchers such as Niemelä (2010, 2011) go beyond discourse strategies into re-enactments and their bodily and space-related dimension in taking stances in storytelling. All these aspects are directly connected with the narrator's capacity for persuasion. Whether disrupting or illuminating, the role of emotion in persuasion is paramount. Since persuasion is an interactive process, its emotional charge depends on the persuader's skill in mutually aligning her emotions with those of her audience (Cockcroft et al. [1992] 2014: 101), but this alignment will mainly depend on whether they share a common stance which generates a common and intensifying emotional reaction. As will become apparent in our analysis in Section 17.4.2, this kind of emotional connection is precisely what Oprah manages to achieve with her audience.

What Haugh (2013: 61) describes as "one of the most significant developments in im/politeness research", namely "the shift away from a singular focus on the speaker's behaviour or intentions" can also be said about any kind of interaction research, including that of oral narrative. The evaluations and emotions of the participants in any kind of social interaction are crucial for its understanding, and therefore the fundamental questions in this type of analysis should not just be whether the speaker intends to do this or that, but rather questions such as: *For whom is s/he behaving in such a way? What type of participation or role (footing) do speaker(s) and hearer(s) have in the talk? In what kind of environment? What aspects of the personal history of the speaker should be known in order to assess the meanings conveyed? What geographical, historical, situational, etc. aspects should be considered in this assessment?* These considerations are in line with, for instance, Haugh's (2013) argument about the need to account for the complex array of participation footings, foreshadowed in Goffman's ([1979] 1981: 129) seminal claim that we need to deconstruct the "folk categories" of speaker and hearer into "smaller, analytically coherent elements". Goffman suggested that the folk notion of speaker conflates four different *footings* (i.e. sets of roles and responsibilities), namely those of *author, animator, principal* and *figure*, which have their counterpart in various hearer or recipient footings (*ratified* and *unratified recipients/participants*, which are in turn subdivided in different participation statuses).[12] This deconstruction of elements is also necessary

---

[12] See Kadar and Haugh's (cited in Haugh 2013: 62, figure 2) summary of the different types of participation footings.

at other levels of analysis, such as the one having to do with the kind of emotion expressed (as shown in Alba-Juez 2018). If the phenomenon is viewed in terms of *emotion systems* (taking into account their physical, psychological and/or verbal component elements) we will obtain a more complete picture than a simple description based on single categories of discrete emotions or broad appraisal categories.

17.4.2 A Case Study

This section provides an overall sociopragmatic analysis of the emotional content and elements of the oral narrative in (3), told by Oprah Winfrey, the American talk show host and philanthropist.

(3) And I thought of the best Christmas I ever had. The best Christmas I ever had was when I was 12 years old; my mother was on welfare, I was living with my mother, and my brother and sister in Milwaukee. My mother called me, the oldest, to say, into a room to say: "We won't be having Christmas this year". And I said: "we won't be having Christmas this year; what about Santa Claus?" "There is no Santa Claus". I had already figured that out, but >OK. [Pause, winking] I was embarrassed, and I was ashamed, because for the first time I . . . had to . . . face the reality that . . . yeah . . . what I'd been suspecting, that we're not like the other kids, that we really are poor, is true, so we're not gonna have Christmas and there is no Santa Claus. My first thought . . . after being embarrassed to shame, was "what would my story be", "what am I gonna tell everybody" [Pause] When we go back to school, and they're showing their toys and I don't have anything to . . . talk about . . . What am I gonna do, I'm not gonna go outside tomorrow, when everybody is out in the ya:rd showing the toys they got for Christmas, am I gonna pretend I'm sick, what is my sto:ry going to be? [pause] Well – late that night some nun showed up at our house and they brought a basket of . . . food, and they brought toys for >>my uh. . . my brother and my sister . . . [Holding back her tears] >>and I was overwhelmed with joy that those nuns came up, not because they brought me a Tammy doll when I really wanted a Barbie doll (Oprah smiles – audience laughs) I was overwhelmed because somebody remembered that we existed and somebody cared enough . . . > in the middle of the night to come to our house, with food and toys, and also I would now have a story [She wipes her tears] . . . (Oprah's 'Tearful Speech at Power of Women', 2015: www.youtube.com/watch?v=6Rfn94k717U, 3:05)

First, it is important to consider the relational history between Oprah Winfrey and her followers/audience, as well as Oprah's personal biography. All of Oprah's followers know that she was born into poverty in rural Mississippi to a teenage single mother, that she was then raised in

Milwaukee and, among other hardships, was molested during her childhood and adolescence, giving birth to a child (at the age of 14) who died at birth. They also know that because of all her childhood traumatic experiences, she is still fighting with some issues of her personality, such as binge eating (something she openly talks about in her shows). These are aspects that have built up a special emotive relationship between Oprah and her audience, who perfectly align with her feelings by sharing affective practices, one of them being the narration of her personal life experiences. Everyone also knows that she is now North America's first black multi-billionaire, and in 2007 she was named the most influential woman in the world.[13] These two contrasting facts (her poor and disgraceful youth vs her financial and personal success and power later in life) are key to understanding the relational work established between her and her audience, and the fact that she can awaken equally contrasting emotions in them, such as pity and admiration, or compassion and pride, which in their eyes makes Oprah a very humane person with whom everyone can identify.

Because of their knowledge of Oprah's personal emotional context, her audience bear some emotive expectations and can work certain particularized e-implicatures out of her narrative. Thus her audience normally expect that her memories from childhood will have some kind of negative emotive meaning, materialized in (3) when she says that her mother told her they weren't going to have any Christmas that year, an utterance that immediately triggers the e-implicature that Oprah must have experienced some kind of negative emotion on that occasion, as she then admits when she speaks of her feeling of embarrassment and shame. However, the emotion system that transpires in this narrative is more complex than that: Oprah expresses her emotions at the time, which combine with her emotions at the moment of telling the story. There is a physical manifestation (e.g. creaky voice, watery eyes, holding back her tears, hand movement stressing the words *embarrassed* and *ashamed*) and a linguistic expression of her emotions, by stating directly that she was ashamed, invoking a deep feeling of sadness and disappointment (... *what I'd been suspecting, that we're not like the other kids, that we really are poor, is true*). This emotionally negative scenario is eventually turned into a more promising and hopeful one when the nuns come to her house with a basket of food and toys, thereby transforming the initial negative emotional context into a more positive one, where there is even a humorous moment (Oprah smiles and the audience laughs), bringing emotional relief at the narrative stage of the resolution. Thus, we may speak of a multidimensional 'emotionality' throughout the narrative that includes both negative and positive emotions, involving tears as well as laughter, among other (intermediate) manifestations. This mixture of diverse emotions in one affective practice is a relatively frequent feature of narratives of

---

[13] "The Most Influential US Liberals: 1–20", *Daily Telegraph*, 31 October 2007, www.telegraph.co.uk/news/worldnews/1435442/The-most-influential-US-liberals-1-20.html

personal experience, which normally contributes to the *reportability* and *credibility* of the story (Labov 1997).

The footings taken by the participants in this social action are also part of the emotive practice machinery. Oprah's leading role here allows for her participation status being that of animator (utterer), author (creator of the talk) and principal (responsible for the talk) at the same time. Furthermore, at some points during her narrative she acts as figure (the character portrayed by the talk) of her old self as a girl and teenager, enacting the girl's emotional state at that moment (e.g. *"what am I gonna tell everybody"*). As for the audience's participation status, it is assumed that the people in the room where she is delivering her talk are ratified participants who are actively listening to her by evaluating everything she says and thus participating in the practice by, for instance, laughing or making gestures showing their empathy towards the feelings expressed, and for that matter they can be considered *targets*, *interpreters* and *recipients* (Kádár and Haugh 2013) at the same time. But a different group of recipients, other than those present in the room where Oprah delivered her talk, should be taken into account, namely those watching her on TV at that moment or those watching her in the YouTube video. Here we are speaking of mediated interactions in which the spectators are considered meta-recipients in a different meta-level of communication (Dynel 2011) and participate in the emotive practice as overhearers. But as Haugh (2008: 67) explains, in some cases the evaluation (and I would add, the emotions) of meta-recipients "may in fact be much more consequential in the everyday world than those of the initially co-present recipients". This is a fact in Oprah's case, considering the enormous media coverage and reach of every event in which she participates, including the one analysed here.

In the action of telling this narrative of personal experience, Oprah also engages in the social practice of politeness, for in the act of sharing her emotions and opening her heart by telling her audience about her childhood suffering and experiences in general, she constructs a positive politeness atmosphere, where Oprah considers the audience as people "who want her wants" (in Brown and Levinson's terms). In this way she makes them "feel good" by including them within her peer group, for which they are grateful and empathetic. Thus, Oprah's narration is a clear example of a discursive practice through which emotions are shaped, shared and constructed as the social practice develops.[14]

Oprah's videotaped talk allows us to observe a multimodal performance of emotion through all of the above-explained sociopragmatic aspects of her narration (which are key elements and components of this kind of affective practice), together with the linguistic and paralinguistic features of her talk, such as her use of emotion-laden words and expressions (e.g.

---

[14] As opposed to the view of emotions as (uncontrollable) products of human biology and physiology or as primarily inner-psychological phenomena (Harré 1986: 2–5).

embarrassed to shame), the lengthening of vowels at certain points and in certain words (*what is my sto:ry going to be?*), the use of high pitch on some key words (*what about Santa Claus?*), or the strategic use of pauses and body language, allowing for her emotions to surface (*"There is no Santa Claus". I had already figured that out, but >OK [Pause, winking]*).

Apart from looking into the communicative channels through which the emotion is expressed (body, prosody and speech rhythm, lexicon, syntax, pragmatics etc.) and the types of cue (gesture, posture, smile, tears, intonation, voice quality, pitch, expressive words, emotional implicatures etc.), it is also relevant to take into consideration the emotional dimensions of camera work having to do, for instance, with the kind of shot or the lightning. Langlotz's (2017) categories in the analysis of telecinematic fiction prove to be useful in this regard. In Oprah's narrative the camera focuses on her all the time (the audience is not seen; only heard), but we notice there is a close-up (which is then maintained until she finishes her narration) at the moment she starts to speak in a creaky voice because she is holding back her tears. This is clearly done in order to focus on the emotional process she is undergoing. It is also worth noticing that the close-up shot is made from an eye-level angle and the whole talk is filmed with normal lightning, which places Oprah as a person equal to her audience (Langlotz 2017: 537) and also pulls the spectators into the emotional scenario as if they were part of a conversation with her, not mere observers.

It goes without saying that much more could be said of both the pragmalinguistic and sociopragmatic features of this particular affective practice and those described in (1) and (2). In general, in this chapter, I have given special attention to the sociopragmatic variables affecting the emotional, intersubjective content and context of interactions, but I am also aware that many other sociopragmatic variables could have been included and discussed, not only at the local interactional level but also at wider levels including multiple interactions between participants across different relational networks.

17.5 Summary and Future Directions

In this chapter, I have outlined and critically discussed the key theories that have addressed the topic of emotion mainly in language and communication, with some incursions in the psychological theories of emotion and a few interdisciplinary studies. I have discussed the findings of functional and cognitive linguistics, as well as those of social theories which devote special attention to the cultural aspects of emotion, arguing that in order to have a complete sociopragmatic picture of the phenomenon, it is crucial to consider not only cultural aspects but also personal idiosyncratic ones applying to the specific social action being analysed, as well as those related to different social actions involved in distinct discourse systems.

I have also touched on aspects such as the relationship between stance-taking and emotion, (im)politeness, and emotion and embodied discursivity within the field of sensory pragmatics. In that respect, I concluded, in agreement with Siromaa and Rauniomaa (Chapter 6), that it is important to identify the dialogic and reflexive processes in the interacting bodies that have to do with taking stances, to which I would add those processes that have to do with emoting, and thereby called, like them, for a thorough multidisciplinary investigation to disclose such reoccurring practices in versatile sites and contexts.

The workings of emotion in social action have also been illustrated by means of the brief analyses of examples (1), (2) and (3), being conscious of the fact that there are various other sociopragmatic variables that could have been contemplated.

Many other topics could have been explored, such as the relationship between power, gender and emotion or the workings of cyberemotion, among many more, which are here left for future research. Future investigation should consider more studies with multimodal corpora, as well as a multidimensional conception of the phenomenon of emotion in social interaction. An interesting avenue of research can be found in the new discourse types emerging in the social networks or digital media, including so-called *hate speech*, which would embrace the affective practices with respect to phenomena such as racism, sexism, gender identity or any kind of discriminatory social behaviour.

Finally, and as an additional path for future research, this author's opinion is that in order to be able to obtain better and more reliable results, more interdisciplinary studies are needed in which disciplines such as linguistics, psychology, sociology, computer science or philosophy could join their efforts and findings to reach a more complete picture of the workings of emotion in social interaction. Emotion is a dynamic intersubjective phenomenon, and as such it should be explored in all its human dimensions.

Transcription Conventions

... → Short pause
[pause] → Longer pause
Underlining → High pitch
>X → Creaky voice
>> → Creaky, weeping voice in following utterance
a:/ o:, etc. → Lengthening of vowel
/ →Rising intonation
[Overlapping talk. Two people speaking at the same time.
() Incomprehensible speech
CAPITAL LETTERS → Stressed word or phrase

References

Alba-Juez, L. (2016). The variables of the evaluative functional relationship: The case of humorous discourse. In L. Ruiz Gurillo (ed.) *Metapragmatics of Humor: Current Research Trends*. IVITRA Research in Linguistics and Literature. Amsterdam: John Benjamins, pp. 11–34.

Alba-Juez, L. (2018). Emotion and appraisal processes in language: How are they related? In M. Gómez González and J. L. Mackenzie, eds., *The Construction of Discourse as Verbal Interaction*. Amsterdam: John Benjamins, pp. 227–50.

Alba-Juez, L. and Attardo, S. (2014). The evaluative palette of verbal irony. In G. Thompson and L. Alba-Juez, eds., *Evaluation in Context*. Amsterdam: John Benjamins, pp. 93–115.

Alba-Juez, L. and Mackenzie, J. L. (2019). Emotion processes in discourse. In J. L. Mackenzie and L. Alba-Juez, eds., *Emotion in Discourse*. Amsterdam: John Benjamins, pp. 3–26.

Alba-Juez, L. and Pérez-González, J. C. (2019). Emotion and language 'at work': The relationship between Trait Emotional Intelligence and communicative competence as manifested at the workplace. In J. L. Mackenzie and L. Alba-Juez, eds., *Emotion in Discourse*. Amsterdam: John Benjamins, pp. 247–78.

Alba-Juez, L. and Thompson, G. (2014). The many faces and phases of evaluation. In G. Thompson and L. Alba-Juez (eds.), *Evaluation in Context*. Amsterdam: John Benjamins, pp. 3–23.

Alonso Belmonte, I. (2019). Victims, heroes and villains in newsbites: A Critical Discourse Analysis of the Spanish eviction crisis in El País. In J. L. Mackenzie and L. Alba-Juez, eds., *Emotion in Discourse*. Amsterdam: John Benjamins, pp. 335–55.

Attardo, S. (2008). Semantics and pragmatics of humor. *Language and Linguistics Compass*, 2(6), 1203–15.

Attardo, S. (2019). Humor and mirth: Emotions, sustained humor and embodied cognition. In J. L. Mackenzie and L. Alba-Juez, eds., *Emotion in Discourse*. Amsterdam: John Benjamins, pp. 199–211.

Bamberg, M. (1997). Language, concepts and emotions: The role of language in the construction of emotions. www.econgeography.org/~mbamberg/Material_files/1997A.pdf.

Bargiela-Chiappini, F. (2013). Embodied discursivity: Introducing sensory pragmatics. *Journal of Pragmatics*, 58, 39–51.

Bateson, M. C. (1975). Mother–infant exchanges: The epigenesis of conversation interaction. *Annals of the New York Academy of Science*, 263, 101–13.

Bednarek, M. (2008). *Emotion Talk across Corpora*. New York: Palgrave Macmillan.

Bednarek, M. (2019). The multifunctionality of swear/taboo words in television series. In J. L. Mackenzie and L. Alba-Juez, eds., *Emotion in Discourse*. Amsterdam: John Benjamins, pp. 29–54.

Benítez Castro, M. A. and Hidalgo Tenorio, E. (2019). Rethinking Martin and White's AFFECT taxonomy: A psychologically-inspired approach to the linguistic expression of emotion. In J. L. Mackenzie and L. Alba-Juez, eds., *Emotion in Discourse*. Amsterdam: John Benjamins, pp. 29–54.

Bosque, I. (2010). Aspectos individuales y sociales de las emociones. Sobre la noción de 'vergüenza' y sus variantes. *Páginas de Guarda*, 10, 13–27.

Brown, P. and Levinson, S. ([1978] 1987). *Politeness: Some Universals in Language Use*. Cambridge: Cambridge University Press.

Cockcroft, R., Cockcroft, S., Hamilton, C. and Hidalgo Downing, L. ([1992] 2014). *Persuading People: An Introduction to Rhetoric*. New York: Palgrave Macmillan.

Culpeper, J. (1996). Towards an anatomy of impoliteness. *Journal of Pragmatics*, 25, 349–67.

Culpeper, J. (2011). *Impoliteness: Using Language to Cause Offence*. Cambridge: Cambridge University Press.

Culpeper, J., Shauer, G., Marti, L., Mei, M. and Nevala, M. (2014). Impoliteness and emotions in a cross-cultural perspective. *SPELL: Swiss Papers in English Language and Literature*, 30, 67–88.

Damasio, A. (2003). *Looking for Spinoza: Joy, Sorrow, and the Feeling Brain*. London: Heinemann.

Damasio, A. (2018). *The Strange Order of Things*. New York: Pantheon Books.

Darwin, C. (1872). *The Expression of Emotions in Man and Animals*. London: John Murray. http://darwin-online.org.uk/converted/pdf/1872_Expression_F1142.pdf.

Dynel, M. (2011). Revisiting Goffman's postulates on participant statuses in verbal interaction. *Language and Linguistic Compass*, 5, 454–65.

Ekman, P. (2003). *Emotions Revealed: Recognizing Faces and Feelings to Improve Communication and Emotional Life*. Rev. ed. New York: St. Martin's Griffin.

Ekman, P. and Friesen, W. V. (1975). *Unmasking the Face*. Englewood Cliffs, NJ: Prentice Hall.

Escandell-Vidal, V. (2017). Expectations in interaction. In K. Allan, A. Capone and I. Kecskes, eds., *Pragmemes and Theories of Language Use*. Cham: Springer International, pp. 493–503.

Evans, N. (2007). Insubordination and its uses. In I. Nikolaeva, ed., *Finiteness: Theoretical and Empirical Foundations*. Oxford: Oxford University Press, pp. 366–431.

Foolen, A. P. (2012). The relevance of emotion for language and linguistics. In A. Foolen, U. M. Lüdtke, T. P. Racine and J. Zlatev, eds., *Moving Ourselves, Moving Others: Motion and Emotion in Intersubjectivity, Consciousness and Language*. Amsterdam: John Benjamins, pp. 349–68.

Foolen, A. P. (2017). Expressives. In L. de Stadler and C. Eyrich, eds., *The Routledge Handbook of Semantics*. London: Routledge, pp. 473–90.

Frijda, N. H. (1998). The laws of emotion. *American Psychologist*, 43(5), 349–58.

Geeraerts, D. and Grondelaers, S. (1995). Looking back at anger: Cultural traditions and metaphorical patterns. In J. Taylor and R. E. MacLaury, eds., *Language and the Construal of the World*. Berlin: Mouton de Gruyter, pp. 153–80.

Gironzetti, E., Attardo, S. and Pickering, L. (2016). Smiling, gaze and humor in conversation. In L. Ruiz-Gurillo, ed., *Metapragmatics of Humor: Current Research Trends*. Amsterdam: John Benjamins, pp. 235–54.

Goffman, E. (1967). *Interactional Ritual: Essays on Face-to-Face Behavior*. Garden City, NY: Anchor Books.

Goffman, E. (1981). Footing. In *Forms of Talk*. Philadelphia: University of Pennsylvania Press, pp. 124–59.

Goodwin, C. (2007). Participation, stance, and affect in the organization of activities. *Discourse and Society*, 18, 53–73.

Haddington, P. (2005). *The Intersubjectivity of Stance Taking in Talk-in-Interaction*. Oulu: Oulu University Press.

Harré, R. (ed.). (1986). *The Social Construction of the Emotions*. Oxford: Blackwell.

Haugh, M. (2008). Intention and diverging interpretings of implicature in the "uncovered meat" sermon. *Intercultural Pragmatics*, 5, 201–29.

Haugh, M. (2013). Im/politeness, social practice and the participation order. *Journal of Pragmatics*, 58, 52–72.

Kádár, D. Z. and Haugh, M. (2013). *Understanding Politeness*. Cambridge: Cambridge University Press.

Kaufer, D. (1983). Irony, interpretive form and the theory of meaning. *Poetics Today*, 4(3), 451–64.

Labov, W. (1997). Some further steps in narrative analysis. *Journal of Narrative and Life History*, 7(1-4), 3–38.

Lakoff, G. (1987). *Women, Fire and Dangerous Things*. Chicago: University of Chicago Press.

Lakoff, G. (2016). Language and emotion. *Emotion Review*, 8(3), 269–73.

Larina, T. (2015). Culture-specific communicative styles as a framework for interpreting linguistic and cultural idiosyncrasies. *International Review of Pragmatics*, 7(5), 195–215.

Langlotz, A. (2017). Language and emotion in fiction. In M. A. Locher and A. H. Jucker, eds., *Pragmatics of Fiction*. Berlin: Mouton de Gruyter, pp. 515–52.

Langlotz, A. and Locher, M. A. (2013). The role of emotions in relational work. *Journal of Pragmatics*, 58, 87–107.

Le Doux, J. E. (2000). Emotion circuits in the brain. *Annual Review of Neuroscience*, 23, 155–84.

Leech, G. (1983). *Principles of Pragmatics*. London: Longman.

Leech, G. (2014). *The Pragmatics of Politeness*. Oxford: Oxford University Press.

Locher, M. A. and Watts, R. J. (2005). Politeness theory and relational work. *Journal of Politeness Research*, 1, 9–33.

Locher, M. A. and Watts, R. J. (2008). Relational work and impoliteness: Negotiating norms of linguistic behavior. In D. Bousfield and M. Locher, eds., *Impoliteness in Language: Studies on its interplay with Power in Theory and Practice*. Berlin: Mouton de Gruyter, pp. 77–99.

Lutz, C. A. (1988). *Unnatural Emotions: Everyday Sentiments on a Micronesian Atoll and Their Challenge to Western Theory*. Chicago: University of Chicago Press.

Mackenzie, J. L. and Alba-Juez, L. (eds.). (2019). *Emotion in Discourse*. Amsterdam: John Benjamins.

Majid, A. (2013). Discussion note: Making semantics and pragmatics "sensory". *Journal of Pragmatics*, 58, 48–51.

Martin, J. R. and White, P. R. R. (2005). *The Language of Evaluation: Appraisal in English*. Basingstoke, UK: Palgrave Macmillan.

Mayer, J., Salovey, P. and Caruso, D. (2000). Models of emotional intelligence. In R. Sternberg, ed., *Handbook of Intelligence*. Cambridge: Cambridge University Press, pp. 396–420.

McKeon, R. (1941). *The Basic Works of Aristotle*. New York: Random House.

Myers, D. G. (2004). *Theories of Emotion in Psychology*. 7th ed. New York: Worth.

Nash, W. (1985). *The Language of Humour*. London: Longman.

Niemelä, M. (2010). The reporting space in conversational storytelling: Orchestrating all semiotic channels for taking a stance. *Journal of Pragmatics*, 42(12), 3258–70.

Niemelä, M. (2011). *Resonance in Storytelling: Verbal, Prosodic and Embodied Practices of Stance Taking*. Acta Universitatis Ouluensis B95. Oulu: Oulu University Press.

Ochs, E. and Schieffelin, B. (1989). Language has a heart. *Text*, 9(1), 7–25.

Ortony, A. and Turner, T. J. (1990). What's basic about emotions? *Psychological Review*, 97(3), 315-31.

Planalp, S. (1999). *Communicating Emotion: Social, Moral and Cultural Processes*. Cambridge: Cambridge University Press.

Price, M. (2014). Profiles in evolutionary moral psychology: Richard Joyce. https://evolution-institute.org/article/profiles-in-evolutionary-moral-psychology-richard-joyce/?source=.

Quintilian. (AD 35–100). *Institutio Oratoria*. 4 vols. Translated by H. Butler (1920–22). Loeb Classical Library. London: Heinemann.

Rollins, P. R. (2017). Developmental pragmatics. In Y. Huang, ed., *The Oxford Handbook of Pragmatics*. Oxford: Oxford University Press, pp. 300–309.

Romano, M. (2014). Evaluation in emotion narratives. In G. Thompson and L. Alba-Juez, eds., *Evaluation in Context*. Amsterdam: John Benjamins, pp. 367–86.

Russell, J. A. (1991). In defense of a prototype approach to emotion concepts. *Journal of Personality and Social Psychology*, 60(1), 37–47.

Sancho Guinda, C. (2019). Promoemotional science? Emotion and intersemiosis in graphical abstracts. In J. L. Mackenzie and L. Alba-Juez, eds., *Emotion in Discourse*. Amsterdam: John Benjamins, pp. 357–86.

Scherer, K. R. (2009). The dynamic architecture of emotion: evidence for the component process model. *Cognition and Emotion*, 23, 347–85.

Schiff, B. and Noy, C. (2006). Making it personal: Shared meanings in the narratives of Holocaust survivors. In A. de Fina, D. Schiffrin and M. Bamberg, eds., *Discourse and Identity*. Cambridge: Cambridge University Press, pp. 398–425.

Schwarz-Friesel, M. (2010). Expressive Bedeutung und E-Implikaturen – Zur Relevanz konzeptueller Bewertungen bei indirekten Sprechakten: Das Streichbarkeitskriterium und seine kognitive Realität. In W. Rudnitzky, ed., *Kultura Kak Tekst* . Moscow: SGT, pp. 12–27.

Schwarz-Friesel, M. (2015). Language and emotion: The cognitive linguistic perspective. In U. M. Lüdtke, ed., *Emotion in Language*. Amsterdam: John Benjamins, pp. 157–73.

Shakovsky, V. I. (2016). *Dissonance in Communicative Sustainability: People, Language, Emotions*. Volgograd: IP Polikarpov.

Soriano, C., Fontaine, J. R. and Scherer, K. R. (2015). Surprise in the GRID. *Review of Cognitive Linguistics*, 13(2), 436–60.

Spencer-Oatey, H. (2013). Conceptualizing 'the relational' in pragmatics: Insights from metapragmatic emotion and (im)politeness comments. *Journal of Pragmatics*, 43(14), 3565–78.

Stapleton, K. (2010). Swearing. In M. A. Locher and S. L. Graham, eds., *Interpersonal Pragmatics*. Berlin: Mouton, pp. 289–305.

Taboada, M. (2016). Sentiment analysis: An overview from linguistics. *Annual Review of Linguistics*, 2, 1–23.

Terkourafi, M. (2015). The linguistics of politeness and social relations. In K. Allan, ed., *Routledge Handbook of Linguistics*. London: Routledge, pp. 221–35.

Terkourafi, M., Weissman, B. and Roy, J. (2020). Different scalar terms are affected by face differently. *International Review of Pragmatics*, 12(1), 1–43.

Thompson, G. (2014). AFFECT and emotion, target-value mismatches, and Russian dolls: Refining the APPRAISAL model. In G. Thompson and L. Alba-Juez, eds., *Evaluation in Context*. Amsterdam: John Benjamins, pp. 47–66.

Tomkins, S. S. (1982). Affect theory. In P. Ekman, W. V. Friesen and P. Ellsworth, eds., *Emotion in the Human Face*, 2nd ed. Cambridge: Cambridge University Press, pp. 353–95.

Trevarthen, C. (1979). Instincts from human understanding and for cultural cooperation: Their development in infancy. In M. V. Cranach, K. Foppa, W. Lepenies and D. Ploog, eds., *Human Ethnology: Claims and Limits of a New Discipline*. Cambridge: Cambridge University Press, pp. 530–71.

Watts, R. J. (1989). Relevance and relational work: Linguistic politeness as politic behaviour. *Multilingua*, 8(2–3), 131–66.

Watts, R. J. (2003). *Politeness*. Cambridge: Cambridge University Press.

Wetherell, M. (2012). *Affect and Emotion: A New Social Science Understanding*. London: Sage.

Wierzbicka, A. ([1991] 2003). *Cross-Cultural Pragmatics: The Semantics of Human Interaction*. 2nd ed. Berlin: Mouton de Gruyter.

Wierzbicka, A. (2009). Language and metalanguage: Key issues in emotion research. *Emotion Review*, 1(1), 3–14.

18

Power

Michiel Leezenberg

18.1 Introduction

Power is a Protean and elusive phenomenon that pervades our social life, and hence our linguistic practices. In most if not all forms of communication – whether oral written, or technologically mediated, whether informal or institutionalized – different kinds of power, authority, or domination are articulated: between man and woman, between parent and child, between teacher and pupil or student, between employer and employee, between rich and poor, between members of different classes, ethnic groups or cultures, or between speakers of different languages or language varieties.

Yet, power is surprisingly absent in most linguistic theorizing. Whereas different forms, modalities and aspects of power have received serious attention in social theory, power has received scant attention in the various linguistic subdisciplines (with the partial exceptions of sociolinguistics and linguistic anthropology) and in the philosophy of language. Generally, power is assumed rather than investigated: most authors take it either as given, or as at best a conceptually primitive contextual parameter or variable, rather than analysing how power may be constituted, reproduced or contested in linguistic practice.

One reason for this lack of attention may be the presence in these approaches of a number of implicit and therefore uncontested language-ideological assumptions about how language functions in the social world. Some of these language-ideological assumptions are the belief that power is normally, or should ideally be, absent in cooperative communicative behaviour (an assumption most explicit in Habermas' (1986) theory of communicative action as informed by an ideal of a power-free speech situation); the belief that any power involved, in communication is normally legitimate; and the belief that the linguistic and the social are two analytically distinct realms, with power exclusively belonging to the latter. Another reason may be the fact that, as a number of authors have argued, some modalities of power are not usually seen or recognized as such, and are effective precisely *because* they are misrecognized. Thus, Pierre Bourdieu (1991, 1998) famously distinguishes what he calls 'symbolic power', or the power to constitute the social world in and through symbols, as functioning to the extent that it is mistaken for socially neutral and universally shared forms and norms of communication. Likewise, Michel Foucault ([1978] 1994) suggests that power may be invisible precisely because it is omnipresent, and may be overlooked precisely because it is right in front of our eyes. Thus, it may seem odd or far-fetched to treat the institutionalized authority of, say, civil servants and priests to conclude marriages as a form of social power, or to analyse seemingly structural linguistic phenomena, like standard language as opposed to dialect, or polite speech as opposed to vulgar talk or slang, as involving social domination.

This inability to see, or reluctance to acknowledge power for what it is also informs much work in semantics, pragmatics and the philosophy of language. As a result, the workings of power in language have remained largely unanalysed. Yet, as I will argue in more detail below, various currently dominant frameworks rest on language-ideological assumptions that either take power as legitimate by default (Speech Act Theory); see power as a deviation or distortion of 'rational' or 'normal' communication (Gricean approaches); or deny, neutralize or naturalize the presence of power in language (communitarian approaches). I also hope to show that power is not merely an interesting and important *empirical* aspect of language use, but that it is actually *constitutive* of language.

One omission of the present chapter may strike some readers as odd: I will not be addressing Critical Discourse Analysis (CDA) in this chapter. Although the study of how inequality and exclusion are communicated in and through discourse would seem a prototypical way of studying power in communication, CDA appears to focus on the structure and content of discourse itself, rather than on the principles of its use, thus rendering it a less obvious topic in a volume on sociopragmatics; but I realize others may disagree on this point. Moreover, CDA generally presumes a rather monolithic, Marxist-inspired concept of power as a feature of a reified class consciousness, which is problematic in its own right. For a more detailed critique of the power concept presupposed by CDA, see Leezenberg (2013: 279–81).

18.2 Concepts of Power in Linguistic and Social Theory

Because of this lack of theorizing, it is not even clear at present with what conceptual tools power relations in communication should be analysed. How should power be represented theoretically? Is it part of what is communicated in language, or is it an aspect of the non-linguistic setting within which linguistic communication takes place? If the former, should it be represented as (part of) propositional content, as illocutionary force, as a perlocutionary effect or as another aspect of the utterance? Is whatever information it involves asserted or presupposed by sentences, or conversationally or conventionally implied by speakers? If the latter, should we model power as a property *of* the various participants in a conversation, as a relation *between* participants, or as a structural feature of the broader social or cultural context? Put differently: is power part of the micro- or the macro-context? And exactly where should any such contextual factors be located? In, respectively, the consciousness of language users, in institutions like the state, or elsewhere?

It is not to be excluded a priori that power may be articulated at all of these levels; perhaps it is not a unitary phenomenon in the first place. Hence, it may be useful to start by distinguishing a number of different concepts or modalities of power. First, there is the well-known Weberian characterization of power as the ability to constrain other people's actions; call this 'subjective' power, as it is phrased in terms of individual actors' actions and intentions. Second, we may distinguish an 'objective' or 'structural' mode of power; it appears, albeit unobtrusively, in the writings of Durkheim (1982) and Marx (1976: 270–306).[1]

Subjective and structural modes of power differ not only in accessibility to individual consciousness or intentionality, but also in scale: the former appears at the micro-level of face-to-face interaction, whereas the latter functions at the macro-level. There appears to be no good reason for reducing either to the other. Eric Wolf (1990) has tried to refine this distinction by identifying four types or modalities of power: first, a Nietzschean or individual sense of power as capability, which implies that power is an individual property; second, a Weberian or interpersonal (or what one might call 'relational') mode of power, as individuals' ability to impose their will on others; third, a 'tactical' or 'organizational' mode of power, which is not interpersonal or intentional but captures how actors 'circumscribe the actions of others within determinate settings' (presumably, close to what Marx in the *Grundrisse* (McLellan 1971: 65–9) calls 'social power' in processes of production or exchange); and fourth, 'structural' power as the ability to organize those settings themselves and thus to 'structure the possible field of action of others' (Wolf 1990: 586–7). Despite an emphasis on political economy, this typology is not based on any single coherent, let alone explanatory, principle. Wolf's notion of structural power, in particular, captures quite heterogeneous forms and modes of power, ranging from Marx's 'relations of production' and Foucault's 'government' to the Chinese doctrine of the 'correction of names' (*zheng ming*). Wolf's characterization does imply, however, a rejection of the autonomy of linguistic meaning, or symbolism more generally:

---

[1] Thus, Durkheim appears to talk of power when he talks of the 'coercive force' of social facts, adding in a footnote that this coercive power is 'so small a part of its totality' that we often take it for its opposite (Durkheim 1982: 16n4).

power, he argues, 'inhabits' meaning, as it upholds one set of meanings as true, correct or beautiful (1990: 593).

Wolf's four-fold typology suggests that power may function both at the micro-level of individual agency and intentions and at the macro-level of (economic, linguistic and other) structure. Perhaps, however, such attempts at classification are premature if not misguided. Foucault (1978: 93) has warned, famously, against reifying power relations: power, he argues, is not a stable and reified (let alone recognized or legitimate) institution or structure, but 'the name of a complex strategic situation in a particular society'. Power is omnipresent, he adds, not because it is a unitary and sovereign, transcendent or transcendental entity or condition of possibility, but because it is produced in every social relation, and as such, is always local, unstable and contested (Foucault 1978). It is not the possession of or emanation from a sovereign and antecedently given subject, but is actualized in social practices that may also produce truths, subjects and knowledge. Foucault proceeds to characterize, but not strictly define, power as 'both intentional and nonsubjective' (94); meaning, presumably, that power is a relation *between* actors rather than a property *of* actors; that it involves aims and meanings; and that it does not presuppose subjects as foundational. In other words, according to Foucault, power relations are not only internal to linguistic meanings, but also constitutive of language-using subjects; his practice approach also appears to crosscut the structure-agency divide to which Wolf still seems beholden.

Another theorization of power, and an important attempt to bridge the gap between structure and agency and between micro- and macro-levels in its own right, may be found in Pierre Bourdieu's sociology; of particular relevance here are his notions of habitus and symbolic power. According to Bourdieu, social practices are neither driven by conscious calculation nor fully determined by structures outside of individual consciousness; instead, they are generated by what he calls 'habitus', that is, the actor's semi-conscious dispositions to act in a particular way. For example, in many societies, men's habitus disposes them to look up, and to act assertively, whereas women's habitus disposes them to look down and act modestly. Such practices involve what Bourdieu calls 'symbolic power', a form of domination exercised by symbolic rather than physical means, or through communication rather than coercion; it involves the power to constitute social reality by determining which meanings are correct or legitimate, for example by distinguishing which forms of language are authoritative, correct and/or civilized. Hence, Bourdieu argues, it is simultaneously *recognized* as legitimate and *misrecognized*, or mistaken for a relation of communication rather than domination (Bourdieu 1991: chapter 7).

Bourdieu's notion of symbolic power would seem highly relevant for discussions in pragmatics and philosophy of language; but this potential has remained largely untapped. In the literature on politeness, and in some forms of post-Gricean pragmatics, the notion of habitus as an intermediary between structure and agency has gained some currency (see e.g. Levinson 2000: 386n; Leezenberg 2002; Terkourafi 2001; Watts 2003); but this exclusive focus on habitus has generally led to overlooking the fact that Bourdieu sees habitus as internalized structure, involving the acquisition, reproduction and indeed naturalization of domination and inequality.

Another way of mediating between linguistic microanalysis and political-economic macro-processes and of explicating the interconnections between the linguistic and the political may be found in linguistic anthropology, in particular in the notions of 'language regime', i.e. the relation between linguistic practices and forms of governance, and of 'language ideology', i.e. the beliefs and legitimations concerning words and their societal functioning developed by language users (cf. Kroskrity 2000: 1–2). Language ideologies both represent and rationalize group interests; as such, they need not be uniform across social divisions of, for example, class or gender. One important effect of such language-ideological research has therefore been the denaturalization of homogeneous and community-wide standard languages assumed as the self-evident object of theorizing in structural linguistics, and as the unproblematic end-product of successful national movements, as presented by early scholars of nationalism, like Ernest Gellner (1983) and Benedict Anderson (1991). The former's idea of shared languages as a prerequisite for successful modern industrialized societies and the latter's notion of an 'imagined community' both overlook the inherently political process of standardization, the concomitant marginalization of non-standard dialects and the heterogeneity – often accompanied by violent conflicts and struggles – within any supposedly homogeneous and harmonious national linguistic community (Silverstein 2000).

In theoretical linguistics and the philosophy of language, it is only in recent years that questions of power have started to attract more systematic attention; and this attention has often been a side effect of the study of phenomena like impoliteness, slurs, hate speech, pornography, and propaganda (cf. Butler 1997; Culpeper 2011; Langton 2009). Hence, in what follows, I will discuss a number of recent studies of these topics, asking how they conceptualize power. It will emerge that many of these studies reproduce a number of largely implicit assumptions about societies and the social functioning of language. Such political-ideological and language-ideological assumptions are not only debatable once made explicit; they also seem to prejudice or preclude raising the very question of how power functions in linguistic communication. For example, Habermas' (1986) theory of communicative action is informed by a strongly normative notion of an 'ideal speech situation' of power-free communication, which, he argues, is constitutive of communicative rationality as opposed to egocentric goal rationality. This notion of an ideal speech situation as power-free implies that power ideally *should* be absent from relations of communication; but it is not at all clear that this is a viable ideal. Methodologically, this and similar normative assumptions may have the effect of making any actual power expressed in linguistic practices appear as abnormal or theoretically secondary.

18.3 Positioning Power: The Linguistic and the Social

One seemingly intuitive reply to the question of why linguistics has shown so little concern with power is that the linguistic is autonomous with respect to the social, and that only the latter is a domain of power. One influential formulation of such a conceptual division of labour, in fact, comes from Geoffrey Leech, the very author who coined the term *sociopragmatics*. In his well-known 1983 pragmatics textbook, Leech distinguishes 'general pragmatics', which explores the general conditions of the communicative use of language, from the "less abstract" field of 'sociopragmatics', or the "sociological interface of pragmatics", as the study of local conditions of language use. As a third item, he also distinguishes what he calls 'pragmalinguistics', at the interface of pragmatics and grammar, which studies the "particular resources a given language provides for conveying particular illocutions" (Leech 1983). Thus, he argues that general pragmatic principles, like the Cooperative Principle and the Politeness Principle, "operate variably in different cultures and different language communities" (10). Unlike pragmalinguistics and sociopragmatics, that is, general pragmatics is neither language-specific nor culture-specific. One of the main tasks of pragmatics, Leech (1983: 84) continues, is to study how different language communities realize and articulate universal principles, like the Principle of Politeness.

This idiosyncratic definition not only presumes an unproblematic distinction between the linguistic as the domain of grammatical structure, the pragmatic as the domain of general or universal principles of language use, and the social as the specific sphere of the 'merely socially or culturally specific'; it also implies that linguistics and pragmatics as such have nothing to do with the social. Put differently: Leech presumes a level of purely linguistic structure and language use, which he sees as distinct from, and perhaps prior to, social action. Thus, his characterization not only reproduces the familiar structuralist belief that linguistic structure is *sui generis*, and is in itself autonomous with respect to the social; it also implies that there is such a thing as language use in itself, in isolation from particular social conditions and cultural conventions.

It should be emphasized, however, that structural concepts of language themselves rest on a rather ambiguous methodological exclusion of the social. Thus, in his *Course in General Linguistics*, Ferdinand de Saussure (1983: chapters II–III) sets out to define the science of linguistics in such a way that it is autonomous with respect to, say, history and social psychology, and follows its own, purely linguistic, laws. But despite this attempt to create an autonomous linguistics, Saussure states that "language is a social fact" (*la langue est un fait social*) and speaks of langue as a matter of "collective consciousness".[2] That is, the key structuralist concept of *langue*, or the language system, as the proper object of study for linguistics, appears to be formulated in large part in the terms of Durkheim's (1982) sociology. Although Saussure nowhere elaborates on this idea, his characterization of a language (tacitly identified, moreover, with a unified and standardized state language) as a social fact does seem to reflect a consensus-oriented view of societies as essentially unified, harmonious and geared towards social integration, as opposed to the conflict views of, for example, Marxists. The very assumption, however, that *langue* is a shared and anonymous 'collective representation' rather than, say, a set of norms or standards imposed by socially dominant individuals or groups, appears to prejudice the very attempt to raise questions concerning conflict or domination in language. Similar objections may be raised against other structuralist conceptions of language, such as those found in Generative Grammar or Cognitive Linguistics. Thus, Chomsky (1965) appears to naturalize standard languages to the extent that he characterizes them in terms of a biologically endowed 'language organ', and represents grammaticality judgements as the purely cognitive acts of a 'linguistic competence', rather than the recognition or reproduction of social norms.

Bourdieu (1991: 43–4) has pointed out the ambiguity in authors like Saussure and Chomsky, arguing that the former, in the very act of separating *langue* from *parole*, also separates language from its social conditions of production and reproduction; while Chomsky, in postulating that linguistic competence is the perfect knowledge of an ideal speaker-listener belonging to a perfectly homogeneous linguistic community, converts the 'immanent law of legitimate discourse' into universal norms of correct linguistic practice, while sidestepping the social conditions underlying the establishment and imposition of this legitimacy (Bourdieu 1991: 44). Put differently: these and other authors tacitly legitimize and naturalize standard language as opposed to substandard varieties, like dialects, slang or patois.[3]

If Bourdieu's argument holds, the structural features of languages are not quasi-naturally given but constituted by social relations – that is, by relations of power. Seen in this way, structuralist and cognitive approaches not only represent public and culture-specific practices as purely linguistic, universal and/or cognitive structures; they also presume a very specific – and debatable – consensus view of society, which sees conflict and – illegitimate – power as socially abnormal and/or theoretically secondary phenomena.

Bourdieu thus criticizes the autonomy of the linguistic with respect to the social. In turn, Judith Butler (1999) teases out the ambiguities in

---

[2] *Cours*, ch. I.i; tr. Harris: 6.

[3] Although a number of later authors working in the generative framework have analyzed dialects as distinct from standard language, the normative (and indeed political) questions underlying the very opposition between standard and dialect have remained largely untouched.

Bourdieu's own argument, and in particular in his appropriation of Saussure's (as cited by Bourdieu 1991: 34) claim that "the social nature of language is one of its inherent characteristics", arguing that the linguistic and the social are more deeply and more radically mutually implicated than Bourdieu allows for.

Bourdieu claims that the illocutionary effect of words is located not in linguistic rules but in the extralinguistic social power of speakers; in doing so, however, he appears to imply that the linguistic is wholly secondary to, if not constituted by, the social. Against this, Butler argues that social positions and institutions are constituted performatively. Her analysis undermines the idea that 'the social' is simply an extralinguistic context in which the habitus achieves its effects, and amounts to a complex analysis of the performative constitution – and contestation – of linguistic rules, social power, and gendered and other identities (see also Section 18.5). Analytically minded readers may balk at this deconstruction of the seemingly obvious opposition between the linguistic and the social; but for now, it may serve as a useful reminder that the apparently purely linguistic is in fact socially constituted, and may be based on a very particular conception of the social – and that vice versa, the social may be linguistically constituted. Either way, social power appears to be performatively – that is, linguistically – structured; and conversely, language is at least in part constituted by social power. This implies the more concrete methodological question of whether we should analyse power as a form of information that is communicated, or instead see language as merely an instrument for exercising power, and consequently set out to unmask relations of communication as relations of domination. There is no easy answer to these questions – but the views discussed below all appear to take the former option.

18.4 Power, Authority and Speech Acts

With the above considerations in mind, let us discuss how a number of influential frameworks in pragmatics treat, or may be construed as treating, the articulation of power in language use. Do they see power as part *of* the utterance? If so, what part exactly? Or is it perhaps an aspect of the (non-linguistic) context *in* which utterances are made? Speech Act Theory is an obvious starting point for studying such questions. For classical speech act theorists, like Austin and Searle, the answer seems rather straightforward: for them, whatever power is involved in speech acts primarily belongs to their conventional illocutionary force, rather than to their locution, or propositional content, or to their (primarily non-conventional) perlocutionary effects. That is, they locate whatever social power is involved in speech acts in their constitutive, that is, conventional linguistic rules rather than in the speaker (cf. Bourdieu 1991: 170). Thus, in his original discussion, J. L. Austin ([1962] 1975) shows himself well aware that the felicitous utterance of performative speech acts like naming children and concluding marriages may involve specific forms of social power, either by requiring a specific authority on the part of the speaker or by conferring a particular authority on the addressee. He nowhere discusses these forms of power in any detail, however, instead generically heading them under the label of 'authority'. Moreover, he clearly appears to assume that the authority of priests and civil servants is institutionalized and recognized, that is, legitimate.[4]

There is one class of speech acts, however, which Austin explicitly characterizes in terms of 'the exercise of power' (151), viz., the class of *exercitives*, like naming, appointing, ordering, voting and bequeathing.[5] Unlike verdictives like convicting and acquitting, he argues, exercitives are legislative rather than judicial acts. They are decisions rather than judgements, and as such they cannot be correct or incorrect in the light of the facts: they involve a decision that something *be* so, or a normative proclamation that it *should* be so, rather than a descriptive judgement that it *is* so. All exercitives involve the assertion of influence or the exercising of powers, in that they amount to a decision in favour of or against a particular course of action.[6] To the extent that they may allow or compel others to act in particular ways, they may be said to confer rights and powers on others, or may take rights and powers away from them.

Austin's characterization of exercitives, as of other kinds of speech acts, is enumerative and inductive rather than based on theoretical principles or general criteria. Nor does he discuss exactly what powers are involved in exercitives. From his account, however, it becomes clear that the uttering of an exercitive both has the conventional illocutionary force of bestowing particular rights or powers on the addressee, and requires or presupposes as a preparatory condition a specific institutionalized or conventional authority on the part of the speaker. Thus, the very fact that performative utterances like exercitives can be used to create or change social realities points to the social powers these utterances, or the speakers using them, may have.

It is not at all obvious, however, whether this power should be located in the speakers, in the linguistic rules constituting performatives, or elsewhere. This ambivalent role of power emerges especially in what one might call 'contested performatives'. Austin's examples are restricted to settings where the authority or power involved is tacitly or explicitly recognized as legitimate; but it is not clear how power or authority functions in performatives uttered in less clearly institutionalized or more conflictual situations.

---

[4] See e.g. Austin ([1962] 1975: 28, 29, 57, 59, 156, 161).

[5] See in particular Austin ([1962] 1975: 155–7). My discussion of exercitives owes much to Sbisà (1984) and to still unpublished work which Marina Sbisà has kindly put at my disposal.

[6] In itself, the insight that some kinds of language use involve power is not new or very surprising. Thus, the link between naming and political power was known already to pre-Han thinkers in ancient China; for example, in the *Analects* (13.3), Confucius states that the so-called correction of names (*zheng ming*) is the first task of government (cf. Leezenberg 2006).

In such settings, it appears, the authority involved in a felicitous speech act need not be supported by institutions, nor need it be recognized by all participants involved; rather, this power may be arrogated and/or contested. For example, when the Founding Fathers uttered the words that constituted the American Declaration of Independence,

> "We, the Representatives of the united States of America ..., do, in the Name, and by Authority of the good People of these Colonies, solemnly publish and declare, That these united Colonies are, and of Right ought to be Free and Independent States; that they are Absolved from all Allegiance to the British Crown".

They did not *possess* the authority to do so (nor, of course, had they been named the 'Founding Fathers' yet); rather, they *claimed* or *arrogated* the very power to represent the 'good peoples'. More precisely, their declarative power appears to be presupposed rather than asserted; and by the very act of its being uttered successfully, the power it presupposes comes into existence. This suggests that the speaker's power or authority need not exist prior to the utterance, but may in some contexts be *accommodated*, much as some presuppositions may not obtain prior to an utterance but come into being just by being required at a particular moment.

Generalizing from this, one might argue that the power required for the felicitous utterance of performatives involves presupposed information rather than asserted information, and that consequently, it may be analysed as analogous to linguistic presupposition.[7] This opens up all sorts of questions, however, which we have not even begun to explore; for example, should we analyse such presupposed power in terms of semantic presuppositions, i.e. as necessary conditions on meaningfulness, or of pragmatic presuppositions, i.e. as the information a speaker takes for granted? How does power-as-presupposition interact with conversational principles, like Grice's maxims? The latter assume that language use is normally rational and cooperative, and thus seem to deny or neutralize power differences in communication (cf. Leezenberg 2006). And, perhaps most importantly, exactly when is the power presupposed by an utterance accommodated, rather than leading to a presupposition failure or an infelicitous utterance? In other words: when is the power claimed by the speaker *recognized* or *accepted* by the addressee? These are difficult questions; and in different settings, the answer may have to be sought in semantics, in pragmatics or in extralinguistic factors.

A good case can be made that exercitives are central to Austin's entire undertaking: as his editors note, all explicit performative utterances with which he opens his argument are in fact exercitives, invokviung a speaker

---

[7] The original study that introduced accommodation as a particular kind of pragmatic inferencing is Lewis (1979), but the subsequent literature has considerably nuanced and enriched Lewis' original sketch. See e.g. Beaver and Zeevat (2007) for an overview.

endowed with an institutionalized authority and granting the addressee specific rights and duties (Austin [1962] 1975: 5n). This would make the development of a fuller account of what power is and how it functions in speech acts an all the more desirable goal; but this desideratum was hardly taken up by later scholars working on Speech Act Theory.[8]

Thus, in his 1969 study and in later works, John Searle ignores the social dimension of linguistic practices, and instead focuses on what he takes to be the purely linguistic rules constituting speech acts.[9] In doing so, he rejects the category of exercitives altogether, arguing that Austin classifies not illocutionary *acts* but only English-language illocutionary *verbs*; moreover, this classification is not based on any clear or consistent principles (Searle 1975: 8). Hence, he concludes, Austin's categories are heterogeneous within themselves, and display considerable overlap with each other. Next, Searle himself distinguishes a broader category of *directives*, the illocutionary point of which is the speaker's "attempt to get the hearer to do something" (Searle 1975: 11). This classification is formulated entirely in – supposedly purely linguistic – terms of illocutionary point and direction of fit between words and the world, and accordingly leaves out social factors.

As a result, in Searle's approach to speech acts, the dimension of social power drops out completely. Much later, however, social power reappears in Searle's speech act-theoretical analyses, in particular in his account of social or institutional facts, *The Construction of Social Reality* (Searle 1995). Here, Searle sets out to give an account of 'social' or 'institutional facts'. Such facts, he argues, are as objective as any, but they exist only by human agreement; thus, things like money and marriages only exist because people *believe* that they do. Many of these institutional facts may have been created by explicit performatives, or declarations; but Searle makes the rather stronger claim that all of institutional reality is created by exactly one logical operation. This operation may, but need not be, explicit; moreover, it may be superimposed on the result of earlier operations. According to Searle, this operation has the form:

We accept (S has power (S does A))

By the (possibly repeated or superimposed) exercise of such operations, particular powers – or what Searle, tellingly, calls 'status functions' – are conferred on an individual. For example, by conferring the status-function of president of the United States on an individual, the people who do so accept that that person has the right to present the federal budget, declare wars, etc. (Searle 1995: 104–11).

At first blush, this suggests that institutional reality is based on a series or a superimposition of exercitives, as distinguished by Austin. Searle's

---

[8] But see Sbisà (1984) for a defence of the distinct characteristics and importance of exercitives.
[9] In *Speech Acts*, Searle does acknowledge that a theory of speech acts is, or should be, part of a general theory of action; but he does not start developing this line of thinking until several decades later.

account, however, displays some significant – and problematic – features of its own. First, it suggests that the 'we' involved in this operation rests on collective intentionality – a phenomenon which, Searle claims, is primitive and cannot be reduced to any combination of individual intentions (Searle 1995: 24–6). But this *presumes*, rather than accounts for, the rational agreement of language users as free and equal actors. Second, the speaker's authority presupposed by this operation is not restricted or limited to particular institutional settings as it is in Austin's exercitives; rather, it is the general mechanism underlying *all* forms of social power. But that implies that the members of a community already have the power to grant specific powers to others. Thus, Searle's account not only presupposes a collective or a community, as expressed in a 'we', as a conceptual primitive; it also turns out to presuppose the very phenomenon of social power it sets out to explain.

18.4.1 A Case Study: Power and Pornography

Speech act theory has also been applied to – and in the process, transformed by – the study of pornography. Early feminist critics, such as, most famously, Catharine MacKinnon, have argued that pornography not only *depicts* but also *constitutes* oppression of women: in construing a woman's *no* as a *yes*, they argue, pornography effectively silences women and deprives them of the right to consent. This implies that defending pornography in the name of free speech would amount to granting men the freedom to deprive women of *their* right to free expression. In speech act-theoretical terms, this means that oppression is a conventional illocutionary force of pornography. One may object that such an analysis is too coarse-grained, as it tacitly identifies pornography with the representation of heterosexual intercourse, and assumes that it is *inherently* oppressive, regardless of the context in which it is uttered, by which 'speakers' (the actors, the director, etc.), and with what intentions.

For the sake of argument, however, let us assume that pornography can indeed be unproblematically analysed as a speech act with more or less determinate 'speakers' and 'addressees' and explore the forms of power it may involve.

In a series of articles, Rae Langton (2009: 30) has argued that the ability to perform particular speech acts can mask political power: "powerful speakers can generally do more, say more and have their speech count for more than can the powerless". Building on McKinnon's argument, she then explores exactly what kind of speech act pornography amounts to, and exactly where its effect should be located. She argues that pornography may indeed be an illocutionary speech act of subordinating or silencing, as it undermines the felicity conditions of women's speech by taking the woman's 'no' as a 'yes'. More specifically, she argues that earlier discussions of pornography overlook this illocutionary force by focusing on its locutionary dimension and perlocutionary effects.

Judith Butler, however, has criticized Langton for allegedly reifying the effects of pornography. In *Excitable Speech* (1997), she rejects reductionist analyses that unambiguously locate the effects of such utterances either in the words or in the speakers, or in, respectively, conventional illocutionary force or perlocutionary effects.[10] Against any such attempt, Butler suggests that performatives are not fully conscious acts by sovereign subjects endowed with authority prior to their utterance; rather, she argues, "the subject who 'cites' the performative is temporarily produced as ... the origin of the performative" (49). Speech acts, she argues, are bodily acts and as such are never fully controlled by the intentions of the speaker; moreover, because they can be quoted or iterated, they cannot be controlled by their original context of utterance, but may acquire new meanings in new contexts, witness the reappropriation by homosexuals of the word *queer*, or by African Americans of the N-word. A felicitous performative, that is, is neither governed by speaker's intentions nor constrained by its (original) context of utterance; rather, it *acquires* the 'force of authority' through the repetition or citation of a prior and authoritative set of practices (51). The very repetition by which it does so, however, opens up the possibility of iteration, quotation and subversive re-signification. In line with these considerations, Butler criticizes Langton's speech act-theoretical account of the silencing effect of pornography. The latter's analysis of pornographic images as imperatives that *order* women to be subordinated, she argues, turns pornography into 'a subject who speaks and, in speaking, brings about what it names'. That is, echoing Althusser's view of the subject-constituting power of ideology as a 'divine voice', she argues that one should not ascribe such a performative agency, and indeed 'divine authority', to pornography (69).

Against this criticism, Langton (2009: chapter 6) has retorted that she does not analyse pornography as an imperative that *commands* women, but as a verdictive that *declares* women inferior, analogously to the way a jury declares a defendant guilty in a court case. The self-fulfilling or performative aspect of verdictives, she argues, is typically illocutionary or constitutive in that the addressee's social status changes itself to fit the speaker's words; but on occasion, verdictives may also have a perlocutionary or causal effect of the world itself rearranging itself to what the powerful say (Langton 2009: 106). Butler, she continues, is too sceptical about the ability of pornography to silence women, and too optimistic about the possibility of the subversive acts of parody, reappropriation or re-signification to help or empower silenced or oppressed women.

In more recent years, Mary Kate McGowan (2004) has argued that there is another way in which speech may enable people to speak or, conversely,

---

[10] Butler also rejects the – understandable – calls for greater regulation of hate speech by the state, claiming that 'the state produces hate speech'; i.e. what language may be spoken in public is decided by state power. Thus, she argues, the allegedly sovereign power of hate speech 'is itself modeled on the speech of a sovereign state' (77).

silence them and in particular contribute to the silencing of women. She does so by distinguishing what she calls 'Austinian exercitives' from 'conversational exercitives'; the former, she argues, require institutional settings and a specific and recognized authority, whereas the latter occur in more informal settings and involve a less visible form of power. The former *explicitly* express the content of the permissibility fact, as in "Playing music after 11PM is not permitted"; in the latter, what is permitted in the subsequent conversation is *tacitly* changed, just as happens with presuppositions that are accommodated. For example, if I make a statement presupposing that I have children, and this is not challenged by the hearer, this presupposition becomes part of the conversational score, and changes what may subsequently be uttered. This points to a more general fact about conversational exercitives: they do not require that the speaker already has a conventionalized or institutionalized power before making an utterance; nor do they depend on either speaker's intentions or on recognition by the hearer. Rather, they invoke a rule of *accommodation* (cf. Lewis 1979).

McGowan (2004: 93) not only argues that pornography may be analysed as involving accommodated conversational exercitives, and thus rendered immune to much of the criticisms raised against MacKinnon and Langton; she also makes the stronger claim that *any* conversational contribution that invokes a rule of accommodation is an exercitive speech act. This analysis recalls how the relevant power to declare independence came into being in the very act of being uttered by the Founding Fathers, as discussed in Section 18.4; but it need not imply that *all* social power works in this way. Subsequently, however, McGowan (2009: 396) has generalized her analysis to the claim that all speech constituting a move in a rule- or norm-governed activity is exercitive, in that it may *change* the rules, by enacting facts about what is subsequently permissible in that activity. Thus, McGowan's analyses raise questions concerning the articulation of power presupposed in speech acts, and the role of accommodation in such presuppositions. In short, in particular the notions of exercitives and accommodation seem promising for the further study of the workings of power in language use; but at present, it is undecided whether these questions are best answered in linguistic or in social-scientific terms.

18.5 Politeness, Impoliteness and Power

Another area of pragmatics that touches on questions of power without really addressing them systematically or in detail is Politeness Theory. The basis for much of this work, and arguably still the single most influential model, is Brown and Levinson's (1987) pioneering study, which presents all language users as rational actors endowed with 'face', and all linguistic exchanges as inherently face-threatening acts; accordingly, polite language use is one of the main strategies to deal with such threats (cf.

Chapter 16). The most important ingredient of this approach is undoubtedly Grice's theory of conversational implicature. From Grice, Brown and Levinson inherit a Kantian or contractarian view of speakers as free, equal, and rational; or, put differently: a linguistic ideology that views language use as normally cooperative, power-free, and geared towards social integration.[11] Hence, they suggest that their conception of politeness is universal, in that it reflects general principles of rational communication (4–5, 58). Against this view, Sachiko Ide (1992, 1993) and various authors in her wake have argued that, in languages like Japanese and Korean, politeness is encoded in grammatical structure, and hence not an optional strategy of communication.[12]

Both approaches appear to make rather different, but equally strong and equally debatable assumptions about the kind and status of power in language use, and in society at large. Brown and Levinson (1987: 77) presume a Weberian, or subjective, conception of relative power as the degree to which one actor can impose their own plans and self-evaluations at the expense of those of others; this power, they add, may be authorized or unauthorized, and may result from both material and metaphysical control; a greater power difference leads to more 'deference' in interaction by the weaker side. By thus locating power squarely in speakers, rather than in, say, rules of illocutionary force, they render it an entirely extralinguistic phenomenon; accordingly, they pay little if any attention to possible performative effects of polite or impolite language use in reproducing, arrogating or contesting power for speakers and hearers. Later refinements and modifications have generally not directly addressed Brown and Levinson's underlying Weberian concept of power. Ide's and other approaches that treat norms of politeness as grammatically encoded and shared by an entire community appear to skirt questions of power and social domination altogether.

More recently, a so-called discursive approach to politeness has been developed, according to which no act is inherently polite or impolite; what is crucial is that actors *perceive* or *interpret* it as polite or other in the light of existing social norms (cf. Locher 2006). Thus, a discursive approach mitigates the strict dichotomy between polite and impolite language use; it also emphasizes the inherently norm-dependent character of politeness. It also conceives of power as negotiated rather than possessed; but it does not engage in a more radical questioning of the modalities, scale and workings of power involved in communication. This becomes clear from Locher (2004), one of the few studies that explicitly link politeness to questions of power, which focuses on power in cases of verbal disagreement.

---

[11] For more discussion of the Kantian assumptions in Brown and Levinson, and in Grice, see Leezenberg ([2006] 2010).
[12] Often, such claims are backed by essentializing orientalist oppositions between an 'individualist' West that has ideals of rational calculation as self-interest, and a 'communitarian' East, allegedly driven by values of social harmony and collectivity. Even authors who reject the idea of an East–West divide in politeness, like Leech (2007), do not contest the individualist–communitarian opposition that informs it.

Following Steven Lukes' 'three-dimensional' concept of power as one actor's affecting another against the latter's interests, Locher characterizes power as relational, dynamic and contestable. But although she makes a number of useful conceptual distinctions between, among others, power-over and power-to and between power and force, coercion and influence, her conception of power remains recognizably Weberian and strongly normative: it views power as essentially negative, distortive or repressive.

It seems that it was only with the rising interest in *im*politeness that questions of power started to emerge among politeness scholars.[13] Thus, criticizing Leech and Brown and Levinson, Jonathan Culpeper (2011) adduces some empirical evidence concerning the importance of power asymmetries in establishing whether particular instances of directness or indirectness are polite or impolite. Others have cautiously suggested that impolite language may involve the assertion of power or the resistance against authority; but even these discussions often appear to proceed from the tacit assumption that impoliteness and the assertion of power in language use are marked, exceptional and/or abnormal.[14] Far rarer are explorations of the possibility that politeness *itself* is a communicative ideal created and reproduced by socially dominant groups, and may thus contribute to the reproduction of that domination.[15] Indeed, many existing frameworks would seem to militate against the very possibility of exposing social domination in polite communication. Scholars inspired by Brown and Levinson's approach see linguistic actors as rational, equal and free; while Ide and other communitarian-oriented authors appear to elide questions of power altogether, tacitly assuming that the cultures or traditions they are dealing with are agentless and anonymous, and result in homogeneous and harmonious, communities. In its most extreme form, such a position would amount to an outright denial of social domination, whether through language or by other means. Both approaches thus appear to make a number of very specific, and debatable, language-ideological assumptions: to the extent that polite communication (say, between older and younger speakers, between noblemen and commoners, or between men and women) involves authority at all, both seem to hold, and this authority is generally or normally perceived as legitimate.

Yet, against both positions, it may be argued that notions, norms and principles of politeness are neither universal and timeless nor agentless. Rather, specific forms and conceptions of politeness have emerged in very specific historical and social circumstances, and appear to have been

---

[13] See e.g. Leezenberg (2005); Culpeper (2008, 2011: 186–94); and the various papers collected in Bousfield and Locher (2008).

[14] See in particular the papers by Bousfield and Schnurr a.o. in Bousfield and Locher (eds.) 2008.

[15] Watts (2003) seems to go some way in this direction, but does not address the question of social domination in detail. Moreover, his 'social model' of politeness repeatedly refers to Bourdieu's work, but proceeds to use notions like symbolic power and symbolic violence in a rather idiosyncratic way that does no justice to Bourdieu's more radical suggestions.

produced by specific forms of social power. In fact, the very etymology of various folk terms for politeness already indicates its link to dominant social classes, and hence to domination (cf. Ehlich 1992). German *Höflichkeit* (literally 'courtliness') clearly reflects its origins in court culture. Likewise, in seventeenth-century England, the ideal of polite language use emerged as a means of avoiding religious conflict if not outright civil war; moreover, it was perceived as the language of urban, and urbane, 'gentlemen', as opposed both to women and to lower-class males. Various authors have discussed the historical development of forms and norms of politeness (see e.g. Watts 2002; Jucker 2011; Terkourafi 2011); but few if any of them acknowledge that the history of politeness is also, and perhaps even primarily, a history of power.

Against this, however, it may be objected that these historical changes reflect developing folk theories or linguistic ideologies rather than analytical notions of politeness. In the later literature, as is well known, it has become customary to distinguish folk conceptions of politeness, or politeness$_1$, from theoretical conceptions, or politeness$_2$ (e.g. Watts 2003). None of the authors who make this distinction, however, address the question of what social imaginaries or linguistic ideologies may be at work in the latter. Even Eelen (2001), perhaps the most radical critique of the ideological and other assumptions in dominant approaches to politeness, stops short of explicating the power concept and the societal and linguistic ideologies presupposed in the various theoretical frameworks.

One may well ask why politeness research has on the whole been so reluctant to tackle the question of power. This reluctance is all the more surprising as one of the most influential authors on the sociology of language, Pierre Bourdieu, has explicitly linked politeness to social power. Polite speech as opposed to rude language or slang, he argues, is a kind of 'legitimate language' much like standard language as opposed to dialect or patois; as such, it is an integral if normally not recognized aspect of social domination (Bourdieu 1991: 80, 88; cf. 47–8). More specifically, Bourdieu analyses both standard language and polite speech as forms of what he calls 'symbolic violence', that is, the exercise of power by seemingly harmonious social behaviour. The most familiar case of such violence is the exchange of gifts, which seemingly cements friendly social relations, but also and simultaneously amounts to a challenge of the recipient's honour. Likewise, Bourdieu analyses polite speech as seemingly expressing harmonious social relations while simultaneously marginalizing the language of oppressed groups as 'rude' or 'vulgar' (see in particular Bourdieu 1991: 80, 88).

Bourdieu's analysis suggests a complex relation between politeness, impoliteness and social power. If correct, it implies that rude or impolite language as used by dominated groups need not involve either the bare assertion of power or resistance against linguistically encoded forms of social domination: on the contrary, Bourdieu argues that, precisely in appearing to reject the dominant or authoritative form of language, speakers using 'coarse' or 'vulgar' forms tacitly accept and reproduce the very distinction between authoritative and subordinate forms of language.

It is quite astonishing to note that this dimension of social power in Bourdieu's work has been consistently if not systematically overlooked even in discussions of politeness that explicitly appeal to his work. I have no good explanation for this silence; but I suspect that different currents in politeness studies remain beholden to powerful, if largely tacit, linguistic ideologies which deny the presence, or importance, of domination in cooperative, rational, and/or polite communication; or which tends to see societies as harmonious, inspired by communitarian values that place the (anonymous, classless and ungendered) collective over the individual, and social integration.[16]

One significant recent exception to this general neglect is Sara Mills' (2017) recent study, *English Politeness and Class*. Mills proposes to replace Brown and Levinson's Gricean rationalist account of politeness by what she calls a 'materialist discursive approach', inspired by Marxist theoreticians like, most importantly, Louis Althusser; to some extent, this enables her to explicate the role of power in polite linguistic behaviour. Her approach is materialist in its focus on class and class conflict, and on ideology as class-based distortion; it is discursive in that it treats cultural norms as locally negotiated rather than generically given. Thus, it criticizes the widely held assumption that cultures are homogeneous, and rejects oft-made distinctions between individualist and collectivist cultures, and between negative-politeness and positive-politeness cultures, as both reductionist and ideological. Although she does not thematize or define any particular concept of power, she does acknowledge the importance of a generic notion of 'authority'. Only certain speakers, she argues, can judge what counts as polite behaviour, and they can do so 'because of their authoritative position as members of an elite class, institution, or government' (54) – that is, because of their institutionalized power. Although it is far from complete, Mills' analysis thus invites us to further explore social power in linguistic behaviour judged to be polite.

18.6 Conclusion

The examples of speech acts, pornography and politeness discussed above suggest that power remains a sorely undertheorized and inadequately investigated topic in the study of language and language use. Other topics that are currently starting to attract attention – like slurs, hate speech and propaganda – would similarly benefit from a more systematic focus on the factor of power. Attempts to confront power in language use are rendered

---

[16] For a fuller statement of this argument, see Leezenberg (in prep.).

more difficult by the fact that many of the currently dominant frameworks rest on language-ideological assumptions that deny, neutralize or naturalize domination in language, or even actively reproduce the marginalization of dominated groups, thus precluding these matters from even being raised almost from the start. In particular, many approaches turn out to rest on the liberal assumption that power is normally, or should ideally be, absent from communication; or alternatively, that whatever power *is* involved in speech actions is normally legitimate. Others tacitly appeal to a communitarian assumption that social collectives are essentially harmonious, anonymous and consensual. Against such assumptions, we have seen that much if not all linguistic communication involves different forms or modalities of power; that power need not be recognized as legitimate; and that power need not even be recognized as such at all.

A first step in further research, then, might be the further study of linguistic ideologies at work in the currently dominant theoretical frameworks, continuing – and radicalizing – a task initiated by authors like Eelen (2001) and Watts (2002). Furthermore, it is to be hoped that pragmatics scholars will conduct more detailed empirical research aimed at exposing systems of domination and mechanisms of exclusion, especially when they are least recognized for what they are. An equally urgent task is to develop the conceptual tools that do justice to the multifarious forms of power and the various ways in which they function. Although some valuable work has been done on both fronts, many questions – even elementary ones – remain unanswered. These challenges are formidable indeed, but that is no reason to leave this phenomenon out of consideration, or to relegate it to other disciplines. Power is involved in the articulation, and indeed the mutual constitution, of both the linguistic and the social; hence the study of power in linguistic practices should be a prime object of concern in sociopragmatics.

References

Anderson, B. (1991). *Imagined Communities*. 2nd ed. London: Verso.
Austin, J. L. ([1962] 1975). *How to Do Things with Words*. 2nd ed. Edited by J. O. Urmson and M. Sbisà. Cambridge, MA: Harvard University Press.
Beaver, D. and Zeevat, H. (2007). Accommodation. In G. Ramchand and C. Reiss, eds., *The Oxford Handbook of Linguistic Interfaces*. Oxford: Oxford University Press, pp. 503–37.
Bourdieu, P. (1991). *Language and Symbolic Power*. Cambridge: Polity Press.
Bourdieu, P. (1998). *Practical Reason: On the Theory of Action*. Stanford, CA: Stanford University Press.
Bousfield, D. and Locher, M. (eds.). (2008). *Impoliteness in Language: Studies on Its Interplay with Power in Theory and Practice*. Berlin: Mouton de Gruyter.
Brown, P. and Levinson, S. C. (1987). *Politeness: Some Universals in Language Usage*. Cambridge: Cambridge University Press.

Butler, J. (1999). Performativity's Social Magic. In R. Shusterman, ed., *Bourdieu: A Critical Reader*. Oxford: Blackwell, pp. 113–28.

Butler, J. (1997). *Excitable Speech: A Politics of the Performative*. New York: Routledge.

Chomsky, N. (1965). *Aspects of the Theory of Syntax*. Cambridge, MA: MIT Press.

Culpeper, J. (2008). Reflections on impoliteness, relational work and power. In D. Bousfield and M. Locher, eds., *Impoliteness in Language*. Berlin: Mouton de Gruyter, pp. 17–44.

Culpeper, J. (2011). *Impoliteness*. Cambridge: Cambridge University Press.

Durkheim, É. ([1895] 1982). *The Rules of Sociological Method*. Edited by S. Lukes. London: Palgrave Macmillan.

Eelen, G. (2001). *A Critique of Politeness Theories*. Manchester, UK: St Jerome.

Ehlich, K. (1992). On the historicity of politeness. In R. J. Watts, S. Ide and K. Ehlich, eds., *Politeness in Language: Studies in Its History, Theory, and Practice*. Berlin: de Gruyter, pp. 71–108.

Foucault, M. (1978). *The Will to Knowledge*. The History of Sexuality vol. 1. New York: Pantheon Books.

Foucault, M. ([1978] 1994). La philosophie analytique de la politique. In *Dits et écrits*, vol. III. Paris: Gallimard, pp. 538–54.

Gellner, E. (1983). *Nations and Nationalism*. Oxford: Oxford University Press.

Habermas, J. (1986). *The Theory of Communicative Action*. 2 vols. Cambridge: Polity Press.

Ide, S. (1992). On the notion of Wakimae: Toward an integrated framework of linguistic politeness. In *Mosaic of Language*. Mejiro Linguistic Society, pp. 298–305.

Ide, S. (1991). Comments from Outside Europe for *Politeness: Some Universals in Language Usage*. *Sociolinguistica: International Yearbook of European Sociolinguistics*, pp. 160–61.

Jucker, A. (2011). Positive and negative face as descriptive categories in the history of English. *Journal of Historical Pragmatics*, 12, 178–97.

Kroskrity, P. V. (ed.). (2000). *Regimes of Language: Ideologies, Polities, and Identities*. Santa Fe, NM: School of American Research Press.

Langton, R. (2009). *Sexual Solipsism: Philosophical Essays on Pornography and Objectification*. Oxford: Oxford University Press.

Langton, R. (2018). The authority of hate speech. In J. A. O. Gardner, ed., *Oxford Studies in Philosophy of Law*, vol. 3. Oxford: Oxford University Press, pp. 123–52.

Leech, G. (1983). *Principles of Pragmatics*. London: Longmans.

Leech, G. (2007). Politeness: Is there an East–West divide? *Journal of Politeness Research*, 3(2), 167–206.

Leezenberg, M. (2002). Power in communication: Implications for the semantics–pragmatics interface. *Journal of Pragmatics*, 34, 893–908.

Leezenberg, M. (2005). Greek tragedy as impolite conversation: Towards a practice approach in linguistic theory. In S. Marmaridou and M. Drossou, eds., *Reviewing Linguistic Thought: Converging Trends for the Twenty-first Century*. Berlin: Mouton de Gruyter, pp. 191–208.

Leezenberg, M. (2006). Gricean and Confucian pragmatics: A contrastive analysis. *Journal of Foreign Languages*, November 2006, 2–21. (Reprinted in D. F. Shu and K. P. Turner (eds.). (2010). *Contrasting Meaning in Languages of the East and West*. Berlin: Peter Lang, pp. 3–32)

Leezenberg, M. (2013). Power in speech actions. In M. Sbisà and K. P. Turner, eds., *Pragmatics of Speech Actions*, Handbooks of Pragmatics 2. Berlin: Mouton de Gruyter, pp. 263–88.

Leezenberg, M. (in prep.). Politeness as symbolic violence.

Levinson, S. C. (2000). *Presumptive Meanings: The Theory of Generalized Conversational Implicature*. Cambridge, MA: MIT Press.

Lewis, D. (1979). Scorekeeping in a language game. *Journal of Philosophical Logic*, 8, 339–59.

Locher, M. A. (2004). *Power and Politeness in Action: Disagreements in Oral Communication*. Berlin: Mouton de Gruyter.

Locher, M. A. (2006). Polite behaviour within relational work: The discursive approach to politeness. *Multilingua*, 25, 249–67.

McGowan, M. K. (2004). Conversational exercitives: Something else we do with our words. *Linguistics and Philosophy*, 27, 93–111.

McLellan, D. (ed.). (1971). *Marx's Grundrisse*. London: Macmillan.

Marx, K. (1976). *Capital*. Vol. 1. Translated by Ben Fowkes. Harmondsworth, UK: Penguin.

McGowan, M. K. (2009). On pragmatics, exercitive speech acts and pornography. *Lodz Papers in Pragmatics*, 5(1), 133–55.

Mills, S. (2017). *English Politeness and Class*. Cambridge: Cambridge University Press.

Saussure, F., de. ([1916] 1983). *Course in General Linguistics*. Translated by Roy Harris. London: Duckworth.

Sbisà, M. (1984). Illocutionary types. *Journal of Pragmatics*, 8, 93–112.

Searle, J. (1969). *Speech Acts: An Essay in the Philosophy of Language*. Cambridge: Cambridge University Press.

Searle, J. (1975). A classification of illocutionary acts. *Language in Society*, 5(1), 1–23.

Searle, J. (1995). *The Construction of Social Reality*. New York: Penguin Books.

Silverstein, M. (2000). Whorfianism and the linguistic imagination of nationality. In P. V. Kroskrity, ed., *Regimes of Language: Ideologies, Polities, and Identities*. Santa Fe, NM: School of American Research Press, pp. 85–138.

Terkourafi, M. (2001). Politeness in Cypriot Greek: A frame-based approach, unpublished PhD diss., University of Cambridge, Department of Linguistics.

Terkourafi M. (2011). From Politeness$_1$ to Politeness$_2$: Tracking norms of im/politeness across time and space. *Journal of Politeness Research*, 7(2), 159–85.

Watts, R. J., Ide, S. and Ehlich, K. (eds.). (1992). *Politeness in Language: Studies in Its History, Theory, and Practice*. Berlin: de Gruyter.

Watts, R. J. (2002). From polite language to educated language: The re-emergence of an ideology. In R. Watts and P. Trudgill, eds., *Alternative Histories of English*. London: Routledge, pp. 155–72.

Watts, R. J. (2003). *Politeness*. Cambridge: Cambridge University Press.

Weber, M. ([1925] 1978). *Economy and Society: An Outline of Interpretive Sociology*. Berkeley: University of California Press.

Wolf, E. R. (1990). Distinguished lecture: Facing power — old insights, new questions. *American Anthropologist*, 92(3), 586–96.

19

Morality in Sociopragmatics

Pilar Garcés-Conejos Blitvich and Dániel Z. Kádár

19.1 Introduction

This aim of this chapter is to present an overview of sociopragmatic research on morality. Recent sociopragmatic related research has devoted significant attention to the phenomenon of morality and the ways in which it influences language use. In particular, morality has become an important focus of im/politeness research.

In this chapter, we review relevant research on the notion of moral order and its relationship with morality. After we review the extant literature on this latter topic, much of which has been from the perspective of moral psychology, we propose a working definition of morality (see Section 19.2). We further argue that understandings of morality can complement notions of the moral order, or serve in themselves as the basis of insightful analyses of im/politeness and related phenomena, such as in/civility (see Section 19.3).

Importantly, we discuss what, in our view, are important synergies between morality and im/politeness, including their common interest and focus on notions such as Autonomy, Community, Rights, Fairness/ Reciprocity, In-group Loyalty; Authority/Respect; Unity, Hierarchy, Equality, Proportionality, among others. In our illustrative case study, which further challenges the binary conceptions of civility/politeness as good/moral and incivility/impoliteness as bad/immoral (see Watts 1999 among others), we apply Rai and Fiske's (2011) relational taxonomy of moral concepts and relate assessments of in/civility and im/politeness to those concepts (see Section 19.4). As has been previously argued (e.g. Kádár and Márquez Reiter 2015), incivility and impoliteness emerge as more morally salient behaviour than their counterparts civility and politeness. In Section 19.5, we offer some

---

Dániel Z. Kádár would like to acknowledge the funding of the Momentum (Lendület) Research Grant (LP2017/5) of the Hungarian Academy of Sciences.

concluding remarks on the main issues addressed and claims made in this chapter and provide recommendations for future avenues of research on the intersection between morality and sociopragmatics.

19.2 An Overview of the Moral Order and Morality

Since both the moral order and morality are relatively new concepts for sociopragmatics, in the present section we provide a detailed overview of different understandings of these notions. Before we proceed, however, we would like to clarify our understanding of certain key concepts (i.e. norms and values) that come up in the overview below, and indeed throughout the paper, but can be susceptible to multiple interpretations. Along with Frese (2015), we understand norms and values in relation to cultural practices. Thus, we see norms as entities that define how people think and behave in a particular context/interpersonal relationship. In that sense, norms encompass routinized practices.[1] Furthermore, we understand values as more abstract entities. Thus, we see values as being inside the person, whereas norms and cultural practices are seen as largely person-external (see also Chapter 9). One could summarize the difference between norms and values by arguing that values are abstract and are not necessarily tied to behaviour, whereas norms are more specific.

19.2.1 The Moral Order

Garfinkel's (1964) definition of the moral order is grounded in his ethnomethodological approach to social order. For Garfinkel (1967: 35) the moral order consists of "the rule governed activities of everyday life ... perceivedly normal courses of action – familiar scenes of everyday affairs, the world of daily life known in common with others and with others taken for granted". Ethnomethodology focuses on how the existence of social constructs can be evidenced with the aid of interactional data. From this perspective, the existence of the moral order should be made evident through interactional practices. To that end, Garfinkel studied cases drawn from everyday activities, such as interaction among family members, in which routines are highly important. As Garfinkel (1964: 225) states, such scenes are:

> treated by members as the "natural facts of life", [and] are massive facts of the members' daily existence both as a real world and as the product of activities in a real world. They furnish the "fix", the "this is it" to which the waking state returns one, and are the points of departure and return for every modification of the world of daily life that is achieved in play, dreaming, trance, theatre, scientific theorising, or high ceremony.

---

[1] It is relevant to note that recent pragmatic research (Kádár, 2020) distinguishes descriptive norms prescribing routines and injunctive norms influencing evaluations.

Garfinkel demonstrated, with the aid of "breaching experiments", that violations of the routine of an interaction triggered strong reactions. These reactions, in turn, were seen as evidence of everyday activities being regulated by a moral order.

Since then, a body of research has deployed the moral order in a somewhat different sense. For example, social anthropologists such as Wuthnow (1989) and Douglas (2001) anchored their explorations in Goffman's (1963) understanding of the interactional order as morally loaded or "sacred" (for an overview, see Horgan 2019). For their part, Pearce and Littlejohn (1997) saw the moral order as a socially constructed set of understandings we carry from situation to situation, which is moral because it guides our sense of (contextual) "right" and "wrong", and an order because it instantiates itself in patterned actions. In sum, social anthropology research focuses on the relationship between the interactional order and the broader social context and, as a result, it mainly studies interactional contexts not associated with routinized areas of daily life. Thus, this approach views morality as both an interactional and extra-interactional phenomenon. Having an extra-interactional nature, however, does not imply that morality is rigid or "universal" in social anthropological research. In this respect, as Spencer-Oatey and Kádár (2016; 2020) point out, it would be fruitful to engage in interdisciplinary explorations of whether or how moral values, as described by cross-cultural psychologists, manifest themselves in language use.

19.2.2 Morality

In this subsection, we review some of the frameworks applied to the study of morality as a way of unpacking the concept of the moral order.

Morality has been a prominent focus of study in philosophy, sociology, cognitive psychology, theology and anthropology, among other fields. Philosophers like Kant were major influences on sociologists such as Durkheim who is, in turn, credited with inspiring psychologists like Piaget who most moral psychologists (whose work this section will focus on) view as the main precursor to current scholarship in the field (Haidt 2008: 66). In view of the complexity of morality and moral issues in previous research, positing morality as a unified construct, univocally understood and defined, would be erroneous. For example, according to Haidt (2008), the most widely accepted definition of morality in psychology is the one by Turiel (1983). In an attempt to explain the distinction between the social order and the moral order, Turiel (1983: 211–26) defined morality as the individual's prescriptive judgements of justice, rights and welfare affecting how people ought to relate to each other. This definition is a reflection of a strong tradition that connects understandings of morality with issues of harm, rights or justice. Justice ethics, as this tradition is commonly known in moral psychology, represents Western secular views of morality and operates within an ethics of autonomy.

In later research, this interpretation of morality was questioned. One of the first to do so was Gilligan (1982). Gilligan argued that morality is not autonomous and its research should: (1) acknowledge that a morality of care, focused on interpersonal interactions, is a major concern for individuals; and (2) consider a relational conception of the self in connection to others as central to self-definition. Importantly, Plessner Lyons (1983), who conducted empirical research that garnered support for Gillian's theory, concluded that the language of morality is subject to discursive struggle; i.e. she claimed that the language of morality in everyday speech has different meanings for different people and these differences may have behavioural implications. In this respect, the work of Plessner Lyons (1983) raised similar issues to those raised by social anthropologists, such as Wuthnow (1989), regarding moral conflicts in the context of research on the moral order.

Turiel's work was also questioned from a cross-cultural perspective.[2] Turiel and his colleagues argued that particular rules may vary from culture to culture but in *all* cultures moral issues involve matters of harm, rights or justice, that is, there is a sense of core moral values that dominate human lives across cultures (Schwartz 1994). However, cross-cultural psychologists saw morality as culturally variable and as going beyond harm, rights and justice; this strand of research raises the problem that the concept of "moral norm" – i.e. how one is supposed to behave in a particular situation – can neither be strictly separated from "ideology" (Shweder et al. 1997: 140–42) nor from the moral values of the individual. For example, Shweder et al. (1997) claimed there are three codes of moral thought and discourse which different cultures elaborate and rely on to different degrees:

- Ethics of autonomy: conceptualizes the self as an individual structure and sees moral regulations as the way to increase choice, autonomy and control. The ethics of autonomy lies at the core of the legal systems and moral philosophies of many secular societies.
- Ethics of community: conceptualizes the self as holding an office or a role in a larger interdependent and collective organization. It requires duty, respect, obedience to authority and actions consistent with one's gender, social status, age or other elements of one's social role.
- Ethics of divinity: conceptualizes the self as a spiritual entity who seeks to avoid pollution and achieve purity and sanctity. Within this code, acts that are degrading to one's spiritual self are rejected even if they result in no harm to others. This moral code and its emphasis on bodily practices tends to be perceived as alien by members of modern urbanized societies.

---

[2] To date, research on morality in sociopragmatics has been limited mainly to what are, it could be argued, Western understandings and perceptions of this concept, but see Ran and Zhao (2018) for an important step toward a more inclusive view.

Inspired by Shweder et al.'s (1997) work, Haidt and colleagues (see among others Graham et al. 2009; Haidt and Graham 2007; Haidt and Joseph 2004, 2008) formulated the Moral Foundations Theory as an extension of these three moral codes. Adopting a more evolutionary, phylogenetic perspective, Moral Foundations Theory posits that there are five innately prepared foundations to our moral psychology, each of them responding to an adaptive challenge. These foundations and their challenges are as follows:

(1) Harm/Care – protect and care for young, vulnerable or injured kin.
(2) Fairness/Reciprocity – reap benefits of dyadic cooperation with non-kin.
(3) In-group/Loyalty – reap benefits of group cooperation.
(4) Authority/Respect – negotiate hierarchy, defer selectively.
(5) Purity/Sanctity – avoid microbes and parasites.

(Haidt and Joseph 2007: 382)

Moral Foundations Theory does not argue these foundations are hardwired into the human brain, but rather that our brain is *prepared* for them, i.e. organized ahead of social experience. Although it has been strongly problematized (for a challenge of the theory's basic tenets see Suhler and Churchland 2011 and Haidt and Joseph 2011), Moral Foundations Theory is still a work in active progress.

What can be garnered from this brief overview is that morality has been, for the most part, seen as operating within overarching principles or foundations which are both culture-based and universal.

> The view that morality is, in any sense, universal was challenged by Rai and Fiske's (2011, 2012, 2016) socio-relational approach to moral psychology. Their Relationship Regulation Theory (RRT, henceforth) sees itself as extending the Moral Foundations Theory of Shweder et al. (1997) by grounding those foundations in a theory of social relationships and predicting when and how people will rely on one foundation over another. According to Rai and Fiske, moral intuitions are defined "by the particular types of social relationships in which they occur. In its strongest form, a social-relational approach to moral psychology posits that the moral status of actions cannot be determined independent of the social-relational contexts in which they take place. Rather, any given action will be judged as right, just, fair, honorable, pure, virtuous, or morally correct when it occurs in some social-relational contexts and will be judged as wrong when it occurs in other social-relational contexts" (Rai and Fiske 2011: 57).

Thus, judgements about morality are relationship and context bound rather the result of universal principles that influence the judgements of individuals as autonomous entities. This implies that the primordial function of morality is to sustain social relationships. RRT posits that there are four key moral motives that drive individuals to generate and maintain social relations.

- Unity: directed towards supporting the integrity of social groupings guided by a sense of responsibility and common fate.
- Hierarchy: guided to creating and maintaining linear ranking in social groups. Subordinates are motivated to respect, obey and pay deference to superiors, while superiors feel pastoral responsibility for their subordinates and are motivated to lead, guide, direct and protect them.
- Equality, directed towards enforcing even balance and in-kind reciprocity in social relations.
- Proportionality: "directed towards calculating in accord with ratios or rates for otherwise distinct goods to ensure that rewards or punishment for each party are proportional to their costs, contribution, effort, merit or guilt" (64).

Rai and Fiske (2011: 58) argued that these moral motives – which regulate social relationships – are universal but different social-relational models influence how they influence the behaviour and judgements of individuals, social groups and cultures in any given domain of life. Furthermore, in the authors' views, there may be both individual and ideological variation as regards which moral motif or value is important in a particular interpersonal context. This will be illustrated in the discussion of the data analysed in our case study.

Before concluding this section, let us propose a tentative definition of morality, building on the theoretical backdrop we have reviewed. Morality is, in our view, constructed through language use when we attribute (non)linguistic good or bad behaviour to others. However, these are usually non-binary evaluations, as they often occur along a cline. (For an overview, see Schwartz 1970.) Furthermore, these are situated evaluations regarding others' choices that are never independent of the practice and the type of relationships we are involved in and are guided by overarching principles that can be subject to discursive struggle. This is of interest to the pragmatician as it is evident there is a strong correlation between morality and the phenomenon of valence (Leach et al. 2007), i.e. language use and evaluation are often loaded with implicit or explicit references to moral values, norms, and ideologies (Kádár and Ning 2019).[3]

19.2.3 Morality and the Moral Order

Although the moral order and morality have not often been used on a par in sociopragmatics (but see Kádár et al. 2019 for a discussion of the interconnections between morality, the moral order and language aggression), it seems appropriate to provide a working definition of how we envision the

---

[3] Regarding ideology, we agree with van Dijk (1998) and Verschueren (2012), who see it in fundamentally discursive terms. More specifically, van Dijk (1998) argues that ideology is the basis of the social representations of a group, its functions in terms of social relations between groups, and its reproduction as enacted by discourse.

relationship between these concepts. As we have mentioned, some researchers have applied to their analysis the concept of the moral order, defined as a "socially constructed set of understandings we carry with us from situation to situation" (Domenici and Littlejohn, cited in Culpeper 2011: 38). The main reason behind this choice is that the moral order can never be separated from interaction, whereas morality is more abstract, in the sense that it guides both individuals and interactions.

As a corollary of foregrounding the moral order, one may argue that the primary way for morality "to exert a huge influence on the way people function in society" is "interactionally constituted moral orders" (Parvaresh and Tayebi 2018: 93); i.e. one may regard the moral order as a situated manifestation of morality. In other words, while morality and moral values are thought to be universal concepts, yet subject to cross-cultural variation (see Spencer-Oatey and Kádár 2020), moral orders are best viewed as practice-based instantiations of morality.

19.3 The Interface of Im/morality and Im/politeness

As discussed, morality and especially the related concept of moral order have become particularly important in recent im/politeness research (e.g. see among others Culpeper 2011; Davies 2018; Graham 2018; Georgakopoulou and Vasilaki 2018; Jay 2018; Kádár and Haugh 2013; Kádár and Fukushima 2018; Kádár et al. 2019; Márquez Reiter and Haugh 2019; Márquez Reiter and Orthaber 2018; Sinkeviciute 2018; Spencer-Oatey and Xing 2019; Parvaresh and Tayebi 2018). Important in this respect is the publication of two special issues on the interconnections between morality and im/politeness (*Internet Pragmatics*, 1.2 and the *Journal of Language Aggression and Conflict*, 7.1, published in 2018 and 2019, respectively). In view of this growing interest, Xie (2018) described what seems to be a "moral turn" in im/politeness research that explores the link between evaluations of linguistic forms and behaviour and the moral order or morality. Common to all this work is the fundamental influence attributed to the moral order on the evaluation (and also the production) of im/politeness.

A case in point is Culpeper (2011: 37) who relates the violation of the norms of social behaviour, via impoliteness, for example, to attributions of immorality. He further argues that morality can be understood as a "moral order" (38). Along the same lines, Kádár and Haugh (2013) state that evaluations of im/politeness are "rooted in the expectations that constitute the moral order" (94). Similarly, Haugh (2013: 57), discusses how "social actions and pragmatic meanings are not simply the means and basis for accomplishing the multitude of interactions through which we constitute our daily lives, they are also 'inexorably moral'" (see also Kádár and Haugh 2013). For its part, the social anthropological approach to the moral order mentioned in the previous section also seems to be appealing to im/politeness scholars, fundamentally because it is interested in morally loaded contexts and often uses morality as a lay concept. For instance, Kádár and Márquez Reiter (2015: 246) studied instances of bystander intervention in public places where debates on how an interaction should unfold are anchored in popular (extra-interactional) notions of what counts as morally right/acceptable behaviour in public. The social anthropological interpretation of the moral order also recurs in Kádár (2017) who brings together im/politeness, ritual and the moral order and presents the most elaborate analysis of morality vis-à-vis im/politeness to date.

Importantly, work that relates im/politeness and morality suggests that insights from disciplines that have looked at morality in depth, such as social psychology or philosophy would be particularly useful to better understanding im/politeness. For instance, Spencer-Oatey and Kádár (2016) see the application of insights from social psychology as useful in unveiling the moral foundations of im/politeness evaluations (see also Kádár 2017). Without resorting to the use of other concepts such as motivation (for an overview, see Hardy and Carlo 2005); it may be difficult to study certain pragmatic behaviours, such as moral panics (Moulinou 2019). Additionally, if a person fails to give over their seat to a pregnant mom on a crowded bus and this becomes an incident (e.g. it gets aired on TV or becomes viral online), people may become psychologically and socially motivated to talk about the incident, go after the perpetrator on online forums, etc. (Horgan 2019).

Although scholarly interest in the relationship between im/politeness and morality, as we have seen above, is relatively recent, in/civility has often been theorized in moral terms. Despite their conceptual proximity, with a few relatively recent exceptions (Lakoff 2005; Mills 2009; Papacharissi 2004; Sifianou 2019; Terkourafi et al. 2018) we find little cross-pollination between research on in/civility and im/politeness – to the point that major linguistic projects dedicated to civility have been carried out entirely outside of the politeness paradigm (e.g. Truss 2005), and vice-versa in the bulk of linguistic politeness research.[4] Another important exception to this trend has been in historical pragmatics (e.g. Jucker 2012; Werkhofer 1992) in which politeness and civility are often discussed together in the context of European data; however, this strand of research predominantly aligns with the linguistic politeness paradigm and usually pursues interest in civility as a historical concept. Indeed, as Sifianou (2019) states, (in)civility seems to be the preferred term in many disciplines such as sociology, philosophy, and political science whereas im/politeness scholars hardly ever mention the term. It is beyond the scope of this chapter to theorize on the similarities/differences between civility and

---

[4] Interestingly the concepts of 'politeness' and 'civility' are used jointly in fields like history (e.g. Peltonen 2003); however, such research does not usually capitalize on pragmatics, or the linguistic politeness paradigm.

im/politeness (for a detailed discussion, see Sifianou 2019; Terkourafi et al. 2018). Nonetheless, it is worth noting that Sifianou (2019: 59) who argues that "in/civility is a broader concept than im/politeness in that it includes not only verbal behavior, which is the major terrain of im/politeness, but also much that is non-verbal".

What is relevant for the present discussion is that morality is seen by many scholars to be at the heart of conceptions of civility. Billante and Saunders (2004: 33–4) argue that the fact that civility requires us to show respect for people we do not know is what invests it with a strong moral quality. Thus, they characterize civility as a moral value: it is morally better to be civil than uncivil. Along the same lines, Pearson et al. (2001) claim that being uncivil is immoral: an indication of moral decay. Moreover, citing Carter (1998), they describe civility as the way through which we display our humanity. Calhoun (2000: 225), for her part, contends that "the function of civility is to communicate basic moral attitudes of respect, tolerance, and considerateness". Hwang et al. (2018) discuss moral indignation (which includes anger, disgust, and contempt) and link it to uncivil commentary. Moral indignation is a reaction to the violation of social and interpersonal norms, i.e. others' failure to adhere to the moral code (see e.g. Márquez Reiter and Orthaber 2018; Moulinou 2014).

The notion that there is a fundamental relationship between politeness and morality also has a background in philosophy. Buss (1999) relates good [verbal] manners to the maintenance of a person's dignity. Buss' good manners are equivalent to the verbal realization of politeness. Crucially, she disagrees with Hume and others who view morals and good manners as two different things, by arguing that not only are good manners essential to treating people with respect, indeed the moral significance of good manners is that "appearing to respect people is essential to *really* respecting them" (805). In this view, politeness is a manifestation of morality as there is no difference between being polite/appropriate and abiding by moral codes. Rawls (1987: 140) expressed similar beliefs when she argued that it is "not only moral, but also prudent to act in accordance with the working consensus" because violating it would upset the interaction upon which the maintenance of self depends. Accepting this line of argumentation implies that morality does not only emerge on the level of how people talk about im/politeness (i.e. the *metapragmatics* of politeness; see e.g. Kádár and Haugh 2013), but also at the level of how im/politeness is verbally realized.

An interesting exception, from a moral order perspective, would be to think of situations in which one expresses moral indignation or anger (Kádár and Márquez Reiter 2015; Kádár 2017) via impoliteness or other types of conflictual language. In such cases, the moral order of the interaction (see Section 19.2) may call for rudeness. In other cases, such as complaining phone calls, the moral order of the interaction may be polite but face threatening. This claim coincides with the approach to im/politeness that sees it as a phenomenon that comes into existence vis-à-vis interactional evaluative moments (Eelen 2001). This relationship between im/politeness and morality also accords with the sociopragmatic phenomenon of moral agency (Kádár et al. 2019); i.e. language users tend to frame their own and others' interactional behaviour in terms of attributed moral decisions/responsibility (even though the person who is evaluated as im/moral may not have actually made a moral *decision* in the particular instance of language use being evaluated). For instance, offences often trigger morally loaded evaluations anchored in cruelty. While moral agency is not always relevant in social interaction, it becomes so in certain moments, such as in conflictual scenarios, or instances when interactants evaluate, positively or negatively, the behaviour of a third party.

An intriguing question for sociopragmatics is whether all attributed *decisions* in interpersonal interaction can be described as moral. Irrespective of whether the attributed norms of social behaviour (and the related moral order) were trespassed intentionally (i.e. whether there has been a *decision* at all), it remains unclear whether, at the level of im/politeness evaluations, such trespasses were meant to be morally associated. To answer this question, Churchland's (2006) study is relevant. As she argues,

> within the huge domain of practical decision-making, no sharp line demarcates the moral from the non-moral issues. Instead, decisions fall on a continuum, with prototypically non-moral decisions at one end (e.g. Should I have grapefruit or bananas for breakfast?), and prototypically moral decisions at the other end (e.g. How should we punish a juvenile capital offender?). (4)

Indeed, it may be difficult to reliably demarcate morally loaded and non-moral im/politeness evaluations, mainly because of the attributed nature of morality discussed above. As a result, im/polite behaviour tends to be perceived within the frame of moral agency. Potential exceptions to this may be morally complex scenarios, such as cases of institutional discourse, in which sociopragmatic behaviour is not individualistic. In those scenarios, linguistic behaviour cannot be evaluated purely in terms of agency (see e.g. Archer 2011 on the relativity of impoliteness in legal settings).

Another point of connectivity between morality and im/politeness is their similar evolution from being theorized in terms of universal principles (Brown and Levinson 1987; Haidt and Joseph 2007, among others) to being seen as context bound assessments, tied to relationships and practices (Locher and Watts 2005; Mills 2003; Rai and Fiske 2011; Watts 1989) . As seen above, traditional approaches such as the one postulated by Turiel (1983) defined morality as the prescriptive judgements of justice, rights and welfare affecting how people ought to relate to each other. For his part, Durkheim ([1925] 1973) mainly saw morality as a system of rules and maxims that prescribe to individual ways of behaving in certain situations. More recent approaches, such as Rai and Fiske (2011), however, argue that the moral status of actions cannot be determined independent of the socio-relational contexts in which they take place. According to this view, it is difficult to claim that morality exists outside the social practices wherein relationships and identities are constructed (Garcés-Conejos Blitvich 2010, 2013; Haugh 2013). Practices raise certain expectations of morality associated with the relational identities constructed therein that guide participants in their behaviour. These expectations, nonetheless, are open to discursive struggle just as norms themselves, which also applies to im/politeness. If one agrees that politeness is the verbal realization of morality, then this is to be expected as evaluations of what counts as politeness are always subject to discursive struggle (Eelen 2001).

Another powerful reason to bring conceptualizations of morality into the study of im/politeness is the fact that many of the concepts used to study and describe morality (Autonomy, Community, Rights, Fairness/Reciprocity, In-group Loyalty; Authority/Respect; Unity, Hierarchy, Equality, Proportionality, etc.: see, among others, Haidt and Joseph 2007; Rai and Fiske 2011) resonate and overlap with concepts used to theorize and describe im/politeness (especially with those concepts found in im/politeness approaches, such as Brown and Levinson's, who talk about negative face/politeness, related to Autonomy, Hierarchy, Respect), positive face (In-group Loyalty, Community, Reciprocity, Unity). Again, if we assume a primordial relationship between the two, this is to be expected.

In studies of morality, there is a sense that morality is related to the understanding and cognitive evolution of the self (Kohlberg 1969; Gilligan 1982). Im/politeness is essentially related to the presentation of the self (Goffman 1956). The difference between scholarship in morality and im/politeness, however, is that in those descriptions of the self espoused by morality scholars, there is a sense that self is a unitary entity. However, im/politeness as above has experienced both a discursive and a practice turn (Eelen 2001; Garcés-Conejos Blitvich 2013; Haugh 2013; Locher and Watts 2005). From a discursive or practice view, the self is seen as a conglomerate of co-constructed roles or identities. It is the agent who is at the heart of practice (Reckwitz 2002) and the agent can be instantiated in multiple co-constructed roles, identities, and faces (researcher, teacher, parent, customer, friend, boss etc.), whose moral expectations may vary depending on the practice the agent is engaged in. This is yet another argument in favour of situating morality in practices.

19.4 Case Study

This case study analyses one of (many) recent instances in which national conversation in the United States has focused on in/civility. In/civility, besides being the term of choice in disciplines such as sociology, law, communications, is also widely used in the US media and in lay usages by the public or politicians (Mills 2009). As mentioned, along with Sifianou

(2019), we do not see politeness and civility as being one and the same thing. Civility seems to be an umbrella term that covers a broader spectrum of behaviour (including both verbal and non-verbal communication), whereas politeness tends to circumscribe the relevant verbal manifestations. Thus, politeness is part of what it is referred to as civility. Therefore, and importantly for our study, claims of uncivil behaviour, as the ones discussed in this case study, may include or be exclusively about impolite (i.e. verbal) behaviour.

We have also seen, in Section 19.3, how in/civility has almost always been described as imbued with im/morality: civility is seen as moral, incivility as immoral. Based on the relationship established above, then if civility is seen as moral, so is politeness; if incivility is seen as immoral, so is impoliteness. In our case study, we will see, however, that the unidirectional relation between morality–politeness/civility and immorality–impoliteness/incivility is not straightforward (for similar arguments, see Sell 1992; Watts 1999).

As the moral order has often been used as an analytical conceptual tool to research im/politeness (but see Parvaresh 2019; Spencer-Oatey and Kádár 2016; Spencer-Oatey and Xing 2019 for an application of Haidt and colleagues' work on moral foundations and Schwartz et al.'s 2020 basic values), our goal here is to show how Rai and Fiske's (2011) RRT that focuses on morality and the four key moral motives (namely Unity, Hierarchy, Equality and Proportionality) that drive individuals to generate and maintain social relations can also be useful when applied to the study of im/politeness or related construals. Besides incorporating insights of previous theories, Rai and Fiske's (2011) RRT is appealing to us and appropriate for our data for its socio-relational orientation, specifically for their view that the moral status of actions cannot be determined independent of the social-relational contexts in which they take place

In the US digital public sphere, morality[5] has been an important focus of discussion since Donald Trump was a presidential candidate and later elected in 2016, focusing on whether he has the moral standards expected of the highest office in the land. By association, those who work or have worked with and for him are not immune to being accused of lacking morals, i.e. standards of behaviour or beliefs regarding what is/is not acceptable for them to do.

In June 2018, former White House Press Secretary Sarah Huckabee Sanders was having a quiet lunch with a small party at a restaurant in Lexington, a small town in rural Virginia. When the staff recognized her,

---

[5] Issues of morality and religion have traditionally played a more explicit role in public and political life in the US, especially in conservative politics (representing the US as a homogenous, mono-cultural society would be erroneous, however), than in other parts of the world, Europe for example. In the past, public assessments of moral and religious issues were in a way top down (institutional), although they may have also represented a general sentiment or, at least, the sentiment of some part of the population. The demotic turn (Turner 2010) associated with digital technologies has allowed bottom up manifestations of understandings of morality to reach the public sphere in an unprecedented number.

they informed the owner, Stephanie Wilkinson. In her own words, Wilkinson believed that "Sarah Huckabee Sanders work[ed] in the service of an *'inhumane and unethical'* administration. That she publicly defend[ed] the president's cruelest policies, and that that [could] not stand". And although, as a business owner she did not like confrontation and wanted her business to thrive: "This feels like the moment in our democracy when people have to make uncomfortable actions and decisions to uphold their *morals*" (our emphasis). After consulting with staff, she told Sanders she would like to have a private word and asked her to leave the restaurant. Sanders and her party left quietly; however, the next day, Sanders posted the following on her official twitter account: "Last night I was told by the owner of Red Hen in Lexington, VA to leave because I work for @POTUS and I politely left. Her actions say far more about her than about me. I always do my best to treat people, including those I disagree with, respectfully and will continue to do so".

Making this incident public online triggered a national discussion regarding incivility (although we can see that it clearly relates to impoliteness in the verbal sense discussed above). The debate, mostly divided along ideological lines, was between those who saw Wilkinson's behaviour as an unjustified act of incivility and those who agreed that "desperate times call for desperate measures"; thus, her actions were justified as a way to uphold her moral values in the face of a corrupt and immoral administration. Indeed, a day after the incident was made public, Congresswoman Maxine Waters (Democrat-California) encouraged Americans to publicly shame all members of the Trump administration whenever they appeared in public. Once again, a moral issue, the welfare of immigrant children separated from their parents and left in camps at the border, was at stake. The members of the Trump administration, Waters claimed, needed to be harassed into breaking their alliance with the president and telling him "No, I can't hang with you. This is wrong. This is unconscionable, and we can't keep doing this to children".

Although this discussion focuses on a small number of examples, it is worth exploring user-generated comments triggered by an article in the *New York Post* (n#24,300) about the Sanders' incident[6] in order to get a sense of first order evaluations regarding the connection between im/politeness/in/civility and im/morality. What these comments indicate is the situatedness of in/civility, im/politeness and im/morality. Whereas many scholars have argued that incivility is necessarily immoral (Pearson et al. 2001, among others), this case study brings to the fore the fact that citizens may resort to uncivil, impolite behaviour in order to uphold moral values (see Kádár and Márquez Reiter 2015 for similar conclusions regarding the function of impoliteness in this respect); here, it is civility and politeness

---

[6] www.washingtonpost.com/news/local/wp/2018/06/23/why-a-small-town-restaurant-owner-asked-sarah-huckabee-sanders-to-leave-and-would-do-it-again/?noredirect=onandutm_term=.3223aa127f15

that are not moral, but seen as complicit of an immoral administration. This was the position of the poster in example 1 who implicitly agreed with Wilkinson's decision to ask Sanders to leave as s/he – a restaurant owner, too – also refuses service to patrons who espouse ideologies detrimental to minorities, as many in the Trump administration do, in her/his view. Refusing service, which may be considered (im)polite, is seen as a way to resist bigotry and racism.

Example 1[7]
As a small business owner, all I can say is I reserve the right to refuse service to anyone who exposes or supports a philosophical idiology of bigotry, predudice or exclusion based on nationality, race, skin colour, sex, creed, sexual orientation or disability.
Many individuals in this administration fit that description. (or anyone with a red MAGA hat)

Furthermore, it was argued, as in examples 2 and 3, that you cannot act immorally and debase public discourse and expect civility and politeness in return. Again, incivility was seen as just retribution for the administration's past and on-going discourse and policies:

Example 2
Expect nothing less, or more, depending on your outlook. in the Age of Trump. 'As ye sow, so shall ye reap'. Trump and Sanders have debased political discussion and polite discourse to crass, barroom language and the type of boorish behaviour common at a drunken frat party. And then they expect civility in return? I honestly don't agree with the owner's decision, but I understand the impetus, and further see the 'outrage' on the right as hypocritical at best.

Example 3
In normal times, this might have been considered extreme and rude. However, given the vileness and absolute corruption of this administration, I applaud the owner of this restaurant. We're way beyond differing viewpoints. If you support trump you have no soul. I hope this trend continues. Its' that bad. This is what trump has brought our country to.

As is the case with im/politeness (Garcés-Conejos Blitvich 2009, 2010, 2012; Lorenzo-Dus et al. 2011), who does what to whom, along with the diverse ideologies of those judging the same action will render it, in usually polarized views, either moral or immoral, polite or impolite. Furthermore, as opposite sides claim, it is always the other side that exhibits the less moral behaviour. Therefore, even if you can accuse a Republican or a Democrat of acting uncivilly and not having high moral standards, examples of much

---

[7] All examples have been left as they appeared in the original thread. Spelling, grammatical or other types of errors have not been corrected.

worse transgressions by the other side can be found that result in the action being evaluated as "mild", as we can see in examples 4 and 5:

Example 4
These PC, liberal, born again losers don't get it ... I love it when they praise the Red Hen for morals and standing up for what's right. Meanwhile, democrats believe in abortion and homosexuality, which are totally against what Christianity stands for. But they know everything about morality.
I also think the Women's Rights movement has gone too far. If these politically correct ignoramuses want to learn anything from the Red Hen, they need to "count their chickens before they hatch".

Example 5
Republicans drive cars into crowds of protesters, blow up women's health care clinics, and kill OB/GYN doctors, in addition to discriminating against minorities and LGBTQ people on a regular basis. Wilkinson's actions were pretty mild in comparison.

Yet, for many others, making a call on Wilkinson's action was not easy. People showed their understanding, as we see in comment 6, but could not offer complete support. This comes to show that moral evaluations are not necessarily binary (right/wrong) but tinted by many shades of grey and seen as part of a situated cline:

Example 6
I'm torn.
On the one hand, I thin that public establishments should serve everyone. Including gay couples who want wedding cakes.[8]
On the other hand, the Trump people are teetering on the edge of crimes against humanity.
– sigh – [sic]

We also find a quite nuanced response in example 7 whose poster, although finding Wilkinson's asking Sanders to leave the restaurant immoral and impolite, vowed to support her business anytime s/he visits Virginia:

Example 7
As much as I loathe Trump, the owner of the restaurant and staff were wrong in the treatment of Ms Sanders and her friends. The first assumption was the Sanders' party were all of one mind politically. Suppose this was not the case. People who were not morally bankrupt would have been treated the same as if they were ... What the Stephanie did was morally questionable – no matter what her actual intention was. It was bad

---

[8] This refers to the case of a gay couple who were refused service by a bakery whose owner was against gay marriage. This case went all the way up to the US Supreme Court who ruled, by a narrow margin, in favour of the baker.

manners, but perhaps forgivable ... That said, if I am in Virginia – I'll make a beeline for Lexington ... [sic]

This short discussion and the wide range of views expressed make clear that, much like im/politeness, im/morality is subject to discursive struggle and tied to personal ideology. However, the practices agents are engaged in, along with the expectations regarding obligations and behaviour associated with certain roles and identities (restaurant owner, member of government administration etc.) and the intersubjective relations between those and other roles and identities (customer, citizens, voters) are key. Behaviours are assessed on the bases of expectations attached to practices and to specific relations.

Following Rai and Fiske (2011), we can also see moral motives at work in this discussion. For example, Unity (which is geared towards supporting the integrity of groups by a sense of responsibility and common fate) seems to be quite relevant. In this respect, both Wilkinson and Sanders acted in accordance with the ideological beliefs of the groups they associate with. Some members of Wilkinson's staff belonged to minorities that have been targeted by policies of the Trump administration that had been defended publicly by Sanders. Wilkinson conferred with her staff and made the decision to ask Sanders to leave thus preserving the unity of her in-group.

The principle of Hierarchy may have had a role here as well: as the owner she felt a pastoral responsibility to protect her subordinates, members of minority groups wronged by Trump and other members of his administration. Sanders, in her tweet, also positioned herself as preserving Unity with Trump and his administration. For their part, the posters supported the Unity of their in-groups by claiming that it was always the other (Republicans or Democrats) who were less civil, and had lower moral standards. Furthermore, a substantial part of the discussion focuses on the motive of Proportionality (calculating rewards and punishments for different parties proportional to their costs, contributions, effort, merit or guilt) and Equality (pondering reciprocity, what actions require retaliation and what retaliatory behaviour should be). Posters argued for and against Wilkinson's having asked Sanders to leave and related their positions to their views on whether this retribution was justified, in view of past actions and policies put in place by the Trump administration and Sanders' public support of those.

With this brief case study, we hope to have shown the applicability of morality-based frameworks can further our understanding of evaluations of im/politeness and in/civility and fact that just as is the case for im/politeness, what constitutes moral or immoral behaviour is subject to discursive struggle and should be understood along a cline within situated practice.

19.5 Discussion and Future Directions

In the present chapter, we have provided an overview of the phenomenon of morality in sociopragmatic research. As we have argued, a growing body of current sociopragmatic research approaches the role of morality in language use by using (various interpretations of) the concept of the moral order, drawn from the ethnomethodological and sociological disciplines. This is certainly key, as the moral order connects pragmatic research on interpersonal and interactional data with the well-established ethnomethodological and sociological traditions. We have also shown, briefly in Section 19.3, that the moral order becomes relevant to discussions on a variety of morality-related issues, such as whether im/politeness is the verbal realization of in/civility.

Furthermore, we have maintained that morality as a concept (and phenomenon) is highly relevant to sociopragmatics. It may be the case that answers to questions such as, (1) Why is morality so important in interpersonal interaction? and (2) What are the reasons why a specific behaviour is judged as im/moral in a particular context? may reside outside of the boundaries of language understood in structural terms. However, those answers are always connected to the genres and discourses that situate language use. In this respect, the multidisciplinary nature of academic inquiry into morality is crucial, since it is often difficult to assess issues of morality regarding language use without resorting to the application of postulates from social and cross-cultural psychology and sociology, among others. As an example, in this paper, we have mostly drawn insights from moral psychology. We have also argued that morality is such an fundamental part of language use that no sociopragmatic approach – in particular, im/politeness frameworks – can afford to ignore it. As Section 19.4 has illustrated, our daily lives and assessments of in/appropriate interpersonal relationships are imbued with morality.

It is important to reiterate here that sociopragmatic research on morality is in its infancy, and there are various major areas awaiting exploration:

- While research on morality is a multidisciplinary area, little attempt has been made by other fields to bring pragmatic postulates into their research traditions. However, the study of meticulously transcribed and analysed interactional data would certainly contribute to further research in other disciplines, as it has been the case of discursive psychology
- More research needs to be devoted to the interface between im/morality, in/civility, and im/politeness. While in the present chapter (Section 19.3), we have briefly examined the relationship among these phenomena, further research is needed. Such research could open up new academic vistas. For instance, it may be a useful uptake to incorporate the concept

of respect – which has been a central phenomenon in academic work on civility (e.g. Carter 1998) – into the analytic repertoire of im/politeness research (see e.g. Placencia 2001, 2010).
- Further academic work that theorizes im/politeness and morality through the lens of the moral order is still needed. It remains to be seen whether the various approaches to the moral order can be brought together in the attempt to *moralize* sociopragmatics.
- Finally, more cross-cultural and intercultural pragmatic research needs to target issues of morality and language use. While cross-cultural psychology and other related fields have extensively studied cultural variation, little is currently known about how cultural differences may impact on the interface between im/politeness and im/morality (but see Spencer-Oatey and Xing 2019).

The significance of these and other potential questions demonstrates that morality is a highly relevant phenomenon for sociopragmatics to delve into. We see our chapter as a step in that direction.

References

Archer, D. (2011). Facework and im/politeness across legal contexts: An introduction. *Journal of Politeness Research*, 7(1), 1–19.

Beer, D. (2009). Power through the algorithm? Participatory web cultures and the technological unconscious. *New Media and Society*, 11(6), 985–1002.

Billante, N. and Saunders, P. (2004). Why civility matters. *Policy*, 18(3), 32–36.

Brown, P. and Levinson, S. (1987). *Politeness: Some Universals in Language Usage*. Cambridge: Cambridge University Press.

Buss, S. (1999). Appearing respectful: The moral significance of manners. *Ethics*, 109(4), 795–826.

Calhoun, C.. (2000). The virtue of civility. *Philosophy and Public Affairs*, 29(3), 251–75.

Carter, S. L. (1998). *Civility: Manners, Morals, and the Etiquette of Democracy*. New York: Basic Books.

Churchland, P. (2006). Moral decision-making and the brain. In J. Illes, ed., *Neuroethics: Defining the Issues in Theory, Practice, and Policy*. Cambridge: Cambridge University Press, pp. 1–16.

Culpeper, J. (2011). *Impoliteness: Using Language to Cause Offence*. Cambridge: Cambridge University Press.

Culpeper, J., Haugh, M. and Kádár, D. (2017). Introduction. In J. Culpeper, M. Haugh and D. Kádár, eds., *The Palgrave Handbook of Linguistic (Im)Politeness*. Basingstoke, UK: Palgrave Macmillan, pp. 1–8.

Davies, B. (2018). Evaluating evaluations: What different types of metapragmatic behaviour can tell us about participants' understandings of the moral order. *Journal of Politeness Research*, 14(1), 121–51.

Douglas, M. (2001). *Implicit Meanings*. 2nd ed. London: Routledge.
Durkheim, É. ([1925] 1973). *Moral Education*. Translated by E. Wilson and H. Schnurer. New York: The Free Press.
Eelen, G. (2001). *A Critique of Politeness Theories*. Manchester, UK: St. Jerome.
Garcés-Conejos Blitvich, P. (2010). A genre approach to the study of im-politeness. *International Review of Pragmatics*, 2(1), 46–94.
Garcés-Conejos Blitvich, P. (2013). Face, identity, and im/politeness: Looking backwards, moving forward – From Goffman to Practice Theory, *Journal of Politeness Research*, 9(1), 1–33.
Garcés-Conejos Blitvich, P., Bou-Franch, P. and Lorenzo-Dus, N. (2010). A genre-approach to im-politeness in a Spanish TV talk show: Evidence from corpus-based analysis, questionnaires and focus groups. *Intercultural Pragmatics*, 7(4), 689–723.
Georgakopoulou, A. and Vasilaki, M. (2018). The personal and/as the political: Small stories and impoliteness in online discussions of the Greek crisis. *Internet Pragmatics*, 1(2), 215–40.
Graham, S. L. (2018). Impoliteness and the moral order in online gaming. *Internet Pragmatics*, 1(2), 303–28.
Frese, M. (2015). Cultural practices, norms, and values. *Journal of Cross-Cultural Psychology*, 46(10), 1327–30.
Garcés-Conejos Blitvich, P. (2009). Impoliteness and identity in the American news media: The 'culture wars'. *Journal of Politeness Research*, 5(2), 273–303.
Garcés-Conejos Blitvich, P. (2012). 'Politics, "lies" and YouTube: A genre approach to assessments of im/politeness on Obama's 9/9/2009 presidential address'. In L. Fernández-Amaya, M. Hernández López, R. Gómez Morón, M. Padilla Cruz, M. Mejias Borrero and M. Relinque Barranca, eds., *New Perspectives on (Im)politeness and Interpersonal Communication*. Newcastle, UK: Cambridge Scholars, pp. 62–90.
Garfinkel, H. (1964). Studies of the routine grounds of everyday activities. *Social Problems*, 11(3), 225–50.
Garfinkel, H. (1967). *Studies in Ethnomethodology*. Englewood Cliffs, NJ.: Prentice Hall.
Gilligan, C. (1982). *In a Different Voice*. Cambridge, MA: Harvard University Press.
Goffman, E. (1956). *The Presentation of Self in Everyday Life*. New York: Doubleday.
Goffman, E. (1963). *Behaviour in Public Places: Notes on the Social Organization of Gatherings*. New York: Free Press.
Graham, J., Haidt, J. and Nosek, B. (2009). Liberals and conservatives rely on different sets of moral foundations. *Journal of Personality and Social Psychology*, 96, 1029–46.
Hardy, S. and Carlo, G. (2005). Identity as a source of moral motivation. *Human Development*, 48, 232–56.
Haidt, J. (2008). Morality. *Perspectives on Psychological Science*, 3(1), 65–72.

Haidt, J. (2012). *The Righteous Mind: Why Good People Are Divided by Politics*. London: Penguin.
Haidt, J. and Craig, J. (2011). How moral foundations theory succeeded in building on sand: A response to Suhler and Churchland. *Journal of Cognitive Neuroscience*, 23(9), 2117–22.
Haidt, J. and Graham, J. (2007). When morality opposes justice: Conservatives have moral intuitions that liberals may not recognise. *Social Justice Research*, 20, 98–116.
Haidt, J. and Joseph, C. (2004). Intuitive ethics: How innately prepared intuitions generate culturally variable virtues. *Daedalus*, 133, 55–66.
Haidt, J. and Joseph, C. (2008). The moral mind: How five sets of innate moral intuitions guide the development of many culture-specific virtues, and perhaps even modules. In P. Carruthers, S. Laurence and S. Stich, eds., *The Innate Mind: Vol. 3. Foundations and the Future*. Oxford: Oxford University Press, pp. 367–91.
Haugh, M. (2013). Im/politeness, social practice and the participation order. *Journal of Pragmatics*, 58, 52–72.
Horgan, M. (2019). Strangers and everyday incivilities: Towards a theory of moral affordances in ritualised interaction. *Journal of Language Aggression and Conflict*, 7(1), 31–54.
Hwang, H., Kim, Y. and Kim, Y. (2018). Influence of discussion incivility on deliberation: An examination of the mediating role of moral indignation. *Communication Research*, 45(2), 213–40.
Jay, T. (2018). Swearing, moral order, and online communication. *Journal of Language Aggression and Conflict*, 6(1), 107–26.
Jones, R. H. (2017). Surveillant landscapes. *Linguistic Landscape*, 3(2), 149–86.
Jucker, A. (2012). Changes in politeness cultures. In T. Nevelainen and E. Closs Traugott, eds., *The Oxford Handbook of The History of English*. Oxford: Oxford University Press, pp. 422–431.
Kádár, D. Z. (2017). *Politeness, Impoliteness and Ritual: Maintaining the Moral order in Interpersonal Interaction*. Cambridge: Cambridge University Press.
Kádár, D. Z. (2020). Capturing injunctive norm in pragmatics: Meta-reflective evaluations and the moral order. *Lingua* 237: 102814.
Kádár, D. Z. and Haugh, M. (2013). *Understanding Politeness*. Cambridge: Cambridge University Press.
Kádár, D. Z. and Márquez-Reiter, R. (2015). (Im)politeness and (im)morality: Insights from intervention. *Journal of Politeness Research*, 11(2), 239–60.
Kádár, D. Z. and Fukushima, S. (2018). The meta-conventionalisation and moral order of e-practices: A Japanese case study. *Internet Pragmatics*, 1(2), 352–78.
Kádár, D. Z. and Ning, P. (2019). Ritual public humiliation – A case study of Chinese adulterous couples. *Acta Linguistica Academica*, 66(2),189–208.
Kádár, D. Z., Parvaresh, V. and Ning, P. (2019). Morality, moral order, and language conflict and aggression – A position paper. *Journal of Language Aggression and Conflict*, 7(1), 6–30.

Kádár, D. Z., Ran, Y. and Ning, P. (2018). Public ritual apology – A case study of Chinese. *Discourse, Context and Media,* 26, 21–31.

Kohlberg, L. (1969). Stage and sequence: The cognitive-developmental approach to socialization. In D. A. Goslin, ed., *Handbook of Socialization Theory and Research.* Chicago: Rand McNally, pp. 387–480.

Lakoff, R. T. (2005). Civility and its discontents: or getting in your face. In R. T. Lakoff and S. Ide, eds., *Broadening the Horizon of Linguistic Politeness.* Amsterdam: John Benjamins, pp. 23–43.

Leach, C., Ellemers, N. and Barreto, M. (2007). Group virtue: The importance of morality (vs. competence and sociability) in the positive evaluation of in-groups. *Journal of Personality and Social Psychology,* 93(2), 234–49.

Locher, M. A. and Watts, R. J. (2005). Politeness theory and relational work. *Journal of Politeness Research,* 1, 9–33.

Lorenzo-Dus, N., Garcés-Conejos Blitvich, P. and Bou-Franch, P. (2011). Online polylogues and impoliteness: The case of postings sent in response to the Obama Reggaeton YouTube video. *Journal of Pragmatics,* 43, 2578–93.

Márquez-Reiter, R. and Orthaber, S. (2018). Exploring the moral compass. *Internet Pragmatics,* 1(2), 241–70.

Márquez-Reiter, R. and Haugh, M. (2019). Denunciation, blame and the moral turn in public life. *Discourse, Context and Media,* 28, 35–43.

Mills, S. (2003). *Gender and Politeness.* Cambridge: Cambridge University Press.

Mills, S. (2009). Impoliteness in a cultural context. *Journal of Pragmatics,* 41(5), 1047–60.

Moulinou, I. (2014). Striving to make the difference: Linguistic devices of moral indignation. *Journal of Language Aggression and Conflict,* 2(1), 74–98.

Molinou, I. (2019). Moral 'tropes', moral panic against witnesses and victim in court: explicit and implicit discursive strategies of moral aggression. *Journal of Language Aggression and Conflict,* 7(1), 103–30.

Papacharissi, Z. (2004). Democracy online: Civility, politeness, and the democratic potential of online political discussion groups. *New Media and Society,* 6(2), 259–83.

Parvaresh, V. (2019). Moral impoliteness. *Journal of Language Aggression and Conflict,* 7(1), 79–104.

Parvaresh, V. and Tayebi, T. (2018). Impoliteness, aggression and the moral order. *Journal of Pragmatics,* 132, 91–107.

Pearce, W. B. and Littlejohn, S. W. (1997). *Moral Conflict: When Social Worlds Collide.* Thousand Oaks, CA: Sage.

Pearson, C., Anderson, L. and Wegner, J. (2001). When workers flout convention: A study of workplace incivility. *Human Relations,* 54(11), 1387–1419.

Peltonen, M. (2003). *The Duel in Early Modern England: Civility, Politeness and Honour.* Cambridge: Cambridge University Press.

Placencia, M. E. (2001). Inequality in address behavior at public institutions in La Paz, Bolivia. *Anthropological Linguistics,* 43, 198–217.

Placencia, M. E. (2010). (Des)cortesía, migración y comunicación intercultural. In F. Orletti and L. Mariottini, eds., *(Des)cortesía en español. Espacios teóricos y metodológicos para su estudio*. Rome: Roma Universidad Roma Tre – Programa EDICE, pp. 399–430.

Plessner Lyons, N. (1983). Two perspectives: On self, relationships, and morality. *Harvard Educational Review*, 53(2), 125–45.

Rai, T. S. and Fiske, A. P. (2012). Beyond harm, intention, and dyads: Relationship regulation, virtuous violence, and metarelational morality. *Psychological Inquiry*, 23, 189–93.

Rai, T. S. and Fiske, A. P. (2011). Moral psychology is relationship regulation: Moral motives for unity, hierarchy, equality, and proportionality. *Psychological Review*, 118, 57–75.

Rai, T. S. and Fiske, A. P. (2016). The morality of violence. In T. Sommers, ed., *A Very Bad Wizard: Morality behind the Curtain*, 2nd ed. New York: Routledge, pp. 253–71.

Ran, Y. and Zhao, L. (2018). Building mutual affection-based face in conflict mediation: A Chinese relationship management model. *Journal of Pragmatics*, 129, 185–98.

Rawls, A. W. (1987). The interaction order sui generis: Goffman's contribution to social theory. *Sociological Theory*, 5, 136–49.

Reckwitz, A. (2002). Toward a theory of social practice. *European Journal of Social Theory*, 5(2), 243–63.

Schwartz, S. H. (1970). Moral decision making and behaviour. In M. Macauley and L. Berkowitz, eds., *Altruism and Helping Behaviour*. New York: Academic Press, pp. 127–41.

Schwartz, S. (1994). Are there universal aspects in the structure and contents of human values? *Journal of Social Issues*, 50(4), 19–45.

Schwartz, S. (2007). Universalism values and the inclusiveness of our moral universe. *Journal of Cross-Cultural Psychology*, 38, 711–28.

Schwartz, S. H., Cieciuch, J., Vecchione, M., Davidov, E., Fischer, R., Beierlein, C. and Konty, M. (2012). Refining the theory of basic individual values. *Journal of Personality and Social Psychology*, 103(4), 663–88.

Shweder, R. A., Much, N. C., Mahapatra, M. and Park, L. (1997). The "big three" of morality (autonomy, community, and divinity) and the "big three" explanations of suffering. In A. Brandt and P. Rozin, eds., *Morality and Health*. New York: Routledge, pp. 119–69.

Sell, R. (1992). Literary texts and diachronic aspects of politeness. In R. J. Watts, S. Ide and K. Ehlich, eds., *Politeness in Language: Studies in Its History, Theory and Practice*. Berlin: de Gruyter, pp. 109–29.

Sifianou, M. (2019). Im/politeness and in/civility: A neglected relationship? *Journal of Pragmatics*, 147, 49–64.

Sinkeviciute, V. (2018). "Ya bloody drongo!!!": Impoliteness as situated moral judgement on Facebook. *Internet Pragmatics*, 1(2), 271–302.

Spencer-Oatey, H. and Kádár, D. (2016). The bases of (im)politeness evaluations: Culture, the moral order and the East-West debate. *East Asian Pragmatics*, 1(1), 73–106.

Spencer-Oatey, H. and Kádár, D. (2020). *Intercultural Politeness: Relating across Cultures*. Cambridge: Cambridge University Press.

Spencer-Oatey, H. and Xing, J. (2019). Interdisciplinary perspectives on interpersonal relations and the evaluation process: Culture, norms, and the moral order. *Journal of Pragmatics*, 151, 141–54.

Suhler, C. L. and Churchland, P. (2001). Can innate, modular "foundations" explain morality? Challenges for Haidt's moral foundations theory. *Journal of Cognitive Neuroscience*, 23(9), 2103–16.

Terkourafi, M., Catedral, L., Haider, I., Karimzad, F., Melgares, J., Mostacero, C., Nelson, J. and Weissman, B. (2018). Uncivil Twitter: A sociopragmatic analysis, *Journal of Language Aggression and Conflict*, 6(1), 26–57.

Turner, G. (2010). *Ordinary People and the Media: The Demotic Turn*. Newbury Park, CA: Sage.

Truss, L. (2005). *Talk to the Hand: The Utter Bloody Rudeness of the World Today; or, Six Good Reasons to Stay Home and Bolt the Door*. London: Penguin.

Turiel, E. (1983). *The Development of Social Knowledge: Morality and Convention*. Cambridge: Cambridge University Press.

Varis, P. and van Nuenen, T. (2017). The Internet, language, and virtual interactions. In O. García, N. Flores and M. Spotti, eds., *The Oxford Handbook of Language and Society*. Oxford: Oxford University Press, pp. 473–88.

van Dijk, T. A. (1998). *Ideology: A Multidisciplinary Approach*. Newbury Park, CA: Sage.

Verschueren, J. (2012). *Ideology in Language Use: Pragmatic Guidelines for Empirical Research*. Cambridge: Cambridge University Press.

Watts, R. J. (1989). Relevance and relational work: Linguistic politeness as politic behavior. *Multilingua. Journal of Cross-Cultural and Interlanguage Communication*, 8(2–3), 131–66.

Watts, R. J. (1999). Language and politeness in early eighteenth century Britain. *Pragmatics*, 9(1), 5–20.

Watts, R. (2003). *Politeness*. Cambridge: Cambridge University Press.

Werkhofer, K. T. (1992). Traditional and modern views: The social constitution and power of politeness. In R. Watts, S. Ide and K. Ehlich, eds., *Politeness in Language: Studies in Its History: Theory and Practice*. Berlin: Mouton de Gruyter, pp. 155–99.

Wuthnow, R. (1989). *Meaning and Moral Order: Explorations in Cultural Analysis*. Berkeley: University of California Press.

Xie, C. (2018). (Im)politeness, morality and the internet. *Internet Pragmatics*, 1(2), 205–14.

20

Conversational Humour

Marta Dynel and Valeria Sinkeviciute

20.1 Introduction

Conversational humour is perceived as a blanket term for all manner of verbal forms and communicative practices that may cause amusement in the speaker and/or in the hearer(s). As the very term suggests, such humour occurs in human conversations across various modes of communication and discourse domains. Whilst usually produced intentionally, conversational humour may also be an unplanned consequence of a speaker's utterance (see Dynel 2016a). Thus, conversational humour encompasses not only various concepts that have been studied independently as types of humour, but also, for instance, (at least) some slips of the tongue or bitingly critical comments that become the source of vicarious pleasure (and hence humour) for non-targeted unratified participants. Here, we focus on the former, i.e. recognized forms of conversational humour.

This chapter gives an overview of diversified language studies pertinent to the sociopragmatics of conversational humour. However, it must be underscored that it is also sociological and psychological investigations that adduce findings relevant to this perspective. We begin by addressing the key concepts and theoretical approaches to humour in interaction, concentrating on different forms of humour that have been studied from a sociopragmatic perspective. Then, we provide a critical overview of the data sources for humour analysis and of sociopragmatic variables such as age, gender and culture. Furthermore, we outline the sociopragmatic functions of humour in interaction, paying special attention to discursive and interpersonal aspects, which are illustrated in the case study that focusses on how language users engage in humorous practices in a specific interactional setting. Finally, in the concluding section, we identify promising areas for future research.

20.2 Key Concepts and Theories

20.2.1 Categories of Conversational Humour

Conversational humour encompasses a wide range of categories, typically determined by the function and form of the verbal practice at hand. New forms and labels keep being added and new analyses of previously recognized forms keep being carried out. The different humorous forms frequently overlap (fully or in part), which is why a neat classification of verbal practices falling under the umbrella term "conversational humour" is hardly possible. Moreover, one label may pertain to markedly different phenomena, as epitomized by "teasing" (see Keltner et al. 2001).

Teasing is traditionally regarded as involving overtly feigned hostility/aggression that in actual fact testifies to real friendliness (Radcliffe-Brown 1940), premised on what Bateson ([1955] 1972) calls a meta-communicative "this is play" message. However, some authors claim that teasing may actually carry genuine aggression and may be oriented towards insulting the target (Straehle 1993; Boxer and Cortés-Conde 1997). An alternative proposal is that this hurtful kind of teasing should perhaps be seen as a different form of conversational humour (see Keltner et al. 2001; Dynel 2011), such as *disaffiliative humour* (see Dynel 2013a and references therein), i.e. a conversational species of *disparaging* humour, which is a blanket term for any humour that pokes fun at the butt of the joke and encompasses also other forms not coinciding with conversational humour, notably canned jokes (see Ford and Ferguson 2004). In order to be distinguishable from disaffiliative humour (i.e. disparaging conversational humour), teasing instances essentially need to be benevolent even if a serious and potentially aggressive message is to be communicated as well (e.g. Holmes and Schnurr 2005; Sinkeviciute 2013).

Disaffiliative humour may be an adequate label to capture conversational humour that centres on denigrating the target/butt, frequently in front of other participants in interaction, who reap humorous rewards, together with the speaker. Therefore, this blanket term will encompass humorous forms that involve genuine aggression and pejorative meanings, such as *sarcasm* and *insults* (on both, see below), as well as *putdowns* (Zillmann and Stocking 1976; but see Terrion and Ashforth 2002, who seem to equate putdown humour with playful teasing). What makes these distinctions problematic is that there is often no way of ascertaining (whether from an interactant's or a researcher's perspective) what a given speaker's intentions categorically are and whether any genuine aggression is meant (see e.g. Zajdman 1995; Dynel 2011, 2016b).

Besides teasing, banter is another polysemous label that denotes a category of humour and/or *mock impoliteness*, i.e. overtly pretended politeness, which may carry humorous effects (see Dynel 2018a). More often, it is considered a category of friendly humorous exchanges devoid of aggression (e.g. Chiaro

1992; Norrick 1993; Haugh and Bousfield 2012). Banter may thus materialize as *joint fantasizing* (e.g. Kotthoff 2007; Stallone and Haugh 2017; Tsakona 2018 and references therein), which relies on participants' joint construction of a fictional scenario or narrative in an ongoing interaction.

Teasing and banter are very close to, and sometimes explicitly presented as encompassing, *jocular mockery* (e.g. Haugh 2010) and *jocular abuse* (e.g. Hay 1994; Haugh and Bousfield 2012). Both of these notions are anchored in the assumption of the speaker's friendly attitude to the target who is mocked or abused but is not the object of genuine aggression (Haugh 2010).

Self-mockery is jocular mockery's close relative, and it concerns the cases of the speaker being the target of his/her own mockery (e.g. Haugh 2010; Zare 2016). It is essentially synonymous with *self-denigrating* or *self-deprecating* humour, as well as *self-directed joking* (see Dynel and Poppi 2020 for an overview and references), blanket terms referring to all kinds of self-directed humorous remarks or personal stories whereby speakers poke fun at themselves and build a positive self-image as a result.

Jocular abuse, in turn, bears strong similarity to the notion of *ritual insults*, which were originally studied in the context of Afro-American male interactions and labelled 'sounds or dozens' (Abrahams 1962; Kochman 1983; Labov 1972) or to the interactional practices of rubbishing your mates in Australian English. Ritual (jocular) insults are understood as competitive exchanges that are not intended to "be taken seriously" or offend; rather, they should be seen as being oriented towards building rapport and showing off the abuser's wit (e.g. Eder 1990; see Dynel and Poppi 2019 and references therein). Similarly, while rubbishing mates, the speaker denigrates the target by insulting him/her, but it also implies that this behaviour should not be taken seriously (Goddard 2006: 92). Jocular/ritual insults must not be mistaken for genuine insults, which are truly meant to offend the target (e.g. Mateo and Yus 2013; Sinkeviciute 2015; Dynel and Poppi 2020). Whether or not genuine insults are produced with an intention to amuse anybody, they may indeed invite humorous effects in the hearers who are not the targets of the abuse, but who affiliate with the speaker. Thus they qualify as a manifestation of disaffiliative humour (Dynel 2013a).

Apart from these mainly function-driven distinctions, several forms of conversational humour can be discerned based primarily on the form of expression, a case in point being humorous *irony* (see e.g. Kotthoff 2009; Kapogianni 2011; Dynel 2014, 2013b and references therein). Contrary to popular opinion, the figure of irony cannot be taken for granted as inhering in humour and it must present a combination of characteristics in order to qualify as such (see Dynel 2013b). However, "irony" has also been used as a label for various conversational practices that involve jocularity and "not meaning what one is saying" (e.g. Goddard 2006; Gibbs et al. 2014), which can be theoretically conceptualized as a form of overt untruthfulness (see Dynel 2018b). On the other hand, the figure of irony tends to be labelled *sarcasm*, which may also be humorous. Whilst some authors apply the label "sarcasm" to the rhetorical figure of irony, others argue in favour of differentiating between the two concepts. (For an overview, see Dynel 2017b.) Regardless of its relationship with irony, sarcasm is typically considered a type of verbal aggression, which may coincide with disaffiliative humour.

Finally, *punning*, which has received a lot of attention in semantic and cognitive studies on humour, is another form that conversational humour may take. Essentially, puns reside in the ambiguity of meanings. Apart from humorous comments (e.g. "Better late than pregnant"), puns in conversation may manifest themselves as *interactional puns* (Norrick 1993) or *reformulation puns* (Partington 2006), which can be seen as a type of *trumping* (Veale et al. 2006; Brône 2008). Trumping is an "adversarial" language game based on the speaker's overtly pretended misunderstanding of the preceding turn, which prompts him/her to skew the intended meaning and activate an alternative one, which may be facilitated by the ambiguity of meaning in the trumped utterance (e.g. "Are you coming?" "No, just breathing hard").

Numerous authors often refer to these and other forms of humour as they examine conversational data. What also reverberates across the literature is a range of theoretical assumptions underlying the workings of humour in human interaction.

20.2.2 Concepts and Approaches

Whilst early studies on humour seem to have treated instances (especially canned jokes and puns) as isolated artefacts subject to different semantic or cognitive analysis, conversational humour is typically approached as a joint interactional product, the (intentional) creation of the speaker as received by the hearer (see Hay 2001). This is what most interactional-pragmatic research (often using conversational-analytic tools) seems to take as a point of departure. Thus, attention is paid not only to how and why humour is produced but also whether and how it is received.

What is intended to be humour may invite different responses classified as either humorous reactions, notably laughter or humour reciprocation; or serious reactions, which typically indicate *failed humour*, such as: responses testifying to the hearer's having taken offence, defensive explanation, silence, return to topical talk, or topic change (e.g. Sinkeviciute 2013). What may occasion failed humour is lack of success at any of the four communicative stages proposed by Hay (2001), that is recognizing the humour, understanding the humour, appreciating the humour and agreeing with any message associated with it. An item of humour that the speaker produces may fail for various speaker- or hearer-dependent reasons (see Hay 2001; Bell 2009, 2015; Priego-Valverde 2009).

While various non-verbal cues, such as smiling or laughter, may help others to appreciate the speaker's humorous intention (e.g. Boxer and Cortés-Conde 1997; Keltner et al. 2001; Kotthoff 2007), they are by no means unequivocal. Moreover, cues need not override the power of potentially hurtful words (Sinkeviciute 2013, 2015). In addition, the response may not testify to how the hearer actually finds the interlocutor's contribution, especially in the cases when the former chooses not to admit to having taken offence (Sinkeviciute 2016, 2017c). Thus, what is meant as humour may be taken as being serious.

According to a well-entrenched view going back to traditional philosophy, humour is associated with *non-seriousness,* and hence juxtaposed with seriousness (e.g. Drew 1987; Holt 2013); it is thus considered as an autotelic activity, that is an activity performed for its own sake (see Dynel 2017a, 2018b). Along these lines, humour is often connected with a special mode of communication, labelled "play frame" or "humorous/non-serious" frame/key (see Dynel 2017a, 2018b for an overview of the field). However, many studies have abundantly shown that interactants can swiftly enter and leave the humorous frame or may be thought to merge the two frames while aiming to amuse the hearer(s) and simultaneously to communicate non-humorous/serious meanings (e.g. Emerson 1969; Drew 1987; Dynel 2011; see Dynel 2018b for a state-of-the-art view). Moreover, humour can be used as a strategic tool that confers on the speaker the right to convey serious meanings, while appearing to be "only joking" and/or holding the right to disavow responsibility for having communicated any such meanings (e.g. Haddington 2011; Dynel 2018b). In this sense, humour may be thought to serve politeness, for it helps save face or prevent face damage.

Generally speaking, humour has frequently been associated with *(im)politeness* effects. Numerous studies address specific manifestations of conversational humour with the use of notions and postulates derived from (im)politeness studies, such as the face threat or solidarity politeness (e.g. Antonopoulou and Sifianou 2003; Holmes 2000; Haugh 2010). Some authors also examine specific forms of conversational humour with reference to (im)politeness. Notably, jocular mockery and jocular abuse are conceived of as involving mock impoliteness (Haugh and Bousfield 2012). Moreover, a few consistent attempts have been made at conceptualizing conversational humour in the light of (im)politeness theory (Zajdman 1995; Dynel 2013a, 2016b; Sinkeviciute 2013, 2019b).

Zajdman (1995: 333) puts forward four configurations of agreement and disagreement between the speaker and the hearer as they produce and receive humorous face-threatening acts. This proposal is based on the speaker's intention (meaning/not meaning offence) and expectations (insult/amusement), and the hearer's interpretation (taking/not taking offence) and reactions (insult/amusement). On the other hand, Sinkeviciute (2013) proposes a production-evaluation model for interpreting acts of teasing, based on the form of a tease (potentially polite or impolite), and the hearer's reaction. Consequently, an ostensibly impolite utterance is conducive to impoliteness if the hearer perceives it as such, or to mock impoliteness if the hearer considers it "non-impolite". By contrast, a potentially polite (face-saving) utterance, which carries no overt aggression, gives rise to either politeness or mock politeness if the hearer finds the utterance impolite. For her part, Dynel (2016b) gives a critical overview of humour and impoliteness research. Also taking account of the production and reception ends, she shows that conversational humour may bring about politeness or impoliteness effects, or sometimes both for different hearers in multi-party interactions. Overall, these three proposals bring into focus the importance of the interactional aspect in the study of conversational humour.

Another burgeoning strand of linguistic research in humour studies concerns language users' perceptions, evaluations and labelling of humorous behaviours. These studies address the *metapragmatics* of humour. (For more on metapragmatics, see Caffi 1994.) Metamessages such as "only joking" or "just kidding" are used as the basis of evaluations of interactional goings-on (cf. Kane et al. 1977; Haddington 2011;). Other works are based on qualitative interviews (Plester and Sayers 2007; Lundquist 2014; Sinkeviciute 2017b), post-interaction questionnaires with quantitative findings (Bippus 2009) or lexical corpus studies (Dynel 2017b). Emic labels and understandings also lie at the heart of the ethnopragmatic approach to humour, which examines lexicalized metalanguage in order to capture native speakers' understandings of humour-related culture-specific concepts (e.g. Goddard 2006).

20.3 Sources of Data

Sociopragmatic studies on conversational humour encompass conversation-analytic discussions or other qualitative studies and, more rarely, quantitative investigations, as well as theoretic research into the mechanics of conversational humour interspersed with illustrative data.

Whilst some of the oft-quoted classical research on conversational humour presents random examples (overheard or fabricated by the authors themselves), recent work has been based on corpora of naturally occurring interactions. Such corpora and specific datasets are either compiled by the researchers themselves or culled from previously existing corpora, such as the BNC corpus. The selection of a corpus, together with the discourse domain/setting to which it belongs, is frequently inextricably connected with the selected research topic. These different discourse domains include private informal interactions among friends and colleagues or leaders' and employees' discourse in the workplace (which some of the works quoted in the course of this chapter show). These are the contexts studied most frequently, while other venues for conversational humour include: political talk (Partington 2006); therapy sessions (Buttny 2001); interactions in prison, involving both staff (Nielsen 2011) and inmates (Terry 1997) and in detention homes (Gradin et al. 2013); as well as hospital settings (Coser 1959; Grainger 2004; McCreaddie 2016; Chimbwete-Phiri and Schnurr 2017; see the overview of socio-psychological literature in Cuervo et al. 2018).

Although conversational humour is traditionally associated with oral communication in everyday face-to-face encounters, it is prevalent in various types of traditional and new media discourse, which are worthy of investigation. Whether spoken or written, human interactions that contain humour may be private or public, being available to wide audiences (e.g. television viewers or internet users). For instance, reality television shows offer publicly available spontaneous natural language data (Sinkeviciute 2014, 2017a; see case study). Conversational humour is present also in (partly) scripted genres such as TV documentaries (Chovanec 2017) or televised interviews or debates (Dynel 2011).

A rather new trend, based on the presumption of verisimilitude of fictional discourse (i.e. their similarity to real-life interactions), is to analyse conversational humour in the discourse of films and series (both comedy and drama), so far primarily British and American (see Davies 2006; Dynel 2013a, 2013b, 2016b, 2017a). These studies examine the workings of conversational humour of the characters treated as if they are real human beings with their communicative intentions and other mental states, about which viewers (and researchers alike) can make conjectures.

Moreover, written interactions online seem to have been attracting more and more academic attention over the past years; and so does humour present therein. The research so far has concerned conversational humour in personal emails (Schnurr and Rowe 2008; Dynel 2011) and Facebook exchanges (Maíz-Arévalo 2015), as well as publicly available online forums and social media interactions (Demjén 2016, 2018; Chovanec 2012; Vásquez and Creel 2017; Dynel and Poppi 2018, 2020).

20.4 Sociopragmatic Variables

Besides focusing on different contexts, research on conversational humour sometimes takes account of specific sociopragmatic variables, such as age, gender and culture. Among these factors, age has generated the least attention, even though some research has been done on the humour of the elderly (Matsumoto 2011; Damianakis and Marziali 2011), as well as on children's teasing that has been mainly associated with bullying (e.g. Lightner et al. 2000). In comparison, gendered humour has proved a much more productive topic of investigation. Early studies on gender and humour reinforce the idea of gendered use of humour, pointing to the specificity of humour used in male, female and mixed gender groups (see e.g. Hay 2000; Ervin-Tripp and Lampert 1992; Kotthoff 2006; Crawford 2003; Davies 2006; Ardington 2006; Lampert and Ervin-Tripp 2006). However, more recent work is orientated towards undermining the well-entrenched male versus female humour style divisions (e.g. Ferreira 2012; Reichenbach 2015). Such studies may be indicative of social changes going on in contemporary societies.

Overall, the body of academic literature on conversational humour seems to show a strong Anglo-centric bias, even though some authors do use data in other languages, whether or not focusing on the cultural specificity of the humour involved. The focus is on the seemingly universal workings of humour, for instance in Greek (Antonopoulou and Sifianou 2003), Japanese (Geyer 2010), Galician Spanish (Ferreira 2012), Brazilian Portuguese (Stallone and Haugh 2017) or Italian (Dynel and Poppi 2018). However, some ink has been devoted to the specificity of humour in select cultural contexts. For instance, Australian interactants tend to jocularly mock each other in various contexts (Haugh 2010; Goddard 2006). Apart from intracultural studies like these, there have also been a number of projects on humour in cross-cultural and intercultural contexts (see Sinkeviciute and Dynel 2017), two areas of investigation which are worth distinguishing.

While the notion of "cross-cultural communication" may be seen as encompassing "comparative or contrastive studies of native speakers' interactions within their own cultural contexts, intercultural communication brings together participants from different cultural and linguistic backgrounds and the focus of analysis is their interaction in a common language" (Sinkeviciute and Dynel 2017: 2). Intercultural studies have focused on English-Italian couples (Chiaro 2009), English native speakers and learners of English as a second language (Davies 2003; Bell 2007a, 2007b; Habib 2008; Moalla 2015). Many studies concern workplace, interactions between, for instance: the Māori, that is indigenous New Zealanders, and the Pākehā, that is New Zealanders of European (particularly British) descent (Holmes and Hay 1997), Hong Kong Chinese and English speakers (Cheng 2003), English native speakers and ethnic Chinese speakers (Rogerson-Revell 2007), as well as Danes working in France and the French working in Denmark (Lundquist 2014). Another research strand concerns humour in bilingual conversations, such as those of the Muslim community of Rhodes (Georgalidou and Kaili 2018).

There are relatively few cross-cultural studies that aim specifically to compare and/or contrast humorous practices in two cultures, the notable exception being Béal and Mullan's (2017) investigations into Australian and French contexts, Sinkeviciute's (e.g. 2014, 2016, 2017a, 2017b) studies on British and Australian humorous practices, as well as Haugh and Bousfield's (2012) investigation in jocular mockery and jocular abuse in British and Australian data and Maíz-Arévalo's (2015) examination of jocular mockery in British English and Peninsular Spanish. Some cross-cultural conclusions can also be drawn about teasing performed by speakers of American English and of Argentinian Spanish (Boxer and Cortés-Conde 1997), as well as the humour in the workplace interactions of the Māori's and Pākehā (Holmes and Hay 1997).

20.5 Functions of Humour

A lot has been written about the interpersonal – psychological, social and linguistic – functions of humour which facilitate the achievement of both transactional and relational objectives. Almost each and every analysis of conversational humour data yields some evidence about the function(s) that humour may perform, whether or not authors emphasize this fact. This ample body of interdisciplinary research is relevant to sociopragmatic studies on humour. It is practically impossible to exhaustively summarize or classify the plethora of specific (frequently overlapping) functions that humour can perform in various conversational contexts, as reported by numerous studies accumulated mainly since the 1970s. What complicates this task even more is the diversified terminology and potential synonymy of various labels, and hence a lot of overlap between seemingly independent notions describing specific functions of humour, typically with regard to its chosen forms, such as variously called manifestations of teasing or banter.

Nonetheless, some attempts have been made to present the whole gamut of the functions of humour (e.g. Martineau 1972; Kane et al. 1977; Ziv 1984; Long and Grasser 1988; Graham et al. 1992; Attardo 1994; Martin 2007). For instance, Martineau (1972) addresses three groups of functions related to consensus, conflict and control. In his influential book, Attardo (1994) presents the primary functions as follows: *social management* (e.g. facilitating in-group bonding and out-group rejection), *mediation* (the communication of "serious" messages and attaining serious goals, see Mulkay 1988), which is related to *decommitment* (i.e. *retractability* of messages, see Kane et al. 1977) and can be juxtaposed with *defunctionalization* (essentially, the use of humour for its own sake, see Dynel 2017a). These fundamental (but, it must be stressed, not mutually exclusive) functions of humour, have been validated by ample empirical research, with the focus on specific functions and applications of humour, or the consequences of it, which language users may feel intuitively.

The central unquestionable function of humour that has been amply demonstrated is its *bonding* capacity. It has been abundantly shown that humour helps build and reinforce *solidarity* and group cohesion among interactants across all manner of conversational contexts (e.g. Apte 1985; Holmes 2000; Lennox et al. 2002; Demjén 2016). Whilst promoting solidarity among particular interactants – representative of a chosen social group, frequently conceptualized as a *community of practice*, a term originally proposed by Lave and Wenger (1991) – humour can simultaneously be used for out-group exclusion (e.g. Holmes and Hay 1997; Fine and de Soucey 2005; Rogerson-Revell 2007; Plester and Sayers 2007). Moreover, based on their frequent use of humour, interactants are sometimes regarded as constituting "joking relationships" (Radcliffe-Brown 1940) or "joking cultures" (Fine and de Soucey 2005). It is especially in close relationships that humour increases intimacy and testifies to interactants' affection, interpersonal attraction and likeability (e.g. Cann et al. 1997; Alberts et al. 1996; Zajdman 1995). Humour also testifies to people's mutual understanding and helps build common ground on both conceptual and linguistic levels (see Ziv 1984; Coser 1959, 1960; Norrick 1993; Antonopoulou and Sifianou 2003; Fine and de Soucey 2005).

On the other hand, humour may be deployed as a tool for testifying to the speaker's power and sustaining the hierarchical structure (Coser 1960; Holmes 2000; Hay 2001; Rogerson-Revell 2007), for enforcing social order (Gradin Franzén and Aronsson 2013) or for subverting the status quo, and thereby building power over an interlocutor (Collinson 1988; Rodrigues and Collinson 1995; Holmes 2000). Even in such hierarchical contexts, however, humour is frequently employed to mitigate face-threatening (imposing or corrective) messages. This function of humour, sometimes labelled "decommitment", involves, for instance, "probing" the hearer's reactions or "salvaging" a previous utterance under the pretext that one was only joking (Kane et al. 1977).

Indeed, many studies indicate that conversational humour easily carries "serious" meanings, which may be difficult to communicate otherwise (e.g. Emerson 1969; Pizzini 1991; Young and Bippus 2001), such as gauging personal values, addressing intimate, taboo topics (e.g. Kane et al. 1977; Demjén 2016), expressing criticism (Holmes and Marra 2002a) or frustration (Schnurr and Rowe 2008), making requests (Holmes and Marra 2002b) or "disarming resistance" (Buttny 2001). In all these and many other situations humour helps the speaker mitigate the face threat to the hearer as the former is performing "serious" communicative acts. This is because the intertwining of humour and seriousness (which may be seen through the lens of the speaker's (un)truthfulness) seems to soften the blow on the hearer, who (ideally) recognizes both the humour and the non-humorous message (see Dynel 2017a and references therein). In other cases, thanks to the communicative ambiguity that humour affords, the speaker cannot be held fully accountable for the messages he/she is communicating, being able to retroactively withdraw them on the "only joking" pretext (see Dynel 2011, 2017a). This ambiguity and merging of humour with seriousness allows for interactants' joint negotiation of the communicative actions at hand (see Holt 2013).

Furthermore, whether or not language users are aware of this, humour is also a means of identity construction (e.g. Lennox et al. 2002; Norrick and Klein 2008, Nielsen 2011; Vine et al. 2009; Sinkeviciute 2019a), an issue which is most pronounced in the context of how social identity (e.g. professional or gender) is claimed and negotiated. In terms of professional identities, humour can help negotiate leadership and power relations in the workplace (Holmes and Marra 2002b; Schnurr and Chan 2011). Humour can also mark gender boundaries, for instance by reinforcing the idea of male humour styles (e.g. Schnurr and Holmes 2009) or when women challenge identities and display stereotypically masculine behaviours of controlling and silencing subordinates (Schnurr 2008).

Finally, what falls under the umbrella term of the "social management" function is a long and open-ended list of socio-psychological effects of conversational humour (for an overview, see Martin 2007), some of which have also garnered linguistic evidence. For example, humour helps cope with insults (Dynel and Poppi 2020), handle awkward situations (Kane et al. 1977; Grainger 2004) and conflictual interactions (Bippus 2009) by ending/resolving existing conflicts or forestalling impending ones (Norrick and Spitz 2008) between intimates and strangers (Boxer and Cortés-Conde 1997). Humour is also frequently presented as a coping mechanism in grave circumstances, such as serious illness (Demjén 2016) or political oppression. (For socio-psychological evidence, see Martin 2007; Martin and Ford 2018; Dynel and Poppi 2018.) Different types of humour can also function as a form of social corrective, i.e. when the speaker jocularly indicates that some behaviour is inappropriate. A case in point is the interactional practice of *taking the piss out of someone* (Goddard 2009) that is frequently encountered in the English-speaking world but particularly often used in an Anglo-Australian cultural context in order to point out "an alleged infringement of normative behaviour on the part of the target" (Haugh and Bousfield 2012: 1106).

20.6 Case Study: Teasing among Speakers of Australian English and Its Local Functions

In order to illustrate how humour works in a localized context in a particular community of practice, we present here an extract from a naturally occurring conversation that comes from the reality television game show *Big Brother* Australia 2012. The extract shows an interaction between the housemates that takes place on day 7. We will focus on the two main interlocutors: Ben and George. Prior to this conversation, the housemates have just found out that George is a millionaire. All the housemates are in the shared bedroom and Ben initiates a conversation with George in front of other participants. In terms of interactional roles, Ben is seen as the main instigator of this humorous sequence and George as the butt of the humour.

(1) Day 7 (AU)
Ben: George you know you know you made a million dollars
            can you start a class I'm sure I'm gonna say
            that 80 per cent of us are gonna go to
            every day (.) and it's just 5 to 10 minutes
            that says you're not a millionaire
            and I am = [smiles looking around] =
George: = [laughs] =
HMs: = [laugh] =

Sara:	= and this is your next move =
Ben:	this is how we all gonna live being really happy instead of just two of us cause that's you and the other person who wins the money [smiles]
George:	= [laughs] =
HMs:	= [laugh] =
part omitted	
George:	if if I win I'll shout you all a trip to Perth {[smile voice] my shout}
HMs:	o::h yay
Ben:	and you know if you don't win {[smiling] can you shout us all a trip = to Perth =}
HMs:	= [hahaha] =
	= [hahaha] =
George:	= [rolls on the bed laughing] =

Ben starts his deadpan teasing by suggesting that George should 'start a [daily] class' to provide the others with useful tips on how to become a millionaire, with the punchline being that George would only need to state the fact: 'you're not a millionaire and I am'. This immediately gives rise to the housemates' (including George) laughter, which indicates that they (and the target) could recognize and appreciate the funny side of what is said (see e.g. Goddard 2009). Ben continues referring to the game situation, where only one housemate can win, which would leave everyone else without an opportunity to become a millionaire. In that case, only George and the winner would be happy, which, as Ben jokingly suggests, can be fixed if George shares his secret on how to get all that money. This, again, generates loud laughter from all the housemates present. After a few jocular turns (not in the transcript), George decides to show his generosity if he should win the show, i.e. 'shout[ing] ... all a trip to Perth'. While it is possible to hear the positive genuinely excited reaction from the housemates ('o::h' and 'yay'), it is Ben who once more initiates another humorous turn. From the analytical perspective, it can be labelled as taking the piss out of George, as it points out that George, being a millionaire, does not need to win the show in order to 'shout' other housemates a trip to Perth. This receives an extended laughing reaction from everyone, including the target, for the third time. The comment-reaction pattern becomes quite obvious in this sequence, with Ben projecting his 'joker' identity (Plester and Orams 2008) and trying to amuse other housemates, including the target himself, who is the first to react with laughter. This can indicate that he does not take himself too seriously, a quality that is particularly valued in the Anglo-Australian society (Goddard 2009; Sinkeviciute 2014, 2017b).

What is essential to understanding Ben's humorous turns is the social values that seem to be promoted in an Australian cultural context. When communicating with other people, interlocutors are seen to engage in 'egalitarianism of manners', i.e. projecting social and interactional equality among them (Hirst 2009). This 'egalitarianism' can be threatened by some interactants being superior in their ways (for example, George's financial status), as a result of which, the interactional practice of taking the piss out of someone usually takes place in order to attempt and bring everyone to the same level (e.g. Haugh and Bousfield 2012; Sinkeviciute 2014, 2017a). When this cultural and societal dimension is taken into account, it becomes clearer why Ben might have decided to tease George in the first place, i.e. to point out his financial superiority. Up until this point in conversation, however, George has not made any clear reference in interaction to him being more advantageous than his fellow housemates. The indication of this can be seen towards the end when he promises to pay for everyone's trip to Perth if he wins the game. Ben might, however, see this as an unfair situation and decides to tease George (who is a millionaire) by asking him to 'shout' them all a trip to Perth even if he does not win the show. Even though what Ben does can certainly be classified as playful teasing, it is based on the difference between George and all other housemates that Ben seems to highlight in order to promote equality in the house. In other words, by jokingly drawing everyone's attention to the fact that George is financially superior, Ben manages to establish a bonding situation in which, while having George as the target of humour, he and other housemates are able to laugh at their own less advantageous situation and their willingness to win the prize money. This humorous exchange from reality television discourse not only highlights the importance of not taking yourself too seriously in an Australian cultural context, with George as the target laughing at Ben having a go at him, but also shows how interpersonal relationships can be promoted through humorous practices.

20.7 Summary and Future Directions

This chapter has aimed to present an overview of research on conversational humour as a vital sociopragmatic phenomenon in human interaction. Whether we look at teasing, banter, humorous irony or ritual insults, the production and perception of these and other categories of humour are highly dependent on social and situational contexts and interpersonal relationships between interlocutors. Due to these dynamic elements, instances of humour can easily fail or even be perceived as inappropriate, leading, for example, to evaluations of impoliteness.

Even though, as the chapter has shown, conversational humour has been attracting much academic attention for several decades and many topics have been thoroughly examined, we can still identify at least a few promising areas for future research. First and foremost, there seems to be a need for more intercultural and cross-cultural studies of different types of humour in interaction. While analyses of humour in English shed much light on how conversational humour is constructed and negotiated, findings based on studies of other linguistic and cultural contexts would bring a more versatile perspective on such a multi-faceted phenomenon. Analysing humour sequences by focusing on the researcher's conceptualizations is essential from a theoretical perspective. However, it is also important to investigate how instances of conversational humour are *actually* understood and judged by language users themselves. A metapragmatic approach to conversational humour can be a useful tool, since it concentrates on the interactants' evaluations of the appropriateness of verbal behaviours, thus allowing for a further exploration of the complexities of humour in interaction. Finally, while most of the existing research on conversational humour concerns oral interactions, the continually developing world of internet communication keeps offering more and more interesting venues for the occurrence of humour manifesting a wide variety of new forms and functions, which deserve to be examined.

References

Abrahams, R. (1962). Playing the dozens. *Journal of American Folklore, 75*, 209–20.

Alberts, J., Kellar-Guenther, Y. and Corman, S. (1996). That's not funny: Understanding recipients' responses to teasing. *Western Journal of Communication, 60*, 337–57.

Antonopoulou, E. and Sifianou, M. (2003). Conversational dynamics of humour: The telephone game in Greek. *Journal of Pragmatics, 35*(5), 741–69.

Apte, M. L. (1985). *Humor and Laughter: An Anthropological Approach*. London: Cornell University Press.

Ardington, A. (2006). Playfully negotiated activity in girls' talk. *Journal of Pragmatics, 38*, 73–95.

Attardo, S. (1994). *Linguistic Theories of Humor*. New York: Mouton.

Bateson, G. ([1955] 1972). A theory of play and fantasy. In G. Bateson, ed., *Steps to an Ecology of Mind*. San Francisco, CA: Chandler, pp. 177–93.

Béal, C. and Mullan, K. (2017). The pragmatics of conversational humour in social visits: French and Australian English. *Language and Communication, 55*, 24–40

Bell, N. (2007a). Humor comprehension: Lessons learned from cross-cultural communication. *Humor, 20*(4), 367–87.

Bell, N. (2007b). How native and non-native English speakers adapt to humor in intercultural interaction. *Humor, 20*(1), 27–48.

Bell, N. (2009). Responses to failed humour. *Journal of Pragmatics, 41*(9), 1825–36.

Bell, N. (2015). *We Are Not Amused: Failed Humor in Interaction*. Berlin: Mouton de Gruyter.

Bippus, A. M. (2009). Making sense of humor in young romantic relationships: Understanding partners' perceptions. *Humor, 13*(4), 395–418.

Boxer, D. and Cortés-Conde, F. (1997). From bonding and biting: Conversational joking and identity display. *Journal of Pragmatics, 23*, 275–95.

Brône, G. (2008). Hyper- and misunderstanding in interactional humour. *Journal of Pragmatics, 40*, 2027–61.

Buttny, R. (2001). Therapeutic humor in retelling the clients' tellings. *Text, 21*(3), 303–26.

Caffi, C. (1994). Metapragmatics. In *Encyclopedia of Language and Linguistics*, vol. 5. New York: Pergamon Press, pp. 2461–6.

Cann, A., Calhoun, L. G. and Banks, J. (1997). On the role of humour appreciation in interpersonal attraction: It's no joking matter. *Humor, 10*(1), 77–89.

Cheng, W. (2003). Humor in intercultural conversations. *Semiotica, 146*, 287–306.

Chiaro, D. (1992). *The Language of Jokes: Analysing Verbal Play*. London: Routledge.

Chiaro, D. (2009). Cultural divide or unifying factor? Humorous talk in the interaction of bilingual, cross-cultural couples. In N. R. Norrick and D. Chiaro, eds., *Humor in Interaction*. Amsterdam: John Benjamins, pp. 211–32.

Chimbwete-Phiri, R. and Schnurr, S. (2017). Negotiating knowledge and creating solidarity: Humour in antenatal counselling sessions at a rural hospital in Malawi. *Lingua, 197*, 68–82.

Chovanec, J. (2012). Conversational humour and joint fantasizing in online journalism. In J. Chovanec and I. Ermida, eds., *Language and Humour in the Media*. Newcastle: CSP, pp. 139–61.

Chovanec, J. (2017). Interactional humour and spontaneity in TV documentaries. *Lingua, 197*, 34–49.

Coates, J. (2007). Talk in a play frame: More on laughter and intimacy. *Journal of Pragmatics, 39*, 29–49.

Collinson, D. (1988). "Engineering humour": Masculinity, joking and conflict in shop-floor relations. *Organization Studies, 9*(2), 181–99.

Coser, R. L. (1959). Some social functions of laughter. *Human Relations, 12*, 171–82.

Coser, R. L. (1960). Laughter among colleagues: A study of the social functions of humour among the staff of a mental hospital. *Psychiatry, 23*, 81–95.

Crawford, M. (2003). Gender and humor in social context. *Journal of Pragmatics, 35*, 1413–30.

Cuervo, P., Vinita Mahtani-Chugani, M. A., Sanchez Correas, M. A. and Sanz Rubiales, A. (2018). The use of humor in palliative care: A systematic literature review. *American Journal of Hospice and Palliative Medicine, 35*(10), 1–13.

Damianakis, T. and Marziali, E. (2011). Community-dwelling older adults' contextual experiencing of humour. *Ageing and Society, 31*(1), 110–24.

Davies, C. E. (2003). How English-learners joke with native speakers: An interactional sociolinguistic perspective on humor as collaborative discourse across cultures. *Journal of Pragmatics, 35*, 1361–85.

Davies, C. E. (2006). Gendered sense of humor as expressed through aesthetic typifications. *Journal of Pragmatics, 38*, 96–113.

Demjén, Z. (2016). Laughing at cancer: Humour, empowerment, solidarity and coping online. *Journal of Pragmatics, 101*, 18–30.

Demjén, Z. (2018). Complexity theory and conversational humour: Tracing the birth and decline of a running joke in an online cancer support community. *Journal of Pragmatics, 133*, 93–104.

Drew, P. (1987). Po-faced receipts of teases. *Linguistics, 25*, 219–53.

Dynel, M. (2011). Joker in the pack: Towards determining the status of humorous framing in conversations. In M. Dynel, ed., *The Pragmatics of Humour across Discourse Domains. Pragmatics and Beyond New Series*. Amsterdam: John Benjamins, pp. 217–41.

Dynel, M. (2012a). Humour on the house: Interactional construction of metaphor in film discourse. In J. Chovanec and I. Ermida, eds., *Language and Humour in the Media*. Newcastle: Cambridge Scholars, pp. 83–106.

Dynel, M. (2013a). Impoliteness as disaffiliative humour in film talk. In M. Dynel, ed., *Developments in Linguistic Humour Theory*. Amsterdam: John Benjamins, pp. 105–44.

Dynel, M. (2013b). When does irony tickle the hearer? Towards capturing the characteristics of humorous irony. In M. Dynel, ed., *Developments in Linguistic Humour Theory*. Amsterdam: John Benjamins, pp. 298–320.

Dynel, M. (2014). Isn't it ironic? Defining the scope of humorous irony. *Humor: International Journal of Humor Research, 27*, 619–39.

Dynel, M. (2016a). With or without intentions: Accountability and (un)intentional humour in film talk. *Journal of Pragmatics, 95*, 67–98.

Dynel, M. (2016b). Conceptualising conversational humour as (im)politeness: The case of film talk. *Journal of Politeness Research, 12*(1), 117–47.

Dynel, M. (2017a). But seriously: On conversational humour and (un)truthfulness. *Lingua, 197*, 83–102.

Dynel, M. (2017b). Academics vs. American scriptwriters vs. Academics: A battle over the etic and emic "sarcasm" and "irony" labels. *Language and Communication, 55*, 69–87.

Dynel, M. (2018a). Theoretically on Mock Politeness in English and Italian. *Journal of Aggression and Conflict, 6*(1), 149–65.

Dynel, M. (2018b). *Irony, Deception and Humour: Seeking the Truth about Overt and Covert Untruthfulness*. Mouton Series in Pragmatics. Berlin: Mouton de Gruyter.

Dynel, M. and Poppi, F. I. M. (2018). In tragoedia risus: Analysis of dark humour in post-terrorist attack discourse. *Discourse and Communication, 12*(4), 382–400.

Dynel, M. and Poppi, F. I. M. (2019). Risum teneatis, amici?: The sociopragmatics of RoastMe humour. *Journal of Pragmatics, 139*, 1–21.

Dynel, M. and Poppi, F. I. M. (2020). Arcana imperii: The power of humorous retorts to insults on Twitter. *Journal of Language Aggression and Conflict*, 8(1), 57–97.

Eder, D. (1990). Serious and playful disputes: Variation in conflict talk among female adolescents. In A. D. Grimshaw, ed., *Conflict Talk: Sociolinguistic Investigations of Arguments and Conversations*. Cambridge: Cambridge University Press, pp. 67–84.

Emerson, J. P. (1969). Negotiating the serious import of humor. *Sociometry*, 32, 169–81.

Ervin-Tripp, S. M. and Lampert, M. D. (1992). Gender differences in the construction of humorous talk. In K. Hall, E. Buchholtz and B. Moonwomon, eds., *Locating Power: Proceedings of the Second Berkeley Women and Language Conference*. Berkeley: University of California Press, pp. 108–17.

Ferreira, A. V. A. (2012). The humorous display of transgressor femininities: 'Sharing a laugh' in Spanish/Galician friendly talk among young women. *Sociolinguistic Studies*, 6(1), 121–47.

Fine, G. A. and De Soucey, M. (2005). Joking cultures: Humor themes as social regulation in group life. *Humor*, 18, 1–22.

Ford, T. E. and Ferguson, M. A. (2004). Social consequences of disparagement humor: A prejudiced norm theory. *Personality and Social Psychology Review*, 8(1), 79–94.

Georgalidou, M. and Kaili, H. (2018). The pragmatics of humour in bilingual conversations. In V. Tsakona and J. Chovanec, eds., *The Dynamics of Interactional Humor*. Amsterdam: John Benjamins, pp. 77–103.

Geyer, N. (2010). Teasing and ambivalent face in Japanese multi-party discourse. *Journal of Pragmatics*, 42, 2120–30.

Gibbs, R., Bryant, G. and Colston, H. (2014). Where's the humor in irony? *Humor: International Journal of Humor Research*, 27, 575–95.

Goddard, C. (2006). "Lift your game Martina!": Deadpan jocular irony and the ethnopragmatics of Australian English. In C. Goddard, ed., *Ethnopragmatics: Understanding Discourse in Cultural Context*. New York: Mouton de Gruyter, pp. 65–97.

Goddard, C. (2009). "*Not taking yourself too seriously* in Australian English: Semantic explications, cultural scripts, corpus evidence." *Intercultural Pragmatics*, 6(1), 29–53.

Gradin Franzén, A. and Karin, A. (2013). Teasing, laughing and disciplinary humor: Staff–youth interaction in detention home treatment. *Discourse Studies*, 15(2), 167–83.

Graham, E., Papa, M. and Brooks, G. (1992) Functions of humour in conversation: Conceptualization and measurement, *Western Journal of Communication*, 56(2), 161–83.

Grainger, K. (2004). Verbal play on the hospital ward: Solidarity or power? *Multilingua*, 23(1–2), 39–59.

Habib, R. (2008). Humor and disagreement: Identity construction and cross-cultural enrichment. *Journal of Pragmatics, 40*, 1117–45.

Haddington, P. (2011). Serious or non-serious? Sequential ambiguity and disavowing a prior stance. *Functions of Language, 18*(2), 149–82.

Haugh, M. (2010). Jocular mockery, (dis)affiliation, and face. *Journal of Pragmatics, 42*, 2106–19.

Haugh, M. (2017). Jocular language play, social action and (dis)affiliation in conversational interaction. In N. Bell, ed., *Multiple Perspectives on Language Play*. Boston: Mouton de Gruyter, pp. 143–68.

Haugh, M. and Bousfield, D. (2012). Mock impoliteness in interactions amongst Australian and British speakers of English. *Journal of Pragmatics, 44*, 1099–1114.

Hay, J. (1994). Jocular abuse patterns in mixed-group interaction, *Wellington Working Papers in Linguistics, 6*, 26–55.

Hay, J. (2000). Functions of humour in the conversations of men and women. *Journal of Pragmatics, 32*, 709–42.

Hay, J. (2001). The pragmatics of humor support. *Humor, 14*(1), 55–82.

Hirst, J. (2009). *Sense and Nonsense in Australian History*. Melbourne: Blanc Inc Agenda.

Homes. J. (2000). Politeness, power and provocation: How humour functions in the workplace. *Discourse Studies, 2*, 159–85.

Holmes, J. and Hay, J. (1997). Humour as an ethnic boundary market in New Zealand interaction. *Journal of Intercultural Studies, 18*(2), 127–51.

Holmes, J. and Marra, M. (2002a). Over the edge? Subversive humor between colleagues and friends. *Humor, 15*(1), 65–87.

Holmes, J. and Marra, M. (2002b). Having a laugh at work: How humour contributes to workplace culture. *Journal of Pragmatics, 34*, 1683–1710.

Holmes, J. and Schnurr, S. (2005). Politeness, humor and gender in the workplace: Negotiating norms and identifying contestation. *Journal of Politeness Research, 1*, 121–49.

Holt, E. (2013). "There's many a true word said in jest": Seriousness and nonseriousness in interaction. In P. Glenn and E. Holt, eds., *Studies of Laughter in Interaction*. London: Bloomsbury, pp. 69–89.

Kane, T. R., Suls, J. and Tedeschi, J. T. (1977). Humor as a tool of social interaction. In A. J. Chapman and H. C. Foot, eds., *It's a Funny Thing, Humour*. Elmsford, NY: Pergamon, pp. 13–16.

Kapogianni, E. (2011). Irony via "surrealism". In M. Dynel, ed., *The Pragmatics of Humour across Discourse Domains*. Amsterdam: John Benjamins, pp. 51–68.

Keltner, D., Capps, L., Kring, A., Young, R. and Heerey, E. (2001). Just teasing: A conceptual analysis and empirical review. *Psychological Bulletin, 127*, 229–48.

Kochman, T. (1983). The boundary between play and nonplay in black verbal duelling. *Language in Society, 12*, 329–37.

Kotthoff, H. (2006). Gender and humor: The state of the art. *Journal of Pragmatics, 38*, 4–25.

Kotthoff, H. (2007). Pragmatics of performance and the analysis of conversational humor. *Humor*, 19(3), 271–304.

Kotthoff, H. (2009). An interactional approach to irony development. In N. R. Norrick and C. Delia, eds., *Humor in Interaction*. Amsterdam: John Benjamins, pp. 49–78.

Labov, W. (1972). Rules for ritual insults. In D. Sudnow, ed., *Studies in Social Interaction*. New York: The Free Press, pp. 120–69.

Lampert, M. and Ervin-Tripp, S. M. (2006). Risky laughter: Teasing and self-directed joking among male and female friends. *Journal of Pragmatics*, 38, 51–72.

Lave, J. and Wenger, E. (1991). *Situated Learning: Legitimate Peripheral Participation*. Cambridge: Cambridge University Press.

Lennox Terrion, J. and Ashforth, B. E. (2000). From 'I' to 'we': The role of putdown humour and identity in the development of a temporary group. *Human Relations*, 55(1), 55–88.

Lightner, R. M., Bollmer, J. M., Harris, M. J., Milich, R. and Scambler, D. J. (2000). What do you say to teasers? Parent and child evaluations of responses to teasing. *Journal of Applied Developmental Psychology*, 21(4), 403–27.

Long, D. L. and Graesser, A. C. (1988). Wit and humour in discourse processing. *Discourse Processes*, 11, 35–60.

Lundquist, L. (2014). Danish humor in cross-cultural professional settings: Linguistic and social aspects. *Humor*, 27(1), 141–63.

Maíz-Arévalo, C. (2015). Jocular mockery in computer-mediated communication: A contrastive study of a Spanish and English Facebook community. *Journal of Politeness Research*, 11(2), 289–327.

Martin, R. (2007). *The Psychology of Humor. An Integrative Approach*. Burlington, MA: Elsevier.

Martin, R. and Ford, T. (2018). *The Psychology of Humour. An Integrative Approach*. 2nd ed. New York: Academic Press.

Martineau, H. W. (1972). A model for the social function of humour. In J. H. Goldstein and P. E. McGhee, eds., *The Psychology of Humour*. New York: Academic Press, pp. 101–25.

Mateo, J. and Yus, F. (2013). Towards a cross-cultural pragmatic taxonomy of insults. *Journal of Language Aggression and Conflict*, 1(1), 87–114.

Matsumoto, Y. (2011). Painful to playful: Quotidian frames in the conversational discourse of older Japanese women. *Language in Society*, 40(5), 591–616.

McCreaddie, M. A. (2016). Poor wee souls and fraggle rock: The visceral humor of nurse-peers in a non-accomplishment setting. *Humor*, 29(2), 175–96.

Moalla, A. (2015). Intercultural strategies to co-construct and interpret humor. *International Journal of Applied Linguistics*, 25(3), 366–85.

Mulkay, M. (1988). *On Humour: Its Nature and Its Place in Society*. Cambridge: Polity Press.

Nielsen, M. M. (2011). On humour in prison. *European Journal of Criminology*, 8, 500–514.

Norrick, N. R. (1993). *Conversational Joking: Humor in Everyday Talk*. Bloomington: Indiana University Press.

Norrick, N. and Klein, N. (2008). Class clowns: Talking out of turn with an orientation toward humor. *Lodz Papers in Pragmatics*.

Norrick, N. R. and Spitz, A. (2008). Humor as a resource for mitigating conflict in interaction. *Journal of Pragmatics, 40*(10), 1661–86.

Partington, A. (2006). *The Linguistics of Laughter. A Corpus-Assisted Study of Laughter-Talk*. Oxon, UK: Routledge.

Pizzini, F. (1991). Communication hierarchies in humour: Gender differences in the obstetrical/gynaecological setting. *Discourse and Society, 2*, 477–88.

Plester, B. A. and Sayers, J. (2007). "Taking the piss": Functions of banter in the IT industry. *Humor, 20*(2), 157–87.

Plester, B. and Orams, M. (2008). Send in the clowns: The role of the joker in three New Zealand IT companies. *Humor, 21*(3), 253–81.

Priego-Valverde, B. (2009). Failed humor in conversation: A double voicing analysis. In N. R. Norrick and D. Chiaro, eds., *Humor in Interaction*. Amsterdam: John Benjamins, pp. 165–86.

Radcliffe-Brown, A. R. (1940). On joking relationships. *Africa, 13*, 195–210.

Reichenbach, A. (2015). Laughter in times of uncertainty: Negotiating gender and social distance in Bahraini women's humorous talk. *Humor, 28*(4), 511–39.

Rodrigues, S. and Collinson, D. (1995) 'Having fun?' Humour as resistance in Brazil. *Organization Studies, 16*(5), 739–68.

Rogerson-Revell, P. (2007). Humour in business: A double-edged sword. A study of humour and style shifting in intercultural business meetings. *Journal of Pragmatics, 39*, 4–28.

Schnurr, S. (2008). Surviving in a man's world with a sense of humour: An analysis of women leader's use of humour at work. *Leadership, 4*(3), 299–319.

Schnurr, S. and Chan, A. (2011). When laughter is not enough: Responding to teasing and self-denigrating humor at work. *Journal of Pragmatics, 43*(1), 20–35.

Schnurr, S. and Holmes, J. (2009). Using humour to do masculinity at work. In N. R. Norrick and D. Chiaro, eds., *Humor in Interaction*. Amsterdam: John Benjamins, pp. 101–23.

Schnurr, S. and Rowe, C. (2008). The "dark side" of humour: An analysis of subversive humour in workplace emails. *Lodz Papers in Pragmatics, 4*, 109–30.

Sinkeviciute, V. (2013). Decoding encoded (im)politeness: 'Cause on my teasing you can depend'. In M. Dynel, ed., *Developments in Linguistic Humour Theory*. Amsterdam: John Benjamins, pp. 263–88.

Sinkeviciute, V. (2014). "When a joke's a joke and when it's too much": *Mateship* as a key to interpreting jocular FTAs in Australian English. *Journal of Pragmatics, 60*, 121–39.

Sinkeviciute, V. (2015). "There's definitely gonna be some serious carnage in this house" or how to be genuinely impolite in *Big Brother* UK. *Journal of Language Aggression and Conflict*, 3(2), 317–48.

Sinkeviciute, V. (2016). "Everything he says to me it's like he stabs me in the face": Frontstage and backstage reactions to teasing. In N. Bell, ed., *Multiple Perspectives on Language Play*. Amsterdam: Mouton de Gruyter, pp. 169–98.

Sinkeviciute, V. (2017a). What makes teasing impolite in Australian and British English? "Step[ping] over those lines [...] you shouldn't be crossing". *Journal of Politeness Research: Language, Behaviour, Culture*, 13(2), 175–207.

Sinkeviciute, V. (2017b). Funniness and "the preferred reaction" to jocularity in Australian and British English: An analysis of interviewees' metapragmatic comments. *Language and Communication*, 55, 1–9.

Sinkeviciute, V. (2017c). "It's just a bit of cultural [...] lost in translation": Australian and British intracultural and intercultural metapragmatic evaluations of jocularity. *Lingua*, 197, 50–67.

Sinkeviciute, V. (2019a). Juggling identities in interviews: The metapragmatics of 'doing humour'. *Journal of Pragmatics*, 152, 216–27.

Sinkeviciute, V. (2019b). *Conversational Humour and (Im)politeness: A Pragmatic Analysis of Social Interaction*. Amsterdam: John Benjamins.

Sinkeviciute, V. and Dynel, M. (2017). Approaching conversational humour culturally: A survey of the emerging area of investigation. *Language and Communication*, 55, 1–9.

Stallone, L. and Haugh, M. (2017). Joint fantasising as relational practice in Brazilian Portuguese interactions. *Language and Communication*, 55, 10–23.

Straehle, C. (1993). 'Samuel?' 'Yes dear?' Teasing and conversational rapport. In D. Tannen, ed., *Framing in Discourse*. New York: Open University Press, pp. 210–29.

Terrion, J. and Ashforth, B. (2002). From 'I' to 'we': The role of putdown humour and identity in the development of a temporary group. *Human Relations*, 55(1), 55–88.

Terry, C. M. (1997). The function of humor for prison inmates. *Journal of Contemporary Criminal Justice*, 13(23), 23–40.

Tsakona, V. (2018). Online joint fictionalization. In V. Tsakona and J. Chovanec, eds., *The Dynamics of Interactional Humor: Creating and Negotiating Humor in Everyday Encounters*. Topics in Humor Research 7. Amsterdam: John Benjamins, pp. 229–55.

Vásquez, C. and Creel, S. (2017). Conviviality through creativity: Appealing to the reblog in Tumblr Chat posts. *Discourse, Context and Media*, 20, 59–69.

Veale, T., Feyaerts, K. and Brône, G. (2006). The cognitive mechanisms of adversarial humor. *Humor*, 19, 305–40.

Vine, B., Kell, S., Marra, M. and Holmes, J. (2009). Boundary-marking humor: Institutional, gender and ethnic demarcation in the workplace.

In N. R. Norrick and D. Chiaro, eds., *Humor in Interaction*. Amsterdam: John Benjamins, pp. 125–39.

Young, L. S. and Bippus, A. M. (2001). 'Does it make a difference if they hurt you in a funny way? Humorously and non-humorously phrased hurtful messages in personal relationships.' *Communication Quarterly*, 49(1), 35–53.

Zajdman, A. (1995). Humorous face-threatening acts: Humor as strategy. *Journal of Pragmatics*, 23, 325–39.

Zare, J. (2016). Self-mockery: A study of Persian multi-party interactions. *Text andTalk*, 36(6), 789–81.

Zillmann, D. and Stocking, H. (1976). Putdown humor. *Journal of Communication*, 26, 154–63.

Ziv, A. (1984). *Personality and Sense of Humour*. New York: Springer.

21

Gesture and Prosody in Multimodal Communication

Lucien Brown and Pilar Prieto

21.1 Introduction

Human interaction does not occur only on the verbal dimension. Speakers use gestures and prosodic features to clarify meaning, manage the structure of the interaction and to express their emotions and stances. For instance, a speaker might use a pause or an outstretched hand gesture to signal that they are inviting the other participant to take a turn. Similarly, a speaker might use a louder voice and large gestures to signal aggression, and/or impoliteness. When used regularly, certain ways of speaking or gesturing may become stylized as markers of a speaker's identity.

Despite the obvious potential for prosody and gestures to communicate these kinds of meanings, sociopragmatics as a field has been dominated by the analysis of verbal correlates. Culpeper (2011: 151) notes that "non-verbal cues ... [receive] relatively little attention in communication and pragmatic studies". The tendency to overlook non-verbal behaviour is now being challenged, however. Recent years have seen multimodality rise to prominence within pragmatics, spearheaded by ground-breaking research using state-of-the-art methodologies. Still, prosody and gesture tend to be studied separately and in a non-integrated fashion.

Following the tenets of audio visual prosody, we will start with the assumption that both prosody and gesture can be considered as two sides of the same coin in the sociopragmatic marking of human communication (see Swerts and Krahmer 2005). In this chapter, we provide a thorough overview of multimodal research in sociopragmatics by focusing on the joint contributions of prosody and gesture to meanings such as information structure, epistemic information, politeness or turn-taking.

21.2 Key Concepts and Theories

21.2.1 Gesture

Gesture refers to visible bodily action that is used as an utterance, or as part of an utterance (Kendon 2004: 7). Gestures may be used to substitute speech, for example, when a speaker makes a "telephone" gesture to somebody across a crowded room to communicate "I'll call you". But gestures are more commonly characterized by the way that they are closely integrated with talk, such as when a speaker performs a rolling motion with their fingers in accompaniment to saying "the ball rolled down the street". Gestures are most commonly made by the arms, but movements of the face and other body parts can also be considered gestures if they convey referential meaning and/ or if they are closely synchronized with speech (see Bavelas et al. 2014). For instance, speakers can make pointing gestures not just with the hands but also with the feet, lips (Wilkins 2003) and eye gaze (Bavelas et al. 2014: 18).

Gestures may function in a variety of different ways. McNeill (1992) proposed a four-way functional coding system that distinguished between (1) iconics (gestures which represent features of the referent in a transparent way, such as framing the shape of a person while speaking about him/ her), (2) metaphorics (which refer to abstract notions, such as touching your heart while speaking about love), (3) beats (hand movements which typically align with prominent positions in speech and have an emphatic function in discourse), and (4) deictics (e.g. gestures signalling locations).

The term "gesture" is reserved for the types of bodily actions described in the previous paragraph, which typically convey or accompany referential meaning and which are closely synchronized with speech. However, speakers may use a wider range of facial expressions, as well as bodily movements, postures and orientations when engaged in communication, which are not tightly coordinated with speech and which do not contribute to the communicative content. For instance, a speaker may choose to keep the arms crossed, and to stand far away from the interlocutor while avoiding eye contact. Although these are not gestures and do not convey referential meanings, they still convey pragmatic meanings related to the speaker's affective stance (i.e. how he/she feels about the interlocutor and/or the topic of conversation) and potentially other considerations such as power or hierarchy. Factors such as speaker posture, bodily orientation, interpersonal distance, facial expressions and so forth are referred to as "non-verbal behaviours". In this chapter, we will jointly assess the role of gestures together with that of other bodily movements as important signals of sociopragmatic meaning.

21.2.2 Prosody

Prosody refers to suprasegmental features of speech; in other words, vocal effects that accompany the sounds of individual segments of speech, and that extend over words, phrases or utterances. Prosody allows for the same word, phrase or utterance to be delivered in different ways, such as louder/quieter, faster/slower, with higher or lower pitch, or with different intonation contours. Four important acoustic dimensions (and perceptual correlates) have been included in the study of the prosodic correlates of sociopragmatic meanings:

(1) *Fundamental frequency (or F0) parameters*. Fundamental frequency is the acoustic feature that measures the rate of vibration of the vocal cords and is the reflection of perceived pitch. It is typically measured in Hertz, or cycles per second. The most common phonetic measures of pitch are pitch height (or highest F0 value in the utterance, also called topline), pitch register or average pitch (a measure of contour pitch raising or lowering in the F0 space, which is calculated by the mean pitch value of the pitch contour), and pitch span or pitch range (a measure of pitch excursion, typically calculated by the difference between the lowest and the highest F0 measures in the utterance). Variations in pitch range can be measured globally (at the level of the utterance) or locally (measuring the difference between the lowest and the highest point in a given pitch accent, e.g. an F0 movement associated with a prosodically prominent unit).

(2) *Duration (perceived length)*. Duration and duration variability, as well as speech rate, correspond to the perception of length and rhythm of the utterance. Duration is commonly measured in milliseconds and milliseconds per unit. Some of the measures that have been used to characterize polite prosody are mean syllable length, speech rate and mean length of pauses.

(3) *Intensity (loudness)*. Intensity is the acoustic correlate of perceived loudness, and is typically reported in decibels (dB). The most frequent measure reported in several studies is mean utterance intensity.

(4) *Voice quality*. Voice quality has been defined as the "characteristic auditory colouring" of a speaker's voice, and it is derived from a variety of laryngeal and supralaryngeal configurations. Supralaryngeal changes can induce a nasalized, dentalized and velarized voice, while different vocal fold configurations lead to different phonation types, such as breathy, whispery, creaky, falsetto, as well as harsh voices. In order to characterize such phonation types, researchers have used acoustic parameters like jitter (the percentage of change in the duration of pitch periods) and shimmer (the percentage of change in speech amplitude between pitch periods). Creaky voice, for example, exhibits high indexes of jitter and shimmer.

Regarding the analysis of *intonation contours*, there is an ample consensus among intonation researchers on the basic tenets of the autosegmental-metrical (or AM) model of intonation and its application to the ToBI annotation conventions developed for a number of typologically diverse languages. (See Ladd 2008; Gussenhoven 2002, 2004 for a review of the AM model of intonation.) The ToBI conventions establish four layers of labelling (words, tones, break indices, and miscellaneous information) which are aligned with the speech signal. In the tones tier, and following the AM model, a set of phonologically contrastive pitch events – pitch accents and boundary tones – may be defined for each system. For example, the intonation contours of English are described as a sequence of phonologically distinctive tonal units (e.g. pitch accents and boundary tones, represented with high and low targets and their combinations) that are associated with metrically prominent units and with phrasal boundaries, respectively. This phonological representation of tones is mapped onto the phonetic representation through language-particular implementation rules. The break index tier represents the phrase grouping structure of the language through numerical indices that indicate degrees of disjuncture between any two adjacent words. Break index 4 represents intonational phrases (IPs) and break index 3 represents intermediate phrases (ips). Readers who are interested in knowing more about the application of the ToBI conventions to different languages can refer to Jun (2005, 2014).

21.2.3 Other Multimodal Resources

Speakers may also use non-verbal speech sounds for sociopragmatic functions, including affective vocalizations (laughter, sobs, screams) that communicate emotions and which have intrinsic sound-to-meaning connections (Lima Castro and Scott 2013). There are also vegetative sounds such as coughing, belching, and breathing sounds) that can be strategically employed for communicative purposes, such as when a speaker coughs to let someone know they are there, or belches to show appreciation for a meal (which may be polite in some cultures).

In written, televised or computer-mediated communication a range of audio and visual resources may be used for sociopragmatic effects. The use of multimodal features in computer-mediated communication (CMC) is covered elsewhere in this handbook (see Chapter 22).

21.3 Critical Overview of Research

This section presents a state-of-the-art review of the literature on the contribution of prosodic and gestural patterns to the encoding of a set of sociopragmatic meanings. Since very few studies have adopted a multimodal perspective that includes a joint analysis of verbal resources alongside prosodic, facial and body signals, our review of the literature will generally rely on studies coming from separate traditions. It is our goal in this chapter to bring together those traditions and to argue for the need to incorporate a truly multimodal perspective.

The majority of work to date has tended to be quantitative in nature, with data most typically being collected via elicitation tasks and experiments, or culled from corpora. However, recent years have witnessed movements towards using semi-spontaneous or naturalistic data, and to include qualitative techniques.

21.3.1 Information Status

Information status involves the way that information is packaged within a sentence in relation to the extent that the information is new, old, shared, expected or so forth. New information that updates the listener's stored knowledge is referred to as *focus*, whereas relationally old information is called *topic*. Focal information can be contrary to the presuppositions of interlocutor ("contrastive focus"), and can differ in its scope ("broad/narrow focus").

Many languages use prosody to mark focused constituents within discourse. Typically, focal elements are produced with prosodic prominence by means of pitch accentuation through the use of louder amplitude, longer duration and higher F0. (See Gussenhoven 2002 for a review of the use of the cross-language utilization of F0; see also Ohala 1984.) Ito and Speer (2008) demonstrated through the use of an experimental study using eye-tracking (i.e. measuring participants' point of gaze) that English participants associated more prominent accent peaks with contrastive interpretations. For instance, when given instructions to hang a *blue drum* on a Christmas tree, prominent accents ('Hang the green drum, now hang the BLUE *drum*') would make participants fixate on suitable alternatives, thus showing that they interpreted the stress as contrastive. This was less likely to happen when the accent was less prominent ('Hang the green drum, now hang the *blue drum*'). Gussenhoven (2002: 5) proposed that the "tendency for focused information to be characterized by relatively wide pitch excursions" can be explained as the grammaticalization of a specific universal related to pitch production that he calls the Effort Code. Despite this general tendency, cross-linguistic differences have been reported in the way languages encode contrastive focus prosodically. Vanrell et al. (2013) used an experimental research design to investigate contrastive focus in Catalan, Italian and Spanish and reported that the three languages differed in the selection of pitch accent type (reflected in pitch scaling and alignment patterns), as well as duration patterns.

Speakers also use gestures to signal focal information, including beat gestures and other repetitive hand movements. Often times, when speakers produce a beat gesture, they accompany their rhythmic hand movements with other "visual beats" (Krahmer and Swerts 2007): coordinated head nod and eyebrow rising-falling movements, as well as torso movements and eye openings. Iconics and pointing gestures tend also to be temporally associated with prosodic prominence (see Prieto et al. 2018). Figure 21.1 (from

Figure 21.1 Coordinating eyebrow movements with hand gestures. Adapted from Prieto et al. (2018).

Prieto et al. 2018) shows a speaker raising his eyebrows in coordination with hand movements when uttering focal information. Interestingly, the more articulators a visual beat involves (and the larger and more intense their movements are), the higher the spoken emphasis of the accompanying word. Independent evidence shows that, similarly to hand beat gestures, "head nods/beats" and "eyebrow beats" show a tight temporal alignment with prosodic prominence (see Shattuck-Hufnagel and Ren 2018; Prieto et al. 2015). These movements are in turn likely to be synchronized with prosodic markers of focus. In a quantitative analysis, Cavé et al. (1996) showed that rapid eyebrow rising-falling movements were associated with F0 rises in 71 per cent of cases.

In Figure 21.1, a speaker coordinates eyebrow movements with hand gestures while uttering focal information. The four selected images represent key points at the gesture phases, namely (from left to right), start of the preparation phase, beginning of the stroke, gesture apex (in this case end of the stroke), and end of the recovery phase.

Speakers may use precision grip gestures involving the thumb touching the tip of the index finger to mark various types of focus. Lempert (2011) qualitatively analysed the precision grip gestures used by Barack Obama in presidential debates. In one instance, Obama used the gesture repeatedly when conveying that his adversary John McCain is planning "$300 billion" in tax relief for wealthy individuals and corporations. In this case, the precision grip gestures marked contrastive focus, in that Obama was emphasizing that "$300 billion" differed both from his own tax plans, and from the lower figure that McCain himself had quoted. Lempert (2011: 251) concludes that precision grip gestures can be viewed as a type of gestural highlighting.

Prosodic and visual signals encoding information status are crucial for successful speech processing and comprehension. The absence of pitch accentuation in focal elements or the introduction of incongruous pitch accentuation can tax speech processing (Dimitrova et al. 2012). Using a video-viewing experimental task, Dimitrova et al. (2016) found that the inclusion of beat gestures on prosodically prominent focal elements facilitated speech processing, whereas inclusion on non-focused information led to difficulties. The same processing difficulties were not found for hand-grooming movements, which were included as a control.

21.3.2 Phrase Structure, Discourse Structure and Turn-Taking

This section looks at how gesture and prosody play roles in marking the way that speech is internally structured. Sentences have distinct phrase structures that control the way that they are structured and processed in natural speech. When multiple sentences come together to form discourse, speakers need to establish what elements of the discourse are prominent, and which parts are related to each other. In conversation, speakers need to organize turn-taking so that participants speak in alternating turns.

A clear function of prosody in natural languages is that of marking phrase groupings or phrasing structure in speech. Typically, speakers use prosodic markers such as tonal continuation rises or falling F0 patterns, together with final lengthening and pauses to mark the end of sentences. These prosodic patterns help hearers to process speech (e.g. Gussenhoven 2002; Ladd 2008). Gesture movements also accompany prosodic phrasing and syntactic structure in speech (e.g. Shattuck-Hufnagel and Ren 2018; Guellaï Langus and Nespor 2014; Krivokapic et al. 2016). Guellaï et al. (2014) showed by means of an experimental research design that hearers were able to perceive the congruency between low-pass filtered (unintelligible) speech and the gestures of the speaker. The second experiment showed that when faced with ambiguous sentences like *Quando Giacomo chiama suo fratello è sempre felice* 'When Giacomo calls his brother he is always happy', mismatched prosody and gestures lead participants to choose more often the phrasing signalled by gestures. These results demonstrate that prosodic phrasing has a clear correlate in gesture movements, which is strongly used by hearers to disambiguate phrasing structure.

Speakers also use prosody and gesture to highlight discourse structure. Researchers have found that prosodic markers can provide independent specification of hierarchical discourse structure and the relative boundary strength of discourse phrases (Ladd 2008 for a review). According to McNeill (1992: 16), beat gestures, together with iconic, metaphoric or pointing gestures, can have cohesive functions too because they "tie together thematically related but temporally separated parts of the discourse".

Regarding turn-taking, studies have identified a number of linguistic features that perform pragmatic functions such as holding and/or giving the turn, or facilitating smooth turn transitions in conversation. These features include prosodic means such as final falling intonational patterns, and phonation and lengthening patterns, as well as gestural features such as hand gestures or eye gaze (e.g. Gravano and Hirschberg 2011; Zellers et al. 2016). Tessendorf (2007) used qualitative analysis of videotaped conversations and TV shows to show that Spanish speakers use a "brushing aside" gesture to organize turn-taking, among other functions. Zellers et al.

(2016) used quantitative and qualitative analysis of video data to show that gesture cues and prosodic cues to turn transitions in Swedish face-to-face conversation function in a complementary way.

21.3.3 Epistemic Stance

Epistemic stance refers to the expression of the commitment of the interlocutors to the propositional content. Whereas evidentiality (or "epistemic modality") refers to "the marking of the source of the information of the statement", epistemicity is "the degree of confidence the speaker has in his or her statement" (de Haan 2001: 201).

Speakers use various linguistic cues to mark uncertainty or even ignorance, such as lexical and morphosyntactic marking, as well as prosodic cues (e.g. delays, hesitations, elongations, higher pitch, specific final rising intonation contours) and gestures (e.g. shoulder shrugging, eye squinting, brow furrowing) (see Krahmer and Swerts 2005; Roseano et al. 2016). Krahmer and Swerts (2005) collected video data via experimental methodology and showed that when adults and children are uncertain or unknowing they produce 'funny faces', that is, a kind of "marked facial expression" that includes some lip corner depression, or lip stretching or pressing combined with brow and shoulder movements (see also Hübscher 2018). Similarly, gestures can also mark changes in the illocutionary force of the epistemic stance adopted by the speaker. In Figure 21.2 (from Prieto et al. 2018), while open palms facing the audience (left) shows low epistemic commitment, the grip gesture (right) represent high commitment.

In Figure 21.2, we can see two types of epistemic gestures in Keith's TED Talk: Left panel (03m 19s): Open palm gesture over "oh **yes**, I think it's bad" referring to climate change. Right panel: Grip gesture over "That rep**ort** that landed on President Johnson's desk ..." (**bold** indicates pitch accented syllable)

Regarding evidential meaning, intonation and gesture patterns can be recruited to encode information source. Vanrell et al. (2017) showed that specific intonation patterns in Majorcan Catalan (the sentence-initial particle *que* combined with the pitch contour L+H* L%) are used by listeners to

Figure 21.2 Two types of epistemic gestures. Adapted from Prieto et al. (2018).

infer direct sensory evidence as opposed to reported evidence in a sentence like *Que hi has posat pebre bo?* '[Que] there's pepper in the soup?' Escandell (2017) showed that specific types of question intonation in Spanish (e.g. the high-rise pattern and the rise-fall pattern) encode evidential distinctions so that the high-rise pattern indicates that the "Self" is the source of the information, and the rise-fall tone indicates the "Other". Regarding gesture, Roseano et al. (2016) analysed a corpus of opinion reports in Catalan and found that two kinds of pointing gestures (point to self and point to an absent referent) reinforce a direct (personal) evidential and an indirect mediated evidential, respectively.

Intonation and gesture encode not only speaker commitment but also speaker agreement or disagreement. A specific type of intonational contour (the so-called contradiction contour) has been documented with the production of sentences conveying the speaker's rejection or disagreement with the previous turn (Prieto et al. 2013 for Catalan). With respect to questions, Prieto and Borràs-Comes (2018) used an acceptability judgement task to show that Catalan speakers use distinct intonational pitch patterns to encode epistemic commitments in two complementary directions, i.e. speaker commitments to the speaker's own proposition and speaker agreement with the addressee's proposition.

Recently, some studies have jointly analysed the use of the so-called disagreement prosodic and gestural patterns. Crespo-Sendra et al. (2013) showed via a perception experiment that while Catalan and Dutch speakers use very similar facial expressions while uttering an incredulity question (e.g. eyebrow furrowing and eyelid closure), they produce language-particular incredulity intonation contours. Prieto et al. (2013) investigated the preferred interpretation of negative words meaning either 'nobody' or 'everybody' in Catalan and Spanish for an auditory-only condition, a video-only condition and an audio-visual condition with congruent and incongruent multimodal matches. In the audio-visual condition, double negation readings were picked up when prosody and gesture converged on the rejection interpretation; otherwise, single negation was preferred, with an increase in reaction times. Interestingly, a recent experimental study by Benitez-Quiroz et al. (2016) documented a common facial expression of disagreement across four languages – Spanish, English, Mandarin Chinese and American Sign Language – suggesting a universal grammaticalized pattern. This common disagreement face is characterized by eyebrows slightly furrowed, lips pursed and chin raised.

In sum, this section has shown how prosodic and gestural features can be regarded as conventional markers of epistemicity and evidentiality across languages. Recent empirical evidence using intonation–gesture matching tasks has shown that epistemic intonation and epistemic gesture are mutually co-expressive and dependent on each other (Borràs-Comes et al. 2019).

Case Study 1: Communicating epistemic stance: How speech and gesture patterns reflect epistemicity and evidentiality

The goal of Roseano et al. (2016) is two-fold: first, to assess the use of prosodic and gesture features expressing epistemic stance used in 30 videotaped opinion reports uttered by 15 Catalan speakers; second, to assess the extent to which these prosodic and gestural features potentially affect the listeners' assessments of the epistemic stance conveyed by these opinion reports.

Two experimental studies were conducted with these two goals in mind. The first study consisted of a production task in which 15 participants performed two oral opinion reports after reading two short articles. In order to elicit different degrees of epistemic certainty, one of the articles dealt with a controversial issue (the properties and effects of acupuncture) and the other with a less controversial issue (the properties and effects of aspirin). By controlling the issue under discussion (debatable vs non-debatable issue), two types of opinion reports were obtained for each participant which encoded two distinct epistemological positionings (high certainty vs low certainty). The elicitation procedure was as follows. The speaker was given the first of the two target articles to read for 5 minutes and was told that he or she would have to convey the contents of the text verbally to a confederate listener who was not aware about the contents. After the description report, the confederate listener was instructed to ask the speaker the following question: 'And what is YOUR opinion about acupuncture/aspirin?', and again instructed to listen in silence and show positive feedback by nodding. The same procedure was repeated for the second text. The audio-visual recordings of the 30 opinion reports were transcribed semantically (for evidentiality and epistemicity features, based on previous work on pragmatic labelling of epistemic stance). Since the main goal was to assess the contribution of textual versus multimodal marking to epistemic expression, textual and multimodal analyses were performed independently. The results of the production study showed that speakers communicate epistemic stance both verbally and non-verbally and that specific prosodic and gestural patterns were frequently used to express a range of epistemic and evidential meanings. For example, rising pitch at phrase boundaries and head nodding were frequent high certainty epistemic markers, as well as pointing gestures for first person and third person evidentials. Importantly, the number of gestural and prosodic epistemic markers in this corpus of opinion reports almost doubled the epistemic markers found at the textual level (and frequently they appeared independently from lexical marking), something that indicates the important amount of epistemic information encoded by prosody and gesture in discourse.

In order to assess the perceptual relevance of these prosodic and gestural markings on epistemic assessments by listeners, the second study consisted of a rating task with 12 independent listeners. These listeners rated the speaker's degree of certainty in each of the 30 opinion reports from the first experiment by means of a seven-point Likert scale. The main goal of this perception task was to empirically test whether the relative density of lexical versus gestural markers plays an important role in the perception and assessment of epistemic stance by Catalan listeners. Results showed that even though the integration of lexical, prosodic and gestural markers was useful to convey a speaker's epistemic stance, the number of gestural high certainty markers used by a speaker when expressing an opinion was a particularly good predictor of the perception of epistemic high certainty.

In sum, the findings of this paper show both from a production and a perception perspective that prosodic and gestural features of language can be regarded as important conventional markers of epistemicity and evidentiality in discourse, being especially effective in the communication and assessment of epistemic stance by listeners.

21.3.4 (Im)politeness

(Im)politeness refers to a range of behaviours for maintaining interpersonal relationships, encompassing conventionalized acts of etiquette (e.g. making a formal apology), the ritualized marking of formality and hierarchy (e.g. "Doctor" or "Professor"), as well other behaviours "through which we take into account the feelings of others as to how they think they should be treated" (Kádár and Haugh 2013: 1). Non-verbal features play a crucial role in determining whether an utterance is perceived as polite or impolite. Culpeper (2011a: 57) points out that an utterance that appears normatively polite at the verbal level (e.g. "Do you know anything about yo-yos?") can be rendered impolite through gesture or prosody (e.g. heavily stressing the beginning of "anything" and delivering the remainder of the utterance with sharply falling intonation).

It has been widely claimed that there is a relationship between high pitch and politeness. This claim was first made in Brown and Levinson ([1979] 1987: 268) and was fleshed out by Ohala (1984), who noted that there is a "frequency code" by which "such social messages as deference, politeness, submission, lack of confidence, are signaled by high and/or rising F0" (Ohala 1984: 327). Ohala claims that these social messages are mediated through the biological association between high pitch and small physical size, in other words, that smaller animals make higher-pitched noises. When speakers adopt a higher-pitched voice, they thus appear less threatening and more submissive. Another claim is that high pitch associates with politeness due to it being more effortful than lower pitch (Gussenhoven's 2002 "effort code").

The claim that high pitch is universally associated with politeness has found support. Orozco (2008) found that Mexican Spanish speakers used a high initial and a high final boundary tone in the production of polite requests. Similarly, Devís and Cantero (2014) found in corpus data that the use of high or suspended utterance-final and utterance-medial melodic inflections in Catalan was one of the most successful politeness attenuators, capable of converting commands into requests or confrontation into cooperation.

However, some recent research has shown evidence that conflicts with such claims. Winter and Grawunder (2012) followed by Brown et al. (2014) showed in quantitative analysis of elicited speech that low pitch (rather than high pitch) correlated with the usage of a polite speech register in Korean, which is prototypically used to index that the hearer is of superior age or social status. The findings were then replicated for Japanese (Idemaru et al. 2019) and similar results were obtained for Catalan requests (Hübscher et al. 2017). These studies claim that in some situations (such as addressing a status superior) and/or in some cultures, politeness is expressed through adopting a lower-pitched voice that sounds calmer, softer and less animated, as part of a strategy of "prosodic mitigation" (Hübscher et al. 2017). Conversely, in some contexts high pitch may actually be associated with meanings related to impoliteness, such as aggression (Stadler 2007) or disagreement (Goodwin et al. 2002).

Recent studies point to the need to consider the role of a wider range of phonetic, gestural and non-verbal features of politeness. In a perception study using manipulated speech, Idemaru et al. (2020) found that intensity was a stronger cue for politeness in Korean than pitch. The authors did not necessarily reject the frequency code however, since they point out that quieter speech may also communicate smaller body size. Elsewhere, research has also shown that politeness may be communicated through a decrease in speech rate (e.g. Lin et al. 2006 for Taiwanese) and through increased breathiness (Ito 2004 for Japanese).

Gestural and non-verbal behaviours may also play vital roles in the way that politeness is communicated. Nadeu and Prieto's (2011) perception experiments showed that politeness ratings based just on acoustic information could be reversed by the provision of facial gestural information. Increased pitch height was only perceived as more polite when a picture of a smiling face was provided to the participants.

Polite speech addressed to status superiors and/or used in formal situations features constrained gestures and non-verbal behaviours. Brown and Winter's (2019) analysis of a corpus of TV dramas found that Korean speakers were more likely to maintain direct bodily orientation and gaze on the line of sight when addressing status superiors, whereas they suppressed manual and facial gestures, as well as self-touches and haptics. Similarly, Hübscher et al. (submitted) found that Catalan speakers used fewer gestures and other facial and body cues when making requests to an older person of higher status. The way that gesture is constrained during formal interactions somewhat mirrors the way that prosody is also constrained, leading Hübscher et al. (submitted) to claim that politeness also features "gestural mitigation".

The appropriate marking of social status is also manifest through non-verbal greeting behaviours, including head bows and differences in handshake behaviours. In East Asian cultures such as Korea it is customary for inferiors to offer non-reciprocal bows to status superiors, but to wait for the superior to initiate handshakes (Brown and Winter 2019). In contrast, Hillewaert's (2016) ethnographic study of Muslim communities in coastal Kenya shows that it is the inferior who should initiate the hand greeting by offering their hand palm up. After the superior has placed their hand on top of the inferior's, the inferior is expected to kiss the back of the superior's hand.

Research on gestures has found that ways in which bodily action is perceived as polite or impolite is due to culture-specific beliefs. For instance, gesturing with the left hand or pointing with the index finger may be restricted in some parts of Africa and Asia due to cultural taboos. (See Kita and Essegby 2001 for discussion of Ghana and Ola Orie 2009 for Yoruba.)

Case Study 2: Cross-cultural Multimodal Politeness: The Phonetics of Japanese Deferential Speech in Comparison to Korean

Idemaru et al. (2019) carried out an exploratory production study of the acoustic differences between deferential and non-deferential speech in Japanese. They then conducted a perception study to see whether Japanese listeners could use these acoustic differences as perceptual cues for differentiating between these two registers of speech. The paper compared the findings for Japanese with previous results for Korean collected using the same methodologies in Winter and Grawunder (2012) and Brown et al. (2014).

"Deferential speech" should be understood here as language used when "submitting to or showing regard to a superior or someone else deserving of respect" (Haugh et al. 2015: 81). The contrast between deferential and non-deferential speech is linguistically salient in Japanese and Korean since it is marked systematically in the morphology and lexicon through developed systems of honorifics.

Production data was collected from 20 Japanese speakers, who participated in two tasks. The first was a reading task where they read utterances simulating conversational situations. There were 10 situations and two versions of each situation: one version where the assumed interlocutor was a friend, and one version where the assumed interlocutor was a professor. The utterances were structured so that each of the two versions of the same situation contained a middle clause that was lexically and morphologically identical across the two versions. The second task was an oral Discourse Completion Task featuring six scenarios, again with two versions for each (friend version and professor version). Participants were provided with a prompt, but were required to devise and produce their own utterances.

The results showed that deferential speech in Japanese was quieter and breathier than non-deferential speech, and showed a smaller degree of variation in pitch within each utterance. Contrary to claims that high pitch is universally associated with politeness, deferential speech was slightly lower pitched (but the result was not statistically significant). The results essentially repeated those for Korean reported in Winter and Grawunder (2012), except that Korean showed more pronounced results than Japanese, including a significant effect for pitch (low pitch = deferential).

The authors then conducted a perception study to see if Japanese listeners were sensitive to the acoustic differences between honorific and non-honorific speech. This involved extracting the middle clauses from the reading task data produced by eight of the speakers in the production study, which featured identical lexical and morphological content produced in deferential and non-deferential situations. These speech fragments were then played to 20 Japanese listeners in pairs, with each pair featuring lexically and morphologically identical fragments produced in the two different situations. The task was to decide which of the two utterances was the deferential one.

Results showed that Japanese participants could successfully identify the deferential utterance 56 per cent of the time. This performance was reliably better than 50 per cent (chance level), but lower than the the result obtained for Korean in Brown et al. (2014), which was 70 per cent. Since the stimuli were devoid of verbal honorific markers, the above chance performances of the Japanese and Korean listeners shows that the stimuli contained phonetic features that signalled deferential and non-deferential meanings, although weakly in the case of Japanese.

In sum, the findings of this paper show that both Japanese and Korean exploit a number of phonetic features in addition to the obligatory grammatical markings to signal (non-)deferential meanings.

21.3.5 Irony

Attardo (2000: 817) defines irony (or sarcasm)[1] as language usage that "violates the conditions for contextual appropriateness", typically because the literal meaning is the opposite to the intended. For example, when a speaker utters a positive remark such as *Fantastic!* after the car breaks down. Ironic utterances may differ in the degree to which the irony is explicit or potentially ambiguous: *dry sarcasm* is often ambiguous on the verbal level, whereas *dripping sarcasm* is obviously sarcastic even in written form (Bryant and Fox Tree 2005: 260).

Speakers in many languages hold a belief that there is a specific ironic tone of voice. Indeed, when researchers ask participants to produce ironic speech they explicitly indicate sarcasm by lowering their pitch, raising their amplitude, and speaking more slowly (Rockwell 2000; González-Fuente 2017). TV actors use similar techniques (Bryant and Fox Tree 2005). However, studies of spontaneous speech find that speakers do not always use these "signature" features (Bryant and Fox Tree 2002), and that irony may be marked more subtly, if at all. Bryant's (2010) analysis of spontaneous speech found that speakers made prosodic contrasts within sentence pairs when the first utterance was non-ironic and the second ironic. These contrasts were not as frequent when both sentences were non-ironic. However, the actual acoustic differences between the sentence pairs were not consistent across speakers, except that ironic utterances were spoken by all speakers significantly slower than preceding speech. Bryant and Fox Tree (2002) concluded that the acoustic marking of sarcasm in spontaneous speech is unpredictable due to the fact that speakers are often simultaneously marking other stances and the complex interaction with the context.

Regarding gesture, speakers often use so-called ironic gestures (ironic winks, facial expressions involving specific eye and eyebrow configurations, raised eyebrows, laughter or smiles), together with head tilts or shoulder shrugs. Using examples from spontaneous conversations, Bryant (2011) observed that laughter is also used by speakers to indicate the presence of an ironic statement, as well as by listeners to mark comprehension of the ironic intention of the speaker (both in response laughter, as well as in laughter that occurs during or immediately after a social partner's laugh, e.g. so-called antiphonal laughter). In contrast, other studies have reported that a very common visual cue to irony in TV sitcoms is in fact the absence of any facial expression, i.e. a "blank face" (Attardo et al. 2003: 243).

Despite the lack of systematicity in the use of prosody and gesture in the expression of ironic intent, it is clear that the expression of irony is a multimodal affair. Clearly, irony comprehension is helped when prosodic and gestural features contrast with the meaning of the propositional

---

[1] We discuss irony and sarcasm together and do not enter the complex debate as to whether there is a difference between the two. Attardo (2000: 795) concludes that there is "no consensus on whether sarcasm and irony are essentially the same thing, with superficial differences, or if they differ significantly".

content of the utterance. For example, uttering *Fantastic* with a sad facial expression or with prosodic features conveying negative emotion such as slow tempo and low pitch and intensity, and a sad voice, will help in the conveyance of negative emotion and thus ironic intent (see González-Fuente 2017). Another case of reverse ironic intent can be perceived in the phenomenon of mock impoliteness, whereby negative verbal remarks can be understood as positive under certain social circumstances. As McKinnon and Prieto (2014) showed, prosodic and gestural features conveying positive emotions help listeners to comprehend the positive ironic intent.

21.3.6 Speaker Identity

Speakers manipulate language to dynamically construct aspects of their identities (see Chapter 15). Linguistic forms rarely if ever directly equate with identity. Rather, the identity-related meanings emerge when linguistic resources are used in particular contexts and in co-occurrence with other resources. Identity-related meanings are thus "second order" or "indirect" indexical meanings (e.g. Silverstein 2003; Ochs 1993) which are derived only in certain contexts.

The sound of the speaker's voice has the potential to signal whether the speaker belongs to different social groups in relation to factors including gender. In addition to the general tendency for women to speak with higher F0, women also tend to produce breathier phonation, whereas men produce more creaky voice (Podesva and Callier 2015: 178). However, these general patterns show variegation according to culture-specific gender roles, changing ideologies and other individual factors. Japanese women speak on average with higher pitch than American and Swedish women (Yamazawa and Hollien 1992) as well as Dutch women (Van Bezooijen 1995). In addition, some Japanese-English bilinguals use higher pitch when speaking Japanese (Ohara 2001). In experimental data reported in Van Bezooijen (1995), Japanese listeners found higher-pitched female voices attractive, whereas Dutch listeners did not. Van Bezooijen (1995: 264) concludes that Japanese women raise their pitch "in order to conform to sociocultural expectations stressing femininity". Meanwhile, more recently in the United States, women are producing higher rates of creaky voice than their male counterparts (Yuasa 2010).

Gendered patterns of speech are also variegated according to factors such as social class, race and sexuality. For instance, men in England who speak a variety of received pronunciation use less creaky voice than working class men from northern England (Henton and Bladon 1985). African American women use falsetto at high rates not typically found in white American women (Podesva 2007). Speakers can vary or manipulate the sound of their voice across different contexts in order to foreground different aspects of their identity. Podesva (2007) investigated the stylistic use of falsetto phonation by a gay medical student, Heath, across different situations. While attending a barbecue with intimate friends, Heath's falsetto was more frequent, longer and displayed higher f0 and wider f0 ranges, which he used to construct a diva persona (see Podesva and Callier 2015).

Gestures are also indexical resources for constructing speaker identity. In Section 21.3.1, we mentioned how Barack Obama uses finger-to-thumb precision grip gestures to highlight focal information. Lempert (2011) argues that this underlying, "first order" indexical meaning has in political debate taken on extra "second order" indexical meanings. Namely it has become discursively and iconically connected with an argumentative strategy colloquially known as "making a 'sharp' point" and ultimately with being a speaker who has sharp points to make, and is thus crisp, decisive and strong on details. Lempert (2011) shows how Obama's sharply increased use of precision grip gestures in the latter stages of the primaries accompanied an increasing perception that he was a substantial candidate. In this way, precision grip gestures rise through the indexical order from simple markers of linguistic focus, to key components of candidate brand.

Speakers may use subtle changes in non-verbal behaviour to negotiate their identities vis-à-vis established roles and social hierarchies. As noted in Section 21.3.4, position in the social hierarchy may lead to different expectations regarding the use of non-verbal behaviours. Hillewaert (2016) shows how interactants in Muslim communities in coastal Kenya manipulate the sensory details of handshakes to navigate shifting norms of conduct and new social positions. For instance, professional women may be careful to perform full hand kisses to female community elders to defy accusations that they have lost piety due to their entry into the world of work. In turn, female elders may subtly refuse the hand-kissing gesture by resisting the upward lifting of the hand in order to indicate that they recognize the valued position in society that the professional women have gained. Alternatively, women who do not approve of these shifts in social status may choose to receive the hand kiss, even when they are socially expected to reject it. In short, these subtle manipulations in greeting behaviour mark how speakers position their own identities vis-à-vis shifting societal norms.

21.3.7 Overview

Section 21.3 has overviewed previous research on how prosody and gesture are involved in six different areas of pragmatics: information status, phrase/discourse structure and turn-taking, epistemic stance, (im)politeness, irony and speaker identity. Table 21.1 in the next page summarizes the main findings of this section.

21.4 Summary and Future Directions

In recent decades, gesture studies have demonstrated that speech and gesture constitute a single communicative system which is well integrated

Table 21.1 *Main findings of sociopragmatic research on gesture and prosody*

	Area	Prosody	Gestures
1	Information status	• Prosodic prominence occurs on focal elements	• Beat gestures, head nods and eyebrow movements accompany focal information
2	Phrase structure, discourse structure and turn-taking	• Prosodic markers (e.g. tonal continuation rises, falling F0, final lengthening and pauses) mark the end of sentences • Prosodic means (e.g. final falling intonational patterns) are signals for turn holding/giving	• Gesture movements accompany syntactic structure • Hand gestures and eye gaze are used for turn holding/giving
3	Epistemic stance	• Delays, hesitations, elongations, higher pitch and specific final rising intonation contours mark degrees of speaker conviction • Language-specific intonation patterns are used for "disagreement prosody"	• Shoulder shrugging and facial gestures involving eye squinting and brow furrowing mark speaker certainty • Eyebrow furrowing and eyelid closure are used for disagreement
4	(Im)politeness	• There are claims that high pitch is universally associated with politeness • However, some politeness-related contexts may feature low pitch and a calmer, softer and less animated voice	• Politeness features more constrained gestures and non-verbal behaviours
5	Irony	• Lower pitch, raised amplitude and slower speech are prototypically associated with irony	• Winks, raised eyebrows, laughter or smiles, head tilts and shoulder shrugs may accompany ironic speech
6	Speaker identity	• Speakers manipulate pitch and other prosodic means to index aspects of their identities	• Gestures can be manipulated as indexical resources for constructing speaker identity

semantically, pragmatically and temporally with speech (Kendon 2004; Levinson and Holler 2014; McNeill 1992). In this chapter, we have shown that a specific linguistic trait, prosody, is more closely integrated with gesture than previously thought. We have reviewed empirical evidence from sociopragmatic communication studies showing that prosodic features of speech are intertwined with gestures at different levels. First, at the temporal level, gesture prominence is tightly coordinated with prosodic prominence in speech. Typically, prosodic prominence units (as pitch accents) and prosodic phrasing domains (as intonational phrases) function as anchoring domains for gestural movements (e.g. Ambrazaitis and House 2017; Esteve-Gibert et al. 2017; Krahmer and Swerts 2007; Guellaï et al. 2014; Krivokapic et al. 2016). Second, we have shown that speakers use prosodic and gestural patterns to jointly convey various communicative functions that include semantico-pragmatic functions such as epistemic positioning and information status, as well as politeness and speaker identity.

Future work in this field needs to look at prosody and gesture as integrated systems in multimodal communication. This is particularly important given that recent studies adopting a developmental view have shown that prosody and gesture overlap and also act as precursors of language development (e.g. Hübscher and Prieto 2019; Esteve-Gibert and Guellaï 2018). The ways that gesture interacts and coordinates with prosody lends support for the position of Gibbon (2009) as well as Zellers et al. (2016) that gesture should be regarded as an important part of the prosodic system, particularly in the context of discourse-level and sociopragmatic information. We believe that future studies need to capture the ways in which prosodic and gestural features are tightly integrated in speech from a sociopragmatic perspective.

Going forward, research will need to look in more depth at the complex ways in which speakers manipulate and coordinate multiple gestural and pragmatic resources during communication. Throughout the different areas covered in this chapter, we see that sociopragmatic meanings are created by the confluence of different cues, with no one-to-one relationship between linguistic features and sociopragmatic meanings. Although we may normatively consider certain words, prosodic patterns or gestures to mark certain pragmatic meanings, these meanings can be overridden when cues are mismatched with each other. In addition, the same multimodal cues can have a variety of different complementary sociopragmatic meanings. Grip gestures, for example, are related to contrastive focus, high epistemic commitment, as well as indexical meanings. Beat gestures have also been claimed to have an information structure and conversational interaction functions, as well as an epistemic function (see Prieto et al. 2018). Future studies need to work towards understanding how sociopragmatic meanings are communicated when multiple cues with underspecified and/or mismatched meanings converge during interaction. In this regard, there is a particular need for more studies that use naturalistic data to complement the experimental focus in the field to date.

Future work will also need to look at data from a wider range of languages and cultural contexts in order to better assess the universality or cultural specificity of prosodic and gestural features. Throughout the chapter, we have seen that research has tried to establish universal cross-linguistic patterns. For example, authors have proposed the so-called frequency and the effort codes for the expression of information status, speech act marking and politeness through high pitch (e.g. Ohala 1984; Gussenhoven 2002). Likewise, in studies of gesture, there have been recent claims about the universal nature of "disagreement face" (e.g. Benitez-Quiroz et al. 2016). However, these universalist claims have not always been supported when applied to new languages, raising the need to look for language-specific markers. The focus of these universalist claims on certain features (such as pitch) also potentially overlooks the importance of other prosodic and gestural features (Hübscher et al. 2017; Idemaru et al. 2019), which need more attention. All in all, we argue for the need to incorporate a multimodal view of language into sociopragmatic inquiry and investigate prosodic and gestural systems in tandem. From a methodological point of view, we claim that this multimodal analysis needs to include a flexible analysis not only of manual gestures but also facial expressions and other bodily movements as important signals of sociopragmatic meanings. Similarly, phonetic and phonological features of prosody should be included in order to fully embrace the holistic nature of sociopragmatic expression.

References

Ambrazaitis, G. and House, D. (2017), Multimodal prominences: Exploring the patterning and usage of focal pitch accents, head beats and eyebrow beats in Swedish television news readings. *Speech Communication*, 95, 100–113.

Attardo, S. (2000). Irony as relevant inappropriateness. *Journal of Pragmatics*, 32, 793–826.

Attardo, S., Eisterhold, J., Hay, J. and Poggi, I. (2003). Multimodal markers of irony and sarcasm. *International Journal of Humor Research*, 16, 243–60.

Bavelas, J. B., Gerwing, J. and Healing, S. (2014). Including facial gestures in gesture-speech ensembles. In M. Seyfeddinipur and M. Gullberg, eds., *From Gesture in Conversation to Visible Action as Utterance: Essays in Honor of Adam Kendon*. Amsterdam: John Benjamins, pp. 15–34.

Benitez-Quiroz, F. C., Wilburb, R. B. and Martinez, A. M. (2016). The not face: A grammaticalization of facial expressions of emotion. *Cognition*, 150, 77–84.

Boersma, P. and Weenink, D. (2017). Praat: Doing Phonetics by Computer [Computer program]. Version 6.0.35.

Borràs-Comes, J., Kiagia, E. and Prieto, P. (2019). Epistemic intonation and epistemic gesture are mutually co-expressive: Empirical results from two intonation–gesture matching tasks. *Journal of Pragmatics*, 150, 39–52.

Breen, M., Fedorenko, E., Wagner, M. and Gibson, E. (2010). Acoustic correlates of information structure. *Language and Cognitive Processes*, 25(7–9), 1044–98.

Brown, L. and Winter, B. (2019). Multimodal indexicality in Korean: "Doing deference" and "performing intimacy" through nonverbal behavior. *Journal of Politeness Research*, 15(1), 25–54.

Brown, L., Winter, B., Idemaru, K. and Grawunder, S. (2014). Phonetics and politeness: Perceiving Korean honorific and non-honorific speech through phonetic cues. *Journal of Pragmatics*, 66, 45–60.

Brown, P. and Levinson, S. C. (1987). *Politeness: Some Universals in Language Usage*. Cambridge: Cambridge University Press.

Bryant, G. A. (2010). Prosodic contrasts in ironic speech. *Discourse Processes*, 47(7), 545–66.

Bryant, G. A. and Fox Tree, J. E. (2002). Recognizing verbal irony in spontaneous speech. *Metaphor and Symbol*, 17(2), 99–119.

Bryant, G. A. and Fox Tree, J. E. (2005). Is there an ironic tone of voice? *Language and Speech*, 48(3), 257–77.

Bryant, G. A. (2011). Verbal irony in the wild. *Pragmatics and Cognition*, 19(2), 291–309.
Cavé, C., Guaïtella, I., Bertrand, R., Santi, S., Harlay, F. and Espesser, R. (1996). About the relationship between eyebrow movements and F0 variations. *Proceedings of ICSLP, 96*, 2175–9.
Crespo-Sendra, V., Kaland, K., Swerts, M. and Prieto, P. (2013). Perceiving incredulity: The role of intonation and facial gestures. *Journal of Pragmatics*, 47, 1–13.
Culpeper, J. (2011a). *Impoliteness: Using Language to Cause Offence*, Cambridge: Cambridge University Press.
Culpeper, J. (2011). "It's not what you said, it's how you said it!": Prosody and impoliteness. In Linguistic Politeness Research Group, ed., *Discursive Approaches to Politeness*. Mouton Series in Pragmatics 8. Berlin: Mouton de Gruyter, pp. 57–83.
Devís, E. and Cantero, F. (2014). The intonation of mitigating politeness in Catalan. *Journal of Politeness Research*, 10, 127–49.
de Haan, F. (2001). The relation between modality and evidentiality. In R. Müller and M. Reis, eds., *Modalität und Modalverben im Deutschen*. Linguistische Berichte 9. Hamburg, Germany: H. Buske, pp. 201–16.
Dimitrova, D. V., Stowe, L. A., Redeker, G. and Hoeks, J. C. (2012). Less is not more: Neural responses to missing and superfluous accents in context. *Journal of Cognitive Neuroscience*, 24(12), 2400–2418.
Dimitrova, D., Chu, M., Wang, L., Özyürek, A. and Hagoort, P. (2016). Beat that word: How listeners integrate beat gesture and focus in multimodal speech discourse. *Journal of Cognitive Neuroscience*, 28(9), 1255–69.
Escandell, V. (2017). Intonation and evidentiality in Spanish polar interrogatives. *Language and Speech*, 60(2), 224–41.
Esteve-Gibert, N., Borràs-Comes, J., Asor, E., Swerts, M. and Prieto, P. (2017). The timing of head movements: The role of prosodic heads and edges. *The Journal of the Acoustical Society of America*, 6(141), 4727–39.
Esteve-Gibert, N. and Guellaï, B. (2018). Prosody in the auditory and visual domains: A developmental perspective. *Frontiers in Psychology, 9*.
Gibbon, D. (2009). Gesture theory is linguistics: On modelling multimodality as prosody. *Proceedings of the Twenty-third Pacific Asia Conference on Language, Information and Computation*, pp. 9–18.
González-Fuente, S. (2017). *Audiovisual Prosody and Verbal Irony*. Universitat Pompeu Fabra, Departament of Translation and Language Sciences.
Goodwin, M., Goodwin, C. and Yaeger-Dror, M. (2002). Multi-modality in girls' game disputes. *Journal of Pragmatics*, 34, 1621–49.
Gravano, A. and Hirschberg J. (2011). Turn-taking cues in task-oriented dialogue, *Computer Speech and Language*, 25, 601–34.
Guellaï, B., Langus, A. and Nespor, M. (2014). Prosody in the hands of the speaker. *Frontiers in Psychology*, 5, 700.
Gussenhoven, C. (2002). Intonation and interpretation: Phonetics and phonology. In B. Bel and I. Marlien, eds., *Proceedings of the Speech Prosody*. Aix-en-Provence, France: Université de Provence, pp. 47–57.

Gussenhoven, C. (2004). *The Phonology of Tone and Intonation*, Cambridge: Cambridge University Press.

Haugh, M., Chang, W. and Kádár, D. (2015). Doing deference: Identities and relational practices in Chinese online discussion boards. *Pragmatics*, 25(1), 73–98.

Henton, C. G. and Bladon, R. A. W. (1985). Breathiness in normal female speech: Inefficiency versus desirability. *Language and Communication*, 5, 221–7.

Hillewaert, S. (2016). Tactics and tactility: A sensory semiotics of handshakes in coastal Kenya. *American Anthropologist*, 118(1), 49–66.

Hübscher, I. (2018). Preschoolers' pragmatic development: How prosody and gesture lend a helping hand. Unpublished doctoral dissertation, Universitat Pompeu Fabra, Barcelona, Spain.

Hübscher, I., Borràs-Comes, J. and Prieto, P. (2017). Prosodic mitigation characterizes Catalan formal speech: The Frequency Code reassessed. *Journal of Phonetics*, 65, 145–59.

Hübscher, I. and Prieto, P. (2019). Gestural and prosodic development act as sister systems and jointly pave the way for children's sociopragmatic development. *Frontiers in Psychology*, 10.

Hübscher, I., Sánchez-Conde, C., Borràs-Comes, J., Vincze, L. and Prieto, P. (submitted). Multimodal mitigation: How facial and body cues index social meaning in Catalan requests.

Idemaru, K., Winter, B. and Brown, L. (2019). Cross-cultural multimodal politeness: The phonetics of Japanese deferential speech in comparison to Korean. *Intercultural Pragmatics*, 16(5), 517–56.

Idemaru, K., Winter, B., Brown, L. and Oh, G. E. (2020). Loudness trumps pitch in politeness judgments: evidence from Korean deferential speech. *Language and Speech*, 60, 123–48.

Ito, M. (2004). Politeness and voice quality – The alternative method to measure aspiration noise. *Proceedings of the Second International Conference on Speech Prosody*. Nara, Japan: International Speech Communication Association pp. 213–16.

Ito, K. and Speer, S. R. (2008). Anticipatory effects of intonation: Eye movements during instructed visual search. *Journal of Memory and Language*, 58(2), 541–73.

Jun, S. (2005). *Prosodic Typology: The Phonology of Intonation and Phrasing*, Oxford: Oxford University Press.

Jun, S. (2014). *Prosodic Typology 2: The Phonology of Intonation and Phrasing*, Oxford: Oxford University Press.

Kádár, D. Z. and Haugh, M. (2013). *Understanding Politeness*. Cambridge: Cambridge University Press.

Kendon, A. (2004). *Gesture: Visible Action as Utterance*, Cambridge: Cambridge University Press.

Kita, S. and Essegbey, J. (2001). Pointing left in Ghana: How a taboo on the use of the left hand influences gestural practice. *Gesture*, 1(1), 73–95.

Krahmer, E. and Swerts, M. (2005). How children and adults produce and perceive uncertainty in audiovisual speech. *Language and Speech*, 48(1), 29–53.

Krahmer, E. and Swerts, M. (2007). The effects of visual beats on prosodic prominence: Acoustic analyses, auditory perception and visual perception. *Journal of Memory and Language*, 57(3), 396–414.

Krivokapic, J., Tiede, M. K., Tyrone, M. E. and Goldenberg, D. (2016). Speech and manual gesture coordination in a pointing task. *Proceedings of the Eighth International Conference on Speech Prosody*, pp. 1240–44.

R Core Team. (2016). R: A Language and Environment for Statistical Computing. R Foundation for Statistical Computing, Vienna, Austria. www.R-project.org/.

Swerts, M. and Krahmer, E. (2005). Audiovisual prosody and feeling of knowing. *Journal of Memory and Language*, 53(1), 81–94.

Ladd, D. R. (2008). *Intonational Phonology*. 2nd ed. Cambridge: Cambridge University Press.

Lempert, M. (2011). Barack Obama, being sharp: Indexical order in the pragmatics of precision-grip gesture. *Gesture*, 11(3), 241–70.

Levinson, S. C. and Holler, J. (2014). The origin of human multi-modal communication. *Philosophical Transactions of the Royal Society of London, Series B*, 369(1651), 20130302.

Lima, C. F., Castro, S. L. and Scott, S. K. (2013). When voices get emotional: A corpus of nonverbal vocalizations for research on emotion processing. *Behavior Research Methods*, 45(4), 1234–45.

Lin, H., Kwock-Ping, J. T. and Fon, J. (2006). An acoustic study on the paralinguistic prosody in the politeness talk in Taiwan Mandarin. *Proceedings from ISCA Tutorial and Research Workshop on Experimental Linguistics*, pp. 173–6.

McNeill, D. (1992). *Hand and Mind: What Gestures Reveal about Thought*, Chicago: University of Chicago Press.

McKinnon, S. and Prieto, P. (2014). The role of prosody and gesture in the perception of mock impoliteness. *Journal of Politeness Research*, 10(2), 185–219.

Nadeu, M. and Prieto, P. (2011). Pitch range, gestural information, and perceived politeness in Catalan. *Journal of Pragmatics*, 43(3), 841–54.

Ochs, E. (1993). Constructing social identity: A language socialization perspective. *Research on Language and Social Interaction*, 26(3), 287–306.

Ohala, J. J. (1984). An ethological perspective on common cross-language utilization of F0 of voice. *Phonetica*, 41, 1–16.

Ohara, Y. (2001). Finding one's voice in Japanese: A study of the pitch levels of L2 users. In A. Pavlenko, A. Brackledge, I. Piller and M. Teutsch-Dwye, eds., *Multilingualism, Second Language Learning, and Gender*. New York: Mouton de Gruyter, pp. 231–54.

Ola Orie, O. (2009). Pointing the Yoruba way. *Gesture*, 9(2), 237–61.

Orozco, L. (2008). Peticiones corteses y factores prosódicos. In Z. E. Herrera and P. Martín Butragueño, eds., *Fonología instrumental. Patrones fónicos y variación*. México DF: El Colegio de México, pp. 335–55.

Podesva, R. J. (2007). Phonation type as a stylistic variable: The use of falsetto in constructing a persona. *Journal of Sociolinguistics*, 11(4), 478–504.

Podesva, R. J. and Callier, P. (2015). Voice quality and identity. *Annual Review of Applied Linguistics*, 35, 173–94.

Prieto, P., Borràs-Comes, J., Tubau, S. and Espinal, T. (2013). Prosody and gesture constrain the interpretation of double negation. *Lingua*, 131, 136–50.

Prieto, P. and Borràs-Comes, J. (2018). Question intonation contours as dynamic epistemic operators. *Natural Language and Linguistic Theory*, 36(2), 563–86.

Prieto, P., Cravotta, A., Kushch, O., Rohrer, P. L. and Vilà-Giménez, I. (2018). Deconstructing beat gestures: A labelling proposal. *Proceedings of the International Conference on Speech Prosody 2018*, Poznan, Poland, 13–16 June.

Prieto, P., Puglesi, C., Borràs-Comes, J., Arroyo, E. and Blat, J. (2015). Exploring the contribution of prosody and gesture to the perception of focus using an animated agent. *Journal of Phonetics*, 49(1), 41–54.

Rockwell, P. (2000). Lower, slower, louder: Vocal cues of sarcasm. *Journal of Psycholinguistic Research*, 29(5), 483–95.

Roseano, P., González, M., Borràs-Comes, J. and Prieto, P. (2016). Communicating epistemic stance: How speech and gesture patterns reflect epistemicity and evidentiality. *Discourse Processes*, 53(3), 135–74.

Shattuck-Hufnagel, S. and Ren, A. (2018). The prosodic characteristics of non-referential co-speech gestures in a sample of academic-lecture-style speech. *Frontiers in Psychology*, 9, 1514.

Silverstein, M. (2003). Indexical order and the dialectics of social life. *Language and Communication*, 23, 193–229.

Stadler, S. (2007). *Multimodal (Im)politeness: The Verbal, Prosodic and Non-Verbal Realization of Disagreement in German and New Zealand English*. Hamburg, Germany: Verlag Dr. Kovac.

Swerts, M. and Krahmer, E. (2005). Audiovisual prosody and feeling of knowing. *Journal of Memory and Language*, 53, 81–94.

Tessendorf, S. (2007). Pragmatic functions of gestures: The case of the 'brushing aside gesture' in Spanish conversation. *Proceedings of the International Pragmatics Association Conference 2007*, Gothenburg, Sweden, 8–12 July.

Van Bezooijen, R. (1995). Sociocultural aspects of pitch differences between Japanese and Dutch women. *Language and Speech*, 38(3), 253–65.

Vanrell, M. M., Stella, A., Gili-Fivela, B. and Prieto, P. (2013). Prosodic manifestations of the Effort Code in Catalan, Italian, and Spanish contrastive focus. *Journal of the International Phonetics Association*, 43(2), 195–220.

Vanrell, M. M., Armstrong, M. and Prieto, P. (2017). Experimental evidence for the role of intonation in evidential marking. *Language and Speech*, 60(2), 242–59.

Wilkins, D. (2003). Why pointing with the index finger is not a universal (in sociocultural and semiotic terms). In S. Kita, eds., *Pointing: Where Language, Culture, and Cognition Meet*. Mahwah, NJ: Erlbaum, pp. 171–215.

Winter, B. and Grawunder, S. (2012). The phonetic profile of Korean formal and informal speech registers. *Journal of Phonetics*, *40*(6), 808–15.

Yamazawa, H. and Hollien, H. (1992). Speaking fundamental frequency pattern of Japanese women. *Phonetica*, *49*, 128–40.

Yuasa, I. P. (2010). Creaky voice: A new feminine voice quality for young urban-oriented upwardly mobile American women? *American Speech*, *85*(3), 315–37.

Zellers, M., House, D. and Alexanderson, S. (2016). Prosody and hand gesture at turn boundaries in Swedish. *Proceedings of the International Conference on Speech Prosody*, pp. 831–5.

22

Digitally Mediated Communication

Chaoqun Xie and Francisco Yus

22.1 Introduction

It may be no exaggeration to say that with the rise of the internet and the advent of the always-available, seamless connectivity of mobile devices, human beings are now living a substantial part of their lives in digital environments (see Rainie and Wellman 2012). Labels for the impact of the internet on human lives include *digital body* (Broadhurst and Price 2017), *digital citizen* (Ohler 2010), *digital communication* (Tagg 2015), *digital consumption* (Belk and Llamas 2013), *digital culture* (Creeber and Martin 2009), and *digital existence* (Lagerkvist 2019), to name just a few. Although the boundaries between the online world and the offline world are becoming more and more blurred, and with more and more interconnections and interactions between them, the digital revolution has spread to almost every corner of the globe, impacting dramatically almost every aspect of human life. Digital connectivity and mobility are indispensable to the social and communicative life of human beings, and digitally mediated communication is now normal for most societies (Herring et al. 2013; Georgakopoulou and Spilioti 2016; Hoffmann and Bublitz 2017; Xie and Yus 2018). Lane (2019: 3) expresses similar ideas when he notes that "the rise of digitally networked technologies has radically changed the ways people connect and relate, presence and awareness of others, access and exposure to information, and the very structure of everyday life". The advent of the digital revolution has contributed to the emergence of a bigger and augmented world, or rather, a more extensive and expansive world by providing both fascinating opportunities and serious challenges for social and interpersonal interaction (see e.g. Bou-Franch and Garcés-Conejos Blitvich 2019).

This chapter is mainly about digitally mediated communication and how internet-mediated communication (henceforth IMC), may fit the underlying assumptions of sociopragmatics. This IMC label is more suitable than other alternative acronyms such as CMC (computer-mediated communication) which looks more outdated to us.

As a starting point, we agree with Márquez Reiter and Placencia (2005: 192) that one of the goals of sociopragmatics is "to uncover the cultural norms which underlie the interactional features of a given social group in a given social context; that is to say, to make the interactants' implicit sociocultural knowledge and values explicit". Therefore, sociopragmatics, or societal pragmatics (see e.g. Mey 2016), is concerned about sociocultural contexts and how these are enacted, assumed, fostered, unveiled or reacted upon through interaction. Speaking of interaction, we are committed to the view that "the roots of human sociality lie in a special capacity for social interaction" (Levinson 2006: 39).

The term interaction is itself conceptualized as a dynamic process, in which intended meanings and inferred interpretations are constantly negotiated between the interlocutors according to certain contextual parameters including the context of situation and broader contextual margins such as the interlocutors' speech community. Hence, for analysts of sociopragmatics, the ways in which interlocutors ascribe meanings to utterances in socially contextualized situations gives us analysts information about their sociocultural knowledge and social norms of behaviour. Interestingly, these sociocultural norms and values are explicitly sought by the analyst, but often stored and enacted by the interlocutors themselves in ways that are normally beyond their full awareness. Within *cyberpragmatics* (Yus 2011) or internet pragmatics (Xie and Yus 2017, 2018; Xie et al. 2021), cultural and social information is conceptualized as *filtering* into the individual's mind and *leaking* from meaning in interaction. A nice proposal in this direction is Escandell-Vidal's (2004), which proposes, within a broad relevance-theoretic stance, a picture of human cognition as capable of processing, almost simultaneously, both the specific information from utterances and the social information obtained from the processing of verbal stimuli. Basically, two *cognitive skills* (or *faculties*) of the human mind are pictured, namely the *inferential cognitive system* responsible for processing the utterance, and the *social cognitive system*, which contrasts the information obtained in the interpretation of utterances to already-stored social information. The *social system*, the most interesting for sociopragmatics, is devoted to obtaining and stabilizing social and cultural features that are assessed during daily interactions with others, a universal inferential procedure. However, the *social system* is also culture-specific, since every culture has a particular way of organizing shared social and cultural representations and there are even different ways of conceptualizing the world we live in depending on the culture, together with different rules for engaging in communication and interaction.

Of course, this duality of cognitive and social systems connects to the traditional distinction by Leech (1983) between *pragmalinguistics* and *sociopragmatics*. As summarized in Marmaridou (2011: 77), the former is typically interested in the study of the particular resources that a given language provides for conveying pragmatic meaning (illocutionary and interpersonal), whereas sociopragmatics addresses the relationship between pragmatic meaning and the assessment of participants' social distance, the language community's social rules and appropriateness norms, discourse practices and accepted behaviours. This methodological distinction, Marmaridou contends, has been widely adopted in work in pragmatics ever since Leech's initial proposal in 1983.

22.2 Sociopragmatics, Ethnography and Data Gathering on the Internet

In theory, sociopragmatics should be straightforwardly applicable to IMC, since storing and enacting social information through interactions are two highly relevant mental and communicative tasks both in their universal and culture-specific attributes, and therefore these are also bound to be at work in internet-mediated interactions. But the specific qualities of the internet, with its ubiquity beyond the physical, cultural and social boundaries and with its capacity to bring together both *anonymous* and *nonymous* interactants, pose a challenge for analysts.

Besides, IMC is constantly evolving and sites or *apps* for interaction, together with options for coding and interpreting utterances, are also changing constantly. Take sociopragmatic variation, for example. It may be defined as "the way in which speakers vary their use of language in similar situational contexts with similar communicative purposes and thus exhibit different interactional features/patterns. These, in turn, possibly reflect different cultural norms" (Márquez Reiter and Placencia 2005: 192–3). The primary focus when studying sociopragmatics is to identify and/or compare the interactional patterns of given social groups in given situational contexts. These "given social groups" are also found on the internet, with similar linguistic markers, vocabulary or interactive rules that act as barriers of group specificity (Yus 2015), as happens with the Tunisian letter-based (and not Arabic-based) social media discourses illustrated in example (11) below. However, the Net also brings together heterogeneous users from radically different cultural backgrounds. This poses a challenge for sociopragmatics, since the Net is accessible from everywhere and producing discourses online is not limited by social or regional constraints.

A related issue is how to gather naturally occurring data from interactions, which is not only faced by sociopragmatics but also by sociolinguistics (more interested in broad social issues such as dialects, age and gender constraints, among others, than in how social issues are enacted or leak from everyday social practices), discourse analysis (more concerned with language than with the underlying intentions or leaked social information) and offline ethnography (more interested in direct access to social phenomena), among others. Furthermore, the very term "natural" is not devoid of discussion, either (see e.g. Potter 2002; Speer 2002; Golato 2017; Jucker 2018; Culpeper and Gillings 2019). In general, though, the idea or rather, the ideal, is to record interactions beyond the interactants' acknowledgement that these are being used for linguistic or pragmatic research. In this case, some asynchronous forms of IMC may be less challenging for sociopragmatics, since very often the data is easier to gather (as in Twitter or Facebook, as long as permission is granted), because of the persistent nature of the data. Other types of internet-mediated interaction pose other challenges. For example, there are ethical issues involving instant messaging conversations, which are private and users are often unwilling to provide the researcher with sample conversations. Similar ethical issues are found in synchronous video-mediated oral conversations through the Net (e.g. Skype), whose data should not be recorded without the users' awareness that these interactions are being used for research purposes.

The extent of these data-gathering challenges has varied as the interactions themselves have evolved from the initial text-based conversations that were so popular in the early years of the 1990s to today's interactions filled with visual and multimodal content. In this sense, Androutsopoulos (2006: 420) identifies three main *waves*, phases in sociolinguistic research on IMC. In the first one, language use on the internet is treated as distinct, homogeneous, and indecipherable to "outsiders". The Net is conceptualized as a whole, and individual modes or genres are regarded as linguistically uniform due to shared technological properties, and these properties are seen to determine language use (Bolander and Locher 2014: 16). In this first phase, there is an emphasis on "descriptive accounts" of online language, with special focus on the hybrid combination of written and spoken features, and differences between synchronous and asynchronous forms of IMC. In the second wave, there is a move into the acknowledgement of how technological, social and contextual factors interplay in the shaping of computer-mediated language practices. Finally, in the third wave, research becomes more focused on the role of linguistic variability in the formation of social interaction and social identities on the internet. This last phase is most tightly connected with the interest of sociopragmatic research.

Besides the problem of data gathering, analysts of sociopragmatics face an incredibly varied amount of content produced and exchanged on the Net, through desktop programs and mobile phone *apps*. Indeed, the IMC discourses produced and inferred exhibit qualities that cross-cut dichotomies such as synchronous-asynchronous, written-oral, visual-verbal and human- versus system-generated, among others, and much of the internet-mediated content does not fit neatly into the aforementioned pairs. For example, discourse of chats and instant messaging conversations often exhibit a mixture of written (i.e. typed) and oral qualities, what has been labelled *oralized written text* (see Yus 2005, 2011) and *orthographic emotive expression* (Albritton 2017) among other proposals (see also Georgakopoulou 2006: 549–50; Herring 2007). Besides, typically asynchronous forms of communication such as email often feel as if the users are engaged in a synchronous conversation if the connection is fast enough. Finally, many discourses on the internet do not fit neatly the label of *verbal* or *visual*, but in general are made of multimodal combinations of text, image, sound and text, as in the case of many memes that spread across populations (see Yus 2018a, 2019a).

As has already been mentioned, sociopragmatics is related to sociolinguistics and ethnography in its interest in how social information emerges from social interactions. In Yus (2018b), the ethnographic approach is underlined as a crucial form of social information gathering, but its application to virtual settings entails a revision of its objectives, methodology and even the way data are gathered from sample dialogues and interactions. One problem is that the analyst cannot *live* among the users to conclude what social aspects are assumed and reinforced through online interactions; instead, partial logging onto the social sites is expected. Besides, identity play and anonymity are frequent on the Net and the ethnographer may well be deceived in the research. Indeed, identity exhibits multiple, hybrid, fluid, relational, situated and even contested qualities. For instance, users of messaging apps such as WhatsApp are able to divide their contacts or friends into different groups and share different types of content with different groups, thus presenting, invoking or even manipulating different identities and group-centred discourses within different groups. Of course, it should be noted that identity construction and self-presentation on the internet are partly influenced by technological affordances (i.e. the discursive resources made available by the program or app for identity shaping, as happens for example with some messaging *apps* that were initially text-based but later added the possibility of using visual discourses, audio files or even video-mediated calls), and this may be regarded as an example of how the internet both contributes to and constrains social interaction. Here, we may also find that identity can be, or rather, is actually, linked to morality in that the identity a person projects can tell us something about the very person's morality (see Xie and Yus 2017; Xie 2018a; Chapter 15).

22.3 Digital Communication and Research Interests for Sociopragmatics

22.3.1 Discourse Used in Digital Communication

In Yus (2011: 17–18), it is proposed that internet discourses may be placed on a *scale of contextualization* ranging from highly context-saturated media (video conferencing, internet-enabled phone calls, chat rooms with web cam etc.) to highly cues-filtered text-based media (traditional chat rooms, email, SMS etc.). In this sense, the discourse typically exchanged among users in conversations mediated by typed texts is a hybrid of written (typed) and oral modes of communication (see Jucker and Dürscheid 2012), with frequent discursive strategies such as repetition of letters, creative use of punctuation marks, strategic use of capitalization, and also the use of emoticons and *emoji* (Danesi 2017). Within *cyberpragmatics* (Yus 2011), it is assumed that these alterations of default, unmarked text possess communicative value and increase the eventual relevance of the text, either because "addressee users" obtain a clearer picture of the sender users' feelings, emotions and impressions, or because they find it easier to access interpretations that depart more or less substantially from the interpretations that are literally coded in the text, as happens with irony, joking, teasing and banter. As Fussell and Moss (1998) state, the conventional affective lexicon does not suffice for expressing the nuances of specific emotional experiences. Many affective terms are used loosely and therefore may not have the precision speakers desire. Faced with this limitation, users tend to resort to text alterations (*oralized written text*) and *emoji* in order to ensure a more adequate coding (and the addressee user's eventual inference) of this non-propositional information, although some more ludic uses of *emoji* and oralized text may also be found in messaging *apps*.

In general, users assume that departures from default standard typed text, regardless of how intense these departures might be, possess some communicative value which is not obtainable from plain typed text. In Wiseman (2013: 29), for example, there are quotes by young mobile users which indicate that both text oralization and *emoji* use can radically alter the eventual interpretation of the message, and are inferred as such by the users when they come across these strategies in the messages that they interpret:

> Dre Gambrell (18 years old): "You can tell what she wants pretty much by how she texts. The dry "Hey" is O.K. But then there's some that have the "Heyyy" with the extra y's and the winky face, and that means this conversation could possibly go somewhere. They.re probably the hooking-up type".

> Ian Davis (19 years old): "When I see a smiley face, it's the opening of the doorway to emotions. That first emoticon is significant. When it comes, it means something".

In the bibliography, *oralized written text* and the use of *emoji* have been signalled as a useful discursive tools to obtain the communication of a number of effects and propositions that typed text alone would be unable to convey. In Yus (2005), several communicative uses are listed specifically for texts exchanged in chat rooms, among others the following are worth commenting briefly:

1. To function as a procedural device guiding the reader towards the kind of inferential processing that should be applied to the subsequent stretch of discourse. Consider (1):

    (1) <stefany> jooooooo pronto empieza el curso.
    [Jeez! The school term starts soon].

In (1) "jooooooo" would encode procedural information activating various attitudinal schemas into which the utterance following them would be embedded. The reader of (1) would be instructed not to infer that the subsequent stretch of discourse is to be interpreted as encoding an assertive higher-level explicature (<stefany> believes that the school term starts soon) but that this stretch is produced with a different attitudinal schema, which is interpreted as an "S regrets that *p*" schema.

2. Textual alteration should be a good resource for chat users when they intend to communicate the higher-level attitude-connoted explicature of the utterance, especially when the propositional attitude is not coded by conventional linguistic means. In (2), for instance, textual alteration is useful in pinning down the user's propositional attitude (I regret that *p*), since the proposition expressed by the utterance could well be interpreted as an assertion, unless textual alteration underlines the attitude:

    (2) <saratogo> estoy gorrrrrrrrrddddoooooooooooooooooooooooo [gordo].
    [I am fat].

3. Users have feelings which they want to communicate to the other users and they resort to textual alteration in an attempt to favour both an identification and a measurement of these feelings. Therefore, while some chat users simply type the closest – and more conventional – way of coding their feelings, as in (3a), others frequently rely on textual alteration, as in (3b):

    (3) a. <ferrari> me siento solo.
    [I feel lonely].
    b. <morena> me aburrooooooooooooooooooooooooooooooo.
    [I am bored].

Concerning the use of emoticons and *emoji*, some pragmatic uses have also been proposed. In Yus (2014a), for example, up to eight functions were proposed (1) to signal the propositional attitude that underlies the utterance and which would be difficult to identify without the aid of the emoticon, as in (4a); (2) to communicate a higher intensity of a propositional attitude which has already been coded verbally, as in (4b); (3) to strengthen/mitigate the illocutionary force of a speech act, as in (4c); (4) to contradict the explicit content of the utterance (joking), as in (4d); (5) to contradict the explicit content of the utterance (irony), as in (4e); (6) to add a feeling or emotion towards the propositional content of the utterance (affective attitude towards the utterance), as in (4f); (7) to add a feeling or emotion towards the communicative act (feeling or emotion in parallel to the communicative act), as in (4g); and (8) to communicate the intensity of a feeling or emotion that has been coded verbally, as in (4h):

(4)   a. I have no time to get bored, nor to read :(([*sad face emoticon*].
[I regret that I have no time to get bored, nor to read].
        b. I hope you'll always remember my Spanish lessons :-) [*smile emoticon*].
        c. Stop writing about me! You're obsessed! XDDDDDD [*wide smile emoticon*].
[the force of the directive is softened by the emoticon].
        d. [Text commenting on a photo of a shop with the same name as the addressee user]. I didn't know you had a shop in Alicante :)))))) [*connoted smile emoticon*]. Kisses.
        e. What a hard life you lead xD [*wide smile emoticon*].
        f. Saturday at home :-) [*smile emoticon*].
[Spending Saturday at home makes me happy].
        g. How pretty!!! Some parties, uh! You never stop!!!! :-) [*smile emoticon*].
        h. Sounds great!! So excited to see you!! :-) [*smile emoticon*].

Crucially for sociopragmatics, text alteration and *emoji* may be used in order to communicate social information beyond the propositional content coded in the text. Indeed, in many synchronous internet interactions, for example on messaging *apps*, the messages exchanged are often devoid of objective relevance (i.e. they do not provide substantial information) but raise the interlocutor's interest precisely in their phatic quality. For example, these innovative textual strategies and the use of accompanying *emoji* may be an ideal means to remind addressee users of the kind of social position that they occupy in the physical-virtual group and the feelings associated with this group membership, an important source of identity shaping and self-expression on the internet. Consider (5), taken from a Facebook conversation and translated into English in (6):

(5)   Usuaria 1: que guapa!!! pedazo fiestas que te pegas, no paras!!!! ☺
        Usuaria 2: La próxima t aviso a ver si te animas!!!!!! ☺
(6)   User 1: how pretty!!! Great parties you go to, you never stop!!!! ☺
        User 2: Next time I'll let you know, in case you feel like it!!! ☺

In this example, in which the original yellow *emoji* of a smiling face has been replaced with the text-processing default equivalent icon for practical editing reasons, two young female users 1 and 2 are having a casual, phatic conversation on Facebook. As is always the case with coded content, the proposition literally communicated by User 2 has to be inferentially enriched so as to yield a relevant explicit (and/or implicated) interpretation. In other words, coded content *underdetermines* communicated (i.e. inferred) interpretations (the coded content in the utterance always communicates less information than is eventually inferred in its interpretation). In the specific case of (5–6), User 1 will be expected to enrich inferentially User 2's utterance into roughly the proposition quoted in (7), the *explicature* in relevance-theoretic terms (Sperber and Wilson 1995), in which added inferred content appears between square brackets:

(7) CONTEXTUALIZED EXPLICIT INTERPRETATION
Next time [I go to a party] I'll let you know in case you feel like [coming] [with me] [to that party].

User 1 is also expected to infer User 2's *higher-level explicature*. These are further characterizations of explicatures by adding, for example, the speaker's attitude when saying an utterance or the utterance's underlying speech act schema. For example if someone asks "Can you help me to find work?" and the interlocutor answers, with sadness, that she cannot help him, we could establish an explicature of her answer (She cannot help him to find work) and several higher-level explicatures expressed by the same answer, such as "she says that she cannot help him to find work; she believes that she cannot help him to find work; or she regrets not being able to help him to find work" (see Yus 1998). In the specific case of (5–6) above, a possible higher-level explicature would be (8):

(8) PROPOSITIONAL ATTITUDE (towards content of utterance)
[I inform you that] next time [I go to a party] I'll let you know in case you feel like [coming] [with me] [to that party].

Now, a question arises: is that all that User 2 intends to communicate to User 1? Obviously not. She also wants her to know that she would love User 1 to join her at the party (in other words, she wants to communicate her *affective attitude*), and the *emoji* of the smiling face helps User 2 to convey this feeling. Besides, User 2 wants to show her that this is not an open-ended question; she wants to convey the idea that some insistence and urge underlie this invitation, and she resorts to the repetition of the exclamation mark so as to achieve her communicative purposes. The resulting proposition would be the one quoted in (9) below:

(9) AFFECTIVE ATTITUDE (towards whole communicative act)
[I inform you that] [I am happy to tell you that] next time [I go to a party] I'll let you know in case you feel like [coming] [with me] [to that party] [and I insist that you accept to come].

This latest proposition is the one that would be more interesting to a sociopragmatics of IMC. Indeed, from this exchange, the analyst can infer, with the aid of text alteration and the use of *emoji*, aspects of the social relationship existing between User 1 and User 2, the joy of group membership and the importance of social bonding.

22.3.2 Digitally Mediated Interactions

Digitally mediated interactions are essential for the users' assessment of their personal qualities against those of the collectivity of users (personal identity, self-concept, identity management etc.) and also for the reinforcement of the user's status within certain social groups, either the ones that the user *chooses* to be part of, or macro-social collectivities in terms of gender, occupation, nationality etc. Additionally, personal and social issues (i.e. the individual related to the group and the individual within the group) are an inherent research interest of sociopragmatics as this information is typically embedded in broad cultural contexts. This is so despite the fact that the Net often exhibits a fragmentary social background of interlocutors, who can log onto the system (e.g. a chat room) from a myriad of places all over the world.

Digitally mediated interactions are highly heterogeneous, and discursively variable, and this poses a challenge for sociopragmatic analysis. For example, Bolander and Locher (2014: 16) list a number of attributes that make the analysis of digitally mediated interaction a challenging endeavour:

(a) People in different numbers engage in various forms of interaction (dyadic vs multi-party interactions); (b) with other users who bring to the interaction their differing backgrounds and characteristics. (c) These interactions exhibit different rates of intensity; (d) and follow varied purposes intended to satisfy group requirements or be delimited to particular interactions. (e) The virtual group itself may pursue a specific topic or chat freely without pre-established goals in the interaction; and (f) the goals may entail various interactional activities. (g) The "tone" of these activities may also vary, ranging from friendly chat to very formal exchanges. (h) The participants are also strongly guided by "norms" for language use and socialization, which may be imposed on the users by some form of authority, and/or emerge as the interaction is sustained in time. (i) Finally, the interaction is carried out by using a specific writing system and performed in a particular language variety. All of these factors, Bolander and Locher contend, need to be considered when collecting and analysing data, as any number of them (in isolation or combination) may influence the way interlocutors use language. This diversity of language use online is a challenge for researchers. In any case, our opinion is that we can still find on the internet tightly uniform patterns of socialization, as happens, for example, in fora of migrants or certain blogs, and these should pose no problem of a sociopragmatic analysis.

For us, the most important quality of digitally mediated interactions, as has been stressed above, is how personal and the collective information unfold or *leak* from online interactions, often without an explicit reference to this person- or group-related information (see Yus 2014b, 2016), which is especially pervasive in casual interactions such as the ones through instant messaging and social networking sites. Consider this dialogue, on a user's Facebook wall, among several girls in their twenties (originally in Spanish, our translation and reproduced with permission). Again, smiling *emoji* have been replaced with word-processing default icons for editing purposes:

(10) User 1: I've just been accepted as teacher-in-training at the Secondary School!!!! and I am going with my mate User 2!!! I cannot be happier!!! ☺ ☺

User 2: Congrats User 1!!! These two girls on the loose at the School, what a danger! We'll have a jolly good time!! ☺

User 3: I am happy for you

User 4: You are the best!

User 1: let's see if I can get my students to love me even if it's just a bit of how much they love you!!

User 5: congratulations! ☺

User 4: It will be your best experience of life, unforgettable, enriching and full of learning . . . I'm sure you'll get a lot of love from them . . .

User 1: thanks User 5!!!xx

User 6: User 1!!! these pupils should get ready for what is about to come! haha only joking, you know, enjoy it, it's the best experience there is (ah let's talk, when? today?? tomorrow???)

User 1: not today because I am having supper with the gang in the gym . . . hehe, I rarely go to the gym but I couldn't miss the supper! :-) tomorrow evening-night is fine by me! when are you available, goatface ☺?

User 7: Sure you'll succeed . . . welcome to the guild!!!!

User 8: Congratulations!!! So good, User 1!! You deserve it!!!

User 9: You don't know how happy I am!!! . . . well, you do! ☺ Beware of the students, because I'm a teacher! I adore you beauty ;-x

This example shows how personal and social information overlay and are intertwined as the textual interaction unfolds, with similar impacts on the user's identities to the ones found in intense face-to-face interactions among friends. The dialogue starts with what in Yus (2014b) was labelled *interactivity trigger*, a text that is intended to *trigger* a number of responses from friends and acquaintances, which will themselves generate an offset of rewarding effects for the initial user. Some of the comments do indeed flatter User 1 and impact her personal identity. At the same time, however, the analyst may uncover some interesting information about these girls and their social groups or cultural backgrounds. User 1 and User 2 are part of the group of girls within a certain age (their twenties) and shared cultural background (Spain, Valencia), but they also belong to the job-related community of secondary school teachers. They are also flattered by the other girls even though they do not belong to that group. Furthermore, User 1 belongs to the social group of the gym, and even though she rarely attends the gym, she does feel part of the group and is willing to join them in a social gathering.

Notice, also, how this Facebook interaction is not only used as a means to describe the users' social groups but also to arrange a gathering or conversation offline. Besides, the vocabulary and expressions used are also interesting data for the sociopragmatics analyst concerning the kind of social bonding that unites them, including the affectionate nickname *goat-face*, the inclusion of emoticon/emoji and onomatopoeias, among others.

Furthermore, users exhibit and manage their social identity by uploading verbal, visual or multimodal content that links the user with activities involving peers and collectivities (photos of friends having a meal, teachers gathered at a conference . . .), and sometimes use these utterances as interactivity triggers. In these cases, there is as much relevance in the "audience validation" (i.e. its positive reaction), as in the interpretation of the content uploaded. This is so essential that when users upload content, they are constantly predicting their peers' reaction and also expecting it (Stern 2008: 106; Maghrabi et al. 2014: 370, Vitak and Kim 2014: 466; Greitemeyer 2016: 185). This is especially pervasive in content uploaded by youngsters, always desperate to get legitimation through comments and reactions (Salimkhan et al. 2010).

22.3.3 The Social Side of Internet Communication

Not surprisingly, this social aspect of digitally mediated communication is the one that mostly suits a sociopragmatics of IMC, especially concerning social identities as enacted, inferred and stored through internet-mediated interactions. However, the interplay of physical and virtual social identities has shifted as the Net itself has acquired more prominence in people's lives. In Yus (2018c), up to five stages of physical-virtual relationships are proposed:

1. *Online identity as irrelevant*. This happened mainly in the 1990s, when the internet had hardly any impact on users' identity.
2. *Offline inverted triangle versus online re-inverted triangle*. As can be seen in Figure 22.1, this stage occurred at the end of last century, in which offline sources of identity can be pictured as an inverted triangle, the broad top part devoted to social, inherited sources of identity – nationality, race, sex – the middle part for interactions within optional groups and acquaintances, and the narrow bottom part for the user as holder of a unique identity and parallel idiolect. On the Net, this triangle would be re-inverted, the former broad top becoming narrowed due to the capacity of the internet to filter out "inherited" social aspects, the middle part being roughly the same though this time developed and sustained online, and the former narrow part of the self would now be broad, due to the possibility to play with different identities online.
3. *Real virtualities*. At the beginning of this century a process of growing virtualization of physical places for interaction was perceived (i.e. people shying away from physical contexts for interaction) in parallel to a growing importance of online sources of identity management (i.e. people increasingly managing their interactions through the internet, see Yus 2007).

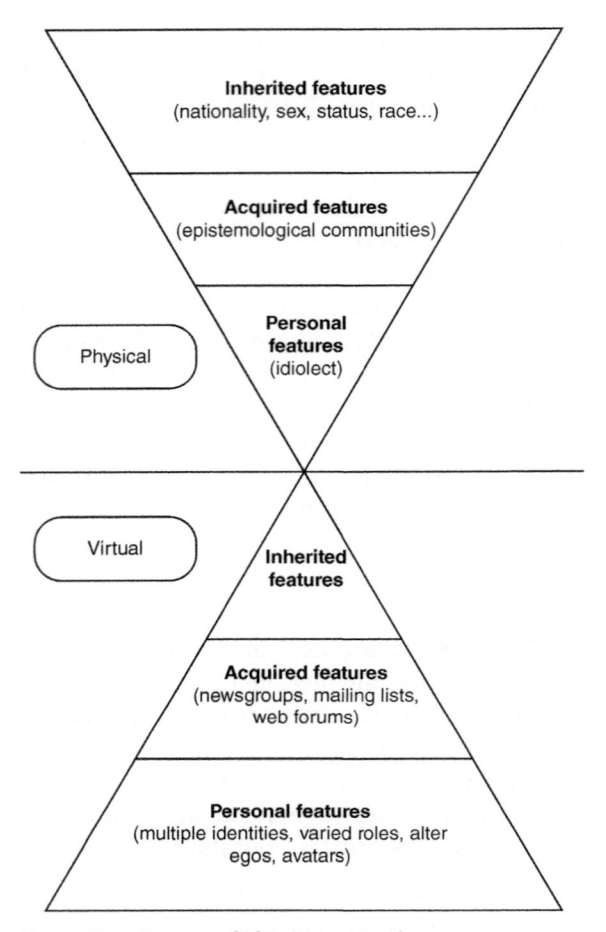

Figure 22.1 Sources of identity as triangles.

4. The *user as a node* of intersecting online-offline interactions. This is the typical scenario nowadays, with the users seamlessly shaping their identities online and offline without really differentiating them in their functions or management.
5. The same pattern as (4), but this time with a *presumption of online-offline congruence*, since now the user is expected to remain the same in both environments, as happens with social networking sites such as Facebook or Instagram.

Undoubtedly, the main source of data for sociopragmatic analysis is the virtual community, which has become more and more imbricated and hybridized with physical communal counterparts as people's reliance on the Net for their social needs has increased across the aforementioned stages (Yus 2007). Undoubtedly, these virtual communities and the language used therein may be an important marker of social identity and an important source of information for analysts within sociopragmatics. For example, certain types of online discourse (or some form of online code of behaviour, interface use etc.) are only comprehensible to those who belong to a specific social group within some delimited space of the Net, thus generating feelings of community membership and parallel feelings of being excluded by those unable to understand the discourse properly (Yus 2014a). An example of discourse fitting this role of community bonding is the use of Roman letters and numbers (instead of Arabic language) among the Tunisian youth, and these texts are only comprehensible to them, and not to others such as some adults with whom they do not want to share the information from their posts, and in this case the discourse exhibited strengthens their group membership and feelings of community bonding. An example from a Facebook dialogue among several Tunisian girls is quoted in (11):

(11) User 1: Nharek zin ya mezyana ... nharek as3ad layam.
[Have a nice day my friend. Good morning].
User 2: Ma7leeehaaaa 9e3ayeda trois erouuh sahaaa.
[I love it, what a beautiful atmosphere].
User 1: 7ata commenterek yrod rou7 ye fatouna hh.
[Your comment is more beautiful than the garden haha].
User 3: Bjr les fifis saha likommm.
[Good morning girls, have a nice time].
User 1: samsoum lik wa7cha.
[Many thanks; I miss you].
User 3: Ntouma zeda.
[Thanks. Me too].
User 4: Sa7aa les fifis w nchallah nharkom zin.
[Have a nice day, girls].
User 1: yaatik saha w far7a amouuul.
[Wish you happiness, my friend].

Dialogues like this generate a strong feeling of collective identity which emanates from exchanges which are often casual and trivial, but not devoid of importance for the social group (and for the analyst of sociopragmatics). As was argued in Yus (2016), this identity is shaped by this kind of discursive marker that indicates membership to broad collectivities and communities. People store a number of common-sense assumptions that emanate from the human environment and our trust in these assumptions is not easily altered by other in-coming stimuli. The fact that we belong to a specific community entails the creation and storage of certain archetypical assumptions that we accept as "normal" in the ordinary life of the community (Yus 2007; Parks 2011: 106–11). For those belonging to a community it is interesting to assess which information is shared by the whole community, as happens with the command of the type of language used by Tunisian youth in dialogues such as the one quoted in (11) above. And interactions are a good means to determine this area of mutuality. Besides, the reiterative assessment of this area generates *community stereotypes,* made up of highly accessible stereotypical schemas. This is part of the tendency of human cognition to form and maintain ties, to weigh one's social prestige against other people's, to assess the effect of our actions on other people's opinions and to predict their plausible replies.

22.4 Future Directions

So far in this chapter, we have analysed the social qualities of IMC as communicated propositionally, mainly as coded (typed) content that is inferred and from which certain social aspects of the user's social background and cultural environment emerge and end up stored as part of the user's social background knowledge. However, in recent research, a different research direction has been proposed concerning effects that are generated out of non-propositional information and are also devoid of intentionality. In a nutshell, nowadays we witness a huge number of internet-mediated exchanges whose interest does not lie in the content communicated, but in what the act of communication *as a whole* generates in users, producing an offset of non-propositional effects that compensate for the lack of interest that the content objectively possesses. Internet interactions are filled with (apparently) irrelevant utterances if we analyse them from a purely informative point of view, but they do provide relevance in foregrounding or generating non-propositional assumptions such as awareness of co-presence inside the group or network of friends who are synchronously inter-connected, as well as relevance in the mutual manifestness of being acknowledged in the conversation, even if not actively participating. In mobile instant messaging conversations, for instance, there is an interest in demonstrating that the user is part of the interaction, part of the collectivity, and very often, arising from the posting of photos, videos and recorded audios, there is an offset of feelings associated with being noticed and acknowledged by friends or collectivities (Yus 2017).

Needless to say, non-propositional effects may be both positive and negative. Among the latter, we can list effects associated with *flaming, trolling* and *cyberbullying,* among other aggressive strategies on the internet. However, we are more interested in the positive non-propositional effects that add to or even compensate for the lack of interest provided by verbal content itself. Some of the positive *social non-propositional effects* that may *leak* unintentionally for IMC include the following (Yus 2017, 2018c):

1. Feelings of connectedness, social awareness, feeling of being part of the interactions and friendships. Many users engage in "chained" acts of communication (typically trivial ones) because they eventually obtain an awareness of friends and peers and a feeling of connectedness. What used to be obvious in situations of physical co-presence is managed

nowadays through persistent online interactions, many of which are casual and utterly uninformative from an objective point of view.
2. Feelings of being noticed by the network of friends, by the user's community, of feedback, of social support. Sustained interactions not only generate connectedness, but also feelings of in-group membership and communal support, of being "attached" to the other members of the group), that is, an awareness of the group members' affective connection to and caring for a virtual community in which they become involved (Cheng and Guo 2015: 232).
3. Feelings out of sharing mutual areas of interest and finding support in sustained interactions, from which users get an offset of positive effects associated with virtual communication. They find support and the reward of connection from their peers through non-stop trivial interactions. Certainly, its use grants users – especially adolescents – a relatively cheap, readily available solution from among existing communication alternatives with their peer group and these apparently useless conversations strengthen the feeling of closeness to their groups and reduce loneliness (cf. John 2017).
4. Feelings of group membership and social capital. Internet-mediated interactions, especially through the feature that allows for multi-party conversations inside a group of contacts, can create non-propositional feelings of group membership, of belonging to a community of users, of the generation of social capital.
5. Feelings of narrowed gap between the physical and the virtual. Today's social media are filled with messages concerning the users' physical activities that they want to share with their peers. An example is the non-stop updating of one's and other users' daily activities, which provides a feeling of closeness and even of co-presence (White and White 2007: 89; Hannam et al. 2014: 179).

In fact, the increasing importance of non-propositional effects is one of the research issues for the future of internet pragmatics proposed by Yus (2019b). Some other issues also pertinent to the current discussion include application of pragmatic research to multimodal discourses, typed messages with visual support, identity on social networking sites, online polylogues, media convergence and multiple simultaneous areas of interaction, blurring of traditional elements in communication, big data's impact on users' interactions etc. We believe these issues, among others, are worth further exploration and investigation. For instance, although much has been written about issues of identity in online interactions (see e.g. Tanis and Postmes 2007; Upadhyay 2010; Guegan and Michinov 2011; Walther et al. 2011; Danesi 2014; Georgalou 2017; Petroni 2019; Reyes 2019), more effort should be made to investigate, for example, how digital affordances both facilitate and constrain identity performance and how identity constructions and identity struggles are both related to and different from each other (Xie 2018c). Also, as Garcés-Conejos Blitvich and Bou-Franch (2019: 11) rightly point out, "to move the field forward, further studies of ways of doing sociability, of entextualizing identity and relational practices in social media, are still needed". It may be said that where there is interaction, there is identity performance, and digital interactions are no exception. Besides, given the fact that there is already a chapter devoted to (im)politeness in this handbook (see Chapter 16), this present chapter does not address the topic. Still, it needs to be pointed out that recent years have witnessed a growing body of research on (im)politeness in digitally mediated communication (see e.g. Haugh 2010; Haugh et al. 2015; Graham and Hardaker 2017; Terkourafi et al. 2018; Xie 2018b; Sifianou and Bella 2019). Undoubtedly, digital communication has not only brought about new ways of thinking about (im)politeness, but also helped to revisit or revise classic or traditional topics in the field. It will continue to be a topic of much concern in future research on digitally mediated communication.

References

Albritton, A. (2017). Emotions in the ether: Strategies for effective emotional expression in text-messages. *Online Journal of Communication and Media Technologies*, 7(2), 50–58.
Androutsopoulos, J. (2006). Introduction: Special issue on sociolinguistics and computer-mediated communication. *Journal of Sociolinguistics*, 10(4), 419–38.
Belk, R. W. and Llamas, R. (eds.). (2013). *The Routledge Companion to Digital Consumption*. Abingdon, UK: Routledge.
Bolander, B. and Locher, M. (2014). Doing sociolinguistic research on computer-mediated data: A review of four methodological issues. *Discourse, Context & Media*, 3, 14–26.
Bou-Franch, P. and Garcés-Conejos Blitvich, P. (eds.). (2019). *Analyzing Digital Discourse: New Insights and Future Directions*. London: Palgrave Macmillan.
Broadhurst, S. and Price, S. (eds.). (2017). *Digital Bodies: Creativity and Technology in the Arts and Humanities*. London: Palgrave Macmillan.
Cheng, Z. and Guo, T. (2015). The formation of social identity and self-identity based on knowledge contribution in virtual communities: An inductive route model. *Computers in Human Behavior*, 43, 229–41.
Creeber, G. and Martin, R. (eds.). (2009). *Digital Cultures: Understanding New Media*. Berkshire, UK: Open University Press.
Culpeper, J. and Gillings, M. (2019). Pragmatics: Data trends. *Journal of Pragmatics*, 145, 4–14.
Danesi, M. (2014). Forging a linguistic identity in the age of the internet. *Forum Italicum*, 48(2), 227–37.

Danesi, M. (2017). *The Semiotics of Emoji: The Rise of Visual Language in the Age of the Internet*. London: Bloomsbury.

Escandell-Vidal, V. (2004). Norms and principles: Putting social and cognitive pragmatics together. In R. Márquez-Reiter and M. E. Placencia, eds., *Current Trends in the Pragmatics of Spanish*. Amsterdam: John Benjamins, pp. 347–71.

Fussell, S. R. and Moss, M. M. (1998). Figurative language in emotional communication. In S. R. Fussell and R. J. Kreuz, eds., *Social and Cognitive Approaches to Interpersonal Communication*. New York: Erlbaum, pp. 113–41.

Garcés-Conejos Blitvich, P. and Bou-Franch, P. (2019). Introduction to analyzing digital discourse: New insights and future directions. In P. Bou-Franch and P. Garcés-Conejos Blitvich, eds., *Analyzing Digital Discourse: New Insights and Future Directions*. London: Palgrave Macmillan, pp. 3–22.

Georgakopoulou, A. (2006). Postscript: Computer-mediated communication in sociolinguistics. *Journal of Sociolinguistics*, 10(4), 548–57.

Georgakopoulou, A. and Spilioti, T. (eds.). (2016). *The Routledge Handbook of Language and Digital Communication*. Abingdon, UK: Routledge.

Georgalou, M. (2017). *Discourse and Identity on Facebook: How We Use Language and Multimodal Texts to Present Identity Online*. London: Bloomsbury.

Golato, A. (2017). Naturally occurring data. In A. Barron, Y. Gu and G. Steen, eds., *Routledge Handbook of Pragmatics*. Abingdon, UK: Routledge, pp. 21–26.

Graham, S. L. and Hardaker, C. (2017). (Im)politeness in digital communication. In J. Culpeper, M. Haugh and D. Z. Kádár, eds., *Palgrave Handbook of Linguistic (Im)politeness*. London: Palgrave Macmillan, pp. 785–814.

Greitemeyer, T. (2016). Facebook and people's state self-esteem: The impact of the number of other users' Facebook friends. *Computers in Human Behavior*, 59, 182–6.

Guegan, J. and Michinov, E. (2011). Internet communication and identities dynamics: A psychosocial analysis. *Psychologie Française*, 56(4), 223–38.

Hannam, K., Butler, G. and Paris, C. M. 2014. Developments and key issues in tourism mobilities. *Annals of Tourism Research*, 44, 171–85.

Haugh, M. (2010). When is an email really offensive? Argumentativity and variability in evaluations of impoliteness. *Journal of Politeness Research*, 6(1), 7–31.

Haugh, M., Chang, W. M. and Kádár, D. Z. (2015). Doing deference: Identities and relational practices in Chinese online discussion boards. *Pragmatics*, 25(1), 73–98.

Herring, S. C. (2007). A faceted classification scheme for computer-mediated discourse. *Language@Internet* 4.

Herring, S. C., Stein, D. and Virtanen, T. (eds.). (2013). *Pragmatics of Computer-Mediated Communication*. Berlin: Mouton de Gruyter.

Hoffmann, C. R. and Bublitz, W. (eds.). (2017). *Pragmatics of Social Media*. Berlin: Mouton de Gruyter.

John, N. A. (2017). *The Age of Sharing*. Cambridge: Polity Press.

Jucker, A. H. (2018). Data in pragmatic research. In A. H. Jucker, K. P. Schneider and W. Bublitz, eds., *Methods in Pragmatics*. Berlin: Mouton de Gruyter, pp. 3–36.

Jucker, A. H. and Dürscheid, C. (2012). The linguistics of keyboard-to-screen communication. A new terminological framework. *Linguistik Online*, 56, 39–64.

Lagerkvist, A. (2019). *Digital Existence: Ontology, Ethics and Transcendence in Digital Culture*. Abingdon, UK: Routledge.

Lane, J. (2019). *The Digital Street*. Oxford: Oxford University Press.

Leech, G. (1983). *Principles of Pragmatics*. London: Longman.

Levinson, S. C. (2006). On the human "interaction engine". In N. K. Enfield and S. C. Levinson, eds., *Roots of Human Sociality*. Oxford: Berg, pp. 39–69.

Maghrabi, R. O., Oakley, R. L. and Nemati, H. R. (2014). The impact of self-selected identity on productive or perverse social capital in social network sites. *Computers in Human Behavior*, 33, 367–71.

Marmaridou, S. (2011). Pragmalinguistics and sociopragmatics. In W. Bublitz and N. R. Norrick, eds., *Foundations of Pragmatics*. Berlin: Mouton de Gruyter, pp. 77–106.

Márquez Reiter, R. and Placencia, M. E. (2005). *Spanish Pragmatics*. Basingstoke, UK: Palgrave Macmillan.

Mey, J. L. (2016). Pragmatics seen through the prism of society. In A. Capone and J. L. Mey, eds., *Interdisciplinary Studies in Pragmatics, Culture and Society*. Cham, Switzerland: Springer, pp. 15–41.

Ohler, J. B. (2010). *Digital Community, Digital Citizen*. Thousand Oaks, CA: Sage.

Parks, M. R. (2011). Social network sites as virtual communities. In Z. Papacharissi, ed., *A Networked Self: Identity, Community, and Culture on Social Network Sites*. London: Routledge, pp. 105–23.

Petroni, S. (2019). How social media shape identities and discourses in professional digital settings: Self-communication or self-branding? In P. Bou-Franch and P. Garcés-Conejos Blitvich, eds., *Analyzing Digital Discourse: New Insights and Future Directions*. London: Palgrave Macmillan, pp. 251–81.

Potter, J. (2002). Two kinds of natural. *Discourse Studies*, 4(4), 539–42.

Rainie, L. and Wellman, B. (2012). *Networked: The New Social Operating System*. Cambridge, MA: The MIT Press.

Reyes, A. (2019). Virtual communities: Interaction, identity and authority in digital communication. *Text and Talk*, 39(1), 99–120.

Salimkhan, G., Manago, A. M. and Greenfield, P. M. (2010). The construction of the virtual self on MySpace. *Cyberpsychology*, 4(1), Article 1.

Sifianou, M. and Spiridoula Bella, S. (2019). Twitter, politeness, self-presentation. In P. Bou-Franch and P. Garcés-Conejos Blitvich, eds., *Analyzing Digital Discourse: New Insights and Future Directions*. London: Palgrave Macmillan, pp. 341–65.

Speer, S. A. (2002). "Natural" and "contrived" data: A sustainable distinction? *Discourse Studies*, 4(4), 511–25.

Sperber, D. and Wilson, D. (1995). *Relevance: Communication and Cognition*. 2nd ed. Oxford: Blackwell.

Stern, S. (2008). Producing sites, exploring identities: Youth online authorship. In D. Buckingham, ed., *Youth, Identity, and Digital Media*. Cambridge, MA: The MIT Press, pp. 95–118.

Tagg, C. 2015. *Exploring Digital Communication: Language in Action*. Abingdon, UK: Routledge.

Tanis, M. and Postmes, T. (2007). Two faces of anonymity: Paradoxical effects of cues to identity in CMC. *Computers in Human Behavior*, 23(2), 955–70.

Terkourafi, M., Catedral, L., Haider, I., Karimzad, F., Melgares, J., Mostacero-Pinilla, C., Nelson, J. and Weissman, B. (2018). Uncivil Twitter: A sociopragmatic analysis. *Journal of Language Aggression and Conflict*, 6(1), 26–57.

Upadhyay, S. R. (2010). Identity and impoliteness in computer-mediated reader responses. *Journal of Politeness Research*, 6(1), 105–27.

Vitak, J. and Kim, J. (2014). "You can't block people offline": Examining how Facebook's affordances shape the disclosure process. In *Proceedings of CSCW'14: Proceedings of the 17th ACM Conference on Computer Supported Cooperative Work & Social Computing*, pp. 461–74.

Walther, J. B., Liang, Y. H., DeAndrea, D. C., Tong, S. T., Carr, C. T. Sppottswood, E. L. and Amichai-Hamburger, Y. (2011). The effect of feedback on identity shift in computer-mediated communication. *Media Psychology*, 14(1), 1–26.

White, N. R. and White, P. B. (2007). Home and away: Tourists in a connected world. *Annals of Tourism Research*, 34(1), 88–104.

Wiseman, R. (2013). What boys want. *Time*, 12 February.

Xie, C. (2018a). (Im)politeness, morality and the internet. *Internet Pragmatics*, 1(2), 205–14.

Xie, C. (2018b). (Im)politeness and moral order in online interactions. Special issue. *Internet Pragmatics*, 1(2).

Xie, C. (2018c). What's in a photo? Identity struggles on WeChat. Keynote speech presented at the First International Conference on Internet Pragmatics, Fujian Normal University, 21–23 September.

Xie, C. and Yus, F. (2017). An internet dialogue on internet pragmatics. *Foreign Language and Literature Studies*, 34(2), 75–92.

Xie, C. and Yus, F. (2018). Introducing internet pragmatics. *Internet Pragmatics*, 1(1), 1–12.

Xie, C., Yus, F. and Haberland, H. (eds.). (2021). *Approaches to Internet Pragmatics: Theory and Practice*, Amsterdam: John Benjamins.

Yus, F. (1998). A decade of relevance theory. *Journal of Pragmatics*, 30, 305–45.

Yus, F. (2005). Attitudes and emotions through written text: The case of textual deformation in internet chat rooms. *Pragmalingüística*, 13, 147–74.

Yus, F. (2007). *Virtualidades reales. Nuevas formas de comunidad en la era de Internet* [Real Virtualities: New Norms of Community at the internet Age]. Alicante: University of Alicante.

Yus, F. (2011). *Cyberpragmatics: Internet-Mediated Communication in Context*. Amsterdam: John Benjamins.

Yus, F. (2014a). Not all emoticons are created equal. *Linguagem em (Dis)curso*, 14(3), 511–29.

Yus, F. (2014b). El discurso de las identidades en línea: El caso de Facebook [The discourse of online identity: The case of Facebook]. *Discurso and Sociedad*, 8(3), 398–426.

Yus, F. (2015). Discourse and identity. In J. D. Wright, ed., *International Encyclopedia of the Social and Behavioral Sciences*, 2nd ed., vol. 6. Oxford: Elsevier, pp. 498–502.

Yus, F. (2016). Discourse, contextualization and identity shaping: The case of social networking sites and virtual worlds. In M. L. Carrió-Pastor, ed., *Technology Implementation in Higher Education for Second Language Teaching and Translation Studies: New Tools, New Approaches*. Singapore: Springer, pp. 71–88.

Yus, F. (2017). Contextual constraints and non-propositional effects in WhatsApp communication. *Journal of Pragmatics*, 114, 66–86.

Yus, F. (2018a). Identity-related issues in meme communication. *Internet Pragmatics*, 1(1), 113–33.

Yus, F. (2018b). The interface between pragmatics and internet-mediated communication: Applications, extensions and adjustments. In C. Ilie and N. Norrick, eds., *Pragmatics and Its Interfaces*. Amsterdam: John Benjamins, pp. 267–90.

Yus, F. (2018c). Relevance from and beyond propositions: The case of online identity. In H. Nasu and J. Strassheim, eds., *Relevance and Irrelevance: Theories, Factors and Challenges*. Berlin: Walter de Gruyter, pp. 119–40.

Yus, F. (2019a). Multimodality in memes: A cyberpragmatic approach. In P. Bou-Franch and P. Garcés-Conejos Blitvich, eds., *Analyzing Digital Discourse: New Insights and Future Directions*. Cham, Switzerland: Palgrave Macmillan, pp. 105–32.

Yus, F. (2019b). An outline of some future research issues for internet pragmatics. *Internet Pragmatics*, 2(1), 1–33.

23

Workplace and Institutional Discourse

Meredith Marra and Shelley Dawson[*]

23.1 Introduction

Language use in workplace settings has become an increasingly important area of investigation over the past 20–30 years. The original focus of this analysis was conversations between professional and laypeople (institutional talk), a focus which quickly expanded to interactions between colleagues that take place as part of normal, everyday workplace activities (workplace discourse). This change reflects ongoing developments in theory, innovative methodological advancements and shifting priorities for workplace researchers who are often motivated by real world applications and the potential to make a difference, especially to the lives of those from marginalized groups.

Throughout this progression there has been strong interest in issues of sociopragmatics, most notably (im)politeness. In line with wider developments in pragmatics, analyses adopting a Brown and Levinsonian model ([1978] 1987) are now outnumbered by interactional and discursive approaches. This has meant a shift in focus from the instantiation of speech acts in cross-cultural workplace settings, to the co-construction of professional, gender and ethnic identities in context. Throughout the research there is an emphasis on workplace teams (viewed through the lens of the Community of Practice; Wenger 1998), including the enactment of sociocultural norms and the negotiation of meaning between group members.

In this contribution we outline chronological changes within the field of workplace and institutional discourse since its emergence in the early 1990s, highlighting the way in which (im)politeness and appropriacy has been a central concern, as well as the methods adopted to access the naturally occurring data that drives the field. This discussion is illustrated

---

[*] Our thanks to colleagues from the Language in the Workplace project, especially Janet Holmes, Bernadette Vine and Jo Angouri, who contributed ideas and insights for the chapter.

by analyses from workplace discourse scholars, including examples from our own research. We conclude by offering suggestions for future directions based on evolving trends, specifically the use of metapragmatics as a method for gaining more nuanced perspectives on sociopragmatic issues.

23.2 Key Theoretical Issues

The major interest within sociopragmatic research in the workplace setting can be summed up as the intersection between power and politeness. The focus on power reflects not only the hierarchies inherent to organizations, but also the more dynamic negotiation of status, authority and expertise as it becomes relevant in talk. Depending on the theoretical stance adopted by the analyst, power can be foregrounded as a theoretical lens, or left to emerge as the interaction unfolds. The focus on politeness is equally diffuse, ranging from more fixed understandings of what is seen as polite, to interpretations which recognize the different norms that may exist within groups for ascertaining appropriacy. Theoretical stance affects the analytic approach as well as the term (institutional or workplace) with which scholars align.

23.2.1 Institutional Talk versus Workplace Discourse

Even though the popularity of workplace interaction as a research interest is comparatively recent, there has been considerable change and diversification within the area over its short lifetime. One of the most interesting developments has been the separation of *institutional* and *workplace* talk, representing a theoretical divide between conversation analysts and discourse analysts, the two dominant strands of analysis in the field. The distinction between the two throws light on the differing treatment of context: while those in Conversation Analysis (CA) restrict their interest to the local context (and specifically the context made relevant by participants in their talk), those who align with a discursive approach actively draw on wider societal understandings to interpret the (typically naturally occurring) workplace interactions that characterize the shared interest between the two branches.

In the early 1990s, Drew and Heritage produced a highly influential edited collection which created a solid foundation for research in the area: *Talk at Work* (1992). This is a thick tome, offering dozens of chapters that approach workplace talk from a CA perspective, exploring the sequential organization of talk-in-interaction. Grouped around 'questions' and 'answers', the contributions exemplify our understanding of the workplace as an institutional setting in which interactions take place between a representative of an institution (e.g. a doctor, a lawyer, a reporter, an interviewer) and a layperson (e.g. a patient, a witness, a story source, a job interviewee). Interaction is understood as highly patterned and ordered, comprising multiple and embedded sequences. Certain turns are pre-allocated to the professional, and meaning is negotiated through first and second pair parts of the sequence – a question followed by an answer, or a request for advice and the advice, an offer and a refusal/acceptance. Data extracts are chosen to represent a sequence type. They are typically short, transcribed in considerable detail and then compared in order to identify patterns, repeated structures and key features of the sequence under investigation. It is thus the sequence and generalizations about the sequence that are of most interest, rather than the wider contribution this sequence makes to the ongoing interaction between the participants.

This approach continues today. Analysts offer enormous detail about the instantiation of specific repeated action and their research increasingly recognizes paralinguistic contributions to meaning, such as the role of gaze. This extension has been augmented by the affordances of video data. Many researchers have moved into multimodal analyses, while retaining the techniques and theoretical foundations provided by this strong theoretical stance (see e.g. Mondada 2011, 2018).

In its initial stages of development, CA made use of telephone recordings, an ideal interactional setting for scholars who had access to audio, but not video data – the participants did not have access to visual cues and neither did the analysts. While, as noted, current research incorporates many more paralinguistic and gestural features, telephone data still features in research, including in Heritage and Clayman's (2010) influential analysis of institutional talk which exemplifies the strength of the approach. Within their updated summary of CA research in institutional contexts, a section is devoted to calls for emergency services. Illustrating the thorough attention to linguistic detail that is the hallmark of CA investigations, the authors offer fine-grained interpretations of the ways in which callers gain help from emergency call operators and the complexities around the calls. The mundane nature of the calls (even when they occur in an emergency context) emphasize that they are highly ordered as the careful analysis demonstrates. And while the goal may not have been applications per se, it is good example of how workplace research offers insights outside the theoretical.

As early as the mid to late 1990s, there were parallel and growing moves from other language scholars to explore the intricacies of interaction and to go beyond the prevailing conclusions offered by management scholars about the way we communicate at work. The arguments being made about workplace communication at the time were commonly based on self-reported data gathered through questionnaires, surveys and interviews, often resulting in large data sets analysed quantitatively to provide generalizations. Linguists were keen to take up the focus on audio recordings that those in CA were using in order to check the validity of what people thought they did in the workplace through the analysis of actual practices. Rather than following the sociological origins of CA, however, they typically followed an Interactional Sociolinguistic (IS) approach (Gumperz 1982). This analytic approach takes the position that there is always potential for miscommunication based on contextualization cues which vary across different 'cultural' groups. Rather than investigating the ordered nature of talk, attention turned to the way people engage with each other in the workplace setting and the norms that underpin these interactions. Whether it was the evidence of discrimination in job interviews identified through close linguistic analysis by Roberts et al. (1992), or the gender differences at work described by Tannen (1994), these early discourse analyses aimed to shed light on everyday practices and the effect of difference.

A dominant early player in the IS approach to workplace talk was Michael Clyne whose project on new migrants entering the Australian workplace became the model for a number of international projects. The groundbreaking research by Clyne and his colleagues brought attention to the workplace as an overlooked setting in wider sociolinguistics, ripe for further investigation. The findings testified to the importance of pragmatic issues, including the centrality of overlooked discourse activities such as small talk to successful workplace interaction. Using recordings of authentic talk accompanied by ethnographic details which provided information about the contextual and societal environment (well beyond the local context used in CA), the impetus in this new approach was to recognize root causes of interactional trouble and in doing so identify opportunities for improving workplace communication.

Clyne and his colleagues were the inspiration for the long-standing Language in the Workplace project (LWP) team which has been investigating effective workplace communication in New Zealand workplaces since 1996 (see Holmes and Stubbe [2003] 2015), again grounded in an IS approach and motivated by the implications and potential applications of the research findings. Over more than two decades, the team has worked with organizations across a wide range of different settings. While Clyne's research included blue-collar environments, the LWP team began their investigations of everyday talk in white-collar workplaces such as government departments and corporate organizations before moving on to IT workplaces, hospital and eldercare settings and blue-collar Tig environments including building sites and garden centres. They also returned to the factory setting that Clyne had investigated, but with an expectation that the New Zealand context would differ from the Australian.

The LWP philosophy and data collection methods, which prioritize *researching with* participants as co-researchers and handing control over the recording process to volunteers in the collaborating organizations, have come to represent a dominant approach which has been replicated in the United Kingdom (e.g. Angouri 2007; Mullany 2007), continental Europe (e.g. Franziskus 2013; Franziskus et al. 2013; Lønsmann 2011) and Asia (e.g. Schnurr and Chan 2009; Murata 2011).

At its most basic, the approach can be described in four steps:

(1) Contact is made with an organization/team/leader that has been identified as representing best practice based on recommendations from their industry or colleagues. Once agreement for collaboration is reached, a mutually beneficial focus for research is negotiated.

(2) Following a period of participant observation (during which important background information, logistical details and common practices are identified), volunteers in the organization audio record a data set of their everyday practices over a period of two or more weeks. In addition to the audio recordings, the research team typically video record larger group interactions such as weekly meetings over longer periods of time, and there are many informal debriefing discussions and more formal interviews.
(3) The data is described, transcribed and analysed, making use of the ethnographic material collected during the data collection phase. Participants may be approached for member checking and clarification, and where there is interest they may be more actively involved in listening to recordings and commenting on transcripts and interpretations.
(4) Feedback is given to the organizations in a form that best suits the shared goal of research. For some this might be a report expressed in an appropriately accessible style. For others, a hands-on workshop or collaborative discussion is more desirable.

An overarching philosophy for this ethnographic approach is to be responsive to the needs of the group, to capture an emic or participant perspective in order to support the analysts' interpretations, and to acknowledge the ongoing social relationship between the analysts and participants as co-researchers (see Vine and Marra 2017).

As with the data used in CA, emphasis is placed on authentic, naturally occurring talk. The IS-informed branch of workplace discourse analysis includes a number of theoretically distinct forms of discourse analysis, ranging from more micro to more macro attention to language, and from descriptive to critical frameworks.[1] In each of the discourse analytic approaches, the contextual setting (including the team culture, the organizational culture and the sociocultural norms of the wider society) plays a key role in the process of interpretation. While the data is understood as embedded within its own particular contextual setting, the widespread sharing of a common approach to data collection has also created opportunities for some cross-cultural comparisons (see e.g. Angouri and Marra 2010 on meetings as genre).[2]

23.2.2 Cross-Cultural Analysis of Speech Acts

Due to the foundations provided by IS, cultural difference is a concern of all the analyses conducted under the umbrella of workplace discourse analysis, albeit it with a very broad understanding of what counts as 'culture'. More

---

[1] While IS provides the (often-implicit) foundations for most of the research within workplace discourse analysis, the higher-level theoretical frameworks range from the more macro Critical Discourse Studies to the more micro social constructionism, often differing according to the analyst's stance on the relationship between structure and agency.

[2] Due to the growth of contextualized, qualitative corpora, other comparisons are beginning to appear more regularly.

explicit attention to cross-cultural differences can be seen in research which takes speech acts as its focus (see also Chapter 5). Speech acts were a particularly important part of the field of workplace discourse analysis as it was being established, because they offered a recognizable and specific focus at a time when the boundaries of workplace communication were wide open, researchers' interests all-encompassing and the setting underexplored.

Because of the well-recognized hierarchies inherent in organizational settings, it should be of no surprise that meeting management and the role of the chair, as well as directives from superiors to superordinates, quickly gained prominence as productive areas of interest. Workplace communication is rife with what Vine (2004) labels 'control acts', i.e. directives and requests, categories distinguished by the power differences between speakers; while a manager *tells* an employee what to do when giving a directive, a subordinate *asks* a superior/equal, i.e. as a request. Speech act research considers the enactment of a range of different acts, initially at the utterance level and now more commonly recognizing that these acts are negotiated across wider stretches of talk.

Early forays within a speech act approach made use of standard data collection methods in cross-cultural pragmatics, including elicitation techniques such as Discourse Completion Tasks (DCTs), role plays and reports of perceived practices. This has been a strong and fruitful area of research and supports some of the more quantitative findings that have emerged within the new area of variational pragmatics (see Barron and Schneider 2009). In line with the turn to discourse which became so prominent in the 1990s/2000s, however, most current approaches within the area of workplace discourse aim to identify these kinds of speech acts as they occur naturally within everyday talk.

The control acts discussed above fulfil one side of the transactional-relational duality that has come to characterize the conceptualization of workplace talk. Directives are the way we 'get things done' at work and are thus exemplars of task-focused discourse strategies (in contrast to small talk and humour which have come to represent the relational or people-focused side of the fused coin). Directives have thus been a frequent focus in workplace research, especially in studies which consider management style and leadership, and those which employ an intercultural or cross-cultural lens (see e.g. chapter 3 in Holmes et al. 2011). Others have defended elicitation methods for speech acts based on the amount of data that would be needed to gather an appropriate sample (see Morrison and Holmes 2003). Workplace interactions are, however, a fertile environment for certain acts; the use of authentic speech has not been too much of a barrier for research in the workplace context, and analyses have regularly demonstrated that the naturally occurring enactment of speech acts is sometimes quite different to (and typically more indirect than) stereotypical realizations which are often at the core of the experimental and self-reported data that has been used in the past, and which can frequently be found in pedagogical materials.

Other speech acts which have gained particular traction in the workplace context include advice giving (e.g. Locher and Limburg 2012), refusals and complaints (e.g. Riddiford and Holmes 2015) and disagreements which we use as illustration in Section 23.3.

23.2.3 (Im)politeness in the Workplace

The switch from a focus on speech acts at the utterance level to their negotiation between participants according to locally relevant cultural norms aligned with corresponding developments in politeness which were occurring within pragmatics more widely (see also Chapter 16). As a field of inquiry, (im)politeness (vs lay understandings of politeness) has been in a process of rapid change. The various theoretical approaches can usefully be summarized as three waves (Kadar and Haugh 2013):

(1) the analysis of utterances (speech acts) separate from the speakers and the context (as best exemplified by Brown and Levinson's (1987) attempt at a universal approach to politeness);
(2) an extension into a discourse-focused approach which accounts for participants' perspectives and broader social meaning in interaction (e.g. Spencer-Oatey's 2000 rapport management and Watts 2003, who called for greater emphasis on the lay (politeness1) dimension over the analyst (politeness2) understandings);
(3) the negotiation and struggle around norms for appropriacy, whether polite or impolite (dominated by Locher and Watts 2005 in terms of unmarked 'politic' behaviour, and Culpeper 2011, who introduced a much greater focus on the role of impoliteness).

Each of the three waves is seemingly matched by theoretical developments within the field of workplace discourse research. In particular there has been increasing exploration of sociocultural norms and their micro instantiation as evidenced in practices.

At the heart of the universal approach to politeness proposed by Brown and Levinson ([1978] 1987) are face and face threatening acts (FTAs), the very same directives, requests, disagreements etc. discussed above (see also Chapter 13). And like the utterance-level focus in early speech act research, the focus in this more cognitive approach to politeness was similarly the speaker's attention to the hearer's face and the linguistic realizations of this concern as demonstrated through the choice of politeness strategy.

Because of the productive and clear-cut strategies suggested by Brown and Levinson for ways in which speakers attend to face when enacting acts (e.g. 'state the FTA as a general rule', 'be pessimistic', 'minimize the imposition'), workplace researchers were drawn to the approach. It offered useful categories for coding and for ascertaining common strategies used for enacting goals. Examples include Waldvogel's (2002) analysis of workplace emails and the formulaic rituals of requests in small shops in France by Kerbrat-Orecchioni (2006).

However, a challenging critique of the universal approach developed among politeness researchers, because it was seen as neglecting cultural difference outside of western societies (see e.g. Eelen 2001; Ide 1989). The resulting shift towards a sociocultural and discursive approach did not escape the notice of those in workplace research. Some applied a revised version of the Brown and Levinsonian approach in the form of Neo-politeness (see Mullany 2007; Holmes et al. 2012; Kerbrat-Orecchioni 2006). This adapted approach recognized the importance of the analyst in interpreting politeness in context and incorporated variability in sociocultural enactment, moving towards a more emic, participant perspective. Even though the neo-Brown and Levinson approach to politeness intended to go beyond the traditional utterance-focused model towards a postmodern approach which embraced the dynamic, negotiated and contextually sensitive priorities of social constructionism, the past decade has seen a much greater alignment with discursive politeness and a move away from considerations of face towards the relational aspects of politeness.

As part of this journey, Spencer-Oatey's (2000) Rapport Management (a response to the perceived limitations of Brown and Levinson's treatment of face and the prioritization of the individual) offered a useful avenue for research. Spencer-Oatey proposed an extension to the categories of positive and negative face (which comprise the Brown and Levinson's perspective), fleshing out the basis of rapport beyond these limited face sensitivities by adding sociality rights and obligations as well as interactional goals. The focus on rapport found favour with a new generation of workplace discourse scholars who recognized the centrality of rapport to harmonious interactions. Examples include an interdisciplinary approach to a 'climate of care' in organizations (Fletcher 2014) and the importance of building trust and establishing relationships when successfully navigating call centre discourse (Hui 2014), each of which followed Spencer-Oatey's own work on British-Chinese negotiations in welcome meetings (Spencer-Oatey and Xing 2003).

This research still views culture at a more macro, often national, level. The increasingly nuanced approaches to politeness that prioritized contextualized, emic understandings of group norms requires more tightly defined groups to determine which norms were relevant. The model proposed by Locher and Watts (2005) offered a more attractive solution for workplace discourse analysts who were by then highly engaged with the concept of the Community of Practice (Wenger 1998) as a mediating lens between wider society and the micro instantiation of norms and which was also being used as a contextual constraint by Locher and Watts.

Workplace research was and continues to be dominated by an interest in identity construction (see Angouri and Marra 2011; van de Mieroop and Schnurr 2017; Chapter 15), especially gender, ethnic and professional identities.[3]

---

[3] Narrative has provided a particularly fruitful discourse context for these investigations and dominated early analyses in particular (see de Fina et al. 2006).

The social constructionist approach (informed by IS) that guides much of the analysis views identity as dynamic, fluid and in ongoing negotiation with others in context. As the field progressed, analysts were looking for a way to understand identity construction that allowed for a narrowing of the contextual constraints on this negotiation. The Community of Practice (CofP) offered a solution. Analysts draw on the notion that team members are demonstrating their identities as members of the community in the way that they interact, signalling their membership through indexical choices (Silverstein 1976; Ochs 1992). This includes following group norms about how to be interactionally polite or impolite.

23.2.4 Community of Practice

The CofP was now being applied in both workplace discourse analysis and in the discursive approach to politeness promoted by Locher and Watts. This convergence on group understandings for how to be appropriate or 'politic' resonated with workplace researchers. The focus on relational work that this approach represents also addressed the relational side of the task versus people-focused functions that have guided workplace research since the outset of the field. This became a satisfying and rewarding space for those interested in (im)politeness. The resulting analyses of doing (im)politeness included consideration of ethnicized norms in workplace talk (Schnurr et al. 2007) and the negotiation of power in context (Schnurr et al. 2008).

As with any field, however, there is always room for reflection. Embracing the concept of the CofP for its perceived benefits to the analytic goals of researchers did not always mean thorough engagement with the theoretical basis of the concept. As noted by King (2019a), many researchers mistakenly declared a group to be a CofP without consideration of whether the team met the criterial requirements established by Wenger, namely (1) a joint, negotiated enterprise (2) mutual engagement and (3) a shared repertoire of resources built up over time. Not every workplace team is a CofP and this has ramifications for our understanding of norms. Third wave politeness approaches rely on established patterns for ascertaining a participant perspective concerning what is understood as appropriate. The approach means that expletive use, blunt directives and direct complaints which might stereotypically be seen as 'rude' can instead be interpreted with some confidence as being unmarked and appropriate (Daly et al. 2004). To make these claims, however, means understanding if the norms really are specific to the group. The focus on norms remains a challenging and problematic issue for the field and offers exciting opportunities for future theoretical work in coming years.

23.3 Critical Overview of Research through Case Studies

As a field, workplace research is strongly data-driven, using authentic interactions to make sense of theoretical issues. The preference for bottom up theorizing is particularly significant to provide evidence and justifications for the arguments being made about the importance and subtleties of group norms in more recent research. In line with this stance, we provide some examples to illustrate work in the field. To narrow our scope, we have chosen to focus on the treatment of one particular discourse activity, namely disagreements. The research we refer to emphasizes both workplace identities and the enactment of (im)politeness to demonstrate the developing understandings.

23.3.1 Case Studies of Disagreement

We begin our illustrations with an example from early work by Miriam Locher who offered analyses of disagreements in a range of contexts, including the workplace. The underlying concerns that led to the disagreement are reasonably opaque to us as outsiders. Locher points to subtle negotiations around a decision about deadlines, with some arguing the need to go beyond procedural issues to consider relational issues in reaching a decision.

(1) (Context: A research committee in an institution disagree on the cut off dates for applications.)
1. Jack: /because what happens\\ if [name 1] is at the verge of
2. getting great data at +
3. december twenty fifth or whenever you shut down
4. Ron: he's out of luck +
5. it's a hard tear down date +
6. I mean
7. X: tsss
8. [...]
9. Bill: well it's easy for us to //sit here\ and say that
10. X: /yeah\\
11. Ron: well that's true on [name 3]

(Locher 2004: 246–7)[4]

In this example the conflict and divide between Ron and his fellow committee members Bill and Jack is reasonably accessible for us as readers. While Ron sees a decision as having been reached, Bill and Jack use various strategies to keep the decision under negotiation, an indirect method of

---

[4] All examples have been simplified and adjusted to LWP transcription conventions for ease of reading.

[laughs]: :	Paralinguistic features and editorial information in square brackets; colons indicate beginning and end
+	Pause of up to one second
...//.....\ /......\\...	Simultaneous speech
( )	Unclear utterance
yes	Underlining indicates emphasis
[...]	Section of transcript omitted

Names of workplace participants and workplaces are pseudonyms

signalling disagreement without having to go fully 'on record' as registering an opposing point of view. Jack raises a hypothetical scenario which should, in his view, require a change to the *tear down date* (lines 1–3) and Bill offers support by suggesting that if they were in the same situation they would not be happy with the decision (*it's easy for us to sit here and say that*). This section of disagreement follows a number of other attempts at challenging the proposal that has been put forward by Ron, and Locher highlights the implicit and indirect ways in which Bill continues to challenge the decision without directly criticizing Ron.

This example (and the related extracts) are a helpful illustration of the way the field considers more extended sequences of disagreement than found in a standard speech act approach which might only focus on a single utterance; it is hard to know exactly which utterance is most relevant here, especially since it is the collaboration between Jack and Bill as an 'interactional team' (Locher 2004: 246) that helps identify the disagreement. It thus also demonstrates the importance of co-construction in the discursive approach, as well as the identities that the various participants are constructing as members of the committee and as relationally-focused versus process-focused individuals.

Timing and dates are also the focus in the following example taken from work by Jo Angouri and involving participants from a multinational organization.

(2) (Context: A formal meeting in which the CEO (Paul) and regional manager (Sam, chair) negotiate the timing of various activities in their engineering project, especially in terms of the work being undertaken by subcontractor Garry which is behind schedule.)
1. Sam: are you confident you can do it
2. Garry: if the weather is good + and if [the company] +
3. assists me //+ i can do it\
4. Paul: /we always assi //st you\\ \
5. Sam: /what kind o\\f assistance
6. do you mean
7. Garry: for example crane //s + \
8. Paul: /you alrea\\dy have the
9. [details] crane and the [details] one will be
10. ready within //the day\
11. Garry: /ok then\\
12. Sam: paul is there anything you need to clarify
13. [provides details]
14. Paul: yes + as we discussed earlier we think that + in
15. order uhm to speed up the works and not leave the
16. rest of the project + behind + you need uhm to
17. have more workers + uhm one more [details]
18. operator + at least one more fore//man\
19. Sam: /certai\\ nly you need
20. mo//re people\
(Angouri 2012: 1571)

In the article from which this extract is taken, Angouri argues that there needs to be a separation between conflict and disagreement, again troubling the speech act approach which would typically collapse these two categories. She takes the stance that conflict in problem-solving talk (which the example represents) need not undermine the rapport that exists between the participants. In the analysis she notes that there is no evidence that the relationship is challenged, rather that this kind of talk has been established as normal for the goals of problem solving. Paul and Sam are explicit and direct with Garry (lines 14–20) that he must change his practices if he is to meet the agreed deadline, and that his confidence (*if the weather is good and [the company, i.e. you] assist me I can do it*) is not accepted as a solution to them. While there is quite explicit disagreement at the surface level (both the locution and the illocution), the perlocutionary effect does not include a breaking down of the group relationships. Instead this can be seen as problem talk which serves to (re)negotiate the group's norms for ways to engage with their shared goal.

The two extracts presented so far represent data from Europe, albeit involving participants from multinationals in the case of example 2. In the next example we call on data collected at the opposite end of the world. This national context is relevant because of the perceived (Anglo) universality of the Brown and Levinsonian approach, and also because of the assumed cultural differences that are fundamental to the IS approach.

(3) (Context: Clara is chairing the regular meeting of a project team in the absence of the team leader. While Clara is the section manager, she normally sits in as a participant rather than leader in these meetings.)

1.	Clara:	okay well we might just start without Seth
2.		he can come in and can review the minutes from last week
3.	Renee:	are you taking the minutes this week
4.	Clara:	no I'm just trying to chair the meeting
5.		who would like to take minutes this week
6.	Renee:	who hasn't taken the minutes yet
7.	Benny:	I haven't yet I will
8.	Clara:	thank you //Benny\
9.	Renee:	/oh Benny\\ takes beautiful minutes too
10.	Benny:	don't tell them they'll want me doing it every week
11.		[general laughter]
12.	Clara:	it's a bit of a secret
13.		okay shall we kick off and just go round the room um doing an update
14.		[...]

(Holmes and Marra 2004: 442–3)

In this example, the role of the CofP is salient. The team has been working together over a number of weeks and are actively engaged with a project to establish a new call centre for the organization. Part of the disagreement that is occurring in this example is a challenge to Clara's authority to manage the meeting as represented by Renee's contributions in lines 3 and 6: Renee raises the issue of who will take the minutes and she seems to announce the group norm for deciding who takes the rotating role of minute taker by calling for someone who hasn't taken the minutes yet. In the original article from which this extract was used to illustrate how leaders navigate conflict (Holmes and Marra 2004: 443), we analysed Clara as

> [managing] Renee's contestive behaviour good-humouredly but firmly. She re-asserts her role at line 8 by ratifying Benny as minute-taker, and then after a brief acknowledgement of the humorous exchange between Renee and Benny, she very firmly announces the agenda.

For this team, the LWP's ethnographic observations and extensive recordings highlight the importance of humour to all interactions, the prioritization of people-focused strategies and typical mitigation of power asymmetries in talk. This does not mean that status is not an important consideration for the team, as evident in the subversive and contestive behaviour exhibited here, but rather that the enactment of power was often 'smoothed out' interactionally and softened. In this case, other CofP members recognize the breach by Renee and work to rectify the sense of group cohesion: not only does Benny quickly volunteer to take the minutes to dissipate the tension but introduces humorous self-effacing comments about his abilities, which are ratified by Clara and the disagreement is resolved.

In all three examples, relational factors are a crucial consideration in the interpretations offered by the various analysts. All rely on interaction among participants rather than single utterances. All cases require investigation beyond surface level instantiations to consider the emic perspective, and in the last case, the CofP model offers more nuance and subtlety to the interpretations of appropriacy. These short case studies speak to the importance of contextualization in the workplace analyses of pragmatic features of talk.

23.3.2 Social Impact of Workplace Research

As noted in the opening of the chapter, researchers in the discourse analytic tradition are typically motivated by the ways in which their findings can be used by the organizations with whom they collaborate, or in wider society. One of the ways the LWP team has managed to address this motivation is through collaborations with ESOL teachers and relevant government agencies. On the basis of an extensive data set and analyses of New Zealanders interacting in a range of workplace settings, analytic categories for pragmatic priorities have been identified and form the basis for materials used in a successful course entitled Workplace Communication for Skilled Migrants, which recently graduated its twenty-eighth cohort. The course emphasizes pragmatic instruction with a focus on teaching interpretation skills so that participants can analyse their own contexts and interactions when entering New Zealand workplaces (especially in a supported internship which makes up half the 12-week course content). So, for example, participants work with scenarios to develop an understanding of how colleagues might give a directive to a subordinate, then reflect on how they would have done this in the past (i.e. making their existing pragmatic norms explicit), analyse transcriptions of naturally occurring talk in effective workplace situations and make comparisons that raise their awareness of sociopragmatic differences and similarities. Armed with these analytic skills, the class members engage with colleagues in their internships, get feedback from mentors and reflect on their experiences with the class teacher.[5] The high success rate in graduates securing satisfying work in their chosen areas and commensurate with their qualifications and expertise suggests strong potential in the use of research findings (see Prebble 2009). The impact has been recognized by Immigration New Zealand who now fund the course and make use of the LWP team's advice in the creation of resources which are distributed more widely. Importantly for both the government and for the theoretical stance of the research team, resources are created for both potential employees *and* their employers. This two-way approach engages with interaction as a collaboration and negotiation.

This is just one illustrative example of the social impact that workplace discourse research can and does have. As the (relatively young) field develops further, we can expect many more examples.

23.4 Summary and Future Directions

As this chapter has indicated, research in the areas of institutional and workplace discourse analysis continues to develop and grow. Each year there are more researchers working in the area and we learn from theoretical developments in cognate and related areas. The three waves of politeness research described earlier have paralleled the developments in workplace research; from stereotypical perceptions of workplace behaviour and isolated utterances our focus has turned towards the negotiation of identities between participants as we go about our everyday working lives, always searching for more nuance and sophistication to deepen our understandings of the practices with which we engage on a daily basis. In line with theoretical developments, the research agenda has moved from the enactment of speech acts at the level of utterance (notably directives,

---

[5] For an example of the interactions which take place between the skilled migrant class members and their colleagues during these internships, see Marra (2012), where the focus is sociopragmatic issues surrounding disagreement as a co-construction, i.e. 'disagreeing without being disagreeable'.

disagreements and aspects of meeting management) to the impact of interactional context/s (especially the workplace CofP) and the role of wider discourses in the negotiation of meaning making between interactants.

A particularly promising area for future research in workplace talk and pragmatics lies in the area of metapragmatics, that is talk about what speech *does* in a particular context (much in the same way as metalanguage is explicit talk about language) (see Chapter 7). Metapragmatic signalling functions to aid comprehension of meaning (Silverstein 1976). In other words, during the unfolding of an interaction, direct and indirect signalling in talk provides interlocutors with clues as to what is happening moment-by-moment, to what the norms are in a particular context, and (in the best case scenario) ensuring sociocultural understanding. Recent work has seen renewed analytic attention to the concept (e.g. King 2019b, drawing on Woolard 1998; Coupland and Jaworski 2004). Arguments have been made for attention to signalling within the stream of discourse as a way to access the doxa (Bourdieu 1977) of a situation, or the taken-for-granted norms and beliefs in any particular community (Holmes et al., 2020). This is a way that we can add a further layer to our analyses, especially extending the limits of the current CofP approach by expanding into the ideologies in which group practices are embedded.

Accessing these taken-for-granted, 'commonsense' assumptions in an interaction requires in the first instance a shared understanding of the particular metapragmatic signalling. If implicit, this relies on interlocutors being able to access indexical layers of meaning (Silverstein 2003), or rather peeling back the layers of an utterance to access the contextual intent and meaning. This process is compounded by the fact that linguistic features may well index multiple meanings (Eckert 2008) depending on context. We bring our sociocultural 'knowledge' (Holmes 2007) along with us to interactions and deploy it to make sense of linguistic and pragmatic behaviour. If both interlocutors share these intertextual understandings of indexical features, then mutual understanding may well be achieved.

As a process, these shared understandings develop in workplace CofPs, forming an important aspect of choosing to belong. By way of illustration we offer an example of a skilled migrant intern from the course described above. Here, we see an instance of indirect metapragmatic signalling, functioning as an instance of workplace socialization.

(4) (Context: Carl is a skilled migrant originally from Taiwan on an internship and Nerissa his mentor at a New Zealand workplace.)
1. Carl: oh Nerissa I just um
2. you know tomorrow is my last //day here\
3. Nerissa: /mm mm\\
4. Carl: so um I'm thinking I um I will bring some finger food
5. Nerissa: oh yep
6. Carl: er for the morning tea

7.	Nerissa:	oh yeah
8.	Carl:	yep and how what do you think?
9.	Nerissa:	um yep well we were going to do lunch any way
10.		for you for relieving things
11.		so I don't know if you need to
12.		um they have um forecasting have their meeting
13.		//on friday morning don't they at eleven to twelve
14.		you should bring something for that
15.		that would be a good idea\
16.	Carl:	/yep mhm yep that's right mhm + oh okay\\
17:	Nerissa:	what kind of things were you thinking?
18.	Carl:	mm I think just some tai- taiwanese um cake
19:	Nerissa:	oh yeah
20.	Carl:	and er and a sweets
21.	Nerissa:	oh yeah cool
22.	Carl:	yeah I think I //will bring some of that
23.		and a put on the morning tea table
24.		and er everyone can help by their self\
25:	Nerissa:	/I think they'd like that + yep yeah yeah yeah yep yep
26.		yep + yep themselves\\ yep yep
27:		and then take some of it to their meeting
28.		they'll like that if you take that there
29.		yeah that's a good idea mm
30:	Carl:	okay

Carl has been told in his class that a common way of marking the final day at work in New Zealand organizations is to provide morning tea for your colleagues as a way of thanking them for their collegial support. In the example he navigates the enactment of this practice with Nerissa as his coach, at the same time ensuring that there is space for his own individualized practice by highlighting his national Taiwanese identity. He thus proposes bringing *Taiwanese cake* (line 18) and putting it out for colleagues to share. Initially Nerissa rejects this idea to some degree by announcing that they would be taking him to lunch (line 9–11) but after further discussion she reassures Carl that this is something the others will appreciate and can be managed within their current plans (lines 25–9). Carl has successfully navigated the enactment of a politeness1 norm and found a space for it within the group norms for appropriate workplace behaviour. Along the way, however, there are many metapragmatic signals of acceptable practice that are referenced by the two participants. Through Nerissa's largely indirect explanations, her implicit metapragmatic signalling is working to explain how things are done, namely how one is expected to thank others on the last day of work.

What is particularly of interest to discourse analysts seeking to deepen understandings of pragmatics in the workplace is the link from metapragmatic signalling to ideologies. In other words, a focus on metapragmatics allows access to the outermost layer of the wider sociocultural discourses we are interested in. What is happening in the interactional 'now' connects indexically to the norms and expectations of the workplace, and these in turn are tethered to ideologies. Through the lens of the doxa, we see what is taken for granted, what assumptions are underpinning workplace talk, and what is appropriate in a particular setting. Access to ideologies lifts the veil on these hidden aspects of discourse that can reveal so much about the way we talk at work. To return to Carl and Nerissa, the emphasis (albeit indirect) on thanking colleagues by bringing food to them is indexical to commonly shared New Zealand values of reciprocity and gratitude, but this workplace also has a way to thank Carl which is specific to them. Both layers are important to our interpretations.

As well as the emic affordances that a focus on metapragmatics offers (an ability to see things from an insider perspective), there is equally valuable potential for etic understandings to be harnessed, for researchers to draw on their own knowledge of the sociocultural research context. This combination allows for greater analytical depth and, as such, we see it as an important future scholarly direction. It is the potential for social impact; however, that remains the most exciting line of further development. Deeper and more nuanced understandings of the role of ideologies (and how these are 'given voice' through metapragmatic signalling) has implications for workplace practices themselves. In understanding the ideological roots of expectations and norms, there is more potential to be able to share these with the workplace community. The 'way things are done' is, of course, always changing, but if people in a workplace CofP have access to these ideological guides (including those of insiders and those of newcomers), there is a higher likelihood of mutual understanding. Fellow workmates may be seen not only as individuals with their own particular ways of getting things done at work, but as socially embedded in wider discourses and ingrained ways of thinking, doing and being.

While the aim of inclusive and respectful workplaces can certainly be assisted by such a focus, we would also argue that the potential for problematization is important. Just because things are done a certain way in a workplace, and have been for a long time, does not equate to best practice. Enhanced understandings of ideologies may well help with understanding some of these 'commonsense' practices and norms, and how they have come to establish themselves, and they may also lead to eventual change (for the better) through the processes of reflection and problematization. This is a very exciting avenue to be pursuing.

Workplace talk is multifaceted and does not lend itself to clear and non-contestable analyses applicable across all contexts under investigation. Context is crucial; interactions are embedded not only in the particular organizational order of the workplace, but in wider social-cultural discourses. The way we talk with our colleagues has implications for 'getting things done' at work (the transactional elements of talk) as well as for the social relationships within which we operate in a workplace (relational elements). Across our data, (im)politeness manifests as a pragmatic function in both transactional and relational realms. It follows that greater understandings of the dynamism and complexities involved in workplace interactions can extend our interpretive reach.

References

Angouri, J. (2007). Language in the workplace: A multimethod study of communicative activity in seven multinational companies situated in Europe. Unpublished PhD thesis, University of Essex.
Angouri, J. (2012). Managing disagreement in problem solving meeting talk. *Journal of Pragmatics*, 44, 1565–79.
Angouri, J. and Marra, M. (2010). Corporate meetings as genre: A study of the role of the chair in corporate meeting talk. *Text and Talk*, 30, 615–36.
Angouri, J. and Marra, M. (eds.). (2011). *Constructing Identities at Work*. Basingstoke, UK: Palgrave Macmillan.
Barron, A. and Schneider, K. P. (2009). Variational pragmatics: Studying the impact of social factors on language use in interaction. *Intercultural Pragmatics*, 6(4), 425–42.
Brown, P. and Levinson, S. C. ([1987] 1987). *Politeness: Some Universals in Language Usage*. Cambridge: Cambridge University Press.
Bourdieu, P. ([1972] 1977). *Outline of a Theory of Practice*. Vol. 16, Translated by R. Nice. Cambridge: Cambridge University Press.
Clyne, M. (1994). *Inter-Cultural Communication at Work: Discourse Structures across Cultures*. Cambridge: Cambridge University Press.
Coupland, N. and Jaworski, A. (2004). Sociolinguistic perspectives on metalanguage: Reflexivity, evaluation and ideology. In A. Jaworski, N. Coupland and D. Galasinski, eds., *Metalanguage: Social and Ideological Perspectives*. Berlin: Mouton de Gruyter, pp. 15–51.
Culpeper, J. (2011). *Impoliteness: Using Language to Cause Offence*. Cambridge: Cambridge University Press.
Daly, N., Holmes, J., Newton, J. and Stubbe, M. (2004). Expletives as solidarity signals in FTAs on the factory floor. *Journal of Pragmatics*, 36(5), 945–64.
De Fina, A., Schiffrin, D. and Bamberg, M. (2006). *Discourse and Identity*. Cambridge: Cambridge University Press.
Drew, P. and Heritage, J. (eds.). (1992). *Talk at Work: Interaction in Institutional Settings*. Cambridge: Cambridge University Press.
Eckert, P. (2008). Variation and the indexical field. *Journal of Sociolinguistics*, 12(4), 453–76.
Eelen, G. (2001). *A Critique of Politeness Theories*. Manchester, UK: St Jerome.
Fletcher, J. (2014). Social communities in a knowledge enabling organizational context: Interaction and relational engagement in a community of

practice and a micro-community of knowledge. *Discourse and Communication*, 8(4), 351–69.

Franziskus, A. (2013). Getting by in a multilingual workplace: Language practices, ideologies and norms of cross-border workers in Luxembourg. Unpublished PhD thesis, University of Luxembourg.

Franziskus, A., de Bres, J. and Gilles, P. (2013). 'I learnt English – the wrong thing, eh'. Power, interests and language practices among cross-border workers in Luxembourg. In P. Gilles, H. Koff, C. Maganda and C. Schulz, eds., *Theorizing Borders through Analyses of Power Relationships*. Brussels: Peter Lang, pp. 249–70.

Gumperz, J. J. (1982). *Discourse Strategies*. Cambridge: Cambridge University Press.

Heritage, J. and Clayman, S. (2010). *Talk in Action: Interactions, Identities, and Institutions*. Chichester, UK: John Wiley

Holmes, J. (2007). Social constructionism, postmodernism and feminist sociolinguistics. *Gender and Language*, 1(1), 51–65.

Holmes, J. and Marra, M. (2004). Leadership and managing conflict in meetings. *Pragmatics*, 14(4), 439–62.

Holmes, J., Marra, M. and Vine, B. (2011). *Leadership, Discourse, and Ethnicity*. Oxford: Oxford University Press.

Holmes, J., Marra, M. and Vine, B. (2012). Politeness and impoliteness in New Zealand English workplace discourse. *Journal of Pragmatics*, 44, 1063–76.

Holmes, J., Marra, M. and Vine, B. (2020). Contesting the culture order: Contrastive pragmatics in action. *Contrastive Pragmatics*, 1(1), 1–27.

Holmes, J. and Stubbe, M. ([2003] 2015). *Power and Politeness in the Workplace*. 2nd ed. Abingdon, UK: Routledge.

Hui, S. Y. (2014). Analysing interpersonal relations in call-centre discourse. Unpublished PhD thesis, Victoria University of Wellington.

Ide, S. (1989). Formal forms and discernment: Two neglected aspects of universals of linguistic politeness. *Multilingua – Journal of Cross-Cultural and Interlanguage Communication*, 8(2–3), 223–48.

Kádár, D. Z. and Haugh, M. (2013). *Understanding Politeness*. Cambridge: Cambridge University Press.

Kerbrat-Orecchioni, C. (2006). Politeness in small shops in France. *Journal of Politeness Research*, 2(1), 79–103.

King, B. W. (2019a). *Communities of Practice in Language Research: A Critical Introduction*. London: Routledge.

King, B. W. (2019b, December). Finding ideologies in talk about talk. Paper presented at the New Zealand Discourse Conference, Wellington.

Locher, M. A. (2004). *Power and Politeness in Action: Disagreements in Oral Communication*. Berlin: Mouton de Gruyter.

Locher, M. A. and Limburg, H. (eds.). (2012). *Advice in Discourse*. Amsterdam: John Benjamins.

Locher, M. A. and Watts, R. J. (2005). Politeness theory and relational work. *Journal of Politeness Research*, 1(1), 9–33.

Lønsmann, D. (2011). English as a corporate language: Language choice and language ideologies in an international company in Denmark. Unpublished PhD thesis, Roskilde University.

Marra, M. (2012). Disagreeing without being disagreeable: Negotiating workplace communities as an outsider. *Journal of Pragmatics, 44*, 1580–90.

Mondada, L. (2011). The organization of concurrent courses of action in surgical demonstrations. In J. Streeck, C. Goodwin and C. LeBaron, eds., *Embodied Interaction, Language and Body in the Material World*. Cambridge: Cambridge University Press, pp. 207–26.

Mondada, L. (2018). The multimodal interactional organization of tasting: Practices of tasting cheese in gourmet shops. *Discourse Studies, 20*(6), 743–69.

Morrison, A. and Holmes, J. (2003). Eliciting refusals: A methodological challenge. *Te Reo, 46*, 47–66.

Mullany, L. (2007). *Gendered Discourse in the Professional Workplace*. Basingstoke, UK: Palgrave Macmillan.

Murata, K. (2011). A contrastive study of the discourse of business meetings in New Zealand and Japan. Unpublished PhD thesis, Victoria University of Wellington.

Ochs, E. (1992). Indexing gender. In A. Duranti and C. Goodwin, eds., *Rethinking Context: Language as an Interactive Phenomenon*. Cambridge: Cambridge University Press, pp. 335–58.

Prebble, J. (2009). A cost/benefit analysis of the Skilled Migrant programme: 2005–2008.Victoria University of Wellington Language in the Workplace Project Occasional Paper 9.

Riddiford, N. and Holmes, J. (2015). Assisting the development of sociopragmatic skills: Negotiating refusals at work. *System, 48*, 129–40.

Roberts, C., Davies, E. and Jupp, T. (1992). *Language and Discrimination*. London: Longman.

Schnurr, S. and Chan, A. (2009). Politeness and leadership discourse in New Zealand and Hong Kong: A cross-cultural case study of workplace talk. *Journal of Politeness Research, 5*(2), 131–57.

Schnurr, S., Marra, M. and Holmes, J. (2007). Being (im)polite in New Zealand workplaces: Māori and Pākehā leaders. *Journal of Pragmatics, 39*, 712–29.

Schnurr, S., Marra, M. and Holmes, J. (2008). Impoliteness as a means of contesting power relations in the workplace. In D. Bousfield and M. Locher, eds., *Impoliteness in Language: Studies on Its Interplay with Power in Theory and Practice*. Berlin: Mouton de Gruyter, pp. 211–30.

Silverstein, M. (1976). Shifters, linguistic categories and cultural description. In K. H. Basso and H. A. Selby, eds., *Meaning in Anthropology*. Albuquerque: University of New Mexico Press, pp. 11–55.

Silverstein, M. (2003). Indexical order and the dialectics of sociolinguistic life. *Language and Communication, 23*(3–4), 193–229.

Spencer-Oatey, H. (2000). Rapport management: A framework for analysis. In H. Spencer-Oatey, ed., *Culturally Speaking: Managing Rapport through Talk across Cultures*. London: Continuum, pp. 11–46.

Spencer-Oatey, H. and Xing, J. (2003). Managing rapport in intercultural business interactions: A comparison of two Chinese–British welcome meetings. *Journal of Intercultural Studies*, 24(1), 33–46.

Tannen, D. (1994). *Talking from 9 to 5: Women and Men at Work*. New York: William Morrow.

Van de Mieroop, D. and Schnurr, S. (eds.). (2017). *Identity Struggles: Evidence from Workplaces Around the World*. Amsterdam: John Benjamins.

Vine, B. (2004). *Getting Things Done at Work: The Discourse of Power in Workplace Interaction*. Amsterdam: John Benjamins.

Vine, B. and Marra, M. (2017). The Wellington Language in the Workplace Project: Creating stability through flexibility. In M. Marra and P. Warren, eds., *Linguist at Work: Festschrift for Janet Holmes*. Wellington: Victoria University Press, pp. 181–201.

Waldvogel, J. (2002). Some features of workplace emails. *New Zealand English Journal*, 16, 42–52.

Watts, R. J. (2003). *Politeness*. Cambridge: Cambridge University Press.

Wenger, E. (1998). *Communities of Practice: Learning, Meaning and Identity*. Cambridge: Cambridge University Press.

Woolard, K. A. (1998). Introduction: Language ideology as a field of inquiry. In B. B. Schiefflin, K. A. Woolard and P. V. Kroskrity, eds., *Language Ideologies: Practice and Theory*. Oxford: Oxford University Press, pp. 3–47.

24

Service Encounter Discourse

J. César Félix-Brasdefer and Rosina Márquez Reiter

24.1 Introduction

We buy everyday products at supermarkets or convenience stores, interact with telephone companies to request or complain about services, and engage in online commerce (e-commerce). Buyers and sellers are offered an array of options regarding the contexts in which they respectively receive and deliver services, including diverse lingua-cultural environments. This includes sales transactions in online environments (e.g. eBay, Amazon) that offer the possibility of connecting with billions of potential buyers across the world. Service encounters are thus everyday interactions in which some kind of commodity (i.e. goods, information, or both) is exchanged between a service provider (e.g. clerk, vendor) and a service seeker (e.g. customer, visitor) (Ventola 2005).

Research on service encounters has examined different aspects of transactional and non-transactional discourse, particularly concerning face-to-face interactions (e.g. Félix-Brasdefer 2015, 2017; Márquez Reiter and Placencia 2004; Márquez Reiter and Stewart 2008), online environments (e.g. Garcés-Conejos Blitvich et al. 2019; Placencia 2015), intercultural service encounters (e.g. Bailey 1997; Lee 2015; Márquez Reiter 2011; Ramírez-Cruz 2017), (im)politeness in social media platforms (e.g. Antonopoulou 2001; Hernández López and Fernández Amaya 2015; Márquez Reiter et al. 2015; Márquez Reiter and Bou-Franch 2017; Márquez Reiter and Orthaber 2019), and non-verbal communication (Dorai and Webster 2015).

This chapter is organized as follows. First, we provide an overview of key concepts, describe the scope of service encounter discourse, and problematize the transactional versus interpersonal talk distinction. Second, we describe how service encounter discourse is constructed in three predominant contexts, namely small shops, bars and cafés and call centres. Third, we

---

See Félix-Brasdefer and Placencia's (2020) volume for an overview of service encounter interactions in face-to-face and online environments.

describe some instances of sociopragmatic variation, including the effects of globalization in service encounter settings. We end this chapter with methodological issues and future directions.

24.2 Key Elements of Service Encounters

24.2.1 Towards a Multidisciplinary Understanding of Service Encounters

The goal-oriented nature of service encounters has led to qualifying the construction of the talk that emerges in these encounters as institutional. Service encounter discourse has thus been described as a type of institutional (e.g. library front desk; online call centre) or quasi-institutional (e.g. small shop or street vendors) talk, which takes place in a particular physical or virtual setting between a service provider and a service seeker who have specific roles and concomitant rights and responsibilities. Service encounters comprise the following components: (1) *setting* (e.g. telephone transaction at a bank; sales transaction through eBay); (2) task or goal-orientedness (the participants in a service encounter show an orientation towards some task/goal that is conventionally related to the setting); (3) *participants' roles* (i.e. each participant is expected to play a specific role, such as service provider or service seeker); (4) *constrained topic* (i.e. the topic of the encounter is constrained by what participants consider to be allowable for the sales transaction) (Drew and Heritage 1992: 22; see also Félix-Brasdefer 2017).

Initial research on service encounter discourse focused on the organizational characteristics that make up the genre of verbal interactions during the face-to-face negotiation of service. For example, Mitchell (1957) analysed the language of buying and selling in Cyrenaica (Libya) and examined the social actions that occurred in three types of encounters: (1) market sales transactions; (2) market auctions and (3) shop transactions. With regard to market (non-auction) and shop transactions, Mitchell identified five stages: (1) salutation; (2) inquiry as to the object for sale; (3) investigation of the object for sale; (4) bargaining and (5) conclusion. The author showed how service encounters are sequentially organized, how social actions (e.g. requests for service, bargaining) are accomplished, and how each sub-genre (market vs shop transactions) varies with regard to its generic structure.

From a Systemic Functional Linguistics perspective, Halliday and Hasan (1980) and Hasan (1985) looked at the generic structure of service encounters in small shops selling fruit. The authors concluded that the genre of service encounters is defined by these obligatory elements: sale request, sale compliance, sale, purchase, and purchase closure (60). Furthermore, Ventola (1987) examined the conversational structure of service encounters in post offices and small shops, and proposed a generic structure for service encounters with the following elements: greeting, attendance-allocation (e.g. "who's next?"), service bid (e.g. "can I help you?"), service (e.g. "could I have …"), resolution (i.e. decision to buy or not to buy), handover of goods, payment, closing and goodbye. In her more recent work, Ventola (2005) argued for an interdisciplinary approach to analysing service encounters, including the multi-modal analysis of verbal and non-verbal actions.

Merritt's (1976) work influenced our understanding of service encounters at both the organizational and sequential level. In her analysis of over 1,000 interactions at a self-service convenience store, the author identified four stages in the structure of service encounters: (1) the customer's presence, which summons the vendor; (2) the decision stage (e.g. "can I have ..."); (3) the exchange of product and money; and (4) the closing stage, including the exchange of goodbyes (cf. Ventola 1987). She examined the data through pragmatic inferences with regard to the assumptions, contextual presuppositions and appropriateness required during the interpretation of a speech act sequence. Merritt's (1976) work thus determined the basic activities involved in service encounters.

From a cross-cultural pragmatic perspective, the PIXI project (Pragmatics of Italian/English Cross-Cultural Interaction) looked at bookshop interactions in Southern England and Northern Italy. Its main objective was to identify similarities and differences in the social practices, pragmalinguistic forms, and structural patterns of bookshop encounters (e.g. openings, closings, request-response sequences, role of laughter, preference/dispreference). Aston (1995) stressed the need for contrastive pragmatics to consider the sequential organization of the discourse as a whole, seen as a process of progressive negotiation, rather than just isolated speech acts – or indeed two or three-part exchanges, as it had been mainly approached thus far. With regard to data analysis, investigators used a mixed methodology that incorporated both quantitative approaches (analysis of recurrent similarities) and qualitative approaches (sequential analysis). Although the focus of the PIXI project was on those activities essential for the service to be accomplished, some aspects of what we term here as "strictly non-essential talk" were examined during the negotiation of service, such as impersonal solidarity and laughter (Aston 1988; Gavioli 1995).

Despite their different approaches, researchers coincide in pointing out the primarily goal-oriented nature of the talk or text (e-commerce) that emerges from service encounters and the sequences that are essential for transactions to be effected. These transactions entail (1) the opening, where the participants acknowledge each other's presence or co-presence (in telephone mediated encounters or those mediated by the internet) and their roles in the relevant setting; (2) the negotiation of a service request, involving the decision to purchase/request information and the exchange of money; followed by (3) the closing, which may or may not include a thank-you or goodbye exchange (Antonopoulou 2001; Haakana and Sorjonen 2011; Félix-Brasdefer 2015: chapter 3), as the closing may be indexed non-verbally (e.g. head nod, hand waving). This last point may reside in the non-essentiality of verbal goodbyes to coordinate interactional cessation in face-to-face to encounters, especially when compared to telephone encounters. In the latter, participants often orient to their co-presence and physical absence to manage the encounter in the absence of other non-verbal communicative signs (cf. Márquez Reiter 2011). Similarly, traditional interpersonally signs, such as laughter, have often been considered to be non-essential for the transaction to be effected. This, as we argue in the next section, denotes a theoretical distinction that is not necessarily empirically demonstrable.

24.2.2 On the Dichotomy between Interpersonal and Transactional Talk

Service encounters are permeated by elements that orient them to the sociability and efficiency with which they are expected to be managed (cf. Márquez Reiter and Bou-Franch 2017; Goodwin 1996; Goodwin and Frame 1989). This is particularly evident in the way in which the goal-oriented talk, which is typically constructed in these kinds of encounters, is imbued with features reminiscent of what is generally conceived of as "interpersonal talk". The presence of interpersonal talk often indicates an existing relationship between the participants, such as in those cases in which the customer has a buying history with the company (cf. Márquez Reiter 2011), or in which a relationship between the parties, albeit often a temporary one, is sought in pursuit of a sale or the obtaining of a given commodity (Márquez Reiter 2006). The literature on service encounters have identified many interpersonal elements, such as phatic exchanges (e.g. greetings and partings), small talk, or individualized talk (Félix-Brasdefer 2015, 2017; Márquez Reiter 2010; McCarthy 2000; Placencia and Mancera Rueda 2011), many of which are representative of the synthetic personalization that characterizes modern customer relationship management (Fairclough 1989). This synthetic personalization has arguably become increasingly unmarked, especially in the West, as is demonstrated through customers' self-disclosure in complaint calls (Márquez Reiter 2005) and interactional closeness for task-oriented purposes (Márquez Reiter 2006). Synthetic personalization entails the adoption of a personal footing in interactions with the customer (Goffman 1981), so that the service encounter more closely resembles a conversation between friends, rather than a business transaction (e.g. Cameron 2000; Márquez Reiter 2006). A prime example of this can be found in telemarketing calls.

Telemarketing calls are unrequested calls from a salesperson that attempts to sell a product to a prospective customer who may not be remotely interested. The prospective customer's name is typically one of many on a list through which the salesperson works in the hope of striking gold and obtaining a sale. Given the unsolicited and essentially intrusive nature of these calls (e.g. Lakoff 2005), which are characteristic of the postmodern blurring of the private–public boundaries (Habermas 1989), and more recently, of the invasion of individual privacy (i.e. unsolicited calls to mobile telephones), salespersons adopt what is generally known as a "warm approach". A warm approach minimizes the chances of obtaining an unwelcome response. It entails an effort to establish some sort of "intimacy" with the prospective customer, such as anticipating the customer's needs based on their service history, and typically features synthetic personalization strategies (Fairclough 1989). This is observed in the presence of strictly non-essential activities for the transaction to be effected, such as "how-are-you" exchanges and the engagement in small talk – that is, the presence of activities that have been traditionally associated with interpersonal rather than goal-oriented talk. Interpersonal talk is thus intimately related to goal-oriented talk and should not be understood separately. Besides the presence of activities that are, strictly speaking, not necessary for the transaction to be effected, interpersonal-oriented talk also often emerges within transactional talk as the service provider balances efficiency and sociability to enhance the chances of obtaining his or her goal. Typical examples can be found in service telephone calls, when the customers are asked to wait in line while the call agent does a product search, as shown in interaction (1) below.

Example (1) was taken from a small corpus of English calls collected by the second author in 2011 as part of an ethnographic study of communication at an outsourced call centre specializing in time-shares. The conversation/exchange in question has not been previously examined. It is used here to illustrate that the boundaries of transactional and non-transactional talk are not clear-cut.

Following the opening sequence and confirmation of the reason for the call, the telephone agent and the customer engage in the negotiation of the business exchange (see Section 24.2.1); in this case, the agent is helping to choose the right holiday accommodation for the customer based on her needs.

(1)
32	Customer:	How deep is the pool,
33	Service provider:	Um (.) let me check for you Susan (4.0)
34	Service provider:	they're great for doing exercise on holiday (.) aren't they
35	Customer:	= I'm more of a paddler
36	Service provider:	Oh (.) would you prefer a hotel with a pool with a shallow end then,
37	Customer:	No that's fine (.) it's for the children <it's best if they can't touch the bottom>
38	Service provider:	=that's right (0.2) I actually taught my children how to swim in a Olympic size pool
39	Customer:	Were [you able to
40	Service provider:	[here it is it's a shallow end (.) close to a meter and then it goes onto two
41	Customer:	me[ters [that's perfect

42	Service provider:	You'll be able to touch the bottom while they do lengths hhh
43	Customer:	=Hh That's handy hh
44	Service provider:	Is there anything else you'd like to know about the facilities Susan,

Example (1) contains features that are generally associated with interpersonally oriented talk, such as the use of vocatives; in this case the service provider addresses the customer by first name (lines 33, 44) and attempts at engaging in small talk (lines 34–5, 42–3). These strategies, however, are part and parcel of the goal-oriented activities that they are helping to construct (i.e. a product search and an offer of assistance aimed at progressing the service encounter from the business exchange to the closing sequence).

If we look at the example more closely, we will notice that during the business exchange, the customer requests further details about the time-share facilities (i.e. the size of the pool, line 32). The service provider thus proceeds to check the relevant information on the system (line 33). Four seconds into the search, he initiates interpersonal talk to indicate co-presence and attentiveness to the customer. The topic is still, however, related to the information search (line 34). The tag question (… "aren't they?") proffered by the service provider inferentially conveys his interpretation that the customer is interested in accommodation that features a swimming pool rather a splashing pool. Likewise, earlier in the conversation, the ages of the customer's children (i.e. 14 and 15 years old) and the need for accommodation with a pool had been established. The likelihood of non-swimmers in the family is thus high. The customer immediately reacts (notice the latch in line 35) by specifying that she is not a strong swimmer. The service provider orients to this as new information (notice the presence of "Oh" in turn initial position; Heritage 1998) and proceeds to determine the customer's pool preference. Later, in lines 38–9, he initiates further interpersonally oriented talk while doing the relevant search. The customer attempts to engage in this talk until the service provider, in a non-competitive overlap, announces that the right product has been found, and the customer acknowledges her satisfaction. The service provider then proceeds to produce an upshot of the requested product in line with the customer's needs followed by laughter (hhh, line 42). The customer immediately reacts with laughter followed by an expression that summarizes her swimming ability relative to that of her children in a humorous manner. From this point on, the service provider engages in unambiguous task-oriented talk.

Example (1) illustrates that interpersonal and transactional talk are on a continuum. The elements of what is usually termed "interpersonal talk" are servicing the overarching business at hand and, in some cases, also help to avoid the gaps that would ensue while searching for relevant information. It then follows that any attempt at differentiating between interpersonal and transactional talk would have to take into account the activities that they help to construct and the participants' agendas.

24.3 Contexts of Service Encounters

In this section, we offer a selective account of research in service encounter interactions in three contexts: small shops, bars and cafés and call centres (telephone service encounters).

24.3.1 Small Shops

Francophone researchers made significant contributions through their data collected in bakeries, butcher shops and jewellery stores and at newspaper stands. For example, Kerbrat-Orecchioni and Traverso (2008) investigated politeness practices and sequential organization (e.g. openings, closings, request-response sequence) in small shops. They defined commercial encounters as "one type of social situation that is characterized by regulations of different orders (of what we can and cannot buy, where, when etc.), and for which there exist specific places: commercial sites" (Kerbrat-Orecchioni and Traverso 2008: 24). The authors proposed the following levels of analysis (15–23):

(i) The organization of interactions in commercial settings:
   a. overall organization (top-down approach);
   b. sequential organization (e.g. structural elements of the request-response sequence);
   c. micro-analysis of sequential interactions (bottom-up approach);
(ii) The transactional component;
(iii) Multi-modal analysis (*La dimension praxique*) (gesture; audio- and videotaped data);
(iv) The roles of the participants; and
(v) The relational level (e.g. small talk, humour, jokes, polite behaviour).

This model aims at examining different aspects of the transactional and non-transactional elements that permeate service encounter talk. It takes both a top-down approach, looking at the overall organization of the encounter (generic structure), and a bottom-up approach, analysing the sequential structure of social actions (e.g. openings and closings, request-response sequence). Furthermore, Filliettaz (2004) examined service encounters in bookshops and small stores in Geneva from a multi-modal perspective. In his multimodal approach to service encounter discourse, Filliettaz examined the complex realization of gesture, action and setting. Specifically, he looked at the impact of non-verbal behaviour during the construction of the negotiation of service using audio-taped face-to-face interactions, complemented with field-note data to gather information on non-verbal cues during the interaction. He focused on how gesture (e.g. hand movements) and speech co-occur both during the negotiation and in the successful outcome of the transaction. His analysis underscores the importance of the multimodal negotiation of service encounters of "nonverbal actions [that] are deeply interwoven with communicative process" (Filliettaz 2004: 98).

Francophone discourse analysts examined politeness practices, the sequential structure of actions (e.g. openings and requests), and the organizational structure of service encounters in small shops (e.g. Kerbrat-Orecchioni 2001, 2004, 2006). Research has looked at the participants' roles, pragmatic variation of the request for service, and the presence or absence of internal modifiers. For example, Traverso's (2001, 2006, 2007) work made important contributions to contrastive pragmatics by focusing on two different linguacultures: that of France and that of Syria. Traverso's work, in line with that of the authors we cite in this chapter, has helped to further attest the usefulness of the service encounter arena to examine an array of linguistic pragmatic features, ranging from politeness orientations to activity formation.

Service encounters have also been analysed, among others, in Finnish (e.g. Haakana and Sorjonen 2011; Isosävi and Lappalainen 2015), Turkish (e.g. Bayyurt and Bayraktaroğlu 2001), Greek (Antonopoulou 2001; Sifianou and Tzanne 2018), French (Kerbrat-Orechionni 2006) and most extensively in varieties of Spanish following the sociopragmatic variation venture within contrastive pragmatics at the time, the diversity of the Spanish language and its global remit (Márquez Reiter and Placencia 2005; Márquez Reiter 2002; Placencia 1998). Márquez Reiter and Placencia (2004) analysed 56 audio-taped interactions (clothing and accessory shops) in lower-middle class shopping areas in Montevideo and in Quito. The different ways of offering and requesting service, including the negotiation of the exchange and the closings, were interpreted as orientations to interactional closeness (Montevideans) and respectful distance (Quiteños) and reported as statistically significant. The results of their study were further corroborated by Placencia's (2005) analysis of intra-lingual pragmatic variation in small shop interactions in Quito and Madrid. Although customer requests reflected an overall preference for direct requests internal modification of the request (e.g. diminutives and politeness markers), was more frequent in Ecuadorian Spanish. Similarly, in a contrastive study of service encounters at household appliances stores in Montevideo and Edinburgh, Márquez Reiter and Stewart (2008) report a tendency towards interactional closeness by Montevideans. Montevidean service providers engaged in proactive selling strategies, such as offering unsolicited products and information, with a higher level of personal involvement (Tannen 1984) relative to their counterparts in Edinburgh. In both cities, service providers engaged in interpersonal talk in pursuit of their goal. From a pragmatic variational perspective, Félix-Brasdefer and Yates (2020) looked at intra-lingual pragmatic variation during the negotiation of service in corner stores in three regions, namely Mexico City, Buenos Aires and Seville. Results showed differences with regard to the type of request for service: Mexicans showed a preference for assertion statements (e.g. *Me da* ... 'you give me ...'), Spaniards favoured imperatives (e.g. *Ponme una barra de pan* 'You give me a loaf of bread'), and Argentines predominantly selected ellipticals (e.g. *Un pancho* 'one hot dog'). At the stylistic level, the second person informal pronoun (T) was more frequent among Spanish and Argentine buyers and sellers, while the formal address form (V) predominated among Mexican customers irrespective of age and gender differences.

Furthermore, service encounters have also been analysed at the subnational level in corner stores: Placencia (2008) looked at pragmatic variation in two regions of Ecuador (Quito and Manta). The study employed Spencer-Oatey's (2000) classification of discourse domains: illocutionary (requests), discourse (openings and closings), stylistic (variation in T/V address forms), and participatory domains (turn-taking/relational talk). With regard to the illocutionary level, although both groups used direct requests (e.g. imperatives, elliptical), imperative requests predominated among the Quiteño customers. Internal modification of the request was more frequent and varied in the Quiteño data than in the Manteño data, such as diminutives, politeness forms, lexical downgrading, and hedges (e.g. *Regáleme un pancito por favor* 'Give me bread^{DIM} for free please'). At the discourse domain, openings in the form of greeting or greeting exchanges were more frequent among the Quiteño customers and almost completely absent among the Manteño customers. Placencia concluded that Quiteños show an orientation for an interpersonal style (e.g. phatic exchanges, longer greeting sequences) more frequently than Manteños, who are more task-oriented and less concerned about the interpersonal demands of the interaction. Félix-Brasdefer (2015) examined subnational variation in two Mexican regions, central (Mexico City) and Northern Mexico (Guanajuato). With regard to the pragmalinguistic realization of the request for service, while customers from both regions predominantly selected assertions (e.g. *Me da* ... 'you give me ...'), ellipticals were preferred by customers from the Northern region (e.g. *Medio kilo de jamón* 'half a kilo of ham'), and implicit requests predominated among customers of Mexico City. Bataller (2020) looked at regional variation (request for service and pronominal address) in two Colombian regions: Cartagena de Indias (Caribbean Coast) and Bucaramanga (Easter Andean Region). Overall, while customers from both regions preferred direct strategies, customers from Cartagena were more direct than the Bucaramanga customers, as shown by their frequent use of imperatives and elliptical requests. At the stylistic level, customers from Cartagena were more informal with a preference for the informal address pronoun (*tú* 'you') and casual terms to express affiliation, while customers from Bucaramanga preferred the formal pronominal form (*usted* 'you formal') and the use of formal address terms, such as (*Doña* 'Ma'am').

Two recent studies analysed the selection of pronominal address in small shops in Central America, Costa Rica (Murillo Medrano 2020) and Nicaragua (Michno 2020). Murillo Medrano (2020) looked at variation in the use of personal pronouns and vocatives in Costa Rican service encounter interactions in grocery stores and call centres, considering gender, the participants' role, the goal of the transaction, and the context and its relation with (im)politeness strategies. In both settings, the singular formal address form *usted* predominates over *vos*, along with high levels of deference and respect. The type of setting conditioned the orientation of the transaction: while in call centres the interactions were more deferent and gave more attention to transactional talk, customers in grocery stores showed an orientation to interpersonal talk by means of solidarity markers, such as colloquial address forms and a preference of informal markers between male speakers. Michno (2020) examined pragmatic variation according to gender during service encounters in a rural Nicaraguan community. Results showed that address form selection by both vendor and customer was primarily conditioned by customer gender; female customers were more likely to use *usted* with a male service provider, while males were more likely to use *vos*. Females were also more likely than males to use *usted* and to opt for employing more direct requests, such as assertions and commands.

24.3.2 Cafés and Bars

The transactional and interpersonal dimension of service encounter interactions has also been analysed in cafés and bars. Fink and Félix-Brasdefer (2015) examined the realization of politeness and pragmalinguistic variation in requests for service among male and female clients at a US café. In their study, the following actions were used to build rapport on the part of the client: a preference for conventionally indirect requests (more frequent among female clients), the politeness marker 'please', and the predominant use of greeting formulas. The authors concluded that female clients appeared more polite than males because of the high indices of conventional indirectness in female requests, and that the gender of the interlocutor determined request production.

Three studies examined the realization of service between customers and baristas in Starbucks cafés. Taylor (2015) looked at pragmalinguistic variation of request forms in 820 Starbucks café service encounters in the northwestern United States. Results showed that both participant gender and the modality of the interaction affect the request forms produced in Starbucks service encounters. Customer gender greatly influenced request forms in face-to-face encounters, and yet this difference disappeared in drive-through encounters where both male and female customers most frequently employed conventional indirect requests. The author concluded that the visual impact of the participant gender in a face-to-face encounter renders gender-based variation null in drive-through encounters due to the lack of the face-to-face contact with the barista. Although Taylor's work focused on service requests and their pragmalinguistic formulation, the synthetic personalization that accompanies coffee consumption at Starbucks (e.g. inquiring the customer's name and writing it on a personalized disposable coffee cup) is a classic example of both the continuum between interpersonal and transactional talk as well as the way in which talk is regulated via prescribed rules of interaction (cf. Márquez Reiter 1998 on ordering food at a traditional Montevidean bar). Furthermore, using posts from different blogs, Isosävi and Lappalainen (2015) looked at the issue of globalization, specifically in how multinational companies, such as Starbucks or IKEA, adopt first names when addressing customers in Finland and France, a practice typical of synthetic personalization (see Section 24.2.2). According to the authors, in these social contexts, first names are associated with America and Americans. These practices break the norms of politeness of non-US countries. Thus, globalization is helping to change discursive practices in certain sociocultural settings.

Finally, Downey Barlett (2005) looked at the transactional nature of service encounters of novice and expert buyers when buying coffee in three different Starbucks cafés in Hawaii (168 audio-taped interactions), including the sequential structure of beginnings, request-response-sequences and endings. The author looked at the interactional features of buyers and baristas (e.g. Barista: Can I help you ma'am?; Customer: Can I try an iced Macadamia latte?; Barista: Did you want that blended or on the rocks?; Customer: Blended). Although the organization of the turn-taking structure of these interactions is symmetric with little overlap or interruption, some differences were observed; short interactions and succinct orders predominated with regular customers, while longer interactions occurred with novice customers who did not know the expected conventional expressions used by expert customers as part of the acculturation process that the Starbucks experience entails: "A double shot 2 per cent mocha latte, please, with whip".

A few studies have examined the negotiation of service in bars. Placencia and Mancera Rueda (2011) looked at the realization of rapport-building talk in bars in Seville, Spain. The data included 140 interactions, including bars frequently visited by customers (70) and bars where the customer and the bartender had infrequent interaction (70). Although the requests for service were direct and mitigated (e.g. *Dame un cafélito para llevar cuando tú puedas* 'Give me a coffee^{DIM} to go when you can'), the data showed that during the negotiation of service, both the customer and the bartender engaged in individualized creative forms expressing humour and teasing activities, such as *piropos* or flirting. Furthermore, Bataller (2015) compared the norms of interaction in Spanish bars in Valencia (Valencian Spanish) and near Granada (Andalusian Spanish). With regard to the request for service, customers from both regions showed a preference for direct requests; those from Valencia employed elliptical requests, while customers in the Granada region selected both elliptical constructions and imperatives (e.g. *Échame un vasito de vino blanco* 'Pour me a little glass of white wine'). Finally, in a more recent study, Padilla Cruz (2020) examined interpersonal aspects of humour to promote rapport between the customer and the bartenders in Seville, Spain. The author found that the manifestation of humour was influenced by the age of the participants and the type of setting. These findings offer further evidence of the empirical inseparability of interpersonal and transactional talk that characterize service provision.

24.3.3 Call Centres: Service Encounters over the Telephone

International companies with a global remit need to connect at a local level. One way in which they do so is by offering their services via the telephone. Telephone mediated service exchanges are institutional, synchronous, real-time encounters that involve a degree of planning by the service provider or the customer. The proliferation and establishment of call centres around the world has mainly revolved around similarities in language and culture and low operational costs. These factors, among others, would make a location attractive. Staff, especially telephone agents, are typically locally procured and trained in culturally appropriate ways so as to manage efficiency and sociability. This would, at least in theory, make it possible for participants who may not share cultural assumptions or values to (re)negotiate their relations and identities. While multinational companies are aware of the need to fit in in diverse lingua-cultural markets and modify their communicative practices on the local level, their efforts at doing so are typically characterized by minimum expenditure. This is illustrated in the way in which they seek service provision standardization across the various locales in which they operate with only partially customized aspects to avoid formulating differences in procedures that are resonant with local expectations. One such example can be found in the in-house rules for opening calls in which greetings, despite their non-essential nature for the transaction to take place, have been found (Márquez Reiter 2010, 2011). In her analyses of service calls across and within different varieties of Latin American Spanish, Márquez Reiter (2005, 2006, 2010, 2011, 2019) reported an overwhelming presence of greeting exchanges in the opening calls. The author argued that the presence of greeting exchanges indicates an orientation to interpersonal connectedness, that is, an aspect of the sociability with which these encounters need to be managed in the lingua-cultures examined in these studies. Yet another example can be observed in the presence of offers of assistance such as *How can I help you?* Despite the fact that they constitute a pragmatically redundant element, they are, nonetheless, pervasive. The presence of greetings and offers of assistance is illustrative of the way in which multinational companies partially customize aspects of the service in order to attend to local expectations while maintaining their identity and avoiding incurring any extra costs.

When telephoning a customer or a company, call initiators "have to relate to the preparation of presence from the situation of absence given that the encounter is carried out at a distance" (Márquez Reiter 2011: 2). This is especially relevant in the case of telephone agents making a call rather than receiving it. Telephone agents, particularly those in outsourced call centres, have to schedule calls, taking into account the time difference between the place where the call is made and the corner of the world where the customer is in, the normal working hours in the customer's respective country, and the agenda of the call, while all the while calibrating the need for efficiency and sociability.

Interactions between telephone agents and customers at call centres have received significant scholarly attention, especially by discourse analysts interested in the feminization of the workforce (e.g. Cameron 2000, 2008), where discursive features that have been associated with the language of females have been adopted to personalize service provision, thus becoming conventionalized and unmarked. Call centre interactions have also received attention by scholars interested in the management of multilingualism (e.g. Dûchene 2009; Márquez Reiter and Martín Rojo 2010) and critical sociolinguists (e.g. Budach Roy and Heller 2003) interested in shedding light on the way in which the management and commodification (Heller 2003) of language practices is ideologically and contextually conditioned by a service-based economy. Interactions at call centres have also been examined by applied linguists interested in the linguistic patterns and communication problems that emerge, especially at outsourced call centres where agents whose first language is not English communicate in English with English-speaking customers and receive relevant training to this end (e.g. Forey and Lockwood 2007; Friginal 2009; Lockwood et al. 2009).

In addition, the different ways in which sociability and efficiency are managed in telephone mediated service encounters, coupled with the formalized nature of service encounters with rule-bound structures have also attracted the attention of (im)politeness scholars. Varcasia (2013) examined requests and their responses in British English, Italian and German at an array of local companies – from pharmacies to fruit and vegetable suppliers – and reported a preference for brevity in the responses. Economidou-Kogetsidis (2005) analysed requests by Greek customers to an airline company, finding that more complex response types were preferred. Specifically, she found that telephone agents offered more information than that requested by the customer. Although not addressed by Economidou-Kogetsidis, the difference observed in the results also reveal the different contexts where the data came from, such as small shops that are not necessarily subject to the exigencies of the new economy, versus large airline companies. Thus, communication in local shops is primarily oriented towards efficiency, whereas the training that airline agents are likely to receive enhances customer experience by calibrating efficiency and sociability, particularly in light of the various possibilities that may be available in terms of flights.

24.4 Globalization and Sociopragmatic Variation

The impact of globalization has affected the way we negotiate service for the exchange of goods or information in a variety of sociocultural contexts. According to Blommaert (2010), globalization concerns "the intensified flows of capital, goods, people, images and discourses around the world" (13). It includes the technological advances and interconnectedness of people around the world in a variety of sociocultural settings. Thus, the expansion of multinational companies (e.g. Starbucks, IKEA) to cultures that do not share the same sociocultural expectations (e.g. politeness norms, informality and deference) has influenced discursive practices and the ways in which people perceive and engage in transactional and interpersonal talk.

Globalization has also impacted our understanding of sociopragmatic variation. Sociopragmatics focuses on the study of discourse in a variety of sociocultural contexts. According to Márquez Reiter and Placencia (2005), sociopragmatics examines meaning in interaction; specifically, the aim of sociopragmatics is to "uncover the cultural norms which underlie the interactional features of a given social group in a given social context; that is to say, to make interactants' implicit sociocultural knowledge and values explicit" (192). More importantly, the factors that influence discursive practices may include the kind of store in which the encounter takes place (e.g. national or multinational stores, call centres or open-air markets), the location of the site (a store in a rural vs an urban community), the situation, and the degree of familiarity or lack thereof between the interlocutors (Félix-Brasdefer 2015; Félix-Brasdefer and Placencia 2020).

Sifianou and Tzanne (2018) examined sociocultural discursive practices during the negotiation of service in three face-to-face service encounter settings in Greece (total of 579 encounters): multinational chain stores (Benetton, Starbucks), Greek chain stores (Hondos Center, Plaisio), and independently owned local shops. Formality (74 per cent) predominated across the three settings by means of the deferential V form used in offers of assistance, interrogatives and imperatives. On the other hand, informality (26 per cent) was realized by means of the diminutive and the informal pronoun of address T-form, and first names accompanied by formal V forms. T-forms, common in the small shops, were used by young employees to address a person of similar age or an older employee addressing a young customer. According to the authors, although service providers in Starbucks cafés prefer an informal style through referring to the customer by first name, this practice is viewed as inappropriate in the Greek sociocultural context. The authors claim that "there seems to be no global adherence to a given script and thus interlocutors may change and reconstruct imported global discourse practices in ways that seem more appropriate for the specific socio-cultural context" (Sifianou and Tzanne 2018: 167). Similar conclusions were reached by Isosävi and Lappalainen (2015) in

Finnish and French Starbucks cafés. Bayyurt and Bayraktaroğlu (2001) analysed variation of pronominal forms and vocatives in Turkish service encounters using a Discourse Completion Test with six situations. The selection of address forms varied according to the setting (e.g. open market, local shops, kiosks, and two stores of high reputation and even higher price points), the degree of social distance between the seller and the buyer, and the socioeconomic level of the buyers. For example, the highest occurrence of pronouns and vocatives took place at the local grocery store and were less frequent at the fashion shop (higher socioeconomic level). Sociopragmatic variation was conditioned by the socioeconomic level of the shoppers and their degree of familiarity with the service providers: the familiar pronoun T (*Sen*), was more frequent in the local shops, while the V form (*siz*) was the preferred form in the more affluent sites, such as in reputable supermarkets and fashion shops.

24.5 Computer-Mediated Discourse: Online Service Encounters in a Global World

Computer-Mediated Discourse Analysis (CMDA) studies language use in online interaction. In these interactions, participants interact through verbal language that is either typed on a keyboard and read on a computer screen, as is the norm for email, chat, Facebook, or negotiated through live video and audio (e.g. Skype). In their model of CMDA, Herring and Androutsopoulos (2015) proposed four domains of language: structure, meaning, interaction and social behaviour. Of these, two (meaning and interaction) can be applied to the negotiation of online service. Herring and Androutsopoulos regard one or more ordered speech acts (e.g. a clarification question or a series of speech acts in an email message) to be at the level of meaning. At the interactive level, sequences of speech acts are negotiated by means of "'interactive exchanges'" by two or more participants (e.g. Skype [spoken discourse] or chat [written discourse]).

These levels of language can be applied to the analysis of the emerging genre of e-service encounters. Placencia (2015) examined the negotiation process of online service among native speakers of Spanish with regard to the address forms used during the online transaction. Garcés-Conejos Blitvich (2015) provided a programmatic agenda for the analysis of e-service encounters. Finally, Zahler (2016) offered a contrastive analysis of online personal ads with regard to the speech act strategies used to request a personal encounter among users in Mexico City and London. The negotiation of e-service presents a rich research field since many current consumers prefer sales transactions conducted through internet sites such as eBay, Vivastreet and as many department stores also offer online sales.

E-service encounters have been broadly defined as web-based services or interactive services that are delivered through online technology, such as a website. Given the emerging field of computer-mediated communication and the various ways to negotiate the online delivery of services, researchers focus on the discourse structure of the e-service encounter genre in modalities such as eBay, Amazon, Craigslist and Facebook, and of online sales in the context of internet retailing, particularly in Latin America, investigating sites such as *Mercado Libre* Ecuador and Argentina (Placencia 2015; Powell and Placencia 2020). Rowley (2006) offers a critical overview of e-service encounters in commercial and non-commercial settings. According to Rowley, e-service is defined as deeds, efforts or performances whose delivery is mediated by information technology (including the Web, information kiosks and mobile devices). Such e-service includes the service element of e-tailing ("electronic retailing"), customer and service and service delivery. Current research in e-service encounters includes the negotiation of meaning through online service in a variety of online environments; such research includes studies on commercial and non-commercial interactions in web-mediated service encounters SEs (e.g. Bou-Franch and Garcés-Conejos Blitvich 2020), online buying and selling in a Mexican market through Facebook (Merino Hernández 2020), e-commerce and selection of forms of address in Ecuadorian (Placencia 2015) and Argentinean markets (Powell and Placencia 2020), the negotiation of service through hyperlinks (Stommel and te Molder 2015), and requests for service through personal ads in *Vivastreet* (Zahler 2016). In these studies, Herring and Androutsopoulos' (2015) Computer-Mediated Discourse model is the predominant framework utilized to examine the e-service encounter discourse.

24.6 Methodological Considerations

For the analysis of service encounter interactions, researchers predominantly rely on authentic data in face-to-face interactions and in online environments. Although audio-recorded methods predominate in the literature, video recording should also be considered to examine non-verbal actions during the negotiation of service. This is especially relevant when considering that various activities, such as the exchange of goodbyes we discussed earlier (Section 24.2.2) or the exchange of money, do not always require verbal communication and frequently (if not always) consist of non-verbal communicative elements (see also Antonopoulou 2001). This, in turn, will not only help us to gain a more encompassing picture of how service encounters unfold, but will also provide evidence as to the applicability of the models that have been put forward and discussed above.

In addition to audio-recorded data, researchers should consider data triangulation to account for the unavoidable sources of error inherent in the methods used (Márquez Reiter and Placencia 2005; Schneider 2018). One way of doing this is to conduct post-performance interviews to better establish the perception of service on the part of both the clerk and the customer, or by playing the recording back to gauge the participants' or others' evaluations of service. Furthermore, an ethnographic approach can help to identify discrepancies between what people say they do and what they actually do, as well as reveal unarticulated phenomena. Ethnography, despite being rarely used in service encounter research (cf. Márquez Reiter 2011), offers a self-reflective element that is virtually absent in extant research on the subject. An ethnographically informed approach allows the researcher's personal experience to describe and critique the very practices and experiences that the participants engage in or report having engaged in Duranti (1997). Ethnography also accounts for the researcher's presence from a critical stance and helps to develop a 'thick' description of the lived experience of parties to commercial encounters. This, in turn, offers the potential to inform marketing and customer service research, thus giving pragmatic knowledge a practical applicability to service encounters.

24.7 Conclusion

This chapter offered an account of general topics related to service encounter interactions. Since the discourse of service encounters depends heavily on the research site, we reviewed the literature in three contexts, namely small stores, bars and cafés, and call centres. In addition to the negotiation of service in verbal interactions, we examined the discursive structure of online service encounters. We also looked at two types of talk that are embedded in service encounter interactions, namely transactional and interpersonal talk. Although most research has focused on the negotiation of the sales transaction (see Félix-Brasdefer 2015: chapter 2; Félix-Brasdefer and Placencia 2020), we have shown the interweaving of the transactional and the interpersonal in service encounter talk. Furthermore, the integrative approach to analysing service encounters allows the researcher to examine different dimensions of service encounter interactions, including the analysis of transactional and interpersonal talk. The structure of service encounter discourse can be analysed from both a top-down (generic structure) and bottom-up perspective (sequential structure and the organization of turn-taking). This model opens the door to examining pragmatic variation, including macro-social (e.g. region, age, gender, socioeconomic class) and microsocial factors (e.g. situation, social power and distance) that impact communicative language use across languages and across varieties of a language (Félix-Brasdefer 2021; Schneider 2020).

References

Antonopoulou, E. (2001). Brief service encounters: Gender and politeness. In A. Bayraktaroğlu and M. Sifianou, eds., *Linguistic Politeness across Boundaries: The Case of Greek and Turkish.* Amsterdam: John Benjamins, pp. 241–69.

Archer, D. and Jagodziński, P. (2015). Call centre interaction: A case of sanctioned face attack? *Journal of Pragmatics,* 76, 46–66.

Aston, G. (Ed.). (1988). *Negotiating Service: Studies in the Discourse of Bookshop Encounters.* Bologna: CLUEB.

Aston, G. (1995). In reference to the role of openings in service encounters. *Cahiers de Linguistique Française,* 16, 89–112.

Bailey, B. (1997). Communication of respect in interethnic service encounters. *Language in Society,* 26, 327–56.

Bataller, R. (2015). ¡Enrique, échame un tintillo! A comparative study of service encounter requests in Valencia and Granada. In L. Fernández-Amaya and M. Hernandez-Lopez, eds., *Service Encounters and Cross-Cultural Communication.* Leiden, Netherlands: Brill, pp. 113–37.

Bataller, R. (2020). Corner-store interactions in Cartagena and Bucaramanga: A variational pragmatics study. In J. C. Félix-Brasdefer and M. E. Placencia, eds., *Pragmatic Variation in Service Encounter Interactions across the Spanish-Speaking World.* Abingdon, UK: Routledge, pp. 35–54.

Blommaert, J. (2010). *The Sociolinguistics of Socialization.* Cambridge: Cambridge University Press.

Bayyurt, Y. and Bayraktaroğlu, A. (2001). The use of pronouns and terms of address in Turkish service encounters. In A. Bayraktaroğlu and M. Sifianou, eds., *Linguistic Politeness across Boundaries: The Case of Greek and Turkish.* Amsterdam: John Benjamins, pp. 209–40.

Bou-Franch, P. and Garcés-Conejos Blitvich, P. (2020). Socioeconomic variation and conflict in Spanish retailer-consumer interactions on Facebook. In J. C. Félix-Brasdefer and M. E. Placencia, eds., *Pragmatic Variation in Service Encounter Interactions across the Spanish-Speaking World.* Abingdon, UK: Routledge, pp. 189–206.

Budach, G., Roy, S. and Heller, M. (2003). Community and commodity in French Ontario. *Language in Society,* 32, 603–27.

Cameron, D. (2000). Styling the worker: Gender and the commodification of language in the globalized service economy. *Journal of Sociolinguistics,* 4, 323–47.

Cameron, D. (2008). Talk from the top down. *Language and Communication,* 28, 143–55.

Dorai, S. and Webster, C. (2015). The role of nonverbal communication in service encounters. In M. Hernández López and L. Fernández Amaya, eds., *A Multidisciplinary Approach to Service Encounters.* Leiden, Netherlands: Brill, pp. 215–33.

Downey Bartlett, N. J. (2005). A double shot 2% mocha latte, please, with whip: Service encounters in two coffee shops and at a coffee cart. In

M. H. Long, ed., *Second Language Needs Analysis*. Cambridge: Cambridge University Press, pp. 305–43.

Drew, P. and Heritage, J. (eds.). (1992). *Talk at Work: Interaction in Institutional Settings*. Cambridge: Cambridge University Press.

Dûchene, A. (2009). Marketing, management and performance: Multilingualism as commodity in a tourism call centre. *Language Policy*, 8, 27–50.

Duranti, A. (1997). *Linguistic Anthropology*. Cambridge: Cambridge University Press.

Economidou-Kogetsidis, M. (2005). 'Yes, tell me please, what time is the midday flight from Athens arriving?': Telephone service encounters and politeness. *Intercultural Pragmatics*, 2, 253–73.

Fairclough, N. (1989). *Language and Power*. London: Longman.

Félix-Brasdefer, J. C. (2015). *The Language of Service Encounters: A Pragmatic-Discursive Approach*, Cambridge: Cambridge University Press.

Félix-Brasdefer, J. C. (2017). Service encounters. In B. Vine, ed., *The Routledge Handbook of Language in the Workplace*. Berlin: Mouton de Gruyter, pp. 162–74.

Félix-Brasdefer, J. C. (2021). Pragmatic variation across varieties of Spanish. In D. A. Koike & J. C. Félix-Brasdefer (eds.), *The Routledge Handbook of Spanish Pragmatics*. Oxford & New York: Routledge. pp. 269–287.

Félix-Brasdefer, J. C. and Placencia, M. E. (2020). *Pragmatic Variation in Service Encounter Interactions across the Spanish-Speaking World*. Abingdon, UK: Routledge.

Félix-Brasdefer, J. C. and Yates, A. (2020). Regional pragmatic variation in small shops in Mexico City, Buenos Aires, and Seville, Spain. In J. C. Félix-Brasdefer and M. E. Placencia, eds., *Pragmatic Variation in Service Encounter Interactions across the Spanish-Speaking World*. Abingdon, UK: Routledge, pp. 15–34.

Fink, L. and Félix-Brasdefer, J. C. (2015). Pragmalinguistic and gender variation in U.S. café service encounters. In K. Beeching and H. Woodfield, eds., *Researching Sociopragmatic Variability: Perspectives from Variational, Interlanguage and Contrastive Pragmatics*. Basingstoke, UK: Palgrave Macmillan, pp. 19–48.

Filliettaz, L. (2004). The multimodal negotiation of service encounters. In P. Le Vine and R. Scollon, eds., *Discourse and Technology: Multimodal Discourse Analysis*. Washington, DC: Georgetown University Press, pp. 88–100.

Forey, G. and Lockwood, J. (2007). "I'd love to put someone in jail for this": An initial investigation of English in the business processing outsourcing (BPO) industry. *English for Specific Purposes*, 26, 308–26.

Friginal, E. (2009). Threats to the sustainability of the outsourced call center industry in the Philippines: Implications for language policy. *Language Policy*, 8, 51–68.

Garcés-Conejos Blitvich, P. (2015). Setting the linguistics research agenda for the e-service encounters genre: Natively digital versus digitized perspectives. In M. de la O Hernández-López and L. Fernández-Amaya, eds., *A Multidisciplinary Approach to Service Encounters*. Boston: Brill, pp. 15–36.

Garcés-Conejos Blitvich, P., Fernández-Amaya, L. and Hernández-López, M. (2019). (eds.). *Technology Mediated Service Encounters*. Amsterdam: John Benjamins.

Gavioli, L. (1995). Turn-initial and turn-final laughter: Two techniques for initiating remedy in English/Italian bookshop service encounters. *Discourse Processes*, 19, 369–84.

Goffman, E. (1981). *Forms of Talk*. Philadelphia: University of Pennsylvania Press.

Goodwin, C. (1996). Communality as a dimension of service relationships. *Journal of Consumer Psychology*, 5, 387–415.

Goodwin, C. and Frame, C. D. (1989). Social distance within the service encounter: Does the consumer want to be your friend? *Advances in Consumer Research*, 16, 64–71.

Habermas, J. (1989). *The Structural Transformation of the Private Sphere: An Enquiry into a Category of Bourgeois Society*. Translated by Thomas Burger. Cambridge, MA.: MIT Press.

Halliday, M. A. K. and Hasan, R. (1980). Text and context: Aspects of language in a social-semiotic perspective. *Sophia Linguistica*, 6, 4–107.

Hasan, R. (1985). The structure of a text. In M. A. K. Halliday and R. Hasan, eds., *Language, Context, and Text: Aspects of Language in a Social-Semiotic Perspective*. Oxford: Oxford University Press, pp. 52–69.

Haakana, M. and Sorjonen, M. L. (2011). Invoking another context: Playfulness in buying lottery tickets at convenience stores. *Journal of Pragmatics*, 43, 1288–1302.

Heller, M. (2003). Globalization, the new economy, and the commodification of language and identity. *Journal of Sociolinguistics*, 7, 473–92.

Hernández López, M. and Fernández Amaya, L. (eds.). (2015). *A Multidisciplinary Approach to Service Encounters*. Leiden, Netherlands: Brill.

Heritage, J. (1998). Oh-prefaced responses to inquiry. *Language in Society*, 27, 291–334.

Herring, S. and Androutsopoulos, J. (2015). Computer-mediated discourse 2.0. In D. Tannen, H. E. Hamilton and Deborah Schiffrin, eds., *The Handbook of Discourse Analysis*, 2nd edn. Malden, MA: Wiley-Blackwell, pp. 127–51.

Isosävi, J. and Lappalainen, H. (2015). First names in Starbucks: A clash of cultures? In C. Norrby and C. Wide, eds., *Address Practice as Social Action: European Perspectives*. Basingstoke, UK: Palgrave Macmillan, pp. 97–118.

Kerbrat-Orecchioni, C. (2001). Je voudrais un p'tit bifteck: la politesse à la française en site commercial [I would like a small steak: French-style politeness in commercial sites]. *Les Carnets du Cediscor*, 7. http://cediscor.revues.org/307.

Kerbrat-Orecchioni, C. (2004). Politeness in France: How to buy bread politely. In L. Hickey and M. Stewart, eds., *Politeness in Europe*. Clevedon, UK: Multilingual Matters, pp. 29–44.

Kerbrat-Orecchioni, C. (2006). Politeness in small shops in France. *Journal of Politeness Research*, 2, 79–103.

Kerbrat-Orecchioni, C. and Traverso, V. (2008). *Les interactions en site commercial: Invariants et variations* [Interactions in Commercial Sites: Invariants and Variations]. Lyon: Ens Éditions.

Lakoff, R. (2005). Civility and its discontents: Or, getting in your face. In R. T. Lakoff and S. Ide, eds., *Broadening the Horizon of Linguistic Politeness*. Amsterdam: John Benjamins, pp. 23–43.

Lee, H. (2015). Does a server's attentiveness matter? Understanding intercultural service encounters in restaurants. *International Journal of Hospitality Management*, 50, 134–44.

Lockwood, J., Forey, G. and Elias, N. (2009). Call centre communication: Measurement processes in non-English speaking contexts. In D. Belcher, ed., *English for Specific Purposes in Theory and Practice*. Ann Arbor: University of Michigan Press, pp. 143–65.

Márquez Reiter, R. (1998). The teaching of 'politeness' in the language classroom. In I. Vázquez Orta and I. Guillén Galve, eds., *Perspectivas Pragmáticas en Lingüística Aplicada*. Anubar: Zaragoza, pp. 290–97.

Márquez Reiter, R. (2002). A contrastive study of conventional indirectness in Spanish: Evidence from Peninsular and Uruguayan Spanish. *Pragmatics*, 12, 135–51.

Márquez Reiter, R. (2005). Complaint calls to a caregiver service company: The case of *desahogo*. *Intercultural Pragmatics*, 2, 481–513.

Márquez Reiter, R. (2006). Interactional closeness in service calls to Montevidean carer service company. *Research on Language and Social Interaction*, 39, 7–39.

Márquez Reiter, R. (2008). Intra-cultural variation: Explanations in service calls to two Montevidean service providers. *Journal of Politeness Research*, 4, 1–29.

Márquez Reiter, R. (2010). A ella no le gusta que le digan María y a mí que me traten de tú: A window into Latin American diversity. *Sociolinguistic Studies*, 4, 413–42.

Márquez Reiter, R. (2011). *Mediated Business Interactions: Intercultural Communication between Speakers of Spanish*. Edinburgh: Edinburgh University Press.

Márquez Reiter, R. (2019). Navigating commercial constraints in a Spanish service call. In P. Garcés Conejos Biltvich, M. Hernández López and L. Amaya, eds., *Mediated Service Encounters*. Amsterdam: John Benjamins, pp. 121–44.

Márquez Reiter, R. and Bou-Franch, P. (2017). (Im)politeness in service encounters. In J. Culpeper, M. Haugh and D. Kádár, eds., *The Palgrave Handbook of (Im)politeness*. London: Palgrave Macmillan, pp. 661–87.

Márquez Reiter, R. and Placencia, M. (2004). Displaying closeness and respectful distance in Montevidean and Quiteño service encounters. In R. Márquez Reiter and M. E. Placencia, eds., *Current Trends in the Pragmatics of Spanish*. Amsterdam: John Benjamins, pp. 121–55.

Márquez Reiter, R. and Placencia, M. E. (2005). *Spanish Pragmatics*. New York: Palgrave Macmillan.

Márquez Reiter, R. and Stewart, M. (2008). Interactions en site commercial à Montevideo et à Édimbourg (Royaume Uni): "engagement" et "considération enver autri". In C. Kerbrat-Orecchioni and V. Traverso, eds., *Les interactions en site commercial: Invariants et variants*. Paris: ENS Editions, pp. 277–303.

Márquez Reiter, R. and Martín Rojo, L. (eds.). (2010). Service encounters in multilingual and multicultural contexts. Special issue. *Sociolinguistic Studies*, 4.

Márquez Reiter, R., Orthaber, S. and Kádár, D. (2015). Disattending customer dissatisfaction on Facebook: A case study of a Slovenian public transport company. In E. Christopher, ed., *International Management and Intercultural Communication: A Collection of Case Studies*. Basingstoke, UK: Palgrave/Macmillan, pp. 108–26.

Márquez Reiter, R. and Orthaber, S. (2019) Exploring the moral compass: Denunciations in a Facebook carpool group. *Internet Pragmatics*, 1(2), 241–70.

McCarthy, M. (2000). Mutually captive audiences: Small talk and the genre of close-contact service encounters. In J. Coupland, ed., *Small Talk*. Harlow, UK: Pearson, pp. 84–109.

Merino Hernández, L. M. (2020). The role of gender in Mexican e-service encounters. In J. C. Félix-Brasdefer and M. E. Placencia, eds., *Pragmatic Variation in Service Encounter Interactions across the Spanish-Speaking World*. Abingdon, UK: Routledge, pp. 115–29.

Merritt, M. (1976). On questions following questions in service encounters. *Language in Society*, 5, 315–57.

Michno, J. (2020). Gender variation in address form selection in corner store-interactions in a Nicaraguan community. In J. C. Félix-Brsadefer and M. E. Placencia, eds., *Pragmatic Variation in Service Encounter Interactions across the Spanish-Speaking World*. Abingdon, UK: Routledge, pp. 77–98.

Mitchell, T. F. (1957). The language of buying and selling in Cyrenaica: A situational statement. *Hesperis*, 26, 31–71.

Murillo Medrano, J. (2020). Forms of address and gender in Costa Rican service encounters. In J. C. Félix-Brasdefer and M. E. Placencia, eds., *Pragmatic Variation in Service Encounter Interactions across the Spanish-Speaking World*. Abingdon, UK: Routledge, pp. 130–49.

Orthaber, S. and Márquez Reiter, R. (2016). When routine calls for information become interpersonally sensitive. *Pragmatics and Society*, 7, 638–63.

Padilla Cruz, M. (2020). Verbal humor and age in cafés and bars in Seville, Spain. In J. C. Félix-Brasdefer and M. E. Placencia, eds., *Pragmatic Variation in Service Encounter Interactions across the Spanish-Speaking World*. Abingdon, UK: Routledge, pp. 169–88.

Placencia, M. E. (1998). Pragmatic variation: Ecuadorian Spanish vs. Peninsular Spanish. *Spanish Applied Linguistics*, 2, 71–106.

Placencia, M. E. (2005). Pragmatic variation in corner store interactions in Quito and Madrid. *Hispania*, 88(3), 583–98.

Placencia, M. E. (2008) Requests in corner shop transactions in Ecuadorian Andean and Coastal Spanish. In K. Schneider and A. Barron, eds., *Variational Pragmatics: A Focus on Regional Varieties in Pluricentric Languages*. Amsterdam: John Benjamins, pp. 307–32.

Placencia, M. E. (2015). Address forms and relational work in e-commerce: The case of service encounter interactions in MercadoLibre Ecuador. In M. de la O Hernández-López and L. Fernández Amaya, eds., *A Multidisciplinary Approach to Service Encounters*. Leiden, Netherlands: Brill, pp. 37–64.

Powell, H. and Placencia, M. E. (2020). Interpersonal work in service encounters in Mercado Libre Argentina: A comparison between buyer and vendor patterns across two market domains. In J. C. Félix-Brasdefer and M. E. Placencia, eds., *Pragmatic Variation in Service Encounter Interactions across the Spanish-Speaking World*. Abingdon, UK: Routledge, pp. 209–29.

Placencia, M. E. and Mancera Rueda, A. (2011). Vaya, ¡qué chungo! Rapport-building talk in service encounters: The case of bars in Seville at breakfast time. In N. Lorenzo-Dus, ed., *Spanish at Work: Analyzing Institutional Discourse across the Spanish Speaking World*, New York: Palgrave/Macmillan, pp. 192–207.

Ramírez Cruz, H. (2017). No manches, güey! Service encounters in a Hispanic American intercultural communication setting. *Journal of Pragmatics*, 108, 28–47.

Rowley, J. (2006). An analysis of the e-service literature: Towards a research agenda. *Internet Research*, 16, 339–59.

Schneider, K. P. (2020). Rethinking pragmatic variation: The case of service encountersfrom a modified variational pragmatics perspective. In J. C. Félix-Brasdefer and M. E. Placencia, eds., *Pragmatic Variation in Service Encounter Interactions across the Spanish-Speaking World*. Abingdon, UK: Routledge, pp. 251–64.

Schneider, K. and Barron, A. (eds.). (2008). *Variational Pragmatics: A Focus on Regional Varieties in Pluricentric Languages*, Amsterdam: John Benjamins.

Schneider, K. (2010). Variational pragmatics. In M. Fried, ed., *Variation and Change: Pragmatic Perspectives*. Amsterdam: John Benjamins, pp. 239–67.

Schneider, K. (2018). Methods and ethics of data collection. In A. H. Jucker, K. P. Schneider and W. Bublitz, eds., *Methods in Pragmatics*. Berlin: Mouton de Gruyter, pp. 37–93.

Sifianou, M. and Tzanne, A. (2018). The impact of globalization on brief service encounters. *Journal of Pragmatics*, 134, 163–72.

Spencer-Oatey, H. (2000). A problematic Chinese business visit to Britain: Issues of face. In H. Spencer-Oatey, ed., *Culturally Speaking: Managing Rapport through Talk across Cultures*. London: Continuum, pp. 272–88.

Stommel, W. and te Molder, H. (2015). Counseling online and over the phone: When preclosing questions fail as a closing device. *Research on Language and Social Interaction,* 48, 281–300.

Tannen, D. (1984). *Conversational Style: Analyzing Talk among Friends.* Norwood, NJ: Ablex.

Taylor, J. (2015). Coffee: Pragmalinguistic variation of request in Starbucks service encounters. In J. C. Félix-Brasdefer, ed., *Current Issues in Pragmatic Variation.* IU Working Papers 15. https://scholarworks.iu.edu/journals/index.php/iulcwp/issue/view/1715.

Traverso, V. (2001). Syrian service encounters: A case study of shifting strategies within verbal exchange. *Pragmatics,* 11, 421–44.

Traverso, V. (2006). Aspects of polite behaviour in French and Syrian service encounters: A data-based comparative study. *Journal of Politeness Research,* 2, 105–22.

Traverso, V. (2007). Insisting: A goal-oriented or a chatting interactional practice? One aspect of Syrian service encounters. *Intercultural Pragmatics,* 4, 377–98.

Varcasia, C. (2013). *Business and Service Telephone Conversations: An Investigation of British English, German and Italian Encounters.* London: Palgrave.

Ventola, E. (1987). *The Structure of Social Interaction: A Systemic Approach to the Semiotics of Service Encounters.* London: Frances Pinter.

Ventola, E. (2005). Revisiting service encounter genre – some reflections. *Folia Linguistica,* 39, 19–43.

Zahler, S. (2016). Pragmalinguistic variation in electronic personal ads from Mexico City and London. In J. C. Félix-Brasdefer, ed., *Current Issues in Pragmatic Variation.* IU Working Papers 15. https://scholarworks.iu.edu/journals/index.php/iulcwp/issue/view/1715.

25

Argumentative, Political and Legal Discourse

Anita Fetzer and Iwona Witczak-Plisiecka

25.1 Introduction

Pragmatic approaches to discourse are based on the premise that participants do not only know *How to Do Things with Words* (Austin [1962] 1975), but also how to do things with words in discourse and how to do things with words in discourse in context (Fetzer 2018a). Discourse is thus more than some concatenated sequence of utterances which has been produced arbitrarily. Instead, participants intend their production of discourse to count as communicative action and they perform that communicative action in social context. Discourse is an interactional achievement; it is something which participants do and achieve by acting in accordance with particular contextual and discursive constraints and requirements, and by acting in dis-accordance with others, thus interactionally organizing different tokens of discourse which count as the realization of a discourse genre. Against this background, discourse cannot be examined without considering explicitly its contribution to sustaining reality as regards social structure and social organization, as is done in interactional sociolinguistics and ethnomethodological conversation analysis. This is accounted for by their fundamental premise of indexicality of communicative action (Gumperz 1992) and the indexicality of social action (Garfinkel 1994), relating discursive structure with communicative function to perform communicative action, and communicative action with social action and with social context. Despite the rather common assumption that speech act theory should concentrate on individual utterances, or even sentences, this image of rational and actional nature of communication can in fact be traced back to J. L. Austin and his original agenda to elucidate "the total speech act in the total speech situation" (Austin [1962] 1975: 147);[1] it is also well reflected

---

[1] Cf. Witczak-Plisiecka (2013a) for a discussion.

in Mey's (2001) conception of pragmatic acts and Searle's macro conception of speech acts as constitutive of all social reality (cf. Searle 1995).

Discourse pragmatics is firmly anchored in sociopragmatics, sharing the fundamental premises of pragmatics and supplementing them with sociopragmatic particularization, as for generalized rationality and their context-dependent instantiation in practical reasoning. This holds for the production and interpretation of discourse and manifests itself in participants being accountable to other participants for discourse production and discourse interpretation. In any discourse, rationality is presupposed by default and only referred to or made explicit when communicative infelicities surface, which need to be repaired. Closely related to rationality is the premise of intentionality of communicative action which also holds by default. It refers to micro communicative actions and to macro communicative actions, such as discourse genre (cf. Cohen et al. 1991; Fetzer 2004). The production and interpretation of discourse and its constitutive parts requires their contextualization, another fundamental premise related to indexicality which holds by default. This refers to contextualization in linguistic contexts – or pragmatic enrichment – and to contextualization in social contexts, which may undergo sociocultural-context-dependent particularization (cf. sections on legal and political discourse below). While contextualization is generally anchored in the reception format, its production-format-anchored counterpart is entextualization, that is, the encoding and implicating of speaker-intended discursive meaning. The premise which relates participants and the premises of intentionality, rationality and contextualization is the Gricean concept of cooperation as captured by the cooperative principle, which holds for cooperation with respect to the performance of micro communicative actions and for the performance of macro communicative actions, such as discourse genre, across different social and sociocultural contexts.

This chapter argues for argumentation as a constitutive part of theories of discourse as regards meaning-making processes and the negotiation of meaning. It demonstrates that argumentation undergoes social-context-specific particularization in various domains of discourse. Two domains to be examined in this chapter are political discourse and legal discourse.

25.2 The Pragmatics of Argumentative Discourse

Pragmatic theories of communication and pragmatic theories of discourse are based on the premise that participants act in a rational and intentional manner and that they act in accordance with a communicative norm inducing social and discursive entitlements and commitments (e.g. Brandom 1994; Kukla and Lance 2009,), a discourse norm (Gauker 1994, 2007, 2008, 2011), which demands intelligibility, truth, warrant and sincerity (e.g. Grice 1975; Habermas 1987; Searle 1969, 1983, 1995; Millikan 1984,

2004, 2005 on convention; Alston 2000). This norm defines an ideal pragmatic situation in which communication cannot be distorted by social factors. Contrary to the then one directional conception of a speech act in speech act theory (Austin [1962] 1975; Searle 1969), Habermas expands the process and product of producing and understanding communicative action to a dyadic setting: participants postulate and ratify validity claims by negotiating their truth, appropriateness and sincerity. The ratification of a postulated validity claim requires its acceptance or its rejection: an accepted validity claim is assigned the status of a plus-validity claim, and a rejected validity claim is assigned the status of a minus-validity claim (cf. Fetzer 2000, 2002, 2004 for the application of validity claim to the micro and macro domains of communication). Argumentation and felicitous communication are not unilateral, but rather dialogical processes. Both require rational and intentional participants, and both are based on the premise that the production and interpretation of validity claims is carried out in accordance with sociocultural norms, and that their ratification is performed through argumentation. In the case of acceptance, the ratification is a two-move sequence. In the case of rejection, the ratification requires several moves, in which the speaker may make explicit the relevant presuppositions of the rejected claim, thus accounting for their communicative action to their communication partner in order to convince them of its validity and make them accept the postulated claim. The process of justification goes hand in hand with an exchange of opposing views and opposing arguments which are needed to come to a final agreement about the communicative status of the claim.

In studies of discourse, the meaning of a discursive contribution is neither predetermined nor given. Instead, participants infer its meaning with respect to its embeddedness in context, assigning and disambiguating contextual references and calculating conversational implicatures (Grice 1975; Sperber and Wilson 1996). The process of meaning assignment is carried out in accordance with internal socio-cognitive argumentative principles regarding the status of a discursive contribution as true, appropriate and sincere. A speaker postulates a discursive contribution whose communicative meaning is inferred, negotiated and ratified. If the contribution is ratified through an acceptance, the discourse continues in the speaker-intended manner, and if the contribution is ratified through a rejection, the flow of discourse comes to a halt. In that case, the speaker makes explicit the relevant presuppositions, thus providing reasons for the validity of the argument. The process and product of postulating and ratifying communicative meaning is performed in accordance with the fundamental pragmatic premises of intentionality and rationality, and it is at the stage of ratifying and negotiating the truthfulness, appropriateness and sincerity where discourse and argumentation meet – both cognitively with respect to internal reference resolution and meaning negotiation, and socially with respect to the negotiation of meaning in discourse.

Argumentation fulfils a key function in the internal and external relationships between premises and conclusions, in the internal and external relationships between expressed and unexpressed premises, and in the internal and external relationships between expressed and unexpressed standpoints. The internal perspective to argumentation has been introduced by Ducrot (1984) and by Anscombre and Ducrot (1983). They claim that every piece of discourse contains explicit and implicit dialogues. This is signified by the title of their seminal work *Le dire et le dit* (Ducrot 1984). In a sociopragmatic frame of reference, the distinction between *le dire* and *le dit* can be compared and contrasted with the fundamental Gricean (1975) differentiation between 'what is said' and 'what is meant', a differentiation which lies at the heart of the distinction between direct and indirect speech acts (Searle, 1975), explicit and implicit language use (Clark 1996), or explicit and implicit modes of linguistic representation (Fetzer 2002). Anscombre and Ducrot's radical stance towards argumentation sees language and language use as a dialogic and polyphonous activity which is fundamental to the production and interpretation of discourse: internal and external argumentation is expressed through argumentative operators and argumentative connectors, such as *but, since, because, although* and *thus* and *almost, hardly, only, still, few, little, by the way* and *moreover*, through the sequential organization of arguments and through argumentative principles, such as *claim, warrant* or *backing*. The impact of this radical internal shift is described by van Eemeren and Grootendorst (1995: 59) as follows:

> Ducrot and Anscombre's position is unique in the field insofar as they believe that 'argumentativity' is a general feature of all language use. In mainstream contemporary literature, argumentative discourse is seen as a special form of language use with specific communicative and interactional function. Another distinctive characteristic of Ducrot and Anscombre's approach is that they are exclusively descriptive.

The pragma-dialectical perspective on argumentation differentiates between argumentation as pragmatic problem-solving and argumentation as recommendation to invoke a majority (van Eemeren 2017). The differentiation is based on different communicative goals: pragmatic problem-solving is more of a local achievement anchored in the discourse-as-such, while argumentation as recommendation to invoke a majority is a macro goal which goes beyond the discourse-as-such and is primarily anchored in the intended perlocutionary effects beyond the discourse-as-such.

Analogously to speech act theory and its felicity conditions and the Gricean cooperative principle, maxims and conversational implicature (Austin [1962] 1975; Grice 1975; Searle 1969), which have been adapted to the contextual constraints and requirements of conversation (Cohen et al. 1991; Fetzer 2017; Searle 1991; Witczak-Plisiecka 2013a), the pragma-dialectical approach to argumentation has postulated pragma-dialectical rules of communication constraining the negotiation of the intersubjective validity of pragma-dialectical standards for reasonableness. Pragma-dialectical argumentation is sequentially organized in four stages: "The model of a critical discussion specifies the four stages the parties have to go through in resolving their differences of opinion as the confrontation stage, the opening stage, the argumentative stage and the concluding stage and describes the argumentative moves instrumental in each of these stages as speech acts. The standards of reasonableness applying to argumentative discourse are in the pragma-dialectical theory depicted as rules for critical discussion" (van Eemeren 2017: 8). In an argumentation, the initial situation is described as the confrontation stage, the starting points of the argumentation are expressed in the opening stage, argumentative means and criticism are voiced in the argumentation stage, and the outcome of the exchange is reached in the concluding stage. These four stages can be seen as generalized argumentative stages, which may undergo communicative-genre and communicative-activity-type-specific particularization. This may hold for the separate stages to various degrees and for their entire organization: "The model of a critical discussion is a heuristic and analytic tool in reconstructing argumentative discourse by serving as a 'template' that constitutes a point of reference and ensures that the discourse can be reconstructed in terms of argumentative moves relevant to resolving a difference of opinion on the merits" (van Eemeren 2017: 9).

Pragma-dialectical argumentation differentiates between two different strategies: *argumentum ad hominem*, that is criticism and attacks on individuals, and *argumentum ad res*, that is criticism of subject matter attacks. These strategies may be seen as gradient matters and thus be foregrounded or respectively backgrounded at different stages in the argumentative discourse.

Participants in public discourse may also choose to use less frequent eristic strategies that raise little claim to objective reason or pure logic, such as, inter alia, arguments *ad populum*, *ad baculum* or *ad vanitatem*. Adoption of strategies of this kind will typically mark a particular discourse space, where a person wants to use, and sometimes abuse, the power that rests, or at least appears to rest, at his or her disposal. It is not infrequent in the public space, as has been richly demonstrated in Europe in the context of the discourse on refugees or on Brexit in the second decade of the twenty-first century, to hear *ad populum* arguments with prejudice placed over reason. In similar contexts, the strategy of *ad baculum* argumentation will exert pressure by posing a threat, which replaces the logical thought as a motivational factor.

The eristic context where the search for success takes precedence over the search for truth and justice are comfortably accommodated in the ancient, Aristotelian, rhetorical model of communication (Aristotle 2007), which puts emphasis on three main factors, viz. Speaker, Audience and Message, as associated with three sociolinguistic values: ethos, pathos and logos, respectively. In a simplified view, the role of the speaker (alternatively, Producer, Writer etc.) is associated with ethos, which foregrounds the fact that the speaker needs to show authority and adequate moral qualities to be able to influence the audience and to gain their support.[2] Such positive response is secured through an emotional impact on the part of the audience, which, in turn, emerges thanks to the 'logic', i.e. well-formedness and attractiveness of the message. There are thus three main bases on which the effectiveness of the argument in question will rest, viz. the character (ethos) of the Speaker, the emotional state of the Audience (pathos), and the character of the message (logos). It is evident that the Aristotelian model is primarily functional in the context of speeches, a kind of top-down discourse where one of the parties in interaction, i.e. the Speaker, is active in the discourse space, with the relevant feedback emerging on a macro scale. Political and legal discourse, as discussed below, provide many contexts where the Aristotelian perspective is particularly relevant.

Argumentation is context- and discourse-dependent communicative action. It is generally performed in institutional contexts and therefore constrained by institutional preconditions which are categorized as primary and secondary institutional preconditions. Primary institutional preconditions are captured by rules, for instance, the code of conduct in Prime Minister's Question in the British House of Commons; acting in disaccordance with those rules is sanctioned. Should a Member of Parliament insult another member and call them names or misrepresent their motives, the Speaker of the House of Commons may suspend the member. Secondary institutional preconditions are unofficial, informal codes of conducts and are best represented by participants' expectations about how a particular communicative activity should be performed; some of these preconditions are captured by what is considered to be polite behaviour, and what is considered to be impolite or rude behaviour. Acting in disaccordance with those secondary institutional preconditions is only socially sanctioned, for instance by attributing the 'rude' participant to a negative reference group.

The four stages of argumentation can undergo context- and communicative-genre-dependent particularization manifest in variations across argumentative patterns. They may result out of different participant-specific rights and obligations, entitlements and commitments, as has been captured in speech act theory for different speech acts (e.g. Kukla and Lance 2009), and which may undergo genre-specific particularizations, as has been shown for political interviews (Fetzer 2000). On a more local level of analysis, argumentative patterns are of particular importance: "An argumentative pattern is characterized by a constellation of argumentative moves in which, in order to deal with a particular kind of difference of opinion, in defence of a particular type of standpoint a particular argument scheme or combination of argument schemes is used in a particular kind of argumentation structure" (van Eemeren 2017: 19–20).

---

[2] This notion is convergent with "epistemic vigilance" as discussed in relevance theory (Sperber et al. 2010).

Argumentation and its discourse- and context-specific particularization to argumentative patterns and argumentative strategies is constitutive of discourse. Argumentative discourse is thus a superordinate type of discourse which undergoes discourse-domain- and social-context-specific particularization, as for instance in political discourse.

25.3 Political Discourse as Communicative Action

Political discourse is a multifaceted phenomenon which comprises discourse about politics on the one hand, and discourse by politicians on the other. However, not every instance of discourse produced by one or more politicians counts as political discourse, and not every discourse about politics counts as political discourse, either. What are the necessary and sufficient conditions for a stretch of discourse to count as political discourse?

Political discourse in our westernized mass democracies is public discourse, it is institutional discourse, it is media discourse, and it is – to a large extent – professional and elite discourse. As public discourse, political discourse differs from everyday discourse in being 'on record': "Talk-in-public, especially political talk, is 'on record' and this has consequences on what can and cannot be said and for ways of saying and not saying" (Scannell 1998: 260). As institutional discourse, it differs from everyday conversation in being subject to institutional constraints. As media discourse, it is different from other types of institutional discourse by being, above all, public discourse addressed to a heterogeneous mass media audience. As mediated and mediatized political discourse, it is the outcome of the encounter of two different institutional discourses: political discourse and media discourse, feeding on the inherent constraints of mediated discourse, i.e. communication through a medium and thus the uncoupling of space and time, and the movement of meaning from one text, discourse or event to another with the constant transformation of meanings. And it feeds on the inherent constraints of political discourse, i.e. the professionalization of politics, elite political discourse and the management of mediation of political 'messages' by spin doctors or political branding, among others (Fairclough 2006). What is more, mediated and mediatized political discourse interface with micro domains of mundane everyday life, thus entering private-domain-anchored spheres of life through the media. In mediatized mass democracies, this is often the only way for people to encounter politics (cf. Fairclough 1995; Fetzer and Weizman 2006, 2015, 2018; Lauerbach and Fetzer 2007).

Political discourse is communicative action which is constrained by its situatedness in public, institutional and media domains, as is reflected in the choice of public topics, institutional topics, media topics and professional topics, and in the choice of public, institutional and media styles and registers (Fetzer 2000, 2013). Those macro constraints do not only constrain the choice of topic, style and register, but also the location and duration of the communicative exchange, self- and other-selection of speaker and their institutional and interactional roles, and what counts as appropriate argumentation, for instance argumentum ad hominem, ad res or ad populum (Adone 2017; Livnat 2012). The particularized constraints do not only hold for political discourse as a whole, but also for its constitutive parts, such as agent, speech action, topic, style, register or argumentative strategy and move. Thus, political agents bring political topics into the political arena, utilizing political styles and registers and political argumentative strategies.

For the interface between argumentative discourse and political discourse this means that political argumentation is public, i.e. the validity of arguments is negotiated and followed up in the public domains, and political agents account for the validity of their arguments to the public in public domains of life. Political argumentation is institutional, viz. the validity of arguments is negotiated and followed up in accordance with institutional constraints and requirements in institutional domains, and political agents account for the validity of their arguments to the public in institutional domains of society. Political argumentation is mediated, i.e. the validity of arguments is negotiated and followed up in the media and thus is available and accessible across time and space, and political agents account for the validity of their arguments to the media audience in mediated domains of life and in mediated domains of society. Political argumentation is professional, and it is elitist, i.e. the validity of arguments is negotiated and followed up in professional and elitist domains of society, and political agents account for the validity of their arguments to the public, targeting primarily professional and elitist addressees in professional and elitist domains of society.

The pragma-dialectical perspective on argumentation has been applied to the analysis of institutional and professional elite political discourse in the context of the European Parliament, concentrating on the communicative genres of plenary debate and committee on inquiry. Garssen shows that "the same argument scheme may have a different role in different macro-contexts" (Garssen 2017: 31), discussing the reasons which political agents may have for supporting or not supporting a political proposal, and for not-supporting a political proposal. He demonstrates that practical argumentation, i.e. pointing out positive and negative causal consequences of a plan or policy, is not always causal in nature as there is also non-causal practical argumentation. The latter is based on some desired action which is in line with a normative behavioural rule, for instance that members of a society should support those in need, or which argues that a particular person's behaviour should serve as an example, for instance when a particular company donates a substantial sum of money for food banks. In professional and elitist political argumentation, political agents make use of a number of argumentative strategies, such as causal argumentation from cause to effect, causal argumentation from effect to cause, argumentation by authority or argumentation by example. Political argumentation can be pragmatic-problem-solving, and it can be complex problem-solving and refer to relevant stock issues, for instance problem or need, inherency, plan, practicability, advantages and disadvantages or a counterplan. Adone addresses the question whether backstage argumentation as used in preparatory committees differs from on-stage argumentation as employed in the actual debate. The latter utilizes pragmatic argumentation in which a recommendation is made, while explicitly considering arguments which may invoke a majority and appeals to the majority thereby invoking policy claims of legitimacy in order to give support to the policy. In that scenario argumentative strategies of political accountability, in particular argument ad populum, is used. Adone comes to the conclusion that "the expression 'accountability deficit' is used to suggest that those in power do not ultimately explain and justify their actions to the public and, more importantly, do not take the responsibility for the consequences of their behaviour" (Adone 2017: 53).

The pragma-dialectical perspective on political argumentation shares the fundamental sociopragmatic premises of intentionality of communicative action and social action, rationality and practical reasoning as well as accountability and responsibility of communicative and social action. Conceiving political discourse as communicative action is not only of relevance to the analysis of political argumentation but also to communicative strategies used in mundane everyday discourse, which are brought into political discourse. This holds for the deliberate use of face-threatening acts and face aggravation in parliamentary discourse, which is institutional discourse, public discourse and media discourse (Bull and Wells 2012), it holds for the use of quotation as an argumentative strategy to challenge the credibility and ideological coherence of political opponents (Fetzer 2015) and for bringing in ordinary people into elite political discourse (Fetzer and Weizman 2018), and it holds for the use of pronouns to evade difficult questions in political interviews (Fetzer and Bull 2008).

Recent changes in political discourse, for instance the strategic exploitation of references to the private domains of life to enhance the interactional organization of sincerity or credibility (Fetzer 2002) or the bringing in of ordinary people into institutional political discourse have also contributed to ongoing changes in argumentative practices (Fetzer and Weizman 2018; Fetzer and Bull, 2019; Weizman and Fetzer 2018). Research in media studies has examined the strategic use of argumentation in lay-expert communication in the context of talk shows, which is systematized in Table 25.1 (Livingstone and Lunt 1994: 102).

In a digital world, political discourse can no longer be conceived of only as a static notion, produced at some more or less specific location and some more or less specific time. Rather, political discourse in the media – and in particular computer-mediated political discourse – needs to be viewed from a dynamic perspective that accounts for the contextual constraints and requirements in which the discourse has been produced and in which it has been communicated. The dynamization of discourse in general and of political discourse in particular goes hand in hand with the ongoing changes in postmodern societies, especially within our mediatized society. Modern technologies enable us to transmit information instantaneously to anybody who is a member of the web-anchored community and we generally expect instantaneous replies, if only some kind of '+like' or '-like'. This process-orientation is reflected in the transmission of the discourse-as-such, for example in tweets and blogs, in parliamentary discourse and web-based commentaries and comments produced not only by professional journalists, but also by ordinary citizens in discussion forums constituting some kind of participatory or citizen journalism (Fetzer 2018b), in panel interviews with audience participation and follow-up chat sessions with the politicians interviewed, in mediatized party-political conferences with follow-up interviews and web-based discussion forums, in live-reports of mediations concerning controversial decision-making processes, and in rather spontaneously organized – and videoed – demonstrations, marches or sit-ins (cf. Atifi and Marcoccia 2015 for an overview of different types of computer-mediated political discourse). The common mediatized reality has thus become a kind of common ground. This is also reflected in ongoing changes in the conception of political agents with blurred boundaries between 'true professional agents' and 'true grassroot agents' and in the argumentative strategies utilized, as is systematized in Table 25.2 based on

Table 25.1 *Argumentation strategies in expert–lay talk shows*

Lay (traditional)	Expert (traditional)	Lay (participation programmes)	Expert (participation programmes)
Subjective	Objective	Authentic	Alienated
Ungrounded	Grounded in data	Narrative	Fragmented
Emotional	Rational	Hot	Cold
Particular	Replicable / general	Relevant	Irrelevant
Concrete	Abstract	In depth	Superficial
Motivated	Neutral	Grounded in experience	Ungrounded
Supposition	Factual	Meaningful	Empty in meaning
Obvious	Counter-intuitive	Practical / real	Useless / artificial

Table 25.2 *Ordinary and 'new ordinary people'*

Ordinary person and ordinary speech	'New ordinary person' and 'new ordinary speech'
Aggressive	Objective, grounded in data
Evaluative	Rather rational, general, abstract
Accusatory	Emotional dimension, conflict, verbal violence
Informal style	Personal speech – spokesperson

Atifi and Marcoccia's (2017) research on social TV and 'new ordinary persons' and 'new ordinary speech'.

The new kind of ordinariness and the new kind of ordinary speech and the argumentative strategies employed anchored in objectivity grounded in data supplemented by an emotional, subjective dimension has had an impact on political argumentation and on political accountability. From an ethnomethodological perspective (e.g. Garfinkel 1994), political agents 'do' politics in and through their acts of communication as regards politics-as-a-whole and as regards its constitutive parts: they do 'political talk', 'political ideology' and 'political identity'. In Gumperz's (1996) interactional-sociolinguistic terms, political agents can be seen both as bringing their discursive identities into a communicative setting, and as bringing them about in that setting. However, politicians 'do' more than simply 'talk politics in the media'. At the same time, they construct and reconstruct their multiple identities and functions in discourse against the background of others with whom they relate by aligning or dis-aligning with them and aligning and dis-aligning with the ideologies they represent, contributing to the discursive construction, reconstruction and deconstruction of their own identities as well as to those of others. Prototypical occasions for political agents to demonstrate their multiple skills and dedications are political speeches, interviews and debates and new formats emerging in the digital media.

Political discourse uses various discourse genres, such as statements and speeches in the contexts of election campaigns, summit meetings, business meetings or party conferences: interviews in the context of TV or print media, multi-party discourse in the context of panel interviews, parliamentary debates and digital discourse. Political discourse may also be formatted as reports, analyses, commentaries, editorials or letters to the editor, to name but the most prominent ones. All of these discourse genres are employed strategically to talk politics and to talk about politics. Moreover, these discourse genres do not occur context-independently but rather are embedded in journalistic news discourse and may be repeated as sound bites in later programming. Ordinary people may also participate in audience participation programmes in mediated political discourse, for instance panel interviews, standing in for the interviewer and asking questions, or by members of the home audience, calling in or sending emails and texts. Most recently, the evolution of the internet and the professionalization of digital discourse has brought about new forms of communication and opened up new arenas for political discourse, e.g. social networks, online discussion forums, Twitter or blogs.

25.4 Legal Discourse

The complexity found in political discourse is matched by the variety present in the legal discourse domain with its polyphony of voices and varied sociopragmatic constraints. The notion of legal discourse covers sociopragmatic patterns culled from much varied communicative encounters: interactions between legal professionals, and interactions between legal professionals and laypeople, which cross-cut with the discourses of legal texts and both written and spoken legal discourses present in the interpretation and negotiation of the meaning of law. The categories which emerge in such contexts are naturally motivated by sociolinguistic and pragmatic considerations of ethnomethodological nature.

In many contexts it is instructive to draw a distinction between the language of the law and legal language (Wróblewski 1985; Dascal and Wróblewski 1991), where the former embraces the language of legislation and written legal document, and the latter corresponds to lawyers' language as used to discuss the law and law-related issues. Both these varieties are notorious in laypeople's eyes for their non-transparency and departure from common conventions (cf. Witczak-Plisiecka 2007 and references within). The language of the law is typically perceived as "a language apart", a variety used by crafty lawyers in documents with an archaic touch, while legal language is often seen as manipulative and able to put people with less expertise at a disadvantage. Naturally, as there is an expansive interface in which documents, lawyers and laypeople "speak" in legal contexts with the law being disputed and interpreted, the distinction is not at all as clear as it might seem.

One of the most significant features of legal discourse is the fact that law itself, unlike many other fields of expertise, relies on language in a specific way. Law, being a social construct, is simply not conceivable without language; it is constructed through language (with the possible exception of natural law, where it is granted existence), negotiated and interpreted through language, and all legal disputes involve language. In its own special way, even written man-made law is "continually speaking",[3] reaffirming and re-establishing legal social reality. In this perspective law in all its aspects involves discourse, or rather a whole galaxy, a constellation of discourses, both primarily official and primarily private and particularized; discourses with more or less societal impact, with pre-defined structures (as in interrogations) or a considerable degree of freedom.

Table 25.3, adapted from Danet (1980: 471) and related to Joos' (1961) styles of English, summarizes the main contexts in which English legal language may be used.

The four decades that have passed since the publication of the typology created a need for the inclusion of mediated, especially Internet-based, situations, which exhibit a mixed mode with texts, appearing in written form, but displaying certain features of spoken discourse.

---

[3] The idea was reportedly (Elliott 1989: 3) expressed as early as 1842, when George Coode, an English Barrister, wrote: "If the law be regarded while it remains in force as constantly speaking, we get a clear and simple rule of expression."

Table 25.3 *A typology of situations in which English legal language is used*

	Style			
Mode	Frozen	Formal	Consultative	Casual
Written	Documents: 　insurance policies 　contracts 　landlord-tenant leases 　wills	Statutes Briefs Appellate opinion		
Spoken-composed	Marriage ceremonies Indictments Witnesses' oaths Pattern instructions Verdict	Lawyers' examinations of witnesses in trials and depositions Lawyers' arguments, motions in trials Expert witnesses' testimony	Lay witnesses' testimony	
Spoken-spontaneous			Lawyer-client interaction Bench conferences	Lobby conferences Lawyer-lawyer conversations

Source: Joos (1961)

Ethnomethodologically, law provides an overarching frame for all professional and public interactions where it is involved. Legal discourses are defined and constrained by the regulative normative function of law and as such are of actional nature. In a sociopragmatic perspective it would be difficult to find more illustrative examples of speech as a type of action than legal ones, especially in the language of the courtroom, e.g. pleading or a judge delivering a verdict, but also in more open contexts, where speech can blur with other modes of action. In pre-defined contexts there are thus utterances such as:

(1)
A.　How do you plead: guilty or not guilty
B.　(I plead) Not guilty, My Lord".

These leave little space for creativity and rely on well-established pre-defined patterns of linguistic behaviour. Still, they are profoundly operative, i.e. in linguistic terms, performative in nature. It is not accidental that historically there is a link between legal studies and speech act theory, marked by the well-documented cooperation between J. L. Austin and H. L. A. Hart at the time of the emergence of Austin's speech act theory (cf. Hart 1948–9; Sugerman and Hart 2005; Hart 1961; Austin [1962] 1975; discussion in Witczak-Plisiecka 2013a). It is further noteworthy that the sociopragmatic speech act-theoretic approach to legal communication was pioneered at the beginning of the twentieth century in a parallel study by Adolf Reinach ([1913] 1983), a German lawyer and phenomenologist, who in his doctoral project discussed legal "Soziale Akte", i.e. mental acts performed in speaking. Significantly, Reinach also commented on the "distinctive function" of the adverb "hereby", which "refers to an event which is happening along with the performance of the act, ... which ... designates itself" (Reinach [1913] 1983: 30). Reinach's work did not exert much impact on Western Anglo-American research, but the convergence of his theoretical reflections with speech act theory may indicate the universal quality of legal communicative acts.

The actional character of discourse situated in legal settings with its different styles and modes is primarily actional and as such transcends the level of linguistic forms. It may seem rather straightforward that legal discourse as represented in the language of judges or the language used in the courtroom follows predefined patterns of linguistic behaviour and uses formulae which in most cases only need saturation with data relevant for a particular case. It is, however, important to recognise that legal contexts invite interactions which blur the written mode with the spoken-composed, the spoken-spontaneous, and with instances of meaningful silence (cf. Walker 1985; Kurzon 1997). This is often the case because legal practice, including consultations and casual legal profession-oriented interactions, involves reference to and interpretation of legal documents. Thus, there is a constant duality and a certain conflict between legal language as used in legal interpretation and argumentation, and the 'continually speaking' law of the legal, especially legal normative, texts. While the spoken legal language is instantly perceived as actional, written law, due to its presupposed stability, is a better candidate for the conception which sees language as a collection of accurate descriptive images of the world as it is supposed to be. As such images are phrased in language they also carry metaphors which prompt certain conceptualizations. There is then an ongoing conflict in legal semantics, which resembles the two Wittgensteinian (1922, 1953) conceptions of linguistic meaning, an image theory with a firm, although 'lawfully' enacted picture of the world, and an action-based image where the world is inherently dynamic. In the world of legal discourse these two aspects persevere in constant interaction. The conflict may also be related to the powerful metaphor in which law, in the sense of legal order, is perceived as (static) equilibrium, which needs to be maintained and restored in contexts where it has been violated.

Legal discourses are associated with certain expectations and myths about language and the law. One of the generally accepted ideas is the division of powers, which directs that the legislative power creates the law, while the judiciary will only apply it. There is further an expectation that law, e.g. statutory law, will be phrased with clarity and precision, but also with a kind of openness which allows for the application of legal provisions in future in cases which can only generally be envisaged at the time of the drafting of the rules and document in question. Contrary to such a view, language will often resent semantic fossilization, showing that with regard to meaning the agency does not rest solely with the creator of the message.

Smith v United States, 508 US 223 (1993) is an illustrative example. In the case which was eventually decided at the level of the US Supreme Court the dispute concentrated on the meaning of the statutory passage which stipulated that whoever "during and in relation to ... [a] drug trafficking crime[,] uses ... a firearm" (Title 18 USC 924(c)(1)) would face aggravated penalty. The facts of the case were that the defendant had a gun in his rucksack and wanted to exchange it for cocaine, but did not use the said gun to threaten or harm any person. After an extended period of discussions and appeals, the US Supreme Court held that exchanging the gun for cocaine constituted a "use" in the statutory sense. A closer look at the majority opinion delivered by Justice O'Connor and the dissent opinion given by Antonin Scalia shows that what the law 'says' may be seen quite differently even by educated lawyers. Despite emphasizing the role of "context" in establishing the meaning of the verb "use" in the legal act, both lawyers came to opposite conclusions. It is significant that Justice O'Connor pointed to the fact that the Congress could have excluded the uses of gun (such as using it in exchange for drugs) which fell outside that particular law, which they had not. On the other hand Justice Scalia, who incidentally was a confirmed textualist, argued that using a gun in the context of law should not include using it, for instance, to scratch one's head, and similarly not as currency. One of the most interesting aspects of this case in a sociopragmatic view is the fact that judges on both sides appealed to similar factors and agreed that the context in which the words were used in the legislative act was important in finding adequate interpretation, and yet they came to opposite conclusions. The legal argumentation practiced in the case did not recognize the phenomenon that in linguistics is often labelled as "semantic absence" or "impliciture" (e.g. Bach 2001)[4] and the fact that all language use is naturally underdetermined. Consequently, it may be argued that "use of a gun" is supposed to be understood as "use as a weapon", just like an utterance "I haven't had breakfast" is naturally saturated with "today", and "Jack and Jill went up the hill" with "together".

According to H. L. A. Hart (1961: 127–8), legal language necessarily inherits the quality of "open texture", a general feature found in all language. As a result, legislative texts may on occasion produce difficulty with regard to their application to a particular case, leaving a choice between "open alternatives". Hart's "open alternatives", in turn, should not be directly identified with vagueness, another natural feature of legal language, which does not have to be a vice either (cf. Endicott 2000; Dworkin 1986; Witczak-Plisiecka 2009a, 2009b). Irrespective of attempts to stabilize legal semantics, there can always be a prenumbra[5] leaving decisions to judges' discretion and projecting on them agency that goes beyond simple conventions of common law precedents.

---

[4] Cf. Neale (2007) comments on the case.
[5] Cf. Hart's (a legal positivist) 1958's *Harvard Law Review* debate with Lon Fuller (natural law theorist) and Hart's concept of the core and the 'prenumbra' of meaning and his reference to the imaginary rule of "No vehicles in the park", which, while read literally, could potentially affect users of wheelchairs, prams, and similar 'vehicles'.

Legal discourses will often provide contexts which show that there is a forensic dimension in language use, i.e. that users of language may be held responsible for meanings which they did not envisage at the time they produced their speech acts, even though such a meaning is not the meaning they intended to produce and regardless of the fact that they are not able to control its interpretation. Korta and Perry (2007, 2011), who suggested the "forensic" label for the phenomenon, discuss non-legal examples, but Hutton (2009: 169–70) cites cases from defamation law where authors were held responsible for meanings which escaped their control. In fact, in defamation law, in cases of libel or even blasphemy, the intent of the author is usually backgrounded and the relevant legal authority will decide whether the offence was committed because the words would have a harmful effect and lower the plaintiff in the estimation of right-thinking members of society. Interestingly, it is implicit in such reasoning that words can act independently of their author's intention as it is not of prime importance what the writer of an alleged libel or defamation meant, but how the words 'on their own' may act in society. The abstracted, but socially situated meaning takes precedence over the issue of the author's intent. Technological advancements and the growing number of cyberspace-based communicative contexts contribute to aggravating defamation-oriented problems, the case that has already been marked in language with neologisms labelling novel, often still unofficial genres, such as "Twibel", a blend of Twitter and libel. New genres also mark particularization in public spaces, areas being in need of more precise analysis and updated conventional treatment.[6]

An inherently sociolinguistic and a Gricean aspect of legal communication can be found in pragmatic selectivity in the interpretation of utterances in contexts in which one of the parties has more political power and as such is able to control the discourse to the advantage of the party in authority. An illustrative example comes from Tiersma and Solan's (2004) US-based analysis of "selective literalism" related to the language of interrogation of laypeople by police officers. It has been shown that utterances produced by, for example, drivers stopped by traffic police were selectively interpreted as literal or non-literal both on the scene and later in the court of justice. For instance, the police would often ask people to consent to a search of their person or possessions, which is known as consensual searches. People often agree to allow such searches because they interpret the officers' ostensible "requests" as indirect commands. Yet it has been demonstrated that courts routinely interpret police utterances in such situation as genuine requests. In turn, in the context of custodial interrogation people being interrogated are inclined to invoke their right to

---

[6] Cf. The concept of theft as discussed in Larsson (2011) in the context of intellectual property law, where legislative images of theft understood in terms of "removing" a piece of property needed to be adjusted to account for theft of electronic materials. The metaphorical dimension (ornamental, pragmatic and argumentative) has been explored in an analysis of Polish and English legal language imagery in Wojtczak et al. 2017).

counsel in a relatively indirect or tentative way, which is often the function of their being confronted with a more powerful party.[7] Yet in such contexts courts more often conclude that the suspect in question did not really "request" the presence of counsel.

The practice of "selective literalism" (Tiersma and Solan 2004), i.e. selective consideration of pragmatic circumstances, provides another motivational factor for research into the sociopragmatic aspects of contexts in which language mediates between authority-laden party and laypeople. Evidently, at the level of language form, there is little difference between "May I see your driver's licence?" which is effectively an order when uttered by an authorized person, and "May I look in your trunk?", which, legally speaking, is just a request unless strengthened with a search warden, and in such cases a person's consent is voluntary. This, together with a polite phrasing of the utterance may blur the legal difference and make it easier for authorities to tacitly exert pressure on laypeople. In addition, there are sociopragmatic factors, such as politeness-oriented conventions, situation-related emotions and a need to save one's positive face on the part of the interrogated person, which may be operative in the context of discursive constructions of consent (cf. Ehrlich et al. 2016) or the lack of such consent.

In a broader social context, the actional nature of legal discourse, as well as the legal dimension of private discourse, have both been explored in contexts where speech is officially (and legally) recognized as action, and where action can be recognized as speech in critical research that has been ongoing since the 1990s. For instance, there is a clearly discursive dimension in discussing pornography in terms of speech acts, i.e. action and not just representation by authors such as feminist Andrea Dworkin or Catharine MacKinnon, a lawyer and language theorist, and Rea Langton. As MacKinnon claims, "acts speak and ... speech acts" (MacKinnon 1991: 813) and "pornography is at once a concrete practice and an ideological statement" (MacKinnon 1991: 802); an act, a form of mediated effectful representation, rather than a descriptive image. MacKinnon's focus is on what pornography does, being directly injurious and being an act situated in a society which is "made of language" (MacKinnon 1991: 811).

Similarly to defamation contexts, the question of why the image was produced, and what it was intended to mean, would not be of forensic relevance in this context. In a related way feminists argue that contemporary language is oppressive as it carries and reinforces past obsolete conceptualizations in its linguistic images of the world. Due to this obsolete imagery there is a constant re-enactment of patriarchal values and male domination in today's world (cf. MacKinnon 1989, 1993; Langton 1993).

---

[7] Ainsworth (2008: 11) emphasizes the importance of the judge being able to recognize such discursive tendencies: 'a linguistically informed judge could recognize that speakers in powerless positions are quite likely to resort to direct and hedged syntactic forms, in lieu of using unmodified imperatives, but that utterances in a "powerless" register are intended by their users to be no less unequivocal that those that are syntactically more direct'.

The legal authority–laden dimension of discourse is when patterns of linguistic behaviour are themselves judged along with non-linguistic performance under the same law, as has often been the case in the Free Speech Clause context;[8] they are also clearly visible when legal discourse is being politicized.[9]

In the constellation of legal discourses there is significant authority ranking, particular conception of plain meaning, and varied situated conventions, which are not always easy to notice. It is a sociopragmatically dynamic field, in which emerging practices can motivate the appearance of new genres and where people's performances are shaped by social and pragmatic aims and constraints.

25.5 Conclusion

The main linking thread between argumentation, political discourse and legal discourse is their social and public dimension. Most of the situated interactions classified as political, legal and argumentative will take place in a public space and will be on record. Quite naturally, a significant part of political and legal discourse space will involve persuasion and an attempt to influence, or even exert pressure, in which argumentation is a tool. Moreover, in most political and legal settings, linguistic interactions are biased due to the fact that one party holds power over the procedure, and sometimes even life and liberty.

Political discourse is discourse about politics and discourse by politicians, while legal discourse can be understood as a discourse which involves a legal dimension. Due to the fact that both politics and law are such basic aspects of social life, the richness and variety of the related discourses is inevitable. Like discourses of language in general, political and legal discourses in their variety may be discussed with a synchronic and diachronic approach, and, because of their inherent variety, require an ethnomethodological approach.

---

[8] There is an ample body of cases in which the main issue cantered around defining certain patterns of behaviour as either lawful expression of personal opinion or aggressive action beyond linguistic representation. The relevant patterns of behaviour included, for instance, burning of the Army card as protest against the war, burning of the cross in racist contexts, sleeping in the park as a sign of protest against homelessness (cf. e.g. *Texas v Johnson* (1989); *Community for Creative Non-Violence v Watt* (1983); *R.A.V. v St. Paul* (1992), *Virginia v Black et al.* (2003)). Significantly, such actions have on many occasions been evaluated under the Free Speech Clause as parallel to discourse.

[9] In 2018 Polish authorities decided to legally ban, and prosecute, any public use of the phrase "Polish death camps" in case it should unlawfully suggest that Poland organized such camps. The phrase had occasionally appeared over the years after World War II, evidently with varied particularized intentions. It may have been used to unjustly incriminate Poland, or as a shortcut, just to mark the geographic location of Nazi concentration camps, including Auschwitz; the latter use was, inter alia, thoughtlessly performed by President Barack Obama in 2012. The phrase had already been voluntarily censored in numerous public spaces, e.g. listed as banned in certain magazines and publishing houses, but, reportedly, in the first 48 hours after the legislation was enacted, it was recorded on the internet more than a million times. The apparent ban prompted the use of the form, which it was meant to eradicate.

One of the most significant points is that in contexts where law meets language, and further, when law meets sociopragmatics, the language of the law and legal judgements concerning language at large, will not readily reflect the semantics and the theories that linguists normally pursue. The legal intervention will bring about legal functions and conventions, which will necessarily have a bearing on how language is processed. However, the communicative difficulty is that the "legal" element in discourse can be blurred with natural language conventions. Lawyers with a higher level of expertise conduct ongoing disputes about legal issues, and evidently, the knowledge of sociopragmatics may assist them in handling language matters. However, legal culture (speech) acts, providing exciting research material, are situated in a mixed reality whose legal aspects may not be directly visible or accessible for laypeople, and where it may be difficult to tell the spirit of the law from its word.

Data Sources

www.clarity-international.net/journals/56.pdf (accessed March 2018)

References

Adone, C. (2017). The role of pragmatic and majority argumentation in reports of European parliamentary committees of inquiry. In F. van Eemeren, ed., *Prototypical Argumentative Patterns: Exploring the Relationship between Argumentative Discourse and Institutional Context*. Amsterdam: John Benjamins, pp. 53–70.

Ainsworth, J. (2008). "You have the right to remain silent . . ." but only if you ask for it just so: The role of linguistic ideology in American police interrogation law. *International Journal of Speech, Language and the Law*, 15(1), 1–22.

Alston, W. P. (2000). *Illocutionary Acts and Sentence Meaning*. Ithaca, NY: Cornell University Press.

Anscombre, J.-C. and Ducrot, O. (1983). *L'Argumentation dans la langue*. Brussels: Mardaga.

Aristotle. (2007). *Aristotle: On Rhetoric*. 2nd ed. Edited by G. A. Kennedy. Oxford: Oxford University Press.

Atifi, H. and Marcoccia, M. (2015). Follow-ups and dialogue in online discussions on French politics: From internet forums to social TV. In A. Fetzer, E. Weizman and L. N. Berlin, eds., *The Dynamics of Political Discourse: Forms and Functions of Follow-Ups*. Amsterdam: John Benjamins, pp. 109–40.

Atifi, H. and Marcoccia, M. (2017). The fabrication of ordinary people in French media discourse: when ordinary people are not only ordinary. Paper presented at the 15th IPRA conference, Panel on Constructing ordinariness across media genres, organized by E. Weizman and A. Fetzer, Belfast, June.

Austin, J. L. ([1962] 1975). *How to Do Things with Words*. 2nd ed. Oxford: Oxford University Press.

Bach, K. (2000). Quantification, qualification and context: A reply to Stanley and Szabó. *Mind and Language*, 15, 262–83.

Brandom, R. (1994). *Making It Explicit: Reasoning, Representing, and Discursive Commitment*. Cambridge, MA: Harvard University Press.

Bull, P. and Wells, P. (2012). Adversarial discourse in Prime Minister's questions. *Journal of Language and Social Psychology*, 31(1), 30–48.

Charrow, R. P. and Charrow, V. R. (1979). Making legal language understandable: A psycholinguistic study of jury instructions. *Columbia Law Review*, 79(7), 1306–74.

Clark, H. (1996). *Using Language*. Cambridge: Cambridge University Press.

Cohen, P., Morgan, J. and Pollack, M. E. (eds.). (1991). *Intentions in Communication*. Cambridge, MA: MIT Press.

Danet, B. (1980). Language in the legal process. *Law and Society Review*, 14, 445–564.

Dascal, M. and Wróblewski, J. (1991). The rational law-maker and the pragmatics of legal interpretation. *Journal of Pragmatics*, 15, 421–44.

Ducrot, O. (1984). *Le dire et le dit*. Paris: Minuit.

Dworkin, R. (1986). *Law's Empire*. Cambridge, MA: Harvard University Press.

Ehrlich, S., Eades, D. and Ainsworth, J. (eds.). (2016). *Discursive Constructions of Consent in the Legal Process*. Oxford: Oxford University Press.

Elliott, D. C. (1989). Constitutions in a Modern Setting – the Language of the Practice of Law. A paper presented at Lawasia Conference, Hong Kong, September. www.davidelliott.ca/papers/lawasia.htm#section9.

Endicott, T. A. O. (2000). *Vagueness in Law*. Oxford: Oxford University Press.

Fairclough, N. (1995). *Media Discourse*. London: Arnold.

Fairclough, N. (2006). *Language and Globalization*. Oxon, UK: Routledge.

Fetzer, A. (2000). Negotiating validity claims in political interviews. *Text*, 20(4), 1–46.

Fetzer, A. (2002). Communicative intentions in context. In A. Fetzer and C. Meierkord, eds., *Rethinking Sequentiality: Linguistics Meets Conversational Interaction*. Amsterdam: John Benjamins, pp. 37–69.

Fetzer, A. (2004). *Recontextualizing Context: Grammaticality Meets Appropriateness*. Amsterdam: John Benjamins.

Fetzer, A. (2013). The multilayered and multifaceted nature of political discourse. In A. Fetzer, ed., *The Pragmatics of Political Discourse: Explorations across Cultures*. Amsterdam: John Benjamins, pp. 1–18.

Fetzer, A. (2015). 'When you came into office you said that your government would be different': Forms and functions of quotations in mediated political discourse. In A. Fetzer, E. Weizman and L. N. Berlin, eds., *The Dynamics of Political Discourse: Forms and Functions of Follow-Ups*. Amsterdam: John Benjamins, pp. 245–73.

Fetzer, A. (2017). The dynamics of discourse: Quantity meets quality. In P. Cap and M. Dynel, eds., *Implicitness: From Lexis to Discourse*. Amsterdam: John Benjamins, pp. 235–57.

Fetzer, A. (2018a). Discourse pragmatics: Communicative action meets discourse analysis. In C. Ilie and N. Norrick, eds., *Pragmatics and Its Interfaces*. Amsterdam: John Benjamins, pp. 33–57.

Fetzer, A. (2018b). 'Our Chief Political Editor reads between the lines of the Chancellor's Budget speech': The strategic exploitation of conversational implicature in mediated political discourse. *Internet Pragmatics*, 1(1), 29–54.

Fetzer, A. and Weizman, E. (2006). Political discourse as mediated and public discourse. *Journal of Pragmatics*, 38(2), 143–53.

Fetzer, A. and Bull, P. (2008). 'Well, I answer it by simply inviting you to look at the evidence': The strategic use of pronouns in political interviews. *Journal of Language and Politics*, 7(2), 271–89.

Fetzer, A. and Weizman, E. (2015). Introduction. In E. Weizman and A. Fetzer, eds., *Follow-Ups in Political Discourse: Explorations across Discourse Domains*. Amsterdam: John Benjamins, pp. vii–xvii.

Fetzer, A. and Weizman, E. (2018). "What I would say to John and everyone like John is . . .": The construction of ordinariness through quotations in mediated political discourse (with E. Weizman). *Discourse and Society*, 29(5), 1–19.

Fetzer, A. and Bull, P. (2019). Quoting ordinary people in Prime Minister's Questions. In A. Fetzer and E. Weizman, eds., *The Construction of Ordinariness across Media Genres*. Amsterdam: John Benjamins, pp. 73-101.

Garfinkel, H. (1994). *Studies in Ethnomethodology*. Cambridge: Polity Press.

Garssen, B. (2017). The role of pragmatic problem-solving argumentation in plenary debate in the European Parliament. In F. van Eemeren, ed., *Prototypical Argumentative Patterns: Exploring the Relationship between Argumentative Discourse and Institutional Context*. Amsterdam: John Benjamins, pp. 31–51.

Gauker, C. (1994). *Thinking Out Loud*. Princeton, NJ: Princeton University Press.

Gauker, C. (2007). On the alleged priority of thought over language. In S. L. Tsohatzidis, ed., *John Searle's Philosophy of Language: Force, Meaning, and Mind*. Cambridge: Cambridge University Press, pp. 125–42.

Gauker, C. (2008). Zero tolerance for pragmatics. *Synthese*, 165, 359–71.

Gauker, C. (2011). *Words and Images: An Essay on the Origin of Ideas*. Oxford: Oxford University Press.

Grice, H. P. (1975). Logic and conversation. In P. Cole and J. L. Morgan, eds., *Syntax and Semantics*, Vol. III. New York: Academic Press, pp. 41–58.

Gumperz, J. J. (1992). Contextualization and understanding. In A. Duranti and C. Goodwin, eds., *Rethinking Context: Language as an Interactive Phenomenon*. Cambridge: Cambridge University Press, pp. 229–52.

Gumperz, J. J. (1996). The linguistic and cultural relativity of inference. In J. J. Gumperz and S. C. Levinson, eds., *Rethinking Linguistic Relativity*. Cambridge: Cambridge University Press, pp. 374–406.

Habermas, J. (1987). *Theorie des kommunikativen Handelns*. Frankfurt am Main, Germany: Suhrkamp.

Hart, H. L. A. (1948–9). The ascription of responsibility and rights. *Proceedings of the Aristotelian Society (New Series), 49*, 171–94.

Hart, H. L. A. ([1961] 1994). *The Concept of Law*. 2nd ed. Oxford: Oxford University Press.

Hutton, C. (2009). *Language, Meaning and the Law*. Edinburgh: Edinburgh University Press.

Joos, M. (1961). *The Five Clocks: A Linguistic Excursion into the Five Styles of English Usage*. New York: Harcourt, Brace and World.

Korta, K. and Perry, J. (2007). How to say things with words. In S. L. Tsohatzidis, ed., *John Searle's Philosophy of Language: Force, Meaning, and Mind*. Cambridge: Cambridge University Press, pp. 169–89.

Korta, K. and Perry, J. (2011). *Critical Pragmatics*. Cambridge: Cambridge University Press.

Kukla, R. and Lance, M. (2009). *'Yo!' and 'Lo!': The Pragmatic Topography of the Space of Reasons*. Cambridge, MA: Harvard University Press.

Kurzon, D. (1997). 'Legal language': varieties, genres, registers, discourses. *International Journal of Applied Linguistics, 7*(2), 119–39.

Langton, R. (1993). Speech acts and unspeakable acts. *Philosophy and Public Affairs, 22*, 305–30.

Larsson, S. (2011). *Metaphors and Norms: Understanding Copyright Law in a Digital Society*. Lund: Lund University.

Lauerbach, G. and Fetzer, A. (2007). Political discourse in the media: Cross-cultural perspectives. In A. Fetzer and G. E. Lauerbach, eds., *Political Discourse in the Media: Cross-Cultural Perspectives*. Amsterdam: John Benjamins, pp. 3–28.

Livingstone, S. and Lunt, P. (1994). *Talk on Television: Audience Participation and Public Talk*. London: Routledge.

Livnat, Z. (2012). Follow-ups in a loose argumentative context: The pragmatic effectiveness of figurative analogy. In A. Fetzer, E. Weizman and E. Reber, eds., *Proceedings of the ESF Strategic Workshop on Follow-Ups across Discourse Domains: A Cross-Cultural Exploration of Their Forms and Functions, Würzburg (Germany), 31 May–2 June 2012*. Würzburg: Universität Würzburg, pp. 165–77. http://opus.bibliothek.uni-wuerzburg.de/frontdoor/index/index/docId/6116.

MacKinnon, C. (1989). *Towards a Feminist Theory of the State*. Cambridge, MA: Harvard University Press.

MacKinnon, C. (1991). Pornography as defamation and discrimination. *Boston University Law Review, 71*, 793–815.

MacKinnon, C. (1993). *Only Words*. Cambridge, MA: Harvard University Press.

Mey, J. (2001). *Pragmatics: An Introduction*. Oxford: Blackwell.

Millikan, R. G. (1984). *Language, Thought and Other Biological Categories*. Cambridge, MA: MIT Press.

Millikan, R. G. (2004). *Varieties of Meaning*. Cambridge MA: MIT Press.
Millikan, R. G. (2005). *Language: A Biological Model*. Oxford: Oxford University Press.
Neale, S. (2007). On location. In M. O'Rourke and C. Washington, eds., *Situating Semantics: Essays on the Philosophy of John Perry*. Cambridge, MA: MIT Press, pp. 251–393.
Reinach, A. ([1913]1983). The a priori foundations of civil law. Translated by John Crosby. *Aletheia*, 3, 1–142.
Scannell, P. (1998). Media-language-world. In A. Bell and P. Garrett, eds., *Approaches to Media Discourse*. Oxford: Blackwell, pp. 252–67.
Searle, J. R. (1969). *Speech Acts*. Cambridge: Cambridge University Press.
Searle, J. R. (1983). *Intentionality*. Cambridge: Cambridge University Press.
Searle, J. R. (1991). Conversation revisited. In J. R. Searle, H. Parret and J. Verschueren, eds., *(On) Searle on Conversation*. Amsterdam: John Benjamins, pp. 137–47.
Searle, J. R. (1995). *The Construction of Social Reality*. New York: The Free Press.
Sperber, D., Clément, F., Heintz, C., Mascaro, O., Mercier, H., Origgi, G., Sperber, D. and Wilson, D. (1996). *Relevance*. Oxford: Blackwell.
Sperber, D., Clément, F., Heintz, C., Mascaro, O., Mercier, H., Origgi, G., Sperber, D. and Wilson, D. (2010). Epistemic vigilance. *Mind and Language*, 25(4), 359–93.
Sugarman, D. and Hart, H. L. A. (2005). Hart interviewed: H.L.A. Hart in conversation with David Sugarman (interview 1988). *Journal of Law and Society*, 32, 267–93.
Tiersma, P. M. and Solan, L. M. (2004). Cops and robbers: Selective literalism in American criminal law. *Law and Society Review*, 38(2), 229–66.
Van Eemeren, F. (ed.). (2017). *Prototypical Argumentative Patterns: Exploring the Relationship between Argumentative Discourse and Institutional Context*. Amsterdam: John Benjamins.
Van Eemeren, F. (2017). Argumentative patterns viewed from a pragma-dialectical perspective. In F. van Eemeren, ed., *Prototypical Argumentative Patterns: Exploring the Relationship between Argumentative Discourse and Institutional Context*. Amsterdam: John Benjamins, pp. 7–29.
Van Eemeren, F. and Grootendorst, R. (1995). Argumentation theory. In J. Verschueren, J.-O. Östman and J. Blommaert, eds., *Handbook of Pragmatics*. Amsterdam: John Benjamins, pp. 55–61.
Walker, A. (1985). The two faces of silence: The effect of witness hesitancy on lawyers' impressions. In D. Tannen and M. Saville-Troike, eds., *Perspectives on Silence*. Norwood, NJ: Ablex, pp. 55–75.
Weizman, E. and Fetzer, A. (2018). Constructing ordinariness in online journals: A corpus-based study in the Israeli context. *Israel Studies in Language and Society*, 11(1), 22–48.
Witczak-Plisiecka, I. (2007). *Language, Law and Speech Acts: Pragmatic Meaning in English Legal Texts*. Łódź: WSSM.

Witczak-Plisiecka, I. (2009a). A linguistic-pragmatic note on legal indeterminacy in legal language. *Linguistica Copernicana*, *1*, 231–43.

Witczak-Plisiecka, I. (2009b). A note on legal discourse semantics and J.L. Austin's theory of speech acts. In M. Dynel, ed., *Advances in Discourse Approaches*. Newcastle upon Tyne, UK: Cambridge Scholars, pp. 92–111.

Witczak-Plisiecka, I. (2013a). *From Speech Acts to Speech Actions*. Łódź: Łódź University Press.

Witczak-Plisiecka, I. (2013b). Speech action in legal contexts. In M. Sbisa and K. Turner, eds., *Pragmatics of Speech Actions*, Handbook of Pragmatics Part 2. Berlin: Mouton de Gruyter, pp. 613–58.

Wojtczak, S., Witczak-Plisiecka, I. and Augustyn, R. (2017). *Metafory konceptualne jako narzędzia rozumowania i poznania prawniczego* [Conceptual metaphors as instruments of legal cognition and reasoning]. Warsaw: Wolters Kluwer.

Wittgenstein, L. (1922). *Tractatus Logico-Philosophicus*. Edited by C. K. Ogden and K. Paul. London: Routledge.

Wittgenstein, L. ([1953] 1958). *Philosophical Investigations*. 2nd rev. ed. Oxford: Basil Blackwell.

Wróblewski, J. (1985). Legal language and legal interpretation. *Law and Philosophy*, *4*, 239–55.

26

The Pragmatics of Translation

Juliane House

26.1 Introduction: How Context Is Viewed in Different Disciplines

The tradition in philosophical thinking about context is frequently linked with the work of Wittgenstein ([1958] 1967: 35) and his emphasis on language as a type of action. According to Wittgenstein, the meaning of linguistic forms is their use, and language is never used to simply describe the world around us, but functions inside actions, or "language games" (*Sprachspielen*), which are embedded in a "form of life" (*Lebensform*). The idea of analysing language as action was further pursued in the tradition of the British Ordinary Language Philosophy, particularly by Austin (1962), who emphasized the importance of the context of a speech act for linguistic production and interpretation in the form of socio-cultural conventions. It is through these conventions that the force and type of speech act is determined. With his emphasis on conventions as shared norms, Austin gives clear priority to social aspects of language rather than a speaker's state of mind, intentions and feelings.

Particularly influential for further ideas about context has been Grice (1975) in his theory of implicature in language use. Grice assumed the operation of conversational maxims that guide the conduct of talk and stem from fundamental rational considerations of how to realize cooperative ends. These maxims express a general cooperative principle and specify how participants have to behave in order to converse in an optimally efficient, rational and cooperative way: participants should speak sincerely, clearly and relevantly and provide sufficient information for their interlocutors. In Grice's view, speech is regarded as action, and it can be explained in terms of the beliefs and purposes of the actors. Grice's theory is thus in essence a psychological theory of rhetoric. This also holds for Sperber and Wilson's (1986) relevance theory, in which the Gricean maxim of relevance is further developed, and in which context is clearly a psychological concept. Context is defined by Sperber and Wilson as "the set of premises used in interpreting it [an utterance]" ; it is a cognitive construct and a "subset of the hearer's assumptions about the world" (15).

As opposed to such psychological approaches, socio-cognitive approaches to context consider language choices to be intimately connected with social-situational factors. Thus Forgas (1985) stresses the role social situations play for the way human beings use language. He considers verbal communication to be an essentially social communicative act, and points to the fact that interaction between language and social context can be traced back to the early years of language acquisition. Both the meanings of utterances and the shared conceptions of the social context enveloping linguistic units are here regarded as the result of collective, supra-individual, cognitive activities.

But there is also a 'third way' in psychological theorizing about context. This encompasses both individual and social processes. Its propagators (e.g. Clark 1996) focus both on individual cognitive processes and their social conditioning in concrete acts of language use. Language use is regarded as a form of joint action carried out collaboratively by speakers and hearers who form an ensemble. According to Clark, "language use arises in joint activities" (29), which are closely bound up with contexts and vary according to goals and other dimensions of variation such as formal versus informal, egalitarian versus autocratic as well as other participant-related variables. Clark also operates with the concept of 'common ground', taken over from Stalnaker (1978). This is a psychological notion which captures what speakers/hearers bring with them to a joint activity, i.e. their prior knowledge, beliefs, assumptions etc., all of which accumulate in the course of the activity.

In conversation analysis, the focus is on the analysis of talk-in-interaction and on the significance of sequential utterances as both context-creating and context-determined. According to Heritage (1984), talk is in fact 'doubly contextual' since utterances are realized and organized sequentially and linearly in time, such that any subsequent utterance relies on the existing context for its production and interpretation, but also constitutes an event in its own right which itself engenders a new context for the following utterances. There are also recent suggestions that interaction is based on the possibility of 'projection', with the grammar of a language providing speakers and addressees with more extensive shared paths (Auer 2005). In other words, grammar and interaction share the common feature of 'projectability'. This idea is consistent with regarding context in a dynamic relationship with linguistic phenomena, i.e. context and talk stand in a reflexive relationship, with talk and the interpretation it instigates shaping context as much as context shapes talk.

In the tradition of pragmatics, context has played an eminent role. Indeed the very definition of pragmatics is often bound up with the notion of context. Thus Stalnaker (1999: 43) writes that "Syntax studies sentences, semantics studies propositions. Pragmatics is the study of linguistic acts and the contexts in which they are performed". And we might even say, with Levinson (1983: 32), that pragmatics is "a theory of language understanding that takes context into account". The underlying assumption here is that in order to arrive at an adequate theory of the relation between linguistic expressions and what they express, one must consider the context in which these expressions are used. In pragmatics, attention is given to how the interaction of context and content can be represented, how the linguistic expressions used relate to context. The relationship between content and context is however never a one-way street: content expressed also influences context, i.e. linguistic actions influence the context in which they are performed. The effects of this dependency are omnipresent and decisive for the construction and recovery of meaning.

A pragmatic framework would then need to include a general representation of contextual features that determine the values of linguistic expressions, with context being represented by information presumed to be available to the participants in the speech situation. Given the need to specify context as features of this situation, a distinction must be made between actual situations of utterance in all their manifold variety and the selection of only those features that are linguistically and socio-culturally relevant for both the speaker producing a particular utterance and the hearer who interprets it.

It is exactly this distinction that Leech (1983) refers to when he distinguishes between general pragmatics on the one hand and sociopragmatics or pragmalinguistics on the other, and pleads for the usefulness of a narrow view of context as background knowledge shared by addresser and addressee and contributing to the addressees' interpretation of what the addresser means by his or her utterance. Context in this more specific sense would then cover the social and psychological world in which language users act at any given time This includes participants' knowledge, beliefs and assumptions about temporal, spatial and social settings, previous, ongoing and future (verbal and non-verbal) actions, knowledge of the role and status of speaker and hearer, of spatial and temporal location, of formality level, medium, appropriate subject matter, province or domain determining the register of language. As pointed out in particular by Gumperz (1992), context-indexical linguistic features, which he calls "contextualization cues", invoke the relevant contextual assumptions. Among the linguistic features to be accounted for in an adequate notion of context, linguistic context or 'co-text' must also be evoked, i.e. the place of the current utterance in the sequence of utterances in the unfolding text/ discourse must also be considered.

Another example of assuming a decisive influence of context on utterance content is the notion of *framing*, first introduced by Bateson (1972) and significantly further developed by Goffman (1974, 1981). In framing their verbal behaviour, speakers and addressees can transform conventionalized expectations to fit a specific, local context and also invoke genre changes.

As this brief review of classic definitions of context has shown, context is a complex, multi-faceted concept. Most approaches emphasize the notion that utterances and texts can only be explained by reference to their embeddedness in a situation that envelops the utterance and that this embeddedness also has a cognitive substratum. For translation and pragmatics this means that they both build on assumptions about context and the way it connects linguistic forms with socio-cognitive phenomena.

However, in translation matters are rather different. What is of crucial importance in translation is the fact that a finished, and in this sense 'static' stretch of written language as text is presented to the translator in its entirety from the start of her translatory action. The task of translating then consists of enacting a discourse out of a written text, i.e. the translator must create a 'living', but essentially not dynamic, cognito-social entity replete with contextual conditions (cf. Widdowson 2004). The 'static' quality of context in translation arises in the very space opened up by the separation in time and space of writer, translator and reader and by means of the ability of the translator herself to define what the context is. This is very different from the type of context invoked in conversational interaction, where spoken text is a direct reflection of the discourse enacted between two or more co-present interactants and a discourse dynamically unfolds, sequentially develops and explicitly and overtly involves speaker and hearer turns-at-talk. For translation, the availability of a written text at once in its entirety (as opposed to the bit-by-bit unfolding of negotiable discourse) is indeed constitutive. From this it follows that context in translation cannot be regarded as dynamic. True to the nature of written language, the realization of a discourse out of a text presented in writing only involves imaginary, hidden interaction between writer and reader in the mind of the translator, where the natural unity of speaker and hearer in oral interaction is replaced by the real world separateness in space and time of writer and reader. The only way in which the translator can overcome this separateness and create a new unity is to transcend the givenness of the text with its immutable arrangement of linguistic elements by (mentally) activating its contextual connections, by linking the text he is about to translate to both its old and new context, which the translator must imagine and unite in her mind.

26.2 Overview of Linguistic Approaches to Translation

26.2.1 Early Linguistic, Textual and Communicative Approaches

One of the earliest schools of translation which gave language, text and communication a pride of place is the Leipzig school of 'translation science' (*Uebersetzungswissenschaft*), as it was called. It originated in the 1950s in the East German city of Leipzig. Many of the concepts scholars of the Leipzig school developed, most importantly 'equivalence,' have influenced translation studies to this day.

Under the influence of the then developing disciplines of text linguistics and sociolinguistics, the early focus of Leipzig scholars on system-based linguistics and lexico-structural equivalence was soon replaced by a view of the embeddedness of texts in different socio-cultural situations leading to a communicative conception of equivalence which implies that texts in different languages differ in terms of their communicative value. Communicative equivalence exists whenever the communicative value can be maintained in translation (Jäger 1975: 36).

The Leipzig translation school has also early on described pragmatic aspects of translation stressing that functional equivalence would obtain when the translation of a text that belongs to a certain text type and a concrete communicative situation has the same communicative effect as the one achieved with the source text.

Not only for the Leipzig school of translation, but also for the entire discipline of translation studies has text linguistics had an important impact early on, only to be replaced later (from the mid 1980s onwards) by discourse analysis.

An important early work in text linguistics relevant for translation is by Halliday and Hasan (1976). Prime concern is the 'texture' of a text that resulted from the connectedness of individual textual units through processes of reference, substitution, ellipsis, conjunction and lexical cohesion as well as semantic relations which "enable one part of a text to function as context for another" (Halliday and Hasan 1989: 48). Other fields of interest within text linguistics are the distribution of information as old information (known *per se* or mentioned previously) and new information (new for the addressee), referred to as theme and rheme or topic and comment, as well as related studies of lexico-grammatical and phonological devices employed to produce marked word order patterns for certain effects. All of these were later recognized as highly relevant for translation, e.g. by Baker (1992).

Particularly influential for translation studies was the work of de Beaugrande and Dressler (1981). In trying to determine what it is that makes a text a text, i.e. a unified meaningful whole rather than a mere string of unrelated words and sentences, they set up seven standards of textuality: cohesion, coherence, intentionality, acceptability, informativity, situationality and intertextuality. These were famously made relevant for translation by Hatim and Mason (1990).

Other early, in Western translation studies often ignored, linguistically oriented work on translation was done in Russia by Andrei Fedorov (1958) and in the Prague school of functional linguistics with its early emphasis of functional styles and information organization. One of the members of the Prague school was Roman Jakobson who, following his move to the United States, made an important contribution to the linguistically oriented view of translation as early as 1959, distinguishing basic types of translation and presenting convincing arguments for the very possibility of translation.

An early, complete linguistic theory of translation was presented by J. C. Catford (1965). For Catford, meaning cannot be simply transferred from a source text to its translation text, rather meaning can only be replaced, so that it can function in a comparable way in its new context. While the idea of a transference of meaning implies that there is meaning in the original text that can be taken out and given a new and different expression, the idea of replacement suggests that the meaning of a text is a function of the relationship between text and context, and can therefore only be replaced by, in some specifiable way, replicating the relationship. Such a view of meaning as inextricably enmeshed in the context of use of a linguistic unit based on the recognition that it is only through relating linguistic items to their context of situation that meaning can be replicated, was very new at the time. Catford also makes an important distinction between formal correspondence and textual equivalence in translation. He regards formal correspondence as a matter of the language system (langue), textual equivalence as a matter of the realization of that system (parole). Formal correspondence between linguistic units in the original and its translation exists when a TL category has approximately the same position in its system of langue as the corresponding category in the SL. However, in many cases involving typologically distant languages translation shifts will be necessary. They involve departures from formal correspondence using shifts from lexis to grammar or grammar to lexis.

Another influential, early linguistic theory of translation is Eugene Nida's (1964) sociolinguistic account of translation. Nida's interest in translation stems from Bible translation. In his view, translation is first and foremost an act that is directed at certain recipients, whose different knowledge sets, linguistic-cultural conventions and expectation norms need to be taken into account in translation. In Nida's view, it is only when a translated text is adapted to the needs of the new recipients that it can have the intended effect. But despite the necessity of adaptation, the original message remains important and must be maintained in the translation. In order to resolve this dilemma, Nida identified two different measures for making and evaluating a translation: Formal equivalence and dynamic equivalence, categories not too different from Catford's distinction between formal correspondence and textual equivalence. Nida's hypothesized three phases of any translation process – analysis, transfer and reconstruction. In Nida's view, the message presented in the original text is first linguistically analysed and broken down into observed grammatical relationships and the meanings of words and word combinations. The translator then mentally transfers this analysed material from the source language to the target language. Finally, she restructures the transferred material so as to make the message adequate for reception by the intended readers in the target language.

26.2.2 Discourse, Pragmatic and Functional Approaches to Translation

The usage-oriented approaches of discourse, pragmatic and functional analyses are particularly appropriate for translation. The historical roots of discourse analysis range from classical rhetoric, Russian formalism, French structuralism to semiotics. In the 1970s, discourse analysis began to establish itself as a discipline in its own right. It was influenced by sociolinguistics with its emphasis on language variation and the crucial role of the social context; speech act theory, where a discourse is seen as a form of social action and cooperative achievement such that a speaker's intention and her relationship with her addressee(s) are taken into account as added features of meaning; anthropology, where studies on the 'ethnography of speaking' link up with linguistics and stylistics. All these played an important part in widening our understanding of discourse.

Branches of discourse analysis that are of immediate relevance for translation are contrastive rhetoric and contrastive discourse analysis. They compare underlying text conventions in different linguacultures and examine their influence on the production and comprehension of different discourse types. Cross-cultural discourse analyses examined inter alia discourse organization, coherence, cohesive devices and the presence of reader or writer perspective. Findings suggest differences in the sequencing of topical strands in texts (linear or circular), presence or absence of digressions and other arrangements of textual parts in different genres and languages (cf. Connor 1996). The culture specificity of discourse structuring is also exemplified in the work by Clyne (1987) and House (2006) for the typologically close languages of English and German. Contrastive discourse analyses are crucial for translation because they provide translators and translation evaluators with the necessary empirical foundation for justifying and explaining changes in the target text.

The importance of the socio-cultural environment enveloping a text was captured early on by the anthropologist Malinowski in his concept 'context of situation', which strongly influenced British contextualism (cf. Halliday 1994). The concept embraces the human participants in a situation, their verbal and non-verbal actions, the effect of these actions and other relevant features, object and events. These categories have influenced what came to be known as *Register*, i.e. the variety of language according to use. *Register* is a socio-semantic concept referring to configurations of meaning typically associated with particular situational constellations. In Register analysis, texts are related to context such that both are mutually predictable, the outcome being the isolation of different text types or genres. Register analysis has been fruitfully used in translation studies by House (1977, 1997, 2015, 2016a) and Steiner (2004).

Other suggestions of types of texts – a popular quest in translations studies – have involved the concept of 'function of language'. Many different views of functions of language have been proposed, most famously by

Bühler (1934), Jakobson (1960) or Popper (1972). Although they vary considerably, a basic distinction between an informative, cognitive function and an interpersonal function to do with the 'me' and 'you' of language use can be found in all functional classifications. Classifications of language functions were often used to devise 'text typologies' following the equation 'one function – one text type' (Reiss 1971). In translation studies they are very popular because it is often assumed that knowledge of a text type is an important prerequisite for effective translation procedures. However, preferable to any externally motivated text typology seems to be a view of a text as in principle multifunctional (i.e. not embodying a predetermined function), such that each text is to be analysed and translated as an individual 'case', considered in its particular context of situation and culture on the basis of an explicit set of text linguistic procedures for describing and explaining how a text is what it is, how it fares in translation, and what the effect of the translation is in each individual case.

Such a case-study approach to translation can today be combined with reference to large text corpora featuring original texts and translations in many different languages (see Kruger et al. 2011; Zanettin 2014), fruitfully combining qualitative and quantitative methodologies.

26.3 Defining Translation as Re-contextualization

Translation is a means to facilitate communication between people who do not have, or do not choose to use, a common language. It is always a secondary communicative event. Normally, a communicative event occurs once, translation, however, duplicates it for persons otherwise prevented form appreciating the original event. Translation serves to provide interlingual and intercultural understanding.

We can define this understanding as the success with which communication is made to function through the provision of common ground despite the fact that it exists in a 'dilated speech situation' (Ehlich 1984). When a message is transmitted from a writer to a reader, both are not at the same place at the same time, they are caught in a 'dilated speech situation'. Through such a transmission by a text, the original speech situation becomes 'dilated'. However, the situation is even more complex in the case of translation. Here we are faced not only with a dilated, but also a ruptured speech situation. The rupture of the original speech event is due to the linguacultural barrier between the author of the original text and the reader of the translation. This rupture is bridged in translational action, and it is this rupture-mending by the translator which makes translation necessarily a highly reflective action. The inherent reflective nature of translational action reveals itself in the translator's focus on the situatedness of a text and the interconnectedness of text and context.

Translation involves exploring texts in context, which is the only way of exploring texts. Since in translation, texts travel across time, space and different orders of indexicality, they must be re-contextualized. To describe and explain the trajectory of texts in translatory action, a theory of translation as re-contextualization is needed. In what follows I will briefly describe such a theory.

Translated texts are always doubly contextually bound: to their originals and to the new recipients' communicative conditions. This double linkage is the basis of the equivalence relation – the conceptual heart of translation theory. Since appropriate use of language in communicative performance is what matters most in translation, it is functional pragmatic equivalence which is crucial in translation.

A first requirement for this equivalence is that a translation text should have a function equivalent to that of its original text. However, this requirement needs to be differentiated given the existence of an empirically derived distinction into **overt** and **covert** translation, concepts to be discussed below in detail.

The use of the concept of "function" presupposes that there are elements in a text which, given appropriate tools, CAN reveal this function. The use of the concept of function is here not to be equated with functions of language"– different language functions clearly always co-exist inside any text, and a simple equation of language function with textual function/ textual type is overly simplistic. Rather, a text's function – consisting of an ideational and an interpersonal functional component (following Halliday 1994) – is defined pragmatically as the application of the text in a particular context of situation. Text and "context of situation" (Malinowski 1935) should thus not be viewed as separate entities, rather the context of situation in which the text unfolds is encapsulated in the text through a systematic relationship between the social environment on the one hand and the functional organization of language on the other (Halliday and Hasan 1989: 11). This means that the text is to be referred to the particular situation enveloping it, and for this a way must be found for breaking down the broad notion of "context of situation" into manageable parts, i.e. particular features of the context of situation, or pragmatic parameters or situational dimensions. The linguistic correlates of the situational dimensions are the means with which the textual function is realized, and the textual function is the result of a linguistic-pragmatic analysis along the dimensions with each dimension contributing to the two functional components, the ideational and the interpersonal. Opening up the text with these dimensions yields a specific textual profile that characterizes its function, which is then taken as the individual textual norm against which the translated text can be measured.

The relationship between context and language-in-text which can be revealed by breaking down context into manageable situational or contextual parameters, may be concretized using for instance the classic

Hallidayan Register concepts of "Field", "Mode" and "Tenor". Field captures the topic and content of the text, its subject matter, with differentiations of degrees of generality, specificity or granularity in lexical items according to rubrics of specialized, general and popular. It also captures different 'Processes', such as material processes (verbs of doing), mental processes (verbs of thinking, believing, opining) or relational ones (of being and having). Tenor refers to the nature of the participants, the addresser and the addressees, and the relationship between them in terms of social power and social distance, as well as degree of "emotional charge". Included here are the text producer's temporal, geographical and social provenance and his intellectual, emotional or affective stance (his "personal viewpoint") vis-à-vis the content he is portraying and the communicative task he is engaged in. Furthermore, Tenor captures "social attitude", i.e. different styles (formal, consultative and informal). Linguistic indices realizing along Tenor are those of Mood and Modality. Mode refers to both the channel – spoken or written (which can be "simple", i.e. "written to be read" or "complex", e.g. "written to be spoken as if not written"), and the degree to which potential or real participation is allowed for between writer and reader. Participation can also be "simple", i.e. be a monologue with no addressee participation overtly built into the text, or "complex" with various addressee-involving mechanisms characterizing the text. In taking account of (linguistically documentable) differences in texts between the spoken and written medium, reference is also made to the empirically established (corpus-based oral-literate dimensions as, for example, hypothesized by Biber (1988). He suggests dimensions along which linguistic choices may reflect medium, i.e. involved versus informational text production; explicit versus situation-dependent reference; abstract versus non-abstract presentation of information.

The type of (con)textual analysis in which linguistic features discovered in the original and the translation are correlated with the Hallidayan categories Field, Tenor, Mode does not, however, lead directly to a statement of the individual textual function (and its interpersonal and ideational components). Rather, the concept of "Genre" is usefully incorporated into the analytic scheme, "in between", as it were, the register categories of Field, Tenor, Mode. Genre enables one to refer any single textual exemplar to the class of texts with which it shares a common purpose or function. Genre is a category superordinate to Register. While Register captures the connection between texts and their "microcontext", Genre connects texts with the "macrocontext" of the linguacultural community in which a text is embedded, for example the type of institution in which a text conventionally appears (a sermon traditionally happening in a religious locale). Register and Genre are both semiotic systems realized by language such that the relationship between Genre, Register and Language/Text is one between semiotic planes which relate to one another in a Hjelmslevian "content-expression" type, i.e.

Genre is the content plane of Register, and Register is the expression plane of Genre. Register in turn is the content plane of Language, with Language being the expression plane of Register.

26.4 Functional Equivalence in Re-contextualization

In any translational action, translators will have to ask whether the function of the text to be translated CAN be kept equivalent. The answer to this question is that this depends on the type of translation sought. Two basic types of translation as qualitatively different ways of re-contextualization can be distinguished: overt and covert translation (cf. House 1977).

26.4.1 Overt and Covert Translation

The distinction between two fundamentally different types of translation and the terms overt and covert translation go back to the German philosopher Friedrich Schleiermacher's (1813) famous distinction between "verfremdende" (alienating) and "einbürgernde" (integrating) translations, which has had many imitators using different terms. What sets the overt-covert distinction apart from other similar distinctions is the fact that it is part of a coherent theory of translation inside which the origin and function of the two types of translation are theoretically motivated and consistently explicated. The distinction is as follows: In an overt translation, the receptors of the translation are quite "overtly" not being addressed; an overt translation is thus one which must overtly be a translation, not a "second original". The source text is tied in a specific manner to the source linguaculture. The original is specifically directed at source culture addressees but at the same time points beyond it because it is also of general human interest. Source texts that call for an overt translation have an established worth in the source language community. They are either overt historically source texts tied to a specific occasion where a precisely specified source language audience is/was being addressed, or they may be timeless source texts transcending as works of art and aesthetic creations a distinct historical meaning. In overt translation true linguacultural transfer takes place.

A covert translation is a translation which enjoys the status of an original source text in the target culture. The translation is covert because it is not marked pragmatically as a translation text of a source text but may, conceivably, have been created in its own right as an independent text. A covert translation is thus a translation whose source text is not specifically addressed to a particular source culture audience, i.e. it is not firmly tied to the source linguaculture. A source text and its covert translation are pragmatically of comparable interest for source and target language addressees. Both are, as it were, equally directly addressed. A source text and its covert translation have equivalent purposes. They are based on contemporary equivalent needs of a comparable audience in the source and target language communities. In the case of covert translation texts, it is thus both possible and desirable to keep the function of the source text equivalent in the translation text. This can be done by inserting a "cultural filter" between original and translation with which to account for contextual differences between the two linguistic communities.

The distinction between overt and covert translation can be given greater explanatory adequacy by relating it to the concepts of "frame" (Goffman 1981) and "discourse world" (Edmondson 1981). Translation involves a transfer of texts across time and space, and whenever texts move, they also shift cognitive frames and discourse worlds. A frame often operates unconsciously as an explanatory principle, i.e. any message that defines a frame gives the receiver instructions in his interpretation of the message included in the frame. An example is the phrase "Once upon a time ..." which indicates to the addressee that a fairy is now forthcoming. Similarly, the notion of a "discourse world" refers to a superordinate structure for interpreting meaning in a certain way. An example would be a case where a teacher, at the end of a foreign language teaching unit conducted entirely in the foreign language, switches into learners' mother tongue, thus indicating a switch of discourse worlds.

If we apply these concepts to overt and covert translation, we can see that in overt translation, the translated text is embedded in a new speech event, which gives it also a new frame. An overt translation is a case of "language mention", similar to a quotation. Here the original and its overt translation can be equivalent at the levels of Language/Text and Register as well as Genre. At the level of the individual textual function, however, functional equivalence, while still possible, is of a different nature: it can be described as merely enabling access to the function the original has in its discourse world or frame. An example would be a speech by Winston Churchill during the Second World War at a particular time and in a particular location. A translation of this speech from English into any other language can obviously not 'mean the same' to the new addressees in their new context. So a switch in discourse world and frame becomes necessary, i.e. the translation will have to be differently framed, it will operate in its own frame and discourse world, and can thus reach at best 'second-level functional equivalence'. As this type of equivalence is, however, achieved though equivalence at the levels of Language/Text, Register and Genre, the original's frame and discourse world will be co-activated, such that members of the target culture may eavesdrop, as it were, i.e. be enabled to appreciate the original textual function, albeit at a distance. Coming back to the example of Churchill's speech, this distance can be explained not only by the fact that the speech happened in the past, but also by the fact that the translation's addressees belong to a different linguacultural community. In overt translation, the work of the translator is important and clearly visible. Since it is the translator's task to permit target culture members to access the original text and its cultural impact on source culture members in its original context, the translator puts target culture members in a position to observe this text "from outside" so to speak, in a new context.

In covert translation, the translator will attempt to re-create an equivalent speech event. Consequently, the function of a covert translation is to reproduce in the target text the function the original has in its frame and discourse world. A covert translation operates quite "overtly" in the frame and discourse world provided by the target culture. No attempt is made to co-activate the discourse world in which the original unfolded. Covert translation is both psycholinguistically less complex than overt translation and more deceptive: the translated text only 'lives' in the new context. The translator's task in covert translation is to betray the origin, to hide behind the transformation of the original, necessary due to the adaptation to the needs and knowledge levels of the new target audience. The translator in covert translation is clearly less visible, if not totally absent. Since true functional equivalence is aimed at, the original may be legitimately manipulated at the levels of Text and Register using a' cultural filter. The result may be a very real distance from the original.

Overt translations are "more straightforward", the originals being taken over "unfiltered" and "simply" transposed from the source to the target cultural context in the medium of a new language. The major difficulty in translating overtly is, of course, finding *linguistic*-cultural "equivalents" particularly along the dimension of Tenor and its characterizations of the author's temporal, social and geographical provenience. However, here we deal with *overt* manifestations of cultural phenomena that are transferred only because they happen to be manifest linguistically in the original. A judgement whether, for example, a "translation" of a dialect is adequate in overt translation can ultimately not be objectively given: the degree of correspondence in terms of social prestige and status cannot be measured in the absence of complete contrastive ethnographic studies – if, indeed, there will ever be such studies. However, as opposed to the difficulty in covert translation of evaluating differences in cultural presuppositions, and communicative preferences between text production in source and target cultural context, the explicit overt transference in an overt translation is still easier to judge.

In discussing different types of translations, there is an implicit assumption that a particular text may be adequately translated in only one particular way. The assumption that a particular text necessitates either a covert or an overt translation does, however, not hold in any simple way. Thus any text may, for a specific purpose, require an overt translation. text may be viewed as a document which „has an independent value" existing in its own right, e.g. when its author has become, in the course of time, a distinguished figure, and then the translation may need to be an overt one. Furthermore, there may well be source texts for which the choice overt-covert translations is necessarily a subjective one, e.g. fairy tales may be viewed as products of a particular culture, which would predispose the translator to opt for an overt translation, or as non-culture specific texts, anonymously produced, with the general function of entertaining and educating the young, which would suggest a covert translation. Or consider the case of the Bible, which may be treated as either a collection of historical literary documents, in which case an overt translation would be called for, or as a collection of human truths directly relevant to all human beings, in which case a covert translation might seem appropriate.

In covert translation, the application of a "cultural filter" is needed. This construct will be discussed in the following section.

26.5 The "Cultural Filter" and Contrastive Pragmatics

The concept of a "cultural filter" was first suggested by House (1977) as a means of capturing socio-cultural differences in expectation norms and stylistic conventions between the source and target cultural contexts. The concept was used to emphasize the need for an empirical contrastive-pragmatic basis for changes of the original undertaken by the translator. Given the goal of achieving functional equivalence in covert translation, assumptions of cultural difference should be carefully examined before any change in the source text is undertaken. Contrastive-pragmatic research into contextually determined communicative preferences in the source and target communities can give more substance to the concept of a cultural filter than mere reliance on tacit native-speaker knowledge. In the case of the German and Anglophone linguacultural communities, for example, evidence of differences in communicative norms is now available, i.e. the cultural filter has been substantiated through empirical contrastive-pragmatic analyses, as an outcome of which a set of Anglophone and German communicative preferences were hypothesized (summary in House 2006). This type of research demonstrates how the notion of a cultural filter can be used to explain (and justify) re-contextualization measures undertaken by the translator in covert translation.

A series of German–English contrastive-pragmatic analyses were conducted over the past 30 years, in which native German and English texts and discourses using a variety of different subjects and methodologies were compared. These yielded a series of individual results, which together provide converging evidence that points to a set of more general hypotheses about the nature of German-English contextually conditioned differences in text and discourse conventions. For example, in a variety of everyday situations and text types, German subjects tended to prefer expressing themselves in ways that are more direct, more explicit, more self-referenced and more content-oriented; they were also found to be less prone to resorting to the use of verbal routines than Anglophone speakers. This pattern of cross-cultural differences can be displayed along a number of dimensions such as directness versus indirectness, explicitness versus implicitness, orientation towards content versus orientation towards persons. These dimensions are continua rather than clear-cut dichotomies, i.e. they reflect tendencies rather than categorical distinctions. In German discourse, then, a transactional style focussing on the content of a message is frequently preferred, whereas in Anglophone discourse, speakers tend to prefer an interactional, addressee-focused manner of expression. In terms of the two Hallidayan functions of language, the ideational and the interpersonal, German texts and discourse often lean towards the ideational function, whereas Anglophone expressions tend to emphasize the interpersonal function.

By hypothesizing dimensions of cross-cultural difference in discourse conventions, which add substance to the notion of a cultural filter, it is also implicitly suggested that linguistic-textual differences in the realization of discourse can be taken to reflect deeper differences in cultural preference patterns. The following examples of German–English translations illustrate the operation of these dimensions in the process of cultural filtering.

The first example comes from a corpus of German signs placed in different domains of public life b. In many cases, these signs are accompanied by translations which, more often than not, reveal German–English differences of communicative preference, and thus the operation of a German–English cultural filter:

(1) Sign at Frankfurt Airport on display at a building site (original German):

Damit die Zukunft schneller kommt!
[Such that the future comes more quickly!]
versus accompanying English translation:
We apologize for any inconvenience work on our building site is causing you!

The difference in perspective, i.e. a focus on content in German and an interpersonal focus in the English translation, is clearly noticeable here.

The next example is taken from an instruction for using ovenware. A preference for greater explicitness in the German original compare to the English translation is clearly noticeable here:

(2) Instruction leaflet, oven ware (original German)

Kerafour ist in unabhängigen Prüfungsinstituten auf Ofenfestigkeit und Mikrowellenbeständigkeit getestet worden. Damit Sie lange Freude an ihm haben, geben wir Ihnen einige kurze Gebrauchshinweise:

-1. Stellen Sie nie ein leeres, kaltes Gefäß in den erhitzten Ofen (als leer gilt auch ein nur innen mit Fett bestrichenes Gefäß) . . .

[Back translation: Kerafour has been tested for ovenproofness in independent testing institutes. So that you can enjoy it for a long time, we give you some brief instructions for use: 1. Never put an empty cold vessel into the heated oven ("empty" also refers to a vessel which is only rubbed with fat)] versus Kerafour oven-to-table pieces have been tested by independent research institutes and are considered ovenproof and microwave resistant. Here are a few simple rules for using Kerafour.
1. Never put a cold and empty piece into the heated oven ...

In the second sentence, the German original gives an explicit reason for this instruction: "Damit Sie lange Freude an ihm haben", which is left out in the English translation. And under 1., the German original – unlike the translation – explicitly defines the conditions under which the Kerafour pieces are to be considered 'empty'. While one might of course assume that the German text producer was specifically instructed to avoid potentially costly consequences of a customer's misinterpretation of 'empty', the interesting fact remains that the entire explicitizing bracket is left out in the English translation.

In English popular scientific articles, an effort is often made to simulate interaction with the reader. The reader is often addressed directly and 'drawn into' the scenes described in the text, as in the following example from the American popular science magazine *Scientific American*:

(3) Original English taken from the opening passage of Susan Buchbinder "Avoiding infection after HIV-exposure" in *Scientific American*, July 1998.

Suppose YOU are a doctor in an emergency room and a patient tells YOU she was raped two hours earlier. She is afraid she may have been exposed to HIV, the virus that causes AIDS but has heard that there is a "morning-after pill" to prevent HIV infection. Can YOU in fact do anything to block the virus from replicating and establishing infection?

The German translation of this passage which appeared in the German daughter publication of *Scientific American*, *Spektrum der Wissenschaft* in October 1998 reads as follows:

In der Notfallaufnahme eines Krankenhauses berichtet eine Patientin, sie sei vor zwei Stunden vergewaltigt worden und nun in Sorge, AIDS-Erregern ausgesetzt zu sein, sie habe gehört, es gebe eine "Pille danach", die eine HIV-Infektion verhüte. Kann der Arzt überhaupt etwas tun, was eventuell vorhandene Viren hindern würde, sich zu vermehren und sich dauerhaft im Körper einzunisten? (Back translation: In the emergency room of a hospital, a patient reports that she had been raped two hours ago and was now worrying that she had been exposed to the AIDS-Virus. She said she had heard that there was an "after pill" which might prevent an HIV infection. Can THE DOCTOR in fact do anything which might prevent potentially existing viruses from replicating and establishing themselves permanently in the body?)

This translation can be understood as governed by the aim to adapt the American English original to the reading habits of the German target audience. Note that changes have been made in particular concerning the degree of addressee-involvement: The German reader is no longer asked to imagine herself as one of the agents of the scene presented. Instead, the scene in the hospital is presented as it were 'from the outside', the addressee are not asked to actively engage with what is presented.

Cultural filtering in covert translation is also evident in the translations of English children's books into German. Here is an example from an early German translation (in the sixties) of the classic children's book *A Bear called Paddington* by Michael Bond:

(4) "Hello Mrs Bird" said Judy "It's nice to see you again. How's the rheumatism?" "Worse than it's ever been" began Mrs Bird.

This entire exchange is left out in the German translation.
Equally omitted is the utterance by another character in the book: "Delighted to know you, bear. Delighted to know you".

Here we can see that the phatic exchanges in the English original – as a sign of a heightened consideration of addressees – are considered irrelevant in the German translation and thus "filtered away". It is interesting to note, however, that in the more recent German translation of the Paddington books, these phatic exchanges are present. This means that cultural filtering has been abolished, the translations are now overt rather than covert, which shows a greater respect for the original and a philosophy of introducing the child reader to a foreign cultural content with its different conventions and norms.

26.6 Translation as Re-contextualization and English as a Lingua Franca

In the course of today's processes of globalization in many aspects of contemporary life, there is also a rising demand for texts that are simultaneously meant for recipients in many different cultural contexts. These texts are either translated covertly or produced immediately as 'comparable texts' in different languages. In the past, translators and text producers tended to routinely apply a cultural filter in such cases. However, due to the worldwide political, economic, scientific and cultural dominance of the English language – especially in its function as lingua franca – a tendency towards 'cultural universalism' or 'cultural neutralism', which is really a drift towards Anglo-American norms, has now been set in motion. In the decades to come, the conflict between cultural universalism propelled by the need for fast and global dissemination of information on the one hand

and culture specificity catering to local, particular needs on the other hand will become more marked. It is therefore plausible to hypothesize that much less cultural filtering in re-contextualization processes will occur in the future, with many more 'culturally universal', 'contextually homogenized' translation texts being routinely created as carriers of (hidden) Anglophone and West-European/North-Atlantic linguistic-cultural norms.

While the influence of the English language in the area of lexis has long been acknowledged and bemoaned by many (cf. House 2003), Anglophone influence at the levels of pragmatics has hardly been recognized, let alone adequately researched. The effect of the shift in translation and multilingual text production towards neutral contexts in influential genres in many languages and cultures is therefore an important research area for the future. What is needed in this area is empirical, longitudinal corpus-based research into hitherto unidentified problems. One first step in this direction has been made in the project Covert Translation-Verdecktes Übersetzen directed by the present author and generously funded from 1999 to 2012 by the German Research Foundation (DFG). The project examined the influence of English as a global lingua franca on German, French and Spanish translated texts and comparable texts. In this project, quantitative and qualitative diachronic analyses are conducted on the basis of multilingual primary and validation corpora of 550 texts (800,000 words) from popular science and economic genres as well as interviews and background material. The analyses have shown that German communicative preferences – unlike French and Spanish ones – have indeed undergone a process of change under the influence of English over the space of 25 years. Particularly vulnerable to English influence are certain functional categories such as personal deixis, co-ordinate conjunctions and modal particles, which function as a sort of trigger for contextually induced changes in textual norms in both translations and comparable texts (cf. Becher et al. 2009; House 2010, 2017; Kranich et al. 2012). To illustrate this trend, here is an example from the popular science corpus. In this example, it is the subject position in the German translation which points to English influence. Whereas a non-animate noun as agent in the subject position is routinely possible in English, it is marked in German in this genre:

(5) Michael Rose: "Can Human Aging be Postponed?" *Scientific American*, December 1999 (Original English)

Anti-ageing therapies of the future will undoubtedly have to counter many destructive biochemical processes at once.

Michael Rose: „Läßt sich das Altern aufhalten?" *Spektrum der Wissenschaft*, March 2000. (German Translation)

Wirksame Therapien müssen allerdings *den Kampf* gegen viele zerstörerische biochemische Prozesse gleichzeitig *aufnehmen*.

[Effective therapies must however take up the fight against many destructive biochemical processes simultaneously.]

The German translation shows that the Anglophone convention of personalizing inanimate, abstract entities is adopted, adding a persuasive force to the text and eliciting a potentially more emotive-affective response from addressees. In German, the passive would be a less marked construction: "Durch Anti-Altern Therapien der Zukunft muss vielen zerstörerischen biochemischen Prozessen zweifellos gleichzeitg entgegengewirkt werden" ('Through anti-ageing therapies of the future, many destructive biochemical processes will undoubtedly be countered at once').

The results of analyses in the project described above show that re-contextualization processes both in English–German translations and in comparable texts are being transformed under the impact of global English.

Due to globalization, technological progress, the dominance of global English and the massive increase of translations from English, cultural filtering may gradually become extinct giving way to what one my call 'cultural neutralism' or 'universalism' – which is really a drift towards uniform, easily marketable texts embodying Anglophone discourse norms.

26.7 Conclusion

In this chapter, I have traced the connection between translation and pragmatics to their common concern with 'context'. Context was described as an interdisciplinary concept. In translation, texts are doubly contextually bound: to their originals and to the new addressees' communicative and contextual conditions. This 'double-bind' nature of translation means that translation is essentially a procedure of re-contextualization, which involves two basic types of translation: covert and overt translation. The distinction between overt and covert translation was shown to reflect very different ways of solving the task of re-contextualization: in overt translation the original's context is reactivated alongside the target context, such that two different frames and discourse worlds are juxtaposed in the medium of the target language. Covert translation displays an exclusive focus on the target context, employing a cultural filter to take account of the new addressees' context-derived communicative norms. Covert translation is thus more directly affected by contextual and cultural differences than overt translation, the latter showing genuine linguistic-cultural transfer. In covert translation, a so-called cultural filter is routinely employed. It is given substance through empirical contrastive research – another sign of the close connection between translation studies and pragmatics.

Given the importance of English as a global lingua franca, and the concomitant continuous increase of unilateral translations from English into other languages, translation as a phenomenon of re-contextualization is well and alive in overt translation, where linguacultural specificities continue to be maintained in certain genres. For covert translation, the future is less clear: Dominance of global English in the guise of cultural universalism and neutralism may well lead to hitherto unknown forms of re-contextualization.

Translation studies and pragmatics were shown to be closely connected in their common reliance on context, re-contextualization and empirical contrastive-pragmatic research.

Future research in translation as a sociopragmatic phenomenon of re-contextualization should try to make links with neuro- and psycholinguistic research that may provide evidence for the two different types of re-contextualization in the bilingual mind, which I have called overt and covert translation. The neurolinguistic theory by Paradis (2004) looks promising in this regard. As House (2016b) explained, Paradis' theory neatly explains neurological substrates of the two fundamental translation types in the translator's bilingual mind. For the future, a transdisciplinary combination of descriptive, psycholinguistic and neurolinguistic research into translation processes (cf. Halverson 2014) looks most promising.

References

Auer, P. (2005). Projection in interaction and projection in grammar. *Text, 25*, 7–36.

Austin, J. (1962). *How to Do Things with Words*. Cambridge, MA: Harvard University Press.

Baker, M. (1992). *In Other Words: A Course Book on Translation*. London: Routledge.

Baker, M. (2011). *In Other Words: A Coursebook on Translation*. London: Routledge.

Bateson, G. (1972). *Steps to an Ecology of Mind*. New York: Ballantine Books.

De Beaugrande, R. and Dressler, W. (1981). *Einführung in die Textlinguistik*. Berlin: de Gruyter.

Becher, V., House, J. and Kranich, S. (2009). Convergence and divergence of communicative norms through language norms in translation. In K. Braunmüller and J. House, eds., *Convergence and Divergence in Language Contact Situations*. Amsterdam: John Benjamins, pp. 125–52.

Biber, D. (1988). *Variation across Speech and Writing*. Cambridge: Cambridge University Press.

Bühler, K. (1934). *Sprachtheorie. Die Darstellungsfunktion der Sprache*. Jena, Gemany: Fischer.

Catford, J. C. (1965). *A Linguistic Theory of Translation*. Oxford: Oxford University Press.

Clark, H. (1996). *Using Language*. Cambridge: Cambridge University Press.

Connor, U. (1996). *Contrastive Rhetoric*. Cambridge: Cambridge University Press.

Clyne, M. (1987). Cultural differences in the organization of academic texts. *Journal of Pragmatics, 11*, 214–74.

Edmondson, W. (1981). *Spoken Discourse: A Model for Analysis*. London: Longman.
Ehlich, K. (1984). Zum Textbegriff. In A. Rothkegel and B. Sandig, eds., *Text-Textsorten Semantik*. Hamburg, Germany: Buske, pp. 9–25.
Federov, A. (1958). *Introduction to the Theory of Translation*. 2d ed. (in Russian). Moscow: Isdatel'stvo literartury na inostrannikh yazykakh.
Forgas, J. (1985). *Language and Social Situations*. New York: Springer.
Goffman, E. (1974). *Frame Analysis*. New York: Harper and Row.
Goffman, E. (1981). *Forms of Talk*. Philadelphia: University of Philadelphia Press.
Grice, H. P. (1975). Logic and conversation. In P. Cole and J. Morgan, eds., *Syntax and Semantics*, Vol. 3, *Speech Acts*. New York: Academic Press, pp. 41–58.
Gumperz, J. (1992). Contextualisation and understanding. In A. Duranti and C. Goodwin, eds., *Rethinking Context*. Cambridge: Cambridge University Press, pp. 229–52.
Halliday, M. A. K. (1994). *An Introduction to Functional Grammar*. London: Arnold.
Halliday, M. A. K. and Hasan, R. (1976). *Cohesion in English*. London: Longman.
Halliday, M. A. K. and Hasan, R. (1989). *Spoken and Written Language*. Oxford: Oxford University Press.
Halverson, S. (2014). Reorienting translation studies: Cognitive approaches and the centrality of the translator. In J. House, ed., *Translation: A Multidisciplinary Approach*. New York: Palgrave Macmillan, pp. 116–39.
Hatim, B. and Mason, I. (1990). *Discourse and the Translator*. London: Longman.
Heritage, J. (1984). *Garfinkel and Ethnomethodology*. Cambridge: Polity Press.
House, J. (1977). *A Model for Translation Quality Assessment*. Tübingen, Germany: Narr.
House, J. (1997). *Translation Quality Assessment: A Model Revisited*. Tübingen, Germany: Narr.
House, J. (2003). English as a lingua franca: A threat to multilingualism? *Journal of Sociolinguistics*, 7, 556–79.
House, J. (2006). Communicative styles in English and German. *European Journal of English Studies*, 10, 249–67.
House, J. (2010). Discourse and dominance: Global English, language contact and language change. In A. Duszak, J. House and L. Kumiega, eds., *Globalization, Discourse, Media*. Warsaw: University of Warsaw Press, pp. 61–94.
House, J. (2015). *Translation Quality Assessment: Past and Present*. Oxford: Routledge.
House, J. (2016a). *Translation as Communication across Language and Cultures*. Oxford: Routledge.
House, J. (2016b). Towards a new linguistic-cognitive orientation in translation studies. In M. Ehrensberger-Dow, S. Göpferich and S. O'Brien, eds.,

Interdisciplinarity in Translation and Interpreting Process Research. Amsterdam: John Benjamins, pp. 49–63.

House, J. (2017). Global English, discourse and translation: Linking constructions in English and German popular science texts. In J. Munday and M. Zhang, eds., *Discourse Analysis in Translation Studies.* Amsterdam: John Benjamins, pp. 47–62.

Jäger, S. (1975). *Translation und Translationslinguistik.* Halle: VEB Niemeyer.

Jakobson, R. (1959). On linguistic aspects of translation. In R. Brower, ed., *On Translation.* New York: Oxford University Press, pp. 232–9.

Jakobson, R. (1960). Closing statement: Linguistics and poetics. In T. Sebeok, ed., *Style in Language.* Cambridge, MA: MIT Press, pp. 350–77.

Kranich, S., House, J. and Becher, V. (2012). Changing conventions in English and German translations of popular science texts. In K. Braunmüller and C. Gabriel, eds., *Multilingual Individuals and Multilingual Societies.* Amsterdam: John Benjamins, pp. 315–35.

Kruger, A., Wallmach, K. and Mundy, J. (2011). *Corpus-Based Translation Studies: Research and Applications.* London: Bloomsbury.

Leech, G. (1983). *Principles of Pragmatics.* London: Longman.

Levinson, S. (1983). *Pragmatics.* Cambridge: Cambridge University Press.

Malinowski, B. (1935). *Coral Gardens and Their Magic (II).* London: Allen and Unwin.

Nida, E. (1964). *Toward a Science of Translation.* Leiden, Netherlands: Brill.

Paradis, M. (2004). *A Neurolinguistic Theory of Bilingualism.* Amsterdam: John Benjamins.

Popper, K. (1972). *Objective Knowledge: An Evolutionary Approach.* Oxford: Clarendon.

Reiss, K. (1971). *Möglichkeiten und Grenzen der Übersetzungskritik.* Munich, Germany: Hueber.

Schleiermacher, F. (1813). Über die verschiedenen Methoden des Übersetzens. Reprinted in H.-J. Störig, eds., *Das Problem des Übersetzens.* Darmstadt, Germany: Wissenschaftliche Buchgesellschaft, pp. 38–70.

Sperber, D. and Wilson, D. (1986). *Relevance: Communication and Cognition.* Oxford: Blackwell.

Stalnaker, R. (1978). Assertion. In P. Cole, ed., *Syntax and Semantics,* Vol. 9. New York: Academic Press, pp. 315–22.

Stalnaker, R. (1999). *Context and Content.* Oxford: Oxford University Press.

Steiner, E. (2004). *Exploring Texts: Properties, Variants, Evaluations.* Frankfurt, Germany: Peter Lang.

Widdowson, H. (2004). *Text, Context, Pretext.* Oxford: John Wiley.

Wittgenstein, L. ([1958] 1967). *Philosophical Investigations.* Oxford: Blackwell.

Zanettin, F. (2014). Corpora in translation. In J. House, ed., *Translation: A Multidisciplinary Approach.* New York: Palgrave Macmillan, pp. 178–99.

Part III
Approaches and Methods in Sociopragmatics

Part III

27

Interpersonal Pragmatics

Miriam A. Locher and Sage L. Graham[*]

27.1 Introduction

Next to the informational side, language always also has an interpersonal, relational side (Watzlawick et al. 1967), which deserves to be studied in its own right. Paying attention to this side of communication allows us to pursue questions of relationship creation in situ, which will allow us in turn to uncover underlying ideologies that shape our understanding of self and self-in-relation-to-others in particular communities of practice (Eckert and McConnell-Ginet 1992; Lavé and Wenger 1991). In order to zoom in on the relational and interpersonal side of communication, there have been a number of scholars since the 2010s who explicitly work with the term 'interpersonal pragmatics' (see Locher and Graham 2010b; Haugh et al. 2013). Adopting a relational perspective within pragmatics, interpersonal pragmatics is defined as follows:

> The term 'interpersonal pragmatics' is used to designate examinations of the relational aspect of interactions between people that both affect and are affected by their understandings of culture, society, and their own and others' interpretations. (Locher and Graham 2010a: 2)

The purpose of this chapter is to demonstrate how this research interest on the interpersonal and relational side of language is inspired by studies on (im)politeness, identity construction and communication in order to tackle questions about pragmatic variation and interpersonal effects. This view complements research which focuses more on the informational side of language (such as classic speech act studies). Interpersonal pragmatics does not propagate a particular, single methodology nor does it stand for only one theoretical approach. The chapter is therefore not intended to develop a

---

[*] We thank the editors and anonymous reviewers for their constructive and helpful feedback. We also thank the originators of the Hospitalk Project, Dr. Heidi Hamilton, Dr. Elaine Larson and Dr. John Eisenberg.

meta-theory, nor to provide a step-by-step demonstration of how interpersonal pragmatics is better suited than other approaches within pragmatics to address questions about the interpersonal side of language use. Instead, the label is used for research that focuses on the relational side of communication and combines interests that have often been pursued with different approaches in separate studies. The aim of suggesting the label in the first place has always been to bring scholars from different traditions together when discussing interpersonal phenomena. As a consequence, this chapter will have a certain overlap with other contributions to this handbook. Our aim is to show what research has been conducted either under the umbrella term interpersonal pragmatics and/or can be interpreted with this label in mind.

In general, scholars working within interpersonal pragmatics ask questions such as the following:

— In what ways do identities surface in texts and practices and how are they negotiated?
— In what ways are norms of conduct and ideologies made manifest and negotiated?
— In what ways do interpersonal relationships emerge concurrently with (or as a result of) these norms of conduct?

These questions are of course interconnected and lead us to consider the influence of factors such as age, class, gender, seniority, expertise, role understanding etc. that are part of sociolinguistics and interactional sociolinguistics as well as discourse analysis frameworks. They are addressed with a particular community of practice in a particular time and location in mind and are approached from a multi-modal perspective.

Readers may wonder how interpersonal pragmatics is related to the concept of sociopragmatics used in this volume (cf. Chapters 1 and 2):

> Sociopragmatics is positioned on the more social side of pragmatics, standing in contrast to the more linguistic side. It is focussed on the construction and understanding of meanings arising from interactions between language (or other semiotic resources) and socio-cultural phenomena. It is centrally concerned with situated interaction, especially local, meso-level contexts (e.g. frames, activity types, genres). It often considers norms emerging in such contexts, how they are exploited by participants, and how they lead to evaluations of (in) appropriateness. (Chapter 27)

As stated above, our understanding of interpersonal pragmatics is that it is a perspective and not a unified theory. In this way, we feel uncomfortable in subsuming the term under a particular label within pragmatics (which would make it narrower) or claiming that it is the hierarchically more encompassing concept (which it is neither). However, as can be gleaned from Culpeper's definition, there are number of issues highlighted as pertinent for sociopragmatics which are also relevant when pursuing questions inspired by interpersonal pragmatics (situated context, frames etc.). Like the other chapters in this part of the handbook, interpersonal pragmatics can neither be easily equated with nor subsumed under the label of sociopragmatics but is undeniable aligned with it.

The next section explores the history of interpersonal pragmatics and then introduces a number of important concepts (Section 27.2). We will then illustrate key findings within this research field by drawing on examples from health communication (Section 27.3). The chapter ends with an outlook on challenges and advantages.

27.2 History and Key Concepts in Interpersonal Pragmatics

To study the interpersonal or relational side of communication is of course not new and therefore also not exclusive to the term interpersonal pragmatics. In what follows, we will explain why we suggested the term in 2010 nevertheless (Locher and Graham 2010a). The main inspiration for it comes from the pragmatic turn in the 1960s and within it the question of why pragmatic variation occurs in the first place. Exploring why the same speech act is habitually and systematically performed in different linguistic and multi-modal ways led to early politeness theories as proposed by Lakoff (1973), Leech (1983) and especially Brown and Levinson ([1978] 1987). Apart from working with speech acts and drawing on Grice's (1975) Cooperative Principle, these theories have in common that they focus on language in use and context when explaining why people express speech acts (however, often with invented examples). For example, Brown and Levinson (1987) argue that people take each other's face into account when interacting (see Chapter 13), and thus project the consequences of their (linguistic) actions. They identified the distance between speakers, the power difference between speakers and the ranking of the imposition to be engaged in as defining factors that influence how the potential weightiness of a face-threatening act is calculated. The sum of this metaphorical equation is claimed to result in various linguistic strategies which differ in their level of directness and thus in the way that mitigation is used to save the speaker's or addressee's face. Politeness – seen as a technical concept to pay attention to face – is thus understood as an explanatory factor for pragmatic variation (for a longer historical account of this argument, see Locher 2011, 2013, 2015).

Research within the field of politeness studies, however, used the early work from the 1970s as a springboard to elaborate on more ideas concerning pragmatic variation: impoliteness became a central point of interest, methodological and theoretical debates abounded concerning the claim to universality of the early theories as well as the notions of first- and second-order terms (see Locher 2013). One of the central claims of scholars working within a discursive approach to politeness was that politeness is a term that can be used as an etic, theoretical concept which alerts us to the fact that people shape relationships through language; however, the term should not be confused with the emic concept of politeness. The emic notion is culture and community of practice bound and thus may vary from culture to culture as well as historically. This is not the same as saying that "anything goes" since there are indeed societal ideologies about polite conduct, but it alerts scholars to the fact that what is considered polite needs to be discussed in its particular context at a given moment in time since societal ideologies are constantly challenged and/or confirmed and hence negotiated.

The 2000s thus saw a surge in research within historical linguistics (see Culpeper and Kádár 2010). For example, for English, when and how the ideology of politeness came about was discussed by scholars like Fitzmaurice (2010). In addition, the interest in the entire semantic field to which politeness belongs resulted in studies on impoliteness or incivility as well (e.g. Bousfield 2008; Bousfield and Locher 2008; Culpeper 2011; Graham 2007, 2008). In fact, scholars working within politeness studies today usually employ the term (im)politeness to point to this semantic field. As a consequence of this widened interest, Locher and Watts (2005, 2008) proposed to use the concept of relational work rather than politeness when referring to the interpersonal aspect of language:

> Relational work refers to all aspects of the work invested by individuals in the construction, maintenance, reproduction and transformation of interpersonal relationships among those engaged in social practice. (Locher and Watts 2008: 96)

The advantage of the term relational work from our point of view is that it is an etic, technical one, which can be used without invoking the emic notions that politeness also carries. We can describe face-maintaining, face-aggravating or face-enhancing behaviour without yet having to make recourse to ideologically charged terms such as politeness or impoliteness. In a second step, of course, one might ask questions about the ideologies that motivate the pragmatic choices of interactants that might explain the observed patterns and engage in a study of norms of conduct and their ideologies in their own right. To study relational work within interpersonal pragmatics thus means that one may indeed be interested in the negotiation of politeness, but one can also be interested in other ideologies, for example pertaining to gender, class, or age, and how these factors are all related to each other when accounting for pragmatic variation (see also Chapter 31).

When reviewing the literature that is relevant for interpersonal pragmatics, we are faced with the fact that there are many research fields and studies that can be linked to the relational side of language, such as the study of identity construction, persuasion and communication. Scholars in these fields often share an interest in the same or similar research questions, but do not necessarily employ the concept of interpersonal pragmatics per se, nor do they primarily draw on the (im)politeness literature either (Locher 2015). This is not surprising since the term refers neither to a single theory nor to a particular methodology. When we conceptualized the Mouton handbook *Interpersonal Pragmatics* (Locher and Graham 2010b), this is reflected in its design. We first commissioned eight chapters which dealt with (im)politeness studies as well as approaches to relating, gender and identity construction. We then focused on a number of central concepts that are meaningful when describing relational effects in general (humour, mitigation, respect and deference, swearing). At the end – in an eclectic manner – we solicited chapters that focused on the interpersonal side of communication within certain areas of communication (interaction in politics, the workplace, the courtroom, health contexts and dating ads).

From this brief historical account of the genesis of the term interpersonal pragmatics, we can take that scholars working in different research traditions often overlap with their research interests but not necessarily with their technical vocabulary. For example, when recently writing a handbook article on (im)politeness in health settings (Locher and Schnurr 2017), it was striking that there were a large number of relevant articles that described how health professionals engaged with each other and patients in delicate and less delicate ways (e.g. through the use of humour and mitigation), with some scholars never drawing on the (im)politeness literature, while others discussed data only with the (im)politeness terminology. Since this made none of the studies less valid, we made the following argument:

> The term (im)politeness can also be used as a shorthand for referring to facework [Brown and Levinson 1987] / relational work/ rapport management [Spencer-Oatey 2005] in general. With this larger lens in mind, scholars are interested in situated pragmatic rules that show how social interactants negotiate relationships and get 'things done' by means of language without jeopardising the social balance or how people exploit linguistic means in more conflictual situations to get their points of view across and to save, maintain or challenge each other's face.... Studies with such a larger (im)politeness lens often look at particular interpersonal strategies, such as the use of humour, mitigation strategies and address terms, in order to report on patterns in relational work. (Locher and Schnurr 2017: 690)

This means that much of the literature not using the (im)politeness terminology is relevant for (im)politeness scholars nevertheless (and vice versa).

Within interpersonal pragmatics a number of technical terms that allow us to explore the relational side of language in use have wide currency. At the same time scholars are invited to be open to studies in other fields that might ask similar research questions. Research fields that come easily to mind are especially the study of identity construction, style and audience design (see e.g. Bucholtz and Hall 2005; Coupland 2007; Davies and Harré 1990; Hall and Bucholtz 2013; Rampton 1995). We can easily establish a link between the study of identity construction, style and (im)politeness since how persons express themselves will be judged according to social norms (see Locher 2008; Garcés-Conejos Blitvich 2013 for an elaboration of this argument). In fact, (im)politeness studies have long addressed this connection between (im)politeness, identity and societal norms and ideologies, as briefly alluded to above when talking about the historicity of concepts and codes of conduct. The fields of "interpersonal communication" (Haugh et al. 2013: 1), discursive psychology and discourse analysis more generally come to mind as further inspiration as well. In Haugh et al.'s (2013: 2) terms, interpersonal pragmatics is thus of an "inherently interdisciplinary or multidisciplinary" nature.

Since we define interpersonal pragmatics as a perspective within pragmatics which focuses on the relational aspect of communication, we will be able to draw on and point to a number of earlier chapters in this volume dealing with key concepts for this field, among them (im)politeness (Chapter 16), face (Chapter 13), identity and roles (Chapter 15), relationships (Chapter 14), power (Chapter 18), morality (Chapter 19), humour (Chapter 20) as well as the social and historical embeddedness of communication (Chapter 32). We might want to add the key terms of community of practice (Eckert and McConnell-Ginet 1992; Lavé and Wenger 1991), positioning, aligning and disaligning (Davies and Harré 1990), frames of interaction (Goffman 1974; Tannen 1993) or activity type (Levinson 1992; see also Chapter 11), as well as the importance of emotions within relating (Langlotz and Locher 2013 2017; see also Chapter 17). Rather than giving a comprehensive overview of all these key concepts which are discussed by other people in the handbook already, we have chosen to illustrate in the next section how an interpersonal pragmatics lens can be used in the field of health communication.

27.3 Interpersonal Pragmatics in Health Contexts

As O'Driscoll (2013: 172) notes, in interpersonal pragmatics the focus has been "shifting away from understanding the nature of language to the understanding of human relations". Since 'human relations' are influenced by a broad array of factors within any interaction, interpersonal pragmatics allows us to explore the relational work people employ from many perspectives. To illustrate, this section will examine interactions from medical caregiving teams within an urban teaching hospital in the United States. By moving beyond the 'traditional' pragmatic approaches that focused solely on language rather than relations (O'Driscoll 2013), we can employ perspectives from multiple areas of linguistics to arrive at a more complex understanding of the ways that language influences human relations.

As a general comment, we wish to stress that all interaction is relational, and all interaction is multimodal (in the sense that there are multiple aspects ('modes') that go into any communicative event – including eye gaze, body positioning, screen camera angles, a/synchronicity etc.). The approaches to analysis illustrated below, therefore, are not mutually exclusive and, as this section will show, can benefit from cross-pollination. We also wish to stress that the approaches discussed here are only a subset of the possible ways to explore relationship construction. The aim is thus to argue for why it is beneficial to draw on the resources of multiple theoretical constructs. For space reasons, we cannot illustrate further examples of such combinations from our research (see e.g. Locher 2017 and Locher and Thurnherr 2017 for other options).

27.3.1 The Hospitalk Project

The data used here was collected in an urban teaching hospital in the United States in 1997 and included semi-structured one-on-one interviews, observations on hospital floors, observation and recording of weekly 'discharge rounds' and surveys distributed to a random sample of hospital employees. The language involved is English. The goal of the study was to assess whether restructuring daily work assignments so that the same caregivers worked together more frequently (a structure the hospital labelled a 'firm' system) would minimize conflict and create greater cohesion and collaboration among different categories of caregivers (e.g. doctors, nurses, social workers). Using the data from this study, Larson et al. (1998) examined interactions between RNs (registered nurses) and MDs (medical doctors), quantitatively tracking their perceptions of communicative acts such as giving orders, asking for information, giving and providing opinions and providing education. Survey results in this study indicated that differences in perceptions of roles sometimes led to misunderstanding and conflict. Graham (2009), taking a more interpersonal pragmatic perspective, found discrepancies between the institutional hierarchy of the hospital and the social/expertise hierarchy perceived by nurses, social workers and other caregivers who were not doctors; this resulted in non-doctor caregivers interpreting interactions as impolite and caused at least some of the difficulties that the proposed team structure was designed to address. While these studies certainly illuminated some characteristics of interaction in this setting, a more complex picture of the interpersonal strategies and their outcomes could also enhance our understanding of the complexities of caregiver-team relationships (and therefore, ultimately, the quality of patient care). What follows, therefore, is an examination of the data from this study using multiple frameworks/approaches – each of which illuminates different aspects of relational work. By using multiple theoretical and methodological lenses to examine the same set of data, we illustrate the ways that different approaches (which fall under the larger umbrella of interpersonal pragmatics) may be used to examine the negotiation of interpersonal relationships.

27.3.2 An Interactional Sociolinguistic Approach

Examining turn-taking and floor-management allows us to explore the discursive sequences through which caregivers demonstrate and/or challenge the power structures that exist within the hospital (for an introduction to interactional sociolinguistics, consult Schiffrin 1994; Gordon 2011). Once per week in this hospital, caregivers meet to discuss which of the current patients should be discharged and which should remain in the hospital; these meetings are labelled interdisciplinary discharge rounds since they provide the only opportunity for all members of the caregiving team to come together in one place to discuss patients. These sessions are attended by RNs (registered nurses), MDs (medical doctors), social workers (who manage the patient's care resources – e.g. insurance, family, home care – both within the hospital and after discharge), and other caregivers (such as a clinical pharmacologist and in one case a chaplain).

RNs in this hospital were assigned four to five patients for their 10-hour shifts, during which time they gained wide-ranging knowledge of a given patient's situation (personality, fears/concerns, visiting family dynamics). A common complaint among nurses in individual interviews prior to the implementation of the firm system was that they felt that MDs often did not solicit RNs' input or take their knowledge into account when making decisions about treatment. In theory, then, interdisciplinary discharge rounds (hereafter IDR) should be extremely useful in insuring that patients get the best possible care, since they provide an opportunity to take advantage of the different types of knowledge that each type of caregiver brings to the team.

In IDR, one RN (the charge nurse[1] for that day) manages the meeting, identifying each patient in turn so that the team can discuss whether discharge is in order. The charge nurse allocates the turns within the conversation, but makes minimal contributions to the conversation herself unless she needs to fill a 'knowledge gap' when other participants (usually MDs) are unable to answer questions. Rounds are structured with the charge nurse identifying the next patient to be discussed, followed by the diagnosis the patient was given upon check in (given by either the MD or the charge nurse). The charge nurse then gives the conversational floor to the MD who has been assigned to that patient. The MD gives a summary of the patient's care – which may include why s/he came to the hospital, diagnoses, what treatments have been given, and what the current status is regarding whether the patient is ready for discharge. After the MD gives this summary, others may ask questions for clarification or offer other suggestions. The MD's talk in these cases serves primarily as an informational report rather than a negotiable discussion

---

[1] Each day, nurses on a given floor are assigned a specified number of patients for whom they will be responsible. There is also a 'charge nurse', who coordinates these RNs as they work their shifts.

to which other caregivers may contribute. Instead, non-MD caregivers (particularly social workers since they are responsible for creating a plan of care *after* the patient leaves the hospital) most often ask for clarification of the MD's orders. Consistent with the hierarchical structure of the hospital, the MDs make the final decision regarding discharge, and the documents that order the discharge of the patient are authorized and issued by physicians.

While the MDs in these cases make the final determination, there are instances where other caregivers question either the decision to discharge a patient or some other aspect of the patient's treatment. While in some cases the questions are simply requests for information, others contain a challenge to the MD's decision; such cases either prompt repair work by the charge nurse or deferral of the question(s) by the MD. In one such instance, a clinical pharmacologist (hereafter CP) questions the drug and dosage given to a patient. In transcribed examples, all names are pseudonyms and consent has been given by all interactants.

(1)
1   CP (to MD1): Do you know how much kitoralic she's receiving? At
2   this point.
3   MD1:   I don't know
4   CP: Is she receiving /???/
5   MD1:   I don't know.
6   CP: 'Cause the dose is hard. For her age.
7   MD1:   Ok. We will – We will –
8   CP: It's supposed to be 59 on Q6. Is she going home on it?
9   MD1:   We'll – We'll – We'll decide that /???/

In this case, the clinical pharmacologist asks for information about care the MD team has administered (line 1). Upon an unsatisfactory response, she modifies the question to be more specific (line 4) and, when the MD repeats 'I don't know', a justification for the pharmacologist's question is delivered (line 6). In these instances, the MD deflects the questions, saying 'we'll decide that' (line 9). On these occasions, the 'we' is exclusive and refers to the team of *doctors* rather than the comprehensive team of all types of caregivers. The implication is also that the team of doctors will make the decision later, so the CP should not expect to negotiate a resolution with the doctor now. In effect, then, despite the attempt to justify the question (which also implies the pharmacologists' opinion that it might *not* be advisable for the patient to receive that dose), the clinical pharmacologist's questions have been dismissed.

A similar instance occurs with a different MD in example 2. In this case, the MD ends his report by stating that it will still be 'a couple of days' before the patient is ready to be discharged (line 1).

(2)
1   MD2:   It's still gonna be a couple of days I would think.
2   CP: Her magnesium level is 2.2. And she's still on Magalox. How long
3   do you think that –
4   MD2:   – I actually stopped that this morning ... Yeah.

After the MD's report is completed in line 1, which refers to the duration of patient's hospital stay, the CP questions whether the patient should continue a medicine by providing relevant details on the patient's situation ("her magnesium level is a 2.2", line 2). The CP thus implies that the patient's physical condition justifies some modification in the medicine during the rest of the hospital stay. The MD, however, interrupts the CP and pre-emptively dismisses her query (line 3).

Finally, there are markers that reflect the MDs authority through minimal responses, as evidenced in example 3.

(3)[2]
1   MD3:   She was on Cipara ten days. Just finished a while ago.
2   CP: She's also on potassium chloride. Her potassium level is
3   now five.
4   MD3:   Okay.
5   CP: Are you going to [continue on, or –
6   MD3:   (overlap)   [was that – – No, no.
7   CP: Okay. She's receiving 20 mil for her v.i.d.
8   MD3:   Yeah. That was what she came in on. I'll – /???/ She actually
9   came in on twice that dose. I cut it in half [laughing].
10   CP: But it was lower, when I was checking that, it was lower. All of
11   a sudden, it's like five. That was from yesterday.
12   MD3:   'Kay.
13   CP: Um, she is on Macex, 40 milligram q.d., so.
14   MD3:   We'll just follow up while she's here.

The sequence begins with the MD stating that a particular medication was discontinued (line 1). The CP continues by stating that the patient is also on potassium chloride. By identifying the patient's potassium level (line 2), the CP indirectly questions the efficacy of giving the patient a particular dose of medication. Her statement thus implies a question of whether the team should continue to administer potassium chloride to the patient. When the implied question only receives the minimal response "okay" from the MD (line 4), she asks more directly "are you going to continue" (line 5). In subsequent turns the CP continues to elaborate with details about the

---

[2] In all examples, [indicates overlapping talk. [ ] indicates multimodal features and metadata.

patient's medication, expanding her implied request that the MD re-evaluate the doses (lines 10–11, 13). The MD's responses throughout the interaction, however, deflect the request; the MD states that he had reduced the dose (lines 8–9), gives a non-committal acknowledgement (line 12), and finally closes the interaction by saying that "we" (again used exclusively to refer to doctors) will "follow up" (line 14). In these instances, the hierarchy is established/reinforced via both the MD's deflection of the CP's question and his refusal to negotiate the medical decision regarding the medication dose.

In each of these examples, the MD's interruption or deflection of the CP's concerns ends the conversational segment and closes the floor for further questions. While not necessarily extreme enough to be classified as impolite, the fact that the MDs do not take up the CP's concerns for further discussion reinforces their position at the top of the institutional hierarchy – a matter which has a significant impact on the way that interpersonal communication unfolds and interpersonal relationships are established.

27.3.3 A Critical Discourse Approach

Critical Discourse Analysis (CDA) can also be used as a valuable lens through which to examine the hierarchies that affect interpersonal relationships in this setting (see Bloor and Bloor 2014; Cap 2018; Fairclough 2013). As a general rule, American culture assigns greater prestige to MDs than RNs – a view that is consistent with the hierarchical structure of most hospitals. Due to multiple factors, including legal liability, MDs are held accountable for healthcare outcomes to a greater extent than other members of a caregiving team. As Graham (2009) notes, however, there is often a 'knowledge hierarchy' that conflicts with this institutional hierarchy in cases where MDs who are early in their careers and therefore have limited experience have different assessments than RNs who have more years of experience and potentially greater medical knowledge.

In IDRs we see evidence of the hierarchical roles that different types of caregivers are expected to play regarding care decisions. The following excerpt occurs during the discussion of a patient whose care is being overseen by multiple physicians.

(4)
1	MD3:	Nobody really wants to say okay this is what it is and this is
2		what we're gonna do.
3	SW1:	Sure
4	SW2:	She's complex in every way [...]
5		From her personality to her social situation to her medical
6		situation.
7	MD3:	That's the perfect –
8	RN4:	– that's the one.

9	SW2:	The perfect home care patient [...]. And right. So she's set up
10		for whatever, whenever [the attending physician] decides.
11	MD3:	She – /??/ She's just – Basically it's up to us to decide. I mean,
12		everything else is set up and /???/
13	SW2:	You just write the home care orders. I've got notes in the
14		chart as to what needs to go there, okay?

In this case, the discourse reinforces the roles that different categories of caregivers are expected to play. As noted above, MDs are responsible for issuing discharge orders while social workers (SWs) are responsible for orchestrating a plan of care that can be implemented after the patient leaves. In this hospital, discharge orders include post-discharge instructions such as recommended activity level, follow-up plans and plans for home care. By telling MD2 to 'just write the home care orders' (line 13) followed by her statement that she has notes about what needs to go in them (line 14), SW2 is indirectly telling MD2 to leave a section of the orders blank that she will then fill in with the pertinent information. The statement implies that the orders will be signed by the MD and then completed later by the SW, without the MD necessarily being briefed on the full contents before the discharge actually occurs. In doing this, SW2 acknowledges the MD's expected role and responsibilities (e.g. signing discharge orders), but also her own role as the expert on post-discharge (i.e. home) care. This example, then, reinforces a potential difficulty with how different domains of care come together under institutional procedure and how active assessment and negotiation of the institutional responsibilities and relationships at play may be necessary.

The negotiation of relationships involved in deciding who is responsible for recording all pertinent information in the (official) medical chart was also confirmed in other (non-IDR) interactions. In these, multiple RNs stated that negotiating relationships with attending physicians, who had the medical experience, the confidence and the authority to trust RN evaluations and take their recommendations into account, was fundamentally different from interactions with less-experienced doctors. In an individual interview, one RN described an interaction with an Intern as follows:

(5)
RN5: This patient with Krohn's disease had abdominal pain and cramping, but no orders for meds. I approached the MD for medication orders. She kept saying she would do it and she didn't. The patient was on the bell constantly. I'm like, 'I can't make this physician write this order and I can't bug her about it any more than I already have'. **So I was just giving it**. And then, I finally approached her (the MD) a third time. She was very nice about it, but she just wasn't getting around to doing what I needed from her.

In this example, the RN acknowledges that she followed protocol in trying to get orders from the MD (since the MD is the one who is authorized to take this action). By using the word 'just' in 'I was just giving it', however, she acknowledges the fact that she was taking an action that deviated from sanctioned behaviour (which requires that MDs approve medical care decisions before they are implemented). In this case, she acknowledges that the MD was 'very nice about it' when the RN reported (post-facto) what she had done. The example thus points to the hierarchies in place and the problems that may be encountered on an everyday basis on a ward. It also, however, acknowledges that there are cases where the hierarchies are violated without necessarily generating negative responses.

Examples 4 and 5, while occurring at potential moments of conflict, in fact illustrate the potential for trusting relationships among caregivers. While the discourse in examples 1 to 3 illustrate cases where the MD's decisions are questioned/challenged, examples 4 and 5 illustrate the potential collaboration that can take place. The MD's statement in example 4 "it's up to us to decide" (line 11) comes immediately after all caregivers have voiced their agreement that the case is complex, and the "we" is inclusive (referring to all caregivers rather than only MDs). The inclusive pronoun sets the stage for SW2's request that the MD trust her to fill out the home care orders. As with signing a blank check and handing it over to another person, to some degree SW2's assertion that the MD should just write the orders indicates an atmosphere of cooperation in which she proposes that the MD trust her to complete the paperwork (which he has authorized) accurately and appropriately without his intervention.

In these cases, then, the discrepancy between the institutional hierarchy that assigns ultimate responsibility for all aspects of patient care to the physician, also entails some potential problems with regard to how different aspects of care are authorized and documented. This disconnect requires trust between MDs and other caregivers, and is a critical component of the ways that they negotiate interpersonal relationships (via interpersonal pragmatic strategies) in this institutional setting.

27.3.4 A Multimodal Approach

Yet another way to examine interactions between caregivers is to focus on multimodal aspects of the unfolding discourse (see e.g. Bateman 2017; Jewitt 2009; Jones 2013; Mondada 2019). In the case of IDRs, two elements that play a noteworthy role in the communicative event (in addition to speech) are physical positioning and the role of documentation. Both of these play an important role in the ways that hierarchies are displayed and maintained. Figure 27.1 illustrates the position of various caregivers seated around a table during weekly discharge rounds. Positioning around the table reflects participants' roles and the contributions they are expected/ allowed to make. Including awareness of physical positioning not only allows a richer understanding of the relational work being performed, it

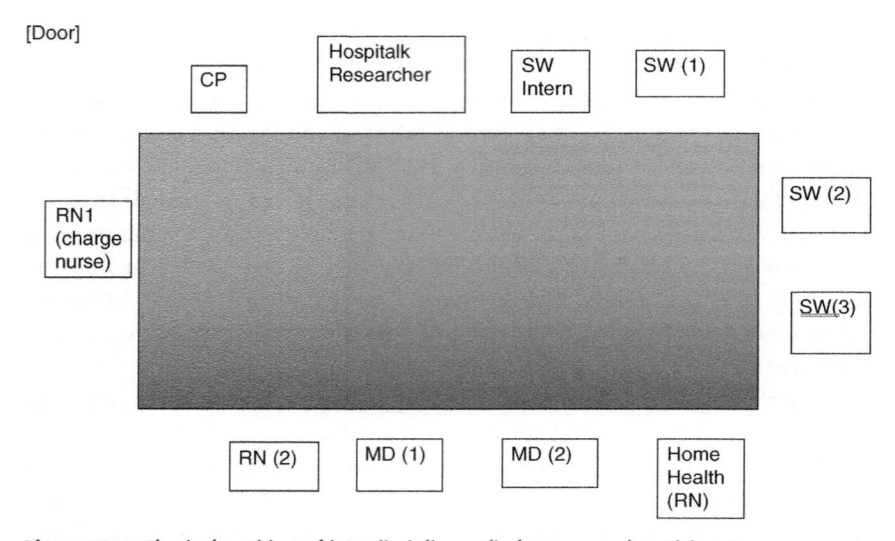

Figure 27.1 Physical position of interdisciplinary discharge round participants.

also provides insights into elements that affect multimodal communicative events like eye gaze and body posture.

In the interdisciplinary discharge rounds sessions included in this study, one RN (the charge nurse for the day) always sat at the head of the table and served as the 'conversation manager', controlling and distributing the conversational floor (Edelsky 1981; Goffman 1971). MDs who would be reporting on individual patients sat near the head of the table and always spoke first. The social workers normally sat at the opposite end of the table furthest from the door and gave their contributions/asked questions at the end of the discussion about a given patient.

In the rounds meeting that Figure 27.1 depicts, the participants are arrayed in such a way that the left end of the table (closest to the door) comprises those who give input on *medical treatments* while the right end of the table (furthest from the door) includes those individuals who plan the patient's care with regard to insurance resources, family and home situation. While both elements are important to patient care, it is the medical assessment and treatment that is given priority (since it is the medical care that ultimately determines whether a patient is ready for discharge regardless of that patient's insurance resources or home care situation). This physical positioning mirrors and/or creates separation between those who provide medical interventions/treatments (who are at the top of the institutional hierarchy) from those who arrange post-discharge care.

It is important to note that, while this arrangement was the norm, there were other factors that influenced physical positioning in other IDR meetings, such as arriving late (and therefore sitting nearer the door regardless of caregiving role). It is also important to note that this configuration was not the result of any procedure or guideline, but it did appear in multiple IDR sessions. Even if the configuration was not intentional, the clustering of types of caregivers together has the potential to play an important role in the ways that information is transferred and power is negotiated.

The interaction in example 6 follows a similar pattern to examples 1 to 3, in which the CP questions the MD in charge of a particular patient about a medication dose. In this case, the CP's gaze is an important element in our understanding of the roles and hierarchies at play.

(6)
1	CP:	I have a question. [Gazing at RN1, then gaze shifts to MD1]
2	RN1:	Yeah.
3	CP:	Her fentinoid? Um. Her total fentinoid level was kind of low.
4		[Gazing at MD1]
5	RN1:	Right.
6	CP:	Then I checked the albulin. The albulin is wa:y low. Have you
7		thought about checking for fentinoid on her to see how she's
8		doing? [Gaze stays on MD1]
9	MD2:	No. Um.
10	CP:	'Cause she's receiving IV 100 milligrams d.i. of the /???/
11	MD2:	What –
12	CP:	– When the albulin is low, usually 3/10/20 is
13		recommended.
14	MD2:	Ok.
15	CP:	To see how the patient is doing. Because the 3.6 of total /??/ doesn't
16		mean anything.. When the albulin is low.
17	MD2:	Ok.
18	CP:	So if you –
19	MD2:	– We'll – We'll check it out.

In this example, which occurs after the MD has given her report on the patient's status, the CP begins with the statement "I have a question" (line 1), which serves as a request for the conversational floor. She gazes at the RN while the request is granted (line 2), then shifts her gaze to the MD as she asks about the patient's fentinoid (line 4). The RN responds to the CP's question in line 5 ("Right"), which would ordinarily cause the CP to shift her gaze back to the RN as the speaker. The CP continues to gaze at the MD throughout the rest of this exchange, however, until the MD deflects her question by promising that the MDs managing the patient's care will "check it out" (line 19).

The gaze of the CP after the RN allocates the conversational floor (line 1) reinforces the expected roles within the team where MDs are the primary reporters of patient medical information. The RN, however, in responding "Right" to the CP's question (line 5) has selected herself as the appropriate responder. The fact that the CP's gaze stays on the MD instead of shifting to acknowledge the RNs claim (line 5) reflects the fact that MDs are expected to provide (and perhaps justify) the medical care decisions that have been made, even in cases where other caregivers (RNs) indicate that they may also have the knowledge to do so. The CP's ultimate goal appears to be to have the patient's medication dose re-evaluated or changed. She not only questions the dose, but also makes a declarative statement that a different dose is the norm (line 12) and then justifying her reasoning (line 15). Given the hierarchy in place, the charge nurse would be unable to authorize any changes in care that the CP's questions initiate, and it therefore makes sense from a strategic point of view for the CP to keep her gaze on the individual (MD) who has the power to accomplish her request.

In these cases, the multimodal factors of gaze/physical positioning reflect and reinforce the hierarchical structures that exist and therefore the negotiation of interpersonal relationships between the team members. These insights can thus be added to the previous observations gained from an Interactional Sociolinguistic Approach and Critical Discourse Analysis by adding further detail to linguistic interaction and complementing this with non-linguistic observations.

27.3.5 An Ethnographic Approach

Finally, an ethnographic approach is also well suited to examining interpersonal relationships. (For foundational concepts, see Hymes 1974; Schiffrin 1994.) An ethnographic perspective differs from an Interactional Sociolinguistic/Pragmatic perspective primarily with regard to expanding the scope of data and including a wider array of contextual factors. Using Hymes' (1974) SPEAKING grid, we see that, not only speech, but also physical objects in the environment, other (potential) participants, aspects of the physical environment such as furniture arrangement etc. all count as data that contribute to our analysis. In the data from the Hospitalk study, IDRs are only one piece of a much larger kaleidoscope of caregiver interactions, all of which determine and reinforce the roles and hierarchies at play. Ethnographic knowledge of the structure of hospitals, duties performed by various types of employees, hospital layout (e.g. general trauma floors vs oncology treatment floors), whether visitors are allowed and how frequently, types of treatment for different conditions, typical insurance coverage for various ailments, social work resources etc. – all of these influence the ways that relational work occurs.

On a general trauma floor, for example, patients are admitted with acute conditions and have relatively short stays before being discharged. This means that there is less opportunity to work extensively with a given patient to get a better understanding of concerns outside the purely symptomatic. For MDs, this often means that they focus on getting patients discharged as quickly as possible. Their assessments, however, are often based on their morning rounds, which comprise 10–15 minutes with a patient followed by a group discussion in the hallway outside the patient's room about treatment options moving forward. In contrast, RNs often work 10-hour shifts in which they are assigned four to five patients. Since they are responsible for seeing that all of the patient's needs are met (i.e. they are 'on call' to respond when a patient rings the call bell and ensure that the patient receives the care that was specified in the medical notes). The RN is also responsible for contacting the doctor if needed to address a medical situation. Because of the longer shifts and higher involvement of RNs, they have different knowledge of the patient's comprehensive situation (i.e. beyond the symptomatic and including aspects such as family relationships, patient fears and concerns etc.).

The amount of time spent with a patient or knowledge of a patient's resources after discharge fall outside the realm of what would count as 'traditional linguistic data', yet in this context they play a role in the ways that caregivers enact relational work with one another. In this hospital, an attending physician escorts medical interns[3] on 'morning rounds' in which they all enter each patient's room, assess his/her current condition, answer any questions the patient might ask, and then return to the hall. These rounds are used as one tool to train interns; after seeing the patient, the team (comprising attending physician, interns, and RN assigned to that patient) gathers in the hallway where the attending physician asks for diagnoses and treatment recommendations. Unlike IDRs, which function primarily as a place to report information, morning rounds are used for teaching purposes, and the only caregivers present are doctors and the RN who is caring for the patient on that given day. Examining these rounds, then, particularly in conjunction with the IDRs, allows us a more complex understanding of the relationships that are being negotiated.

In morning rounds, the interns arrange themselves in a circle facing the attending physician, who asks them questions and evaluates their responses. In most morning rounds sessions, the RN assigned to the patient stood outside the circle and to one side – present, but not physically within the circle. In one case, however, one RN physically stood and participated in the circle. She was the only RN observed to do this, but in these cases the interns moved away from her and did not look at her during the rounds discussion, even when she was commenting on the patient and held the conversational floor. In this case, the RN's body positioning and her willingness to participate verbally demonstrated her perception of her role as that of an equal to the interns. Their responses indicated a discomfort with this enactment of role understanding and power. In this case, the RN's perception of herself within a social hierarchy that positioned her as (at least) an equal to the medical students in terms of knowledge and ability to contribute, came into conflict with their reliance on the institutional hierarchy that placed them

---

[3] An intern is a doctor-in-training. After graduating from medical school, MDs work a 'residency' in the United States of America. The first year in their residency, these MDs are called interns, in subsequent years they are referred to as residents. Both groups are labeled "house staff" and are directed by an attending physician – an MD who has completed medical school, his/her residency, and is fully licensed to practice medicine.

above the RN. It is through negotiating this type of mismatch that relational work is accomplished (with either a positive or negative outcome).

In another instance, an RN enters the morning rounds discussion in support of an intern. In this case, the attending physician is discussing a patient with breast cancer who is also a drug addict. The team has seen the patient and discussed a problem with a previous surgery site. The Acting Intern (who oversees the case) has also confessed that he does not like the patient personally. When the discussion moves to whether to give the patient methadone (the patient's drug of addiction) for pain, the Acting Intern and the RN both discuss their similar reservations about not enabling the patient's addiction.

(7)
1	MD6:	She was screaming for it (methadone) at 6 this morning and
2		she was supposed to get it once a day. She got it late
3		yesterday afternoon. So.
4	[...]	
5	RN5:	Right. I wouldn't give it to her this time. I can't – I – really
6		have a problem with this patient, too.
7	MD10	(attending physician): Why?
8	RN:	[Because –
9	MD6:	[Too manipulative.
10	MD10:	Why? /???/ Why start a war on something you don't really
11		give a shit about? It's a control issue. Give a shit about
		controlling her pain.

In this instance, the RN and MD6 have a similar response to treating the patient's pain with a particular drug because they are both concerned about being manipulated by an addict who is simply trying to get more of the addictive substance. While the RN's participation in the rounds overall is minimal, in at least this instance, MD6 does not appear to be uncomfortable by the RN's presence and participation and the two together present a consistent concern to MD10 (the overseeing physician). MD6 and RN5 again present a united front when they both assert that they have comprehensive knowledge of the patient since they interact with her all day. Finally, the fact that MD10 dismisses both of their concerns together and instructs them both to focus on treating the patient's pain (lines 10 to 11), making no distinction between the two, further reinforces the MD/RN alignment created in this interaction.

In order to fully understand the interaction in example 7, ethnographic knowledge of the hospital structure is necessary. This interaction occurs on the oncology floor of the hospital (rather than either of the general trauma floors). The oncology floor in this hospital has more consistent teams of caregivers who work together, and patients receiving treatment often have longer or more frequent stays than patients on other floors. Throughout the course of this study, the overall climate of the oncology floor was more collaborative and cohesive than the general trauma floors, a fact which may explain the united front that MD6 and RN5 present. The ethnographic knowledge of the context and structure of the hospital, in this case can give us greater insights into the overall patterns of caregiver interactions by comparing sub-groups (i.e. different floors) to one another.

In the Hospitalk study, not only is the data complex, the potential approaches to analysing it are equally varied. If our goal is to explore how caregivers interact with one another so that we can improve their relations with one another (i.e. to assess their relational work), we must recognize the breadth of influences that affect the negotiation of roles and identities involved through a variety of methodologies and approaches, each of which could come under the umbrella of interpersonal pragmatics.

The mixed methodology and multiple data types in the Hospitalk Project allowed the researchers to gain a more holistic understanding of human relations and shows that the project is also well suited for an interpersonal pragmatic approach. While each of the methodologies illustrated here (as well as many others) has value in illuminating the formation of relationships in its own right, the cross-fertilization of methods and analytical practices that interpersonal pragmatics proposes has the potential to provide a much more comprehensive picture of the relational work being done.

27.4 Challenges and Opportunities

In the introduction, we highlighted that the research questions asked within interpersonal pragmatics include negotiations of how identities surface in texts and practices, how these patterns can be linked to societal norms, and how this shapes relationships. The focus on negotiations is important since the processes of identity construction and relationship creation are dynamic in nature. The definition of relational work entails a pointer to this dynamic nature in referring to the "construction, maintenance, reproduction and transformation of interpersonal relationships" (Locher and Watts 2008: 96). Working within interpersonal pragmatics, we believe that this perspective on the interpersonal and relational side of communication offers an enriching avenue of research since as a result we also can understand communication in general better.

However, this is not to say that the informational side of communication ought to be neglected in one's research design. In order to better understand how something is said, we also need to be aware of what is being said. In the Hospitalk Project briefly introduced in the previous section, this was accounted for by mixing Interactional Sociolinguistics with Critical Discourse Analysis, Multimodal Analysis and Ethnography.

Throughout this chapter, we have made a strong case for mixed methodologies in order to find the best ways to answer one's research questions. We thus explicitly propagate that scholars should be open to looking into related fields for inspiration and cross-pollination. The Hospitalk examples in Section 27.4 demonstrate one possibility for selection and combination of methodologies. Others are possible. For example in Locher (2017), the author works on written reflective writing texts by UK and Swiss medical students and doctors. The data is thus of a written, non-interactive nature, which, however, does not mean that there are not many voices involved which bear exploration from an interpersonal perspective. The methodology is mixed and draws on content analysis, corpus linguistics, genre analysis and narrative studies. The relational perspective comes to the fore throughout the different research steps and each methodological step is a stepping stone for the next. While content analysis, corpus linguistics, genre analysis and narrative studies are not necessarily associated with a relational lens, these methodologies can be used to discover and explore interpersonal issues nevertheless. Having said this, this mixing of methodologies also comes with its own challenges. For one, scholars cannot be current with all literature traditions to the same extent so that there is the danger of selective coverage, i.e. of missing out when you decide what to include and what to leave out. This challenge of breadth needs to be explicitly addressed when blending multiple perspectives.

From a writing perspective, merging different perspectives bears the risk of not having enough space within our traditional journal and chapter outlets to give justice to all the concepts to the same extent. Having readers who are unfamiliar with at least some of the theoretical bases for your study will either need to be told (which might add unmanageable length) or you may end up with extremely long lists of parenthetical citations that are cumbersome when providing the groundwork for your analysis. Scholars taking this approach thus need to find a good balance in how to address these concerns in their writings. Despite these challenges, which are true for any interdisciplinary work, we believe that the lens of interpersonal pragmatics is valuable and bears many possibilities for further research.

References

Bateman, J., Wildfeuer, J. and Hiippala, T. (2017). *Multimodality: Foundations, Research and Analysis – A Problem-Oriented Introduction*. New York: Mouton.

Bloor, M. and Bloor, T. (2014). Critical discourse analysis. In K. P. Schneider and A. Barron, eds., *Pragmatics of Discourse*. Berlin: Mouton de Gruyter, pp. 189–213.

Bousfield, D. (2008). *Impoliteness in Interaction*. Amsterdam: John Benjamins.

Bousfield, D. and Locher, M. A. (eds.). (2008). *Impoliteness in Language: Studies on Its Interplay with Power in Theory and Practice*. Berlin: Mouton de Gruyter.

Brown, P. and Levinson, S. C. (1978). Universals in language usage: Politeness phenomena. In E. N. Goody, ed., *Questions and Politeness*. Cambridge: Cambridge University Press, pp. 56–289.

Brown, P. and Levinson, S. C. (1987). *Politeness: Some Universals in Language Usage*. Cambridge: Cambridge University Press.

Bucholtz, M. and Hall, K. (2005). Identity and interaction: A sociocultural linguistic approach. *Discourse Studies*, 7(4–5), 585–614.

Cap, P. (2018). Critical discourse analysis. In A. H. Jucker, K. P. Schneider and W. Bublitz, eds., *Methods in Pragmatics*. Berlin: de Gruyter, pp. 425–52.

Coupland, N. (2007). *Style: Language Variation and Identity*. Cambridge: Cambridge University Press.

Culpeper, J. (2011). *Impoliteness: Using Language to Cause Offence*. Cambridge: Cambridge University Press.

Culpeper, J. and Kádár, D. (eds.). (2010). *Historical (Im)politeness*. Vol. 65. Bern, Switzerland: Peter Lang.

Davies, B. and Harré, R. (1990). Positioning: The discursive production of selves. *Journal for the Theory of Social Behaviour*, 20(1), 43–63.

Eckert, P. and McConnell-Ginet, S. (1992). Communities of practice: Where language, gender, and power all live. In K. Hall, M. Bucholtz and M. Birch, eds., *Locating Power: Proceedings of the Second Berkeley Women and Language Conference*. Berkeley, CA: Women and Language Group, pp. 89–99.

Edelsky, C. (1981). Who's got the floor? *Language and Society*, 10(3), 383–421.

Fairclough, N. (2013). *Critical Discourse Analysis: The Critical Study of Language*. New York: Routledge.

Fitzmaurice, S. (2010). Changes in the meanings of *politeness* in eighteenth-century England: Discourse analysis and historical evidence. In J. Culpeper and D. Kádár, eds., *Historical (Im)politeness*. Bern, Switzerland: Peter Lang, pp. 87–115.

Garcés-Conejos Blitvich, P. (2013). Introduction: Face, identity and im/politeness. Looking backward, moving forward: From Goffman to practice theory. *Journal of Politeness Research*, 9(1), 1–33.

Goffman, E. (1971). *Relations in Public*. New York: Harper and Row.

Goffman, E. (1974). *Frame Analysis: An Essay on the Organization of Experience*. Cambridge, MA: Harvard University Press.

Gordon, C. (2011). Gumperz and interactional sociolinguistics. In R. Wodak, B. Johnstone and P. Kerswill, eds., *The SAGE Handbook of Sociolinguistics*. Los Angeles, CA: SAGE, pp. 67–84.

Graham, S. L. (2007). Disagreeing to agree: Conflict, (im)politeness and identity in a computer-mediated community. *Journal of Pragmatics*, 39(4), 742–59.

Graham, S. L. (2008). A manual for impoliteness? The impact of the FAQ in an electronic community of practice. In D. Bousfield and M. A. Locher, eds., *Impoliteness in Language: Studies on Its Interplay with Power in Theory and Practice*. Berlin: Mouton de Gruyter, pp. 281–304.

Graham, S. L. (2009). Hospitalk: Politeness and hierarchical structures in interdisciplinary discharge rounds. *Journal of Politeness Research*, 5(1), 11–31.

Grice, H. P. (1975). Logic and conversation. In P. Cole and J. L. Morgan, eds., *Syntax and Semantics*, Vol. 3, *Speech Acts*. New York: Academic Press, pp. 41–58.

Hall, K. and Bucholtz, M. (2013). Epilogue: Facing identity. *Journal of Politeness Research*, 9(1), 123–132.

Haugh, M., Kádár, D. and Mills, S. (2013). Interpersonal pragmatics: Issues and debates. *Journal of Pragmatics*, 58, 1–11.

Hymes, D. (1974). *Foundations in Sociolinguistics: An Ethnographic Approach*. Philadelphia: University of Pennsylvania Press.

Jewitt, C. (ed.). (2009). *The Routledge Handbook of Multimodal Analysis*. New York: Routledge.

Jones, R. (2013). Multimodal discourse analysis. In C. E. Chapelle, ed., *The Encyclopedia of Applied Linguistics*. Oxford: Wiley-Blackwell, pp. 3992–6.

Lakoff, R. T. (1973). The logic of politeness, or minding your p's and q's. *Chicago Linguistics Society*, 9, 292–305.

Langlotz, A. and Locher, M. A. (2013). The role of emotions in relational work. *Journal of Pragmatics*, 58, 87–107.

Langlotz, A. and Locher, M. A. (2017). (Im)politeness and emotion. In J. Culpeper, M. Haugh and D. Z. Kádár, eds., *Palgrave Handbook of Linguistic (Im)Politeness*. London: Palgrave, pp. 287–322.

Larson, E., Hamilton, H. E. and Eisenberg, J. (1998). Hospitalk: An exploratory study to assess what is said and what is heard between physicians and nurses. *Clinical Performance and Quality Health Care*, 6(4), 183–9.

Lave, J. and Wenger, E. (1991). *Situated Learning: Legitimate Peripheral Participation*. Cambridge: Cambridge University Press.

Leech, G. N. (1983). *Principles of Pragmatics*. New York: Longman.

Levinson, S. C. (1992). Activity types and language. In P. Drew and J. Heritage, eds., *Talk at Work: Interaction in Institutional Settings*. Cambridge: Cambridge University Press, pp. 66–100.

Locher, M. A. (2008). Relational work, politeness and identity construction. In G. Antos, E. Ventola and T. Weber, eds., *Handbooks of Applied Linguistics*, Vol. 2, *Interpersonal Communication*. Berlin: Mouton de Gruyter, pp. 509–40.

Locher, M. A. (2011). Situated impoliteness: The interface between relational work and identity construction. In B. L. Davies, M. Haugh and A. J. Merrison, eds., *Situated Politeness*. New York: Continuum International, pp. 187–208.

Locher, M. A. (2013). Politeness. In C. E. Chapelle, ed., *The Encyclopedia of Applied Linguistics*. Oxford: Wiley-Blackwell, pp. 4457–63.

Locher, M. A. (2014). The relational aspect of language: Avenues of research. In S. Mergenthal and R. M. Nischik, eds., *Anglistentag 2013 Konstanz: Proceedings*. Trier: Wissenschaftlicher Verlag Trier, pp. 309–22.

Locher, M. A. (2015). Interpersonal pragmatics and its link to (im)politeness research. *Journal of Pragmatics*, 86, 5–10.

Locher, M. A. (2017). *Reflective Writing in Medical Practice: A Linguistic Perspective*. Bristol: Multilingual Matters.

Locher, M. A. and Graham, S. L. (2010a). Introduction to interpersonal pragmatics. In M. A. Locher and S. L. Graham, eds., *Interpersonal Pragmatics*. Berlin: Mouton, pp. 1–13.

Locher, M. A. and Graham, S. L. (eds.). (2010b). *Interpersonal Pragmatics*. Vol. 6. Berlin: Mouton.

Locher, M. A. and Schnurr, S. (2017). (Im)politeness in health settings. In J. Culpeper, M. Haugh and D. Kádár, eds., *Palgrave Handbook of Linguistic (Im)Politeness*. London: Palgrave, pp. 689–711.

Locher, M. A. and Thurnherr, F. (2017). Typing yourself healthy: Introduction to the special issue on language and health online. *Linguistics Online, 87*(8/17), 3–24.

Locher, M. A. and Watts, R. J. (2005). Politeness theory and relational work. *Journal of Politeness Research, 1*(1), 9–33.

Locher, M. A. and Watts, R. J. (2008). Relational work and impoliteness: Negotiating norms of linguistic behaviour. In D. Bousfield and M. A. Locher, eds., *Impoliteness in Language: Studies on Its Interplay with Power in Theory and Practice*. Berlin: Mouton de Gruyter, pp. 77–99.

Mondada, L. (2019). Contemporary issues in conversation analysis: Embodiment and materiality, multimodality and multisensoriality in social interaction. *Journal of Pragmatics, 145*, 47–62.

O'Driscoll, J. (2013). The role of language in interpersonal pragmatics. *Journal of Pragmatics, 58*, 170–81.

Rampton, B. (1995). *Crossing: Language and Ethnicity among Adolescents*. London: Longman.

Schiffrin, D. (1994). *Approaches to Discourse*. Malden, MA: Blackwell.

Spencer-Oatey, H. (2005). (Im)politeness, face and perceptions of rapport: Unpackaging their bases and interrelationships. *Journal of Politeness Research, 1*(1), 95–119.

Tannen, D. and Wallat, C. (1993). Interactive frames and knowledge schemas in interaction: Examples from a medical examination/interview. In D. Tannen, ed., *Framing in Discourse*. Oxford: Oxford University Press, pp. 57–76.

Watzlawick, P., Beavin, J. H. and Jackson, D. D. (1967). *Pragmatics of Human Communication: A Study of Interactional Patterns, Pathologies and Paradoxes*. New York: W. W. Norton.

28

Sociocognitive Pragmatics

Istvan Kecskes

28.1 Introduction

The sociocognitive approach (SCA) is an alternative to the two main lines of pragmatics research: linguistic-philosophical pragmatics and sociocultural-interactional pragmatics. What is common in these three lines of thinking is that they all originate from the Gricean pragmatics but they represent three different perspectives on it (cf. Horn and Kecskes 2013). Linguistic-philosophical pragmatics seeks to investigate speaker meaning within an utterance-based framework focusing mainly on linguistic constraints on language use. Socio-cultural interactional pragmatics, which is basically the main theoretical frame for sociopragmatics, maintains that pragmatics should include research into social and cultural constraints on language use as well. The sociocognitive approach (SCA) to pragmatics initiated by Kecskes (2008, 2010, 2014) integrates the pragmatic view of cooperation and the cognitive view of egocentrism and emphasizes that both cooperation and egocentrism are manifested in all phases of communication, albeit to varying extents.

Sociopragmatics is a subdiscipline of pragmatics while the sociocognitive approach to pragmatics is a third theoretical perspective in addition to linguistic-philosophical pragmatics and sociocultural-interactional pragmatics. Culpepper in Chapter 2 underlines that sociopragmatics is on the more social side of pragmatics, standing in contrast to the more linguistic side. This view puts more emphasis on the societal factors of pragmatics than on the linguistic and cognitive individual factors. This is where there is a basic difference between SCA and sociopragmatics. SCA places equal importance on the social and cognitive individual factors in pragmatics. The basic element of Gricean pragmatics is cooperation which represents the social side of communication. SCA emphasizes that individually privatized social experience that, most of the time, subconsciously motivates intention and communicative action is as important as the effect of the socio-cultural environment and social factors in which the interaction takes place. SCA claims that while (social) cooperation is an intention-directed practice that is governed by relevance, (individual) egocentrism is an attention-oriented trait dominated by salience which is a semiotic notion that refers to the relative importance or prominence of information and signs. SCA pulls together these seemingly antagonistic factors (cooperation and egocentrism) to explain production and comprehension in the communicative process.

What is especially important for the SCA is the interplay of three types of knowledge in meaning construction and comprehension: *collective prior knowledge, individual prior knowledge and actual situationally co-created knowledge* (Kecskes 2008, 2010, 2014). What is co-constructed and co-developed in practice contains prior social and material experience of the individual and the given speech community as well as situationally, socially constructed knowledge. Both sides are equally important. Practice can hardly work without the presence of relevant cultural mental models with which people process the observed practice, or which they use to actually create practice. Even when we pass along simple routines by sharing them in practice (e.g. how to use a razor or make coffee) we rely on the presence of a large amount of pre-existing knowledge. Social practices are conventionalized routines that may develop into expectations and norms. They are shared and conventional ways of doing social things in talk, such as the way transactions are completed in a store, phone calls are closed or servers take an order in a restaurant.

The social character of communication and knowledge transfer should not put community-of-practice theory at odds with individualistic approaches to knowledge. After all, social practices pass 'through the heads of people, and it is such heads that do the feeling, perceiving, thinking, and the like' (Bunge 1996:303). While communities of practice exist, members of those communities may still interpret shared practices differently. This is a key issue to understand what communication is all about. Collective knowledge exists but it is interpreted, "privatized" (subjectivized) differently by each individual (see Kecskes 2008, 2014). Collective cultural models are distributed to individuals in a privatized way. In order for members to share the meaning of a particular practice a huge amount of shared knowledge must already be present to assure common ground. Pragmatic theories have tried to describe the relationship of the individual and social factors by putting specific emphasis on the idealized social side, and focusing on cooperation, rapport and politeness.

In the following sections I will first discuss the idealized view of communication. Then I will analyse how communication is understood in the sociocognitive approach. Intention and salience are in the focus of Section 28.4. The final sections examine the effect of context and common ground.

28.2 The Idealized View of Communication in Pragmatics

Grice did in pragmatics what Chomsky did in linguistics but, of course from a different perspective and with a different goal in mind. While Chomsky focused on the linguistic system, Grice focused on language use. What is common in their approach is the idealization of a knowledge system (Chomsky) and the systematization of a usage system (Grice). Grice developed an idealized description of communication in order for us to better understand what actually happens when human beings communicate. That was an important step forward in the field of pragmatics. Science requires idealizations. For example, physicists or chemists often work with ideal models of reality that abstract from the existence of friction. Basically this kind of abstraction also happens when we analyse the semantics-pragmatics division. Carnap (1942) was quite specific about the relationship of the two by saying: "If in an investigation explicit reference is made to the speaker, or, to put it in more general terms, to the user of a language, then we assign it to the field of pragmatics.... If we abstract from the user of the language and analyze only the expressions and their designata, we are in the field of semantics" (Carnap 1942: 9). Carnap's approach clearly handles semantics as an abstraction of pragmatics because it is said to abstract away from the specific aspects of concrete discourse situations in which utterances are used. The theory of meaning, both in philosophy and linguistics, is no different. Basically all work in the theory of meaning presupposes an idealized model, which we can call the standard model. In that model various idealizations have been made to focus attention on the most central aspects of linguistic communication. So there is nothing wrong with idealization. But we should know that what happens in real life is not the idealized version of communication. The question is: can we offer something beyond just criticizing the ideal view? Can we offer an alternative approach or theory that absorbs and can explain "messy" communication too? Well, there have been attempts to that extent.

In a paper from 2010, I argued that recent research in pragmatics and related fields shows two dominant tendencies: an idealistic approach to communication and context-centredness. According to views dominated by these tendencies (RT and Neo-Griceans), communication is supposed to be a smooth process that is constituted by recipient design and intention recognition (e.g. Clark 1996; Grice 1989; Sperber and Wilson 1995; Capone 2020). The speaker's knowledge involves constructing a model of the hearer's knowledge relevant to the given situational context; conversely, the hearer's knowledge includes constructing a model of the speaker's knowledge relevant to the given situational context. The focus in this line of research is on the "positive" features of communication: cooperation, rapport, politeness.[1] The emphasis on the decisive role of context, socio-cultural factors and cooperation is overwhelming, while the role of the individual's prior experience, existing knowledge and egocentrism is almost completely ignored, although these two sides are not mutually exclusive.

The idealistic view on communication and the over-emphasis placed on context-dependency give a lopsided perspective on interactions by focusing

---

[1] Positive in a sense that ensures smooth communication and mutual understanding.

mainly on the positive features of the process. But, in fact, communication is more like a trial-and-error, try-and-try-again, process that is co-constructed by the participants. It appears to be a non-summative and emergent interactional achievement (Arundale 1999, 2008; Mey 2001; Kecskes and Mey 2008). Consequently, due attention should be paid to the less positive aspects of communication including breakdowns, misunderstandings, struggles and language-based aggression – features which are not unique, but seem to be as common in communication as are cooperation and politeness.

Similar criticism of idealized communication has been formulated by Beaver and Stanley (forthcoming) and Stanley (2018) but from a different perspective. In their co-authored work Beaver and Stanley isolated five idealizations (cooperativity, rationality, intentionality, alignment, propositionality) that are made by the vast majority of work in the theory of meaning, and argued that these idealizations are scientifically problematic and politically flawed. Stanley uses the critique of the standard model to develop a new programme for the theory of meaning, one that places at the centre of inquiry into linguistic communication precisely the features of communication (such as impoliteness, misunderstandings) that the idealizations of the standard model seem to almost deliberately occlude. Political discourse is the main focus of Beaver's and Stanley's programme.

What is common in Beaver and Stanley's and Kecskes' approach described above is that they both emphasize that the idealized Gricean theory cannot explain the messy reality of communication. However, while Beaver and Stanley make an attempt to change the Gricean approach and develop a new theory of "messy communication", SCA acknowledges the need for the ideal theory that provides us with a basic understanding of the communicative process. SCA uses the Gricean theory as a starting and reference point to describe and better understand what actually happens in communicative encounters. It has been developing an approach that does not want to be the counterpart of the ideal theory of communication. Rather it offers a theoretical frame that considers ideal and messy not like a dichotomy but a continuum with two hypothetical ends incorporating not only the Gricean theory but also the criticism of the Gricean approach by cognitive psychologists such as Barr and Keysar (2005), Giora (2003), Gibbs and Colston (2012) and Keysar (2007). These scholars claimed that speakers and hearers commonly violate their mutual knowledge when they produce and understand language. Their behaviour is called "egocentric" because it is rooted in the speakers' or hearers' own knowledge instead of in mutual knowledge. Other studies in cognitive psychology (e.g. Keysar and Bly 1995; Giora 2003; Keysar 2007), have shown that speakers and hearers are egocentric to a surprising degree, and that individual, egocentric endeavours of interlocutors play a much more decisive role, especially in the initial stages of production and comprehension than is envisioned by current pragmatic theories. This egocentric behaviour is rooted in speakers' and hearers' reliance more on their own knowledge than on mutual knowledge. People turn out to be poor estimators of what others know. Speakers usually underestimate the ambiguity and overestimate the effectiveness of their utterances (Keysar and Henly 2002).

Findings about the egocentric approach of interlocutors to communication have also been confirmed by Giora's (1997, 2003) Graded Salience Hypothesis and Kecskes' (2003, 2008) dynamic model of meaning. Interlocutors seem to consider their conversational experience more important than prevailing norms of informativeness. Giora's (2003) main argument is that knowledge of salient meanings plays a primary role in the process of using and comprehending language. She claimed that "privileged meanings, meanings foremost on our mind, affect comprehension and production primarily, regardless of context or literality" (Giora 2003: 103). Kecskes' (2008) dynamic model of meaning also emphasizes that what the speaker says relies on prior conversational experience, as reflected in lexical choices in production. Conversely, how the hearer understands what is said in the actual situational context depends on her prior conversational experience with the lexical items used in the speaker's utterances.

Cognitive psychologists claim that cooperation, relevance, and reliance on possible mutual knowledge come into play only after the speaker's egocentrism is satisfied and the hearer's egocentric, most salient interpretation is processed. Barr and Keysar (2005) argued that mutual knowledge is most likely implemented as a mechanism for detecting and correcting errors, rather than as an intrinsic, routine process of the language processor.

The studies mentioned above and many others (e.g. Giora 2003; Arundale 1999, 2008; Scheppers 2004) warrant some revision of traditional pragmatic theories on cooperation and common ground. However, a call for revision of the ideal abstraction should not mean its absolute denial as we already argued above. If we compare the pragmatic ideal version and the cognitive coordination approach, we may discover that these two approaches are not contradictory but complementary to each other. The ideal abstraction adopts a top-down approach, and produces a theoretical construct of pragmatic tenets that warrant successful communication in all cases. In contrast, the cognitive coordination view adopts a bottom-up approach which provides empirical evidence that supports a systematic interpretation of miscommunication. From a dialectical perspective cooperation and egocentrism are not conflicting, and the a priori mental state versus post facto emergence of common ground may converge to a set of integrated background knowledge for the interlocutors to rely on in pursuit of relatively smooth communication. So far no research has yet made an attempt to combine the two, at least to our knowledge.

Therefore, the aim of SCA is to eliminate the ostensible conflicts between common ground notions as held by the two different views, and propose an approach that integrates their considerations into a holistic concept that envisions a dialectical relationship between intention and attention in the construal of communication.

28.3 Communication in the Sociocognitive Approach

The sociocognitive approach (Kecskes 2008, 2010, 2012, 2014; Kecskes and Zhang 2009) emphasizes the complex role of socio-cultural and private mental models, explains how these are applied categorically and/or reflectively by individuals in response to socio-cultural environmental feedback mechanisms, and describes how this leads to and explains different meaning outcomes and knowledge transfer. In meaning construction and comprehension, individuals rely both on pre-existing encyclopaedic knowledge and knowledge created (emergent) in the process of interaction.

SCA is based on two important claims. First, speaker and hearer are equal participants in the communicative process. They both produce and comprehend, while relying on their most accessible and salient knowledge both in production and comprehension. They are not different people when they produce language and interpret language. They are the same person with the same mind-set, knowledge and skills. However, their goals and functions are different when acting as a speaker or as a hearer. Interlocutors should be considered as "complete" individuals with various cognitive states, with different commitments and with different interests and agenda. *One of the main differences between current pragmatic theories and SCA is that there is no "impoverished" speaker meaning in SCA.* The speaker utterance is a full proposition with pragmatic features reflecting the speaker's intention and preferences and expressing the speaker's commitment and egocentrism (in the cognitive sense). The proposition expressed is "underspecified" only from the hearer's perspective but not from the speaker's perspective.

Second, communication is a dynamic process, in which individuals are not only constrained by societal conditions but they also shape them at the same time. As a consequence, communication is characterized by the interplay of two sets of traits that are inseparable, mutually supportive, and interactive:

Individual traits:	*Social traits:*
prior experience	actual situational experience
salience	relevance
egocentrism	cooperation
attention	intention

Individual traits (prior experience → salience → egocentrism → attention) interact with societal traits (actual situational experience → relevance → cooperation → intention). Each trait is the consequence of the other. Prior experience results in salience which leads to egocentrism that drives attention. Intention is a cooperation-directed practice that is governed by relevance which (partly) depends on actual situational experience. In the SCA communication is considered the result of the interplay of intention and attention motivated by socio-cultural background that is privatized individually by interlocutors. The socio-cultural background is composed of environment (actual situational context in which the communication occurs), the encyclopaedic knowledge of interlocutors deriving from their "prior experience", tied to the linguistic expressions they use, and their "current experience", in which those expressions create and convey meaning. In communication we demonstrate the combination of our two sides. On the one hand, we cooperate by generating and formulating intention that is relevant to the given actual situational context. At the same time our egocentrism (prior experience) activates the most salient information to our attention in the construction (speaker) and comprehension (hearer) of utterances.

A pivotal element of SCA is *privatalization* (making something private, subjectivize something). Privatalization is the process through which the interlocutor "individualizes" the collective. S/he blends his/her prior experience with the actual situational (current) experience, and makes an individual understanding of collective experience. This approach is supported by the Durkheimian thought according to which cultural norms and models gain individual interpretation in concrete social actions and events (Durkheim 1982).

Before describing the main tenets of SCA, we have to make a clear distinction between SCA and Van Dijk's understanding of the sociocognitive view in language use. A major difference is that SCA is an extended utterance-centred pragmatic view, while Van Dijk's approach is a discursive view on communication. Van Dijk (2008)argues in his theory that it is not the social situation that influences (or is influenced by) discourse, but the way the participants define the situation. He goes further and claims that contexts are not some kind of objective conditions or direct cause, but rather (inter)subjective constructs designed and ongoingly updated in interaction by participants as members of groups and communities (Van Dijk 2008: 56). In Van Dijk's approach, everything is co-constructed by participants in the socio-cultural environment (context). Emphasis is placed on how meaning is co-constructed in the communicative process, but what is somewhat neglected is the "baggage" that the participants bring into the process based on their previous experience. SCA adopts a more dialectical perspective by considering communication a dynamic process in which individuals are not only constrained by societal conditions, but they also shape them at the same time. They rely not only on what they co-construct synchronically in the communicative process, but also on what is subconsciously motivated by their prior experience. It is very important for us to realize that there are social conditions and constraints (contexts) which have some objectivity from the perspective of individuals. So it is not that everything is always co-constructed in the actual situational context as claimed in Van Dijk's approach. Of course, there may always be slight differences in how individuals process those relatively objective societal factors based on their prior experience. *In SCA blending is considered the main driving force of interactions which is more than just a process of co-constructing*. It is combining the interlocutors' prior experience with the actual situational experience which creates a blend that is more than just a merger. In blending, the constituent parts are both distinguishable and indistinguishable from one another when needed. Blending incorporates the dynamic interplay of crossing (parts are distinguishable) and merging (parts are indistinguishable). Depending on the dynamic moves in the communicative process, either crossing or merging becomes dominant to some extent.

Now we will need to examine the main tenets of SCA that concern intention, salience, context and common ground.

28.4 Intention and Salience

28.4.1 Types of Intention

In the SCA the interplay of the cooperation-directed intention and the egocentrism governed attention is the main driving force in meaning production and comprehension. Cooperation means that attention is paid to others' intention. Attention is driven by individual egocentrism that is the result of salience.

Successful communication requires communicators to recognize that others' perspectives may differ from their own and that others may not always know what they mean (cf. Keysar and Henly 2002). As previously argued, the pragmatic view is concerned about intention while the cognitive view is more about attention. But in current pragmatic theories, there is no explicit explanation of the relations between the two. Relevance Theory defines relevance with respect to the effects of both attention and intention, but does not distinguish these two effects and never clarifies their relations explicitly. RT theoreticians claim that "an input (a sight, a sound, an utterance, a memory) is relevant to an individual when it connects with background information he has available to yield conclusions that matter to him" (Wilson and Sperber 2004: 608). SCA not only considers the centrality of intention in conversation, but also takes into account the dynamic process in which the intention can be an emergent effect of the conversation. So intention, on the one hand can be private, individual, pre-planned and a precursor to action, or somewhat abruptly planned or unplanned, or emergent, ad hoc generated in the course of communication. Here, it should be underlined that we are not talking about a trichotomy. Rather, *a priori intention, salience-charged intention* and *emergent intention* are three sides of the same phenomenon that may receive different emphasis at different points in the communicative process. When a conversation is started, the private and pre-planned nature of intention may be dominant, or a subconscious, salience-charged intention may occur. However, in the course of conversation the emergent and social nature of intention may come to the fore. These three sides of intention are always present; the question is only *to what extent* they are present at any given moment of the communicative process.

Intention with its three faces in SCA is more complicated than it is described in current pragmatic theories. From the speaker's perspective, intention is something that s/he bears in mind prior to the utterance, or something that is just abruptly formulated, usually subconsciously as a result of salience effect. Or alternatively, it is generated and/or co-constructed in the course of conversation and expressed in the form of utterances. From the hearer's or analyst's perspective, intention is something that is processed by the hearer simultaneously with the utterance, or after it has been completed.

Emergent intention is co-constructed by the participants in the dynamic flow of conversation. This dynamism is reflected in emerging utterances: they may be interrupted and started again. It is not only the context, but also the dynamism of the conversational flow and the process of formulating an utterance that likewise affect and change the intention. The following exchange between several international students demonstrates this point.

(1) HKM: Hong Kong Male, CZM: Chinese Male, TYF: Turkish Female; GMF: German Female; BIF: Bolivian Female

HKM: Do you think it's ... it's kind of difficult for you to make friends here with Americans?
CZM: Hmm.
HKM: ... enerally, you know ...
BSF: Yeah.
HKM: ... or it's more directly than it is in China ...
TYF: Yeah.
HKM: ... in Singapore or that ... it's more difficult ... What do you think so?
Why it's more difficult?
GMF: I am maybe, thinking, it's because ... I don't know ...
CZM: I would say the culture issue is the most thing. Because, you know,
the background is different and errh ... even the value is maybe different.
BIF: Yeah. But we have a lot of friends from other countries.
CZM: Aha.
BIF: and we ... we really met with each other ...
BNF: Yeah.
BIF: ... we aren't from Americans, I don't know why.
CZM: Oh.
BSF: The Americans all the times[2] I guess would know how are you but they
don't really want to know how you are.
CZM: Yeah.
BIF: Yeah. Yeah.

HKM starts the conversation with a *pre-planned intention* to talk about how to make friends here with Americans. When he sees that the exchange takes off with difficulties a *salience-triggered intention* leads to an utterance "or it's more directly than it is in China". with the goal to provoke responses. CZM's intention is to explain the issue with cultural differences. BIF's *emergent intention* is triggered by CZM's utterance. She wants to say that they (the international students) have many friends who are not Americans. In the course of this short encounter we have examples for each of the three types of intentions.

As we saw above, SCA adds a *third type of intention* in between a priori intention and emergent intention: *salience-charged intention*. How does that differ from the other two? As we discussed earlier salience leads to egocentrism that drives attention which refers to those cognitive resources available to interlocutors that make communication a conscious action. When intention is formed, expressed and interpreted in the process of communication, attention contributes to the various stages of the process in varying degrees. Three factors affect the salience of knowledge and ease of attentional processing in all stages: (1) interlocutors' knowledge based on prior experience; (2) frequency, familiarity, or conventionality of knowledge tied to the situation; and (3) the interlocutors' mental state and/or the availability of attentional resources. Based on these three factors, the knowledge most salient to the interlocutors in a particular situation is the information that is included in their knowledge base, is pertinent to the current situation, and is processed by the necessary attentional resources. No matter what mental state the interlocutors are in, and at which stage of the communication they are operating, the most salient knowledge will be available as a result of the interplay of these three factors.

A priori intention and emergent intention are somewhat controlled by the interlocutor. However, salience-charged intention is not necessarily. It is mostly subconscious and automatic, and can take the place of either of the other two intentions as we saw in example (1) where HKM referred to direct friend-making that was triggered by actual situational relevance and relied on prior pertinent information. Salience-charged intention means that interlocutors act under the influence of the most salient information that comes to their mind in the given actual situational context.

28.4.2 Linguistic Salience: Inter-label Hierarchy and Intra-label Hierarchy

Now we need to discuss how salience affects linguistic production and comprehension. The focus of SCA on the interlocutor as a speaker-hearer results in a claim according to which there is a difference in salience effect between scenarios when the interlocutor acts as speaker and when s/he acts as hearer (Kecskes 2008: 401). When a lexical unit (labelled for private context) is used by a speaker to produce an utterance, private contexts (prior experience of the speaker) attached to this lexical expression are activated top-down in a hierarchical order by salience. For the speaker, there is primarily an inter-label hierarchy (which item to select out of all possible), while for the hearer intra-label hierarchy (which out of all possible interpretations of the particular lexical item) hits first. The inter-label hierarchy operates in the first phase of production, when a speaker looks for words to express her/his intention. As a first step, s/he has to select words or expressions from a group of possibilities in order to express his/her communicative intention. This selection goes consciously or subconsciously. These words or expressions constitute a hierarchy from the best fit to those less suited to the idea s/he is trying to express. To explain how this works we will analyse an excerpt from a movie.

(2) This is an excerpt from the film "Coogan's Bluff":
(A man and a young woman are sitting in a restaurant after meal. The woman stands up and with a short move reaches for her purse.)
W: I have to be going.
M: (seeing that she reaches for her purse) What are you doing?
W: Dutch.
M: You are a girl, aren't you?
W: There have been rumors to that effect.
M: Sit back and act like one.
W: Oh, is that the way girls act in Arizona?

When the girl wants to leave, she says "I have to be going". She has had a number of choices (inter-label hierarchy) to express the same meaning: "I must go now", "it's time to go", "I have to leave" etc. There does not seem to be any particular reason for her to use "I have to be going". This is what has come to her mind first out of all possible choices.

When she wants to pay, the man expresses his objection by asking "what are you doing?" This hardly looks like salience effect. The man knew exactly what he wanted to say and how he wanted to say it. The girl perfectly understands what the man is referring to, so she tells him "Dutch", which means she wishes to pay for her share of the bill. Again, this does not look like salience effect rather a well-planned expression from the girl. The man has no difficulty in processing the expression although "Dutch" could mean a number of different things (language, people of the Netherlands). "To split the expense" is not very high on the intra-label hierarchy list. This is why it is important that salience effect and contextual effect run parallel as the Graded Salience Hypothesis (Giora 1997) says. A less salient meaning gets the right interpretation because of the contextual force.

The man indicates his dislike in a very indirect but still expressive way: "You are a girl, aren't you?" The inter-label hierarchy is governed in this instance by a well-planned recipient design. The girl's response shows that she follows where the man is getting to. Then the man hints at what he expects the girl to do: "Sit back and act like one". The intra-label hierarchy helps the girl identify the figurative meaning of "sit back" which means that he does not want her to pay the bill. This inductively developed sequence in the segment is a good example for elaborated recipient design where nothing is said directly, still there is no misunderstanding because the speaker adequately alerts the hearer to what he means.

28.4.3 Shaping Speaker's Utterance

As discussed earlier, recipient design in current pragmatic theories and conversational analysis, according to which the speaker constructs a model of the hearer's knowledge relevant to the given situational context, is considered too idealistic in SCA. Everyday communication appears to be a mixture of consciously designed and subconsciously, automatically and ad hoc generated utterances. The cognitive approach is not quite right when it claims that the initial planning of utterances ignores common ground, and that messages are adapted to addressees only when adjustments are required (Horton and Keysar 1996; Keysar et al. 1998). According to SCA what really happens is that there are usually both conscious planning and/or subconscious formulating in communicative encounters. Fitting words into actual situational contexts speakers are driven not only by the intent (conscious) that the hearer recognize what is meant as intended by the speaker (cooperation), but also by speaker individual salience that affects production subconsciously (egocentrism). However, the two factors affect the communicative process to a varying degree. The interplay of these social (recipient design) and individual (salience) factors shapes the communicative process. This can be demonstrated through the following two excerpts. In (3) I am going to use an excerpt from Sacks, but I have no intention of comparing SCA to conversational analysis. I just want to demonstrate how recipient design works.

(3) Sacks (1992: II: 147)
1   Ann: I'm reading one of uh Harold Sherman's books.
2   Bea: Mm hm,
3   Ann: I think we read one, one time, about life after death'r
4   something.
5   Bea: Mm hm,
6   Ann: And uh, this is How Tuh Make uh ESP Work For You.
7   Bea: Mm hm,
8   Ann: And it's excellent.
9   Bea: Well, when you get through [with it
10 Ann: [And he talks about-

According to the recipient design view, in order to succeed speakers must correctly express intended illocutionary acts by using appropriate words, and make their attempt in an adequate context. In this process speakers relate propositional contents to the world (actual situational context; audience) with the intention of establishing a correspondence between words and things from a certain direction of fit. This is what happened in the Sacks example (3). The description is a well-built inductive sequence by Ann. However, excerpt (4) from the movie "Angel Eyes" demonstrates an entirely different process which is a deductively built-up sequence (used in Kecskes 2017).

(4) A policewoman in uniform is driving the car, and the man sitting beside her is starring at her
PW: What?
M: I was trying to picture you without your clothes on.
PW: Excuse me?
M: Oh no, I did not mean like that. I am trying to picture your without your uniform.
PW: Okaay?
M: I mean, on your day off, you know, in regular clothes.

Here we see a deductive sequence where the speaker has something on his/her mind, and this intention is formulated abruptly, rather carelessly without specific planning, as seems to be the case in example (4). This excerpt demonstrates salience effect and supports the claim of cognitive psychologists according to which the initial planning of utterances ignores common ground (egocentric approach), and messages are adapted to addressees only when adjustments are required (Horton and Keysar 1996; Keysar and Henly 2002). It looks like *recipient design* usually requires an inductive process that is carefully planned, while *salience effect* generally appears in the form of a deductive process that may contain repairs and adjustments.

Let us return to example (4) and explore how salience effect works. Why were the man's first two attempts unsuccessful in the conversation? Subconscious salience affected how the man formulated his intention. As a result, the word selection was wrong. Why was word selection wrong? Because it was not directed by recipient design but was prompted by salience. "I was trying to picture you without your clothes on". Is this what the speaker wanted to say and mean? Yes, this is exactly what he wanted to mean but not necessarily what he wanted to say. Wording, i.e. expressing intention in words, is a tricky thing. Conceptualization is one thing, wording is another and meaning is a third one. There is no one-to-one relationship between any of the three.

Salience effect may result in subconscious, automatic formulation of intention that prompts expressions that are unwanted, uncontrolled and unfit for the actual situational context. This, of course, does not mean that salience effect always results in problematic utterances. Most of the time subconscious, automatic reactions prompt perfectly fine utterances. However, this was not the case in example (4) where prior context (sexual connotation encoded in the used expressions) cancelled the selective role of actual situational context. This leads us to the issue of context that has a unique interpretation in SCA.

28.5 Contextual Effects on Meaning

There are several different definitions of "context". What is common in these definitions is that they usually refer to the actual situational context of the linguistic sign(s) or utterance. Goodwin and Duranti (1992) argued that in semiotics, linguistics, sociology and anthropology, context usually refers to those objects or entities which surround a focal event, in these disciplines typically a communicative event, of some kind. Context is "a frame that surrounds the event and provides resources for its appropriate interpretation". According to George Yule (1996: 128), 'context' is "the physical environment in which a word is used". Most definitions stick to framing context as the actual situational background. Leech (1983: 13) argued that context refers to "any background knowledge assumed to be shared by speaker and hearer and which contributes to his interpretation of what speaker means by a given utterance". However, this is just one side of context. I usually refer to this side of context as "actual situational context" (Kecskes 2008, 2014) that combines linguistic and extra-linguistic factors in a given situational frame. My problem with this definition is that it refers only to "actual situational context" and there is no mention of "prior context", which is an important notion in SCA.

SCA claims that context is a dynamic construct that appears in different forms in language use both as a repository and/or trigger of knowledge. Consequently, it plays both a selective and a constitutive role. Several current theories of meaning (e.g. Coulson 2000; Croft 2000; Evans 2006) argue that meaning construction is primarily dependent on what I call actual situational context. SCA, however, points out that the meaning values of linguistic expressions, encapsulating prior contexts of experience, play as important a role in meaning construction and comprehension as actual situational context. *What SCA attempts to do is to bring together individual cognition with situated cognition.* This view recognizes the importance of an individual's background and biases (often prompted by prior contexts, prior experience) in information processing (Finkelstein et al. 2008; Starbuck and Milliken 1988), but at the same time it also suggests that the context in which individuals are situated is equally strong enough to direct attention and shape interpretation (Elsbach et al. 2005; Ocasio 1997). In other words, the context in which individuals are located has a major effect on what they notice and interpret as well as the actions they take. Based on this view, *SCA emphasizes that there are two sides of context: prior context and actual situational context.* Prior context is a repository of prior contextual experiences of individuals. Prior context makes things/information salient in a communicative encounter and actual situational context makes things/information relevant. Our experience is developed through the regularity of recurrent and similar situations which we tend to identify with given contexts and frames. The standard (prior recurring) context can be defined as a regular situation that we have repeated experience with, and about which we have expectations as to what will or will not happen, and on which we rely to understand and predict how the world around us works. Gumperz (1982: 138) says that utterances somehow carry with them their own context or project a context. Justifying Gumperz's stance, Levinson (2003) claimed that the message versus context opposition is misleading because the message can carry with it or forecast the context. Prior, reoccurring context may cancel the selective role of actual situational context. We can demonstrate this through an example taken from Culpeper (2009).

(5) Culpeper: Example 3: Creative deviation from the default context (cf. "mock impoliteness")
(Lawrence Dallaglio, former England Rugby captain, describing the very close family he grew up in)
"As Francesca and John left the house, she came back to give Mum a kiss and they said goodbye in the way they often did. "Bye, you bitch", Francesca said. "Get out of here, go on, you bitch", replied Mum. (*It's in the Blood: My Life*, 2007)".

Culpeper explained that the reason why the conversation between the mother and daughter does not hurt either of them is due to the context ("mock impoliteness"), meaning "actual situational context". However, a closer look at the example reveals that actual situational context plays hardly any role here. The real defining element is the strong effect of prior context, prior experience that overrides actual situational context: "they said goodbye in the way they often did". Reoccurring context, frequent use may neutralize the impolite conceptual load attached to expressions. This is exactly what happens here.

Context represents two sides of world knowledge: one that is already "encoded" with different strength in our mind (prior context) as declarative knowledge and the other (actual situational context) that is out there in the world occurring in situated conversational events (see Kecskes 2008). These two sides of world knowledge are interwoven and inseparable. Actual situational context is viewed through prior context, and vice versa, prior context is viewed through actual situational context when communication occurs. Their encounter creates a unique blend of knowledge that supports interpretation of linguistic signs and utterances. According to this approach, meaning is the result of the interplay of prior experience and current, actual situational experience. Prior experience that becomes declarative knowledge is tied to the meaning values of lexical units constituting utterances produced by interlocutors, while current experience is represented in the actual situational context (procedural knowledge) in which communication takes place, and which is interpreted (often differently) by interlocutors. Meaning formally expressed in the utterance is co-constructed "online" as a result of the interaction and mutual influence of the private contexts represented in the language of interlocutors and the actual situational context interpreted by interlocutors.

Now that we have discussed the two sides of context we should examine how this relates to common ground that basically unites salience with contextual relevance.

28.6 Common Ground

28.6.1 What Is Common Ground in SCA?

Common ground refers to the 'sum of all the information that people assume they share' (Clark 2009: 116) that may include worldviews, shared values, beliefs and situational context. Much of the success of natural language interaction is caused by the participants' mutual understanding of the circumstances surrounding the communication. The new element that SCA brings into the understanding of common ground is *emergent common ground*. In the SCA common ground is directly related to prior context (core common ground) and actual situational context (emergent common ground). The question is how much of this common ground is the result of prior experience (core) and how much of it is emergent, growing out of actual situational experience.

People usually infer "common ground" from their past conversations, their immediate surroundings and their shared cultural background and experience. In the SCA we distinguish between three components of the common ground: information that the participants share, understanding the situational context and relationships between the participants – knowledge about each other and trust and their mutual experience of the interaction. Similar prior contexts, prior experience and similar understanding of the actual situational context will build common ground. It is important to note that *we should not equate prior context with core common ground*. Prior context is a privatized understanding, privatized knowledge of the individual based on his/her prior experience. Common ground is assumed shared knowledge. Individual prior context is a part of core common ground that is assumed to be shared by interlocutors. The same way emergent common ground is that part of actual situational context that is assumed to be understood similarly by interlocutors in a given situation.

Clark et al (1983: 246) defined common ground as follows: "The speaker designs his utterance in such a way that he has good reason to believe that the addressees can readily and uniquely compute what he meant on the basis of the utterance along with the rest of their common ground". This means that the speaker assumes or estimates the common ground between speaker and hearer with respect to the utterance. Assumed common ground from the speaker's perspective is based on an assessment of the hearer's competence to understand the utterance. Common ground makes it possible for speakers to be economical in wording utterances in a given speech community.

Research in intercultural pragmatics (e.g. Kecskes 2014, 2019; Liu and You 2019; García-Gómez 2020), and the application of Kecskes' sociocognitive approach (e.g. Mildorf 2013; Macagno and Capone 2017; Macagno 2018) with its emphasis on emergent common ground, calls attention to the fact that current pragmatic theories (e.g. Stalnaker 2002; Clark and Brennan 1991; Clark 1996) may not be able to describe common ground in all its complexity because they usually consider much of common ground as the result of prior experience and pay less attention to the emergent side of common ground. In the meantime current cognitive research (e.g. Barr and Keysar 2005; Colston and Katz 2005) may have overestimated the egocentric behaviour of the dyads and argued for the dynamic emergent property of common ground while devaluing the overall significance of cooperation in the process of verbal communication and the prior experience-based side of common ground. The SCA attempts to eliminate this conflict and proposes to combine the two views into an integrated concept of common ground, in which both core common ground (assumed shared knowledge, a priori mental representation) and emergent common ground (emergent participant resource, post facto emergence through use) converge to construct a socio-cultural background for communication.

Both cognitive and pragmatic considerations described above are central to common ground. While attention (through salience, which is the cause for interlocutors' egocentrism) explains why emergent property unfolds, intention (through relevance, which is expressed in cooperation) explains why presumed shared knowledge is needed. Based on this way of thinking, in SCA common ground is perceived as an effort to merge the mental representation of shared knowledge that is present as declarative memory that we can activate, shared knowledge that we can seek, and rapport, as well as knowledge that we can create and co-construct in the communicative process. The core components (shared based on the knowledge of target language, let it be either L1 or L2) and emergent components join in the construction of common ground in all stages, although they may contribute to the construction process in different ways, in various degree, and in different phases of the communicative process as demonstrated by studies based on the application of SCA (e.g. Mildorf 2013; Macagno and Capone 2017; Macagno 2018; La Mantia 2018).

28.6.2 Nature and Dynamism of Common Ground

Core common ground is something like collective salience, a repertoire of knowledge that can be assumed to be shared among individuals of a speech community independent of the situational circumstances, such as when and where the conversation occurs or between whom it occurs. In contrast, emergent common ground is knowledge that is aroused, co-constructed and/or involved as shared enterprises in the particular situational context that pertains to the interlocutors exclusively. This contingent circumstance draws attention of the interlocutors to the same entities or states and, with the formation of particular intentions therein, activates some of their prior individual experiences that join in this intention-directed action.

Core common ground is a general assumption in two ways. First, although core common ground is relatively static and shared among people, it usually changes diachronically. During a certain period, say a couple of years, we may safely assume that interlocutors have access to relatively similar common knowledge because components of core common ground in a given speech community won't change dramatically. However, in the long run it definitely will change. People's social lives, both material and spiritual, will experience some changes over a long period of time, and as a consequence their core common ground will also be changed. For instance:

(6)   At the check-out desk in a department store: the customer is about to pay
      Sales associate: Credit or debit?
      Customer: Debit.

It is part of core common ground what the terms "credit" and "debit" refer to. No more words are need. However, 30 years ago that conversation would not have made much sense, since credit and debit cards did not exist as a part of core common ground.

Second, core common ground may also vary among different groups of individuals within a speech community. Types of shared knowledge may be determined by different factors such as geography, life style, educational, financial and racial factors. This fact may restrain the accessibility of certain elements of core common ground to particular groups only within that speech community.

Emergent common ground is assumptive in that it is contingent on the actual situational context, which reflects a synchronic change between common grounds in different situations. However, emergent common ground is not only new shared knowledge created in the course of communication but also the use and modification of shared prior knowledge or experience. There is a dialectical relationship between core common ground and emergent common ground. The core part may affect the formation of the emergent part in that it partly restricts the way the latter occurs. In many cases the emergent part may partly originate in instances of information that are predictable in the core part. On the other hand, the emergent part may contribute to the core part in that the contingent emergent part in a frequent ritual occurrence potentially becomes public disposition that belongs to the core part. In other words, core common ground and emergent common ground are two different components of assumed common ground, which are interconnected and inseparable.

In SCA there are three different ways intention and attention affect the construction of common ground in the process of communication (Kecskes and Zhang 2009). One is when the interlocutors activate mental representations of shared information that they already have as in example (7).

(7) Co-workers in the office talking about vacation
 Jim: Where will you leave Rex while you are away?
 Bill: Oh, he will be OK with our neighbors.

Both Jim and Bill know that they are talking about Bill's dog, Rex. Since this information is available to both, no more wording is needed.

The second way of constructing common ground is that interlocutors seek information that potentially facilitates communication as mutual knowledge. Before the speaker makes the seeking effort, the piece of information is not salient in the hearer as background underlying the upcoming conversation as in example (8).

(8)
 Sally: How are you planning to get to Hilton Head?
 Emma: Well, John has made the old Volvo ready.
 Sally: Oh, you still have that one.

Both Sally and Emma know what "old Volvo" refers to. However, its relevance had to be put forth in the given situation.

The third contribution to common ground is when the speaker brings in her private knowledge and makes it a part of CG. The speaker has some private information that she knows is non-accessible to the hearer. She adopts it as common ground in the belief that it facilitates the conversation and that the hearer will accept it willingly. Example (9) demonstrates this case.

(9) Andy is having his second date with Ashley in a restaurant.
 Andy: Ashley, would you be interested in coming with me to the office party on Saturday evening?
 Ashley: I am sorry, I cannot. I will need to pick up my sister at the airport.
 Andy: Oh, I did not know that you have a sister.

Since that was their second date Andy did not seem to know much about Ashley. She did not find it important so far to mention to Andy that she has a sister. That was her private matter. However, the situation made it necessary to make this private information part of common ground.

28.7 Summary and Future Research

SCA offers an alternative approach to communication. It does not idealize the communicative process, but rather makes an attempt to describe it with its ups and downs. SCA claims that individual egocentrism is just as part of human rationality as socially based cooperation is. It takes into account both the societal and individual factors in communication and considers interlocutors social beings searching for meaning with individual minds embedded in a socio-cultural collectivity.

The central idea in SCA is that there is a dialectical relationship between prior experience and actual situational experience that affect how meaning is created and interpreted. Prior experience results in salience which leads to egocentrism that drives attention. Intention is a cooperation-directed practice that is governed by relevance which (partly) depends on actual situational context.[2] As a result relatively static elements blend with ad hoc generated elements in meaning production and comprehension. Collective salience – emergent situational salience, a priori intention – emergent intention, and core common ground and emergent common ground are all essential elements of the dynamism of communication. But they function not as dichotomies. Rather they operate like continuums with constant movements between the two hypothetical ends of those continuums resulting in both positive and negative effects in dynamic communication such as cooperation – egocentrism, politeness – impoliteness, understanding – non-understanding, rapport – disaffection etc. One of the major projects of SCA within the confines of sociopragmatics should be the experimental and corpus-based investigation of the interplay of dynamic elements of communication such as collective salience and emergent situational salience or prior intention and emergent intention.

SCA considers assumed common ground a central factor of communication that pulls together the other crucial factors; intention, salience and context. The approach offers a transparent description of sources and components of common ground, and the specific manners in which they join to influence the process of communication. In the dynamic creation and constant updating of CG speakers are considered as "complete" individuals with different possible cognitive status, evaluating the emerging interaction through their own perspective. Constructing CG occurs within the interplay of intention and attention, and in turn the interplay of the two concepts is enacted on the socio-cultural background constructed by common ground. In this sense CG plays not only a regulative but also a constitutive role in communication. The approach of SCA to common ground has been in the centre of several studies in health communication (e.g. Biggi 2016; Rossi 2016), and dialogue research (e.g. Mildorf 2013; Macagno and Biggi 2017). Researchers focus on the interplay of core CG and emergent CG in different social interactions. This line of research feeds into and broadens the scope of sociopragmatics.

SCA as a theoretical frame has been playing a growing role in different branches of pragmatics research in general and sociopragmatics in

---

[2] Actual situational context makes things, events, pieces of knowledge, information, etc. relevant.

particular. Researchers apply SCA not only as a theoretical underpinning of their work but also develop it further by modifying or clarifying some of its tenets or claims. Several studies have focused on the interpretation of context and the dynamic model of meaning in the SCA (e.g. Romero-Trillo and Maguire 2011; Mildorf 2013; Moss 2013; Wojtaszek 2016), and intercultural communication (e.g. Kecskes 2014; Liu and You 2019). Khatib and Shakouri (2013) used SCA to explain certain processes in language acquisition. Some theoretical papers on issues like meaning argumentation, presupposition, and miscommunication also relied on SCA as theoretical support (e.g. Gil 2019; La Mantia 2018; Macagno and Capone 2017; Macagno 2018; Rossi 2016; Capone 2020; Martin de la Rosa and Romero 2019). These studies all underline the potential of SCA to explain important phenomena and processes in communication. However, the theory is still under development and needs further improvement.

References

Arundale, R. B. (1999). An alternative model and ideology of communication for an alternative to politeness theory. *Pragmatics, 9*, 119–54.

Arundale, R. B. (2008). Against (Gricean) intentions at the heart of human interaction. *Intercultural Pragmatics, 5*(2), 231–56.

Bandura, A. (1986). *Social Foundations of Thought and Action: A Social Cognitive Theory*. Englewood Cliffs, NJ: Prentice Hall.

Barr, D. J. and Keysar, B. (2005). Making sense of how we make sense: The paradox of egocentrism in language use. In H. Colston and A. Katz, eds., *Figurative Language Comprehension*. Mahwah, NJ: Lawrence Erlbaum, pp. 21–43.

Beaver, D. and Stanley, J. (forthcoming). *Hustle: The Politics of Language*. Princeton, NJ: Princeton University Press.

Bigi, S. (2016). *Communicating (with) Care: A Linguistic Approach to the Study of Doctor-Patient Interactions*. Amsterdam: IOS Press.

Bunge, M. (1996). *Finding Philosophy in Social Science*. New Haven, CT: Yale University Press.

Capone, A. (2020). Presuppositions as pragmemes: The case of exemplification acts. *Intercultural Pragmatics, 17*(1), 53–77.

Carnap, R. (1942). *Introduction to Semantics*. Cambridge, MA: Harvard University Press.

Clark, H. H. (1996). *Using Language*. Cambridge: Cambridge University Press.

Clark, H. H. (2009). Context and common ground. In J. L. Mey, ed., *Concise Encyclopedia of Pragmatics*. Oxford: Elsevier, pp. 116–19.

Clark, H. H. and Brennan, S. E. (1991). Grounding in communication. In L. B. Resnick, J. M. Levine and S.D. Teasley, eds., *Perspectives on Socially Shared Cognition*. Washington, DC: American Psychological Association, pp. 127–49.

Clark, H. H., Schreuder, R. and Buttrick, S. (1983). Common ground and the understanding of demonstrative reference. *Journal of Verbal Learning and Verbal Behavior, 22*, 245–58.

Colston, H. L. and Katz, A. N. (eds.). (2005). *Figurative Language Comprehension: Social and Cultural Influences*. Hillsdale, NJ: Erlbaum.

Coulson, S. (2000). *Semantic Leaps: Frame-Shifting and Conceptual Blending in Meaning-Construction*. Cambridge: Cambridge University Press.

Croft, W. (2000). *Explaining Language Change: An Evolutionary Approach*. London: Longman.

Culpeper, J. (2009). Impoliteness: Using and understanding the language of offence. ESRC project. www.lancs.ac.uk/fass/projects/impoliteness/.

Durkheim, E. (1982). *The Rules of Sociological Method*. New York: Simon and Schuster.

Elsbach, K. D., Barr, P. S. and Hargadon, A. B. (2005). Identifying situated cognition in organizations. *Organization Science, 16*(4), 422–33.

Evans, V. (2006). Lexical concepts, cognitive models and meaning construction. *Cognitive Linguistics, 17*(4), 491–534.

Finkelstein, S., Hambrick, D. C. and Cannella, B. (2008). *Strategic Leadership: Theory and Research on Executives, Top Management Teams, and Boards*. Oxford: Oxford University Press.

García-Gómez, A. (2020). Intercultural and interpersonal communication failures: Analyzing hostile interactions among British and Spanish university students on WhatsApp. *Intercultural Pragmatics, 17*(1), 27–53.

Garfinkel, H. (1967). *Studies in Ethnomethodology*. Englewood Cliffs, NJ: Prentice Hall.

Gibbs, R. and Colston, H. (2012). *Interpreting Figurative Meaning*. Cambridge: Cambridge University Press.

Gil, J. M. (2019). A relational account of communication on the basis of slips of the tongue. *Intercultural Pragmatics, 16*(2), 153–85.

Giora, R. (1997). Understanding figurative and literal language: The graded salience hypothesis. *Cognitive Linguistics, 7*, 183–206.

Giora, R. (2003). *On Our Mind: Salience, Context and Figurative Language*. Oxford: Oxford University Press.

Goodwin, C. and Duranti, A. (eds.). (1992). Rethinking context: An introduction. In A. Duranti and C. Goodwin, eds., *Rethinking Context: Language as an Interactive Phenomenon*. Cambridge: Cambridge University Press, pp. 1–42.

Grice, P. (1989). *Studies in the Way of Words*. Cambridge, MA: Harvard University Press.

Gumperz, J. (1982). *Discourse Strategies*. Cambridge: Cambridge University Press.

Horn, L. and Kecskes. I. (2013). Pragmatics, discourse and cognition. In A. Stephen, R. J. Moeschler and F. Reboul, eds., *The Language–Cognition Interface*. Geneva: Librairie Droz, pp. 353–75.

Horton, W. S. and Keysar, B. (1996). When do speakers take into account common ground? *Cognition, 59*, 91–117.

Kecskes, I. (2003). Szavak és helyzetmondatok értelmezése egy dinamikus jelentésmodell segitségével [Interpretation of words and situation-bound utterances in a dynamic model of meaning]. In *Általános Nyelvészeti Tanulmányok*. Budapest: Akadémiai Kiadó, pp. 79–105.

Kecskes, I. (2012). Is there anyone out there who is interested in the speaker? *Language and Dialogue*, 2(2), 285–99.

Kecskes, I. (2008). Dueling contexts: A dynamic model of meaning. *Journal of Pragmatics*, 40(3), 385–406.

Kecskes, I. (2010). The paradox of communication: A socio-cognitive approach. *Pragmatics and Society*, 1(1), 50–73.

Kecskes, I. (2014). *Intercultural Pragmatics*. Oxford: Oxford University Press.

Kecskes, I. (2017). The effect of salience on shaping speaker's utterance. *Reti, Saperi, Linguaggi*, 6(11), 5–32.

Kecskes, I. (2019). Impoverished pragmatics? The semantics–pragmatics interface from an intercultural perspective. *Intercultural Pragmatics*, 16(5), 489–517.

Kecskes, I. and Mey, J. (eds.). (2008). *Intention, Common Ground and the Egocentric Speaker-Hearer*. Berlin: Mouton de Gruyter.

Kecskes, I. and Zhang, F. (2009). Activating, seeking and creating common ground: A socio-cognitive approach. *Pragmatics and Cognition*, 17(2), 331–55.

Keysar, B., Barr, D. and Horton, W. (1998). The egocentric basis of language use: Insights from a processing approach. *Current Directions in Psychological Science*, 7(2), 46–50.

Keysar, B. (2007). Communication and miscommunication: The role of egocentric processes. *Intercultural Pragmatics*, 4(1), 71–84.

Keysar, B. and Bly, B. (1995). Intuitions of the transparency of idioms: Can one keep a secret by spilling the beans? *Journal of Memory and Language*, 34, 89–109.

Keysar, B. and Henly, A. (2002). Speakers' overestimation of their effectiveness. *Psychological Science*, 13, 207–12.

Khatib, M. and Shakouri, N. (2013). On situating the stance of socio-cognitive approach to language acquisition. *Theory and Practice in Language Studies*, 3(9), 1590–95.

La Mantia, F. (2018). Where is meaning going? Semantic potentials and enactive grammars. *Acta Structuralica*, 1, 89–113.

Leech, G. (1983). *Principles of Pragmatics*. London: Longman.

Levinson, S. C. (2003). Language and mind: Let's get the issues straight! In G. Dedre and S. Goldin-Meadow, eds., *Language in Mind: Advances in the Study of Language and Cognition*. Cambridge, MA: MIT Press, pp. 25–46.

Liu, P. and You, X. Y. (2019). Metapragmatic comments in web-based intercultural peer evaluation. *Intercultural Pragmatics*, 16(1), 57–85.

Macagno, F. (2018). A dialectical approach to presuppositions. *Intercultural Pragmatics*, 15(2), 291–313.

Macagno, F. and Capone, A. (2017). Presuppositions as cancellable inferences. In K. Allan, A. Capone and I. Kecskes, eds., *Pragmemes and Theories of Language Use*. Cham, Switzerland: Spinger, pp. 45–68.

Macagno, F. and Bigi, S. (2017). Analyzing the pragmatic structure of dialogues. *Discourse Studies, 19*(2), 148–68.

Martin de la Rosa, M. V. and Romero, E. D. (2019). A modality-based approach to the United Nations Security Council's ambiguous positioning in the resolutions on the Syrian armed conflict. *Intercultural Pragmatics, 16*(4), 363–89.

Mey, J. (2001). *Pragmatics: An Introduction.* 2nd ed. Malden, MA: Blackwell.

Mildorf, J. (2013). Reading fictional dialogue: Reflections on a cognitive-pragmatic reception theory. *Anglistik: International Journal of English Studies, 24*(2), 105–16.

Moss, M. (2013). Rhetoric and time: Cognition, culture and interaction. Unpublished PhD thesis, Chase Western University.

Ocasio W. (1997). Towards an attention-based view of the firm. *Strategic Management Journal, 18*, 187–206.

Romero-Trillo, J. and Maguire, L. (2011). Adaptive context: The fourth element of meaning. *International Review of Pragmatics, 3*, 228–41.

Rossi, M. G. (2016). Metaphors for patient education: A pragmatic-argumentative approach applying to the case of diabetes care. *Rivista Italiana di Filosofia del Linguaggio, 10*(2), 34–48.

Scheppers, F. (2004). Notes on the notions of 'communication' and 'intention' and the status of speaker and addressee in linguistics. *Circle of Linguistics Applied to Communication, 19*.

Sperber, D. and Wilson, D. (1995). *Relevance: Communication and Cognition.* 2nd ed. London: Blackwell.

Stalnaker, R. C. (2002). Common ground. *Linguistics and Philosophy, 25*, 701–21.

Stanley, J. (2018). Precis of how propaganda works. *Philosophy and Phenomenological Research, 96*(2), 470–74.

Starbuck, W. H. and Milliken, F. J. (1988). Executive's perceptual filters: What they notice and how they make sense. In D. C. Hambrick, ed., *The Executive Effect: Concepts and Methods for Studying Top Managers.* Greenwich, CT: JAI Press, pp. 35–65.

Van Dijk, T. (2008). *Discourse and Context: A Sociocognitive Approach.* Cambridge: Cambridge University Press.

Yule, G. (1996). *Pragmatics.* Oxford: Oxford University Press.

Wojtaszek, A. (2016). Multimodel integration in the perception of press advertisements within the dynamic model of meaning. *Lodz Papers in Pragmatics, 12*(1), 77–101.

29

Conversation Analysis and Sociopragmatics

Rebecca Clift and Michael Haugh

29.1 Introduction

In this chapter, we consider what methods and research in Conversation Analysis (CA) can bring to sociopragmatics. In focusing on the co-ordination of action and how particular interactional practices – both linguistic and embodied – implement actions, CA attempts to uncover the generic, context-free procedural infrastructure of interaction (Schegloff 2000) through close, case-by-case analysis of collections of recordings of naturally occurring, spontaneous interaction. With its origins in sociology (Sacks 1992a, 1992b) and its focus on the organization of social life, it does not accord language any principled primacy in the investigation of interaction. However, its methods have done more than any other to identify the means by which language is used in interaction. A central working principle in this respect has been the insistence that both 'position and composition' are equally constitutive in the understanding of action (Schegloff 1993: 121). That is, while linguistic theory has focused overwhelmingly on the compositional elements of language (Clift 2005) – the linguistic features of an utterance – CA gives equal analytic attention to the fact that the utterance has been produced after some specific other utterance in a particular interactional sequence; thus "the construction of talk designed to conduct a certain action is responsive to and bound up with the sequence in which the action is being done" (Drew 2018a: 66). In short, we cannot understand what a particular interactional resource is doing without considering its position within sequences of actions.

Sociopragmatics, in contrast, is located firmly within the analysis of language use. It attempts to uncover the interpersonal and contextual mechanisms driving the use of language by examining a range of different data types, including not only naturally occurring spoken interaction, but also fictional data, written data, and elicited data through a variety of different methods (discourse analytic, corpus-based and experimental methods). In essence, it involves person-centred analysis of language use, with a particular focus on meaning and the composition of linguistic units. Research in sociopragmatics thus emphasizes that we cannot understand what a particular linguistic unit is doing without considering who is using it and for what purposes (see Chapter 1).

At first glance CA and sociopragmatics may seem like quite distinct endeavours. They traditionally differ with respect to their main research questions, what counts as data and their method(s) of choice. Our argument in this chapter, however, is that the methods of CA can supply an alternative way into the concerns of sociopragmatics. Evans and Levinson (2009) make the point that "All sciences search for underlying regularities – that's the game, and there is no branch of linguistics ... that is not a player... The art is to find the highest level generalization that still has empirical 'bite'" (475); in giving us analytic traction on interactional data, CA arguably offers compelling empirical 'bite' through its methods. We begin, therefore, by focusing on the two aspects of CA method that make it so distinct from other approaches to language use: transcription and the use of collections. We then go on, in Section 29.3, to illustrate through two case studies how CA work can help us leverage open areas of ongoing interest in sociopragmatics. It is shown that the raison d'être of a CA-grounded approach is that sociopragmatic phenomena should emerge in the course of data analysis, rather than the analyst starting with pre-existing categories, such as particular speech acts or identities, and looking for instances of them in the data. We conclude by reflecting on the intersection between CA and sociopragmatics, and possible directions for future research.

29.2 The Fundamentals of CA Method: Transcription and Collections

In this section, we discuss two fundamental features of CA methods: the transcription of the data, and the organization of that data into collections of instances of interactional phenomena. We further examine how CA uses collections of instances to furnish both external (exogenous) and internal (endogenous) evidence to bring to bear on the analysis of interaction.

29.2.1 Transcription

Perhaps the most visibly distinctive aspect of CA method from all others in the social sciences is the detailed transcription of audio and/or video-recorded data. To those unfamiliar with these transcription conventions, the spelling of what is said, and the symbols – many repurposed from those in standard orthography – capturing how it is said, such details might initially appear to be dense and distracting.[1] However, to understand the rationale for such transcription is to grasp the fundamental basis of the CA approach: that is, that nothing in the data is treated *a priori* as irrelevant or inconsequential to the building of action in interaction. Sacks' (1984: 22) injunction that we proceed as if there is "order at all points" is pertinent here. The treatment of but one interactional phenomenon – laughter – provides us with useful insights into the CA approach to the transcription of data.

Gail Jefferson, tasked by Sacks with transcribing calls from the suicide helpline that furnished the earliest CA data, notes that in standard transcriptions "laughter is named, not quoted" (Jefferson 1985: 28), such as can be seen in line 7 in the transcript she cites below:

```
(1)   GTS:I:1:14, 1965
1        Ken:      And he came home and decided he was gonna play
2                  with his orchids from then on in.
3        Roger:    With his what?
4        Louise:   heh heh heh heh
5        Ken:      With his orchids. [He has an orchid-
6   ->   Roger                       [Oh heh hehheh
7   ->   Louise:   ((though bubbling laughter)) Playing with
8                  his organ yeah I thought the same thing!
9        Ken:      No hes got a great big [glass house-
10       Roger:                           [I can see him
11                 playing with his organ hehh hhhh
```
(Jefferson 1985: 28)

In this transcript, Louise's laughter at line 7 is conveyed much like a stage direction.

In contrast, Jefferson then offers us a re-transcription of the above extract using the conventions she devised for capturing interactional phenomena. The orthography is not standardized, but what Jefferson calls modified standard orthography, designed to look to the eye as it sounds to the ear (Schenkein 1978: xi). Note here at lines 8–9 the transition from what Jefferson calls 'naming' to 'quoting' in her treatment of the laughter:

```
(2)   GTS:I:2:33:R2, 1977
1        Ken:      An' e came home' n decided' e wz gonna play
2                  with iz o:rchids. from then on i:n.
3        Roger:    With iz what?
```

---

[1] We list the key CA transcription conventions we use in this chapter in an appendix. For a more detailed list of these conventions, see Jefferson (2004a). For a more extended account of CA transcription, see Hepburn and Bolden (2017).

```
4        Louise:   mh hih hih[huh
5        Ken:                [With iz orchids.==
6        Ken:      =Ee[ z got an orchi[id-
7  ->    Roger:    [Oh:.            [hehh[h a h ˙he:h]  ˙heh
8  ->    Louise:                              [heh huh.hh] PLAYN(h)
9                  W(h) IZ O(h) RN
10       Louise:   ya:h I[thought the [same
11       Roger:         [˙uh::       [˙hunhh ˙hh˙hh
12       Ken:                        [Cz eez gotta=
13                 =great big[gla:ss house]=
14       Roger              [I c' n s(h)ee]
15       Ken      =[(      )
16       Roger    =[im pl(h)ay with iz o(h)r(h)g(h)n uh
```

(Jefferson 1985: 29)

In now quoting, rather than naming, the laughter – that is, representing how it is produced rather than simply registering that it is produced – the transcript makes available (to us as analysts) the relationship of the laughter to the utterance. This second transcript captures the production of the laughter in only discrete portions of the utterance: that is, in the course of producing an obscenity. Jefferson (1985) subsequently reflects that:

> It may, then, be no happenstance occurrence that the explicit obscenity is slurred, and accountably slurred with the presence of laughter, and that the complex and delicate proposal about the authorship of the obscenity is produced with utter felicity, free of the laughter which can make an utterance difficult to "hear". (Jefferson 1985: 33)

As Jefferson then shows across a range of exemplars, both the presence and absence of laughter are salient; for the first time, laughter is not treated as an uncontrolled flooding out (Goffman 1961), but rather revealed as a methodical device that obscures delicate components of an utterance, thereby implicating a recipient in its authorship. It is the choice to transcribe in this way that makes Jefferson's analysis possible. And indeed her subsequent work on laughter (Jefferson 1979, 1984, 1985, 2004b; Jefferson et al. 1987), stands as a testament to her design of a transcription system which, in her words, "warrants and rewards more than a naming of (laughter's) occurrence" (Jefferson 1985: 34).

Laughter is one phenomenon among many that may not, at first glance at least, seem like a natural focus of sociopragmatics, except perhaps in the context of studies of conversational humour (see Chapter 20). However, Clift's (2012) study of laugh-infiltrated reported speech illustrates how paying close attention to the occurrence of laughter can have considerable analytical payoffs with respect to identifying the action accomplished by that turn (see Chapter 5), as well as for deepening our understanding of stance-taking (see Chapter 6) vis-à-vis speaker identities (see Chapter 15). Our more general point is that without detailed transcription of both linguistic and non-linguistic features, the analyst is left blind to the array of resources that can be deployed by participants in interaction.

29.2.2 Collections

Alongside the specific transcription system that makes CA so distinct, an emphasis on collections-based analysis lies at the roots of CA. Collecting numerous instances of a given phenomenon makes it possible for the analyst to identify the generic features of that phenomenon – to show that it is produced in a particular sequential environment. It is the use of collections that allows for technical *analysis* of the action being pursued rather than interpretation of what the speaker may (or may not) have meant on particular occasions. (For more on the distinction between action and linguistic meaning, see Clift 2016: 6–9.) In one of his earliest lectures, Sacks (1992a) displays this method in his observation that, in calls to a suicide helpline, callers at the beginning of their calls are often claiming to not be able to hear the call-taker; the following is one such instance of the three he gives:

```
(3)
1   A:   This is Mr. Smith, may I help you.
2   B:   I can't hear you.
3   A:   This is Mr. Smith.
4   B:   Smith.
```

(Sacks 1992a: 3)

The collection of instances he subsequently builds is evidence that there is potentially a systematic practice being deployed that has nothing to do with the claimed hearing problem. In solving the puzzle of what it is that these callers might be doing, Sacks demonstrates that it is a systematic solution to an interactional fix. It is a solution grounded in the apprehension of sequential position as critical to our understanding of action in interaction: the fact that, standardly, one gives one's name at the beginning of an encounter with an unfamiliar, and, further, that one gives one's name in response to the proffer of a name. But a caller in such a situation may have good reasons for remaining anonymous; so how to do so without being seen to do so? Sacks reasons that the callers claiming not to hear are finding a solution to the problem of "having to avoid giving one's name in response to the proffering of another's while not being seen to avoid doing so" (Clift 2014: 99). If Sacks' reasoning regarding this practice is grounded in an understanding of sequential position, his confidence that it is a systematic practice is grounded in his collection of instances. In this way, building and analysing a collection of cases enables the analyst to identify the context-free procedural infrastructure of interaction (i.e. the practice works in the same way across different contexts by different speakers), whilst also being able to account for context-sensitive deployment of the practice in question in particular situated contexts. Practices in CA thus encompass assemblages of compositional and positional features of (embodied) talk that make social actions recognizable and accountable to members across contexts (Garfinkel and Sacks 1970).

In seminal work on social action, Schegloff (1996, 1997) argues that these practices should be analysed through building collections so that one can establish not only what are canonical instances, but also boundary cases and deviant cases. Boundary cases refer to cases that look like an instance of the practice in question but turn out not to be canonical, while deviant cases refer to instances where there are particular interactional constraints that involve departures from the canonical pattern. The value of boundary cases is that they enable the analyst to zero in on the canonical compositional and positional features of that practice. The value of deviant cases is that they provide evidence that members do indeed orient to it as a practice. The classic instance of a deviant case is in one of the earliest CA collection-based studies, Schegloff's (1968) study of phone call openings. In this study, onr deviant instance out of 500 of a caller, rather than the recipient of a phone call, speaking first, prompted Schegloff to reconsider the rules of sequencing in conversational openings more generally – not just in telephone talk. As Clift and Raymond (2018) note, then, "the particular methodological power of collections is located just as much in what they throw into relief. In a search for 'empirical bite', the biting point for CA is not solely in the empirical skewing that emerges through collections of practices, but also in the deviant case: the exception that proves the rule" (94). So evidence for the existence of particular practices may be furnished by means of comparing instances within a collection. But the value of collections goes beyond the comparison of cases to encompass sequence-internal evidence from the data themselves.

29.2.3 External versus Internal Evidence in Collections

Two CA studies of requests in social interaction show the value of this bottom-up, data-driven method to the top-down concerns of sociopragmatics. Curl and Drew's (2008) study of the differential deployment of different formats for making requests – although not designed specifically as such – speaks to a central concern of sociopragmatics: politeness. Brown and Levinson's (1987) theory of politeness claims that, in contrast to direct requests, indirect requests reduce the potential threat to the recipient's negative face in making that request (Brown and Levinson 1987; cf. Chapter 16). Curl and Drew's (2008) focus is not 'indirect' versus 'direct' requests as such, or at least, it is not stated in such terms, but rather two distinct formats that were identified in their data: those requests prefaced by "would/could you" and those prefaced by "I wonder if". A key finding that emerged from their analysis was that these "different formats were used by speakers to display or claim *entitlement* to make a request and to display (or conversely, not acknowledge) an understanding of the *contingencies* associated with granting their requests" (Curl and Drew 2008: 139, emphasis added). In short, speakers implicitly claim a higher entitlement to make the request in question and that the contingencies of granting that request are low through the use of modal verbs (e.g. *can/could I ...*), while speakers index a lower entitlement to make the request and that there are greater contingencies associated with granting that request through the use of more contingent forms (e.g. *I wonder if ...*). The fact that these regularities hold across the two datasets investigated by Curl and Drew – one of phone calls amongst friends and family, the other a corpus of after-hours calls to family doctors – suggest that these orientations are generic and irrespective of individual differences.[2]

Curl and Drew's (2008) work on requests is a paradigmatic study of how exogenous evidence from language use can be gathered from collections revealing participant orientations. Such empirical skewing towards a particular format in a specific context is made possible by the existence of the parallel cases that constitute a collection. But the data can also itself supply endogenous evidence of participant orientations. In subsequent work on requests, Drew et al. (2013) use evidence from an analysis of a collection of self-repairs – where speakers work to address 'problems in speaking, hearing and understanding' (Schegloff et al. 1977: 361) – to illustrate how participants may orient to changing contingencies in selecting different formats for making those requests. In the following excerpt, Leslie is negotiating with her daughter Kath, who lives away at college, as to when Kath will return home for Christmas.

```
(4)    Field X(C)85:2:1:4
01     Les:   Anyway when d' you think you' d like
02            t' come home ↓love.
03            (.)
04     Kat:   Uh:m (.) we:ll Brad' s goin' down on Monday.
05            (0.7)
06     Les:   Monday we:ll ah-:hh .hh w:Monday we can' t manage
07            becuz (.) Granny' s ↓coming Monday.↓
08            (0.4)
09     Kat:   Oh;,
10            (0.5)
11  -> Kat:   C' d- (0.3) Dad couldn' t pick me up fr' m:: (.) ee-
12            even fr' m Glastonbury could' e
13     Les:   .hh I CAN' T HEAR you very well cz a' this damn
```

---

[2] As we discuss in the following section, this context-free procedural infrastructure can then be used to empirically ground a sociopragmatic analysis of "embodied actors, bringing the elements of the organization of human sociality just mentioned into being moment by moment in a particular place, with particular others, vying with or yielding to one another, etc." (Schegloff 2010: 38).

```
14                  machine tht's attached to this telephone say it
15                  again,
16    -> Kat:       Would it be possible: for Dad t' pick me up fr' m
17                  Glastonbury on [Monday.
18       Les:                     [Ye:s yes THAT would be ↓alright if
19                  the Kidwells don't mi↓:nd.
```
(Drew et al. 2013: 89–90)

In response to her mother's response that they can't pick up Kath on Monday (lines 6–7), Kath begins her request, in line 11, with a modal (i.e. "C'd"), but she then aborts this and replaces it with what is initially a negative declarative statement that is transformed ultimately into a negative interrogative by dint of the tag question ("Dad couldn't... could'e"). In so doing, Kath "more firmly orients to the difficulty that has arisen (that her father may not be able to collect her), and hence to the changed contingencies" (Drew et al. 2013: 90). Following a claim from her mother that she is unable to hear her properly (lines 13–15), Kath uses a more contingent form ("would it be possible") that orients to the compromise that her father pick her up from somewhere closer rather than driving all the way to her college (lines 16–17). This elicits conditional granting, in turn, from her mother (lines 18–19). The take-home point here is that there is data-internal evidence, through self-repair, of a speaker's orientation to a range of contingencies.

Thus we have both exogenous and endogenous evidence, through collections-based analysis, of a speaker's orientation to different contexts in her selection of specific formats. While not initially designed to interrogate the claims in Brown and Levinson (1987), the work in both Curl and Drew (2008) and Drew et al. (2013) serves to illuminate the claims made by politeness theory by reference to the data of actual language usage.

Having discussed two central features of CA method – transcription and collections – we now turn in the following section to pursue further the means by which CA has been able to lever open sociopragmatic concerns. We illustrate this through case studies focusing on two key topics in sociopragmatics: (1) speech acts and indirectness, and (2) inference and identity.

29.3 CA-Grounded Sociopragmatics

In CA-grounded sociopragmatics, the aim is for the analyst to pay close attention to the details of actual talk – through transcription – in order to identify recurrent patterns in the production of that talk – through collections. This approach is the classic 'bottom-up' approach to data which allows sociopragmatic phenomena to emerge in the course of data analysis, rather than, as with 'top-down' approaches, starting with pre-existing categories and searching for examples of them in data.[3] CA methods thus encourage us to go beyond the study of vernacularly named phenomena, while the procedural account of social action in CA offers a *tertium comparationis* or "common platform of reference" (Krzeszowski 1990: 15; cf. Chapters 10 and 31) across languages and cultures. A procedural account of social action is grounded in the analysis of the recurrent practices by which actions are interactionally accomplished. In identifying context-free, and thus potentially universal dimensions of this procedural infrastructure, CA thereby provides an empirical basis for comparative work across languages.[4]

CA-grounded approaches have been implemented in the study of a range of different sociopragmatic phenomena, including 'face' (e.g. Arundale 2010, 2020; Merrison 2011), 'politeness' (e.g. Cook 2006; Ferenčik 2007; Haugh 2013), 'impoliteness' (e.g. Bayraktaroğlu and Sifianou 2012; Hutchby 2008; Piirainen-Marsh 2005) and 'relationships' (e.g. Pomerantz and Mandelbaum 2005; Flint et al. 2019). In what follows we illustrate what methods in CA can offer through two case studies that touch upon selected areas of ongoing interest in sociopragmatics: indirectness and identities. We begin by considering how a CA-informed approach to action can recast our understanding of the kind of action categories familiar to us from Speech Act Theory (Austin [1962] 1975; Searle 1969; see also Chapter 5), and the implications of this for the study of what has traditionally come under the rubric of 'indirectness'. This motivates our subsequent discussion of the role played by identities in attributing inferences to talk.

29.3.1 Case Study 1: Social Action and Indirectness

Our first case study shows what is entailed in a CA-grounded approach to sociopragmatics by examining the following data extract. This piece of data has been selected because through it we can see very clearly how actions and indirectness are conceptualized in Speech Act Theory–based approaches to language use, and how CA methods can further illuminate the nature of the actions being prosecuted across the sequence. The excerpt comes from a longer exchange between Mike with his old music teacher Mary at her home. Prior to this excerpt, Mary, who is not particularly mobile, has prepared tea for them both, and they have both just sat down to start eating some biscuits:

---

[3] An important point of departure for our overview of CA-grounded sociopragmatics is the repeated cautioning in CA about the problems that can arise when we use vernacular categories in analysis. These include folk terms for actions in talk (e.g. requests, apologies etc.) and various kinds of identities (e.g. cultural, gender etc.). Schegloff (2017: 437), for instance, argues that we should not rely on such categories, except and insofar as they are invoked by the participants themselves as we attempt to start to make sense of our data. This is not to say, however, that systematic studies of how people talk about language use and its bearing on evaluations of it are not useful (see Chapter 7).

[4] For studies that illustrate recurrent aspects of the sequential organization of social action across a diverse range of languages; for instance, see Floyd et al. (2020) and Kendrick et al. (2020).

```
(5)     DS30007
1   Mary:   ((while eating)) ↑o:h.
2           (0.8)
3   Mike:   [°m:m°
4   Mary:   [I haven't gotten y' a bread 'n butter plate
5           but (0.4) there's one in the cupboard if you want one.
6   Mike:   mm? o::h ↑sho:uld be okay?
7   Mike:   I'll j[u-
8   Mary:        [yo[:u alright?]
9   Mike:           [d' yu d' yu ] do you want one?
10  Mary:   u::m yea- (.) well it's le- less messier actually.
11  Mike:   okay.
12  Mike:   ((gets up and goes to the kitchen))
13  Mary:   u:m. on the bottom shelf,
14  Mike:   mhm.
15  Mary:   just above the stove.
16  Mike:   ((takes two plates and brings them back to the table))
```
(adapted from Haugh 2017: 189)

The outcome of the above exchange is that Mike and Mary end up with plates from which to eat their biscuits. But how is this course of action achieved? A broad gloss of what is apparent in the above exchange might be that, in the course of 16 lines, Mary indirectly offers Mike a plate (line 5) by informing him as to where he can find one (as opposed to a direct offer, e.g. of the form 'would you like a plate?'), and Mike declines the offer (line 6), subsequently producing an indirect counter-offer to get a plate for her (line 9). Mary indirectly accepts the offer (line 10), whereupon Mike, under Mary's direction, finds the plates for them to use (line 16). It might be further proposed, under a pragmatic analysis, that Mary's initial indirect offer – 'there's [a bread and butter plate] in the cupboard if you want one' is subsequently revealed to be a 'hint'. Approaches grounded in the analysis of speech acts, such as Brown and Levinson's (1987) politeness theory would call such a strategy an 'off-record indirect request' for a plate – a strategy oriented to the addressee's 'negative face' and desire to preserve his autonomy in a way that, for example, 'Could you get us some plates?' would not. Such an account initially seems plausible to capture what we see in the exchange.

However, such an account only serves, in Schegloff's (2007) words, to "invoke and parlay 'the reader's experience' without having to offer a definition, explanation, or evidence" (88); 'offers' and 'requests' are familiar enough categories in both lay and Speech Act Theory terms, and the notions of 'direct' and 'indirect' utterances are derived from a purely compositional approach to the study of language, where the sole focus is trying to establish what an utterance might be doing with reference to its form. Such a 'top-down' gloss makes no reference, however, to the orientations of the participants *themselves* in deriving the categories of action. In contrast, CA's 'bottom-up' approach puts participants' own displayed understandings as shown in 'next turn' at the centre of the analysis. In so doing, it moves beyond a speech act focus on the individual utterance or utterance pair to focus on the wider interactional sequence in which the actions are embedded; it recognizes that utterances are not unilateral but necessarily implemented across sequences. Drew and Holt (1998) capture this focus in their observation that

> the components of a turn's construction – at whatever level of linguistic production – are connected with the activity which the turn is being designed to perform in the unfolding interactional sequence of which it is a part, and to the further development of which it contributes. (497)

The immediate upshot of focusing on the wider sequence of action in which any given turn is embedded is thus to see that, to take but one example, Mike's offer to get a plate at line 9 cannot but be seen in the context of his immediately prior declination of Mary's offer, and, as he moves to expand on and account for that declination (with what is projectably about to be something like 'I'll just do without'), Mary's line 8, in which she pursues the matter, having received a declination of her offer ('should be okay?', line 6), effectively disattends that declination. Note also the contrastive stress on 'want' in Mike's offer: 'do you want one', which topicalizes Mary's wishes, in contrast to Mary's prior topicalization of Mike's wishes in her original offer (line 5). A speech act analysis essentially shows us that this sequence contains two offers: Mary's (lines 4–5), which is declined, and Mike's (lines 9–10), which is accepted. But it cannot tell us the relationship between these offers, and the visible evidence that comes from the positioning of Mike's offer as it intersects with Mary's pursuit at line 8, that it is motivated by Mary's initial offer. In trying to understand actions in interaction we can, however, bring to bear on this extract evidence from collections-based CA work to show that there are specific practices in interaction that implement particular practices. In this respect, work by Kendrick and Drew (2016) on what they call 'recruitments' is directly pertinent to this exchange. Recruitments constitute a category of practices by which participants enlist assistance from others. Requests form one such subset. As the work of Curl and Drew (2008) shows, these involve a range of different request formats that are responsive to different interactional entitlements and contingencies. Enlisting assistance through reporting troubles, difficulties, needs or noticeable absences is another type of recruitment practice (Kendrick and Drew 2014). In this light, it is possible to hear Mary's 'I haven't gotten y'a bread 'n butter plate' (line 4), as clearly formulating an absence; and, in her pursuit of the matter even in the face of Mike's refusal, and in her ultimate assent to his offer in line 10, we can see evidence that the exchange above constitutes a recruitment sequence. In this respect, we can see that, by examining actions in their unfolding production across sequences, we can arrive at the general category of recruitments by working 'bottom-up', in reference to participants' own orientations, achieving empirical 'bite' – and in so doing, discover a hitherto unidentified category of action.

From the very beginning of the sequence, with the noticing that registers, with 'oh', a change-of-state from not-knowing to knowing in line 1 (Heritage 1984), CA also offers us a wealth of analytic leverage to open up what these two participants are doing beyond simply glossing it as an instance of "negative politeness". Let us take but one instance of a turn, line 10, Mary's acceptance of Mike's offer. In examining the moral and interpersonal implications of its occurrence here in this particular situated context, we attempt to further illustrate what detailed transcription and collections-based analysis of social action can bring to our understanding of 'indirectness'.

Mike's offer, in line 9, is delivered through a polar interrogative, that is, using what Curl (2006) terms a DYW (*do you want me to* ...?) syntactic form, which frames it as responsive to a problem that can be deduced from their prior talk: if Mike does not have a plate (line 4), then neither does Mary. While a speech act–based approach such as Brown and Levinson's (1987) politeness theory might just note that Mary accepts the offer, attention to the detail of the production of the talk, captured in the detail of the transcription, reveals that the acceptance of this offer is accomplished in anything but a straightforward manner. We note, for instance, the stretched 'U::m' that constitutes the immediate response, the cut-off on Mary's 'yea-', and then the micropause that follows in its wake, before Mary reformulates her turn, prefaced by 'well'. In the first instance, the initial 'U::m' in response to an offer, as the second part of an adjacency pair (Schegloff 2007) indicates that a dispreferred response is upcoming (Pomerantz 1984) – that is, a response which disaligns with the activity proposed in the first pair part (Schegloff 2007: 59). However, she then starts to produce a type-conforming response (Raymond 2003) – that is, a 'yes' response to a 'yes'-'no' question – but then subsequently initiates a self-repair to delete acceptance of the offer in favour of an account ("well it's less messier actually") (Robinson 2016). The latter is delivered through three key components: *well*-prefacing, the account itself and turn-final *actually*. Drawing on CA studies of collections of each of these components, it becomes evident that they are delicately shaping the benefactive stance Mary is enacting in the course of accepting Mike's offer (Clayman and Heritage 2014). For example, a study of *well*-prefaced responses to 'yes'-'no' questions by Schegloff and Lerner (2009), argues that turn-initial "well" is used in response to questions to indicate that the following answer will be non-straightforward, while accounts are canonically associated with dispreferred turn formats (Pomerantz and Heritage 2013). In this case, the account proposes the grounds for acceptance of this offer ("it's less messier") as based in a practical, rather than personal, motivation. Finally, a fine-grained analysis of "actually" in different positions within turns by Clift (2001) has found that turn-final "actually" is associated with responses that are counter to the attributed expectations of the recipient. So, through this highly granular turn design (Schegloff 2000), Mary construes herself not as the beneficiary of an offer that addresses a 'desire' to eat with a plate, but rather the beneficiary of an offer that addresses the 'trouble' that can be engendered by eating without a plate – a 'trouble' that applies as equally to Mike as it does to Mary. This non-straightforward response thus enacts a stance in which both her and Mike are beneficiaries, substituting for the one previously enacted by Mike in which she was the sole beneficiary of the plate-getting. In responding in this way, Mary also neatly avoids being held accountable for the agenda that Mike appears to be attributing to her prior inquiry in line 8 through his DYW-formatted offer in line 9 (Pomerantz 2017). In the course of this sequence, then, Mary recruits assistance from Mike, that is, he gets plates for them both, but accepts this assistance in such a way that leaves it equivocal as to whether that was her design all along. This has important moral implications, as Mike is positioned as volunteering, rather than being requested to offer, assistance (Haugh 2017).

A collection-based analysis of responses to prompted offers of the type identified above found, in English at least, that they were "recurrently granular, designed in ways that avoided straightforward acceptance of the offer of assistance" (Haugh 2017: 196). This reflects, in turn, an orientation to a complex set of entitlements and contingencies (Curl and Drew 2008), which the practice of prompting offers appears designed to address. We take these issues up in the next section – but register for now that examining the very different ways in which Mary and Mike choose to package their offers has revealed the means by which participants make choices from the interactional resources available to them. In Mary's choice to report an absence that establishes the relevance of a solution, that is, an offer of assistance (Kendrick and Drew 2014), and her acceptance of Mike's offer with a dispreferred turn format, we see the means by which participants conduct collaborative courses of action while remaining alert to the contingencies of their particular situation.

In sum, a CA perspective highlights the sequential practices by which participants make available and contest the ascription of actions – in the case above, the type of "offer" is Mary accepting here and the terms on which she is accepting that "offer" – and the interpersonal and moral implications of construing actions in just those ways (Haugh 2015, 2017, forthcoming). In short, what CA offers is an empirically grounded way of linking the accomplishment of action with what comes under the broader rubric of politeness in sociopragmatics. It thus offers a method of advancing Brown and Levinson's (1987) original insight that politeness is tied to the composition of particular speech acts (e.g. "bald-on-record imperatives" versus "off-record indirect requests") in a way that addresses the subsequent shift in sociopragmatics towards examining politeness in naturally occurring interaction rather than at the utterance level. What CA adds to this discursive turn in sociopragmatics is the insight that paying close attention to the position of utterances, in addition to their composition, is important. One way of doing so is through detailed transcription and collections-based analysis of the various practices by which actions are interactionally achieved.

29.3.2 Case Study 2: Inference and Identity

In the previous section we pointed to a complex set of entitlements and contingencies that may shape the actions being implemented across sequences. We noted in passing that Mary has prepared tea for Mike at her home, but did not otherwise invoke aspects of identity in the analysis of the exchange. However, participant orientations to one or another aspect of their identities is surely displayed in their positioning of themselves with respect to each other in talk; note, for example, that it is Mary who registers the absence of a plate, rather than Mike. But how do we systematically ground orientations to identity in talk? In what follows, we elaborate on these by reference to work in CA on identities in interaction, and the link between identity and a central feature of work in sociopragmatics: inference.

The link between identities and inference has long been noted in work on what Harvey Sacks termed membership categorization (Sacks 1972).[5] In a famous observation, Sacks notes that anyone hearing 'The X cried. The Y picked it up' – taken from a story told by a two-year-old (1992a: 243–51) could immediately grasp that 'X' would be the category 'baby' and 'Y' would be 'mummy' (rather than, say, 'dentist' and 'footballer', to take two random examples). Moreover, the 'mummy' is understood to be the 'mummy' of the 'baby', and picking up the baby is understood to be a consequence of the baby crying.[6] Such categories are thus inference-rich, a point also well noted by Levinson (2000) in his discussion of generalized conversational implicatures (see Chapter 3).

Consider, for example, how the referent of a pronoun is derived by inference in the following exchange, through familiarity with British social norms regarding husband-and-wife couples. Lesley's 'We have friends in Bristol' (line 3) allows her to refer subsequently to 'he' (lines 7 and 13) as one member of the invoked couple, the husband:

---

[5] See Clift (2016: 186–95) for an overview of how identity has been studied through the lens of the membership categorization device in CA.

[6] We note that 'Y' might now potentially include 'daddy' reflecting the ways in which inferences from categories can be shaped by changing social norms.

(6) Holt 2:3
1   Les   ..hh (.) Uhm (0.3) .tch Well I don't know how
2   that went, .h uh (.) It's just thet I wondered if he
3 →   hasn:' t (0.3) uh we have **friends in Bristol**
4   Mar   Ye:s?
5   Les   who:- (.) uh: thet u- had the same experience.
6   Mar   Oh↑::.
7 → Les   And they uhm: .t (0.2) .hh **He** worked f' r a printing an:'
8   paper (0.9) uh firm [u-
9   Mar   [Ye:s,
10   Les   uh[:- which ih puh- uh: part' v the Paige Group.
11   Mar   [Yeh,
12   (.)
13 → Les   .hh And **he** now has: u- a:: um (1.1) I don' t think you' d
14   call it a consultancy (0.2) They find positions for
15   people: in the printing'n paper industry:,
                                    (Kitzinger 2005: 249)

'He', then, is derived by pragmatic inference; and, as the sequence shows, the recipient displays no trouble in accessing the referent (as displayed in her 'Yes' in line 9, rather than, say, 'Who?'). We thus have evidence in the data itself of the inference-generating nature of membership categories.

The ways in which orientations to particular category labels can shape sequences of action is further brought out by the work of Kitzinger and Mandelbaum (2013) who investigate how the categories 'expert' as distinct from the 'layperson' are invoked across two sequences of action. Expectable sets of knowledge and competencies are part of the attribution of category membership. In the following extract, the call-taker on a Birth Crisis helpline uses the term 'doulas' (line 4), but adumbrates it with an inbreath and produces it with try-marking, that is, upward intonation (Sacks and Schegloff 1979), and then checks the caller's understanding of the term ('D'you know what doulas are', lines 4–6), thus showing her understanding that she is not talking to someone occupying the identity category 'childbirth expert':

(7) (CT = call-taker on a Birth Crisis helpline, here listing the occupations of the other call-takers servicing the helpline. DAW is the caller)
1   CT   I mean they' re N-C-T teache:rs a:[nd] u:m=
2   DAW   [yeah]
3   CT   .hhhhh post-natal (.) people' n breastfeeding
4 →   people' n [.hhhh] doulas? D' you know what=.
5   [Yes]
6   CT   =doulas are.

```
7      DAW   No:.=
8      CT    =Well they offer (.) woman-to-woman care in childbirth
9            along wi- you know just being another woman friend.
```
(Kitzinger and Mandelbaum 2013: 6)

The call-taker's decision to check her recipient's familiarity with the term is clearly justified in this case, and the sequence gets further expanded as the call-taker provides an explanation (lines 8–9). Compare this sequence, expanded in its course with question and answer at lines 4–5, with the following use of the same term, used with no understanding check by the speaker – a confidence endorsed by the recipient:

```
(8)    (Pau=Caller to Birth Crisis Helpline; CT=Call-taker)
1      Pau   Hi:: uhm (.) I wonder if you could help
2   →        me.=I'm working as a doula i[n (.)] in=
3      CT                                 [mm hm]
4      Pau   =West London and (.) a baby has just die:d.
5      CT    Oh I'm so so:rry:. Tell me about it.
```
(Kitzinger and Mandelbaum 2013: 7)

Here, the announcement in line 4, 'a baby has just died', gets immediate condolences in the next turn, and the term 'doula' is not treated as problematic by either party, with the call-taker receipting the term with a continuer in line 3. We can thus see that the orientation to one or another category – 'expert' or 'layperson' has a consequential effect on the progression of the sequence. In (7) it is temporarily halted; in (8) it is not. Note, in particular, that nowhere are such categories explicitly named, but rather implicitly invoked through speakers' orientations. Thus, rather than imposing pre-existing categories onto the data, CA shows the relevance and salience of identity categories to participants through the talk itself.

In a ground-breaking study of identity in CA, Raymond and Heritage (2006: 681) note that: "there can be direct links between the identities of participants and the rights and responsibilities associated with those identities that are directly implicated in practices of speaking". Raymond and Heritage demonstrate these links by reference to their work on epistemic rights in interaction, in which they show how the producers of first and second assessments[7] in talk can, through particular grammatical practices, index the relative primacy and subordination of their assessments relative to that of co-participants. So, note how in the exchange from a phone call below, Jenny's assessment in line 1 of Vera's son and his family, 'They're a lovely family now" is appended, turn-finally,

---

[7] First assessments are those that initiate sequences, while second assessments are responsive to a (just) prior assessment.

with a tag question, and is met, in line 2, by a confirmation plus an agreement from Vera ("They are, yes"):

(9)   Rahman: B:2: JV(14):4
(Jenny and Vera are talking about Vera's son Bill, his wife Jean, and their children)
```
1 → Jen:  They're [a lovely family now aren't [they.
2 → Ver:          [°Mm:.°                     [They
3                                      are: ye[s.
4     Jen:                                   [eeYe[s::,
5     Ver:                                        [Yes,
6     Jen:  Mm: All they need now is a little girl tih
7           complete i:t.
```

As Heritage and Raymond (2005) make clear, the syntactic form of lines 1 and 2–3 make specific claims vis-à-vis the rights of their speakers to make their relative assessments. Heritage and Raymond show that the speaker going first with an assessment by default claims primary rights to assess, and the speaker going second, by the same token, claims subordinate rights to make that assessment. But speakers in those positions can upgrade or downgrade those claims by means of particular grammatical resources. In excerpt (9), Jenny's first position assessment ('They're a lovely family now') is downgraded by means of the tag question, which transforms the declarative format into an interrogative in asking her recipient for confirmation; in doing so, Jenny cedes epistemic primacy to Vera. In turn, although Vera is in second position with respect to the assessment, she upgrades her rights to assess by producing a confirmation ('they are'), followed by an agreement ('yes'). As Heritage and Raymond (2005: 23) note, in treating confirming as the priority, a speaker can propose that one held this position prior to, and independently of, her co-participant. What the exchange above thus shows us is a speaker in first position downgrading her rights to assess and a speaker in second position upgrading hers. By negotiating their respective rights to assess the family, these two speakers show the relevance to themselves of particular identity categories. As in examples (7) and (8), nowhere is the relevant category explicitly invoked or referred to, but the relevance of Vera's identity as 'grandparent' is, as Raymond and Heritage (2006) make clear, indexed throughout the conversation.

In this way, then, CA finds, in the details of the talk itself, participants' own orientations to particular category memberships. The role of identities in generating inferences about who knows what, who has more rights to know that and so forth, is empirically grounded in detailed collections-based analysis of the practices by which participants make such inferences recognizable and relevant to each other. The notion of epistemic rights may be as abstract a concept as politeness, but this 'bottom-up' method of data analysis allows us to achieve 'empirical bite', as part of the highest-level generalization demanded of all science.

29.4 Conclusion

While CA's place with respect to pragmatics has sometimes been contested, we have argued in this chapter that detailed transcription and collections-based analysis can contribute to leveraging open important areas of interest in sociopragmatics.

One important insight from CA is that underlying order in the ways in which sociopragmatic phenomena are interactionally accomplished can be found through detailed case-by-case analysis. While work in sociopragmatics often favours distributional analyses that investigate correlations between particular linguistic formats and sociopragmatic variables, CA offers a methodological alternative in its focus on the analysis of collections of individual cases. Analysing the idiosyncratic details of individual cases may seem to be moving us a long way from achieving the kind of empirical bite that is the aim of all scientific endeavour. However, as Jefferson (2002: 1377) argues, when "one begins to work with the materials on a case-by-case basis – where one might think that the further into the details one gets the murkier things become ... in fact the manifest order intensifies". A second key insight from CA is the importance of paying attention to *sequential* context as part of the broader attention to context in sociopragmatics. While in pragmatics there is considerable emphasis placed on the intentions of speakers in analysing what is meant, in CA "the focus shifts from speakers' intentions – the implication(s) that a speaker may (putatively) have intended in uttering a sentence – to the implications that recipients find in or attribute to a speaker's utterance in an empirical – i.e. sequential – context" (Drew 2018b: 244). A third overarching insight from CA for sociopragmatics is the importance of making discoveries through examining data in a bottom-up fashion in the first instance, not by assuming the necessary relevance of politeness, identity or other sociopragmatic touchstones in a particular situated context. The relevance of such issues emerges from the data and is discovered in it.

Looking forward, then, how might CA continue to productively inform sociopragmatics? Over the past decade, it can be seen that CA and sociopragmatics have been simultaneously converging and diverging as disciplines. On the one hand, the two fields are converging in calls to draw from a more diverse range of methods. The methodological distinctions that distinguish CA from pragmatics are arguably being challenged, as there are increasing attempts to bring other methods into CA. On the other hand, CA is increasingly moving towards multimodal analyses of interaction that do not privilege language in that analysis (Mondada

2019), thus moving away from the central focus placed on language use in pragmatics. We would suggest that the middle ground mediating between CA and sociopragmatics is increasingly likely to lie in the growth of interactional linguistics (Couper-Kuhlen and Selting 2018), and the push for increased methodological eclecticism within CA itself (Kendrick 2017). While they will no doubt continue to remain distinct endeavours, this does not mean to say, as Schegloff (2010) has previously argued, that a mutually beneficial fellowship between them cannot be cultivated.

Appendix: Key CA Transcription Conventions

[ ]	overlapping speech
(0.5)	gap (in tenths of a second)
(.)	micropause
.	falling or final intonation
,	'continuing' intonation
=	latched utterances
?	rising intonation
↓ ↑	sharply falling/rising intonation
underlining	contrastive stress or emphasis
:	elongation of vowel or consonant sound
-	word cut-off
CAPS	markedly louder
° °	markedly soft
.hhh	in-breathing
(hh)	interpolated laughter/aspiration
> <	talk is compressed or rushed
< >	talk is markedly slowed or drawn out

References

Arundale, R. B. (2010). Constituting face in conversation: Face, facework, and interactional achievement. *Journal of Pragmatics*, 42, 2078–2105.

Arundale, R. B. (2020). *Communicating and Relating: Constituting Face in Everyday Interacting*. Oxford: Oxford University Press.

Austin, J. L. ([1962] 1975). *How to Do Things with Words*. 2nd ed. Edited by J. O. Urmson and M. Sbisà. Cambridge, MA: Harvard University Press.

Bayraktaroğlu, A. and Sifianou, M. (2012). The iron fist in a velvet glove: How politeness can contribute to impoliteness. *Journal of Politeness Research, 8*(2), 143–60.

Brown, P. and Levinson, S. (1987). *Politeness: Some Universals in Language Usage*. Cambridge: Cambridge University Press.

Clayman, S. and Heritage, J. (2014). Benefactors and beneficiaries: Benefactive status and stance in the management of offers and requests. In E. Couper-Kuhlen and P. Drew, eds., *Requesting in Interaction*. Amsterdam: John Benjamins, pp. 55–86.

Clift, R. (2001). Meaning in interaction: The case of *actually*. *Language, 77*(2), 245–91.

Clift, R. (2005). Discovering order. *Lingua, 115*, 1641–65.

Clift, R. (2012). Identifying action: Laughter in non-humorous reported speech. *Journal of Pragmatics, 44*, 1303–12.

Clift, R. (2014). Conversation analysis. In K. P. Schneider and A. Barron, eds., *Pragmatics of Discourse*. Berlin: Mouton de Gruyter, pp. 97–124.

Clift, R. (2016). *Conversation Analysis*. Cambridge: Cambridge University Press.

Clift, R. and Raymond, C. (2018). Actions in practice: On details in collections. *Discourse Studies, 20*(1), 90–119.

Cook, H. M. (2006). Japanese politeness as an interactional achievement: Academic consultation sessions in Japanese universities. *Multilingua, 25*, 269–91.

Couper-Kuhlen, E. and Selting, M. (2018). *Interactional Linguistics*. Cambridge: Cambridge University Press.

Curl, T. (2006). Offers of assistance: Constraints on syntactic design. *Journal of Pragmatics, 38*, 1257–80.

Curl, T. and Drew, P. (2008). Contingency and action: A comparison of two forms of requesting. *Research on Language and Social Interaction, 41*, 129–53.

Drew, P. (2018a). The interface between pragmatics and conversation analysis. In C. Ilie and N. Norrick, eds., *Pragmatics and Its Interfaces*. Amsterdam: John Benjamins, pp. 59–83.

Drew, P. (2018b). Inferences and indirectness in interaction. *Open Linguistics, 4*, 241–59.

Drew, P. and Holt, E. (1998). Figures of speech: Figurative expressions and the management of topic transition in conversation. *Language in Society, 27*, 495–522.

Drew, P., Walker, T. and Ogden, R. (2013). Self-repair and action construction. In M. Hayashi, G. Raymond and J. Sidnell, eds., *Conversational Repair and Human Understanding*. Cambridge: Cambridge University Press, pp. 71–94.

Evans, N. and Levinson, S. (2009). The myth of language universals: Language diversity and its importance for cognitive science. *Behavioral and Brain Sciences, 32*, 429–92.

Ferenčik, M. (2007). Exercising politeness: Membership categorisation in a radio phone-in programme. *Pragmatics, 17*(3), 351–70.

Flint, N., Haugh, M. and Merrison, A. J. (2019). Modulating troubles affiliating in initial interactions. *Pragmatics*, 29(3), 384–409.

Floyd, S., Rossi, G. and Enfield, N. J. (2020). *Getting Others to Do Things: A Pragmatic Typology of Recruitments*. Berlin: Language Science Press.

Garfinkel, H. and Sacks, H. (1970). On formal structures of practical actions. In J. C. McKinney and E. A. Tiraykian, eds., *Theoretical Sociology*. New York: Appleton Century Crofts, pp. 338–66.

Goffman, E. (1961). *Encounters: Two Studies in the Sociology of Interaction*. Indianapolis, IN: Bobbs-Merrill.

Haugh, M. (2013). Im/politeness, social practice and the participation order. *Journal of Pragmatics*, 58, 52–72.

Haugh, M. (2015). *Im/politeness Implicatures*. Berlin: Mouton de Gruyter.

Haugh, M. (2017). Prompting offers of assistance in interaction. *Pragmatics and Society*, 8, 183–207.

Haugh, M. (forthcoming). Action ascription, accountability and inference. In A. Deppermann and M. Haugh, eds., *Action Ascription*. Cambridge: Cambridge University Press.

Hepburn, A. and Bolden, G. (2017). *Transcribing for Social Research*. Thousand Oaks, CA: Sage.

Heritage, J. (1984). A change of state token and aspects of its sequential placement. In J. M. Atkinson and J. Heritage, eds., *Structures of Social Action*. Cambridge: Cambridge University Press, pp. 299–345.

Heritage, J. (1998). Oh-prefaced responses to inquiry. *Language in Society*, 27, 291–334.

Heritage, J. and Raymond, G. (2005). The terms of agreement: ndexing epistemic authority and subordination in talk-in-interaction. *Social Psychology Quarterly*, 68, 15–38.

Hutchby, I. (2008). Participants' orientations to interruptions, rudeness and other impolite acts in talk-in-interaction. *Journal of Politeness Research*, 4(2), 221–41.

Jefferson, G. (1979). A technique for inviting laughter and its subsequent acceptance-declination. In G. Psathas, ed., *Everyday Language: Studies in Ethnomethodology*. New York: Irvington, pp. 79–95.

Jefferson, G. (1984). On the organization of laughter in talk about troubles. In J. M. Atkinson and J. Heritage, eds., *Structures of Social Action*. Cambridge: Cambridge University Press, pp. 346–69.

Jefferson, G. (1985). An exercise in the transcription and analysis of laughter. In T. van Dijk, ed., *Handbook of Discourse Analysis*, Vol. 3, *Discourse and Dialogue*. London: Academic Press, pp. 25–34.

Jefferson, G. (2002). Is 'no' an acknowledgement token? Comparing American and British uses of (+)/(−) tokens. *Journal of Pragmatics*, 34, 1345–83.

Jefferson, G. (2004a). Glossary of transcript symbols with an introduction. In G. Lerner, ed., *Conversation Analysis: Studies from the First Generation*. Amsterdam: John Benjamins, pp. 13–23.

Jefferson, G. (2004b). A note on laughter in 'male–female' interaction. *Discourse Studies*, 6, 117–33.

Jefferson, G., Sacks, H. and Schegloff, E. (1987). Notes on laughter in the pursuit of intimacy. In G. Button and J. R. E. Lee, eds., *Talk and Social Organisation*. Clevedon, UK: Multilingual Matters, pp. 152–205.

Kendrick, K. (2017). Using conversation analysis in the lab. *Research on Language and Social Interaction*, 50, 1–11.

Kendrick, K., Brown, P., Dingemanse, M., Floyd, S., Gipper, S., Hayano, K., Hoey, E., Hoymann, G., Manrique, G., Rossi, G. and Levinson, S. C. (2020). Sequence organization: A universal infrastructure for social action. *Journal of Pragmatics*, 168, 119–38.

Kendrick, K. and Drew, P. (2014). The putative preference for offers over requests. In P. Drew and E. Couper-Kuhlen, eds., *Requesting in Social Interaction*. Amsterdam: John Benjamins, pp. 87–113.

Kendrick, K. and Drew, P. (2016). Recruitments: Offers, requests, and the organization of assistance in interaction. *Research on Language and Social Interaction*, 49, 1–19.

Kitzinger, C. (2005). Speaking as a heterosexual: (How) does sexuality matter for talk-in-interaction? *Research on Language and Social Interaction*, 38(3), 221–65.

Kitzinger, C. and Mandelbaum, J. (2013) Word selection and social identities in talk-in-interaction. *Communication Monographs*, 80(2), 176–98.

Krzeszowski, T. (1990). *Contrasting Languages: The Scope of Contrastive Linguistics*. Berlin: Mouton de Gruyter

Levinson, S. C. (2000). *Presumptive Meanings: The Theory of Generalized Conversational Implicature*. Cambridge, MA: MIT Press.

Merrison, A. J. (2011). Doing aphasia – 'are you with me?': Analysing facework around issues of (non-)competence. In LPRG, ed., *Discursive Approaches to Politeness*. Berlin: Mouton de Gruyter, pp. 221–44.

Mondada, L. (2019). Contemporary issues in conversation analysis: Embodiment and materiality, multimodality and multisensoriality in social interaction. *Journal of Pragmatics*, 145, 47–62.

Piirainen-Marsh, A. (2005). Managing adversarial questioning in broadcast interviews. *Journal of Politeness Research*, 1(1), 193–217.

Pillet-Shore, D. (in press). When to make the sensory social: Registering in face-to-face openings. *Symbolic Interaction*.

Pomerantz, A. (1984). Agreeing and disagreeing with assessments: Some features of preferred/dispreferred turn shapes. In J. M. Atkinson and J. Heritage, eds., *Structures of Social Action: Studies in Conversation Analysis*. Cambridge: Cambridge University Press, pp. 57–101.

Pomerantz, A. (2017). Inferring the purpose of a prior query and responding accordingly. In G. Raymond, G. Lerner and J. Heritage, eds., *Enabling Human Conduct*. Amsterdam: John Benjamins, pp. 61–77.

Pomerantz, A. and Heritage, J. (2013). Preference. In J. Sidnell and T. Stivers, eds., *Handbook of Conversation Analysis*. Malden, MA: Wiley-Blackwell, pp. 210–28.

Pomerantz, A. and Mandelbaum, J. (2005). Conversation analytic approaches to the relevance and uses of relationship categories in interaction. In K. Fitch and R. Sanders, eds., *Handbook of Language and Social Interaction*. Mahwah, NJ: Erlbaum, pp. 149–71.

Raymond, G. (2003). Grammar and social organization: Yes/no interrogatives and the structure of responding. *American Sociological Review*, 68, 939–67.

Raymond, G. and Heritage, J. (2006). The epistemics of social relations: Owning grandchildren. *Language in Society*, 35, 677–705.

Robinson, J. (2016). Accountability in social interaction. In J. Robinson, ed., *Accountability in Social Interaction*. Oxford: Oxford University Press, pp. 1–44.

Sacks, H. (1972). An initial investigation of the usability of conversational data for doing sociology. In D. Sudnow, ed., *Studies in Social Interaction*. New York: The Free Press, pp. 31–75.

Sacks, H. (1984). Notes on methodology. In J. M. Atkinson and J. Heritage, eds., *Structures of Social Action*. Cambridge: Cambridge University Press, pp. 21–27.

Sacks, H. (1992a). *Lectures on Conversation*. Vol. 1. Oxford: Blackwell.

Sacks, H. (1992b). *Lectures on Conversation*. Vol. 2. Oxford: Blackwell.

Sacks, H. and Schegloff, E. (1979). Two preferences in the organization of reference to persons in conversation and their interaction. In G. Psathas, ed., *Everyday Language: Studies in Ethnomethodology*. New York: Irvington, pp. 15–21.

Schegloff, E. (1968). Sequencing in conversational openings. *American Anthropologist*, 70(6), 1075–95.

Schegloff, E. (1993). Reflections on quantification in the study of conversation. *Research on Language and Social Interaction*, 26, 99–128.

Schegloff, E. (1996). Confirming allusions: Toward an empirical account of action. *American Journal of Sociology*, 102, 161–216.

Schegloff, E. (1997). Practices and actions: Boundary cases of other-inititated repair. *Discourse Processes*, 23, 499–545.

Schegloff, E. (2000). On granularity. *Annual Review of Sociology*, 26, 715–20.

Schegloff, E. (2007). *Sequence Organization in Interaction*. Cambridge: Cambridge University Press.

Schegloff, E. (2010). Commentary on Stivers and Rossano: 'Mobilising response'. *Research on Language and Social Interaction*, 43, 38–48.

Schegloff, E. (2017). Conversation analysis. In Y. Huang, ed., *The Oxford Handbook of Pragmatics*. Oxford: Oxford University Press, pp. 435–49.

Schegloff, E., Jefferson, G. and Sacks, H. (1977). The preference for self-correction in the organisation of repair in conversation. *Language*, 53(2), 361–82.

Schegloff, E. and Lerner, G. (2009). Beginning to respond: *Well*-preface responses to *wh*-questions. *Research on Language and Social Interaction*, 42, 91–115.

Schenkein, J. (ed.). (1978). *Studies in the Organization of Conversational Interaction*. New York: Academic Press.

Searle, J. R. (1969). *Speech Acts: An Essay in the Philosophy of Language*. Cambridge: Cambridge University Press.

30

Corpus Pragmatics

Svenja Adolphs and Yaoyao Chen

30.1 Introduction

Pragmatics is often defined as a field of study focusing on the investigation of linguistic communication in context, thereby establishing meaning in use (Leech 1983; Mey 2001; Thomas 1995). Leech (1983: 10–11) further distinguishes between general pragmatics, pragmalinguistics and sociopragmatics. Pragmalinguistics focuses on 'the particular resources which a given language provides for conveying particular illocutions' while sociopragmatics is concerned with 'more specific "local" conditions on language use'. The two sub-divisions together are separated from general pragmatics, which deals with 'the general conditions of the communicative use of language', or the philosophical and cognitive aspects of pragmatics (Leech 1983:10). According to Leech (1983), pragmalinguistics primarily relates to the grammatical side of pragmatics, whereas sociopragmatics primarily concerns the social side of pragmatics. To further explain sociopragmatics, he states that the politeness principle and cooperative principle 'operate variably in different cultures or language communities, in different social situations, among different social classes, etc.' (Leech 1983:10). This illustrates the focus of sociopragmatics as being on the study of language use in relation to all kinds of sociocultural variables such as culture, social activity, class, speaker role, power, religion, race or age. Further defining Leech's concept of 'local', Culpeper (Chapter 2 in this volume) puts forward three levels of contexts, i.e. micro, meso and macro, and specifies that sociopragmatics is particularly associated with the meso or medial level of context, which is usually related to concepts such as activity types, frames, genres or discourses. Thomas' (1983) definition of pragmatic failure in the context of cross-cultural pragmatics is also relevant in this context: 'sociopragmatic failure stems from cross-culturally different perceptions of what constitutes appropriate linguistic behaviour' (99). It suggests that sociopragmatics very much concerns the general social norms, values and evaluations of appropriate behaviour in a certain context. It will become clear later that it is this interest in the general patterns of linguistic behaviour in different contexts where corpus pragmatics has the most to offer to the field of sociopragmatics.

Historically, the area of pragmatics has not been too concerned with sociocultural aspects, or actual language usage, and most of the early theories and concepts around speech acts and utterance function developed by Austin and Searle (Austin 1962; Searle 1971, 1976) were based on invented sentences or utterances. This was not with a view to ignore language as used in real context, but rather because the focus of those early pragmatic explorations was more concerned with philosophical frameworks and theories. However, with the fast-growing attention to sociopragmatics over the past two decades, corpus pragmatics becomes particularly relevant as an area that investigates patterns of language use based on real language as recorded in corpora. The rich metadata available as part of large spoken and written corpora (such as text types, speaker age, sex, relationship, ethnicity, linguistic variations, formality) offer ideal platforms for conducting sociopragmatic research on language use in different situations. As sociopragmatics is often concerned with the norms of language use in certain contexts, corpus-based quantitative analysis of a large dataset (ideally collected from a large population representative of a particular context) enables pragmaticians to observe and discover general patterns of language use in a given context. Drawing on corpus data and textual analytical tools also allows functional disambiguation by examining patterns in context and co-text. The example we discuss below of the phrase *do you know/see what I mean* can be used as a discourse marker or as a device for checking understanding depending on the discourse environment in which it is used. The area of corpus pragmatics has therefore both tested and extended more traditional pragmatic theory and practice, and enabled a series of additional insights into the relationship between form and function in different contexts

Despite the increase in transcribed 'text-based' research in corpus pragmatics, there is still a distinctive lack of multimodal corpus pragmatic research that explores the interplay between speech and other modes, such as gesture, in meaning-making. This is possibly the combined result of the scarcity of large multimodal corpora and (semi-)automatic multimodal tools. Situated at the intersection between corpus pragmatics and multimodal pragmatics, multimodal corpus pragmatics adopts research methods that typify both areas. At the time of writing, multimodal corpus pragmatic research typically does not involve an investigation of a very large number of instances. This is a direct result of the extremely labour-intensive nature of multimodal analysis in the absence of fully automated capabilities for gesture analysis. Multimodal corpus pragmatics draws on both qualitative and quantitative methods, where appropriate and possible, to identify emerging patterns based on actual instances and numbers in multimodal corpora. In this chapter, drawing on a small number of instances, we will present a multimodal corpus-based approach for exploring the functional relationship between speech and gesture. Implications for the field of sociopragmatics and future research will also be discussed.

In the remainder of the chapter, we will first illustrate some basic textual corpus linguistic methods that have proven useful for sociopragmatic research and pragmatic research in general. We will then review existing research in corpus pragmatics with a focus on sociopragmatics, before presenting a case study that explores a multimodal corpus-based approach for establishing a speech-gesture functional profile for a multiword expression. Our case study serves here as an exemplar of a multimodal corpus pragmatic investigation that integrates methods used in the fields of corpus linguistics, pragmatics and multimodality.

30.2 Corpus Methods and Pragmatic Analysis

Below we illustrate three basic techniques of corpus analysis that are applicable and widely used in the area of pragmatics. These types of investigations can be performed with most corpus software tools such as *WordSmith*,[1] *AntConc*[2] and *Sketch Engine*,[3] in which more complex analysis may also be provided. Throughout our chapter, we draw on specific multiword units to illustrate methods and approaches.

One of the most common corpus linguistic analyses is the study of the concordance, or KWIC (key word in context) analysis, which generates a list of all the instances of the searched item, or the node, aligned in the centre of the concordance lines (Kennedy 1998). For pragmatic research, concordance lists are particularly useful for discovering emerging functional variations of words and phrases, along with other information such as the number of instances that occur across different contexts and sociolinguistic variables.

Table 30.1 shows the result of a search for all the instances of *do you know what I mean* in the supervision meeting sub-corpus of the Nottingham Multimodal Corpus. In addition to the useful information of the number of instances (column 1) and their source files (mostly from S06FF), preliminary concordance analysis of those instances reveals three types of positions of occurrence: initial, medial and final. These three positions indicate the potential functional variations of the phrases: the function of a discourse marker in turn-initial position (9, 14, 15, 23, 24, 27, 29, 30); of checking understanding in turn-final position, usually followed by a listener response *Yeah* (6, 10, 12, 16, 21, 30); of combining the function of a discourse marker and checking understanding in turn-medial position (1, 2, 3, 4, 5 etc.). Although assigning the function of each instance requires further

---

[1] https://lexically.net/wordsmith/   [2] www.laurenceanthony.net/   [3] www.sketchengine.eu/

Table 30.1 *All the concordance lines of* do you know what I mean *in NMMC*

Hit	Left	Node	Right	File
1	possibilities that weren't afforded	do you know what I mean	to writers early	S06FF.txt
2	a a historical chapter which just goes back	do you know what I mean	using basic contextual	S06FF.txt
3	to be written which actually links Bowen	do you know what I mean	in a funny	S06FF.txt
4	literally how how you get into this chapter	do you know what I mean	it's literally	S06FF.txt
5	do this is the aim of this chapter	do you know what I mean	set out in	S06FF.txt
6	get into the very beginning of this chapter	do you know what I mean	+ <$2> Mm.	S06FF.txt
7	stuff that's possibly a different chapter	do you know what I mean	you c= having	S06FF.txt
8	Simplify. <$2> +simplify it down	do you know what I mean	get rid of	S06FF.txt
9	<$2> <$E>Laughs</$E> <$1> +	do you know what I mean	down a different	S06FF.txt
10	by going and finding the good examples.	Do you know what I mean	?+ <$2> Yeah <$E> laughs <	S03MF.txt
11	you you can perhaps have some footnotes	do you know what I mean	and fill in	S06FF.txt
12	is that this change actually has happened	do you know what I mean	+<$2> Yeah	S06FF.txt
13	to actually allow you to investigate	do you know what I mean	. What approaches+	S06FF.txt
14	century lead in? <$2> Mhm. <$1>	Do you know what I mean	in this particular	S06FF.txt
15	ally different+ <$2> Mhm. <$1> +	do you know what I mean	so instead of	S06FF.txt
16	past is always trying to put too much	do you know what I mean	+ <$2> Yeah true. <$1> +i	S06FF.txt
17	as high modernists neglecte=	do you know what I mean	t= how important	S06FF.txt
18	applied to the twentieth century novel	do you know what I mean	the chapter somehow	S06FF.txt
19	references to nineteenth century novels	do you know what I mean	you might have	S06FF.txt
20	it's a transition which is taking place	do you know what I mean	over a long	S06FF.txt
21	that is the material on erm town planning	do you know what I mean	+ <$2> Yeah that that	S06FF.txt
22	's been raised here but try and resist	do you know what I mean	resist the temptation	S06FF.txt
23	to novelists+ <$2> Right. <$2> +	do you know what I mean	just forget the	S06FF.txt
24	tic men. <$2> Mhm. <$2> So it's	do you know what I mean	you you could	S06FF.txt
25	really quite uninteresting it's not a sig=	do you know what I mean	it's not	S06FF.txt
26	simply grown out of modernist spaces	do you know what I mean	is it very	S06FF.txt
27	of space theory? <$1> Yeah that	do you know what I mean	that could be	S06FF.txt
28	want to put the historical stuff in then	do you know what I mean	cos one argument	S06FF.txt
29	next step+ <$2> I think+ <$1> +	do you know what I mean	you a completely	S06FF.txt
30	<$2> Right. <$1>	Do you know what I mean	+ <$2> Yeah. <$1> +and ju	S06FF.txt

qualitative analysis of a larger discourse context, the concordance lines provide an initial overview of possible functions.

Another important corpus method that is not usually taken into account in more traditional pragmatic research is the analysis of the mutual attraction between the node and its surrounding lexical items, or the node's collocations. Corpus tools may offer various statistics for measuring co-occurrence and identifying collocations such as Mutual Information (MI), chi-squared, log-likelihood, c-score, t-score or z-score (Gablasova et al. 2017; Hunston 2002; McEnery and Hardie 2011). The analysis of collocational patterns can be particularly valuable for disambiguating the functions of the searched item and for exploring form-function associations. This point can be illustrated by the collocations of the speech act expression *why don't you* in the CANCODE corpus (Table 30.2) (Adolphs 2008: 56). After noting the collocates of *said, saying, say, says*, further concordance analysis of *why don't you* co-occurring with lemma SAY shows that, when this node does not occur in sentence initial position, it tends to occur in a reported structure such as *And so I **said** Well **why don't you** give her a ring*. Relating to politeness, the directness of the suggestion is thus largely reduced as the hearer of the suggestion is not the same as the addressee of the suggestion.

The third method often used within corpus linguistics is the automatic generation of single or multiword wordlists based on frequency. The former can be generated with the Word List function and the latter by N-grams/Clusters analysis. Wordlists can help foreground the most frequently used words and clusters of a particular corpus, and thus help describe language features in a particular context represented by that corpus. Subsequent comparative analysis of wordlists generated by different corpora can also be conducted. A case in point is Diani's (2015) research on the realization of politeness in different cultural contexts. Her research compares the frequency and forms of mitigated criticism in the two corpora that represent English and Italian academic book reviews in history. She adopts a data-driven approach by identifying the inherently critical expressions in the wordlists of the two corpora, such as *failure* and *objection* in English, and *vago* (vague) and *riduttivo* (simplistic) in Italian. After selecting and sorting the words manually, she then conducts further concordance analysis of all the chosen critical expressions.

Table 30.2 *Collocates to the left of* why don't you *in CANCODE*

Collocate	C-score	Main position in span
said	6.95	−1
saying	6.16	−1
keep	5.79	−4
say	5.56	−1
says	5.47	−1
said	6.95	−1
don't	4.90	−1
her	4.53	−1
him	4.49	−1
you	4.08	−1

From Adolphs (2008: 56).

30.3 Research in Corpus Pragmatics

Corpus pragmatics has become a popular area of research with an ever increasing number of specialist publications, such as a series of yearbooks of corpus linguistics and pragmatics (Romero-Trillo 2013, 2014, 2015, 2016), and the handbook of corpus pragmatics (Aijmer and Rühlemann 2015). Research in corpus pragmatics covers a wide variety of key topics and issues in pragmatics such as discourse markers (Aijmer 2013; Fraser 2015; Fung and Carter 2007; Gray and Biber 2015; Irvine et al. 2016; Martín-Laguna and Alcón-Soler 2018; Werner 2017), speech acts (Adolphs 2008; Aijmer 1996; Jautz 2008; Kohnen 2015; Maíz-Arévalo 2017; Ronan 2015), deixis (Rühlemann and Clancy 2018; Rühlemann and O'Donnell 2015), vocalizations (e.g. *uh, um*) (Tottie 2011, 2015), response tokens (O'Keeffe and Adolphs 2008) and (im)politeness (Diani 2015; Haugh and Culpeper 2018), among many others. However, not all corpus pragmatic studies have a sociopragmatic focus. As corpus methods have become mainstream in linguistic research, many studies in corpus pragmatics align to other strands in pragmatics, especially variational pragmatics (Aijmer 2013; Schneider and Barron 2008), intercultural pragmatics and second language/interlanguage pragmatics (Romero-Trillo 2018a). We will now introduce some research relating to the above topics and beyond that exemplifies the use of a corpus pragmatic approach in sociopragmatic research.

Among the extensive research on pragmatic markers (PMs, including discourse markers, DMs, as a sub-category of PMs), much previous research either compares the differences of their uses (both frequency and variety) among native speakers and language learners, or the development of PMs in language learners (Fung and Carter 2007; Martín-Laguna and Alcón-Soler 2018; Werner 2017). These studies tend to interpret the data in relation to the learner's proficiency level (e.g. low proficiency level may lead to over/ under-use of certain PMs, or a restricted variety of PMs). Gablasova and Brezina (2015), however, investigate how the learner's role in different speaking activities affects the use of adverbial epistemic markers (ADMs) indicating certainty (e.g. *certainly, clearly*) and uncertainty (e.g. *maybe, perhaps*). They find that the candidates overall produce more ADMs (both certainty and uncertainty markers) than the examiners, but this difference is only significant in one task, an interactive task, where the candidates are required to recommend and suggest, hence taking on a leading role in managing information exchange and interpersonal relationship. Further qualitative analysis of the functions of ADMs reveals that candidates dominantly use certainty ADMs serving the subjective function (i.e. indicating the certainty of their own opinions) in the discussion task, where they are the expert of the topic. In contrast, they use far more intersubjective certain ADMs that stress their shared experience/opinion in the interactive task, where the candidates take on the role of an information-seeker instead of an expert. Gablasova and Brezina (2015) emphasize that understanding the learner's use of PMs solely based on their proficiency level might be too simplistic, other pragmatic factors such as their role in communication, politeness, age may also be relevant.

Aijmer (2013) offers a detailed corpus investigation into the use of *well, in fact* and *actually* (adversative pragmatic markers), and *and things* and *and stuff like that*, all of which are sociopragmatic in nature. She explores them in various text types available in large corpora such as the BNC and the British component of the International Corpus of English corpus (ICE). Her recent work on *I think* based on the British component of ICE demonstrates the functional variations of this PM in terms of frequency, key collocations in different spoken text types (broadcast debate vs conversation) (Aijmer 2015). She compares the frequencies of *I think* based on corpus analysis and then selecting 100 instances from each text type for further qualitative analysis of their pragmatic functions. The overall results show that whereas *I think* in conversation is more strongly associated with a spontaneous and friendly speech style (e.g. used to mitigate opinions, signal word-search, self-repair and hesitation), it tends to be used in broadcast discussion to express relatively pre-prepared opinions, and demonstrate knowledge and authority on the subject matter. This study is a good illustration of how prevalent PMs such as *I think* function differently in accordance with the contexts of communication such as the participants, the social relationship and the agenda of communication.

Focusing on speech acts and politeness, Jautz (2008) compares the uses of expressions of gratitude in radio programmes in British English and New Zealand English, drawing on the sub-corpus of the spoken BNC and the Wellington Corpus of Spoken New Zealand English. General frequency analysis seems to indicate a higher level of politeness and formality in British English due to the significantly higher number of occurrences of gratitude expressions in total, and of more formal expressions such as *Thank you* rather than *Thanks* in the BNC. However, further qualitative analysis of the co-texts and functions of the expressions of gratitude suggests otherwise. New Zealand English uses more gratitude for contributions (i.e. stating the reasons for their gratitude), and for interpersonal purposes (i.e. replying to interlocuters' inquiry of health, good wishes, compliments). On the other hand, the British corpus shows a significantly higher number of occurrences of gratitude used to appreciate some form of service, financial support or material goods.

O'Keeffe and Adolphs (2008) compare backchannels, or response tokens, in CANCODE (British English) and the Limerick Corpus of Irish English (LCIE) (Irish English). They use wordlists and clusters analysis to identify the forms of response tokens (that occur five times or above) in the first 5,000 words in both corpora. The results bring to light some sociopragmatic implications, suggesting a lower level of formality in Irish English due to the absence of more formal lexical response token words (e.g. *quite*), and more religious references as part of the backchannel expressions in the Irish corpus.

The use of corpora has thus revolutionized our descriptions of pragmatic phenomena. In addition, corpus pragmatics has opened up a lens for investigating social phenomena, such as identity, politics, education, economics and conflict, which is in parallel with the fast growth of sociopragmatic research. This is well reflected in the 2016 Yearbook of Corpus Linguistics and Pragmatics (Romero-Trillo 2016), which includes scholarly works addressing challenges in digital on-line communication and education. For instance, drawing on on-line discussion boards for victims of domestic violence, Mestre-Mestre (2016) explores the way in which participants express their emotion and support for each other by analysing the frequency and uses of positive and negative adjectives, social words and self-references. Avila-Ledesma and Amador-Moreno (2016) carry out corpus pragmatic and sociolinguistic research concerning the conceptualization of Irish identity and immigration in male and female post-famine emigrants. Their analysis concentrates on the nouns *home* and *country* in the discourse captured in the Corpus of Irish English Correspondence.

30.4 Issues in Corpus Pragmatics

As outlined above, the synergy between corpus linguistics and pragmatics has proven fruitful, however, several issues remain. To begin with, whereas corpus methods, such as concordance analysis are robust in analysing the frequency, distribution and collocation of certain words or phrases, the interpretation of the pragmatic function of each item requires qualitative analysis of the larger discourse context beyond the concordance. That is, concordance lines do not contain sufficient context for interpreting functions, and therefore manual discourse analysis and annotation of pragmatic functions are normally required. To the present date, there are few agreed pragmatic annotation schemes, or technologies that can assist automatic pragmatic annotation. Indeed, some researchers such as Weisser (2016) are working towards a more automated way of extracting speech acts from corpora, often via pragmatic annotation. For example, DART (the Dialogue Annotation and Research Tool) can conduct pragmatic annotation at different levels (semantic, syntactic, speech acts etc.) with a relatively high degree of precision. Also, a few corpora such as the SPICE-Ireland Corpus (based on the spoken component of ICE-Ireland) (Kallen and Kirk 2008, 2012) are pragmatically annotated, which allow for automatic retrieval of speech act functions. Nonetheless, there is still a long way before precise automatic retrieval of pragmatic functions (e.g. apology, thanking) can be accomplished.

In part due to the lack of pragmatic annotations in corpora, it is common practice among corpus pragmatic studies to choose routinized expressions as a way in to investigate pragmatic functions (e.g. using *how about* as an entry to study suggestion) (Adolphs 2008). Combined with manual filtering of the concordance lines, such a method may well lead to a high precision of instances (e.g. by identifying all the instances of *how about* performing the function of suggestion). However, this can lead to bad recall in the sense that other expressions that can perform the same function will not be identified (Rühlemann and Aijmer 2015).

Another issue that seems more problematic is the lack of multimodal corpus pragmatic research. Much of the current research on corpus pragmatics focuses on recorded spoken discourse that is rendered into a textual record (or transcript). Transcripts of spoken discourse tend to include various levels of detail in terms of other modes (such as gesture, prosody, facial expressions). Yet, these modes are crucial when it comes to performing speech acts and other pragmatic functions. Treating a transcript of spoken interaction in the same way as we would treat a corpus of texts that originate from a written record is therefore problematic in a number of respects. Indeed, we may find that the pragmatic functions we have assigned on the basis of a transcript, are deemed to be incorrect when we consider the accompanying prosody or gestures.

Early work on multimodal corpora illustrates these points, including research on response tokens and head nods (Adolphs and Carter 2007, 2013; Knight 2011), gesture and backchanneling in turn taking (Tsuchiya 2013), and pragmatic markers and prosody (Romero-Trillo 2018b). These research projects rely heavily on the development of digital data collection methods and software, digital storage capacity, and on advances in multimodal annotation software such as *ELAN*[4] (Wittenburg et al. 2006). Multimodal annotation tools play a key role for multimodal corpus pragmatics in terms of enabling the alignment and mark-up of audio and visual data streams in the same interface, as well as in supporting basic statistics.

For the remainder of this chapter, we will present an example of a multimodal corpus-based analysis of a conventionalized pragmatic marker *(do) you know/see what I mean*. We will use this example to illustrate two things: first of all, we will show how a corpus investigation can assist us in our description of this particular function in use. Second, we will demonstrate that a monomodal, or purely textual, approach to this phrase does not allow us to carry out a functional disambiguation between a discourse marker and checking understanding. We argue that the analysis of the gesture profiles that co-occur with this phrase, on the other hand, does allow for functional disambiguation, and highlights that this kind of multimodal analysis suggests that we rely less on contextual variables in our interpretation of function and meaning than a traditional pragmatic approach or textual corpus pragmatic approaches would suggest.

---

[4] https://tla.mpi.nl/tools/tla-tools/elan/citing_elan/

30.5 Multimodal Corpus Pragmatics: A Case Study of *(Do) You Know/See What I Mean*

The basis for our study is the Nottingham Multimodal Corpus (NMMC). This is a specialized English academic corpus with 250,000 running words. The corpus comprises of two sub-corpora: lectures and post-graduate supervision meetings. Specifically, we use one supervision session in the corpus that contains a high number of our target multiword expressions (MWEs) *(do) you know/see what I mean* with 64 instances occurring in 47:52 minutes of recorded supervision (11,705 running words in total for the supervision). The supervision meeting is between a female supervisor and female PhD student, both of whom are native speakers of English. All the instances were found in the supervisor's speech. It is important to point out that the student has not used any variation of *(do) you know/see what I mean*. Thus, the study becomes a case study of an individual speaker regarding the use of this particular group of sequences. The dataset is, therefore, greatly biased towards the supervisor. However, given that the purpose of the analysis is to illustrate a general multimodal corpus approach, rather than to generalize from the use by a particular speaker, this was not deemed to be a serious issue for the purpose of this chapter.

We should also clarify that the search for this MWE was conducted in all the 13 supervision meetings (9 supervisors and 12 students) using *AntConc* (Anthony, 2019) at the outset. We did not use the lecture sub-corpus due to the interactive nature of this MWE. In total, except for the chosen video containing 64 instances, only 12 instances were found in the rest of the 12 videos, all used by supervisors. Due to the extremely small number of instances from the other speakers, we decided to conduct a case study focusing on one speaker as an illustration of the analytical approach itself.

There are four potential variations of *(do) you know/see what I mean*, including *you see what I mean, you know what I mean, do you know what I mean* and *do you see what I mean*. Hence, all these variations have been included here. However, only two forms are present in our supervision session. They are *do you know what I mean* with 29 instances and *do you see what I mean* with 35 (see Table 30.3).

Table 30.3 *Frequency of variations of* (do) you know/see what I mean

Variations	Amount
you see what I mean	0
you know what I mean	0
do you know what I mean	29
do you see what I mean	35
Total	64

The sequence, *(do) you know/see what I mean*, often occurs as an extended version of *you know* and *I mean* (Adolphs and Carter 2013). Previous research has explored the various meanings of *you know* and *I mean* (Stubbe and Holmes 1995; Tree and Schrock 2002), whereas the full expression described here remains underexplored. In Stubbe and Holmes' (1995) description of New Zealand spoken language, they highlight that pragmatic markers such as *you know* and *I mean* are prevalent in everyday speech, and, while they may appear redundant and informal, they perform a vital role of 'oil(ing) the wheels of interaction' (63) and monitoring the common ground between the interlocutors. Similar comments have been made by Tree and Schrock (2002), claiming speakers' uses of *you know* and *I mean* are usually tied to speaker's clarification and modification of speech, inviting the addressees' involvement and confirmation of understanding.

Particularly relevant to the current study, Carter and McCarthy (2006) argue that frequently occurring multiword expressions such as *you know*, *I mean*, *you know what I mean* and *do you know what I mean* are used to reinforce common ground between participants in communication. From a slightly different perspective, Woods' (1991) study of Canadian English underlines the pragmatic function of *you know* as an appeal for sympathy, indicating an important interpersonal role. In view of these findings, we can assume that the targeted expression is multifunctional in aspects such as discourse cohesion, negotiation of mutual understanding and interpersonal affiliation. This is largely confirmed by the results of our own research.

30.5.1 Coding the Data

The approach we take here involves, first, identifying the various contexts in which different multiword expressions (MWEs) occur from a discourse analytical perspective (Adolphs 2008), and then describing the gestures that co-occur with them from a semiotic perspective, i.e. their form and different semantic derivations (Calbris 2011). We mainly use the free corpus software *AntConc* for concordance analysis. The gesture annotation is carried out with the use of established software for multimodal discourse analysis, i.e. *ELAN*.

30.5.1.1 Coding Speech Function Based on Co-text

The first step in our analysis of speech function is to pinpoint all the instances of the MWEs in the transcription and then identify the functional variations that occur across these items. As is shown in the section on corpus techniques (refer back to Table 30.2), we use *AntConc* to retrieve all instances of the MWEs in the transcripts of all supervision meetings in the corpus, and to observe their positions and co-texts in the concordance lines. (Refer back to that section for some preliminary observations of the positions and functions based on concordance analysis). While the literal meaning of the MWEs indicates a function of checking understanding on the part of the speaker, concordance observation and discourse analysis allow for a more systematic and nuanced description. Using this approach, we find that the MWEs are positioned alongside a scale that has checking understanding on the one end and the function of a discourse marker on the other. To distinguish between the two main functions, we need to consider the discourse structure, i.e. the position of the expressions in the utterance, and the wider discourse co-text. The latter allows us to identify those contexts where challenges of mutual understanding trigger the use of this expression as a means of establishing common ground between interlocutors.

A relatively clear-cut example of checking understanding is provided in the following extract:

SUPERVISOR: I think I think that might give you the focus better and then this chapter will become more a chapter that's setting up the theorisation of space <u>do you see what I mean</u>+
STUDENT: Yeah.

The key criterion for coding the function of checking understanding is to identify a speaker-eliciting-and-listener-confirming sequence. However, while observing the videos, it becomes clear that the confirmation from the student can be verbal, but also non-verbal, in this case realized by nodding of the head. Hence, to achieve a more accurate coding of speech function, we code all the head nods that follow right after the MWEs, adding them to the original speech transcripts. A multimodal discourse analysis of the functions of the expressions reveals that a lack of consideration of the non-verbal elements in interaction limits our understanding of the dynamic functional variations across these items. Although we decided to include head-nodding responses in the coding of speech function for their special role here, we only use speech transcripts for speech coding, excluding hand-and-arm gestures. The separation between speech and hand-and-arm gesture coding is crucial for avoiding circularity in the analysis, i.e. coding speech function based on both speech and gesture, and then investigating the functional relationship between speech and gesture.

Those instances that are used as discourse markers usually occur at the beginning of an utterance or in dysfluent speech that is marked by false starts, repetition, an incomplete utterance etc. Also, there tend to be no verbal or non-verbal responses from the other party in those instances. The following example illustrates this observation:

SUPERVISOR: +and utility of space theory for a literary critic as opposed to the chapter being about hotels
STUDENT: Right.

SUPERVISOR: do you see what I mean and why are hotels an important issue cos I think you've you've got to make a decision are you using space theory as a mechanism to help you understand what's going in the hotel+
STUDENT: Mhm.

Another functional type of the MWEs seems to combine both functions of checking understanding and discourse markers. These are usually inserted in the middle of a sentence where the meaning of the utterance is still incomplete, but followed by an instant or delayed student response. The position of the expression indicates the function of discourse marking, whereas the wider discourse structure and contents point to the function of checking understanding.

SUPERVISOR: it's a it's a transition which is taking place do you know what I mean (Student: head nods) over a long longish period of time just as hotel buildings are taking place over a longish period of time (Student: head nods) so I think if you (turn continued)

Our analysis (see Figure 30.1) shows that more than half of the expressions (34 out of 64) are adopted by the supervisor as a way of ensuring the understanding of the student on a particular issue. Only 11 of them are discourse markers, and the remaining 19 instances appear to combine both functions.

30.5.1.2 Demarcating Gesture Phases

Following the identification of the MWEs and their functions in our data, we then focus on investigating hand-and-arm gestures co-occurring with the MWEs. The gestures surrounding each expression were segmented using a time-based analytical framework that has been widely adopted by researchers such as Kendon (2004), McNeill (1992, 2005) and Kita's team (Kita et al. 1998). Based on those established models, we demarcate gestures into five phases: preparation, pre-stroke hold, stroke, post-stroke hold, and retraction in *ELAN*, and annotate the speech co-occurring with

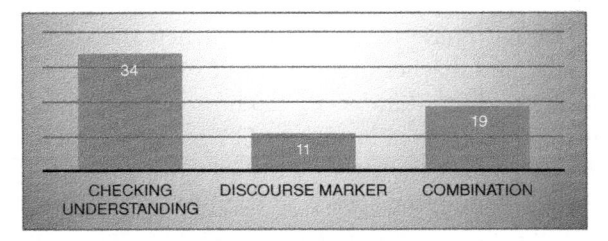

Figure 30.1 Distribution of speech functions in the MWE.

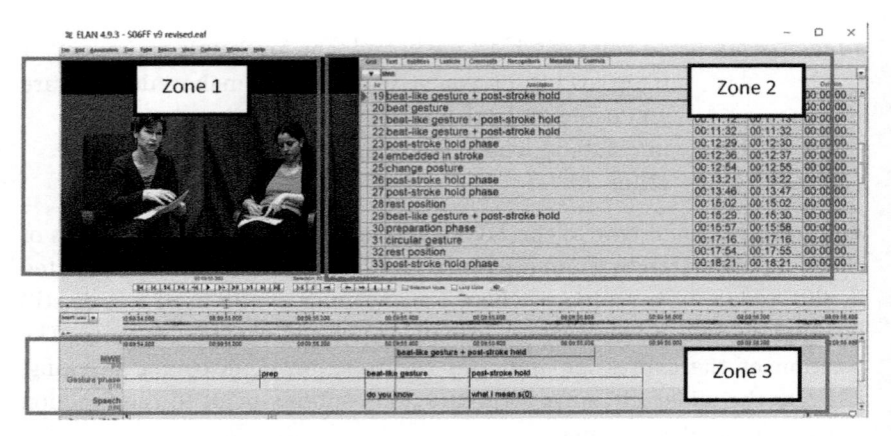

Figure 30.2 A screenshot of ELAN.

each phase. Figure 30.2 is a screen shot of the *ELAN* interface after segmenting all the gestures co-occurring with the MWEs.

Zone 1 is the video area where gestures can be observed, and Zone 2 is the area where all the instances and annotations are listed and numbered. The researcher can select any instance for analysis and observe gesture patterns. Zone 3 is the annotation area, where the MWEs, speech and gestures were annotated in separate tiers. The exact speech and each gesture phase were aligned, transcribed and annotated in the second and third tiers.

The stroke phase (Kendon 2004; Kita et al. 1998; McNeill 2005) is the only mandatory phase for a gesture to exist, which is closest to the apex, and the most salient and emphatic part of the entire gesture. Stroke is also the only meaningful gesture phase that achieves the closest temporal and semantic coordination with the speech it relates to (e.g. the hand rapidly moving downwards while saying 'going down'). The preparation phase (McNeill 1992) refers to the stage that comes before the stroke, which can start from a rest position where the hand is relaxed, for instance, lying on the arm of a chair or a desk. It can also begin when the hand is only partially relaxed after a stroke before the hand could retract to a potential rest position. It can even start instantly after the last stroke without any other gesture phases occurring in-between them.

A pre-stroke hold phase (Kita et al. 1998) emerges when the hand remains still after reaching the starting point of a stroke, i.e. the delayed period from the end of the preparation phase to the moment when the stroke motion actually starts. If the hand reaches the end of a stroke, but freezes for a while, a post-stroke hold phase (Kita et al. 1998) occurs. The post-stroke hold phase performs a crucial role in terms of aligning the stroke with its associated speech part when the stroke finishes earlier than the speech, i.e. the hand freezes, awaiting the speech to complete. Thus, post-stroke hold phases constitute an integral part of stroke and the same applies to the pre-stroke hold phase. Retraction (Kendon 2004) is defined as the period when the hand relaxes and reaches an actual or potential rest position.

As we are focusing specifically on the speech-gesture profile of this MWE produced by the speaker, the gestures in our case study refer exclusively to spontaneous hand-and-arm movements. Any other forms of movements, such as self-adapting, changing posture, self-touching and head movements, were excluded from analysis. Among the 64 instances, 49 of them co-occur with certain gesture phases. After annotating the main gesture phases co-occurring with each instance, we can then analyse the main gesture patterns in each speech function, the results of which will be reported in the next section.

30.5.1.3 Interrater Reliability Test

An interrater reliability test has been conducted with a second researcher, who was provided with both the speech and gesture coding schemes. The researcher coded the speech function of all the instances based on the speech transcript (with head-nodding responses transcribed). The result shows a 70 per cent degree of agreement with the original coding. In terms of the gesture coding, the coder checked all the instances of gesture segmentation, and the rate of agreement here is 96 per cent. This outcome is within expectation as the coding of speech function is more nuanced and less clear than gesture coding. It also illustrates that an analysis of gestures enables more decisive assignment of a specific function, which in turn suggests that reference to gestures is vital in our descriptions of language in use.

30.5.2 Data Analysis: Identifying Gesture Patterns in Each Speech Function

This section illustrates the finding that there is a tendency for certain speech functions to co-occur with certain gesture phases. In the current case study, three main categories of such relationships have been identified, and we report on each of them in turn.

(a) *The MWEs as checking understanding with beat/beat-like strokes, beat/beat-like strokes with long post-stroke holds and post-stroke hold phases.*

Table 30.4 shows all the gesture phases and corresponding expressions as a means of checking understanding. The results show that the MWEs, when used to check understanding, tend to co-occur with particular types of gestures. Except for the seven instances that are not being accompanied by any gesture, it is evident that a significant number of those expressions that function as a device for checking understanding are synchronized with beat/beat-like strokes, with 16 instances in total. Eleven of the beat gestures emerged without long post-stroke hold phases, and five of them have post-stroke hold phases. In addition, the post-stroke hold phase (seven instances)

Table 30.4 *Gesture phases co-occur with the MWEs as checking understanding*

Beat/beat-like stroke	11
Beat/beat-like stroke with long post-stroke hold	5
Post-stroke hold phase	7
Circular stroke	2
Preparation phase	1
Retraction phase	1
No gesture	7
Total	34

also tends to co-occur with this function. Only two instances are accompanied by circular strokes (i.e. rotating hand); one in a preparation phase and the other in a retraction phase.

Beat/beat-like strokes refer to those motions that mainly involve up and/or down, left and/or right, inward and/or outward movements etc., which could be performed single-handed or bi-handed. The movements and velocity of the hand are mostly symmetric in standard beat gestures, but asymmetric in beat-like gestures. As a well-documented gesture, beats are metaphoric gestures (McNeill 1992, 2005) that usually synchronize with the tonic centre of an utterance and mark-up the relatively more salient, noteworthy component(s) in speech (Duncan et al. 2007; Gullberg 2006; McNeill 2005). Although beat gestures do not have any referential meaning, they are pragmatically significant in terms of adding extra emphasis to the important information in discourse (Gullberg 1998; McNeill 2005). This kind of pragmatic role played by the beat gestures is well aligned with the function of checking understanding performed here.

For the many instances where checking understanding is coordinated with long post-stroke hold phases, previous studies have suggested that holding serves the purpose of sustaining the communicative intention of the speaker and eliciting responses from the listener (Brookes 2005; Kendon 1995). For instance, Kendon (1995) found out that, after performing a conventionalized *purse hand gesture* (which has the meaning of questioning) throughout the entire question, the speaker maintains the hand in a post-stroke hold phase, extending the intention of questioning and seeking an answer from the interlocutor. Such a function is largely equivalent to the function of checking understanding performed by those MWEs.

(b). The MWEs as a combination of checking understanding and discourse marker and embedded in stroke phases

The tendency of the expressions to mainly co-occur with certain gesture phases has also been identified in those instances where we find a combination of checking understanding and a discourse marker. As shown in Table 30.5, more than one-third of these are aligned with bodily movements emerging in the midst of large-sized stroke phases (7/19).

Table 30.5 *Gesture types co-occurring with the MWEs as a combination of checking understanding and discourse marker*

Embedded in stroke phase	7
Preparation phase	4
Post-stroke hold phase	2
Beat/beat-like stroke	2
Circular gesture	1
Retraction	1
No gesture	2
Total	19

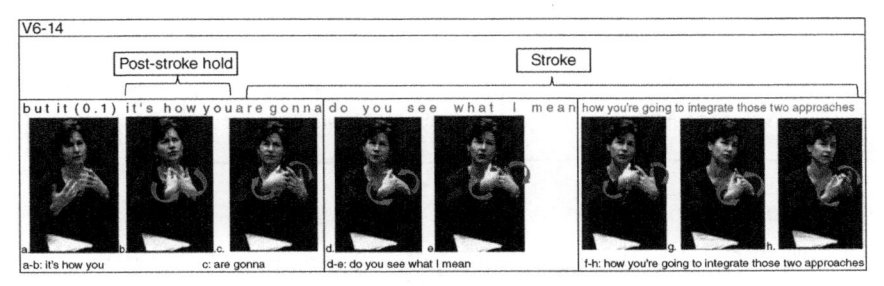

Figure 30.3 An instance of embedded in stroke phase.

Figure 30.3 shows an instance where both the MWE and its co-occurring gesture (d-e) are embedded in a long multimodal utterance. Specifically, this stroke is a series of two-handed movements consisting of outward-inward motions in turn by rotating the wrists (c-h): the right hand moves outwards, the left inwards and vice versa. The intertwined fingers are iconic of the meaning of "integrate the two approaches", which means incorporate separate things into a unity.

(c). *The expressions as discourse marker with no gesture*

Whereas the previous sections illustrate how the expressions of checking understanding and the combination of checking understanding and discourse markers are likely to co-occur with certain types of gestures, Table 30.6 shows that no gesture type is particularly foregrounded for the expression as a discourse marker.

All gesture types only occur once. This might also be the result of the small number of instances in the current case study, and further exploration of this matter with a much larger corpus may reveal different patterns. However, what can be inferred from the current figures is that more than half of the instances (6/11) used as discourse markers occur without the speaker performing any gesture. Furthermore, considering all the instances across the entire video, this means that 6 out of 15 instances without gestures function as discourse markers. These observations, therefore, suggest that, when the expressions are adopted by the speaker as a

Table 30.6 *Gesture types co-occurring with the MWEs as a discourse marker*

Beat-like stroke	1
Preparation phase	1
Retraction phase	1
Post-stroke hold phase + retraction phase	1
Post-stroke hold phase + preparation phase	1
No gesture	**6**
Total	11

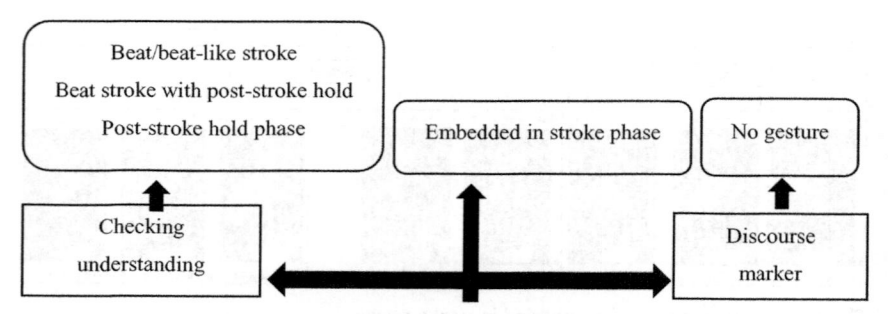

Figure 30.4 Gesture–speech functional profile for the MWEs.

discourse marker with little intention of checking understanding, they tend not to be accompanied by any gesture.

30.5.3 The Functional Speech–Gesture Profile for '(Do) You Know/See What I Mean'

According to the dominant gesture types emerging from each functional variation of the MWEs, Figure 30.4 represents a tentative gesture–speech profile. This profile attempts to demonstrate *the general tendency* of speech-gesture coordination mostly in accordance with the figures. Admittedly, these are merely tendencies, and the factors that lead to uncommon uses could be valuable to investigate. However, surfacing overall tendencies is in line with a corpus linguistic approach and has value for a number of applications such as supporting dictionary and textbook development and design (Sinclair 1991).

The profile shows that, on the left side of the continuum, the MWEs as checking understanding tend to be accompanied by beat/beat-like strokes, beat-like strokes with post-stroke holds, and post-stroke holds, all of which represent the most salient and meaningful gesture types. On the other hand, those that function as discourse markers tend to occur without any gesture. Situated in the middle of the continuum are the instances that tend to perform both functions, with the majority of them co-occurring with motions embedded in stroke phases. In general, as the salience and significance in the speech functions and gesture phases decreases from the left to the right, so do the entire multimodal units.

In addition to reflecting the dominant tendency in gesture–speech associations for most instances, this continuum also illustrates some of the complications involved in positioning those instances with overlapping gesture types. For instance, the function of an instance as checking understanding with no gesture moves slightly more towards the other side of the continuum. On the other hand, for an instance functioning as a discourse marker that co-occurs with a beat-like gesture, its function moves, to a certain extent, to the direction of checking understanding.

The case study also has implications for sociopragmatics in light of the nature of the multimodal corpora, i.e. academic supervision meetings at postgraduate level. The fact that this MWE is only used by supervisors in the corpus indicates a more powerful position held by them, and reflects the supervisor's role of ensuring the learning and development of the student while involving them in the process of academic supervision. This may also relate to the main goal of this context, which is to help the student to make good progress in their postgraduate study. We believe that this result may well be replicated in future research and similar studies are worthwhile doing drawing on much larger multimodal corpora where one party is in a more powerful position than the other. It is also worth investigating the ways in which this MWE will be used differently in those contexts where the status of the participants is relatively equal. A comparative study of this MWE in different genres may thus shed light on the use of language in relation to contextual variables such as role, identity or communicative goals.

Our small-scale case study presented here has a number of limitations. First of all, we have only analysed the language of one speaker and as such we are likely to have described, at least to a certain extent, the idiosyncratic discourse patterns of that speaker. Secondly, we have only investigated one particular interaction in a specific context, and we are unable to make any generalizations on the basis of this. However, with this case study, we are able to show that a multimodal corpus pragmatic approach can help us reach a more nuanced interpretation of utterance function, and conduct more fine-grained research on the pragmatic function of MWEs. We hope that we have at least shown an approach to corpus pragmatics that allows us to investigate the potential for functional disambiguation on the basis of patterning in a multimodal dataset.

30.6 Conclusion

In this chapter, we have shown that a corpus pragmatic approach is helpful in investigating sociopragmatic norms and values in particular social contexts. We have illustrated corpus methods for conducting pragmatic research, and provided an overview of research in corpus pragmatics with a focus on sociopragmatics. We have also emphasized the particular lack of multimodal corpus pragmatic research drawing on large multimodal corpora. We have presented a case study that exemplifies a multimodal corpus pragmatic approach for establishing a speech-gesture functional profile for an MWE, which can potentially generate meaningful insights for sociopragmatics. Notable here is the importance that we assign to context, or variables outside of the immediate text and co-text, when it comes to performing and understanding utterance function. With an increase in corpus data, and the addition of new multimodal corpora, we find that utterance function is encoded in the text and co-text to a much larger degree than traditional pragmatics might have suggested, where an overreliance on context has sometimes detracted from analysing linguistic patterns in use. In future, it might be possible to extend the meaning-based description of words and phrases that have become a mainstay of written corpus linguistics, to include core pragmatic functions and values. To do this, we will need a multimodal approach to functional corpus analysis and a commitment to the development of a fully multimodal unit of meaning that includes form (including gesture, prosody etc.), function and contextual information.

References

Adolphs, S. (2008). *Corpus and Context: Investigating Pragmatic Functions in Spoken Discourse*. Amsterdam: John Benjamins.

Adolphs, S. and Carter, R. (2007). Beyond the word. *European Journal of English Studies*, 11(2), 133–46.

Adolphs, S. and Carter, R. (2013). *Spoken Corpus Linguistics: From Monomodal to Multimodal*. London: Routledge.

Aijmer, K. (1996). *Conversational Routines in English: Convention and Creativity*. London: Longman.

Aijmer, K. (2013). *Understanding Pragmatic Markers: A Variational Pragmatic Approach*. Edinburgh: Edinburgh University Press.

Aijmer, K. (2015). Pragmatic markers. In K. Aijmer and C. Rühlemann, eds., *Corpus Pragmatics: A Handbook*. Cambridge: Cambridge University Press, pp. 195–218.

Aijmer, K. and Rühlemann, C. (eds.). (2015). *Corpus Pragmatics: A Handbook*. Cambridge: Cambridge University Press.

Austin, J. L. (1962). *How to Do Things with Words*. Oxford: Clarendon Press.

Avila-Ledesma, N. E. and Amador-Moreno, C. P. (2016). "The more please [places] I see the more I think of home": On gendered discourse of Irishness and migration experiences. In J. Romero-Trillo (ed.), *Yearbook* of *Corpus Linguistics and Pragmatics 2016: Global Implications for Society and Education in the Networked Age*. Cham, Switzerland: Spinger, pp. 85–105.

Brookes, H. (2005). What gestures do: Some communicative functions of quotable gestures in conversations among Black urban South Africans. *Journal of Pragmatics*, 37(12), 2044–85.

Calbris, G. (2011). *Elements of Meaning in Gesture*. Amsterdam: John Benjamins.

Carter, R. and McCarthy, M. (2006). *Cambridge Grammar of English: A Comprehensive Guide*. Cambridge: Cambridge University Press.

Diani, G. (2015). Politeness. In K. Aijmer and C. Rühlemann, eds., *Corpus Pragmatics: A Handbook*. Cambridge: Cambridge University Press, pp. 169–91.

Duncan, S. D., Cassell, J. and Levy, E. (eds.). (2007). *Gesture and the Dynamic Dimension of Language: Essays in Honor of David McNeill*. Amsterdam: John Benjamins.

Fraser, B. (2015). The combining of discourse markers – a beginning. *Journal of Pragmatics*, 86, 48–53.

Fung, L. and Carter, R. (2007). Discourse markers and spoken English: Native and learner use in pedagogic settings. *Applied Linguistics*, 28(3), 410–39.

Gablasova, D. and Brezina, V. (2015). Does speaker role affect the choice of epistemic adverbials in L2 speech? Evidence from the Trinity Lancaster Corpus. In J. Romero-Trillo, ed., *Yearbook of Corpus Linguistics and Pragmatics: Current Approaches to Discourse and Translation Studies*. Cham, Switzerland: Springer, pp. 117–36.

Gablasova, D., Brezina, V. and McEnery, T. (2017). Collocations in corpus-based language learning research: Identifying, comparing, and interpreting the evidence. *Language Learning*, 67, 155–79.

Gray, B. and Biber, D. (2015). Stance markers. In K. Aijmer and C. Rühlemann, eds., *Corpus Pragmatics: A Handbook*. Cambridge: Cambridge University Press, pp. 219–48.

Gullberg, M. (1998). *Gesture as a Communication Strategy in Second Language Discourse: A Study of Learners of French and Swedish*. Lund, Sweden: Lund University Press.

Gullberg, M. (2006). Some reasons for studying gesture and second language acquisition (Hommage à Adam Kendon). *International Review of Applied Linguistics in Language Teaching*, 44(2), 103–24.

Haugh, M. and Culpeper, J. (2018). Integrative pragmatics and (im)politeness theory. In C. Ilie and N. R. Norrick, eds., *Pragmatics and Its Interfaces*. Amsterdam: John Benjamins, pp. 213–39.

Hunston, S. (2002). *Corpora in Applied Linguistics*. Cambridge: Cambridge University Press.

Irvine, C. A., Eigsti, I. M. and Fein, D. A. (2016). Uh, Um, and autism: Filler disfluencies as pragmatic markers in adolescents with optimal outcomes from autism spectrum disorder. *Journal of Autism and Developmental Disorders*, 46(3), 1061–70.

Jautz, S. (2008). Gratitude in British and New Zealand radio programmes: Nothing but gushing? In K. P. Schneider and A. Barron, eds., *Variational Pragmatics: A Focus on Regional Varieties in Pluricentric Languages*. Amsterdam: John Benjamins, pp. 141–78.

Kallen, J. L. and Kirk, J. M. (2008). *ICE-Ireland: A User's Guide*. Belfast: Cló Ollscoil na Banríona.

Kallen, J. L. and Kirk, J. M. (2012). *SPICE-Ireland: A User's Guide*. Belfast: Cló Ollscoil na Banríona.

Kendon, A. (1995). Gestures as illocutionary and discourse structure markers in Southern Italian conversation. *Journal of Pragmatics, 23*(3), 247–79.

Kendon, A. (2004). *Gesture: Visible Action as Utterance*. Cambridge: Cambridge University Press.

Kennedy, G. (1998). *An Introduction to Corpus Linguistics*. London: Longman.

Kita, S., van Gijn, I. and van der Hulst, H. (1998). Movement phases in signs and co-speech gestures, and their transcription by human coders. In I. Wachsmuth and M. Fröhlich, eds., *Gesture and Sign Language in Human–Computer Interaction: International Gesture Workshop Bielefeld, Germany, September 17–19, 1997 Proceedings*, pp. 23–35. https://doi.org/10.1007/BFb0052986

Knight, D. (2011). *Multimodality and Active Listenership: A Corpus Approach*. London: Bloomsbury.

Kohnen, T. (2015). Speech acts: A diachronic perspective. In K. Aijmer and C. Rühlemann, eds., *Corpus Pragmatics: A Handbook*, pp. 52–83. Cambridge: Cambridge University Press.

Leech, G. N. (1983). *Principles of Pragmatics*. London: Routledge.

Maíz-Arévalo, C. (2017). Expressive speech acts in educational e-chats. *Soprag, 5*(2), 151–78.

Martín-Laguna, S. and Alcón-Soler, E. (2018). Development of discourse-pragmatic markers in a multilingual classroom: A mixed method research approach. *System, 75*, 68–80.

McEnery, T. and Hardie, A. (2011). *Corpus Linguistics: Method, Theory and Practice*. Cambridge: Cambridge University Press.

McNeill, D. (1992). *Hand and Mind: What Gestures Reveal about Thought*. Chicago: University of Chicago Press.

McNeill, D. (2005). *Gesture and Thought*. Chicago: University of Chicago Press.

Mestre-Mestre, E. M. (2016). Healing and comfort on the net: Gender and emotions in violent domestic environments. In J. Romero-Trillo, ed., *Yearbook of Corpus Linguistics and Pragmatics 2016: Global Implications for Society and Education in the Networked Age*. Cham, Switzerland: Spinger, pp. 51–84.

Mey, J. L. (2001). *Pragmatics: An Introduction*. 2nd ed. Oxford: Blackwell.

O'Keeffe, A. and Adolphs, S. (2008). Response tokens in British and Irish discourse: Corpus, context and variational pragmatics. In K. P. Schneider and A. Barron, eds., *Variational Pragmatics: A Focus on Regional Varieties in Pluricentric Languages*. Amsterdam: John Benjamins, pp. 69–98.

Romero-Trillo, J. D. (ed.). (2013). *Yearbook of Corpus Linguistics and Pragmatics: New Domains and Methodologies*. Dordrecht, Netherlands: Springer.

Romero-Trillo, J. (ed.). (2014). *Yearbook of Corpus Linguistics and Pragmatics: New Empirical and Theoretical Paradigms*. Cham, Switzerland: Springer.

Romero-Trillo, J. (ed.). (2015). *Yearbook of Corpus Linguistics and Pragmatics: Current Approaches to Discourse and Translation Studies*. Cham, Switzerland: Springer.

Romero-Trillo, J. (ed.). (2016). *Yearbook of Corpus Linguistics and Pragmatics: Global Implications for Society and Education in the Networked Age*. Cham, Switzerland: Springer.

Romero-Trillo, J. (2018a). Corpus pragmatics and second language pragmatics: A mutualistic entente in theory and practice. *Corpus Pragmatics*, 2(2), 113–27.

Romero-Trillo, J. (2018b). Prosodic modeling and position analysis of pragmatic markers in English conversation. *Corpus Linguistics and Linguistic Theory*, 14(1), 169–95.

Ronan, P. (2015). Categorizing expressive speech acts in the pragmatically annotated SPICE Ireland corpus. *ICAME Journal*, 39(1), 25–45.

Rühlemann, C. and Aijmer, K. (2015). Introduction: Corpus pragmatics: Laying the foundations. In K. Aijmer and C. Rühlemann, eds., *Corpus Pragmatics: A Handbook*. Cambridge: Cambridge University Press, pp. 1–26.

Rühlemann, C. and Clancy, B. (2018). Corpus linguistics and pragmatics. In C. Ilie and N. R. Norrick, eds., *Pragmatics and Its Interfaces*. Amsterdam: John Benjamins, pp. 241–66.

Rühlemann, C. and O'Donnell, M. B. (2015). Deixis. In K. Aijmer and C. Rühlemann, eds., *Corpus Pragmatics: A Handbook*. Cambridge: Cambridge University Press, pp. 331–59.

Schneider, K. P. and Barron, A. (eds.). (2008). *Variational Pragmatics: A Focus on Regional Varieties in Pluricentric Languages*. Amsterdam: John Benjamins.

Searle, J. R. (1971). *The Philosophy of Language*. Oxford: Oxford University Press.

Searle, J. R. (1976). A classification of illocutionary acts 1. *Language in Society*, 5(1), 1–23.

Sinclair, J. (1991). *Corpus, Concordance, Collocation*. Oxford: Oxford University Press.

Sloetjes, H. and Wittenburg, P. (2008). Annotation by category-ELAN and ISO DCR. In *The Sixth International Conference on Language Resources and Evaluation (LREC 2008)*, pp. 816–20.

Stubbe, M. and Holmes, J. (1995). You know, eh and other "exasperating expressions": An analysis of social and stylistic variation in the use of pragmatic devices in a sample of New Zealand English. *Language and Communication*, 15(1), 63–88.

Thomas, J. (1983). Cross-cultural pragmatic failure. *Applied Linguistics*, 4(2), 91–112.

Thomas, J. A. (1995). *Meaning in Interaction: An Introduction to Pragmatics*. New York: Routledge.

Tottie, G. (2011). *Uh* and *Um* as sociolinguistic markers in British English. *International Journal of Corpus Linguistics*, 16(1), 173–97.

Tottie, G. (2015). Turn management and the fillers uh and um. In K. Aijmer and C. Rühlemann, eds., *Corpus Pragmatics: A Handbook*. Cambridge: Cambridge University Press, pp. 381–407.

Tree, J. E. F. and Schrock, J. C. (2002). Basic meanings of you know and I mean. *Journal of Pragmatics*, 34(6), 727–47.

Tsuchiya, K. (2013). *Listenership Behaviours in Intercultural Encounters: A Time-Aligned Multimodal Corpus Analysis*. Amsterdam: John Benjamins.

Weisser, M. (2016). DART – The dialogue annotation and research tool. *Corpus Linguistics and Linguistic Theory*, 12(2), 355–88.

Werner, V. (2017). Adversative pragmatic markers in learner language: A cross-sectional perspective. *Corpus Pragmatics*, 1(2), 135–58.

Wittenburg, P., Brugman, H., Russel, A., Klassmann, A. and Sloetjes, H. (2006). Elan: A professional framework for multimodality research. In *Proceedings of LREC 2006, Fifth International Conference on Language Resources and Evaluation*.

Woods, H. B. (1991). Social differentiation in Ottawa English. In J. Cheshire, ed., *English around the World: Sociolinguistic Perspectives*. Cambridge: Cambridge University Press, pp. 134–50.

31

Variational Pragmatics

Klaus P. Schneider[*]

31.1 Introduction

Variational pragmatics is conceptualized as the intersection of pragmatics with sociolinguistics. The relevant area in sociolinguistics is also referred to as dialectology. In this context, dialectology is not reduced to traditional dialect geography focusing on regional variation within the boundaries of a nation-state alone. The broad notion of dialectology adopted in variational pragmatics also includes types of social variation, e.g. socioeconomic and ethnic variation (cf. Wolfram and Schilling 2016).

Variational pragmatics addresses complementary research gaps in pragmatics and dialectology. Researchers in sociolinguistics interested in regional and social variation have predominantly concentrated on pronunciation, vocabulary and grammar, whereas pragmatics has been largely ignored. Researchers in pragmatics, on the other hand, have either focused on pragmatic universals (e.g. speech act theory) or on differences between languages (e.g. contrastive pragmatics), but not on differences between varieties of the same language. The aim of variational pragmatics is therefore two-fold. It is aimed at adding pragmatic phenomena to the research agenda of sociolinguistics, and regional and social variation to the agenda of pragmatics.

The basic tenet of variational pragmatics is that macro-social factors such as ethnicity, gender and age impact language use in interaction in systematic ways, resulting in divergent sociopragmatic norms and language use conventions. Macro-social factors are distinguished from micro-social factors such as power and distance. While the latter characterize relationships between participants in an interaction (e.g. as asymmetrical, or as distant), the former characterize identities as they are displayed and

---

[*] I thank an anonymous reviewer for their most helpful comments. As always, any remaining infelicities are, of course, my own.

perceived by the participants. Variational pragmatics can thus be defined as the study of macro-social variation in language use conventions across social groups sharing the same language.

It is a relatively recent development in pragmatics research (on the history of variational pragmatics, cf. Schneider 2010; Barron 2017). Work pre-dating the introduction of the term 'variational pragmatics' include the examination of speech acts across national varieties of Spanish. In Hispanic studies, this field of inquiry was referred to as the study of sociopragmatic variation (cf. Márquez Reiter and Placencia 2005).

The present chapter provides a state-of-the-art overview of variational pragmatics. It includes an outline of the original framework (Section 31.2), a summary of recent modifications of this framework (Section 31.3), a discussion of theoretical issues (Section 31.4) and methodological principles (Section 31.5), and a survey of studies carried out in variational pragmatics (Section 31.6). In the conclusion (Section 31.7), a summary is provided and perspectives for future research are sketched out.

31.2 The Original Framework

The framework originally proposed for variational pragmatics comprises two component parts, reflecting the cross-disciplinary nature of this field of inquiry. These are a variational component, specifying relevant macro-social factors, and a pragmatic component, specifying relevant levels of analysis. These two components will now be briefly outlined.

31.2.1 The Variational Component: Macro-social Factors

In the variational component of the original framework, five macro-social factors are specified. These are region, social class, ethnicity, gender, and age. (For a detailed discussion of these factors, cf. Schneider and Barron 2008a; Barron and Schneider 2009; Schneider 2010; Barron 2017.) It is assumed that these same factors systematically impact how language is used in interaction, specifically pragmatic phenomena such as the choice of discourse markers, the realization speech acts, turn-taking and so on.

In variational pragmatics, the concept of region is more flexible than in traditional dialect geography. It pertains not only to sub-national varieties of languages, but also to national varieties of pluricentric languages, e.g. Austrian German and Swiss German. Further distinctions include the local and the sub-local level, i.e. differences between cities and between districts in the same city, often correlating with social class differences. Transnational regions have also been suggested, e.g. North America or North-Western Europe (cf. Section 31.4). Finally, the urban–rural divide, i.e. differences between life in relative anonymity in cities as opposed to village life with a high degree of social control, also constitutes a relevant aspect of regional variation which merits investigation in the framework of variational pragmatics.

While social class has played a crucial role in the development of sociolinguistics, this concept has been problematized as an undertheorized concept (e.g. Ash 2002: 419–20; cf. also Wolfram and Schilling 2016: 159–79). Hence, some researchers in variational pragmatics have preferred a more differentiated view, distinguishing such factors as level of education, occupation or income (e.g. Plevoets et al. 2008).

Age has played only a subordinate role in variational pragmatics; in some studies generations are contrasted. More commonly, perhaps, reference is made to stages in the life cycle, i.e. most prominently, children, adolescents, and adults and sometimes some further differentiations such as young adults, old speakers and old old speakers (for further discussion, cf. Georgakopoulou and Charalambidou 2011).

It has been argued that studies in sociolinguistics involving male and female speakers do not, as a rule, examine gender variation but sex variation, and that the term 'gender' is only used because it is considered more politically correct (Cheshire 2002: 423). Yet treating sex as a broad and unrefined macro-social variable avoids the deployment of a careful ethnographic case study approach necessary to adequately examine complex social concepts such as gender and the influence of gender construction on language use (cf. Murphy 2011; also Queen 2013), and essentially the same applies to race and ethnicity. Also this more simplistic approach makes studies more easily comparable (Cheshire 2002: 424–5). At least in the early days of variational pragmatics this reduced complexity approach to macro-social factors was considered useful, maybe even inevitable (Barron and Schneider 2009: 432).

No claim has been made that the five factors distinguished in the original framework of variational pragmatics are the only conceivable macro-social factors which have a systematic impact on language use in communication and may be responsible for specific patterns of use and interactional practices.

31.2.2 The Pragmatic Component: Levels of Analysis

In the pragmatic component of the original framework, five levels of analysis are distinguished. These are the formal, actional, interactional, topic and organizational level (cf. Schneider and Barron 2008a; Barron and Schneider 2009; Schneider 2010; Barron 2017). Distinguishing these five levels shows that variational pragmatics is based on a broad notion of pragmatics which integrates micro- and macro-pragmatic perspectives. That is to say that the analysis is not limited to individual utterances or speech acts, but also considers interaction, longer stretches of discourse and entire speech events.

On the formal level, the analysis is focused on individual words or short phrases that serve specific communicative functions and can be summarized as pragmatic markers. Examples include discourse markers such as *well* and *you know*, and question tags such as *isn't it?* and *eh?*. The aim of analysis is to identify the functions these forms may have in interaction, and which of the functions is relevant under what contextual circumstances.

The actional level of analysis is the level of speech acts. Work on this level is aimed at establishing how speech acts are realized and how realizations differ in terms of (in)directness, (im)politeness, (in)formality etc. A further parameter is speech act modification. Each realization strategy can be aggravated or mitigated (cf. Blum-Kulka et al. 1989). The goal is not only to identify the realization strategies and modificational devices that are available (pragmalinguistic perspective), but also which strategies and devices are chosen and considered appropriate under which circumstances (sociopragmatic perspective).

Analysis on the actional level was initially characterized as function-to-form mapping, taking illocutions as a starting point and looking for their realizations, whereas analysis on the formal level was characterized as form-to-function mapping, taking linguistic forms as a starting point and attempting to determine their possible functions (Schneider and Barron 2008a: 20). Both perspectives are, however, relevant to either level (e.g. Schneider 2014). On both levels, there is a many-to-many relationship between linguistic forms and communicative functions.

Analysis on the interactional level goes beyond the individual speech act, accounting for the fact that speech acts do not normally occur in isolation, but combine into larger units of discourse. These units may be adjacency pairs or larger units, as many speech acts are negotiated over a number of turns-at-talk, e.g. offer sequences or remedial interchanges (cf. Barron 2005; Owen 1983). Also, entire speech events may be analysed on this level, for instance small talk or service encounters (e.g. Schneider 2008; Félix-Brasdefer 2015).

On the topic level, the analysis is focused on discourse content. This includes both propositional content of individual speech acts and macro-propositions as larger discourse-structuring content units negotiated across a number of turns and exchanges. The analysis concerns various aspects of topic management including topic selection and topic development (cf. Schneider 1988: 81–97). The analysis also concerns classes of propositional content in individual speech acts, establishing meaningful subclasses of illocutions which behave in markedly different ways in interaction, concerning not only the realization of these speech act subtypes, but also continuation patterns. For instance, subclasses of requests include, among others, requests for action, for material goods, for information, for permission, and for patience (cf. Schneider 2003: 160–78).

Finally, analysis on the organizational level deals with the "machinery of interaction" (Clift 2014: 101). Phenomena studied on this level include various aspects of turn-taking, notably types of simultaneous speech, including overlap and interruptions, and types of silence in interaction, including gaps, lapses and pauses. It has been found that communities and cultures using the same language may also differ regarding these basic mechanics (cf. Wolfram and Schilling 2016: 86–93).

From the discussion of the five levels of pragmatic analysis, it should be clear that variational pragmatics does not subscribe to any particular tradition in pragmatics research, but that it attempts to synthesize a range of approaches, among them speech act analysis, conversation analysis, and discourse analysis, in order to provide a more comprehensive picture of human communication.

31.3 Modifying the Framework

Ever since its inception, variational pragmatics has been modified in a number of ways. These modifications concern both parts of the original framework, i.e. the variational as well as the pragmatic component. These modifications are discussed in the ensuing subsections.

31.3.1 Modifying the Variational Component

Modifications of the variational component concern different aspects of macro-social variation. These are (1) the number of macro-social factors; (2) the status of macro-social factors and (3) the interaction of macro-social variation with other types of pragmatic variation.

Regarding the number of macro-social factors, no claim was made that the five factors originally specified are a closed set and that no other factors are conceivable that might also systematically impact language use in interaction. Religion, for example, seems to be a further relevant factor (e.g. Al-Ali 2006). That this factor was not taken into consideration from the start may reflect a bias in early work in variational pragmatics, which was initially focused on Indo-European languages and Western societies exclusively (cf. Section 31.6). If more work is carried out on languages, societies and cultures, e.g. in the Arab world, in sub-Saharan Africa or East Asia, additional factors may emerge which are socially significant and have an influence on language use.

Regarding the status of the macro-social factors, it has been assumed from the start that these factors have a systematic influence on language use, but that they do not determine language use. This means that researchers in variational pragmatics do not adopt the deterministic view of essentialism. Nor do they, however, subscribe to constructionism. They reject the idea that identities are entirely fluid and can be constructed and negotiated anew in each interaction. As Grant and MacLeod (2016: 54) note, writing about assumed identities from a forensic perspective: "identity performances are necessarily constrained.... Any individual's identity performances are not boundless". As one sociolinguistic constraint, these authors identify "a particular language variety". More importantly, language users go by appearances. Identities are ascribed according to how people look, how they are dressed and how they speak (e.g. Bieswanger 2015: 536; Dinkin 2018: 197).

Based on these insights, an approach has been proposed which is neither essentialist nor constructionist, but can be characterized as an emic first-order approach to the status of macro-social factors in variational pragmatics. This means that "all macro-social factors [are treated] as identities as they are displayed and perceived by participants (in the emic sense) in an interaction" (Haugh and Schneider 2012: 1017). The methodological consequences of this approach are, in fact, quite challenging. Instruments required include perception studies and laypeople's metapragmatic discourse, as can be found for instance in discussions of appropriate language use in blogs or in focus group discussions (e.g. Schröder and Schneider, forthcoming). To date, however, not much work has been carried out in this area.

All research in variational pragmatics shows that the members of a social group (i.e. nation, generation, community etc.) do not behave in uniform ways, highlighting the fact that macro-social factors do not *determine* language use. There are, however, dominant patterns, which have been the main focus of all empirical research in this field of inquiry. To provide just one example, in one study it was found that 56.7 per cent of English English speakers opened party small talk with strangers with an exchange of bare greetings, whereas 60.0 per cent of American English speakers initially introduced themselves, and 73.3 per cent of Irish English speakers assessed the situation (e.g. *Great party, isn't it?*) (Schneider 2008). Yet, other practices also occurred, demonstrating that not only inter-varietal but also intra-varietal variation exists, i.e. variation within a social group. Furthermore, there is inter-situational variation, i.e. the same speech act, for example, may be realized in different ways in different situations, depending on such micro-social factors as power and distance. For instance, there is recent work on responses to thanks in Canadian English illustrating how macro-social and micro-social variation interact (Dinkin 2018).

Finally, it has been established that the same individuals do not behave consistently even in the same type of situation. In their study of initial encounters between strangers from Australia and America, Haugh and Carbaugh (2015) observe not only intra-varietal, but also intra-individual variation. The same participants display different interactional practices in the same type of situation, depending on who they talk to. All types of variation and the interaction between them need to be taken into account in a theory of pragmatic variation yet to be developed.

31.3.2 Modifying the Pragmatic Component

Modifications of the pragmatic component concern different aspects of the analytical approach. These are (1) the number of levels of analysis; (2) the status of the levels of analysis and (3) the focus on spoken language.

Regarding the number of analytical levels, no claim was made that the five levels originally proposed form an exhaustive list. It is therefore not surprising that further levels have been suggested. Most importantly, Félix-Brasdefer (2015) has suggested to add a stylistic, a prosodic, and a non-verbal level (Félix-Brasdefer 2015: 43–8). Relevant distinctions on the stylistic level include formal – informal, serious – non-serious, transactional – interactional, and pertain, for example, to the choice of address terms. On the prosodic level, features such as intonation, pitch, stress, loudness and speech rate are investigated as pragmatic resources. Finally, the non-verbal level permits the inclusion of multimodal elements of interaction, e.g. facial expressions, gaze, gestures and posture.

The presentation of the levels of analysis seems to suggest an additive bottom-up approach, yet this is misleading. What is advocated instead is an integrative top-down approach. It must always be borne in mind that all levels are interdependent, although they can be distinguished analytically and treated separately to reduce the complexities of interactions to a manageable degree in a given study. This entails that investigations of, for example, discourse markers or adjacency pairs should be sensitive to the discourse context these phenomena occur in and take the discourse genre into account (Félix-Brasdefer 2015; Schneider 2019). The genre level may not even be the top-most level, as disjunct communicative events and shared discourse history may also be relevant.

So far, variational pragmatics has been overwhelmingly focused on spoken discourse. Yet, "how to do things with written words" should also be included (Schneider 2019). Complaints are a good example, as they can be made in face-to-face encounters or on the telephone as well as in letters or in emails. Including written discourse may necessitate some minor modifications of the levels of analysis. For instance, speech acts and speech events ought to be referred to more generally as communicative acts and communicative events. Turn-taking is not limited to talk-in-interaction, but essentially also relevant in, for example, email exchanges, threads in blogs and discussion forums. Finally, prosodic features (e.g. SHOUTING!!!!!!!!) and non-verbal elements (e.g. emojis) can also be analysed in at least some written genres.

Finally, a metapragmatic level can be added to the analysis. On this level, researchers examine how ordinary language users think and talk about pragmatic phenomena, e.g. speech acts. Discussions in focus groups and forums on the internet reveal a high degree of metapragmatic awareness of social norms and conventions in general, and an awareness of intra-lingual variation and cross-varietal differences in particular (Schneider 2018; Schröder and Schneider, forthcoming). Work on this particular level of analysis adds a first-order dimension to variational pragmatics.

31.4 Theoretical Issues

In this section, two theoretical issues are addressed. One pertains to pragmatic universals and pragmatic variation, pragmatic variables and their variants. Relevant questions include which pragmatic features are shared across languages, which vary across languages and across varieties of a language. The other issue concerns the status of languages and language varieties, i.e. whether they are spoken by native or non-native speakers, by second language users or foreign language learners.

Universals were the focus of early work in pragmatics. Speech act philosophers were interested in the foundations of human communication (Austin 1962; Searle 1969). Similarly, the proponents of conversation analysis, analysing conversations in American English, were not interested in the specific features of this variety (e.g. Schegloff and Sacks 1973: 291). Finally, Brown and Levinson ([1978] 1987), in their theory of politeness, made explicit claims at universality. These approaches were criticized by Wierzbicka (1985) as being ethnocentric, "mistaking Anglo-Saxon conversational conventions for 'human behaviour' in general" (Wierzbicka 1985: 146).

Her article gave rise to work in contrastive pragmatics examining pragmatic variation between different languages (e.g. Blum-Kulka et al. 1989). Yet Wierzbicka's (1985: 146) remark, made more or less in passing, that "cultural norms reflected in speech acts differ not only from one language to another, but also from one regional and social variety to another", remained largely unheeded before variational pragmatics entered the scene.

Some years before Wierzbicka's article had been published, in 1978, Schlieben-Lange and Weydt had proposed to put pragmatics on the research agenda of traditional dialectology (cf. Schneider and Barron 2008a: 8–11). Interestingly, the differences they observed between different regions in Germany are very similar to differences between different languages observed later on in contrastive pragmatics and differences between national varieties of English observed in variational pragmatics. For example, Schlieben-Lange and Weydt (1978: 261) note that typically compliments are gladly accepted in the Rhineland (in the west of Germany) and rejected in Swabia (in the south-west of Germany). Essentially the same preferences were found by Chen (1993) among Americans and Chinese speakers, respectively.

It can be assumed that there are genuine pragmatic universals, shared by all languages (e.g. the existence of speech acts, the indispensability of requests), and also "culturoversals", i.e. patterns of language use common to languages in close cultural proximity (cf. the analogous concept of areoversals in language typology; Szmrecsanyi and Kortmann 2009). Apparently, this is what Kasper had in mind when postulating a North-Western European area of shared cultural values, manifested, for example, in similar complimenting behaviour (Kasper 1990: 199), and what Nilsson et al. (2018: 81) had in mind when hypothesizing a "pragma-cultural area" including all Nordic countries.

Language use conventions shared across varieties of, for example, English can be regarded as pragmatic Angloversals (cf. Szmrecsanyi and Kortmann 2009: 33 on uses of the term pertaining to morphosyntactic features), whereas other language use conventions are variety-specific. Variety-specific conventions can be established empirically, if comparable data are available (cf. Section 31.5.1). For instance, if under the same circumstances speakers of English deploy an elliptical construction of the type [ADJ EVALpos + Nparty] + question tag (e.g. *Great party, isn't it?*), and speakers from England and Ireland use *isn't it?*, speakers from the United States use *huh?*, and speakers from Canada *eh?* (Schneider 2014), then this specific question tag position is a pragmatic variable, and the three realizations are the variants of this variable. Similarly, alternative realizations of responses to thanks in the same situation (e.g. asking directions) are variants of the same variable (cf. Bieswanger 2015 on American and Canadian preferences). Furthermore, to give a sociopragmatic example, introducing yourself (American English) and assessing the situation (Irish English) are variants of the variable opening small talk with a stranger at a party (cf. Section 31.3.1; for more details on the notion of pragmatic variables, cf. Barron 2017; also Jucker and Taavitsainen 2012; Terkourafi 2012 on a diverging view). Which variants are generally expected in a given situation is specified in the social norms of groups and communities speaking a particular variety, which have been theorized as cultural models acquired in socialization and stored in the long-term memory (Schneider 2012c). In general, most variety-specific variants are variety-preferential rather than variety-exclusive; i.e. they do not occur in only one, but in several or all varieties, yet with different frequencies.

The second theoretical issue concerns language status. Variational pragmatics is standardly defined as the study of intra-lingual macro-social pragmatic variation. From the start, intra-lingual variation has, as a default, been understood as variation between native speakers of a language and the varieties they speak. However, now there is also work explicitly grounded in the framework of variational pragmatics in which native speakers are compared to second language users of the same language. Mulo Farenkia (2014) comparing Canadian French and Cameroonian French is a case in point. Such studies resemble work in post-colonial pragmatics, conceptualized by Anchimbe and Janney (2011) as dealing with the pragmatics in post-colonial societies.

A further development in variational pragmatics is exemplified in a project on the pragmatics of English in Namibia (e.g. Schröder and Schneider 2018). English is the official language of Namibia, although the country was never under British rule. Hence, English is spoken at many levels of proficiency, ranging from very elementary to (near-)native-like. This situation shows that classifying national varieties of English as native, second, and foreign language varieties is overly simplistic (cf. Kachru 1985). In many post-colonial societies today, all types of varieties coexist. The project on Namibia thus contributes to ongoing debates about the fuzzy boundaries between second and foreign language varieties in the multilingual realities in most parts of the world (cf. Mukherjee and Hundt 2011).

Other projects combining variational pragmatics and contrastive pragmatics include, for example, Félix-Brasdefer's (2015) monograph-length study of service encounters in the United States and in Mexico. A further synthesis of approaches is documented in the volume *Researching Sociopragmatic Variability*, edited by Beeching and Woodfield (2015), in which *Perspectives from Variational, Interlanguage and Contrastive Pragmatics* (subtitle) are combined.

These examples demonstrate that, increasingly, the distinctions between native, second and foreign languages are called into question, and the boundaries between variational, post-colonial, interlanguage and contrastive pragmatics seem to become more and more irrelevant. In the light of these trends it appears to be desirable to develop a theory of pragmatic variation in and across languages and language varieties which also takes different categories of pragmatic universals into account.

31.5 Methodological Issues

31.5.1 Three Methodological Principles

In variational pragmatics, three methodological principles have been formulated. These have been termed empiricity principle, contrastivity principle and comparability principle (cf. Barron and Schneider 2009; Schneider 2010, 2014).

The gist of the empiricity principle is that language use cannot be invented, but can only be examined in language data. Researchers in the field of variational pragmatics do not rely on their own language competence and communicative experience alone, but make use of existing data collections such as corpora or collect data themselves. They do not employ armchair methods, but field or laboratory methods, or combinations thereof (cf. Jucker 2009). Observational or experimentational data, gathered by employing collection procedures from a range of different options (cf. Section 31.5.2), are indispensable in work in variational pragmatics.

The contrastivity principle stipulates that at least two varieties of the same language are explicitly compared. In other words, the focus is not on one particular variety alone, e.g. Irish English or youth language. In order to identify specific pragmatic features of a variety, it is not (implicitly) compared to an abstract norm, e.g. Standard English or adult language, but contrasted with one or more further varieties of the same language, e.g. Irish English versus English English. In short, in variational pragmatics explicit comparison of at least two varieties of the same language is required.

Finally, the comparability principle demands that varieties of the same language which are contrasted are in fact comparable. This means that the varieties have the same status, e.g. female speakers of one variety are compared to female speakers of another variety, so that one type of variation can be focused on in direct comparison. Also, it must be borne in mind that speakers of, for example, national varieties belong to various social groups and communities, by virtue of the fact that identities involve all macro-social factors, and that these factors interact. Furthermore, macro-social factors interact with micro-social factors, including those pertaining to the relationship between participants such as power and distance, and those pertaining to context such as discourse genre and circumstances (cf. Section 31.3.1). Ideally, all relevant variables are controlled and systematically manipulated to take into account the multiple interaction of social factors, be it in experimentational work or in the choice of observational contexts. If these issues are ignored, the danger is that apples are compared to oranges (cf. Schneider 2017).

The principles of empiricity, contrastivity and comparativity are not particular to variational pragmatics alone, but should be observed in any type of comparison in language studies, including contrastive, cross-cultural, post-colonial, interlanguage, historical and diachronic pragmatics and, more generally, contrastive, historical and diachronic linguistics as well as language typology (cf. Schneider and Schröder 2014).

31.5.2 Data Types and Data Collection

Variational pragmatics is a pluri-method approach, i.e. it is not limited to using one particular method. This does not mean that any method can be used for any purpose. It does mean, however, that variational pragmatics does not subscribe to methodological totalitarianism witnessed in some areas of pragmatics research. The basic methodological position subscribed to instead is that a wide range of data types and data collection procedures exists which can be used for a range of research purposes. It is furthermore accepted that all methods have strengths as well as weaknesses, and that accordingly there is no best method as such, or a method that could be used for all purposes. The choice of method first and foremost depends on the research question. A method which may be suitable for addressing one particular question may not be suitable for addressing other questions. To compensate the disadvantages of a chosen method triangulation is recommended, i.e. the combination of data collected by employing different methods (Schneider 2018).

Most generally, two types of research goals can be distinguished. These are, on the one hand, a focus on language use conventions, i.e. normative aspects such as social conventions and cultural values underlying communicative behaviour in specific types of situations, and, on the other hand, a focus on interpersonal issues, i.e. actual communicative behaviour under particular circumstances. These two complementary goals have been referred to as the generic and the interactional perspective (Decock and Spiessens 2017: 87–8). Most research in variational pragmatics to date has adopted the generic perspective.

31.6 Research in Variational Pragmatics

The present section provides an overview of work carried out in variational pragmatics by addressing four questions: (1) Which languages and language varieties have been examined? (2) Which social factors have been studied? (3) Which levels of pragmatic analysis have been focused on? (4) Which methods have been employed? (For further surveys, cf. Schneider 2010, 2012b; Schneider and Placencia 2017.)

Prototypically, early research in variational pragmatics is focused on regional variation on the actional level in Indo-European languages, studied by employing experimentational methods. This may have contributed to perceiving variational pragmatics as the study of regional variation alone. Circumstances supporting this reduced perception include the original definition of variational pragmatics as the interface of pragmatics with dialectology, inviting too narrow interpretations of dialectology. Furthermore, the foundational volume by Schneider and Barron (2008b) concentrates on regional variation across national varieties of pluricentric languages.

The languages studied in variational pragmatics so far include, first and foremost, Spanish and English. Both are pluricentric languages, i.e. spoken natively as majority languages in several nation-states. Further languages investigated include French and German, and less frequently Swedish and Dutch. So overwhelmingly Indo-European languages have been examined, specifically Romance and Germanic languages, and there is a clear Western bias. Chinese has, however, also received attention, and in September 2019, a conference will be held on "Variational Pragmatics in East Asian Languages" (cf. *LINGUIST List* 29: 4912).

Among the macro-social factors, region clearly dominates. Most studies of regional variation compare two or more national varieties. For Spanish, these include the varieties spoken in Latin America, specifically in Argentina, Chile, Colombia, Costa Rica, Dominican Republic, Ecuador, Mexico, Nicaragua, Panama, Peru, San Salvador and Venezuela. These varieties are compared to each other or to Peninsular Spanish. As a rule, the data for these comparisons were collected in one particular location in each of the countries involved and are therefore not representative of language use across the respective country. Examples include Félix-Brasdefer (2009) on requests in San José (Costa Rica), Santiago (Dominican Republic), and Mexico City; and Placencia et al. (2015) on nominal address in Santiago (Chile), Quito (Ecuador), and Seville (Spain). Less frequently, locations within the same country are contrasted, e.g. in Lázaro Ruiz and Ramajo

Cuesta (2015) on compliments in five regions of Spain (Andalusia, Castile-Leon, Catalonia, Madrid and Valencia).

For English, the national varieties studied are American, Australian, British/English, Canadian, Irish, and New Zealand English and also Cameroonian, Ghanaian and Namibian English. As a rule, two native-language varieties are compared, rarely three or more. Examples include Barron (2008) comparing English and Irish English; Jautz (2013) comparing British and New Zealand English; Anchimbe (2018) comparing Cameroonian and Ghanaian English; Schneider (2005) comparing English, Irish and American English; and Schröder and Schneider (2018) comparing English, Irish, American and Namibian English.

Work on other languages includes comparisons of French French and Canadian French (e.g. Schölmberger 2008); German German and Austrian German (e.g. Muhr 2008); German German and Swiss German (e.g. Schüpbach 2014); Netherlandic Dutch and Belgian Dutch (e.g. Plevoets et al. 2008); Swedish Swedish and Finnish Swedish (e.g. Nilsson et al. 2018) and Mainland Chinese and Taiwanese Chinese (e.g. Ren 2015).

Investigations on the impact of social class, ethnicity, gender and age are much fewer. Staley's monograph-length analysis of three pragmatic phenomena (address forms, offers, and responses to thanks) across three categories of restaurants in Los Angeles is a unique investigation of socioeconomic variation (Staley 2018). Clancy's comparison of hedging in family discourse among settled Irish families and families of Irish Traveller, an ethnic minority, is a rare study of ethnic variation (Clancy 2011). Holmes' pioneering work on gender differences in New Zealand compliments and apologies (e.g. Holmes 1995) is a forerunner of gender studies in variational pragmatics (e.g. Farr and Murphy 2009, comparing religious references in British and Irish English, and also examining the interaction of gender and age in Irish English). The interaction of age and gender variation is also analysed in Schneider (2012a). Finally, Dinkin (2018) is a recent study on age variation and pragmatic change in Canadian English.

With a focus on the actional level, a wide range of speech acts have been examined, both initiating and responding acts. Among these are the following:

- Apologies (e.g. Wagner and Roebuck 2010)
- Compliments (e.g. Lin 2015)
- Responses to compliments (e.g. Lázaro Ruiz and Ramajo Cuesta 2015)
- Invitations (e.g. García 2008)
- Responses to invitations (e.g. Mulo Farenkia 2015)
- Offers (e.g. Staley 2018)
- Responses to offers (e.g. Anchimbe 2018)
- Requests (e.g. Warga 2008)
- Responses to requests (e.g. Félix-Brasdefer 2008)
- Thanks (e.g. Jautz 2013)
- Responses to thanks (e.g. Bieswanger 2015)

With a focus on the formal level, different types of pragmatic markers have been examined. Among these are:

- Discourse markers such as *well*, *in fact*, *actually* (e.g. Aijmer 2013)
- Hedging (e.g. Clancy 2011)
- Listener responses such as *definitely, are you serious?* (e.g. Murphy 2012)
- Question tags (e.g. Barron et al. 2015)
- Religious references such as *damn, hell, God Almighty* (e.g. Farr and Murphy 2009)

The interactional level has not been studied extensively. Three studies, for example, analyse initial encounters between strangers across national varieties of English. These are Schneider (2008) on English, Irish and American English, Goddard (2012) on English, American and Australian English and Haugh and Carbaugh (2015) on American and Australian English. Schneider (2008) examines especially the opening exchanges and some pragmalinguistic features. Goddard (2012) deals with the underlying cultural scripts in the fashion of ethnopragmatics, and Haugh and Carbaugh (2015) concentrate on self-disclosures. There is also a growing body of research on service encounters. While most work in this area focuses on individual phenomena, some work emphasizes generic aspects (e.g. Félix-Brasdefer 2015).

Studies on the topic level and the organizational level are very rare (but cf. O'Keeffe and Adolphs 2008 on listener responses). There is some work on the prosodic level (e.g. Félix-Brasdefer 2009), and some more work the stylistic level. On this level, the focus is predominantly on forms of address (e.g. Norrby and Kretzenbacher 2014; Schüpbach 2014; Placencia et al. 2015; Staley 2018). Nilsson et al. (2018) is a recent study of the non-verbal/multimodal level, specifically of gaze in service encounter openings.

Work on variation in written discourse is still scarce. The few examples include Merrison et al. (2012), contrasting student request emails to staff from Australia and the United Kingdom; Burmeister (2013), comparing death notices from Scotland, Wales and Ireland; and Zahler (2016), comparing online personal advertisements from heterosexual and homosexual men and women in London (and in Mexico City). Moreover, an attempt has been made to establish what could be considered an analogous field called 'variational text linguistics' (Schubert and Sanchez-Stockhammer 2016). Some of the contributions to this volume examine variation across registers and/or regional, inter-lingual or diachronic register variation.

Concerning methodological choices, a wide range of data types and procedures of data collection have been employed. These include the following:

- Discourse completion tasks (e.g. Anchimbe 2018)
- Dialogue production tasks (e.g. Schneider 2008)
- Role-plays (e.g. Fuentes-Rodríguez et al. 2016)

- Ethnographic field notes (e.g. Wagner and Roebuck 2010)
- Elicited conversation (e.g. Haugh and Carbaugh 2015)
- Existing corpora (e.g. O'Keeffe and Adolphs 2008)
- Self-recorded corpora (audio) (e.g. Placencia 2008)
- Self-recorded corpora (video) (e.g. Nilsson et al. 2018)
- Focus group discussions (e.g. Schröder and Schneider, forthcoming)

The general picture is that both experimentational and observational methods have been used. The selection of a method largely depends on the level of analysis. Large machine-readable corpora are particularly suitable for studies on the formal level, as automatic corpus searches can be performed with individual markers such as *actually, I mean, you know*. Large corpora have also been used in work on the actional level, although to a much more limited extent, given the challenges of function-to-form matching. Hence large corpora have only been used in examinations of highly formulaic speech acts such as thanking (e.g. Jautz 2013), or they have been sifted manually (e.g. Flöck and Geluykens 2018). Corpora which have been employed include the British National Corpus (BNC), the Limerick Corpus of Irish English (LCIE), the Michigan Corpus of Academic Spoken English (MICASE), the Wellington Corpus of Spoken New Zealand English, and national components of the International Corpus of English. Self-recorded corpora, tailored to the specific needs of individual studies and focused on particular types of situations or communicative events have also been used in studies on both the formal and the actional level as well as on the stylistic level (e.g. in Clancy 2011 on hedging in family discourse; Placencia 2008 on requests in corner shops; Staley 2018 on offers, responses to thanks and terms of address in restaurant discourse).

Discourse completion tasks (DCTs), avoiding the challenges of corpus searches, have been used extensively in work of the actional level. While this method has been criticized for not providing data about what people actually say (i.e. for interactional analysis), it has been argued that DCTs reveal pragmatic norms, social conventions and underlying cultural models (e.g. Schneider 2012c; cf. Ogiermann 2018: 247) and are thus particularly suitable for generic analysis (cf. Section 31.5.2). Taking ethnographic field notes is another method deployed in studies on the actional level. Yet, while this method provides authentic data and circumvents the observer's paradox which cannot be avoided when audio- or videotaping data, it is also relatively unreliable and has only been used in studies of highly formulaic speech acts, specifically apologies (Wagner and Roebuck 2010) and responses to thanks (Bieswanger 2015; Dinkin 2018). It goes without saying that DCTs and ethnographic field notes are unsuitable for the purposes of investigating the interactional and the prosodic level. In either case, spoken dialogical material is needed, i.e. transcripts and sound files in corpora, or audio-recordings of role-plays, elicited conversation or naturally occurring discourse. Dialogue production tasks have also been used for examining interactional phenomena, but have similar advantages and disadvantages as DCTs and cannot be used for examining prosodic features. Finally, focus group discussions can be used in work on the metapragmatic level. To balance out the disadvantages of any chosen method, triangulation is recommended (Schneider 2018: 39–40).

Some of the work mentioned here is not explicitly carried out in variational pragmatics, probably because the authors have a limited perception of this field, while in effect they are actually doing variational pragmatics. Examples include Burmeister (2013), who apparently is not aware of variational pragmatics at all, Flöck and Geluykens (2018), who refer to and quote studies explicitly placed in variational pragmatics, but obviously do not consider their own study a contribution to this field, Haugh and Carbaugh (2015), who discuss variational pragmatics, but base their own study on a combination of interactional pragmatics and cultural discourse analysis, Anchimbe (2018), who places his work in post-colonial pragmatics, but does not convincingly bring out the postulated differences between the two approaches, and finally Dinkin (2018), who is a sociolinguist who replicates a study in variational pragmatics which in turn adopted a sociolinguistic method. There are, in fact, many interfaces of work in variational pragmatics with work in sociolinguistics on discourse variation (cf. the contributions in Pichler 2016).

31.7 Conclusions

Variational pragmatics, at the intersection of pragmatics and sociolinguistics, provides a framework for comparing pragmatic phenomena across regional and social varieties of the same language. In this framework, five macro-social factors are identified which impact language use. These are region, social class, ethnicity, gender and age; further factors are conceivable. Also, five levels of pragmatic analysis are distinguished, namely the formal, actional, interactional, topic and organizational level. These have been supplemented by the levels of prosody, style, non-verbal behaviour and metapragmatics.

Much work in variational pragmatics has concentrated on regional variation, and especially on differences between national varieties of pluricentric languages. All other types of macro-social variation have received less attention so far, in particular socioeconomic and ethnic variation. The languages examined are first and foremost Spanish and English. Further languages include, for example, French, German and Chinese. It would be desirable to include many more languages, in particular Arabic, African and Asian languages. This would be a prerequisite for formulating a theory of pragmatic variation, distinguishing pragmatic universals from pragmatic variables and their variants.

Apart from regional variation, only gender and age variation have received a certain amount of attention. Studies of socioeconomic variation are rare, and studies of ethnic variation almost non-existent. Age variation has also been discussed in relation to ongoing pragmatic change. More research is needed on the interdependence of macro-social factors and on the interplay of macro-social and micro-social variation. Intra-varietal and intra-individual variation also need to be taken into account. Considering these different types of variation and the interaction between them would form an important part of a theory of pragmatic variation.

Concerning the influence of macro-social factors, researchers in variational pragmatics do not take an essentialist stance, nor do they subscribe unreservedly to a constructionist position. What is suggested instead is a first-order approach to identities as they are displayed and perceived by participants, bearing in mind that both displays and perception are constrained by language use conventions and behavioural norms, which are theorized as internalized cultural models stored in the long-term memory.

As regards the levels of pragmatic analysis, most work has concentrated on the actional level, focusing on a range of different speech acts. Yet it would seem desirable to cover a wider range of speech actions. There is also a considerable body of work on the formal level, focusing on pragmatic markers. Studies on the interactional level are fewer in number and have mainly been concerned with individual speech action in the context of an interaction rather than with speech act sequences or the macrostructure of entire speech events or discourse genres. The topic level and the organizational level, by contrast, have been neglected almost completely, and studies of the prosodic, stylistic, non-verbal and metapragmatic level are still relatively scarce. It is argued that the interactional level is the most crucial level of analysis, given that neither speech acts nor discourse markers occur in isolation. Consequently, studies of the formal and actional level always have to consider the interactional context of the pragmatic marker or speech act under inspection. Furthermore, it seems necessary to introduce a higher degree of differentiation. On the one hand, it is crucial to distinguish different subtypes of a speech acts (e.g. requests for action versus requests for permission), because they may be realized and used in different ways. On the other hand, it is essential to distinguish between discourse genres. Analysing a particular speech act in a range of genres and not paying attention to the genres they occur in may blur significant distinctions. Moreover, the analysis of written discourse, so far largely neglected, must be fully integrated into the framework of variational pragmatics.

In studies of the actional level, experimentational methods have been employed, predominantly discourse completion tasks and role-plays. Studies of the formal level, by contrast, are typically based on observational data, specifically data from large existing corpora. Studies of the interactional level are also based on observational data, usually self-recorded corpora. Ethnographic methods have also been used. Needless to say, non-verbal behaviour can only be analysed in video-taped material. In general, methodological pluralism is promoted in variational pragmatics and methodological dogmatism rejected. It is firmly believed that all methods have strengths and weaknesses, and that each method can be used for some purpose but not for others. Consequently, methods have to be chosen according to their suitability for a particular purpose.

The three methodological principles formulated in variational pragmatics are the principles of empiricity, contrastivity and comparability. That is to say that research has to be based on data other than the researcher's intuitions, that data sets have to be contrasted in order to establish variety-specific patterns of language use, and that the contrasted data sets are actually comparable. These three principles are in fact not particular to variational pragmatics but relevant to all research involving contrast and comparison in linguistics and beyond.

The framework of variational pragmatics has been adopted in studies outside the original domain of variational pragmatics, e.g. in the analysis of pragmatic variation between native speaker varieties and non-native speaker varieties of the same language, and also between different languages. The approach developed in variational pragmatics thus contributes to ongoing discussions about the fuzzy boundaries between native speakers, second language users and foreign language learners, additionally underscoring the fact that there is no one-to-one relationship between languages and cultures, and that language users who do not share the same native language may share the same culture, i.e. behavioural norms and language use conventions. Conversely, speakers sharing the same native language do not necessarily share the same culture. Against this background, both contrastive pragmatics and variational pragmatics are areas of inquiry within cross-cultural pragmatics.

Finally, metapragmatics is an area which merits further research in variational pragmatics, too. It is interesting to see to what extent ordinary language users are aware of pragmatic variation across varieties of the same language, how they perceive inter-varietal pragmatic differences and how they evaluate behaviours that are different from their own. Focus group discussions as well as discussions in the media provide interesting material for analysis.

References

There is a constantly updated bibliography on variational pragmatics at www.applied-linguistics.uni-bonn.de/en/research/bibliographies/variational-pragmatics. On regional pragmatic variation in particular, also refer to www.bbk.ac.uk/languages/our-staff/maria-elena-placencia/bibliography-on-regional-pragmatic-variation.

Aijmer, K. (2013). *Understanding Pragmatic Markers: A Variational Pragmatic Approach*. Edinburgh: Edinburgh University Press.

Al-Ali, M. (2006). Religious affiliations and masculine power in Jordanian wedding invitation. *Discourse and Society*, *12*(6), 691–714.

Anchimbe, E. A. (2018). *Offers and Offer Refusals: A Postcolonial Pragmatics Perspective on World Englishes*. Amsterdam: John Benjamins.

Anchimbe, E. A. and Janney, R. W. (2011). Postcolonial pragmatics: An introduction. *Journal of Pragmatics*, 43, 1451–9.

Ash, S. (2002). Social class. In J. K. Chambers, P. Trudgill and N. Schilling-Estes, eds., *The Handbook of Language Variation and Change*. Malden, MA: Blackwell, pp. 402–22.

Austin, J. L. (1962). *How to Do Things with Words*. Cambridge, MA: Harvard University Press.

Barron, A. (2005). Offering in Ireland and England. In A. Barron and K. P. Schneider, eds., *The Pragmatics of Irish English*. Berlin: Mouton de Gruyter, pp. 141–77.

Barron, A. (2008). The structure of requests in Irish English and English English. In K. P. Schneider and A. Barron, eds., *Variational Pragmatics: A Focus on Regional Varieties in Pluricentric Languages*. Amsterdam: John Benjamins, pp. 35–67.

Barron, A. (2017). Variational pragmatics. In A. Barron, Y. Gu and G. Steen, eds., *The Routledge Handbook of Pragmatics*. London: Routledge, pp. 91–104.

Barron, A., Pandarova, I. and Muderack, K. (2015). Tag questions across Irish English and British English: A corpus analysis of form and function. *Multilingua*, 34(4), 495–524.

Barron, A. and Schneider, K. P. (2009). Variational pragmatics: Studying the impact of social factors on language use in interaction. *Intercultural Pragmatics*, 6(4), 425–42.

Beeching, K. and Woodfield, H. (eds.). (2015). *Researching Sociopragmatic Variability: Perspectives from Variational, Interlanguage and Contrastive Pragmatics*. Basingstoke, UK: Palgrave Macmillan.

Bieswanger, M. (2015). Variational pragmatics and *responding to thanks* – revisited. *Multilingua*, 34(4), 527–46.

Blum-Kulka, S., House, J. and Kasper, G. (1989). Investigating cross-cultural pragmatics: An introductory overview. In S. Blum-Kulka, J. House and G. Kasper, eds., *Cross-Cultural Pragmatics: Requests and Apologies*. Norwood, NJ: Ablex, pp. 1–34.

Brown, P. and Levinson, S. C. ([1978] 1987). *Politeness: Some Universals in Language Usage*. Cambridge: Cambridge University Press.

Burmeister, M. (2013). Variability in death notices from Scotland, Wales and the Republic of Ireland: A comparative perspective. In M. Bieswanger and A. Koll-Stobbe, eds., *New Approaches to the Study of Linguistic Variability*. Frankfurt, Germany: Lang, pp. 65–88.

Chen, R. (1993). Responding to compliments: A contrastive study of politeness strategies between American English and Chinese speakers. *Journal of Pragmatics*, 20, 49–75.

Cheshire, J. (2002). Sex and gender in variationist research. In J. K. Chambers, P. Trudgill and N. Schilling-Estes, eds., *The Handbook of Language Variation and Change*. Malden, MA: Blackwell, pp. 423–43.

Clancy, B. (2011). 'Do you want to do it yourself like?' Hedging in Irish traveller and settled family discourse. In B. L. Davies, M. Haugh and A. J. Merrison, eds., *Situated Politeness*. London: Continuum, pp. 129–46.

Clift, R. (2014). Conversation analysis. In K. P. Schneider and A. Barron, eds., *Pragmatics of Discourse*. Berlin: Mouton de Gruyter, pp. 97–124.

Decock, S. and Spiessens, A. (2017). Customer complaints and disagreements in a multilingual business environment: A discursive-pragmatic analysis. *Intercultural Pragmatics*, 14(1), 77–115.

Dinkin, A. J. (2018). It's no problem to be polite: Apparent-time change in responses to thanks. *Journal of Sociolinguistics*, 22(2), 190–215.

Farr, F. and Murphy, B. (2009). Religious references in contemporary Irish English: 'For the love of God almighty ... I'm a holy terror for turf'. *Intercultural Pragmatics*, 6(4), 535–59.

Félix-Brasdefer, J. C. (2008). Sociopragmatic variation: Dispreferred responses in Mexican and Dominican Spanish. *Journal of Politeness Research*, 4(1), 81–110.

Félix-Brasdefer, J. C. (2009). Pragmatic variation across Spanish(es): Requesting in Mexican, Costa Rican and Dominican Spanish. *Intercultural Pragmatics*, 6(4), 473–515.

Félix-Brasdefer, J. C. (2015). *The Language of Service Encounters: A Pragmatic-Discursive Approach*. Cambridge: Cambridge University Press.

Flöck, I. and Geluykens, R. (2018). Preference organization and cross-cultural variation in request responses: A corpus-based comparison of British and American English. *Corpus Pragmatics*, 2, 57–82.

Fuentes Rodríguez, C., Placencia, M. E. and Palma-Fahey, M. (2016). Regional pragmatic variation in the use of the discourse marker *pues* in informal talk among university students in Quito (Ecuador), Santiago (Chile) and Seville (Spain). *Journal of Pragmatics*, 97, 74–92.

García, C. (2008). Different realizations of solidarity politeness: Comparing Venezuelan and Argentinean invitations. In K. P. Schneider and A. Barron, eds., *Variational Pragmatics: A Focus on Regional Varieties in Pluricentric Languages*. Amsterdam: John Benjamins, pp. 269–305.

Georgakopoulou, A. and Charalambidou, A. (2011). Doing age and ageing: Language, discourse and social interaction. In G. Andersen and K. Aijmer, eds., *Pragmatics of Society*. Berlin: Mouton de Gruyter, pp. 31–51.

Goddard, C. (2012). Early interactions in Australian English, American English, and English English: Cultural differences and cultural scripts. *Journal of Pragmatics*, 44(9), 1038–50.

Grant, T. and MacLeod, N. (2016). Assuming identities online: Experimental linguistics applied to policing of online paedophile activity. *Applied Linguistics*, 37(1), 50–70.

Haugh, M. and Carbaugh, D. (2015). Self-disclosure in initial interactions amongst speakers of American and Australian English. *Multilingua*, 34(4), 461–94.

Haugh, M. and Schneider, K. P. (2012). Editorial: Im/politeness across Englishes. *Journal of Pragmatics*, 44(9), 1017–21.

Holmes, J. (1995). *Women, Men and Politeness*. London: Longman.
Jautz, S. (2013). *Thanking Formulae in English: Explorations across Varieties and Genres*. Amsterdam: John Benjamins.
Jucker, A. (2009). Speech act research between armchair, field and laboratory: The case of compliments. *Journal of Pragmatics, 41*(8), 1611–35.
Jucker, A. and Taavitsainen, I. (2012). Pragmatic variables. In J. M. Hernández-Campoy and J. C. Conde-Silvestre, eds., *The Handbook of Historical Sociolinguistics*. Oxford: Wiley-Blackwell, pp. 293–306.
Kasper, G. (1990). Linguistic politeness: Current research issues. *Journal of Pragmatics, 14*(1), 193–218.
Kachru, B. (1985). Standards, codification and sociolinguistic realism: The English language in the outer circle. In R. Quirk and H. Widdowson, eds., *English in the World: Teaching and Learning the Language and Literatures*. Cambridge: Cambridge University Press, pp. 11–30.
Lázaro Ruiz, H. and Ramajo Cuesta, A. (2015). Compliment responses in peninsular Spanish: Exploratory and contrastive study conducted on women from Madrid, Valencia, Catalonia, Andalusia and Castile-Leon. *Procedia: Social and Behavioral Sciences, 212*, 93–8.
Lin, C.-Y. (2015). The role of gender in Taiwan and Mainland Chinese compliments. In K. Beeching and H. Woodfield, eds., *Researching SocioPragmatic Variability: Perspectives from Variational, Interlanguage and Contrastive Pragmatics*. Houndmills, UK: Palgrave Macmillan, pp. 49–71.
Lin, C.-Y., Woodfield, H. and Ren, W. (2012). Compliments in Taiwan and mainland Chinese: The influence of region and compliment topic. *Journal of Pragmatics, 44*(11), 1486–1502.
Márquez Reiter, R. and Placencia, M. E. (2005). *Spanish Pragmatics*. Basingstoke, UK: Palgrave Macmillan.
Merrison, A. J., Wilson, J. J., Davies, B. L. and Haugh, M. (2012). Getting stuff done: Comparing e-mail requests from students in higher education in Britain and Australia. *Journal of Pragmatics, 44*(9), 1077–98.
Muhr, R. (2008). The pragmatics of a pluricentric language: A comparison between Austrian German and German German. In K. P. Schneider and A. Barron, eds., *Variational Pragmatics: A Focus on Regional Varieties in Pluricentric Languages*. Amsterdam: John Benjamins, pp. 211–44.
Mukherjee, J. and Hundt, M. (eds.). (2011). *Exploring Second-Language Varieties of English and Learner Englishes: Bridging a Paradigm Gap*. Amsterdam: John Benjamins.
Mulo Farenkia, B. (2014). *Speech Acts and Politeness in French as a Pluricentric Language: Illustrations from Cameroon and Canada*. Münster: LIT Verlag.
Mulo Farenkia, B. (2015). Invitation refusals in Cameroon French and Hexagonal French. *Multilingua, 34*(4), 577–603.
Murphy, B. (2011). Gender identities and discourse. In G. Andersen and K. Aijmer, eds., *Pragmatics of Society*. Berlin: Mouton de Gruyter, pp. 53–77.
Murphy, B. (2012). Exploring response tokens in Irish English – a multi-disciplinary approach: Integrating variational pragmatics, sociolinguistics

and corpus linguistics. *International Journal of Corpus Linguistics*, 17(3), 325–48.

Nilsson, J., Norrthon, S., Lindström, J. and Wide, C. (2018). Greetings as social action in Finland Swedish and Sweden Swedish service encounters – a pluricentric perspective. *Intercultural Pragmatics*, 15(1), 57–88.

Norrby, C. and Kretzenbacher, H. L. (2014). Address in two pluricentric languages: Swedish and German. In A. Soares da Silva, ed., *Pluricentricity: Language Variation and Sociocognitive Dimensions*. Berlin: Mouton de Gruyter, pp. 243–67.

Ogiermann, E. (2018). Discourse completion tasks. In A. Jucker, K. P. Schneider and W. Bublitz, eds., *Methods in Pragmatics*. Berlin: Mouton de Gruyter, pp. 229–55.

O'Keeffe, A. and Adolphs, S. (2008). Response tokens in British and Irish discourse: Corpus, context and variational pragmatics. In K. P. Schneider and A. Barron, eds., *Variational Pragmatics: A Focus on Regional Varieties in Pluricentric Languages*. Amsterdam: John Benjamins, pp. 69–98.

Owen, M. (1983). *Apologies and Remedial Interchanges: A Study of Language Use in Social Interaction*. Berlin: Mouton.

Pichler, H. (ed.). (2016). *Discourse-Pragmatic Variation and Change in English: New Methods and Insights*. Cambridge: Cambridge University Press.

Placencia, M. E. (2008). Requests in corner shop transactions in Ecuadorian Andean and Coastal Spanish. In K. P. Schneider and A. Barron, eds., *Variational Pragmatics: A Focus on Regional Varieties in Pluricentric Languages*. Amsterdam: John Benjamins, pp. 307–22.

Placencia, M. E., Fuentes Rodríguez, C. and Palma-Fahey, M. (2015). Nominal address and rapport management in informal interactions among university students in Quito (Ecuador), Santiago (Chile) and Seville (Spain). *Multilingua*, 34(4), 547–75.

Plevoets, K., Speelman, D. and Geeraerts, D. (2008). The distribution of T/V pronouns in Netherlandic and Belgian Dutch. In K. P. Schneider and A. Barron, eds., *Variational Pragmatics: A Focus on Regional Varieties in Pluricentric Languages*. Amsterdam: John Benjamins, pp. 181–209.

Queen, R. (2013). Gender, sex, sexuality, and sexual identities. In J. K. Chambers and N. Schilling, eds., *The Handbook of Language Variation and Change*, 2nd ed. Chichester, UK: Wiley-Blackwell, pp. 368–87.

Ren, W. (2015). Sociopragmatic variation in mainland and Taiwan Chinese refusals. In K. Beeching and H. Woodfield, eds., *Researching Sociopragmatic Variability: Perspectives from Variational, Interlanguage and Contrastive Pragmatics*. Basingstoke, UK: Palgrave Macmillan, pp. 72–93.

Schegloff, E. A. and Sacks, H. (1973). Opening up closing. *Semiotica*, 8, 289–328.

Schlieben-Lange, B. and Weydt, H. (1978). Für eine Pragmatisierung der Dialektologie. *Zeitschrift für Germanistische Linguistik*, 6(3), 257–82.

Schneider, K. P. (1988). *Small Talk: Analysing Phatic Discourse*. Marburg, Germany: Hitzeroth.

Schneider, K. P. (2003). *Diminutives in English*. Tübingen, Germany: Niemeyer.

Schneider, K. P. (2005). 'No problem, you're welcome, anytime': Responding to thanks in Ireland, England, and the USA. In A. Barron and K. P. Schneider, eds., *The Pragmatics of Irish English*. Berlin: Mouton de Gruyter, pp. 101–39.

Schneider, K. P. (2008). Small talk in England, Ireland, and the USA. In K. P. Schneider and A. Barron, eds., *Variational Pragmatics: A Focus on Regional Varieties in Pluricentric Languages*. Amsterdam: John Benjamins, pp. 99–139.

Schneider, K. P. (2010). Variational pragmatics. In M. Fried, J.-O. Östman and J. Verschueren, eds., *Variation and Change: Pragmatic Perspectives*. Amsterdam: John Benjamins, pp. 239–67.

Schneider, K. P. (2012a). Appropriate behaviour across varieties of English. *Journal of Pragmatics*, 44(9), 1022–37.

Schneider, K. P. (2012b). Pragmatics. In R. Hickey, ed., *Topics in English Linguistics: Areal Features of the Anglophone World*. Berlin: Mouton de Gruyter, pp. 463–86.

Schneider, K. P. (2012c). Pragmatic variation and cultural models. *Review of Cognitive Linguistics*, 10(2), 346–72.

Schneider, K. P. (2014). Comparability and sameness in variational pragmatics. In S. Mergenthal and R. M. Nischik, eds., *Anglistentag 2013 Konstanz: Proceedings*. Trier, Germany: Wissenschaftlicher Verlag Trier, pp. 361–72.

Schneider, K. P. (2017). Pragmatic competence and pragmatic variation. In R. Giora and M. Haugh, eds., *Doing Pragmatics Interculturally: Cognitive, Philosophical, and Sociopragmatic Perspectives*. Berlin: Mouton de Gruyter, pp. 315–33.

Schneider, K. P. (2018). Methods and ethics of data collection. In A. Jucker, K. P. Schneider and W. Bublitz, eds., *Methods in Pragmatics*. Berlin: Mouton de Gruyter, pp. 37–93.

Schneider, K. P. (2019). Re-thinking pragmatic variation: The case of service encounters from a modified variational pragmatics perspective. In J. C. Félix-Brasdefer and M. E. Placencia, eds., *Pragmatic Variation in Service Encounter Interactions across the Spanish-Speaking World*. Oxford: Routledge, pp. 251–62.

Schneider, K. P. and Barron, A. (2008a). Where pragmatics and dialectology meet: Introducing variational pragmatics. In K. P. Schneider and A. Barron, eds., *Variational Pragmatics: A Focus on Regional Varieties in Pluricentric Languages*. Amsterdam: John Benjamins, pp. 1–32.

Schneider, K. P. and Barron, A. (eds.). (2008b). *Variational Pragmatics: A Focus on Regional Varieties in Pluricentric Languages*. Amsterdam: John Benjamins.

Schneider, K. P. and Placencia, M. E. (2017). (Im)politeness and regional variation. In J. Culpeper, M. Haugh and D. Kádár, eds., *The Palgrave Handbook of Linguistic (Im)politeness*. London: Palgrave Macmillan, pp. 539–70.

Schneider, K. P. and Schröder, A. (2014). Comparison and comparability in language studies. In S. Mergenthal and R. M. Nischik, eds., *Anglistentag 2013 Konstanz: Proceedings*. Trier, Germany: Wissenschaftlicher Verlag Trier, pp. 303–7.

Schölmberger, U. (2008). Apologizing in French French and Canadian French. In K. P. Schneider and A. Barron, eds., *Variational pragmatics: A focus on regional varieties in pluricentric languages*. Amsterdam: John Benjamins, pp. 333–54.

Schröder, A. and Schneider, K. P. (2018). Variational pragmatics, responses to thanks, and the specificity of English in Namibia. *English World-Wide*, 39(3), 338–63.

Schröder, A. and Schneider, K. P. (forthcoming). A variational pragmatics approach to responses to thanks in Namibian English: From quantitative to qualitative analysis. In A. Schröder, ed., *The Dynamics of English in Namibia*. Amsterdam: John Benjamins.

Schubert, C. and Sanchez-Stockhammer, C. (eds.). (2016). *Variational Text Linguistics: Revisiting Register in English*. Berlin: Mouton de Gruyter.

Schüpbach, D. (2014). German or Swiss? Address and other routinised formulas in German-speaking Switzerland. In J. Hajek and Y. Slaughter, eds., *Challenging the Monolingual Mindset*. Bristol: Multilingual Matters, pp. 63–77.

Searle, J. R. (1969). *Speech Acts*. Cambridge: Cambridge University Press.

Staley, L. (2018). *Socioeconomic Pragmatic Variation: Speech Acts and Address Forms in Context*. Amsterdam: John Benjamins.

Szmrecsanyi, B. and Kortmann, B. (2009). Vernacular universals and anglo-versals in a typological perspective. In M. Filppula, J. Klemola and H. Paulasto, eds., *Vernacular Universals and Language Contacts: Evidence from Varieties of English and Beyond*. New York: Routledge, pp. 33–54.

Terkourafi, M. (2012). Between pragmatics and sociolinguistics: Where does pragmatic variation fit it? In J. C. Félix-Brasdefer and D. A. Koike, eds., *Pragmatic Variation in First and Second Language Contexts: Methodological Issues*. Amsterdam: John Benjamins, pp. 295–318.

Wagner, L. and Roebuck, R. (2010). Apologizing in Cuernavaca, Mexico and Panama City, Panama: A cross-cultural comparison of positive- and negative-politeness strategies. *Spanish in Context*, 7(2), 254–78.

Warga, M. (2008). Requesting in German as a pluricentric language. In K. P. Schneider and A. Barron, eds., *Variational Pragmatics: A Focus on Regional Varieties in Pluricentric Languages*. Amsterdam: John Benjamins, pp. 245–66.

Wierzbicka, A. (1985). Different cultures, different languages, different speech acts. *Journal of Pragmatics*, 9(2–3), 145–78.

Wolfram, W. and Schilling, N. (2016). *American English: Dialects and Variation*. 3rd ed. Chichester, UK: Wiley-Blackwell.

Zahler, S. L. (2016). Pragmalinguistic variation in electronic personal ads from Mexico City and London. *IULC Working Papers*, 15(1), 208–30.

32

Historical Sociopragmatics

Magdalena Leitner and Andreas H. Jucker

32.1 Introduction

Sociopragmatics is particularly relevant for historical pragmatics because of the reliance of historical studies on contextual information. Historical pragmatics in general, as an independent subfield of pragmatics, started out in the last decade of the previous century when pragmaticists increasingly began to be interested in earlier stages of individual languages and when historical linguists started to develop an interest in pragmatic research questions. Jucker (1995) is an early collection of papers written partly by pragmaticists with a historical interest and partly by historical linguists with an interest in pragmatics. Most articles in that volume include social aspects of language use, as, for instance, Nevalainen and Raumolin-Brunberg's (1995) analysis of politeness phenomena and terms of address in private correspondence from the fifteenth to the seventeenth century with a careful consideration of the social standing and the personal relationships between the writers and recipients of these letters. With hindsight, such approaches can be classified as historical sociopragmatics. But there were also some contributions which focused on pragmatic developments independent of the social embedding (e.g. Schwenter and Traugott 1995).

In subsequent work in the area of historical pragmatics, there continued to be a tradition that relied more systematically on the social context of language use in earlier periods of specific languages and a tradition that focused more on the theoretical underpinnings of pragmatic aspects of language use in the past. These two traditions in historical pragmatics correspond to the traditions in pragmatics in general, called Continental European pragmatics and Anglo-American pragmatics (Huang 2007: 4) or social pragmatics and theoretical pragmatics[1] (Chapman 2011: 5),

---

[1] The use of the label 'theoretical' seems rather unfortunate as it may wrongly imply that social pragmatics somehow lacks a theoretical foundation.

respectively. It is probably fair to say that in historical pragmatics the Continental European or social tradition has always been stronger, not only in the early volume mentioned above but also in subsequent work over the past two and a half decades. Because of the widespread applications of context-sensitive approaches in historical pragmatics it has been argued that the prefix *socio-* is not needed to define the Continental European tradition as a subfield within the field (see Włodarczyk and Taavitsainen 2017: 160). Nevertheless, the term *historical sociopragmatics* has gained currency in historical pragmatics. The label first came into prominence in a special issue of the *Journal of Historical Pragmatics* guest-edited and introduced by Culpeper (2009).[2] This raises the question of how to position historical sociopragmatics within historical pragmatics. The Continental European tradition, although being dedicated to the social dimension, is not synonymous with historical sociopragmatics. The former still integrates the Anglo-American[3] tradition, which examines language change at the semantic-pragmatic interface without locating the changes in the social and interactional context. Historical sociopragmatics, as it has been defined (e.g. Culpeper 2010: 87; Marmaridou 2011: 95–8), puts an even stronger focus on the specific social context of language use. Thus, the concerns of the Anglo-American tradition are in our view outside of the scope of historical *socio*pragmatics. The Anglo-American perspective is particularly evident in diachronic form-to-function mappings, that is, studies that take linguistic forms, such as discourse markers, as their starting point and examine their pragmatic developments over time (Jacobs and Jucker 1995: 13–18). However, form-to-function mappings can be sociopragmatic if diachronic changes are embedded in their wider or more specific social and interactional contexts (e.g. Claridge 2018; Lutzky 2012). Historical sociopragmatics is not a question of whether the starting point of an investigation is a linguistic form or function but whether the social and situational context is systematically taken into account when analysing language use in the past and changes over time.[4]

Context in historical sociopragmatics can be conceptualized at different levels of granularity, as Culpeper has shown in several publications (Culpeper 2009, 2010, Chapter 2). Based on ideas first proposed in Culpeper et al. (2008: 320), he distinguishes between the micro level of the actual use and interpretation of speech acts and discursive practices, the meso level of situated interactions in specific activity types, frames or genres and the macro level of socio-cultural phenomena relating to different cultures, nationalities or

---

[2] The issue was subsequently republished as an independent volume (Culpeper 2011a).
[3] Seminal publications on Continental European historical pragmatics include chapters on topics associated with the Anglo-American tradition, e.g. grammaticalization and pragmaticalization (e.g. Jucker and Taavitsainen 2010, 2013).
[4] We take a different line here from Culpeper (e.g. 2010: 76–8) and Marmaridou (2011: 95–8), who define form-to-function mappings as *pragmalinguistic* approaches and function-to-form mappings and pragmaphilology as part of historical *sociopragmatics*. While we agree that pragmaphilology exemplifies historical sociopragmatics, the distinctions for diachronic pragmatics should be defined by the context-sensitivity of studies. For the general distinction between pragmalinguistics and sociopragmatics, see Culpeper (Chapter 2).

genders (Chapter 2). The label historical sociopragmatics as we are going to use it in this contribution can be applied to studies on all these levels and thus covers a lot of research with a long history.

In the following, we will introduce some of the key concerns and concepts of historical sociopragmatics, which apply to historical pragmatics more generally, as, for instance, the issues of choosing suitable historical data, the units of analysis and the social dimension. Afterwards, we will give an outline of the discursive turn in historical sociopragmatics. We will illustrate the result of this turn and the new way of looking at data with a detailed analysis of a sixteenth-century letter exchange between members of a Scottish Highland clan. The analysis will show how the letter-writers negotiate their relationships and roles and the significance of the events that led to growing tensions between them. We will finish the chapter with an overview of recent trends in historical sociopragmatics and concluding remarks.

32.2 Key Concepts in Historical Sociopragmatics

The first key concept that we want to introduce is the status of data in historical pragmatics. In the early days of historical pragmatics, in the 1990s, the status of the data that could be used for historical pragmatic investigation was a major issue and was regularly discussed in the literature, often in an apologetic way. In fact, entire papers were published that dealt exclusively with data problems in historical pragmatics (see Kytö 2010 and references cited there). It was seen as a problem that for historical periods, apart from the very recent past, the researcher had to rely on written sources. Only a very small proportion of all the language produced in the past was *written* language and only a small part of the written records of the past has survived to the present day. Historical linguistics in general has been seen as an 'art to make the best use of bad data' (Labov 1994: 11). This was felt to be even more true for historical pragmatics. The ideal in pragmatics, at that time, was still natural spoken interaction, and data that deviated from this ideal generally required extensive justifications. Preferred types of data for historical pragmaticists were therefore written texts that could be argued to be as close as possible to spoken language. Trial records were taken to be relatively faithful representations of words spoken in a courtroom even if the formality of the situation produced interactions that could not be taken to represent everyday conversation. Plays present language to be spoken on a stage with many pragmatically interesting features of interaction but they were seen as problematic because of their contrived and artificial nature. In real life, nobody speaks in iambic pentameters, for instance. Letters, and in particular private letters, were seen as interactive and personal and therefore as '*speech-like*' but not as spoken language (Culpeper and Kytö 2010: 17, original emphasis). As a result, historical pragmaticists regularly discussed the implications of what were seen as data limitations.

In recent years, however, attitudes towards different types of data have changed considerably. Pragmatics in general has moved away from considering spoken everyday interaction as the ideal or perhaps the only legitimate type of data and has increasingly recognized all kinds of language use and interaction as legitimate data for pragmatic research. Written language and even fictional language has come to be appreciated for what it is and not as an imperfect substitute of spoken interaction (Jucker and Locher 2017: 4–6; Jucker and Taavitsainen 2013: 25–6). Thus, an investigation of terms of address in a play by Shakespeare, to take just one example, is no longer seen as an attempt to get as close as possible to the everyday spoken language at the turn from the sixteenth to the seventeenth century but as an investigation of how Shakespeare chose to represent the use of address terms in the exchanges between his fictional characters. As a result, pragmaticists have to be more modest. The claims based on their research cannot easily be generalized beyond the specific data of the investigation. But at the same time, there is no need anymore to apologize for specific data choices. On the contrary, different types of data add to an appreciation of the boundless variability and diversity of language use.

The second important concept to be briefly introduced is the unit of analysis. Initially the focus of historical pragmatics was generally on specific linguistic elements that were pragmatically significant, such as discourse markers, terms of address and speech acts. Good examples of early book-length studies of such elements are Brinton (1996), Busse (2002) and Arnovick (1999). Brinton (1996) investigated discourse markers, or pragmatic markers as she called them – such as *gan, anon, hwæt* or *I gesse* – in the history of English. Busse (2002) investigated terms of address (*ye* and *thou* and their morphological variants) in Shakespeare's plays, and Arnovick (1999) traced the histories of seven speech acts, such as insults, promises or curses in the history of English. The extent to which these works consider the social context in which the investigated elements are being used varies considerably, and thus it is not always easy to assign them clearly to historical sociopragmatics or to historical theoretical[5] pragmatics. Brinton and Arnovick are both primarily interested in the theoretical processes of grammaticalization, pragmaticalization and discursization (i.e. the ways in which lexical material in the course of time comes to serve grammatical, pragmatic or discourse functions), while Busse is more interested in the social relationships between the fictional characters in Shakespeare's plays and how these relationships influence their language use.

Some other early work focused on issues of politeness and impoliteness. It did not take long for the ground-breaking work by Brown and Levinson (1987) to be applied to historical data. Brown and Gilman (1989) tested their politeness theory on four major tragedies by Shakespeare, and Kopytko

---

[5] See note 1.

(1995) extended their work with an additional four comedies and more sophisticated statistics. Nevala (2004) used the same framework for her research on terms of address in Early English correspondence. Culpeper (1996) developed a mirror-image impoliteness theory, which he applied in a qualitative case study to Shakespeare's *Macbeth*. In all these cases, taking Brown and Levinson as a lead, the analysis focused on specific linguistic forms and strategies to which specific politeness, or – in the case of Culpeper – impoliteness, values were assigned. Indirect formulations, such as *could you please*, or the use of honorifics (e.g. titles of courtesy, such as *your Ladyship*) were seen to carry specific politeness values.

In more recent work in historical pragmatics the unit of analysis has often been extended. The focus is no longer on an isolated element, such as terms of address or discourse markers, but on communicative practices which can be understood as conventionalized ways of carrying out a communicative task (Jucker 2017: 557). Such tasks can be relatively small, as for instance in the task of entering into a conversation (a greeting), but they can also be larger, as for instance cross examinations in courtrooms (e.g. Archer 2005, and her subsequent publications). The largest units are genres and types of discourse, with investigations into their macrostructures and 'meaning-making practices' (e.g. Taavitsainen 2017: 253). These units – whether small or large – can be understood as more or less conventionalized solutions to specific tasks, and crucially they must be analysed in their wider contexts and with due consideration of their status as being partly conventionalized and partly re-negotiated every time they are being used.

32.3 The Discursive Turn in Historical Sociopragmatics

In this section, we describe what we would like to call the discursive turn in historical pragmatics. It is a development that has been noted and described for approaches on politeness and impoliteness, but we want to argue that this development can also be observed in historical pragmatics and especially in historical sociopragmatics. In Section 32.3.1, we briefly sketch the theoretical background to this development, and in Section 32.3.2, we will provide a case study to demonstrate how such an approach focuses on the interaction in an analysis of a letter exchange between principal members of a Scottish Highland clan of the sixteenth century.

32.3.1 Theoretical Background

Grainger (2011) describes the development of politeness scholarship in terms of three waves (see also Culpeper and Hardaker 2017: 206–8). In the first wave, which she calls Gricean approaches, investigations into politeness were very much modelled on second-order politeness, in particular on the work by Brown and Levinson (1987). Impoliteness was seen – in some sense – as the 'flip-side' or the opposite of politeness. The second wave, called postmodern or discursive approach, focused on participants' evaluations of (im)politeness in interaction. It moved away from speaker intentions and theoretically conceived conceptualizations of politeness (or impoliteness) and concentrated on the lay-person's conceptualizations of these concepts, i.e. first-order politeness. Values of politeness or impoliteness were argued not to be inherent in specific linguistic elements but to be discursively negotiated between the participants. The third and current wave, called sociological or interactional approaches by Grainger (2011), encompasses what can be seen as a rapprochement between the two previous approaches. It takes the speaker and the hearer equally into consideration and examines the management of interpersonal relationships in interactions and their sequential organization. It maintains the discursive concern for participants' evaluations of (im)politeness but also allows for conventionalized and therefore relatively stable politeness or impoliteness values of specific linguistic forms.

We find it useful to extend the metaphor of the three waves to the developments in historical sociopragmatics. It is important to stress, however, that the differences between the three waves are not clear-cut (see Culpeper and Hardaker 2017: 208). They are more a matter of emphasis and focus.

The first wave, or early phase, of historical sociopragmatics was characterized by a focus on the mapping of specific linguistic forms to specific communicative functions or vice versa. In fact, overviews of research at that time regularly categorized different approaches on the basis of whether they started with a specific linguistic form and investigated how their functions changed over time, the so-called form-to-function mapping; or whether they started with a specific communicative function and investigated the various linguistic forms with which it could be performed, the so-called function-to-form mapping (see Jacobs and Jucker 1995, who were probably responsible for introducing these terms). Much of the early work in historical sociopragmatics can easily be classified according to this distinction. While many form-to-function mappings do not pay much attention to the social context of language use, there are early studies that investigate the diachronic functional shifts of linguistic forms from a sociopragmatic perspective. Busse (2002), for instance, starts with second person pronouns in Shakespeare's plays and investigates their functional profiles in connection with the genre context and social parameters of the interlocutors. Examples for function-to-form mapping are Jucker and Taavitsainen's (2000) diachronic study of insults in the history of English and Culpeper's (1996) investigation of the linguistic elements that are used to express the communicative function of attacking face.

The second wave, or discursive approach, rejected the simple mapping patterns of the first wave and argued that linguistic elements cannot be assigned any inherent meaning values. Such values only emerge in the interaction between participants. In other words, they are always discursively negotiated. The focus shifted away from the speaker to the communicative interaction. This trend was particularly noticeable in the area of (im)politeness work. Discursive (im)politeness researchers – in particular Eelen (2001), Mills (2003) and Locher and Watts (2005) – were critical of earlier politeness work and argued strongly for a more comprehensive view in which politeness and impoliteness were no longer seen as mirror images of each other but as behaviours on a continuum of interaction that also includes less marked forms of behaviour. Furthermore, they argued for a shift away from academically defined concepts of different types of behaviour to everyday conceptualizations and discursive negotiations of such behaviour.

The discursive approach has gained ground in historical sociopragmatics. In the subfield of historical (im)politeness studies, historical texts have been analysed without imposing any pre-existing notions of (im)politeness. Instead, (im)politeness values are reconstructed through examining participants' interactive negotiations of meanings, for example, in the fictional dialogues of medieval romance (Jucker 2014), or participants' ritual use and exploitations of conventionalized linguistic strategies in letter-writing (e.g. Bax 2010; Kádár 2010). Discursive investigations have become established beyond historical (im)politeness. Petikó (2017), for example, analyses how participants in eighteenth-century Hungarian witchcraft trials discursively construct witchcraft identities and communities. Moreover, discursive approaches have been developed and applied in historical speech-act research, for example, to examine participants' negotiations of speech-act functions in trial proceedings (Leitner 2017) or participants' use of speech acts to exercise power in parliamentary debates (Reutner 2016). A discursive turn may also be noted in a broader sense, namely in the recent revival of philology in historical sociopragmatics as a means of examining the material dynamics of text production and reception from the perspective of the participants involved in these processes (Włodarczyk and Taavitsainen 2017: 164–5; see Section 32.4).

In a wider sociopragmatic context, the trend away from speaker-produced pragmatic units to interactions between speakers and hearers can be exemplified by the papers in a volume devoted to a range of different communities of practice (Kopaczyk and Jucker 2013). A community of practice is seen as a group of people with a common purpose who share linguistic resources for their specific communicative needs. A focus on such communities, it is argued, provides a new perspective on the social processes involved in language change. Cruickshank (2013), for instance, examines a group of eighteenth-century Scottish letter-writers and how the epistolary exchange contributed to the emergence of Scottish Standard English. Her analysis shows that a Scottish aristocrat's use of Standard English – the prestige variety – was interspersed with Scotticisms, which reflected the communicative needs when writing to members of his local network.

The second wave in historical sociopragmatics is further attested by investigations into metacommunicative expressions, in other words, how participants talk about (im)politeness, speech acts or other aspects of communication. Metacommunicative expressions are the focus of all contributions in Busse and Hübler's (2012) edited volume. A more recent example is Sairio's (2017) study of lexemes associated with the concept of shame in eighteenth-century letters. Her results show that explicit terms of shame occur in formulaic apologies in situations of a perceived breach of social conventions, whereas direct expressions of shame are rare when correspondents talked about situations with a high risk of inducing shame, which suggests emerging taboo connotations of shame.

The third wave, as mentioned above, can be seen as a rapprochement between the first and the second wave. In such a view, the second wave is a strong version of a discursive approach, i.e. one which suggests that linguistic elements do not have inherent meanings. All meanings are always negotiated in a discursive process by speaker and addressee. It is doubtful whether there are any researchers who maintain a strong version of a discursive approach, but the third wave pays more systematic attention not only to the dynamics of the interaction (as defined above) but also to 'more stable meanings arising from particular linguistic forms' (Culpeper and Hardaker 2017: 208). Culpeper and Hardaker (2017: 210) propose the notion of conventionalized expressions or routinized formulae to capture relatively stable politeness or impoliteness values for specific linguistic forms while still allowing for discursive adjustments or re-negotiations of these values in specific interactions. Culpeper (2011b: chapter 4) offers an empirical, corpus-based, method to retrieve such formulae.

In historical sociopragmatics, third-wave approaches are just emergent. Jucker (2012), for example, shows how an analysis of the deception and intrigue depicted in Ben Jonson's *Volpone, Or the Fox* requires both default values and discursively negotiated values. The characters treat each other with superficially exceedingly polite and polished language, which is used to hide their underlying devious motives and intentions. Włodarczyk (2013) combines a first-order with a second-order approach in her study of nineteenth-century British colonial office correspondence to examine the letter as an analytic category from different angles. She concludes that neither approach on its own can fully conceptualize letter-writing in the past. Leitner (2015) applies the interactional focus of the third wave to sixteenth-century Scottish correspondence and examines how participants managed individual and collective aspects of their social roles and relationships in conflicts across sequences of letters.

The following case study illustrates key topics of third-wave sociopragmatics. The approach on historical letter-writing uncompromisingly considers not just the production side of language use but the interaction between writers and readers who take turns in adopting these roles. It demonstrates the way in which linguistic expressions have default meanings that are also regularly negotiated and the implications of these negotiations on the relationships and status of the participants and the groups that they represent.

32.3.2 Case Study

The present case study focuses on a sequence of four letters from the *Breadalbane Collection, 1548–1583* (Dawson 2004/2007), a manuscript-based online edition of Scottish correspondence that offers rare insights into sixteenth-century Highland clan management (Dawson 1997: 1–2). The selected sequence of letters gives evidence of a multi-layered conflict, which starts out as a skirmish between two clans, the Campbells and the Buchanans, whose chiefs were allies. Figure 32.1 gives an overview of the clans involved in the conflict, or mentioned in the exchange, and their leading figures.

The chief of Clan Campbell – Archibald Campbell, the fifth Earl of Argyll (henceforth Argyll) – initiated the letter exchange to settle the conflict, which in turn triggered an internal clan dispute between Argyll and one of his most trusted principal members, Colin Campbell, the sixth Laird of Glenorchy (henceforth Grey Colin, according to his nickname; Dawson 1997: 14). Argyll was told that some of Grey Colin's men had raided the lands of Clan Buchanan and killed a man there. The complaint was made by George Buchanan (henceforth Buchanan), laird and head of Clan Buchanan, whose territories were in The Lennox, a neighbouring area to the Glenorchy lands in Breadalbane (Keay and Keay 2000: 114). There are no letters between Argyll and Buchanan in the *Breadalbane Collection*. It is not clear how Buchanan informed Argyll about the raid, whether in writing or in a personal meeting, which in sixteenth-century Scotland was still preferred over written correspondence (Dawson 1997: 4). The purpose of Argyll's first letter was to find out if Buchanan's report was true, and if so, to admonish Grey Colin that the raided goods should be restored to the Buchanans (MS NRS GD112/39/3/24). Grey Colin was offended by his chief's letter. In his reply, he criticized Argyll for favouring Buchanan over his most loyal kinsmen (Example (1)).

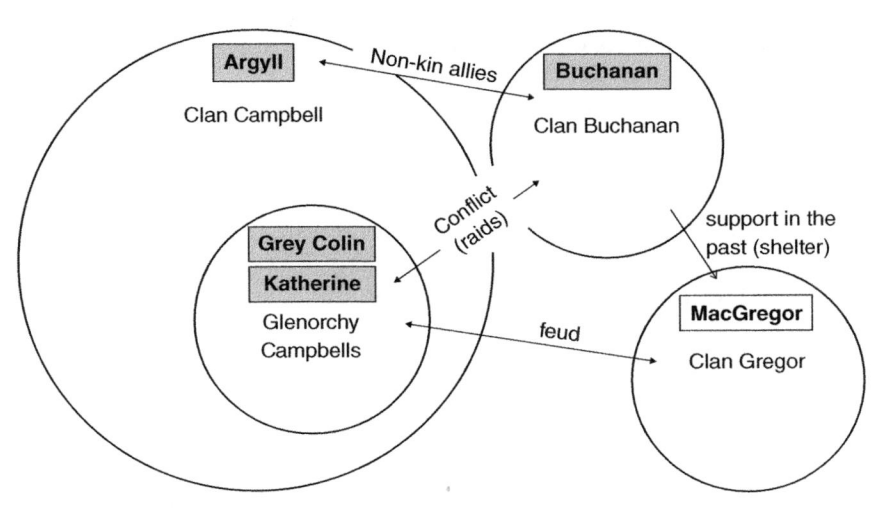

Figure 32.1 Relations between clans and their leaders in the Campbell–Buchanan conflict. Shaded text boxes indicate participants involved in the letter-writing exchange.

(1) I am glaid yat ȝour lordship be servit be boquhennan and siclik honest men nochttheles |
it is na caus to ȝour lordship to lychlie ȝour awin quhilk man be ȝour best quhen
it cummis to ye vpwith For my forbearis servit ȝour lordshipis predecessouris quhen the |
boquhennanis wer to seik and speciallie quhen yair wes mayst ado
'I am glad that your Lordship is served by Buchanan and such honest men; nonetheless, it is no reason to your Lordship to despise your own [i.e. your kinsmen] who are obliged to be your best when difficulties arise. Because my ancestors served your Lordship's predecessors when the Buchanans were not to be found and especially when there was most to do'.
(MS NRS GD112/39/5/2)[6]

Apparently, Grey Colin felt his position and the status of his kin group within Clan Campbell to be threatened by his chief's letter. The wording of Argyll's first letter suggests instead that he put more trust in Grey Colin than in Buchanan's report (Example (2)):

(2) And yis we beleif nocht nor will bel[eif that]
ȝour dewyiss nor consall was <deletion> at yis deid doyng be [rassone]
ȝe maid us na maner of advertisiment
'And this [i.e. the report about the raids] we do not believe nor will believe that your design or counsel was in this act of violence because you gave us no notice of any kind'
(MS NRS GD112/39/3/24)

A discursive close reading of the letter sequence helps to understand Grey Colin's reaction and the delicate situation in which Argyll found himself as mediator in this conflict.

Notably, Argyll's affirmation of trust in Grey Colin is preceded by a praise of Buchanan's loyalty and an implicit threat (Example (3)):

(3) And he hes de
pendit wpoun us and dois ȝit And hes refusit and refussis ony oder to his maister bot us onlie [...]
And we knaw weill yat ye saidis laird
and his freindis wilbe als radelie to put \at/ all ye clangregour at our command as ony off our avyn kynnismen or servanttis
And yairfoir ȝe sall wnderstand yat yairis na man yat will

---

[6] Editing principles for letter excerpts follow Smith's (2012: 71–4) transcription policy for Older Scottish texts. Modern English translations of cited examples are based on the *Dictionary of the Older Scottish Tongue* (DOST) and the *Oxford English Dictionary* (OED).

offend or do skay*th* to ye said*is* laird He offerand ye thyng yat
is werie guid and rasonabill bot quhateuer yai be yat dois
ye say*min* we will no*cht* hald yame na odervayis to us nor the
clangregour

'And he [i.e. Buchanan] has depended on us and still does. And [he] has refused and refuses any other as his master except us only [...] And we know well that the said Laird [i.e. Buchanan] and his friends will be as ready to put all the Clan Gregor at our command as any of our own kinsmen or servants. And therefore, you shall understand that there is no man that will offend or do harm to the said Laird. He is offering the thing that is very good and reasonable but whoever they are who do the same [i.e. offend/attack Buchanan] we will hold them to us in no other ways than the Clan Gregor'.
(MS NRS GD112/39/3/24)

We will examine each of these discursive moves in turn to trace how they afforded the responsive act of taking offence. The emphasis on Buchanan's allegedly undivided loyalty served to foreground Argyll's obligations of lordship over the Buchanans. The Buchanans were bound to Argyll in manrent, which was an important social contract. It consisted of a written agreement that specified obligations of loyalty and protection between the Buchanans as a satellite kin group and Argyll as their lord (Cathcart 2006: 86; Dawson 1997: 43). According to Argyll, Buchanan fulfilled his part of their social contract by promising to put any of his men who were found guilty of raiding Grey Colin's territories under Argyll's judicial authority. Buchanan's readiness to serve Argyll extended to helping with persecuting the Clan Gregor, who were in a feud with the Glenorchy Campbells (see Figure 32.1; Dawson 1997: 55–9).

What stands out in Argyll's letter is his comparison of Buchanan's support to that of his 'own kinsmen' (Example (3) above). This praise evokes the highest level of trust by means of the default value of kinship. Blood relations in sixteenth-century Scotland were regarded as the strongest and closest relationships, which made obligations of mutual support most compelling (Dawson 1997: 9–12). There is no evidence of kinship between Argyll and Buchanan, even though Argyll referred to Buchanan as *our servitour and | cousyng* 'our servant and cousin' (MS NRS GD112/39/3/24). *Cousin* could be used as a term of extended kinship, a social practice rather common at the time to claim a closer relationship than existed (Dawson 1997: 10). By placing Buchanan's non-kin, contract-based, loyalty on the same level as kinship, Argyll exploited the default value of *kinsmen* to claim the closest in-group relationship with Buchanan, which in turn warranted the highest responsibility of protection and served to justify his intervention in the conflict.

Moreover, Argyll implicitly framed Grey Colin and the Glenorchy Campbells as his enemies. He threatened to attack anyone involved in the raid and murder on Buchanan's lands and announced that he would consider them 'in no other ways than the Clan Gregor' (Example (3) above). As Leitner (2015: 134) notes, 'being associated with the Clan Gregor would mark anyone at that time as an enemy to Argyll, because the MacGregors were seen by the Campbells as the rebel clan who defied the lordship of their superiors, Grey Colin and Argyll' (Dawson 1997: 55–6). The threat included Grey Colin's men and by implication Grey Colin himself. Grey Colin was held responsible for the reported raid of his men, according to the collective responsibility of landlords for their inferiors (see Cathcart 2006: 52). Albeit implicit, Argyll's threat worked as an impoliteness formula (see Culpeper 2011b: 136), which is indicated by Grey Colin's 'offensive counter' (Bousfield 2008: 193) as he retaliated with a complaint (Example (1) above).

What Argyll communicated as a justification for acting in his social role of lordship was understood by Grey Colin as a threat to his privileged position within Clan Campbell. The Glenorchy Campbells, of whom Grey Colin was the head, were a cadet branch descended from the house of Argyll (Dawson 1997: 9). Thus, they were bound to the chief by kinship. Grey Colin was one of the members of the chief's fine, i.e. a core circle who stood hierarchically just below the chief. Fine members were heads of cadet branches and heads of minor clans under the chief's lordship. They were the chief's counsellors and assisted him in managing the clan (Cathcart 2006: 75–8). In his reply to Argyll's letter, Grey Colin complained that his chief despised his best kinsmen – by implication, Grey Colin and the Glenorchy Campbells – and overvalued Buchanan's loyalty (Example (1) above). His complaint indicates that Argyll's letter went against his expectation to be acknowledged as a core member in the chief's social network. He perceived himself and his house to be pushed to the edges while Buchanan had been raised to the chief's inner circle.

Correspondents' negotiations of relationships within the clan can be described in terms of Bucholtz's (1999) concepts of association and dissociation. *Associative identity claims*[7] comprise linguistic devices[8] by which participants assert closeness with in-group members and define what unites them as a group. Devices employed by participants 'to distance themselves from a rejected identity' and define what separates them 'from other groups and their values, behaviours, etc.' are called *dissociative identity claims* (Bucholtz 1999: 211–12). As demonstrated by Kádár et al. (2013), Bucholtz's (1999) categories enhance discursive investigations of face in intergroup and intragroup interactions. Applying Bucholtz's (1999) approach to historical data requires the integration of period- and context-specific notions of hierarchy and power, as these aspects are not discussed in her framework.

---

[7] Instead of Bucholtz's (1999: 211) terms 'Negative [... and] positive identity practices', we adopt Kádár et al.'s (2013: 347) renamed labels: *associative/dissociative* identity practices. However, we prefer the term *claim* instead of *practice*. *Practice* has been restricted by Bucholtz and Hall (2004: 377) to habitual behaviour, while *claim* comprises habitual and strategic behaviour.

[8] People construct identities and group membership not only through language but also through other means, such as dress or leisure activities (Bucholtz 1999: 213). The focus in this case study, however, is on language.

Key values that determined in-group status in Scottish clans were kinship and loyalty shown to superiors (Cathcart 2006: 25–6; Dawson 1997: 8–11). The value of kinship was changing in the sixteenth century. As kinship by blood was not always sufficient to achieve clan cohesion, extended forms of kinship, such as marriage alliances and 'fictive kinship' created through fosterage or bonds of manrent, gained importance in strengthening group relations (Cathcart 2006: 25–6, 90). Argyll's and Grey Colin's letters present a case-in-point for the negotiability of in-group relations. Both drew on the default value of kinship but in different ways. Argyll acknowledged Buchanan as a core member of his group by evaluating his non-kin, contractual, loyalty as kin-like (Example (3) above). Grey Colin contested this definition of core group status by foregrounding kinship combined with generational loyalty (Example (1) above). The Glenorchy Campbells also had a bond of manrent with the house of Argyll (Campbell 2002: 6). It seems noteworthy that Grey Colin did not mention this social contract – although he referred to written agreements in other epistolary conflicts with his chief – but asserted closeness to the chief solely on the grounds of the traditional values associated with blood kinship. In a move of dissociation, he challenged Argyll's praise of Buchanan by reminding his chief of Buchanan's lack of loyalty in the past. Thus, he claimed a more peripheral position for his rival in the chief's network. Buchanan was indeed not always as loyal as Argyll claimed him to be: he and his clan were known for offering shelter to the MacGregors, thereby supporting the enemies of Clan Campbell (Dawson 1997: 43; see Figure 32.1). It is possible that Grey Colin's expression 'Buchanan and such honest men' was meant ironically (Example (1) above). Grey Colin's complaint about being despised by his chief suggests that the perceived offence was not only about expected rights and obligations, but also about positive values attributed to in-group relations, and thus a face[9] threat. Since he was acting as representative of his house, his negotiation of in-group relations also had collective implications.

The face threat perceived by Grey Colin was probably aggravated by Argyll's implied threat. Being associated with an out-group like the MacGregors functions as dissociation. Argyll's implicit distancing from the Glenorchy Campbells might have been intended as a warning that they would no longer be entitled to their chief's protection but would have to face punishment if Buchanan's report were true.

Argyll's affirmation of trust (Example (2) above) was not enough to mitigate the threat to Grey Colin's face. Affirmations of trust seem to have been a conventional feature of conflict letters at the time. They 'consist of

---

[9] Face in this case study is defined as a first-order concept. It concerns participants' perceptions of sensitive aspects of identity and social relationships which are negotiated by participants in interaction. The definition is based on Culpeper's (2011b) and Spencer-Oatey's (2002, 2005, 2007) concept of face (and references there cited), but also extended to account for the collective dimensions of face in sixteenth-century Scottish correspondence. (See Leitner 2015 for further discussion.)

an epistemic verb phrase such as *I believe* followed by asserting the other person's conformance to social norms or a denial of his or her violation of those norms' (Leitner 2015: 104). Further evidence from the *Breadalbane Collection* and other sixteenth-century Scottish correspondence shows that affirmations of trust were not perceived as 'a genuine expression' of one's trust in the addressee (Leitner 2015: 109–19). Although employed as mitigation strategies in conflict letters, they appear to have been conventionalized to such a degree that they were no longer powerful enough to neutralize impoliteness formulae such as Argyll's implied threat.

The sequentiality of praising Buchanan, implicitly threatening Grey Colin but then affirming trust in him reflects on the risks at stake for Argyll as mediator in this conflict. The chief had to balance the conflicting obligations of his role of lordship. On the one hand, he had to act as protector of the Buchanans. In his second letter to Grey Colin, Argyll expressed his concerns that Buchanan would cancel their alliance and make an official complaint at the royal court about Argyll's failure to keep law and order in his territories (Example (4)):

(4) And yat
haiffing \respect/ to 30ur hono*ur* yat ye said laird suld no*cht* haif occasioun
to c*o*mplene vpoun 30w to ye quenis ma*iestie* for we wald no*cht* yat 30ur s*er*wantis or ony yat dependis vpoun 30w suld incur sik bruit And ye laird of boquha*n*nan said planlie yat gif he
hald dependit vpoun ony vy*er* except ws yat his guidis or geir wald no*cht* be tane away but law or ordo*ur*.
'And that having respect to your honour that the said Laird [i.e. Buchanan] should not have occasion to complain about you to her Majesty the Queen because we would not want that your servants or any who depend on you should incur such rumours. And the Laird of Buchanan said plainly that if he had depended on any other except us that his goods or possessions would not have been taken away but [there would have been] law and order'.
(MS NRS GD112/39/3/26)

Buchanan held Argyll responsible for the raid and saw him as incapable of fulfilling his duties of lordship. His criticism must have been a heavy blow on those aspects of Argyll's face that were defined by his social role. On the other hand, Argyll had to secure Grey Colin's loyalty. Argyll needed the support of his cadet heads to maintain his power of lordship (Dawson 1997: 38). Cadet branches could break off from the parent clan, either by submitting themselves to the lordship of another chief or by becoming independent, especially if they thought that the chief was not fulfilling his role (Cathcart 2006: 133–34, 216). In a later conflict with his chief, Grey Colin did exert pressure on Argyll by announcing that he would seek support elsewhere (MS NRS GD112/39/12/13). Thus, there was a potential risk for

Argyll of losing Grey Colin and his cadet branch, next to the risk of losing the Buchanans as allies and the risk of face damage for the chief himself as a representative of his clan.

Argyll responded to Grey Colin's complaint with a 'defensive counter-move' (Bousfield 2008: 198) of explaining the motivation behind his first letter. He wrote a second letter to Grey Colin and a letter to Katherine Ruthven, Grey Colin's wife. Katherine played an active part in handling the affairs of the Glenorchy Campbells (Dawson 1997: 22–6). Her inclusion in this letter exchange indicates that Argyll attributed to her a significant role of being a mediator in the interpersonal conflict between him and Grey Colin. In both letters, Argyll emphasized that he had written to Grey Colin out of concern for his cadet head (Example (4) above, Example (5)):

(5) And in deid we wald be leathe to heir ony thing yat war
dishono*u*r to him bot we wald advertis him y*air*off [...]
we will *per*forme ye sami*n* to our awin
hono*u*r and his honor and ye weill of his houss And gif
ye laird be no*cht* co*n*tent yat we advertist him of ye bruit yat
we hard we sall no*cht* writt to him agane in sik ane ma*ner*
for trewlie it was for his awin hono*u*r and weill and es
shewing of ewill bruit yat we wret to him and for vyir
causs quhilk we think to be our dwete

'And it would indeed be hateful to us to hear anything that were dishonour to him [i.e. Grey Colin] but we would inform him about it. [...] We will perform the same to our own honour and his honour and the wellbeing of his house. And if the Laird [i.e. Grey Colin] may not be content that we warned him about the rumours that we heard, we shall not write to him again in such a way, because truly it was for his own honour and wellbeing and keeping clear of evil rumours that we wrote to him and for other reasons which we think to be our duty'.
(MS NRS GD112/39/3/27)

At the heart of Argyll's expressed concern was the reputation of Grey Colin, himself and the whole clan, as reflected in his repeated use of *(dis-)honour*. As one of the core social values of early modern Highland clans, *honour* was intertwined with kinship and hierarchy and had individual as well as collective dimensions (Dawson 1997: 8). It was a face sensitivity for those of superior status. At the individual level, it projected default expectations of fulfilling one's responsibilities as lord/laird towards one's kin group and vassals. The honour of individuals, however, was also determined by the behaviour of their inferiors. Moreover, kin groups had collective honour, which depended on the actions of individual group members or the whole group (Dawson 1997: 8, 12–13, 237). This interweaving of individual and collective aspects is reflected in Argyll's letters. His use of possessive determiners, e.g. *ȝour/his (awin) honour* 'your/his (own) honour' (Examples (4) and

(5) above), indicates that he ascribed honour to Grey Colin as an individual representative of the Glenorchy Campbells. Grey Colin's honour was impugned by the actions of his men. In his reply to Argyll's first letter, Grey Colin acknowledged to have given the orders for the attack on Buchanan's territories but clarified that his men only confiscated the goods that one of Buchanan's men had previously stolen from the Glenorchy Campbells. Additionally, Grey Colin defended his honour by telling his chief that he had his attack legitimized by a royal commission (MS NRS GD112/39/5/2). Through the epistolary interaction, Grey Colin's honour was co-constructed as somehow separate from the honour of his chief, yet nonetheless connected to it. To Katherine, Argyll explained that his motivation was to save *our awin | honour and his* [i.e. Grey Colin's] *honor and ye weill of his houss* (Example (5) above). Evidently, Argyll felt his own honour as representative of Clan Campbell to be threatened by Buchanan's report of the raid and the abovementioned consequences on Argyll's reputation of lordship. Argyll's use of first-person plural pronouns conveyed the collective aspects of his face defined by his social role of lordship and at the same time the group face[10] of Clan Campbell, which by implication had also been damaged by the rumours about the raid. His status as a magnate allowed Argyll to choose between singular and plural pronouns for self-reference. An important factor encouraging the use of the so-called royal *we* was probably the employment of amanuenses for writing his letters (Leitner 2015: 131); however, mixed pronoun usage in some of his letters suggests that the choice of *I* and *we* had additional pragmatic functions, such as distinguishing between matters that concerned him as an individual and matters of his role as a group representative.

This case study demonstrates the potentials of historical sociopragmatics in its richly contextualized analysis of language use in the past. In line with the third wave, it has examined how the sequentiality of discursive moves in a letter and their conventionalized meanings could prime certain readings. It was shown that participants discursively evoked the default values of kinship and loyalty to claim and contest their roles and positions in clan networks. The conflict letters reflect the multiple, interconnected, levels of honour, ranging from individual to group-based face sensitivities.

32.4 Recent Trends

Recent work in historical sociopragmatics has been dominated by several different trends. There has been the move to more discursive approaches, which we have described and illustrated in this article. As a result, recent work increasingly focuses on the complexities of interaction between

---

[10] See Kádár et al. (2013) for the concept of group face as distinct from individual face.

speakers and writers and their (sometimes complex) audiences rather than on speaker meanings alone. In addition, there are two trends that – at first sight – seem to be contradictory. On the one hand, scholars search for larger generalization, which leads to larger and also to more specialized corpora. On the other hand, they search for richer contextualization, i.e. a richer understanding of the specific circumstances in which language is being used, including not only the textual and situational context but also the material context. In the former case, they opt for the wide lens angle to see the larger picture; in the latter case, they opt for the microscope to detect the minute details. In both cases, they are driven by a desire for a deeper understanding of language use in social contexts in the past, and in both cases increased computer capabilities are a driving force behind some of these advances as we will briefly show below.

The last 10–20 years have seen unprecedented progress in the development of both ever larger and ever more specialized corpora. More mega-size corpora have recently become available not only for present-day data but also for historical material (the *Corpus of Historical American English* (COHA), the *Corpus of Late Modern English Texts* (CLMET), the *Old Bailey Corpus*), and some present-day corpora include a historical dimension (e.g. the *Corpus of Contemporary American English* (COCA) from 1990 up to the present day), in which the shallow time depth is offset by an unprecedented corpus size and breadth of genres. This growth of corpus size leads to an increased need for more sophisticated search algorithms to automatically retrieve relevant instances from these vast corpora, and it leads to an increased need for pragmatically annotated corpora. The annotations code the contextual details in the corpus and thus make them accessible to search algorithms which are needed to retrieve pragmatic entities, such as, for instance, specific speech acts (e.g. the Sociopragmatic Corpus; Culpeper and Archer 2008).

This trend to ever richer contextualization of historical analysis also includes the material context. It has become widely acknowledged that meaning is communicated not only through the language of historical texts but also through their visual and physical appearance. Two previously separate research traditions, historical sociopragmatics and 'materialist philology', were brought together to examine the 'pragmatics on the page', that is, the sociopragmatic functions of the various material elements of historical texts (Carroll et al. 2013: 54–5).

The material elements of historical texts that have been examined are various. Studies have focused on paratextual features such as the layout of manuscript or printed pages, the use of space, illustrations and the choice of script or type, and how these visual elements carried meanings and were used by text producers with their readers in mind (e.g. Carroll et al. 2013; Suhr 2011; Williams 2013; see also contributions in Pahta and Jucker 2011). Moreover, linguistic features have been analysed by considering the scribal context. Early modern letters, for example, show practices of collaborative authorship, which raise the question of whose language use it is that we are examining and thus call for careful distinctions between holograph (i.e. writing in the author's own hand) and scribal handwriting (e.g. Williams 2013; Marcus 2018).

The philological revival has also drawn attention to easily overlooked features such as punctuation practices, and their pragmatic functions of structuring texts for their readers (e.g. Claridge and Kytö 2020; Williams 2013). The link between punctuation and reading practices becomes particularly evident when texts move from manuscript to print (e.g. Smith 2017) or when present-day conventions are absent in historical texts, such as the lack of quotation marks for marking direct speech in early modern texts (e.g. Moore 2011). The pragmatic analysis of punctuation and other scribal features, such as corrections or abbreviations, is becoming facilitated by a new generation of text editions which show new standards in historical sociopragmatics for faithful transcriptions of manuscripts and printed texts and the inclusion of facsimile images to study visual features (e.g. Kytö et al. 2011; Taavitsainen and Pahta 2013; Rosenthal et al. 2009).

What ties all the studies together at the interface between philology and historical sociopragmatics is a broadly discursive perspective that written texts represent interactions between writers and their readers. Any textual feature, whether linguistic, visual or material, served communicative needs specific to the socio-historical contexts in which texts were produced and received. For an enhanced understanding of historical texts, it is important to describe the different 'communicative layers' and how they work together in meaning-making processes (Jucker and Pahta 2011: 3).

32.5 Conclusion

Historical sociopragmatics has come a long way since the inception of historical pragmatics in the mid 1990s. It grew out of a merging of research interests between historical linguistics and pragmatics. It happened at a time when the first small-scale historical corpora were released and became more widely available and when pragmaticists extended their views of what was legitimate data for pragmatic theorizing and analysis. Since then, the processing powers and storage capabilities of computers have increased at an unprecedented rate, which has given rise to new and exciting research opportunities. It allows for much larger datasets to be considered and it allows for more sophisticated search algorithms. At the same time, these possibilities also create new challenges. It is important to combine the large-scale diachronic investigations with detailed discursive analyses of individual communicative interactions. Discursive approaches focus on the interaction between speakers and hearers, or – in a historical context – writers and their audiences, and on the dynamic nature of linguistic units and the discursive negotiations of meanings. As illustrated in our case study, default values and the sequential organization of communication play an important role in the discursive negotiations of meanings as participants contest meanings that were established in previous interactions rather than referring only to the 'here and now' of the specific ongoing interaction. Capturing the dynamics between default values and their discursive readjustments as well as participants' management of social relationships and identities is what we have called the emergent third-wave approaches in historical sociopragmatics.

Sources

Dawson, J. (ed.). (2004/2007). *The Breadalbane Collection, 1548–1583*. Edinburgh: University of Edinburgh. www.ed.ac.uk/divinity/research/resources/breadalbane.

National Records of Scotland, Edinburgh. Papers of the Campbell Family, Earls of Breadalbane (Breadalbane Muniments), MS NRS GD112/39/3/24, MS NRS GD112/39/3/26, MS NRS GD112/39/3/27, MS NRS GD112/39/5/2.

References

Archer, D. E. (2005). *Questions and Answers in the English Courtroom (1640–1760)*. Amsterdam: John Benjamins.

Arnovick, L. K. (1999). *Diachronic Pragmatics: Seven Case Studies in English Illocutionary Development*. Amsterdam: John Benjamins.

Bax, M. (2010). Epistolary presentation rituals: Face-work, politeness, and ritual display in Early Modern Dutch letter-writing. In J. Culpeper and D. Z. Kádár, eds., *Historical (Im)politeness*. Bern: Peter Lang, pp. 37–85.

Bousfield, D. (2008). *Impoliteness in Interaction*. Amsterdam: John Benjamins.

Brinton, L. J. (1996). *Pragmatic Markers in English: Grammaticalization and Discourse Functions*. Berlin: Mouton de Gruyter.

Brown, P. and Levinson, S. (1987). *Politeness: Some Universals in Language Usage*. Cambridge: Cambridge University Press.

Brown, R. and Gilman, A. (1989). Politeness theory and Shakespeare's four major tragedies. *Language in Society*, 18(2), 159–212.

Bucholtz, M. (1999). 'Why be normal?': Language and identity practices in a community of nerd girls. *Language in Society*, 28(2), 203–23.

Bucholtz, M. and Hall, K. (2004). Language and identity. In A. Duranti, ed., *A Companion to Linguistic Anthropology*. Malden, MA: Blackwell, pp. 369–94.

Busse, U. (2002). *Linguistic Variation in the Shakespeare Corpus: Morpho-Syntactic Variability of Second Person Pronouns*. Amsterdam: John Benjamins.

Campbell, A. (2002). *A History of Clan Campbell: From Flodden to the Restoration*. Vol. 2. Edinburgh: Edinburgh University Press.

Carroll, R., Peikola, M., Salmi, H., Varila, M.-L., Skaffari, J. and Hiltunen, R. (2013). Pragmatics on the page. *European Journal of English Studies*, 17(1), 54–71.

Cathcart, A. (2006). *Kinship and Clientage: Highland Clanship 1451–1609*. Leiden, Netherlands: Brill.

Chapman, S. (2011). *Pragmatics*. Houndmills, UK: Palgrave Macmillan.
Claridge, C. (2018). Now in the historical courtroom. *Journal of Historical Pragmatics, 19*(2), 223–42.
Claridge, C. and Kytö, M. (eds.). (2020). *Punctuation in Context – Past and Present Perspectives*. Berlin: Peter Lang.
Cruickshank, J. (2013). The role of communities of practice in the emergence of Scottish Standard English. In J. Kopaczyk and A. H. Jucker, eds., *Communities of Practice in the History of English*. Amsterdam: John Benjamins, pp. 19–49.
Culpeper, J. (1996). Towards an anatomy of impoliteness. *Journal of Pragmatics, 25*, 349–67.
Culpeper, J. (2009). Historical sociopragmatics: An introduction. *Journal of Historical Pragmatics, 10*(2), 179–86.
Culpeper, J. (2010). Historical sociopragmatics. In A. H. Jucker and I. Taavitsainen, eds., *Historical Pragmatics*. Berlin: Mouton de Gruyter, pp. 69–94.
Culpeper, J. (ed.). (2011a). *Historical Sociopragmatics*. Amsterdam: John Benjamins.
Culpeper, J. (2011b). *Impoliteness: Using Language to Cause Offence*. Cambridge: Cambridge University Press.
Culpeper, J. and Archer, D. E. (2008). Requests and directness in Early Modern English trial proceedings and play texts, 1640–1760. In A. H. Jucker and I. Taavitsainen, eds., *Speech Acts in the History of English*. Amsterdam: John Benjamins, pp. 45–84.
Culpeper, J., Crawshaw, R. and Harrison, J. (2008). 'Activity types' and 'discourse types': Mediating 'advice' in interactions between foreign language assistants and their supervisors in schools in France and England. *Multilingua, 27*, 297–324.
Culpeper, J. and Hardaker, C. (2017). Impoliteness. In J. Culpeper, M. Haugh and D. Z. Kádár, eds., *The Palgrave Handbook of Linguistic (Im)politeness*. London: Palgrave Macmillan, pp. 199–225.
Culpeper, J. and Kytö, M. (2010). *Early Modern English Dialogues: Spoken Interaction as Writing*. Cambridge: Cambridge University Press.
Dawson, J. (ed.). (1997). *Campbell Letters 1559–1583*. Edinburgh: Scottish History Society.
DOST = *Dictionary of the Older Scottish Tongue*. (2004/2014). University of Dundee/University of Glasgow. www.dsl.ac.uk/.
Eelen, G. (2001). *A Critique of Politeness Theories*. Manchester, UK: St Jerome.
Grainger, K. (2011). 'First order' and 'second order' politeness: Institutional and intercultural contexts. In Linguistic Politeness Research Group, ed., *Discursive Approaches to Politeness*. Berlin: de Gruyter Mouton, pp. 167–88.
Huang, Y. (2007). *Pragmatics*. Oxford: Oxford University Press.
Jacobs, A. and Jucker, A. H. (1995). The historical perspective in pragmatics. In A. H. Jucker, ed., *Historical Pragmatics: Pragmatic Developments in the History of English*. Amsterdam: John Benjamins, pp. 3–33.

Jucker, A. H. (ed.). (1995). *Historical Pragmatics: Pragmatic Developments in the History of English*. Amsterdam: John Benjamins.

Jucker, A. H. (2012). 'These imputations are too common, sir': Politeness in Early Modern English dialogues: The case of Ben Jonson's *Volpone, or The Fox*. In G. Mazzon and L. Fodde, eds., *Historical Perspectives on Forms of English Dialogue*. Milan, Italy: Franco Angeli, pp. 40–58.

Jucker, A. H. (2014). Courtesy and politeness in *Sir Gawain and the Green Knight*. Studia Anglica Posnaniensia, 49(3), 5–28.

Jucker, A. H. (2017). Pragmatics and language change: Historical pragmatics. In Y. Huang, ed., *Oxford Handbook of Pragmatics*. Oxford: Oxford University Press, pp. 550–66.

Jucker, A. H. and Locher, M. A. (2017). Introducing *Pragmatics of Fiction*: Approaches, trends and developments. In M. A. Locher and A. H. Jucker, eds., *Pragmatics of Fiction*, Handbooks of Pragmatics 12. Berlin: Mouton de Gruyter, pp. 1–21.

Jucker, A. H. and Pahta, P. (2011). Communicating manuscripts: Authors, scribes, readers, listeners and communicating characters. In P. Pahta and A. H. Jucker, eds., *Communicating Early English Manuscripts*. Cambridge: Cambridge University Press, pp. 1–10.

Jucker, A. H. and Taavitsainen, I. (2000). Diachronic speech act analysis: Insults from flyting to flaming. *Journal of Historical Pragmatics*, 1(1), 67–95.

Jucker, A. and Taavitsainen, I. (eds.). (2010). *Historical Pragmatics*. Berlin: Mouton de Gruyter.

Jucker, A. H. and Taavitsainen, I. (2013). *English Historical Pragmatics*. Edinburgh: Edinburgh University Press.

Kádár, D. Z. (2010). Exploring the historical Chinese polite denigration/elevation phenomenon. In J. Culpeper and D. Z. Kádár, eds., *Historical (Im)politeness*. Bern, Switzerland: Peter Lang, 117–45.

Kádár, D. Z., Haugh, M. and Chang, W.-L. M. (2013). Aggression and perceived national face threats in Mainland Chinese and Taiwanese CMC discussion boards. *Multilingua*, 32(3), 343–72.

Keay, J. and Keay, J. (eds.). (2000). *Collins Encyclopedia of Scotland*. Rev. ed. London: HarperCollins.

Kopaczyk, J. and Jucker, A. H. (eds.). (2013). *Communities of Practice in the History of English*. Amsterdam: John Benjamins.

Kopytko, R. (1995). Linguistic politeness strategies in Shakespeare's plays. In A. H. Jucker, ed., *Historical Pragmatics: Pragmatic Developments in the History of English*. Amsterdam: John Benjamins, pp. 515–40.

Kytö, M. (2010). Data in historical pragmatics. In A. H. Jucker and I. Taavitsainen, eds., *Historical Pragmatics*, Handbooks of Pragmatics 8. Berlin: Mouton de Gruyter, pp. 33–67.

Kytö, M., Grund, P. and Walker, T. (2011). *Testifying to Language and Life in Early Modern England*. Amsterdam: John Benjamins.

Labov, W. (1994). *Principles of Language Change, Volume 1: Internal Factors*. Oxford: Blackwell.

Leitner, M. (2015). Conflicts in Early Modern Scottish letters and law-courts. Unpublished PhD thesis, University of Glasgow.

Leitner, M. (2017). Curses or threats? Debating the power of witches' words in 17th-century Scottish courtrooms. *Nordic Journal of English Studies*, 16(1), 145–70.

Locher, M. A. and Watts, R. J. (2005). Politeness theory and relational work. *Journal of Politeness Research*, 1, 9–33.

Lutzky, U. (2012). *Discourse Markers in Early Modern English*. Amsterdam: John Benjamins.

Marcus, I. (2018). *The Linguistics of Spoken Communication in Early Modern English Writing: Exploring Bess of Hardwick's Manuscript Letters*. Houndmills, UK: Palgrave Macmillan.

Marmaridou, S. (2011). Pragmalinguistics and sociopragmatics. In W. Bublitz and N. R. Norrick, eds., *Foundations of Pragmatics*, Handbooks of Pragmatics 1. Berlin: de Gruyter, pp. 77–106.

Mills, S. (2003). *Gender and Politeness*. Cambridge: Cambridge University Press.

Moore, C. (2011). *Quoting Speech in Early English*. Cambridge: Cambridge University Press.

Nevala, M. (2004). *Address in Early English Correspondence: Its Forms and Socio-Pragmatic Functions*. Helsinki: Société Néophilologique.

Nevalainen, T. and Raumolin-Brunberg, H. (1995). Constraints on politeness: The pragmatics of address formulae in early English correspondence. In A. H. Jucker, ed., *Historical Pragmatics: Pragmatic Developments in the History of English*. Amsterdam: John Benjamins, pp. 541–601.

OED = Oxford English Dictionary. (1899–2020). Oxford: Oxford University Press. www.oed.com/.

Pahta, P. and Jucker, A. H. (eds.). (2011). *Communicating Early English Manuscripts*. Cambridge: Cambridge University Press.

Petikó, M. (2017). Discursive (re)construction of 'witchcraft' as a community and 'witch' as an identity in the eighteenth-century Hungarian witchcraft trial records. *Journal of Historical Pragmatics*, 18(2), 214–34.

Reutner, R. (2016). Politisch-parlamentarisches Sprachhandeln am Beispiel der Sprachenfrage in der österreichisch-ungarischen Monarchie. Dargestellt am Sprechhandlungstyp Drohung. In P. Ernst and M. Werner, eds., *Linguistische Pragmatik in Historischen Bezügen*. Berlin: de Gruyter, pp. 313–24.

Rosenthal, B., Adams, G. A., Burns, M., Grund, P., Hiltunen, R., Kahlas-Tarkka, L., Kytö, M., Peikola, M., Ray, B. C., Rissanen, M. and Roach, M. K. (eds.). (2009). *Records of the Salem Witch-Hunt*. Cambridge: Cambridge University Press.

Sairio, A. (2017). 'Now to my distress': Shame discourse in eighteenth-century English letters. *Journal of Historical Pragmatics*, 18(2), 295–314.

Schwenter, S. A. and Traugott, E. C. (1995). The semantic and pragmatic development of substitutive complex prepositions in English. In A. H. Jucker, ed., *Historical Pragmatics: Pragmatic Developments in the History of English*. Amsterdam: John Benjamins, pp. 243–73.

Smith, J. J. (2012). *Older Scots: A Linguistic Reader*. Edinburgh: The Scottish Text Society.

Smith, J. J. (2017). From *secreit* script to public print: Punctuation, news management and the condemnation of the Earl of Bothwell. *Huntington Library Quarterly, 80*(2), 223–38.

Spencer-Oatey, H. (ed.). (2002). *Culturally Speaking: Managing Rapport through Talk across Cultures*. Reprint. London: Continuum.

Spencer-Oatey, H. (2005). (Im)politeness, face and perceptions of rapport: Unpackaging their bases and interrelationships. *Journal of Politeness Research, 1*, 95–119.

Spencer-Oatey, H. (2007). Theories of identity and the analysis of face. *Journal of Pragmatics, 39*, 639–56.

Suhr, C. (2011). *Publishing for the Masses: Early Modern English Witchcraft Pamphlets*. Helsinki: Société Néophilologique.

Taavitsainen, I. (2017). Meaning-making practices in the history of medical English: A sociopragmatic approach. *Journal of Historical Pragmatics, 18*(2), 252–70.

Taavitsainen, I. and Pahta, P. (2013). The Corpus of Early English Medical Writing (1375–1800) – a register-specific diachronic corpus for studying the history of scientific writing. In A. Meurman-Solin and J. Tyrkkö, eds., *Principles and Practices for the Digital Editing and Annotation of Diachronic Data*, Studies in Variation, Contacts and Change in English 14. Helsinki: University of Helsinki, VARIENG. www.helsinki.fi/varieng/series/volumes/14/index.html.

Williams, G. T. (2013). *Women's Epistolary Utterance: A Study of the Letters of Joan and Maria Thynne, 1575–1611*. Amsterdam: John Benjamins.

Włodarczyk, M. (2013). British colonial office correspondence on the Cape Colony (1820–1821): Metatextual keywords vs. analytic categories. *Poznań Studies in Contemporary Linguistics, 49*(3), 399–428.

Włodarczyk, M. and Taavitsainen, I. (2017). Introduction: Historical (socio)pragmatics at present. *Journal of Historical Pragmatics, 18*(2), 159–74.

33

Emancipatory Pragmatics

Scott Saft, Sachiko Ide and Kishiko Ueno

33.1 Introduction

Emancipatory Pragmatics (EP) is a line of inquiry that seeks to develop inclusive research frameworks by explicating features of languages that heretofore have been rarely considered within mainstream Western academia. EP researchers recognize that most of the accepted theories within pragmatics have been derived from Euro-American languages and that embedded within these theories are some of the fundamental beliefs, including a Cartesian separation between body and mind and a division between an individualistic self and other, that have undergirded much of Western science and thought. Through analyses of language usage in different contexts, EP endeavours to describe in detail speech practices in and across multiple languages with the aim of establishing new perspectives that may ultimately allow researchers of lesser-studied languages to free themselves from the limitations and restrictions of Western-based theories. Although EP researchers do sometimes adopt a critical lens towards the current stock of theories, the goal is, as Hanks (2014: 1) states, "not to critique, however important that may be, but to build a forward looking and positive approach that can partly free itself from our received frameworks and move beyond them. Hence the term 'emancipatory'".

EP has its origins in a set of workshops, conference panels, and projects funded by the Japan Society for the Promotion of Science that span back to the mid 1990s. Although the term "emancipatory" was not yet used, these frequent meetings brought together a core group of scholars that included Sachiko Ide, Yasuhiro Katagiri, Yoko Fujii, Scott Saft, Kuniyoshi Kataoka, Kaoru Horie, Keiko Abe and Kishiko Ueno to discuss the relationship among language, social interaction and culture, with a particular focus on East Asian languages. Soon thereafter, the group expanded its reach by inviting participation from, among others, William Hanks, Nick Enfield, Kazuyoshi Sugawara, Krisadawan Hongladarom, Songthama Intachakra, Natthaporn

Panpothong, Siriporn Phakdeephasoon, Mayouf Ali Mayouf, Li Wei and William Beeman, who were doing research on languages such as Mayan, ǀGui (an African language), Thai, Lao, Libyan Arabic, Mandarin and Persian. Seeking an inclusive framework to explain patterns of language usage emerging from their data, the group first publicly employed the term "emancipatory pragmatics" in 2007 in the title of a panel at the tenth IPrA conference in Gotenborg, Sweden. The positive reception of the panel prompted the organization of an EP panel at each subsequent IPrA conference, and it also led to three special issues in the *Journal of Pragmatics* 41 (2009), 44 (2012) and 69 (2014). Moreover, members of the EP group have undertaken data collection of social interaction in Japanese, Mandarin, Korean, Thai, Libyan Arabic and American English, and they have continued exploring an emancipatory approach to pragmatics through workshops in places like Tokyo; Sebha, Libya; and Berkeley, California. EP has received recognition as an innovative approach in Senft's (2014) book *Understanding Pragmatics*, it is referred to as "a variety of cultural pragmatics" in the *Oxford Handbook of Pragmatics* (Huang 2017: 10), and it is described as an approach to the "cultural and psychological relationship between interlocutors" by Crawshaw (2017: 10) in an edited volume focusing on intercultural pragmatics (Kecskes and Assimakopoulos 2017).

Like other scholars (i.e. Ameka and Terkourofi 2019), EP researchers acknowledge the potential drawbacks of categories such as "Euro-American languages" and "non-Euro-American languages". Much like the frequently invoked West-East dichotomy, such distinctions not only suffer from a lack of specificity – Ameka and Terkourofi (2019) wonder, for example, where parts of the world like the Middle East, Eastern Europe, Mexico and Greece fit in – but they also have the potential to further stereotype the communicative styles of people in certain parts of the world as "others" to Western norms of interaction (Hanks et al. 2009; Intachakra 2012). Nonetheless, the EP perspective maintains that languages in the "non-Euro-American" category have been thus far vastly understudied and that it is only through a commitment to the investigation of the diverse languages in the world that we will be able to increase our understanding of the human capacity to employ language and organize social interaction. EP researchers therefore strongly agree with Ameka and Terkourofi's (2019:73) assertion that "there are linguistic practices that are radically different from established views currently on offer in pragmatics and that, in the interest of cognitive justice and the plurality of sciences and knowledge systems, these should be developed to complement the current stock".

In addition to Mayan, ǀGui, Thai, Libyan Arabic, Lao, Mandarin and Persian, the EP panels and special issues to date have featured Tactile American Sign Language, Hawaiian, Japanese, Korean, Kilivila and Tibetan, and they have considered various aspects of language usage such as turn-taking practices (Sugawara 2012), speech acts (Sugawara 2009), repetition (Fujii 2012), deixis (Hanks et al. 2019) and demonstratives

(Naruoka 2014) and pronouns (Saft 2011, 2014). In investigating these linguistic phenomena, EP researchers endeavour first and foremost to situate their descriptions within the sociocultural context in which they occur. By doing so, EP aligns itself with the classic focus in anthropology on an emic perspective that "favors the point of view of the members of the community under study and hence tries to describe how members assign meaning" (Duranti 1997: 172; also see Pike 1966, 1971). There has been a more recent push to place an emphasis within pragmatics on "emic practices" (i.e. Chang and Haugh 2013; Haugh 2013, 2016) and EP hopes to join with other contributors within the area of sociopragmatics to develop approaches that give consideration to the orientations and perceptions of language users (cf. Leech 1983).

In attempting to describe emic practices in various languages, EP studies sometimes take a comparative perspective; for instance, Katagiri (2009) has examined the interactional methods used to build consensus in Japanese, English and Libyan Arabic, Fujii (2012) has compared self-referencing processes in Japanese and English, and Horie (2012) has looked at nominalization strategies across Japanese, Korean and Mandarin. By embedding language practices in sociocultural context and by adopting a comparative approach, EP researchers have produced analyses of a range of languages and have, in the process, raised questions about existing theories. The next section offers a more detailed description of EP studies that relate to two theoretical frameworks that have had a major impact in pragmatics, namely politeness theory and the turn-taking system for social interaction.

33.2 Examples of EP Research Findings

33.2.1 Politeness

Soon after Brown and Levinson proposed a universal theory politeness based on the notion of face (Brown and Levinson 1978, 1987), many readers were critical of their adoption of a rationalist model of interaction that seems to place the individual at the centre and to accord this individual with "autonomy in one's action" (Haugh 2005: 44; see also Fraser 1990; Kasper 2009 for discussion). In particular, scholars such as Matsumoto (1988, 1989) and Ide (1989) argued that it is difficult to apply such a model to Japanese society where there is more of an emphasis on group dynamics than on individual face. In contrast to the expression of politeness in English, which is seen as more of a "volitional" choice, politeness strategies in Japanese are chosen through *wakimae*, which is translated as "discernment" and described as the "almost automatic observation of socially agreed-upon rules" (Hill et al. 1986: 348). Further criticism followed from research on other East Asian languages such as Chinese (Mao 1994) and also from scholars focusing on African languages (Nwoye 1992; de Kadt 1994, 1998). As Ameka and Terkoufari (2019: 76) note, the debate about the application of Brown and Levinson's theory of politeness spans at least "three blocks in the world: West, East, and Africa".

Participants in the EP projects have primarily focused on politeness in the "Eastern block" and thus have simultaneously contributed to and benefitted from other attempts to develop concepts such as impoliteness and face in languages such as Japanese, Korean, Chinese, and Thai (i.e. Chang and Haugh 2013; Gao 1998; Haugh 2013, 2016; Kim 2008; Mao 1994). EP research has been critical of Brown and Levinson's theory, but criticism has generally been offered as part of attempts to promote the development of more comprehensive frameworks. Intachakra's (2012) work on politeness in Thai is one example. Intachakra (2012) acknowledges the "helpful" aspects of Brown and Levinson's theory, but he also suggests that it focuses too much on "means-to-end" rationality and virtually ignores "rapport-oriented" rationality. He refers to Kasher (1982), Havertake (1988) and Allan (1998) to note that rationality may be binary in nature, with "rapport-oriented" rationality serving as a complement to "means-to-end rationality" in its "concern for interpersonal connection and relationship maintenance" (Intachakra 2012: 620).

In order to situate his point within a particular context, Intachakra invokes the Thai concept of *kʰwaːmkreːŋtɕaj*, abbreviated as KKJ, which he describes not as a fear but more of a "concern or anxiety about how others may 'feel' as a result of one's expressed words and actions". Elaborating further, he writes that KKJ leads a Thai speaker "to worry about what he/she thinks will most benefit the hearer (whether materially or otherwise) and thus seeks a measure that would accommodate the hearer's convenience and consequently avoid friction" (Intachakra 2012: 622). He also notes that in contrast to the focus on the role of speech acts and especially indirect speech acts in the "means-to-end" rationality of Western politeness theory, KKJ prompts Thai speakers often to refrain from making speech acts for the benefit of the hearer as part of a rapport-oriented rationality. In his words, "in pursuit of KKJ, personal sacrifice transcends the desire for individual rights and benefits" (Intachakra 2012: 623). He, in fact, places, the idea of self sacrifice at the heart of two defining principles of KKJ: "(1) 'Maximise other-accommodation'; and (2) 'Maximise self-effacement'". These principles often lead to so-called non-communication, in which a participant avoids speaking for the benefit of others, and also to "epistemic displacement", "in which a speaker has certain 'knowledge' or a thought in mind but chooses to communicate something else, for fear that the hidden meaning might cause either physical inconvenience to another person" (Intachakra 2012: 626). Intachakra differentiates "epistemic displacement" from lying because epistemic displacement is done for the benefit of others while lying is frequently done to protect the self.

One interesting aspect of Intachakra's discussion of KKJ is the proposal that instead of the notion of "face", a heart metaphor may be a better fit for understanding politeness in Thai communication. He emphasizes the importance of heart metaphors by noting that the word for heart in Thai, *tɕaj*, is embedded not only in the Thai term for KKJ but also in the terms for "pleased", "relieved", "stunned or shocked" and "taken aback with dismay" that are frequently used in interpersonal communication. In addition, he includes a rhyme recited by children that employs the term KKJ as well as the word for heart in *hŭatɕaj*.

(1) Thai children's rhyme
k^hwa:mkre:ŋtɕaj pen sŏmbàt k^hɔ:ŋ p^hûdi:
trɔ:ŋ du: si: t^húkk^{h}on kɔ: mi: hŭatɕaj
kɤ:t pen k^hon t^hâ:hà:k măj kre:ŋtɕaj k^hraj
k^honnán sáj ráj k^hunnat^{h}am prà?tɕam ton

"KKJ is an attribute pertaining to well-mannered people
Through careful contemplation, we will realise that everyone has a heart of his/her own
Born human beings, one who does not show KKJ to others
Is considered as lacking a sense of morality".
(Intachakra 2012: 623)

Noting that a literal translation of KKJ is "fear of hearts", Intachakra uses this common rhyme to emphasize the importance of paying attention to the hearts of those around them. While the difference between "heart" in the Thai model and "face" in Brown and Levinson (1978, 1987) may appear to be merely a matter of semantics, Intachakra's attempts to situate the "heart" within indigenous Thai expressions underscores the fact that the notion of "face" may very much be a metaphor influenced by Western thought that is not reflective of a universal approach to politeness. Based on Intachakra's work on KKJ, we may want to consider a heart metaphor as a better fit for situations in which interlocutors place more of a concern on the feelings of others than on their own.

Intachakra's view of politeness is supported by other research on Thai that has been published in EP special issues. While not employing the term "politeness", Panpothong and Phakdeephasook (2014) examines the Thai expression *maipenrai*, translated into English as "it's not substantial", which is used to accomplish a wide variety of interactional activities that includes responding to apologies and expressions of thanks, refusing, communication consolation and terminating verbal conflict. Although this short verbal response has been misunderstood to represent indifference and lack of ambition on the part of Thai speakers, Panpothong and Phakdeephasook emphasizes that *maipenrai* has "the objective of detaching the hearer from his/her worries" (104). In this sense, it fits nicely with Intachakra's characterization of KKJ as a rapport-oriented politeness strategy that enables Thai speakers to orient to the feelings of their interlocutors as a part of putting their "hearts" at ease.

Panpothong and Phakdeephasook (2014) suggest that *maipenrai* derives from the Buddhist notion of *Tri Laksana* that, according to them, underpins Thai social interaction. In particular, they link *maipenrai* to the concepts of *aniccang* or *anicca* "impermanence", *dukkhang* or *dukkha* "suffering", and *anatta* "no self, selflessness". In the case of expressing consolation for the passing of loved ones, *maipenrai* speaks to the impermanence of life and reminds those still living "that nothing is truly substantial in this world" (Panpothong and Phakdeephasook 2014: 105). In actions such as expressing refusal and terminating verbal conflict, *maipenrai* works as an expression of suffering in performing a negative act and also a withdrawal of the self from the interaction. Intachakra (2012: 624) draws a similar connection in his work on KKJ to Buddhism; "this tendency of native Thai speakers to subjugate their personal goals, wants and rights is rooted in Buddhism (whose doctrines prevail in Thailand), which discourages self-indulgence". Indirectly referencing the Buddhist principles of "suffering" and "selflessness", he states that "personal fulfillment obtains only if people are prepared to benefit others, even if doing so means we have to surrender what is rightly ours" (Intachakra 2012: 624). Buddhism was also referenced by Hongladarom (2009), another contributor to an EP special journal issue, as she highlighted the necessity of grounding Thai evidential expressions and personal pronouns in the Buddhist principle of contingency. She also makes the same suggestion for some indexical expressions in Tibetan, reminding us in the process of the need to consider various aspects of the cultural context in which language usage is embedded.

In concluding his work, Intachakra (2012: 632) agrees with Brown and Levinson by noting that "politeness is a cultural universal", but he also adds that "the more we move from one culture into the next, the more we tend to find differences in the forms, constraints, interpretations and weights each cultures gives in conceptualizing as well as rationalising politeness". And speaking even more directly to the goal of EP to develop more inclusive theories, he suggests that any universal theory "may need to take into account other politeness notions – to mention just some of the non-Western ones – like Japanese *teinei* (Haugh 2004) and *enryoo* (Miike 2003), Chinese *limao* (Mao 1994) and *keqi* (Gao 1998), Korean *nunchi* (Kim 2008), Persian *tae'arof* (Beeman 2001), Thai KKJ and many others". Although these are separate concepts that must be understood through detailed investigation in context, Intachakra remains optimistic that research that further examines these concepts can fit together in one politeness theory. He states that "with 'consideration of others' as a centripetal point of commonality, these concepts will (one hopes) mutually define and help fill in gaps that have remained in politeness research until now" (632).

33.2.2 Turn-Taking and Overlap

As indicated above, questions had been raised about the universality of Brown and Levinson's theory of politeness from a time that predates the conception of EP. Yet, EP also attempts to reconsider theories that have been accepted by the majority of researchers in the area of pragmatics. The turn-taking system postulated by Sacks et al. (1974) is a case in point. Sacks et al. posited a set of rules through which participants select either others or themselves to take turns at talk. In this exchange of talks, some overlap is expected to occur at so-called turn-relevance points (TRPs) as participants work out the allocation of a next turn, but simultaneous talk is supposed to be limited because of the normative expectation of one speaker at a time. To be sure, there are some situations, for example, debates or arguments, where it is not uncommon for participants to use simultaneous talk attempt to "talk over" co-participants, but participants usually orient to such occurrences as "interruptive" by adopting measures to restore the one-speaker at a time system. Participants' general orientation to this turn-taking system has been taken as evidence for its universality. Sidnell, in fact, claims that it varies only minimally according to culture because it "is grounded in a species-specific adaptation to the contingencies of human social intercourse" (Sidnell 2001: 1263).

However, as part of the EP line of inquiry, Sugawara (2012) reports data from his research on speakers of |Gui, an African language spoken in the Xade settlement in Kxʻoensakene (New Xade) outside of the Central Kalahari Game Reserve, that is difficult to explain in terms of the accepted model of turn-taking. Sugawara does note that "the turn-taking system seems applicable to the temporal organization of |Gui conversations in many instances", but he then goes to describe two types of talk, one termed "prolonged talk" and the other "prolonged simultaneous discourse", which appear to deviate from the norm. Of the two, he spends less time on "prolonged talk" and does not offer any excerpts of data. It is characterized by an extended interval of talk by a participant, sometimes longer than 10 minutes, to which other participants may or may not pay attention to as active "hearers". In cases where a speaker continues speaking to participants who are not paying attention, he suggests that "accommodation to the turn-taking system is only superficial ... because other participants pay little attention to the speaker. It is misleading to describe such a situation as the outcome of hearers' refraining from self-selecting in this case, because participants who might be expected to behave as hearers seem quite indifferent to the TRPs" (Sugawara 2012: 584).

While such instances of the prolonged talk type bring into question our typical conception of interaction as consisting of active speakers and hearers, it is "prolonged simultaneous discourse" that poses the biggest challenge to the universality of the accepted model of turn-taking. Prolonged simultaneous discourse is divided into "antagonistic overlap", "cooperative overlaps", and "parallel overlaps". Of the three, he notes that "antagonistic" and "cooperative" overlaps can potentially be explained in terms of the turn-taking system; antagonistic overlap allows participants to express dissent and disgust for the speech of a current speaker while that speaker is in the midst of talk, and cooperative overlap enables hearers to produce support for the current speaker's line of talk. However, Sugawara explains that "parallel overlaps" are difficult to fit into the Western model. In his words, "in parallel simultaneous discourse, one party talks about some subject while the other party talks about a subject that involves a similar topic but comprises very different details. This type of interaction might seem most curious for a non |Gui observer, who might wonder whether the two parties involved in such a conversation are communicating with each other in the usual sense of the word" (Sugawara 2012: 587). As an example, he offers an English translation of an interaction between two participants, QM and Ho, who had previously been involved in an intimate relationship with each other for about five years.[1] In addition to the two speakers, there were four other participants present at the time of the interaction. Example 2 below is reproduced from Sugawara (2012: 587). The overlapped portions are highlighted in bold.

(2)   Parallel overlap

	QM	Ho
1	I had been [good at] dancing	
2	when I had [been] where the dance had died	
3	In this way, I had stopped dancing,	
4	**I had** been dancing, [but] it died	and then
5.1	!Kobasi's* (......), **I had been dancing,**	They (*m, dl*), then, with my leg, grasped me,
5.2	**then**	[they were] **stepping on my leg,**
6	**and [I] consumed, my money had been collected**	With my leg, grasping me, and
7	**but this had died**	[they were] **stepping on my leg**
8	my money was consumed, [but]	
9	[it let] **me praise it,**	Then, when [the song] stops in that way.
10	**we** (*m, pl*) **call to let him come,**	they (*m, dl*) **made me sit down,**
11	they were money – **it was** [that] of steenbok	And then, I thought
12	**those things were eaten** [– consumed]	"Oh! they (*m, dl*), then, kill you"
13	And again, [it le] **me pay it** – mine	"What will they do to you?"

---

[1] Sugawara (2012) adds an appendix showing the romanized IGui transcription, but for the sake of brevity, we only include the English translation here.

14	I put out them,	As I thought of this in my heart,
15	In this way, all things seem to be	I returned to flee
16	[this is what] I used to talk (+)	and fled and then ... (+)

*!Kobasi's is the name of a dance repertoire characterized by a vigorous stepping like a Cossack dance

Sugawara also adds the following "loose" translation for QM's speech.

QM: I had been good at dancing, but my dancing had ended, as you know. I have stopped dancing; I had danced but it was over. I had been dancing !kobasi, and spent much money, but this had ended. My money was gone, but I praised a good dancer and we invited him to come. I earned much money by selling *steenbok skinds*, but I spent all the money [giving it to the dancer]. Again and again, I gifted and paid my money [to the dancer]. Everything seems to be like this.

(Sugawara 2012: 587–8)

Sugawara further explains that Ho is relating in her part of the interaction a bad dream in which two men attempted to attack her at a dance event. In this example, then, QM and Ho loosely share a topic of conversation related to dance but express very different experiences through prolonged overlap.

In attempting to understand this extended parallel talk, Sugawara notes the emergence of two possible interpretations: (1) given the presence of four others in the same space, the two speakers were speaking to different audiences; and (2) regardless of "hearership", the two speakers remained totally disengaged from one another. However, Sugawara rejects both interpretations by observing that none of the other participants demonstrated any kind of visible response to either speaker and that the two speakers were actually physically in contact with another as they spoke. In other words, the speakers were not speaking to different audiences and they were not disengaged from one another. They merely engaged in prolonged simultaneous speech in close proximity to each other.

After providing one other example of the same phenomenon, Sugawara wonders how we can make sense of a participation structure in which participants sometimes adhere to a one-speaker role but then also employ "another mode in which prolonged and frequent overlaps are not avoided". As a response, he suggests a reconsideration of our basic idea of "hearership" given that listeners in ǀGui are sometimes under only a "vague expectation" to pay attention to the content of talk. And while Sugawara stops short of explicating fully how a revised model of hearership might look, he does emphasize, as part of the EP focus, the need to revisit the accepted turn-taking model based on his study. In his words, "the analysis of the cases of parallel overlap illuminates another possibility in regard to verbal interaction; this possibility has received little attention from the Western-centred theory of conversation insofar as it exemplifies the feasibility of an alternative structure that allows, at least temporarily or intermittently, a cessation in this monitoring activity" (Sugawara 2012: 600).

After his analysis, Sugawara reminds us that there may be other yet-unstudied societies that make use of similar participation structures by making the provocative suggestion that prolonged simultaneous discourse is connected to what he calls the "ego-centric relatedness" of hunter-gatherer societies such as |Gui. He makes such a statement due to the |Gui's mutual agreement, in some situations, to allow multiple speakers to overlap each other as they see fit. According to Sugawara, "this observation strongly suggests that simultaneous discourse or overlap may be correlated with some social attitude specific to the so-called egalitarian way of life prevailing among th[ose] societies" (Sugawara 2012: 599). The validity of such a statement, of course, can only be evaluated through continued research of diverse languages. Testing his hypothesis, though, will be one way of gaining a deeper understanding of the human faculty for engaging in social interaction. Sidnell (2001: 163) may indeed be correct that the turn-taking model proposed by Sacks et al. (1974) is "a species-specific adaptation to the contingencies of human social intercourse", but further investigation of interaction in diverse societies may show us that humans are capable of other participation structures as well.

33.3 EP and Theory

The previous section describes how findings of EP research on politeness theory and turn-taking have brought into question the universality of both. At the same time, the EP authors cited above also made suggestions towards the establishment of more comprehensive theories. And while they stopped short of proposing many of the details of such theories, one of the goals of EP is to develop new frameworks that apply across a wider range of languages and cultures. To do so, EP researchers hold that instead of employing English concepts and terminology, a more emancipatory practice may be to elucidate key concepts from lesser-studied languages and explore the possibility of adding them to the metalanguage used in pragmatic research. One example is Hanks' (2005; also see Hanks et al. 2009) observation that *wakimae* may explain similar phenomena in Yucatec Maya discourse. He likewise wonders whether the Maya concept of *iknal*, explained as "one's perceptual field" or "place" (Hanks 1996: 251), may be used to describe Japanese. And if *wakimae* and *iknal* are found in Japanese and Yucatec Maya, might they also have applications in other societies as well, even those in the western part of the world? Along the same lines, we may want to examine in more depth whether the Thai notion of KKJ (Intachakra 2012) can explain politeness in other sociolinguistic situations in which participants place an emphasis on rapport-oriented rationality. EP researchers note that the practice of using such concepts as a starting point may be crucial to breaking down barriers to understanding linguistic practices in lesser-studied languages.

33.3.1 Ba Theory

Of the non-Western concepts, such as *wakimae*, KKJ or *maipenrai*, that have thus far been employed by EP researchers, the one explored the most is *ba* theory. *Ba* theory is based on the Japanese notion of *ba*, which has been loosely translated into English as "field", and has its origins in the work of the Japanese philosopher Kitaro Nishida (2012) and other philosophers in the Kyoto School as well as the ideas of the bio-physicist Hiroshi Shimizu (1995, 2000). EP researchers began exploring *ba* theory largely due to its innovative approach to context and have worked via workshops, conference panels, and some of the articles in the EP special issues (see especially Fujii 2012; Saft 2014) on applying it to language usage. In addition, some members of the EP group recently published an article on *ba* theory in a different special issue of the *Journal of Pragmatics* in response to the question "Quo Vadis, Pragmatics?" (Hanks et al. 2019).

Unlike Western approaches to context that assume the existence of the individual as well as a division between self and other, *ba* theory assumes "non-separation" and "impermanence" and thus represents an opportunity to approach context "as a single, integrated whole" (Hanks et al. 2019: 63). Hanks et al. (2019: 64) describe it, in fact, as a "theory of contextual interdependence" and view it as a means of attaining a deeper understanding of terms such as "relational", "situated", and "co-present" that have frequently been used to explain the conception of the self in non-Western societies.

To explain *ba* theory, Hanks et al. (2019) make a distinction between "primary *ba*" and "secondary *ba*".[2] In their words, "Primary *ba* is basically an ontology of mutual dependence, impermanence and ultimately non-separation. Japanese scholars describe it in terms of Buddhist (especially Zen) and sometimes Shinto ideas regarding the non-separation of humans from nature" (Hanks et al. 2019: 64). This is the level that Nishida refers to as "*basho* of absolute nothingness". But this "nothingness" does not mean "nothing" in an ordinary sense. Rather it means that no things exist because no distinctions are made (Hanks et al. 2019: 64). At the same time, it is "pregnant of meaning" (Ide 2019), or the origin of presence.

Secondary *ba* is the space in which interaction unfolds, and it is at this level, through actions such as speaking and interacting, that distinctions and categories start to emerge. Use of language inevitably breaks the non-separation of primary *ba* and leads to the emergence of "a universe of

---

[2] There is a third level of *ba*, namely *ba* theory. This is the level used to objectify and explain *ba* as a theory that can be added to the metalanguage of pragmatics (Hanks et al. 2019).

inter-related distinctions" (Hanks et al. 2019: 65). As Hanks et al. state, "whereas primary *ba* is unarticulated, secondary *ba* is a space of articulation, categorization and distinction. Language and social practice produce distinctions, divisions, hierarchies and objects of many kinds (including discrete thoughts)" (65).

According to Hanks et al. (2019: 65), "secondary *ba* is much closer to English 'context' or 'situation'. It is the interactional space in which a process unfolds". Yet, crucial to understanding *ba* theory as an innovative approach is appreciating the link between secondary *ba* and primary *ba* of non-separation. Articulation at the level of secondary *ba* arises from primary *ba*, which essentially means that interaction, including the identities and relationships of the participants, emerges from the nothingness of non-separation (i.e. mutual dependence, impermanence and non-separation).

Also important to understanding the relationship between the levels of *ba* is Shimizu's (1995) conception of *basho*, which in Japanese consists of the two morphemes *ba* and *sho*, with *sho* meaning "place" and *basho* referring to "a place in which a relational process emerges" (Hanks et al. 2019: 65). For Shimizu, *basho* is an alternative to the distantiated subject frequently assumed in Western thought, and for *ba* theory, this means that "the starting point is not distantiated, but interior to the world you hope to grasp". As Hanks et al. further note, "interiority becomes radical if you rephrase it as, 'you are in a relation of non-separation from the context you wish to describe'" (66).

As an illustration, Shimizu (1995) offers an example of a painter before a blank canvas in a room who is asked to draw the room "as accurately as possible in its present state" (Hanks et al. 2019: 65). As explained by Hanks et al., "starting to paint on a blank canvas, the painter adds details, but because the canvas is part of the room, the room is changing as (s)he adds details to the canvas" (65). And because the room is constantly changing as the painter works, the painter can never catch up to the state of the room. This is "the problem of reflexivity. *The painter is in a basho* (emphasis in the original)" (Hanks et al. 2019: 66).

Recognition of the reflexivity problem thus inspires us to conceptualize how a separate self may emerge. Shimizu posits two different representations of *basho*: egocentric and *basho* centric (see Hanks et al. 2019). Egocentric representation of *basho* provides a microscopic sketch of *basho*, which corresponds to second level *ba*, where "separation and articulation emerge". *Basho* centric representation of *basho* provides a holistic transcendental sketch of *basho* in which subjects and objects are non-separable. To explain the intersection of the two types of representation *basho* as the well as the relationship to *ba* theory, Hanks et al. (2019) write the following.

> This non-separability is rooted in primary *ba*, which relates to secondary *ba* as the subsuming room relates to the emergent painting produced in it. The self (the reflexive subject) is the "convergence point" at which

these two kinds of representation articulate. We thus have a model with two levels that are distinct but intersect, in a real-time process that produces the self as an emergent process of articulation.

A separated self, then, is not just a pre-existing aspect of a context but rather is the outcome of a process in which the egocentric representation of *basho* is subsumed within the holistic representation of *basho*. And since the self only emerges from this "real-time process" of articulation, this means that descriptions such as "relational", "contingent" and "situated" seem to fit the idea of self as the convergence point of egocentric and holistic representations of *basho*. Any sense of self that arises from this "convergence point" only does so through a mutually interdependent relationship with other participants.

It is therefore not surprising that the Japanese self has been long described as "relational" and "contingent" (Kondo 1990; Lebra 2004; Rosenberger 1994), with links often made to linguistic strategies such as honorifics and sentential final forms that are chosen based on the participants' discernment of what is called for in a given relationship situation (Fujii 2019; Ide 2011, 2019). In a recent paper presented at the EP panel at the sixteenth IPrA conference in Hong Kong, Ueno (2019) employs *ba* theory to understand why teachers use more questions than students in dyadic interactions between the two. Example (3) provides an example from data that was collected as part of one of the grants from the Japanese Society for the Promotion of Science and also served as the basis for Ueno (2017, 2019).

(3)

01 T: a, ima kinchoo shiteru daijyoobu {laugh}
"oh, are (you) nervous now? (Are you) all right?"
02 S: hai, {laugh} kinchoo shite masu
"Yes, (I)'m nervous".
03 S: {laugh} hai
"Yes".
04 T: ee, jaa, chotto kinchoo shiteru mitai dakara, saisho watashi kara
"Very well, then: (you) seem to be a bit nervous, so first I will ..."
05 S: a, hai
"Oh, yes".
06 T: bikkuri shita hanashi suru n desu keredo mo
"(I will) tell a story in which (I) was surprised, so ..."
07 S: hai
"Yes".

(Ueno 2019)

Noting that the dyad was instructed by researchers to talk freely for approximately five minutes about something that surprised them, Ueno (2019) describes how the teacher takes the initiative in the negotiation of topic by first asking questions to the student about how she feels in line 1 and then by providing the first topic in lines 4 and 6. At the same time, the student offers only responses and avoids asking questions. To explain this occurrence, as well as other instances in the data in which the teacher supportively guides the student to choose and navigate her own topic, Ueno (2019) uses the notion of *wakimae* to point out that teachers and students choose such patterns based on an ingrained recognition of their roles within society. After contrasting the role-oriented basis of *wakimae* with theories of pragmatics that assume rationality as the primary motivator of language usage, Ueno (2019) invokes *ba* theory to understand the *wakimae* process. It is only through interaction that the self begins to emerge as it is subsumed within the relationship between the two participants. In other words, even though one participant is articulated as the self whose role is teacher and the other as the self whose role is student, the two emergent selves do not exist separately from their relationship. Furthermore, much like the reflexive painter alters the room from within with every stroke, the teacher and the student constantly redefine their relationship with each utterance. In this way, then, the teacher and student are speaking as parts of a coherence-generating whole, *ba*. Ultimately, *ba* theory aids not only in comprehending this particular instance of interaction but also in understanding how a role-oriented process such as *wakimae* occupies an important place in a society that is constituted by vertical relationships. Through a convergence of primary *ba* of non-separation with the secondary level, in which the relationship between the participants starts to become articulated, Japanese participants develop a flexibility of self that enables social selves to recognize relationships with others and subsequently fill the different roles necessitated by Japanese society.

That *ba* theory has applications to the Japanese language and interaction is not especially surprising given that *ba* is a Japanese concept. Yet, EP research has also begun showing how *ba* provides explanatory power for language and interaction in other languages. Saft (2011, 2019), for instance, has begun considering the application of *ba* to the Polynesian language of Hawaiian, starting with the simple greetings shown in Example 4.

(4a) Greeting given by one participant to another
 Aloha kāua
 Greetings we (first person, dual, inclusive)
 "Greetings to us".
(4b) Greeting given by one participant to two or more participants
 Aloha kākou
 Greetings we (first person, plural, inclusive)
 "Greetings to us".

As Saft (2017) explains, the usages of *kāua* in 4a and *kākou* in 4b need to be understood in terms of the distinctions made in Hawaiian first person pronouns. Like many other Polynesian languages, Hawaiian first person pronouns consist of a distinction between dual and plural forms and also between inclusivity and exclusivity. Hence, a greeting between two people as in 4a) commonly begins with the usage of the first person dual inclusive form *kāua* (which with the greeting term *aloha* might be translated as "greetings to us"), and a greeting by one person to two or more people as in 4b) would employ the first person plural inclusive form *kākou* (which together with *aloha* might be best translated as "greetings to us all"). Hawaiian does have exclusive forms for both pronouns, *māua* is the exclusive first person dual pronoun and *mākou* is the exclusive first person plural pronoun, and it also has three second person pronouns, *'oe* is singular "you", *'olua* is the dual "you", and *'oukou* is the plural form.

From an English perspective, it is interesting that the inclusive first person forms are used in the greetings instead of the second person forms, hence the awkward English translations "Greetings to us" and "Greetings to all of us". Though difficult to explain from a perspective that assumes separate individuals from the outset, such greetings seem in line with *ba* theory. Since greetings usually serve to initiate interaction at the secondary level of *ba*, this usage of inclusive first person pronouns seems to recognize a state of mergence that starts in primary *ba*.

Indeed, these greetings are consistent with the emphasis in the traditional Hawaiian perspective on non-separation. Crucial to Hawaiian thought is the concept of genealogy, *mo'okū'auhau* in the Hawaiian language, through which Native Hawaiians believe that the self is constituted by the spirits of their ancestors as well as their connections to the land and ocean that sustain them. A human body, in other words, is not seen as an isolated individual (Meyer 2001; Nāone 2008; Wilson-Hokowhitu 2019). As Wilson-Hokowhitu and Meyer (2019: 1) write in the introduction to a book focusing on *mo'okū'auhau*, Hawaiian genealogy "prioritizes human kinship relationships, to encompass the vastness of *Kanaka 'Ōiwi* ["indigenous person"] familial relationships that extend well beyond the human realm to include islands, oceans, planets, and the universe". Moreover, in interviews with elder Hawaiians in English, Meyer (2001) finds that many of them emphasized such connections. Calvin Hoe stated, "The question is, Who is the self? You're not just who you are now. You're aligned with people who have gone through it lots of times". Similarly, Ho'oipo DeCambra related that, "I'm really deeply connected to my mother and ancestors and all the Hawaiians that came before us. And in me I have some of that cellular molecular structure and memory of long ago. How comforting!" In focusing on the human–land connection, Nāone (2008: 319) writes, "so intimate is the relationship between land and people that here we have a story where the people become the land by melting into the rain of the area and by becoming a tree and wind of that place". To understand such statements, the idea of non-separation seems essential as the boundaries among the human body, the land, ocean, and sky and ancestors are blurred.

Given this approach to the person, it is not surprising that Native Hawaiians struggled following contact with the West in the late 1700s, as Europeans and Americans alike arrived to spread Western ideas concerning religion and land ownership. These new ideas separated the Native Hawaiians physically from the land and also made it difficult for them to maintain traditional spiritual connections with their ancestors. Only recently have Native Hawaiian voices become strong again through the revitalization of the Hawaiian language (Wilson and Kamanā 2001) and through an increase in research from an indigenous Hawaiian perspective (i.e. Brown 2016; Silva 2004, 2017; Wilson-Hokowhitu 2019). It is in this struggle to make the Native Hawaiian perspective understood that *ba* theory may be of use as an approach to context. While further research of interaction at a level of secondary *ba* is necessary, *ba* theory underscores that non-separation between human bodies and the natural and spiritual environment can "logically" emerge from primary *ba* of non-separation, and it can therefore help demystify a Hawaiian perspective that has until recently been viewed through a Western lens. Likewise, *ba* theory may empower researchers of Hawaiian language to stress the logic of greetings like *aloha kāua* and *aloha kākou* which do not distinguish the speaking self from others. And given Hawaiian's close connection to other Polynesian languages, such as Māori, Tahitian or Sāmoan, we may find through further research that *ba* theory has the power to show how this type of language usage, which emphasizes mutual interdependence, is much more common in the world's languages that previously thought.

33.3.2 Ba Theory and English

As noted earlier, EP endeavours to explicate patterns of language usage in lesser-studied languages, but in the name of of developing an inclusive metalanguage for pragmatics, EP also hopes to show that frameworks derived from non-Western languages and cultures can be applied to Western languages. Towards such a goal, EP researchers have offered analyses of English data in terms of *ba* theory, suggesting that *ba* can lead to a deeper understanding of interaction as well as the construction of self. More specifically, both Hanks et al. (2019) and Saft (2014) use *ba* theory to discuss an excerpt of data from the work of Charles Goodwin (2004) involving Chil, a man with aphasia. Goodwin describes how Chil and his family members collaborated through the interaction to construct Chil, whose aphasia left him able to utter only the three words "yes", "no", and "and", as the main teller of a story. Among other points, Goodwin emphasizes that the key to understanding Chil's ability to be the lead story teller is recognition that competence does not lie in the brains of individual selves but rather is accomplished through the merged perspectives of participants who constantly monitor the unfolding interaction and design their participation to match their recipients.

From the perspective of *ba* theory, it is possible to understand how Chil can emerge as a competent story teller if we assume that the participants, as family members who know each other well, begin the storytelling episode in the secondary *ba* in a merged relationship (which follows naturally from the non-separation of primary *ba*). Following Chil's initiation of the story, every utterance from him and his family members alters the interaction and further reinforces the merging of the participants. As Hanks et al. (2019: 69) write, "through the merged interdependence of the four participants, Chil, together with the others, is constructed as an individual who is a competent participant to the story-telling activity".

Here, it needs to be emphasized that *ba* is not a substantial entity or a physical state of the context, but rather an emerging order perceived from the inside that subsumes the individuals whose distinctness is not a precondition but instead a product of interaction. Thus, there is no "guarantee" that Chil will be articulated as a competent individual in this family interaction, but every utterance from Chil and his family members, just like the painter and the canvas, alters the *ba* so that Chil is constructed as a competent story teller. This sense of an egocentric self is subsumed by the holistic *basho* that itself enables the emergence of such a constructed self (Hanks et al. 2019: 69).

Our analysis of Chil's story using *ba* theory thus strongly suggests that the Western self is also relational and contingent despite commonly used descriptors like "acontextual", "egotistical" and "uniquely individualistic". Such a suggestion is, in fact, in line with the ideas of some who have been critical of Western approaches. For example, in a critique of Western philosophy, Stawarska (2009: 2) reaches back to the work of Descartes and describes how Cartesian reductionism of natural phenomenon to the "I" and the "ego" shifted "the emphasis from the larger-than-human to the all-too-human realm", thus directing the Western analytic lens to focus on individual humans apart from natural environments saturated with other meaningful elements. From anthropology, too, questions have arisen about the depiction of Western selves in light of observations made about people around the world. Geertz (1984: 126), for one, felt compelled to wonder whether the idea of a unique, individual, and acontexual Western self is a "rather peculiar idea within the context of the world's cultures".

Work on language has likewise begun to point to the relational side of Western patterns of language usage in social interaction. For instance, although pronouns such as "I" and "you" have traditionally been offered as evidence for a strong sense of a separate, independent self (Hallowell 1955; Kashima 2000; Kashima and Kashima 1998; Kondo 1990; Yamada 1997) – as Yamada (1997:26) writes, "as an instrument that maximizes independence in a game of individuals, American English requires the use of personal pronouns", more recent writers have challenged this direct correlation between grammar and the self. Saft (2014) reminds us that English also consists of the plural pronouns "we" and "you" that often emphasize collective groupings of people, and Stawarska (2009) extends her critique of the "egocentric tradition" in Western philosophy by stating that egocentrism has led to a "distortion of the ordinary grammatical category of personal pronouns" and produced an "individualist bias" that "does not simply represent but rather produces a novel conception of the person as a repository of inner private events". As she further notes, such a conception of the person "leads to an exclusion of second person relatedness, and a forgetting of the inseparability of *I* and *you* (emphasis in the original)". Such a statement is congruent with a *ba* theory perspective in which a separate *I* and *you* can only emerge through non-separation in primary *ba*.

To be clear, this attempt to show the application of *ba* theory to Western interaction is not intended to argue that social interaction across languages is necessarily similar. Hanks et al. (2019: 70) provide a statement at the conclusion of their explanation of *ba* theory, namely "we come to the key fact that the *ba* and *basho* concept applies at indefinitely many scales, from the body as *basho* of the mind, to nature as *basho* of the human, to the infinity of time and space as the ultimate, impermanent, non-separated, encompassing *basho* of we, here" that reminds us that we are only just at the beginning stage of understanding the implications of *ba* theory for the construction of self and for the usage of language. Nonetheless, the point to be made here is that as we pursue further research across languages and cultures, *ba* theory can provide an innovative approach to context that recognizes the relational and interdependent properties of the self and also social interaction.

33.4 Future Directions

As just described, the EP line of inquiry is making progress towards its goal of providing a voice to lesser-studied languages within the field of pragmatics. Nonetheless, given the number of languages in the world that remain scarcely investigated, it is easy to see that EP is still in its early stages. Accordingly, a future goal of EP must be to expand its search for insights from researchers of diverse languages as they attempt to understand and explicate emic practices in their sociocultural contexts. Will we find more societies in which people engage in parallel overlap to the extent that the |Gui do? Will we find speakers who regularly engage in other forms of extended overlap? What kinds of politeness strategies exist in other languages and how do they fit together into an integrated universal theory? These are the types of questions that can only be answered by continuing the type of empirical, data-based research that EP researchers have been undertaking. Pursuit of this EP research from the point of view of language users will likewise be important to the general understanding of sociopragmatic topics such as (im)politeness, face, relationships, identities and roles, power and stance.

In addition, EP researchers will continue to explore the applicability of *ba* theory to different linguistic situations in various languages and, at the same time, endeavour to add inclusive theories and frameworks to the already available metalanguage in the field of pragmatics. While research thus far on *ba* theory suggests that it may aid in our understanding of social interaction across languages, there is still much more empirical work that is necessary. Likewise, further study is required of other non-Western terms, including *wakimae* from Japanese, KKJ and *maipenrai* from Thai, and *moʻokūʻauhau* from Hawaiian, as we continue to seek a deeper understanding of patterns of language usage throughout the world.

In the introduction to first EP special issue in the *Journal of* Pragmatics, Hanks et al. (2009: 2) liken the usage of the word "emancipation" to the Brazilian educator Paulo Freire's term *conscientization*, the awakening of critical consciousness, in that "emancipation" in the EP project is considered to be "a process and an ongoing aim, not an event or one-time goal". With this in mind, it is hoped that more researchers will join in this particular process of emancipation by undertaking detailed investigations of language usage in lesser-studied languages and by collectively pushing the area of pragmatics to explore and understand the linguistic and interactional potential of humans.

References

Allan, K. (1998). Speech acts and grammar. In J. Mey, ed., *Concise Encyclopedia of Pragmatics*. Oxford: Elsevier, pp. 942–44.

Ameka, F. and Terkourafi, M. (2019). What if...? Imagining non-Western perspectives on pragmatic theory and practice. *Journal of Pragmatics*, 145, 72–82.

Beeman, W. (2001). Emotion and sincerity in Persian discourse: Accomplishing the representation of inner states. *International Journal of the Sociology of Language*, 148, 31–57.

Brown, M. A. (2016). *Facing the Spears of Change: The Life and Legacy of John Apa Ī ī*. Honolulu: University of Hawaiʻi Press.

Brown, P. and Levinson, S. (1978). Universals in language usage: Politeness phenomena. In E. Goody, ed., *Questions and Politeness: Strategies in Social Interaction*. Cambridge: Cambridge University Press, pp. 56–310.

Brown, P. and Levinson, S. (1987). *Politeness: Some Universals in Language Usage*. Cambridge: Cambridge University Press.

Chang, W-L. M. and Haugh, M. (2013). Face in Taiwanese business interactions: From emic concepts to etic practices. In Y. Pan and D. Kadar, eds.,

Chinese Discourse and Interaction: Theory and Practice. London: Equinox, pp. 127–51.

Crawshaw, R. (2017). Determinacy, distance and intensity in intercultural communication: An emancipatory approach. In I. Kecskes and S. Assimakopoulos, eds., *Current Issues in Intercultural Pragmatics*. Amsterdam: John Benjamins, pp. 9–31.

de Kadt, E. (1994). Towards a model for the study of politeness in Zulu. *South African Journal of African Languages, 14*(3), 103–12.

de Kadt, E. (1998). The concept of face and its applicability to the Zulu language. *Journal of Pragmatics, 29*, 173–91.

Duranti, A. (1997). *Linguistic Anthropology*. Cambridge: Cambridge University Press.

Fraser, B. (1990). Perspectives on politeness. *Journal of Pragmatics, 14*, 219–36.

Fujii, Y. (2012). Differences of situation self in the place/*ba* of interaction between the Japanese and American English speakers. *Journal of Prgmatics, 44*, 636–62.

Fujii, Y. (2019). Japanese as a ba-oriented language: Non-Western perspectives for representation of the world. Presentation at the 16th IPrA conference, Hong Kong.

Gao, G. (1998). 'Don't take my word for it': Understanding Chinese speaking practices. *International Journal of Intercultural Relations, 22*, 163–86.

Geertz, C. (1984). From the natives' point of view: On the nature of anthropological understanding. In R. Shweder and R. Levine, eds., *Culture Theory*. Cambridge: Cambridge University Press, pp. 123–36.

Goodwin, C. (2004). A competent speaker who can't speak: The social life of aphasia. *Journal of Linguistic Anthropology, 14*(2), 151–70.

Hallowell, A. I. (1955). *Culture and Experience*. Philadelphia: University of Pennsylvania Press.

Hanks, W. (1996). *Language and Communicative Practices*. Boulder, CO: Westview Press.

Hanks, W. (2005). Explorations in the deictic field. *Current Anthropology, 46*(2), 191–220.

Hanks, W. (2014). Introduction to emancipatory pragmatics. *Journal of Pragmatics, 69*, 1–3.

Hanks, W., Ide, S. and Katagiri, Y. (2009). Introduction: Toward an emancipatory pragmatics. *Journal of Pragmatics, 41*, 1–9.

Hanks, W., Ide, S., Katagiri, Y., Saft, S., Fujii, Y. and Kishiko, U. (2019). Communicative interaction in terms of *ba* theory: Towards an innovative approach to language practice. *Journal of Pragmatics, 145*, 63–71.

Haugh, M. (2004). Revisiting the conceptualisation of politeness in English and Japanese. *Multilingua, 23*, 85–109.

Haugh, M. (2005). The importance of 'place' in Japanese politeness: Implications for cross-cultural and intercultural analyses. *Intercultural Pragmatics, 2*(1), 41–68.

Haugh, M. (2013). Disentangling face, facework, and impoliteness. *Sociocultural Pragmatics*, 1(1), 46–73.

Haugh, M. (2016). The role of English as a scientific metalanguage for research in pragmatics: Reflections on the metapragmatics of 'politeness' in Japanese. *East Asian Pragmatics*, 1(1), 39–71.

Havertake, H. (1988). Toward a typology of politeness strategies in communicative interaction. *Multilingua*, 7, 385–409.

Hill, B., Ide, S., Ikuta, S., Kawasaki, A. and Ogino, T. (1986). Universals of linguistic politeness: quantitative evidence from Japanese and American English. *Journal of Pragmatics*, 10, 347–71.

Hongladarom, K. (2009). Indexicality in Thai and Tibetan: Implications for a Buddhist grounded approach. *Journal of Pragmatics*, 41, 47–59.

Horie, K. (2012). The interactional origin of nominal predicate structure in Japanese: A comparative and historical pragmatic perspective. *Journal of Pragmatics*, 44, 663–79.

Huang, Y. (2017). Introduction: What is pragmatics? In Y Huang, ed., *Oxford Handbook of Pragmatics*. Oxford: Oxford University Press, pp. 1–12.

Ide, S. (1989). Formal forms and discernment: Two neglected aspects of universals of linguistics politeness. *Multilingua*, 8, 223–48.

Ide, S. (2011). Let the wind blow from the east: Using the *ba*-theory to explain how two strangers co-create a story. Presidential lecture at the Twelfth IPrA Conference, Manchester.

Ide, S. (2019). Toward a theory of linguistics of *ba*. Presentation at the 16th IPrA conference, Hong Kong.

Intachakra, S. (2012). Politeness motivated by the 'heart' and 'binary rationality' in Thai culture. *Journal of Pragmatics*, 44, 619–35.

Kasher, A. (1982). Gricean inference revisited. *Philosophica*, 29, 25–44.

Kashima, Y. (2000). Conceptions of culture and person for psychology. *Journal of Cross-Cultural Psychology*, 31, 14–32.

Kashima, E. and Kashima, Y. (1998). Culture and language: The case of the cultural dimensions and personal pronoun use. *Journal of Cross-Cultural Psychology*, 29, 461–86.

Kasper, G. (2009). Politeness. In S. D'hondt, J.-O. Ostman and J. Verschueren, eds., *The Pragmatics of Interaction*. Amsterdam: John Benjamins, pp. 157–73.

Katagiri, Y. (2009). Finding parameters in interaction: A method in emancipatory pragmatics. Plenary presentation at the Eleventh IPrA Conference, Melbourne.

Kecskes, I. and Assimakopoulos, S. (eds.). (2017). *Current Issues in Intercultural Pragmatics*. Amsterdam: John Benjamins.

Kim, H. (2008). The semantic and pragmatic analysis of South Korean and Australian English apologetic speech acts. *Journal of Pragmatics*, 40, 257–78.

Kondo, D. (1990). *Crafting Selves: Power, Gender, and Discourses of Identity in a Japanese Workplace*. Chicago: University of Chicago Press.

Lebra, T. (2004). *The Japanese Self in Cultural Logic*. Honolulu: University of Hawai'i Press.

Leech, G. (1983). *Principles of Pragmatics*. London: Longman.

Mao, L. M. (1994). Beyond politeness theory: 'Face' revisited and renewed. *Journal of Pragmatics, 21*, 451–86.

Matsumoto, Y. (1988). Reexamination of the universality of face: Politeness phenomena in Japanese. *Journal of Pragmatics, 12*, 403–26.

Matsumoto, Y. (1989). Politeness and conversational universals – observations from Japanese. *Multilingua, 8*, 207–21.

Meyer, M. A. (2001). Our own liberation: Reflections on Hawaiian epistemology. *The Contemporary Pacific, 13*(1), 124–48.

Miike, Y. (2003). Japanese *enryo-sasshi* communication and the psychology of *amae*: reconsideration and reconceptualization. *Keio Communication Review, 25*, 93–115.

Nāone, C. (2008) 'O ka 'Āina, ka 'Ōlelo, a me ke Kaiāulu. *Hūlili: Multidisciplinary Research on Hawaiian Well-Being, 5*, 315–39.

Naruoka, K. (2014). Toward meanings of expressive indexicals: The case of Japanese demonstrative *konna/sonna/anna*. *Journal of Pragmatics, 69*, 4–21.

Nishida, K. (2012). *Place and Dialectic: Two Essays by Nishida Kitaro*. Translated by J. Krummel and S. Nagatomo. Oxford: Oxford University Press.

Nwoye, O. (1992). Linguistic politeness and socio-cultural variations of the notion of face. *Journal Pragmatics, 18*(4), 309–28.

Panpothong, N. and Phakdeephasoon, S. (2014). The wide use of *mai-pen-rai* 'It's not substantial' in Thai interactions and its relationship to the Buddhist concept of *Tri Laksana*. *Journal of Pragmatics, 69*, 99–107.

Pike, K. (1966). Etic and emic standpoints for the description of behavior. In A. G. Smith, ed., *Communication and Culture: Readings in the Codes of Human Interaction*. New York: Holt, Rinehart and Winston, pp. 152–63.

Pike, K. (1971). *Language in Relation to a Unified Theory of the Structures of Human Behaviour*. 2nd ed. The Hague: Mouton.

Rosenberger, N. (ed.). (1994). *Japanese Sense of Self*. Cambridge: Cambridge University Press.

Sacks, H., Schegloff, E. and Jefferson, G. (1974). A simplest systematics for the organization of turn-taking system for communication. *Language, 50*, 696–735.

Saft, S. (2011). Pronouns, *wakimae, ba*, and the "native philosophy" of Hawaiian interaction. Paper presented at the Workshop on Emancipatory Pragmatics, Kyoritsu Women's University, Tokyo.

Saft, S. (2014). Rethinking Western individualism from the perspective of social interaction and from the concept of *ba*. *Journal of Pragmatics, 69*, 108–20.

Saft, S. (2017). Documenting an endangered language: The inclusive first-person plural pronoun *kākou* as a resource for claiming ownership in Hawaiian. *Journal of Linguistic Anthropology, 27*(1), 92–113.

Saft, S. (2019). Exploring the expression of agency in the speech of "new" speakers of the Hawaiian language. Presentation at the Sixteenth IPrA conference, Hong Kong.

Senft, G. (2014). *Understanding Pragmatics*. New York: Routledge.

Shimizu, H. (1995). 'Ba-principle': new logic for the real-time emergence of information. *Holonics*, 5(1), 67–79.

Shimizu, H. (2000). Kyooso to basho [Co-creation and place]. In H. Shimizu, T. Kume, Y. Miwa and Y. Miyake, eds., *Ba to Kyooso* [Ba and co-creation]. Tokyo: NTT Shuppan, pp. 23–177.

Sidnell, J. (2001). Conversational turn-taking in a Caribbean English Creole. *Journal of Pragmatics, 33*, 1263–90.

Silva, N. (2004). *Aloha Betrayed: Native Hawaiian Resistance to American Colonialism*. Durham, NC: Duke University Press.

Silva, N. (2017). *The Power of the Steel-Tipped Pen: Reconstructing Native Hawaiian Intellectual History*. Durham, NC: Duke University Press.

Stawarska, B. (2009). *Between You and I: Dialogical Phenomenology*. Athens: Ohio University Press.

Sugawara, K. (2009). Speech acts, moves, and meta-communication in negotiation: Three cases of everyday conversation observed among ǀGui former foragers. *Journal of Pragmatics, 41*, 93–135.

Sugawara, K. (2012). Interactive significance of simultaneous discourse or overlap in everyday conversations among ǀGui former foragers. *Journal of Pragmatics, 44*, 577–618.

Ueno, K. (2017). Speaking as parts of a whole: Discourse interpretation from *ba*-base thinking. Unpublished PhD dissertation, Japan Women's University.

Ueno, K. (2019). Why teachers ask more questions than students in dyadic conversations: An interpretation of *wakimae* utterances using *ba*-based thinking. Presentation at the Sixteenth IPrA conference, Hong Kong.

Wilson, W. and Kamanā, K. (2001). *Mai loko mai o ka ʻiʻini:* Proceeding from a dream: The ʻAha Pūnana Leo Connection in Hawaiian language revitalization. In L. Hinton and K. Hale, eds., *The Green Book of Language Revitalization in Practice*. New York: Academic Press, pp. 147–76.

Wilson-Hokowhitu, N. (ed.). (2019). *The Past before Us:* Moʻokūʻauhau *as Methodology*. Honolulu: University of Hawaiʻi Press.

Wilson-Hokowhitu, N. and Meyer, M. A. (2019). Introduction. In N. Wilson-Hokowhitu, ed., *The Past before Us:* Moʻokūʻauhau *as Methodology*. Honolulu: University of Hawaiʻi Press, pp. 1–8.

Yamada, H. (1997). *Different Games/Different Rules: Why Americans and Japanese Misunderstand Each Other*. Oxford: Oxford University Press.

34

Cross-Cultural and Intercultural Pragmatics

Troy McConachy and Helen Spencer-Oatey

34.1 Introduction

Since Leech's (1983: 10) characterization of sociopragmatics as the 'sociological interface of pragmatics', many scholars have grappled with the issue of how to best conceptualize and research the ways that elements of the social structure interact with language use. As a field, sociopragmatics has generally aimed to reveal how patterns of language use interconnect with features of sociocultural context, and how participants in interaction interpret and evaluate linguistic actions with respect to notions such as appropriateness, politeness and so on. The focus in this chapter is on 'cross-cultural' and 'intercultural' approaches to sociopragmatics, particularly drawing attention to areas of theoretical and methodological similarity and divergence, while considering the contribution of these approaches to sociopragmatic theorizing as a whole.

The field of cross-cultural pragmatics has traditionally aimed to compare and contrast linguistic behaviours across different languages or different national varieties of the same language, with an emphasis on profiling linguistic realization strategies and understanding the ways that aspects of social context influence linguistic choices. Intercultural pragmatics is a more recent disciplinary development which aims to account for the ways that individuals from different cultural backgrounds use, interpret and evaluate language use. In this sense, intercultural pragmatics can be seen as the domain of intercultural communication that focuses specifically on pragmatic phenomena. Within both of these fields, sociopragmatics is closely related to the ways in which culture influences perceptions of context and notions of appropriate language use.

In Section 34.2, we briefly discuss some of the key concepts in the fields of cross-cultural and intercultural pragmatics – culture, context, and the etic/emic distinction.

34.2 Key Concepts

This section critically discusses several key concepts and issues, as they relate to cross-cultural and intercultural pragmatics.

34.2.1 Culture

Culture is notoriously difficult to define (Spencer-Oatey and Franklin 2009: chapter 2) and even though researchers (e.g. Blommaert 1991; Bond Žegarac and Spencer-Oatey 2000) argued many years ago that culture needs to be conceptualized more fully within pragmatics, little progress has been made. Despite such calls, and despite the centrality of the notion of culture to cross-cultural and intercultural pragmatics, the theoretical relationship between language use and culture has tended to remain underspecified (Wolf and Polzenhagen 2006). Within cross-cultural and intercultural pragmatics, culture is often used as a proxy for national boundary, in the sense that linguistic patterns of a particular language prevalent within an individual nation are seen *ipso facto* as linked to national culture. Much research has aimed to establish the pragmatic norms for speech act realization strategies, politeness markers, and discourse organization for individual language varieties (Blum-Kulka and House 1989). Whilst there is work that links patterns of language use to perceptions of context and underlying cultural values (e.g. Meier 2010; Spencer-Oatey and Kádár 2016; Wierzbicka 2003), the link between pragmatic norms and culture is still in need of further theoretical and empirical development.

Within intercultural pragmatics, the notion of culture takes on slightly different significance due to the framing of communication itself as 'intercultural'. In a sense, the notion of intercultural pragmatics is dependent on a view of communication in which individuals from different (usually national) backgrounds negotiate meaning and construct common ground by bridging differences in communicative preferences, attitudes towards directness/indirectness, and culturally defined role relations (Kecskes 2014). In terms of understanding how culture is implicated in language use, attention to the sociopragmatic domain is crucially important, as it allows for insights into how cultural knowledge, assumptions and values influence the contextual assessments of participants, particularly as pertaining to perceptions of rights and obligations in diverse interpersonal and interactional contexts (Spencer-Oatey and Žegarac 2018).

We return to the interconnected issues of the conceptualization of culture and how culture interrelates with language use towards the end our article, where we consider the challenges facing this area of work. Here we turn next to the notion of 'context', which is central to unpacking the link between culture and language use.

34.2.2 Context

Context has been conceptualized in a number of different ways, including from social and cognitive perspectives and at different levels, such as: macro or societal level; exo or formal institutional level; meso or interactional setting level; and micro or discoursal level (Bronfenbrenner 1979; see also Chapter 16). In cross-cultural and intercultural pragmatics, the focus has traditionally been on the meso or interactional level, where context is seen in terms of sociocultural variables that influence language choices. More recently, however, it has become increasingly common to look at the relationship between language use and context from a more discursive perspective. In essence, this means adopting a view of language and context as co-constitutive rather than as one influencing the other (e.g. Duranti and Goodwin 1992).

From a traditional social pragmatic perspective at the meso level, context is typically seen in terms of two main elements: the participants and the communicative or social activity. There has been a lot of classic work in this area and, in terms of participants, Brown and Fraser (1979) developed a very useful comprehensive taxonomy. They drew a fundamental distinction between the personal characteristics of the individuals involved in an interaction and the relationships between the various participants.

In terms of relational dimensions, attention is typically focused on 'role and category relations' and, in another classic study, R. Brown and Gilman ([1960] 1972) demonstrated that two dimensions, power (P) and distance (D), have a major impact on language use. P and D were included by P. Brown and Levinson ([1978] 1987) and Leech (1983) in their respective conceptualizations of politeness, and numerous subsequent empirical studies have supported this position (e.g. Blum-Kulka and House 1989; Holtgraves and Yang 1990; Lim and Bowers 1991). Most cross-cultural pragmatic research has operationalized P and D in terms of role relations that are identified within brief scenarios, such as teacher–student (unequal relations and distant), mother–child (unequal close), friends (equal and close), strangers on a train (equal and distant). However, as Spencer-Oatey (1996) points out, there can be different interpretations as to what the P and D relations of a given role relationship actually are. Moreover, as P. Brown and Fraser (1979) also maintain, people's sense of P and D relations are context specific, and current pragmatic thinking would also argue that they change dynamically within the duration of an interaction, as the communication unfolds.

This leads us to the second main element of a social pragmatic perspective on context: the communicative or social activity. A number of frameworks have been proposed for elucidating this, including Hymes' (1974) SPEAKING mnemonic (Situation, Participants, Ends, Act sequences, Key, Instrumentalities, Norms, Genre) and Levinson's (1979) concept of activity type. Allwood (2007) has argued that social activities can usefully be analysed in terms of four main elements, as shown in Table 34.1. From a

Table 34.1 *Parameters for analysing social activities*

Purpose, function, procedures	Rationale for the event/activity taking place and the possible procedures that might exist to achieve the purpose and function
Roles: rights, obligations, competence	Expectations (and sometimes formal requirements) which exist concerning the rights, obligations and competence needs that are associated with a particular role in an activity
Artefacts, instruments, tools, media	Instruments, tools and media which are used to pursue the activity
Environment: social, physical	• Physical aspects of the setting that could be influential, e.g. furniture, lighting, heating • Broader social context, including national, organizational, setting

Note: Adapted from Allwood (2007).

cross-cultural and intercultural pragmatic perspective, they provide a useful framework for considering the potential impact of cultural factors on people's assessment of the context.

A cognitive approach to context provides a complementary perspective to a social approach and provides us with greater insights into the impact of prior knowledge on interaction. We hold a large amount of information or knowledge in our brains, both declarative and procedural and, as Kecskes (2014) argues, this internal cognitive context is interwoven and inseparable from people's perceptions of the current social situational contexts. He explains that meaning is produced out of an interplay between internal cognitive context based on prior experience and processes of co-construction within actual situational contexts. As will be discussed later in the chapter, one of the key issues in cross-cultural and intercultural pragmatics is how individuals' internal context influences their perception of sociocultural context and preferences for linguistic selection.

34.2.3 Etic and Emic Research Perspectives

A fundamental issue in any study involving culture, including cross-cultural and intercultural pragmatics, is the question of universalism: what aspects of context, language structure and language use are specific to particular cultural groups and what aspects are universal and apply to all. Since cross-cultural studies are by definition comparative in nature, it is essential to ensure that the features being compared are equivalent so that any comparisons are meaningful, and this requires the careful articulation of pragmatic features and underlying sociopragmatic notions. The concepts of etic and emic research perspectives address this issue, and while there are different interpretations of their meanings (e.g. see Spencer-Oatey and Kádár 2016), the following explanation by Triandis (1994) describes the key distinction:

> Emics, roughly speaking, are ideas, behaviours, items, and concepts that are culture-specific. Etics, roughly speaking, are ideas, behaviours, items, and concepts that are culture general – i.e., universal.... Emic concepts are essential for understanding a culture. However, since they are unique to the particular culture, they are not useful for cross-cultural comparisons.... More formally, emics are studied *within* the system in one culture, and their structure is discovered within the system. Etics are studies *outside* the system in more than one culture, and their structure is theoretical. To develop 'scientific' generalizations about relationships among variables, we must use etics. However, if we are going to understand a culture, we must use emics. (Triandis 1994: 67–8)

It is important to take this distinction into consideration in cross-cultural and intercultural pragmatics research, but it would be a mistake to regard them as completely unrelated. As Hall (2002) points out, emic observations can help form the basis of etic frameworks, and etic research can help identify and enrich emic concepts.

Having considered these three key concepts, culture, context and emic/etic research perspectives, we turn to the main lines of sociopragmatic research.

34.3 Summary of Main Research Findings

In this section, we provide a critical overview of research in cross-cultural and intercultural pragmatics, highlighting conceptual issues and key findings that are most relevant to understanding the sociopragmatic domain.

34.3.1 Cross-Cultural Pragmatics: Main Perspectives and Studies

Due to the emphasis on cross-cultural comparison, the field of cross-cultural pragmatics is uniquely positioned to contribute to wider debates within pragmatics regarding the universality of pragmatic phenomena such as politeness, particularly as researchers have looked at patterns of language use from the perspective of underlying conceptions of social relations and cultural values.

One of the first major projects within the field of cross-cultural pragmatics was the Cross-Cultural Study of Speech Act Realization Patterns (CCSARP), led by Blum-Kulka et al. (1989), which investigated requests and apologies. They collected data from eight different languages/language varieties – three varieties of English (American, Australian and British), Argentinian Spanish, Canadian French, German and Israeli Hebrew – and used a DCT in order to ensure comparability. This comprised an initial description of a situation that would elicit the required speech act, followed by an incomplete dialogue. Participants of the study were asked to complete the dialogue, thereby providing contextualized examples of realizations of the speech act. Demographic information on the participants was also obtained so that the impact of individual variables, such as age, sex or level of education, could be examined.

Findings from the series of studies revealed a very complex picture. The focus was on levels of directness in performing the speech acts, and in relation to requests they found that five situational factors had particular impact: "degree of addressee's obligation to carry out the act, the speaker's right to demand compliance, the level of the speaker's dominance over the hearer, the estimated likelihood for compliance, and the estimated difficulty" (Blum-Kulka et al. 1989: 150). In terms of cross-cultural variation, they found noticeable situational variation, in that differences across languages/language varieties in frequency of different realization patterns were more marked in some contexts than others. For instance, there was very little variation in people's use of impositives when asking someone living on the same street for a lift home (i.e. almost nobody chose to use an impositive), yet when asking a roommate to clear up the kitchen which they had left in a mess, there was considerable variation. About 75 per cent of Spanish speakers chose impositives in this context while only 10 per cent of Australian English speakers did so.

Ever since the publication of this pioneering project, there have been numerous studies comparing the performance of speech acts in different languages and contexts (Barnlund and Yoshioka 1990; Chen et al. 2013; Ogiermann 2009). For many years, the DCT was the most frequently used method, since it allows for maximum control of contextual variables. Yet a major criticism of the DCT is that the data collected is not necessarily what people would actually say; on the other hand, the counterargument is that it yields intuitional data and thus probes people's conceptions of normative behaviour in those contexts. Needless to say, a range of other data collection methods have also been used, including field notes, recordings of authentic interactions and elicited conversations (for a review, see Kasper 2008), with an increasing desire for authentic data. The focus of interest has also expanded from speech acts to other phenomena.

House (2006) has compared Anglo-English and German discourse for communication styles, and identified four additional dimensions, such as verbal routines/*ad-hoc* formulations and orientation towards content/ orientation towards addressees. Recent studies have also used authentic data to examine pragmatic phenomena beyond the sentence level, such as leadership, humour, teasing and other relational practices constructed over multiple turns (e.g. Schnurr and Chan 2009; Sinkeviciute 2017a). Such work helps illuminate the ways that relational practices evident in particular communities of practice serve to instantiate or contest more broadly shared pragmatic norms and underlying sociopragmatic assumptions about power and distance, as well as identity-related sensitivities.

From a sociopragmatic perspective on cross-cultural comparisons, there are three key questions: (1) To what extent and in what ways do cultural factors influence people's assessments or interpretations of the various contextual variables; (2) Are there cultural differences in the extent to which contextual assessments influence people's choices of realization patterns; and (3) Are there cultural differences in the extent to which contextual assessments influence people's evaluations of different realization patterns?

There has been surprisingly little systematic research on the first issue. Within cross-cultural psychology, research by Hofstede (2001), Schwartz (2011) and others indicates that there can be variation across cultural groups in people's attitudes towards power differentials, with strong egalitarian beliefs being more prevalent in some cultural contexts than others. However, there can also be substantial variation both across individuals and across situations within the same cultural context.

One contextual factor that mediates this is people's conceptualizations of role rights and obligations, as this necessarily influences the perception of '(un)reasonable' behaviour. For example, while a teacher might be able to set homework or ask students to work together without further justification, expecting the students to clean the whiteboard or pick up items for the teacher from the library might be seen as unreasonable, depending on the context. People's assessments of the legitimacy of such favour requests are likely to be influenced by culturally shaped perceptions of the nature of the teacher–student relationship and the scope of rights and obligations associated with this relationship, as well as ideologically grounded perceptions of power and distance (Kádár 2017). It might be expected that there would be as much individual and contextual variation within any cultural group in members' conceptualizations of role rights and obligations as there is over values such as hierarchy/egalitarianism. However, there has been little empirical research into such questions (for an exception, see Spencer-Oatey 1997), and this is an area that very much needs substantial further research.

The second issue – the extent to which contextual assessments influence people's choices of realization patterns – has been explored in more detail. More than 30 years ago, Hill et al. (1986) conducted a study that compared Japanese and American assessments of which phrases could be used to ask to borrow a pen when speaking with a range of different people. They plotted their results in a chart and for both nationality groups there was a clear association between role and choice of phrase. However, for the Americans many expressions could be used with a wide range of people, whereas for the Japanese there was a much closer association between role relation and choice of expression. On the basis of their findings, they proposed a distinction between 'volition' and 'discernment' politeness. In volition politeness, speakers can choose actively from a wide range of options, while in discernment politeness (also known as *wakimae*) people are expected to conform to the social norms prevalent in the society, which are closely associated with the occupation of a 'place' in particular social and interactional contexts. Ide (1989:230) explains that "to behave according to *wakimae* is to show verbally and non-verbally one's sense of place or role in a given situation according to social conventions."

Hill et al. (1986) conclude that both discernment and volition operate in both American and Japanese sociolinguistic systems, but that discernment accounts for a greater share of language choices among Japanese speakers than it does for American English speakers.

This volition/discernment distinction seems to have some synergy with a concept in cross-cultural psychology known as societal tightness–looseness (Gelfand 2018). Gelfand and her colleagues have argued that the strength of social norms (number and clarity) and the sanctions for breaching the norms (i.e. how far deviance is tolerated) can vary across cultures. Like Hill et al. (1986) and Ide (1989), they suggest that the extent to which people's behaviour is typically constrained or even controlled by contextual factors can vary noticeably across cultural groups. Within pragmatics, the distinction between volition and discernment has been criticized for leading to a polarized view of politeness systems (Pizziconi 2003) and to analytical stereotyping (Kádár and Mills 2013). Kádár and Mills go on to propose that discernment should be approached through the paradigms of convention/ritual research and that "what we can critically compare across cultures is normative ideological representations of language usage" (154). Interestingly, this could be compatible with Gelfand's approach, insofar as those normative ideological representations may be stronger or weaker in different contexts.

The third issue – the extent to which contextual assessments influence people's evaluations of different realization patterns – has also been rarely explored, despite acknowledgement within pragmatics that this entails evaluative judgements. In the occasional studies that have investigated this, most have used Leech's (1983) politeness maxims as a conceptual framework. Leech has proposed that there are a number of politeness maxims or constraints (e.g. tact, generosity, modesty, agreement) that influence people's behaviour, and that the relative importance of a given politeness maxim can vary across cultures. For example, he suggests (137) that the modesty maxim is more powerful in Japanese society than it is in English-speaking societies, and that this has an impact on how people respond to compliments, with Japanese speakers more likely to deny a compliment than English speakers. In line with this, Spencer-Oatey et al. (2008) explored whether there would be differences between British English, Hong Kong Chinese and Mainland Chinese speakers in their evaluations of acceptance and rejection responses to compliments. They found that indeed there were both statistical and qualitative differences for rejection responses. Nationality had a statistically significant effect on people's evaluations of the appropriateness, level of conceit and impression conveyed (favourable–bad) by the rejection responses, and accounted for 38 per cent, 27 per cent and 35 per cent of the variance, respectively. In terms of the open comments, British participants had difficulty understanding why someone would reject a compliment that was clearly accurate, and tried to attribute meaning to it, such as lack of confidence or fishing for more compliments. The HK and Mainland Chinese respondents, on the other hand, were less negative about the rejection responses, interpreting them in relation to the traditional social requirement to appear modest, even though some felt the responses were too modest.

However, this data was collected with questionnaires, so this once again raises the question of potential discrepancies between these artificial judgements and ones that might occur in real life. Nevertheless, as with DCT data, such data can indicate (some of) the parameters that people pay attention to when making their evaluations. In particular, it helps generate insights into the role of cultural values (such as modesty) in informing pragmatic judgements. The specific link between values and language use has been taken up in detail within research on ethnopragmatics.

Ethnopragmatics is an area of cross-cultural pragmatics research that has made a particular contribution to understanding the sociopragmatic domain from an emic perspective. This area has developed over the last few decades, predominantly based on the cultural scripts approach to pragmatic analysis (e.g. Goddard and Wierzbicka 1997, 2008; Goddard and Ye 2015; Wierzbicka 1985, 2003, 2010). The cultural scripts approach assumes a close relationship between patterns of language use and "tacit norms, values and practices, widely shared, and widely known (on an intuitive level) in a given society" (Wierzbicka 2010: 43). The research therefore aims to explicate the links between pragmatic behaviours and the norms and values that underlie them in terms of 'cultural scripts' that represent insider views (Wierzbicka 2010). In part, this is a reaction to universalist theories within the field of pragmatics (e.g. Brown and Levinson [1978] 1987; Grice 1989) which have been criticized for taking Anglo cultural premises as universal ones. Wierzbicka (2003) argues that sociopragmatic terms which are frequently used to describe and compare pragmatic strategies across cultural groups, including adjectives such as 'formal/informal' or speech act terms such as 'apology', tend to represent Anglo cultural categories and thus can lead to 'terminological ethnocentrism' (xviii) when applied to non-Anglo languages and cultures. The cultural scripts approach therefore utilizes the Natural Semantic Metalanguage (NSM) developed over the last three decades by Anna Wierzbicka and Cliff Goddard to represent culture-specific metapragmatic logic in neutral descriptive language. The NSM utilizes around 60 semantic primes – concepts that are purported to exist as distinct lexemes within a large number of distinct languages – within a mini-grammar to formulate cultural scripts by explicating the component semantic elements. Goddard and Wierzbicka (1997: 236) provide the example below to represent a Japanese cultural script:

> if something bad happens to someone because of me
> I have to say something like this to this person:
> 'I feel something bad because of this'

The authors suggest that the English term 'apology' tends to embody the assumption of fault by the speaker and therefore cannot be unproblematically used to describe other languages, such as the Japanese example here. Instead, the aim of this script is to capture the cultural logic that an 'apology' is expected whenever one person is implicated in a negative situation experienced by another person irrespective of whether or not 'fault' can be attributed. As in this example, the authors argue that the NSM allows cross-cultural researchers to explicate emic perspectives on speech practices in terms of universal terms which will make these perspectives more transparent and avoid the imposition of Anglo-centric metapragmatic terminology. Ethnopragmatics places particular importance on the NSM analysis of linguistic data representing a variety of speech practices across languages and cultures, combined with insights from ethnographic studies and (anecdotal) insider accounts (Goddard and Ye 2015).

As an orientation to cross-cultural pragmatics, ethnopragmatics illuminates the sociopragmatic dimension of language use by representing the cultural thought patterns and assumptions that underlie how speech practices are expected to be carried out. Yet there is some critique of this work which questions whether the complexity of cultural meanings can be reduced to linguistic representations within the NSM (e.g. Quinn 2015; Riemer 2006). Additionally, given the tendency to treat culture as a monolithic entity, it is possible to question whether approaching sociopragmatics through the lens of lexical semantics might lead researchers to overlook the contextual variability of language use and therefore reify cross-cultural differences. However, ethnopragmatics does help address a legitimate need in the field of cross-cultural pragmatics to decentre from Anglo-centric concepts and terminology when carrying out research and carefully clarify the comparability of key terms and notions (e.g. speech acts such as apologies or thanks) related to pragmatic behaviours and associated values (Haugh and Hinze 2003).

In summary, then, work in cross-cultural pragmatics has attempted to compare pragmatic strategies across languages and draw links between observable linguistic patterns, features of context and elements of cultural cognition and values. It is evident that cross-cultural pragmatics embodies a tension between etic and emic perspectives – the need to develop rigorous ways of describing pragmatic features to allow for commensurable comparisons and the need to understand pragmatic features as part of unique sociocultural systems.

34.3.2 Intercultural Pragmatics: Main Perspectives and Studies

Compared to the cross-cultural research tradition, the paradigm of intercultural pragmatics has flourished comparatively recently. Whilst there is a certain degree of overlap, relevant work tends to orient towards (socio) cognitive, interactional, or critical perspectives (Haugh 2017). The sociopragmatic domain is conceptualized and operationalized in different ways depending on the perspective. Below, we deal with each of these in turn.

34.3.2.1 (Socio)cognitive Perspectives

In the last 15 years, a strong 'sociocognitive' tradition has developed within the field of intercultural pragmatics, particularly deriving from the work of Istvan Kecskes (e.g. Kecskes 2014, 2017). One of the major theoretical assumptions of the sociocognitive perspective is that intention-based theories of pragmatic meaning that place 'common ground' as the foundation of understanding are limited in their ability to account for meaning-making in intercultural communication, as common ground cannot be assumed (Kecskes and Zhang 2013). Rather, it is argued that the construction of meaning within intercultural communication is largely dependent on interactive processes whereby participants collaboratively construct common ground and understanding in situ, drawing on their respective cultural knowledge and multilingual repertoire derived from prior experience.

Within the sociocognitive perspective, individuals are continually drawing on cognitive resources such as schema, scripts, presuppositions and cultural models associated with multiple languages as the basis for interpreting and constructing meanings. Rather than seeing the influence of L1-based cultural schema on L2 use in terms of 'transfer', therefore, it advocates a view of intercultural pragmatics which embodies a "multilingual, intercultural, socio-cognitive, and discourse-segment (rather than just utterance) perspective" (Kecskes 2014: 1). Reflecting a discursive orientation, Kecskes emphasizes the need to take into account the ways participants' culturally shaped knowledge is activated and negotiated as speakers work to construct understanding over multiple turns in interaction, drawing on linguistic resources from multiple languages as necessary. This synergy between existing cognitive resources and interactive processes represents the essence of the 'sociocognitive' perspective which he espouses. Within the process of interaction, the prior knowledge and cognitive resources of individual speakers are articulated and negotiated in a synergistic way that serves to establish what Kecskes calls 'intercultures' – a collaboratively constructed frame of reference constituted by emergent shared knowledge and behavioural conventions.

Running along a different trajectory to the research above, there is an increasing amount of work which approaches intercultural pragmatics from the perspective of cultural linguistics, particularly aiming to map more direct links between culture-specific conceptualizations and patterns of language use (e.g. Palmer 1996; Sharifian 2013; Wolf and Polzenhagen 2006). Cultural linguistics has its roots in cognitive linguistics, particularly the work of Robert Palmer, who emphasized the need to understand the co-constitutive relations between culture, cognition and linguistic structures within a broadly relativistic framework. Cultural linguistics makes particular use of culture-specific schemas, conceptual metaphors and cultural models for understanding the cognitive bases of language use, including the interfaces between language use and semantic representations of cultural values (cf. Nishida 2005; Wolf and Polzenhagen 2006). Applied to intercultural pragmatics, research aims to show how L1-based value orientations influence the use and evaluation of pragmatic features in an L2. As an example of this research, Sharifian and Jamarani (2011) examined how the Persian cultural schema of *sharmandegi* (shame/ashamed) influenced the production of English speech acts by speakers of L1 Persian in their interactions with L1 speakers of Australian English. The authors found that explicit statements of feeling 'ashamed', which are common in Persian, were prominent in participants' strategies for expressing gratitude, apologizing, offering and requesting. The authors present the reconstructed example below:

(1)   (Lydia and Mahin (Iranian) are neighbours and their children go to the same school. The following interaction happened between the two mothers on school day)
  Lydia: I can pick your daughter from school today and this way I can spare you a trip.
  Mahin: You make me ashamed, I don't want to bother you. But it would be great if you could do that.

(adapted from Sharifian and Jamarani 2011: 236–7)

The authors argue that the cultural schema of *sharmandegi* typically embodies awareness of imposition incurred by an interlocutor and is therefore conventionally used to index gratitude in Persian, but this can lead to misunderstandings in intercultural communication. The authors draw on interview data from Australian respondents, who generally interpreted the use of 'ashamed' literally and thus did not necessarily understand the indexical meaning of 'gratitude' which was more salient in the minds of the Persian L1-speakers. The authors suggest that when important culture-specific schemata from an L1 manifest in L2 talk, they can lead to confusion and negative relational outcomes.

In summary, work in the (socio)cognitive tradition primarily orients towards the sociopragmatic domain of language use in terms of the underlying knowledge, assumptions and values that lead speakers to attribute meaning and interpersonal significance to language forms within intercultural interaction. Whereas work in the sociocognitive tradition of Kecskes emphasizes the interplay between existing and emergent cognition within interaction, work in cultural linguistics is more focused on explaining the link between language use and culture-specific values which are situated within the broader cognitive structures shared by cultural groups.

34.3.2.2 Interactional and Interpersonal Perspectives

Research within an interactional/interpersonal perspective aims to understand the role of pragmatics in constructing and maintaining interpersonal relationships between individuals and groups from different cultural backgrounds. Haugh (2017) explains that this perspective "treats culture as recurrent or preferred ways of doing, thinking, and categorizing people, and focuses on describing how such practices are implemented and evaluated in intercultural encounters" (3). John Gumperz (e.g. Gumperz et al. 1979; Gumperz and Roberts 1991) was one of the early pioneers of this approach and, through analysing authentic data such as workplace interviews and cafeteria service encounters involving people from different ethnolinguistic backgrounds, he and his co-authors argued that communication difficulties and negative evaluative judgements often derive from culturally specific contextualization conventions.

Since then, many other researchers (e.g. Holmes 2018; House 2000; Miller 2008; Tyler 1995) have taken a broadly similar approach. Tyler (1995), for example, analyses an interaction between a US American student and a Korean teaching assistant (TA) that ends problematically, with each complaining to a supervisor that the other was uncooperative. The student was enrolled in an introductory computer programming class and the Korean TA was a graduate student in Computer and Information Science who was offering free tutoring in his area of expertise as part of an advanced elective course in oral English skills. The student wanted help with an assignment that required her to write a program to score bowling and went to a tutoring session for help. The interaction started as follows:

(2)

1	S:	we have to write a program that scores bowling right?
2	T:	mhm
3	S:	the game of bowling and he want us to be able to put in like how many pins well do you know how to score the game?
4	T:	yeah approximately
5	S:	OK cause he he has a little thing that tells you how (shows pages on handout) See I don't know how to score
6	T:	Oh you don't know how to score the bowling game?
7	S:	unhuh I'm like just I've played like I've scored a couple times but I'm not too good on it

(Then the student asks the tutor to read the assignment to himself)

| 8 | T: | uhmm open, spare, strike |

9	S:	OK that has to do with the bowling game
10	T:	OK can you guess the amount you have to figure out?
11	S:	that's what I need to know

(Tyler 1995: 149)

Tyler points out that a key interchange takes place in turns 3 and 4, where the student asks the TA whether he knows how to score the game of bowling. He replies with 'yeah approximately', which the student interpreted at face value; in other words, that the TA only had a rough idea about it. This interpretation is evidenced in turns 8 and 9, when she clearly feels the need to explain what the terms 'open, spare, strike' refer to. As it turns out, the TA was quite an expert at bowling, but he explained afterwards that he did not reveal this for two reasons: (1) in Korean society "it would be considered rude to baldly state that one is an expert in an area" and (2) "that it might be embarrassing to the student for a foreigner to openly say he knows more about a game from her own culture than she did".. In other words, the TA reported being influenced by a need to display modesty (cf. Leech's 1983 modesty maxim) and concern for the US student's face (cf. Brown and Levinson [1978] 1987), yet the student was completely unaware of this.

As the interaction unfolded, the student spoke as though she was more knowledgeable about bowling than the TA, repeatedly challenging his interpretation of procedures. It seems the student felt justified in doing this, because she thought she had established her superior knowledge of the topic. However, for the TA it was highly offensive and inappropriate for a student to speak in such a manner to her tutor. This is a good example of the ways that self-presentation strategies and the perception of such strategies are closely intertwined with perceptions of roles and associated power differentials (cf. Allwood's 2007 parameters for analysing social activities, outlined earlier).

Other researchers have pointed to cultural differences in the practices or procedures of communicative activities that surface in intercultural interactions. For example, Holmes (Holmes 2018; Holmes and Marra 2011) reports the impact that rules for speaking in meetings have on Pākehā–Māori interactions. Holmes and Marra (2011) point out that when a person is speaking, a certain amount of accompanying noise is normal in Māori public meetings, and that this conveys approval, support and trust in the speaker. In fact, if there is silence when someone else is speaking, as is typical of many Pākehā meetings, this signifies opposition, dissent and mistrust. Holmes (2018) develops the concept of the culture order to help account for the impact of culture on interaction. She explains that "the concept of the culture order encourages analysis of taken-for-granted presuppositions about appropriate cultural behavior which impact interaction, especially in intercultural contexts" (34) and, in relation to Māori and

Pākehā cultures, she identifies the following key cultural elements: egalitarianism–status; modesty; group–individual. She then reports on the impact that these elements of the culture order have on interactions in New Zealand workplaces, including the following:

- Meeting openings
- Speaking rules within meetings
- Criticism and complaint
- Modesty
- Responding to praise
- Doing being an expert

From the discussion above, two (further) fundamental questions for cross-cultural and intercultural pragmatics can be raised: (1) How can culture be conceptualized beyond simply treating it as nationality? and (2) How can we theorize the impact of culture on people's evaluations of others' behaviour, beyond simply relating it to expectations and appropriateness? In relation to the first question, Holmes' (2018) concepts of egalitarianism – status and group – individual correspond to work in cross-cultural psychology on values (Hofstede 2001; Schwartz 2011), yet modesty could be seen as of a different order. Psychologists such as Schwartz see values as "trans-situational goals ... that serve as guiding principles in the life of the person" (Schwartz 2011: 464). In Leech's (1983) terms, it is a politeness maxim, or in Spencer-Oatey's terms, a sociopragmatic interactional principle (Spencer-Oatey 2008; Spencer-Oatey and Jiang 2003) that is more relationally or contextually based than a life value. Yet there are clearly interconnections and more conceptualization is needed to ascertain whether or not they should be treated differently.

In relation to the second question, pragmatics scholars (e.g. Haugh 2013; Kádár and Haugh 2013; Spencer-Oatey and Kádár 2016) have recently started paying more attention to the concept of the moral order. Haugh (2013: 57), building on the work of Garfinkel (1964), explains that "the moral order is what grounds our evaluations of social actions and meanings as "good" or "bad", "normal" or "exceptional", "appropriate" or "inappropriate" and so on, and of course, as "polite", "impolite", "over-polite" and so on". However, further elaboration of the moral order is needed in order to take into account the distinction between two types of norms: descriptive norms that refer to what is typically done, and injunctive norms that refer to what is typically approved of or disapproved of by members of a social group (Cialdini 2012). The moral order seems to relate to the latter. Spencer-Oatey and Kádár (2016) propose turning to Haidt's (e.g. Graham et al. 2011; Haidt and Graham 2007; Haidt and Kesebir 2010) moral foundations for more insight and this could be a useful starting point. However, it is a fairly broad-brush framework and may not be fine-tuned enough to allow the detailed analysis required for meaningful insights into intercultural interactions. Further suggestions are made by

Spencer-Oatey and Xing (2019) and Spencer-Oatey and Kádár (2021) which offer promising new analytic avenues.

34.3.2.3 Critical Perspectives

There is an increasing amount of work informed by post-structuralist and constructionist perspectives that is critical of the ways that the notion of culture has been used in intercultural pragmatics research (e.g. Schnurr and Zayts 2017). Such work is particularly critical of the tendency in early research to posit national culture as an explanatory variable for interactional behaviour simply based on the national belonging of individuals. Very early on, Sarangi (1994) pointed out that when researchers define a communicative situation as 'intercultural' in advance, there is a strong tendency for any misunderstandings or other negative outcomes to be attributed to cultural differences. This kind of 'analytic stereotyping' (413) therefore perpetuates the reification of cultural differences, as well as an overemphasis on 'misunderstanding' rather than the achievement of 'understanding'. In moving away from the notion of culture, Scollon, Scollon and Jones (2012) make the notion of discourse central to their analyses of intercultural communication, pointing out that norms for language use are shaped by complex contextual factors relating to discourse needs rather than being uniformly shaped by national culture. Similarly, Verschueren (1999: 92) suggests that, "a truly pragmatic approach to linguistic behavior does not place social variability at the level of idealized groups, but along a range of intersecting dimensions contributing to interlocutors' *social identities*" (italics in original). Critical scholars therefore call for more nuanced treatment of the notion of culture, caution in treating any particular interaction as 'intercultural', and a greater responsibility for researchers to make explicit their assumptions about culture when operationalizing this term within analysis.

In investigating intercultural pragmatics, recent work from a critical perspective has devoted attention to the ways that first-order notions of culture conflict with empirical accounts of interactional behaviour. Schnurr and Zayts (2017) examine interactional phenomena such as politeness, leadership and decision-making within workplace discourse, pointing out the gap between participant's first-order notions of cultural difference and actual interactional practices observed in the data. This is in line with Mills and Kádár (2011), who point out the stereotypical links individuals tend to construct between culture (whether in a national or regional sense) and pragmatic features. Angouri (2018) focuses on how notions of culture are mobilized as an ideological resource to construct identities and achieve interactional effects. She shows how individuals in workplace contexts tend to construct accounts of problematic workplace interactions through the lens of cultural essentialism, frequently attributing behaviour to national culture, and the cause of interactional or relational problems to cultural differences (cf. Dervin and Machart 2015). The combination of detailed linguistic analysis and ethnographic methods in these works not only allows for the assumed relationship between culture and pragmatics to be interrogated, it also allows for attention to how stereotypical notions of culture are used as an interactional resource to position the other as deficient, evade responsibility and/or construct a positive identity for oneself.

34.4 Challenges and Opportunities

34.4.1 Challenges

Based on the discussion thus far, we identify a number of key challenges in theorizing and researching cross-cultural and intercultural pragmatics. The first challenge is how to identify an 'intercultural' encounter in a principled way. Given the multicultural composition of most nations, as well as the international mobility of the current age, it is difficult to justify the labelling of a particular encounter as 'intercultural' simply based on the nationality profiles of participants. Research demands that scholars carefully articulate the assumptions about cultural difference they bring to the analysis of an interactional scenario which they define as 'intercultural'.

The second challenge relates to how to conceptualize the relationship between culture and language use. It is now very widely accepted within pragmatics that the impact of culture is dynamic, yet there is still surprisingly little unpacking of what is actually meant by culture, especially by those who call for it to be studied (solely) in terms of how it is enacted/constructed in interaction. For instance, while Schnurr and Zayts (2017) illustrate differences between first-order claims about (national) cultural behaviour and specific incidents that contradict such claims, they do not unpack the notion of culture itself and its relationship to language. Similarly, sociocognitive approaches refer to concepts such as schema or frame, yet offer little in the way of clear conceptualization of the types of elements or behaviours that they interface with. Although Holmes (2018) has started to address this issue through her notion of 'the culture order', her depiction is brief and clearly more work needs to be done in this area.

The third challenge concerns ways of researching cross-cultural and intercultural pragmatics that provide reliable insights into the role of culture in communication. In fact, this challenge entails a number of elements. The first is the difficulty of collecting suitable data. Research that relies on data collected through instruments such as DCTs or retrospective comments can be expected to have less validity than research which combines analysis of naturally occurring data and participants' direct views on that data. Yet the latter can suffer from the weakness of being small-scale and local, with many idiosyncratic features at play, making it difficult to put forward any reliable claims about cultural factors. The second is the related difficulty of dealing with the inherent variability in behaviour that occurs within any cultural group (Žegarac 2007). From an analytic point of view, it makes it difficult on the one hand to substantiate links between culture and behaviour, and on the other to use individual encounters to make claims about the (lack of) validity of the existence of general cultural patterns. A third element is the influence of the researcher's own cultural perspective. As Haugh (2017) points out, the analysis of intercultural encounters relies on a large degree of interpretation by the researcher, whose own cultural and professional background inevitably has an impact on what is regarded as significant within interactional data. For this reason, Spencer-Oatey and Franklin (2009: 269–70, 288) argue for the importance of decentring and the value of collaborating with people from different cultural backgrounds. Furthermore, when researching the relationship between culture and language use, there is also a need to critically evaluate the ways that the notion of culture is mobilized to account for differences or misunderstandings within a communicative encounter and whether this can be justified.

34.4.2 Promising Areas

Promising areas in cross-cultural and intercultural pragmatics involve theoretical and methodological innovations within these fields, as well as the application of insights from these fields to applied linguistics.

One area of particular promise for developing insight into the sociopragmatic domain is metapragmatics, which focuses on the evaluative and explanatory comments that language users articulate in relation to particular features of interaction or communicative episodes. Metapragmatic analysis is particularly suited to revealing the ideological basis of evaluative judgements that surface in a range of contexts such as online comments (Davies 2018), interviews (Sinkeviciute 2017b; Spencer-Oatey 2011), newspaper articles and media reports (Davies 2018; Kádár 2017) and language learning contexts (McConachy 2018). Corpus approaches to investigating the meta-communicative lexicon (e.g. Haugh 2018), are particularly suited to revealing the clusters of evaluative terms that signal how pragmatic behaviours are situated in relation to the moral order. There is also potential from interdisciplinary perspectives, such as combining insights from pragmatics with those from moral psychology on morality and person perception (Haidt 2013; Janoff-Bulman and Carnes 2018).

There is also increasing interest in synergies between emotion research and intercultural pragmatics. Chang and Haugh (2017) report on emotional difficulties faced by L2 learners of Mandarin Chinese due to encountering interactional behaviours that challenged their own cultural assumptions. They call for more discussion of the affective dimensions of managing intercultural encounters. This links with recent work by Dewaele (2018), who has examined the challenges faced by intercultural couples in the communication of emotions. This research reveals that sociopragmatic issues are most at play when assumptions diverge as to the desirable expression of verbal affection. Once again, theorizing within psychology (e.g. Parkinson et al. 2005) may be of value.

Recently, there is also a strand of work that aims to incorporate theoretical and empirical insights from intercultural pragmatics into language education (e.g. Liddicoat 2006; McConachy 2018, 2019; McConachy and Liddicoat 2016). McConachy (2018) examines the ways that language learners mobilize cultural frames of reference and assumptions about interpersonal relations when reflecting on L1 and L2 pragmatics. He particularly focuses on the role of collaborative reflection in helping learners problematize taken-for-granted assumptions and stereotypes of self and other that lead to negative interpersonal evaluations. This work thus helps reveal the ways that learners perceive the sociopragmatic norms and broader ideologies that pertain to different languages.

34.5 Conclusion

Cross-cultural and intercultural pragmatics are rather disparate fields, with contributions from various pragmatic approaches, including sociocognitive, interpersonal/interactional and critical perspectives. Adherents to these various approaches differ in their interpretations of both context and culture, and of the ways in which both these elements impact on (linguistic) behaviour, and this necessarily results in noticeably different accounts of the sociopragmatic domain. Hopefully, though, these debates will gradually lead to more insights, especially with the benefit of interdisciplinary insights and new research approaches.

References

Allwood, J. (2007). Activity based studies of linguistic interaction. Gothenburg Papers in Theoretical Linguistics. https://halshs.archives-ouvertes.fr/hprints-00460511/document.

Angouri, J. (2018). *Culture, Discourse, and the Workplace*. Edinburgh: Edinburgh University Press.

Barnlund, D. C. and Yoshioka, M. (1990). Apologies: Japanese and American styles. *International Journal of Intercultural Relations*, 14, 193–206.

Blommaert, J. (1991). How much culture is there in intercultural communication? In J. Blommaert and J. Verschueren, eds., *The Pragmatics of International and Intercultural Communication*. Amsterdam: John Benjamins, pp. 13–31.

Blum-Kulka, S. and House, J. (1989). Cross-cultural and situational variation in requesting behavior. In S. Blum-Kulka, J. House and G. Kasper, eds., *Cross-Cultural Pragmatics: Requests and Apologies*. Norwood, NJ: Ablix, pp. 123–54.

Blum-Kulka, S., House, J. and Kasper, G. (eds.). (1989). *Cross-Cultural Pragmatics*. Norwood, NJ: Ablex.

Bond, M. H., Žegarac, V. and Spencer-Oatey, H. (2000). Culture as an explanatory variable: Problems and possibilities. In H. Spencer-Oatey, ed., *Culturally Speaking: Managing Rapport through Talk across Cultures*. London: Continuum, pp. 47–71.

Bronfenbrenner, U. (1979). *The Ecology of Human Development: Experiments by Nature and Design*. Cambridge, MA: Harvard University Press.

Brown, P. and Fraser, C. (1979). Speech as a marker of situation. In K. R. Scherer and H. Giles, eds., *Social Markers in Speech*. Cambridge: Cambridge University Press, pp. 33–62.

Brown, P. and Levinson, S. C. ([1978] 1987). *Politeness: Some Universals in Language Usage*. Cambridge: Cambridge University Press. Originally published as Universals in language usage: Politeness phenomenon. In E. Goody, ed., *Questions and Politeness: Strategies in Social Interaction*. Cambridge: Cambridge University Press, 1978.

Brown, R. and Gilman, A. ([1960] 1972). Pronouns of power and solidarity. In T. A. Sebeok, ed., *Style in Language*. Cambridge, MA: MIT Press, pp. 253–76. Reprinted in Pier P. Giglioli (ed.), *Language and Social Context*. Harmondsworth, UK: Penguin Books, 1972, pp. 252–82.

Chang, M. and Haugh, M. (2017). Intercultural communicative competence and emotion amongst second language learners of Chinese. In I. Kecskes and C. Sun, eds., *Key Issues in Chinese as a Second Language Research*. London: Routledge, pp. 269–86.

Chen, R., He, L. and Hu, C. (2013). Chinese requests: In comparison to American and Japanese requests and with reference to the 'East-West divide'. *Journal of Pragmatics, 55*(Sep), 140–61.

Cialdini, R. B. (2012). The focus theory of normative conduct. In P. A. M. Van Lange, A. W. Kruglanski and E. T. Higgins, eds., *Handbook of Theories of Social Psychology*, Vol. 2. London: Sage, pp. 295–312.

Davies, B. L. (2018). Evaluating evaluations: What different types of metapragmatic behaviour can tell us about participants' understandings of the moral order. *Journal of Politeness Research, 14*(1), 121–51.

Dervin, F. and Machart, R. (eds.). (2015). *Cultural Essentialism in Intercultural Relations*. London: Palgrave.

Dewaele, J.-M. (2018). Pragmatic challenges in the communication of emotions in intercultural couples. *Intercultural Pragmatics, 15*(1), 29–55.

Duranti, A. and Goodwin, C. (eds.). (1992). *Rethinking Context: Language as an Interactive Phenomenon*. Cambridge: Cambridge University Press.

Garfinkel, H. (1964). Studies of the routine grounds of everyday activities. *Social Problems, 11*(3), 225–50.

Gelfand, M. J. (2018). *Rule Makers, Rule Breakers*. London: Robinson.

Goddard, C. and Wierzbicka, A. (1997). Discourse and culture. In T. A. van Dijk, ed., *Discourse as Social Interaction*. London: Sage, pp. 231–59.

Goddard, C. and Wierzbicka, A. (2008). Universal human concepts as a basis for contrastive linguistic semantics. In M. dl A. G. Gonzalez, J. L. Mackenzie and E. M. Gonzáles-Álvarez, eds., *Current Trends in Contrastive Linguistics: Functional and Cognitive Perspectives*. Amsterdam: John Benjamins, pp. 205–36.

Goddard, C. and Ye, Z. (2015). Ethnopragmatics. In F. Sharifian, ed., *The Routledge Handbook of Language and Culture*. London: Routledge, pp. 66–85.

Graham, J., Nosek, B. A., Haidt, J., Iyer, R., Koleva, S. and Ditto, P. H. (2011). Mapping the moral domain. *Journal of Personality and Social Psychology, 101* (2), 366–85.

Grice, H. P. (1989). *Studies in the Way of Words (The William James Lectures)*. Cambridge, MA: Harvard University Press.

Gumperz, J., Jupp, T. and Roberts, C. (1979). *Crosstalk*. London: National Centre for Industrial Language Training.

Gumperz, J. and Roberts, C. (1991). Understanding in intercultural encounters. In J. Blommaert and J. Verschueren, eds., *The Pragmatics of International and Intercultural Communication* (pp. 51–90). Amsterdam: John Benjamins.

Haidt, J. (2013). Moral psychology for the twenty-first century. *Journal of Moral Education, 42*(3), 281–97.

Haidt, J. and Graham, J. (2007). When morality opposes justice: Conservatives have moral intuitions that liberals may not recognize. *Social Justice Research, 20*(1), 98–116.

Haidt, J. and Kesebir, S. (2010). Morality. In S. Fiske, D. Gilbert and G. Lindzey, eds., *Handbook of Social Psychology*, 5th ed. Hoboken, NJ: John Wiley, pp. 797–852.

Hall, J. K. (2002). *Teaching and Researching Language and Culture*. London: Longman.

Haugh, M. (2013). Im/politeness, social practice and the participation order. *Journal of Pragmatics, 58*, 52–72.

Haugh, M. (2017). Intercultural pragmatics. In Y. Y. Kim, ed., *The International Encyclopedia of Intercultural Communication*. London: John Wiley, pp. 1–14.

Haugh, M. (2018). Corpus-based metapragmatics. In A. Jucker, K. Schneider and W. Bublitz, eds., *Methods in Pragmatics*. Berlin: Mouton de Gruyter, pp. 615–39.

Haugh, M. and Hinze, C. (2003). A metalinguistic approach to deconstructing the concepts of 'face' and 'politeness' in Chinese, English and Japanese. *Journal of Pragmatics, 35*(10–11), 1581–1611.

Hill, B., Ide, S., Ikuta, S., Kawasaki, A. and Ogino, T. (1986). Universals of linguistic politeness: Quantitative evidence from Japanese and American English. *Journal of Pragmatics, 10*, 347–71.

Hofstede, G. (2001). *Culture's Consequences: Comparing Values, Behaviors, Institutions, and Organizations across Nations*. 2nd ed. London: Sage.

Holmes, J. (2018). Negotiating the cultural order in New Zealand workplaces. *Language in Society*, 47(1), 33–56.

Holmes, J. and Marra, M. (2011). Politic talk in ethnicised workplaces. In B. L. Davies, M. Haugh and A. J. Merrison, eds., *Situated Politeness*. London: Bloomsbury, pp. 27–52.

Holtgraves, T. and Yang, J.-N. (1990). Politeness as universal: Cross-cultural perceptions of request strategies and inferences based on their use. *Journal of Personality and Social Psychology*, 59(4), 719–29.

House, J. (2000). Understanding misunderstanding: A pragmatic-discourse approach to analysing mismanaged rapport in talk across cultures. In H. Spencer-Oatey, ed., *Culturally Speaking: Managing Rapport through Talk across Cultures*. London: Continuum, pp. 145–64.

House, J. (2006). Communicative styles in English and German. *European Journal of English Studies*, 10(3), 249–67.

Hymes, D. (1974). *Foundations in Sociolinguistics: An Ethnographic Approach*. Philadelphica: University of Pennsylvania Press.

Ide, S. (1989). Formal forms and discernment: Two neglected aspects of universals of linguistic politeness. *Multilingua*, 8(2/3), 223–48.

Janoff-Bulman, R. and Carnes, N. C. (2018). The model of moral motives: A map of the moral domain. In K. Gray and J. Graham, eds., *Atlas of Moral Psychology*. New York: The Guilford Press, pp. 223–30.

Kádár, D. Z. (2017). The role of ideology in evaluations of (in)appropriate behaviour. *Pragmatics*, 27(1), 35–56.

Kádár, D. Z. and Haugh, M. (2013). *Understanding Politeness*. Cambridge: Cambridge University Press.

Kádár, D. Z. and Mills, S. (2013). Rethinking discernment. *Journal of Politeness Research*, 9(2), 133–58.

Kasper, G. (2008). Data collection in pragmatics research. In H. Spencer-Oatey, ed., *Culturally Speaking: Culture, Communication and Politeness Theory*. London: Continuum, pp. 279–303.

Kecskes, I. (2014). *Intercultural Pragmatics*. Oxford: Oxford University Press.

Kecskes, I. (2017). Context-dependency and impoliteness in intercultural communication. *Journal of Politeness Research*, 13(1), 7–31.

Kecskes, I. and Zhang, F. (2013). On the dynamic relations between common ground and presupposition. In A. Capone, F. L. Piparo and M. Carapezza, eds., *Perspectives on Linguistic Pragmatics*. Berlin: Springer, pp. 375–95.

Leech, G. (1983). *Principles of Pragmatics*. London: Longman.

Leung, K. and Morris, M. W. (2015). Values, schemas, and norms in the culture–behavior nexus: A situated dynamics framework. *Journal of International Business Studies*, 46, 1028–50.

Levinson, S. C. (1979). Activity types and language. *Linguistics*, 17, 365–99.

Liddicoat, A. J. (2006). Learning the culture of interpersonal relationships: Students' understandings of personal address forms in French. *Intercultural Pragmatics*, 3(1), 55–80.

Lim, T.-S. and Bowers, J. W. (1991). Facework: Solidarity, approbation, and tact. *Human Communication Research*, 17(3), 415–50.

McConachy, T. (2018). *Developing Intercultural Perspectives on Language Use: Exploring Pragmatics and Culture in Foreign Language Learning*. Bristol: Multilingual Matters.

McConachy, T. (2019). L2 pragmatics as 'intercultural pragmatics': Probing sociopragmatic aspects of pragmatic awareness. *Journal of Pragmatics*, 151, 167–76.

McConachy, T. and Liddicoat, A. J. (2016). Meta-pragmatic awareness and intercultural competence: The role of reflection and interpretation in intercultural mediation. In F. Dervin and Z. Gross, eds., *Intercultural Competence in Education: Alternative Approaches for Different Times*. London: Palgrave Macmillan, pp. 13–30.

Meier, A. J. (2010). Culture and speech act performance. In A. Martínez and E. Usó, eds., *Speech Act Performance*. Amsterdam: John Benjamins, pp. 75–90.

Miller, L. (2008). Negative assessments in Japanese–American workplace interaction. In H. Spencer-Oatey, ed., *Culturally Speaking: Culture, Communication and Politeness Theory*, 2nd ed., Vol. 31. London: Continuum, pp. 227–40.

Mills, S. and Kádár, D. Z. (2011). Politeness and culture. In D. Z. Kádár and S. Mills, eds., *Politeness in East Asia*. Cambridge: Cambridge University Press, pp. 21–44.

Morris, M. W., Hong, Y.-Y., Chiu, C.-Y. and Liu, Z. (2015). Normology: Integrating insights about social norms to understand cultural dynamics. *Organizational Behavior and Human Decision Processes*, 129, 1–13.

Nishida, H. (2005). Cultural schema theory. In W. B. Gudykunst, ed., *Theorizing about Intercultural Communication*. Thousand Oaks: Sage, pp. 401–18.

Ogiermann, E. (2009). *On Apologizing in Negative and Positive Politeness Cultures*. Amsterdam: John Benjamins.

Palmer, G. B. (1996). *Toward a Theory of Cultural Linguistics*. Austin: University of Texas Press.

Parkinson, B., Fischer, A. H. and Manstead, A. S. R. (2005). *Emotion in Social Relations: Cultural, Group, and Interpersonal Processes*. Hove, UK: Psychology Press.

Pizziconi, B. (2003). Re-examining politeness, face and the Japanese language. *Journal of Pragmatics*, 35(10–11), 1471–1506.

Quinn, N. (2015). A critique of Wierzbicka's theory of cultural scripts: The case of Ifaluk *Fago*. *ETHOS*, 43(2), 165–86.

Riemer, N. (2006). Reductive paraphrase and meaning: A critique of Wierzbickian semantics. *Linguistics and Philosophy*, 29(3), 347–70.

Sarangi, S. (1994). Intercultural or not? Beyond celebration of cultural differences in miscommunication analysis. *Pragmatics*, 4(3), 409–27.

Schnurr, S. and Chan, A. (2009). Politeness and leadership discourse in New Zealand and Hong Kong. *Journal of Politeness Research, 5,* 131–57.

Schnurr, S. and Zayts, O. (2017). *Language and Culture at Work.* Abingdon, UK: Routledge.

Schwartz, S. H. (2011). Values: Cultural and individual. In F. J. R. Van de Vijver, A. Chasiotis and S. M. Breugelmans, eds., *Fundamental Questions in Cross-Cultural Psychology.* Cambridge: Cambridge University Press, pp. 463–93.

Scollon, R., Scollon, S. W., and Jones, R. H. (2012). *Intercultural Communication: A Discourse Approach.* 3rd edition. Oxford, UK: Wiley-Blackwell.

Sharifian, F. (2013). Globalization and developing metacultural competence in learning English as an international language. *Multilingual Education, 3*(7), 1–11.

Sharifian, F. and Jamarani, M. (2011). Cultural schemas in intercultural communication: A study of the Persian cultural schema of sharmandegi 'being ashamed'. *Intercultural Pragmatics, 8*(2), 227–51.

Sinkeviciute, V. (2017a). What makes teasing impolite in Australian and British English? "Step[ping] over those lines [...] you shouldn't be crossing". *Journal of Politeness Research, 13*(2), 175–207.

Sinkeviciute, V. (2017b). Funniness and "the preferred reaction" to jocularity in Australian and British English. *Language and Communication, 55,* 41–54.

Spencer-Oatey, H. (1996). Reconsidering power and distance. *Journal of Pragmatics, 26*(1), 1–24.

Spencer-Oatey, H. (1997). Unequal relationships in high and low power distance societies: A comparative study of tutor-student role relations in Britain and China. *Journal of Cross-Cultural Psychology, 28*(3), 284–302.

Spencer-Oatey, H. (2008). Face, (im)politeness and rapport. In H. Spencer-Oatey, ed., *Culturally Speaking: Culture, Communication and Politeness Theory.* London: Continuum, pp. 11–47.

Spencer-Oatey, H. (2011). Conceptualising the 'relational' in pragmatics: Insights from metapragmatic emotion and (im)politeness comments. *Journal of Pragmatics, 43,* 3565–78.

Spencer-Oatey, H. and Franklin, P. (2009). *Intercultural Interaction: A Multidisciplinary Approach to Intercultural Communication.* Basingstoke, UK: Palgrave Macmillan.

Spencer-Oatey, H. and Jiang, W. (2003). Explaining cross-cultural pragmatic findings: Moving from politeness maxims to sociopragmatic interactional principles (SIPs). *Journal of Pragmatics, 35,* 1633–50.

Spencer-Oatey, H. and Kádár, D. Z. (2016). The bases of (im)politeness evaluations: Culture, the moral order and the East-West debate. *East Asian Pragmatics, 1*(1), 73–106.

Spencer-Oatey, H. and Kádár, D. Z. (2021). *Intercultural Politeness: Managing Relations across Cultures.* Cambridge, UK: Cambridge University Press.

Spencer-Oatey, H., Ng, P. and Dong, L. (2008). British and Chinese reactions to compliment responses. In H. Spencer-Oatey, ed., *Culturally Speaking: Culture, Communication and Politeness Theory*. London: Continuum, pp. 95–117.

Spencer-Oatey, H. and Xing, J. (2019). Interdisciplinary perspectives on interpersonal relations and the evaluation process: Culture, norms and the moral order. *Journal of Pragmatics*, 151, 141–54.

Spencer-Oatey, H. and Žegarac, V. (2018). Conceptualizing culture and its impact on behavior. In C. Frisby and W. T. O'Donohue, eds., *Cultural Competence in Applied Psychology: An Evaluation of Current Status and Future Directions*. New York: Springer, pp. 211–41.

Triandis, H. C. (1994). *Culture and Social Behavior*. New York: McGraw Hill.

Tyler, A. (1995). The coconstruction of cross-cultural miscommunication. *Studies in Second Language Acquisition*, 17(2), 129–52.

Verschueren, J. (1999). *Understanding Pragmatics*. London: Edward Arnold.

Wierzbicka, A. (1985). Different cultures, different languages, different speech acts. *Journal of Pragmatics*, 9, 145–78.

Wierzbicka, A. (2003). *Cross-Cultural Pragmatics*. Berlin: Mouton de Gruyter.

Wierzbicka, A. (2010). Cultural scripts and intercultural communication. In A. Trosborg, ed., *Pragmatics across Languages and Cultures*. Berlin: de Gruyter, pp. 43–78.

Wierzbicka, A. (2012). 'Advice' in English and in Russian: A contrastive and cross-cultural perspective. In H. Limberg and M. A. Locher, eds., *Advice in Discourse*. Amsterdam: John Benjamins, pp. 309–31.

Wolf, H.-G. and Polzenhagen, F. (2006). Intercultural communication in English: Arguments for a cognitive approach to intercultural pragmatics. *Intercultural Pragmatics*, 3(3), 285–321.

Žegarac, V. (2007). A cognitive pragmatic perspective on communication and culture. In H. Kotthoff and H. Spencer-Oatey, eds., *Handbook of Intercultural Communication*. Berlin: Mouton de Gruyter, pp. 31–53.

35

Second Language Pragmatics

Elly Ifantidou

35.1 Introduction

The acquisition of pragmatics is nowadays positioned as the ultimate goal in 'second language pragmatics' and the theoretical strands with which it intersects and overlaps, 'sociopragmatics', 'interlanguage pragmatics' and 'intercultural communicative competence'. Viewing second language pragmatics from the perspective of this intersection, I will consider the boundaries between these domains, placing particular emphasis on (1) the notion of (socio-)*pragmatic competence*, (2) the shift of interest from studying the sociopragmatics of *use* to the sociopragmatics of *development* and (3) the role of figurative speech in SLP.

Clearly, how one defines L2 pragmatics bears on the discussion of the core issues mentioned above. Within Thomas and Leech's pragmalinguistic/sociopragmatic model, comparative aspects of how pragmatics is acquired, namely pragmatic transfer, pragmatic failure, instruction and environment, testing methods, received continued interest with fewer research agendas positioning L2 pragmatics acquisitionally. In presenting the dominant orientations of L2 pragmatics for the last three decades, Section 35.2 surveys earlier accounts of (socio)pragmatic competence compared to the intercultural communicative competence and the discursive, socio-cognitive approach. Section 35.3 advances an approach to second language pragmatics shaped by the important distinction between two points of view in the study of second language pragmatics, the sociopragmatics of L2 *use* and the sociopragmatics of L2 *development*. Surprisingly, second language pragmatics still holds a relatively narrow view of pragmatic inference largely geared by the early speech act agenda and social conditions of use. Therefore, focusing on figurative speech, Section 35.4 addresses the striking gap in the field, which is even more surprising given that the use of metaphors, irony, humour is eminently sociopragmatic in nature.

35.2 (Socio)pragmatic Competence

How pragmatic competence is defined depends on the view of pragmatics, and second language pragmatics in particular, one adopts. By revisiting its sub-fields, in this section I will sketch the trajectory of second language pragmatics, with an emphasis on the way pragmatic competence has evolved to date.

Second language pragmatics has its roots in *cross-cultural pragmatics*, which has been re(de)fined into *intercultural* and *interlanguage pragmatics* over the last three decades. Launched as a project on cultural differences of speech acts and their linguistic realization across languages (Blum-Kulka et al. 1989), today this trend retains its comparative, contrastive orientation and is concerned with how culture-specific differences result in communication difficulties. (See the edited volume by Gass and Neu 2006; see also Taguchi and Roever 2017.)

The implications of this paradigm have been explored in interlanguage pragmatics, which used the findings of cross-cultural studies as an explanatory basis for the learner's unsuccessful use of interlanguage at a particular stage of development. Kasper and Dahl (1991: 216) defined interlanguage pragmatics "in a narrow sense, referring to nonnative speakers' (NNSs') comprehension and production of speech acts, and how their L2-related speech act knowledge is acquired". For example, at various stages of interlanguage, pragmatic failure (Thomas 1983) and pragmatic transfer (Kasper 1992) reveal how the influence of L1 pragmatic behaviours can lead to misunderstandings of the speaker's intentions. In this respect, negative transfer has received a great deal of attention as a cause of miscommunication in L2 and a domain where corrective strategies towards native-like performance were much needed. (See Kasper 1992; for a recent review, see Ifantidou 2017.)

Given its fairly narrow focus on pragmatic transfer, pragmatic failure and the primacy of grammar versus pragmatic knowledge in interlanguage development (for a discussion, see Marmaridou 2011), interlanguage pragmatics was subsequently redefined as "the study of the development and use of strategies for linguistic action by nonnative speakers" (Kasper and Schmidt 1996: 150).

The main criticism put forward by Kasper and Schmidt above is that interlanguage pragmatics motivated primarily cross-sectional studies of *use* based on differences with *native speakers*. (For an overview, see Kasper and Rose 2002.) In this perspective, the influence of Leech's original construal of sociopragmatics versus pragmalinguistics (see original Figure 35.1; Leech 1983: 11) fuelled interest in culture-specific principles used by non-native speakers, e.g. the cooperative and politeness principles, and in 'local' conditions of language use, e.g. strategies of indirectness (Leech 1983: 10).

The problems this distinction ran into were partly due to the lack of clear-cut boundaries. Despite the fact that pragmalinguistics was

```
[Grammar]      Pragmalinguistics      Sociopragmatics      [Sociology]
     ↑              related to         |          related to        ↑
     |_____ _|             |_ _____|
```

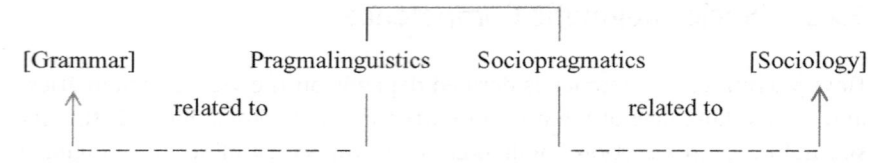

Figure 35.1 General pragmatics, pragmalinguistics and sociopragmatics. Adapted from Leech (1983:11).

originally conceived as a language-specific endeavour complementing sociopragmatics, in effect, the two fields cross-cut each other: if language-specific, acts are bound to make manifest certain culture-specific principles; and if culture-specific (or even universal), principles are applied and conveyed differently, by the linguistic resources of specific language communities. The point has been made convincingly by Marmaridou (2011) who argued that with the exception of L2 teaching, the pragmalinguistics/sociopragmatics divide cannot instigate research which is "theoretically justified, analytically possible, or ideologically desirable", hence viable (Marmaridou 2011: 99). For example, the causes of pragmatic failure are hard to attribute to either pragmalinguistic or sociopragmatic failure whereas the effects on the addressee are the same regardless of the origin of the cause in this case. Moreover, it is not clear which side of the divide the L2 learner is obeying and which side s/he is not conforming to (Marmaridou 2011: 90). Being humble is normative response to compliments in Chinese, which is evaluated as 'arrogance' if intentionally waived by knowledgeable L2 speakers (Chang and Haugh 2017). Being indirect is more tactful by British standards, though not so for Americans (Marmaridou 2011: 83). Both native speakers of English who learn Chinese as L2 and Americans may know the linguistic resources (pragmalinguistic knowledge) and the stereotypes (sociopragmatic knowledge) but may feel 'uncomfortable' to use them and may find complying with cultural norms as 'emotionally challenging' or even 'tiring'. On these grounds, Chang and Haugh (2017: 279) showed that the affective aspects of learning – i.e. L2 learners' feelings and prioritizing their experiences over the actual situational context – influence learners' developing *intercultural communicative competence* and therefore, should be treated as distinct but equally fundamental to knowledge of language and language use.

Clearly, knowing the convention is one thing, conforming to it is another, and there is no failsafe way of attributing the causes of miscommunication to either linguistic inadequacy or social ignorance. Deeply entrenched cultural values are often at play; for example, Americans' life-long exposure to the arts of argument and debate, and Japanese preference for silence and disbelief in arguing can account for varying levels of indirectness, with Japanese being more direct than Americans to lower status addressees (see Barnlund 1989; Beebe and Takahashi 1989; Spees 1994).

As argued above, although interlanguage pragmatics started as the study of the interface of L2 with L1, i.e. of the learning process towards the L2 (Selinker's 1972 definition), it evolved mainly through studies concerned with cross-sectional differences rather than the learning process, focusing on language use rather than development. As Marmaridou (2011: 88) notes (see also Kasper and Schmidt 1996: 150),

> the dominant practice in interlanguage pragmatics concerns the outcome, i.e. the collection and comparison of data from native speakers' linguistic performance in the target language, the learner's use of her native language, and the learner's interlanguage (i.e. her use of the target language at a particular stage of development).

A drastic turn in viewing L1-L2 differences as common ground for co-constructing norms and conventions during interaction (Kecskes 2014), rather than as a cause of communication problems, changed the agendas and developments in the field of second language pragmatics. With the advent of intercultural pragmatics, defined as "the study of interactions among people of different language backgrounds", interest shifted to how L2 speakers of the target language communicate with other L2 speakers of the target language and to their priority to negotiate and interact in order to reach mutual understanding with their interlocutors. Nowadays, with the surge of the discursive approach to pragmatics (see Levinson 2013), linguistic resources and situational factors are more loosely linked, allowing for speakers' attitudes and affect to impact on the dynamic unfolding of the talk.

As part of a definition of pragmatic competence, I would like to return to the guiding question of this section: "How does the trajectory of sub-fields which informed second language pragmatics for more than three decades impact on pragmatic competence?" I will next sketch the main areas pragmatic competence has been held to encompass, in the most dominant fields within SLP (second language pragmatics).

Although well established and widely explored within SLP, pragmatic competence has been mainly associated with an interlanguage, an intercultural or a sociopragmatic approach. In Bardovi-Harlig's (2010) discussion of SLP (185) and her 2012 account, pragmatic competence becomes manifest in learners' conversational talk and their performance as speakers who can "make choices among available linguistic forms to convey social meanings" (Bardovi-Harlig 2012: 150; see also Kasper and Rose 2002: 164–5). If comprehension paves the way to production, it is a mystery why in interlanguage pragmatics, pragmatic competence has been researched primarily as a production ability. 'Speaker bias' in SLA has been criticized (see Culpeper et al. 2018: 30, 90) yet implied meanings are fairly conventionally and straightforwardly retrieved from indirect speech acts and by flouting Gricean maxims (Culpeper et al. 2018: chapters 4 and 5).

From an intercultural perspective, pragmatic competence is described by Kecskes (2014) below:

> I am not in favor of the kind of complex competence taxonomies that talk about different elements of pragmatic competence or communicative competence and separate it from intercultural communicative competence.... The reason I do not support the distinction between pragmatic competence and intercultural communicative competence is that it is almost impossible to draw a dividing line between them. In intercultural communication the existing L1-based pragmatic competence of interlocutors is adjusted as required by the actual situational context and allowed by the preferences of the individual speaker/hearer. This adjustment usually is only temporary and does not have a significant effect on the existing pragmatic competence of language users. Of course, the more a person is engaged in intercultural encounters, the more likely it is that his/her pragmatic competence will change more significantly. (Kecskes 2014: 61).

Kecskes' approach is in line with recent accounts of intercultural communicative competence (Chang and Haugh 2017) which bring individuals' attitudes and emotions to the fore, as underpinning pragmatic competence and shaping the outcome of communicative encounters. This is a novel perspective on SLP with a clear focus on learners' preferences and their need to "feel comfortable between their first and second cultures" (Chang and Haugh 2017: 267–8). Its origins are found in the theoretical tradition of Kramsch's views defined below:

> cultural appropriateness may need to be replaced by the concept of **appropriation** [original emphasis], whereby learners make a foreign language and culture their own by adopting and adapting it to their own needs and interests. The ability to acquire another person's language and understand someone else's culture while retaining one's own is one aspect of a more general ability to mediate between several languages and cultures, called cross-cultural, intercultural, or multicultural communication. (Kramsch 1998: 81)

In narrower definitions, pragmatic competence in L2 is determined by the linguistic context of interaction and its social dimensions (level of formality, orderly turns, transitions, repairs). In Taguchi and Sykes' (2013: 5) interlanguage approach, pragmatic competence involves "knowledge of correct form-function-context mappings and ability to retrieve and use this knowledge efficiently in actual performance". In Culpeper et al.'s (2018: 2) second language pragmatic approach, pragmatic competence draws on "sociopragmatics which is concerned with the contextual features of pragmatics, and pragmalinguistics, which is concerned with the linguistic structure of pragmatics". In both definitions, emphasis is on conventional, formulaic expressions for handling speech encounters, as for example, in the interpretation of "you shouldn't have" when acknowledging and accepting gifts. Pragmatic competence is ultimately examined in terms of a form-context-function mapping, still grounded in its pragmalinguistic/sociolinguistic roots.

Despite the significant body of research in the previously mentioned fields and its significant role in the development of SLP, these approaches leave a number of fundamental questions unanswered: Does pragmatic competence develop in discrete stages? How can it be assessed in the process of its acquisition? Do the dynamics and adjustments in the flow of communication, the interlocutors' attitudes and preferences, resist a more rigid methodological approach to the study of pragmatic competence? Could its different elements facilitate acquiring or testing pragmatic competence (see e.g. Ifantidou 2014)? If we were to accept a broad theoretical divide between approaches positioned on a form-function-context premise, on the one hand, and approaches which allow L2 learners' preferences and emotions to interfere in the learning process, on the other, I believe that the former is a more promising methodological line to testing and teaching, whereas the latter a more realistic account of how communication takes place in real life. Given the lack of a commonly established goal and a framework that encompasses both approaches, most of the questions originally raised by Kasper and Schmidt (1996) – such as, "What are the stages of pragmatic development? How can they be measured by a common means? Does L1 really influence L2 pragmatics?" – remain unanswered to date.

35.3 From Sociopragmatics of *Use* to Sociopragmatics of *Development*

In practice, interlanguage research has been associated with the sociopragmatics of use. As argued in the previous section, the defining skills of pragmatic competence are speech acts and implicatures, and these have been researched as essential in how L2 pragmatics is learnt (see Martínez-Flor and Usó-Juan 2010; Taguchi 2009). Austin's and Searle's taxonomies of the illocutionary purpose of the act (Austin ([1962] 1975); Searle 1969) established the speaker's intention in performing a speech act as the most influential pragmatic paradigm in L2 learning (for criticism, see Taguchi 2009: 8). The learner's ability to communicate successfully requests, apologies, complaints, among many, depended on the use of directness/indirectness, of pragmatic routines and modifiers which can intensify or soften the speech act relative to social factors such as status, social distance and degree of imposition between interlocutors. As a result, culturally specific and socially situated answers were elicited in test items where learners are asked to provide a speech act relative to the setting, social distance and status of participants.

The complex link between universal pragmatic knowledge (found in shared strategies of in/directness and conventionality) and cross-linguistic differences in the realization of speech acts inspired extensive comparative, cross-sectional research within interlanguage pragmatics on how L2 learners can produce speech acts using native speakers' strategies and forms (see Cohen and Olshtain 1993; Cenoz and Valencia 1996; for recent studies, see Wijayanto et al. 2017; Lee 2018; Economidou-Kogetsidis et al. 2018). These studies examined universal principles (e.g. using reasons as an indirect refusal strategy), their role in development and possible L1–L2 differences in speech acts performed by foreign learners of English, with emphasis on how first language and cultural values influence performance.

Interlanguage pragmatics became recently motivated by an acquisitional objective aiming at learner groups' development over time. (See Taguchi 2017 for a historic review; for longitudinal and cross-sectional studies, see Kasper and Rose 2002; Bardovi-Harlig 2010.) This line of studies was implemented by interventionist studies on speech acts, implicatures and conversational strategies which support the effectiveness of explicit over implicit pragmatic instruction. Bardovi-Harlig (2006) raised the importance of developmental work in relation to the acquisition of future in L2 English below:

> The close analysis of individual subsystems of grammar yields information about the development of specific linguistic systems in second language both narrowly in that system, and in second language development more broadly. While this is of great interest to the language analysts among second language researchers, this sort of close analysis – by illuminating the details of acquisition – can also help determine what the effects and limitations of outside influences are. On the other hand, the study of factors that influence acquisition can provide interpretations of some of the differences in the timing, choices, and patterns that can be observed through the careful analysis of the interlanguage of individual learners and in the same learners at different stages. (69)

In her 2010 review of pragmatics in second language acquisition, Bardovi-Harlig stressed the need for more research on the acquisitional side of implicatures, and pointed out the need to embrace a wider range of genuinely pragmatic phenomena while exclude sociolinguistic abilities:

> Within second language studies, work in pragmatics is narrower than it is in the field of pragmatics at large, including the investigation of speech acts and to a lesser extent conversational structure and conversational implicature. It is also broader, investigating areas traditionally considered to be sociolinguistics (Stalnaker 1972). For example, Kasper and Dahl (1991: 216) included speech acts, conversational management, discourse organization, and sociolinguistic aspects of language use such as choice of address forms as part of pragmatics (Bardovi-Harlig 2010: 237).

However, on the developmental strand, the dominant areas investigated are speech acts and implicatures. Conversational implicatures cross-cut speech acts in that they rely, too, on recognizing the speaker's intention by inference when Grice's maxims are flouted or when opinions are indirectly expressed. Early studies investigated the Pope implicature, irony, and indirect speech acts (see Bouton 1994) and to a lesser extent metaphors, sarcasm and hyperbole, as in *What did I do ... well, everything in the world* (Culpeper et al. 2018: 94) (see Bouton 1994; Garcia 2004; Taguchi 2009; Taguchi and Sykes 2013). As with speech acts, the conversational implicatures examined rely largely on conventions of linguistic forms, as in using "would you mind" to make a request, or on conventions of discourse patterns which are customarily used, as in providing a reason for refusing an invitation.

Speech acts and Grice's conversational implicatures were immersed in a conversational frame of analysis studied as sequences of social interaction in longer, developing stretches of discourse (in the tradition of Goffman's 1959 social interaction and Richards and Schmidt's 1983 'conversational analysis') rather than as short, two-part exchanges. In this direction, genre-oriented studies examined telephone conversations, friendly or institutional encounters, classroom interactions with emphasis on naturally occurring discourse, on how speech acts are misinterpreted and how the interlocutor's repair resolves the misunderstanding. In this research strand, claims made during interaction are used as evidence for speakers' intentions, motives or mental states, by drawing on participants' understanding of their interlocutor's statements rather than the analyst's assumptions about the speaker's intentions, mental states and attitudes.

With the outcome of the discursive turns that have taken place throughout the humanities and social sciences since the second half of the twentieth century, discursive pragmatics turned to real communication contexts and real life (Bargiela-Chiappini and Haugh 2009; Culpeper 2011; Félix-Brasdefer 2015). Interest shifted from existing L1-based pragmatic competence to how social actions emerge and how meaning is negotiated during interaction by adjusting to the situational context and to the preferences of interlocutors. This perspective embraced interlocutors' "attitudes" such as "curiosity and openness as well as readiness to see other cultures and the speaker's own without being judgmental" (Byram 1997: 34; see Wiseman and Koester 1993). Within the intercultural communicative approach, Kecskes (2010) treated pragmatic competence as developing from a Common Underlying Conceptual Base and viewed the emerging language in terms of a unique dialectical symbiosis of pragmatic rules and expectations of both languages. A growing concern in the study of L2 pragmatics nowadays is how attitudes affect the behaviour of individual second language learners (see Chang and Haugh 2017; Clouet 2013; Kim 2014). How this strand of research can change the face of pragmatics in applied linguistics is discussed in Section 35.4.

Given how many learn languages in classroom settings, a considerable body of developmental work addressed the issue of whether speech acts, implicatures and conversational skills can be learned within the classroom, or by spending time in the target culture (see Taguchi 2015 for an overview of instructional pragmatics). Specifically for speech acts and implicatures, the evidence is fairly inconclusive, as in Billmyer (1990a, 1990b) whose participants were able to learn to compliment with or without instruction, possibly benefited by the target-language context they lived in (see also Martínez-Flor 2006). Moreover, the mass of available evidence concerns requests, apologies and compliments and hence is fairly limited in scope.

Turning to social interaction skills, although typically not learnt during classroom interaction, the evidence supports the facilitative role of explicit instruction, with real-life educational environments inviting a combination of explicit and implicit instruction (see e.g. Sardegna and Molle 2010). Worth mentioning is that developmental data involves primarily routine formulae, as opposed to pragmatic meaning inferred spontaneously in the absence of pre-fixed linguistic expressions. On study design, the emphasis lies on production with the exception of studies on implicatures where interpretation is assessed instead. The current trend is to create real-life tasks which are experienced as spontaneous encounters while using technology-mediated means (see González-Lloret and Lourdes 2018; Ziegler 2016).

In developmental studies, testing L2 pragmatic competence focuses on tests which can incorporate not only speech acts and routine formulae but implicature, style and extended interaction, too. (For an overview, see Taguchi and Sykes 2013; see also Roever et al. 2014; Roever and Ikeda, 2020; Ross and Kasper 2013.) The central question driving research in SLP testing is "Can valid and reliable measures be designed which meet a number of criteria before they can be used cross-culturally in real-world settings?" In the speech act tradition, it has been observed that when test batteries are designed for a specific L1 background, the test explores cross-linguistic differences with the L2 but loses its wider applicability. A related problem is the low reliability of multiple-choice DCT, for tearing speech acts out of a context of coherent flow. Computer-based tests circumvent a number of problems by decreasing test raters effects, therefore increasing reliability. (See Liu 2006, limited to Mandarin-speaking learners of English, and Tada 2005, limited to the speech acts of request and apology.) Further methodological advances involve developing tasks 'bottom up'; that is, generated and evaluated by EFL learners themselves (see Liu 2006).

The diverse and complex nature of pragmatic competence as outlined in the previous sections and the types of phenomena SLP has covered to date explains why pragmatics tests struggle with practicality, and why they are rarely used in real-life environments. Future challenges in testing include, aiming at interaction with automated speech recognition devices, testing the full range of language proficiency levels and stages of pragmatic competence, covering target languages other than English, achieving balance between construct coverage and instrument practicality, and employing systematic validation to a greater extent. It will then remain to take assessment of pragmatics from research pursuits into real-world, operational testing.

As far as other types of inferential skill are concerned, since Low's (2008) observation that "testing metaphor skills within the construct of general language proficiency presents very different problems from testing metaphor for specific research projects and remains essentially unknown and unexplored territory" (Low 2008: 226), hardly any progress has been made in the domain of inferential second language pragmatics. Next I will turn to pragmatic inference within SLP as it becomes manifest in fairly marginalized types of pragmatic meaning, and to future prospects in exploring these marginalized types, too.

35.4 Pragmatic Inference within Second Language Pragmatics (SLP)

The plethora of studies within interlanguage pragmatics seem to be missing the pragmatics of genuine inference as activated in figurative speech and other expressive types of effect derived from prosody or facial expressions. In this section, I would like to turn to consider whether metaphors, irony, humour can be studied within SLP and if so, how they reveal and strengthen pragmatic competence in a second language.

Research has been fairly balanced between interlanguage comparative studies and teaching of figurative speech (Bell 2005, on humour; Davies 2003; Kim 2014; Lantolf 2018 on sarcasm; Littlemore 2001; Holme 2004, on metaphor). Studies on L2 implicatures which involve irony (Garcia 2004; Lee 2002; Roever et al. 2014) follow Bouton's (1988) first design of testing implicatures to trigger indirectness, politeness, understatements, and irony/sarcasm. Test items comprised either idiosyncratic implicatures which are sensitive to contextual cues (e.g. *Bill is a really good friend*, conveying a sarcastic inference), or formulaic implicatures which are not sensitive to contextual cues (*Is the Pope Catholic?*). L2 learners seem to encounter difficulties when interpreting the former, and significantly fewer difficulties when interpreting the latter which rely on idioms and can, moreover, be linked to expressions with similar functions in L1s (see Lee 2002). Recent studies on conversational implicatures employ, too, Bouton's original tool of fairly straightforward routes and relatively few inferential steps of reasoning (as in John: *How was the wedding? I bet it was exciting.* Mary: *Well ... the cake was OK*; see Taguchi 2013).

When authentic examples are used in naturally occurring language, L2 learners encounter difficulties, as in Littlemore's (2001, 2003) studies on metaphor interpretation; Kim's (2014) study on irony/sarcasm;

Romero-Trillo and Newell's (2012) study on prosodic markers. Humour in SLP is under-explored, too, with cross-sectional evidence limited to its discursive role in beginners' interaction (Davies 2003; Bell 2005; Forman 2011) showing that the discourse context and non-verbal behaviour help L2 learners build on common experience when interpreting humour, despite their limited lexical and syntactic resources. A general tendency revealed in several studies on figurative language is that as proficiency increases, so does utterance comprehension. (On irony, see Shively et al. 2008; Bromberek-Dyzman et al. 2010; on humour, see Bell 2005; but see also Bell 2009; Forman 2011.) In this direction, Taguchi (2013) examined non-conventional implicatures along the lines of *A: Did you like the movie? B: I was glad when it was over*, and found that language knowledge in terms of lexical access speed was significantly associated with speedy comprehension of implicatures.

The non-verbal dimension of SLP is another crucial but under-explored aspect of L2 learners' pragmatic competence. Assumptions about late acquisition of competencies which tap into humour and irony can be challenged if prosody is used as a cue for understanding. Togame (2016) showed that this is the case with ironical utterances which are successfully understood by native speakers and L2 learners (Japanese) of English alike. In recent times, evidence from prosodic features in real interaction has been used by Szczepek Reed (2004: chapter 10) and Couper-Kuhlen (2012) to challenge standard assumptions about patterns of question intonation. Further evidence on underrepresented linguistic and non-linguistic means in SLP comes from interjections (Padilla Cruz 2010), propositional attitudes (Cook 2012) and the pragmatic function of prosodic elements in L2 language learners (Romero-Trillo and Newell 2012).

More specifically, Padilla Cruz (2010) has argued for the multiple expressive roles of interjections (mm!, uh-huh!, yeah!, Yuk! Phew!) as emotive and cognitive markers indicating disgust, surprise, pain, sorrow, volition (I want) or attitude. Yet beginners to advanced L2 learners receive meagre input on interjections as mere *conversational fillers* used to maintain the flow of interaction. On attitudes and preferences, Cook (2012) discussed difficulties by L2 Korean speakers in retrieving speaker-intended meaning which is not linguistically encoded but inferred in the form of higher-level explicatures.

Difficulties at the level of prosody are brought to the fore by Romero-Trillo (2012). In that volume, Nilsenová and Swerts (2012) address prosodic features (pitch, range, register) and how their semantic import is linked to specific communicative effects, for example, a high boundary tone conveying lack of speaker's commitment, a high nuclear pitch accent marking "new" information, lack of final declination signalling incompleteness and overall high pitch being typical for questions. Romero-Trillo and Newell (2012) examine pragmatic markers ('mhm' and 'yeah') whose final pitch was higher in the case of the native group in statistically significant terms. They conclude that prosodic pragmatic markers which function as feedback behave differently in native speakers and L2 learners resulting in different pragmatic functions, e.g. more 'interactional' for natives, more 'transactional' for L2 learners. Studying these features of linguistic performance may minimize misunderstandings at the listener's end and ease some of the discomfort experienced by L2 learners in online communication.

By idealizing away from the properties of context which are hard to formalize and focusing on aspects of interpretation which exhibit a code-driven regularity, genuinely pragmatic phenomena have been discussed at the periphery of SLP. Metaphor, irony, humour, interjections, propositional attitudes, prosodic markers, are types of effect which fall outside the strictly propositional content of an utterance, hence do not affect L2 learners' understanding of linguistically encoded meaning. While they have been of interest to a few scholars, they failed to connect with mainstream frameworks within SLP. As pragmatic theory and the cognitive sciences have matured and expanded (see Cave and Wilson 2018; Wilson and Sperber 2012), expressive, emotive, imagistic, even shallowly processed inferential meaning, is arguably able to establish the relationship between the speaker and the hearer as much as lexically encoded content can. Consider the case of particular tone of voice which might indicate that we want to dissociate ourselves entirely from the proposition we are expressing: that we *mean* the opposite of what we are saying (see Wharton 2012). One can only expect that in the future, SLP will be sensitive to both properly linguistic as well as emotive meaning whose function *is* to convey information about human communicative behaviour interpreted by inference and decoding alike. In view of this prospect, I turn to a current project on metaphor comprehension and its role in SLP in relation to (1) literal meaning and (2) emotions and images as vehicles of communicative effects.

35.5 Case Study: Metaphor Comprehension in Second Language Pragmatics

As argued in this chapter, without figures of speech, L2 pragmatics remains a largely conventional and predictable enterprise with genuine inference, emotions, images and attitudes of L2 users remaining on the fringes of second language pragmatics. Of these, metaphors in L2 are predominantly studied as idioms or conceptual mappings of source and target concepts. (For an overview, see Ifantidou 2019.) Consequently, the growing interest in L2 metaphors has not yet resulted in an alternative framework bringing a novel perspective or methodology to the study of metaphors within SLP. A recent endeavour to capture the role of metaphor when used by L2 learners explored its relation to literal meaning and to individual users' experience, their preferences, emotions or images during interpretation. In this section, I will summarize the findings of recent studies implemented by the author of this chapter and outline implications for future directions which may serve to define further research areas for acquisitional SLP studies.

First insights into the role figurative speech plays in the acquisition of L2 pragmatics and of metaphors in particular are obtained from a study which compared the frequency of four types of inferential route which guided L2 readers in the interpretation process (Ifantidou 2019). When asked to discuss the attitude of the author in opinion articles from broadsheet British and US newspapers, L2 readers used metaphors (94 per cent) significantly more frequently compared to evidentials (63 per cent), referring expressions (43 per cent) and irony (41 per cent) (occurrences in stimuli texts N 29, 28, 29, 27, respectively).

This finding is intriguing given the intuitively easier processing of the linguistic meaning of referring expressions, evidentials and ironical statements as opposed to metaphors, which often include words unknown to L2 learners, as in **plummeting** *living standards*, **crumbling** *public works*, **rigged** *election*. Given this assumption, metaphors randomly selected from the same editorials were put to the test in six comprehension tasks, and was shown that participants noted down a considerable number of unknown words included in the metaphors tested (before interventions: Test 1: 86 per cent, Test 2: 48 per cent, Test 3: 30 per cent, after interventions: Test 1: 53 per cent, Test 2: 33 per cent, Test 3: 53 per cent). Upon checking for correlations, participants' scores in the six tests did not correlate with number of unknown words identified, which suggests that participants interpreted the metaphors correctly regardless of the number of unknown words encountered.

Intrigued by this evidence on preferences for and competence in comprehension of what were identified by participants as semantically fragmented, i.e. not fully linguistically encoded, metaphors I then concentrated on a qualitative discussion of tendencies observed in participants' interpretation of the metaphors tested (Ifantidou 2019). A closer look at the interpretations provided showed that participants relied less on contextual linguistic cues and more on personal experience in inferring the meaning of metaphorical expressions which included unknown words. In the following examples the words 'repugnance', 'crumbling', 'plight', 'grinding' were identified as unknown by the majority of participants (86 per cent, 74 per cent, 68 per cent, 62 per cent, respectively). Therefore the meanings derived could reveal an inclination in L2 learners' behaviour during the interpretation process.

(1) ... a **warfare** which has always **triggered** a special **repugnance** from countries ...
(2) But it could also lead to disaster, if the **crumbling regime** is replaced by the jihadist forces ...

(3) The immigrants' **plight paints a horrific picture** of ... human trafficking.
(4) ... the regime of Bashar al-Assad has appeared to have the upper hand in Syria's **grinding civil war**, ...

Overall, the meanings obtained seem to either approximate the literal content of the word metaphorically used (*repugnance*=disgust, *crumbling*=break down, *plight*=terrible situation, *grinding*=grinder), or to be primed by contextual cues (*repugnance*=undesirable reaction, *grinding*=ongoing), or ignore contextual cues (*repugnance*=dishonour; *plight*=situation, mass of people; *grinding* = widespread, poverty and damage; *crumbling*=troubled). The wide and often disparate range of meanings obtained, as illustrated above, raised the question of whether there was anything which they shared, which was perhaps not very obvious, and perhaps non-linguistic too. Using Bradley and Lang's (1999) norming of emotional ratings for a large number of English words, it turned out that the majority of participants used expressions which have negative or positive valence rates, and overall similar emotional ratings (if we also take into consideration arousal means). On a 1 to 9 scale rating of whether one feels happy or unhappy (valence) while reading individual words, the words 95 per cent and 81 per cent of participants used to define their unknown words in the tests are of clearly negative and clearly positive affective value (see Ifantidou 2019).

This evidence shows that when second language users cope with vague and indeterminate meanings of words metaphorically used, i.e. words they are not capable of fully representing conceptually due to unfamiliar lexical content, they may take an alternative processing route. In other words, when propositional meaning is not fully grasped while interpreting a metaphor, inferential processes may tap into participants' emotional reaction and imagery. This could explain why addressees are attracted to metaphors: by arousing their emotional attitude to images and sensorimotor processes which metaphors evoke, contrary to evidentials, referring expressions and irony. Moreover, processing effort can be reduced because metaphors may create a bond with the readers which is emotion-driven and often autobiographical too.

Compared to evidentials, irony and referring expressions, metaphors seem to convey a certain import which can be broader than the notion of meaning in the sense that they trigger 'beyond-meaning' effects (images and emotions), and hence are able to evoke interpretive effects which are weakly communicated (i.e. neither anticipated nor endorsed by the communicator) (see Wilson 2018). These are not meanings or a message which addressees can easily bring to consciousness and define. They are emotional phenomena (aspects of words, values, states experienced) which, once evoked, help increase the positive rewarding effects conveyed and minimize the processing effort caused by descriptively ineffable types of language use.

To probe further into the nature and role of metaphor comprehension in L2, a reaction time experiment was designed and implemented by Ifantidou and Hatzidaki (2019). Using the same type of fairly conventional metaphors from newspaper editorials, an attempt was made to compare metaphors to literal equivalent sentences and implicatures derived from the original metaphors. Our aim was to explore how literal paraphrases and emotionally arousing content impact metaphorical meaning interpretation. In this direction, we created an experimental setting whereby performance on sentence comprehension and metaphorical meaning-matching, displayed in accuracy and reaction time, was tested across literal equivalents (*historic proportions*) and emotionally loaded implicatures (*amazing proportions*) of target metaphorical expressions (e.g. *Obama presided over a topic of discussion of epochal proportions*).

The results showed that the characteristics of the two types of utterances had the same impact on metaphorical meaning interpretation as both literal paraphrases (*synonymous* condition), and emotion-laden implicatures (*implicature* condition) yielded fewer errors than the control condition, but did not differ between them either in accuracy or in response time. We argued that as emotional arousal relies heavily on episodic memory (Phelps 2004), it may have facilitated metaphorical processing of otherwise challenging content for L2 speakers. That is, the emotional content of the implicature condition might have made the processing of its content as easy as that of the synonymous one. This might also be a reason why differences were not observed in the comparison between these conditions in the behavioural tasks.

A number of conclusions can be drawn from the studies summarized here. On the linguistic level of communication, metaphors are not more effortful to process compared to literal sentences since they did not differ in reading times or comprehension scores in the study above. Secondly, metaphors come with an advantage over literal sentences, since L2 language which is challenging for L2 learners seems to be plausibly interpreted in the metaphorical context. Recent findings (Ifantidou in press) suggest that on asked about the difficulty of a test on metaphors compared to a test on literal sentences involving the same lexical items used metaphorically in the former and literally in the latter, the great majority of respondents considered the metaphorical one easier to cope with.

On the psychological level of communication, metaphors engage readers emotionally, as suggested by the emotion valenced words they used to guess the meaning of unknown words (Ifantidou 2019). Neuroimaging studies on metaphors' emotional salience over literal language (Citron and Goldberg 2014; Citron et al. 2016) have shown that metaphorical sentences activate brain regions associated with emotion processing more strongly than their literal counterparts – which could explain L2 learners' preference of metaphors over other linguistic stimuli. As revealed by Citron and Zervos (2018), metaphors are implicitly perceived as more aesthetically pleasing than their literal renderings. Interestingly, a significant difference was found in beauty ratings between metaphorical and literal sentences, with metaphors perceived as more beautiful than literal sentences despite the fact that metaphors were rated as slightly less familiar than their literal counterparts.

35.6 Implications for Future Research

What are the consequences of these tendencies observed in learners' second language pragmatics? Emotionally engaging language is more riveting and more persuasive, too, and therefore it is expected to yield a greater number of positive cognitive effects, which are more rewarding even when more challenging otherwise. Language stimuli which allow L2 learners' life experience, world knowledge and emotions to contribute equally with their language knowledge can sustain motivation in intercultural communication in ways that pre-fixed language stimuli cannot. It remains to be seen how individual learners' abilities can be more justly catered for in future learning and testing situations.

A related issue which will attract scholars' attention in the future relates to L2 learners' resistance to use the expected L2, which is triggered by negative emotions participants feel when perceiving NS as an authority, while experiencing imposition, lack of flexibility and intolerance against NS who set the rules and the standards for communicative behaviour, but may not follow them themselves. This finding is in line with recent studies which argue that the affective aspects of learning, i.e. L2 learners' feelings and prioritizing their experiences over the actual situational context, influence learners' developing *intercultural communicative competence* (Haugh and Chang 2017) and therefore, should be treated as distinct but equally fundamental to knowledge of language and language use.

Future work should focus on how intercultural communication licences a certain amount of idiosyncrasies in the individual learner's emerging new system of pragmatic competence which is unique, since it reflects their preferences, as well as common, since it reflects elements of their L1 and pragmatic norms informed by the L2. This is a new approach to pragmatic competence as it has been studied for the last three decades or so, to be researched not as a system developing towards L2 native speakers' pragmatic competence but as a complex, non-linear and dynamic process, in the form of a nuanced transition which meshes elements of both L1 and L2. Kecskes' long-standing endeavour in this direction is a promising orientation, known as the Dual Language Model and its Common Underlying Conceptual Base (Kecskes 2010, 2014). A recent encounter with a young Italian in Paris, French resident for the last 15 years, illustrates that the creative, emerging and global nature of communication should reorient second language pragmatics models: "I am proud of my Italian accent; it is

Rome's Italian accent" said twice, implying that he has no inclination of adapting to English or French prosody.

Emotions and autobiographical experience hopefully will be taken more seriously into consideration by second language pragmatists working with verbal or non-verbal communication alike. It is the challenge of 'non-propositional' effects that second language pragmatists need to address in the future, in line with the evolution of general pragmatics to date (see Carston and Wilson, 2019). If second language is co-evolving with the emotional mechanisms or procedures described above, research about the sociopragmatics of L2 *use* and *development* need to be complemented by a new notion of *inference* which is consistent with the influence pragmatic inference has on second language learners' behaviour in real life online (non)-verbal communication.

References

Austin, J. L. ([1962] 1975). *How to Do Things with Words*. 2nd ed. Edited by J. O. Urmson and M. Sbisà. Cambridge, MA.: Harvard University Press.
Barnlund, D. C. (1989). *Communicative Styles of Japanese and Americans: Images and Realities*. Belmont, CA: Wadsworth.
Bardovi-Harlig, K. (2006). Interlanguage development: Main routes and individual paths. *AILA Review, 19*, 69–82.
Bardovi-Harlig, K. (2010). Pragmatics and second language acquisition. In R. B. Kaplan, ed., *The Oxford Handbook of Applied Linguistics*. Oxford: Oxford University Press, pp. 182–92.
Bardovi-Harlig, K. (2012). Pragmatics in SLA. In S. M. Gass and A. Mackey, eds., *The Routledge Handbook of Second Language Acquisition* London: Routledge, pp. 147–62.
Bargiela-Chiappini, F. and Haugh, M. (eds.). (2009). *Face, Communication and Social Interaction*. London: Equinox.
Beebe, L. and Takahashi, T. (1989). Do you have a bag? Social status and patterned variation in second language acquisition. In S. M. Gass, C. Madden, D. Preston and L. Selinker, eds., *Variation in Second Language Acquisition: Discourse and Pragmatics*, Vol. 1. Clevedon: Multilingual Matters, pp. 103–25.
Bell, N. D. (2005). Exploring language play as an aid to SLL: A case study of humour in NS-NNS interaction. *Applied Linguistics, 26*, 192–218.
Bell, N. D. (2009). Learning about and through humor in the second language classroom. *Language Teaching Research, 13*, 241–58.
Billmyer, K. (1990a). The effect of formal instruction on the development of sociolinguistic competence: The performance of compliments. Unpublished doctoral thesis, University of Pennsylvania.
Billmyer, K. (1990b). "I really like your lifestyle": ESL learners learning how to compliment. *Penn Working Papers in Educational Linguistics, 6*, 31–48.

Blum-Kulka, S., House, J. and Kasper, G. (1989). *Cross-Cultural Pragmatics Requests and Apologies*. Norwood, NJ: Ablex.

Bouton, L. (1988). A cross-cultural study of ability to interpret implicatures in English. *World Englishes*, 17, 183–96.

Bouton, L. (1994). Conversational implicature in the second language: Learned slowly when not deliberately taught. *Journal of Pragmatics*, 22, 157–67.

Bradley, M. M. and Lang, P. J. (1999). Affective norms for English words (ANEW): Instruction manual and affective ratings. Technical Report C-1, Center for Research in Psychophysiology, University of Florida.

Bromberek-Dyzman, K., Rataj, K. and Dylak, J. (2010). Mentalizing in the second language: Is irony online inferencing any different in L1 and L2? In I. Witczak-Plisiecka, ed., *Pragmatic Perspectives on Language and Linguistics*, Vol. I, *Speech Actions in Theory and Applied Studies*. New Castle-upon-Tyne, UK: Cambridge Scholars, pp. 197–216.

Byram, M. (1997). *Teaching and Assessing Intercultural Communicative Competence*. Clevedon: Multilingual Matters.

Carston, R. and Wilson, D. (2019). Pragmatics and the challenge of 'non-propositional' effects. *Journal of Pragmatics*, 145, 31–8.

Cave, T. and Wilson, D. (eds.). (2018). *Reading beyond the Code*. Oxford: Oxford University Press.

Cenoz, J. and Valencia, J. F. (1996). Cross-cultural communication and interlanguage pragmatics: American vs. European requests. In L. Bouton and Y. Kachru, eds., *Pragmatics and Language Learning 7*. Urbana-Champaign: Division of English as an International Language, University of Illinois, pp. 85–103.

Chang, W.-L. M. and Haugh, M. (2017). Intercultural communicative competence and emotion among second language learners of Chinese. In I. Kecskes and C. Sun, eds., *Key Issues in Chinese as a Second Language Research*. New York: Routledge, pp. 267–86.

Citron, F. and Goldberg, A. (2014). Metaphorical sentences are more emotionally engaging than their literal counterparts. *Journal of Cognitive Neuroscience*, 26, 2585–95.

Citron, F., Güsten, J., Michaelis, N. and Goldberg, A. (2016). Conventional metaphors in longer passages evoke affective brain response. *NeuroImage*, 139, 218–30.

Citron, F. and Zervos, E. (2018). A neuroimaging investigation into figurative language and aesthetic perception. In A. Baicchi, R. Digonnet and J. Sandford, eds., *Epistemology, Embodiment, and Language: Sensory Perceptions and Representations*. Berlin: Springer, pp. 77–94.

Clouet, R. (2013). Understanding and assessing intercultural competence in an online environment: A case study of transnational education program delivery between college students in ULPGC, Spain, and ICES, France. *Resla*, 26, 139–57.

Cohen, A. D. and Olshtain, E. (1993). The production of speech acts by EFL learners. *TESOL Quarterly*, 27(1), 33–56.

Cook, J. (2012). Why do Korean listeners have difficulty recovering the meaning of casual speech in English? A study in pragmatics. *Asian Social Science*, 8, 40–51.

Couper-Kuhlen, E. (2012). Some truths and untruths about final intonation in conversational questions. In J. P. de Ruiter, ed., *Questions: Formal, Functional and Interactional Perspectives*. Cambridge: Cambridge University Press, pp. 123–45.

Culpeper, J. (2011). *Impoliteness: Using Language to Cause Offence*. Cambridge: Cambridge University Press.

Culpeper, J., Mackey, A. and Taguchi, N. (2018). *Second Language Pragmatics: From Theory to Research*. New York: Routledge.

Davies, C. E. (2003). How English-learners joke with native speakers: An interactional sociolinguistic perspective on humor as collaborative discourse across cultures. *Journal of Pragmatics*, 35, 1361–85.

Economidou-Kogetsidis, M., Soteriadou, L. and Taxitari, L. (2018). Developing pragmatic competence in an instructed setting: The effectiveness of pedagogical intervention in Greek EFL learners' request production. *L2 Journal*, 10(3), 3–30.

Félix-Brasdefer, J. C. (2015). *The Language of Service Encounters: A Pragmatic-Discursive Approach*. Cambridge: Cambridge University Press.

Forman, R. (2011). Humorous language play in a Thai EFL classroom. *Applied Linguistics*, 32, 541–65.

Garcia, P. (2004). Pragmatic comprehension of high and low level language learners. *TESL-EJ*, 8, 1–15.

Gass, S. and Neu, J. (2006). *Speech Acts across Cultures: Challenges to Communication in a Second Language*. New York: Mouton de Gruyter.

Goffman, E. (1959). *The Presentation of Self in Everyday Life*. London: Penguin Books.

González-Lloret, M. and Lourdes, O. (2018). Pragmatics, tasks and technology: A synergy. In N. Taguchi and Y. J. Kim, eds., *Task-Based Approaches to Teaching and Assessing Pragmatics*. Amsterdam: John Benjamins, pp. 191–214.

Holme, R. (2004). *Mind, Metaphor and Language Teaching*. Basingstoke, UK: Palgrave.

Ifantidou, E. (2014). *Pragmatic Competence and Relevance*. Amsterdam: John Benjamins.

Ifantidou, E. (2017). Pragmatic transfer, relevance and procedural meaning in L2. *International Review of Pragmatics*, 9, 82–133.

Ifantidou, E. (2019). Relevance and metaphor understanding in a second language. In K. Scott, B. Clark and R. Carston, eds., *Relevance: Pragmatics and Interpretation*. Cambridge: Cambridge University Press, pp. 218–30.

Ifantidou, E., (in press). Metaphor comprehension: Meaning and beyond. In E. Ifantidou, E., L. de Saussure and T. Wharton, eds., *Beyond Meaning*. Amsterdam: John Benjamins.

Ifantidou, E. and Hatzidaki, A. (2019). Metaphor comprehension in L2: Meaning images and emotions. *Journal of Pragmatics*, 149, 78–90.

Kasper, G. (1992). Pragmatic transfer. *Second Language Research*, 8(3), 203–31.

Kasper, G. and Dahl, M. (1991). Research methods in interlanguage pragmatics. *Studies in Second Language Acquisition*, 13, 215–47.

Kasper, G. and Rose, K. R. (2002). *Pragmatic Development in a Second Language*. Oxford: Blackwell.

Kasper, G. and Schmidt, R. (1996). Developmental issues in interlanguage pragmatics. *Studies in Second Language Acquisition*, 18, 149–69.

Kecskes, I. (2010). Dual and multilanguage systems. *International Journal of Multilingualism*, 7(2), 91–109.

Kecskes, I. (2014). *Intercultural Pragmatics*. New York: Oxford University Press.

Kim, H. Y. (2014). Learner investment, identity, and resistance to second language pragmatic norms. *System*, 45(1), 92–102.

Kim, J. (2014). How Korean EFL learners understand sarcasm in L2 English. *Journal of Pragmatics*, 60, 193–206.

Kramsch, C. (1998). *Language and Culture*. Oxford: Oxford University Press.

Lantolf, J. P. (2018). Developing conceptual understanding of sarcasm in L2 English through explicit instruction. *Language Teaching Research*, 22, 208–29.

Lee, J. S. (2002). Interpreting conversational implicatures: A study of Korean learners of English. *Korea TESOL Journal*, 5, 1–26.

Lee, C. (2018). *Researching and Teaching Second Language Speech Acts in the Chinese Context*. Singapore: Springer.

Leech, G. N. (1983). *Principles of Pragmatics*. London: Longman.

Levinson, S. C. (2013). Action formation and ascription. In T. Stivers and J. Sidnell, eds., *The Handbook of Conversation Analysis*. Malden, MA: Wiley-Blackwell, pp. 103–30.

Littlemore, J. (2001). Metaphoric competence: A possible language learning strength of students with a holistic cognitive style? *TESOL Quarterly*, 35, 459–91.

Littlemore, J. (2003). The effect of cultural background on metaphor interpretation. *Metaphor and Symbol*, 18, 273–88.

Liu, J. (2006). *Measuring Interlanguage Pragmatic Knowledge of EFL Learners*. Frankfurt am Main, Germany: Peter Lang.

Low, G. (2008). Metaphor in education. In R. Gibbs, ed., *The Cambridge Handbook of Metaphor and Thought*. Cambridge: Cambridge University Press, pp. 212–31.

Marmaridou, S. (2011). Pragmalinguistics and sociopragmatics. In B. Wolfram and N. R. Norrick, eds., *Foundations of Pragmatics*. Berlin: Mouton de Gruyter, pp. 77–106.

Martínez-Flor, A. (2006). The effectiveness of explicit and implicit treatments on EFL learners' confidence in recognizing appropriate suggestions. In K. Bardovi-Harlig, C. Félix-Brasdefer and A. Omar, eds.,

Pragmatics and Language Learning, Vol. 11. Honolulu: University of Hawai'i Press, pp. 199–225.

Martínez-Flor, A. and Usó-Juan, E. (eds.). (2010). *Speech Act Performance: Theoretical, Empirical and Methodological Issues*. Amsterdam: John Benjamins.

Nilsenová, M. and Swerts, M. (2012). Prosodic adaptation in language learning. In J. Romero-Trillo, ed., *Pragmatics and Prosody in English Language Teaching*. Dordrecht, Netherlands: Springer, pp. 77–96.

Padilla Cruz, M. (2010). Teaching interjections in the ESL/EFL class: A pragmatic approach. In L. Pérez Ruiz, I. Parrado Román and P. Tabarés Pérez, eds., *Estudios de metodología de la lengua inglesa*, Vol. V. Valladolid, Spain: Universidad de Valladolid, pp. 23–33.

Phelps, E. A. (2004). Human emotion and memory: Interactions of the amygdala and hippocampal complex. *Current Opinion in Neurobiology*, 14, 198–202.

Richards, J. and Schmidt, R. W. (1983). Conversational analysis. In J. C. Richards and R. W. Schmidt, eds., *Language and Communication*. London: Longman, pp. 117–54.

Roever, C., Fraser, C. and Elder, C. (2014). *Testing ESL Sociopragmatics: Development and Validation of a Web-Based Test Battery*. Frankfurt, Germany: Peter Lang.

Roever, C. and Ikeda, N. (2020). Testing pragmatic competence in a second language. In K. Schneider and E. Ifantidou, eds., *Handbook of Developmental and Clinical Pragmatics*. Berlin: Mouton de Gruyter, pp. 475–95.

Romero-Trillo, J. (ed.). (2012). *Pragmatics and Prosody in English Language Teaching*. Dordrecht, Netherlands: Springer.

Romero-Trillo, J. and Newell, J. (2012). Prosody and feedback in native and non-native speakers of English. In J. Romero-Trillo, ed., *Pragmatics, Prosody and English Language Teaching*. Dordrecht, Netherlands: Springer, pp. 117–32.

Ross, S. J. and Kasper, G. (eds.). (2013). *Assessing Second Language Pragmatics*. Basingstoke, UK: Palgrave Macmillan.

Sardegna, V. G. and Molle, D. (2010). Videoconferencing with strangers: Teaching Japanese EFL students verbal backchannel signals and reactive expressions. *Intercultural Pragmatics*, 7, 279–310.

Searle, J. (1969). *Speech Acts: An Essay in the Philosophy of Language*. Cambridge: Cambridge University Press.

Selinker, L. (1972). Interlanguage. *International Review of Applied linguistics*, 10, 209–31.

Shively, R., Menke, M. and Manzón-Omundson, S. (2008). Perception of irony by L2 learners of Spanish. *Issues in Applied Linguistics*, 16, 101–32.

Spees, H. (1994). A cross-cultural study of indirectness. *Issues in Applied Linguistics*, 5, 231–53.

Stalnaker, R. (1972). Pragmatics. In D. Davidson and G. Harman, eds., *Semantics of Natural Language*. Dordrecht, Netherlands: Reidel, pp. 380–97.

Szczepek Reed, B. (2004). Turn-final intonation in English. In E. Couper-Kuhlen and C. Ford, eds., *Sound Patterns in Interaction: Cross-Linguistic Studies from Conversation.* Amsterdam: John Benjamins, pp. 97–118.

Tada, M. (2005). Assessment of EFL pragmatic production and perception using video prompts. Unpublished doctoral thesis, Temple University.

Taguchi, N. (ed.). (2009). *Pragmatic Competence.* Berlin: Mouton de Gruyter.

Taguchi, N. (2013). Comprehension of conversational implicature: What response times tell us. In N. Taguchi and J. Sykes, eds., *Technology in Interlanguage Pragmatics Research and Teaching.* Amsterdam: John Benjamins, pp. 19–41.

Taguchi, N. (2015). Instructed pragmatics at a glance: Where instructional studies were, are, and should be going. *Language Teaching,* 48, 1–50.

Taguchi, N. (2017). Interlanguage pragmatics. In A. Barron, P. Grundy and Y. Gu, eds., *The Routledge Handbook of Pragmatics.* Oxford: Routledge, pp. 153–67.

Taguchi, N. and Sykes, J. (eds.). (2013). *Technology in Interlanguage Pragmatics Research and Teaching.* Amsterdam: John Benjamins.

Taguchi, N. and Roever, C. (2017). *Second Language Pragmatics.* Oxford: Oxford University Press.

Thomas, J. (1983). Cross-cultural pragmatic failure. *Applied Linguistics,* 4(2), 191–12.

Togame, N. (2016). Irony in a second language: Exploring the comprehension of Japanese speakers of English. Unpublished doctoral thesis, Middlesex University.

Wharton, T. (2012). Prosody and meaning: Theory and practice. In J. Romero-Trillo, ed., *Pragmatics, Prosody and English Language Teaching.* Dordrecht, Netherlands: Springer, pp. 97–116.

Wijayanto, A., Prasetyarini, A. and Hikmat, M. H. (2017). Impoliteness in EFL: Foreign language learners' complaining behaviors across social distance and status levels. *SAGE Open,* 7(3), 1–15.

Wilson, D. (2018). Relevance theory and literary interpretation. In T. Cave and D. Wilson, eds., *Reading Beyond the Code.* Oxford: Oxford University Press, pp. 185–204.

Wilson, D. and Sperber, D. (2012). *Meaning and Relevance.* Cambridge: Cambridge University Press.

Wiseman, R. L. and Koester, J. (1993). *Intercultural Communication Competence.* Newbury Park, CA: Sage.

Ziegler, N. (2016). Taking technology to task: Technology-mediated TBLT, performance, and production. *Annual Review of Applied Linguistics,* 36, 136–63.

Index

abduction, 31
accommodation, 376, 713, 716
accountability, 42, 49, 51, 55–7, 60, 85, 87, 193–4, 528, 530
activity type, 6, 25–6, 74–5, 78, 84, 120, 123, 125, 128, 141, 150, 153, 191, 206–18, 221–2, 323, 333, 574, 639, 688, 735
age, 166–7, 185, 188, 190, 193, 238, 350, 414, 440, 456, 507, 509, 645, 663–4, 675, 679
ambiguity, 38, 163, 168–70, 411, 417, 596
Anglo-American pragmatics, 687
apologies, 72
appropriateness, 6, 27, 321, 326, 421, 443, 456, 498, 522, 570, 733, 740, 747, 762
argumentation, 102, 521–8, 533–4, 537
argumentative discourse, 527
attitudes, 95, 97, 101, 307, 393, 761–3, 765, 768–9

blending, 598

collections, 617, 620–1, 623, 626–7, 633, 672
commitment, 48–51, 53–5, 57–9, 64–5
common ground, 36, 54, 74, 78, 81, 129, 301, 324, 417, 529, 545, 551, 596, 604, 607–11, 649–50, 743, 761
communication
 coded, 38
 ostensive-inferential, 32
communicative action, 212, 363, 367, 520, 525–6, 528, 592
community of practice, 23, 176, 228, 231, 316, 327, 416, 418, 475, 482–3, 572, 574, 693
comparability, 188–9, 194–5, 197–8, 672–3, 680, 686, 737, 742
compliments, 72
context, 4, 6, 17, 23–6, 37, 42, 71, 75, 83, 95–6, 207, 209, 212, 215, 273, 317–18, 322, 328, 389, 491, 511, 524, 544–6, 562, 598, 605–7, 641, 688, 721, 735–6
 nonce, 25
 sequential, 71
contextualization, 126, 130, 477, 487, 521, 554, 703
 cue, 126–8, 546

re-contextualization, 551–2, 554, 560, 562–3
 scale, 458
convention, 54, 162, 165, 168, 172–3, 175–8
 ritual, 176–7
 social, 35
conversation analysis, 69–71, 97, 101, 234, 294, 476, 520, 545, 616
 identities, 295
 multimodal, 128
conversational humour, 408–15, 417–18, 420, *See* humour: conversational
Cooperative Principle, 20, 25, 37–8, 49, 208, 368, 521, 571
corpus, 133, 195, 197, 639–46, 648, 657, 703, 750
 multimodal, 648
cross-cultural, 4
cultural filter, 555–8, 560, 562

deduction, 31, 71, 604
deixis, 306
deontics, 78
diachronic pragmatics, 191
dialogic practice, 96–7, 357, 522
disaffiliative humour, 409–11
disagreement, 76, 254, 412, 438, 447, 484–6
Discourse Completion Test (DCTs), 480, 677, 737–8, 741, 749
discourse marker, 131, 182, 184, 191, 193, 641, 644, 656, 676
discursive turn, 95, 98, 250, 629, 691, 693, 765
dynamic model of meaning, 596, 611

egocentric hearer, 596
egocentric speaker, 367, 595–6, 608, 721, 727
embedding, 145, 156
emic, 71, 262, 299, 320, 482, 487, 572, 668, 712, 736–7
emotions, 95, 109, 281, 286, 340, 342, 347–50, 352–3, 356–7, 433, 460, 529, 553, 750, 760, 769, 771–4
English as a *lingua franca*, 560
entailment, 31, 41, 54, 275
epistemics, 69, 74, 78–9, 81, 303, 305, 437, 439, 445, 631–2
ethnicity, 70, 193, 238, 333, 663–4, 675

ethnographic methods, 679, 749
etic, 156, 320, 491, 572, 733, 736
European Continental pragmatics, 15, 17, 190, 478, 687–8
evaluation, 6, 96, 101–3, 105, 109, 111, 129, 341, 343, 347, 350
  attitudinal, 321
  moral, 149
evaluative activity, 110
exercitive, 371–3, 376
experimental, 434–5, 437–9, 480, 611, 616, 772
  pragmatics, 37, 41
experimentational methods, 674, 679
expertise, 303, 488, 531, 538, 570
explicature, 33–4, 460–2
explicit performative, 124, 372–3

face, 234, 249–50, 252–60, 263–4, 280, 299, 322, 412, 481, 571, 698, 712
  emergent, 257
  Face1 and Face 2, 261
  identity, 298, 307
  loss, 252, 348
  management, 233
  save, 233
  threat, 253, 256
  wants, 252
Face Constituting Theory (FCT), 234, 278, 283
face-to-face, 26, 96, 192, 230–1, 240, 282, 365, 414, 505, 511, 669
footing, 95, 124, 140, 144–5, 344, 352, 355, 499
frame, 40, 214, 222, 279, 394, 555

gender, 185, 235, 237, 414, 417, 663–5, 675, 678
general pragmatics, 4, 20–1, 23, 221, 297, 368, 639
genre, 197–8, 206, 208, 210–15, 222, 553
  analysis, 218, 220, 588
  context, 210
  conventions, 183
  equivalence, 198
  macro level, 213

heuristics, 40
  Levinsonian, 40
historical pragmatics, 22, 185, 189–91, 193, 197, 199–200, 392, 687–9, 691, 704
humour, 8, 412
  function, 416–17, *See* conversational humour

identity, 8, 101, 219, 228–30, 235–6, 241, 250, 259, 279–81, 293–4, 296–300, 302, 304–5, 417, 458, 465–7, 469, 482, 569, 573–4, 629, 646
  associative identity claims, 698
  construction, 236, 261, 297, 300, 302, 458, 469, 572, 574
  deixis, 306, 561
  dissociative identity claims, 698
  interaction, 469
  performance, 667
  relational identity display (RID), 233
  social, 101, 103, 234, 259, 417, 465–6
  speaker, 444
  work, 241
ideology, 103, 375, 377, 380, 388
  language, 367
illocutionary force, 195, 365, 370, 460

im/politeness, 262, 298–300, 302, 307, 317, 349, 352, 385, 391–7, 401
  discursive, 302
implicature, 25, 30–2, 34–7, 39, 42, 140, 305, 325
  conversational, 50
  emotional, 345
  generalized, 25
impoliteness, 163, 232, 257, 300, 303, 318–19, 324, 349, 376, 378–9, 385, 396, 412, 444, 571–2, 624, 691–2
  affective, 303
  coercive, 303
  emancipatory pragmatics, 713
  mechanisms, 326
  mock, 351, 409, 412
  prosody, 430, 441
in/civility, 392, 395, 397, 401
incivility, 385, 396–7, 572
indexical, 6, 125–6, 149
  gesture, 445
indexical form, 125
indirectness, 123, 325–6, 558, 624
induction, 31, 371, 604
inference, 30–2, 34, 36–7, 41, 43, 45, 54, 78, 85, 325–6, 629, 758, 767, 769, 774
  conversational, 56
  defeasible, 31
  non-demonstrative, 32
institutional discourse, 210, 304, 394, 475, 526
institutional talk, 475–7
integrative pragmatics, 17
intention, 41–2, 59, 62, 87, 535, 594, 597, 599, 601, 608, 611
  communicative, 32–3, 41, 654
  emergent, 600–1
  speaker, 33, 42, 51, 53, 59, 412, 597, 763
interactional achievement, 49, 55, 57–8, 65, 262, 520, 595
interactional practice, 418, 420, 519
interactional sociolinguistics, 5, 24, 71, 95, 141, 229, 240, 316, 570, 576
interpersonal pragmatics, 272, 296–7, 569–74
intersubjectivity, 76, 87
invitations, 72
iteration, 375
iterative, 333

jocular mockery, 410, 412, 415

language ideologies, 122
laughter, 411, 443, 498, 619
legal action, 534
legal discourse, 9, 520, 525, 530–3, 535–7

macro-social factor, 185–6, 188, 190, 663–4, 667–8, 673–4
meaning
  intentional, 49
  natural, 44
  non-natural, 32, 44, 50
  organic, 44
  speaker, 48–9, 52, 592
media discourse, 102, 414, 526, 528
membership categorization, 629
meta-awareness, 118–19, 125, 128, 133
meta-communication, 732
metalanguage, 27, 117, 119–20, 125, 130, 413, 720

metalinguistic, 40, 119, 125, 130
  activity types, 119–20
  awareness, 117–18
  operators, 131
  quoted/reported speech, 123
  utterances, 119–20
metaphor, 250, 273, 431, 758, 765, 769–72
  conduit, 122
  emotional, 343, 347
  heart, 713–14
  relationships, 279
metapragmatic, 118–19, 121, 195, 261, 413, 489, 491, 680, 750
  awareness, 119, 125, 128–9, 132
  comment, 129
  signalling, 489–90
  universal, 132
methodology, 189, 230, 346
  experimental, 437
  IS, 230
  mixed, 219, 498, 587–8
micro-social factor, 188–9, 663, 673
moral order, 5, 326, 349, 385–8, 391, 393, 396, 747, 750
morality, 322, 385–96, 458, 750
multimodality, 430, 641

networks, 227, 229–32, 234–5, 237, 240, 702
  relational, 227, 230–1, 285
  social, 228, 233
norms, 5–6, 27, 151, 173, 190, 229, 232, 237, 264, 274, 317, 326–8, 369, 378, 386, 391, 455, 481–3, 506, 509, 557, 570, 574, 598, 640, 669–70, 700, 740–1, 747, 760–1

offers, 72, 185, 192, 195–6, 255, 628, 675
  of assistance, 507, 509
online context, 155, 228–9, 231, 237, 239, 241, 392, 414, 454, 465, 469, 496, 510, 750

participant role, 141, 143–4, 146, 149, 156, 305
participation framework, 84, 111, 143, 146–7, 149, 154–5, 157, 176, 281
pluricentric languages, 189, 674
politeness, 21, 24–5, 70, 96, 102, 105, 175, 232, 235, 239, 249, 256–7, 262, 298, 316–19, 325, 348, 377–8, 380, 392–3, 396, 412–13, 482, 503, 505, 571–2, 621, 643, 690, 692, 713, 715, 719
  and humour, 8
  development of, 24–5, 72, 133, 178, 214, 232, 249, 259, 264, 298, 305, 317, 321, 368, 476, 481, 483, 571, 691
  discernment, 739
  emotions, 349
  face, 233, 250, 253, 262–3, 294, 712
  first order, 261, 320, 349
  interaction, 102
  prosody, 440–1
  second order, 261, 320, 349
  strategies, 323, 625
  theory, 70
political discourse, 16, 48, 62, 526, 528, 530, 595
pornography, 367, 374–6, 380
  speech act, 536
positioning, 98, 126, 296, 302

power, 167, 186, 232, 363–4, 366–8, 370–1, 374, 376–80, 524, 574
  asymmetry, 72
  institutionalized, 376
  objective, 372
  politeness, 376, 476
  relations, 24, 70
  relative, 253, 372, 378, 417, 431, 480, 571, 739
  social, 553, 735
  speech genres, 128
  structure, 221, 303, 305, 364
  subjective, 365
pragmalinguistic, 1, 4, 20–2, 189, 191–2, 280, 297, 304, 317, 345, 356, 368, 455, 546, 639, 666, 759, 762
  diachronic, 191
  politeness, 317
pragmatic competence, 758–9, 761–3, 766, 773
pragmatic failure, 21, 163, 639, 758, 760
pragmatic universal, 663, 670, 678
pragmatic variability, 182, 185
pragmatic variable, 22, 185, 193, 196–7, 199, 342, 670–1
production format, 73, 142, 146, 149, 154, 157
public discourse, 526

quotation, 123–4, 528, 555

recipient design, 81, 594, 603–4
recruitment, 72, 626
reflexive awareness, 119–20, 125
reflexivity, 117, 119, 124, 128, 132–3, 147, 721
region, 664
regional variation, 189, 198, 663, 674, 678
relating, 272–5, 279, 281, 283, 288, 520, 573
relational talk, 504
relational work, 259, 281, 297, 348, 572, 587
relationality, 230, 232, 239, 241, 297
Relationship Regulation Theory, 389
relationships, 70, 76, 158, 229, 233–4, 260, 272–6, 278–83, 286, 288–9, 390, 523, 579, 687
Relevance Theory, 33, 41, 51, 59, 64, 544, 599
reported speech, 108–9, 120, 123, 144, 619
request, 72–3, 84, 130, 174, 195, 255, 417, 496, 503, 505–6, 535, 621–2, 626, 666, 675, 737
responsive actions, 72
rhetorical moves, 210, 220

salience, 133, 593, 596–7, 599, 601–4, 608
schema, 214, 216, 749
  cognitive, 214
  theory, 216
script, 214, 216, 288
  cultural, 676, 741
  schema, 216
sequential organization, 476, 523, 624, 692, 704
sequentiality, 74, 295, 702
service encounters, 9, 254, 496–7, 499, 508, 511, 672
shifter, 125
social action, 69, 71, 73–4, 76, 84, 87, 99, 118, 280, 350, 621, 765
  format, 71–3
  implicature, 326
  moral, 391
  service encounter, 497
  social practice, 307
  structure, 502

social class, 379, 664–5, 675
  vernacular spread, 184
social media, 156, 302, 307
  (im)politeness, 303, 496
  communication, 307
  discourse, 38, 456
  interaction, 414
social relationships, 233–4, 256, 316, 333, 389, 491, 699
societal pragmatics, 16, 455
sociolinguistic variables, 238
sociolinguistics, 4, 8, 19, 103, 227, 241, 293, 296, 316, 548, 570, 764, *See* sociopragmatics, *See* interactional sociolinguistics
  dialectology, 663
  historical, 688, 702
sociopragmatics, 1, 22, 192, 227, 229, 231, 235–6, 239–40, 249, 286, 293, 315, 317, 322, 408, 430, 455–6, 458, 463, 509, 624, 639, 733
solidarity, 39, 416, 505
speaker meaning, 50, *See* meaning: speaker
speech act, 18, 69, 140, 168, 252, 374, 480, 522–3, 666, 670
speech event, 6, 121, 125, 141, 212–13, 221, 666
  encounter, 141
stance, 95–9, 101, 103–5, 108, 111, 296, 347
  affective, 431
  epistemic, 78, 437
  marker, 100
  Pierce, 95
stimulus
  ostensive, 32, 40
storytelling, 352
  evaluation, 108
  identity, 108
  sequence, 98, 105
  stance, 108
strategies
  of politeness, 21

strategy, 192, 194, 301, 303, 323, 445, 468, 571, 625, 693, 712, 764
  apology, 188
  argumentation, 524
  argumentative, 528
  comparison, 742
  comprehension, 40
  face threatening act (FTA), 256
  feminine, 237
  humour, 412
  impoliteness, 351
  indirectness, 325
  nonnative, 759
  politeness, 323, 348, 481
  rapport management, 280
  request, 130
  rhetoric, 229
  speech act, 184

teasing, 280, 299, 409, 459, 738
technology mediated communication, 154, 156
telephone mediated, 498, 507–8
transactional talk, 499–501, 505
transcription, 328, 617–20, 623, 627, 633
translation, 554
  covert, 552, 554–5, 557
  overt, 552, 554–6
trust, 284, 482, 607

unfocused interaction, 141, 152

variability, 127, 132, 183–4, 327
variational pragmatics, 22, 185, 189, 199–200, 480, 663–4, 667, 672, 674, 680

web-mediated, 511
workplace discourse, 102, 240, 475, 479, 481, 483, 748
world knowledge, 38–41, 153, 606
written discourse, 104, 197, 218, 510, 669, 676